T0399675

FEEDING GHOSTS

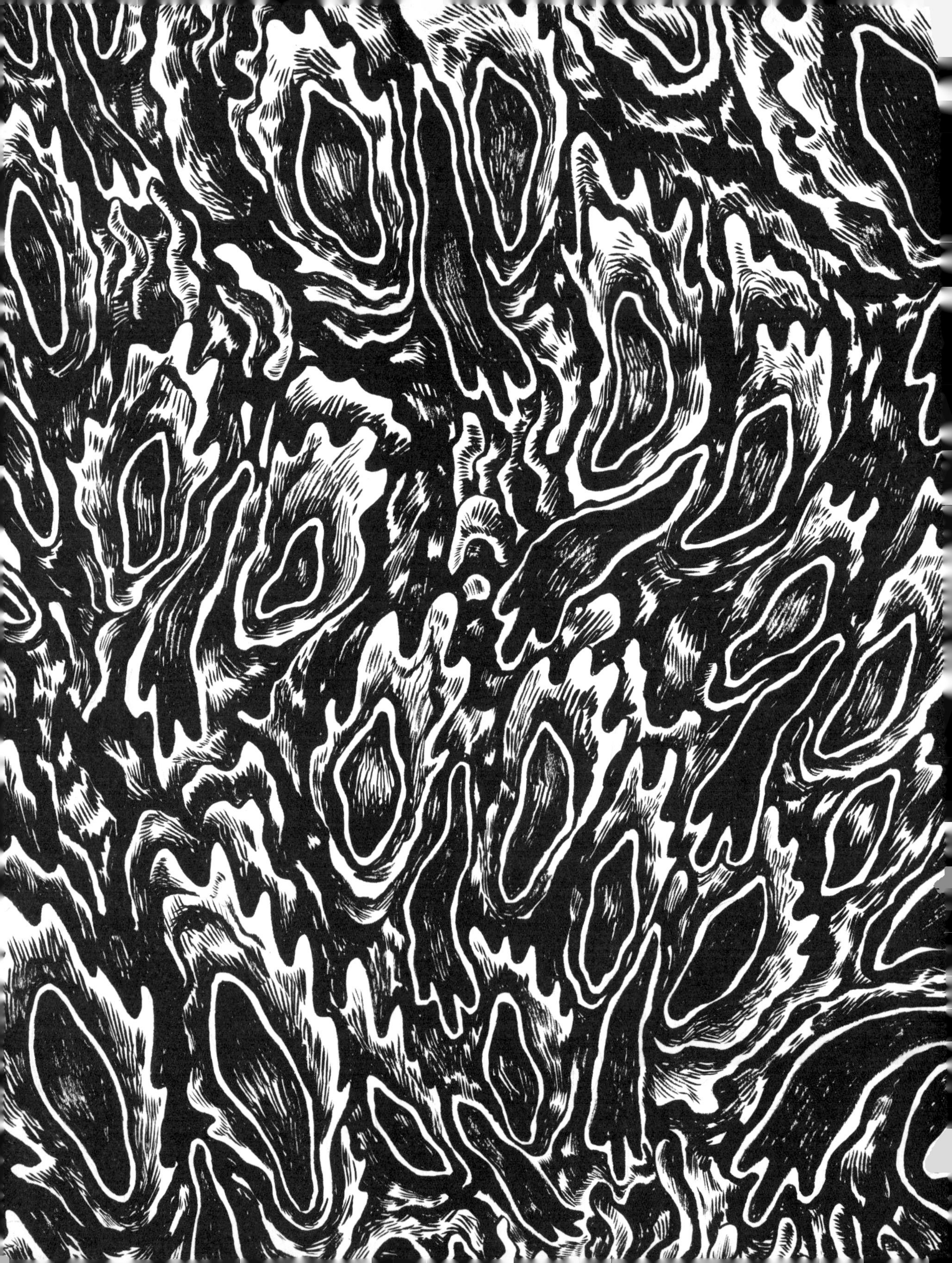

FEEDING GHOSTS

A GRAPHIC MEMOIR

TESSA HULLS

MCD · FARRAR, STRAUS AND GIROUX · NEW YORK

MCD

Farrar, Straus and Giroux

120 Broadway, New York 10271

Printed in the United States of America

First edition, 2024

Grateful acknowledgment is made for permission to reprint the following material:
Lines from "Diving into the Wreck," from *Diving into the Wreck: Poems 1971–1972*, by Adrienne Rich.
Copyright © 1973 by W. W. Norton & Company, Inc. Used by permission of W. W. Norton & Company, Inc.
Lines from "A Litany for Survival," from *The Black Unicorn*, by Audre Lorde.
Copyright © 1978 by Audre Lorde. Used by permission of W. W. Norton & Company, Inc.
Lines from "Cartographies of Silence," from *The Dream of a Common Language: Poems 1974–1977*, by Adrienne Rich.
Copyright © 1978 by W. W. Norton & Company, Inc. Used by permission of W. W. Norton & Company, Inc.
Lines from "Our Daily Bread," by Ocean Vuong, from *Night Sky with Exit Wounds*. Copyright © 2016 by
Ocean Vuong. Reprinted with the permission of The Permissions Company,
LLC on behalf of Copper Canyon Press, coppercanyonpress.org.

Family photographs courtesy of Rose Hulls.

Library of Congress Cataloging-in-Publication Data
Names: Hulls, Tessa, 1984– author.
Title: Feeding ghosts : a graphic memoir / Tessa Hulls.
Description: First edition. | New York : MCD / Farrar, Straus and Giroux, 2024. | Includes bibliographical
  references.
Identifiers: LCCN 2023040893 | ISBN 9780374601652 (hardback)
Subjects: LCSH: Hulls, Tessa, 1984– —Comic books, strips, etc. | Hulls, Rose, 1950– —Comic books, strips, etc. |
  Sun, Yi, 1927–2012—Family—Comic books, strips, etc. | Chinese Americans—Biography—Comic books,
  strips, etc. | Generational trauma—Comic books, strips, etc. | Mothers and daughters—China—Biography—
  Comic books, strips, etc. | Mental illness—Biography—Comic books, strips, etc. | Sun, Yi, 1927–2012.
  Hong se Shanghai ba nian. | China—History—1949–1976—Comic books, strips, etc. | Shanghai (China)—
  Biography—Comic books, strips, etc.
Classification: LCC E184.C5 H8596 2024 | DDC 305.48/89510730922—dc23/eng/20230831
LC record available at https://lccn.loc.gov/2023040893

Our books may be purchased in bulk for promotional, educational, or business use.
Please contact your local bookseller or the Macmillan Corporate and Premium Sales Department at
1-800-221-7945, extension 5442, or by email at MacmillanSpecialMarkets@macmillan.com.

www.mcdbooks.com • www.fsgbooks.com
Follow us on social media at @mcdbooks and @fsgbooks

1   3   5   7   9   10   8   6   4   2

For my mother and her mother

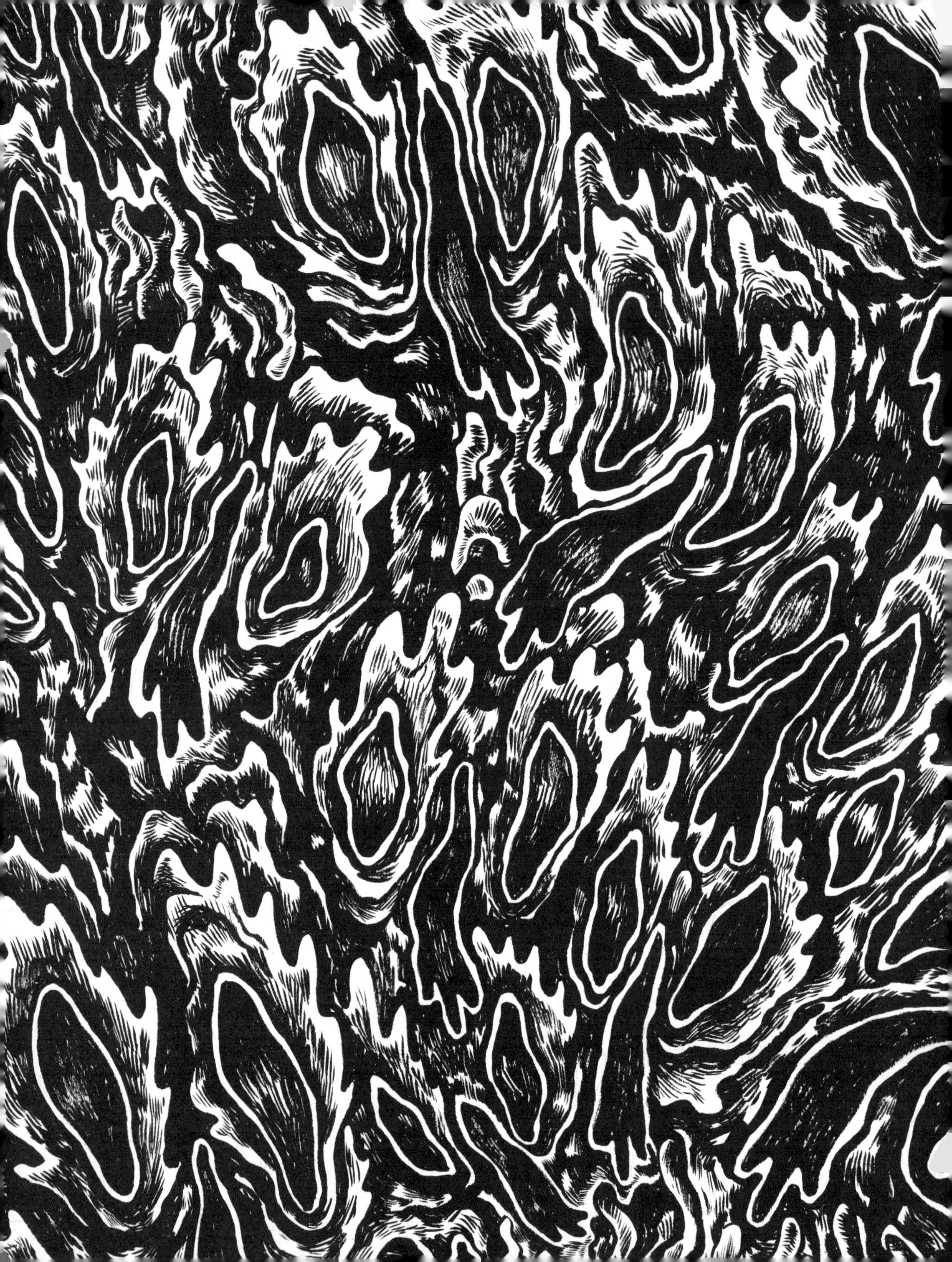

My mother was my first country. The first place I ever lived.

—NAYYIRAH WAHEED, "lands"

So we beat on, boats against the current, borne back ceaselessly into the past.

—F. SCOTT FITZGERALD, *The Great Gatsby*

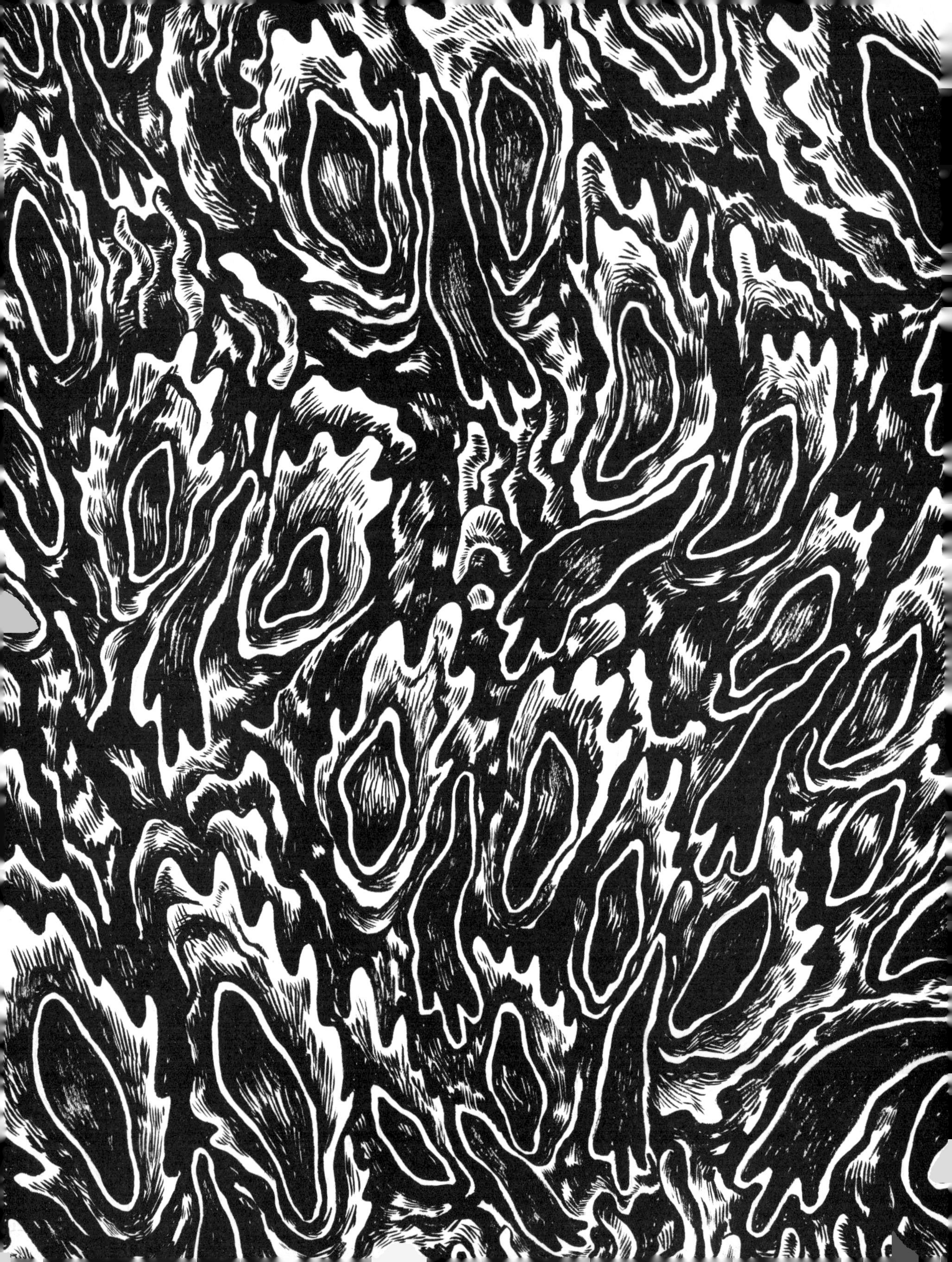

CONTENTS

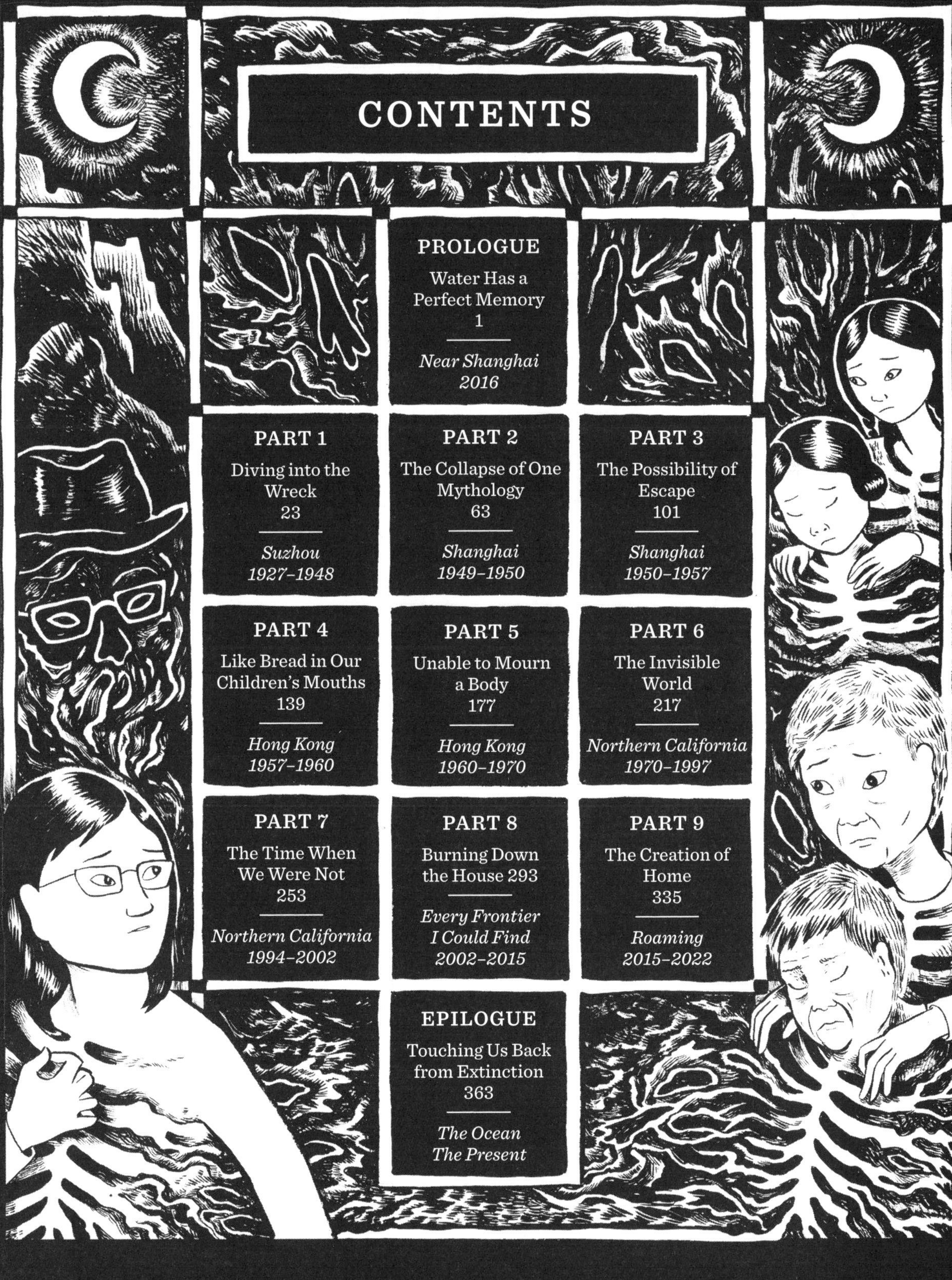

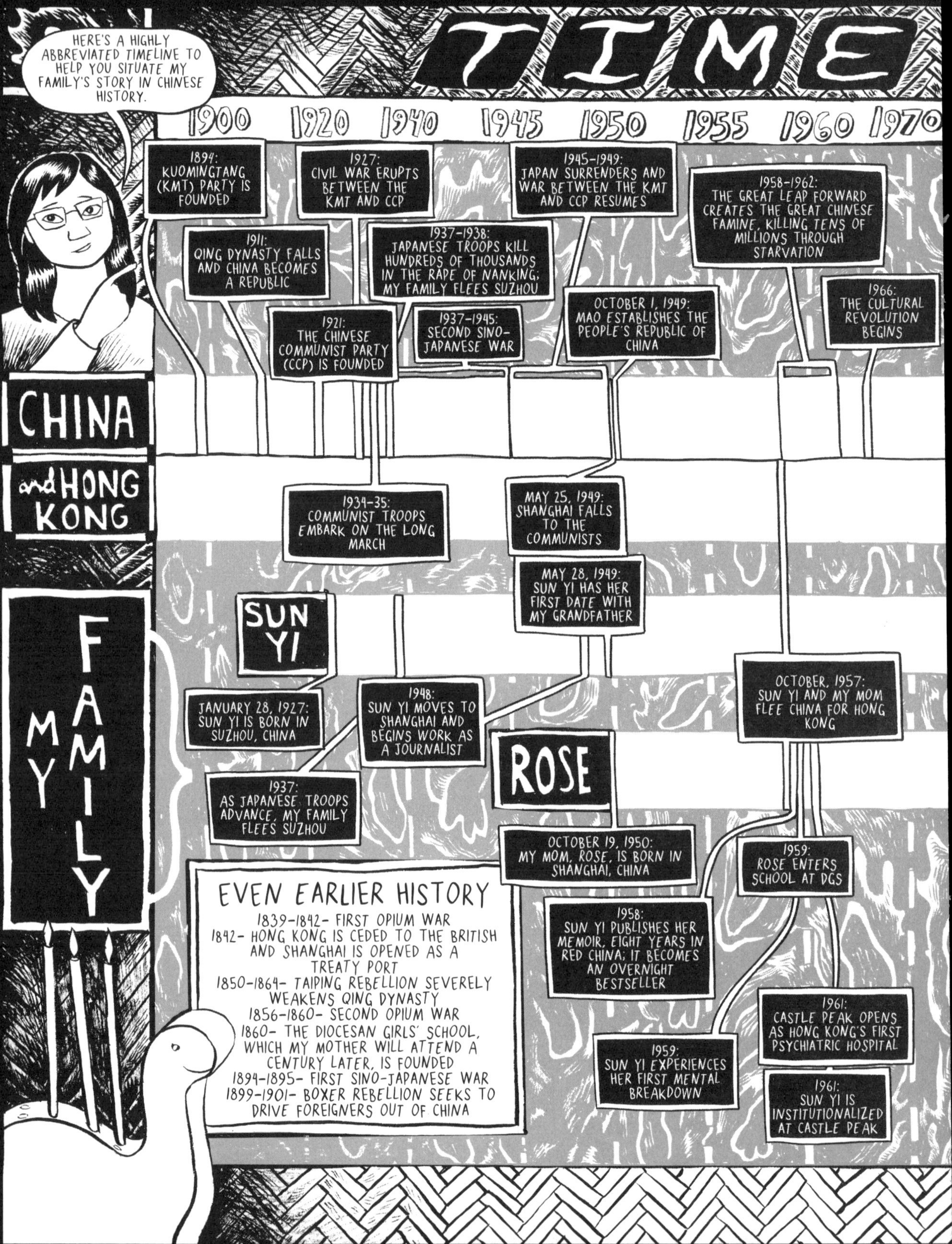
HERE'S A HIGHLY ABBREVIATED TIMELINE TO HELP YOU SITUATE MY FAMILY'S STORY IN CHINESE HISTORY.
TIME
1900 1920 1940 1945 1950 1955 1960 1970
CHINA and HONG KONG
1894: KUOMINGTANG (KMT) PARTY IS FOUNDED
1911: QING DYNASTY FALLS AND CHINA BECOMES A REPUBLIC
1921: THE CHINESE COMMUNIST PARTY (CCP) IS FOUNDED
1927: CIVIL WAR ERUPTS BETWEEN THE KMT AND CCP
1934-35: COMMUNIST TROOPS EMBARK ON THE LONG MARCH
1937-1938: JAPANESE TROOPS KILL HUNDREDS OF THOUSANDS IN THE RAPE OF NANKING; MY FAMILY FLEES SUZHOU
1937-1945: SECOND SINO-JAPANESE WAR
1945-1949: JAPAN SURRENDERS AND WAR BETWEEN THE KMT AND CCP RESUMES
OCTOBER 1, 1949: MAO ESTABLISHES THE PEOPLE'S REPUBLIC OF CHINA
MAY 25, 1949: SHANGHAI FALLS TO THE COMMUNISTS
1958-1962: THE GREAT LEAP FORWARD CREATES THE GREAT CHINESE FAMINE, KILLING TENS OF MILLIONS THROUGH STARVATION
1966: THE CULTURAL REVOLUTION BEGINS
MY FAMILY
SUN YI
JANUARY 28, 1927: SUN YI IS BORN IN SUZHOU, CHINA
1937: AS JAPANESE TROOPS ADVANCE, MY FAMILY FLEES SUZHOU
1948: SUN YI MOVES TO SHANGHAI AND BEGINS WORK AS A JOURNALIST
MAY 28, 1949: SUN YI HAS HER FIRST DATE WITH MY GRANDFATHER
ROSE
OCTOBER 19, 1950: MY MOM, ROSE, IS BORN IN SHANGHAI, CHINA
OCTOBER, 1957: SUN YI AND MY MOM FLEE CHINA FOR HONG KONG
1958: SUN YI PUBLISHES HER MEMOIR, EIGHT YEARS IN RED CHINA; IT BECOMES AN OVERNIGHT BESTSELLER
1959: ROSE ENTERS SCHOOL AT DGS
1959: SUN YI EXPERIENCES HER FIRST MENTAL BREAKDOWN
1961: CASTLE PEAK OPENS AS HONG KONG'S FIRST PSYCHIATRIC HOSPITAL
1961: SUN YI IS INSTITUTIONALIZED AT CASTLE PEAK
EVEN EARLIER HISTORY
1839-1842- FIRST OPIUM WAR
1842- HONG KONG IS CEDED TO THE BRITISH AND SHANGHAI IS OPENED AS A TREATY PORT
1850-1864- TAIPING REBELLION SEVERELY WEAKENS QING DYNASTY
1856-1860- SECOND OPIUM WAR
1860- THE DIOCESAN GIRLS' SCHOOL, WHICH MY MOTHER WILL ATTEND A CENTURY LATER, IS FOUNDED
1894-1895- FIRST SINO-JAPANESE WAR
1899-1901- BOXER REBELLION SEEKS TO DRIVE FOREIGNERS OUT OF CHINA

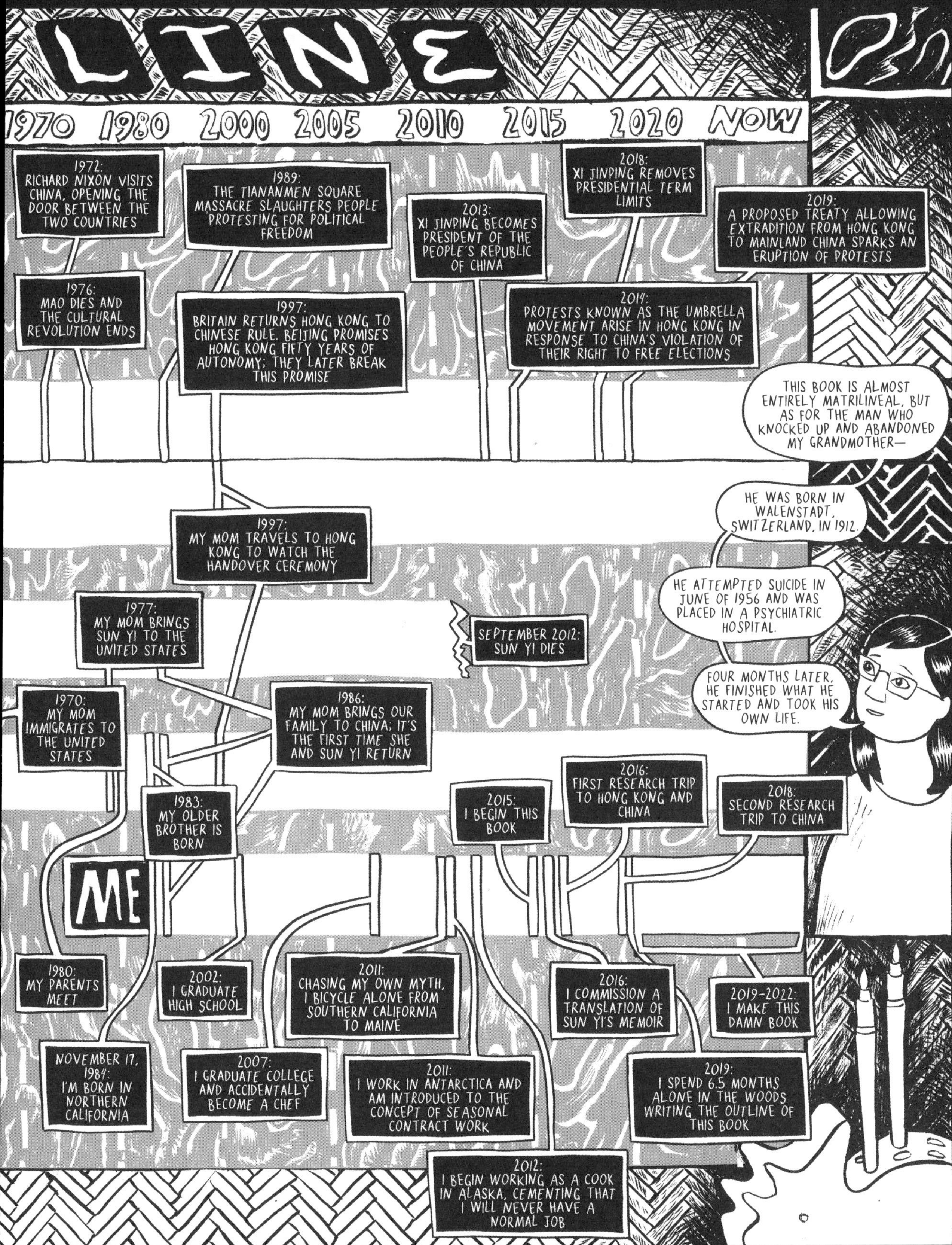
LINE
1970 1980 2000 2005 2010 2015 2020 NOW
1972: RICHARD NIXON VISITS CHINA, OPENING THE DOOR BETWEEN THE TWO COUNTRIES
1976: MAO DIES AND THE CULTURAL REVOLUTION ENDS
1989: THE TIANANMEN SQUARE MASSACRE SLAUGHTERS PEOPLE PROTESTING FOR POLITICAL FREEDOM
1997: BRITAIN RETURNS HONG KONG TO CHINESE RULE. BEIJING PROMISES HONG KONG FIFTY YEARS OF AUTONOMY; THEY LATER BREAK THIS PROMISE
2013: XI JINPING BECOMES PRESIDENT OF THE PEOPLE'S REPUBLIC OF CHINA
2018: XI JINPING REMOVES PRESIDENTIAL TERM LIMITS
2014: PROTESTS KNOWN AS THE UMBRELLA MOVEMENT ARISE IN HONG KONG IN RESPONSE TO CHINA'S VIOLATION OF THEIR RIGHT TO FREE ELECTIONS
2019: A PROPOSED TREATY ALLOWING EXTRADITION FROM HONG KONG TO MAINLAND CHINA SPARKS AN ERUPTION OF PROTESTS
1997: MY MOM TRAVELS TO HONG KONG TO WATCH THE HANDOVER CEREMONY
1977: MY MOM BRINGS SUN YI TO THE UNITED STATES
SEPTEMBER 2012: SUN YI DIES
1970: MY MOM IMMIGRATES TO THE UNITED STATES
1986: MY MOM BRINGS OUR FAMILY TO CHINA; IT'S THE FIRST TIME SHE AND SUN YI RETURN
1983: MY OLDER BROTHER IS BORN
ME
2015: I BEGIN THIS BOOK
2016: FIRST RESEARCH TRIP TO HONG KONG AND CHINA
2018: SECOND RESEARCH TRIP TO CHINA
1980: MY PARENTS MEET
2002: I GRADUATE HIGH SCHOOL
2011: CHASING MY OWN MYTH, I BICYCLE ALONE FROM SOUTHERN CALIFORNIA TO MAINE
2016: I COMMISSION A TRANSLATION OF SUN YI'S MEMOIR
2019–2022: I MAKE THIS DAMN BOOK
NOVEMBER 17, 1984: I'M BORN IN NORTHERN CALIFORNIA
2007: I GRADUATE COLLEGE AND ACCIDENTALLY BECOME A CHEF
2011: I WORK IN ANTARCTICA AND AM INTRODUCED TO THE CONCEPT OF SEASONAL CONTRACT WORK
2019: I SPEND 6.5 MONTHS ALONE IN THE WOODS WRITING THE OUTLINE OF THIS BOOK
2012: I BEGIN WORKING AS A COOK IN ALASKA, CEMENTING THAT I WILL NEVER HAVE A NORMAL JOB
THIS BOOK IS ALMOST ENTIRELY MATRILINEAL, BUT AS FOR THE MAN WHO KNOCKED UP AND ABANDONED MY GRANDMOTHER—
HE WAS BORN IN WALENSTADT, SWITZERLAND, IN 1912.
HE ATTEMPTED SUICIDE IN JUNE OF 1956 AND WAS PLACED IN A PSYCHIATRIC HOSPITAL.
FOUR MONTHS LATER, HE FINISHED WHAT HE STARTED AND TOOK HIS OWN LIFE.

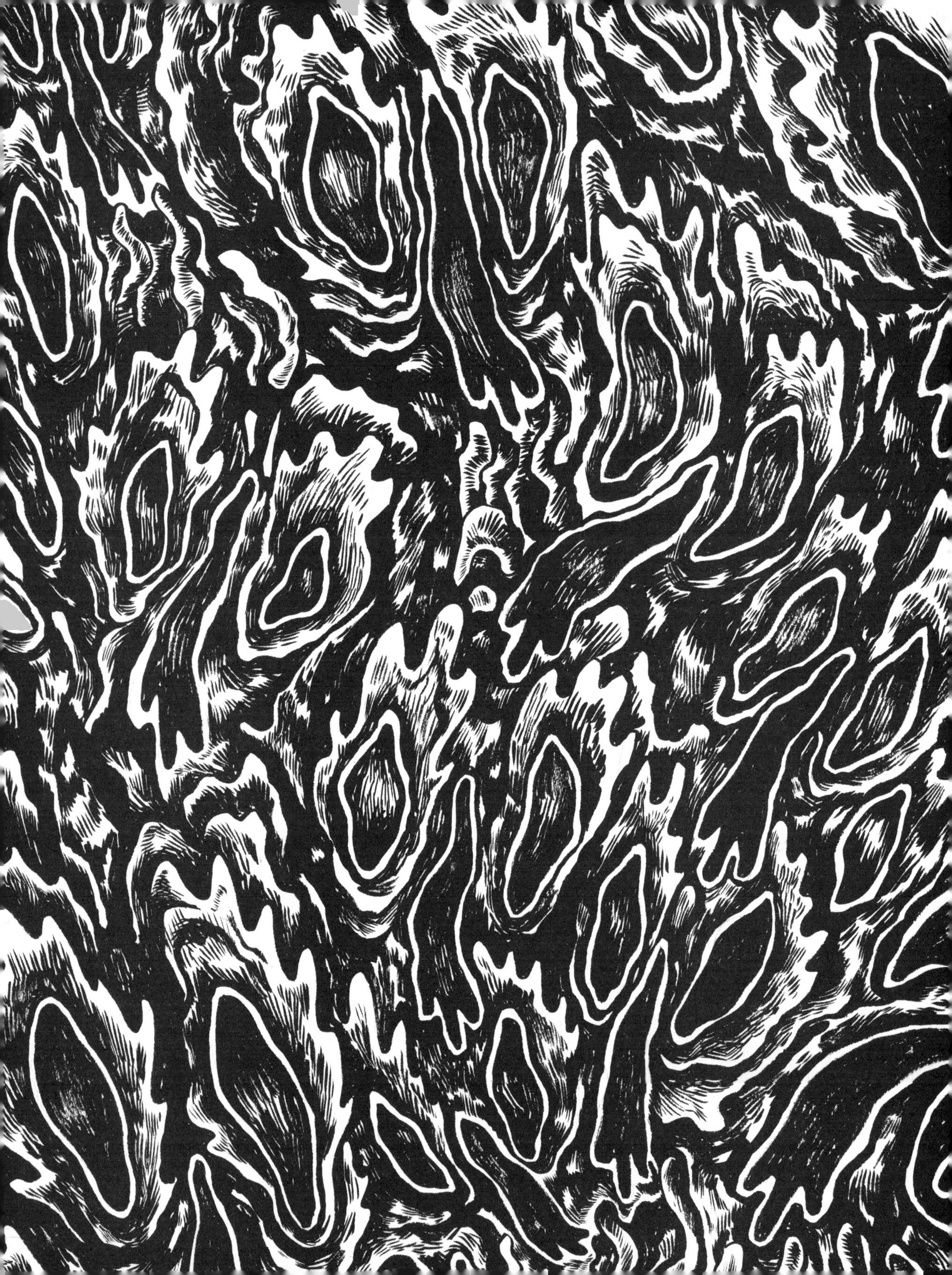

PROLOGUE

WATER HAS A
PERFECT MEMORY

On a Night Train between Shanghai and Guangzhou

2016

*All water has a perfect memory and is forever
trying to get back to where it was.*

—TONI MORRISON

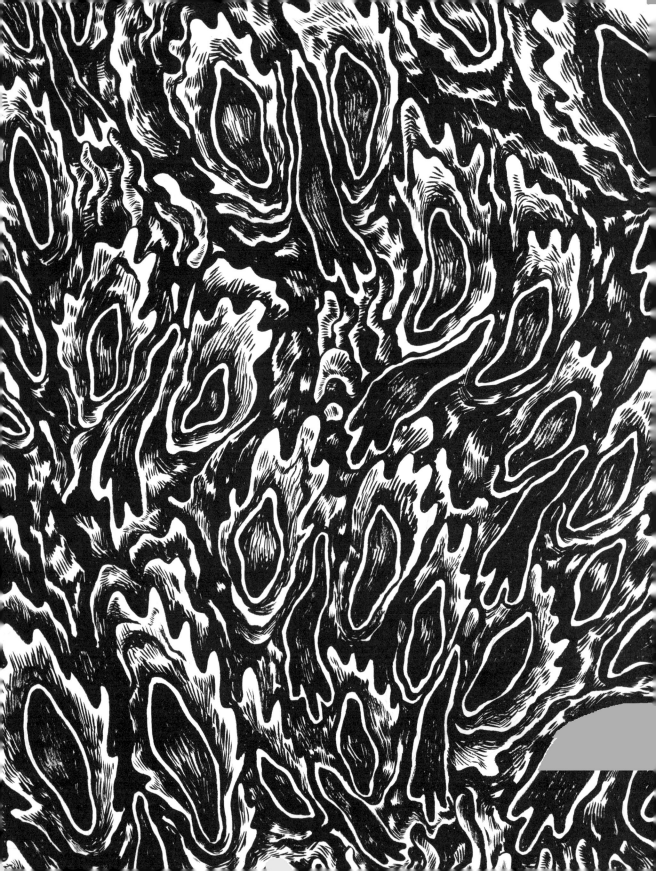

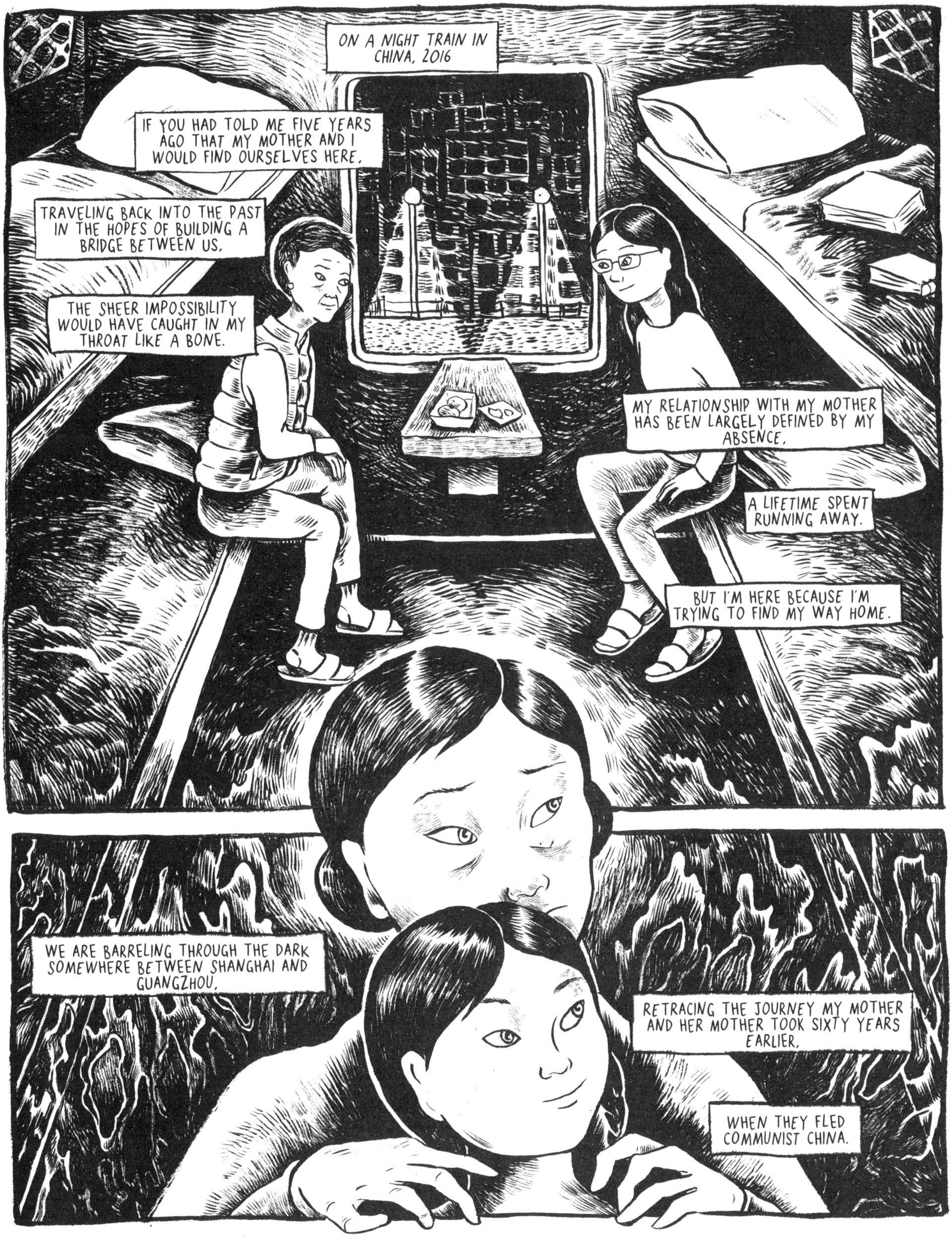
ON A NIGHT TRAIN IN CHINA, 2016
IF YOU HAD TOLD ME FIVE YEARS AGO THAT MY MOTHER AND I WOULD FIND OURSELVES HERE,
TRAVELING BACK INTO THE PAST IN THE HOPES OF BUILDING A BRIDGE BETWEEN US,
THE SHEER IMPOSSIBILITY WOULD HAVE CAUGHT IN MY THROAT LIKE A BONE.
MY RELATIONSHIP WITH MY MOTHER HAS BEEN LARGELY DEFINED BY MY ABSENCE,
A LIFETIME SPENT RUNNING AWAY.
BUT I'M HERE BECAUSE I'M TRYING TO FIND MY WAY HOME.
WE ARE BARRELING THROUGH THE DARK SOMEWHERE BETWEEN SHANGHAI AND GUANGZHOU,
RETRACING THE JOURNEY MY MOTHER AND HER MOTHER TOOK SIXTY YEARS EARLIER,
WHEN THEY FLED COMMUNIST CHINA.

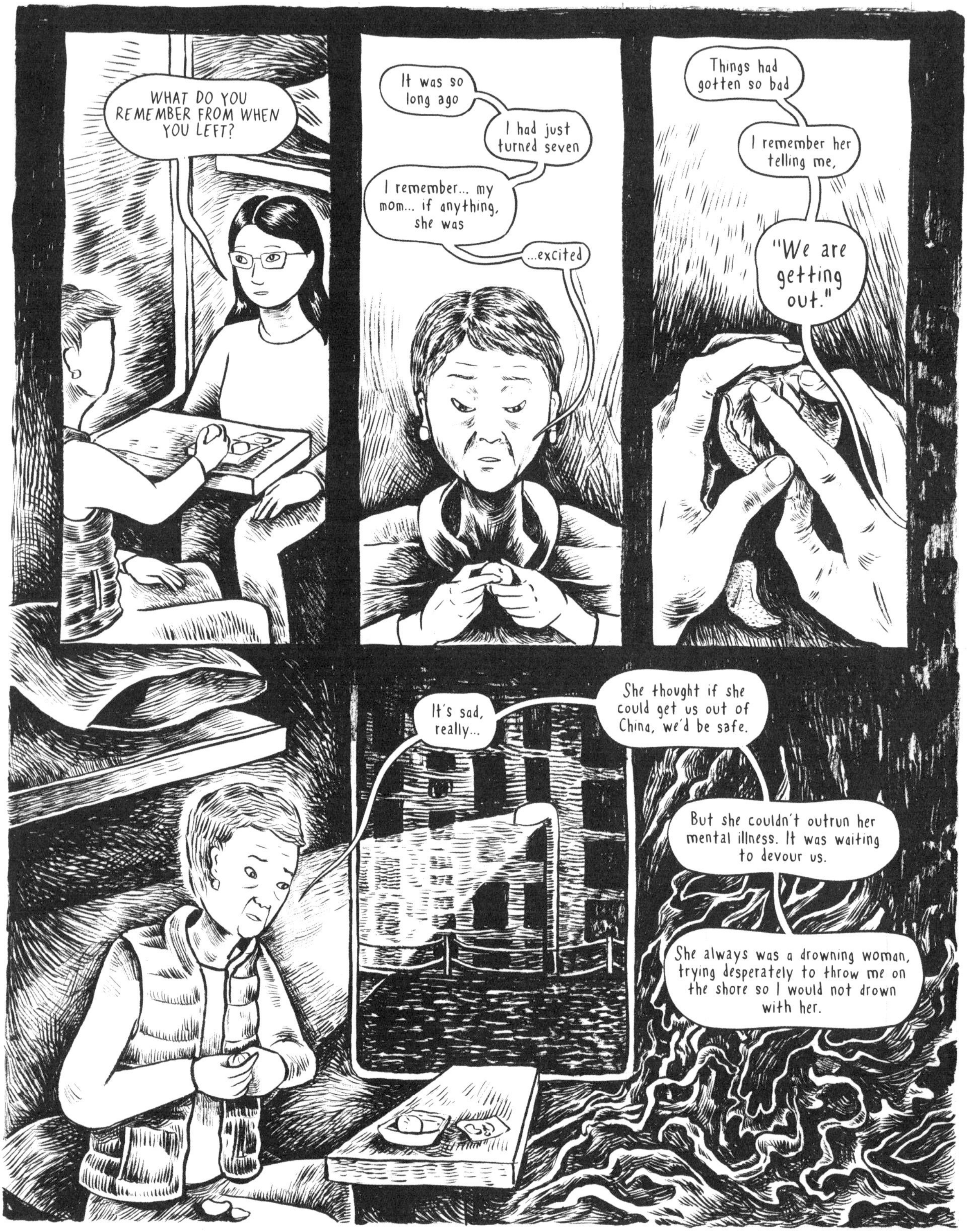
WHAT DO YOU REMEMBER FROM WHEN YOU LEFT?
It was so long ago
I had just turned seven
I remember... my mom... if anything, she was
...excited
Things had gotten so bad
I remember her telling me,
"We are getting out."
It's sad, really...
She thought if she could get us out of China, we'd be safe.
But she couldn't outrun her mental illness. It was waiting to devour us.
She always was a drowning woman, trying desperately to throw me on the shore so I would not drown with her.

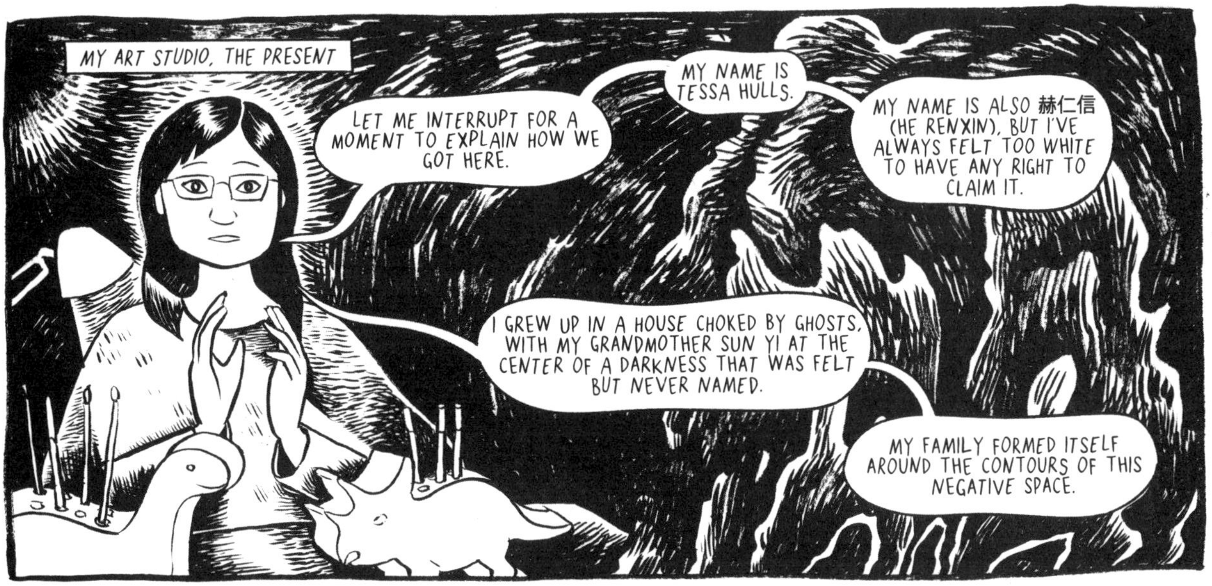
MY ART STUDIO, THE PRESENT
LET ME INTERRUPT FOR A MOMENT TO EXPLAIN HOW WE GOT HERE.
MY NAME IS TESSA HULLS.
MY NAME IS ALSO 赫仁信 (HE RENXIN), BUT I'VE ALWAYS FELT TOO WHITE TO HAVE ANY RIGHT TO CLAIM IT.
I GREW UP IN A HOUSE CHOKED BY GHOSTS, WITH MY GRANDMOTHER SUN YI AT THE CENTER OF A DARKNESS THAT WAS FELT BUT NEVER NAMED.
MY FAMILY FORMED ITSELF AROUND THE CONTOURS OF THIS NEGATIVE SPACE.

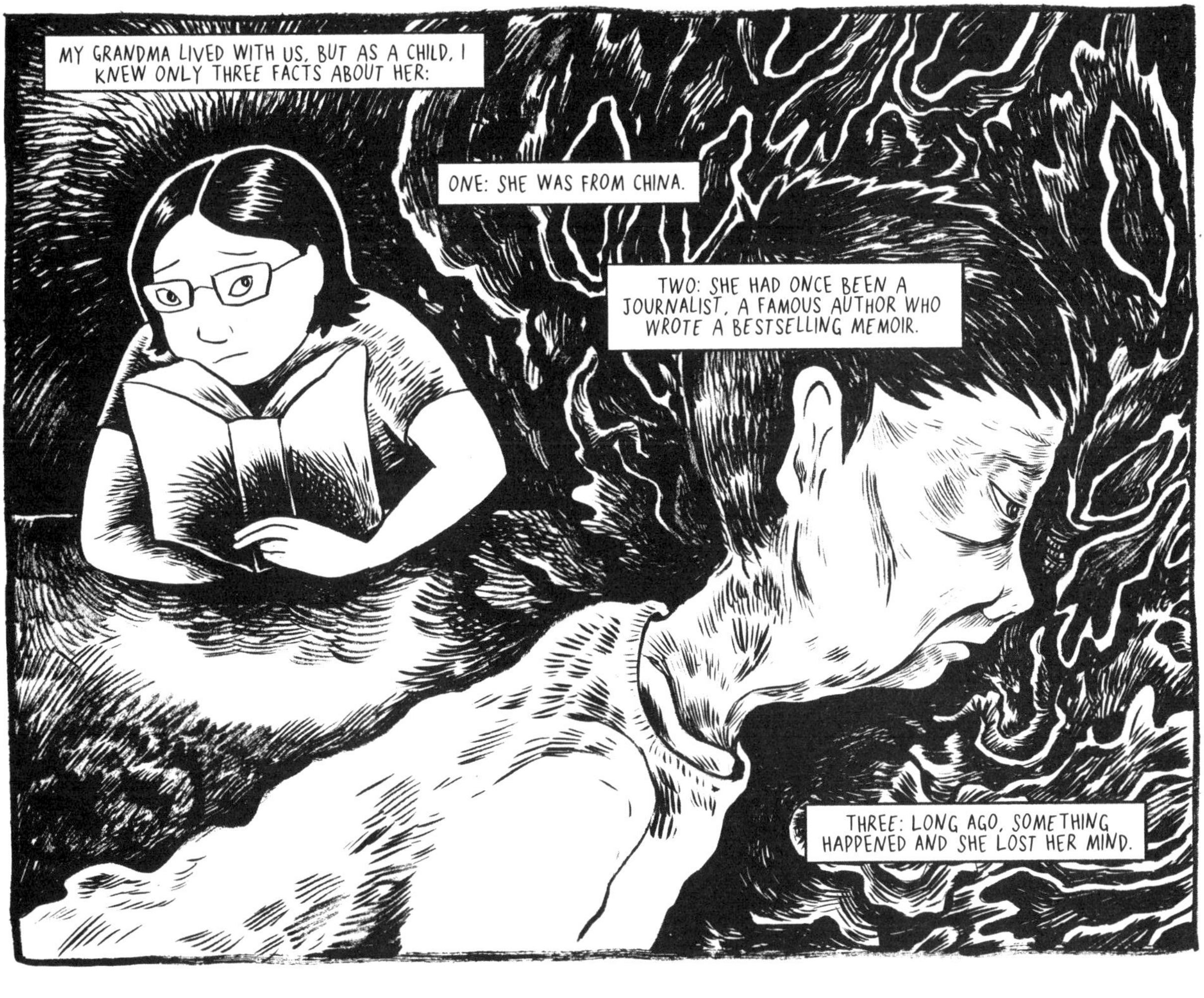
MY GRANDMA LIVED WITH US, BUT AS A CHILD, I KNEW ONLY THREE FACTS ABOUT HER:
ONE: SHE WAS FROM CHINA.
TWO: SHE HAD ONCE BEEN A JOURNALIST, A FAMOUS AUTHOR WHO WROTE A BESTSELLING MEMOIR.
THREE: LONG AGO, SOMETHING HAPPENED AND SHE LOST HER MIND.

MY MOM DIDN'T TEACH ME CHINESE, SO BETWEEN THE LANGUAGE BARRIER AND MY GRANDMA'S MENTAL STATE, I WAS NEVER ABLE TO KNOW HER AS A PERSON—ONLY AS THE BROKEN FRAGMENT OF A CULTURE I DID NOT UNDERSTAND.

I DIDN'T KNOW HOW TO RECONCILE THE STORY OF MY GRANDMA'S PAST WITH THE NINETY-POUND SPECTER WHO SHUFFLED AROUND OUR HOUSE IN GRAY COSTCO SWEATPANTS.

THE FAMILY MYTH

WITHIN MY FAMILY, THE BONES OF HER HISTORY—CHINA, WRITER, MADNESS—WERE RECITED AS THOUGH THEY WERE ANSWERS RATHER THAN QUESTIONS. THE SENSATIONALIZED PLOT POINTS OF HER PAST MADE HER STORY READ LIKE A SOAP OPERA:

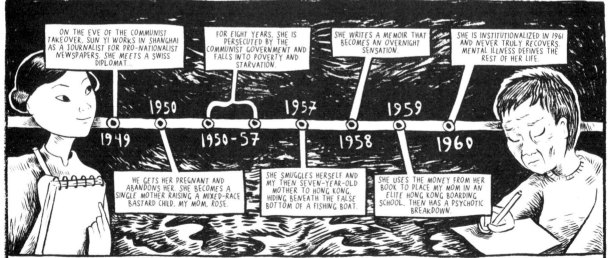

ON THE EVE OF THE COMMUNIST TAKEOVER, SUN YI WORKS IN SHANGHAI AS A JOURNALIST FOR PRO-NATIONALIST NEWSPAPERS. SHE MEETS A SWISS DIPLOMAT...

FOR EIGHT YEARS, SHE IS PERSECUTED BY THE COMMUNIST GOVERNMENT AND FALLS INTO POVERTY AND STARVATION.

SHE WRITES A MEMOIR THAT BECOMES AN OVERNIGHT SENSATION.

SHE IS INSTITUTIONALIZED IN 1961 AND NEVER TRULY RECOVERS. MENTAL ILLNESS DEFINES THE REST OF HER LIFE.

1950   1957   1959

1949   1950-57   1958   1960

HE GETS HER PREGNANT AND ABANDONS HER. SHE BECOMES A SINGLE MOTHER RAISING A MIXED-RACE BASTARD CHILD. MY MOM, ROSE.

SHE SMUGGLES HERSELF AND MY THEN SEVEN-YEAR-OLD MOTHER TO HONG KONG, HIDING BENEATH THE FALSE BOTTOM OF A FISHING BOAT.

SHE USES THE MONEY FROM HER BOOK TO PLACE MY MOM IN AN ELITE HONG KONG BOARDING SCHOOL, THEN HAS A PSYCHOTIC BREAKDOWN.

GROWING UP, I HAD NO KNOWLEDGE OF HOW MY FAMILY'S STORY NESTLED WITHIN THE BROADER STROKES OF CHINESE HISTORY. IT WAS INCONCEIVABLE THAT THE GRANDMOTHER I KNEW—WHO SPENT HER DAYS WITH ZERO HUMAN CONTACT OUTSIDE OUR FAMILY, SITTING AT A WRITING DESK WHERE SHE ENDLESSLY SCRAWLED OUT THE SAME STORIES OF HER PAST—HAD ONCE BEEN A BOLD YOUNG JOURNALIST REPORTING FROM THE FRONT LINES OF CHINA'S CIVIL WAR.

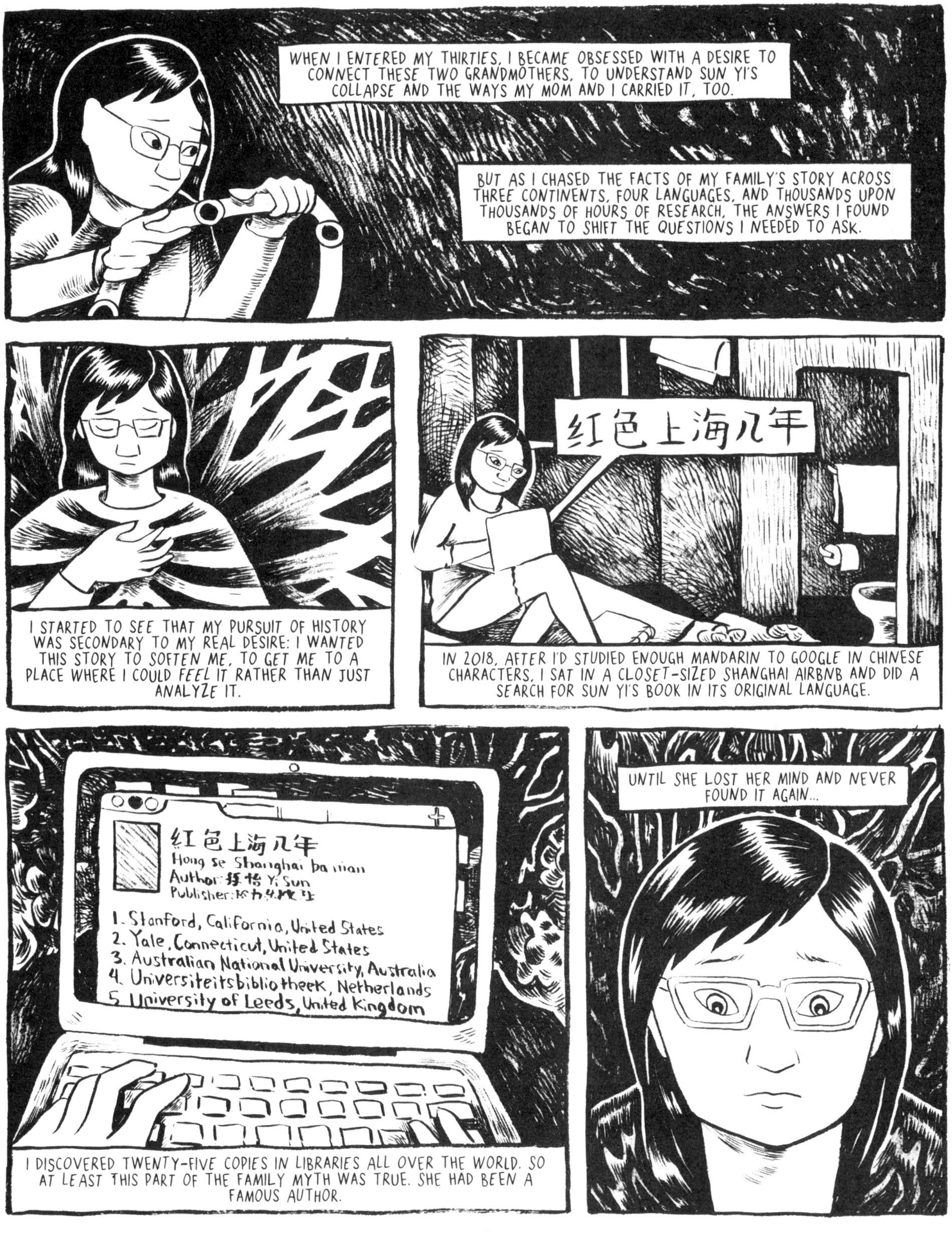

WHEN I ENTERED MY THIRTIES, I BECAME OBSESSED WITH A DESIRE TO CONNECT THESE TWO GRANDMOTHERS, TO UNDERSTAND SUN YI'S COLLAPSE AND THE WAYS MY MOM AND I CARRIED IT, TOO.
BUT AS I CHASED THE FACTS OF MY FAMILY'S STORY ACROSS THREE CONTINENTS, FOUR LANGUAGES, AND THOUSANDS UPON THOUSANDS OF HOURS OF RESEARCH, THE ANSWERS I FOUND BEGAN TO SHIFT THE QUESTIONS I NEEDED TO ASK.
I STARTED TO SEE THAT MY PURSUIT OF HISTORY WAS SECONDARY TO MY REAL DESIRE: I WANTED THIS STORY TO SOFTEN ME, TO GET ME TO A PLACE WHERE I COULD *FEEL* IT RATHER THAN JUST ANALYZE IT.
红色上海几年
IN 2018, AFTER I'D STUDIED ENOUGH MANDARIN TO GOOGLE IN CHINESE CHARACTERS, I SAT IN A CLOSET-SIZED SHANGHAI AIRBNB AND DID A SEARCH FOR SUN YI'S BOOK IN ITS ORIGINAL LANGUAGE.
红色上海几年
Hong se Shanghai ba nian
Author: 孙怡 Yi Sun
1. Stanford, California, United States
2. Yale, Connecticut, United States
3. Australian National University, Australia
4. Universiteitsbibliotheek, Netherlands
5. University of Leeds, United Kingdom
I DISCOVERED TWENTY-FIVE COPIES IN LIBRARIES ALL OVER THE WORLD. SO AT LEAST THIS PART OF THE FAMILY MYTH WAS TRUE. SHE HAD BEEN A FAMOUS AUTHOR.
UNTIL SHE LOST HER MIND AND NEVER FOUND IT AGAIN...

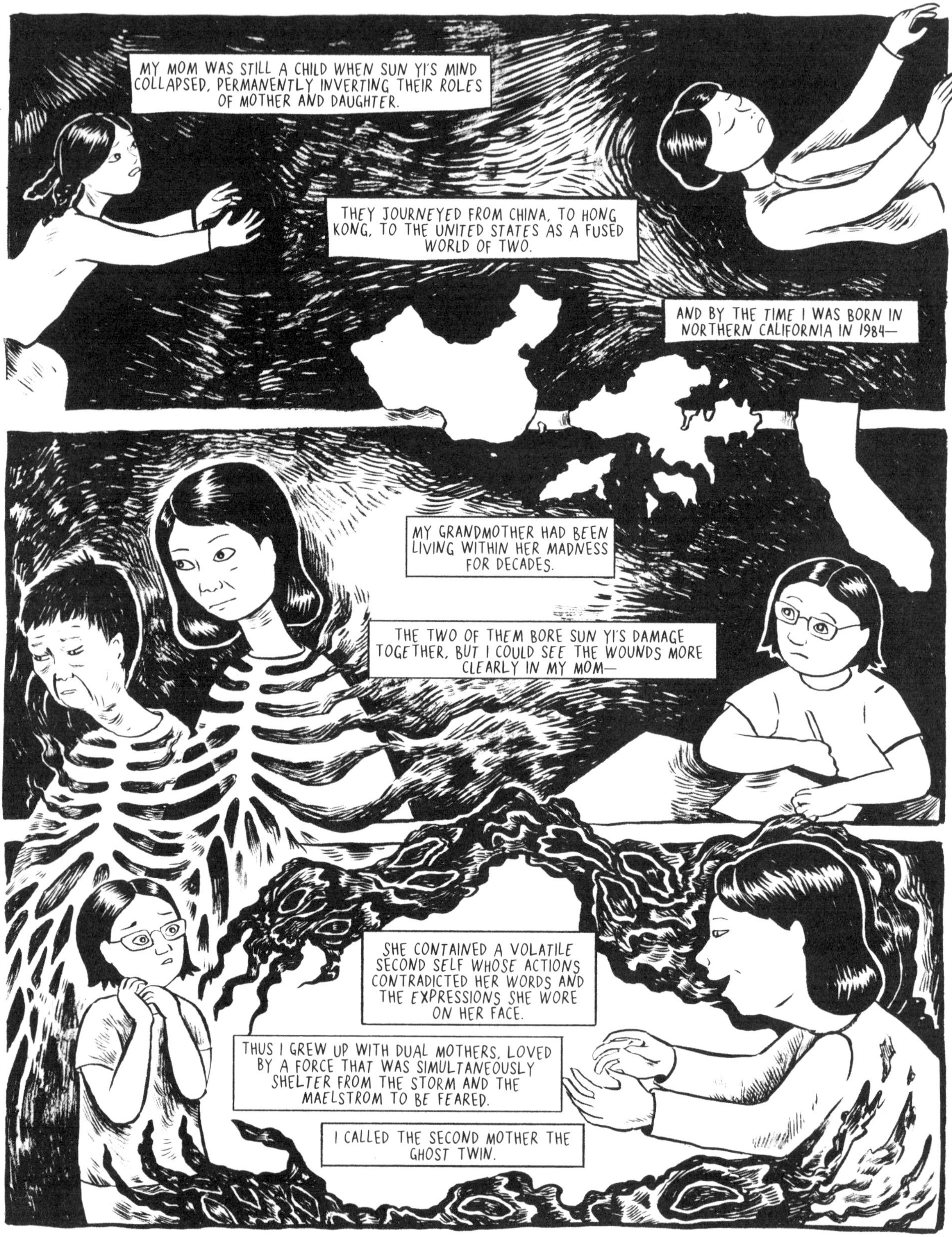

MY MOM WAS STILL A CHILD WHEN SUN YI'S MIND COLLAPSED, PERMANENTLY INVERTING THEIR ROLES OF MOTHER AND DAUGHTER.
THEY JOURNEYED FROM CHINA, TO HONG KONG, TO THE UNITED STATES AS A FUSED WORLD OF TWO.
AND BY THE TIME I WAS BORN IN NORTHERN CALIFORNIA IN 1984—
MY GRANDMOTHER HAD BEEN LIVING WITHIN HER MADNESS FOR DECADES.
THE TWO OF THEM BORE SUN YI'S DAMAGE TOGETHER, BUT I COULD SEE THE WOUNDS MORE CLEARLY IN MY MOM—
SHE CONTAINED A VOLATILE SECOND SELF WHOSE ACTIONS CONTRADICTED HER WORDS AND THE EXPRESSIONS SHE WORE ON HER FACE.
THUS I GREW UP WITH DUAL MOTHERS, LOVED BY A FORCE THAT WAS SIMULTANEOUSLY SHELTER FROM THE STORM AND THE MAELSTROM TO BE FEARED.
I CALLED THE SECOND MOTHER THE GHOST TWIN.

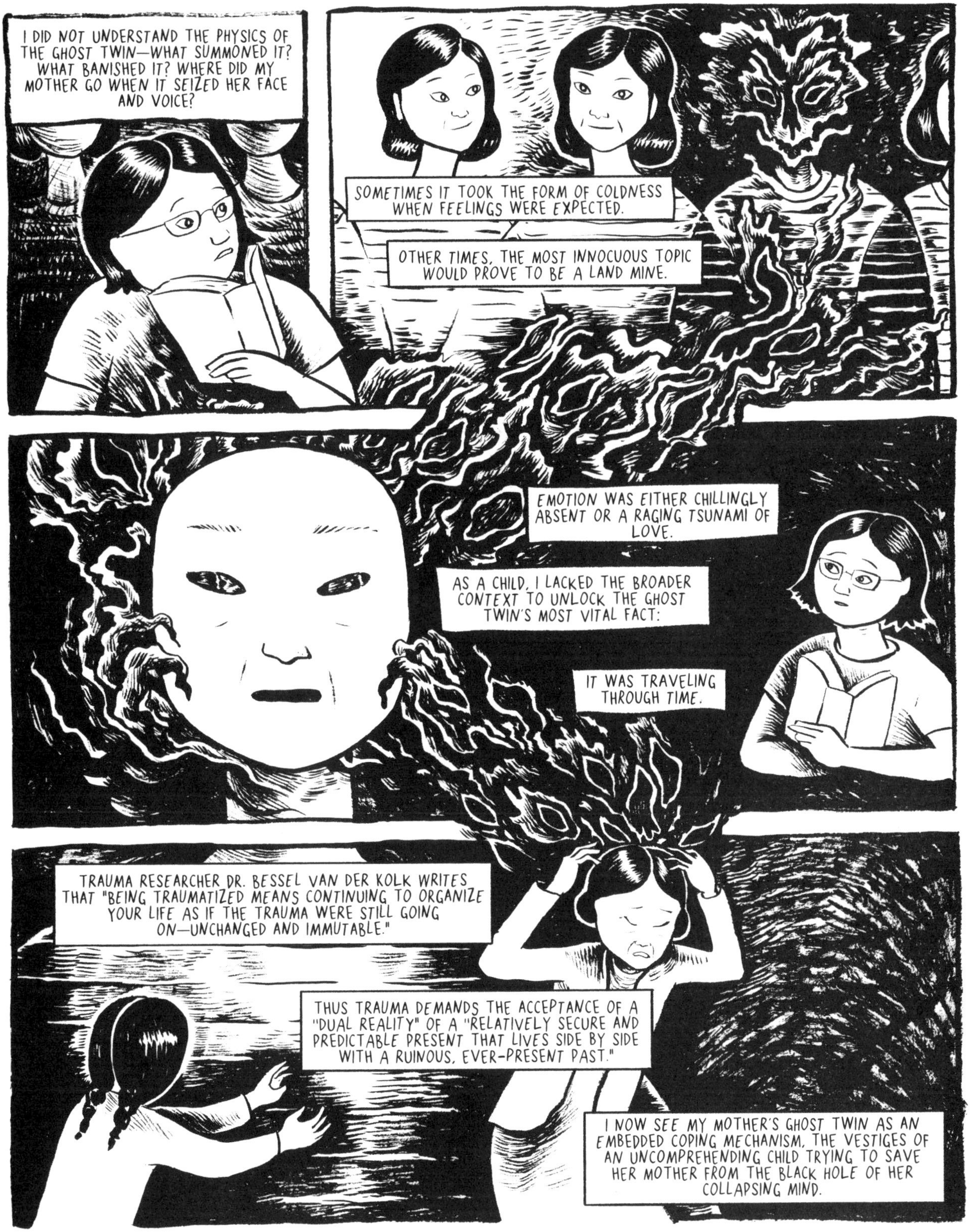
I DID NOT UNDERSTAND THE PHYSICS OF THE GHOST TWIN—WHAT SUMMONED IT? WHAT BANISHED IT? WHERE DID MY MOTHER GO WHEN IT SEIZED HER FACE AND VOICE?
SOMETIMES IT TOOK THE FORM OF COLDNESS WHEN FEELINGS WERE EXPECTED.
OTHER TIMES, THE MOST INNOCUOUS TOPIC WOULD PROVE TO BE A LAND MINE.
EMOTION WAS EITHER CHILLINGLY ABSENT OR A RAGING TSUNAMI OF LOVE.
AS A CHILD, I LACKED THE BROADER CONTEXT TO UNLOCK THE GHOST TWIN'S MOST VITAL FACT:
IT WAS TRAVELING THROUGH TIME.
TRAUMA RESEARCHER DR. BESSEL VAN DER KOLK WRITES THAT "BEING TRAUMATIZED MEANS CONTINUING TO ORGANIZE YOUR LIFE AS IF THE TRAUMA WERE STILL GOING ON—UNCHANGED AND IMMUTABLE."
THUS TRAUMA DEMANDS THE ACCEPTANCE OF A "DUAL REALITY" OF A "RELATIVELY SECURE AND PREDICTABLE PRESENT THAT LIVES SIDE BY SIDE WITH A RUINOUS, EVER-PRESENT PAST."
I NOW SEE MY MOTHER'S GHOST TWIN AS AN EMBEDDED COPING MECHANISM, THE VESTIGES OF AN UNCOMPREHENDING CHILD TRYING TO SAVE HER MOTHER FROM THE BLACK HOLE OF HER COLLAPSING MIND.

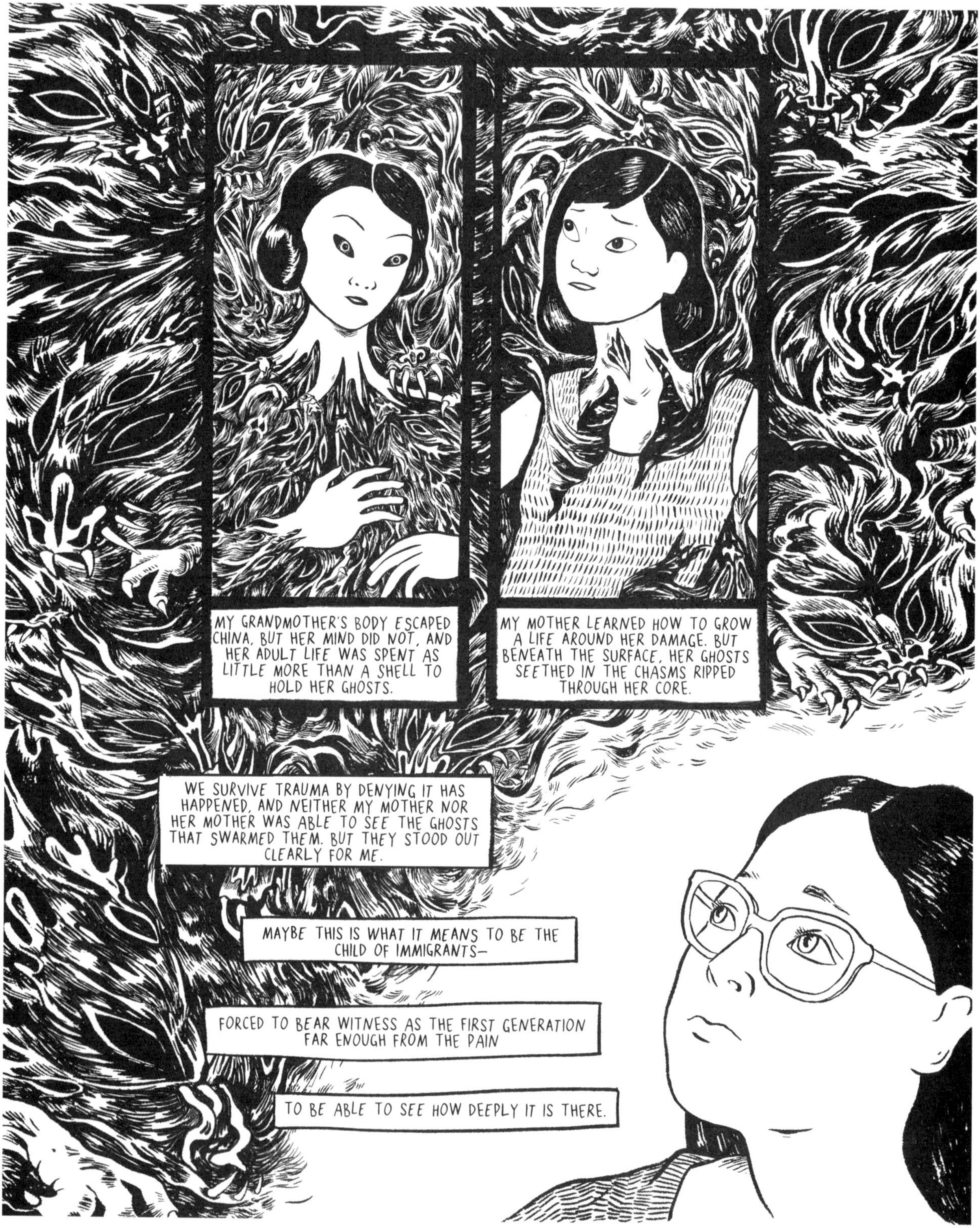

MY GRANDMOTHER'S BODY ESCAPED CHINA, BUT HER MIND DID NOT, AND HER ADULT LIFE WAS SPENT AS LITTLE MORE THAN A SHELL TO HOLD HER GHOSTS.
MY MOTHER LEARNED HOW TO GROW A LIFE AROUND HER DAMAGE. BUT BENEATH THE SURFACE, HER GHOSTS SEETHED IN THE CHASMS RIPPED THROUGH HER CORE.
WE SURVIVE TRAUMA BY DENYING IT HAS HAPPENED, AND NEITHER MY MOTHER NOR HER MOTHER WAS ABLE TO SEE THE GHOSTS THAT SWARMED THEM. BUT THEY STOOD OUT CLEARLY FOR ME.
MAYBE THIS IS WHAT IT MEANS TO BE THE CHILD OF IMMIGRANTS—
FORCED TO BEAR WITNESS AS THE FIRST GENERATION FAR ENOUGH FROM THE PAIN
TO BE ABLE TO SEE HOW DEEPLY IT IS THERE.

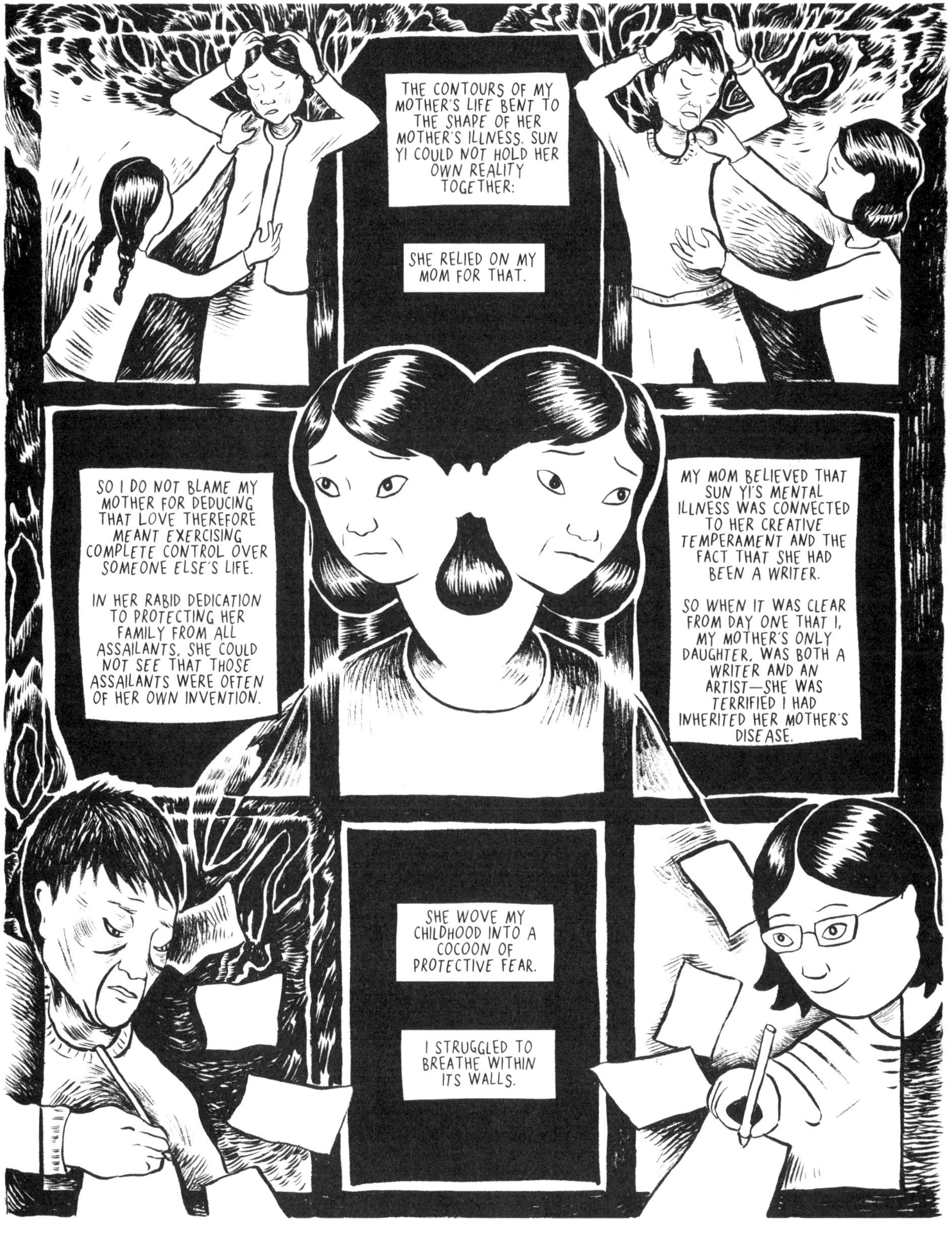
THE CONTOURS OF MY MOTHER'S LIFE BENT TO THE SHAPE OF HER MOTHER'S ILLNESS. SUN YI COULD NOT HOLD HER OWN REALITY TOGETHER:
SHE RELIED ON MY MOM FOR THAT.
SO I DO NOT BLAME MY MOTHER FOR DEDUCING THAT LOVE THEREFORE MEANT EXERCISING COMPLETE CONTROL OVER SOMEONE ELSE'S LIFE.
IN HER RABID DEDICATION TO PROTECTING HER FAMILY FROM ALL ASSAILANTS, SHE COULD NOT SEE THAT THOSE ASSAILANTS WERE OFTEN OF HER OWN INVENTION.
MY MOM BELIEVED THAT SUN YI'S MENTAL ILLNESS WAS CONNECTED TO HER CREATIVE TEMPERAMENT AND THE FACT THAT SHE HAD BEEN A WRITER.
SO WHEN IT WAS CLEAR FROM DAY ONE THAT I, MY MOTHER'S ONLY DAUGHTER, WAS BOTH A WRITER AND AN ARTIST—SHE WAS TERRIFIED I HAD INHERITED HER MOTHER'S DISEASE.
SHE WOVE MY CHILDHOOD INTO A COCOON OF PROTECTIVE FEAR.
I STRUGGLED TO BREATHE WITHIN ITS WALLS.

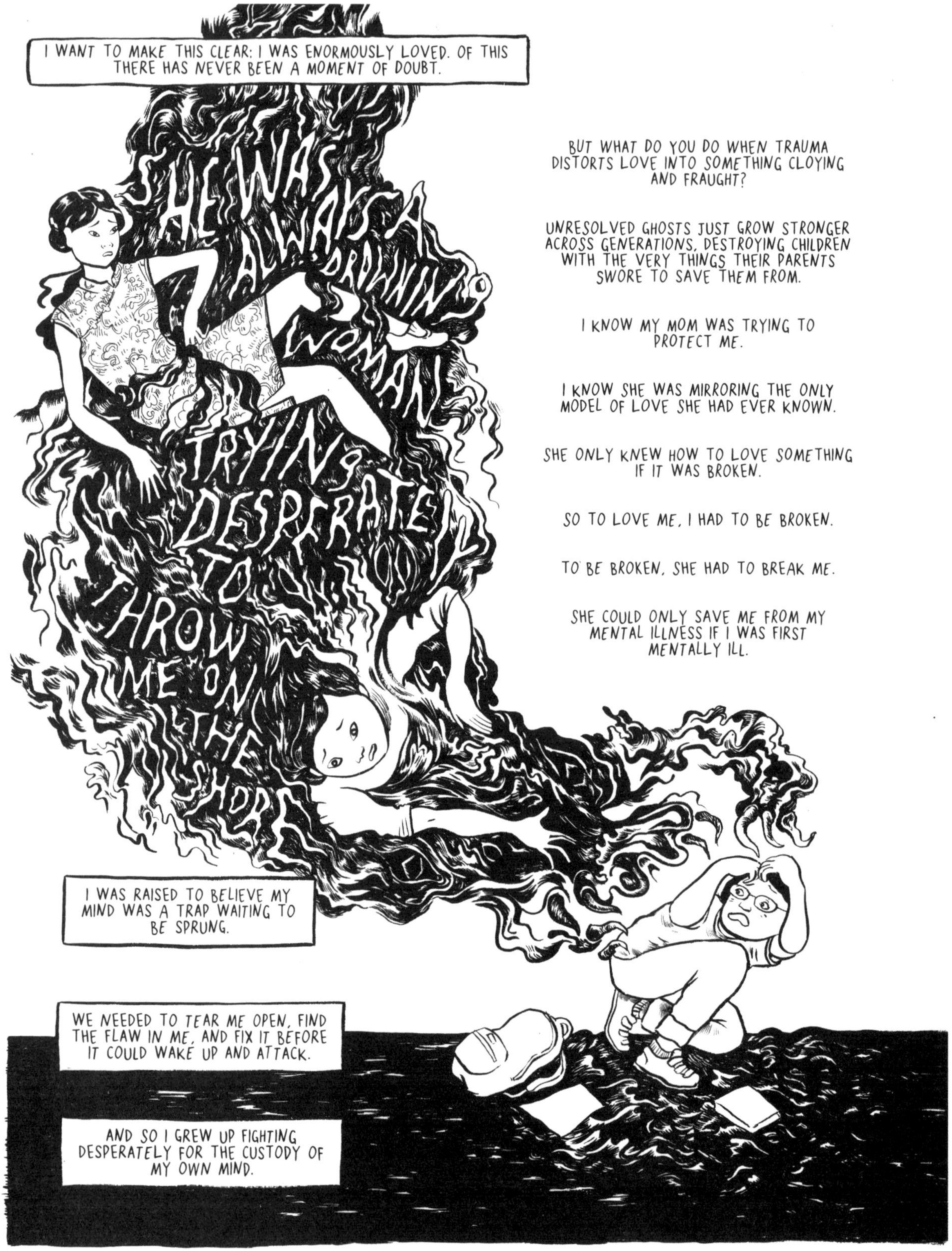
I WANT TO MAKE THIS CLEAR: I WAS ENORMOUSLY LOVED. OF THIS THERE HAS NEVER BEEN A MOMENT OF DOUBT.
SHE WAS ALWAYS A DROWNING WOMAN TRYING DESPERATELY TO THROW ME ON THE SHORE
BUT WHAT DO YOU DO WHEN TRAUMA DISTORTS LOVE INTO SOMETHING CLOYING AND FRAUGHT?
UNRESOLVED GHOSTS JUST GROW STRONGER ACROSS GENERATIONS, DESTROYING CHILDREN WITH THE VERY THINGS THEIR PARENTS SWORE TO SAVE THEM FROM.
I KNOW MY MOM WAS TRYING TO PROTECT ME.
I KNOW SHE WAS MIRRORING THE ONLY MODEL OF LOVE SHE HAD EVER KNOWN.
SHE ONLY KNEW HOW TO LOVE SOMETHING IF IT WAS BROKEN.
SO TO LOVE ME, I HAD TO BE BROKEN.
TO BE BROKEN, SHE HAD TO BREAK ME.
SHE COULD ONLY SAVE ME FROM MY MENTAL ILLNESS IF I WAS FIRST MENTALLY ILL.
I WAS RAISED TO BELIEVE MY MIND WAS A TRAP WAITING TO BE SPRUNG.
WE NEEDED TO TEAR ME OPEN, FIND THE FLAW IN ME, AND FIX IT BEFORE IT COULD WAKE UP AND ATTACK.
AND SO I GREW UP FIGHTING DESPERATELY FOR THE CUSTODY OF MY OWN MIND.

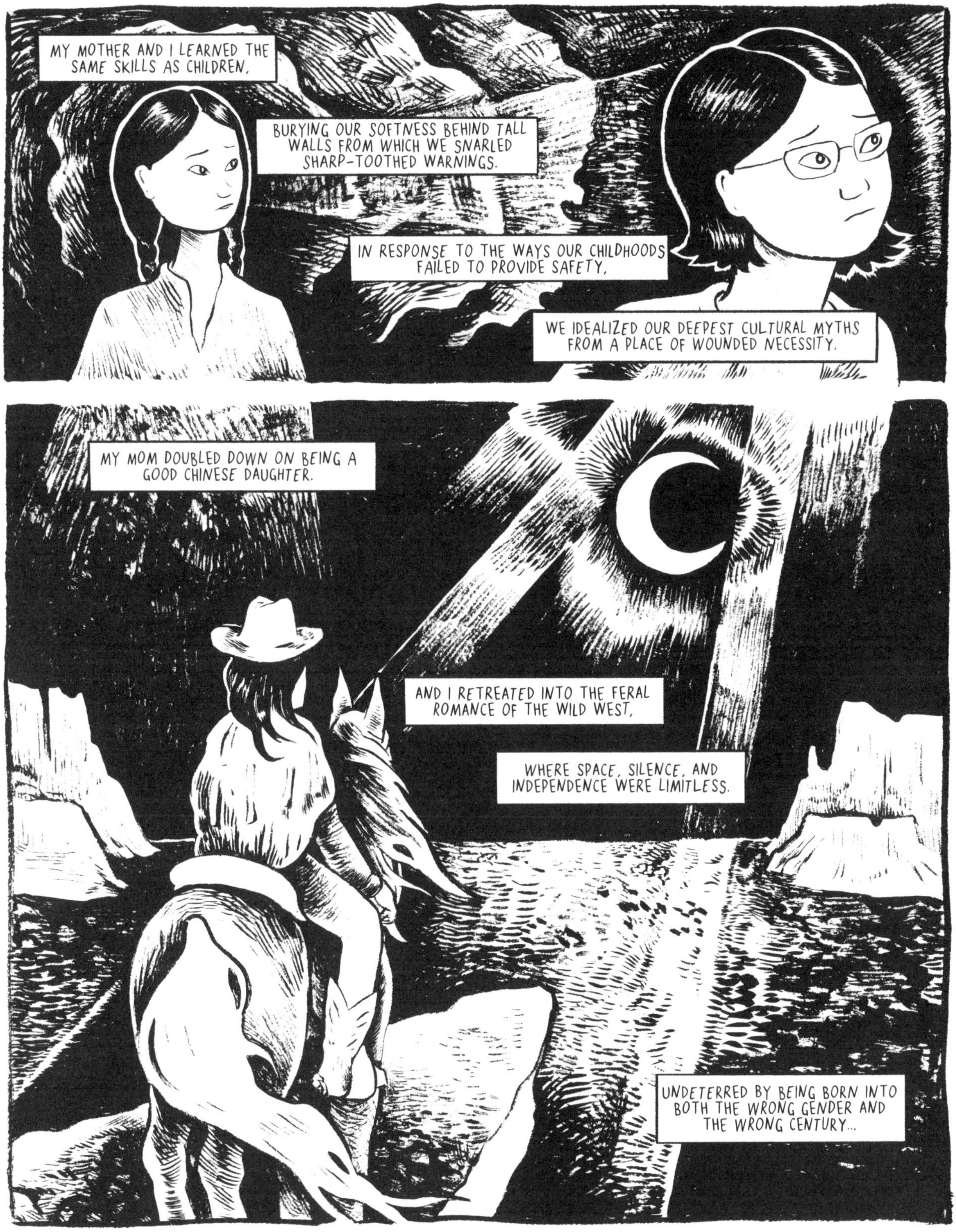
MY MOTHER AND I LEARNED THE SAME SKILLS AS CHILDREN,
BURYING OUR SOFTNESS BEHIND TALL WALLS FROM WHICH WE SNARLED SHARP-TOOTHED WARNINGS.
IN RESPONSE TO THE WAYS OUR CHILDHOODS FAILED TO PROVIDE SAFETY,
WE IDEALIZED OUR DEEPEST CULTURAL MYTHS FROM A PLACE OF WOUNDED NECESSITY.
MY MOM DOUBLED DOWN ON BEING A GOOD CHINESE DAUGHTER.
AND I RETREATED INTO THE FERAL ROMANCE OF THE WILD WEST,
WHERE SPACE, SILENCE, AND INDEPENDENCE WERE LIMITLESS.
UNDETERRED BY BEING BORN INTO BOTH THE WRONG GENDER AND THE WRONG CENTURY...

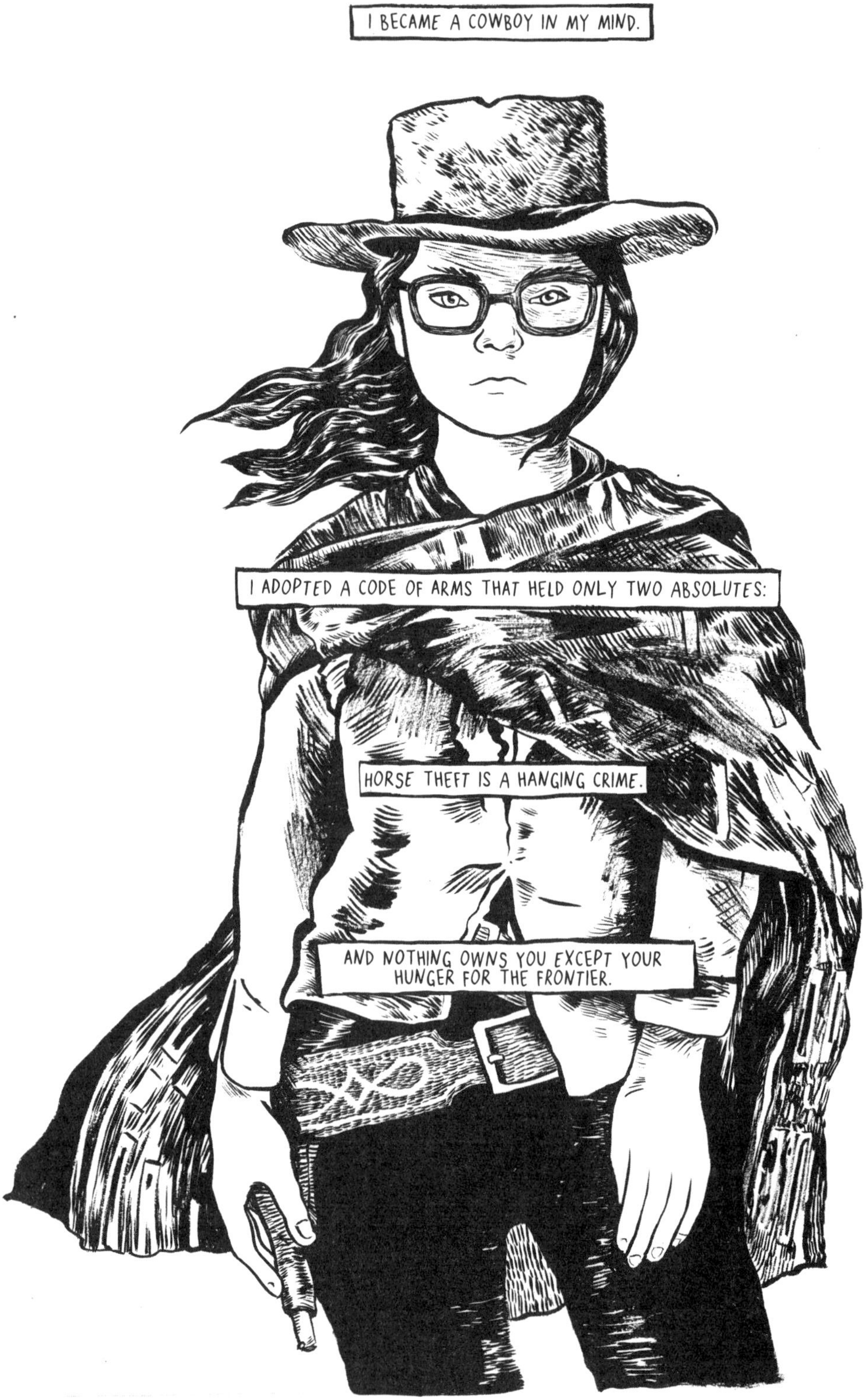
I BECAME A COWBOY IN MY MIND.
I ADOPTED A CODE OF ARMS THAT HELD ONLY TWO ABSOLUTES:
HORSE THEFT IS A HANGING CRIME.
AND NOTHING OWNS YOU EXCEPT YOUR HUNGER FOR THE FRONTIER.

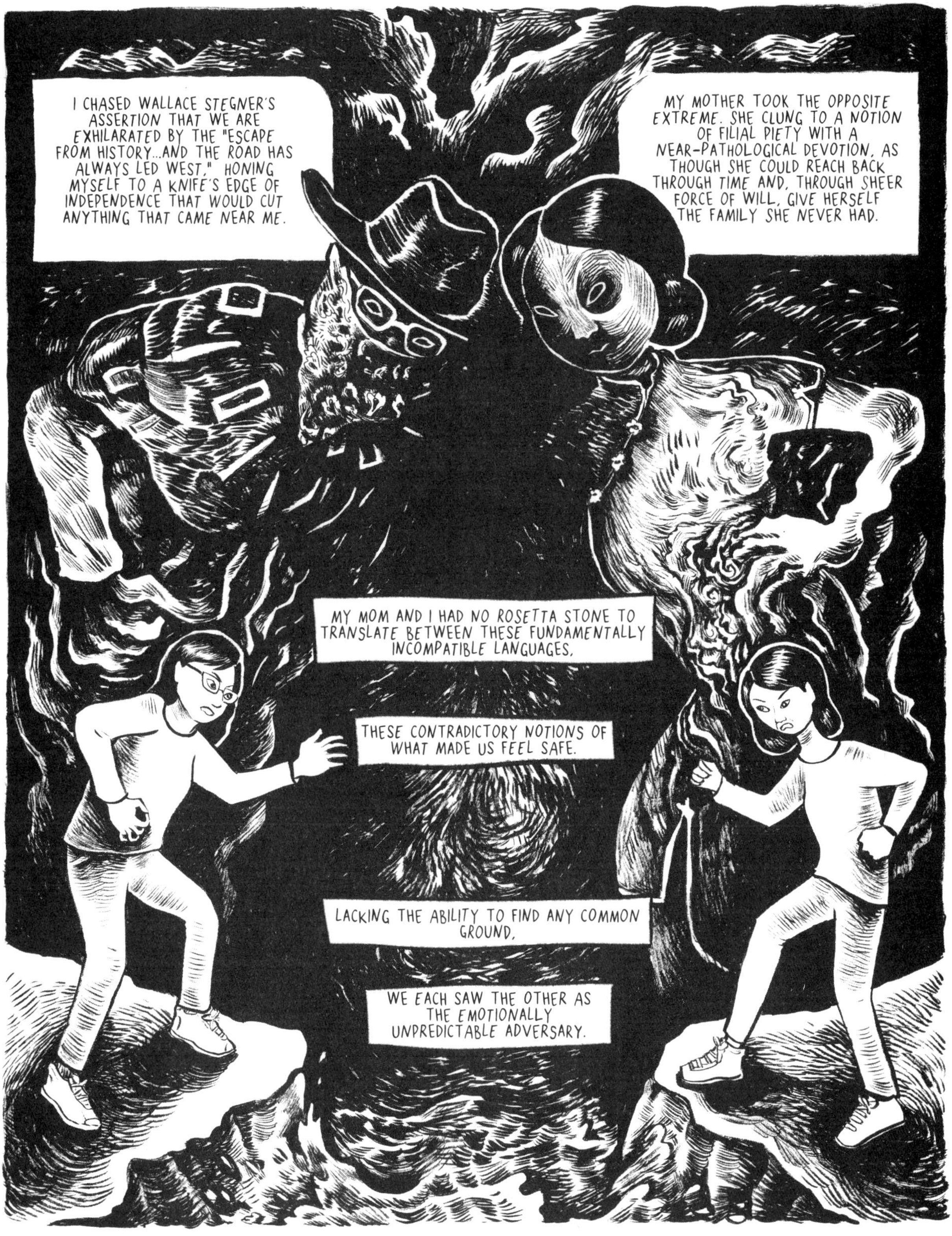
I CHASED WALLACE STEGNER'S ASSERTION THAT WE ARE EXHILARATED BY THE "ESCAPE FROM HISTORY...AND THE ROAD HAS ALWAYS LED WEST," HONING MYSELF TO A KNIFE'S EDGE OF INDEPENDENCE THAT WOULD CUT ANYTHING THAT CAME NEAR ME.
MY MOTHER TOOK THE OPPOSITE EXTREME. SHE CLUNG TO A NOTION OF FILIAL PIETY WITH A NEAR-PATHOLOGICAL DEVOTION, AS THOUGH SHE COULD REACH BACK THROUGH TIME AND, THROUGH SHEER FORCE OF WILL, GIVE HERSELF THE FAMILY SHE NEVER HAD.
MY MOM AND I HAD NO ROSETTA STONE TO TRANSLATE BETWEEN THESE FUNDAMENTALLY INCOMPATIBLE LANGUAGES,
THESE CONTRADICTORY NOTIONS OF WHAT MADE US FEEL SAFE.
LACKING THE ABILITY TO FIND ANY COMMON GROUND,
WE EACH SAW THE OTHER AS THE EMOTIONALLY UNPREDICTABLE ADVERSARY.

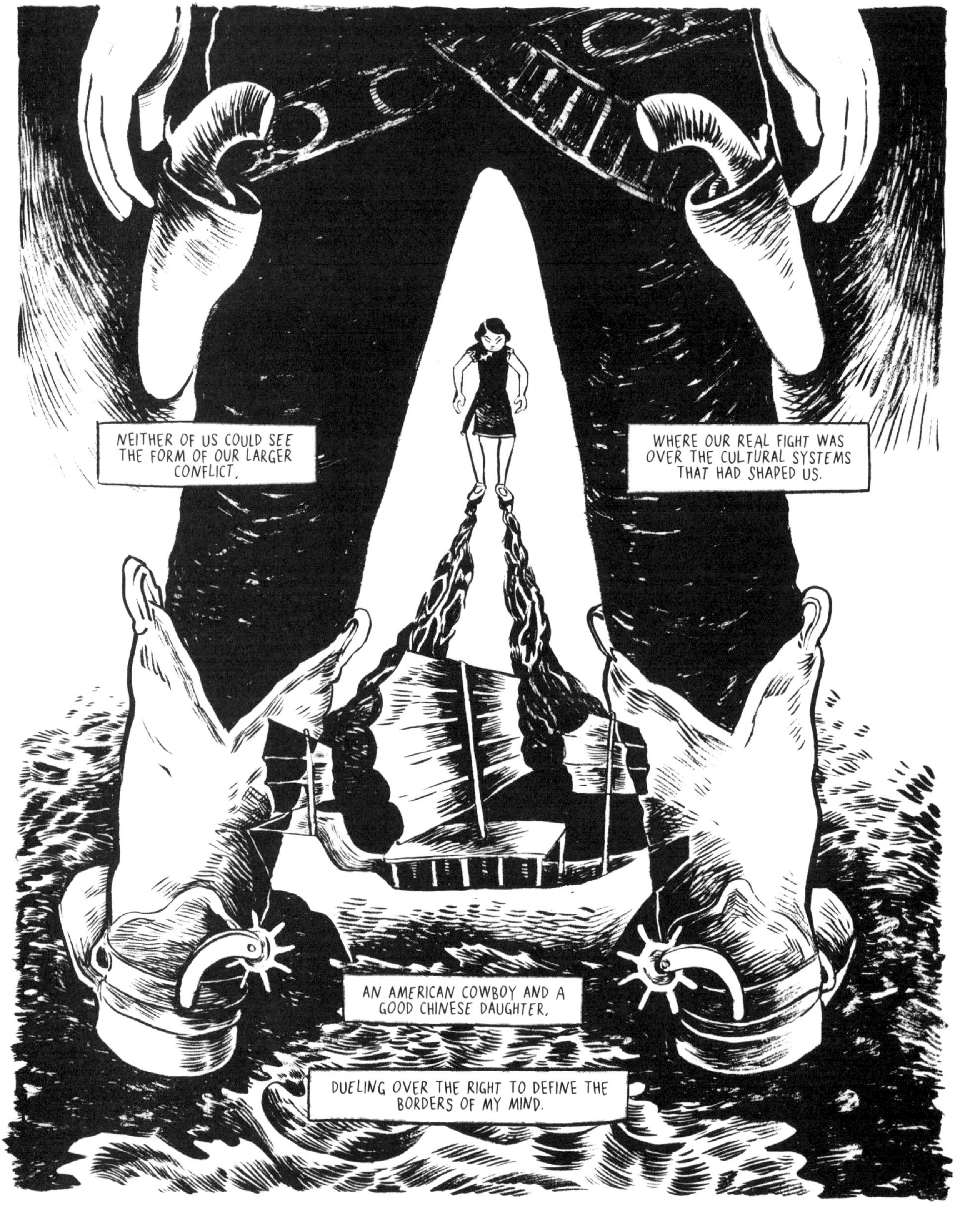
NEITHER OF US COULD SEE THE FORM OF OUR LARGER CONFLICT,
WHERE OUR REAL FIGHT WAS OVER THE CULTURAL SYSTEMS THAT HAD SHAPED US.
AN AMERICAN COWBOY AND A GOOD CHINESE DAUGHTER,
DUELING OVER THE RIGHT TO DEFINE THE BORDERS OF MY MIND.

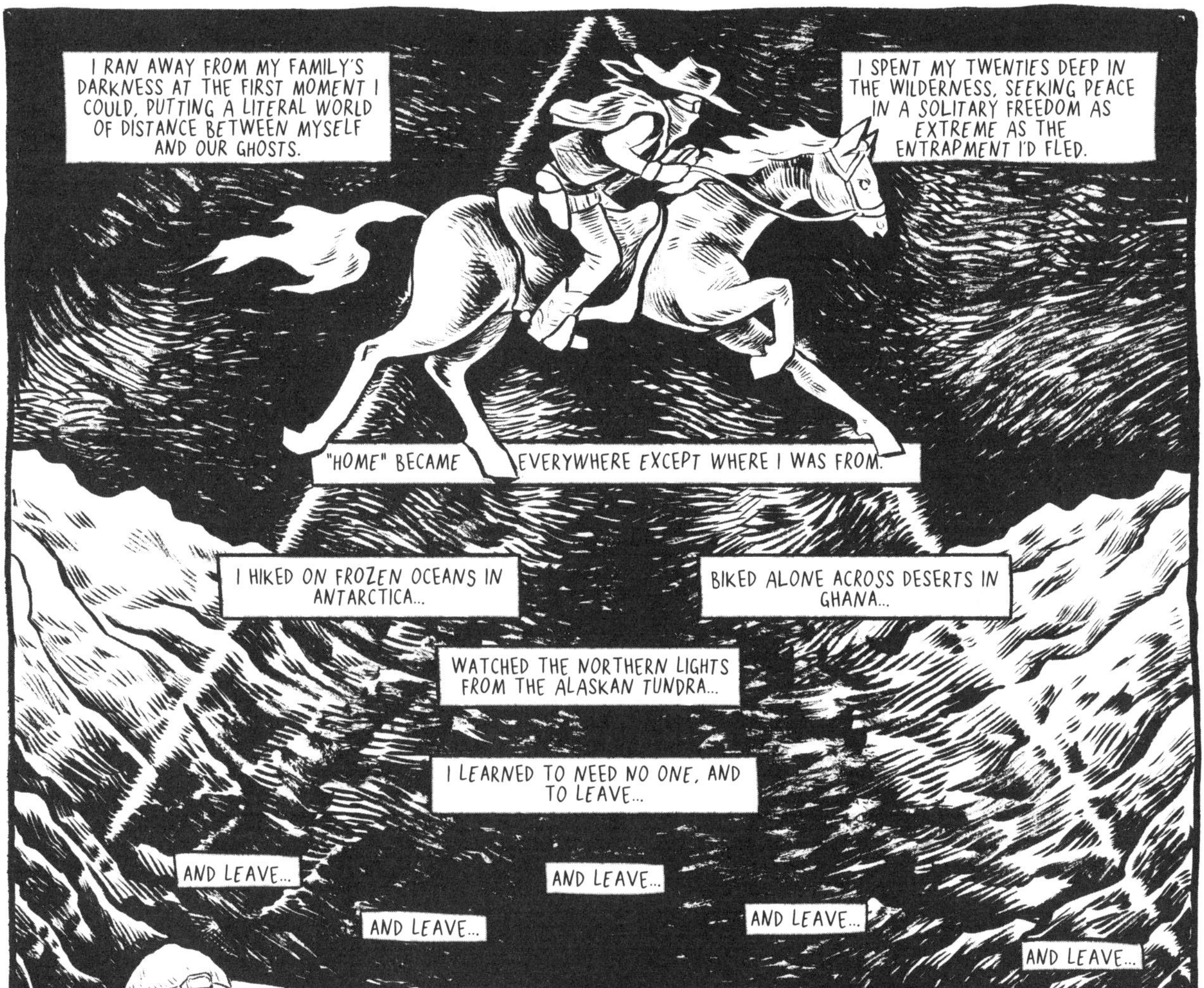
I RAN AWAY FROM MY FAMILY'S DARKNESS AT THE FIRST MOMENT I COULD, PUTTING A LITERAL WORLD OF DISTANCE BETWEEN MYSELF AND OUR GHOSTS.
I SPENT MY TWENTIES DEEP IN THE WILDERNESS, SEEKING PEACE IN A SOLITARY FREEDOM AS EXTREME AS THE ENTRAPMENT I'D FLED.
"HOME" BECAME
EVERYWHERE EXCEPT WHERE I WAS FROM.
I HIKED ON FROZEN OCEANS IN ANTARCTICA...
BIKED ALONE ACROSS DESERTS IN GHANA...
WATCHED THE NORTHERN LIGHTS FROM THE ALASKAN TUNDRA...
I LEARNED TO NEED NO ONE, AND TO LEAVE...
AND LEAVE...
AND LEAVE...
AND LEAVE...
AND LEAVE...
AND LEAVE...

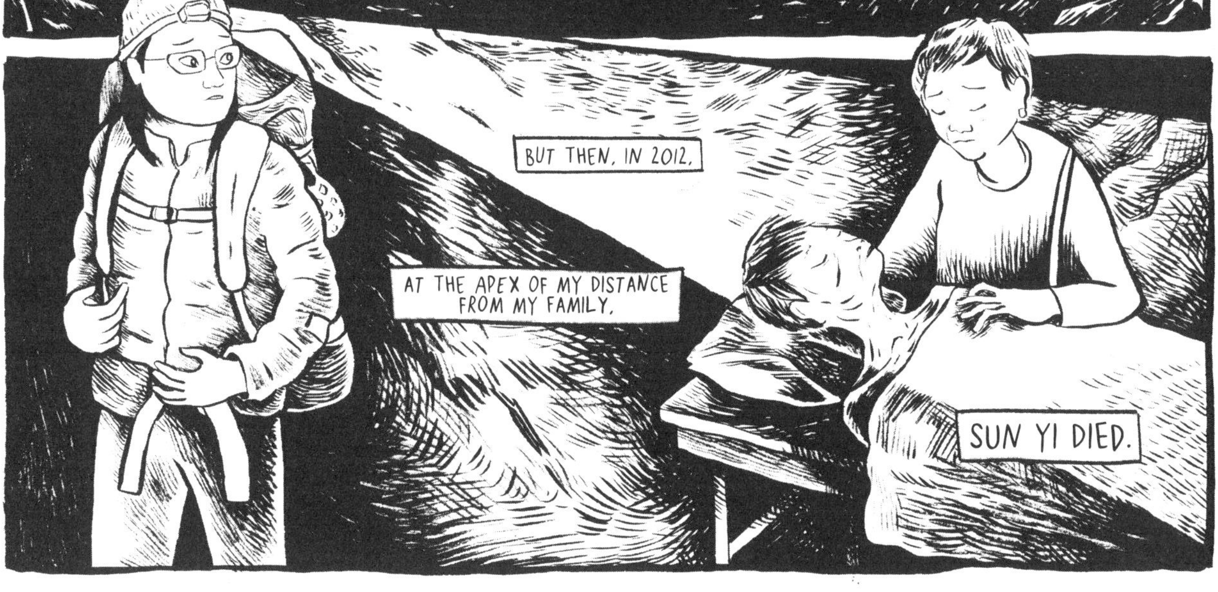
BUT THEN, IN 2012,
AT THE APEX OF MY DISTANCE FROM MY FAMILY,
SUN YI DIED.

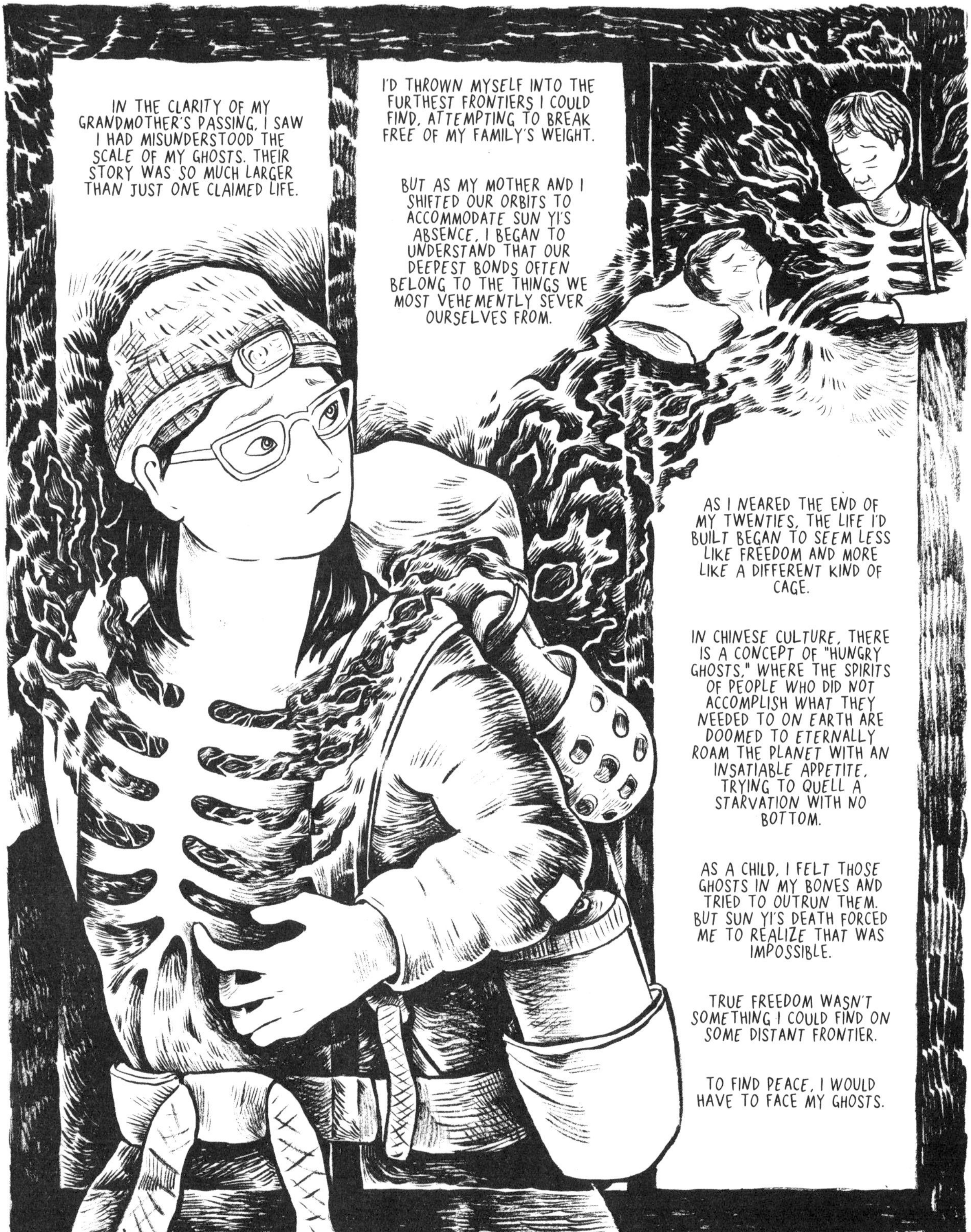
IN THE CLARITY OF MY GRANDMOTHER'S PASSING, I SAW I HAD MISUNDERSTOOD THE SCALE OF MY GHOSTS. THEIR STORY WAS SO MUCH LARGER THAN JUST ONE CLAIMED LIFE.
I'D THROWN MYSELF INTO THE FURTHEST FRONTIERS I COULD FIND, ATTEMPTING TO BREAK FREE OF MY FAMILY'S WEIGHT.
BUT AS MY MOTHER AND I SHIFTED OUR ORBITS TO ACCOMMODATE SUN YI'S ABSENCE, I BEGAN TO UNDERSTAND THAT OUR DEEPEST BONDS OFTEN BELONG TO THE THINGS WE MOST VEHEMENTLY SEVER OURSELVES FROM.
AS I NEARED THE END OF MY TWENTIES, THE LIFE I'D BUILT BEGAN TO SEEM LESS LIKE FREEDOM AND MORE LIKE A DIFFERENT KIND OF CAGE.
IN CHINESE CULTURE, THERE IS A CONCEPT OF "HUNGRY GHOSTS," WHERE THE SPIRITS OF PEOPLE WHO DID NOT ACCOMPLISH WHAT THEY NEEDED TO ON EARTH ARE DOOMED TO ETERNALLY ROAM THE PLANET WITH AN INSATIABLE APPETITE, TRYING TO QUELL A STARVATION WITH NO BOTTOM.
AS A CHILD, I FELT THOSE GHOSTS IN MY BONES AND TRIED TO OUTRUN THEM. BUT SUN YI'S DEATH FORCED ME TO REALIZE THAT WAS IMPOSSIBLE.
TRUE FREEDOM WASN'T SOMETHING I COULD FIND ON SOME DISTANT FRONTIER.
TO FIND PEACE, I WOULD HAVE TO FACE MY GHOSTS.

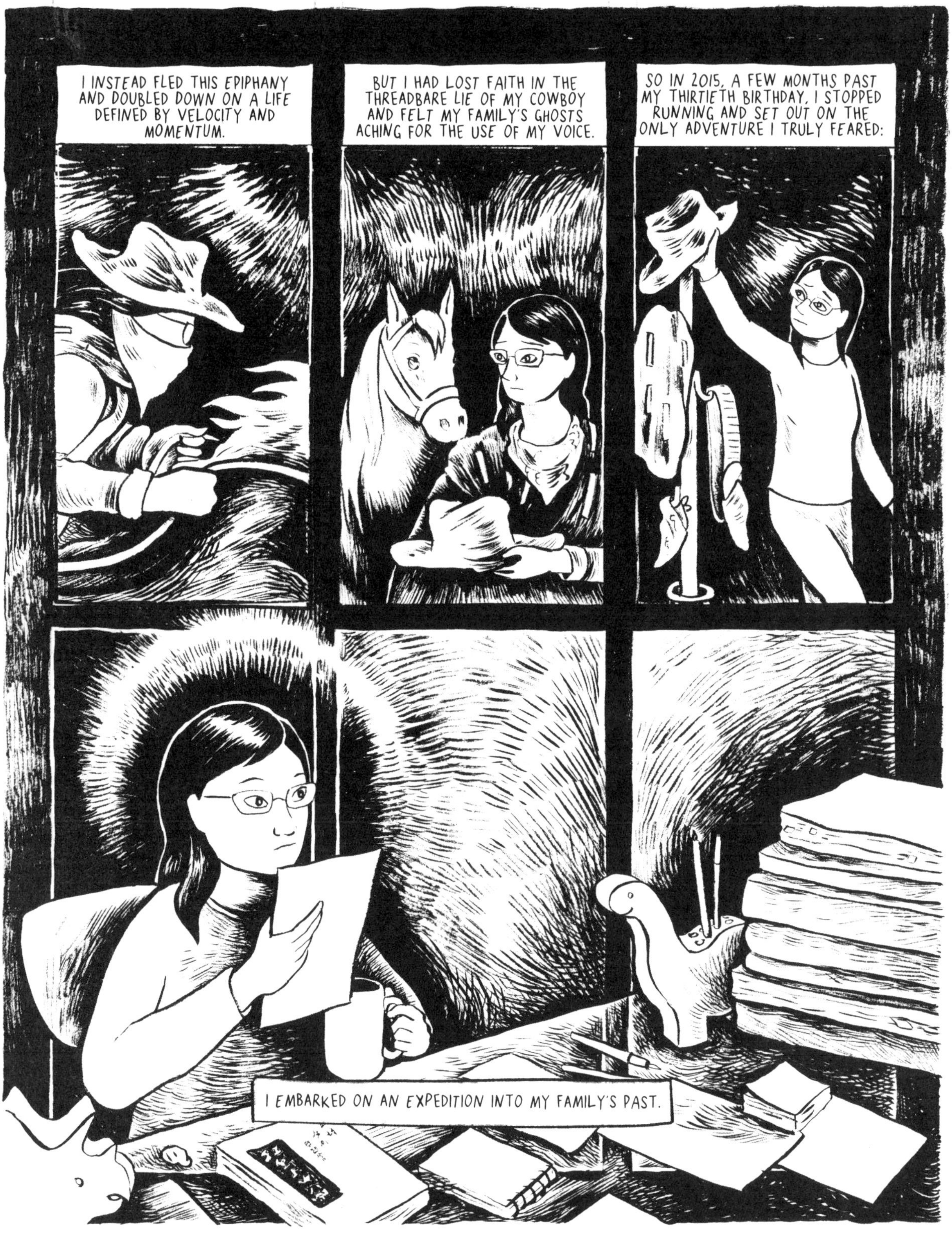
I INSTEAD FLED THIS EPIPHANY AND DOUBLED DOWN ON A LIFE DEFINED BY VELOCITY AND MOMENTUM.
BUT I HAD LOST FAITH IN THE THREADBARE LIE OF MY COWBOY AND FELT MY FAMILY'S GHOSTS ACHING FOR THE USE OF MY VOICE.
SO IN 2015, A FEW MONTHS PAST MY THIRTIETH BIRTHDAY, I STOPPED RUNNING AND SET OUT ON THE ONLY ADVENTURE I TRULY FEARED:
I EMBARKED ON AN EXPEDITION INTO MY FAMILY'S PAST.

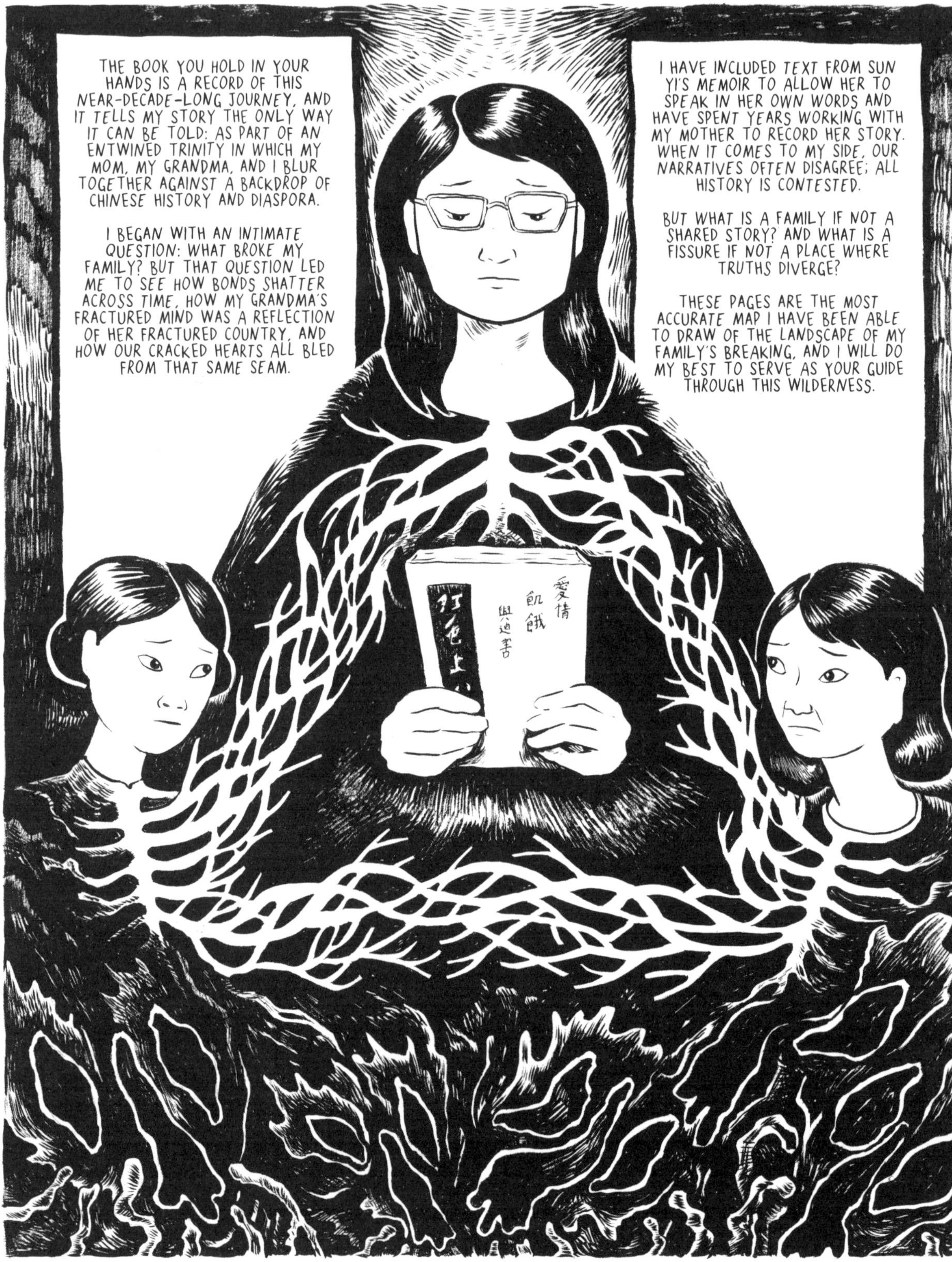
THE BOOK YOU HOLD IN YOUR HANDS IS A RECORD OF THIS NEAR-DECADE-LONG JOURNEY, AND IT TELLS MY STORY THE ONLY WAY IT CAN BE TOLD: AS PART OF AN ENTWINED TRINITY IN WHICH MY MOM, MY GRANDMA, AND I BLUR TOGETHER AGAINST A BACKDROP OF CHINESE HISTORY AND DIASPORA.
I BEGAN WITH AN INTIMATE QUESTION: WHAT BROKE MY FAMILY? BUT THAT QUESTION LED ME TO SEE HOW BONDS SHATTER ACROSS TIME, HOW MY GRANDMA'S FRACTURED MIND WAS A REFLECTION OF HER FRACTURED COUNTRY, AND HOW OUR CRACKED HEARTS ALL BLED FROM THAT SAME SEAM.
I HAVE INCLUDED TEXT FROM SUN YI'S MEMOIR TO ALLOW HER TO SPEAK IN HER OWN WORDS AND HAVE SPENT YEARS WORKING WITH MY MOTHER TO RECORD HER STORY. WHEN IT COMES TO MY SIDE, OUR NARRATIVES OFTEN DISAGREE; ALL HISTORY IS CONTESTED.
BUT WHAT IS A FAMILY IF NOT A SHARED STORY? AND WHAT IS A FISSURE IF NOT A PLACE WHERE TRUTHS DIVERGE?
THESE PAGES ARE THE MOST ACCURATE MAP I HAVE BEEN ABLE TO DRAW OF THE LANDSCAPE OF MY FAMILY'S BREAKING, AND I WILL DO MY BEST TO SERVE AS YOUR GUIDE THROUGH THIS WILDERNESS.
愛情
飢餓
與迫害

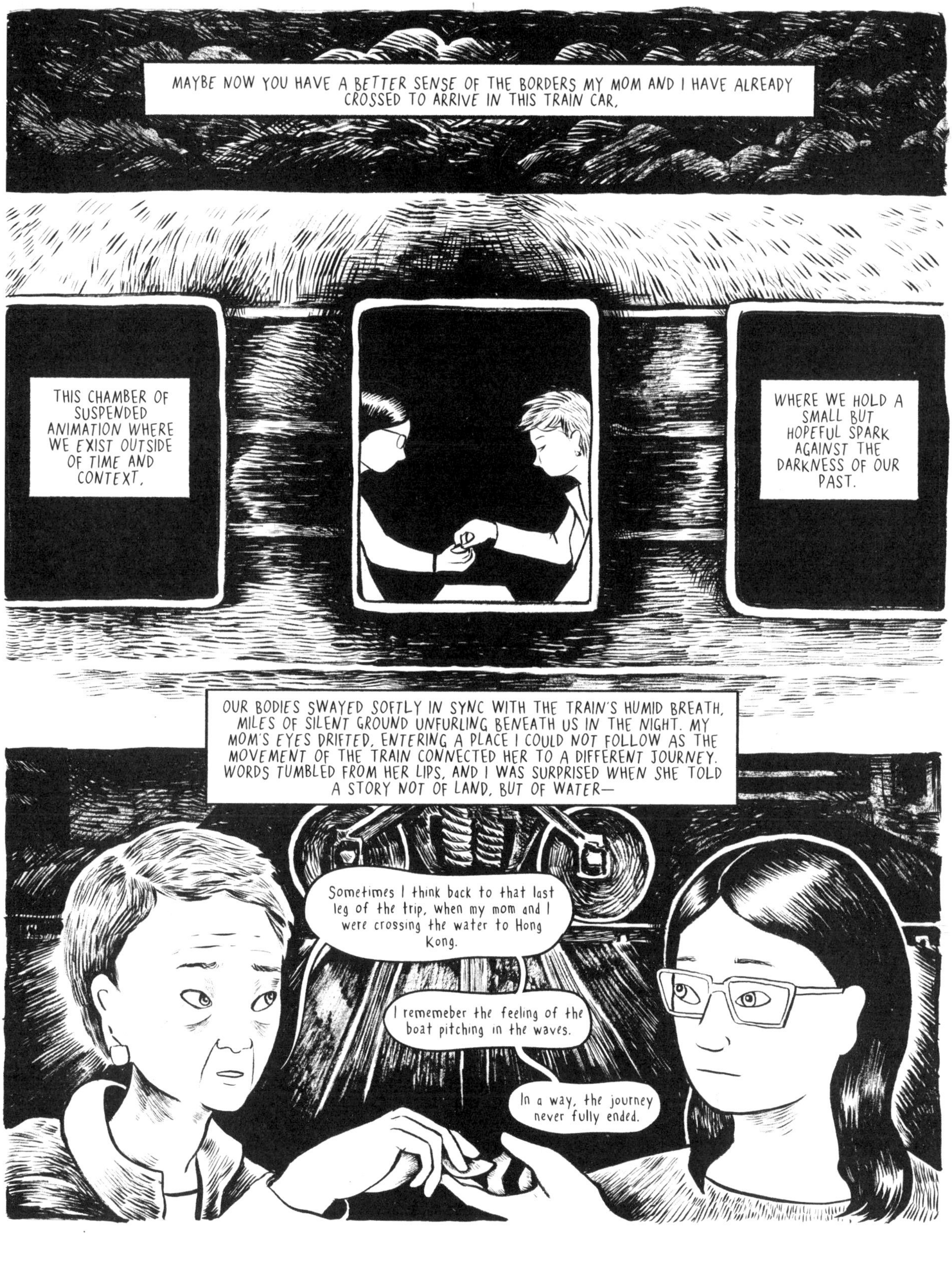
MAYBE NOW YOU HAVE A BETTER SENSE OF THE BORDERS MY MOM AND I HAVE ALREADY CROSSED TO ARRIVE IN THIS TRAIN CAR,
THIS CHAMBER OF SUSPENDED ANIMATION WHERE WE EXIST OUTSIDE OF TIME AND CONTEXT,
WHERE WE HOLD A SMALL BUT HOPEFUL SPARK AGAINST THE DARKNESS OF OUR PAST.
OUR BODIES SWAYED SOFTLY IN SYNC WITH THE TRAIN'S HUMID BREATH, MILES OF SILENT GROUND UNFURLING BENEATH US IN THE NIGHT. MY MOM'S EYES DRIFTED, ENTERING A PLACE I COULD NOT FOLLOW AS THE MOVEMENT OF THE TRAIN CONNECTED HER TO A DIFFERENT JOURNEY. WORDS TUMBLED FROM HER LIPS, AND I WAS SURPRISED WHEN SHE TOLD A STORY NOT OF LAND, BUT OF WATER—
Sometimes I think back to that last leg of the trip, when my mom and I were crossing the water to Hong Kong.
I rememeber the feeling of the boat pitching in the waves.
In a way, the journey never fully ended.

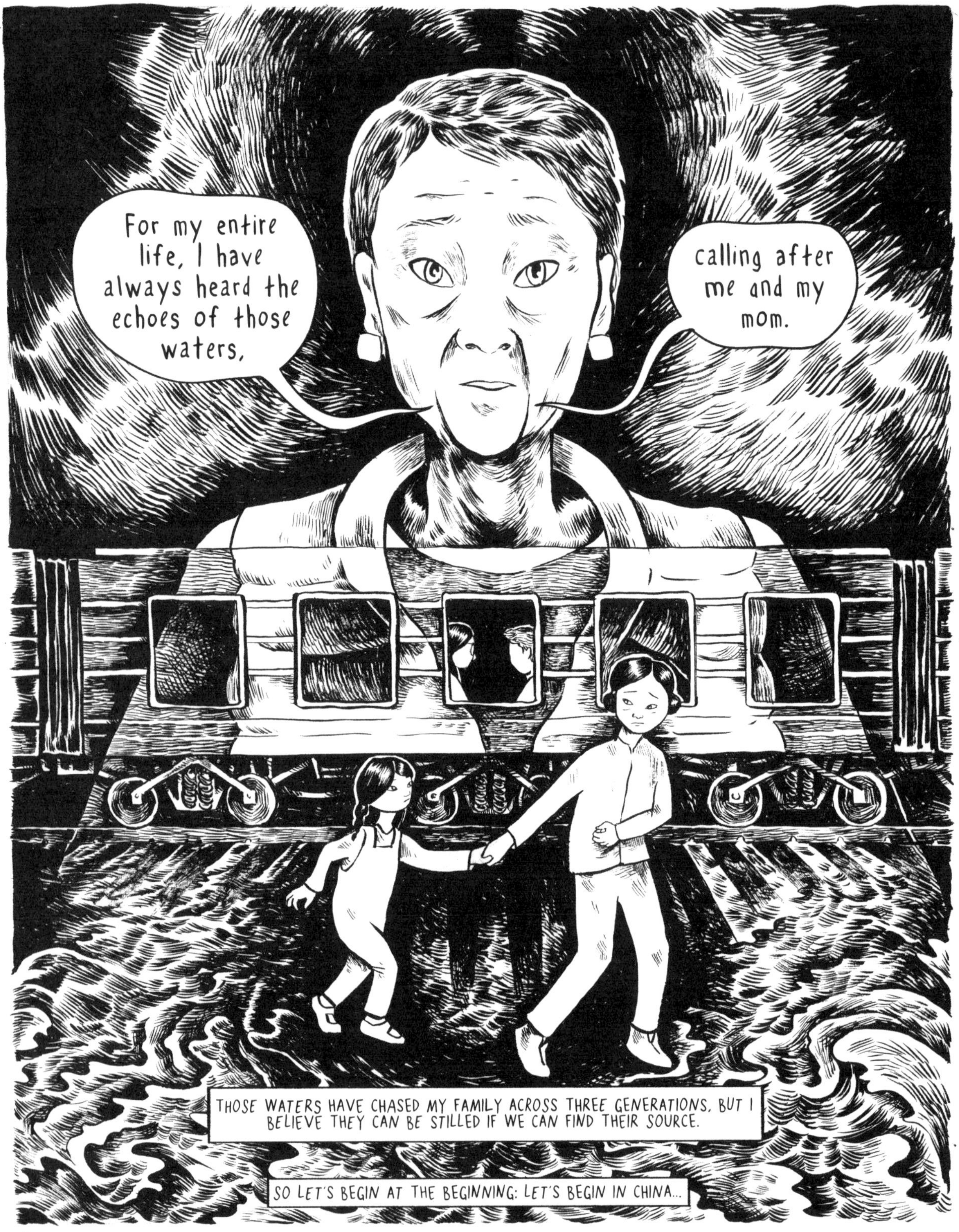
For my entire life, I have always heard the echoes of those waters,
calling after me and my mom.
THOSE WATERS HAVE CHASED MY FAMILY ACROSS THREE GENERATIONS, BUT I BELIEVE THEY CAN BE STILLED IF WE CAN FIND THEIR SOURCE.
SO LET'S BEGIN AT THE BEGINNING: LET'S BEGIN IN CHINA...

PART 1

DIVING INTO THE WRECK

Suzhou • 1927–1948

I came to explore the wreck.
The words are purposes.
The words are maps.
I came to see the damage that was done
and the treasures that prevail.
—ADRIENNE RICH, "Diving into the Wreck"

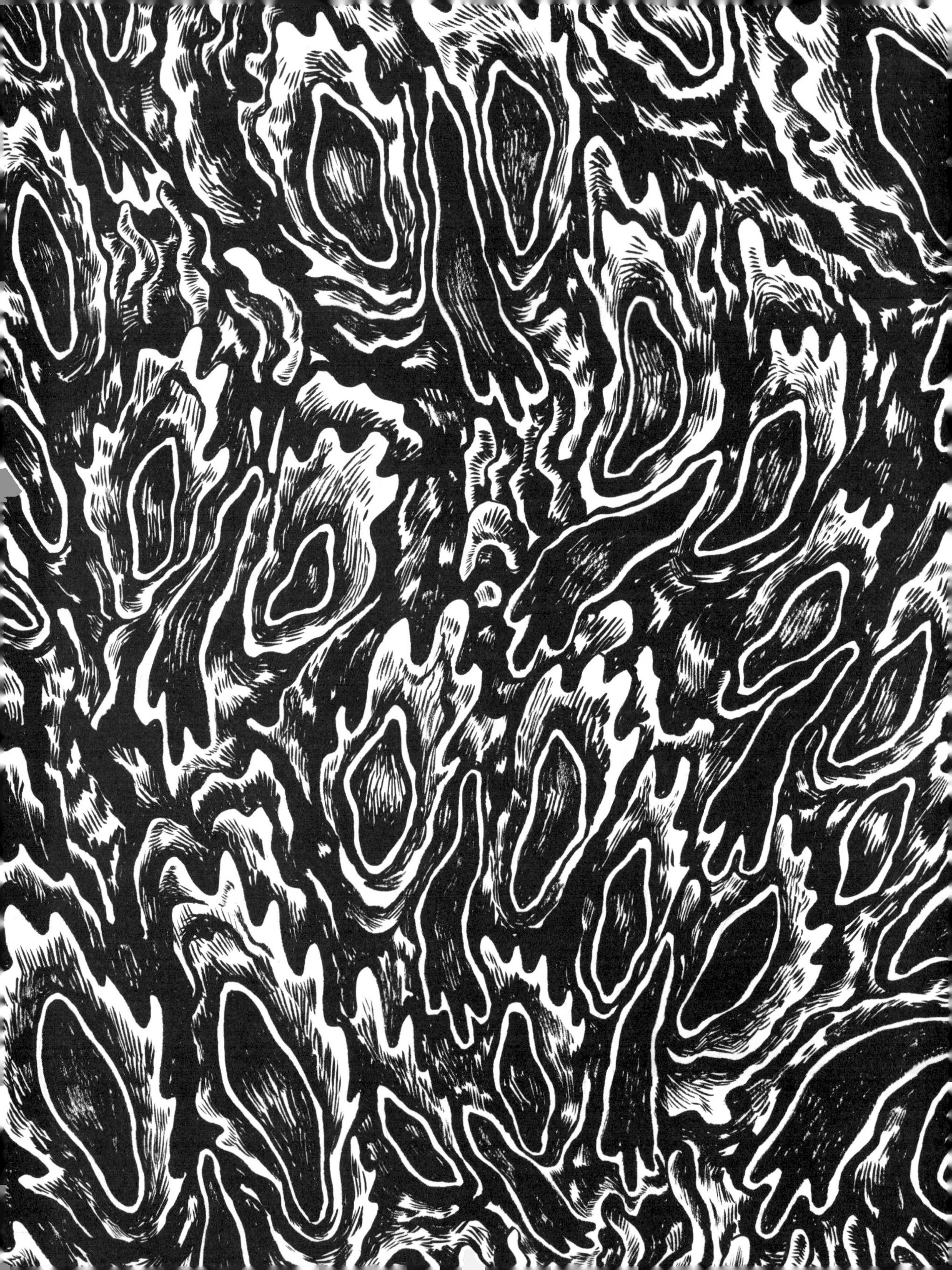

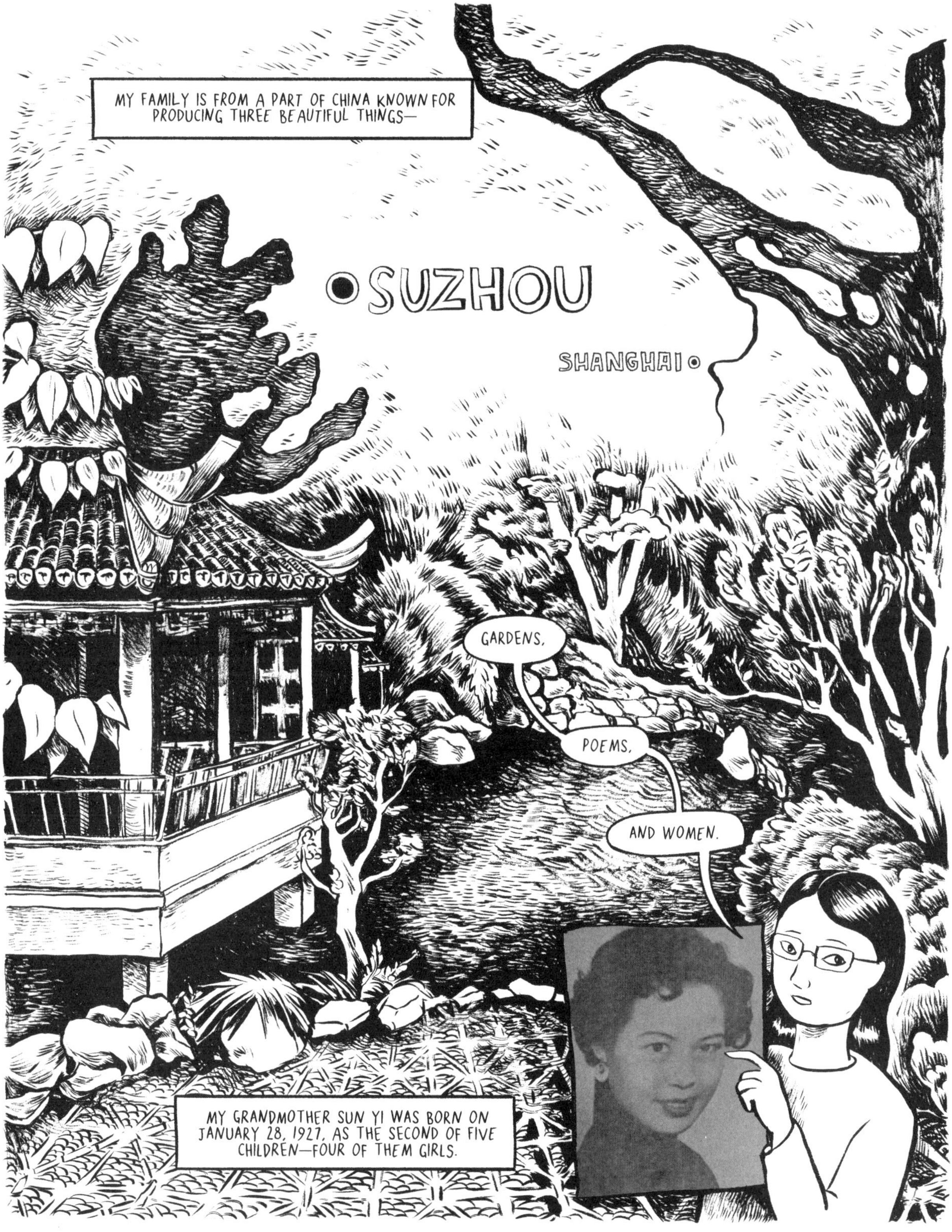
MY FAMILY IS FROM A PART OF CHINA KNOWN FOR PRODUCING THREE BEAUTIFUL THINGS—
SUZHOU
SHANGHAI
GARDENS,
POEMS,
AND WOMEN.
MY GRANDMOTHER SUN YI WAS BORN ON JANUARY 28, 1927, AS THE SECOND OF FIVE CHILDREN—FOUR OF THEM GIRLS.

THE ONLY BOY WAS BORN LAST, A VICTORY PRECEDED BY FOUR FAILURES.

THIS BIRTH ORDER IS IMPORTANT IN EXPLAINING WHY MY FAMILY MADE THE HIGHLY UNUSUAL CHOICE TO EDUCATE THE GIRLS.

OLDEST to YOUNGEST

TO PUT IT BLUNTLY—

"The Chinese girl when she makes her first appearance in the world is very likely to be unwelcome."

VILLAGE LIFE IN CHINA: A STUDY IN SOCIOLOGY, 1889

AS MY MOM IS ALWAYS QUICK TO REMIND ME—

You Americans have no idea what a sexist society really is.

In Chinese culture, girls are worthless. At meals, all the best food would be saved only for the boys.

My friends? Their parents would tell them, "Oh, you're just a girl."

BOYS WERE PRECIOUS TREASURES WHOSE WIVES WOULD EVENTUALLY SERVE THEIR IN-LAWS' FAMILIES.

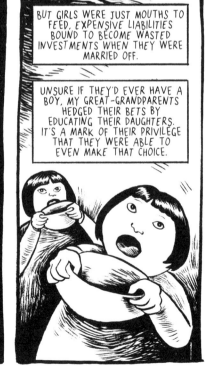

BUT GIRLS WERE JUST MOUTHS TO FEED, EXPENSIVE LIABILITIES BOUND TO BECOME WASTED INVESTMENTS WHEN THEY WERE MARRIED OFF.

UNSURE IF THEY'D EVER HAVE A BOY, MY GREAT-GRANDPARENTS HEDGED THEIR BETS BY EDUCATING THEIR DAUGHTERS. IT'S A MARK OF THEIR PRIVILEGE THAT THEY WERE ABLE TO EVEN MAKE THAT CHOICE.

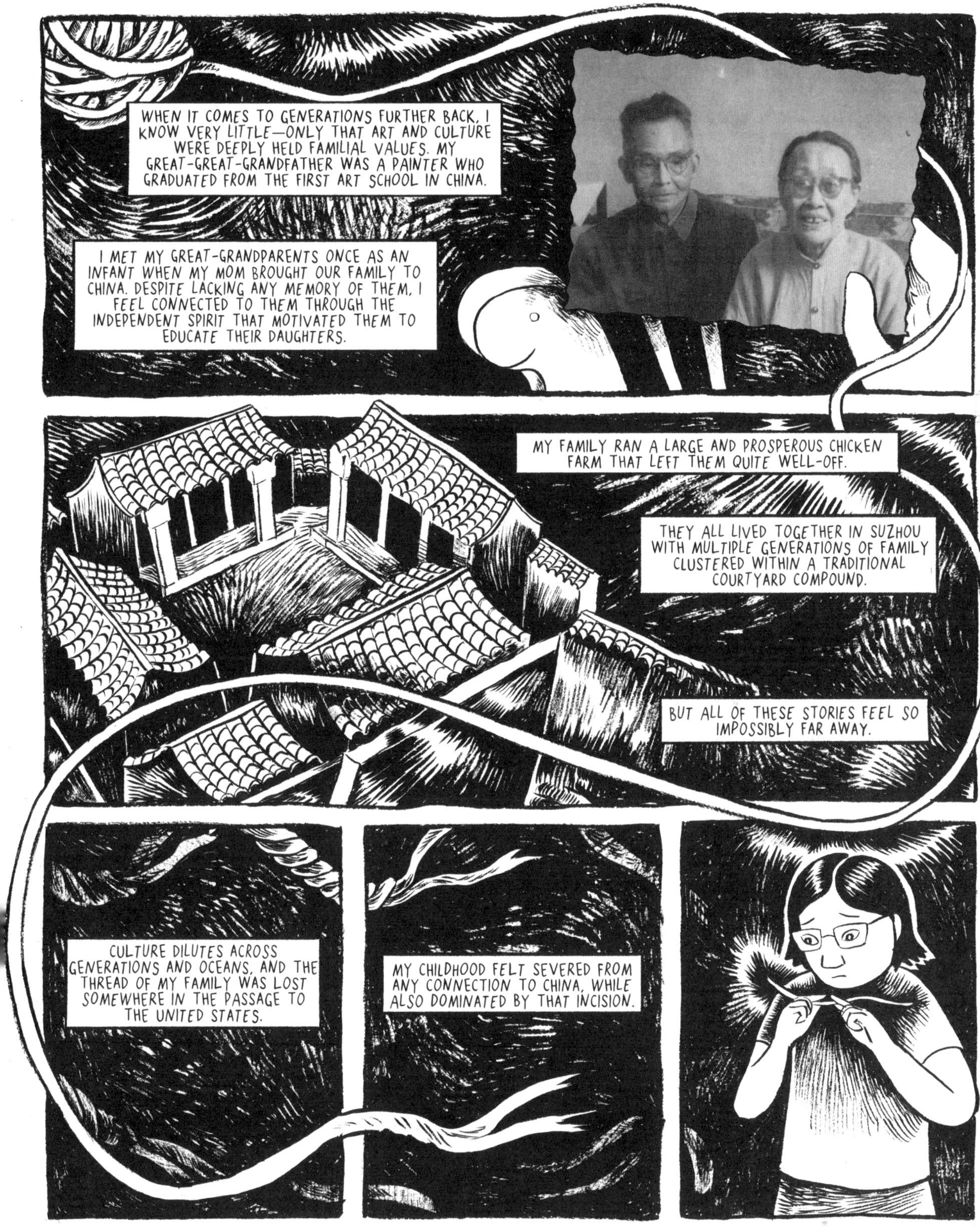
WHEN IT COMES TO GENERATIONS FURTHER BACK, I KNOW VERY LITTLE—ONLY THAT ART AND CULTURE WERE DEEPLY HELD FAMILIAL VALUES. MY GREAT-GREAT-GRANDFATHER WAS A PAINTER WHO GRADUATED FROM THE FIRST ART SCHOOL IN CHINA.
I MET MY GREAT-GRANDPARENTS ONCE AS AN INFANT WHEN MY MOM BROUGHT OUR FAMILY TO CHINA. DESPITE LACKING ANY MEMORY OF THEM, I FEEL CONNECTED TO THEM THROUGH THE INDEPENDENT SPIRIT THAT MOTIVATED THEM TO EDUCATE THEIR DAUGHTERS.
MY FAMILY RAN A LARGE AND PROSPEROUS CHICKEN FARM THAT LEFT THEM QUITE WELL-OFF.
THEY ALL LIVED TOGETHER IN SUZHOU WITH MULTIPLE GENERATIONS OF FAMILY CLUSTERED WITHIN A TRADITIONAL COURTYARD COMPOUND.
BUT ALL OF THESE STORIES FEEL SO IMPOSSIBLY FAR AWAY.
CULTURE DILUTES ACROSS GENERATIONS AND OCEANS, AND THE THREAD OF MY FAMILY WAS LOST SOMEWHERE IN THE PASSAGE TO THE UNITED STATES.
MY CHILDHOOD FELT SEVERED FROM ANY CONNECTION TO CHINA, WHILE ALSO DOMINATED BY THAT INCISION.

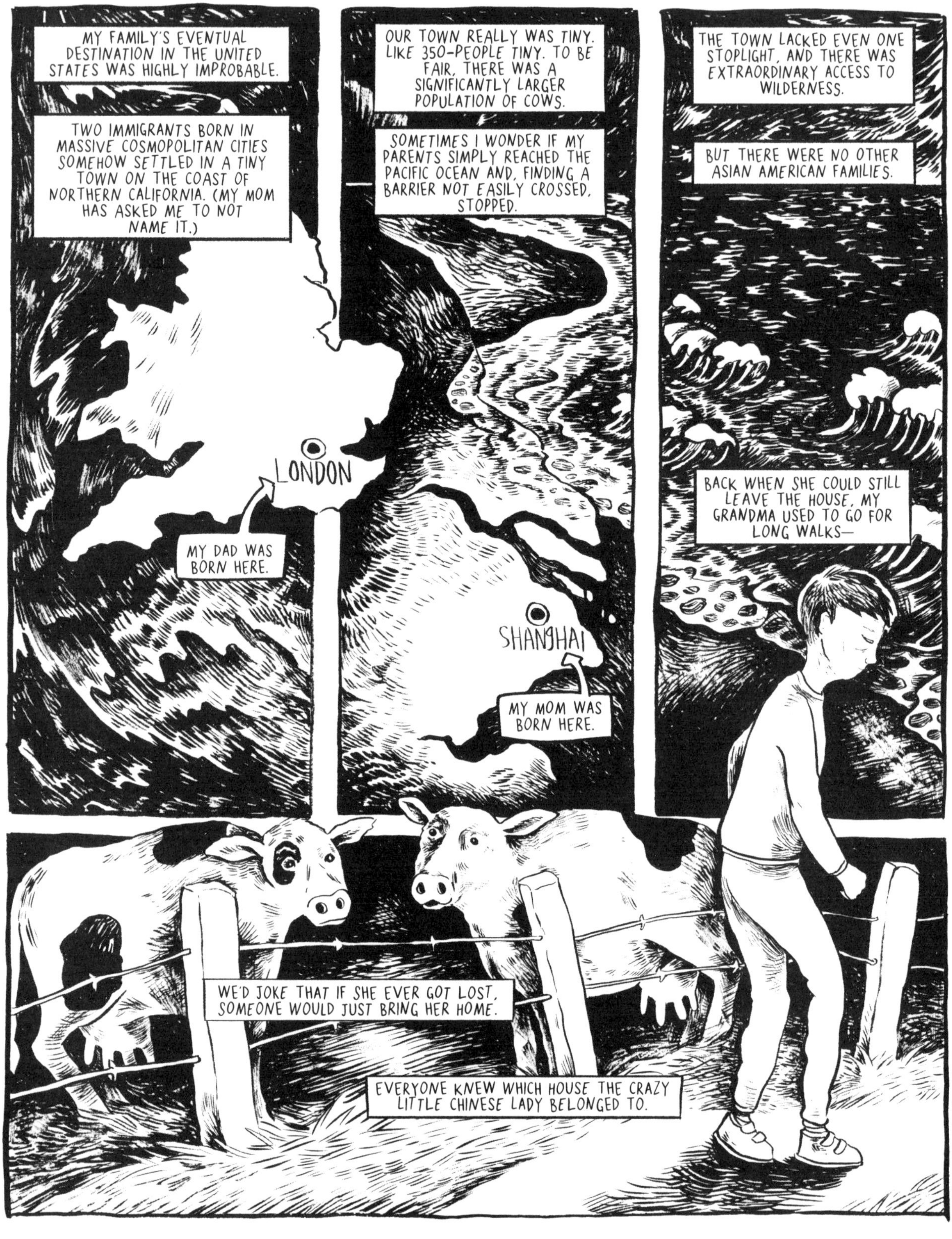
MY FAMILY'S EVENTUAL DESTINATION IN THE UNITED STATES WAS HIGHLY IMPROBABLE.
TWO IMMIGRANTS BORN IN MASSIVE COSMOPOLITAN CITIES SOMEHOW SETTLED IN A TINY TOWN ON THE COAST OF NORTHERN CALIFORNIA. (MY MOM HAS ASKED ME TO NOT NAME IT.)
LONDON
MY DAD WAS BORN HERE.
OUR TOWN REALLY WAS TINY. LIKE 350-PEOPLE TINY. TO BE FAIR, THERE WAS A SIGNIFICANTLY LARGER POPULATION OF COWS.
SOMETIMES I WONDER IF MY PARENTS SIMPLY REACHED THE PACIFIC OCEAN AND, FINDING A BARRIER NOT EASILY CROSSED, STOPPED.
SHANGHAI
MY MOM WAS BORN HERE.
THE TOWN LACKED EVEN ONE STOPLIGHT, AND THERE WAS EXTRAORDINARY ACCESS TO WILDERNESS.
BUT THERE WERE NO OTHER ASIAN AMERICAN FAMILIES.
BACK WHEN SHE COULD STILL LEAVE THE HOUSE, MY GRANDMA USED TO GO FOR LONG WALKS—
WE'D JOKE THAT IF SHE EVER GOT LOST, SOMEONE WOULD JUST BRING HER HOME.
EVERYONE KNEW WHICH HOUSE THE CRAZY LITTLE CHINESE LADY BELONGED TO.

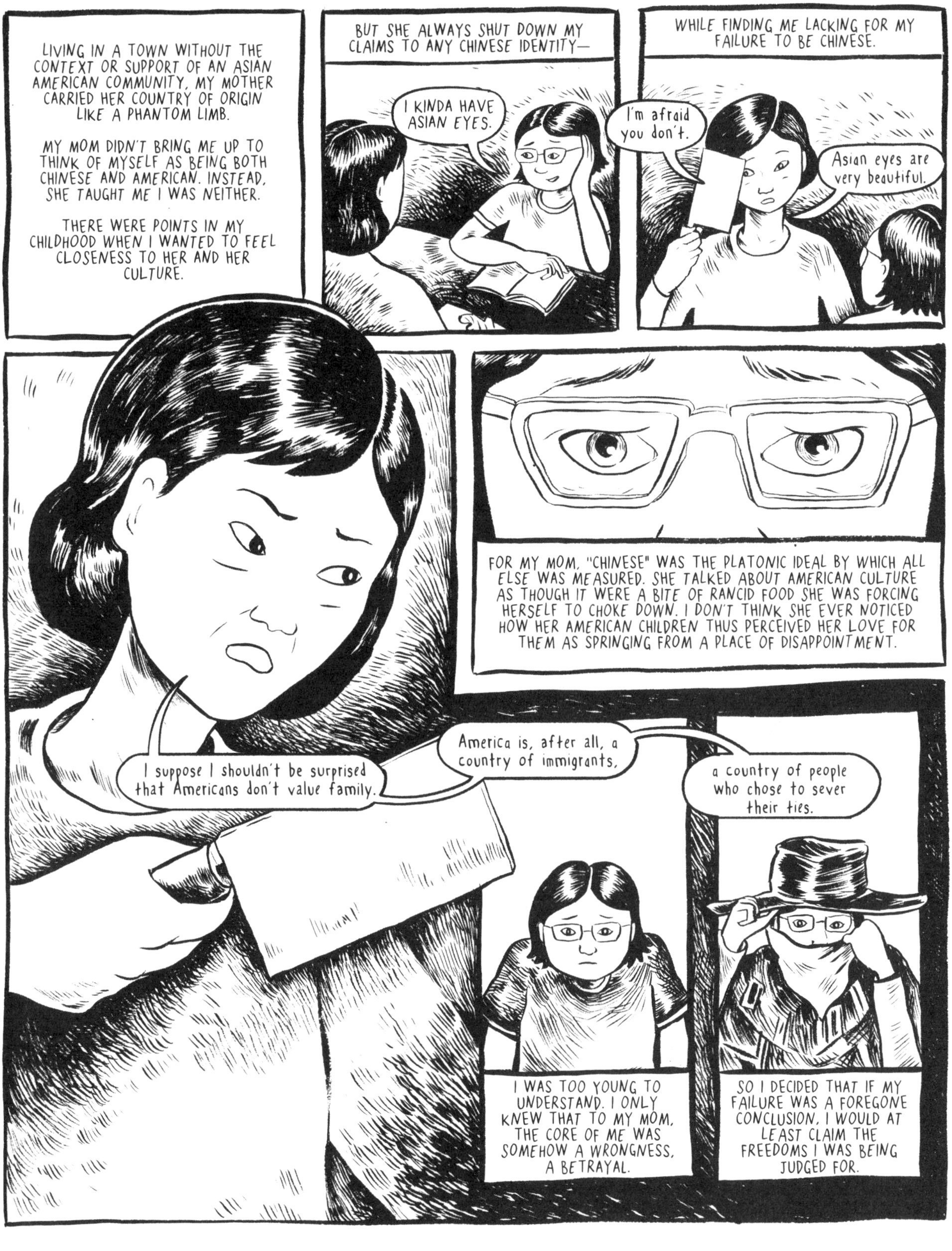
LIVING IN A TOWN WITHOUT THE CONTEXT OR SUPPORT OF AN ASIAN AMERICAN COMMUNITY, MY MOTHER CARRIED HER COUNTRY OF ORIGIN LIKE A PHANTOM LIMB.
MY MOM DIDN'T BRING ME UP TO THINK OF MYSELF AS BEING BOTH CHINESE AND AMERICAN. INSTEAD, SHE TAUGHT ME I WAS NEITHER.
THERE WERE POINTS IN MY CHILDHOOD WHEN I WANTED TO FEEL CLOSENESS TO HER AND HER CULTURE.
BUT SHE ALWAYS SHUT DOWN MY CLAIMS TO ANY CHINESE IDENTITY—
I KINDA HAVE ASIAN EYES.
WHILE FINDING ME LACKING FOR MY FAILURE TO BE CHINESE.
I'm afraid you don't.
Asian eyes are very beautiful.
FOR MY MOM, "CHINESE" WAS THE PLATONIC IDEAL BY WHICH ALL ELSE WAS MEASURED. SHE TALKED ABOUT AMERICAN CULTURE AS THOUGH IT WERE A BITE OF RANCID FOOD SHE WAS FORCING HERSELF TO CHOKE DOWN. I DON'T THINK SHE EVER NOTICED HOW HER AMERICAN CHILDREN THUS PERCEIVED HER LOVE FOR THEM AS SPRINGING FROM A PLACE OF DISAPPOINTMENT.
I suppose I shouldn't be surprised that Americans don't value family.
America is, after all, a country of immigrants,
a country of people who chose to sever their ties.
I WAS TOO YOUNG TO UNDERSTAND. I ONLY KNEW THAT TO MY MOM, THE CORE OF ME WAS SOMEHOW A WRONGNESS, A BETRAYAL.
SO I DECIDED THAT IF MY FAILURE WAS A FOREGONE CONCLUSION, I WOULD AT LEAST CLAIM THE FREEDOMS I WAS BEING JUDGED FOR.

MY FAMILY CONFOUNDED EASY CATEGORIZATION, AND WHEN FRIENDS WOULD COME OVER FOR THE FIRST TIME, I'D WATCH A FAMILIAR PROCESS OF RECLASSIFICATION UNFURL.

YEAH, MY DAD IS FROM ENGLAND.

AND MY MOM IS FROM CHINA.

AS THE STORY OF MY FAMILY...

MY GRANDMA LIVES WITH US.

COLLIDED WITH THE REALITY.

我很緊張 <I AM NERVOUS>

你很安全 <YOU ARE SAFE>

Soon.

Supper's not ready yet?

THICK BRITISH ACCENT

THANKS TO THE GENETICS OF MY UNKNOWN SWISS GRANDPA, I WAS A LARGELY SECRET ASIAN. PEOPLE WOULD VIEW MY APPEARANCE THROUGH THE LENS OF THEIR NEW ASIAN DATA POINTS AND STRUGGLE WITH THE DISCONNECT.

WOK
+2 ASIAN

WEIRD MEAT
(GIBLETS)
+4 ASIAN

ANXIOUS CHINESE GRANDMA
+50 ASIAN

FACE-SIZED GINGER HUNK
+3 ASIAN

DRAGON BOWLS
+2 ASIAN

TESSA'S FACE
???

MANDFIN FFFDU
ASIAN

UNUSUAL NOTES
+10 ASIAN

RECALCULATING

CLEAVER
+5 ASIAN

INDUSTRIAL RICE COOKER

WHITE PARENT HAS HEAVIER ACCENT
??????

ALL NAMED BRITISH POLITICIANS

NOTHING ABOUT ME HAD CHANGED,

BUT THEY NO LONGER KNEW HOW TO CATEGORIZE ME.

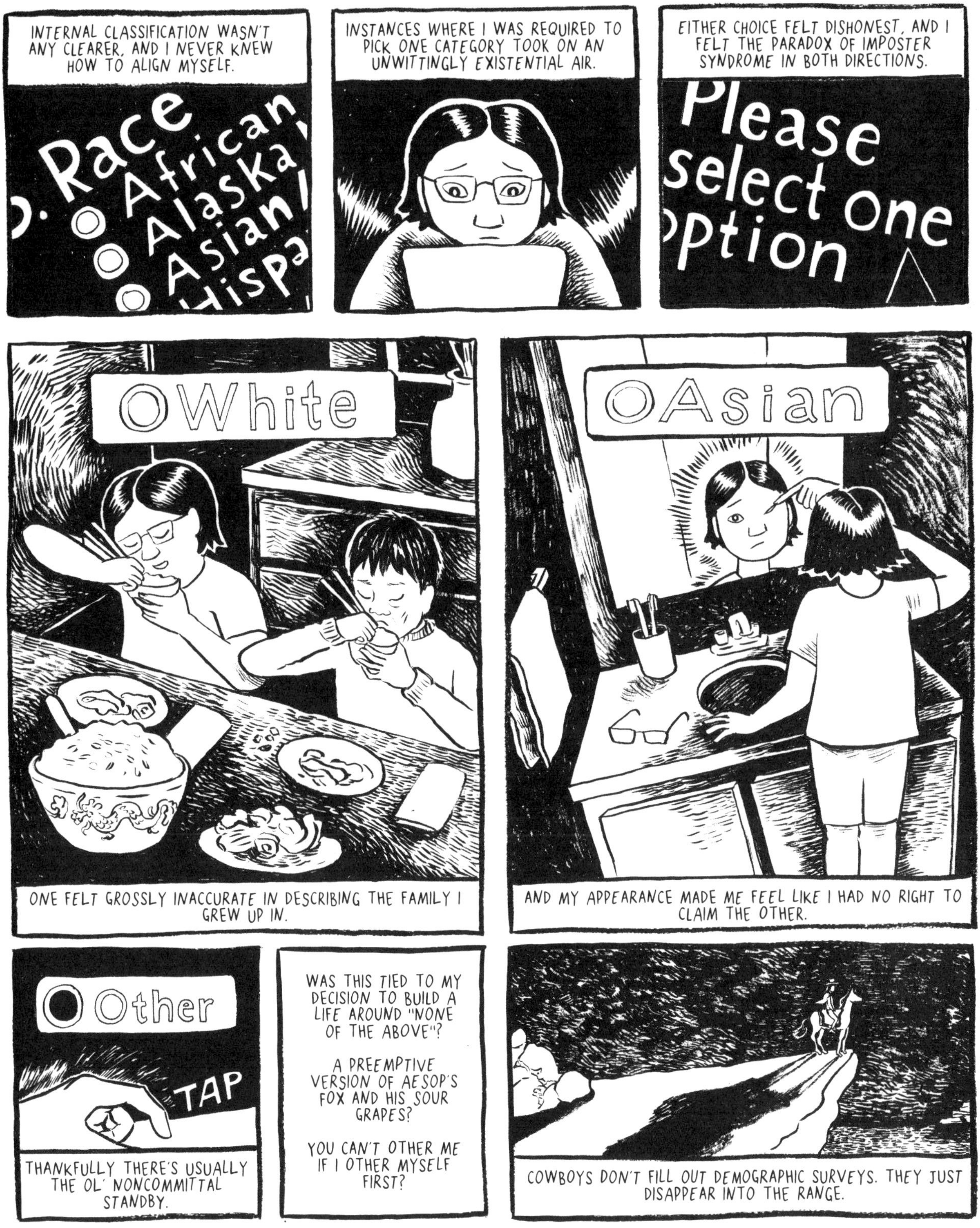
INTERNAL CLASSIFICATION WASN'T ANY CLEARER, AND I NEVER KNEW HOW TO ALIGN MYSELF.
Race
African
Alaska
Asian
Hispa
INSTANCES WHERE I WAS REQUIRED TO PICK ONE CATEGORY TOOK ON AN UNWITTINGLY EXISTENTIAL AIR.
EITHER CHOICE FELT DISHONEST, AND I FELT THE PARADOX OF IMPOSTER SYNDROME IN BOTH DIRECTIONS.
Please select one option
White
ONE FELT GROSSLY INACCURATE IN DESCRIBING THE FAMILY I GREW UP IN.
Asian
AND MY APPEARANCE MADE ME FEEL LIKE I HAD NO RIGHT TO CLAIM THE OTHER.
Other
TAP
THANKFULLY THERE'S USUALLY THE OL' NONCOMMITTAL STANDBY.
WAS THIS TIED TO MY DECISION TO BUILD A LIFE AROUND "NONE OF THE ABOVE"?
A PREEMPTIVE VERSION OF AESOP'S FOX AND HIS SOUR GRAPES?
YOU CAN'T OTHER ME IF I OTHER MYSELF FIRST?
COWBOYS DON'T FILL OUT DEMOGRAPHIC SURVEYS. THEY JUST DISAPPEAR INTO THE RANGE.

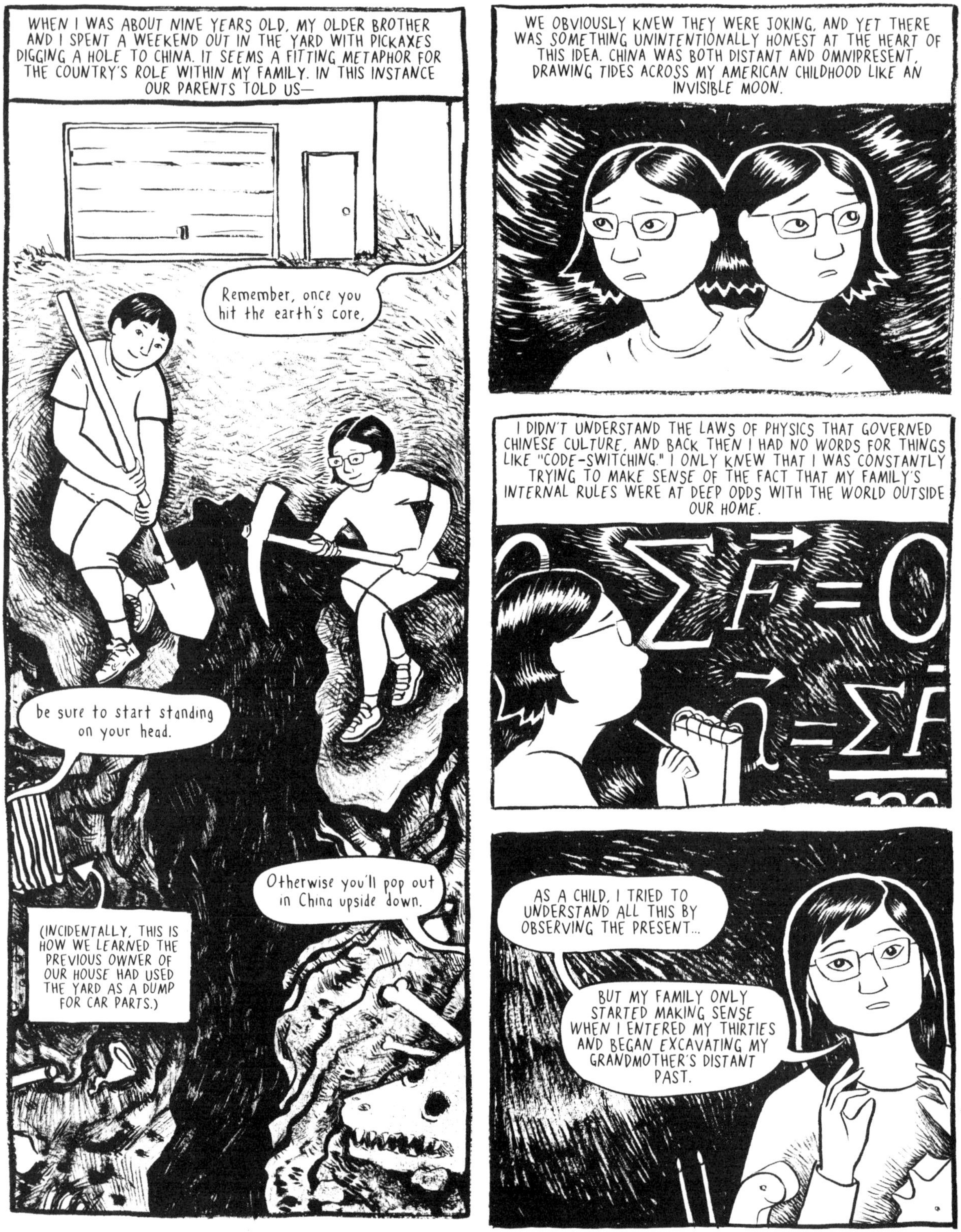
WHEN I WAS ABOUT NINE YEARS OLD, MY OLDER BROTHER AND I SPENT A WEEKEND OUT IN THE YARD WITH PICKAXES DIGGING A HOLE TO CHINA. IT SEEMS A FITTING METAPHOR FOR THE COUNTRY'S ROLE WITHIN MY FAMILY. IN THIS INSTANCE OUR PARENTS TOLD US—
Remember, once you hit the earth's core,
be sure to start standing on your head.
Otherwise you'll pop out in China upside down.
(INCIDENTALLY, THIS IS HOW WE LEARNED THE PREVIOUS OWNER OF OUR HOUSE HAD USED THE YARD AS A DUMP FOR CAR PARTS.)
WE OBVIOUSLY KNEW THEY WERE JOKING, AND YET THERE WAS SOMETHING UNINTENTIONALLY HONEST AT THE HEART OF THIS IDEA. CHINA WAS BOTH DISTANT AND OMNIPRESENT, DRAWING TIDES ACROSS MY AMERICAN CHILDHOOD LIKE AN INVISIBLE MOON.
I DIDN'T UNDERSTAND THE LAWS OF PHYSICS THAT GOVERNED CHINESE CULTURE, AND BACK THEN I HAD NO WORDS FOR THINGS LIKE "CODE-SWITCHING." I ONLY KNEW THAT I WAS CONSTANTLY TRYING TO MAKE SENSE OF THE FACT THAT MY FAMILY'S INTERNAL RULES WERE AT DEEP ODDS WITH THE WORLD OUTSIDE OUR HOME.
AS A CHILD, I TRIED TO UNDERSTAND ALL THIS BY OBSERVING THE PRESENT...
BUT MY FAMILY ONLY STARTED MAKING SENSE WHEN I ENTERED MY THIRTIES AND BEGAN EXCAVATING MY GRANDMOTHER'S DISTANT PAST.

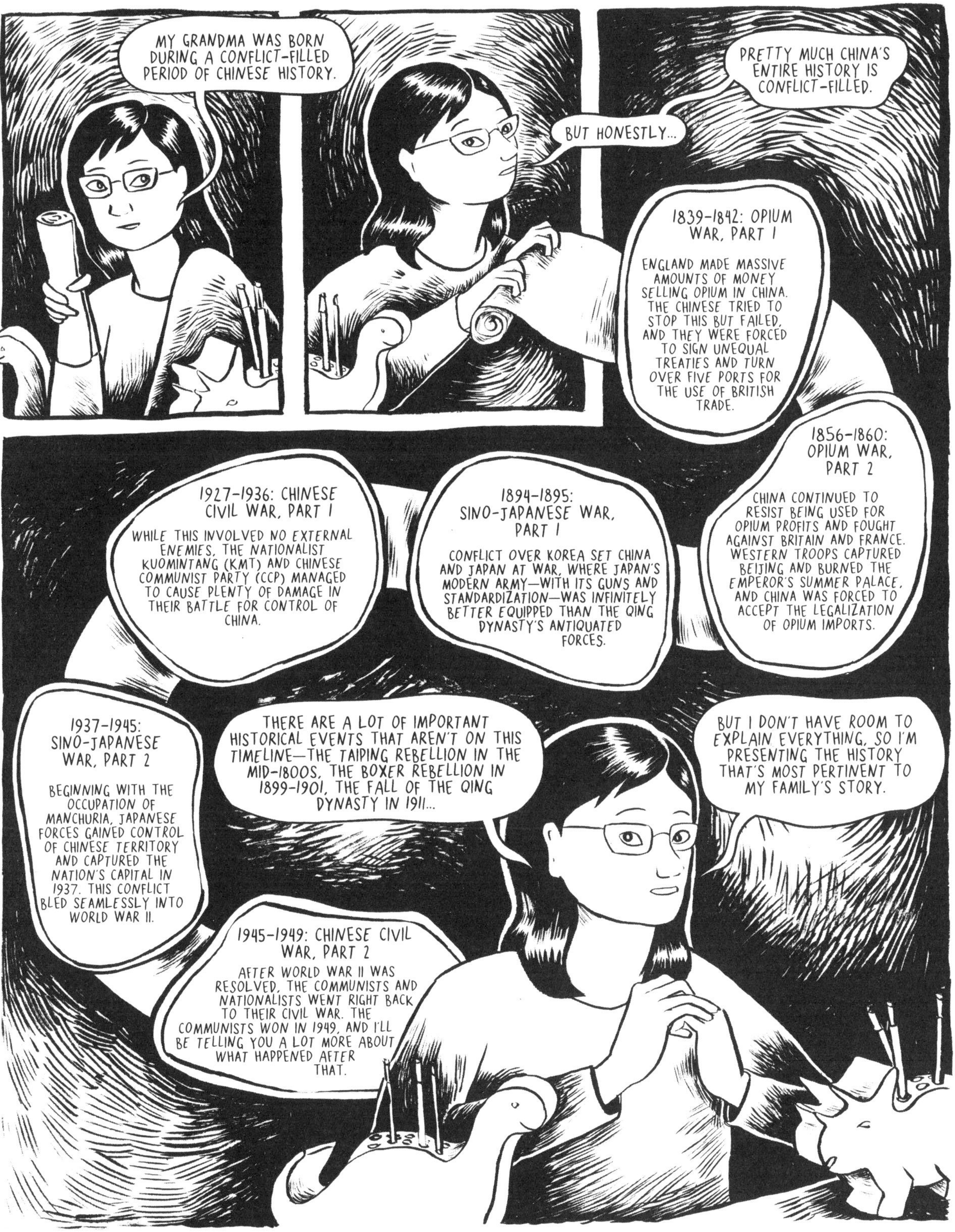

MY GRANDMA WAS BORN DURING A CONFLICT-FILLED PERIOD OF CHINESE HISTORY.
BUT HONESTLY...
PRETTY MUCH CHINA'S ENTIRE HISTORY IS CONFLICT-FILLED.
1839-1842: OPIUM WAR, PART 1
ENGLAND MADE MASSIVE AMOUNTS OF MONEY SELLING OPIUM IN CHINA. THE CHINESE TRIED TO STOP THIS BUT FAILED, AND THEY WERE FORCED TO SIGN UNEQUAL TREATIES AND TURN OVER FIVE PORTS FOR THE USE OF BRITISH TRADE.
1856-1860: OPIUM WAR, PART 2
CHINA CONTINUED TO RESIST BEING USED FOR OPIUM PROFITS AND FOUGHT AGAINST BRITAIN AND FRANCE. WESTERN TROOPS CAPTURED BEIJING AND BURNED THE EMPEROR'S SUMMER PALACE, AND CHINA WAS FORCED TO ACCEPT THE LEGALIZATION OF OPIUM IMPORTS.
1894-1895: SINO-JAPANESE WAR, PART 1
CONFLICT OVER KOREA SET CHINA AND JAPAN AT WAR, WHERE JAPAN'S MODERN ARMY—WITH ITS GUNS AND STANDARDIZATION—WAS INFINITELY BETTER EQUIPPED THAN THE QING DYNASTY'S ANTIQUATED FORCES.
1927-1936: CHINESE CIVIL WAR, PART 1
WHILE THIS INVOLVED NO EXTERNAL ENEMIES, THE NATIONALIST KUOMINTANG (KMT) AND CHINESE COMMUNIST PARTY (CCP) MANAGED TO CAUSE PLENTY OF DAMAGE IN THEIR BATTLE FOR CONTROL OF CHINA.
1937-1945: SINO-JAPANESE WAR, PART 2
BEGINNING WITH THE OCCUPATION OF MANCHURIA, JAPANESE FORCES GAINED CONTROL OF CHINESE TERRITORY AND CAPTURED THE NATION'S CAPITAL IN 1937. THIS CONFLICT BLED SEAMLESSLY INTO WORLD WAR II.
1945-1949: CHINESE CIVIL WAR, PART 2
AFTER WORLD WAR II WAS RESOLVED, THE COMMUNISTS AND NATIONALISTS WENT RIGHT BACK TO THEIR CIVIL WAR. THE COMMUNISTS WON IN 1949, AND I'LL BE TELLING YOU A LOT MORE ABOUT WHAT HAPPENED AFTER THAT.
THERE ARE A LOT OF IMPORTANT HISTORICAL EVENTS THAT AREN'T ON THIS TIMELINE—THE TAIPING REBELLION IN THE MID-1800S, THE BOXER REBELLION IN 1899-1901, THE FALL OF THE QING DYNASTY IN 1911...
BUT I DON'T HAVE ROOM TO EXPLAIN EVERYTHING, SO I'M PRESENTING THE HISTORY THAT'S MOST PERTINENT TO MY FAMILY'S STORY.

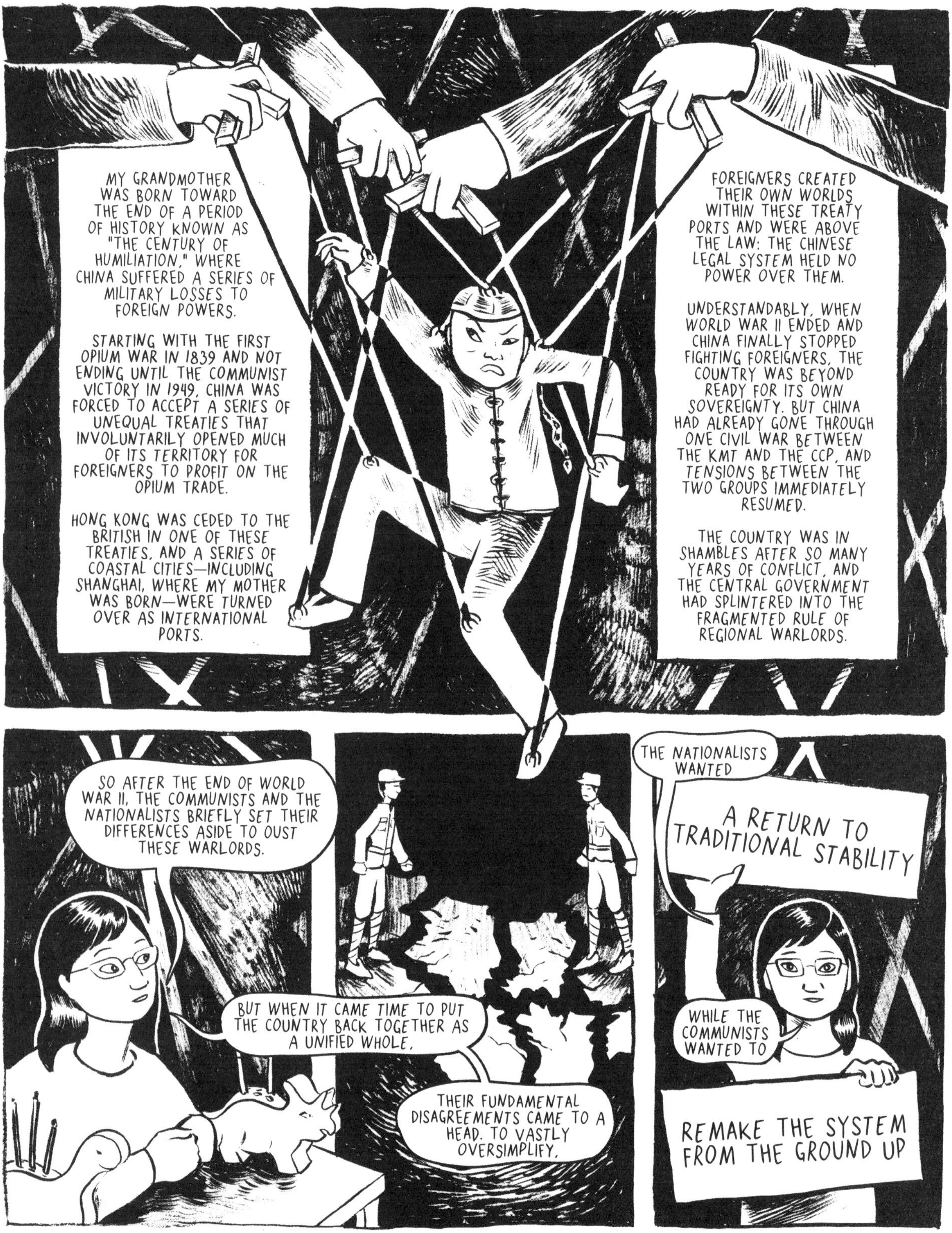
MY GRANDMOTHER WAS BORN TOWARD THE END OF A PERIOD OF HISTORY KNOWN AS "THE CENTURY OF HUMILIATION," WHERE CHINA SUFFERED A SERIES OF MILITARY LOSSES TO FOREIGN POWERS.
STARTING WITH THE FIRST OPIUM WAR IN 1839 AND NOT ENDING UNTIL THE COMMUNIST VICTORY IN 1949, CHINA WAS FORCED TO ACCEPT A SERIES OF UNEQUAL TREATIES THAT INVOLUNTARILY OPENED MUCH OF ITS TERRITORY FOR FOREIGNERS TO PROFIT ON THE OPIUM TRADE.
HONG KONG WAS CEDED TO THE BRITISH IN ONE OF THESE TREATIES, AND A SERIES OF COASTAL CITIES—INCLUDING SHANGHAI, WHERE MY MOTHER WAS BORN—WERE TURNED OVER AS INTERNATIONAL PORTS.
FOREIGNERS CREATED THEIR OWN WORLDS WITHIN THESE TREATY PORTS AND WERE ABOVE THE LAW: THE CHINESE LEGAL SYSTEM HELD NO POWER OVER THEM.
UNDERSTANDABLY, WHEN WORLD WAR II ENDED AND CHINA FINALLY STOPPED FIGHTING FOREIGNERS, THE COUNTRY WAS BEYOND READY FOR ITS OWN SOVEREIGNTY. BUT CHINA HAD ALREADY GONE THROUGH ONE CIVIL WAR BETWEEN THE KMT AND THE CCP, AND TENSIONS BETWEEN THE TWO GROUPS IMMEDIATELY RESUMED.
THE COUNTRY WAS IN SHAMBLES AFTER SO MANY YEARS OF CONFLICT, AND THE CENTRAL GOVERNMENT HAD SPLINTERED INTO THE FRAGMENTED RULE OF REGIONAL WARLORDS.
SO AFTER THE END OF WORLD WAR II, THE COMMUNISTS AND THE NATIONALISTS BRIEFLY SET THEIR DIFFERENCES ASIDE TO OUST THESE WARLORDS.
BUT WHEN IT CAME TIME TO PUT THE COUNTRY BACK TOGETHER AS A UNIFIED WHOLE,
THEIR FUNDAMENTAL DISAGREEMENTS CAME TO A HEAD. TO VASTLY OVERSIMPLIFY,
THE NATIONALISTS WANTED
A RETURN TO TRADITIONAL STABILITY
WHILE THE COMMUNISTS WANTED TO
REMAKE THE SYSTEM FROM THE GROUND UP

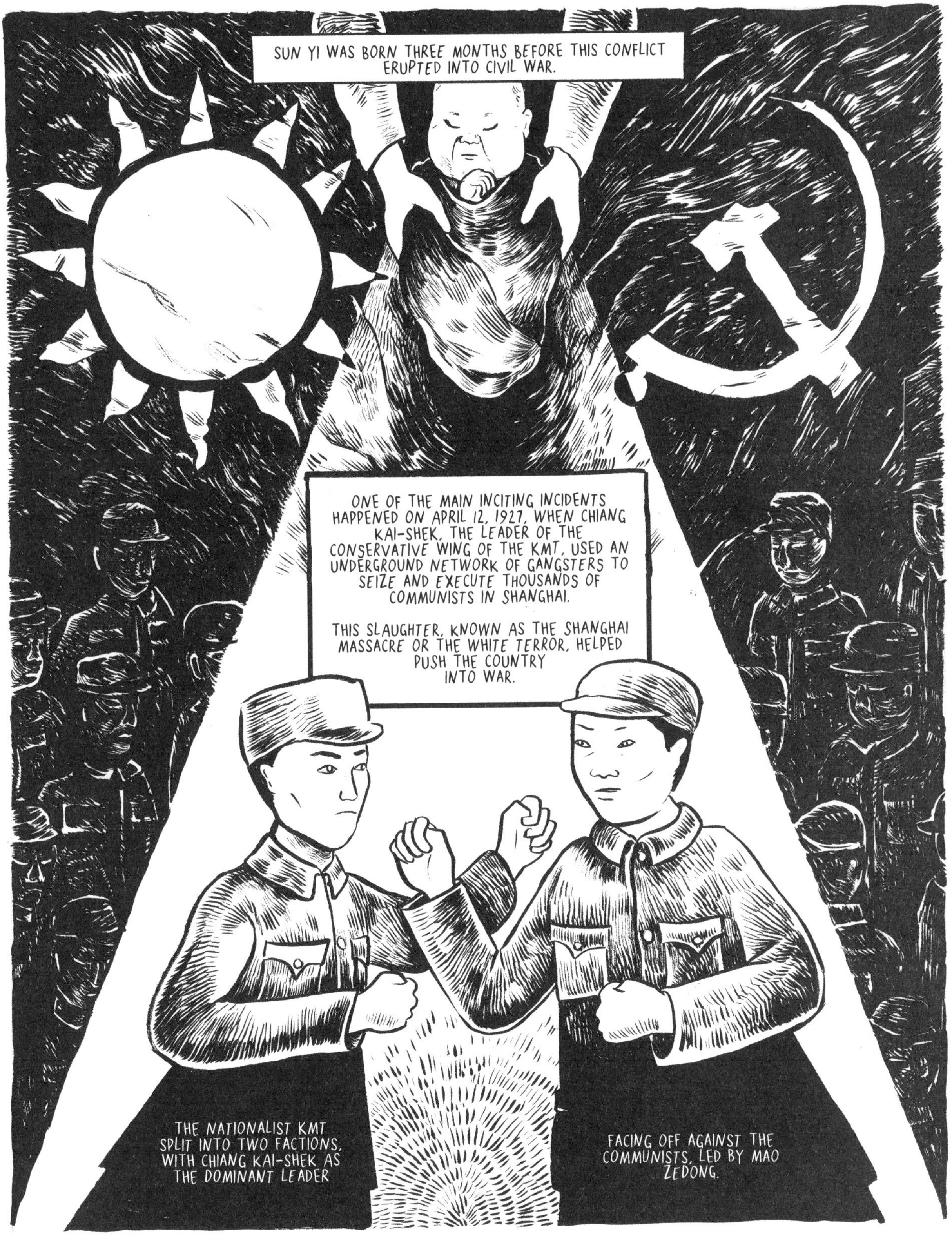
SUN YI WAS BORN THREE MONTHS BEFORE THIS CONFLICT ERUPTED INTO CIVIL WAR.
ONE OF THE MAIN INCITING INCIDENTS HAPPENED ON APRIL 12, 1927, WHEN CHIANG KAI-SHEK, THE LEADER OF THE CONSERVATIVE WING OF THE KMT, USED AN UNDERGROUND NETWORK OF GANGSTERS TO SEIZE AND EXECUTE THOUSANDS OF COMMUNISTS IN SHANGHAI.
THIS SLAUGHTER, KNOWN AS THE SHANGHAI MASSACRE OR THE WHITE TERROR, HELPED PUSH THE COUNTRY INTO WAR.
THE NATIONALIST KMT SPLIT INTO TWO FACTIONS, WITH CHIANG KAI-SHEK AS THE DOMINANT LEADER
FACING OFF AGAINST THE COMMUNISTS, LED BY MAO ZEDONG.

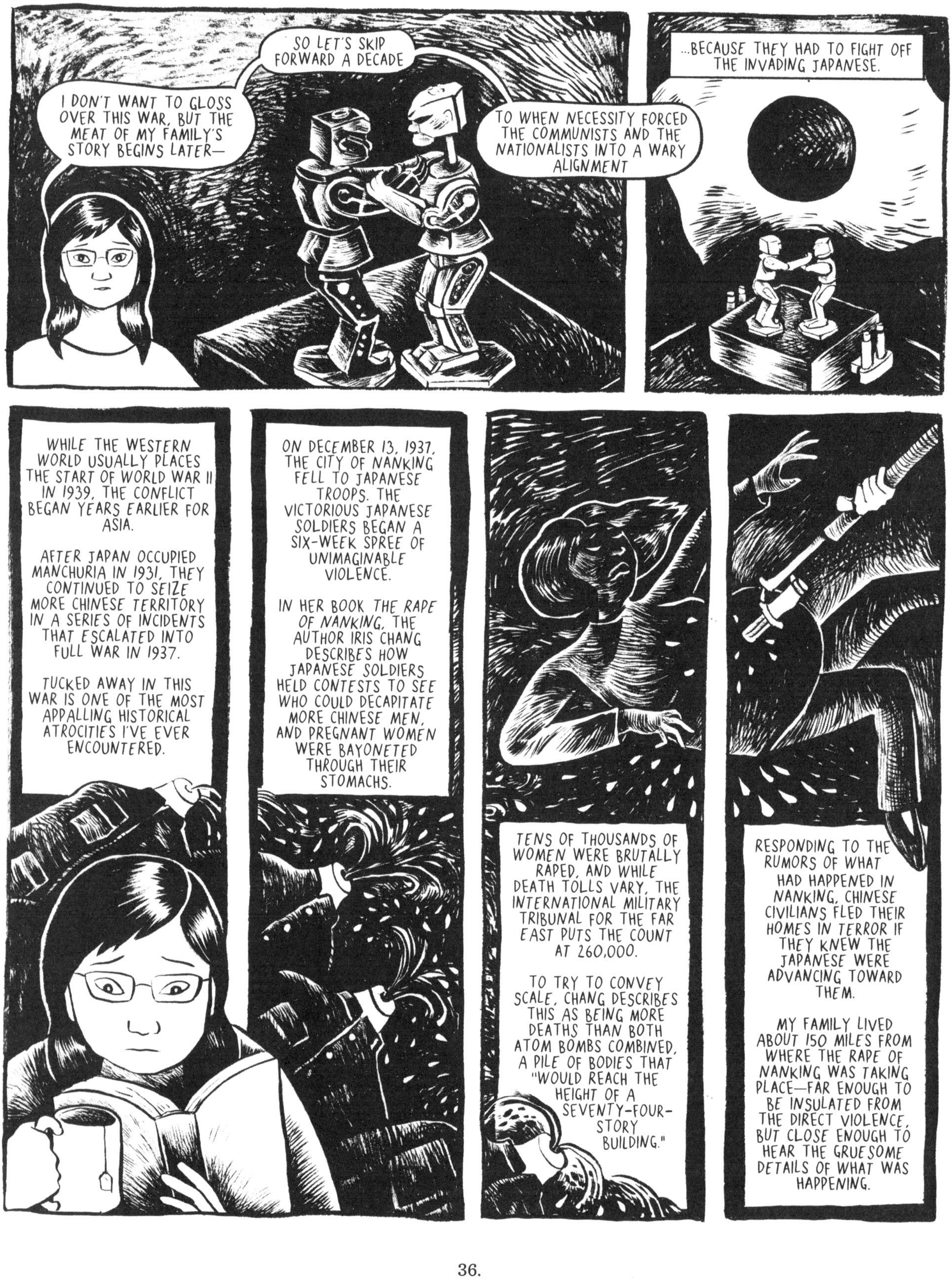
I DON'T WANT TO GLOSS OVER THIS WAR, BUT THE MEAT OF MY FAMILY'S STORY BEGINS LATER—
SO LET'S SKIP FORWARD A DECADE
TO WHEN NECESSITY FORCED THE COMMUNISTS AND THE NATIONALISTS INTO A WARY ALIGNMENT
...BECAUSE THEY HAD TO FIGHT OFF THE INVADING JAPANESE.
WHILE THE WESTERN WORLD USUALLY PLACES THE START OF WORLD WAR II IN 1939, THE CONFLICT BEGAN YEARS EARLIER FOR ASIA.
AFTER JAPAN OCCUPIED MANCHURIA IN 1931, THEY CONTINUED TO SEIZE MORE CHINESE TERRITORY IN A SERIES OF INCIDENTS THAT ESCALATED INTO FULL WAR IN 1937.
TUCKED AWAY IN THIS WAR IS ONE OF THE MOST APPALLING HISTORICAL ATROCITIES I'VE EVER ENCOUNTERED.
ON DECEMBER 13, 1937, THE CITY OF NANKING FELL TO JAPANESE TROOPS. THE VICTORIOUS JAPANESE SOLDIERS BEGAN A SIX-WEEK SPREE OF UNIMAGINABLE VIOLENCE.
IN HER BOOK *THE RAPE OF NANKING*, THE AUTHOR IRIS CHANG DESCRIBES HOW JAPANESE SOLDIERS HELD CONTESTS TO SEE WHO COULD DECAPITATE MORE CHINESE MEN, AND PREGNANT WOMEN WERE BAYONETED THROUGH THEIR STOMACHS.
TENS OF THOUSANDS OF WOMEN WERE BRUTALLY RAPED, AND WHILE DEATH TOLLS VARY, THE INTERNATIONAL MILITARY TRIBUNAL FOR THE FAR EAST PUTS THE COUNT AT 260,000.
TO TRY TO CONVEY SCALE, CHANG DESCRIBES THIS AS BEING MORE DEATHS THAN BOTH ATOM BOMBS COMBINED, A PILE OF BODIES THAT "WOULD REACH THE HEIGHT OF A SEVENTY-FOUR-STORY BUILDING."
RESPONDING TO THE RUMORS OF WHAT HAD HAPPENED IN NANKING, CHINESE CIVILIANS FLED THEIR HOMES IN TERROR IF THEY KNEW THE JAPANESE WERE ADVANCING TOWARD THEM.
MY FAMILY LIVED ABOUT 150 MILES FROM WHERE THE RAPE OF NANKING WAS TAKING PLACE—FAR ENOUGH TO BE INSULATED FROM THE DIRECT VIOLENCE, BUT CLOSE ENOUGH TO HEAR THE GRUESOME DETAILS OF WHAT WAS HAPPENING.

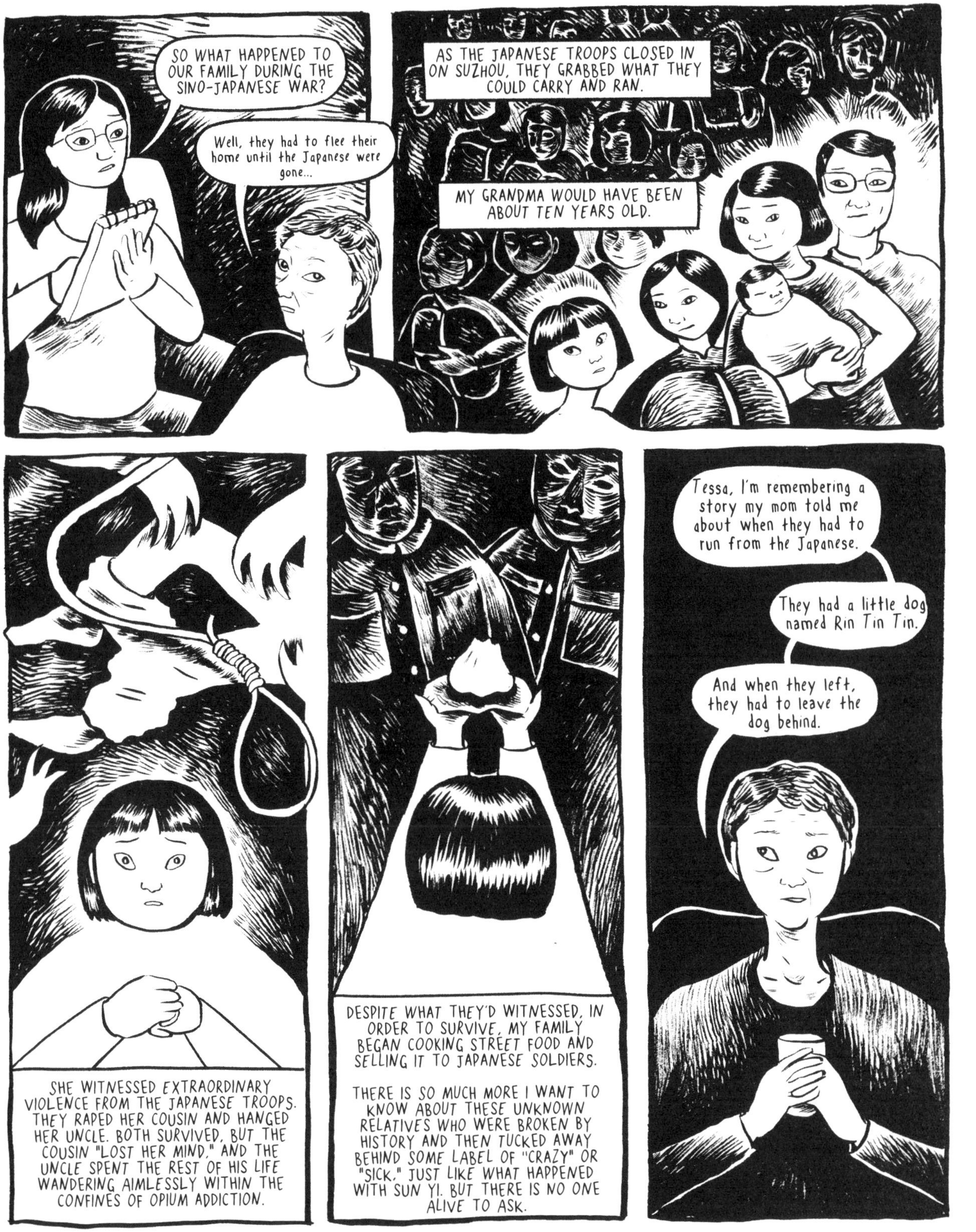

SO WHAT HAPPENED TO OUR FAMILY DURING THE SINO-JAPANESE WAR?
Well, they had to flee their home until the Japanese were gone...
AS THE JAPANESE TROOPS CLOSED IN ON SUZHOU, THEY GRABBED WHAT THEY COULD CARRY AND RAN.
MY GRANDMA WOULD HAVE BEEN ABOUT TEN YEARS OLD.
SHE WITNESSED EXTRAORDINARY VIOLENCE FROM THE JAPANESE TROOPS. THEY RAPED HER COUSIN AND HANGED HER UNCLE. BOTH SURVIVED, BUT THE COUSIN "LOST HER MIND," AND THE UNCLE SPENT THE REST OF HIS LIFE WANDERING AIMLESSLY WITHIN THE CONFINES OF OPIUM ADDICTION.
DESPITE WHAT THEY'D WITNESSED, IN ORDER TO SURVIVE, MY FAMILY BEGAN COOKING STREET FOOD AND SELLING IT TO JAPANESE SOLDIERS.
THERE IS SO MUCH MORE I WANT TO KNOW ABOUT THESE UNKNOWN RELATIVES WHO WERE BROKEN BY HISTORY AND THEN TUCKED AWAY BEHIND SOME LABEL OF "CRAZY" OR "SICK." JUST LIKE WHAT HAPPENED WITH SUN YI. BUT THERE IS NO ONE ALIVE TO ASK.
Tessa, I'm remembering a story my mom told me about when they had to run from the Japanese.
They had a little dog named Rin Tin Tin.
And when they left, they had to leave the dog behind.

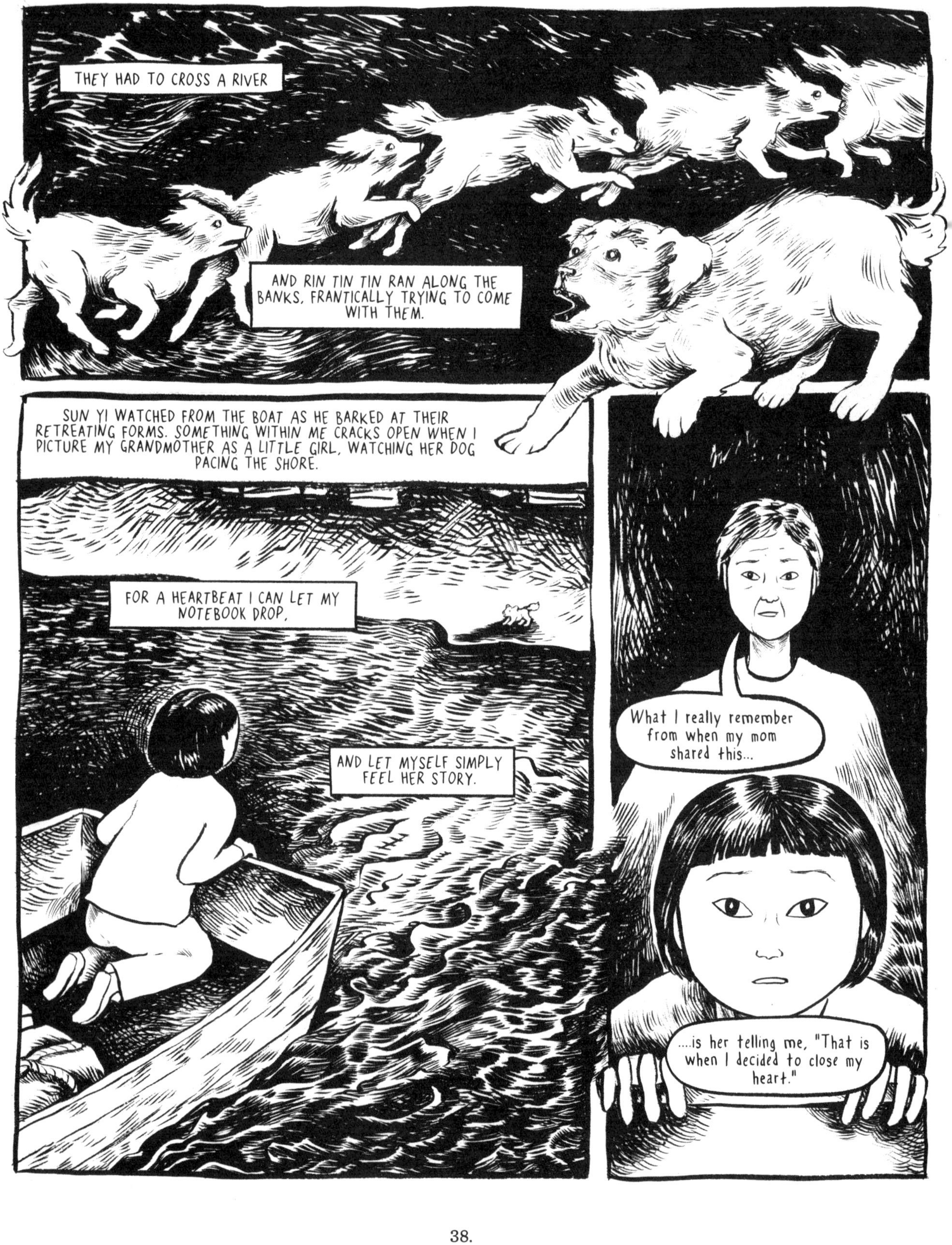

THEY HAD TO CROSS A RIVER
AND RIN TIN TIN RAN ALONG THE BANKS, FRANTICALLY TRYING TO COME WITH THEM.
SUN YI WATCHED FROM THE BOAT AS HE BARKED AT THEIR RETREATING FORMS. SOMETHING WITHIN ME CRACKS OPEN WHEN I PICTURE MY GRANDMOTHER AS A LITTLE GIRL, WATCHING HER DOG PACING THE SHORE.
FOR A HEARTBEAT I CAN LET MY NOTEBOOK DROP,
AND LET MYSELF SIMPLY FEEL HER STORY.
What I really remember from when my mom shared this...
...is her telling me, "That is when I decided to close my heart."

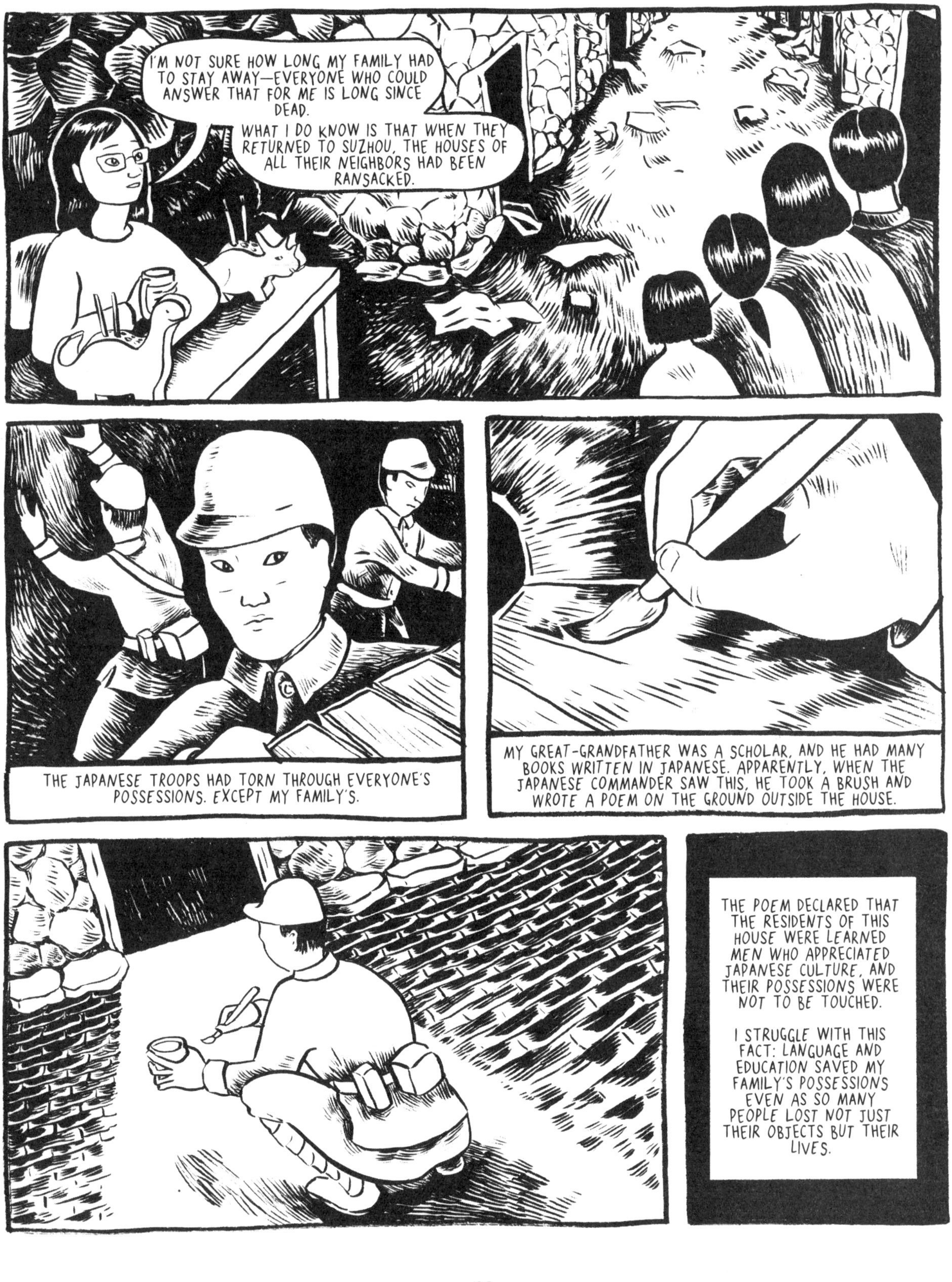
I'M NOT SURE HOW LONG MY FAMILY HAD TO STAY AWAY—EVERYONE WHO COULD ANSWER THAT FOR ME IS LONG SINCE DEAD.
WHAT I DO KNOW IS THAT WHEN THEY RETURNED TO SUZHOU, THE HOUSES OF ALL THEIR NEIGHBORS HAD BEEN RANSACKED.
THE JAPANESE TROOPS HAD TORN THROUGH EVERYONE'S POSSESSIONS. EXCEPT MY FAMILY'S.
MY GREAT-GRANDFATHER WAS A SCHOLAR, AND HE HAD MANY BOOKS WRITTEN IN JAPANESE. APPARENTLY, WHEN THE JAPANESE COMMANDER SAW THIS, HE TOOK A BRUSH AND WROTE A POEM ON THE GROUND OUTSIDE THE HOUSE.
THE POEM DECLARED THAT THE RESIDENTS OF THIS HOUSE WERE LEARNED MEN WHO APPRECIATED JAPANESE CULTURE, AND THEIR POSSESSIONS WERE NOT TO BE TOUCHED.
I STRUGGLE WITH THIS FACT: LANGUAGE AND EDUCATION SAVED MY FAMILY'S POSSESSIONS EVEN AS SO MANY PEOPLE LOST NOT JUST THEIR OBJECTS BUT THEIR LIVES.

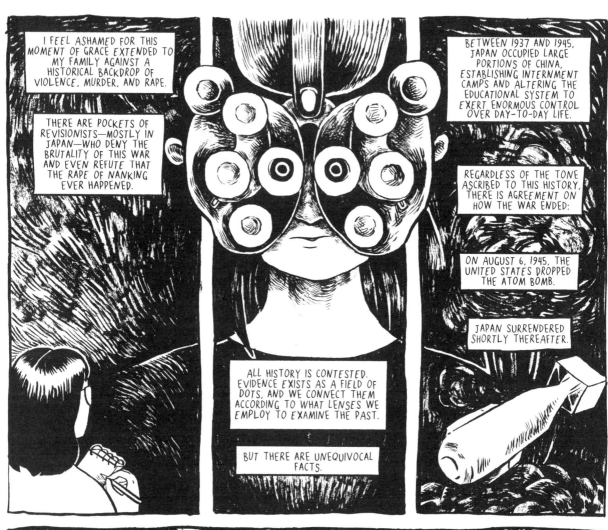

I FEEL ASHAMED FOR THIS MOMENT OF GRACE EXTENDED TO MY FAMILY AGAINST A HISTORICAL BACKDROP OF VIOLENCE, MURDER, AND RAPE.

THERE ARE POCKETS OF REVISIONISTS—MOSTLY IN JAPAN—WHO DENY THE BRUTALITY OF THIS WAR AND EVEN REFUTE THAT THE RAPE OF NANKING EVER HAPPENED.

BETWEEN 1937 AND 1945, JAPAN OCCUPIED LARGE PORTIONS OF CHINA, ESTABLISHING INTERNMENT CAMPS AND ALTERING THE EDUCATIONAL SYSTEM TO EXERT ENORMOUS CONTROL OVER DAY-TO-DAY LIFE.

REGARDLESS OF THE TONE ASCRIBED TO THIS HISTORY, THERE IS AGREEMENT ON HOW THE WAR ENDED:

ON AUGUST 6, 1945, THE UNITED STATES DROPPED THE ATOM BOMB.

JAPAN SURRENDERED SHORTLY THEREAFTER.

ALL HISTORY IS CONTESTED. EVIDENCE *EXISTS* AS A FIELD OF DOTS, AND WE CONNECT THEM ACCORDING TO WHAT LENSES WE EMPLOY TO EXAMINE THE PAST.

BUT THERE ARE UNEQUIVOCAL FACTS.

WHEN I STARTED THIS BOOK, I WAS DETERMINED TO NARRATE DISPASSIONATELY AND KEEP ALL EMOTION OUT OF IT.

I GUESS YOU CAN SEE HOW THAT WORKED OUT...

THE PLAN WAS TO PROTECT MYSELF FROM FEELING TOO MUCH BY STICKING TO HISTORY.

BUT THE DAMN GHOSTS TRICKED ME BY FORCING ME TO REDEFINE WHAT I THOUGHT HISTORY WAS.

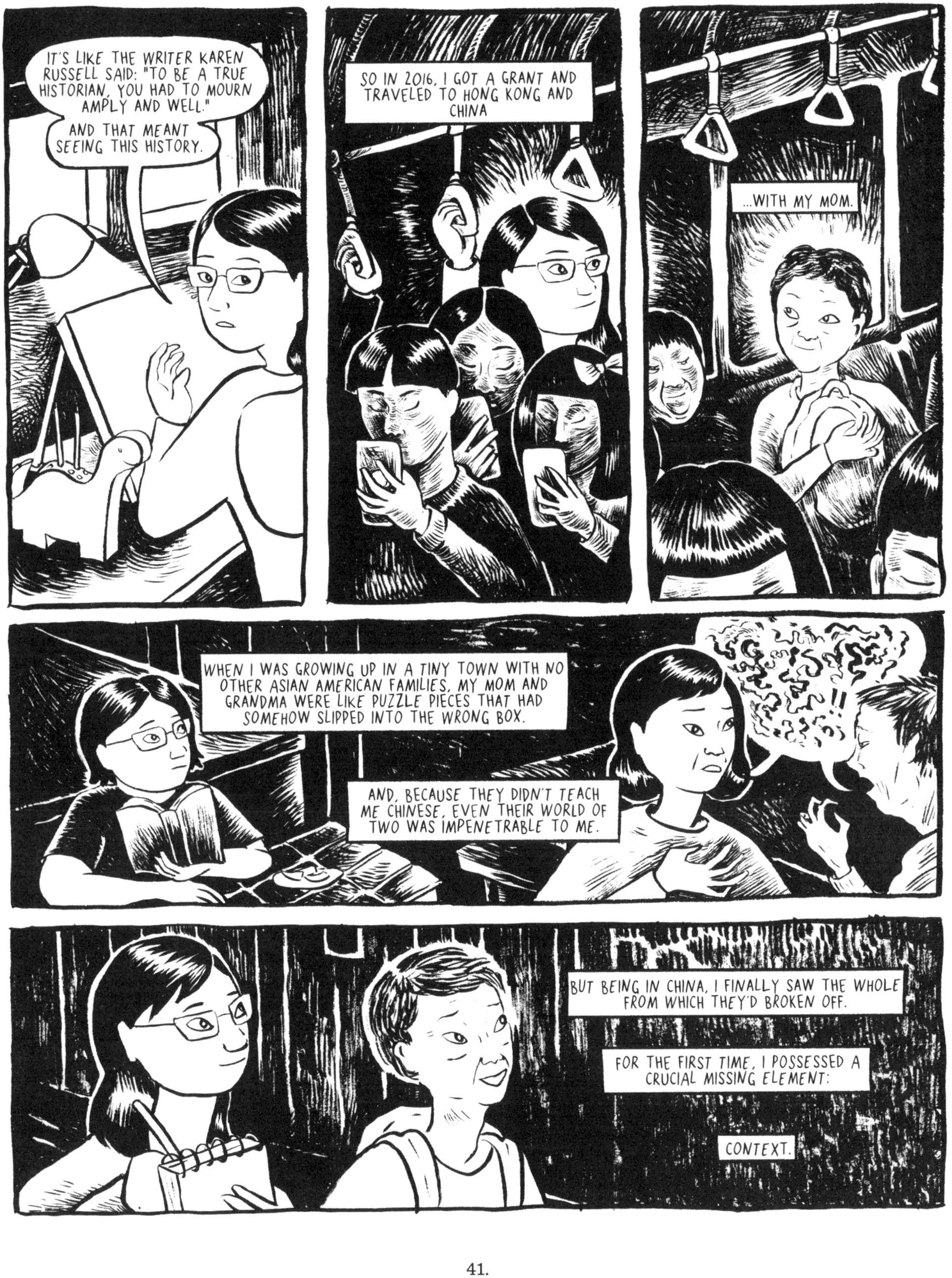
IT'S LIKE THE WRITER KAREN RUSSELL SAID: "TO BE A TRUE HISTORIAN, YOU HAD TO MOURN AMPLY AND WELL."
AND THAT MEANT SEEING THIS HISTORY.
SO IN 2016, I GOT A GRANT AND TRAVELED TO HONG KONG AND CHINA
...WITH MY MOM.
WHEN I WAS GROWING UP IN A TINY TOWN WITH NO OTHER ASIAN AMERICAN FAMILIES, MY MOM AND GRANDMA WERE LIKE PUZZLE PIECES THAT HAD SOMEHOW SLIPPED INTO THE WRONG BOX.
AND, BECAUSE THEY DIDN'T TEACH ME CHINESE, EVEN THEIR WORLD OF TWO WAS IMPENETRABLE TO ME.
BUT BEING IN CHINA, I FINALLY SAW THE WHOLE FROM WHICH THEY'D BROKEN OFF.
FOR THE FIRST TIME, I POSSESSED A CRUCIAL MISSING ELEMENT:
CONTEXT.

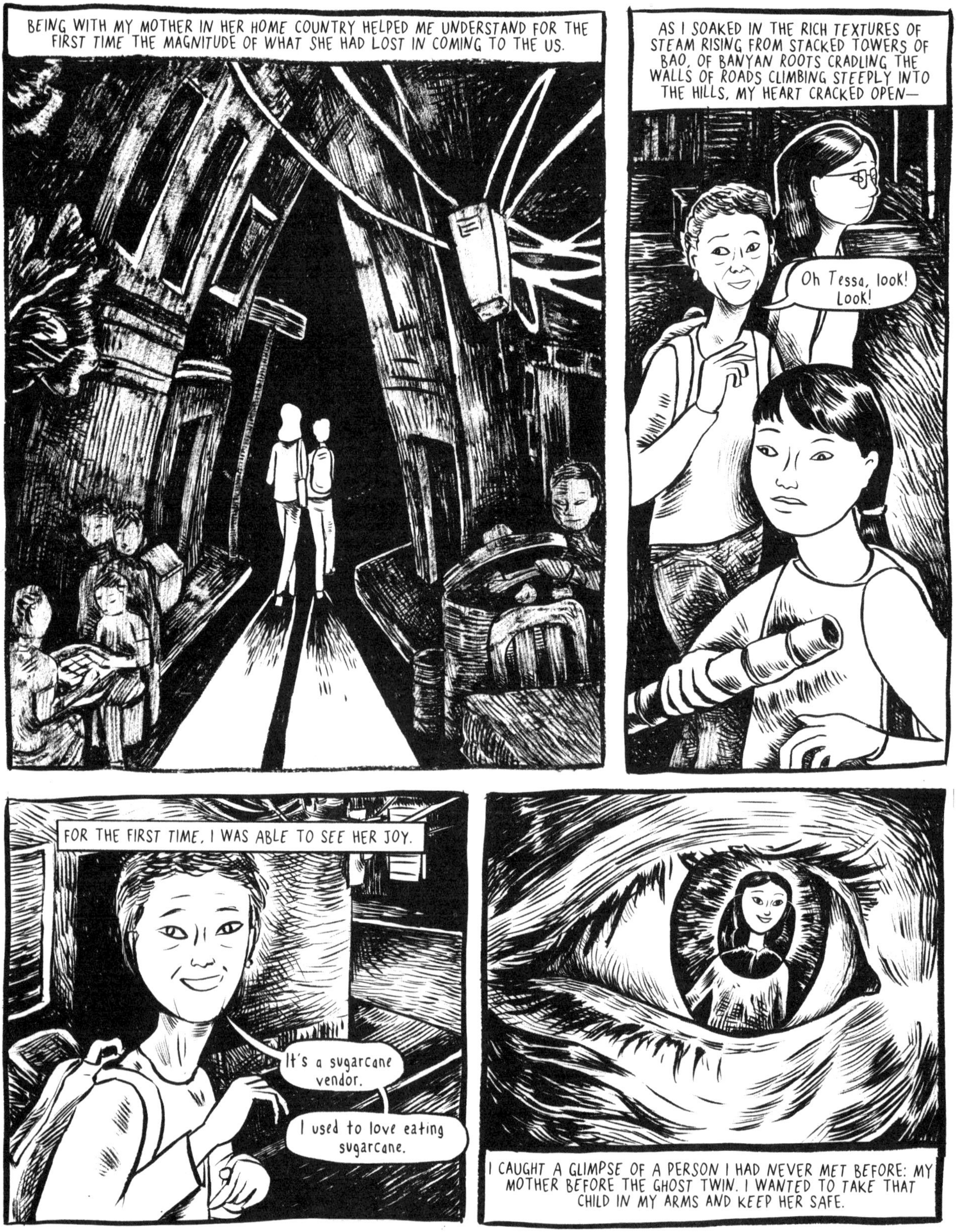
BEING WITH MY MOTHER IN HER HOME COUNTRY HELPED ME UNDERSTAND FOR THE FIRST TIME THE MAGNITUDE OF WHAT SHE HAD LOST IN COMING TO THE US.
AS I SOAKED IN THE RICH TEXTURES OF STEAM RISING FROM STACKED TOWERS OF BAO, OF BANYAN ROOTS CRADLING THE WALLS OF ROADS CLIMBING STEEPLY INTO THE HILLS, MY HEART CRACKED OPEN—
Oh Tessa, look! Look!
FOR THE FIRST TIME, I WAS ABLE TO SEE HER JOY.
It's a sugarcane vendor.
I used to love eating sugarcane.
I CAUGHT A GLIMPSE OF A PERSON I HAD NEVER MET BEFORE: MY MOTHER BEFORE THE GHOST TWIN. I WANTED TO TAKE THAT CHILD IN MY ARMS AND KEEP HER SAFE.

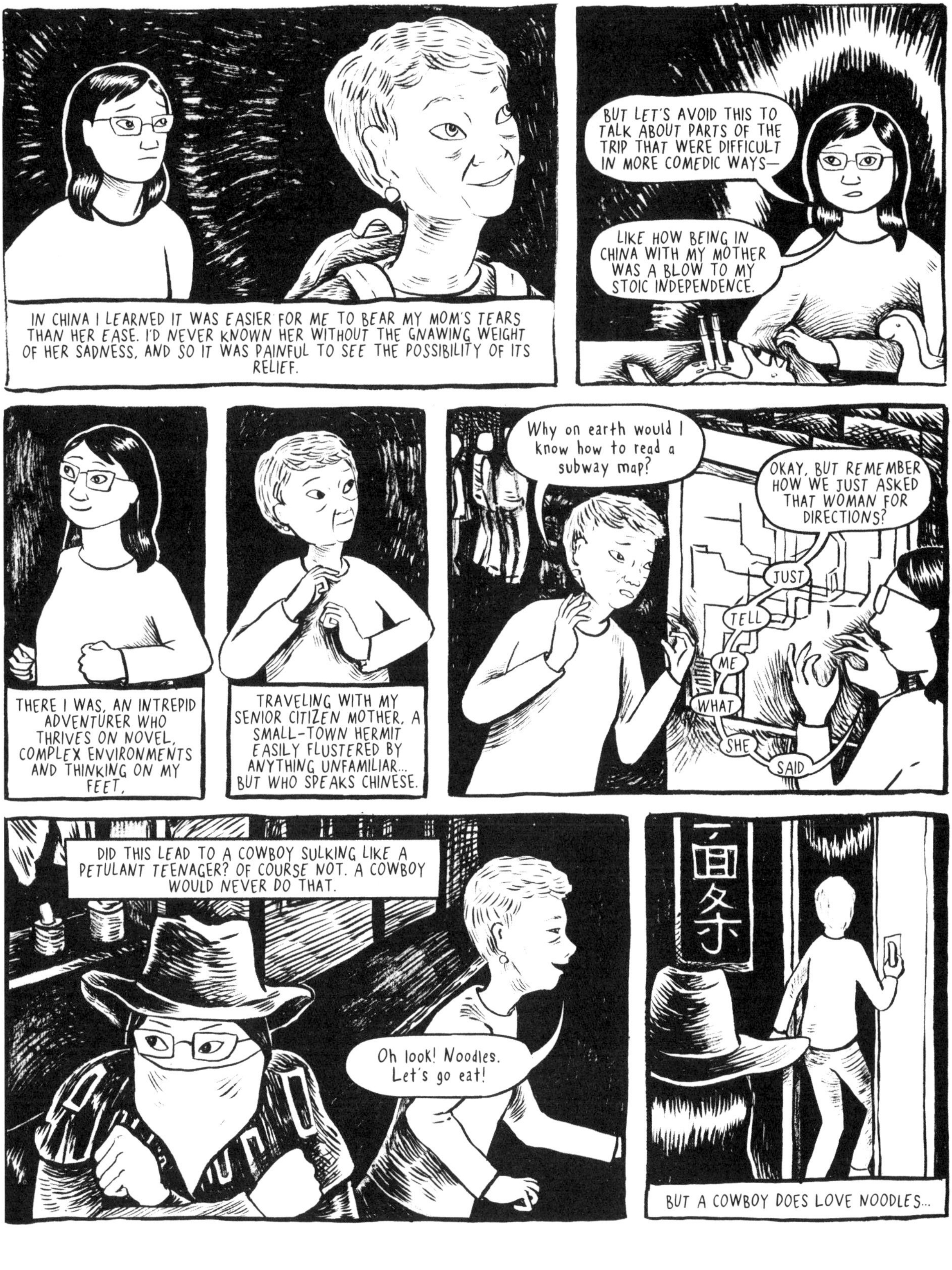
IN CHINA I LEARNED IT WAS EASIER FOR ME TO BEAR MY MOM'S TEARS THAN HER EASE. I'D NEVER KNOWN HER WITHOUT THE GNAWING WEIGHT OF HER SADNESS, AND SO IT WAS PAINFUL TO SEE THE POSSIBILITY OF ITS RELIEF.
BUT LET'S AVOID THIS TO TALK ABOUT PARTS OF THE TRIP THAT WERE DIFFICULT IN MORE COMEDIC WAYS—
LIKE HOW BEING IN CHINA WITH MY MOTHER WAS A BLOW TO MY STOIC INDEPENDENCE.
THERE I WAS, AN INTREPID ADVENTURER WHO THRIVES ON NOVEL, COMPLEX ENVIRONMENTS AND THINKING ON MY FEET,
TRAVELING WITH MY SENIOR CITIZEN MOTHER, A SMALL-TOWN HERMIT EASILY FLUSTERED BY ANYTHING UNFAMILIAR... BUT WHO SPEAKS CHINESE.
Why on earth would I know how to read a subway map?
OKAY, BUT REMEMBER HOW WE JUST ASKED THAT WOMAN FOR DIRECTIONS?
JUST TELL ME WHAT SHE SAID
DID THIS LEAD TO A COWBOY SULKING LIKE A PETULANT TEENAGER? OF COURSE NOT. A COWBOY WOULD NEVER DO THAT.
Oh look! Noodles. Let's go eat!
面条
BUT A COWBOY DOES LOVE NOODLES...

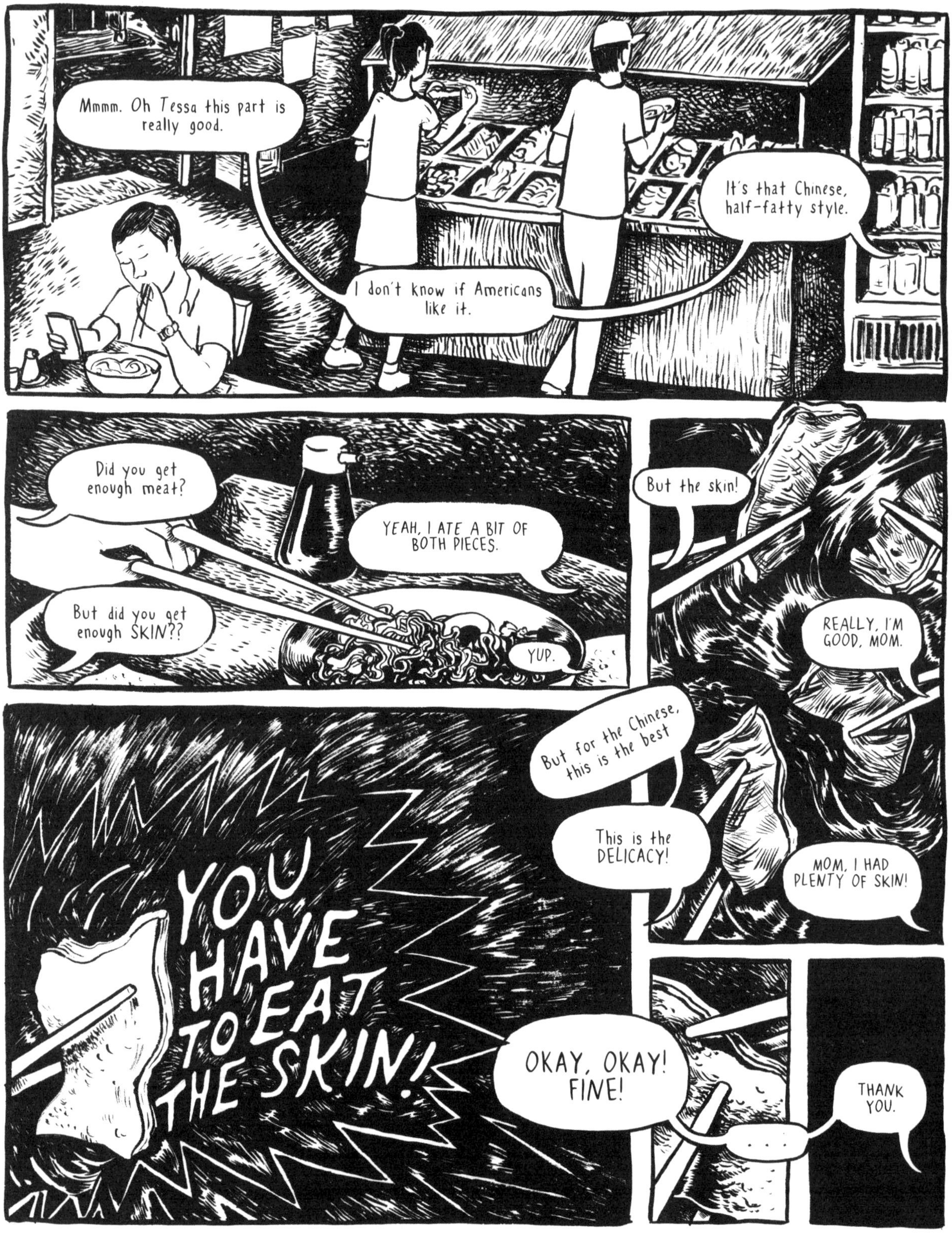
Mmmm. Oh Tessa this part is really good.
It's that Chinese, half-fatty style.
I don't know if Americans like it.
Did you get enough meat?
YEAH, I ATE A BIT OF BOTH PIECES.
But did you get enough SKIN??
YUP.
But the skin!
REALLY, I'M GOOD, MOM.
But for the Chinese, this is the best
This is the DELICACY!
MOM, I HAD PLENTY OF SKIN!
YOU HAVE TO EAT THE SKIN!
OKAY, OKAY! FINE!
. . .
THANK YOU.

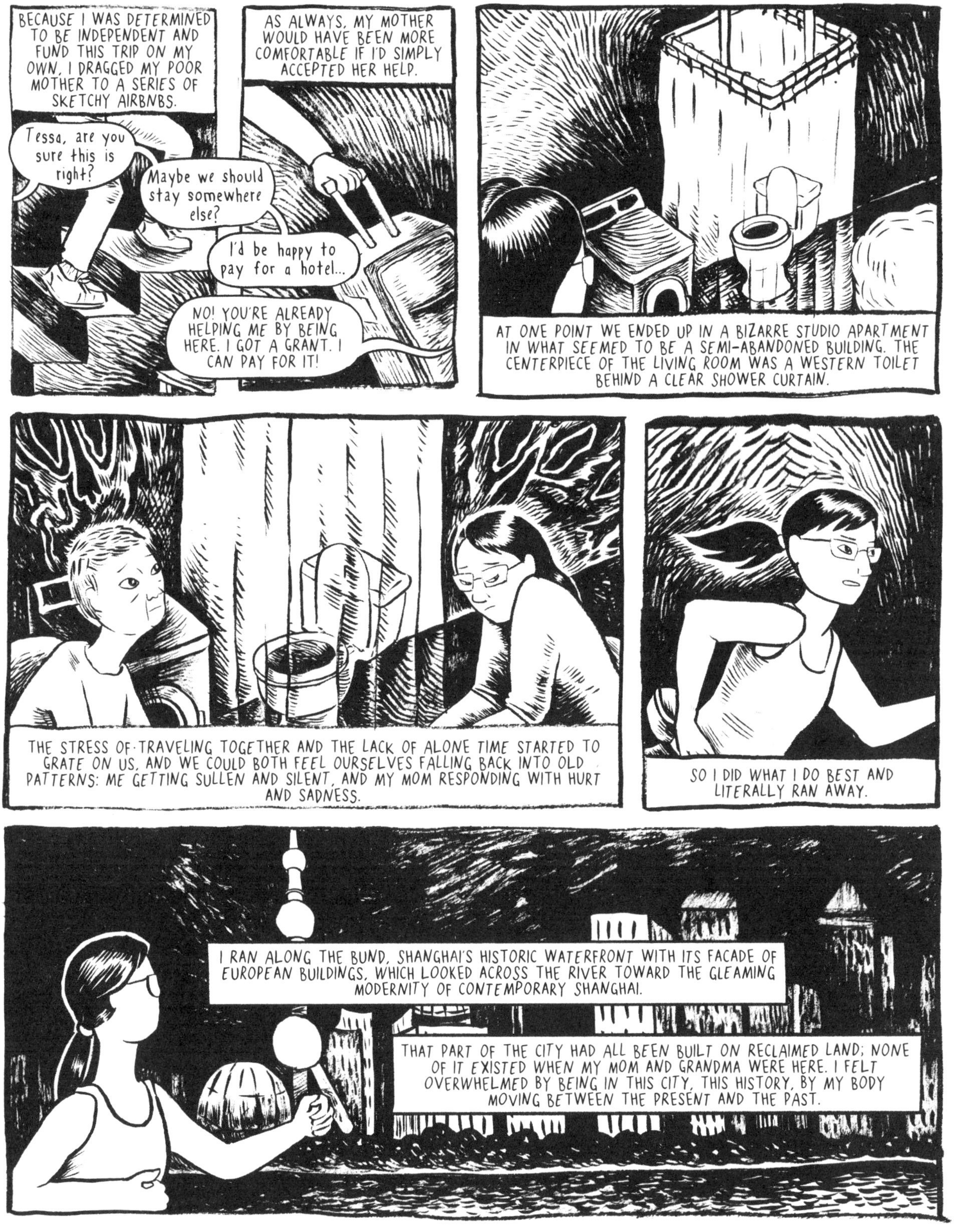
BECAUSE I WAS DETERMINED TO BE INDEPENDENT AND FUND THIS TRIP ON MY OWN, I DRAGGED MY POOR MOTHER TO A SERIES OF SKETCHY AIRBNBS.
Tessa, are you sure this is right?
AS ALWAYS, MY MOTHER WOULD HAVE BEEN MORE COMFORTABLE IF I'D SIMPLY ACCEPTED HER HELP.
Maybe we should stay somewhere else?
I'd be happy to pay for a hotel...
NO! YOU'RE ALREADY HELPING ME BY BEING HERE. I GOT A GRANT. I CAN PAY FOR IT!
AT ONE POINT WE ENDED UP IN A BIZARRE STUDIO APARTMENT IN WHAT SEEMED TO BE A SEMI-ABANDONED BUILDING. THE CENTERPIECE OF THE LIVING ROOM WAS A WESTERN TOILET BEHIND A CLEAR SHOWER CURTAIN.
THE STRESS OF TRAVELING TOGETHER AND THE LACK OF ALONE TIME STARTED TO GRATE ON US, AND WE COULD BOTH FEEL OURSELVES FALLING BACK INTO OLD PATTERNS: ME GETTING SULLEN AND SILENT, AND MY MOM RESPONDING WITH HURT AND SADNESS.
SO I DID WHAT I DO BEST AND LITERALLY RAN AWAY.
I RAN ALONG THE BUND, SHANGHAI'S HISTORIC WATERFRONT WITH ITS FACADE OF EUROPEAN BUILDINGS, WHICH LOOKED ACROSS THE RIVER TOWARD THE GLEAMING MODERNITY OF CONTEMPORARY SHANGHAI.
THAT PART OF THE CITY HAD ALL BEEN BUILT ON RECLAIMED LAND; NONE OF IT EXISTED WHEN MY MOM AND GRANDMA WERE HERE. I FELT OVERWHELMED BY BEING IN THIS CITY, THIS HISTORY, BY MY BODY MOVING BETWEEN THE PRESENT AND THE PAST.

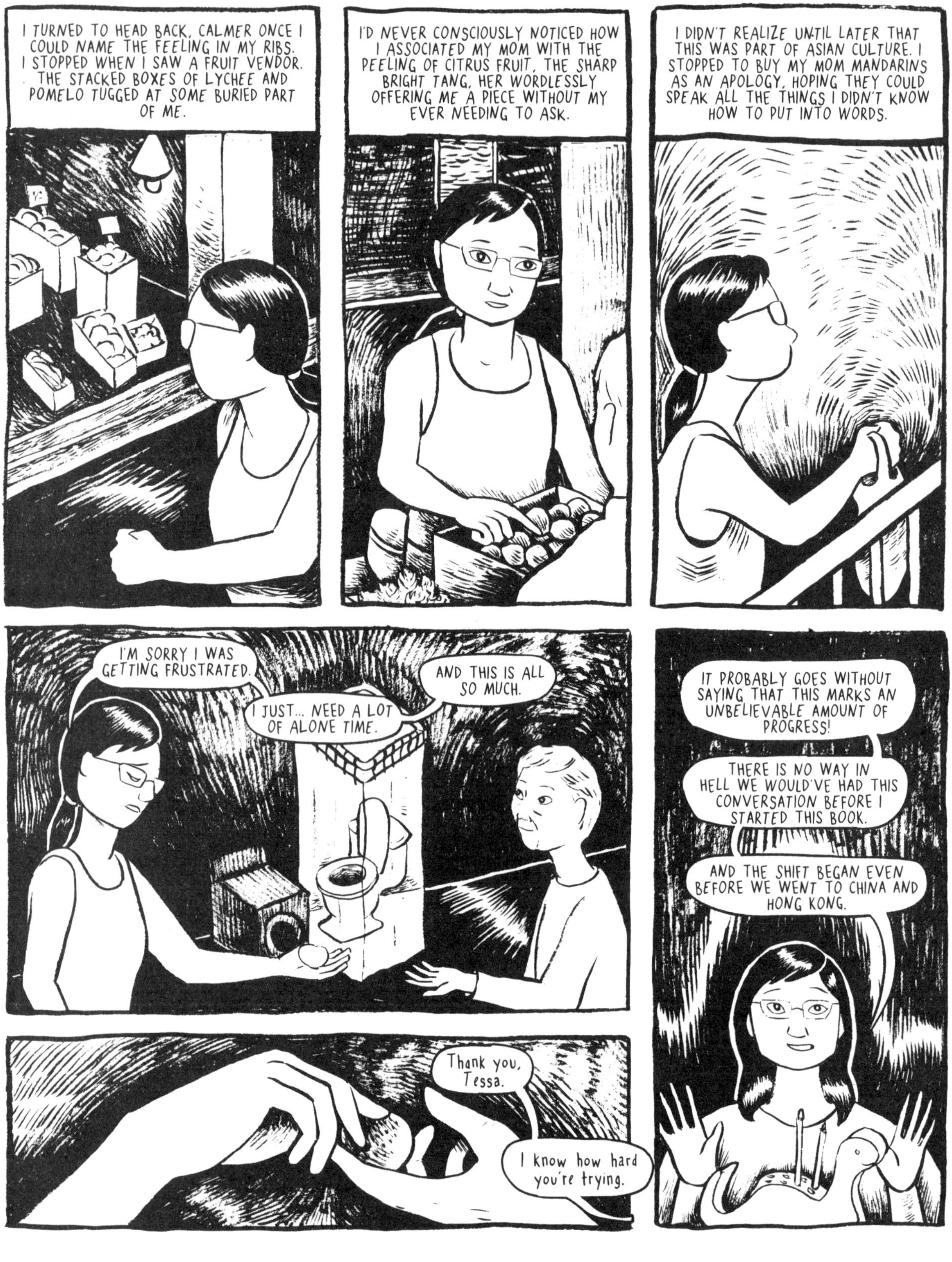
I TURNED TO HEAD BACK, CALMER ONCE I COULD NAME THE FEELING IN MY RIBS. I STOPPED WHEN I SAW A FRUIT VENDOR. THE STACKED BOXES OF LYCHEE AND POMELO TUGGED AT SOME BURIED PART OF ME.
I'D NEVER CONSCIOUSLY NOTICED HOW I ASSOCIATED MY MOM WITH THE PEELING OF CITRUS FRUIT, THE SHARP BRIGHT TANG, HER WORDLESSLY OFFERING ME A PIECE WITHOUT MY EVER NEEDING TO ASK.
I DIDN'T REALIZE UNTIL LATER THAT THIS WAS PART OF ASIAN CULTURE. I STOPPED TO BUY MY MOM MANDARINS AS AN APOLOGY, HOPING THEY COULD SPEAK ALL THE THINGS I DIDN'T KNOW HOW TO PUT INTO WORDS.
I'M SORRY I WAS GETTING FRUSTRATED.
AND THIS IS ALL SO MUCH.
I JUST... NEED A LOT OF ALONE TIME.
Thank you, Tessa.
I know how hard you're trying.
IT PROBABLY GOES WITHOUT SAYING THAT THIS MARKS AN UNBELIEVABLE AMOUNT OF PROGRESS!
THERE IS NO WAY IN HELL WE WOULD'VE HAD THIS CONVERSATION BEFORE I STARTED THIS BOOK.
AND THE SHIFT BEGAN EVEN BEFORE WE WENT TO CHINA AND HONG KONG.

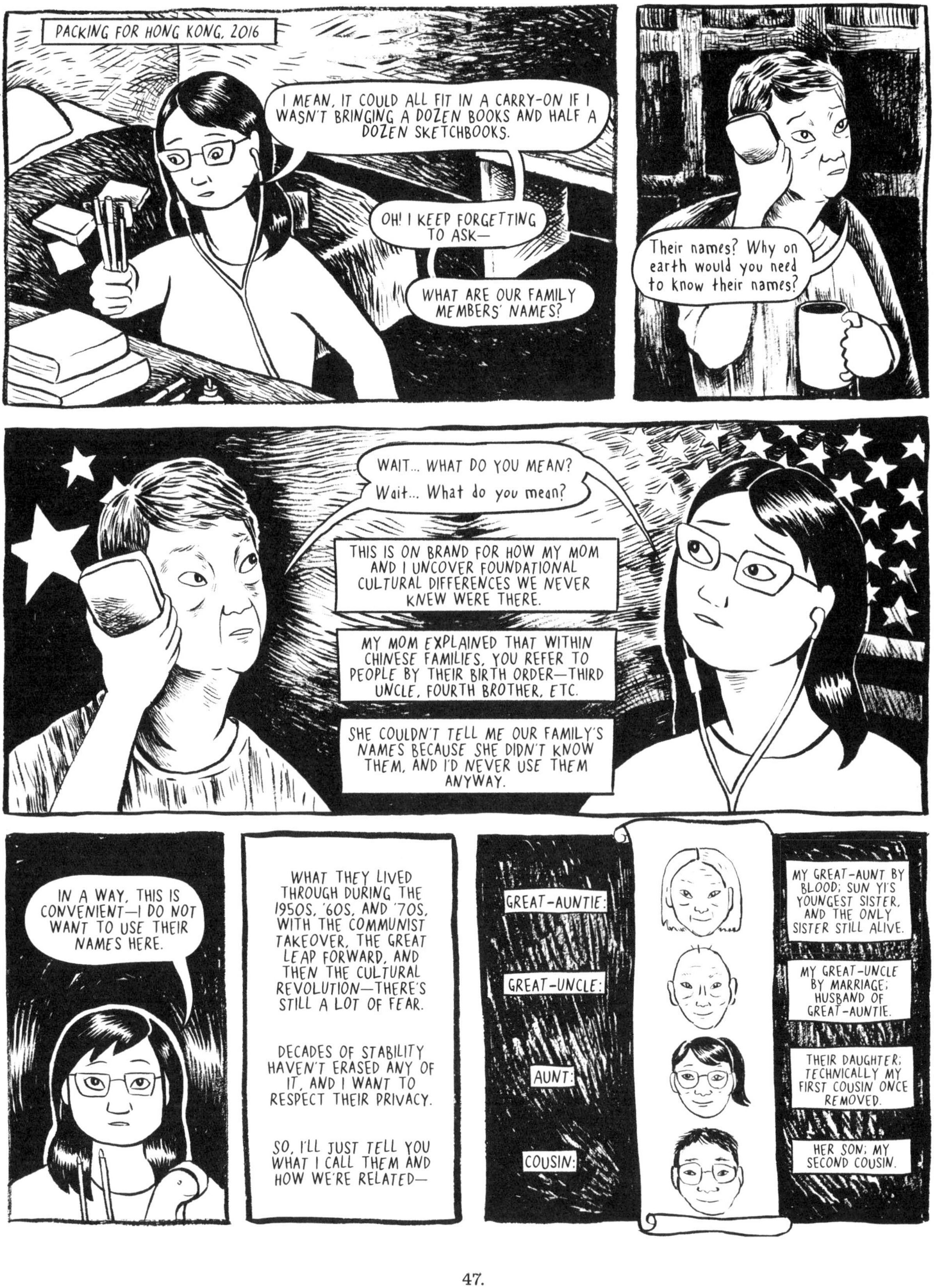

PACKING FOR HONG KONG, 2016
I MEAN, IT COULD ALL FIT IN A CARRY-ON IF I WASN'T BRINGING A DOZEN BOOKS AND HALF A DOZEN SKETCHBOOKS.
OH! I KEEP FORGETTING TO ASK—
WHAT ARE OUR FAMILY MEMBERS' NAMES?
Their names? Why on earth would you need to know their names?
WAIT... WHAT DO YOU MEAN?
Wait... What do you mean?
THIS IS ON BRAND FOR HOW MY MOM AND I UNCOVER FOUNDATIONAL CULTURAL DIFFERENCES WE NEVER KNEW WERE THERE.
MY MOM EXPLAINED THAT WITHIN CHINESE FAMILIES, YOU REFER TO PEOPLE BY THEIR BIRTH ORDER—THIRD UNCLE, FOURTH BROTHER, ETC.
SHE COULDN'T TELL ME OUR FAMILY'S NAMES BECAUSE SHE DIDN'T KNOW THEM, AND I'D NEVER USE THEM ANYWAY.
IN A WAY, THIS IS CONVENIENT—I DO NOT WANT TO USE THEIR NAMES HERE.
WHAT THEY LIVED THROUGH DURING THE 1950S, '60S, AND '70S, WITH THE COMMUNIST TAKEOVER, THE GREAT LEAP FORWARD, AND THEN THE CULTURAL REVOLUTION—THERE'S STILL A LOT OF FEAR.
DECADES OF STABILITY HAVEN'T ERASED ANY OF IT, AND I WANT TO RESPECT THEIR PRIVACY.
SO, I'LL JUST TELL YOU WHAT I CALL THEM AND HOW WE'RE RELATED—
GREAT-AUNTIE:
MY GREAT-AUNT BY BLOOD; SUN YI'S YOUNGEST SISTER, AND THE ONLY SISTER STILL ALIVE.
GREAT-UNCLE:
MY GREAT-UNCLE BY MARRIAGE; HUSBAND OF GREAT-AUNTIE.
AUNT:
THEIR DAUGHTER; TECHNICALLY MY FIRST COUSIN ONCE REMOVED.
COUSIN:
HER SON; MY SECOND COUSIN.

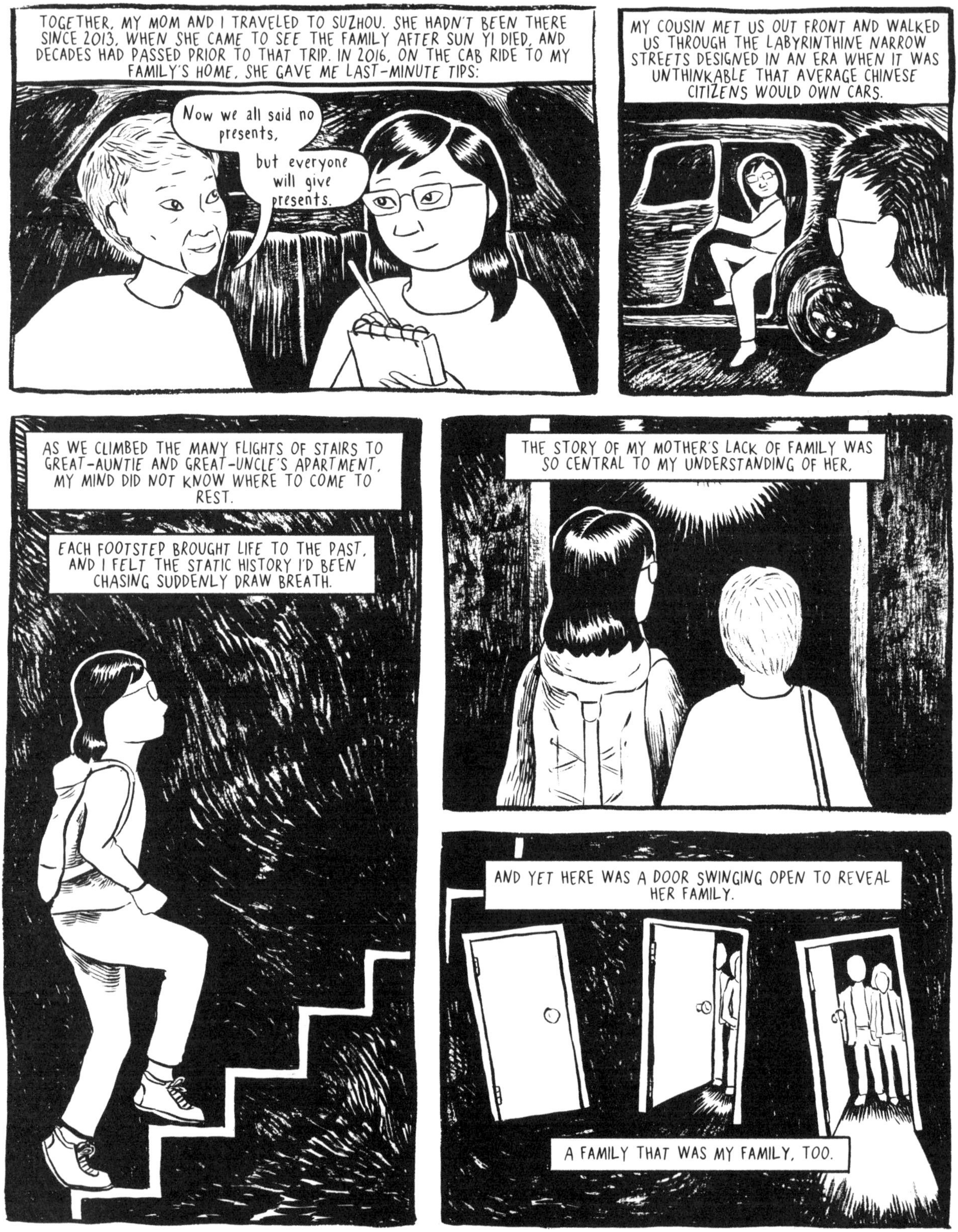
TOGETHER, MY MOM AND I TRAVELED TO SUZHOU. SHE HADN'T BEEN THERE SINCE 2013, WHEN SHE CAME TO SEE THE FAMILY AFTER SUN YI DIED, AND DECADES HAD PASSED PRIOR TO THAT TRIP. IN 2016, ON THE CAB RIDE TO MY FAMILY'S HOME, SHE GAVE ME LAST-MINUTE TIPS:
Now we all said no presents,
but everyone will give presents.
MY COUSIN MET US OUT FRONT AND WALKED US THROUGH THE LABYRINTHINE NARROW STREETS DESIGNED IN AN ERA WHEN IT WAS UNTHINKABLE THAT AVERAGE CHINESE CITIZENS WOULD OWN CARS.
AS WE CLIMBED THE MANY FLIGHTS OF STAIRS TO GREAT-AUNTIE AND GREAT-UNCLE'S APARTMENT, MY MIND DID NOT KNOW WHERE TO COME TO REST.
EACH FOOTSTEP BROUGHT LIFE TO THE PAST, AND I FELT THE STATIC HISTORY I'D BEEN CHASING SUDDENLY DRAW BREATH.
THE STORY OF MY MOTHER'S LACK OF FAMILY WAS SO CENTRAL TO MY UNDERSTANDING OF HER,
AND YET HERE WAS A DOOR SWINGING OPEN TO REVEAL HER FAMILY.
A FAMILY THAT WAS MY FAMILY, TOO.

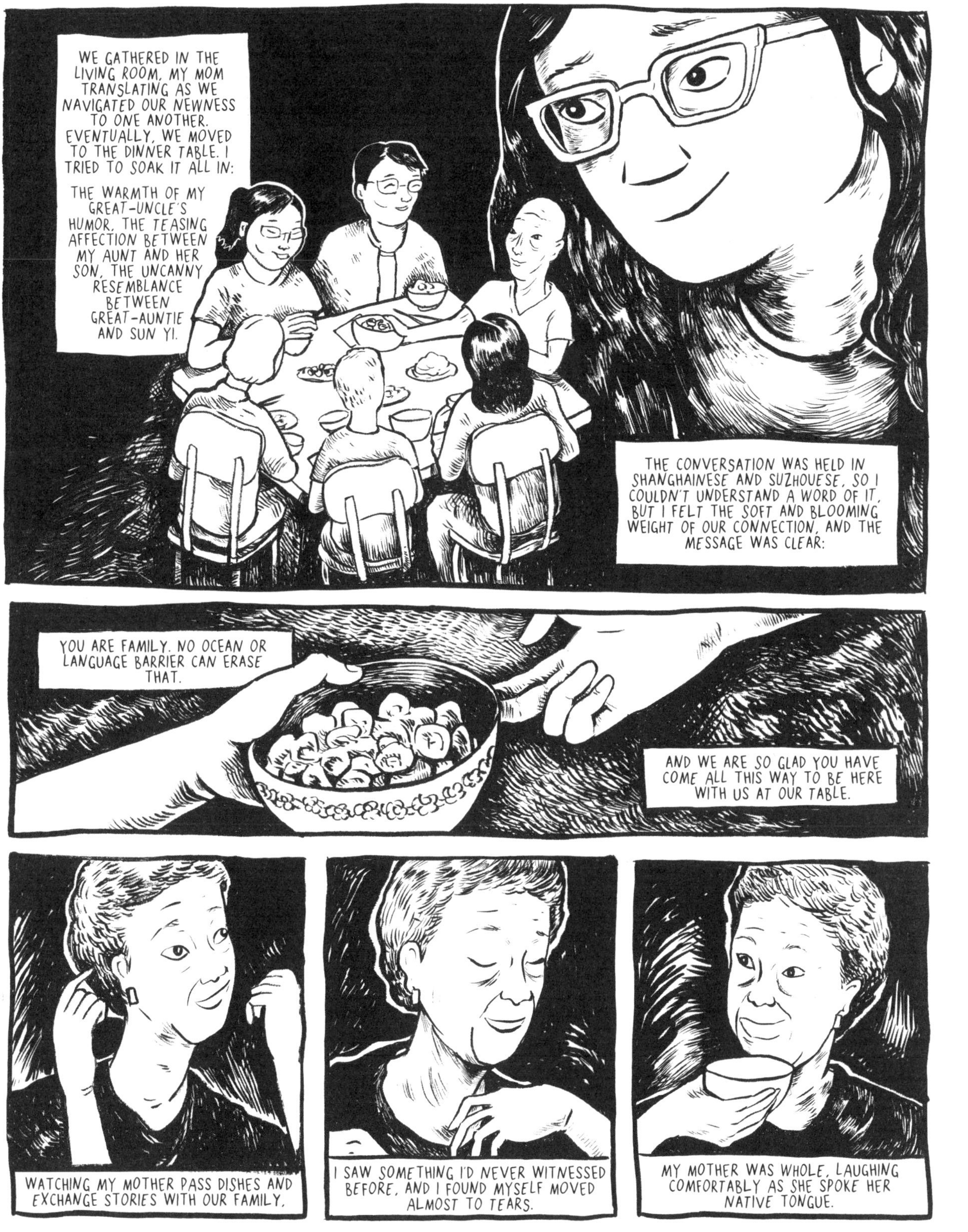
WE GATHERED IN THE LIVING ROOM, MY MOM TRANSLATING AS WE NAVIGATED OUR NEWNESS TO ONE ANOTHER. EVENTUALLY, WE MOVED TO THE DINNER TABLE. I TRIED TO SOAK IT ALL IN:
THE WARMTH OF MY GREAT-UNCLE'S HUMOR, THE TEASING AFFECTION BETWEEN MY AUNT AND HER SON, THE UNCANNY RESEMBLANCE BETWEEN GREAT-AUNTIE AND SUN YI.
THE CONVERSATION WAS HELD IN SHANGHAINESE AND SUZHOUESE, SO I COULDN'T UNDERSTAND A WORD OF IT, BUT I FELT THE SOFT AND BLOOMING WEIGHT OF OUR CONNECTION, AND THE MESSAGE WAS CLEAR:
YOU ARE FAMILY. NO OCEAN OR LANGUAGE BARRIER CAN ERASE THAT.
AND WE ARE SO GLAD YOU HAVE COME ALL THIS WAY TO BE HERE WITH US AT OUR TABLE.
WATCHING MY MOTHER PASS DISHES AND EXCHANGE STORIES WITH OUR FAMILY,
I SAW SOMETHING I'D NEVER WITNESSED BEFORE, AND I FOUND MYSELF MOVED ALMOST TO TEARS.
MY MOTHER WAS WHOLE, LAUGHING COMFORTABLY AS SHE SPOKE HER NATIVE TONGUE.

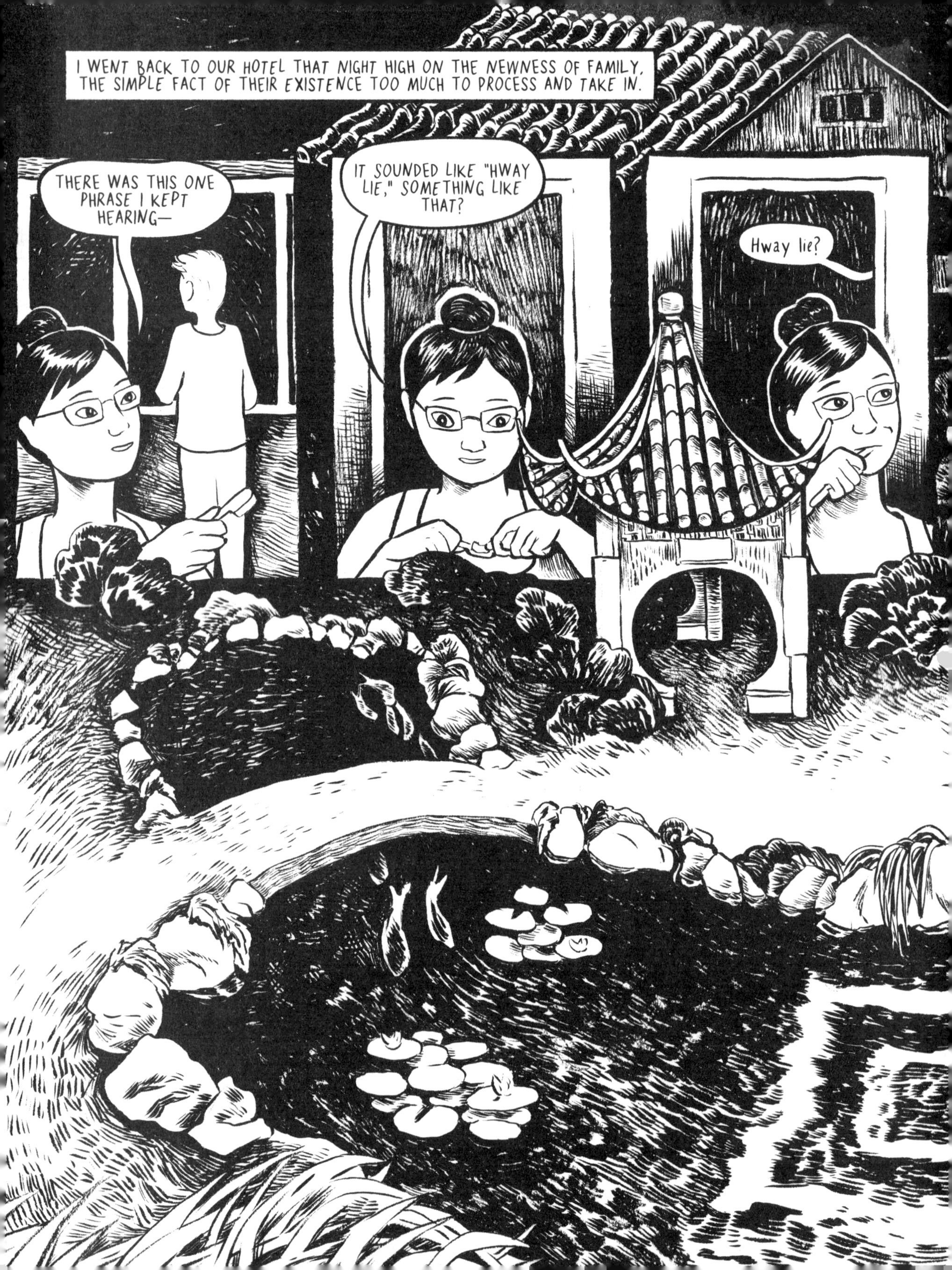
I WENT BACK TO OUR HOTEL THAT NIGHT HIGH ON THE NEWNESS OF FAMILY, THE SIMPLE FACT OF THEIR EXISTENCE TOO MUCH TO PROCESS AND TAKE IN.
THERE WAS THIS ONE PHRASE I KEPT HEARING—
IT SOUNDED LIKE "HWAY LIE," SOMETHING LIKE THAT?
Hway lie?

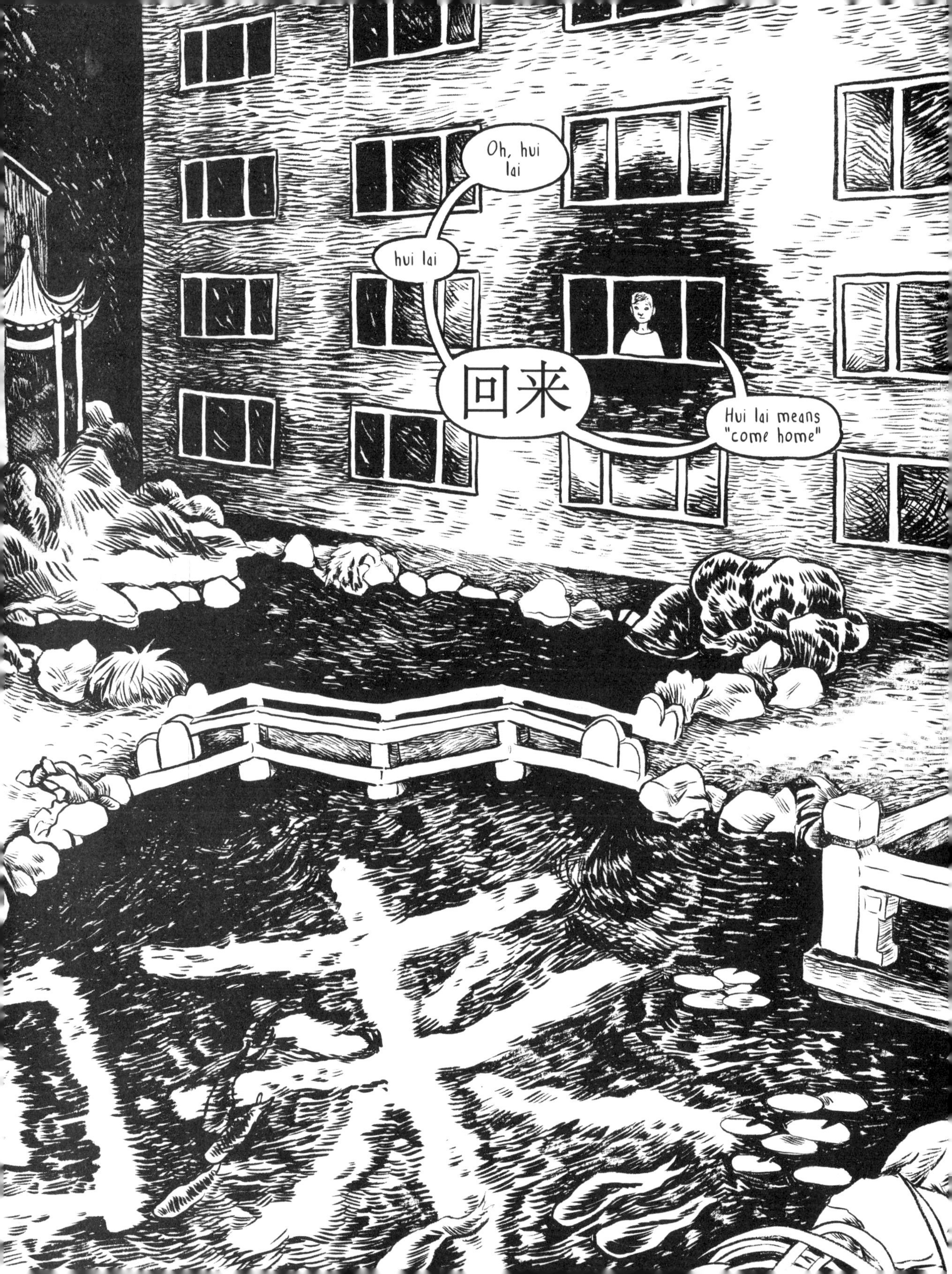
Oh, hui lai
hui lai
回来
Hui lai means "come home"

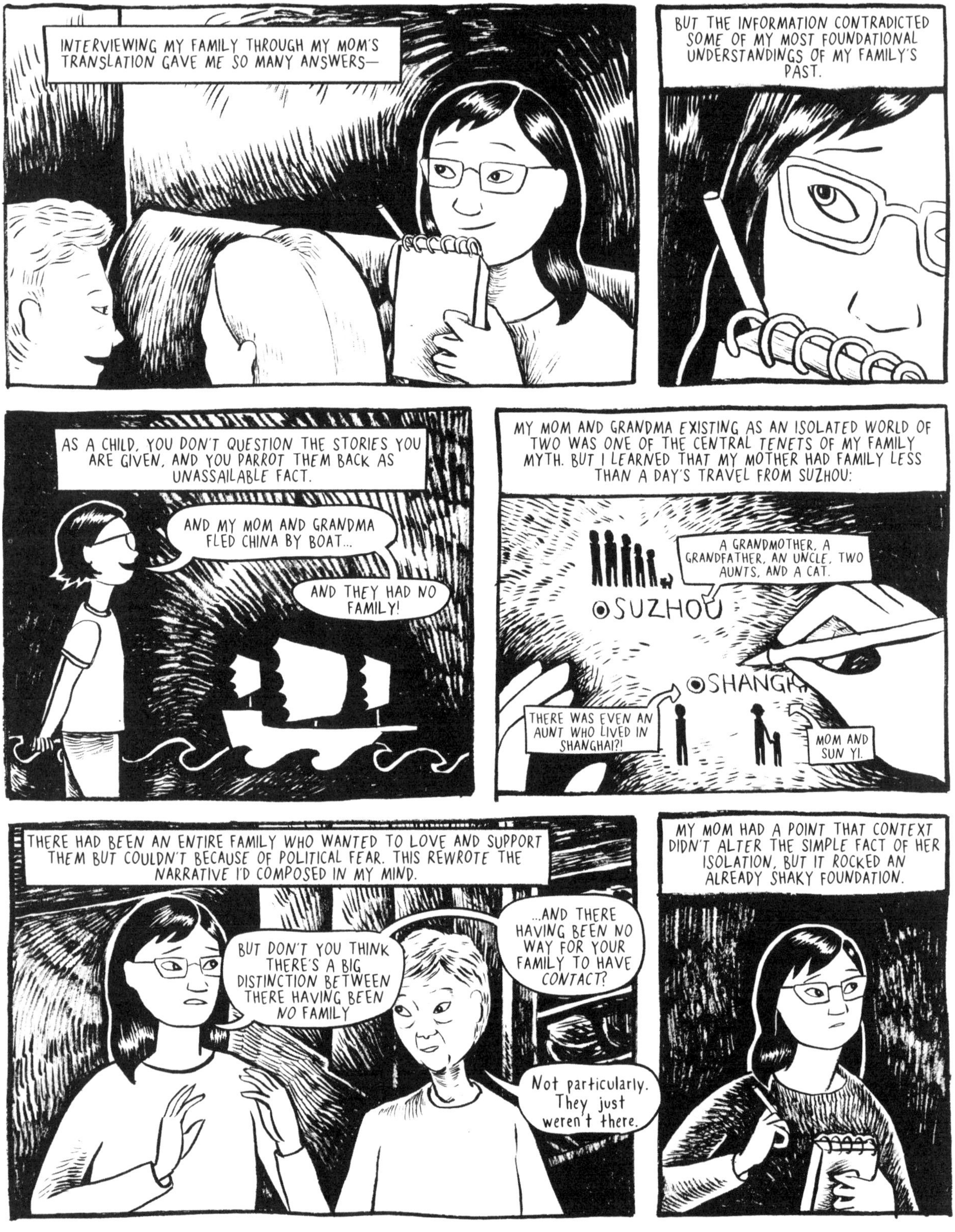
INTERVIEWING MY FAMILY THROUGH MY MOM'S TRANSLATION GAVE ME SO MANY ANSWERS—
BUT THE INFORMATION CONTRADICTED SOME OF MY MOST FOUNDATIONAL UNDERSTANDINGS OF MY FAMILY'S PAST.
AS A CHILD, YOU DON'T QUESTION THE STORIES YOU ARE GIVEN, AND YOU PARROT THEM BACK AS UNASSAILABLE FACT.
AND MY MOM AND GRANDMA FLED CHINA BY BOAT...
AND THEY HAD NO FAMILY!
MY MOM AND GRANDMA EXISTING AS AN ISOLATED WORLD OF TWO WAS ONE OF THE CENTRAL TENETS OF MY FAMILY MYTH. BUT I LEARNED THAT MY MOTHER HAD FAMILY LESS THAN A DAY'S TRAVEL FROM SUZHOU:
A GRANDMOTHER, A GRANDFATHER, AN UNCLE, TWO AUNTS, AND A CAT.
SUZHOU
SHANGH
THERE WAS EVEN AN AUNT WHO LIVED IN SHANGHAI?!
MOM AND SUN YI.
THERE HAD BEEN AN ENTIRE FAMILY WHO WANTED TO LOVE AND SUPPORT THEM BUT COULDN'T BECAUSE OF POLITICAL FEAR. THIS REWROTE THE NARRATIVE I'D COMPOSED IN MY MIND.
BUT DON'T YOU THINK THERE'S A BIG DISTINCTION BETWEEN THERE HAVING BEEN NO FAMILY
...AND THERE HAVING BEEN NO WAY FOR YOUR FAMILY TO HAVE CONTACT?
Not particularly. They just weren't there.
MY MOM HAD A POINT THAT CONTEXT DIDN'T ALTER THE SIMPLE FACT OF HER ISOLATION, BUT IT ROCKED AN ALREADY SHAKY FOUNDATION.

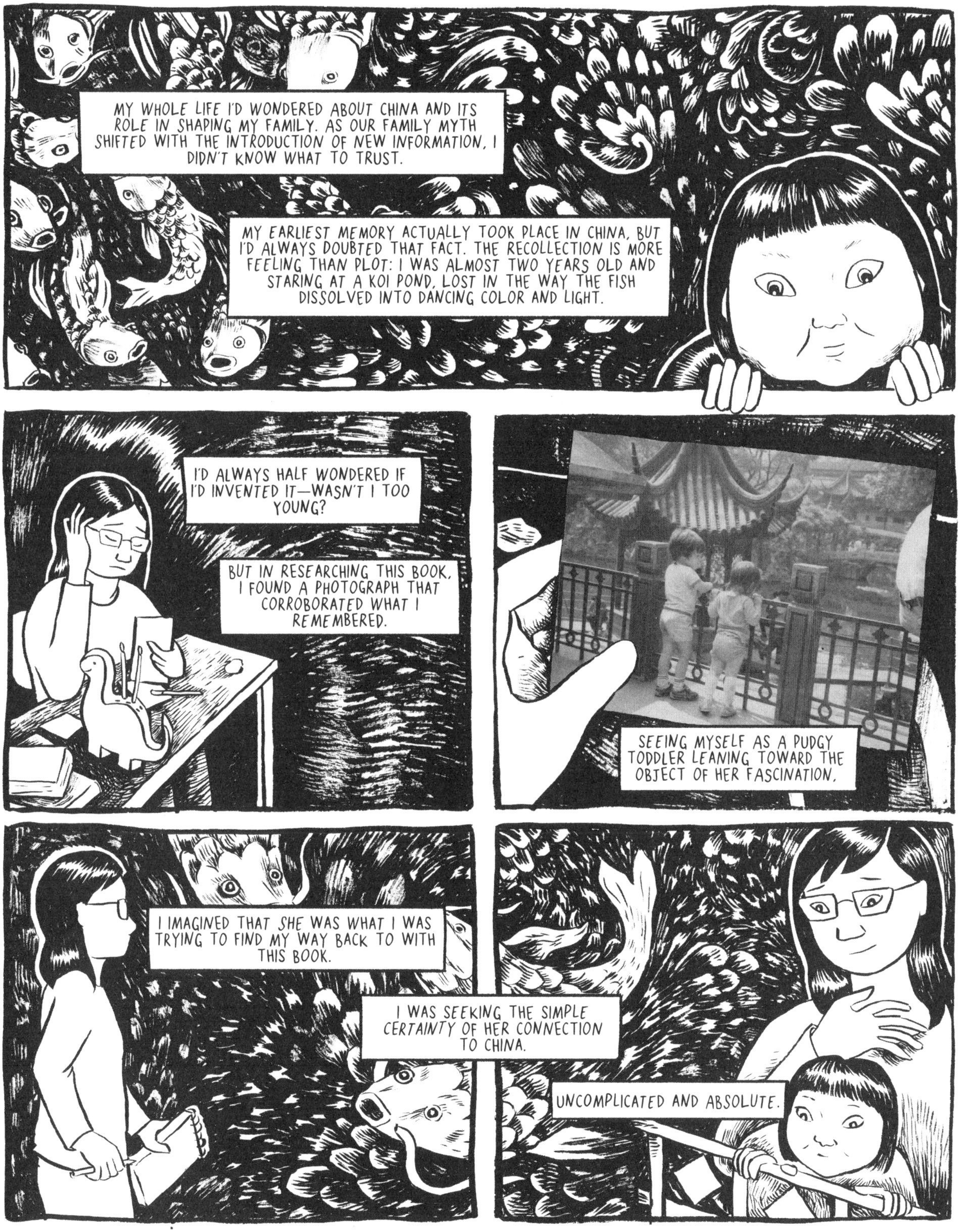

MY WHOLE LIFE I'D WONDERED ABOUT CHINA AND ITS ROLE IN SHAPING MY FAMILY. AS OUR FAMILY MYTH SHIFTED WITH THE INTRODUCTION OF NEW INFORMATION, I DIDN'T KNOW WHAT TO TRUST.
MY EARLIEST MEMORY ACTUALLY TOOK PLACE IN CHINA, BUT I'D ALWAYS DOUBTED THAT FACT. THE RECOLLECTION IS MORE FEELING THAN PLOT: I WAS ALMOST TWO YEARS OLD AND STARING AT A KOI POND, LOST IN THE WAY THE FISH DISSOLVED INTO DANCING COLOR AND LIGHT.
I'D ALWAYS HALF WONDERED IF I'D INVENTED IT—WASN'T I TOO YOUNG?
BUT IN RESEARCHING THIS BOOK, I FOUND A PHOTOGRAPH THAT CORROBORATED WHAT I REMEMBERED.
SEEING MYSELF AS A PUDGY TODDLER LEANING TOWARD THE OBJECT OF HER FASCINATION,
I IMAGINED THAT *SHE* WAS WHAT I WAS TRYING TO FIND MY WAY BACK TO WITH THIS BOOK.
I WAS SEEKING THE SIMPLE *CERTAINTY* OF HER CONNECTION TO CHINA.
UNCOMPLICATED AND ABSOLUTE.

I FELT THAT CONNECTION IN SUZHOU WITH OUR FAMILY. WE FELL INTO AN EASY RHYTHM: EACH NIGHT WE'D EAT TOGETHER, SHARING STORIES.

WE'D TALK UNTIL WE LAPSED INTO A COMFORTABLE SILENCE, THEN I'D MAKE MY MOM PRACTICE NAVIGATING ON THE WAY BACK TO OUR HOTEL.

IT'S NOT MAGIC, IT'S A SKILL YOU HAVE TO LEARN.

I can't!

YES YOU CAN!

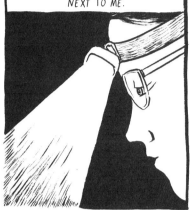

I'D STAY UP LATE, WRITING BY HEADLAMP, CAPTURING THE DAY'S STORIES AS MY MOTHER SNORED SOFTLY IN THE BED NEXT TO ME.

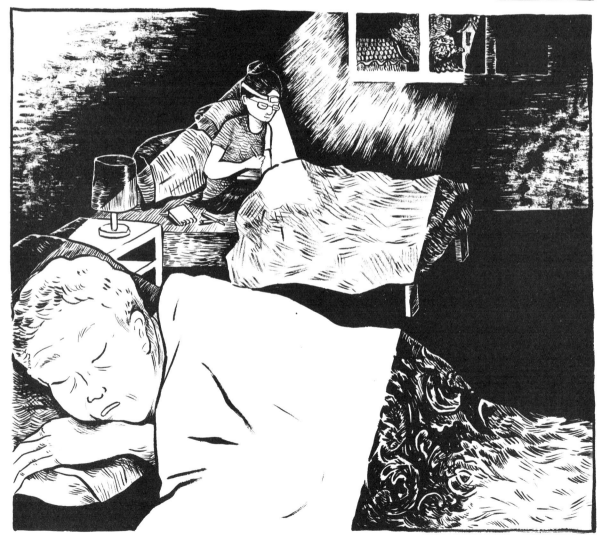

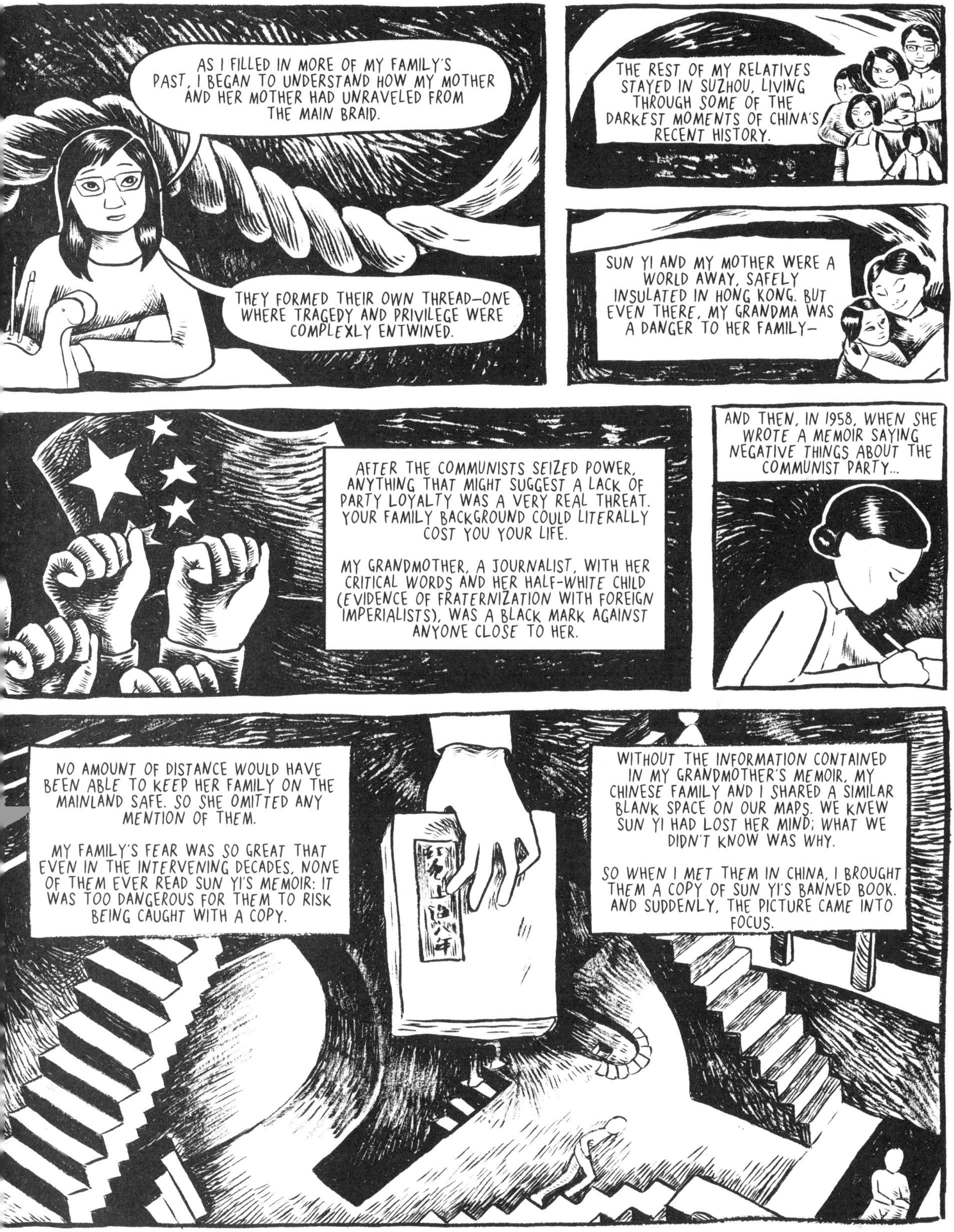
AS I FILLED IN MORE OF MY FAMILY'S PAST, I BEGAN TO UNDERSTAND HOW MY MOTHER AND HER MOTHER HAD UNRAVELED FROM THE MAIN BRAID.
THEY FORMED THEIR OWN THREAD—ONE WHERE TRAGEDY AND PRIVILEGE WERE COMPLEXLY ENTWINED.
THE REST OF MY RELATIVES STAYED IN SUZHOU, LIVING THROUGH SOME OF THE DARKEST MOMENTS OF CHINA'S RECENT HISTORY.
SUN YI AND MY MOTHER WERE A WORLD AWAY, SAFELY INSULATED IN HONG KONG. BUT EVEN THERE, MY GRANDMA WAS A DANGER TO HER FAMILY—
AFTER THE COMMUNISTS SEIZED POWER, ANYTHING THAT MIGHT SUGGEST A LACK OF PARTY LOYALTY WAS A VERY REAL THREAT. YOUR FAMILY BACKGROUND COULD LITERALLY COST YOU YOUR LIFE.
MY GRANDMOTHER, A JOURNALIST, WITH HER CRITICAL WORDS AND HER HALF-WHITE CHILD (EVIDENCE OF FRATERNIZATION WITH FOREIGN IMPERIALISTS), WAS A BLACK MARK AGAINST ANYONE CLOSE TO HER.
AND THEN, IN 1958, WHEN SHE WROTE A MEMOIR SAYING NEGATIVE THINGS ABOUT THE COMMUNIST PARTY...
NO AMOUNT OF DISTANCE WOULD HAVE BEEN ABLE TO KEEP HER FAMILY ON THE MAINLAND SAFE. SO SHE OMITTED ANY MENTION OF THEM.
MY FAMILY'S FEAR WAS SO GREAT THAT EVEN IN THE INTERVENING DECADES, NONE OF THEM EVER READ SUN YI'S MEMOIR: IT WAS TOO DANGEROUS FOR THEM TO RISK BEING CAUGHT WITH A COPY.
WITHOUT THE INFORMATION CONTAINED IN MY GRANDMOTHER'S MEMOIR, MY CHINESE FAMILY AND I SHARED A SIMILAR BLANK SPACE ON OUR MAPS. WE KNEW SUN YI HAD LOST HER MIND; WHAT WE DIDN'T KNOW WAS WHY.
SO WHEN I MET THEM IN CHINA, I BROUGHT THEM A COPY OF SUN YI'S BANNED BOOK. AND SUDDENLY, THE PICTURE CAME INTO FOCUS.

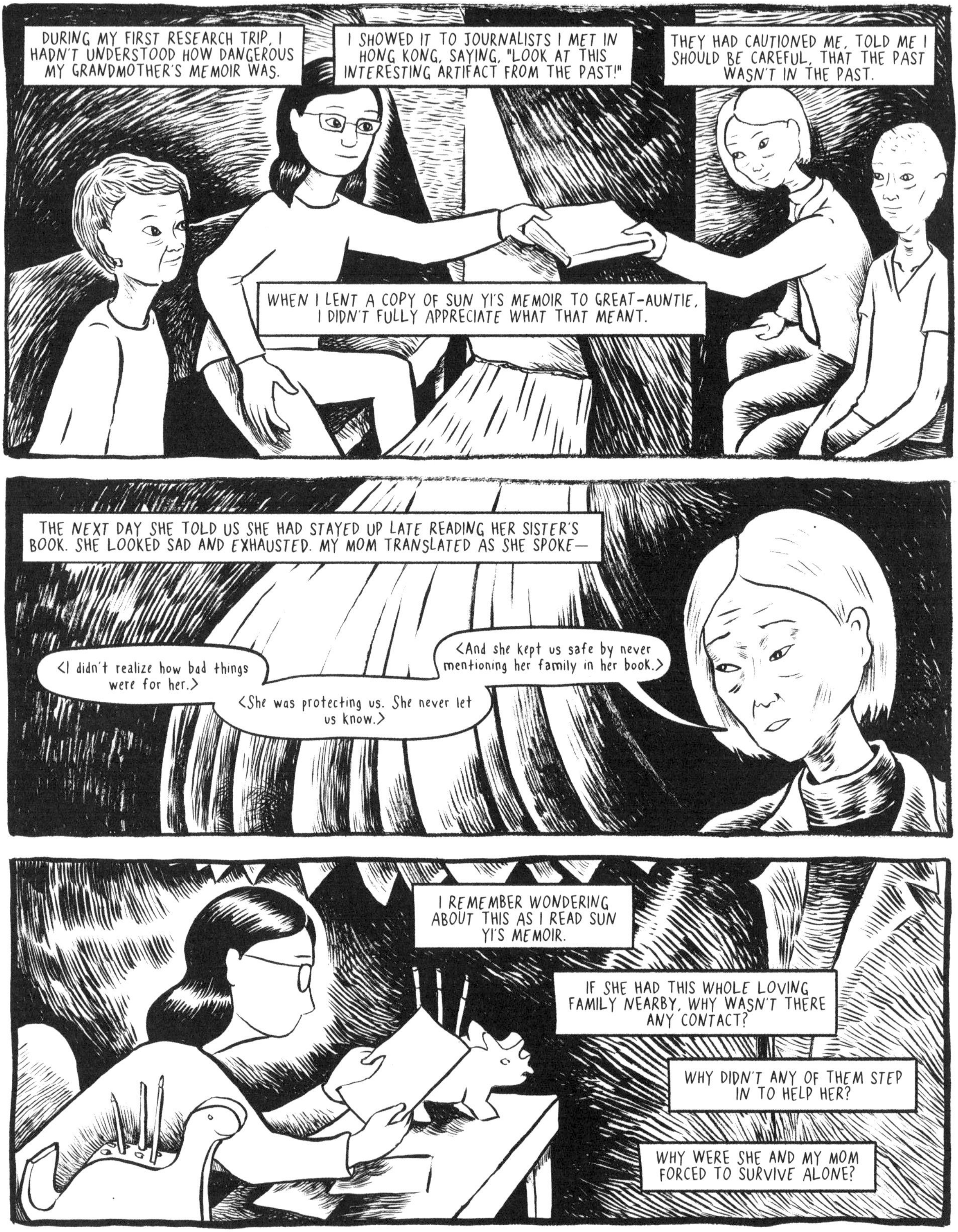
DURING MY FIRST RESEARCH TRIP, I HADN'T UNDERSTOOD HOW DANGEROUS MY GRANDMOTHER'S MEMOIR WAS.
I SHOWED IT TO JOURNALISTS I MET IN HONG KONG, SAYING, "LOOK AT THIS INTERESTING ARTIFACT FROM THE PAST!"
THEY HAD CAUTIONED ME, TOLD ME I SHOULD BE CAREFUL, THAT THE PAST WASN'T IN THE PAST.
WHEN I LENT A COPY OF SUN YI'S MEMOIR TO GREAT-AUNTIE, I DIDN'T FULLY APPRECIATE WHAT THAT MEANT.
THE NEXT DAY SHE TOLD US SHE HAD STAYED UP LATE READING HER SISTER'S BOOK. SHE LOOKED SAD AND EXHAUSTED. MY MOM TRANSLATED AS SHE SPOKE—
<I didn't realize how bad things were for her.>
<She was protecting us. She never let us know.>
<And she kept us safe by never mentioning her family in her book.>
I REMEMBER WONDERING ABOUT THIS AS I READ SUN YI'S MEMOIR.
IF SHE HAD THIS WHOLE LOVING FAMILY NEARBY, WHY WASN'T THERE ANY CONTACT?
WHY DIDN'T ANY OF THEM STEP IN TO HELP HER?
WHY WERE SHE AND MY MOM FORCED TO SURVIVE ALONE?

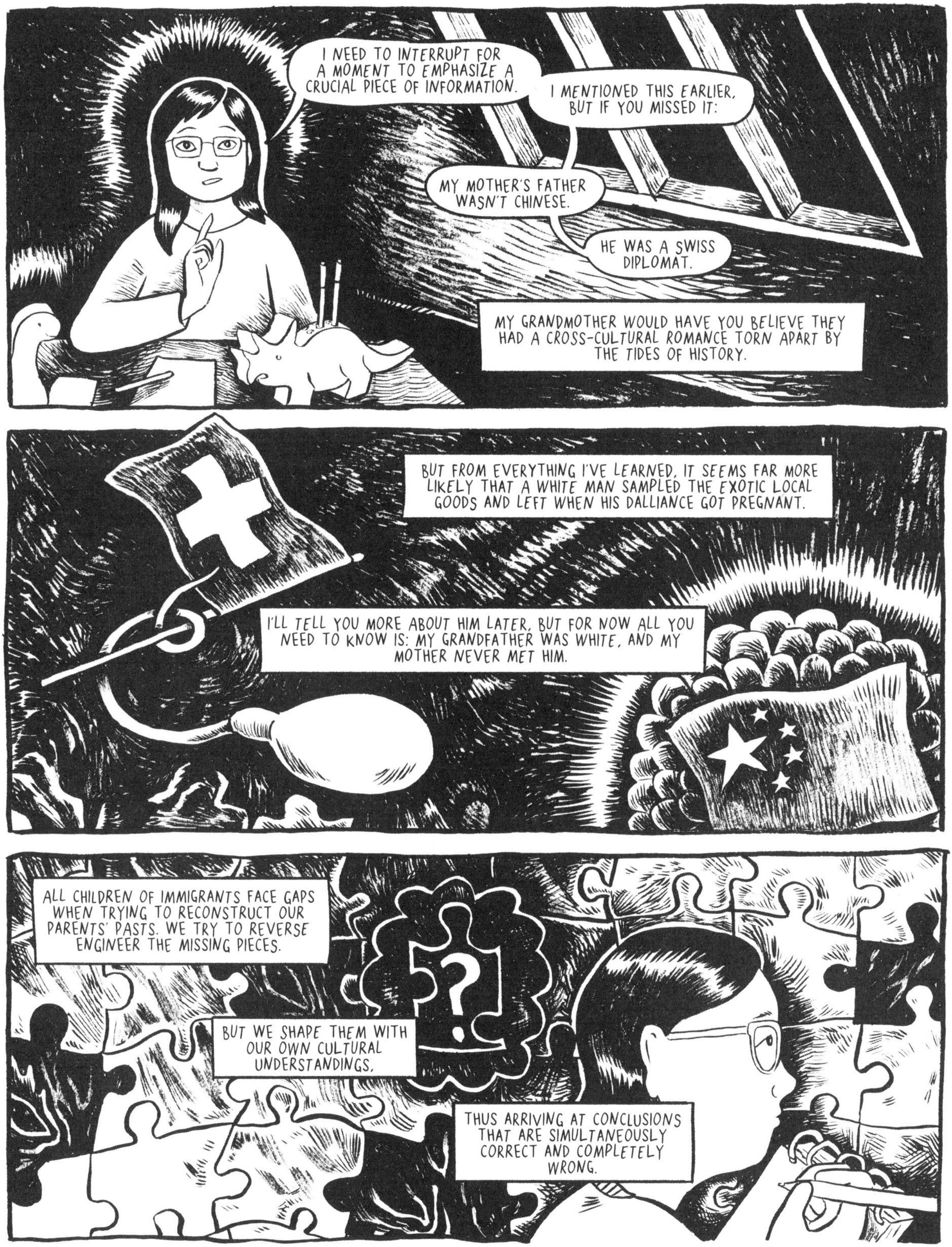
I NEED TO INTERRUPT FOR A MOMENT TO EMPHASIZE A CRUCIAL PIECE OF INFORMATION.
I MENTIONED THIS EARLIER, BUT IF YOU MISSED IT:
MY MOTHER'S FATHER WASN'T CHINESE.
HE WAS A SWISS DIPLOMAT.
MY GRANDMOTHER WOULD HAVE YOU BELIEVE THEY HAD A CROSS-CULTURAL ROMANCE TORN APART BY THE TIDES OF HISTORY.
BUT FROM EVERYTHING I'VE LEARNED, IT SEEMS FAR MORE LIKELY THAT A WHITE MAN SAMPLED THE EXOTIC LOCAL GOODS AND LEFT WHEN HIS DALLIANCE GOT PREGNANT.
I'LL TELL YOU MORE ABOUT HIM LATER, BUT FOR NOW ALL YOU NEED TO KNOW IS: MY GRANDFATHER WAS WHITE, AND MY MOTHER NEVER MET HIM.
ALL CHILDREN OF IMMIGRANTS FACE GAPS WHEN TRYING TO RECONSTRUCT OUR PARENTS' PASTS. WE TRY TO REVERSE ENGINEER THE MISSING PIECES.
?
BUT WE SHAPE THEM WITH OUR OWN CULTURAL UNDERSTANDINGS,
THUS ARRIVING AT CONCLUSIONS THAT ARE SIMULTANEOUSLY CORRECT AND COMPLETELY WRONG.

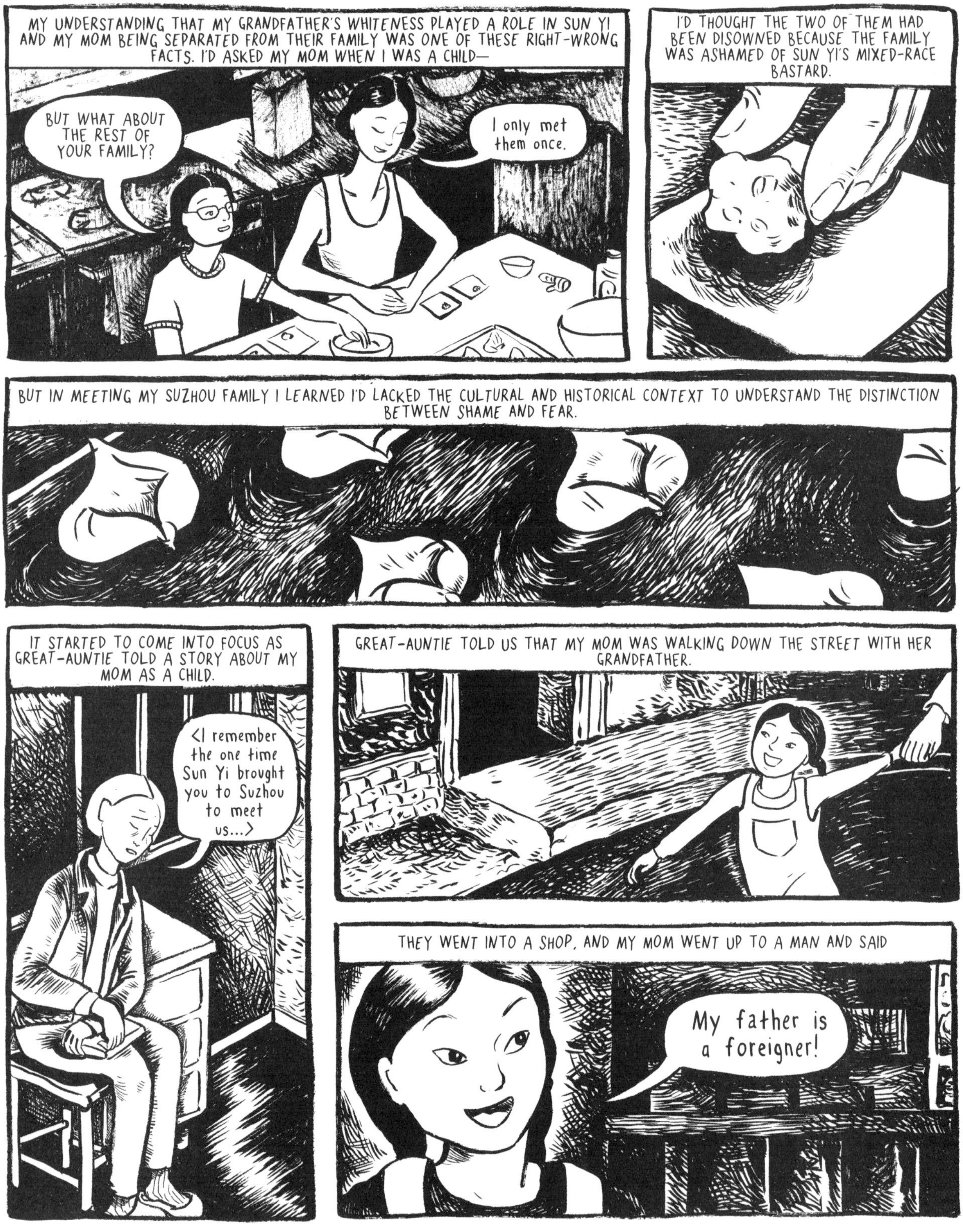

MY UNDERSTANDING THAT MY GRANDFATHER'S WHITENESS PLAYED A ROLE IN SUN YI AND MY MOM BEING SEPARATED FROM THEIR FAMILY WAS ONE OF THESE RIGHT-WRONG FACTS. I'D ASKED MY MOM WHEN I WAS A CHILD—
BUT WHAT ABOUT THE REST OF YOUR FAMILY?
I only met them once.
I'D THOUGHT THE TWO OF THEM HAD BEEN DISOWNED BECAUSE THE FAMILY WAS ASHAMED OF SUN YI'S MIXED-RACE BASTARD.
BUT IN MEETING MY SUZHOU FAMILY I LEARNED I'D LACKED THE CULTURAL AND HISTORICAL CONTEXT TO UNDERSTAND THE DISTINCTION BETWEEN SHAME AND FEAR.
IT STARTED TO COME INTO FOCUS AS GREAT-AUNTIE TOLD A STORY ABOUT MY MOM AS A CHILD.
<I remember the one time Sun Yi brought you to Suzhou to meet us...>
GREAT-AUNTIE TOLD US THAT MY MOM WAS WALKING DOWN THE STREET WITH HER GRANDFATHER.
THEY WENT INTO A SHOP, AND MY MOM WENT UP TO A MAN AND SAID
My father is a foreigner!

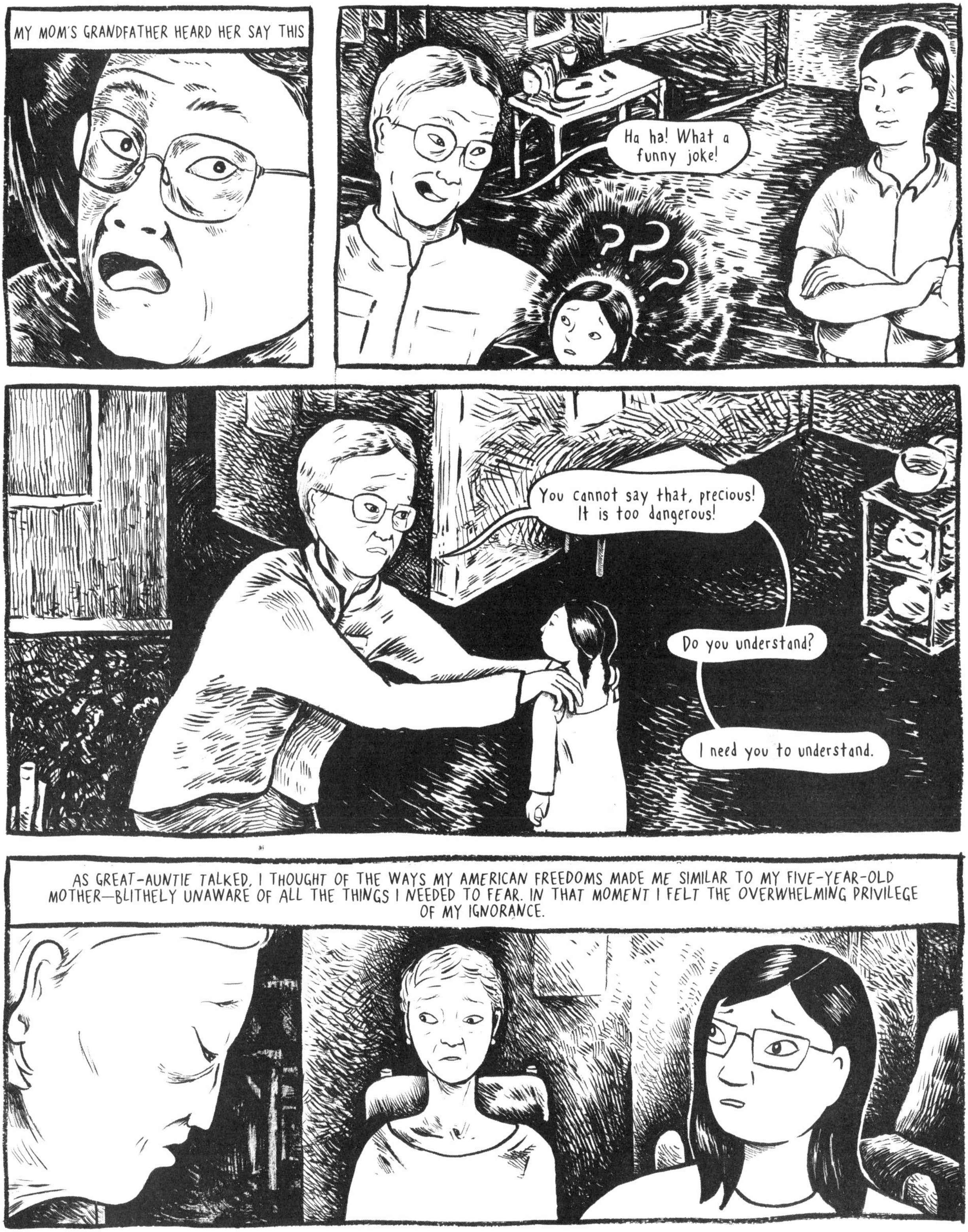
MY MOM'S GRANDFATHER HEARD HER SAY THIS
Ha ha! What a funny joke!
???
You cannot say that, precious! It is too dangerous!
Do you understand?
I need you to understand.
AS GREAT-AUNTIE TALKED, I THOUGHT OF THE WAYS MY AMERICAN FREEDOMS MADE ME SIMILAR TO MY FIVE-YEAR-OLD MOTHER—BLITHELY UNAWARE OF ALL THE THINGS I NEEDED TO FEAR. IN THAT MOMENT I FELT THE OVERWHELMING PRIVILEGE OF MY IGNORANCE.

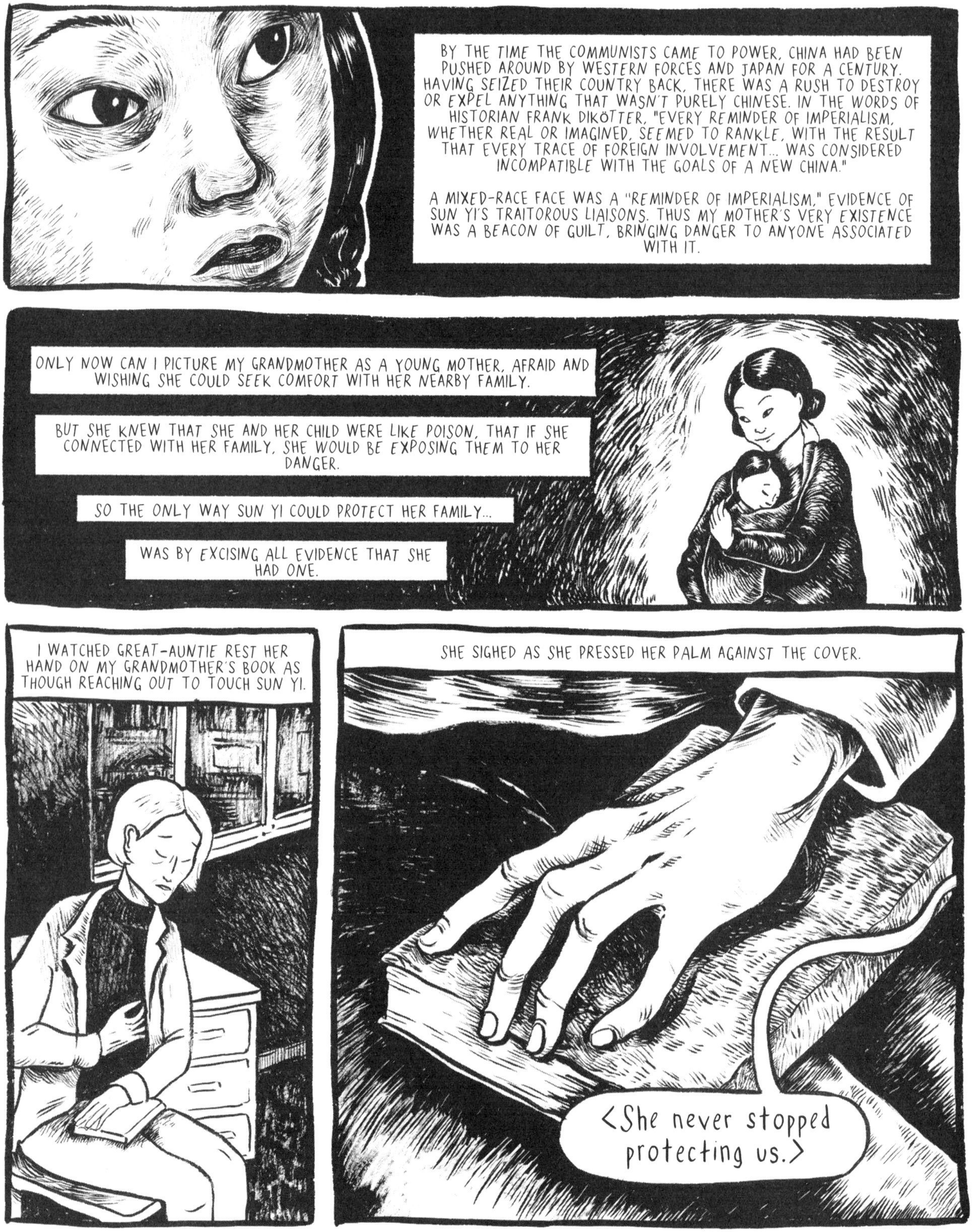

BY THE TIME THE COMMUNISTS CAME TO POWER, CHINA HAD BEEN PUSHED AROUND BY WESTERN FORCES AND JAPAN FOR A CENTURY. HAVING SEIZED THEIR COUNTRY BACK, THERE WAS A RUSH TO DESTROY OR EXPEL ANYTHING THAT WASN'T PURELY CHINESE. IN THE WORDS OF HISTORIAN FRANK DIKÖTTER, "EVERY REMINDER OF IMPERIALISM, WHETHER REAL OR IMAGINED, SEEMED TO RANKLE, WITH THE RESULT THAT EVERY TRACE OF FOREIGN INVOLVEMENT... WAS CONSIDERED INCOMPATIBLE WITH THE GOALS OF A NEW CHINA."
A MIXED-RACE FACE WAS A "REMINDER OF IMPERIALISM," EVIDENCE OF SUN YI'S TRAITOROUS LIAISONS. THUS MY MOTHER'S VERY EXISTENCE WAS A BEACON OF GUILT, BRINGING DANGER TO ANYONE ASSOCIATED WITH IT.
ONLY NOW CAN I PICTURE MY GRANDMOTHER AS A YOUNG MOTHER, AFRAID AND WISHING SHE COULD SEEK COMFORT WITH HER NEARBY FAMILY.
BUT SHE KNEW THAT SHE AND HER CHILD WERE LIKE POISON, THAT IF SHE CONNECTED WITH HER FAMILY, SHE WOULD BE EXPOSING THEM TO HER DANGER.
SO THE ONLY WAY SUN YI COULD PROTECT HER FAMILY...
WAS BY EXCISING ALL EVIDENCE THAT SHE HAD ONE.
I WATCHED GREAT-AUNTIE REST HER HAND ON MY GRANDMOTHER'S BOOK AS THOUGH REACHING OUT TO TOUCH SUN YI.
SHE SIGHED AS SHE PRESSED HER PALM AGAINST THE COVER.
<She never stopped protecting us.>

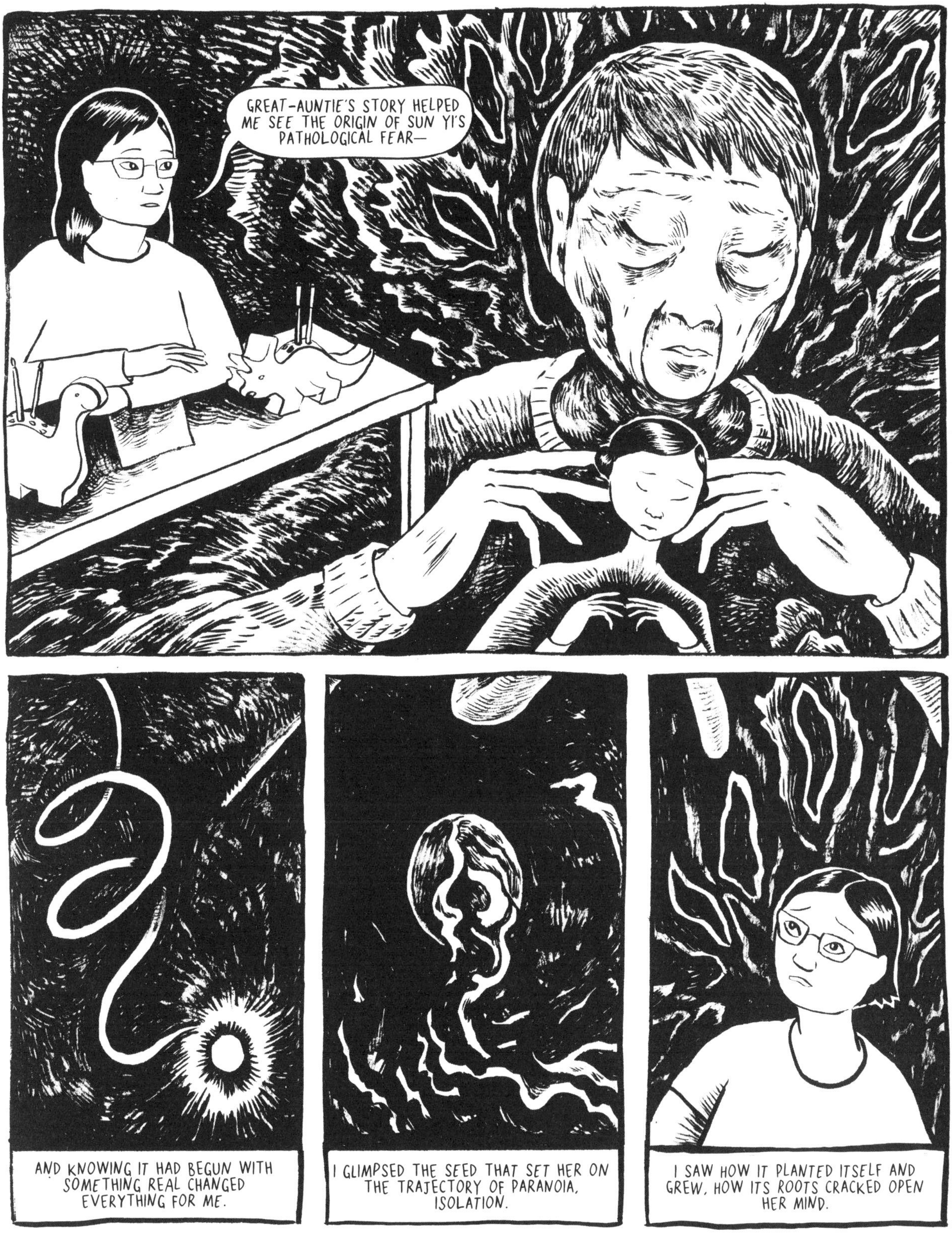
GREAT-AUNTIE'S STORY HELPED ME SEE THE ORIGIN OF SUN YI'S PATHOLOGICAL FEAR—
AND KNOWING IT HAD BEGUN WITH SOMETHING REAL CHANGED EVERYTHING FOR ME.
I GLIMPSED THE SEED THAT SET HER ON THE TRAJECTORY OF PARANOIA, ISOLATION.
I SAW HOW IT PLANTED ITSELF AND GREW, HOW ITS ROOTS CRACKED OPEN HER MIND.

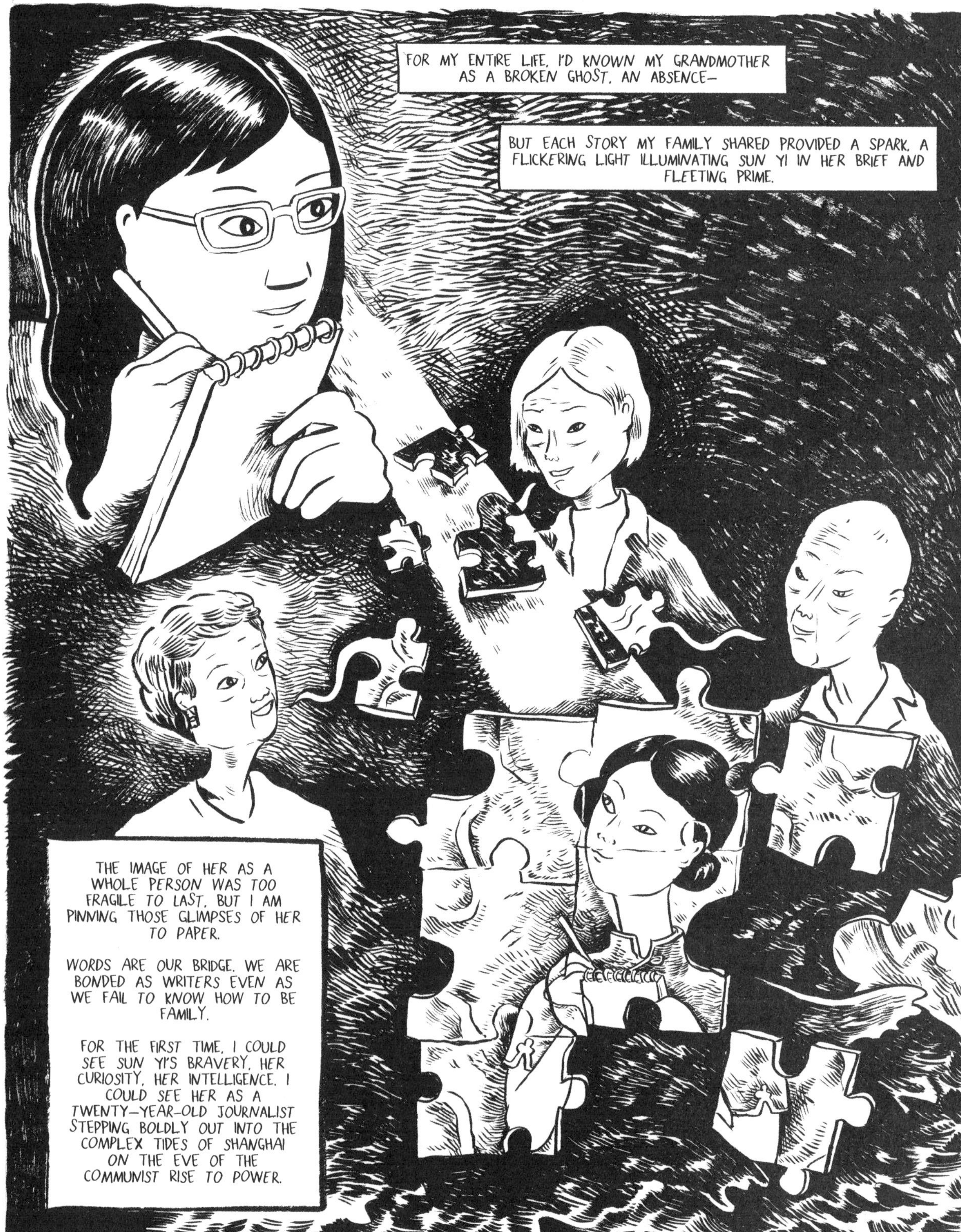
FOR MY ENTIRE LIFE, I'D KNOWN MY GRANDMOTHER AS A BROKEN GHOST, AN ABSENCE—
BUT EACH STORY MY FAMILY SHARED PROVIDED A SPARK, A FLICKERING LIGHT ILLUMINATING SUN YI IN HER BRIEF AND FLEETING PRIME.
THE IMAGE OF HER AS A WHOLE PERSON WAS TOO FRAGILE TO LAST, BUT I AM PINNING THOSE GLIMPSES OF HER TO PAPER.
WORDS ARE OUR BRIDGE. WE ARE BONDED AS WRITERS EVEN AS WE FAIL TO KNOW HOW TO BE FAMILY.
FOR THE FIRST TIME, I COULD SEE SUN YI'S BRAVERY, HER CURIOSITY, HER INTELLIGENCE. I COULD SEE HER AS A TWENTY-YEAR-OLD JOURNALIST STEPPING BOLDLY OUT INTO THE COMPLEX TIDES OF SHANGHAI ON THE EVE OF THE COMMUNIST RISE TO POWER.

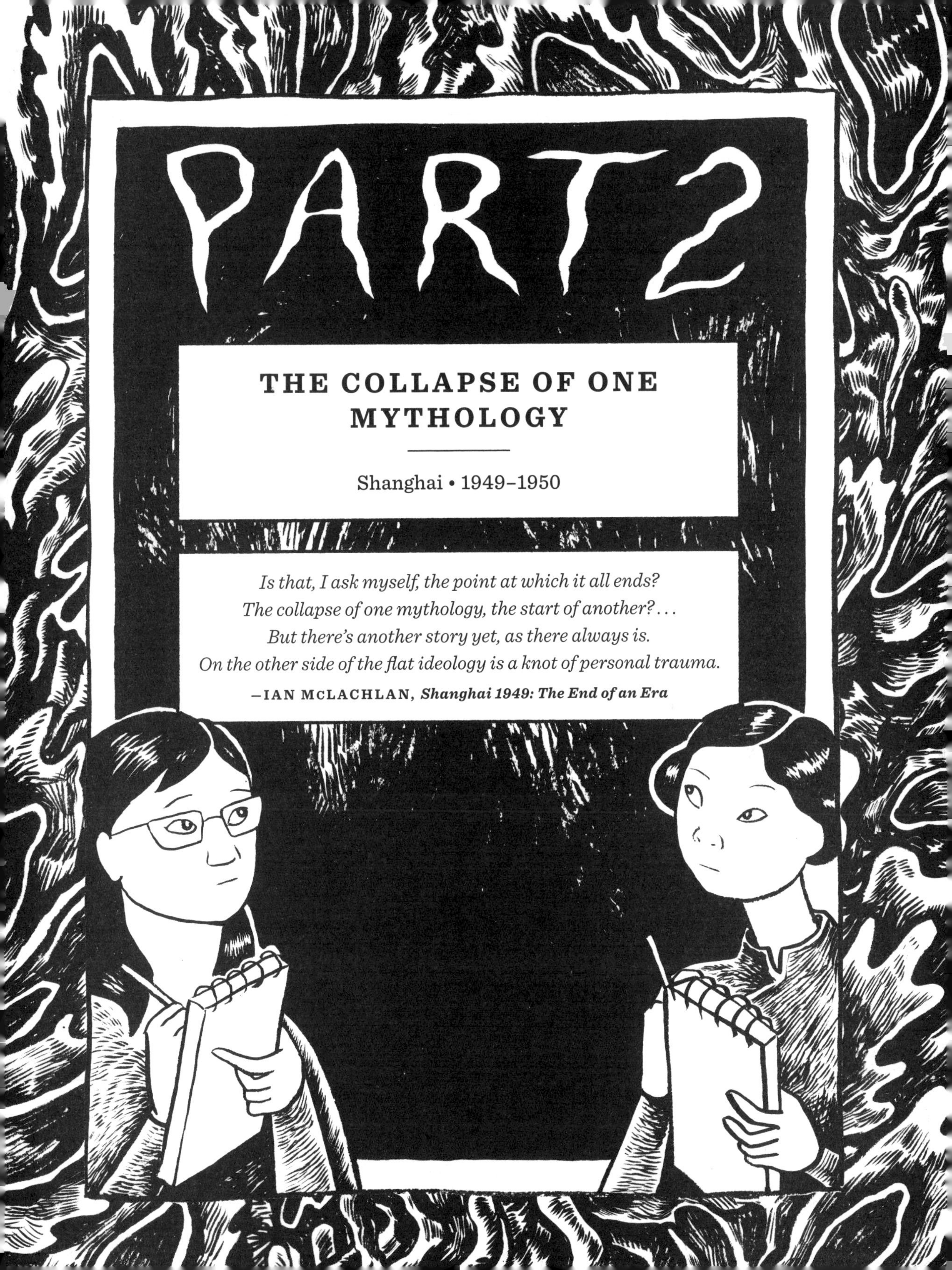

PART 2

THE COLLAPSE OF ONE MYTHOLOGY

Shanghai • 1949–1950

Is that, I ask myself, the point at which it all ends?
The collapse of one mythology, the start of another?...
But there's another story yet, as there always is.
On the other side of the flat ideology is a knot of personal trauma.

—IAN McLACHLAN, ***Shanghai 1949: The End of an Era***

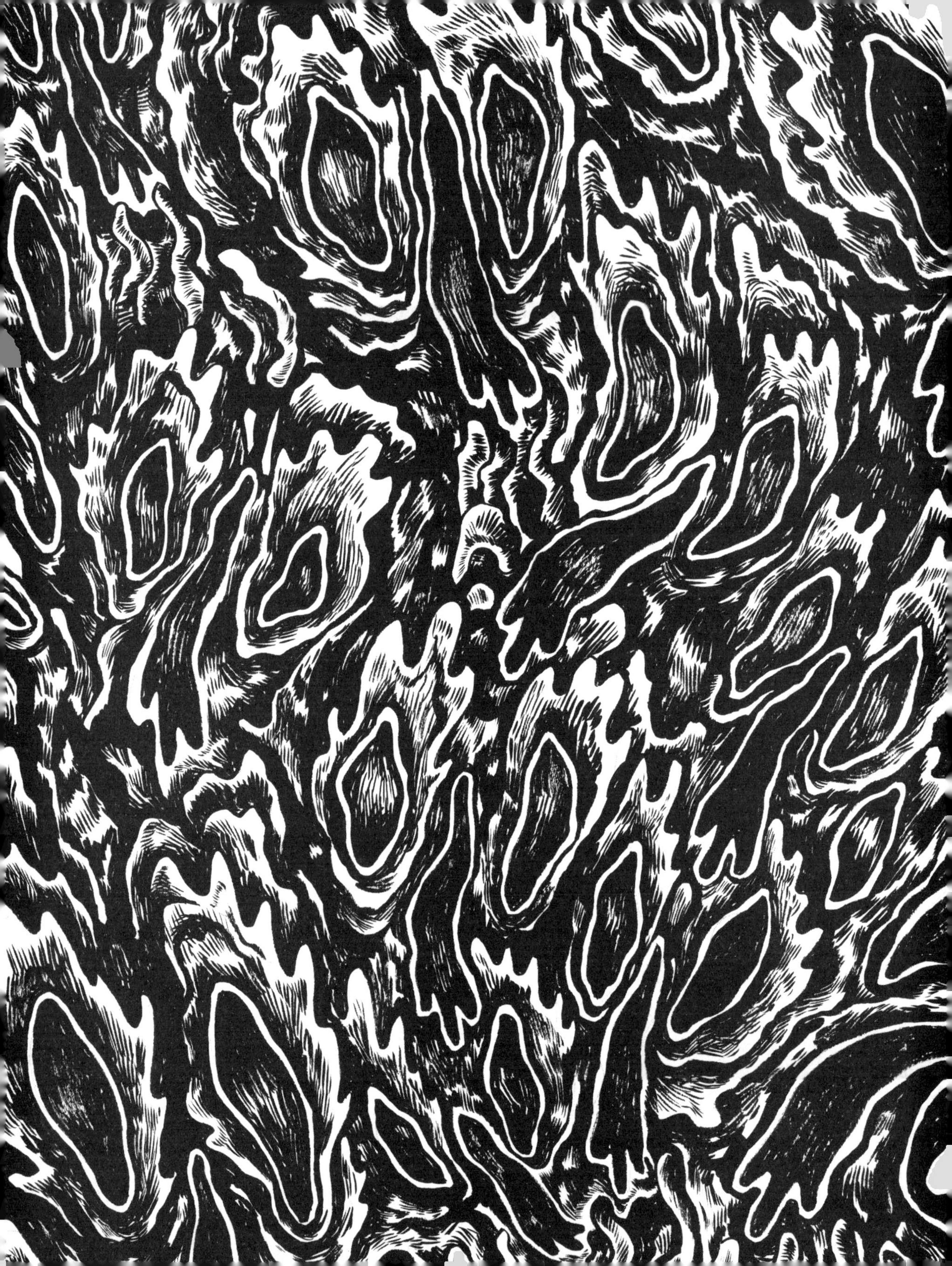

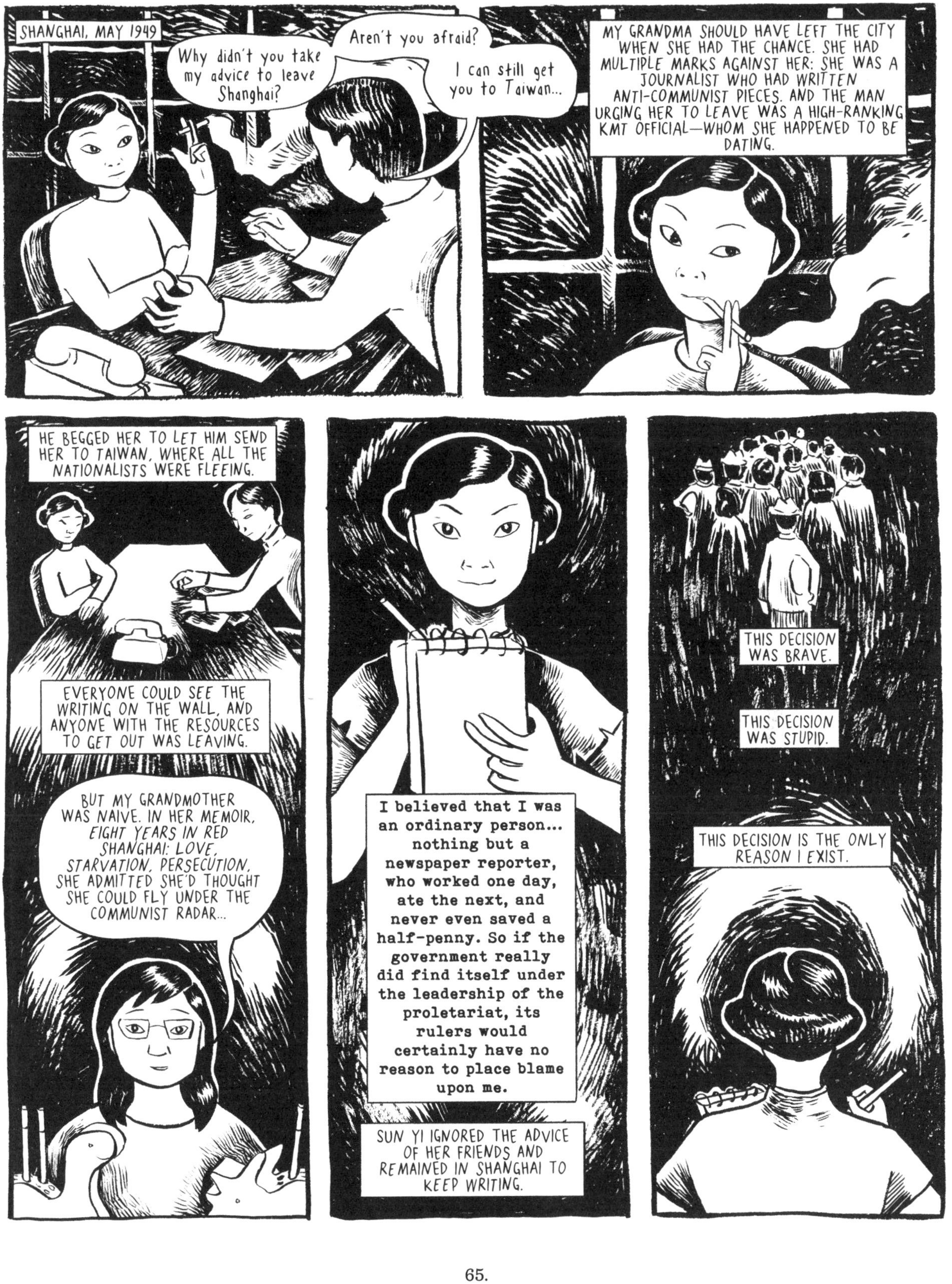
SHANGHAI, MAY 1949
Why didn't you take my advice to leave Shanghai?
Aren't you afraid?
I can still get you to Taiwan...
MY GRANDMA SHOULD HAVE LEFT THE CITY WHEN SHE HAD THE CHANCE. SHE HAD MULTIPLE MARKS AGAINST HER: SHE WAS A JOURNALIST WHO HAD WRITTEN ANTI-COMMUNIST PIECES. AND THE MAN URGING HER TO LEAVE WAS A HIGH-RANKING KMT OFFICIAL—WHOM SHE HAPPENED TO BE DATING.
HE BEGGED HER TO LET HIM SEND HER TO TAIWAN, WHERE ALL THE NATIONALISTS WERE FLEEING.
EVERYONE COULD SEE THE WRITING ON THE WALL, AND ANYONE WITH THE RESOURCES TO GET OUT WAS LEAVING.
BUT MY GRANDMOTHER WAS NAIVE. IN HER MEMOIR, *EIGHT YEARS IN RED SHANGHAI: LOVE, STARVATION, PERSECUTION*, SHE ADMITTED SHE'D THOUGHT SHE COULD FLY UNDER THE COMMUNIST RADAR...
I believed that I was an ordinary person... nothing but a newspaper reporter, who worked one day, ate the next, and never even saved a half-penny. So if the government really did find itself under the leadership of the proletariat, its rulers would certainly have no reason to place blame upon me.
SUN YI IGNORED THE ADVICE OF HER FRIENDS AND REMAINED IN SHANGHAI TO KEEP WRITING.
THIS DECISION WAS BRAVE.
THIS DECISION WAS STUPID.
THIS DECISION IS THE ONLY REASON I EXIST.

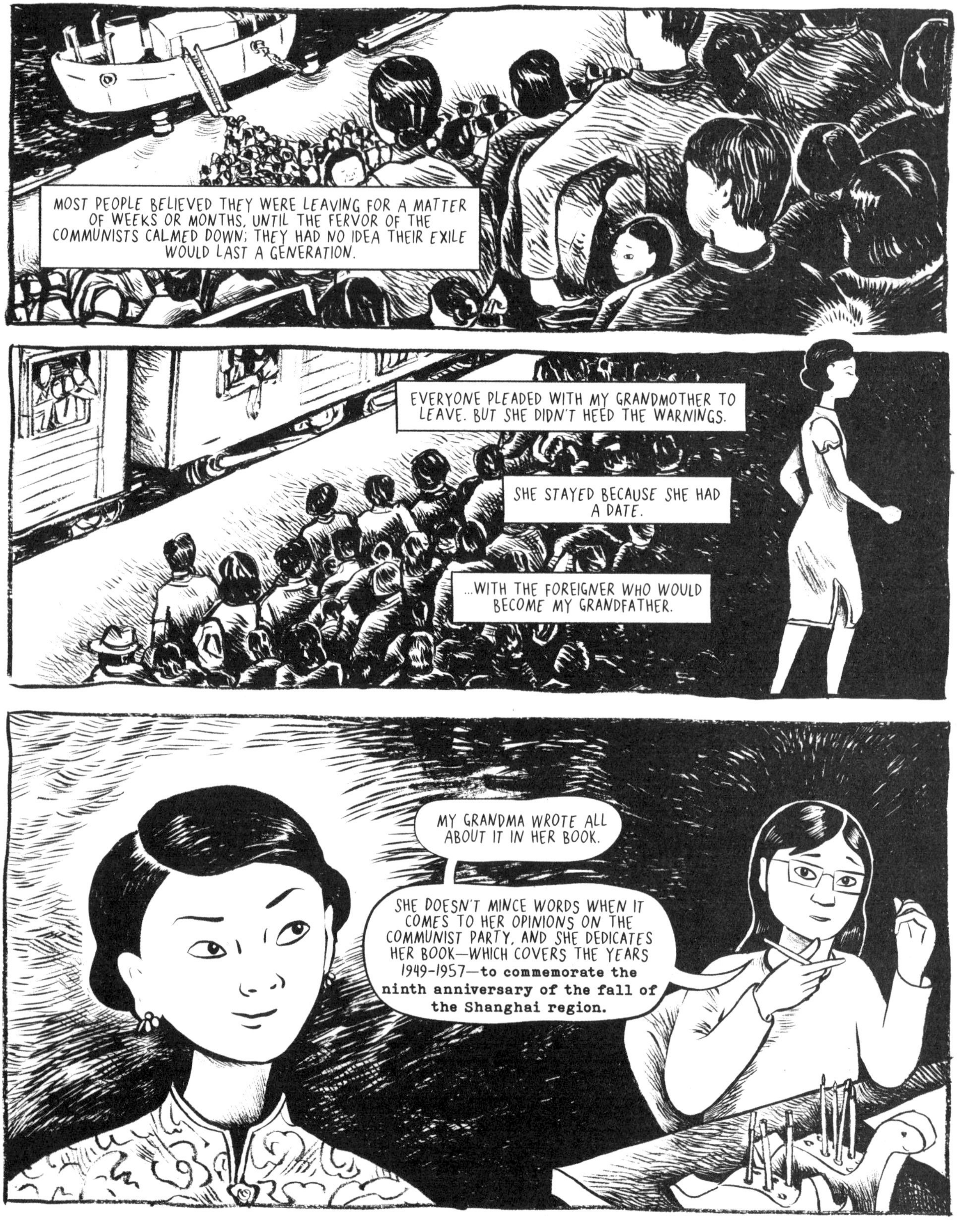

MOST PEOPLE BELIEVED THEY WERE LEAVING FOR A MATTER OF WEEKS OR MONTHS, UNTIL THE FERVOR OF THE COMMUNISTS CALMED DOWN; THEY HAD NO IDEA THEIR EXILE WOULD LAST A GENERATION.
EVERYONE PLEADED WITH MY GRANDMOTHER TO LEAVE. BUT SHE DIDN'T HEED THE WARNINGS.
SHE STAYED BECAUSE SHE HAD A DATE.
...WITH THE FOREIGNER WHO WOULD BECOME MY GRANDFATHER.
MY GRANDMA WROTE ALL ABOUT IT IN HER BOOK.
SHE DOESN'T MINCE WORDS WHEN IT COMES TO HER OPINIONS ON THE COMMUNIST PARTY, AND SHE DEDICATES HER BOOK—WHICH COVERS THE YEARS 1949–1957—**to commemorate the ninth anniversary of the fall of the Shanghai region.**

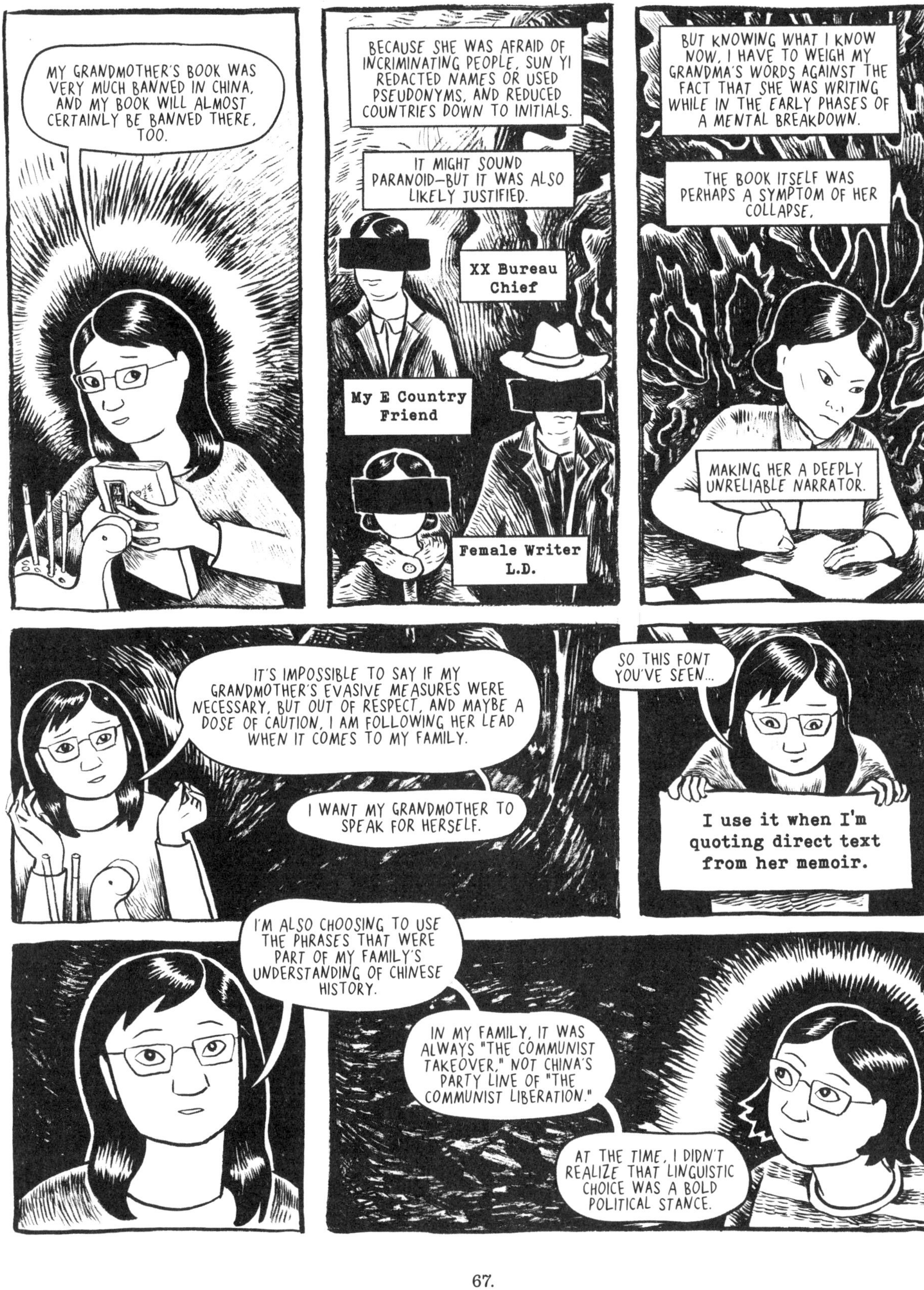
MY GRANDMOTHER'S BOOK WAS VERY MUCH BANNED IN CHINA, AND MY BOOK WILL ALMOST CERTAINLY BE BANNED THERE, TOO.
BECAUSE SHE WAS AFRAID OF INCRIMINATING PEOPLE, SUN YI REDACTED NAMES OR USED PSEUDONYMS, AND REDUCED COUNTRIES DOWN TO INITIALS.
IT MIGHT SOUND PARANOID—BUT IT WAS ALSO LIKELY JUSTIFIED.
XX Bureau Chief
My E Country Friend
Female Writer L.D.
BUT KNOWING WHAT I KNOW NOW, I HAVE TO WEIGH MY GRANDMA'S WORDS AGAINST THE FACT THAT SHE WAS WRITING WHILE IN THE EARLY PHASES OF A MENTAL BREAKDOWN.
THE BOOK ITSELF WAS PERHAPS A SYMPTOM OF HER COLLAPSE,
MAKING HER A DEEPLY UNRELIABLE NARRATOR.
IT'S IMPOSSIBLE TO SAY IF MY GRANDMOTHER'S EVASIVE MEASURES WERE NECESSARY, BUT OUT OF RESPECT, AND MAYBE A DOSE OF CAUTION, I AM FOLLOWING HER LEAD WHEN IT COMES TO MY FAMILY.
I WANT MY GRANDMOTHER TO SPEAK FOR HERSELF.
SO THIS FONT YOU'VE SEEN...
I use it when I'm quoting direct text from her memoir.
I'M ALSO CHOOSING TO USE THE PHRASES THAT WERE PART OF MY FAMILY'S UNDERSTANDING OF CHINESE HISTORY.
IN MY FAMILY, IT WAS ALWAYS "THE COMMUNIST TAKEOVER," NOT CHINA'S PARTY LINE OF "THE COMMUNIST LIBERATION."
AT THE TIME, I DIDN'T REALIZE THAT LINGUISTIC CHOICE WAS A BOLD POLITICAL STANCE.

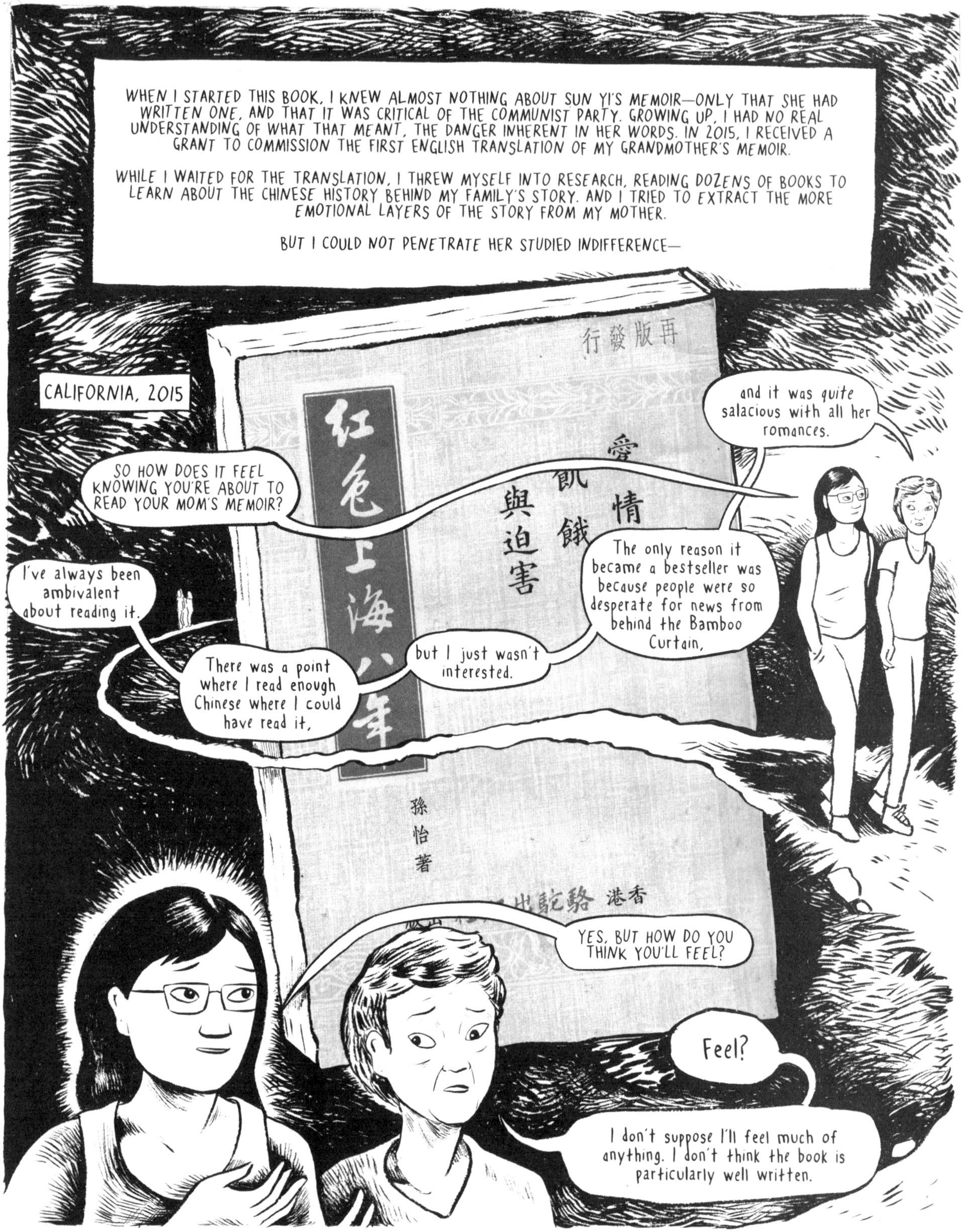

WHEN I STARTED THIS BOOK, I KNEW ALMOST NOTHING ABOUT SUN YI'S MEMOIR—ONLY THAT SHE HAD WRITTEN ONE, AND THAT IT WAS CRITICAL OF THE COMMUNIST PARTY. GROWING UP, I HAD NO REAL UNDERSTANDING OF WHAT THAT MEANT, THE DANGER INHERENT IN HER WORDS. IN 2015, I RECEIVED A GRANT TO COMMISSION THE FIRST ENGLISH TRANSLATION OF MY GRANDMOTHER'S MEMOIR.
WHILE I WAITED FOR THE TRANSLATION, I THREW MYSELF INTO RESEARCH, READING DOZENS OF BOOKS TO LEARN ABOUT THE CHINESE HISTORY BEHIND MY FAMILY'S STORY. AND I TRIED TO EXTRACT THE MORE EMOTIONAL LAYERS OF THE STORY FROM MY MOTHER.
BUT I COULD NOT PENETRATE HER STUDIED INDIFFERENCE—
再版發行
愛情 飢餓 與迫害
孫怡著
CALIFORNIA, 2015
SO HOW DOES IT FEEL KNOWING YOU'RE ABOUT TO READ YOUR MOM'S MEMOIR?
I've always been ambivalent about reading it.
There was a point where I read enough Chinese where I could have read it,
but I just wasn't interested.
The only reason it became a bestseller was because people were so desperate for news from behind the Bamboo Curtain,
and it was quite salacious with all her romances.
YES, BUT HOW DO YOU THINK YOU'LL FEEL?
Feel?
I don't suppose I'll feel much of anything. I don't think the book is particularly well written.

MY MOM'S ASSERTIONS OF DETACHMENT CONVINCED NO ONE EXCEPT HERSELF. I WATCHED AS THE GHOST TWIN PUT ON THE FACE MY MOM WEARS WHEN SHE IS CLOSING HERSELF OFF FROM HER EMOTIONS.

I OBSERVED THIS PROCESS CLINICALLY: HOW THE GHOST TWIN TOOK OVER MY MOTHER'S BODY AND SPOKE WITH HER VOICE, BUT WITH A SEARING CERTAINTY THAT DENIED ALL FEELING. BUT I ALSO KNEW THAT FOR ALL MY MOTHER'S PROFESSED INDIFFERENCE, READING HER MOTHER'S BOOK WOULD BREAK SOMETHING LOOSE IN HER. SHE DIDN'T KNOW THAT SHE WOULD CRY, BUT I DID.

I Don't Suppose I'll FEEL ANYTHING

IN 2016, I HELD THE COMPLETED TRANSLATION IN MY HANDS. WHEN I SAT DOWN TO READ, I REALIZED IT WAS THE FIRST TIME I HAD TRULY HEARD MY GRANDMOTHER'S VOICE.

SUN YI HAD STRUCTURED HER BOOK INTO EIGHTEEN CHAPTERS, EACH WITH A MELODRAMATIC TITLE—

Trapped in Communist Territory

Facing Interrogation About the Child's Origins

With a Gun Pressed to the Chest

Seeking Scarlet-Colored Dreams Within the Red Terror

AS I WADED INTO MY GRANDMOTHER'S WORLD, I FELT MY STOMACH TIGHTEN; I'D WANTED SO BADLY TO KNOW THIS UNKNOWN WOMAN. BUT I HADN'T CONSIDERED THAT SHE MIGHT TURN OUT TO BE A VERY DIFFICULT PERSON TO LIKE.

OUR FAMILY MYTH HAD PAINTED SUN YI AS A VICTIM OF HISTORY, BUT AS I READ HER MEMOIR, I REALIZED THE REALITY WAS INFINITELY MORE COMPLICATED.

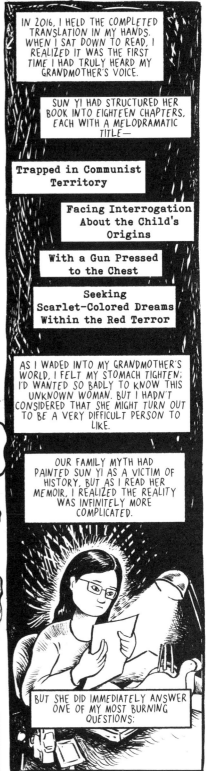

BUT SHE DID IMMEDIATELY ANSWER ONE OF MY MOST BURNING QUESTIONS:

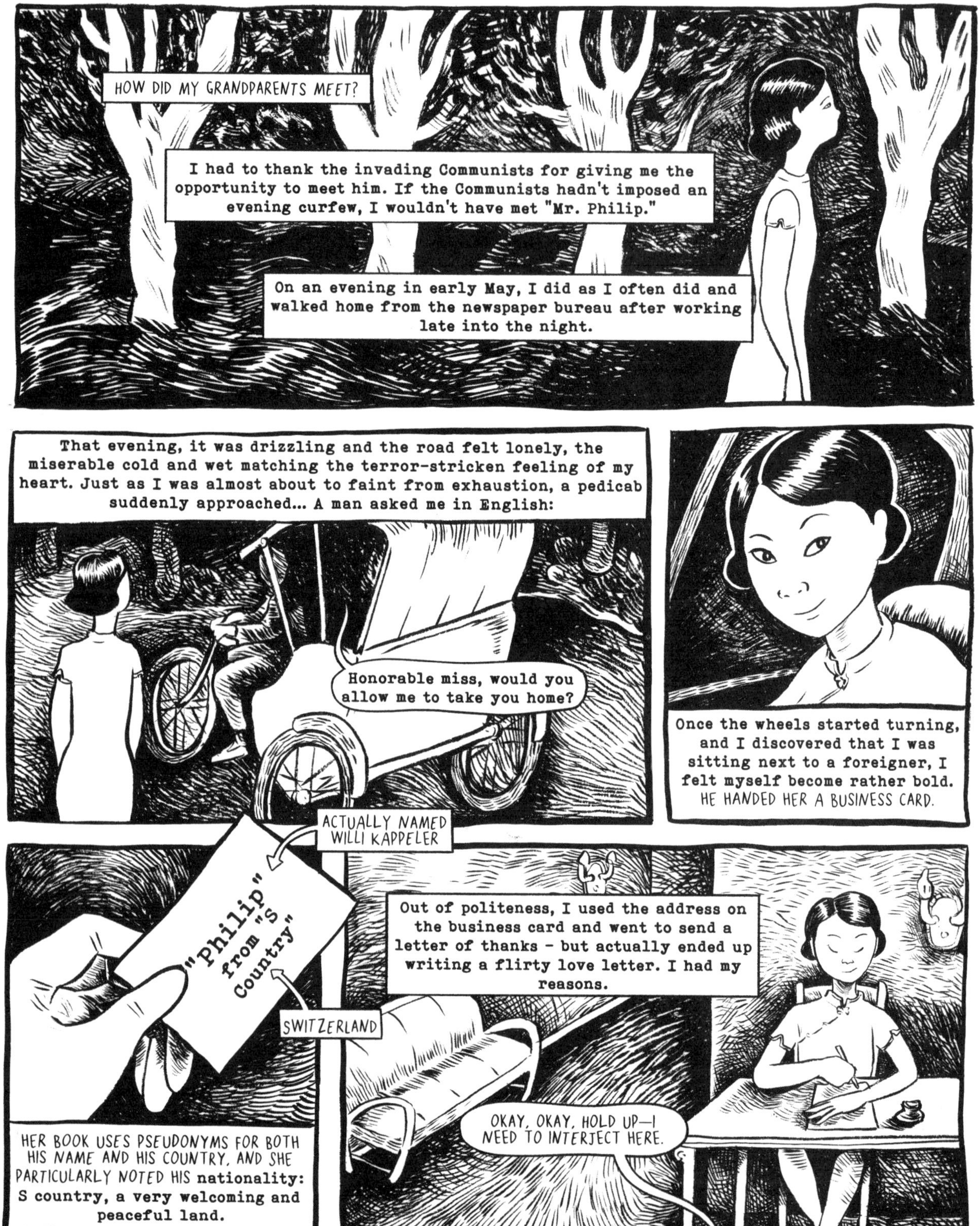

HOW DID MY GRANDPARENTS MEET?
I had to thank the invading Communists for giving me the opportunity to meet him. If the Communists hadn't imposed an evening curfew, I wouldn't have met "Mr. Philip."
On an evening in early May, I did as I often did and walked home from the newspaper bureau after working late into the night.
That evening, it was drizzling and the road felt lonely, the miserable cold and wet matching the terror-stricken feeling of my heart. Just as I was almost about to faint from exhaustion, a pedicab suddenly approached... A man asked me in English:
Honorable miss, would you allow me to take you home?
Once the wheels started turning, and I discovered that I was sitting next to a foreigner, I felt myself become rather bold.
HE HANDED HER A BUSINESS CARD.
ACTUALLY NAMED WILLI KAPPELER
"Philip" from "S Country"
SWITZERLAND
HER BOOK USES PSEUDONYMS FOR BOTH HIS *NAME* AND HIS COUNTRY, AND SHE PARTICULARLY NOTED HIS **nationality: S country, a very welcoming and peaceful land.**
Out of politeness, I used the address on the business card and went to send a letter of thanks - but actually ended up writing a flirty love letter. I had my reasons.
OKAY, OKAY, HOLD UP—I NEED TO INTERJECT HERE.

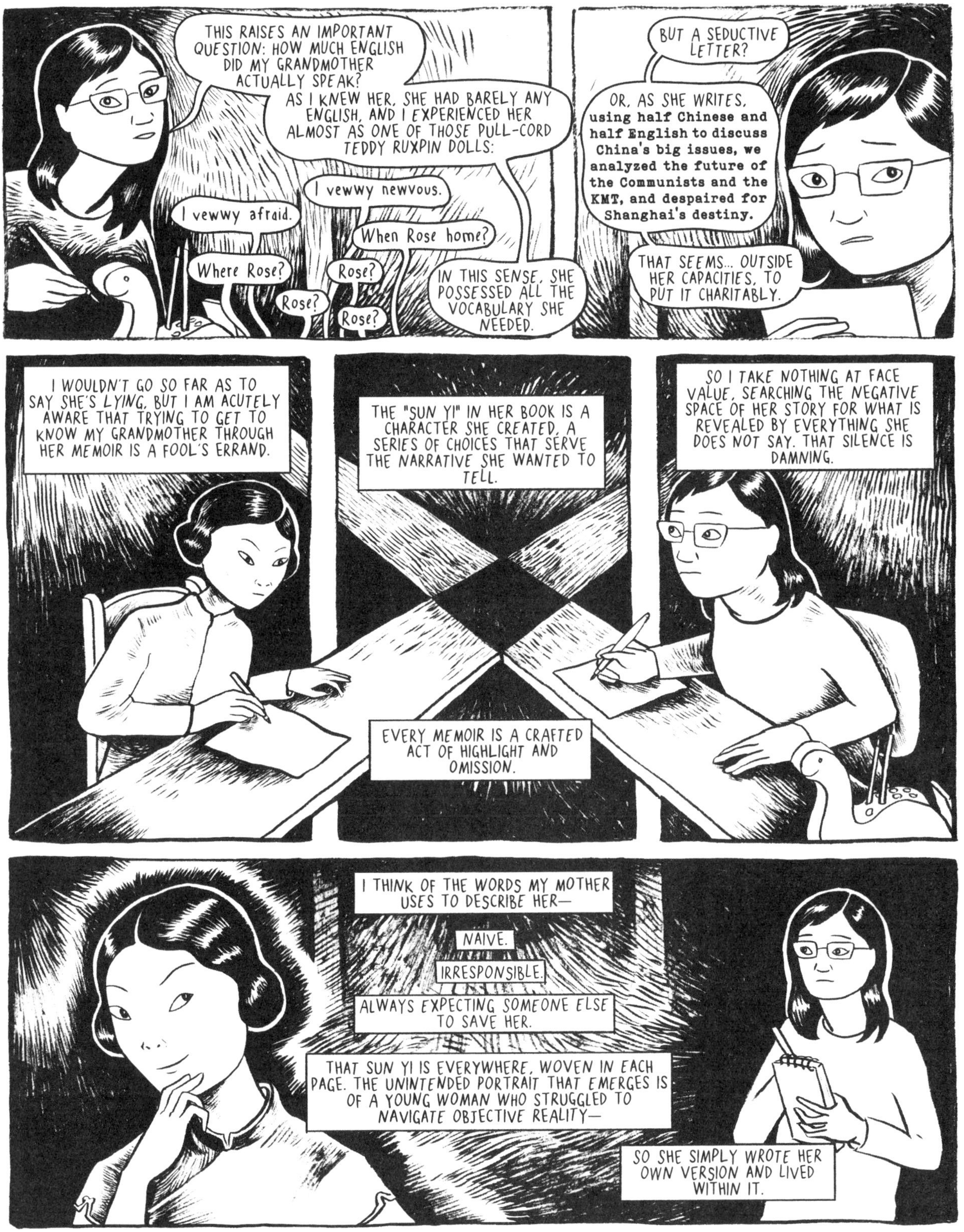
THIS RAISES AN IMPORTANT QUESTION: HOW MUCH ENGLISH DID MY GRANDMOTHER ACTUALLY SPEAK?
AS I KNEW HER, SHE HAD BARELY ANY ENGLISH, AND I EXPERIENCED HER ALMOST AS ONE OF THOSE PULL-CORD TEDDY RUXPIN DOLLS:
I vewwy afraid.
I vewwy newvous.
When Rose home?
Where Rose?
Rose?
Rose?
Rose?
IN THIS SENSE, SHE POSSESSED ALL THE VOCABULARY SHE NEEDED.
BUT A SEDUCTIVE LETTER?
OR, AS SHE WRITES, using half Chinese and half English to discuss China's big issues, we analyzed the future of the Communists and the KMT, and despaired for Shanghai's destiny.
THAT SEEMS... OUTSIDE HER CAPACITIES, TO PUT IT CHARITABLY.
I WOULDN'T GO SO FAR AS TO SAY SHE'S *LYING*, BUT I AM ACUTELY AWARE THAT TRYING TO GET TO KNOW MY GRANDMOTHER THROUGH HER MEMOIR IS A FOOL'S ERRAND.
THE "SUN YI" IN HER BOOK IS A CHARACTER SHE CREATED, A SERIES OF CHOICES THAT SERVE THE NARRATIVE SHE WANTED TO TELL.
EVERY MEMOIR IS A CRAFTED ACT OF HIGHLIGHT AND OMISSION.
SO I TAKE NOTHING AT FACE VALUE, SEARCHING THE NEGATIVE SPACE OF HER STORY FOR WHAT IS REVEALED BY EVERYTHING SHE DOES NOT SAY. THAT SILENCE IS DAMNING.
I THINK OF THE WORDS MY MOTHER USES TO DESCRIBE HER—
NAIVE.
IRRESPONSIBLE.
ALWAYS EXPECTING SOMEONE ELSE TO SAVE HER.
THAT SUN YI IS EVERYWHERE, WOVEN IN EACH PAGE. THE UNINTENDED PORTRAIT THAT EMERGES IS OF A YOUNG WOMAN WHO STRUGGLED TO NAVIGATE OBJECTIVE REALITY—
SO SHE SIMPLY WROTE HER OWN VERSION AND LIVED WITHIN IT.

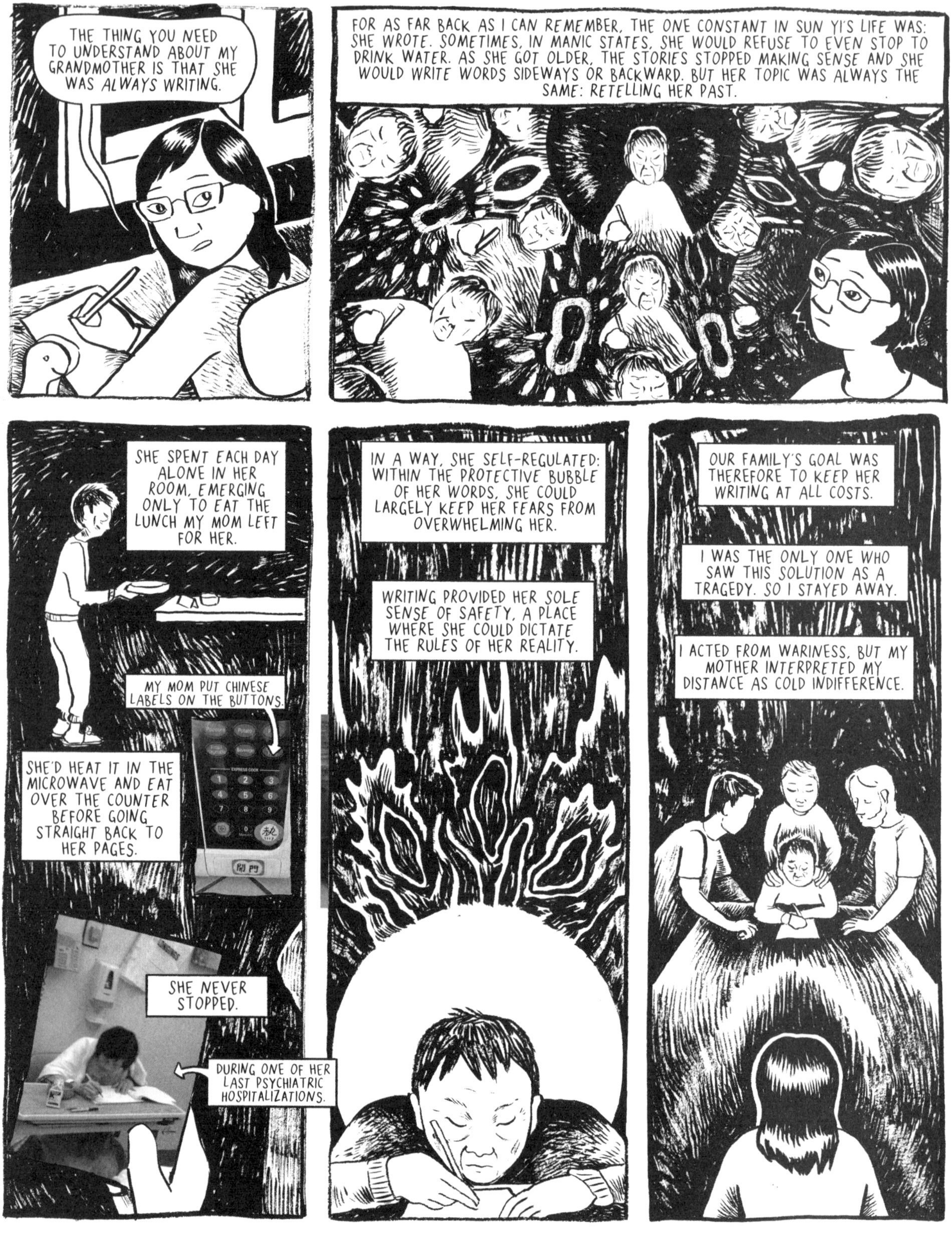
THE THING YOU NEED TO UNDERSTAND ABOUT MY GRANDMOTHER IS THAT SHE WAS *ALWAYS* WRITING.
FOR AS FAR BACK AS I CAN REMEMBER, THE ONE CONSTANT IN SUN YI'S LIFE WAS: SHE WROTE. SOMETIMES, IN MANIC STATES, SHE WOULD REFUSE TO EVEN STOP TO DRINK WATER. AS SHE GOT OLDER, THE STORIES STOPPED MAKING SENSE AND SHE WOULD WRITE WORDS SIDEWAYS OR BACKWARD. BUT HER TOPIC WAS ALWAYS THE SAME: RETELLING HER PAST.
SHE SPENT EACH DAY ALONE IN HER ROOM, EMERGING ONLY TO EAT THE LUNCH MY MOM LEFT FOR HER.
MY MOM PUT CHINESE LABELS ON THE BUTTONS.
SHE'D HEAT IT IN THE MICROWAVE AND EAT OVER THE COUNTER BEFORE GOING STRAIGHT BACK TO HER PAGES.
SHE NEVER STOPPED.
DURING ONE OF HER LAST PSYCHIATRIC HOSPITALIZATIONS.
IN A WAY, SHE SELF-REGULATED: WITHIN THE PROTECTIVE BUBBLE OF HER WORDS, SHE COULD LARGELY KEEP HER FEARS FROM OVERWHELMING HER.
WRITING PROVIDED HER SOLE SENSE OF SAFETY, A PLACE WHERE SHE COULD DICTATE THE RULES OF HER REALITY.
OUR FAMILY'S GOAL WAS THEREFORE TO KEEP HER WRITING AT ALL COSTS.
I WAS THE ONLY ONE WHO SAW THIS SOLUTION AS A TRAGEDY. SO I STAYED AWAY.
I ACTED FROM WARINESS, BUT MY MOTHER INTERPRETED MY DISTANCE AS COLD INDIFFERENCE.

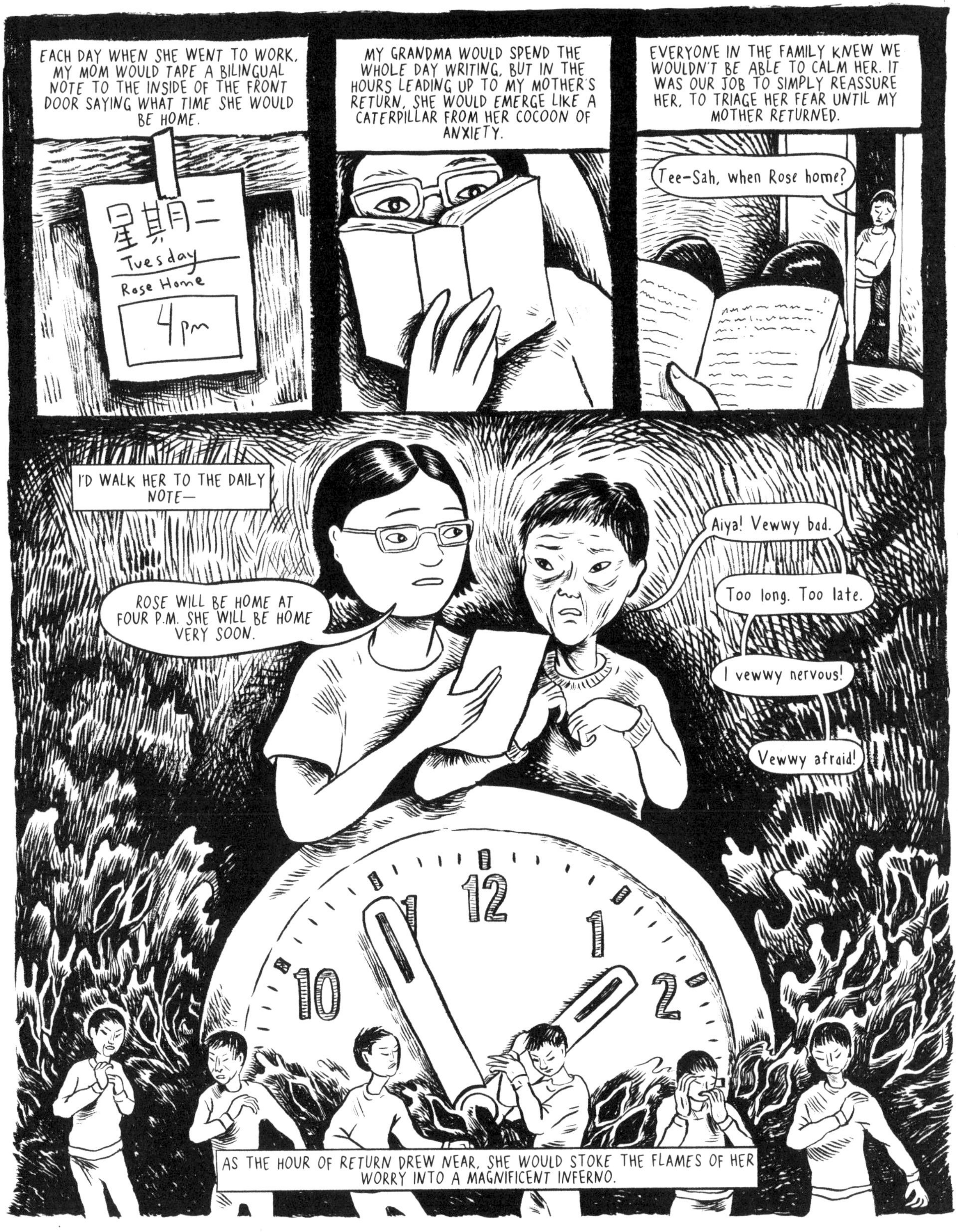
EACH DAY WHEN SHE WENT TO WORK, MY MOM WOULD TAPE A BILINGUAL NOTE TO THE INSIDE OF THE FRONT DOOR SAYING WHAT TIME SHE WOULD BE HOME.
星期二
Tuesday
Rose Home
4pm
MY GRANDMA WOULD SPEND THE WHOLE DAY WRITING, BUT IN THE HOURS LEADING UP TO MY MOTHER'S RETURN, SHE WOULD EMERGE LIKE A CATERPILLAR FROM HER COCOON OF ANXIETY.
EVERYONE IN THE FAMILY KNEW WE WOULDN'T BE ABLE TO CALM HER. IT WAS OUR JOB TO SIMPLY REASSURE HER, TO TRIAGE HER FEAR UNTIL MY MOTHER RETURNED.
Tee-Sah, when Rose home?
I'D WALK HER TO THE DAILY NOTE—
ROSE WILL BE HOME AT FOUR P.M. SHE WILL BE HOME VERY SOON.
Aiya! Vewwy bad.
Too long. Too late.
I vewwy nervous!
Vewwy afraid!
12
1
2
10
AS THE HOUR OF RETURN DREW NEAR, SHE WOULD STOKE THE FLAMES OF HER WORRY INTO A MAGNIFICENT INFERNO.

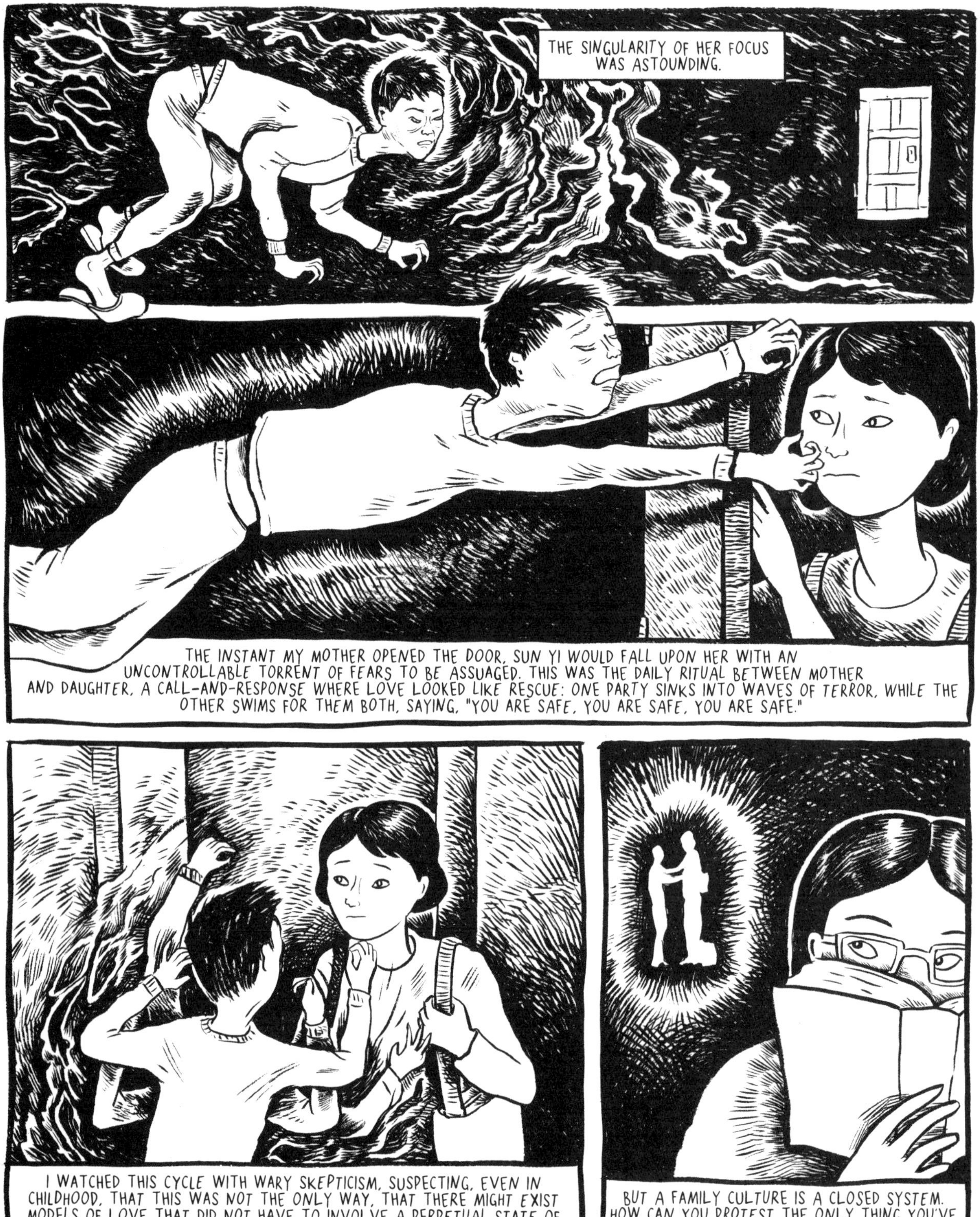
THE SINGULARITY OF HER FOCUS WAS ASTOUNDING.
THE INSTANT MY MOTHER OPENED THE DOOR, SUN YI WOULD FALL UPON HER WITH AN UNCONTROLLABLE TORRENT OF FEARS TO BE ASSUAGED. THIS WAS THE DAILY RITUAL BETWEEN MOTHER AND DAUGHTER, A CALL-AND-RESPONSE WHERE LOVE LOOKED LIKE RESCUE: ONE PARTY SINKS INTO WAVES OF TERROR, WHILE THE OTHER SWIMS FOR THEM BOTH, SAYING, "YOU ARE SAFE, YOU ARE SAFE, YOU ARE SAFE."
I WATCHED THIS CYCLE WITH WARY SKEPTICISM, SUSPECTING, EVEN IN CHILDHOOD, THAT THIS WAS NOT THE ONLY WAY, THAT THERE MIGHT EXIST MODELS OF LOVE THAT DID NOT HAVE TO INVOLVE A PERPETUAL STATE OF NEAR DROWNING.
BUT A FAMILY CULTURE IS A CLOSED SYSTEM. HOW CAN YOU PROTEST THE ONLY THING YOU'VE EVER KNOWN?

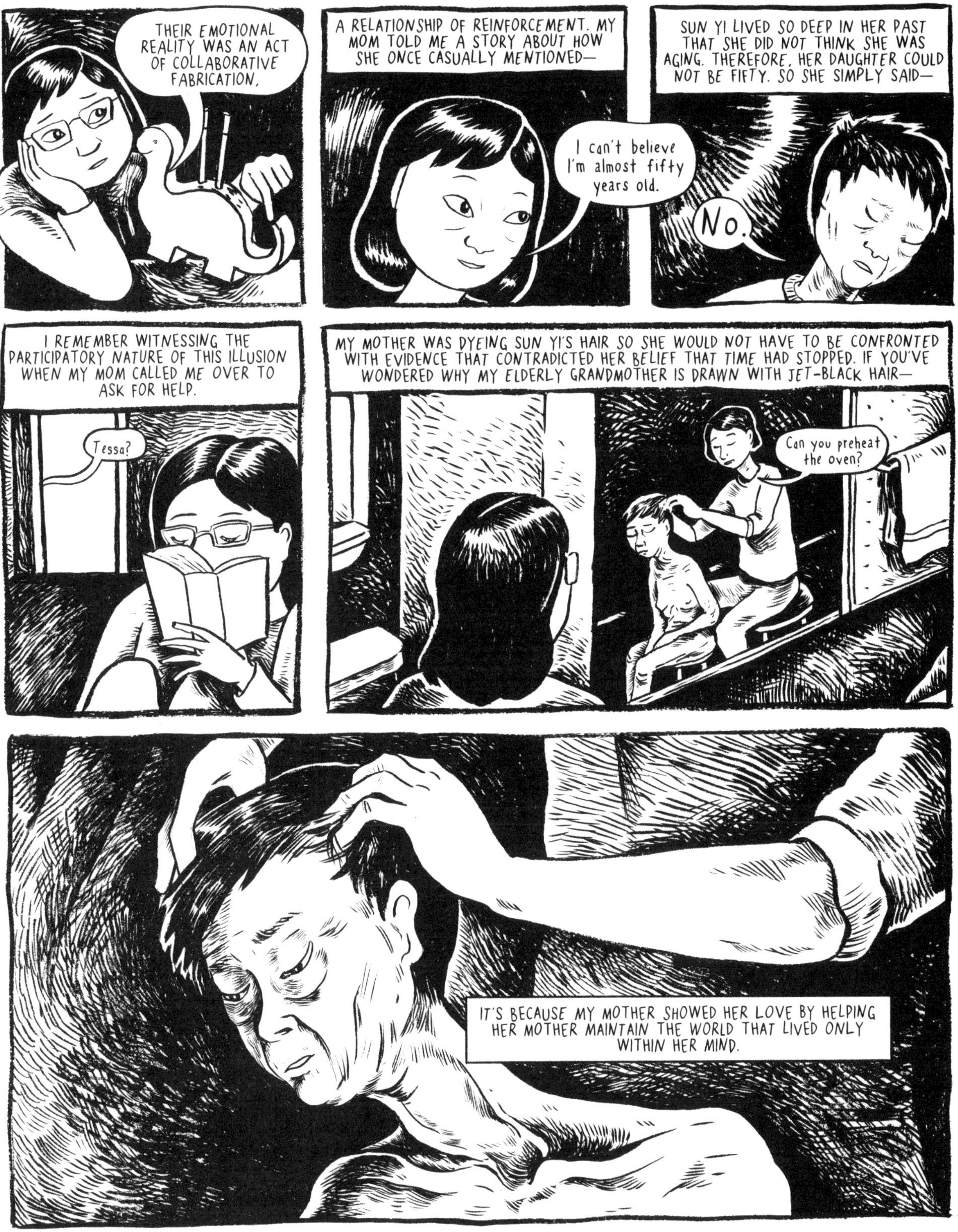
THEIR EMOTIONAL REALITY WAS AN ACT OF COLLABORATIVE FABRICATION.
A RELATIONSHIP OF REINFORCEMENT. MY MOM TOLD ME A STORY ABOUT HOW SHE ONCE CASUALLY MENTIONED—
I can't believe I'm almost fifty years old.
SUN YI LIVED SO DEEP IN HER PAST THAT SHE DID NOT THINK SHE WAS AGING. THEREFORE, HER DAUGHTER COULD NOT BE FIFTY. SO SHE SIMPLY SAID—
No.
I REMEMBER WITNESSING THE PARTICIPATORY NATURE OF THIS ILLUSION WHEN MY MOM CALLED ME OVER TO ASK FOR HELP.
Tessa?
MY MOTHER WAS DYEING SUN YI'S HAIR SO SHE WOULD NOT HAVE TO BE CONFRONTED WITH EVIDENCE THAT CONTRADICTED HER BELIEF THAT TIME HAD STOPPED. IF YOU'VE WONDERED WHY MY ELDERLY GRANDMOTHER IS DRAWN WITH JET-BLACK HAIR—
Can you preheat the oven?
IT'S BECAUSE MY MOTHER SHOWED HER LOVE BY HELPING HER MOTHER MAINTAIN THE WORLD THAT LIVED ONLY WITHIN HER MIND.

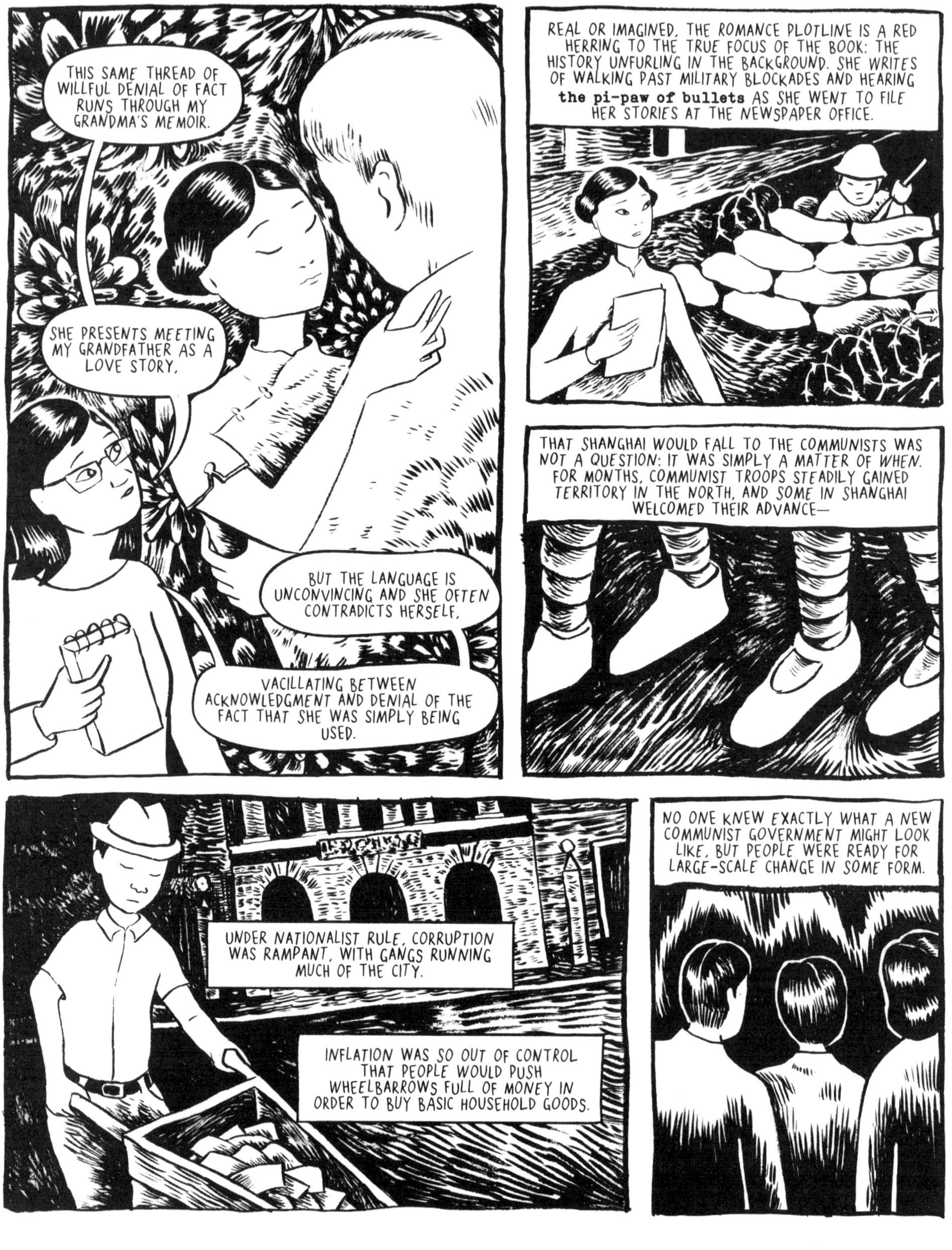
THIS SAME THREAD OF WILLFUL DENIAL OF FACT RUNS THROUGH MY GRANDMA'S MEMOIR.
SHE PRESENTS MEETING MY GRANDFATHER AS A LOVE STORY.
BUT THE LANGUAGE IS UNCONVINCING AND SHE OFTEN CONTRADICTS HERSELF,
VACILLATING BETWEEN ACKNOWLEDGMENT AND DENIAL OF THE FACT THAT SHE WAS SIMPLY BEING USED.
REAL OR IMAGINED, THE ROMANCE PLOTLINE IS A RED HERRING TO THE TRUE FOCUS OF THE BOOK: THE HISTORY UNFURLING IN THE BACKGROUND. SHE WRITES OF WALKING PAST MILITARY BLOCKADES AND HEARING **the pi-paw of bullets** AS SHE WENT TO FILE HER STORIES AT THE NEWSPAPER OFFICE.
THAT SHANGHAI WOULD FALL TO THE COMMUNISTS WAS NOT A QUESTION: IT WAS SIMPLY A MATTER OF WHEN. FOR MONTHS, COMMUNIST TROOPS STEADILY GAINED TERRITORY IN THE NORTH, AND SOME IN SHANGHAI WELCOMED THEIR ADVANCE—
UNDER NATIONALIST RULE, CORRUPTION WAS RAMPANT, WITH GANGS RUNNING MUCH OF THE CITY.
INFLATION WAS SO OUT OF CONTROL THAT PEOPLE WOULD PUSH WHEELBARROWS FULL OF MONEY IN ORDER TO BUY BASIC HOUSEHOLD GOODS.
NO ONE KNEW EXACTLY WHAT A NEW COMMUNIST GOVERNMENT MIGHT LOOK LIKE, BUT PEOPLE WERE READY FOR LARGE-SCALE CHANGE IN SOME FORM.

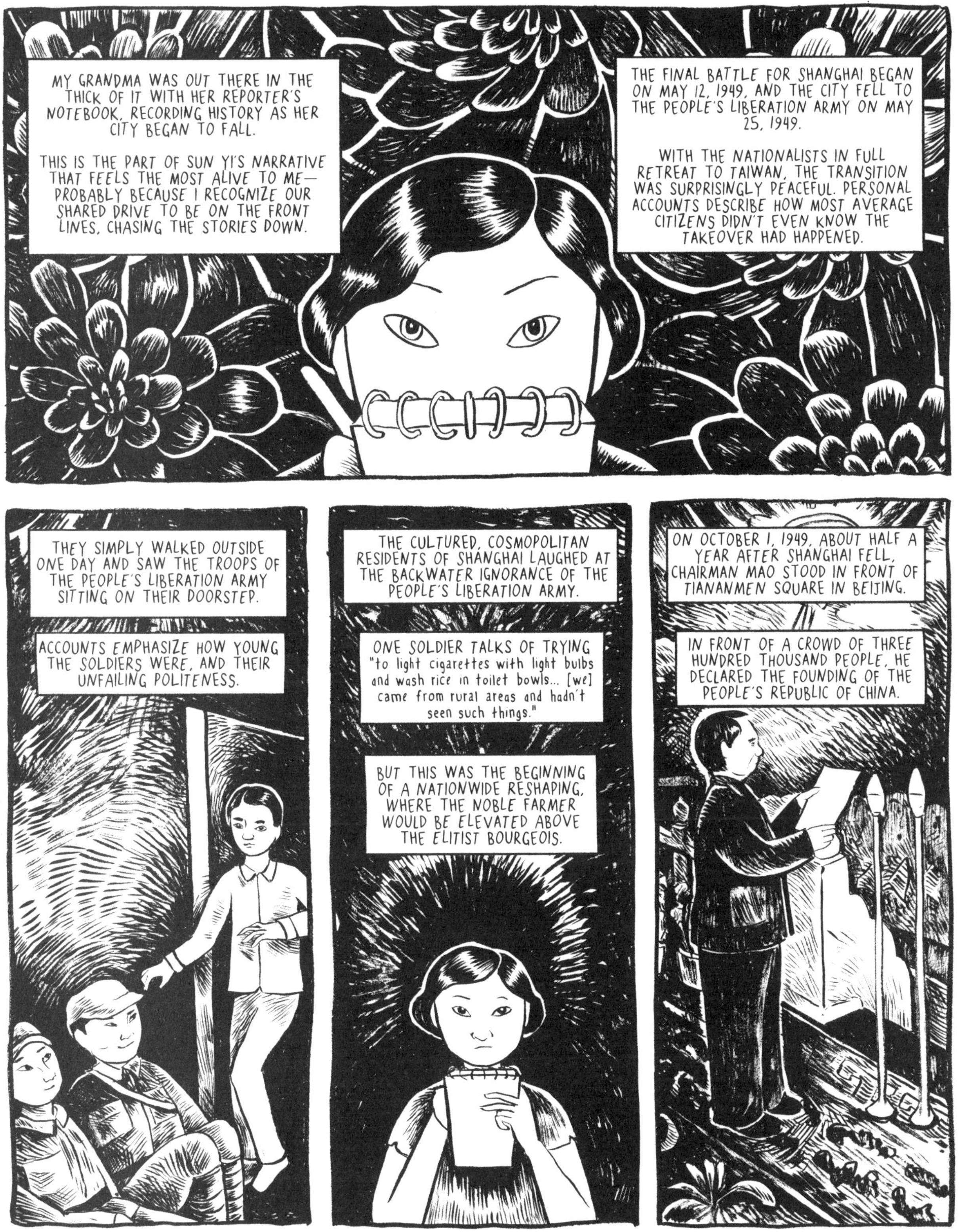
MY GRANDMA WAS OUT THERE IN THE THICK OF IT WITH HER REPORTER'S NOTEBOOK, RECORDING HISTORY AS HER CITY BEGAN TO FALL.
THIS IS THE PART OF SUN YI'S NARRATIVE THAT FEELS THE MOST ALIVE TO ME— PROBABLY BECAUSE I RECOGNIZE OUR SHARED DRIVE TO BE ON THE FRONT LINES, CHASING THE STORIES DOWN.
THE FINAL BATTLE FOR SHANGHAI BEGAN ON MAY 12, 1949, AND THE CITY FELL TO THE PEOPLE'S LIBERATION ARMY ON MAY 25, 1949.
WITH THE NATIONALISTS IN FULL RETREAT TO TAIWAN, THE TRANSITION WAS SURPRISINGLY PEACEFUL. PERSONAL ACCOUNTS DESCRIBE HOW MOST AVERAGE CITIZENS DIDN'T EVEN KNOW THE TAKEOVER HAD HAPPENED.
THEY SIMPLY WALKED OUTSIDE ONE DAY AND SAW THE TROOPS OF THE PEOPLE'S LIBERATION ARMY SITTING ON THEIR DOORSTEP.
ACCOUNTS EMPHASIZE HOW YOUNG THE SOLDIERS WERE, AND THEIR UNFAILING POLITENESS.
THE CULTURED, COSMOPOLITAN RESIDENTS OF SHANGHAI LAUGHED AT THE BACKWATER IGNORANCE OF THE PEOPLE'S LIBERATION ARMY.
ONE SOLDIER TALKS OF TRYING "to light cigarettes with light bulbs and wash rice in toilet bowls... [we] came from rural areas and hadn't seen such things."
BUT THIS WAS THE BEGINNING OF A NATIONWIDE RESHAPING, WHERE THE NOBLE FARMER WOULD BE ELEVATED ABOVE THE ELITIST BOURGEOIS.
ON OCTOBER 1, 1949, ABOUT HALF A YEAR AFTER SHANGHAI FELL, CHAIRMAN MAO STOOD IN FRONT OF TIANANMEN SQUARE IN BEIJING.
IN FRONT OF A CROWD OF THREE HUNDRED THOUSAND PEOPLE, HE DECLARED THE FOUNDING OF THE PEOPLE'S REPUBLIC OF CHINA.

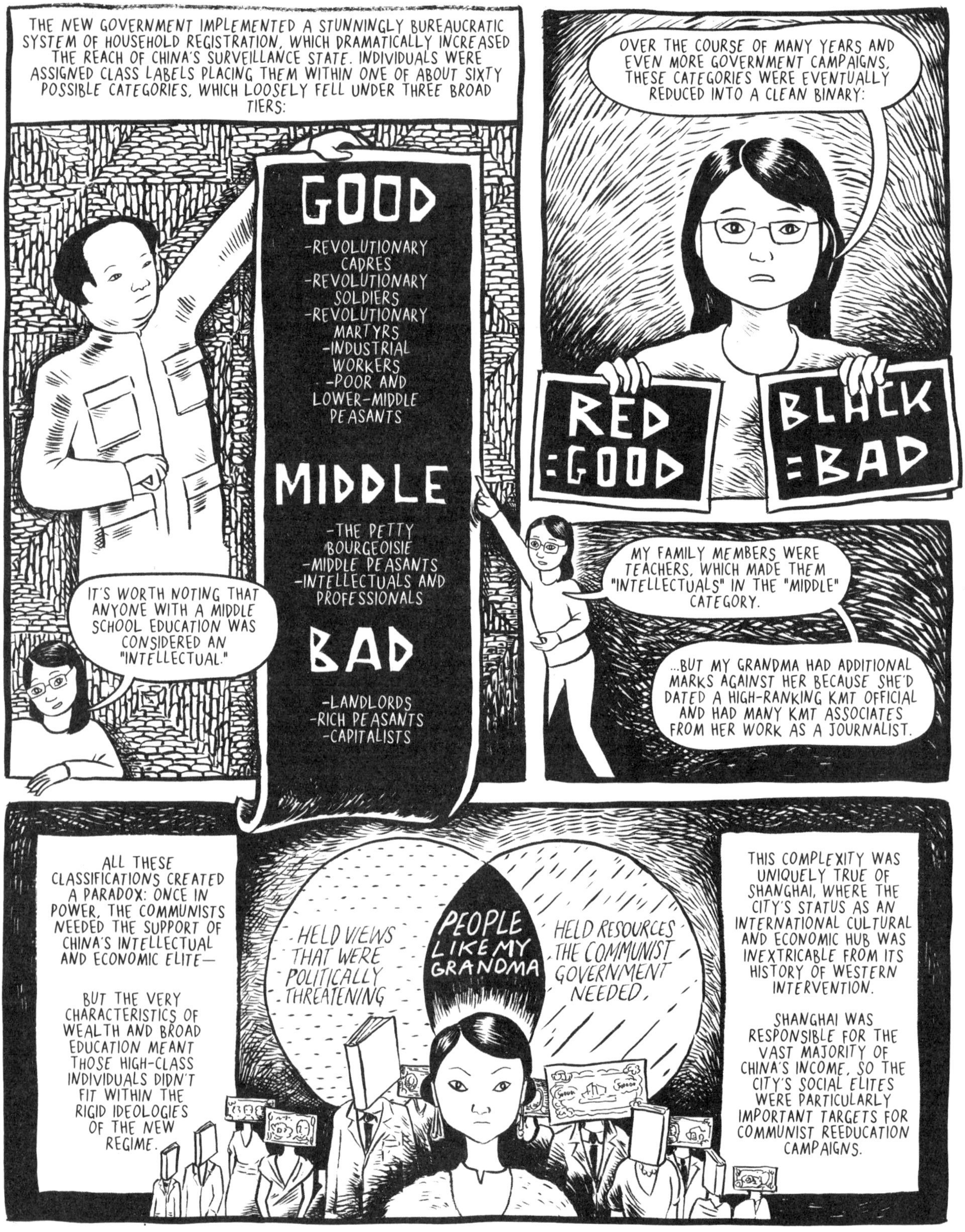
THE NEW GOVERNMENT IMPLEMENTED A STUNNINGLY BUREAUCRATIC SYSTEM OF HOUSEHOLD REGISTRATION, WHICH DRAMATICALLY INCREASED THE REACH OF CHINA'S SURVEILLANCE STATE. INDIVIDUALS WERE ASSIGNED CLASS LABELS PLACING THEM WITHIN ONE OF ABOUT SIXTY POSSIBLE CATEGORIES, WHICH LOOSELY FELL UNDER THREE BROAD TIERS:
GOOD
-REVOLUTIONARY CADRES
-REVOLUTIONARY SOLDIERS
-REVOLUTIONARY MARTYRS
-INDUSTRIAL WORKERS
-POOR AND LOWER-MIDDLE PEASANTS
MIDDLE
-THE PETTY BOURGEOISIE
-MIDDLE PEASANTS
-INTELLECTUALS AND PROFESSIONALS
BAD
-LANDLORDS
-RICH PEASANTS
-CAPITALISTS
IT'S WORTH NOTING THAT ANYONE WITH A MIDDLE SCHOOL EDUCATION WAS CONSIDERED AN "INTELLECTUAL."
OVER THE COURSE OF MANY YEARS AND EVEN MORE GOVERNMENT CAMPAIGNS, THESE CATEGORIES WERE EVENTUALLY REDUCED INTO A CLEAN BINARY:
RED =GOOD
BLACK =BAD
MY FAMILY MEMBERS WERE TEACHERS, WHICH MADE THEM "INTELLECTUALS" IN THE "MIDDLE" CATEGORY.
...BUT MY GRANDMA HAD ADDITIONAL MARKS AGAINST HER BECAUSE SHE'D DATED A HIGH-RANKING KMT OFFICIAL AND HAD MANY KMT ASSOCIATES FROM HER WORK AS A JOURNALIST.
ALL THESE CLASSIFICATIONS CREATED A PARADOX: ONCE IN POWER, THE COMMUNISTS NEEDED THE SUPPORT OF CHINA'S INTELLECTUAL AND ECONOMIC ELITE—
BUT THE VERY CHARACTERISTICS OF WEALTH AND BROAD EDUCATION MEANT THOSE HIGH-CLASS INDIVIDUALS DIDN'T FIT WITHIN THE RIGID IDEOLOGIES OF THE NEW REGIME.
HELD VIEWS THAT WERE POLITICALLY THREATENING
PEOPLE LIKE MY GRANDMA
HELD RESOURCES THE COMMUNIST GOVERNMENT NEEDED
THIS COMPLEXITY WAS UNIQUELY TRUE OF SHANGHAI, WHERE THE CITY'S STATUS AS AN INTERNATIONAL CULTURAL AND ECONOMIC HUB WAS INEXTRICABLE FROM ITS HISTORY OF WESTERN INTERVENTION.
SHANGHAI WAS RESPONSIBLE FOR THE VAST MAJORITY OF CHINA'S INCOME, SO THE CITY'S SOCIAL ELITES WERE PARTICULARLY IMPORTANT TARGETS FOR COMMUNIST REEDUCATION CAMPAIGNS.

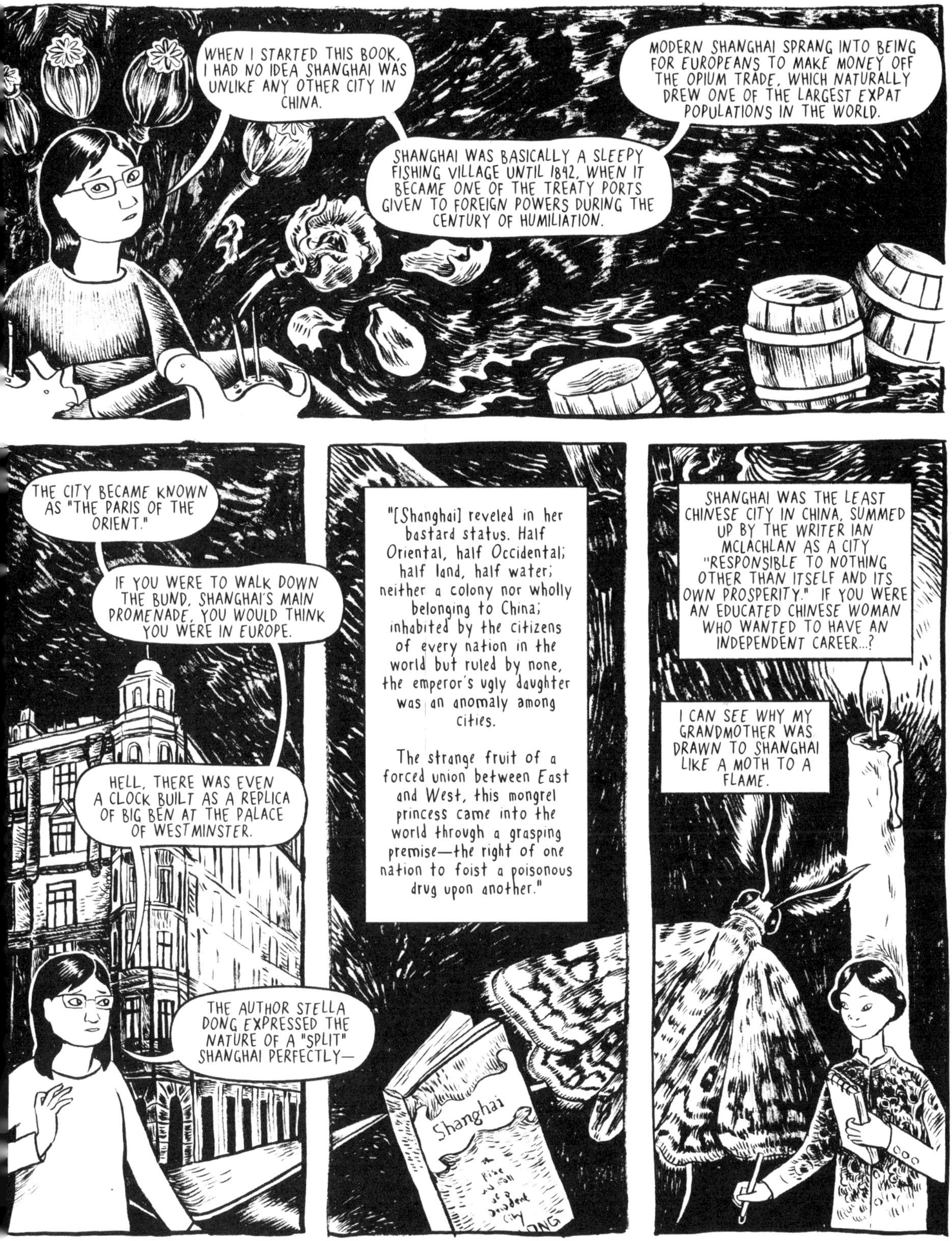
WHEN I STARTED THIS BOOK, I HAD NO IDEA SHANGHAI WAS UNLIKE ANY OTHER CITY IN CHINA.
SHANGHAI WAS BASICALLY A SLEEPY FISHING VILLAGE UNTIL 1842, WHEN IT BECAME ONE OF THE TREATY PORTS GIVEN TO FOREIGN POWERS DURING THE CENTURY OF HUMILIATION.
MODERN SHANGHAI SPRANG INTO BEING FOR EUROPEANS TO MAKE MONEY OFF THE OPIUM TRADE, WHICH NATURALLY DREW ONE OF THE LARGEST EXPAT POPULATIONS IN THE WORLD.
THE CITY BECAME KNOWN AS "THE PARIS OF THE ORIENT."
IF YOU WERE TO WALK DOWN THE BUND, SHANGHAI'S MAIN PROMENADE, YOU WOULD THINK YOU WERE IN EUROPE.
HELL, THERE WAS EVEN A CLOCK BUILT AS A REPLICA OF BIG BEN AT THE PALACE OF WESTMINSTER.
THE AUTHOR STELLA DONG EXPRESSED THE NATURE OF A "SPLIT" SHANGHAI PERFECTLY—
"[Shanghai] reveled in her bastard status. Half Oriental, half Occidental; half land, half water; neither a colony nor wholly belonging to China; inhabited by the citizens of every nation in the world but ruled by none, the emperor's ugly daughter was an anomaly among cities.
The strange fruit of a forced union between East and West, this mongrel princess came into the world through a grasping premise—the right of one nation to foist a poisonous drug upon another."
Shanghai
SHANGHAI WAS THE LEAST CHINESE CITY IN CHINA, SUMMED UP BY THE WRITER IAN MCLACHLAN AS A CITY "RESPONSIBLE TO NOTHING OTHER THAN ITSELF AND ITS OWN PROSPERITY." IF YOU WERE AN EDUCATED CHINESE WOMAN WHO WANTED TO HAVE AN INDEPENDENT CAREER...?
I CAN SEE WHY MY GRANDMOTHER WAS DRAWN TO SHANGHAI LIKE A MOTH TO A FLAME.

I TRIED TO LEARN EVERYTHING I COULD ABOUT SHANGHAI AS MY GRANDMOTHER LIVED IT, PORING THROUGH HER MEMOIR AND EXTRACTING ANY REFERENCE POINT I MIGHT BE ABLE TO TRACK DOWN.

OK SHE WROTE FOR 羅賓漢報社 AND LIVED BY 兆豐花園.

IN 2018, ARMED WITH ALL THE KNOWLEDGE I'D GLEANED FROM BOOKS, PLUS MY GRANDMOTHER'S MEMOIR, I HEADED TO SHANGHAI DETERMINED TO FIND ANYTHING THAT MIGHT STILL EXIST. I ALSO THREW MYSELF INTO MANDARIN IMMERSION CLASSES, AND OVER THE COURSE OF SIX WEEKS I FELL INTO A REGIMENTED SCHEDULE THAT WAS AS EXHAUSTING AS IT WAS FRUITFUL.

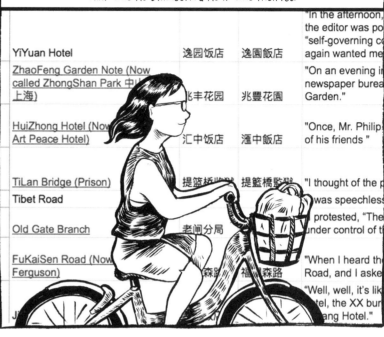

YiYuan Hotel	逸园饭店	逸園飯店	"In the afternoon, the editor was po "self-governing c again wanted me
ZhaoFeng Garden Note (Now called ZhongShan Park 中山 上海)	兆丰花园	兆豐花園	"On an evening i newspaper burea Garden."
HuiZhong Hotel (Now Art Peace Hotel)	汇中饭店	滙中飯店	"Once, Mr. Philip of his friends "
TiLan Bridge (Prison) Tibet Road	提篮桥监狱	提籃橋監獄	"I thought of the p was speechless
Old Gate Branch	老闸分局		protested, "The under control of t
FuKaiSen Road (Now Ferguson)	森路	福 森路	"When I heard the Road, and I aske
			"Well, well, it's li tel, the XX bur ang Hotel."

7AM-10AM

THAT SEWER GRATE LOOKS OLD ENOUGH!

疯老外

<CRAZY FOREIGNER>

I SPENT MY MORNINGS COMBING THE CITY FOR REFERENCE PHOTOS OF MUNDANE OBJECTS FROM THE RIGHT TIME PERIOD SO I COULD ACCURATELY DRAW SUN YI'S WORLD.

10AM-2PM

好的？

<GOT IT?>

我不懂

<I DON'T UNDERSTAND>

FOUR HOURS EACH DAY WENT TOWARD MANDARIN CLASSES, WHERE I CRIED IN FRUSTRATION ONLY TWICE. MANDARIN IS ANTITHETICAL TO HOW MY MIND WORKS.

2PM-6PM

SO WHICH OF THESE GUNS WOULD HAVE BEEN HELD TO MY GRANDMA'S CHEST?

AT THE SHANGHAI PUBLIC SECURITY MUSEUM

AFTERNOONS WERE FOR RESEARCH, TRACKING DOWN INFORMATION IN MUSEUMS AND FINDING LOCATIONS MENTIONED IN MY GRANDMOTHER'S BOOK.

6PM-10PM

我不懂

<I DON'T UNDERSTAND>

NIGHTS WERE FOR STUDYING MORE MANDARIN AND WRITING, USUALLY DONE OVER NOODLES.

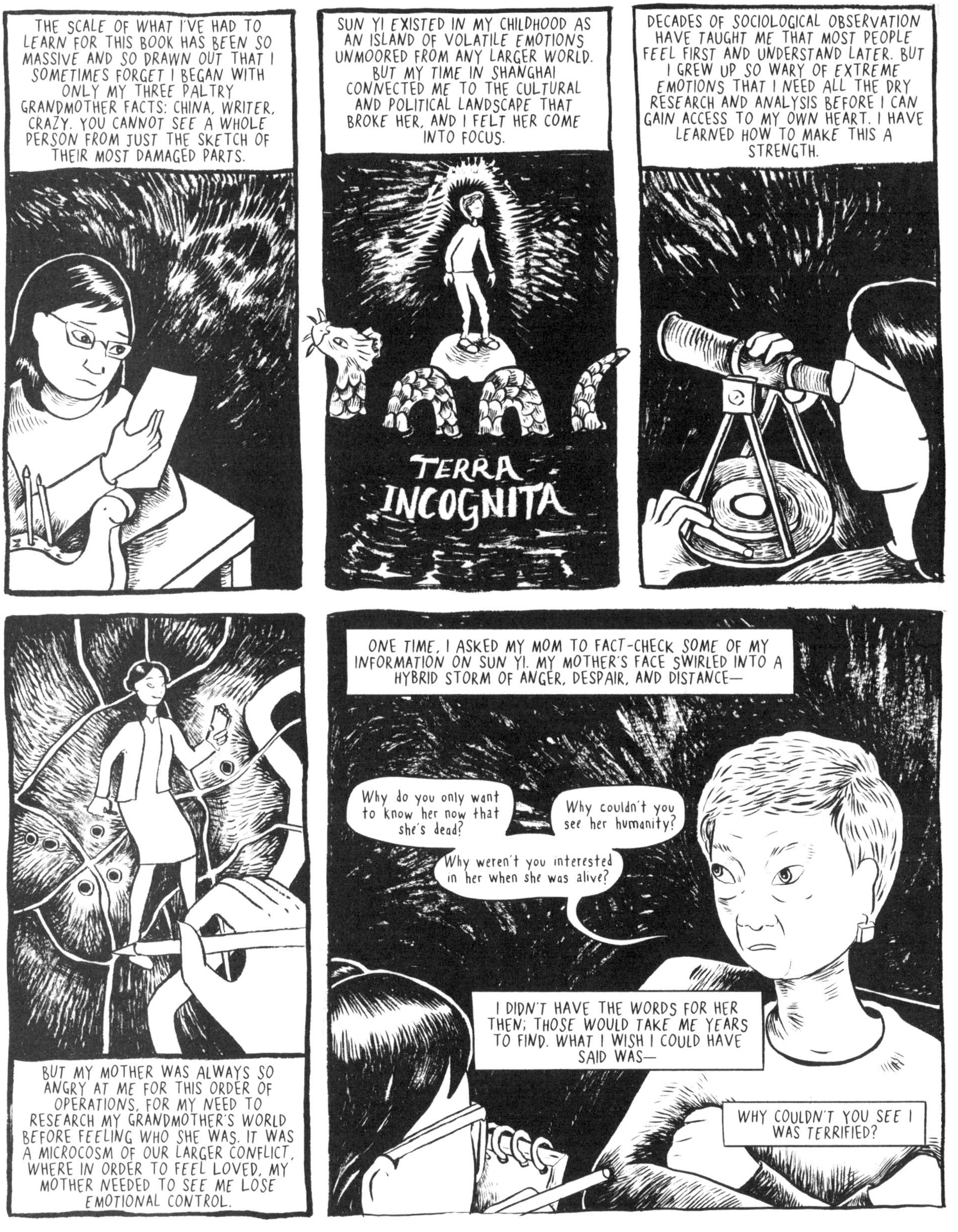
THE SCALE OF WHAT I'VE HAD TO LEARN FOR THIS BOOK HAS BEEN SO MASSIVE AND SO DRAWN OUT THAT I SOMETIMES FORGET I BEGAN WITH ONLY MY THREE PALTRY GRANDMOTHER FACTS: CHINA, WRITER, CRAZY. YOU CANNOT SEE A WHOLE PERSON FROM JUST THE SKETCH OF THEIR MOST DAMAGED PARTS.
SUN YI EXISTED IN MY CHILDHOOD AS AN ISLAND OF VOLATILE EMOTIONS UNMOORED FROM ANY LARGER WORLD. BUT MY TIME IN SHANGHAI CONNECTED ME TO THE CULTURAL AND POLITICAL LANDSCAPE THAT BROKE HER, AND I FELT HER COME INTO FOCUS.
TERRA INCOGNITA
DECADES OF SOCIOLOGICAL OBSERVATION HAVE TAUGHT ME THAT MOST PEOPLE FEEL FIRST AND UNDERSTAND LATER. BUT I GREW UP SO WARY OF EXTREME EMOTIONS THAT I NEED ALL THE DRY RESEARCH AND ANALYSIS BEFORE I CAN GAIN ACCESS TO MY OWN HEART. I HAVE LEARNED HOW TO MAKE THIS A STRENGTH.
BUT MY MOTHER WAS ALWAYS SO ANGRY AT ME FOR THIS ORDER OF OPERATIONS, FOR MY NEED TO RESEARCH MY GRANDMOTHER'S WORLD BEFORE FEELING WHO SHE WAS. IT WAS A MICROCOSM OF OUR LARGER CONFLICT, WHERE IN ORDER TO FEEL LOVED, MY MOTHER NEEDED TO SEE ME LOSE EMOTIONAL CONTROL.
ONE TIME, I ASKED MY MOM TO FACT-CHECK SOME OF MY INFORMATION ON SUN YI. MY MOTHER'S FACE SWIRLED INTO A HYBRID STORM OF ANGER, DESPAIR, AND DISTANCE—
Why do you only want to know her now that she's dead?
Why couldn't you see her humanity?
Why weren't you interested in her when she was alive?
I DIDN'T HAVE THE WORDS FOR HER THEN; THOSE WOULD TAKE ME YEARS TO FIND. WHAT I WISH I COULD HAVE SAID WAS—
WHY COULDN'T YOU SEE I WAS TERRIFIED?

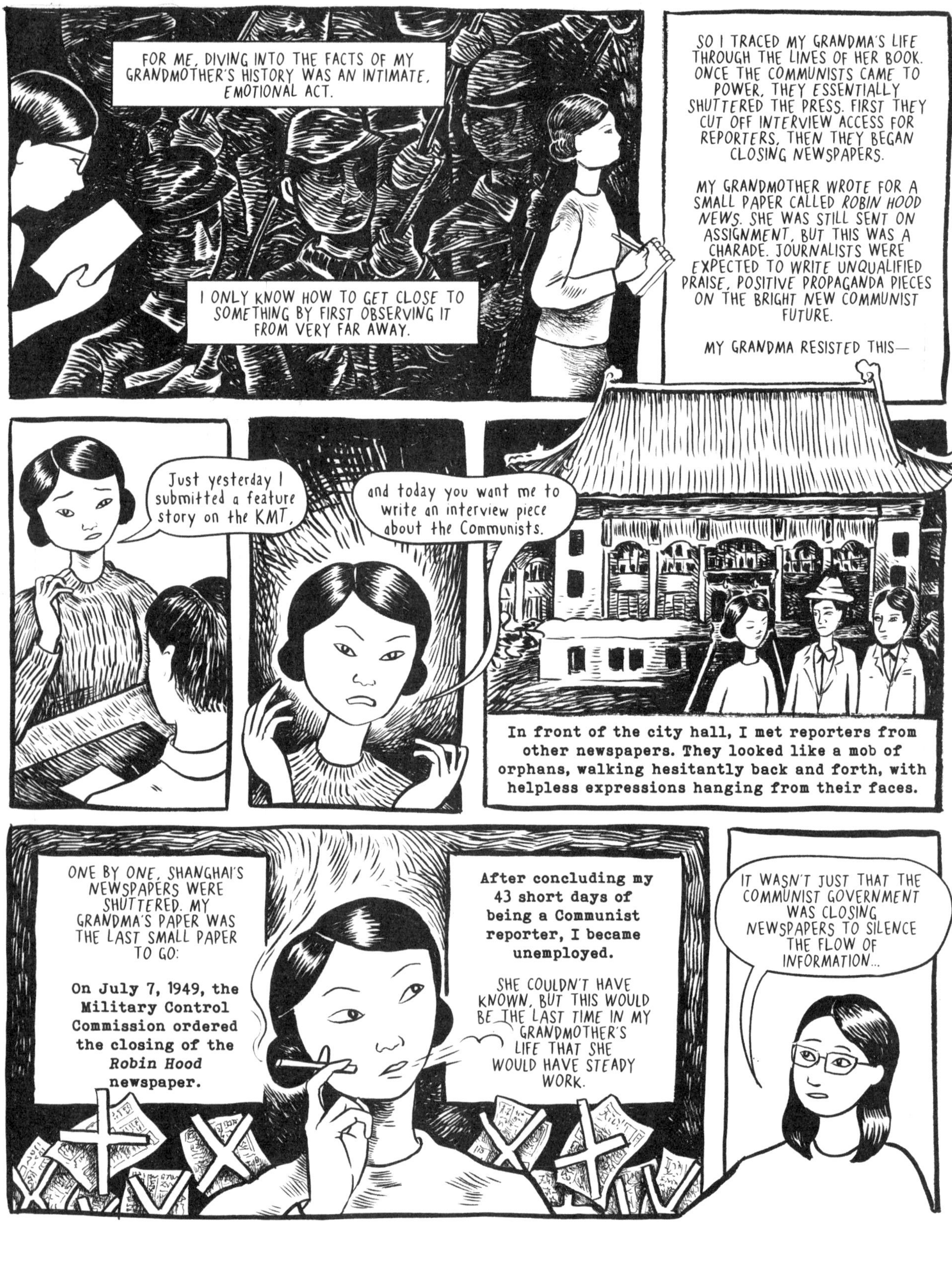
FOR ME, DIVING INTO THE FACTS OF MY GRANDMOTHER'S HISTORY WAS AN INTIMATE, EMOTIONAL ACT.
I ONLY KNOW HOW TO GET CLOSE TO SOMETHING BY FIRST OBSERVING IT FROM VERY FAR AWAY.
SO I TRACED MY GRANDMA'S LIFE THROUGH THE LINES OF HER BOOK. ONCE THE COMMUNISTS CAME TO POWER, THEY ESSENTIALLY SHUTTERED THE PRESS. FIRST THEY CUT OFF INTERVIEW ACCESS FOR REPORTERS, THEN THEY BEGAN CLOSING NEWSPAPERS.
MY GRANDMOTHER WROTE FOR A SMALL PAPER CALLED *ROBIN HOOD NEWS*. SHE WAS STILL SENT ON ASSIGNMENT, BUT THIS WAS A CHARADE. JOURNALISTS WERE EXPECTED TO WRITE UNQUALIFIED PRAISE, POSITIVE PROPAGANDA PIECES ON THE BRIGHT NEW COMMUNIST FUTURE.
MY GRANDMA RESISTED THIS—
Just yesterday I submitted a feature story on the KMT,
and today you want me to write an interview piece about the Communists.
In front of the city hall, I met reporters from other newspapers. They looked like a mob of orphans, walking hesitantly back and forth, with helpless expressions hanging from their faces.
ONE BY ONE, SHANGHAI'S NEWSPAPERS WERE SHUTTERED. MY GRANDMA'S PAPER WAS THE LAST SMALL PAPER TO GO:
On July 7, 1949, the Military Control Commission ordered the closing of the *Robin Hood* newspaper.
After concluding my 43 short days of being a Communist reporter, I became unemployed.
SHE COULDN'T HAVE KNOWN, BUT THIS WOULD BE THE LAST TIME IN MY GRANDMOTHER'S LIFE THAT SHE WOULD HAVE STEADY WORK.
IT WASN'T JUST THAT THE COMMUNIST GOVERNMENT WAS CLOSING NEWSPAPERS TO SILENCE THE FLOW OF INFORMATION...

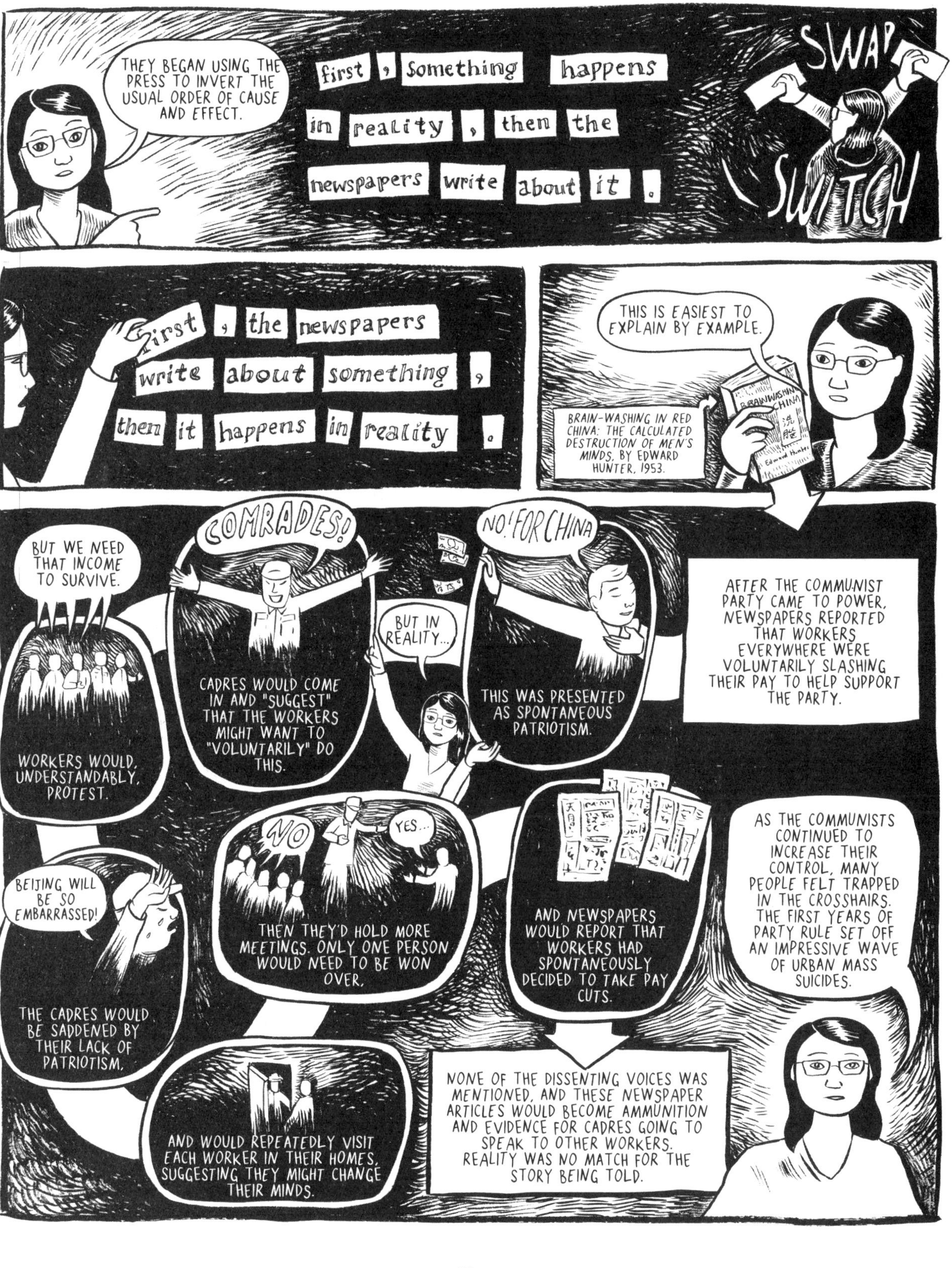

THEY BEGAN USING THE PRESS TO INVERT THE USUAL ORDER OF CAUSE AND EFFECT.
first, something happens in reality, then the newspapers write about it.
SWAP
SWITCH
first, the newspapers write about something, then it happens in reality.
THIS IS EASIEST TO EXPLAIN BY EXAMPLE.
BRAIN-WASHING IN RED CHINA: THE CALCULATED DESTRUCTION OF MEN'S MINDS, BY EDWARD HUNTER, 1953.
AFTER THE COMMUNIST PARTY CAME TO POWER, NEWSPAPERS REPORTED THAT WORKERS EVERYWHERE WERE VOLUNTARILY SLASHING THEIR PAY TO HELP SUPPORT THE PARTY.
NO! FOR CHINA
THIS WAS PRESENTED AS SPONTANEOUS PATRIOTISM.
BUT IN REALITY...
COMRADES!
CADRES WOULD COME IN AND "SUGGEST" THAT THE WORKERS MIGHT WANT TO "VOLUNTARILY" DO THIS.
BUT WE NEED THAT INCOME TO SURVIVE.
WORKERS WOULD, UNDERSTANDABLY, PROTEST.
BEIJING WILL BE SO EMBARRASSED!
THE CADRES WOULD BE SADDENED BY THEIR LACK OF PATRIOTISM.
AND WOULD REPEATEDLY VISIT EACH WORKER IN THEIR HOMES, SUGGESTING THEY MIGHT CHANGE THEIR MINDS.
NO
YES...
THEN THEY'D HOLD MORE MEETINGS. ONLY ONE PERSON WOULD NEED TO BE WON OVER.
AND NEWSPAPERS WOULD REPORT THAT WORKERS HAD SPONTANEOUSLY DECIDED TO TAKE PAY CUTS.
NONE OF THE DISSENTING VOICES WAS MENTIONED, AND THESE NEWSPAPER ARTICLES WOULD BECOME AMMUNITION AND EVIDENCE FOR CADRES GOING TO SPEAK TO OTHER WORKERS. REALITY WAS NO MATCH FOR THE STORY BEING TOLD.
AS THE COMMUNISTS CONTINUED TO INCREASE THEIR CONTROL, MANY PEOPLE FELT TRAPPED IN THE CROSSHAIRS. THE FIRST YEARS OF PARTY RULE SET OFF AN IMPRESSIVE WAVE OF URBAN MASS SUICIDES.

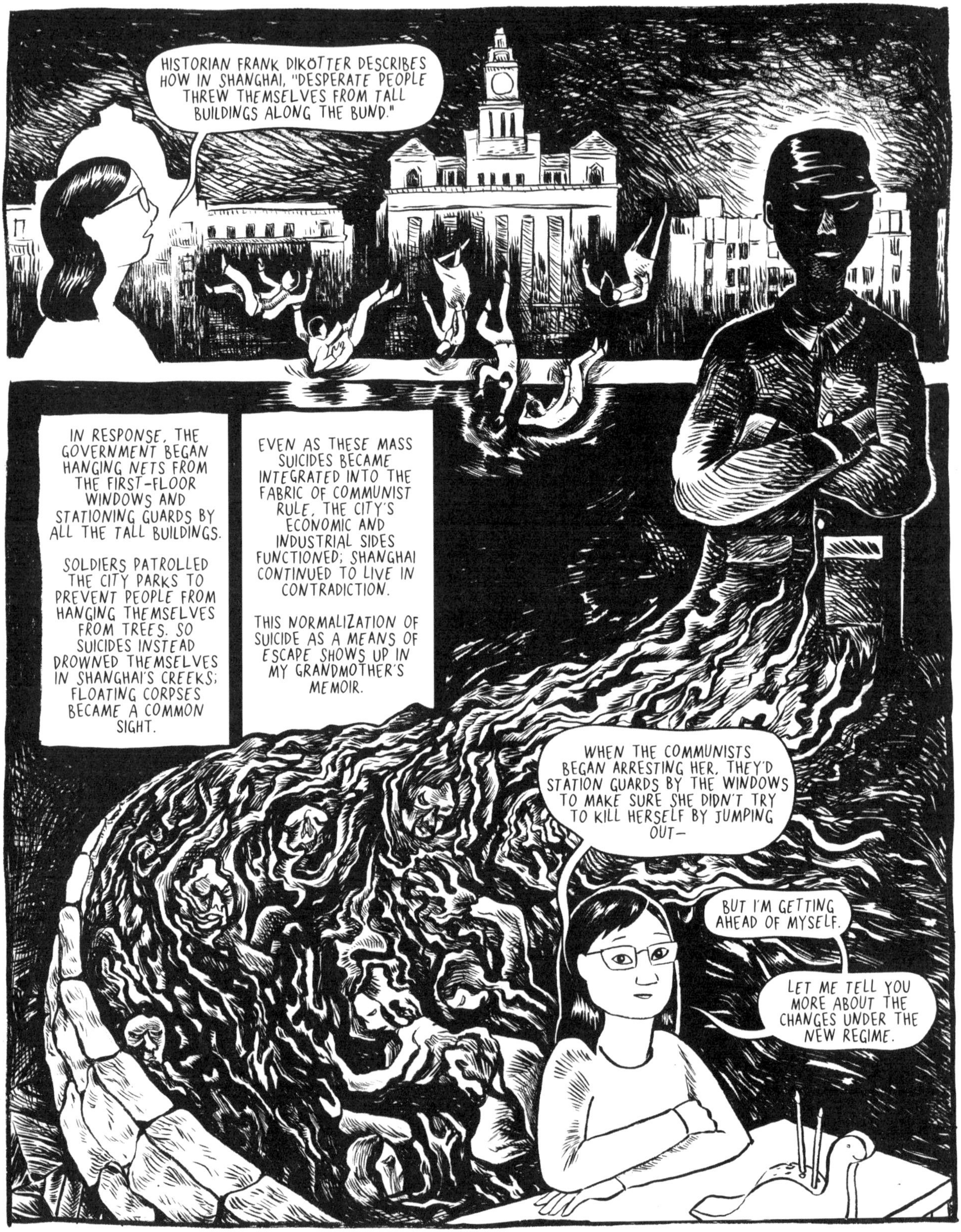
HISTORIAN FRANK DIKÖTTER DESCRIBES HOW IN SHANGHAI, "DESPERATE PEOPLE THREW THEMSELVES FROM TALL BUILDINGS ALONG THE BUND."
IN RESPONSE, THE GOVERNMENT BEGAN HANGING NETS FROM THE FIRST-FLOOR WINDOWS AND STATIONING GUARDS BY ALL THE TALL BUILDINGS.
SOLDIERS PATROLLED THE CITY PARKS TO PREVENT PEOPLE FROM HANGING THEMSELVES FROM TREES. SO SUICIDES INSTEAD DROWNED THEMSELVES IN SHANGHAI'S CREEKS; FLOATING CORPSES BECAME A COMMON SIGHT.
EVEN AS THESE MASS SUICIDES BECAME INTEGRATED INTO THE FABRIC OF COMMUNIST RULE, THE CITY'S ECONOMIC AND INDUSTRIAL SIDES FUNCTIONED; SHANGHAI CONTINUED TO LIVE IN CONTRADICTION.
THIS NORMALIZATION OF SUICIDE AS A MEANS OF ESCAPE SHOWS UP IN MY GRANDMOTHER'S MEMOIR.
WHEN THE COMMUNISTS BEGAN ARRESTING HER, THEY'D STATION GUARDS BY THE WINDOWS TO MAKE SURE SHE DIDN'T TRY TO KILL HERSELF BY JUMPING OUT—
BUT I'M GETTING AHEAD OF MYSELF.
LET ME TELL YOU MORE ABOUT THE CHANGES UNDER THE NEW REGIME.

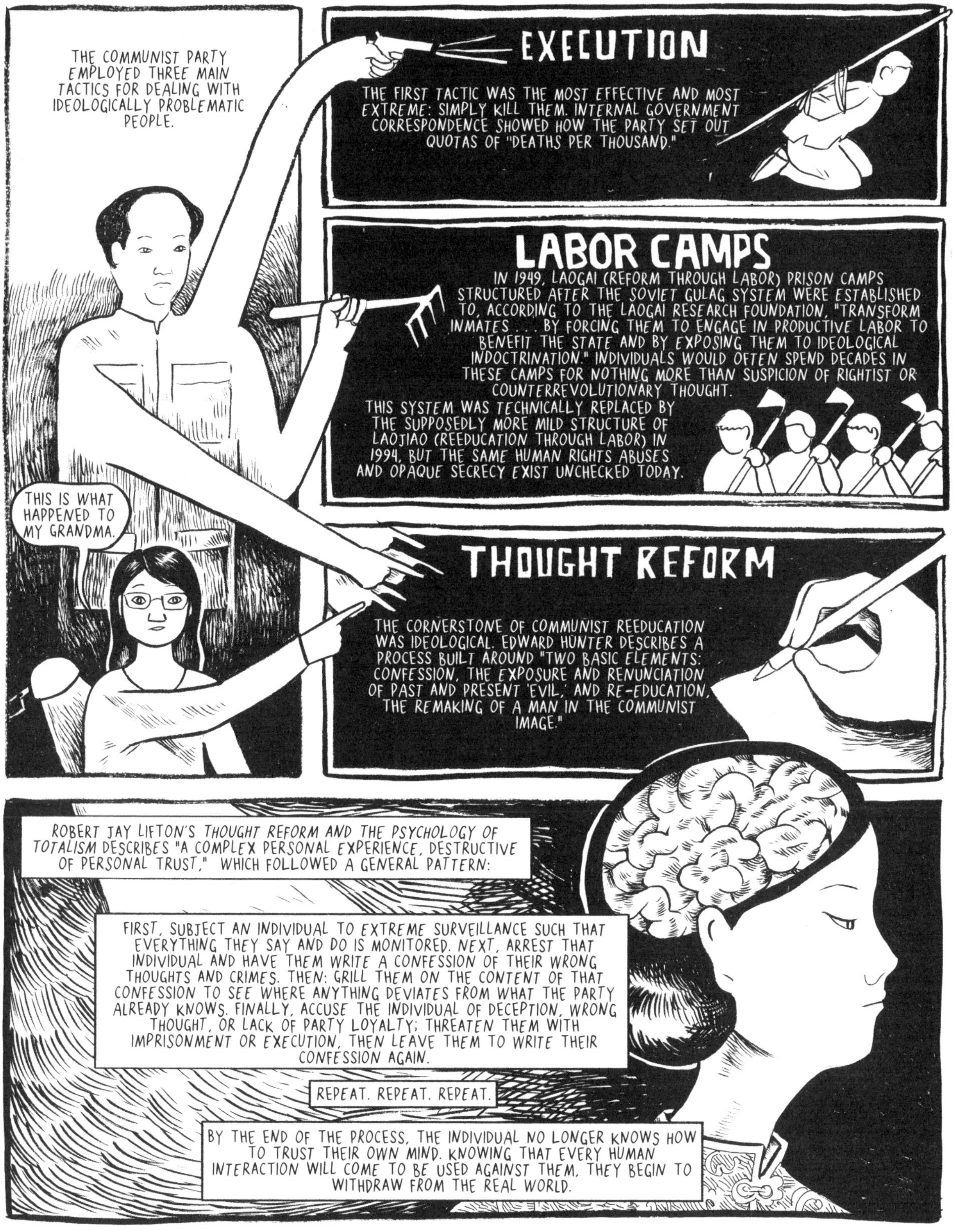

THE COMMUNIST PARTY EMPLOYED THREE MAIN TACTICS FOR DEALING WITH IDEOLOGICALLY PROBLEMATIC PEOPLE.
EXECUTION
THE FIRST TACTIC WAS THE MOST EFFECTIVE AND MOST EXTREME: SIMPLY KILL THEM. INTERNAL GOVERNMENT CORRESPONDENCE SHOWED HOW THE PARTY SET OUT QUOTAS OF "DEATHS PER THOUSAND."
LABOR CAMPS
IN 1949, LAOGAI (REFORM THROUGH LABOR) PRISON CAMPS STRUCTURED AFTER THE SOVIET GULAG SYSTEM WERE ESTABLISHED TO, ACCORDING TO THE LAOGAI RESEARCH FOUNDATION, "TRANSFORM INMATES . . . BY FORCING THEM TO ENGAGE IN PRODUCTIVE LABOR TO BENEFIT THE STATE AND BY EXPOSING THEM TO IDEOLOGICAL INDOCTRINATION." INDIVIDUALS WOULD OFTEN SPEND DECADES IN THESE CAMPS FOR NOTHING MORE THAN SUSPICION OF RIGHTIST OR COUNTERREVOLUTIONARY THOUGHT.
THIS SYSTEM WAS TECHNICALLY REPLACED BY THE SUPPOSEDLY MORE MILD STRUCTURE OF LAOJIAO (REEDUCATION THROUGH LABOR) IN 1994, BUT THE SAME HUMAN RIGHTS ABUSES AND OPAQUE SECRECY EXIST UNCHECKED TODAY.
THIS IS WHAT HAPPENED TO MY GRANDMA.
THOUGHT REFORM
THE CORNERSTONE OF COMMUNIST REEDUCATION WAS IDEOLOGICAL. EDWARD HUNTER DESCRIBES A PROCESS BUILT AROUND "TWO BASIC ELEMENTS: CONFESSION, THE EXPOSURE AND RENUNCIATION OF PAST AND PRESENT 'EVIL,' AND RE-EDUCATION, THE REMAKING OF A MAN IN THE COMMUNIST IMAGE."
ROBERT JAY LIFTON'S THOUGHT REFORM AND THE PSYCHOLOGY OF TOTALISM DESCRIBES "A COMPLEX PERSONAL EXPERIENCE, DESTRUCTIVE OF PERSONAL TRUST," WHICH FOLLOWED A GENERAL PATTERN:
FIRST, SUBJECT AN INDIVIDUAL TO EXTREME SURVEILLANCE SUCH THAT EVERYTHING THEY SAY AND DO IS MONITORED. NEXT, ARREST THAT INDIVIDUAL AND HAVE THEM WRITE A CONFESSION OF THEIR WRONG THOUGHTS AND CRIMES. THEN: GRILL THEM ON THE CONTENT OF THAT CONFESSION TO SEE WHERE ANYTHING DEVIATES FROM WHAT THE PARTY ALREADY KNOWS. FINALLY, ACCUSE THE INDIVIDUAL OF DECEPTION, WRONG THOUGHT, OR LACK OF PARTY LOYALTY; THREATEN THEM WITH IMPRISONMENT OR EXECUTION, THEN LEAVE THEM TO WRITE THEIR CONFESSION AGAIN.
REPEAT. REPEAT. REPEAT.
BY THE END OF THE PROCESS, THE INDIVIDUAL NO LONGER KNOWS HOW TO TRUST THEIR OWN MIND. KNOWING THAT EVERY HUMAN INTERACTION WILL COME TO BE USED AGAINST THEM, THEY BEGIN TO WITHDRAW FROM THE REAL WORLD.

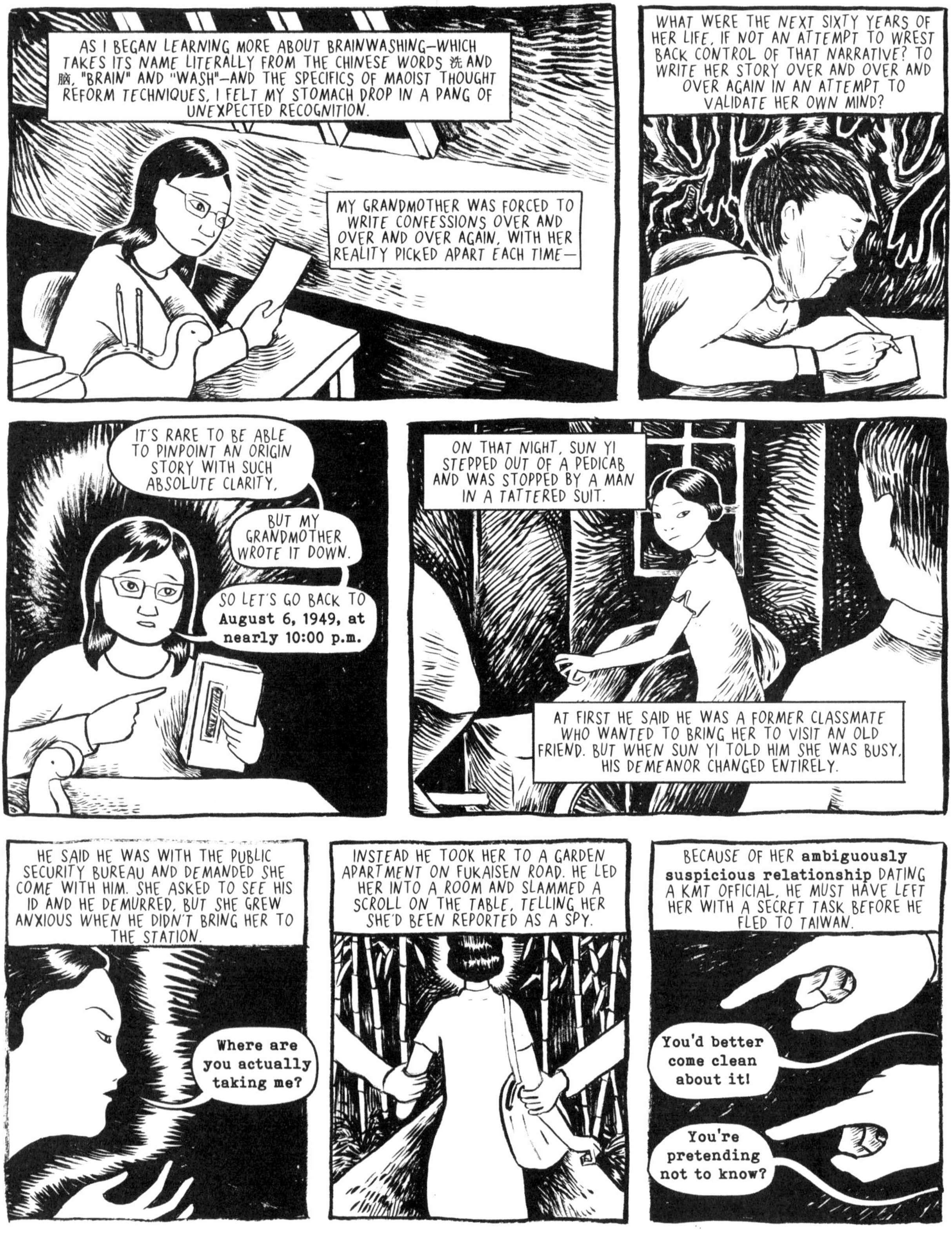
AS I BEGAN LEARNING MORE ABOUT BRAINWASHING—WHICH TAKES ITS NAME LITERALLY FROM THE CHINESE WORDS 洗 AND 脑, "BRAIN" AND "WASH"—AND THE SPECIFICS OF MAOIST THOUGHT REFORM TECHNIQUES, I FELT MY STOMACH DROP IN A PANG OF UNEXPECTED RECOGNITION.
MY GRANDMOTHER WAS FORCED TO WRITE CONFESSIONS OVER AND OVER AND OVER AGAIN, WITH HER REALITY PICKED APART EACH TIME—
WHAT WERE THE NEXT SIXTY YEARS OF HER LIFE, IF NOT AN ATTEMPT TO WREST BACK CONTROL OF THAT NARRATIVE? TO WRITE HER STORY OVER AND OVER AND OVER AGAIN IN AN ATTEMPT TO VALIDATE HER OWN MIND?
IT'S RARE TO BE ABLE TO PINPOINT AN ORIGIN STORY WITH SUCH ABSOLUTE CLARITY,
BUT MY GRANDMOTHER WROTE IT DOWN.
SO LET'S GO BACK TO **August 6, 1949, at nearly 10:00 p.m.**
ON THAT NIGHT, SUN YI STEPPED OUT OF A PEDICAB AND WAS STOPPED BY A MAN IN A TATTERED SUIT.
AT FIRST HE SAID HE WAS A FORMER CLASSMATE WHO WANTED TO BRING HER TO VISIT AN OLD FRIEND. BUT WHEN SUN YI TOLD HIM SHE WAS BUSY, HIS DEMEANOR CHANGED ENTIRELY.
HE SAID HE WAS WITH THE PUBLIC SECURITY BUREAU AND DEMANDED SHE COME WITH HIM. SHE ASKED TO SEE HIS ID AND HE DEMURRED, BUT SHE GREW ANXIOUS WHEN HE DIDN'T BRING HER TO THE STATION.
Where are you actually taking me?
INSTEAD HE TOOK HER TO A GARDEN APARTMENT ON FUKAISEN ROAD. HE LED HER INTO A ROOM AND SLAMMED A SCROLL ON THE TABLE, TELLING HER SHE'D BEEN REPORTED AS A SPY.
BECAUSE OF HER **ambiguously suspicious relationship** DATING A KMT OFFICIAL, HE MUST HAVE LEFT HER WITH A SECRET TASK BEFORE HE FLED TO TAIWAN.
You'd better come clean about it!
You're pretending not to know?

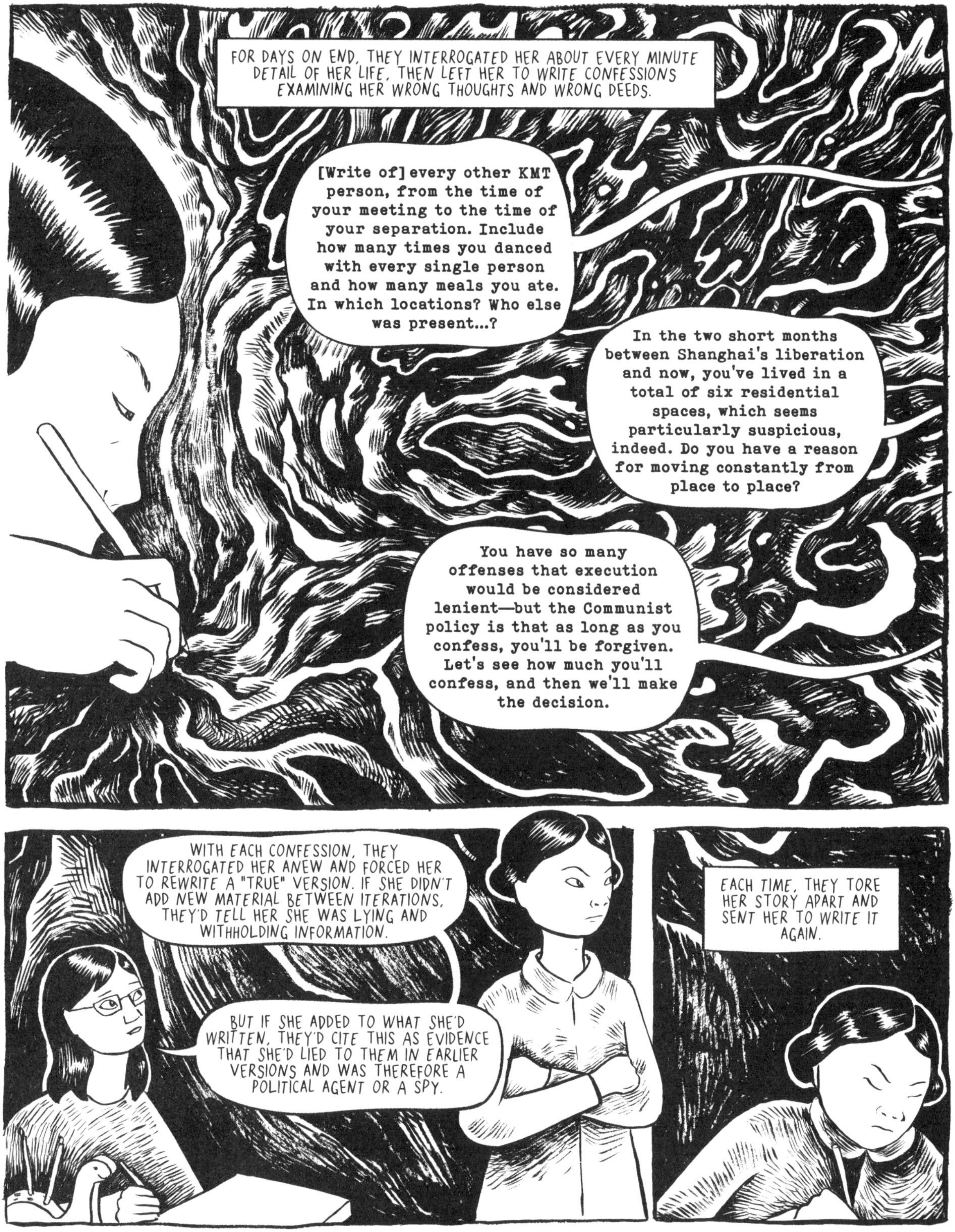

FOR DAYS ON END, THEY INTERROGATED HER ABOUT EVERY MINUTE DETAIL OF HER LIFE, THEN LEFT HER TO WRITE CONFESSIONS EXAMINING HER WRONG THOUGHTS AND WRONG DEEDS.
[Write of] every other KMT person, from the time of your meeting to the time of your separation. Include how many times you danced with every single person and how many meals you ate. In which locations? Who else was present...?
In the two short months between Shanghai's liberation and now, you've lived in a total of six residential spaces, which seems particularly suspicious, indeed. Do you have a reason for moving constantly from place to place?
You have so many offenses that execution would be considered lenient—but the Communist policy is that as long as you confess, you'll be forgiven. Let's see how much you'll confess, and then we'll make the decision.
WITH EACH CONFESSION, THEY INTERROGATED HER ANEW AND FORCED HER TO REWRITE A "TRUE" VERSION. IF SHE DIDN'T ADD NEW MATERIAL BETWEEN ITERATIONS, THEY'D TELL HER SHE WAS LYING AND WITHHOLDING INFORMATION.
BUT IF SHE ADDED TO WHAT SHE'D WRITTEN, THEY'D CITE THIS AS EVIDENCE THAT SHE'D LIED TO THEM IN EARLIER VERSIONS AND WAS THEREFORE A POLITICAL AGENT OR A SPY.
EACH TIME, THEY TORE HER STORY APART AND SENT HER TO WRITE IT AGAIN.

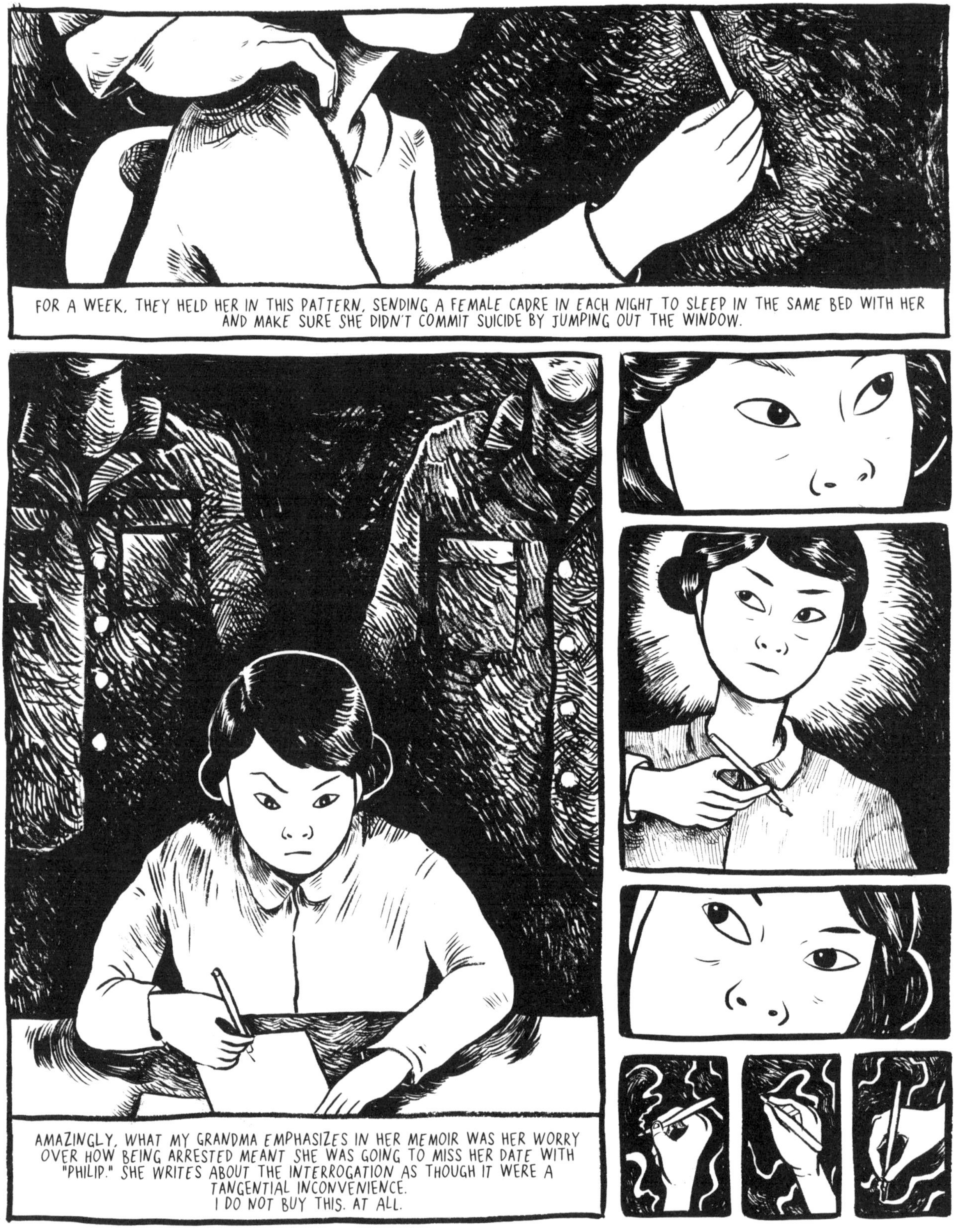
FOR A WEEK, THEY HELD HER IN THIS PATTERN, SENDING A FEMALE CADRE IN EACH NIGHT TO SLEEP IN THE SAME BED WITH HER AND MAKE SURE SHE DIDN'T COMMIT SUICIDE BY JUMPING OUT THE WINDOW.
AMAZINGLY, WHAT MY GRANDMA EMPHASIZES IN HER MEMOIR WAS HER WORRY OVER HOW BEING ARRESTED MEANT SHE WAS GOING TO MISS HER DATE WITH "PHILIP." SHE WRITES ABOUT THE INTERROGATION AS THOUGH IT WERE A TANGENTIAL INCONVENIENCE.
I DO NOT BUY THIS. AT ALL.

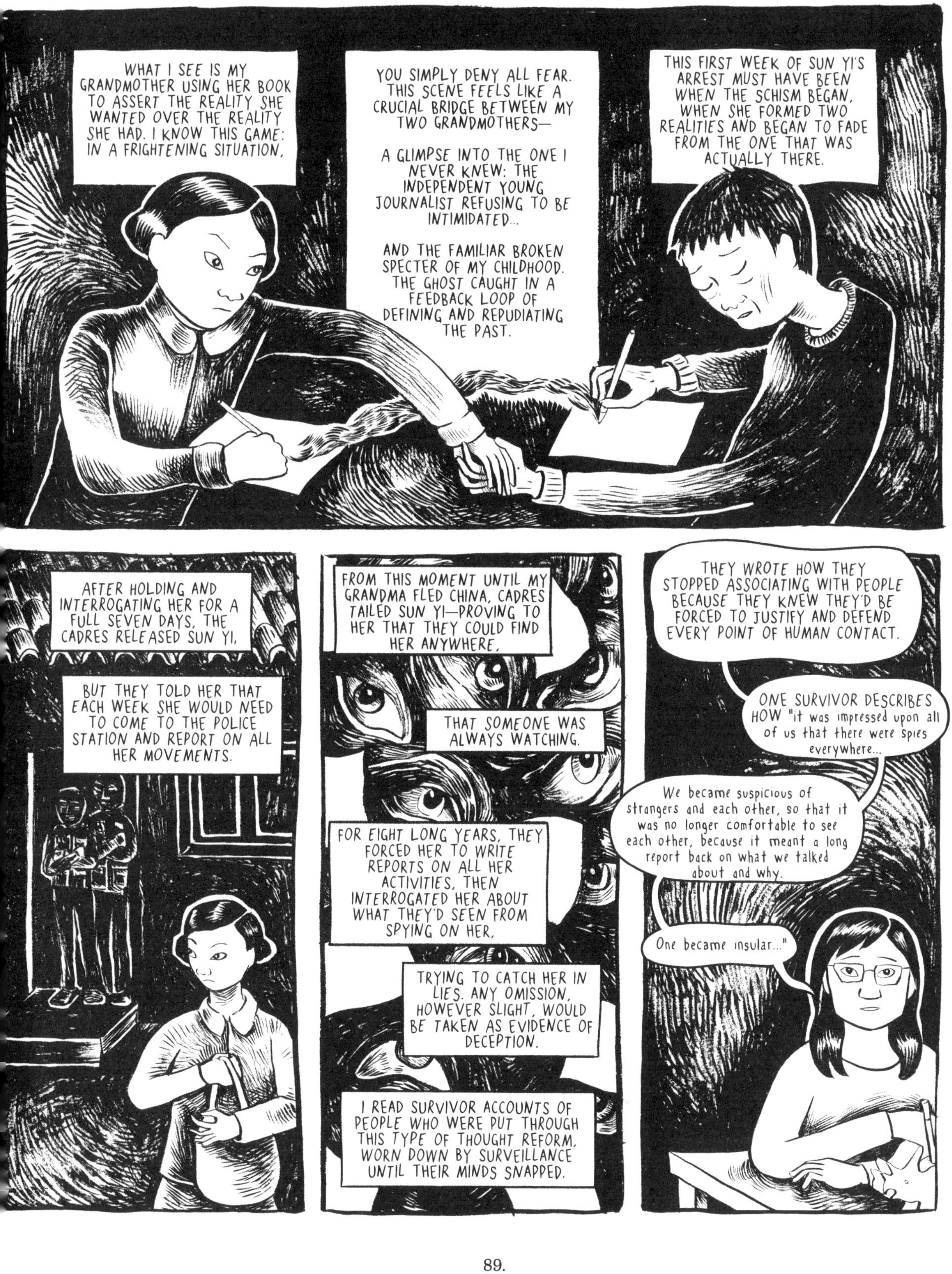

WHAT I SEE IS MY GRANDMOTHER USING HER BOOK TO ASSERT THE REALITY SHE WANTED OVER THE REALITY SHE HAD. I KNOW THIS GAME: IN A FRIGHTENING SITUATION,
YOU SIMPLY DENY ALL FEAR. THIS SCENE FEELS LIKE A CRUCIAL BRIDGE BETWEEN MY TWO GRANDMOTHERS—
A GLIMPSE INTO THE ONE I NEVER KNEW: THE INDEPENDENT YOUNG JOURNALIST REFUSING TO BE INTIMIDATED...
AND THE FAMILIAR BROKEN SPECTER OF MY CHILDHOOD. THE GHOST CAUGHT IN A FEEDBACK LOOP OF DEFINING AND REPUDIATING THE PAST.
THIS FIRST WEEK OF SUN YI'S ARREST MUST HAVE BEEN WHEN THE SCHISM BEGAN, WHEN SHE FORMED TWO REALITIES AND BEGAN TO FADE FROM THE ONE THAT WAS ACTUALLY THERE.
AFTER HOLDING AND INTERROGATING HER FOR A FULL SEVEN DAYS, THE CADRES RELEASED SUN YI,
BUT THEY TOLD HER THAT EACH WEEK SHE WOULD NEED TO COME TO THE POLICE STATION AND REPORT ON ALL HER MOVEMENTS.
FROM THIS MOMENT UNTIL MY GRANDMA FLED CHINA, CADRES TAILED SUN YI—PROVING TO HER THAT THEY COULD FIND HER ANYWHERE,
THAT SOMEONE WAS ALWAYS WATCHING.
FOR EIGHT LONG YEARS, THEY FORCED HER TO WRITE REPORTS ON ALL HER ACTIVITIES, THEN INTERROGATED HER ABOUT WHAT THEY'D SEEN FROM SPYING ON HER,
TRYING TO CATCH HER IN LIES. ANY OMISSION, HOWEVER SLIGHT, WOULD BE TAKEN AS EVIDENCE OF DECEPTION.
I READ SURVIVOR ACCOUNTS OF PEOPLE WHO WERE PUT THROUGH THIS TYPE OF THOUGHT REFORM, WORN DOWN BY SURVEILLANCE UNTIL THEIR MINDS SNAPPED.
THEY WROTE HOW THEY STOPPED ASSOCIATING WITH PEOPLE BECAUSE THEY KNEW THEY'D BE FORCED TO JUSTIFY AND DEFEND EVERY POINT OF HUMAN CONTACT.
ONE SURVIVOR DESCRIBES HOW "it was impressed upon all of us that there were spies everywhere...
We became suspicious of strangers and each other, so that it was no longer comfortable to see each other, because it meant a long report back on what we talked about and why.
One became insular..."

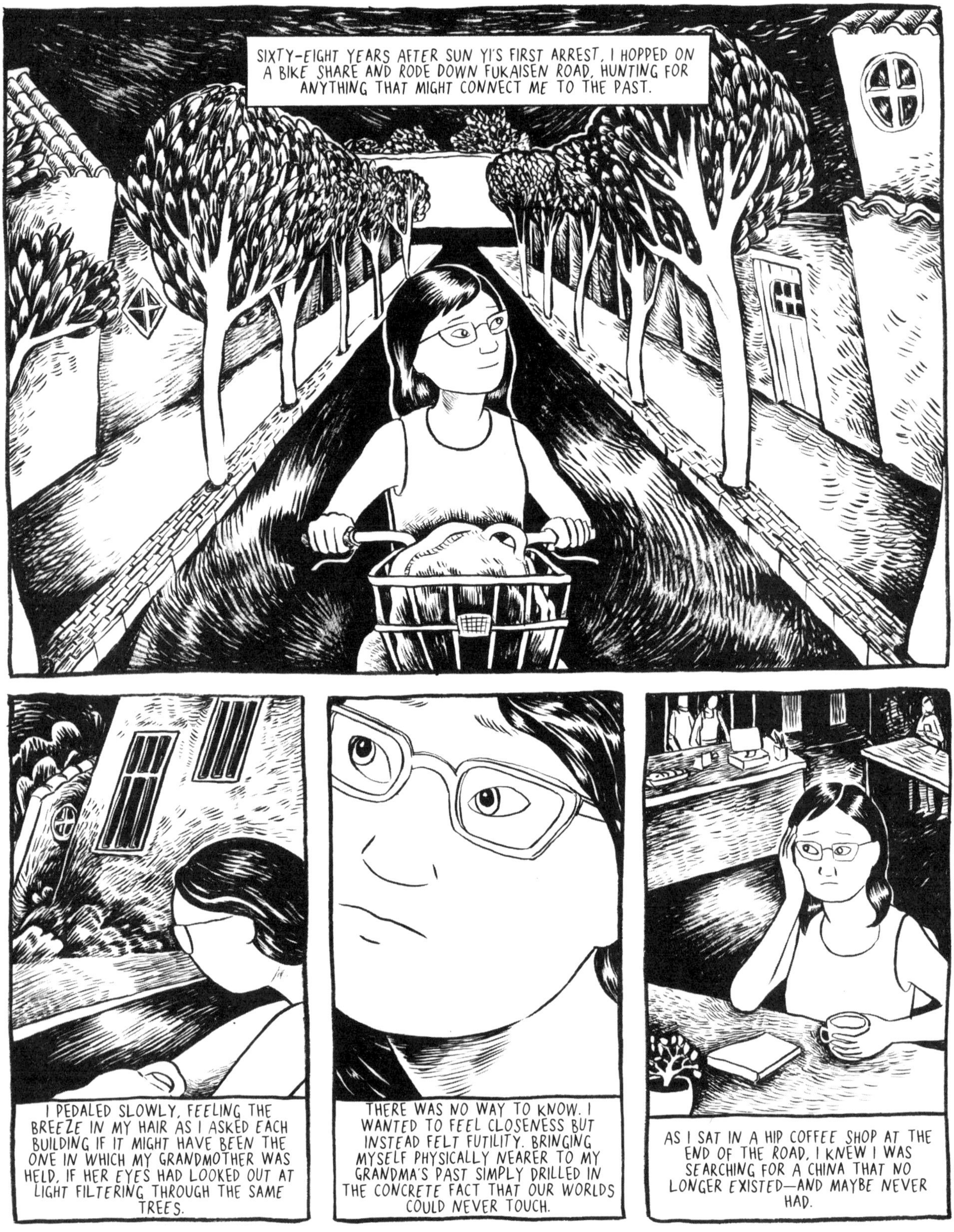
SIXTY-EIGHT YEARS AFTER SUN YI'S FIRST ARREST, I HOPPED ON A BIKE SHARE AND RODE DOWN FUKAISEN ROAD, HUNTING FOR ANYTHING THAT MIGHT CONNECT ME TO THE PAST.
I PEDALED SLOWLY, FEELING THE BREEZE IN MY HAIR AS I ASKED EACH BUILDING IF IT MIGHT HAVE BEEN THE ONE IN WHICH MY GRANDMOTHER WAS HELD, IF HER EYES HAD LOOKED OUT AT LIGHT FILTERING THROUGH THE SAME TREES.
THERE WAS NO WAY TO KNOW. I WANTED TO FEEL CLOSENESS BUT INSTEAD FELT FUTILITY. BRINGING MYSELF PHYSICALLY NEARER TO MY GRANDMA'S PAST SIMPLY DRILLED IN THE CONCRETE FACT THAT OUR WORLDS COULD NEVER TOUCH.
AS I SAT IN A HIP COFFEE SHOP AT THE END OF THE ROAD, I KNEW I WAS SEARCHING FOR A CHINA THAT NO LONGER EXISTED—AND MAYBE NEVER HAD.

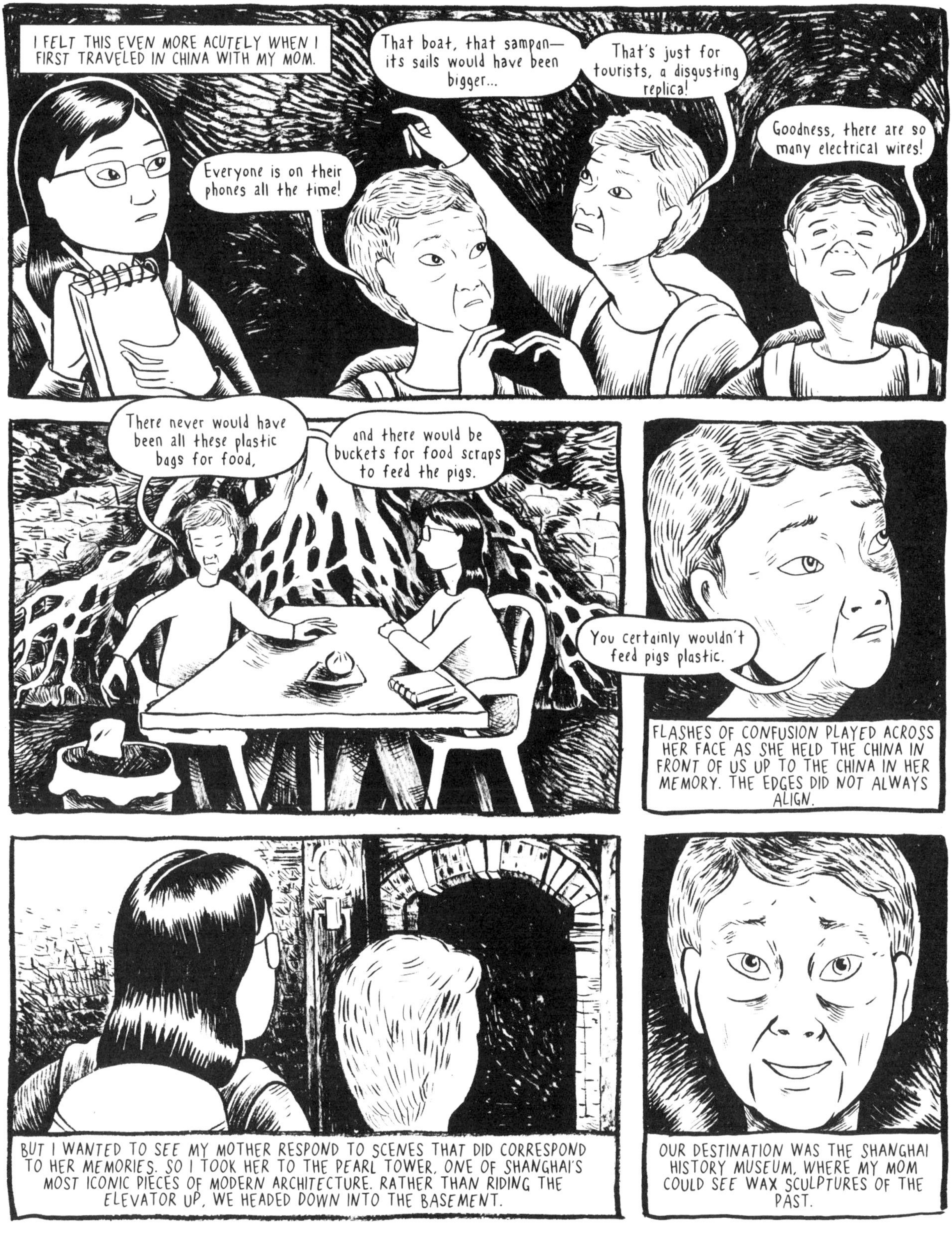
I FELT THIS EVEN MORE ACUTELY WHEN I FIRST TRAVELED IN CHINA WITH MY MOM.
Everyone is on their phones all the time!
That boat, that sampan— its sails would have been bigger...
That's just for tourists, a disgusting replica!
Goodness, there are so many electrical wires!
There never would have been all these plastic bags for food,
and there would be buckets for food scraps to feed the pigs.
You certainly wouldn't feed pigs plastic.
FLASHES OF CONFUSION PLAYED ACROSS HER FACE AS SHE HELD THE CHINA IN FRONT OF US UP TO THE CHINA IN HER MEMORY. THE EDGES DID NOT ALWAYS ALIGN.
BUT I WANTED TO SEE MY MOTHER RESPOND TO SCENES THAT DID CORRESPOND TO HER MEMORIES. SO I TOOK HER TO THE PEARL TOWER, ONE OF SHANGHAI'S MOST ICONIC PIECES OF MODERN ARCHITECTURE. RATHER THAN RIDING THE ELEVATOR UP, WE HEADED DOWN INTO THE BASEMENT.
OUR DESTINATION WAS THE SHANGHAI HISTORY MUSEUM, WHERE MY MOM COULD SEE WAX SCULPTURES OF THE PAST.

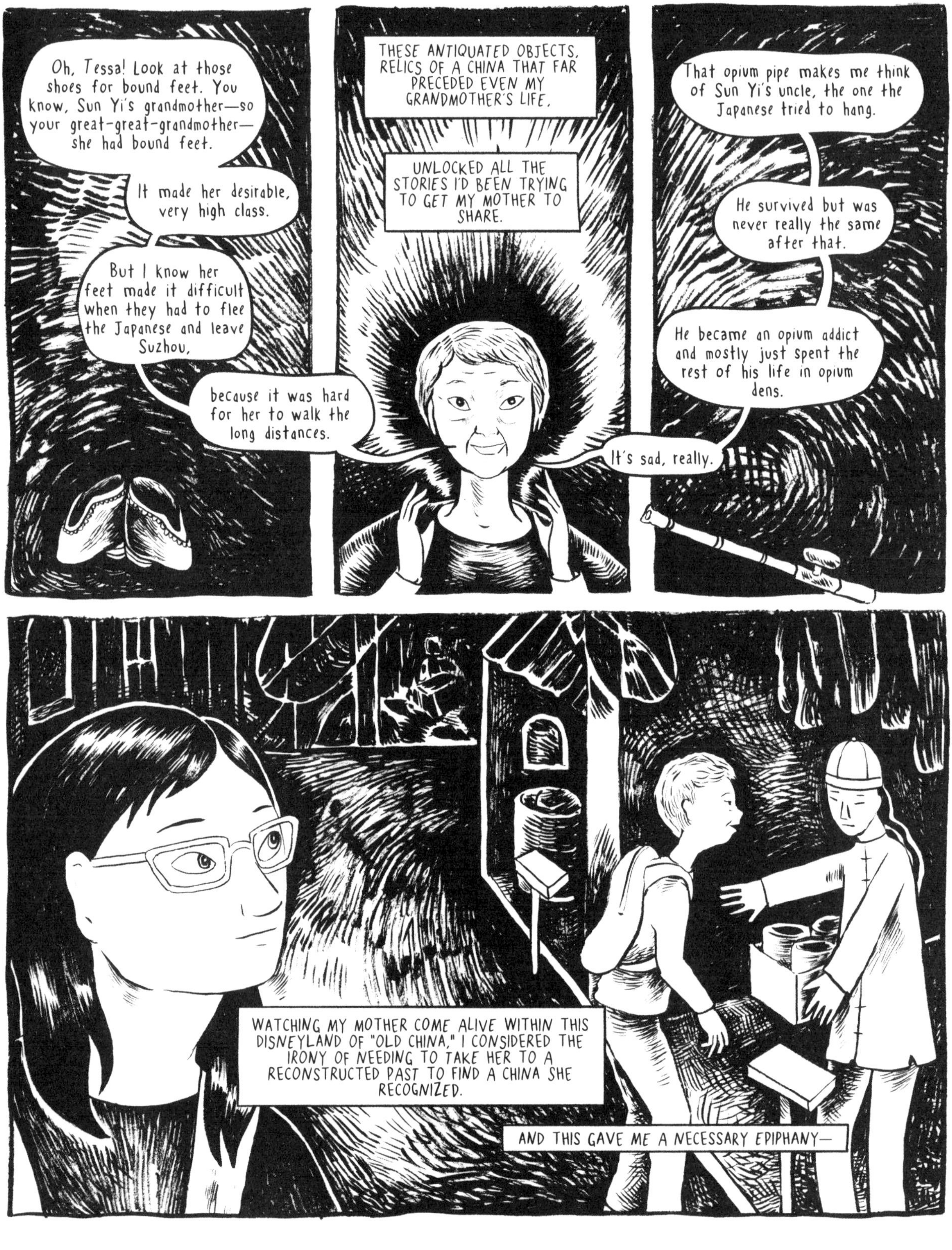
Oh, Tessa! Look at those shoes for bound feet. You know, Sun Yi's grandmother—so your great-great-grandmother—she had bound feet.
It made her desirable, very high class.
But I know her feet made it difficult when they had to flee the Japanese and leave Suzhou,
because it was hard for her to walk the long distances.
THESE ANTIQUATED OBJECTS, RELICS OF A CHINA THAT FAR PRECEDED EVEN MY GRANDMOTHER'S LIFE,
UNLOCKED ALL THE STORIES I'D BEEN TRYING TO GET MY MOTHER TO SHARE.
That opium pipe makes me think of Sun Yi's uncle, the one the Japanese tried to hang.
He survived but was never really the same after that.
He became an opium addict and mostly just spent the rest of his life in opium dens.
It's sad, really.
WATCHING MY MOTHER COME ALIVE WITHIN THIS DISNEYLAND OF "OLD CHINA," I CONSIDERED THE IRONY OF NEEDING TO TAKE HER TO A RECONSTRUCTED PAST TO FIND A CHINA SHE RECOGNIZED.
AND THIS GAVE ME A NECESSARY EPIPHANY—

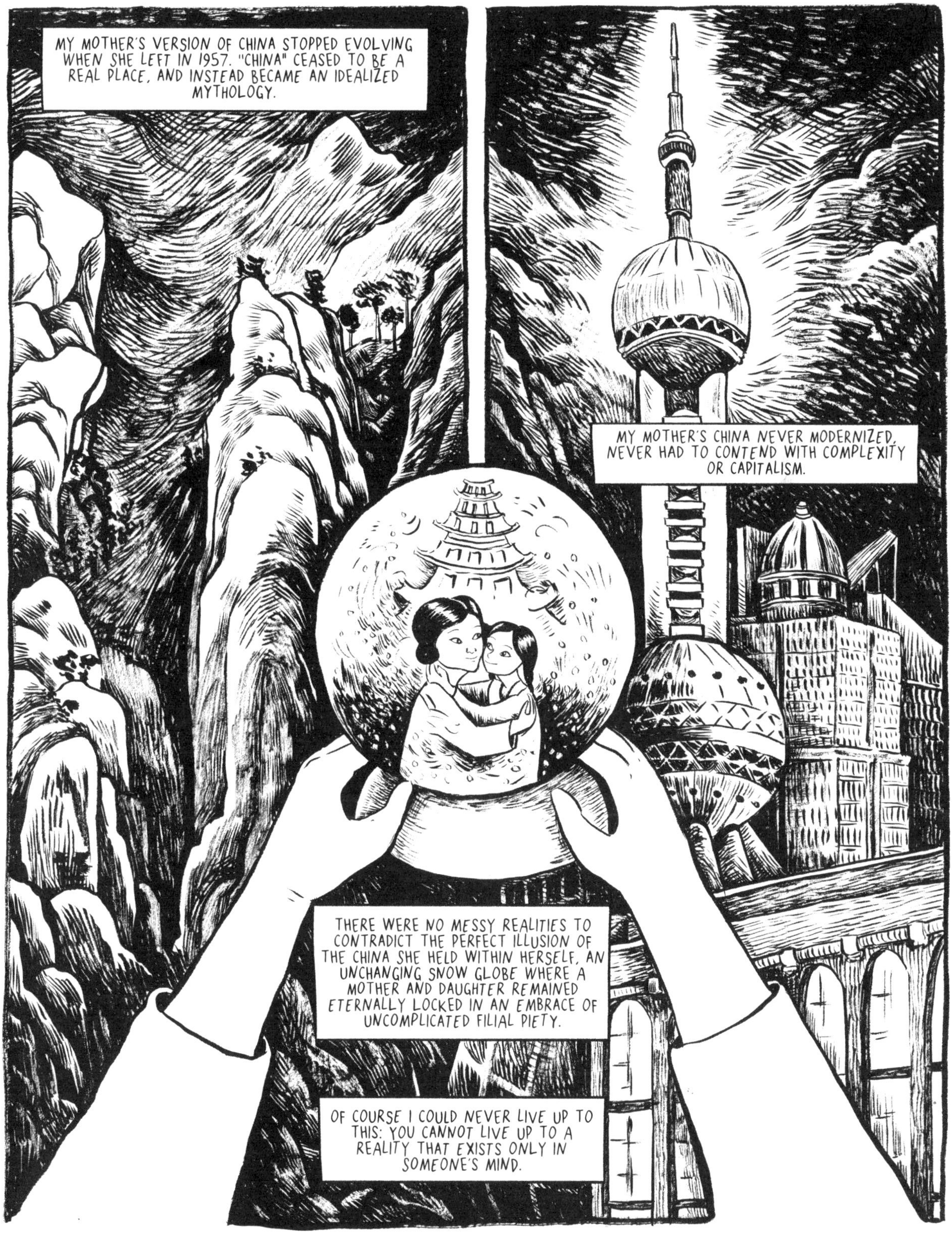

MY MOTHER'S VERSION OF CHINA STOPPED EVOLVING WHEN SHE LEFT IN 1957. "CHINA" CEASED TO BE A REAL PLACE, AND INSTEAD BECAME AN IDEALIZED MYTHOLOGY.
MY MOTHER'S CHINA NEVER MODERNIZED, NEVER HAD TO CONTEND WITH COMPLEXITY OR CAPITALISM.
THERE WERE NO MESSY REALITIES TO CONTRADICT THE PERFECT ILLUSION OF THE CHINA SHE HELD WITHIN HERSELF, AN UNCHANGING SNOW GLOBE WHERE A MOTHER AND DAUGHTER REMAINED ETERNALLY LOCKED IN AN EMBRACE OF UNCOMPLICATED FILIAL PIETY.
OF COURSE I COULD NEVER LIVE UP TO THIS: YOU CANNOT LIVE UP TO A REALITY THAT EXISTS ONLY IN SOMEONE'S MIND.

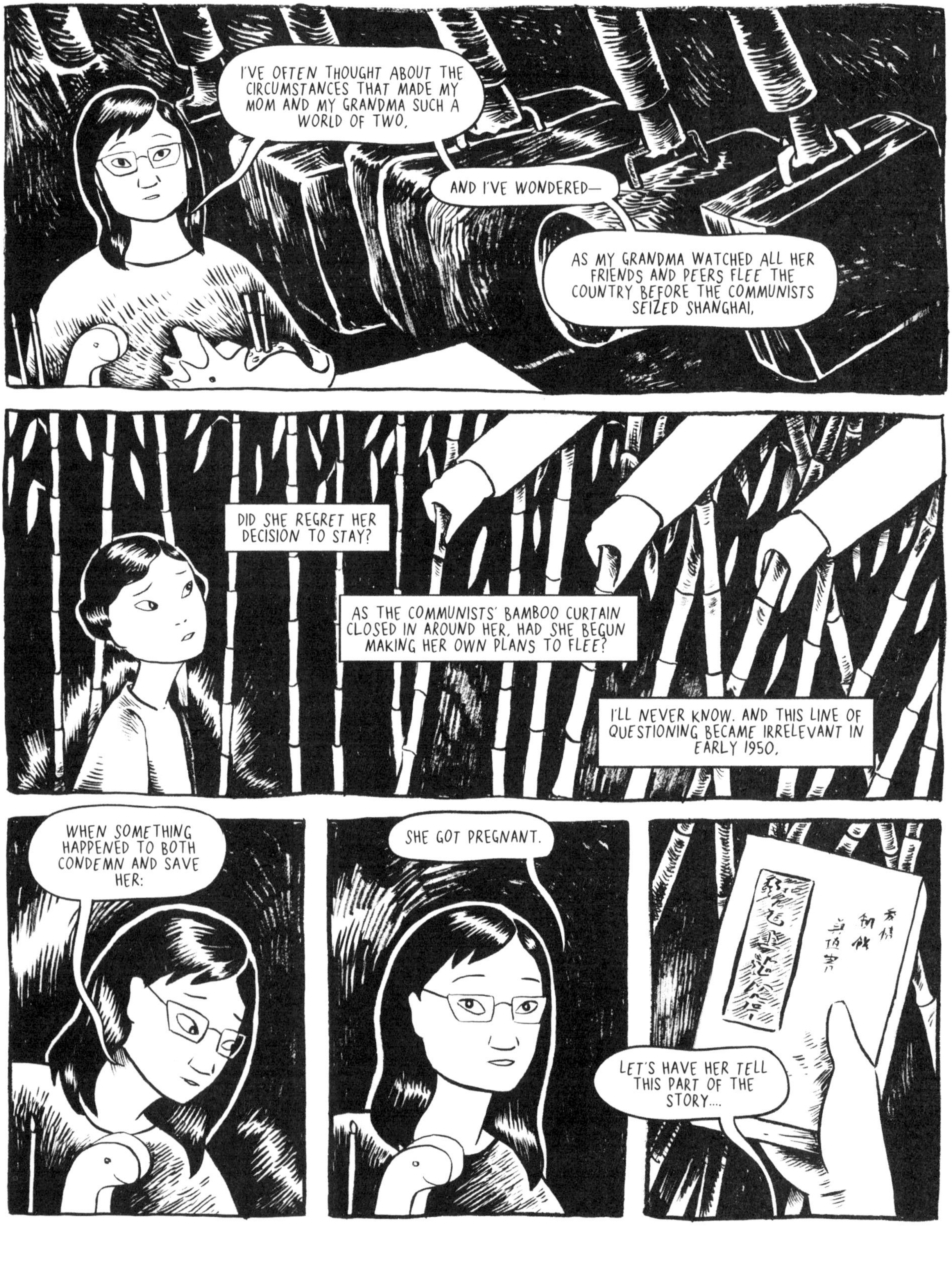
I'VE OFTEN THOUGHT ABOUT THE CIRCUMSTANCES THAT MADE MY MOM AND MY GRANDMA SUCH A WORLD OF TWO,
AND I'VE WONDERED—
AS MY GRANDMA WATCHED ALL HER FRIENDS AND PEERS FLEE THE COUNTRY BEFORE THE COMMUNISTS SEIZED SHANGHAI,
DID SHE REGRET HER DECISION TO STAY?
AS THE COMMUNISTS' BAMBOO CURTAIN CLOSED IN AROUND HER, HAD SHE BEGUN MAKING HER OWN PLANS TO FLEE?
I'LL NEVER KNOW. AND THIS LINE OF QUESTIONING BECAME IRRELEVANT IN EARLY 1950,
WHEN SOMETHING HAPPENED TO BOTH CONDEMN AND SAVE HER:
SHE GOT PREGNANT.
LET'S HAVE HER TELL THIS PART OF THE STORY....

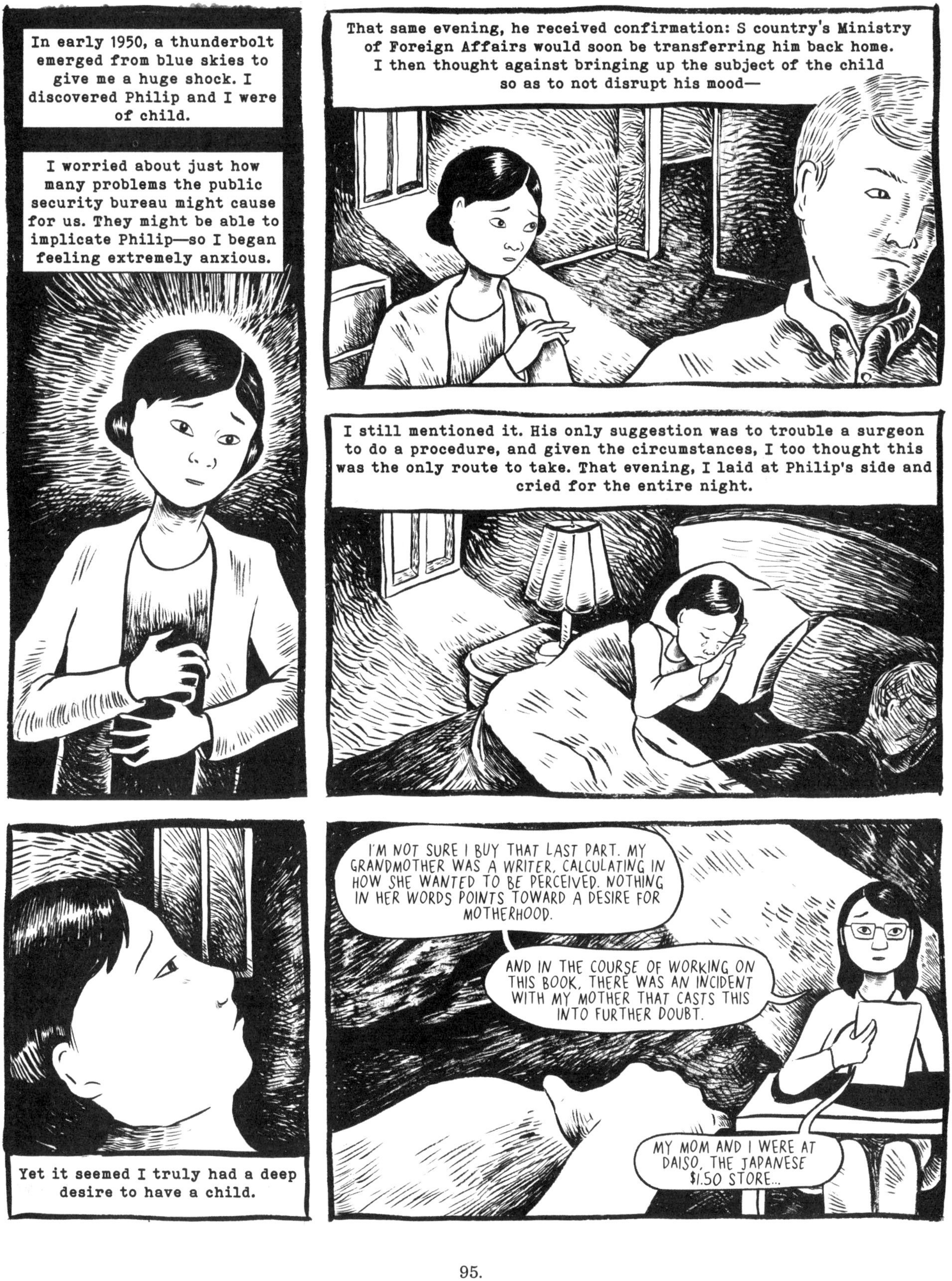

In early 1950, a thunderbolt emerged from blue skies to give me a huge shock. I discovered Philip and I were of child.
I worried about just how many problems the public security bureau might cause for us. They might be able to implicate Philip—so I began feeling extremely anxious.
That same evening, he received confirmation: S country's Ministry of Foreign Affairs would soon be transferring him back home. I then thought against bringing up the subject of the child so as to not disrupt his mood—
I still mentioned it. His only suggestion was to trouble a surgeon to do a procedure, and given the circumstances, I too thought this was the only route to take. That evening, I laid at Philip's side and cried for the entire night.
Yet it seemed I truly had a deep desire to have a child.
I'M NOT SURE I BUY THAT LAST PART. MY GRANDMOTHER WAS A WRITER, CALCULATING IN HOW SHE WANTED TO BE PERCEIVED. NOTHING IN HER WORDS POINTS TOWARD A DESIRE FOR MOTHERHOOD.
AND IN THE COURSE OF WORKING ON THIS BOOK, THERE WAS AN INCIDENT WITH MY MOTHER THAT CASTS THIS INTO FURTHER DOUBT.
MY MOM AND I WERE AT DAISO, THE JAPANESE $1.50 STORE...

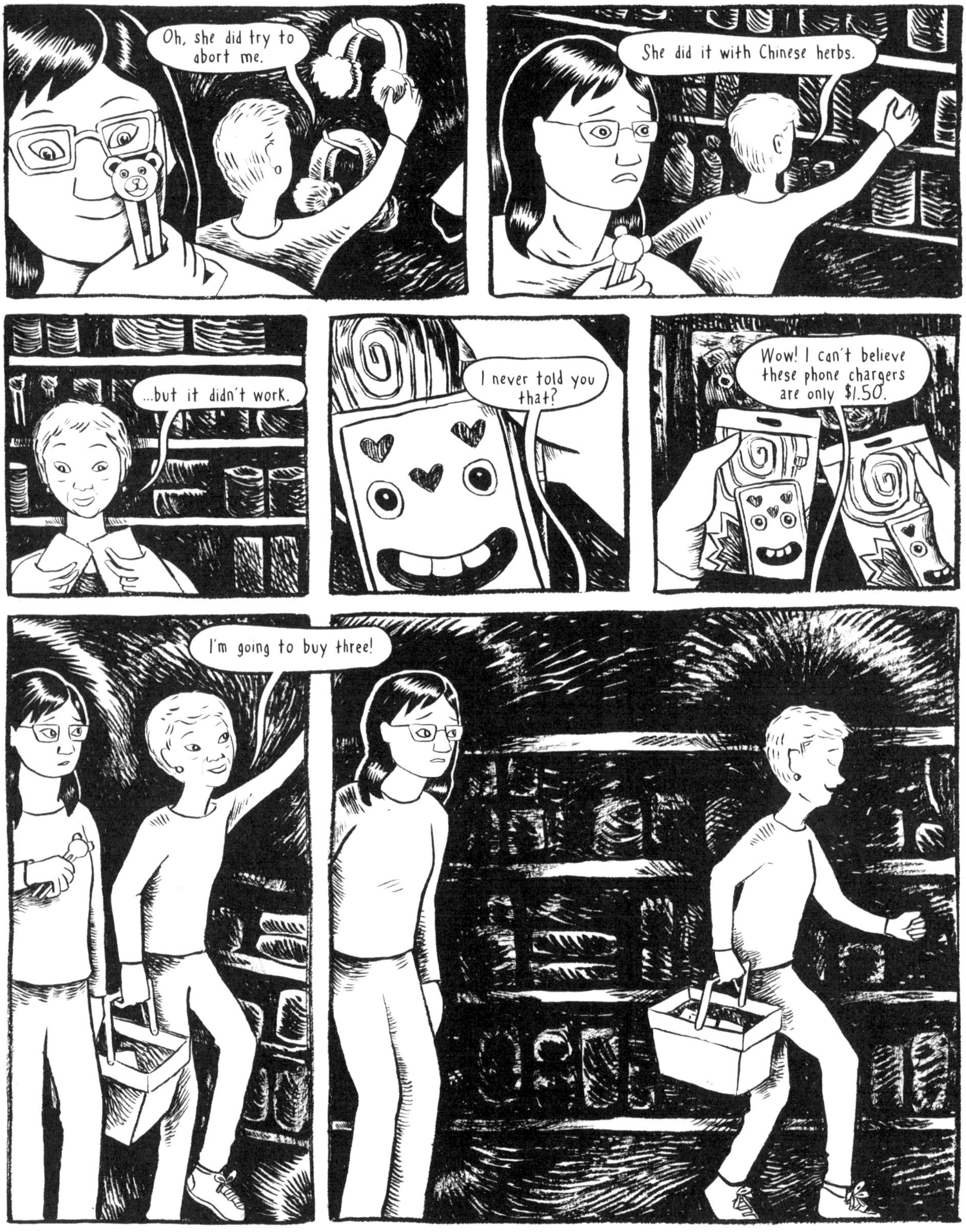
Oh, she did try to abort me.
She did it with Chinese herbs.
...but it didn't work.
I never told you that?
Wow! I can't believe these phone chargers are only $1.50.
I'm going to buy three!

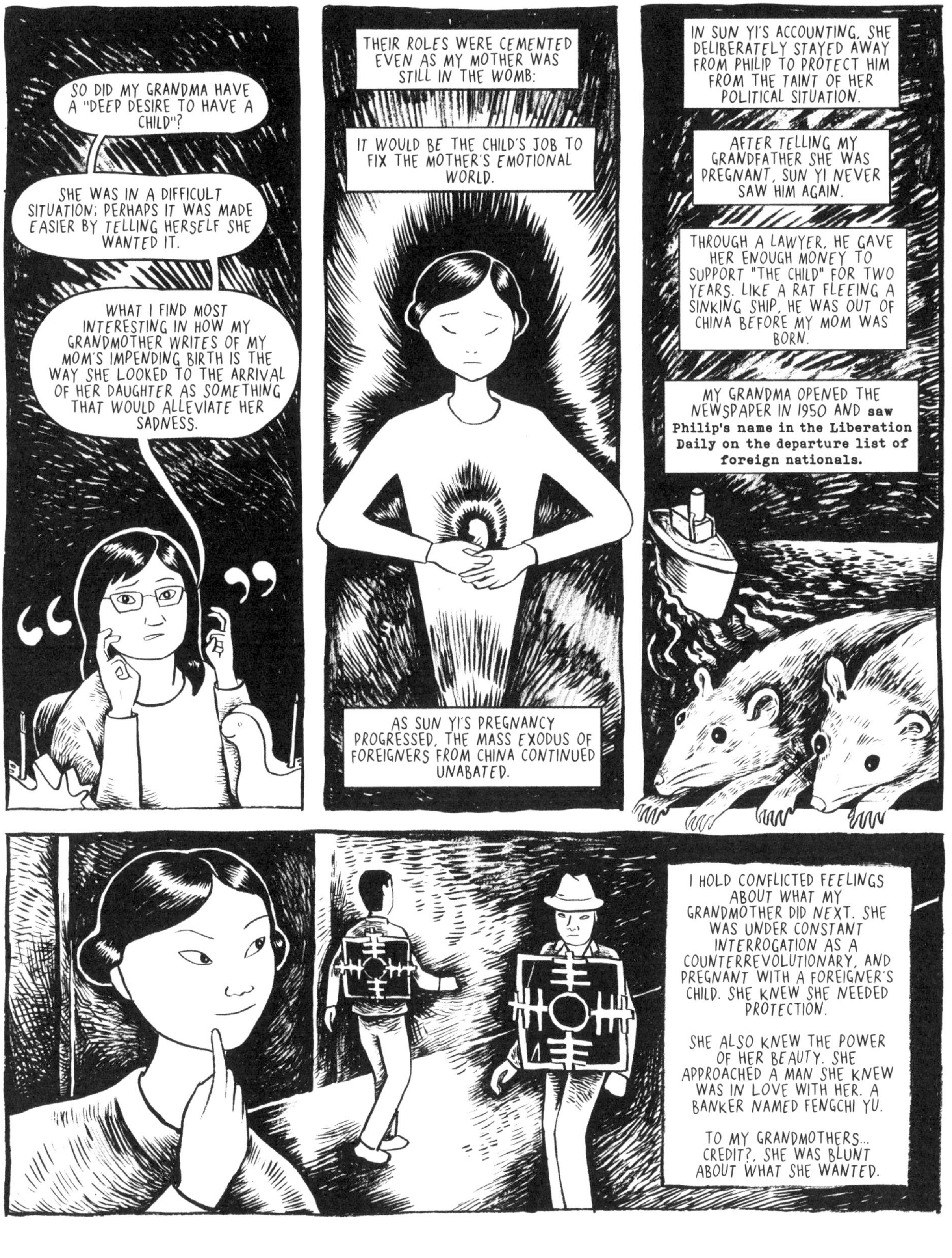
SO DID MY GRANDMA HAVE A "DEEP DESIRE TO HAVE A CHILD"?
SHE WAS IN A DIFFICULT SITUATION; PERHAPS IT WAS MADE EASIER BY TELLING HERSELF SHE WANTED IT.
WHAT I FIND MOST INTERESTING IN HOW MY GRANDMOTHER WRITES OF MY MOM'S IMPENDING BIRTH IS THE WAY SHE LOOKED TO THE ARRIVAL OF HER DAUGHTER AS SOMETHING THAT WOULD ALLEVIATE HER SADNESS.
THEIR ROLES WERE CEMENTED EVEN AS MY MOTHER WAS STILL IN THE WOMB:
IT WOULD BE THE CHILD'S JOB TO FIX THE MOTHER'S EMOTIONAL WORLD.
AS SUN YI'S PREGNANCY PROGRESSED, THE MASS EXODUS OF FOREIGNERS FROM CHINA CONTINUED UNABATED.
IN SUN YI'S ACCOUNTING, SHE DELIBERATELY STAYED AWAY FROM PHILIP TO PROTECT HIM FROM THE TAINT OF HER POLITICAL SITUATION.
AFTER TELLING MY GRANDFATHER SHE WAS PREGNANT, SUN YI NEVER SAW HIM AGAIN.
THROUGH A LAWYER, HE GAVE HER ENOUGH MONEY TO SUPPORT "THE CHILD" FOR TWO YEARS. LIKE A RAT FLEEING A SINKING SHIP, HE WAS OUT OF CHINA BEFORE MY MOM WAS BORN.
MY GRANDMA OPENED THE NEWSPAPER IN 1950 AND saw Philip's name in the Liberation Daily on the departure list of foreign nationals.
I HOLD CONFLICTED FEELINGS ABOUT WHAT MY GRANDMOTHER DID NEXT. SHE WAS UNDER CONSTANT INTERROGATION AS A COUNTERREVOLUTIONARY, AND PREGNANT WITH A FOREIGNER'S CHILD. SHE KNEW SHE NEEDED PROTECTION.
SHE ALSO KNEW THE POWER OF HER BEAUTY. SHE APPROACHED A MAN SHE KNEW WAS IN LOVE WITH HER. A BANKER NAMED FENGCHI YU.
TO MY GRANDMOTHERS... CREDIT?, SHE WAS BLUNT ABOUT WHAT SHE WANTED.

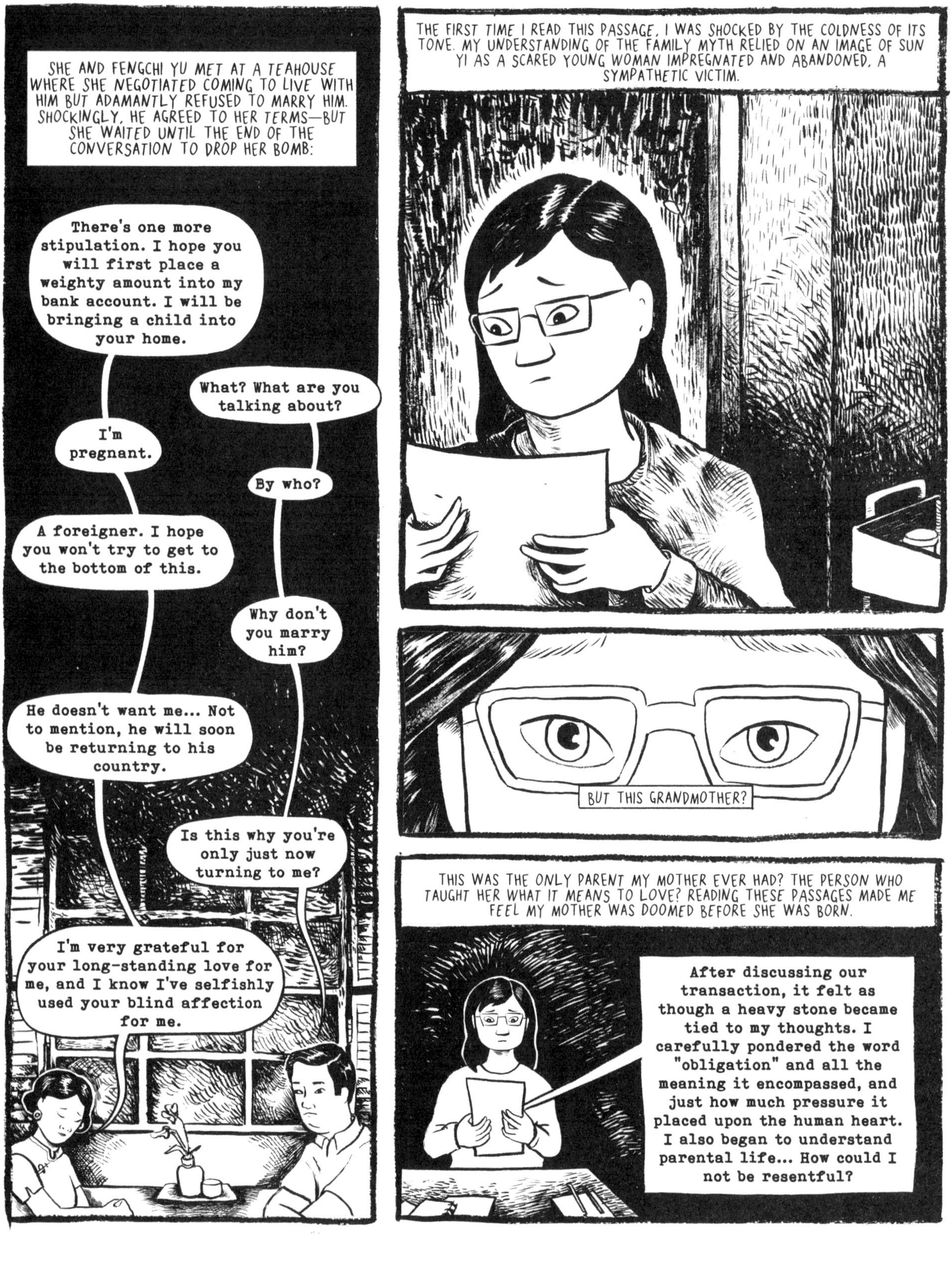
SHE AND FENGCHI YU MET AT A TEAHOUSE WHERE SHE NEGOTIATED COMING TO LIVE WITH HIM BUT ADAMANTLY REFUSED TO MARRY HIM. SHOCKINGLY, HE AGREED TO HER TERMS—BUT SHE WAITED UNTIL THE END OF THE CONVERSATION TO DROP HER BOMB:
There's one more stipulation. I hope you will first place a weighty amount into my bank account. I will be bringing a child into your home.
What? What are you talking about?
I'm pregnant.
By who?
A foreigner. I hope you won't try to get to the bottom of this.
Why don't you marry him?
He doesn't want me... Not to mention, he will soon be returning to his country.
Is this why you're only just now turning to me?
I'm very grateful for your long-standing love for me, and I know I've selfishly used your blind affection for me.
THE FIRST TIME I READ THIS PASSAGE, I WAS SHOCKED BY THE COLDNESS OF ITS TONE. MY UNDERSTANDING OF THE FAMILY MYTH RELIED ON AN IMAGE OF SUN YI AS A SCARED YOUNG WOMAN IMPREGNATED AND ABANDONED, A SYMPATHETIC VICTIM.
BUT THIS GRANDMOTHER?
THIS WAS THE ONLY PARENT MY MOTHER EVER HAD? THE PERSON WHO TAUGHT HER WHAT IT MEANS TO LOVE? READING THESE PASSAGES MADE ME FEEL MY MOTHER WAS DOOMED BEFORE SHE WAS BORN.
After discussing our transaction, it felt as though a heavy stone became tied to my thoughts. I carefully pondered the word "obligation" and all the meaning it encompassed, and just how much pressure it placed upon the human heart. I also began to understand parental life... How could I not be resentful?

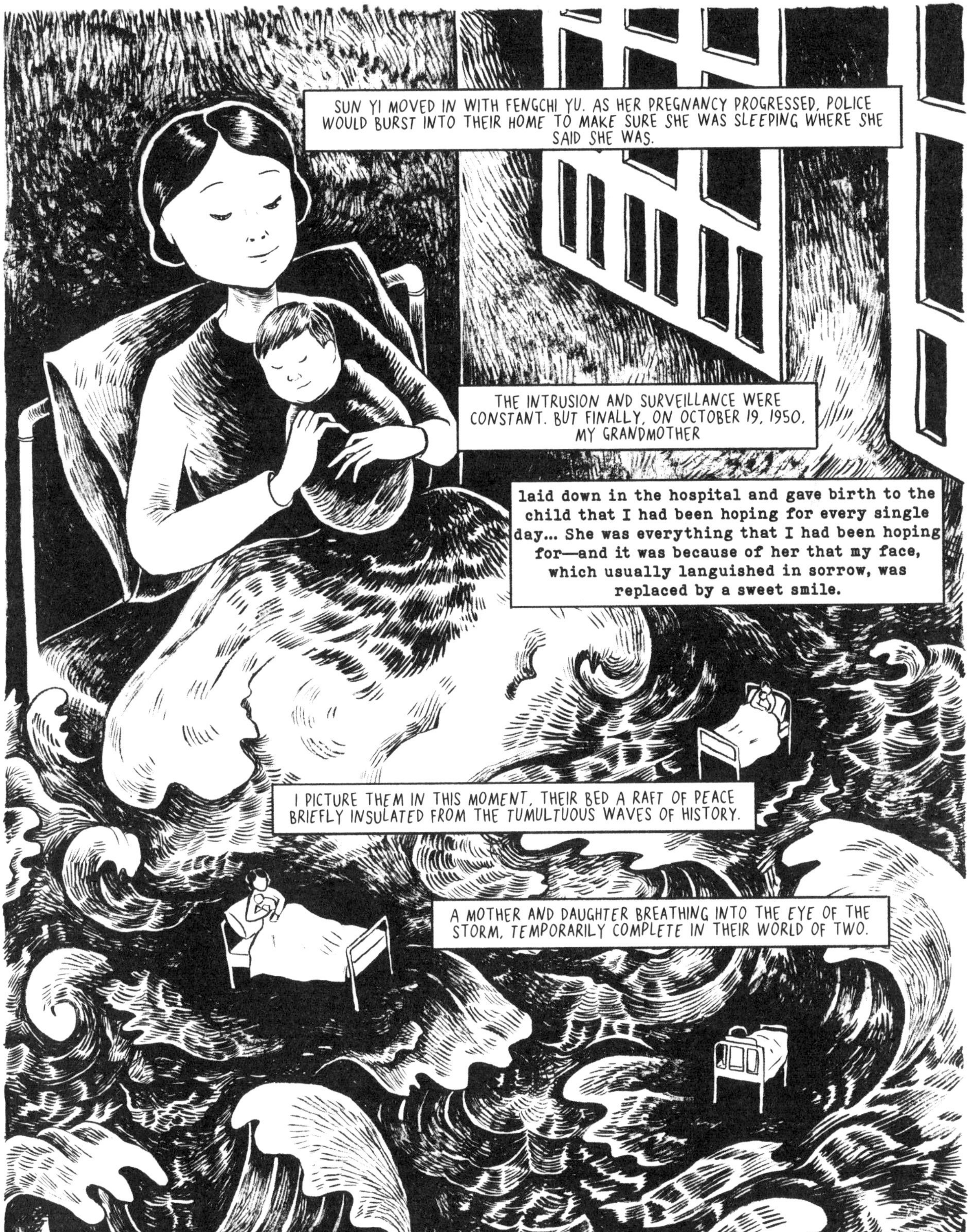
SUN YI MOVED IN WITH FENGCHI YU. AS HER PREGNANCY PROGRESSED, POLICE WOULD BURST INTO THEIR HOME TO MAKE SURE SHE WAS SLEEPING WHERE SHE SAID SHE WAS.
THE INTRUSION AND SURVEILLANCE WERE CONSTANT. BUT FINALLY, ON OCTOBER 19, 1950, MY GRANDMOTHER
laid down in the hospital and gave birth to the child that I had been hoping for every single day... She was everything that I had been hoping for—and it was because of her that my face, which usually languished in sorrow, was replaced by a sweet smile.
I PICTURE THEM IN THIS MOMENT, THEIR BED A RAFT OF PEACE BRIEFLY INSULATED FROM THE TUMULTUOUS WAVES OF HISTORY.
A MOTHER AND DAUGHTER BREATHING INTO THE EYE OF THE STORM, TEMPORARILY COMPLETE IN THEIR WORLD OF TWO.

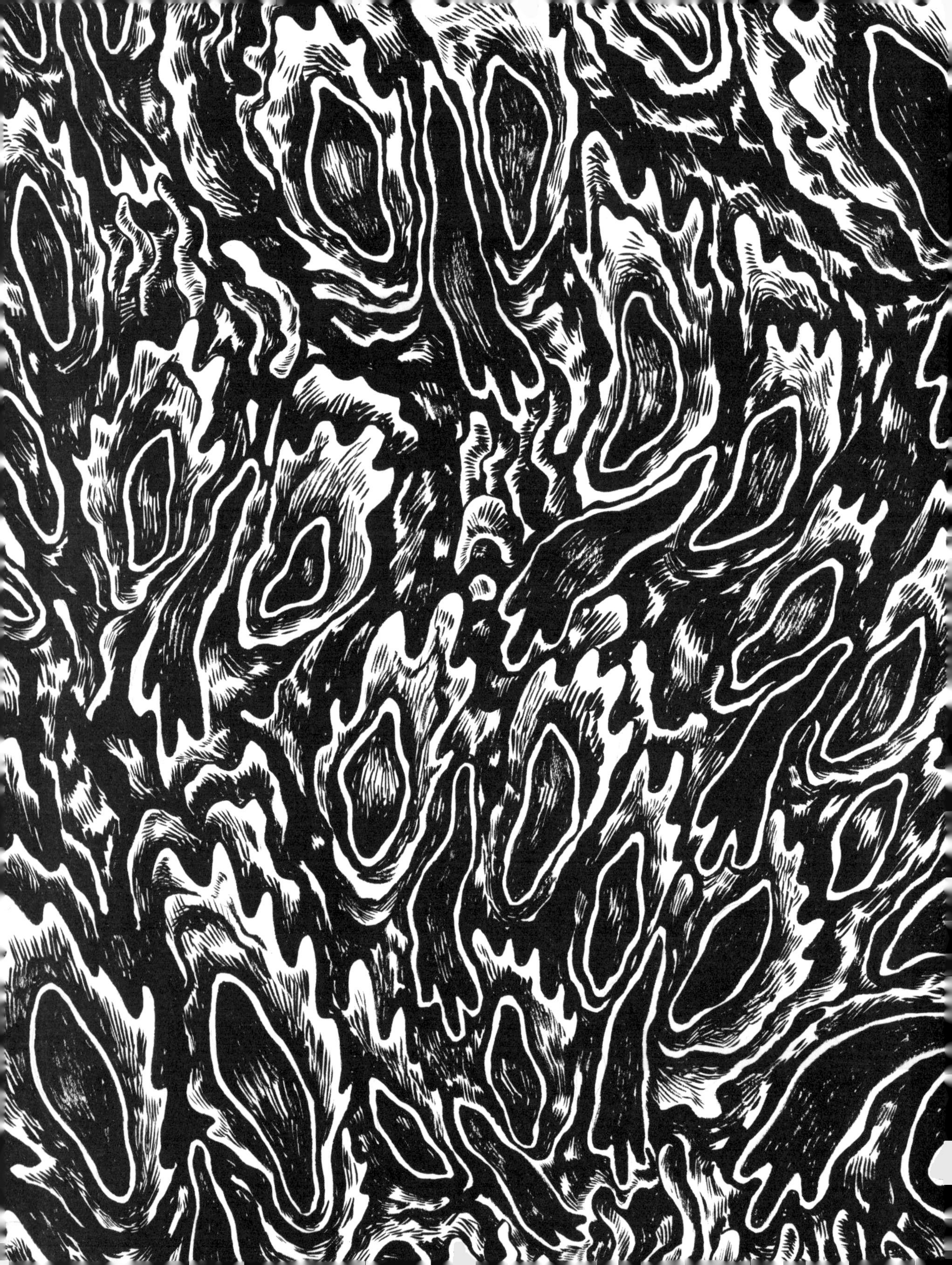

PART 3

THE POSSIBILITY OF ESCAPE

Shanghai • 1950–1957

We need the possibility of escape as surely as we need hope.
—EDWARD ABBEY, *Desert Solitaire*

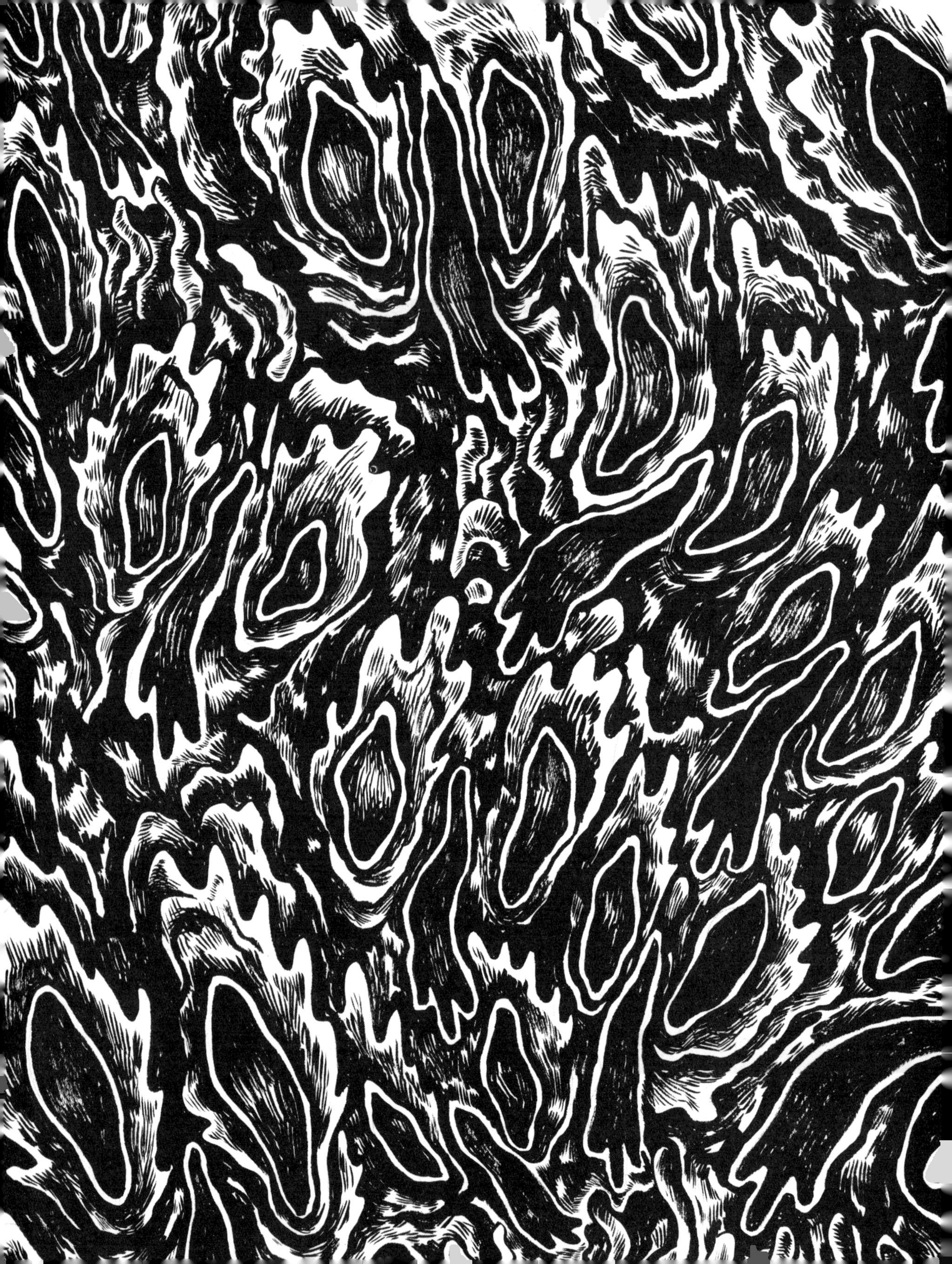

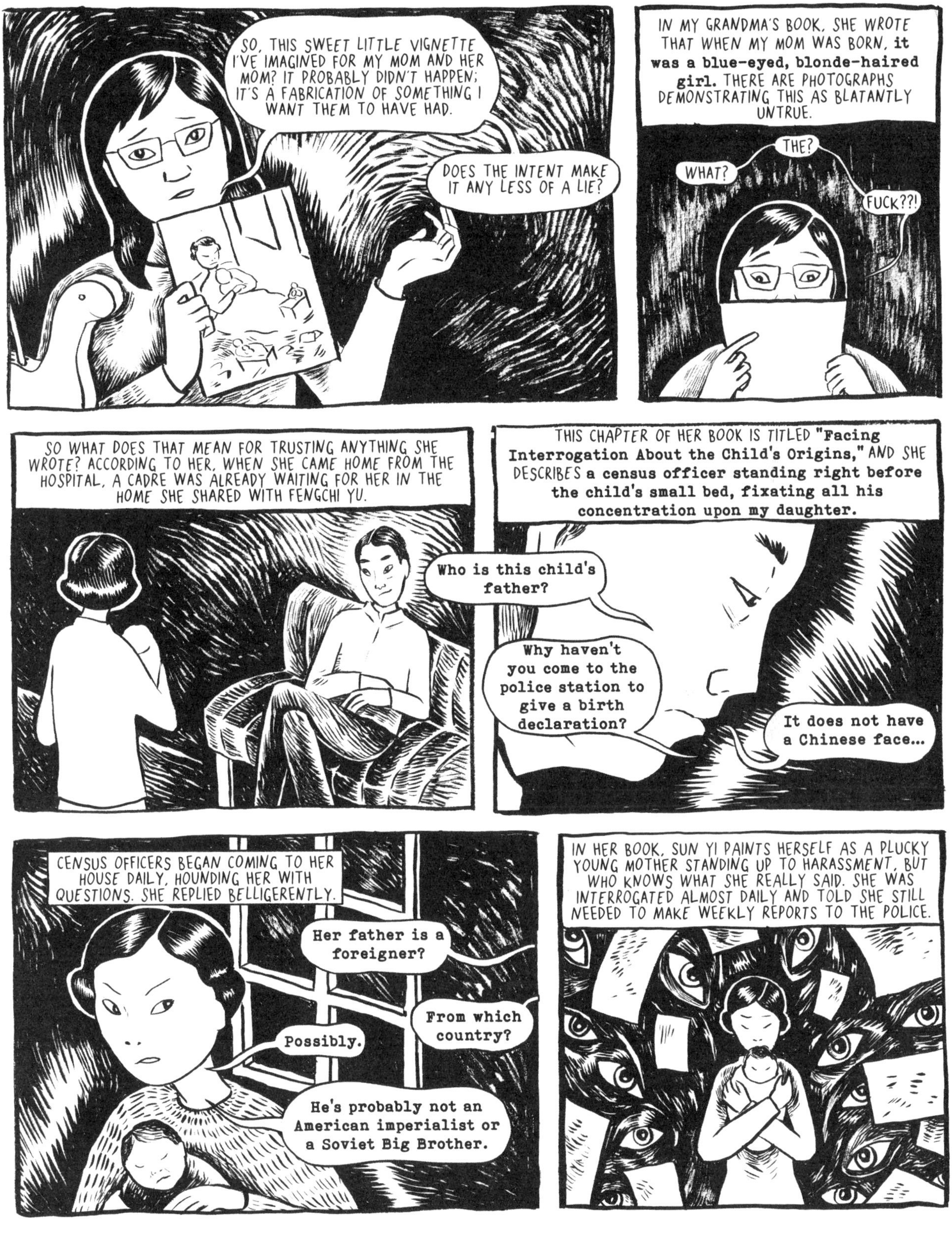

SO, THIS SWEET LITTLE VIGNETTE I'VE IMAGINED FOR MY MOM AND HER MOM? IT PROBABLY DIDN'T HAPPEN; IT'S A FABRICATION OF SOMETHING I WANT THEM TO HAVE HAD.
DOES THE INTENT MAKE IT ANY LESS OF A LIE?
IN MY GRANDMA'S BOOK, SHE WROTE THAT WHEN MY MOM WAS BORN, **it was a blue-eyed, blonde-haired girl.** THERE ARE PHOTOGRAPHS DEMONSTRATING THIS AS BLATANTLY UNTRUE.
WHAT?
THE?
FUCK??!
SO WHAT DOES THAT MEAN FOR TRUSTING ANYTHING SHE WROTE? ACCORDING TO HER, WHEN SHE CAME HOME FROM THE HOSPITAL, A CADRE WAS ALREADY WAITING FOR HER IN THE HOME SHE SHARED WITH FENGCHI YU.
Who is this child's father?
THIS CHAPTER OF HER BOOK IS TITLED **"Facing Interrogation About the Child's Origins,"** AND SHE DESCRIBES **a census officer standing right before the child's small bed, fixating all his concentration upon my daughter.**
Why haven't you come to the police station to give a birth declaration?
It does not have a Chinese face...
CENSUS OFFICERS BEGAN COMING TO HER HOUSE DAILY, HOUNDING HER WITH QUESTIONS. SHE REPLIED BELLIGERENTLY.
Her father is a foreigner?
Possibly.
From which country?
He's probably not an American imperialist or a Soviet Big Brother.
IN HER BOOK, SUN YI PAINTS HERSELF AS A PLUCKY YOUNG MOTHER STANDING UP TO HARASSMENT, BUT WHO KNOWS WHAT SHE REALLY SAID. SHE WAS INTERROGATED ALMOST DAILY AND TOLD SHE STILL NEEDED TO MAKE WEEKLY REPORTS TO THE POLICE.

I FEEL LIKE I SHOULD EMPHASIZE TO YOU THAT I'M CLEARLY NOT AN OBJECTIVE READER OF MY GRANDMA'S MEMOIR.

I ENTERED THIS STORY FROM ITS CONCLUSION, KNOWING IT ENDED IN SUN YI'S MADNESS.

SO I'M MINING HER BOOK FOR CLUES TO REVERSE ENGINEER THE THREAD OF WHAT BROKE.

MY GRANDMOTHER'S MEMOIR CONTAINS SO MANY INFLECTION POINTS OF CHINESE HISTORY—AND I SEE CLEAR LINKS BETWEEN THAT HISTORY AND THE PARANOID FEAR THAT WOULD COME TO DEFINE HER.

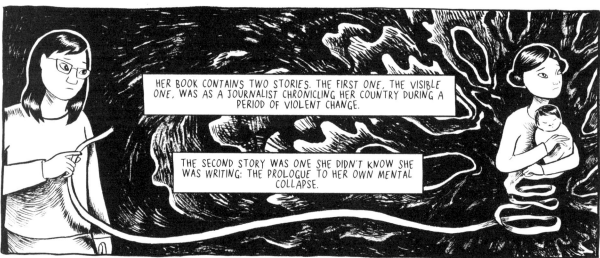

HER BOOK CONTAINS TWO STORIES. THE FIRST ONE, THE VISIBLE ONE, WAS AS A JOURNALIST CHRONICLING HER COUNTRY DURING A PERIOD OF VIOLENT CHANGE.

THE SECOND STORY WAS ONE SHE DIDN'T KNOW SHE WAS WRITING: THE PROLOGUE TO HER OWN MENTAL COLLAPSE.

SO I READ HER MEMOIR TO LEARN THE BACKGROUND OF BOTH THESE STORIES.

AND IT'S ONLY WITH THESE DUAL LENSES THAT THE PICTURE IS COMPLETE.

SO TRY TO HOLD THAT IN YOUR MIND AS WE LET MY GRANDMA TELL YOU WHAT HAPPENED TO HER.

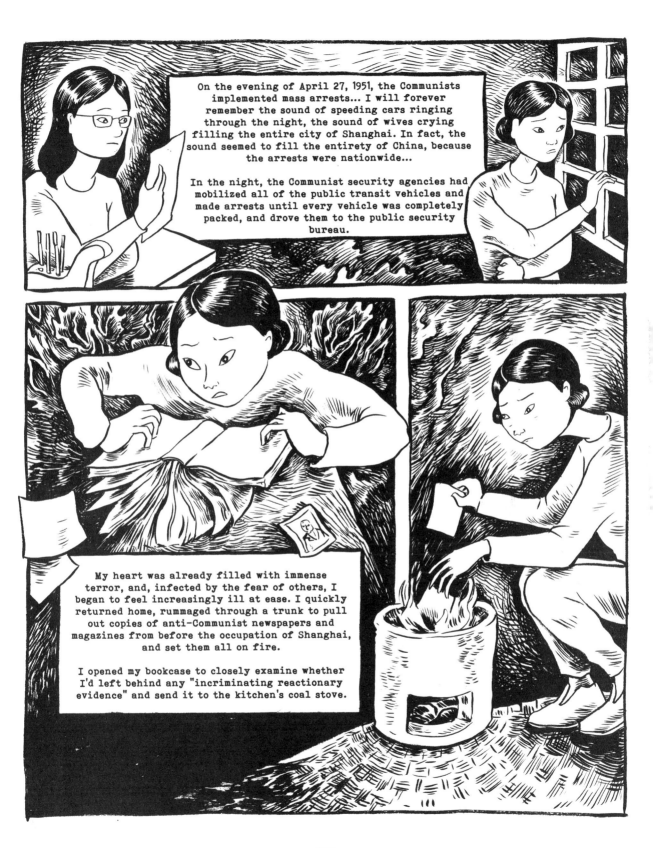

On the evening of April 27, 1951, the Communists implemented mass arrests... I will forever remember the sound of speeding cars ringing through the night, the sound of wives crying filling the entire city of Shanghai. In fact, the sound seemed to fill the entirety of China, because the arrests were nationwide...

In the night, the Communist security agencies had mobilized all of the public transit vehicles and made arrests until every vehicle was completely packed, and drove them to the public security bureau.

My heart was already filled with immense terror, and, infected by the fear of others, I began to feel increasingly ill at ease. I quickly returned home, rummaged through a trunk to pull out copies of anti-Communist newspapers and magazines from before the occupation of Shanghai, and set them all on fire.

I opened my bookcase to closely examine whether I'd left behind any "incriminating reactionary evidence" and send it to the kitchen's coal stove.

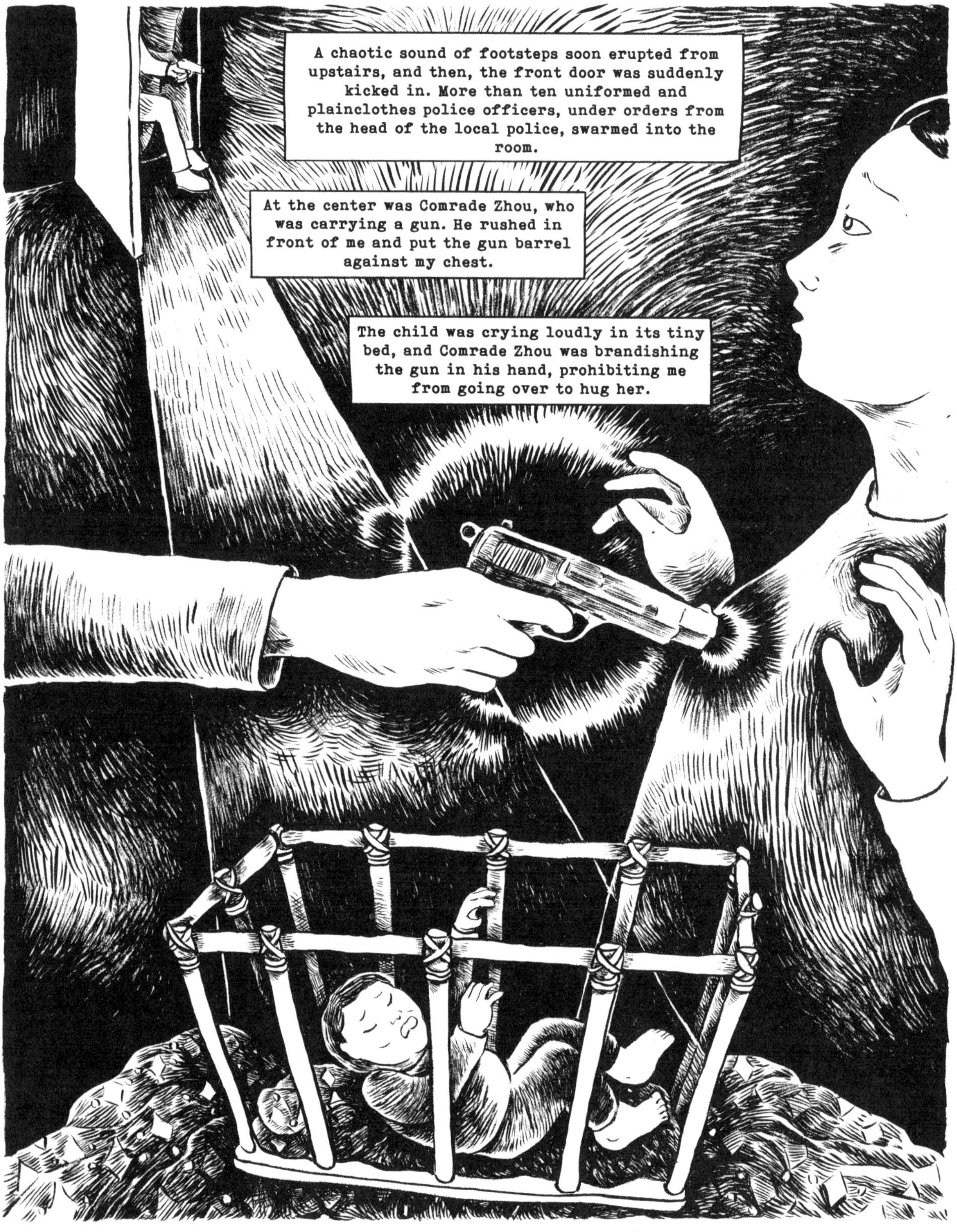
A chaotic sound of footsteps soon erupted from upstairs, and then, the front door was suddenly kicked in. More than ten uniformed and plainclothes police officers, under orders from the head of the local police, swarmed into the room.
At the center was Comrade Zhou, who was carrying a gun. He rushed in front of me and put the gun barrel against my chest.
The child was crying loudly in its tiny bed, and Comrade Zhou was brandishing the gun in his hand, prohibiting me from going over to hug her.

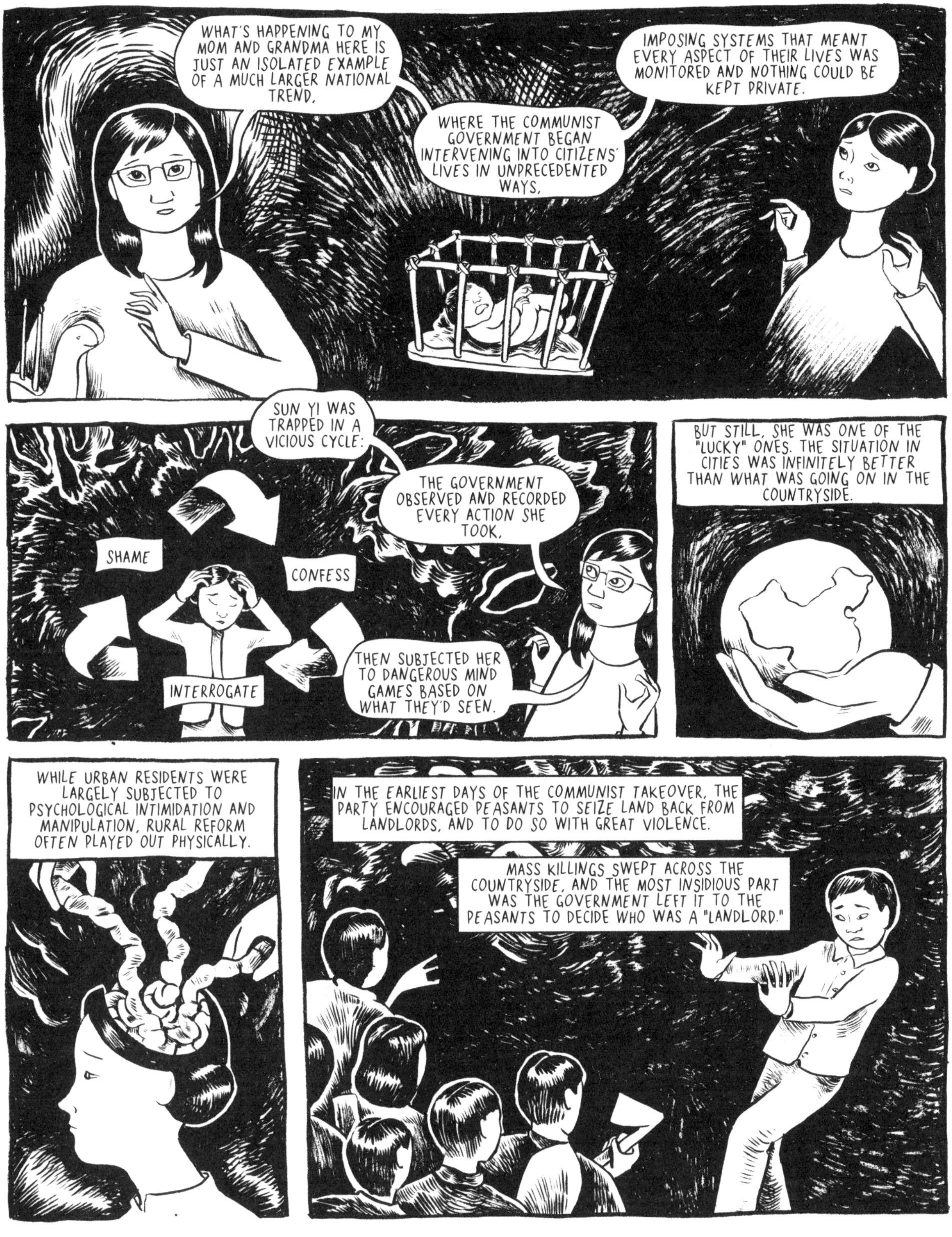
WHAT'S HAPPENING TO MY MOM AND GRANDMA HERE IS JUST AN ISOLATED EXAMPLE OF A MUCH LARGER NATIONAL TREND,
WHERE THE COMMUNIST GOVERNMENT BEGAN INTERVENING INTO CITIZENS' LIVES IN UNPRECEDENTED WAYS,
IMPOSING SYSTEMS THAT MEANT EVERY ASPECT OF THEIR LIVES WAS MONITORED AND NOTHING COULD BE KEPT PRIVATE.
SUN YI WAS TRAPPED IN A VICIOUS CYCLE:
THE GOVERNMENT OBSERVED AND RECORDED EVERY ACTION SHE TOOK,
SHAME
CONFESS
INTERROGATE
THEN SUBJECTED HER TO DANGEROUS MIND GAMES BASED ON WHAT THEY'D SEEN.
BUT STILL, SHE WAS ONE OF THE "LUCKY" ONES. THE SITUATION IN CITIES WAS INFINITELY BETTER THAN WHAT WAS GOING ON IN THE COUNTRYSIDE.
WHILE URBAN RESIDENTS WERE LARGELY SUBJECTED TO PSYCHOLOGICAL INTIMIDATION AND MANIPULATION, RURAL REFORM OFTEN PLAYED OUT PHYSICALLY.
IN THE EARLIEST DAYS OF THE COMMUNIST TAKEOVER, THE PARTY ENCOURAGED PEASANTS TO SEIZE LAND BACK FROM LANDLORDS, AND TO DO SO WITH GREAT VIOLENCE.
MASS KILLINGS SWEPT ACROSS THE COUNTRYSIDE, AND THE MOST INSIDIOUS PART WAS THE GOVERNMENT LEFT IT TO THE PEASANTS TO DECIDE WHO WAS A "LANDLORD."

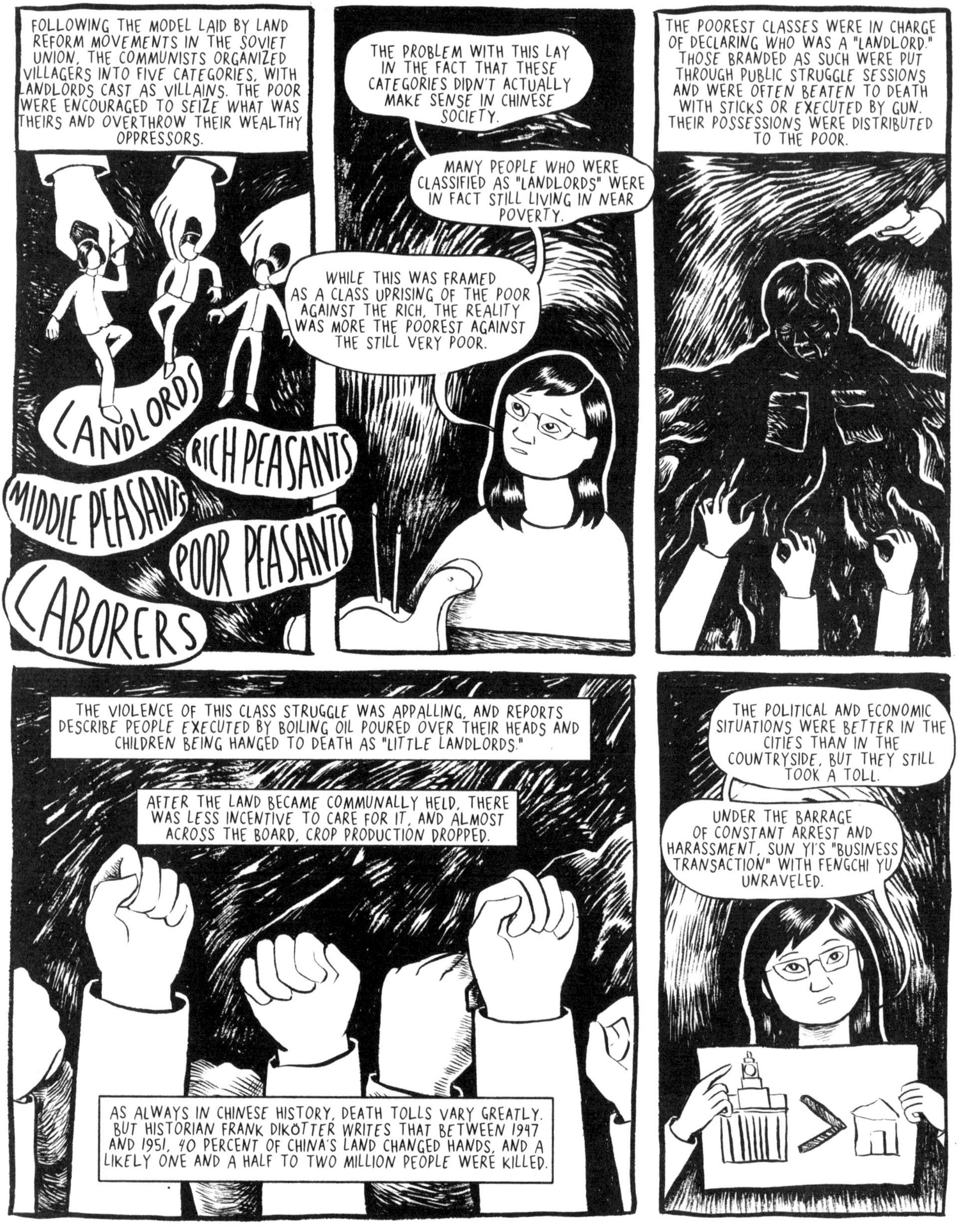
FOLLOWING THE MODEL LAID BY LAND REFORM MOVEMENTS IN THE SOVIET UNION, THE COMMUNISTS ORGANIZED VILLAGERS INTO FIVE CATEGORIES, WITH LANDLORDS CAST AS VILLAINS. THE POOR WERE ENCOURAGED TO SEIZE WHAT WAS THEIRS AND OVERTHROW THEIR WEALTHY OPPRESSORS.
LANDLORDS
RICH PEASANTS
MIDDLE PEASANTS
POOR PEASANTS
LABORERS
THE PROBLEM WITH THIS LAY IN THE FACT THAT THESE CATEGORIES DIDN'T ACTUALLY MAKE SENSE IN CHINESE SOCIETY.
MANY PEOPLE WHO WERE CLASSIFIED AS "LANDLORDS" WERE IN FACT STILL LIVING IN NEAR POVERTY.
WHILE THIS WAS FRAMED AS A CLASS UPRISING OF THE POOR AGAINST THE RICH, THE REALITY WAS MORE THE POOREST AGAINST THE STILL VERY POOR.
THE POOREST CLASSES WERE IN CHARGE OF DECLARING WHO WAS A "LANDLORD." THOSE BRANDED AS SUCH WERE PUT THROUGH PUBLIC STRUGGLE SESSIONS AND WERE OFTEN BEATEN TO DEATH WITH STICKS OR EXECUTED BY GUN. THEIR POSSESSIONS WERE DISTRIBUTED TO THE POOR.
THE VIOLENCE OF THIS CLASS STRUGGLE WAS APPALLING, AND REPORTS DESCRIBE PEOPLE EXECUTED BY BOILING OIL POURED OVER THEIR HEADS AND CHILDREN BEING HANGED TO DEATH AS "LITTLE LANDLORDS."
AFTER THE LAND BECAME COMMUNALLY HELD, THERE WAS LESS INCENTIVE TO CARE FOR IT, AND ALMOST ACROSS THE BOARD, CROP PRODUCTION DROPPED.
AS ALWAYS IN CHINESE HISTORY, DEATH TOLLS VARY GREATLY. BUT HISTORIAN FRANK DIKÖTTER WRITES THAT BETWEEN 1947 AND 1951, 40 PERCENT OF CHINA'S LAND CHANGED HANDS, AND A LIKELY ONE AND A HALF TO TWO MILLION PEOPLE WERE KILLED.
THE POLITICAL AND ECONOMIC SITUATIONS WERE BETTER IN THE CITIES THAN IN THE COUNTRYSIDE, BUT THEY STILL TOOK A TOLL.
UNDER THE BARRAGE OF CONSTANT ARREST AND HARASSMENT, SUN YI'S "BUSINESS TRANSACTION" WITH FENGCHI YU UNRAVELED.

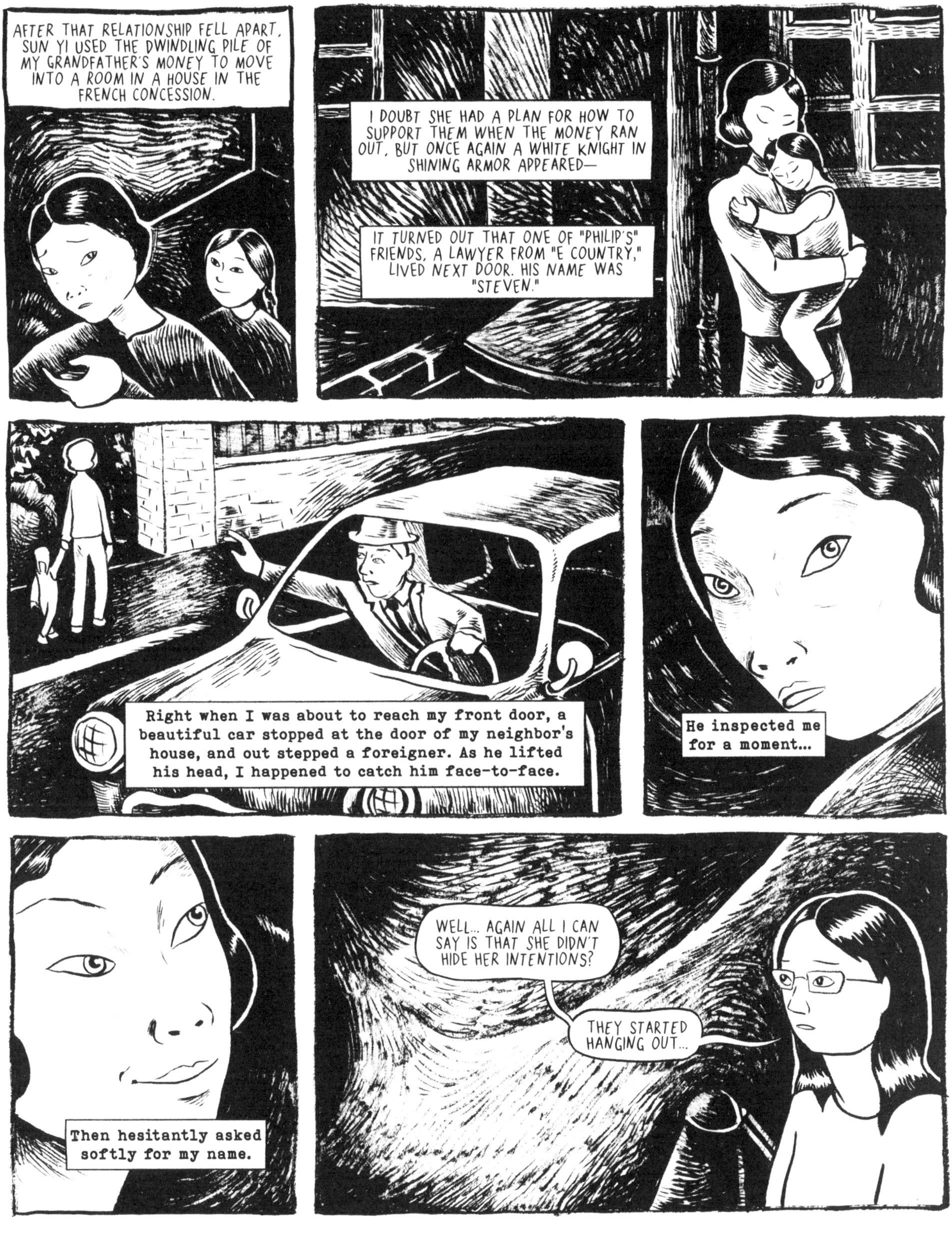
AFTER THAT RELATIONSHIP FELL APART, SUN YI USED THE DWINDLING PILE OF MY GRANDFATHER'S MONEY TO MOVE INTO A ROOM IN A HOUSE IN THE FRENCH CONCESSION.
I DOUBT SHE HAD A PLAN FOR HOW TO SUPPORT THEM WHEN THE MONEY RAN OUT, BUT ONCE AGAIN A WHITE KNIGHT IN SHINING ARMOR APPEARED—
IT TURNED OUT THAT ONE OF "PHILIP'S" FRIENDS, A LAWYER FROM "E COUNTRY," LIVED NEXT DOOR. HIS NAME WAS "STEVEN."
Right when I was about to reach my front door, a beautiful car stopped at the door of my neighbor's house, and out stepped a foreigner. As he lifted his head, I happened to catch him face-to-face.
He inspected me for a moment...
Then hesitantly asked softly for my name.
WELL... AGAIN ALL I CAN SAY IS THAT SHE DIDN'T HIDE HER INTENTIONS?
THEY STARTED HANGING OUT...

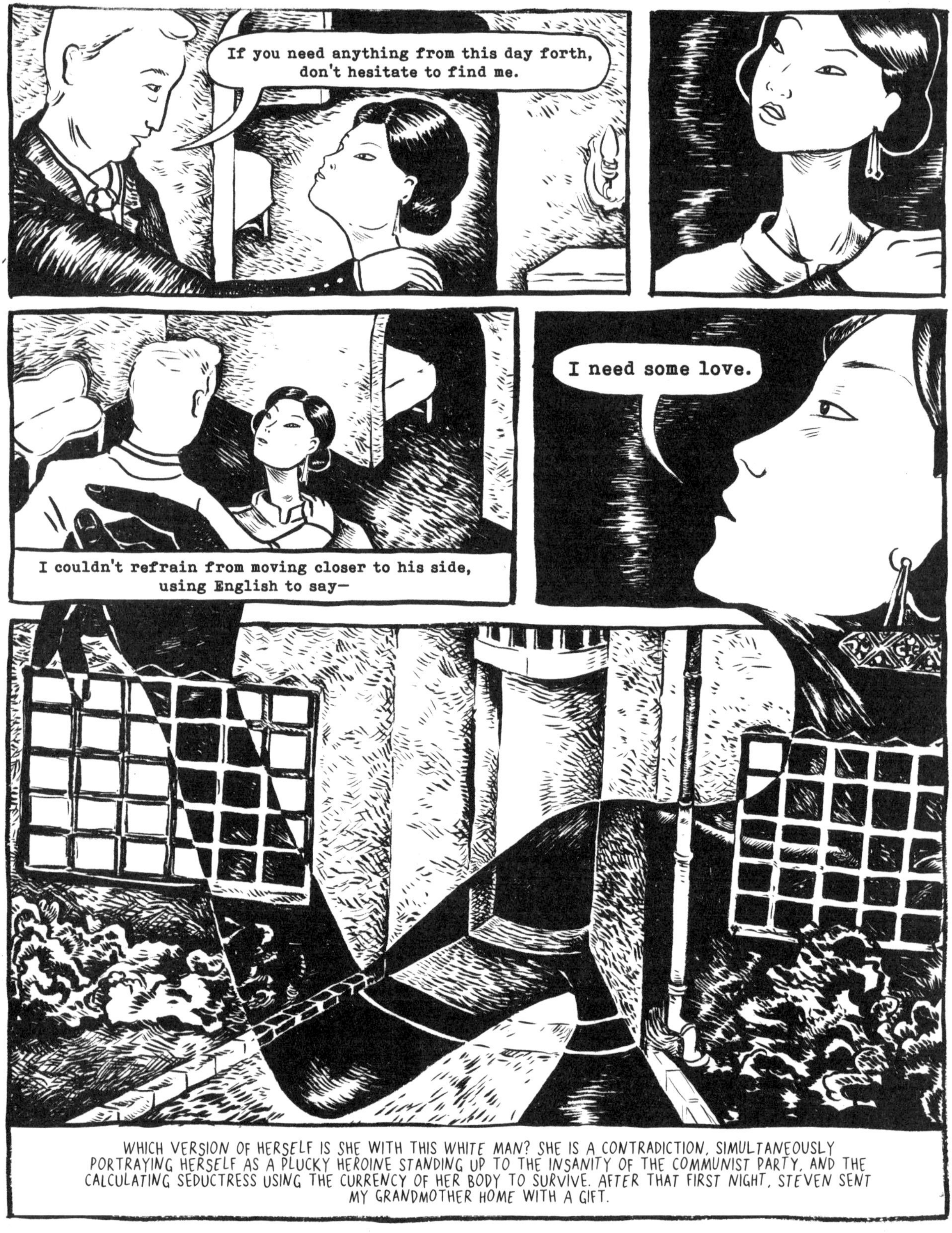
If you need anything from this day forth, don't hesitate to find me.
I couldn't refrain from moving closer to his side, using English to say—
I need some love.
WHICH VERSION OF HERSELF IS SHE WITH THIS WHITE MAN? SHE IS A CONTRADICTION, SIMULTANEOUSLY PORTRAYING HERSELF AS A PLUCKY HEROINE STANDING UP TO THE INSANITY OF THE COMMUNIST PARTY, AND THE CALCULATING SEDUCTRESS USING THE CURRENCY OF HER BODY TO SURVIVE. AFTER THAT FIRST NIGHT, STEVEN SENT MY GRANDMOTHER HOME WITH A GIFT.

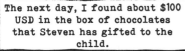
The next day, I found about $100 USD in the box of chocolates that Steven has gifted to the child.

In the days to come, all my financial needs were fulfilled by him.

WELL. ON THE ONE HAND SHE DID FIND A WAY TO PUT FOOD IN THEIR MOUTHS. BUT I ALSO READ THIS THINKING OF MY MOM DESCRIBING SUN YI AS NAIVE, IMPRACTICAL, AND ALWAYS EXPECTING SOMEONE ELSE TO SAVE HER.

ALL OF THIS RESTS ON THE HAPPENSTANCE OF HER BEAUTY. IF SHE HADN'T POSSESSED THAT PHYSICAL CURRENCY, WOULD SHE AND MY MOM HAVE BEEN ABLE TO SURVIVE?

SHE HAD COURTED WHITE SHANGHAI, AND MY MOTHER IS EVIDENCE OF HER SUCCESS—A CHILD WHO BECAME BOTH A DANGEROUS ALBATROSS AND HER GOLDEN TICKET. AS I READ HER BOOK, I WROTE DOWN ALL THE PLACES SUN YI TALKED ABOUT MEETING MEN FOR DATES. WHEN I TRACKED THEM DOWN—

2018

OKAY. SO MY GRANDMA WAS A GOLD DIGGER.

知道怎么说 "GOLD DIGGER"?

<I WONDER HOW YOU SAY "GOLD DIGGER" IN CHINESE?>

THEIR GRANDEUR UNRAVELED THE MYTH OF MY GRANDMA AS A WHOLLY SYMPATHETIC CHARACTER.

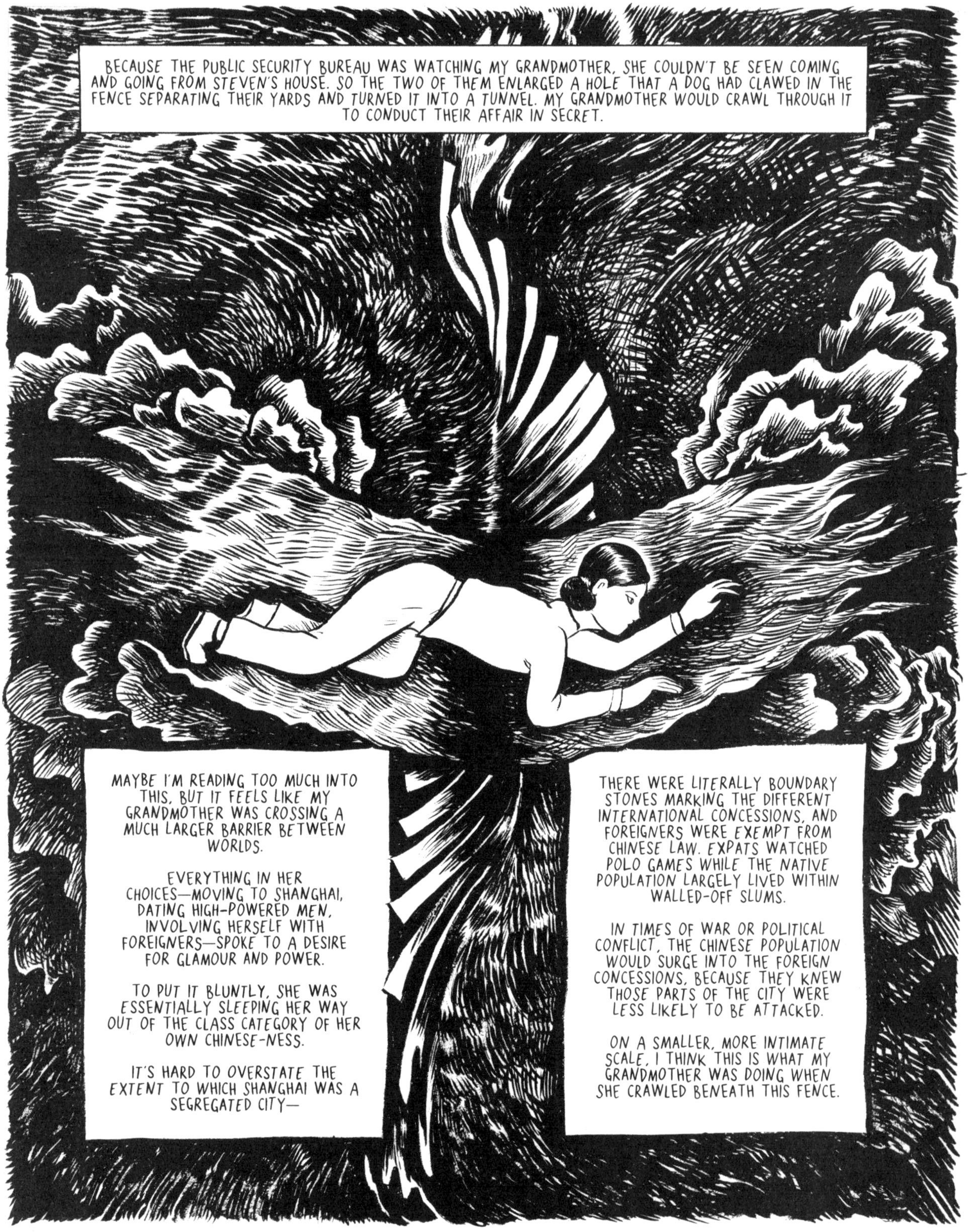
BECAUSE THE PUBLIC SECURITY BUREAU WAS WATCHING MY GRANDMOTHER, SHE COULDN'T BE SEEN COMING AND GOING FROM STEVEN'S HOUSE. SO THE TWO OF THEM ENLARGED A HOLE THAT A DOG HAD CLAWED IN THE FENCE SEPARATING THEIR YARDS AND *TURNED* IT INTO A *TUNNEL*. MY GRANDMOTHER WOULD CRAWL THROUGH IT TO CONDUCT THEIR AFFAIR IN SECRET.
MAYBE I'M READING TOO MUCH INTO THIS, BUT IT FEELS LIKE MY GRANDMOTHER WAS CROSSING A MUCH LARGER BARRIER BETWEEN WORLDS.
EVERYTHING IN HER CHOICES—MOVING TO SHANGHAI, DATING HIGH-POWERED *MEN*, INVOLVING HERSELF WITH FOREIGNERS—SPOKE TO A DESIRE FOR GLAMOUR AND POWER.
TO PUT IT BLUNTLY, SHE WAS ESSENTIALLY SLEEPING HER WAY OUT OF THE CLASS CATEGORY OF HER OWN CHINESE-NESS.
IT'S HARD TO OVERSTATE THE *EXTENT* TO WHICH SHANGHAI WAS A SEGREGATED CITY—
THERE WERE *LITERALLY* BOUNDARY STONES MARKING THE DIFFERENT INTERNATIONAL CONCESSIONS, AND FOREIGNERS WERE *EXEMPT* FROM CHINESE LAW. EXPATS WATCHED POLO GAMES WHILE THE NATIVE POPULATION LARGELY LIVED WITHIN WALLED-OFF SLUMS.
IN TIMES OF WAR OR POLITICAL CONFLICT, THE CHINESE POPULATION WOULD SURGE INTO THE FOREIGN CONCESSIONS, BECAUSE THEY KNEW THOSE PARTS OF THE CITY WERE LESS LIKELY TO BE ATTACKED.
ON A SMALLER, MORE INTIMATE SCALE, I THINK THIS IS WHAT MY GRANDMOTHER WAS DOING WHEN SHE CRAWLED BENEATH THIS FENCE.

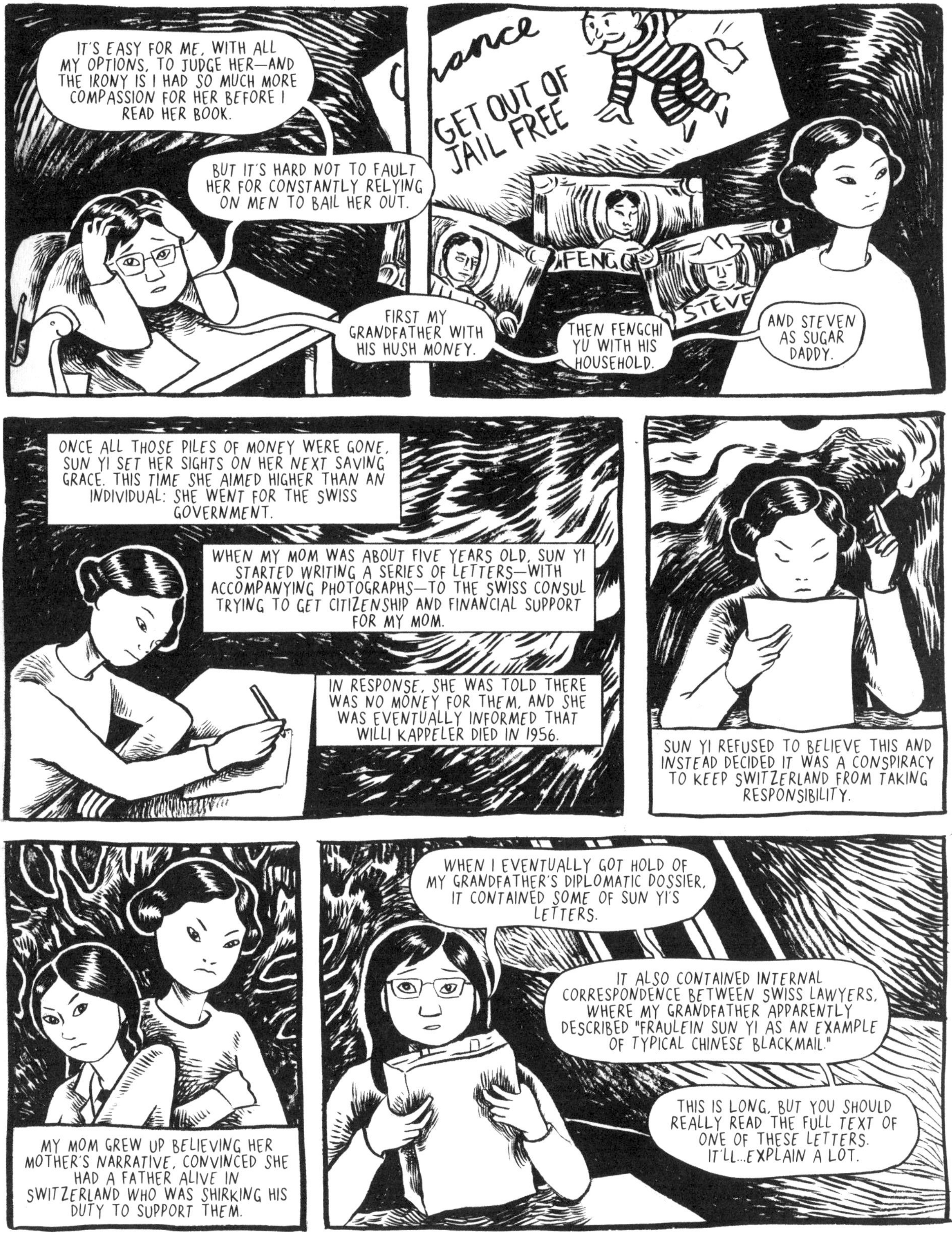
IT'S EASY FOR ME, WITH ALL MY OPTIONS, TO JUDGE HER—AND THE IRONY IS I HAD SO MUCH MORE COMPASSION FOR HER BEFORE I READ HER BOOK.
BUT IT'S HARD NOT TO FAULT HER FOR CONSTANTLY RELYING ON MEN TO BAIL HER OUT.
GET OUT OF JAIL FREE
FENG
STEVE
FIRST MY GRANDFATHER WITH HIS HUSH MONEY.
THEN FENGCHI YU WITH HIS HOUSEHOLD.
AND STEVEN AS SUGAR DADDY.
ONCE ALL THOSE PILES OF MONEY WERE GONE, SUN YI SET HER SIGHTS ON HER NEXT SAVING GRACE. THIS TIME SHE AIMED HIGHER THAN AN INDIVIDUAL: SHE WENT FOR THE SWISS GOVERNMENT.
WHEN MY MOM WAS ABOUT FIVE YEARS OLD, SUN YI STARTED WRITING A SERIES OF LETTERS—WITH ACCOMPANYING PHOTOGRAPHS—TO THE SWISS CONSUL TRYING TO GET CITIZENSHIP AND FINANCIAL SUPPORT FOR MY MOM.
IN RESPONSE, SHE WAS TOLD THERE WAS NO MONEY FOR THEM, AND SHE WAS EVENTUALLY INFORMED THAT WILLI KAPPELER DIED IN 1956.
SUN YI REFUSED TO BELIEVE THIS AND INSTEAD DECIDED IT WAS A CONSPIRACY TO KEEP SWITZERLAND FROM TAKING RESPONSIBILITY.
MY MOM GREW UP BELIEVING HER MOTHER'S NARRATIVE, CONVINCED SHE HAD A FATHER ALIVE IN SWITZERLAND WHO WAS SHIRKING HIS DUTY TO SUPPORT THEM.
WHEN I EVENTUALLY GOT HOLD OF MY GRANDFATHER'S DIPLOMATIC DOSSIER, IT CONTAINED SOME OF SUN YI'S LETTERS.
IT ALSO CONTAINED INTERNAL CORRESPONDENCE BETWEEN SWISS LAWYERS, WHERE MY GRANDFATHER APPARENTLY DESCRIBED "FRAULEIN SUN YI AS AN EXAMPLE OF TYPICAL CHINESE BLACKMAIL."
THIS IS LONG, BUT YOU SHOULD REALLY READ THE FULL TEXT OF ONE OF THESE LETTERS. IT'LL...EXPLAIN A LOT.

TRANSLATION. The Swiss Ambassador to China.
Peking.

Sir,

I am sorry to have to bring to your notice an unpleasant matter, which has oppressed me for nearly six years. I venture to appeal to you in the hope of obtaining your support and assistance in reaching a settlement of the matter.

Please allow me to present my case as briefly as possible in the following, in order to not trespass on your valuable time more than necessary: In 1950 I cohabited with Dr. Willi Kappeler, then Swiss Vice Consul at Shanghai, and became pregnant. Before the birth of the child, Dr. Kappeler was under orders for transfer to Switzerland. Consequently, he commissioned Mr. Henry Ai, then legal adviser to the Swiss Consulate General at Shanghai, to force me, by means of threat and bribery, to sign a document with the object of hashing up the matter privately, but no arrangements whatever were made by Dr. Kappeler as the various questions concerning the child. After the birth of the girl nearly six years ago, I wrote Dr. Kappeler several times, asking him to make, from the viewpoint of law and humanity, the necessary arrangements as to the maintenance of the living and education of the child and for establishing her nationality, but no reply was received from him until last year, when an unpleasant and absurd answer was addressed me by his lawyer. Since then I have again written twice to Dr. Kappeler but nothing has been heard from him. I was a journalist when I cohabited with Dr. Kappeler. Afterwards the care of the child and household affairs rendered it necessary for me to give up my job. At present I have sold all my belongings for the bringing up of the girl and am reduced to such poverty-stricken conditions as to be unable even to provide for our daily needs.

The recent poor health of the child and her frequent illness necessitated my calling on the Swiss Consul General at Shanghai on the 26th of March last, but he flatly refused to take up the matter and expressed his suspicion as to why I should delay for nealy six years before bringing forward the matter. As a matter of fact, during the past six years I have maintained the spirit of a martyr in rearing the child and have spent my own days as an abbess. Had it not been for my inability to continue bringing up the child and also for the necessity of establishing her nationality now that she has attained school age, I would have refrained from taking any drastic measures against Dr. Kappeler although my confidence in him was already shaken. I could apply to the Chinese Embassy in Switzerland for assistance, but as Dr. Kappeler was in the diplomatic service and sent to China by your Government, I consider it better to write you on the subject, in order to protect the reputation of your Shanghai Consulate General.
I earnestly hope that you will lend me a helping hand in settling the matter, so as to enable the child to continue her subsistence and have her nationality established. I shall be very deeply indebted to you for your kindness.

Enclosed herewithin please find a photograph of Dr. Kappeler and one of our girl. Their striking resemblence constitutes definite proof. If other evidences are needed, I can provide them.

I beg you to pardon me for my boldness in addressing you and earnestly hope to have the honour of getting an early reply from you.

Yours faithfully,
Sun Yi

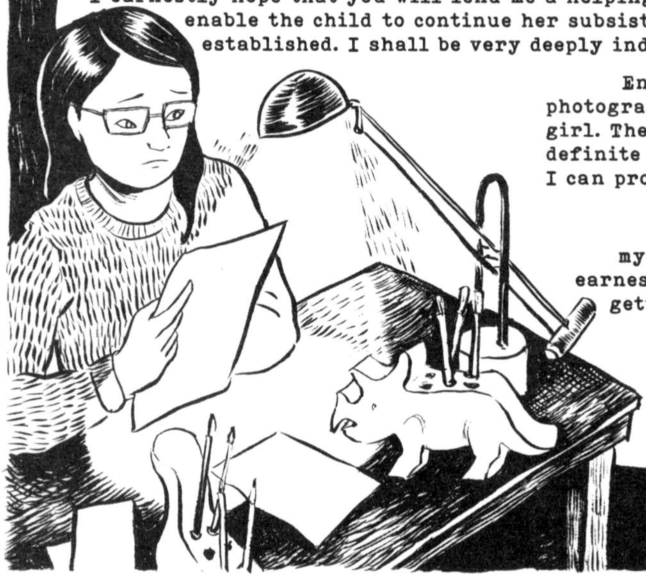

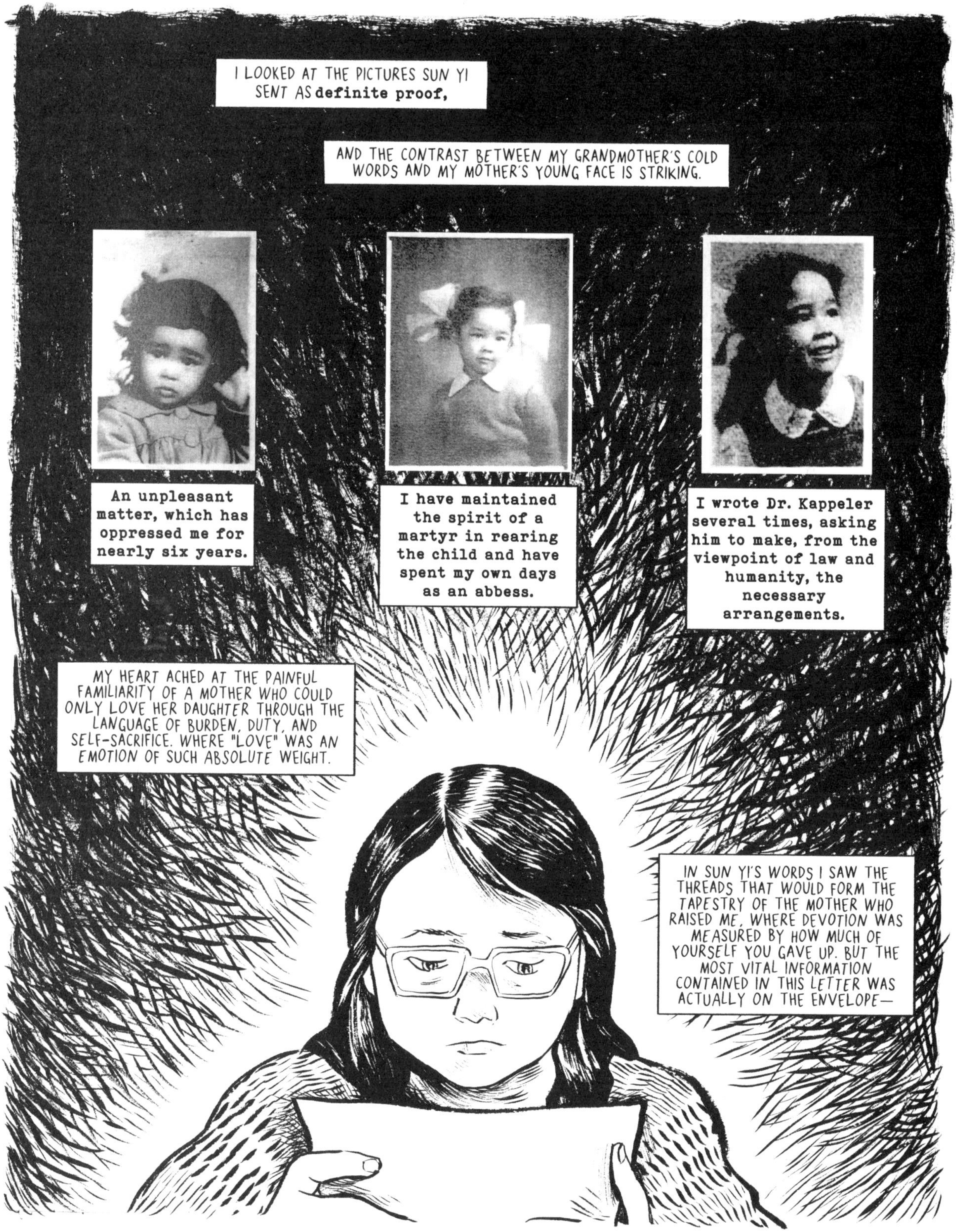

I LOOKED AT THE PICTURES SUN YI SENT AS **definite proof,**
AND THE CONTRAST BETWEEN MY GRANDMOTHER'S COLD WORDS AND MY MOTHER'S YOUNG FACE IS STRIKING.
An unpleasant matter, which has oppressed me for nearly six years.
I have maintained the spirit of a martyr in rearing the child and have spent my own days as an abbess.
I wrote Dr. Kappeler several times, asking him to make, from the viewpoint of law and humanity, the necessary arrangements.
MY HEART ACHED AT THE PAINFUL FAMILIARITY OF A MOTHER WHO COULD ONLY LOVE HER DAUGHTER THROUGH THE LANGUAGE OF BURDEN, DUTY, AND SELF-SACRIFICE. WHERE "LOVE" WAS AN EMOTION OF SUCH ABSOLUTE WEIGHT.
IN SUN YI'S WORDS I SAW THE THREADS THAT WOULD FORM THE TAPESTRY OF THE MOTHER WHO RAISED ME, WHERE DEVOTION WAS MEASURED BY HOW MUCH OF YOURSELF YOU GAVE UP. BUT THE MOST VITAL INFORMATION CONTAINED IN THIS LETTER WAS ACTUALLY ON THE ENVELOPE—

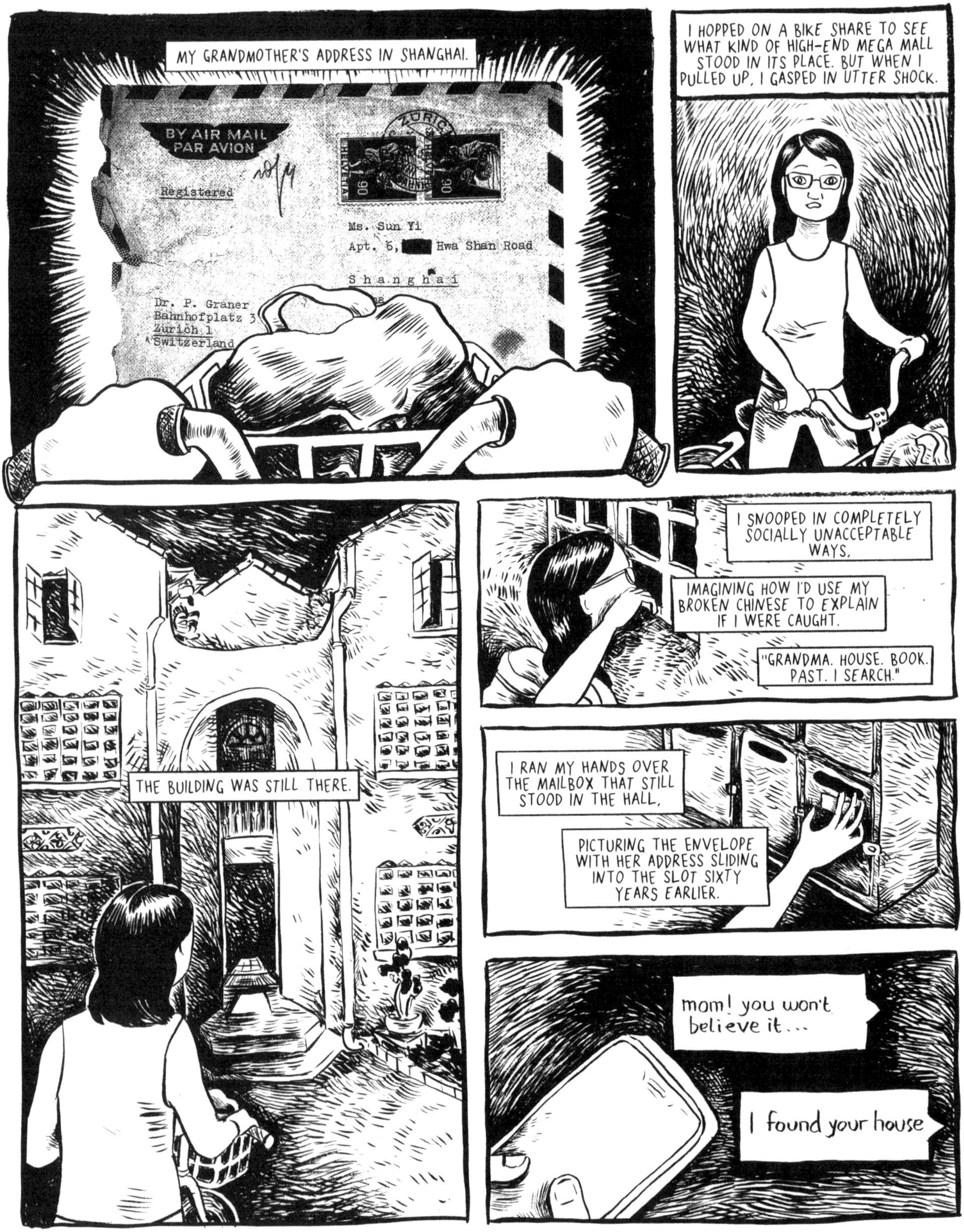
MY GRANDMOTHER'S ADDRESS IN SHANGHAI.
BY AIR MAIL
PAR AVION
Registered
Ms. Sun Yi
Apt. 6, [redacted] Hwa Shan Road
Shanghai
Dr. P. Graner
Bahnhofplatz 3
Zurich 1
Switzerland
I HOPPED ON A BIKE SHARE TO SEE WHAT KIND OF HIGH-END MEGA MALL STOOD IN ITS PLACE. BUT WHEN I PULLED UP, I GASPED IN UTTER SHOCK.
THE BUILDING WAS STILL THERE.
I SNOOPED IN COMPLETELY SOCIALLY UNACCEPTABLE WAYS,
IMAGINING HOW I'D USE MY BROKEN CHINESE TO EXPLAIN IF I WERE CAUGHT.
"GRANDMA. HOUSE. BOOK. PAST. I SEARCH."
I RAN MY HANDS OVER THE MAILBOX THAT STILL STOOD IN THE HALL,
PICTURING THE ENVELOPE WITH HER ADDRESS SLIDING INTO THE SLOT SIXTY YEARS EARLIER.
mom! you won't believe it...
I found your house

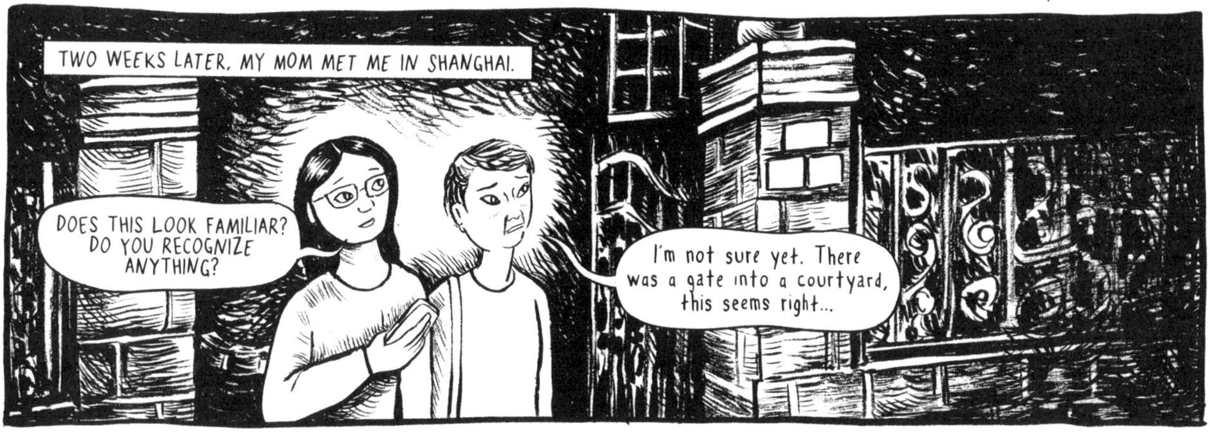
TWO WEEKS LATER, MY MOM MET ME IN SHANGHAI.
DOES THIS LOOK FAMILIAR? DO YOU RECOGNIZE ANYTHING?
I'm not sure yet. There was a gate into a courtyard, this seems right...

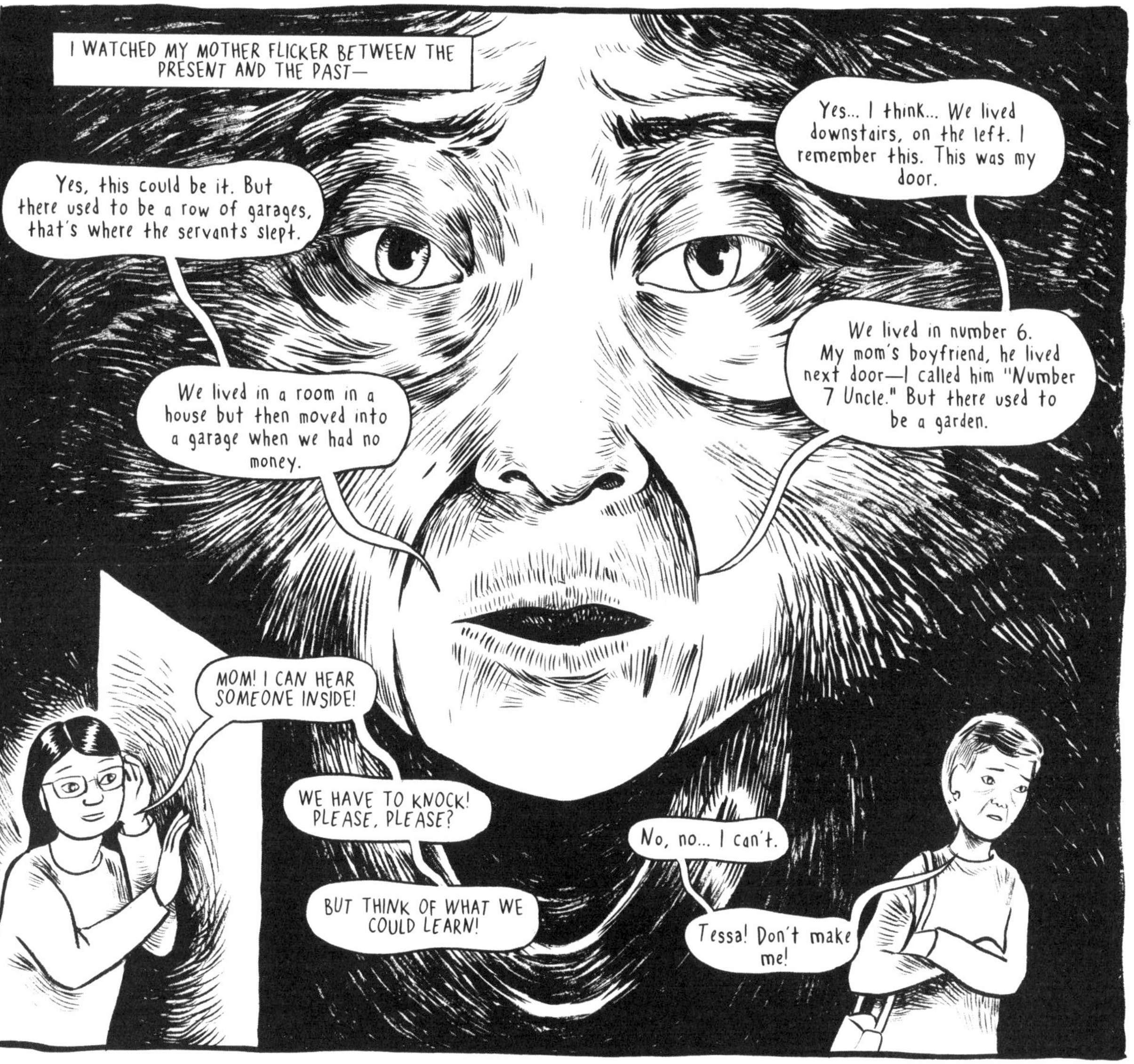
I WATCHED MY MOTHER FLICKER BETWEEN THE PRESENT AND THE PAST—
Yes, this could be it. But there used to be a row of garages, that's where the servants slept.
We lived in a room in a house but then moved into a garage when we had no money.
Yes... I think... We lived downstairs, on the left. I remember this. This was my door.
We lived in number 6. My mom's boyfriend, he lived next door—I called him "Number 7 Uncle." But there used to be a garden.
MOM! I CAN HEAR SOMEONE INSIDE!
WE HAVE TO KNOCK! PLEASE, PLEASE?
No, no... I can't.
BUT THINK OF WHAT WE COULD LEARN!
Tessa! Don't make me!

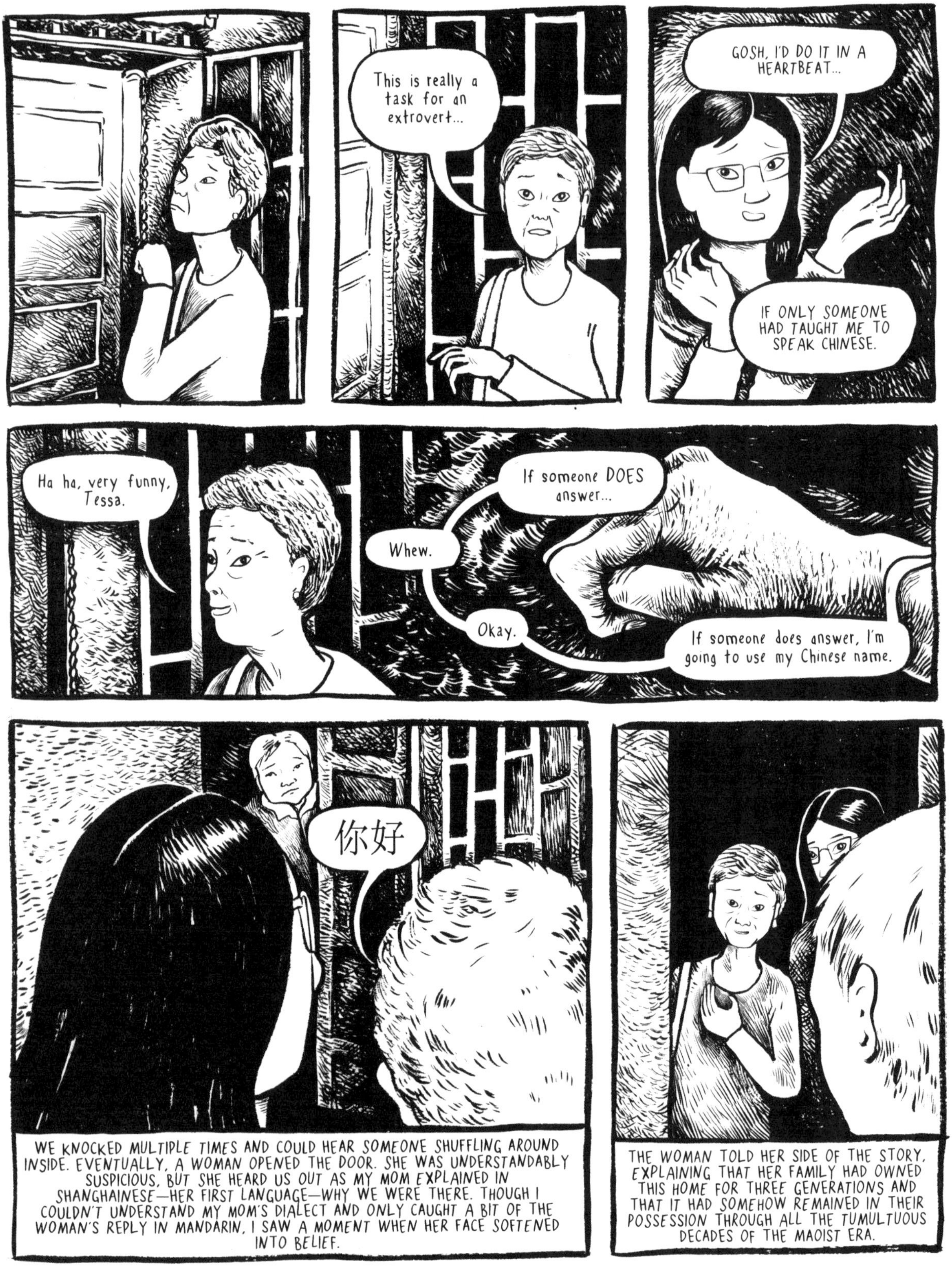
This is really a task for an extrovert...
GOSH, I'D DO IT IN A HEARTBEAT...
IF ONLY SOMEONE HAD TAUGHT ME TO SPEAK CHINESE.
Ha ha, very funny, Tessa.
If someone DOES answer...
Whew.
Okay.
If someone does answer, I'm going to use my Chinese name.
你好
WE KNOCKED MULTIPLE TIMES AND COULD HEAR SOMEONE SHUFFLING AROUND INSIDE. EVENTUALLY, A WOMAN OPENED THE DOOR. SHE WAS UNDERSTANDABLY SUSPICIOUS, BUT SHE HEARD US OUT AS MY MOM EXPLAINED IN SHANGHAINESE—HER FIRST LANGUAGE—WHY WE WERE THERE. THOUGH I COULDN'T UNDERSTAND MY MOM'S DIALECT AND ONLY CAUGHT A BIT OF THE WOMAN'S REPLY IN MANDARIN, I SAW A MOMENT WHEN HER FACE SOFTENED INTO BELIEF.
THE WOMAN TOLD HER SIDE OF THE STORY, EXPLAINING THAT HER FAMILY HAD OWNED THIS HOME FOR THREE GENERATIONS AND THAT IT HAD SOMEHOW REMAINED IN THEIR POSSESSION THROUGH ALL THE TUMULTUOUS DECADES OF THE MAOIST ERA.

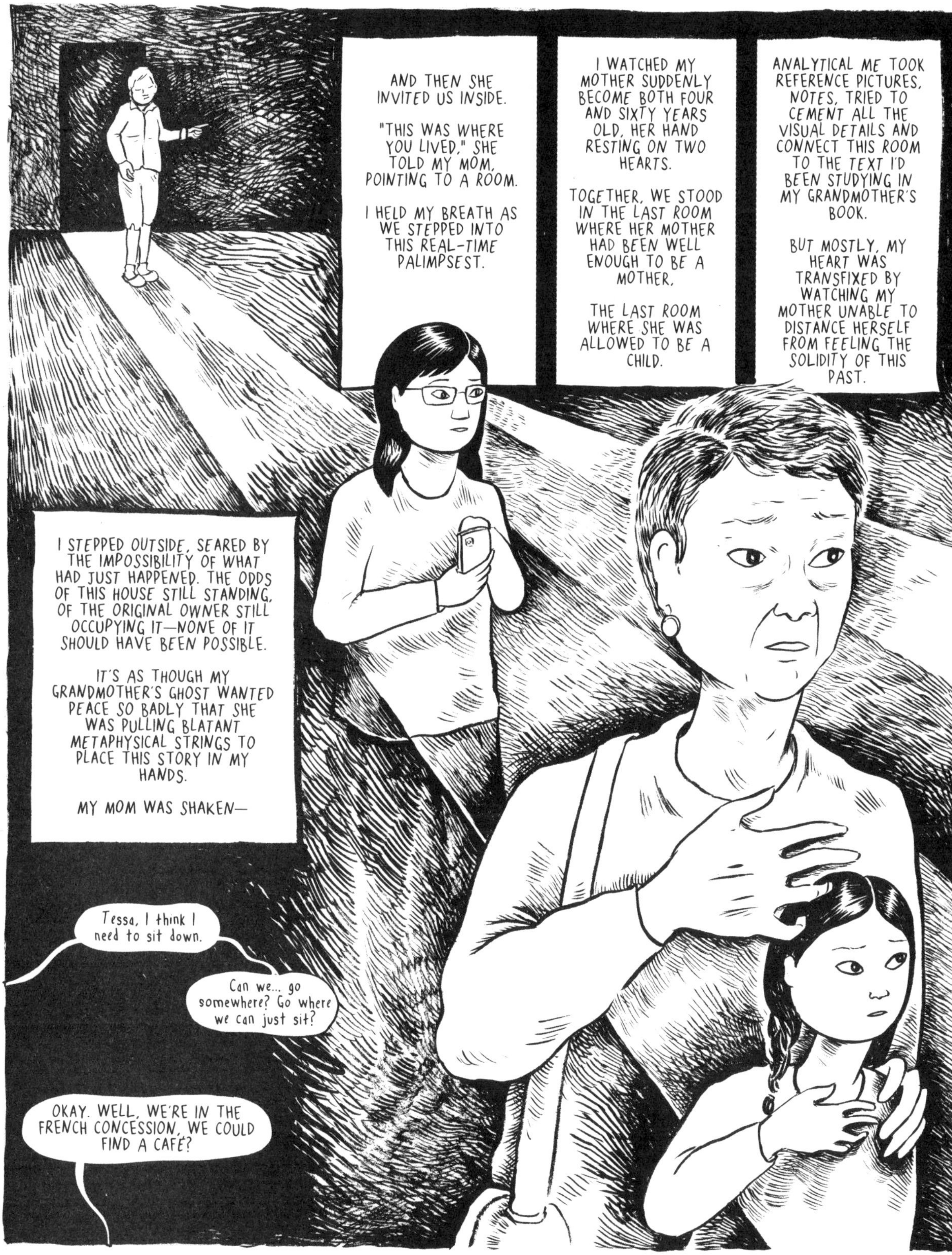
AND THEN SHE INVITED US INSIDE.
"THIS WAS WHERE YOU LIVED," SHE TOLD MY MOM, POINTING TO A ROOM.
I HELD MY BREATH AS WE STEPPED INTO THIS REAL-TIME PALIMPSEST.
I WATCHED MY MOTHER SUDDENLY BECOME BOTH FOUR AND SIXTY YEARS OLD, HER HAND RESTING ON TWO HEARTS.
TOGETHER, WE STOOD IN THE LAST ROOM WHERE HER MOTHER HAD BEEN WELL ENOUGH TO BE A MOTHER,
THE LAST ROOM WHERE SHE WAS ALLOWED TO BE A CHILD.
ANALYTICAL ME TOOK REFERENCE PICTURES, NOTES, TRIED TO CEMENT ALL THE VISUAL DETAILS AND CONNECT THIS ROOM TO THE TEXT I'D BEEN STUDYING IN MY GRANDMOTHER'S BOOK.
BUT MOSTLY, MY HEART WAS TRANSFIXED BY WATCHING MY MOTHER UNABLE TO DISTANCE HERSELF FROM FEELING THE SOLIDITY OF THIS PAST.
I STEPPED OUTSIDE, SEARED BY THE IMPOSSIBILITY OF WHAT HAD JUST HAPPENED. THE ODDS OF THIS HOUSE STILL STANDING, OF THE ORIGINAL OWNER STILL OCCUPYING IT—NONE OF IT SHOULD HAVE BEEN POSSIBLE.
IT'S AS THOUGH MY GRANDMOTHER'S GHOST WANTED PEACE SO BADLY THAT SHE WAS PULLING BLATANT METAPHYSICAL STRINGS TO PLACE THIS STORY IN MY HANDS.
MY MOM WAS SHAKEN—
Tessa, I think I need to sit down.
Can we... go somewhere? Go where we can just sit?
OKAY. WELL, WE'RE IN THE FRENCH CONCESSION, WE COULD FIND A CAFÉ?

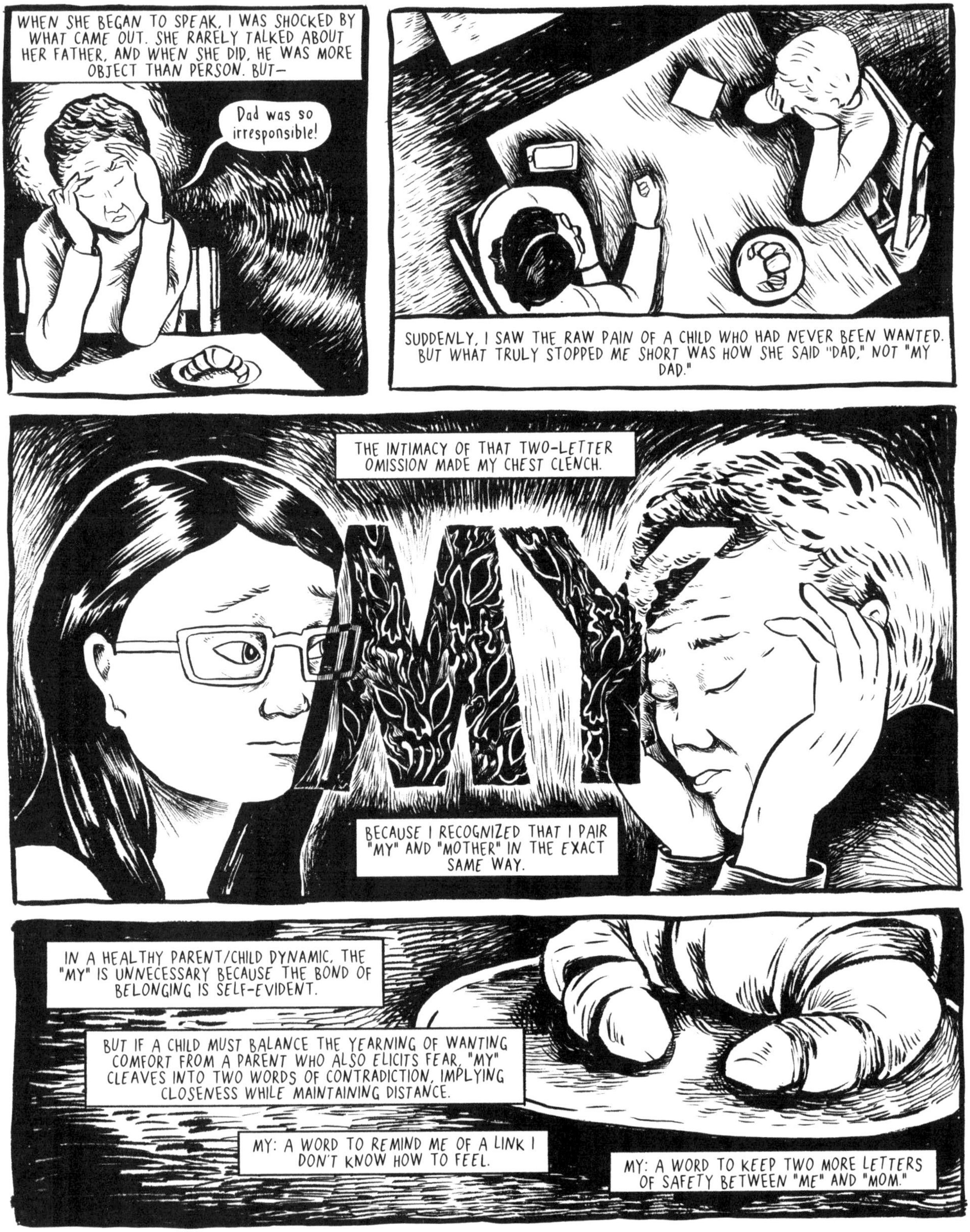
WHEN SHE BEGAN TO SPEAK, I WAS SHOCKED BY WHAT CAME OUT. SHE RARELY TALKED ABOUT HER FATHER, AND WHEN SHE DID, HE WAS MORE OBJECT THAN PERSON. BUT—
Dad was so irresponsible!
SUDDENLY, I SAW THE RAW PAIN OF A CHILD WHO HAD NEVER BEEN WANTED. BUT WHAT TRULY STOPPED ME SHORT WAS HOW SHE SAID "DAD," NOT "MY DAD."
THE INTIMACY OF THAT TWO-LETTER OMISSION MADE MY CHEST CLENCH.
MY
BECAUSE I RECOGNIZED THAT I PAIR "MY" AND "MOTHER" IN THE EXACT SAME WAY.
IN A HEALTHY PARENT/CHILD DYNAMIC, THE "MY" IS UNNECESSARY BECAUSE THE BOND OF BELONGING IS SELF-EVIDENT.
BUT IF A CHILD MUST BALANCE THE YEARNING OF WANTING COMFORT FROM A PARENT WHO ALSO ELICITS FEAR, "MY" CLEAVES INTO TWO WORDS OF CONTRADICTION, IMPLYING CLOSENESS WHILE MAINTAINING DISTANCE.
MY: A WORD TO REMIND ME OF A LINK I DON'T KNOW HOW TO FEEL.
MY: A WORD TO KEEP TWO MORE LETTERS OF SAFETY BETWEEN "ME" AND "MOM."

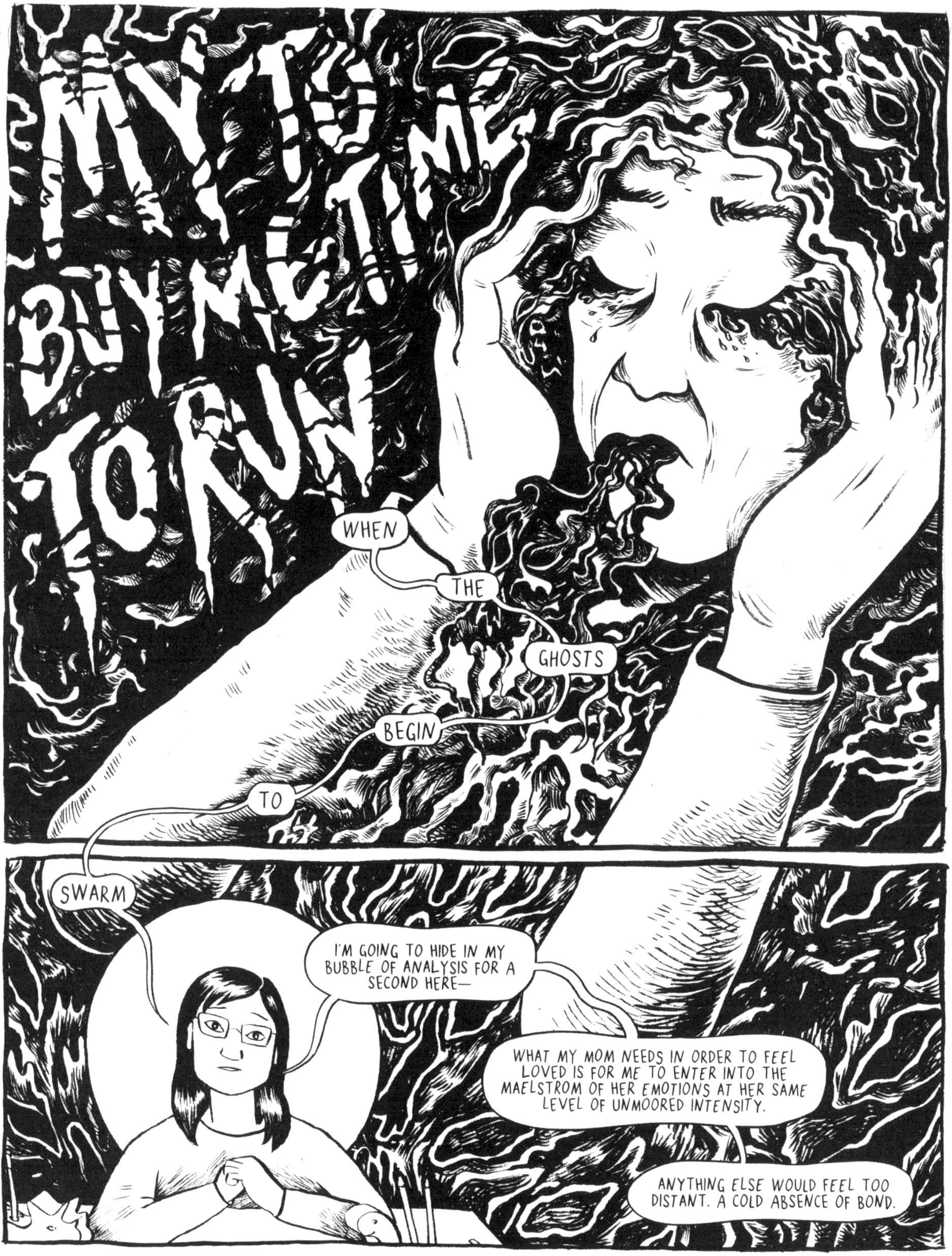
BUY ME TIME
TO RUN
WHEN
THE
GHOSTS
BEGIN
TO
SWARM
I'M GOING TO HIDE IN MY BUBBLE OF ANALYSIS FOR A SECOND HERE—
WHAT MY MOM NEEDS IN ORDER TO FEEL LOVED IS FOR ME TO ENTER INTO THE MAELSTROM OF HER EMOTIONS AT HER SAME LEVEL OF UNMOORED INTENSITY.
ANYTHING ELSE WOULD FEEL TOO DISTANT. A COLD ABSENCE OF BOND.

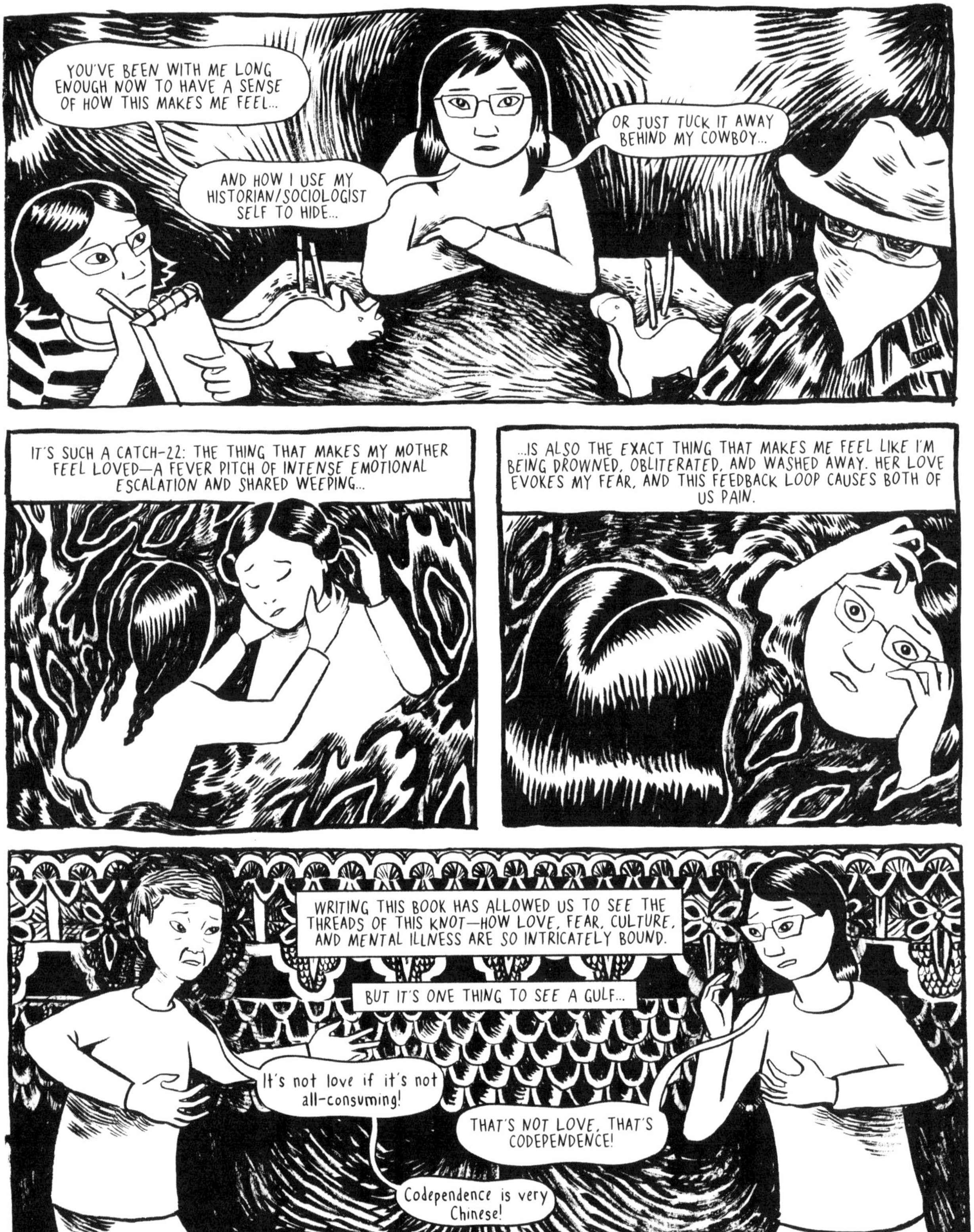
YOU'VE BEEN WITH ME LONG ENOUGH NOW TO HAVE A SENSE OF HOW THIS MAKES ME FEEL...
AND HOW I USE MY HISTORIAN/SOCIOLOGIST SELF TO HIDE...
OR JUST TUCK IT AWAY BEHIND MY COWBOY...
IT'S SUCH A CATCH-22: THE THING THAT MAKES MY MOTHER FEEL LOVED—A FEVER PITCH OF INTENSE EMOTIONAL ESCALATION AND SHARED WEEPING...
...IS ALSO THE EXACT THING THAT MAKES ME FEEL LIKE I'M BEING DROWNED, OBLITERATED, AND WASHED AWAY. HER LOVE EVOKES MY FEAR, AND THIS FEEDBACK LOOP CAUSES BOTH OF US PAIN.
WRITING THIS BOOK HAS ALLOWED US TO SEE THE THREADS OF THIS KNOT—HOW LOVE, FEAR, CULTURE, AND MENTAL ILLNESS ARE SO INTRICATELY BOUND.
BUT IT'S ONE THING TO SEE A GULF...
It's not love if it's not all-consuming!
THAT'S NOT LOVE, THAT'S CODEPENDENCE!
Codependence is very Chinese!

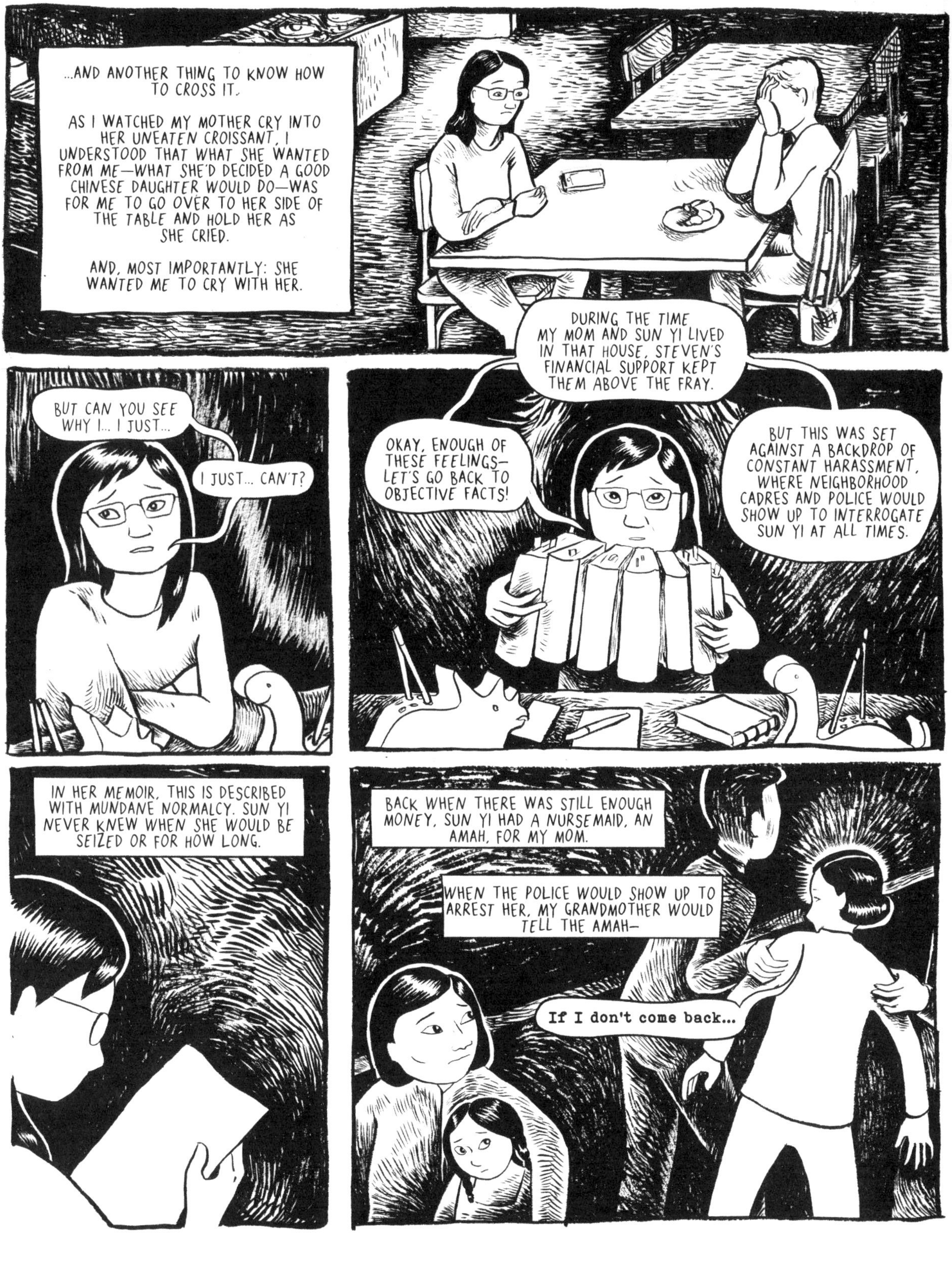
...AND ANOTHER THING TO KNOW HOW TO CROSS IT.
AS I WATCHED MY MOTHER CRY INTO HER UNEATEN CROISSANT, I UNDERSTOOD THAT WHAT SHE WANTED FROM ME—WHAT SHE'D DECIDED A GOOD CHINESE DAUGHTER WOULD DO—WAS FOR ME TO GO OVER TO HER SIDE OF THE TABLE AND HOLD HER AS SHE CRIED.
AND, MOST IMPORTANTLY: SHE WANTED ME TO CRY WITH HER.
BUT CAN YOU SEE WHY I... I JUST...
I JUST... CAN'T?
DURING THE TIME MY MOM AND SUN YI LIVED IN THAT HOUSE, STEVEN'S FINANCIAL SUPPORT KEPT THEM ABOVE THE FRAY.
OKAY, ENOUGH OF THESE FEELINGS—LET'S GO BACK TO OBJECTIVE FACTS!
BUT THIS WAS SET AGAINST A BACKDROP OF CONSTANT HARASSMENT, WHERE NEIGHBORHOOD CADRES AND POLICE WOULD SHOW UP TO INTERROGATE SUN YI AT ALL TIMES.
IN HER MEMOIR, THIS IS DESCRIBED WITH MUNDANE NORMALCY. SUN YI NEVER KNEW WHEN SHE WOULD BE SEIZED OR FOR HOW LONG.
BACK WHEN THERE WAS STILL ENOUGH MONEY, SUN YI HAD A NURSEMAID, AN AMAH, FOR MY MOM.
WHEN THE POLICE WOULD SHOW UP TO ARREST HER, MY GRANDMOTHER WOULD TELL THE AMAH—
If I don't come back...

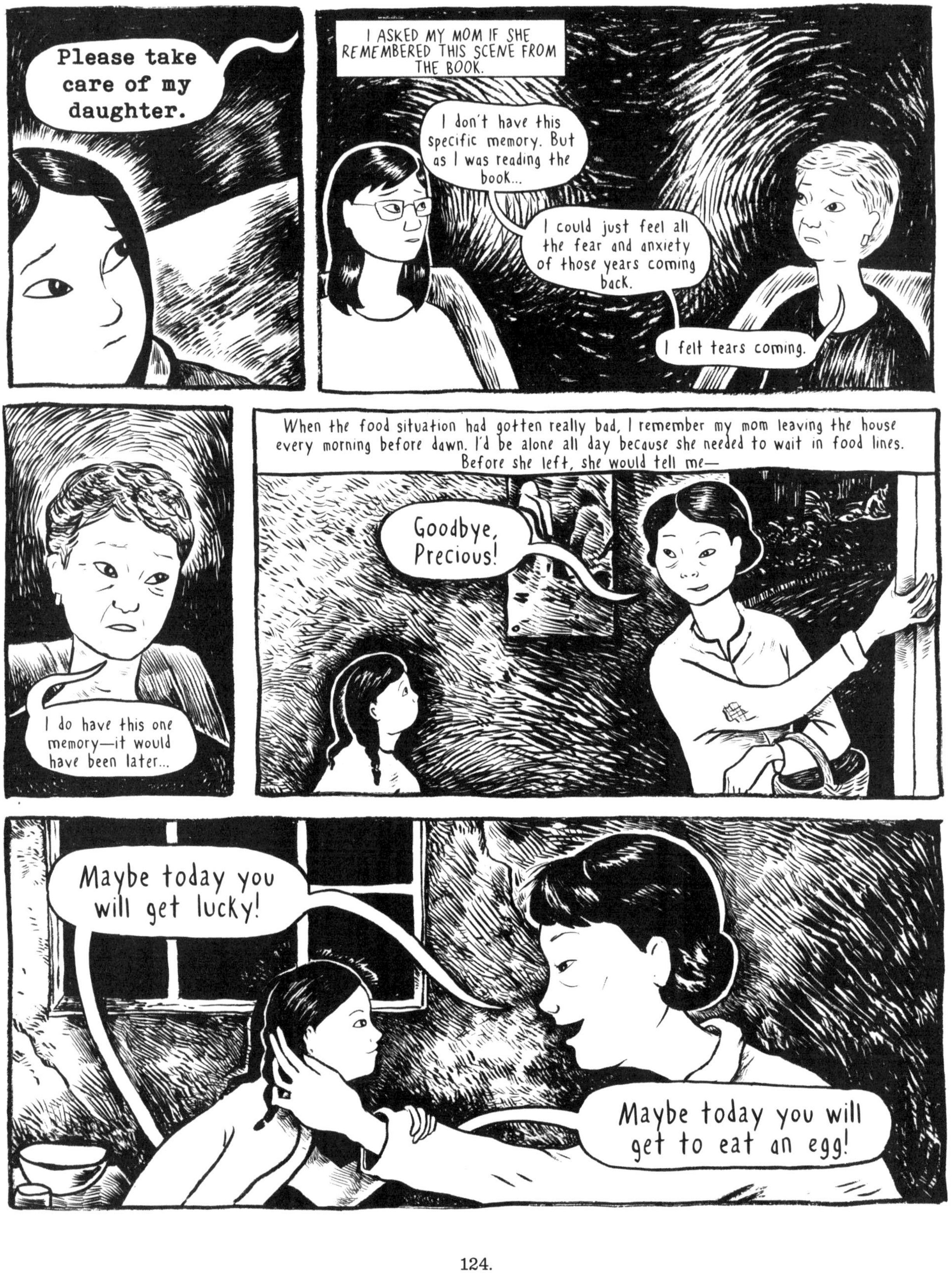

Please take care of my daughter.
I ASKED MY MOM IF SHE REMEMBERED THIS SCENE FROM THE BOOK.
I don't have this specific memory. But as I was reading the book...
I could just feel all the fear and anxiety of those years coming back.
I felt tears coming.
I do have this one memory—it would have been later...
When the food situation had gotten really bad, I remember my mom leaving the house every morning before dawn. I'd be alone all day because she needed to wait in food lines. Before she left, she would tell me—
Goodbye, Precious!
Maybe today you will get lucky!
Maybe today you will get to eat an egg!

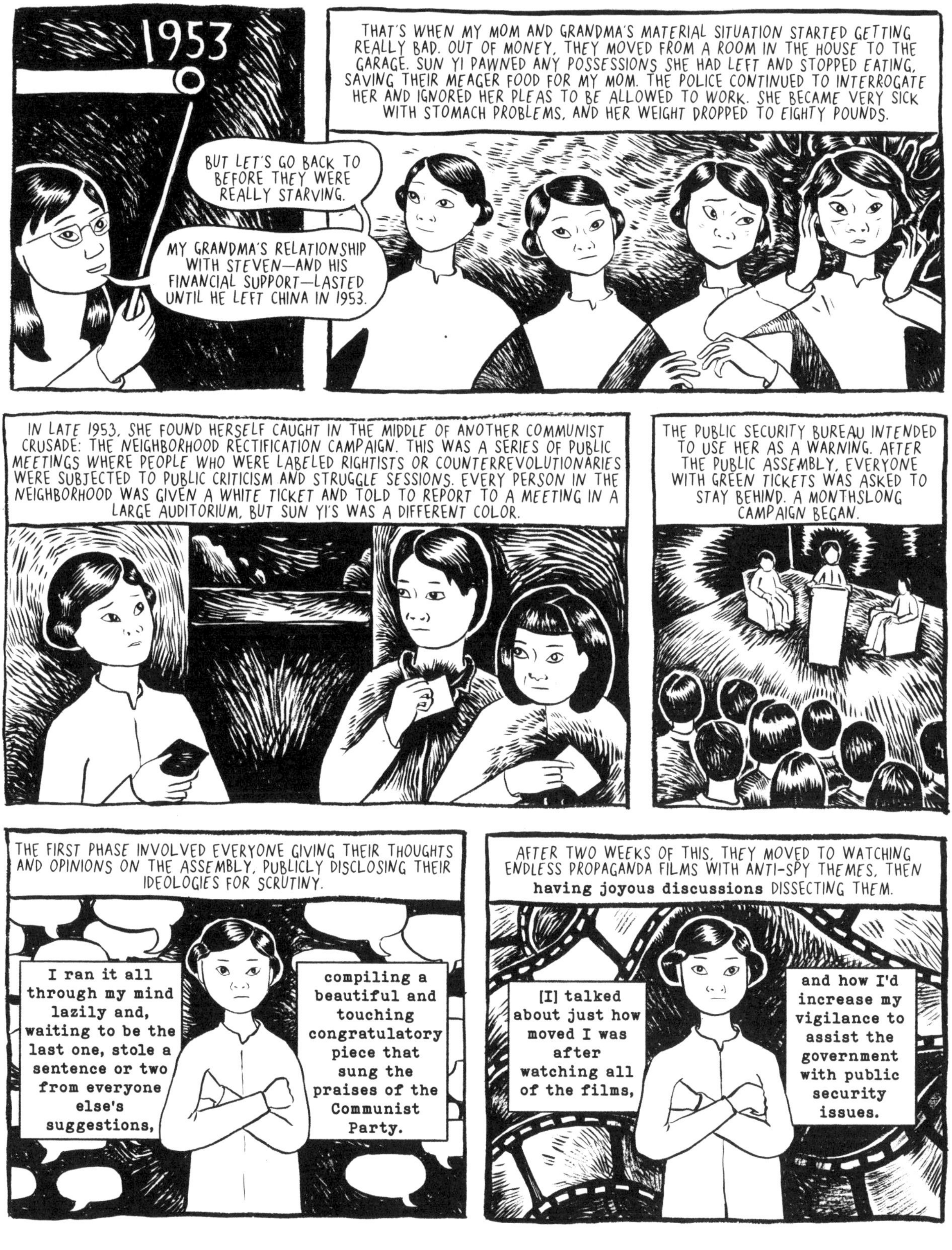
1953
THAT'S WHEN MY MOM AND GRANDMA'S MATERIAL SITUATION STARTED GETTING REALLY BAD. OUT OF MONEY, THEY MOVED FROM A ROOM IN THE HOUSE TO THE GARAGE. SUN YI PAWNED ANY POSSESSIONS SHE HAD LEFT AND STOPPED EATING, SAVING THEIR MEAGER FOOD FOR MY MOM. THE POLICE CONTINUED TO INTERROGATE HER AND IGNORED HER PLEAS TO BE ALLOWED TO WORK. SHE BECAME VERY SICK WITH STOMACH PROBLEMS, AND HER WEIGHT DROPPED TO EIGHTY POUNDS.
MY GRANDMA'S RELATIONSHIP WITH STEVEN—AND HIS FINANCIAL SUPPORT—LASTED UNTIL HE LEFT CHINA IN 1953.
BUT LET'S GO BACK TO BEFORE THEY WERE REALLY STARVING.
IN LATE 1953, SHE FOUND HERSELF CAUGHT IN THE MIDDLE OF ANOTHER COMMUNIST CRUSADE: THE NEIGHBORHOOD RECTIFICATION CAMPAIGN. THIS WAS A SERIES OF PUBLIC MEETINGS WHERE PEOPLE WHO WERE LABELED RIGHTISTS OR COUNTERREVOLUTIONARIES WERE SUBJECTED TO PUBLIC CRITICISM AND STRUGGLE SESSIONS. EVERY PERSON IN THE NEIGHBORHOOD WAS GIVEN A WHITE TICKET AND TOLD TO REPORT TO A MEETING IN A LARGE AUDITORIUM, BUT SUN YI'S WAS A DIFFERENT COLOR.
THE PUBLIC SECURITY BUREAU INTENDED TO USE HER AS A WARNING. AFTER THE PUBLIC ASSEMBLY, EVERYONE WITH GREEN TICKETS WAS ASKED TO STAY BEHIND. A MONTHSLONG CAMPAIGN BEGAN.
THE FIRST PHASE INVOLVED EVERYONE GIVING THEIR THOUGHTS AND OPINIONS ON THE ASSEMBLY, PUBLICLY DISCLOSING THEIR IDEOLOGIES FOR SCRUTINY.
I ran it all through my mind lazily and, waiting to be the last one, stole a sentence or two from everyone else's suggestions,
compiling a beautiful and touching congratulatory piece that sung the praises of the Communist Party.
AFTER TWO WEEKS OF THIS, THEY MOVED TO WATCHING ENDLESS PROPAGANDA FILMS WITH ANTI-SPY THEMES, THEN having joyous discussions DISSECTING THEM.
[I] talked about just how moved I was after watching all of the films,
and how I'd increase my vigilance to assist the government with public security issues.

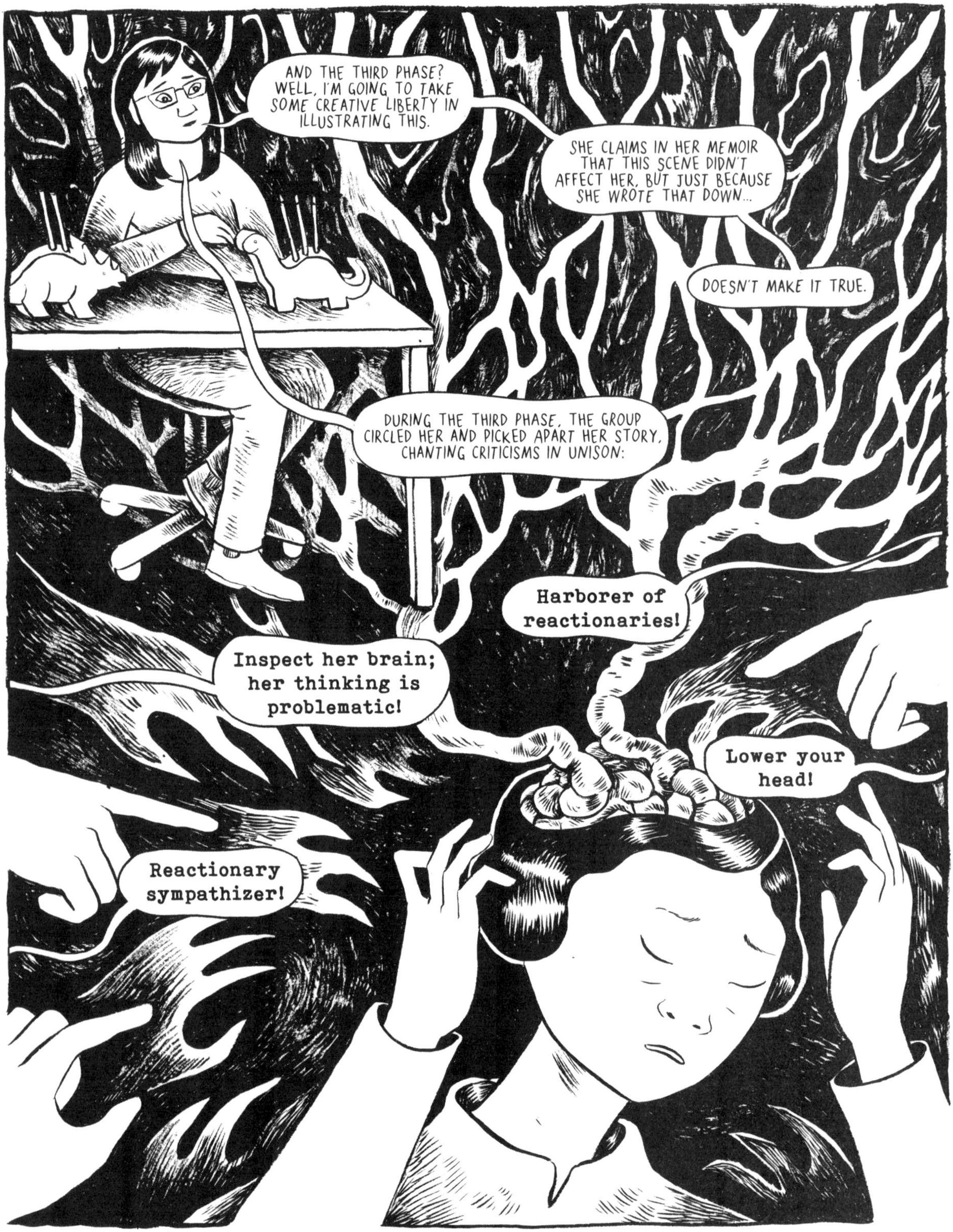
AND THE THIRD PHASE? WELL, I'M GOING TO TAKE SOME CREATIVE LIBERTY IN ILLUSTRATING THIS.
SHE CLAIMS IN HER MEMOIR THAT THIS SCENE DIDN'T AFFECT HER, BUT JUST BECAUSE SHE WROTE THAT DOWN...
DOESN'T MAKE IT TRUE.
DURING THE THIRD PHASE, THE GROUP CIRCLED HER AND PICKED APART HER STORY, CHANTING CRITICISMS IN UNISON:
Harborer of reactionaries!
Inspect her brain; her thinking is problematic!
Lower your head!
Reactionary sympathizer!

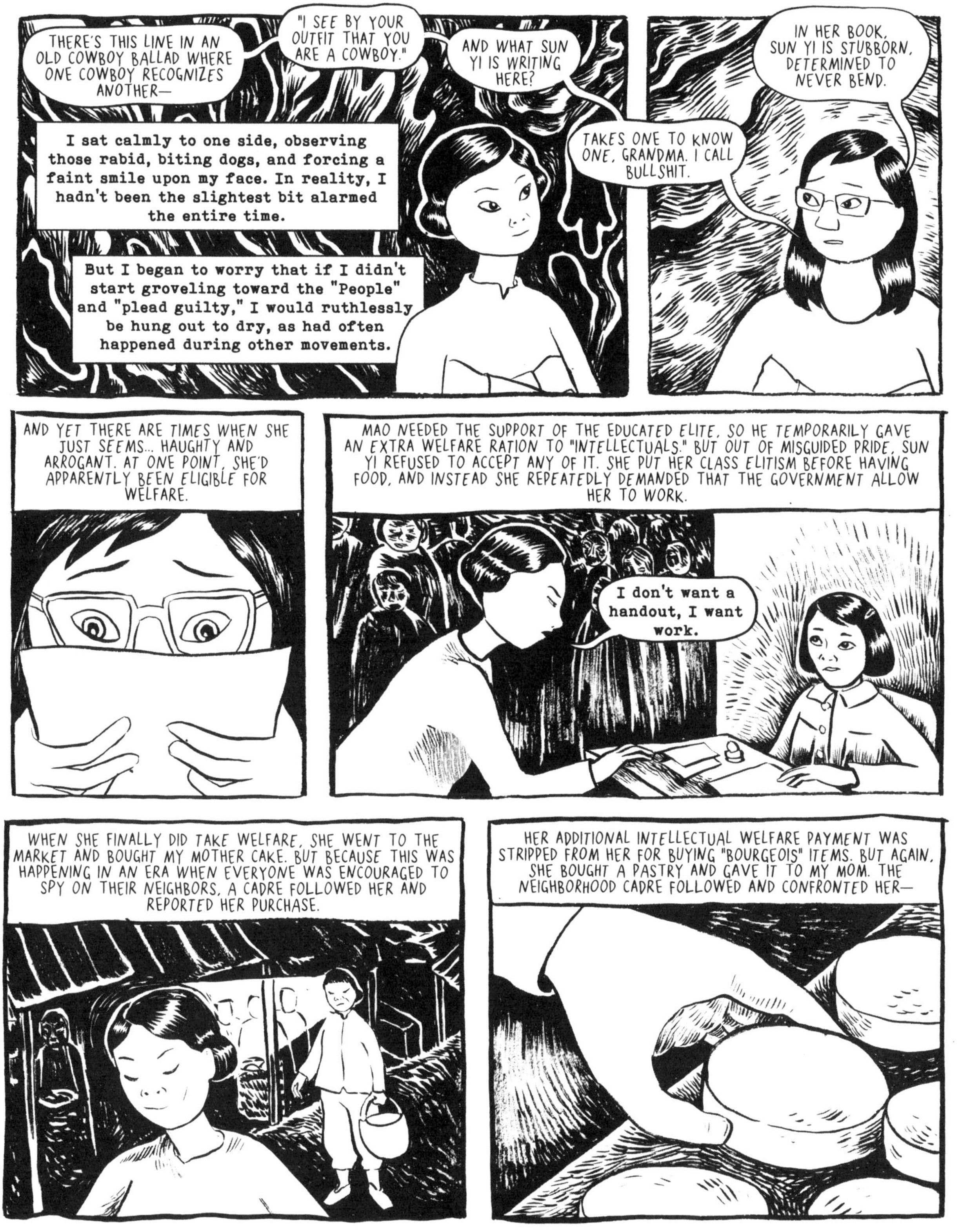
THERE'S THIS LINE IN AN OLD COWBOY BALLAD WHERE ONE COWBOY RECOGNIZES ANOTHER—
"I SEE BY YOUR OUTFIT THAT YOU ARE A COWBOY."
AND WHAT SUN YI IS WRITING HERE?
I sat calmly to one side, observing those rabid, biting dogs, and forcing a faint smile upon my face. In reality, I hadn't been the slightest bit alarmed the entire time.
But I began to worry that if I didn't start groveling toward the "People" and "plead guilty," I would ruthlessly be hung out to dry, as had often happened during other movements.
TAKES ONE TO KNOW ONE, GRANDMA. I CALL BULLSHIT.
IN HER BOOK, SUN YI IS STUBBORN, DETERMINED TO NEVER BEND.
AND YET THERE ARE TIMES WHEN SHE JUST SEEMS... HAUGHTY AND ARROGANT. AT ONE POINT, SHE'D APPARENTLY BEEN ELIGIBLE FOR WELFARE.
MAO NEEDED THE SUPPORT OF THE EDUCATED ELITE, SO HE TEMPORARILY GAVE AN EXTRA WELFARE RATION TO "INTELLECTUALS." BUT OUT OF MISGUIDED PRIDE, SUN YI REFUSED TO ACCEPT ANY OF IT. SHE PUT HER CLASS ELITISM BEFORE HAVING FOOD, AND INSTEAD SHE REPEATEDLY DEMANDED THAT THE GOVERNMENT ALLOW HER TO WORK.
I don't want a handout, I want work.
WHEN SHE FINALLY DID TAKE WELFARE, SHE WENT TO THE MARKET AND BOUGHT MY MOTHER CAKE. BUT BECAUSE THIS WAS HAPPENING IN AN ERA WHEN EVERYONE WAS ENCOURAGED TO SPY ON THEIR NEIGHBORS, A CADRE FOLLOWED HER AND REPORTED HER PURCHASE.
HER ADDITIONAL INTELLECTUAL WELFARE PAYMENT WAS STRIPPED FROM HER FOR BUYING "BOURGEOIS" ITEMS. BUT AGAIN, SHE BOUGHT A PASTRY AND GAVE IT TO MY MOM. THE NEIGHBORHOOD CADRE FOLLOWED AND CONFRONTED HER—

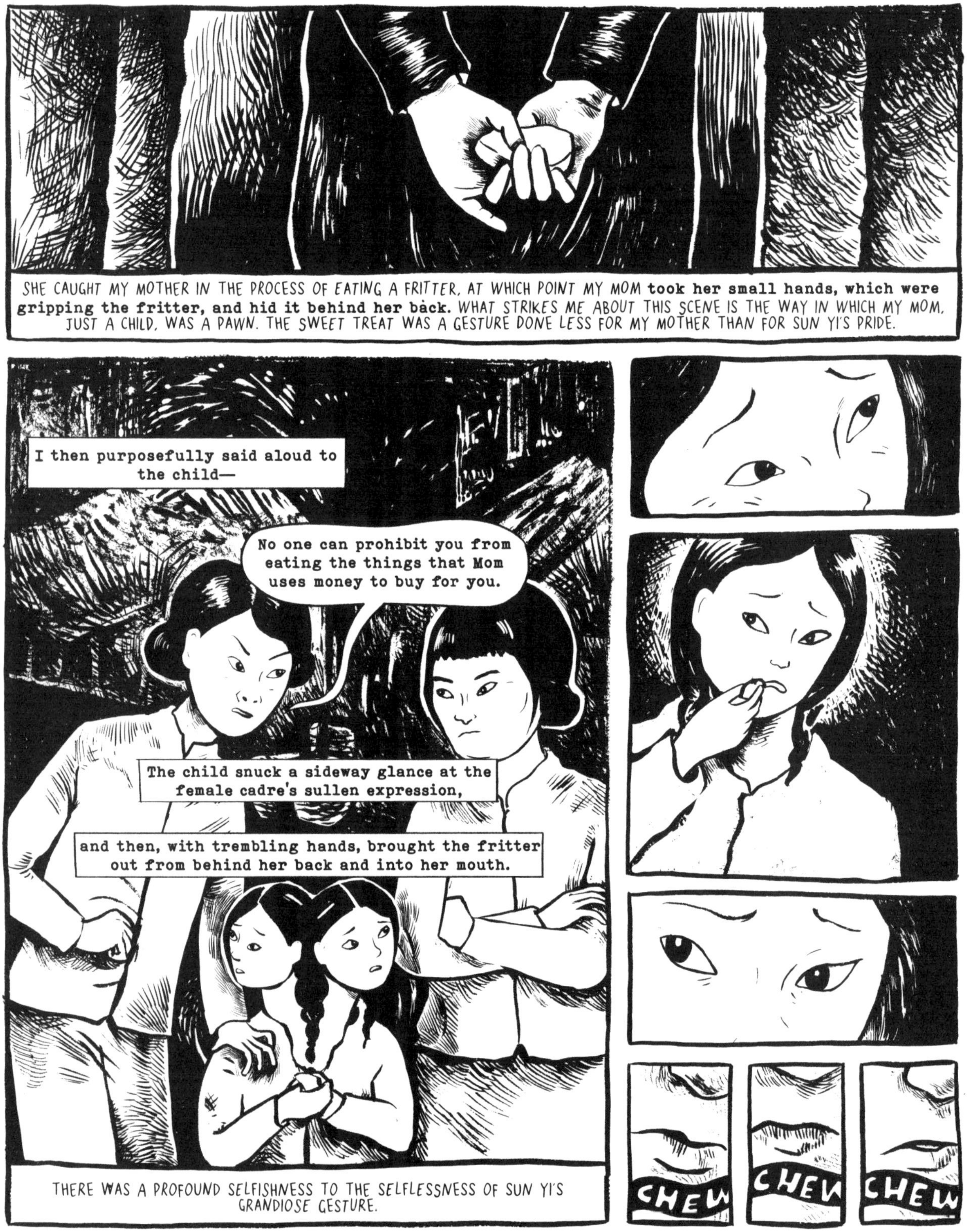
SHE CAUGHT MY MOTHER IN THE PROCESS OF EATING A FRITTER, AT WHICH POINT MY MOM took her small hands, which were gripping the fritter, and hid it behind her back. WHAT STRIKES ME ABOUT THIS SCENE IS THE WAY IN WHICH MY MOM, JUST A CHILD, WAS A PAWN. THE SWEET TREAT WAS A GESTURE DONE LESS FOR MY MOTHER THAN FOR SUN YI'S PRIDE.
I then purposefully said aloud to the child—
No one can prohibit you from eating the things that Mom uses money to buy for you.
The child snuck a sideway glance at the female cadre's sullen expression,
and then, with trembling hands, brought the fritter out from behind her back and into her mouth.
THERE WAS A PROFOUND SELFISHNESS TO THE SELFLESSNESS OF SUN YI'S GRANDIOSE GESTURE.
CHEW
CHEW
CHEW

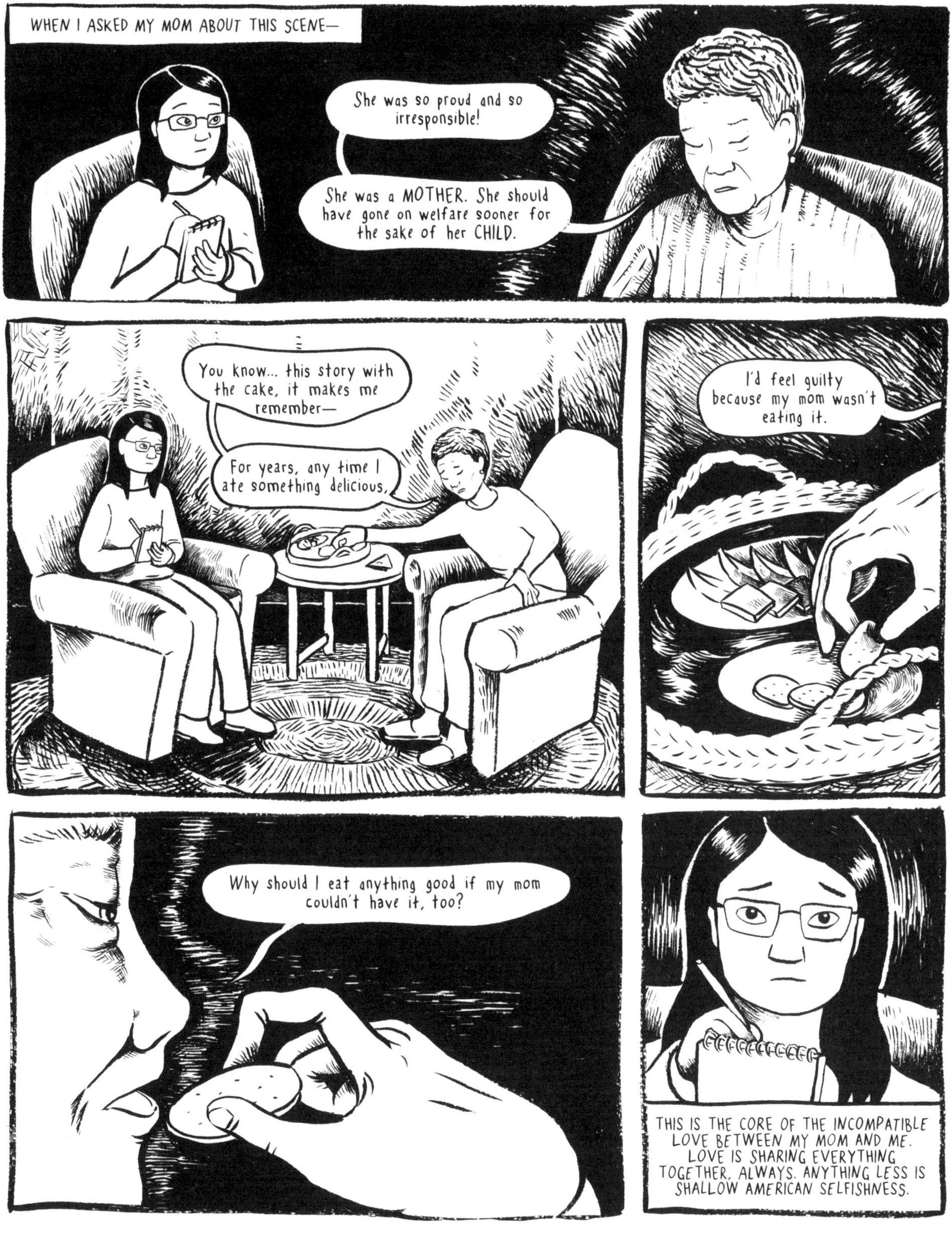
WHEN I ASKED MY MOM ABOUT THIS SCENE—
She was so proud and so irresponsible!
She was a MOTHER. She should have gone on welfare sooner for the sake of her CHILD.
You know... this story with the cake, it makes me remember—
For years, any time I ate something delicious,
I'd feel guilty because my mom wasn't eating it.
Why should I eat anything good if my mom couldn't have it, too?
THIS IS THE CORE OF THE INCOMPATIBLE LOVE BETWEEN MY MOM AND ME. LOVE IS SHARING EVERYTHING TOGETHER, ALWAYS. ANYTHING LESS IS SHALLOW AMERICAN SELFISHNESS.

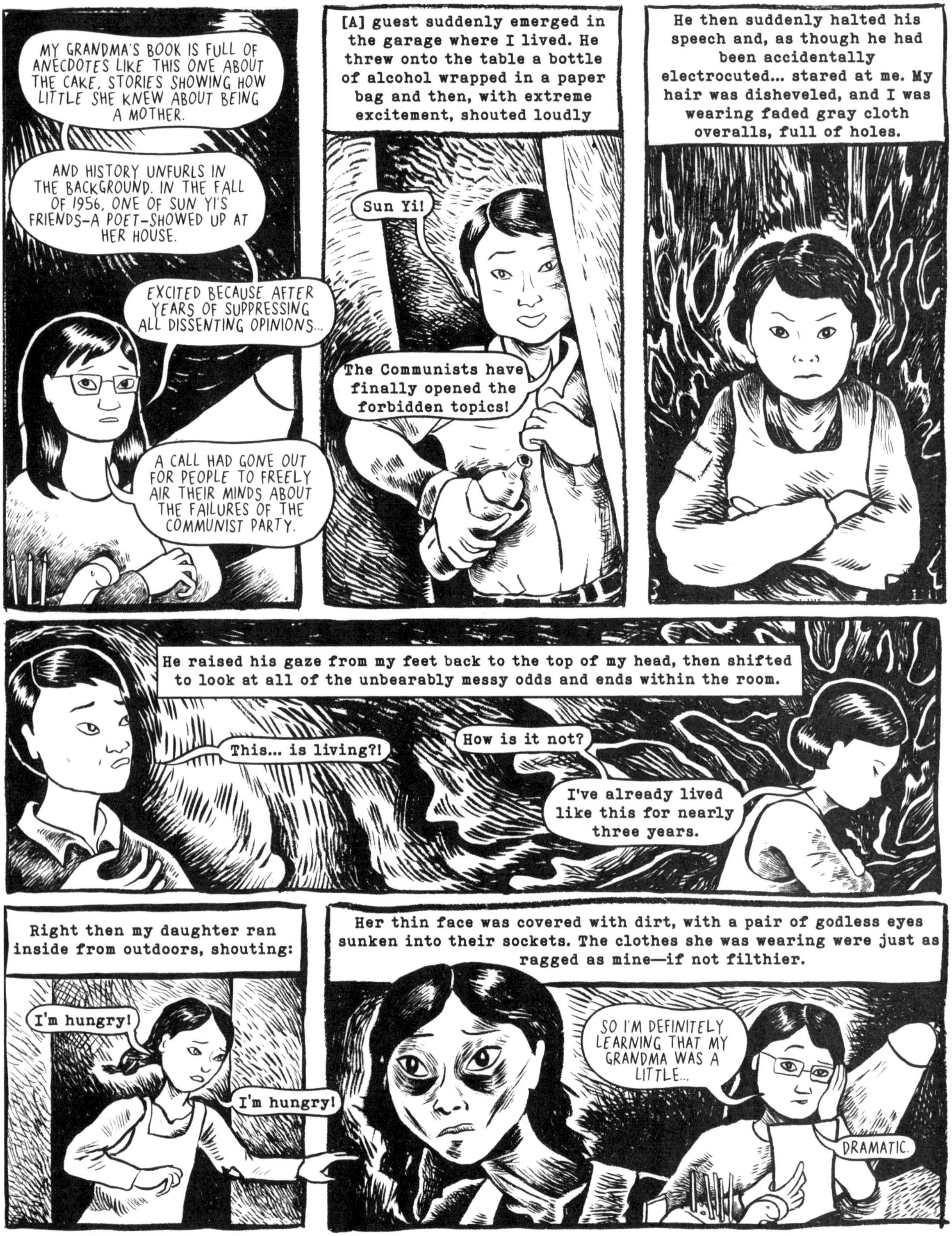
MY GRANDMA'S BOOK IS FULL OF ANECDOTES LIKE THIS ONE ABOUT THE CAKE, STORIES SHOWING HOW LITTLE SHE KNEW ABOUT BEING A MOTHER.
AND HISTORY UNFURLS IN THE BACKGROUND. IN THE FALL OF 1956, ONE OF SUN YI'S FRIENDS—A POET—SHOWED UP AT HER HOUSE.
EXCITED BECAUSE AFTER YEARS OF SUPPRESSING ALL DISSENTING OPINIONS...
A CALL HAD GONE OUT FOR PEOPLE TO FREELY AIR THEIR MINDS ABOUT THE FAILURES OF THE COMMUNIST PARTY.
[A] guest suddenly emerged in the garage where I lived. He threw onto the table a bottle of alcohol wrapped in a paper bag and then, with extreme excitement, shouted loudly
Sun Yi!
The Communists have finally opened the forbidden topics!
He then suddenly halted his speech and, as though he had been accidentally electrocuted... stared at me. My hair was disheveled, and I was wearing faded gray cloth overalls, full of holes.
He raised his gaze from my feet back to the top of my head, then shifted to look at all of the unbearably messy odds and ends within the room.
This... is living?!
How is it not?
I've already lived like this for nearly three years.
Right then my daughter ran inside from outdoors, shouting:
I'm hungry!
I'm hungry!
Her thin face was covered with dirt, with a pair of godless eyes sunken into their sockets. The clothes she was wearing were just as ragged as mine—if not filthier.
SO I'M DEFINITELY LEARNING THAT MY GRANDMA WAS A LITTLE...
DRAMATIC.

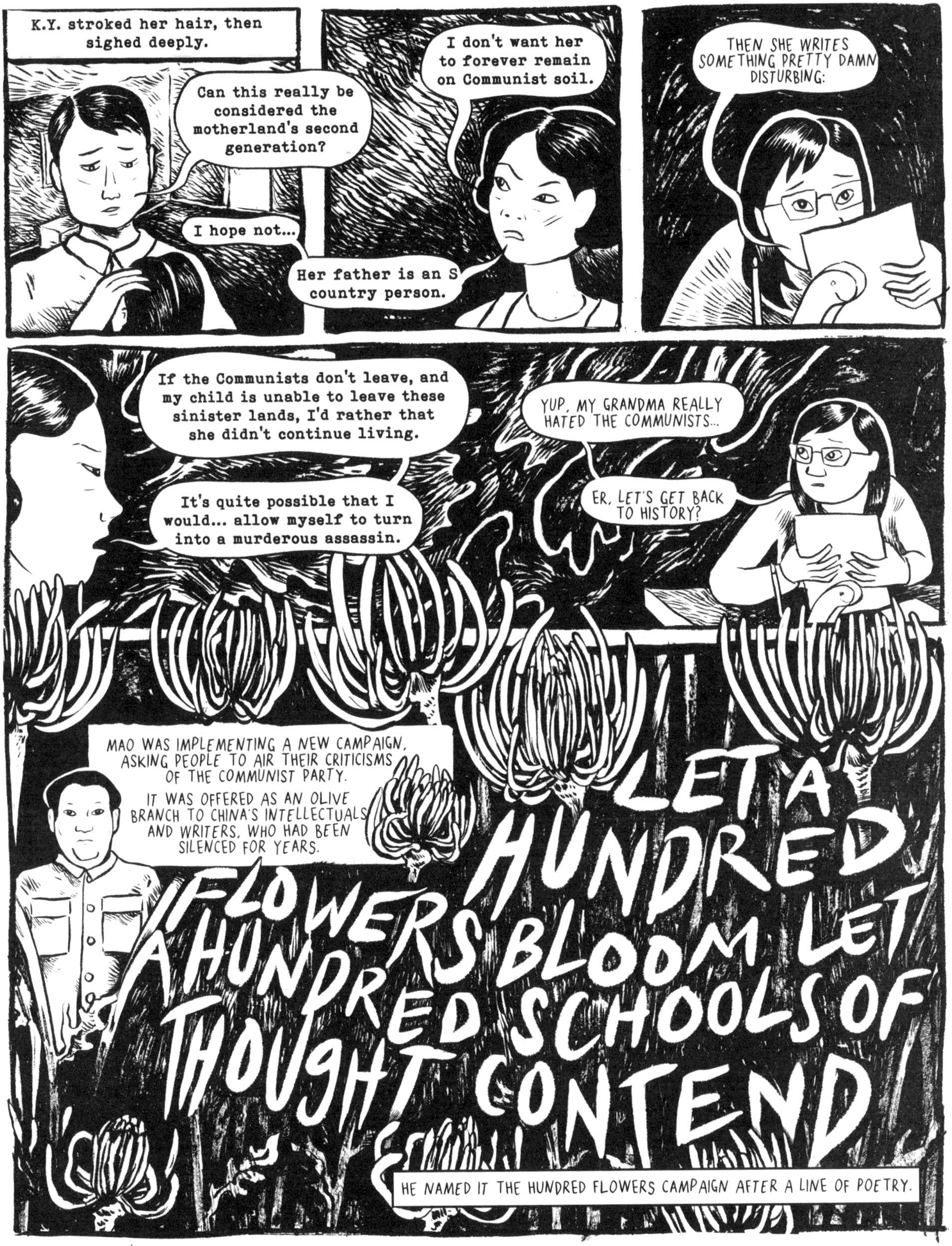

K.Y. stroked her hair, then sighed deeply.
Can this really be considered the motherland's second generation?
I hope not...
Her father is an S country person.
I don't want her to forever remain on Communist soil.
THEN SHE WRITES SOMETHING PRETTY DAMN DISTURBING:
If the Communists don't leave, and my child is unable to leave these sinister lands, I'd rather that she didn't continue living.
It's quite possible that I would... allow myself to turn into a murderous assassin.
YUP, MY GRANDMA REALLY HATED THE COMMUNISTS...
ER, LET'S GET BACK TO HISTORY?
MAO WAS IMPLEMENTING A NEW CAMPAIGN, ASKING PEOPLE TO AIR THEIR CRITICISMS OF THE COMMUNIST PARTY.
IT WAS OFFERED AS AN OLIVE BRANCH TO CHINA'S INTELLECTUALS AND WRITERS, WHO HAD BEEN SILENCED FOR YEARS.
LET A HUNDRED FLOWERS BLOOM LET A HUNDRED SCHOOLS OF THOUGHT CONTEND
HE NAMED IT THE HUNDRED FLOWERS CAMPAIGN AFTER A LINE OF POETRY.

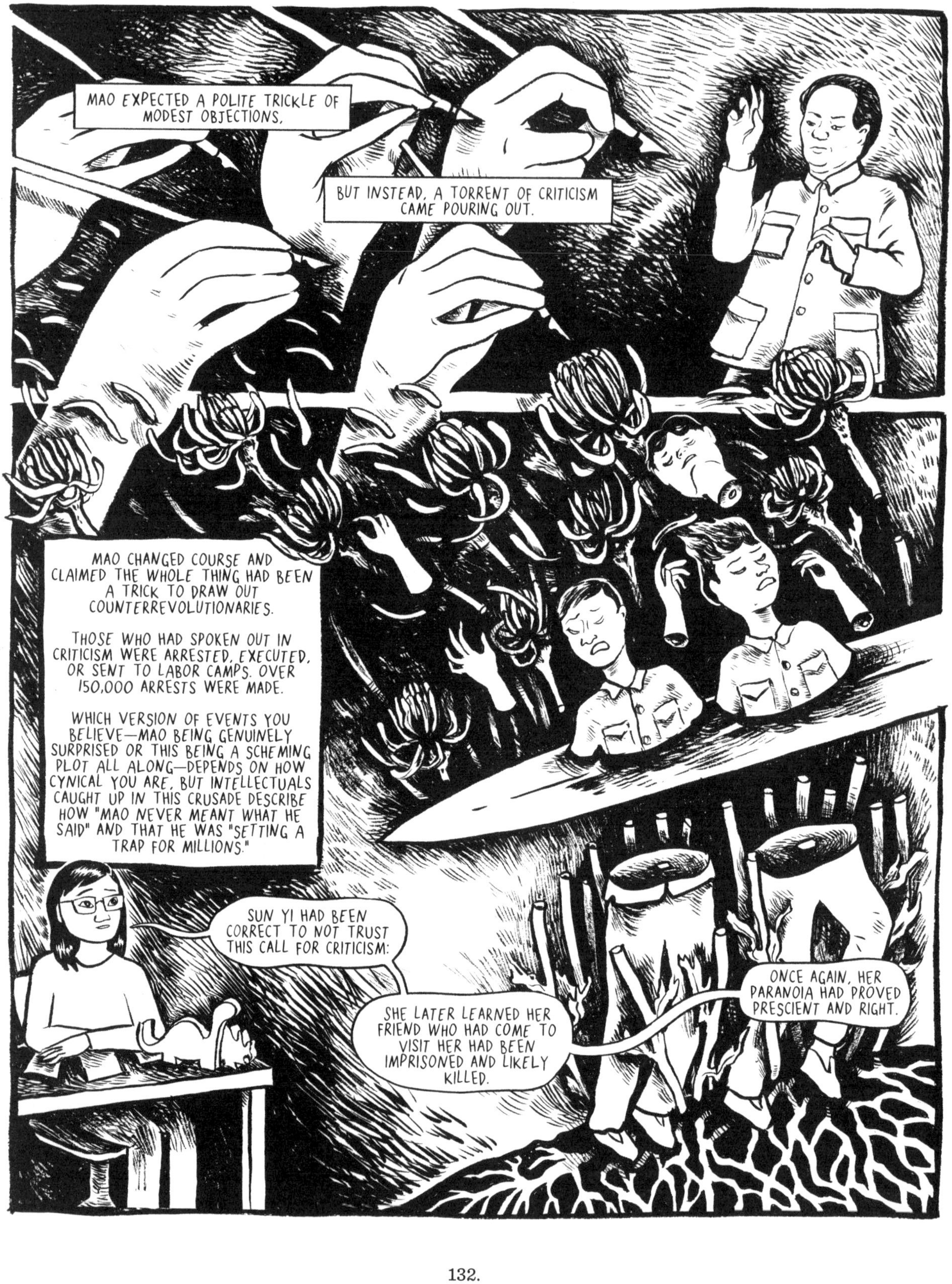
MAO EXPECTED A POLITE TRICKLE OF MODEST OBJECTIONS,
BUT INSTEAD, A TORRENT OF CRITICISM CAME POURING OUT.
MAO CHANGED COURSE AND CLAIMED THE WHOLE THING HAD BEEN A TRICK TO DRAW OUT COUNTERREVOLUTIONARIES.
THOSE WHO HAD SPOKEN OUT IN CRITICISM WERE ARRESTED, EXECUTED, OR SENT TO LABOR CAMPS. OVER 150,000 ARRESTS WERE MADE.
WHICH VERSION OF EVENTS YOU BELIEVE—MAO BEING GENUINELY SURPRISED OR THIS BEING A SCHEMING PLOT ALL ALONG—DEPENDS ON HOW CYNICAL YOU ARE, BUT INTELLECTUALS CAUGHT UP IN THIS CRUSADE DESCRIBE HOW "MAO NEVER MEANT WHAT HE SAID" AND THAT HE WAS "SETTING A TRAP FOR MILLIONS."
SUN YI HAD BEEN CORRECT TO NOT TRUST THIS CALL FOR CRITICISM:
SHE LATER LEARNED HER FRIEND WHO HAD COME TO VISIT HER HAD BEEN IMPRISONED AND LIKELY KILLED.
ONCE AGAIN, HER PARANOIA HAD PROVED PRESCIENT AND RIGHT.

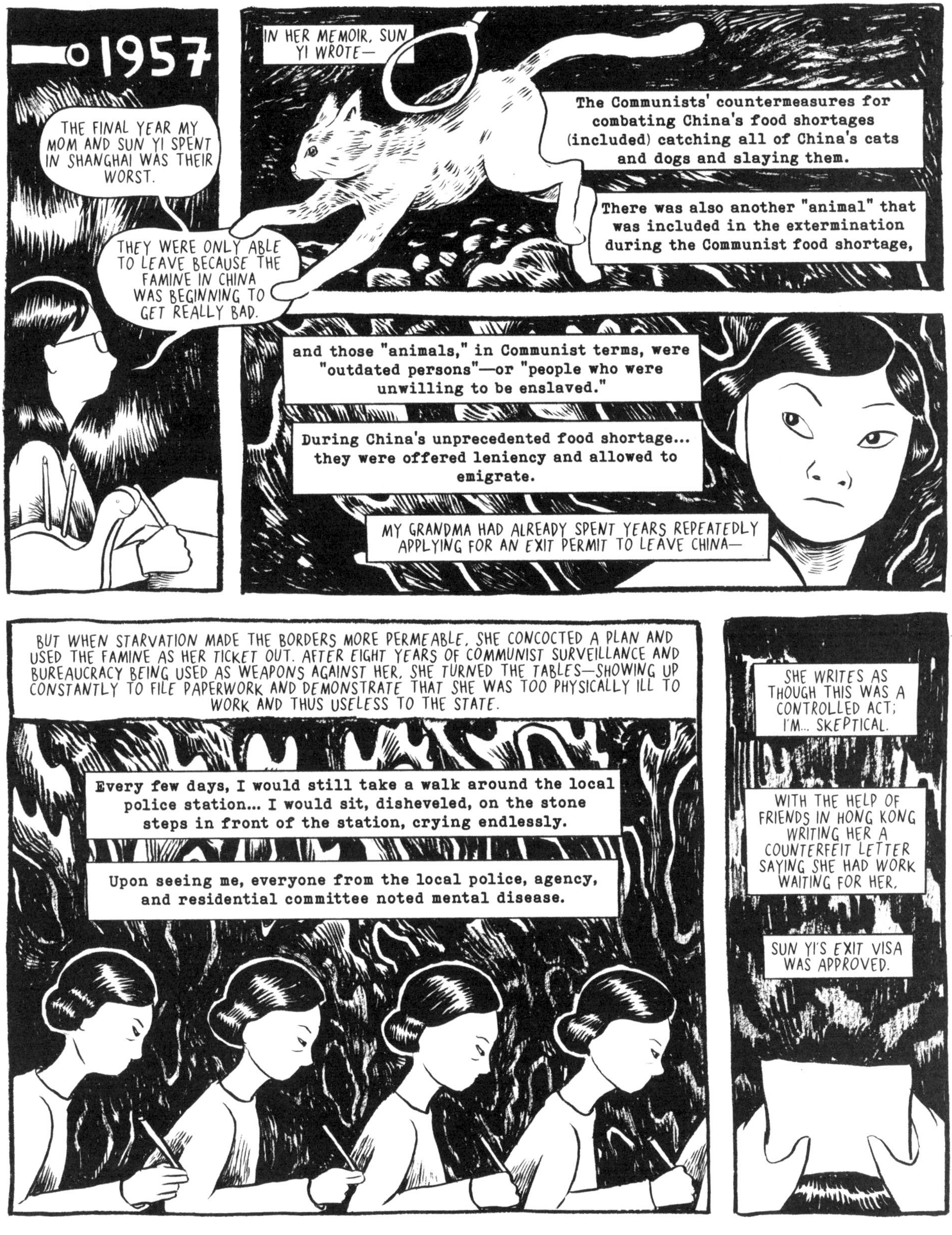
1957
THE FINAL YEAR MY MOM AND SUN YI SPENT IN SHANGHAI WAS THEIR WORST.
THEY WERE ONLY ABLE TO LEAVE BECAUSE THE FAMINE IN CHINA WAS BEGINNING TO GET REALLY BAD.
IN HER MEMOIR, SUN YI WROTE—
The Communists' countermeasures for combating China's food shortages (included) catching all of China's cats and dogs and slaying them.
There was also another "animal" that was included in the extermination during the Communist food shortage,
and those "animals," in Communist terms, were "outdated persons"—or "people who were unwilling to be enslaved."
During China's unprecedented food shortage... they were offered leniency and allowed to emigrate.
MY GRANDMA HAD ALREADY SPENT YEARS REPEATEDLY APPLYING FOR AN EXIT PERMIT TO LEAVE CHINA—
BUT WHEN STARVATION MADE THE BORDERS MORE PERMEABLE, SHE CONCOCTED A PLAN AND USED THE FAMINE AS HER TICKET OUT. AFTER EIGHT YEARS OF COMMUNIST SURVEILLANCE AND BUREAUCRACY BEING USED AS WEAPONS AGAINST HER, SHE TURNED THE TABLES—SHOWING UP CONSTANTLY TO FILE PAPERWORK AND DEMONSTRATE THAT SHE WAS TOO PHYSICALLY ILL TO WORK AND THUS USELESS TO THE STATE.
Every few days, I would still take a walk around the local police station... I would sit, disheveled, on the stone steps in front of the station, crying endlessly.
Upon seeing me, everyone from the local police, agency, and residential committee noted mental disease.
SHE WRITES AS THOUGH THIS WAS A CONTROLLED ACT; I'M... SKEPTICAL.
WITH THE HELP OF FRIENDS IN HONG KONG WRITING HER A COUNTERFEIT LETTER SAYING SHE HAD WORK WAITING FOR HER,
SUN YI'S EXIT VISA WAS APPROVED.

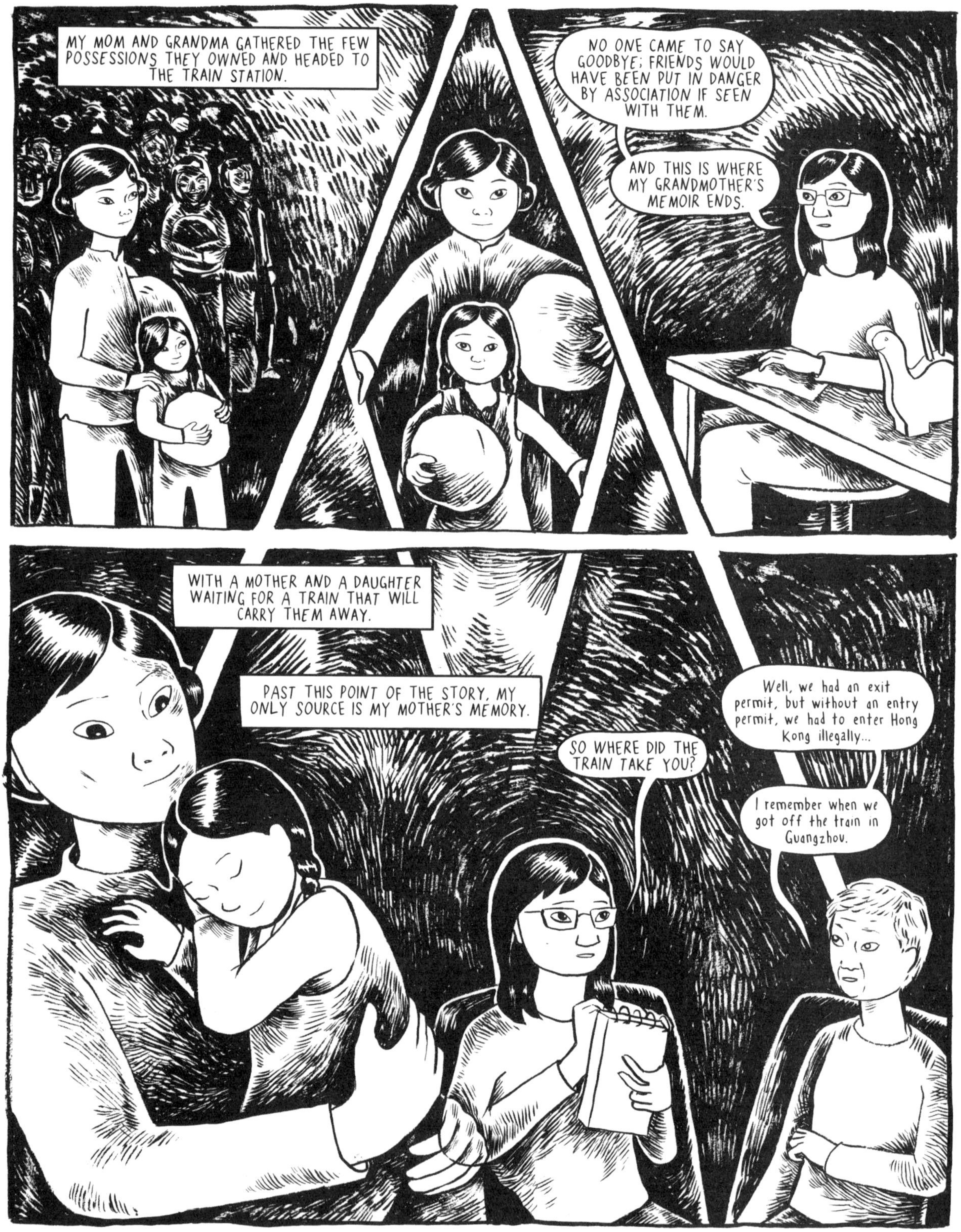
MY MOM AND GRANDMA GATHERED THE FEW POSSESSIONS THEY OWNED AND HEADED TO THE TRAIN STATION.
NO ONE CAME TO SAY GOODBYE; FRIENDS WOULD HAVE BEEN PUT IN DANGER BY ASSOCIATION IF SEEN WITH THEM.
AND THIS IS WHERE MY GRANDMOTHER'S MEMOIR ENDS.
WITH A MOTHER AND A DAUGHTER WAITING FOR A TRAIN THAT WILL CARRY THEM AWAY.
PAST THIS POINT OF THE STORY, MY ONLY SOURCE IS MY MOTHER'S MEMORY.
SO WHERE DID THE TRAIN TAKE YOU?
Well, we had an exit permit, but without an entry permit, we had to enter Hong Kong illegally...
I remember when we got off the train in Guangzhou.

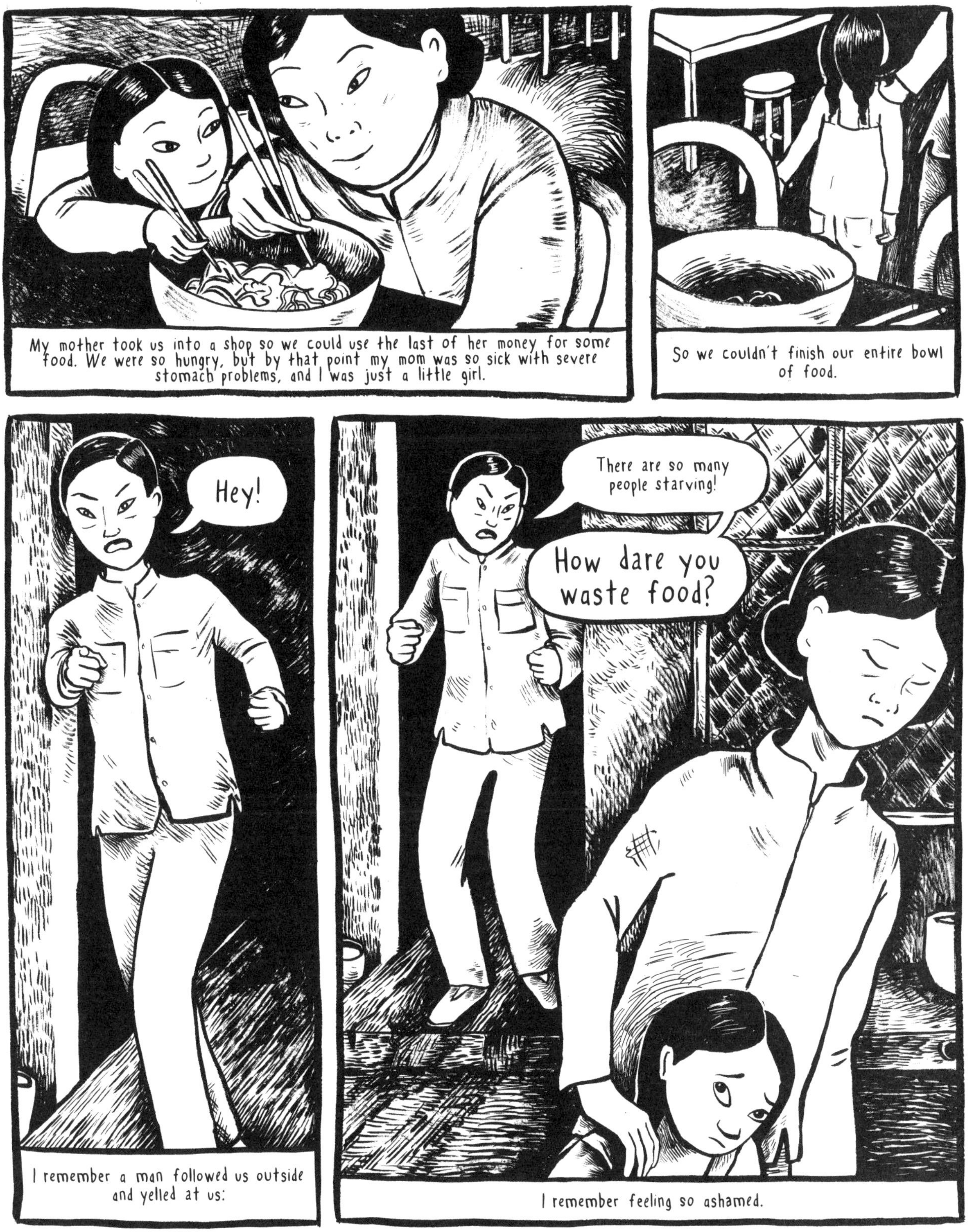
My mother took us into a shop so we could use the last of her money for some food. We were so hungry, but by that point my mom was so sick with severe stomach problems, and I was just a little girl.
So we couldn't finish our entire bowl of food.
Hey!
I remember a man followed us outside and yelled at us:
There are so many people starving!
How dare you waste food?
I remember feeling so ashamed.

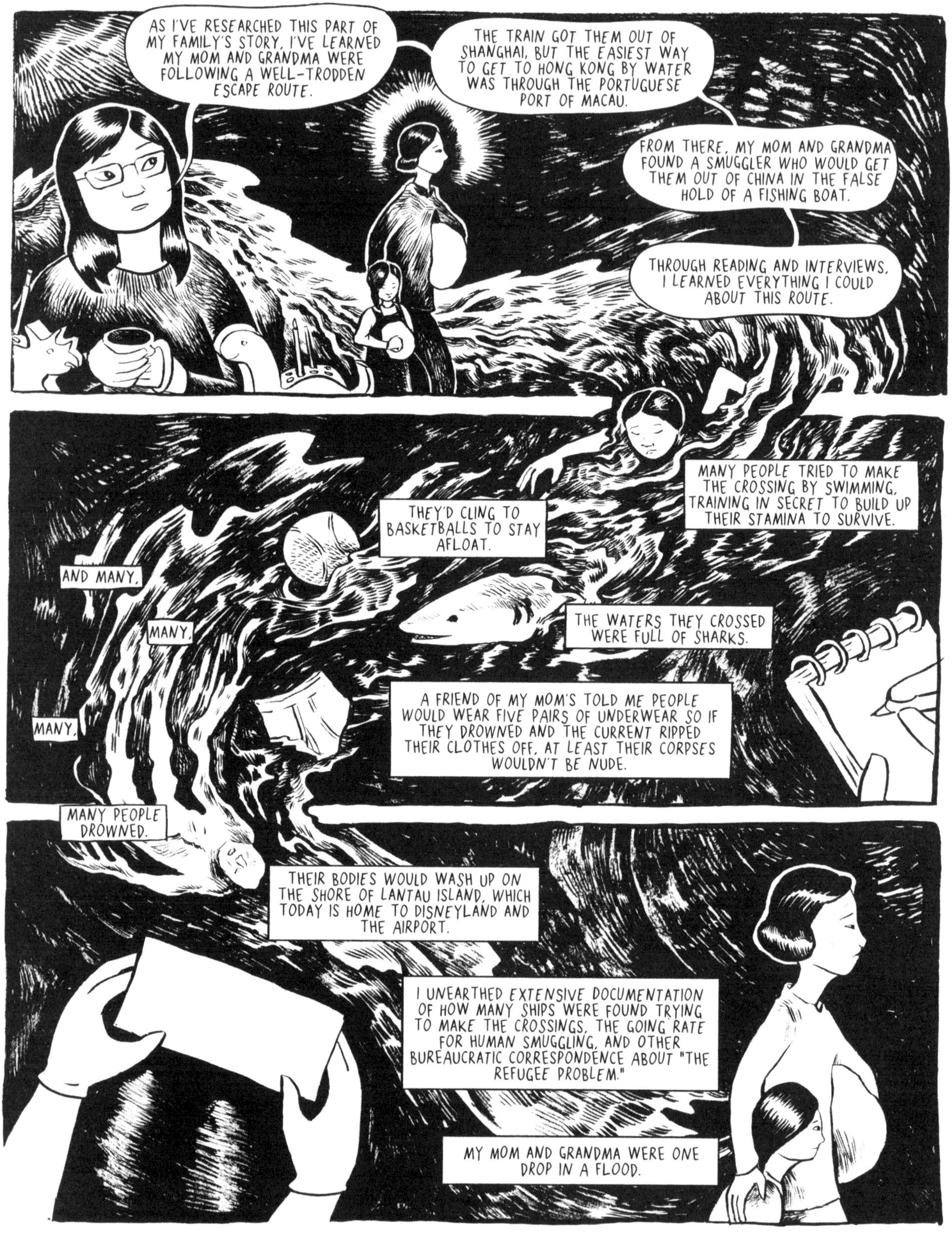
AS I'VE RESEARCHED THIS PART OF MY FAMILY'S STORY, I'VE LEARNED MY MOM AND GRANDMA WERE FOLLOWING A WELL-TRODDEN ESCAPE ROUTE.
THE TRAIN GOT THEM OUT OF SHANGHAI, BUT THE EASIEST WAY TO GET TO HONG KONG BY WATER WAS THROUGH THE PORTUGUESE PORT OF MACAU.
FROM THERE, MY MOM AND GRANDMA FOUND A SMUGGLER WHO WOULD GET THEM OUT OF CHINA IN THE FALSE HOLD OF A FISHING BOAT.
THROUGH READING AND INTERVIEWS, I LEARNED EVERYTHING I COULD ABOUT THIS ROUTE.
MANY PEOPLE TRIED TO MAKE THE CROSSING BY SWIMMING, TRAINING IN SECRET TO BUILD UP THEIR STAMINA TO SURVIVE.
THEY'D CLING TO BASKETBALLS TO STAY AFLOAT.
THE WATERS THEY CROSSED WERE FULL OF SHARKS.
A FRIEND OF MY MOM'S TOLD ME PEOPLE WOULD WEAR FIVE PAIRS OF UNDERWEAR SO IF THEY DROWNED AND THE CURRENT RIPPED THEIR CLOTHES OFF, AT LEAST THEIR CORPSES WOULDN'T BE NUDE.
AND MANY,
MANY,
MANY,
MANY PEOPLE DROWNED.
THEIR BODIES WOULD WASH UP ON THE SHORE OF LANTAU ISLAND, WHICH TODAY IS HOME TO DISNEYLAND AND THE AIRPORT.
I UNEARTHED EXTENSIVE DOCUMENTATION OF HOW MANY SHIPS WERE FOUND TRYING TO MAKE THE CROSSINGS, THE GOING RATE FOR HUMAN SMUGGLING, AND OTHER BUREAUCRATIC CORRESPONDENCE ABOUT "THE REFUGEE PROBLEM."
MY MOM AND GRANDMA WERE ONE DROP IN A FLOOD.

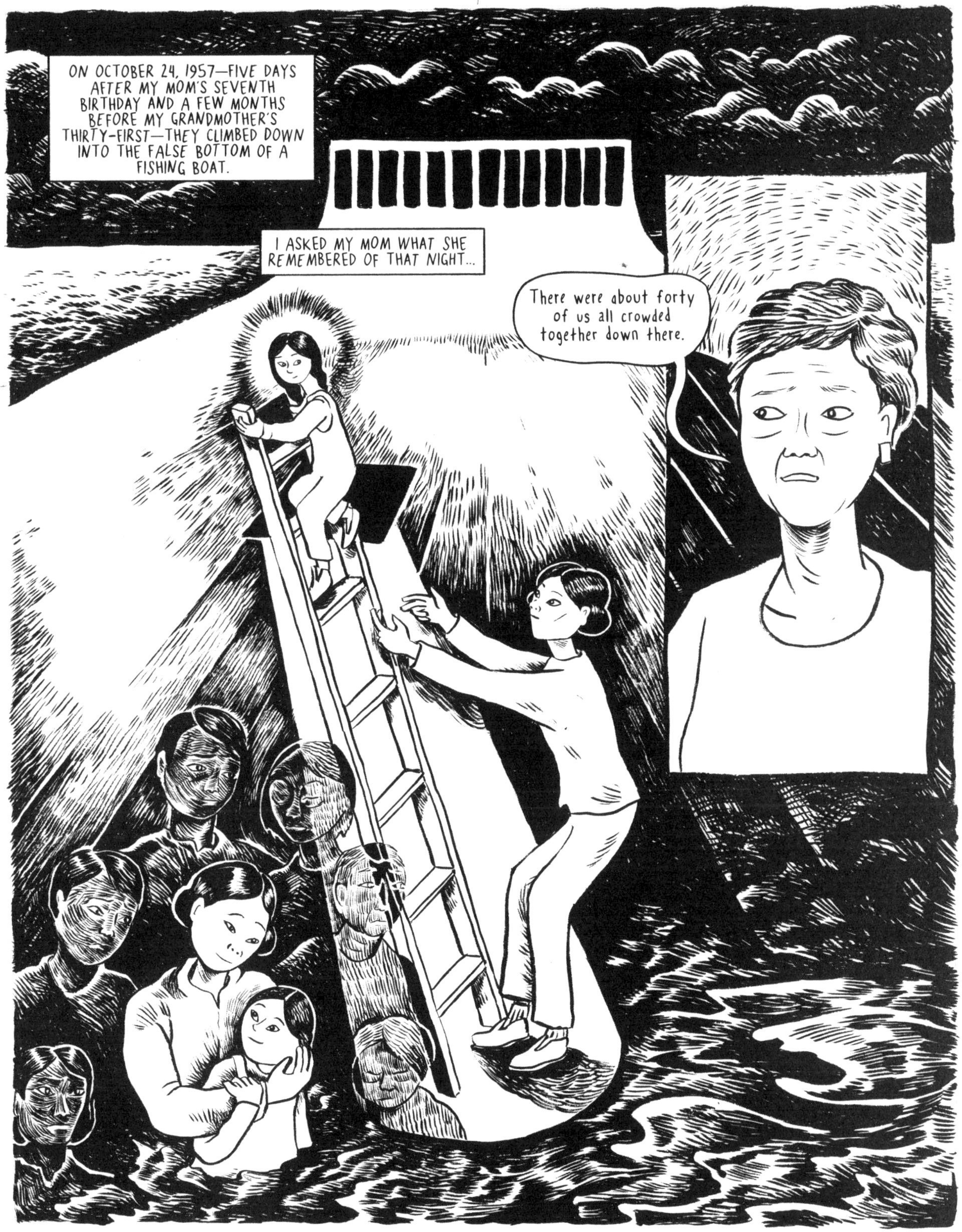
ON OCTOBER 24, 1957—FIVE DAYS AFTER MY MOM'S SEVENTH BIRTHDAY AND A FEW MONTHS BEFORE MY GRANDMOTHER'S THIRTY-FIRST—THEY CLIMBED DOWN INTO THE FALSE BOTTOM OF A FISHING BOAT.
I ASKED MY MOM WHAT SHE REMEMBERED OF THAT NIGHT...
There were about forty of us all crowded together down there.

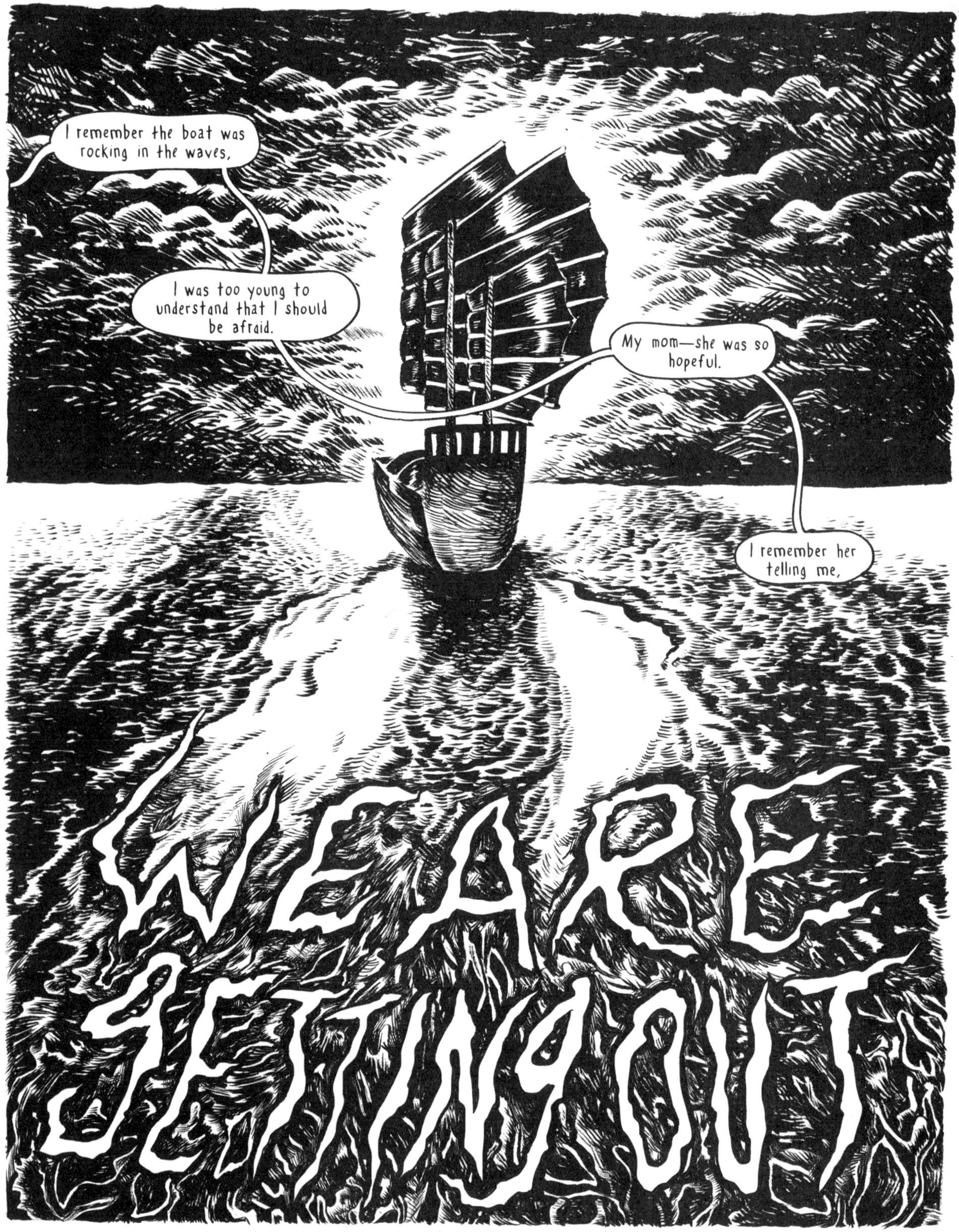

I remember the boat was rocking in the waves,
I was too young to understand that I should be afraid.
My mom—she was so hopeful.
I remember her telling me,
WE ARE GETTING OUT

PART 4

LIKE BREAD IN OUR CHILDREN'S MOUTHS

Hong Kong • 1957–1960

seeking a now that can breed
futures
like bread in our children's mouths
so their dreams will not reflect
the death of ours.

—AUDRE LORDE, **"A Litany for Survival"**

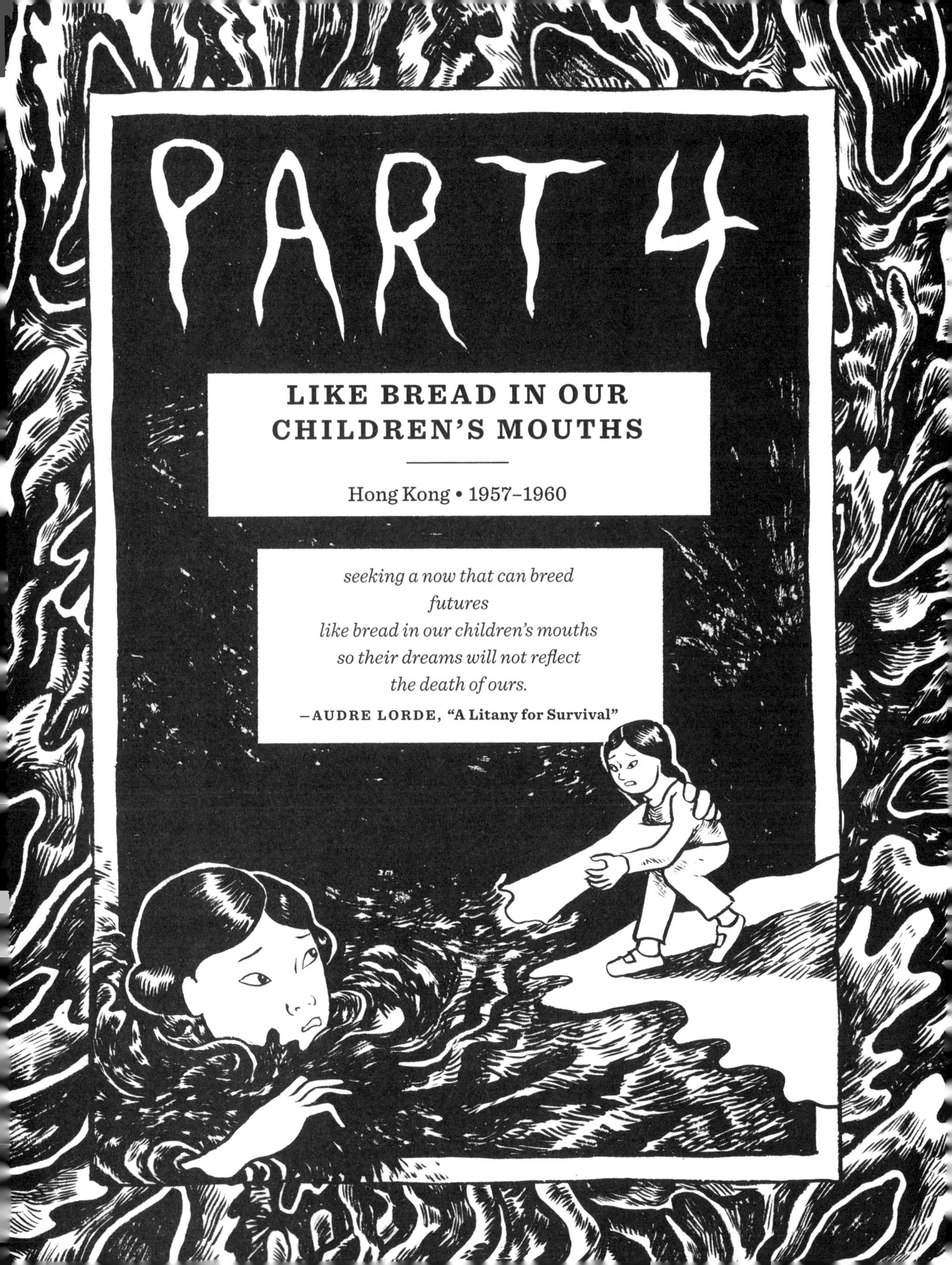

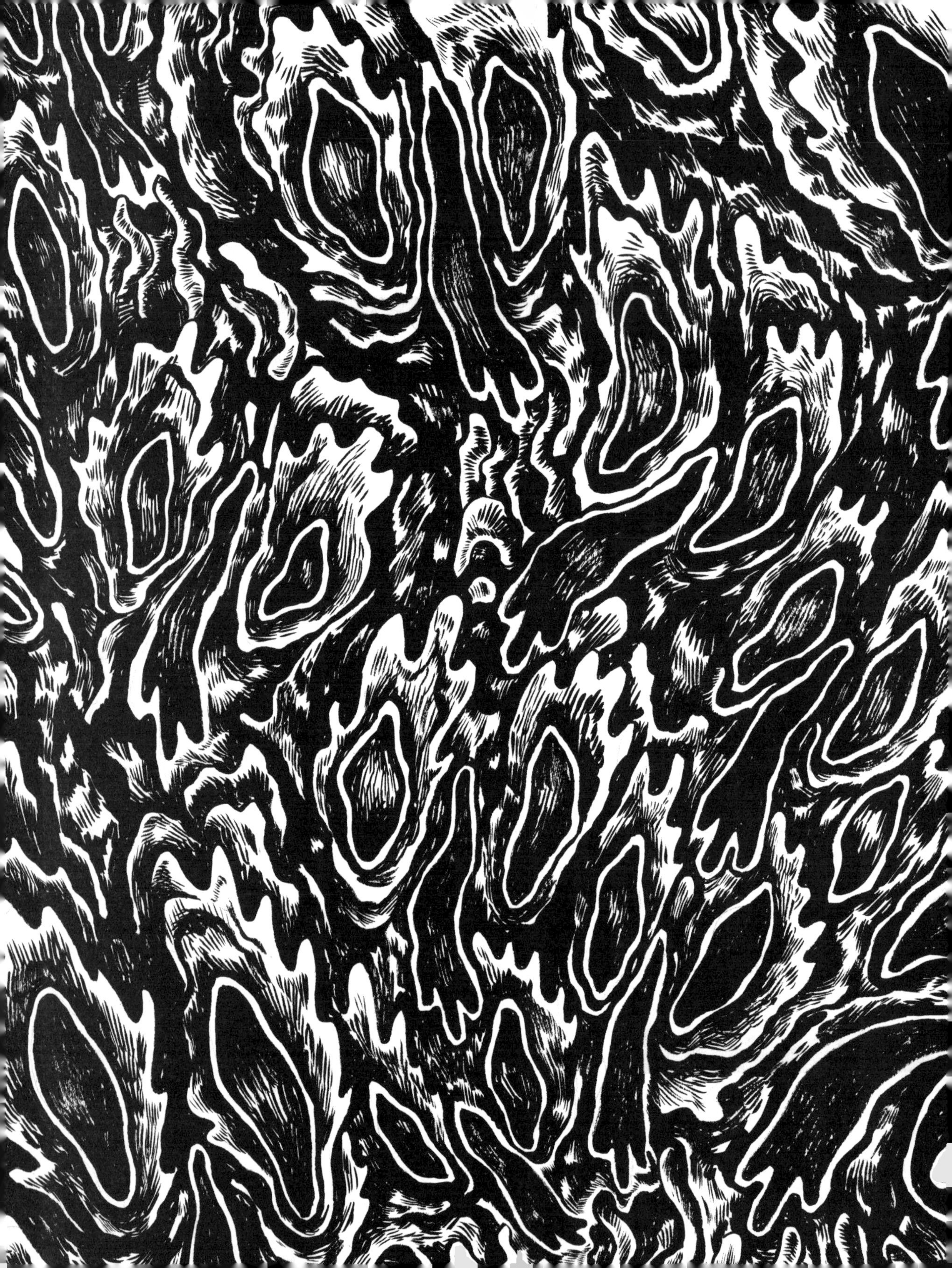

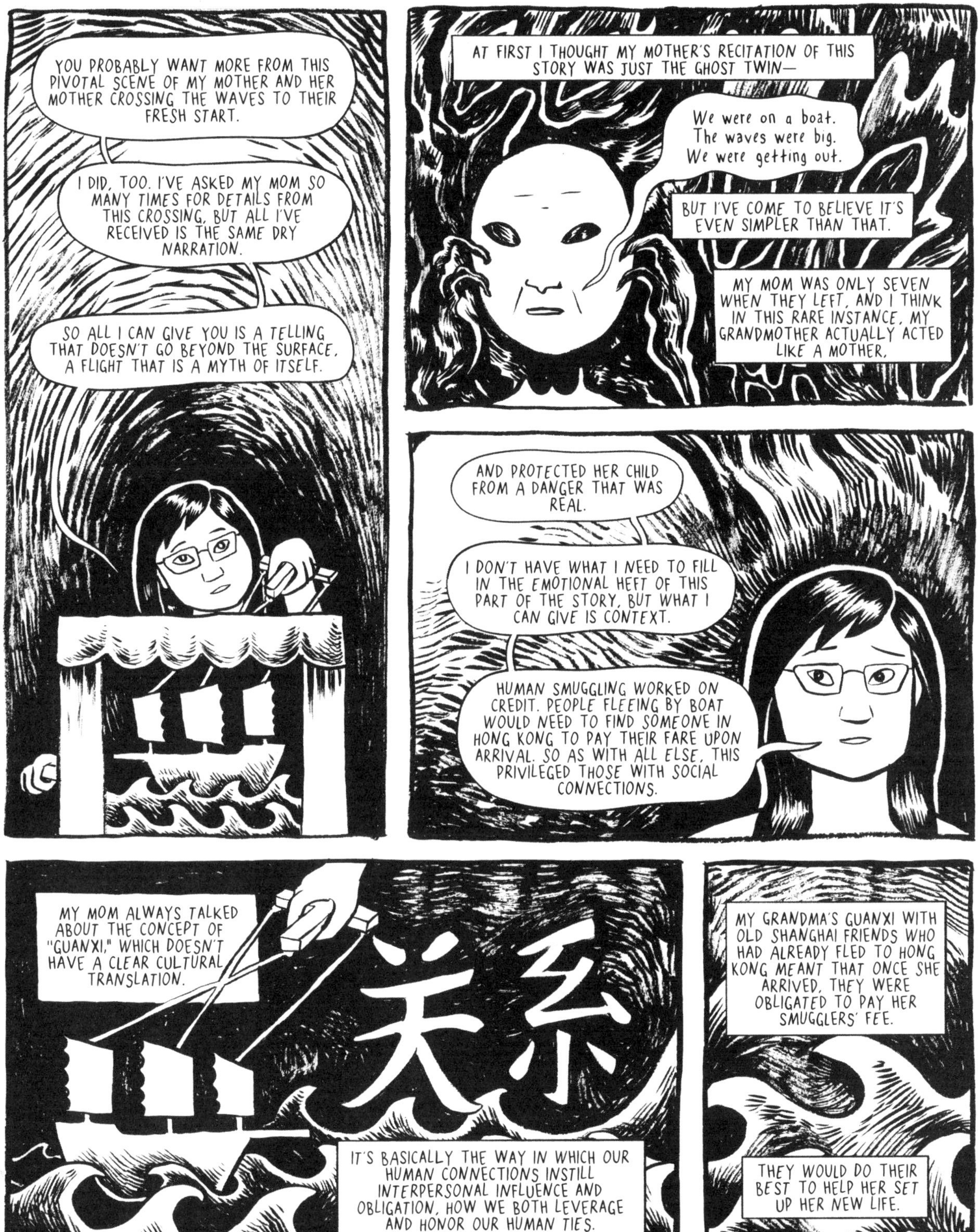
YOU PROBABLY WANT MORE FROM THIS PIVOTAL SCENE OF MY MOTHER AND HER MOTHER CROSSING THE WAVES TO THEIR FRESH START.
I DID, TOO. I'VE ASKED MY MOM SO MANY TIMES FOR DETAILS FROM THIS CROSSING, BUT ALL I'VE RECEIVED IS THE SAME DRY NARRATION.
SO ALL I CAN GIVE YOU IS A TELLING THAT DOESN'T GO BEYOND THE SURFACE, A FLIGHT THAT IS A MYTH OF ITSELF.
AT FIRST I THOUGHT MY MOTHER'S RECITATION OF THIS STORY WAS JUST THE GHOST TWIN—
We were on a boat. The waves were big. We were getting out.
BUT I'VE COME TO BELIEVE IT'S EVEN SIMPLER THAN THAT.
MY MOM WAS ONLY SEVEN WHEN THEY LEFT, AND I THINK IN THIS RARE INSTANCE, MY GRANDMOTHER ACTUALLY ACTED LIKE A MOTHER,
AND PROTECTED HER CHILD FROM A DANGER THAT WAS REAL.
I DON'T HAVE WHAT I NEED TO FILL IN THE EMOTIONAL HEFT OF THIS PART OF THE STORY, BUT WHAT I CAN GIVE IS CONTEXT.
HUMAN SMUGGLING WORKED ON CREDIT. PEOPLE FLEEING BY BOAT WOULD NEED TO FIND SOMEONE IN HONG KONG TO PAY THEIR FARE UPON ARRIVAL. SO AS WITH ALL ELSE, THIS PRIVILEGED THOSE WITH SOCIAL CONNECTIONS.
MY MOM ALWAYS TALKED ABOUT THE CONCEPT OF "GUANXI," WHICH DOESN'T HAVE A CLEAR CULTURAL TRANSLATION.
关系
IT'S BASICALLY THE WAY IN WHICH OUR HUMAN CONNECTIONS INSTILL INTERPERSONAL INFLUENCE AND OBLIGATION, HOW WE BOTH LEVERAGE AND HONOR OUR HUMAN TIES.
MY GRANDMA'S GUANXI WITH OLD SHANGHAI FRIENDS WHO HAD ALREADY FLED TO HONG KONG MEANT THAT ONCE SHE ARRIVED, THEY WERE OBLIGATED TO PAY HER SMUGGLERS' FEE.
THEY WOULD DO THEIR BEST TO HELP HER SET UP HER NEW LIFE.

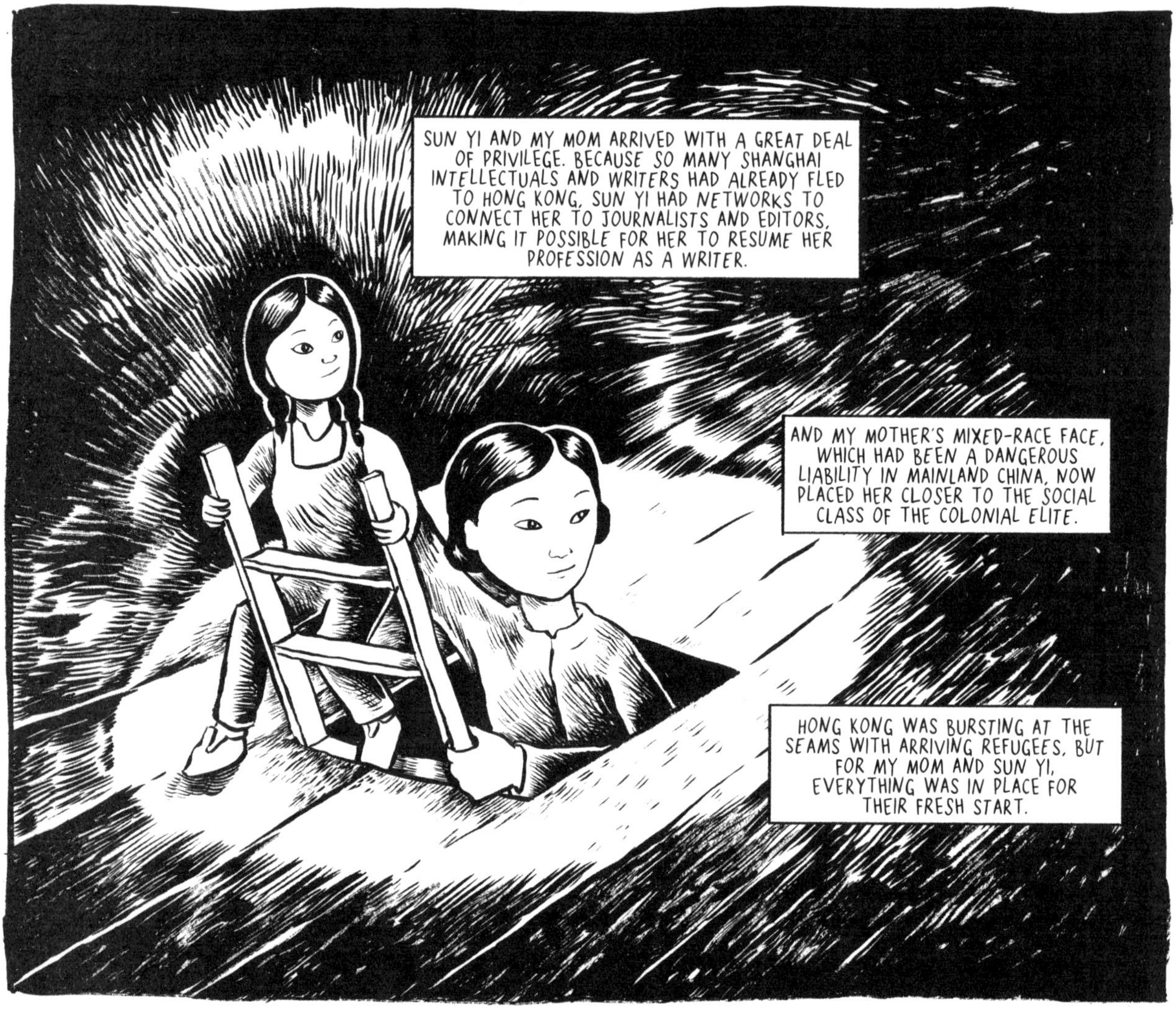
SUN YI AND MY MOM ARRIVED WITH A GREAT DEAL OF PRIVILEGE. BECAUSE SO MANY SHANGHAI INTELLECTUALS AND WRITERS HAD ALREADY FLED TO HONG KONG, SUN YI HAD NETWORKS TO CONNECT HER TO JOURNALISTS AND EDITORS, MAKING IT POSSIBLE FOR HER TO RESUME HER PROFESSION AS A WRITER.
AND MY MOTHER'S MIXED-RACE FACE, WHICH HAD BEEN A DANGEROUS LIABILITY IN MAINLAND CHINA, NOW PLACED HER CLOSER TO THE SOCIAL CLASS OF THE COLONIAL ELITE.
HONG KONG WAS BURSTING AT THE SEAMS WITH ARRIVING REFUGEES, BUT FOR MY MOM AND SUN YI, EVERYTHING WAS IN PLACE FOR THEIR FRESH START.

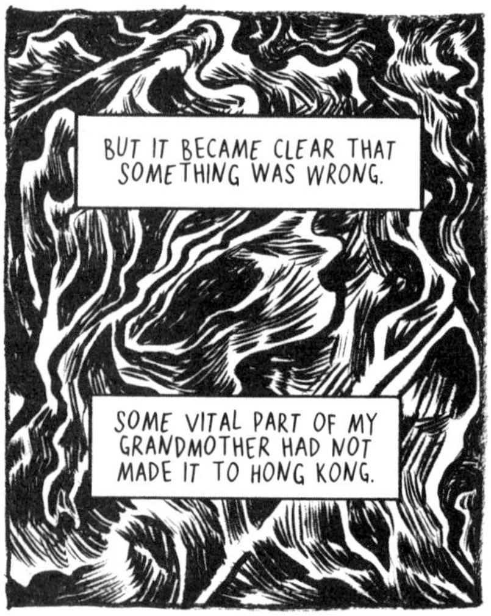
BUT IT BECAME CLEAR THAT SOMETHING WAS WRONG.
SOME VITAL PART OF MY GRANDMOTHER HAD NOT MADE IT TO HONG KONG.

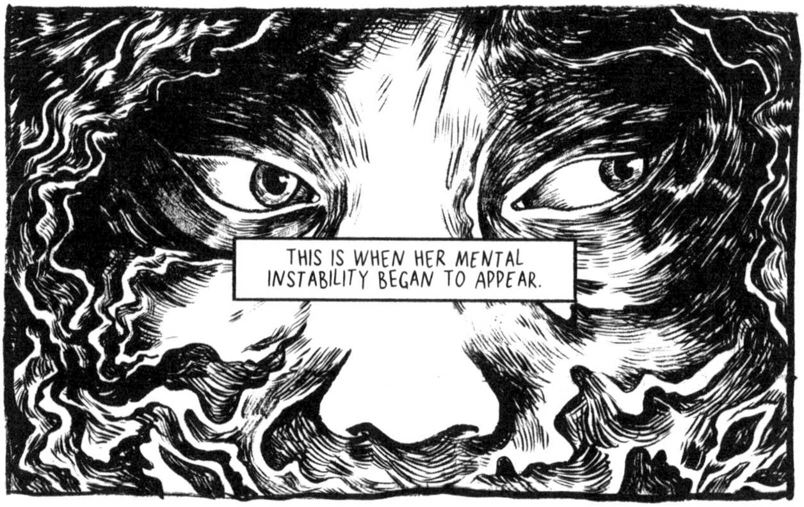
THIS IS WHEN HER MENTAL INSTABILITY BEGAN TO APPEAR.

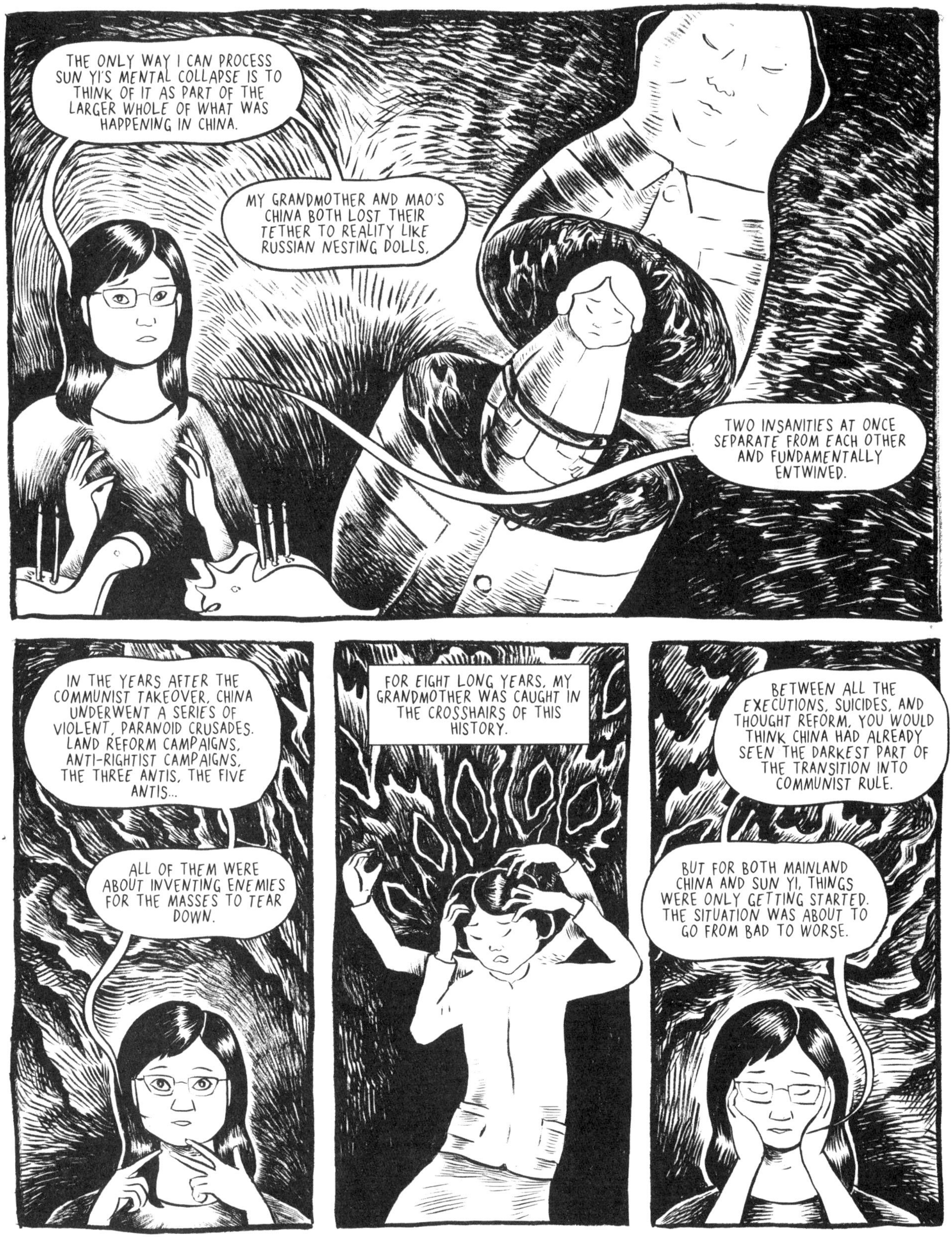
THE ONLY WAY I CAN PROCESS SUN YI'S MENTAL COLLAPSE IS TO THINK OF IT AS PART OF THE LARGER WHOLE OF WHAT WAS HAPPENING IN CHINA.
MY GRANDMOTHER AND MAO'S CHINA BOTH LOST THEIR TETHER TO REALITY LIKE RUSSIAN NESTING DOLLS,
TWO INSANITIES AT ONCE SEPARATE FROM EACH OTHER AND FUNDAMENTALLY ENTWINED.
IN THE YEARS AFTER THE COMMUNIST TAKEOVER, CHINA UNDERWENT A SERIES OF VIOLENT, PARANOID CRUSADES. LAND REFORM CAMPAIGNS, ANTI-RIGHTIST CAMPAIGNS, THE THREE ANTIS, THE FIVE ANTIS...
ALL OF THEM WERE ABOUT INVENTING ENEMIES FOR THE MASSES TO TEAR DOWN.
FOR EIGHT LONG YEARS, MY GRANDMOTHER WAS CAUGHT IN THE CROSSHAIRS OF THIS HISTORY.
BETWEEN ALL THE EXECUTIONS, SUICIDES, AND THOUGHT REFORM, YOU WOULD THINK CHINA HAD ALREADY SEEN THE DARKEST PART OF THE TRANSITION INTO COMMUNIST RULE.
BUT FOR BOTH MAINLAND CHINA AND SUN YI, THINGS WERE ONLY GETTING STARTED. THE SITUATION WAS ABOUT TO GO FROM BAD TO WORSE.

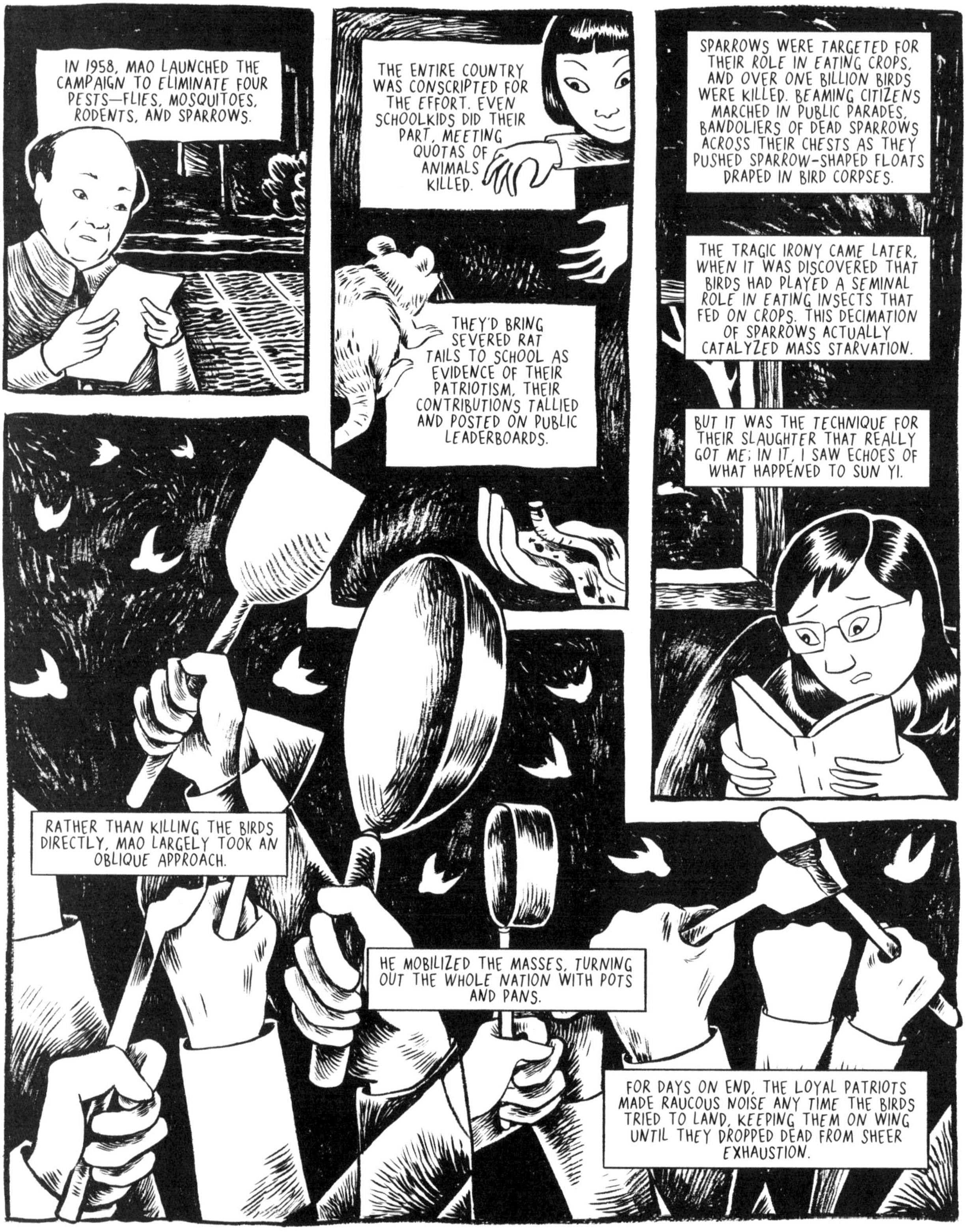
IN 1958, MAO LAUNCHED THE CAMPAIGN TO ELIMINATE FOUR PESTS—FLIES, MOSQUITOES, RODENTS, AND SPARROWS.
THE ENTIRE COUNTRY WAS CONSCRIPTED FOR THE EFFORT. EVEN SCHOOLKIDS DID THEIR PART, MEETING QUOTAS OF ANIMALS KILLED.
THEY'D BRING SEVERED RAT TAILS TO SCHOOL AS EVIDENCE OF THEIR PATRIOTISM, THEIR CONTRIBUTIONS TALLIED AND POSTED ON PUBLIC LEADERBOARDS.
SPARROWS WERE TARGETED FOR THEIR ROLE IN EATING CROPS, AND OVER ONE BILLION BIRDS WERE KILLED. BEAMING CITIZENS MARCHED IN PUBLIC PARADES, BANDOLIERS OF DEAD SPARROWS ACROSS THEIR CHESTS AS THEY PUSHED SPARROW-SHAPED FLOATS DRAPED IN BIRD CORPSES.
THE TRAGIC IRONY CAME LATER, WHEN IT WAS DISCOVERED THAT BIRDS HAD PLAYED A SEMINAL ROLE IN EATING INSECTS THAT FED ON CROPS. THIS DECIMATION OF SPARROWS ACTUALLY CATALYZED MASS STARVATION.
BUT IT WAS THE TECHNIQUE FOR THEIR SLAUGHTER THAT REALLY GOT ME; IN IT, I SAW ECHOES OF WHAT HAPPENED TO SUN YI.
RATHER THAN KILLING THE BIRDS DIRECTLY, MAO LARGELY TOOK AN OBLIQUE APPROACH.
HE MOBILIZED THE MASSES, TURNING OUT THE WHOLE NATION WITH POTS AND PANS.
FOR DAYS ON END, THE LOYAL PATRIOTS MADE RAUCOUS NOISE ANY TIME THE BIRDS TRIED TO LAND, KEEPING THEM ON WING UNTIL THEY DROPPED DEAD FROM SHEER EXHAUSTION.

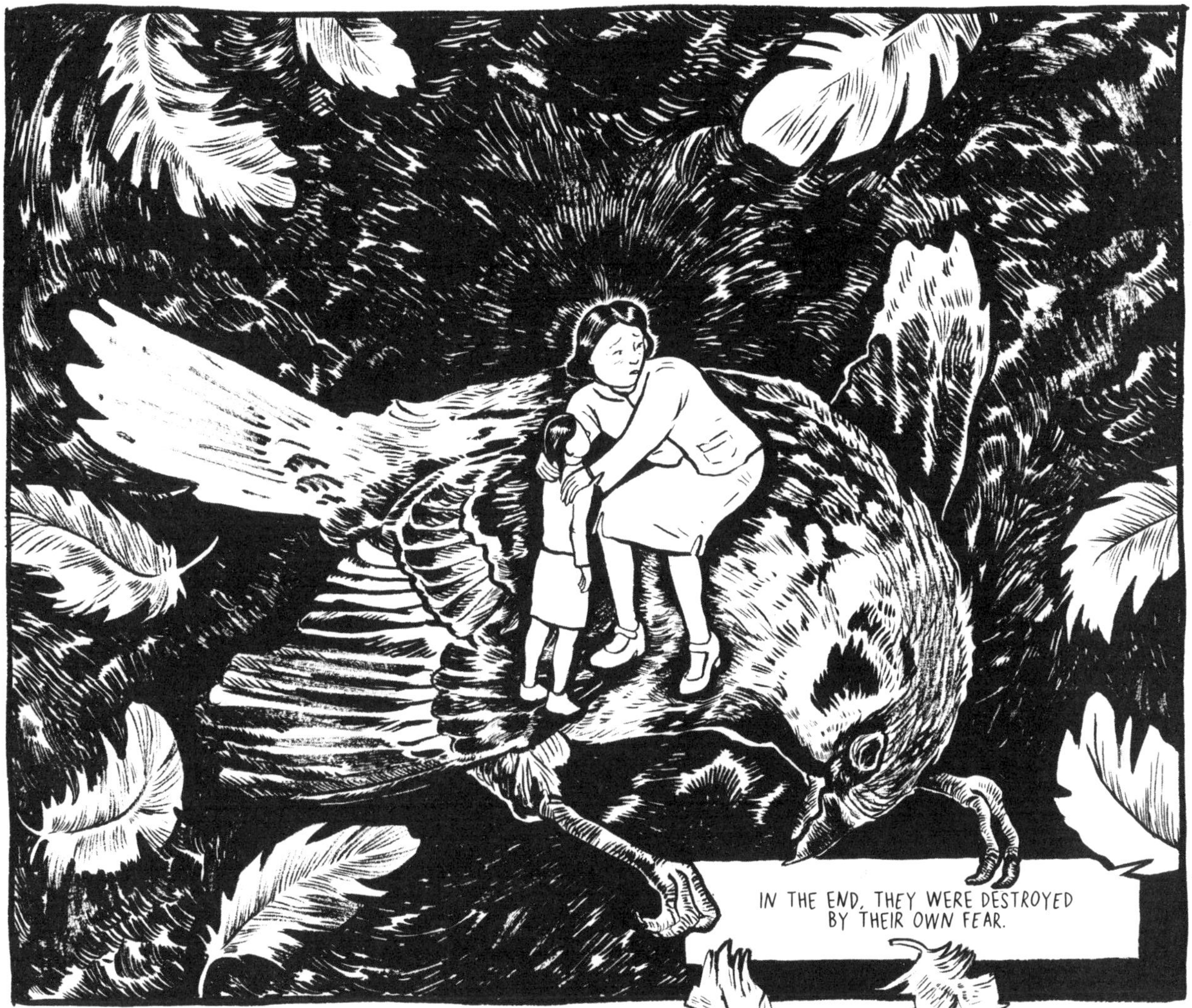
IN THE END, THEY WERE DESTROYED BY THEIR OWN FEAR.

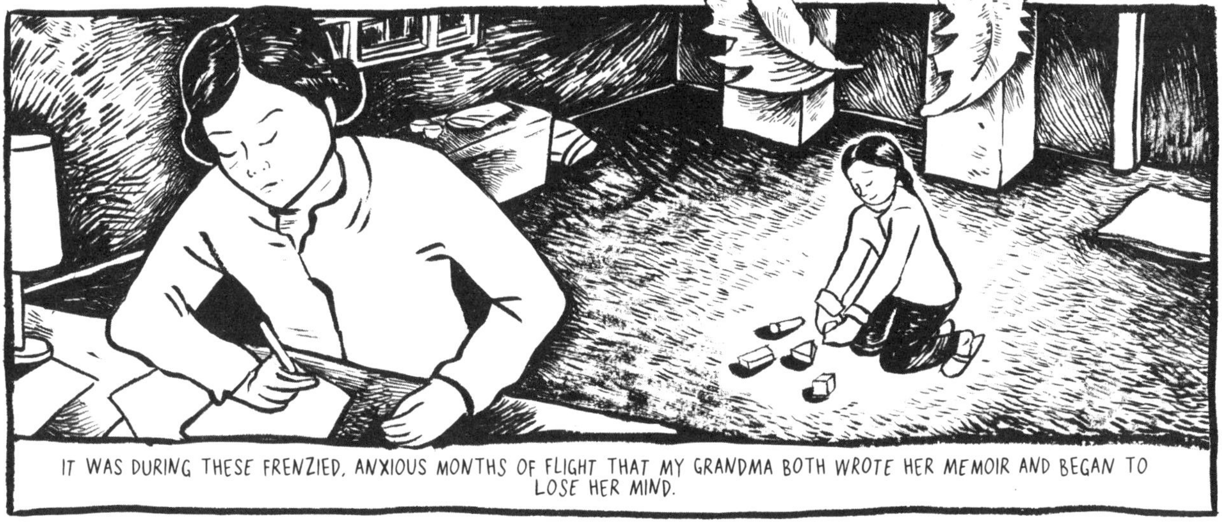
IT WAS DURING THESE FRENZIED, ANXIOUS MONTHS OF FLIGHT THAT MY GRANDMA BOTH WROTE HER MEMOIR AND BEGAN TO LOSE HER MIND.

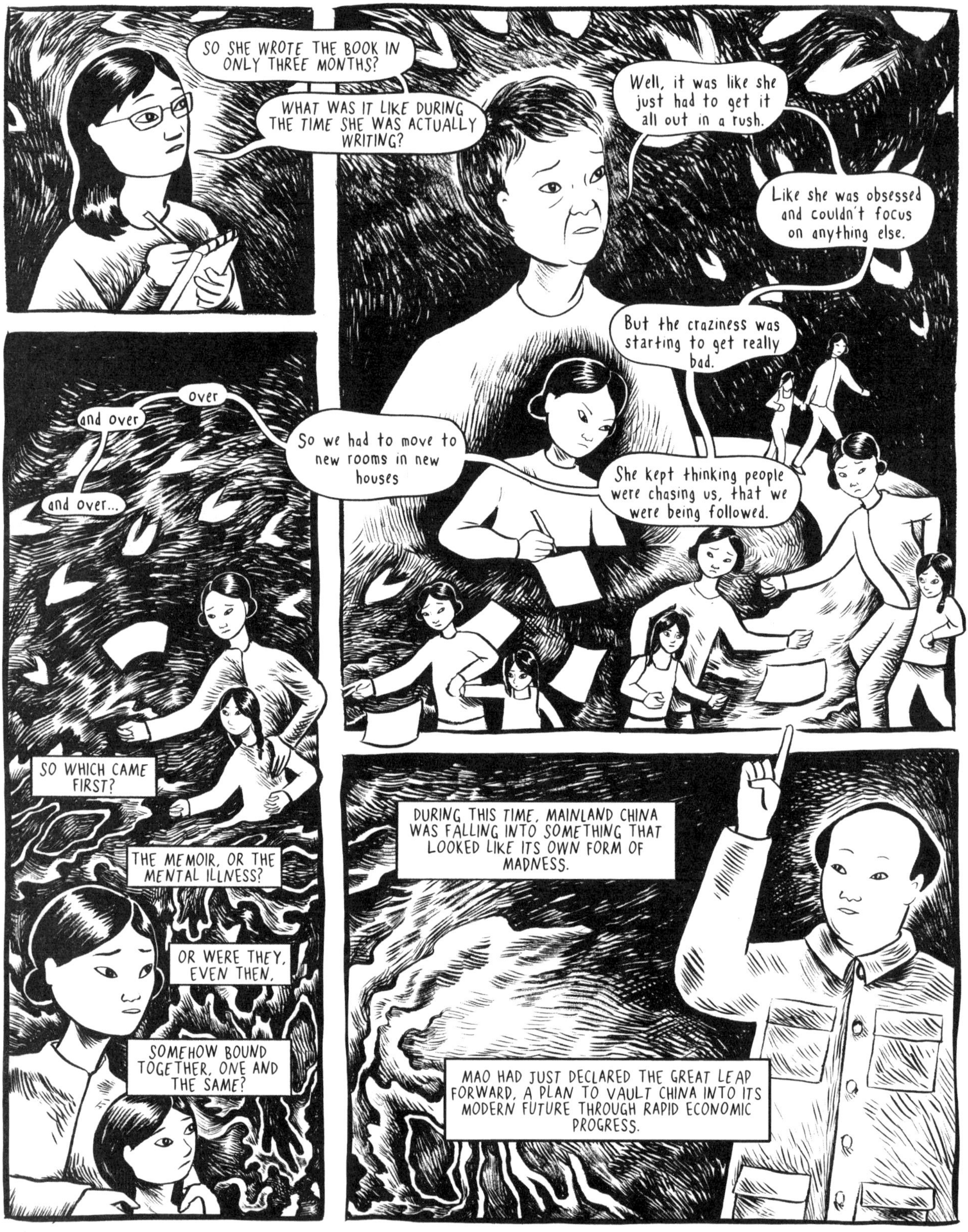
SO SHE WROTE THE BOOK IN ONLY THREE MONTHS?
WHAT WAS IT LIKE DURING THE TIME SHE WAS ACTUALLY WRITING?
Well, it was like she just had to get it all out in a rush.
Like she was obsessed and couldn't focus on anything else.
But the craziness was starting to get really bad.
So we had to move to new rooms in new houses
over
and over
and over...
She kept thinking people were chasing us, that we were being followed.
SO WHICH CAME FIRST?
THE MEMOIR, OR THE MENTAL ILLNESS?
OR WERE THEY, EVEN THEN,
SOMEHOW BOUND TOGETHER, ONE AND THE SAME?
DURING THIS TIME, MAINLAND CHINA WAS FALLING INTO SOMETHING THAT LOOKED LIKE ITS OWN FORM OF MADNESS.
MAO HAD JUST DECLARED THE GREAT LEAP FORWARD, A PLAN TO VAULT CHINA INTO ITS MODERN FUTURE THROUGH RAPID ECONOMIC PROGRESS.

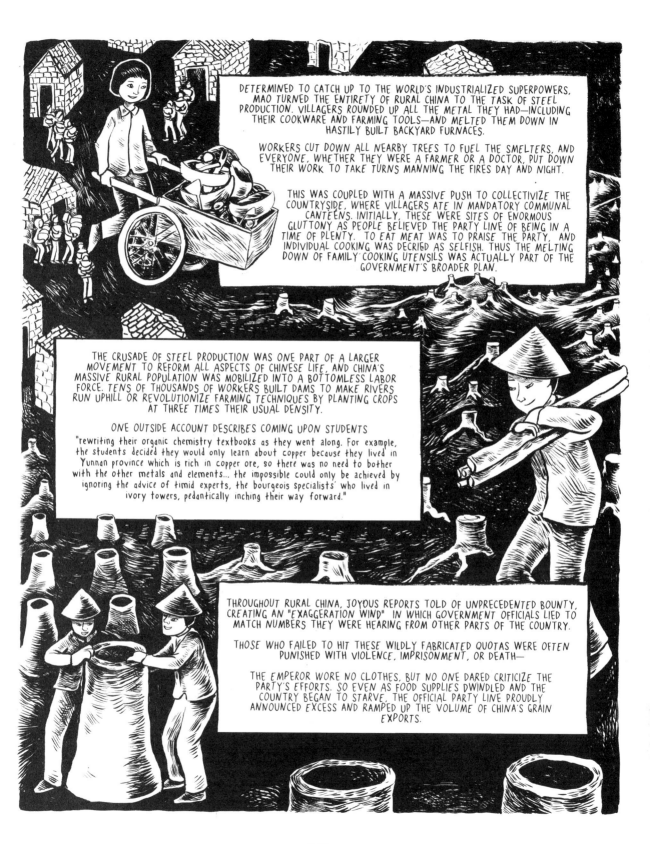

DETERMINED TO CATCH UP TO THE WORLD'S INDUSTRIALIZED SUPERPOWERS, MAO TURNED THE ENTIRETY OF RURAL CHINA TO THE TASK OF STEEL PRODUCTION. VILLAGERS ROUNDED UP ALL THE METAL THEY HAD—INCLUDING THEIR COOKWARE AND FARMING TOOLS—AND MELTED THEM DOWN IN HASTILY BUILT BACKYARD FURNACES.

WORKERS CUT DOWN ALL NEARBY TREES TO FUEL THE SMELTERS, AND EVERYONE, WHETHER THEY WERE A FARMER OR A DOCTOR, PUT DOWN THEIR WORK TO TAKE TURNS MANNING THE FIRES DAY AND NIGHT.

THIS WAS COUPLED WITH A MASSIVE PUSH TO COLLECTIVIZE THE COUNTRYSIDE, WHERE VILLAGERS ATE IN MANDATORY COMMUNAL CANTEENS. INITIALLY, THESE WERE SITES OF ENORMOUS GLUTTONY AS PEOPLE BELIEVED THE PARTY LINE OF BEING IN A TIME OF PLENTY. TO EAT MEAT WAS TO PRAISE THE PARTY, AND INDIVIDUAL COOKING WAS DECRIED AS SELFISH. THUS THE MELTING DOWN OF FAMILY COOKING UTENSILS WAS ACTUALLY PART OF THE GOVERNMENT'S BROADER PLAN.

THE CRUSADE OF STEEL PRODUCTION WAS ONE PART OF A LARGER MOVEMENT TO REFORM ALL ASPECTS OF CHINESE LIFE, AND CHINA'S MASSIVE RURAL POPULATION WAS MOBILIZED INTO A BOTTOMLESS LABOR FORCE. TENS OF THOUSANDS OF WORKERS BUILT DAMS TO MAKE RIVERS RUN UPHILL OR REVOLUTIONIZE FARMING TECHNIQUES BY PLANTING CROPS AT THREE TIMES THEIR USUAL DENSITY.

ONE OUTSIDE ACCOUNT DESCRIBES COMING UPON STUDENTS

"rewriting their organic chemistry textbooks as they went along. For example, the students decided they would only learn about copper because they lived in Yunnan province which is rich in copper ore, so there was no need to bother with the other metals and elements... the impossible could only be achieved by ignoring the advice of timid experts, the bourgeois specialists who lived in ivory towers, pedantically inching their way forward."

THROUGHOUT RURAL CHINA, JOYOUS REPORTS TOLD OF UNPRECEDENTED BOUNTY, CREATING AN "EXAGGERATION WIND" IN WHICH GOVERNMENT OFFICIALS LIED TO MATCH NUMBERS THEY WERE HEARING FROM OTHER PARTS OF THE COUNTRY.

THOSE WHO FAILED TO HIT THESE WILDLY FABRICATED QUOTAS WERE OFTEN PUNISHED WITH VIOLENCE, IMPRISONMENT, OR DEATH—

THE EMPEROR WORE NO CLOTHES, BUT NO ONE DARED CRITICIZE THE PARTY'S EFFORTS. SO EVEN AS FOOD SUPPLIES DWINDLED AND THE COUNTRY BEGAN TO STARVE, THE OFFICIAL PARTY LINE PROUDLY ANNOUNCED EXCESS AND RAMPED UP THE VOLUME OF CHINA'S GRAIN EXPORTS.

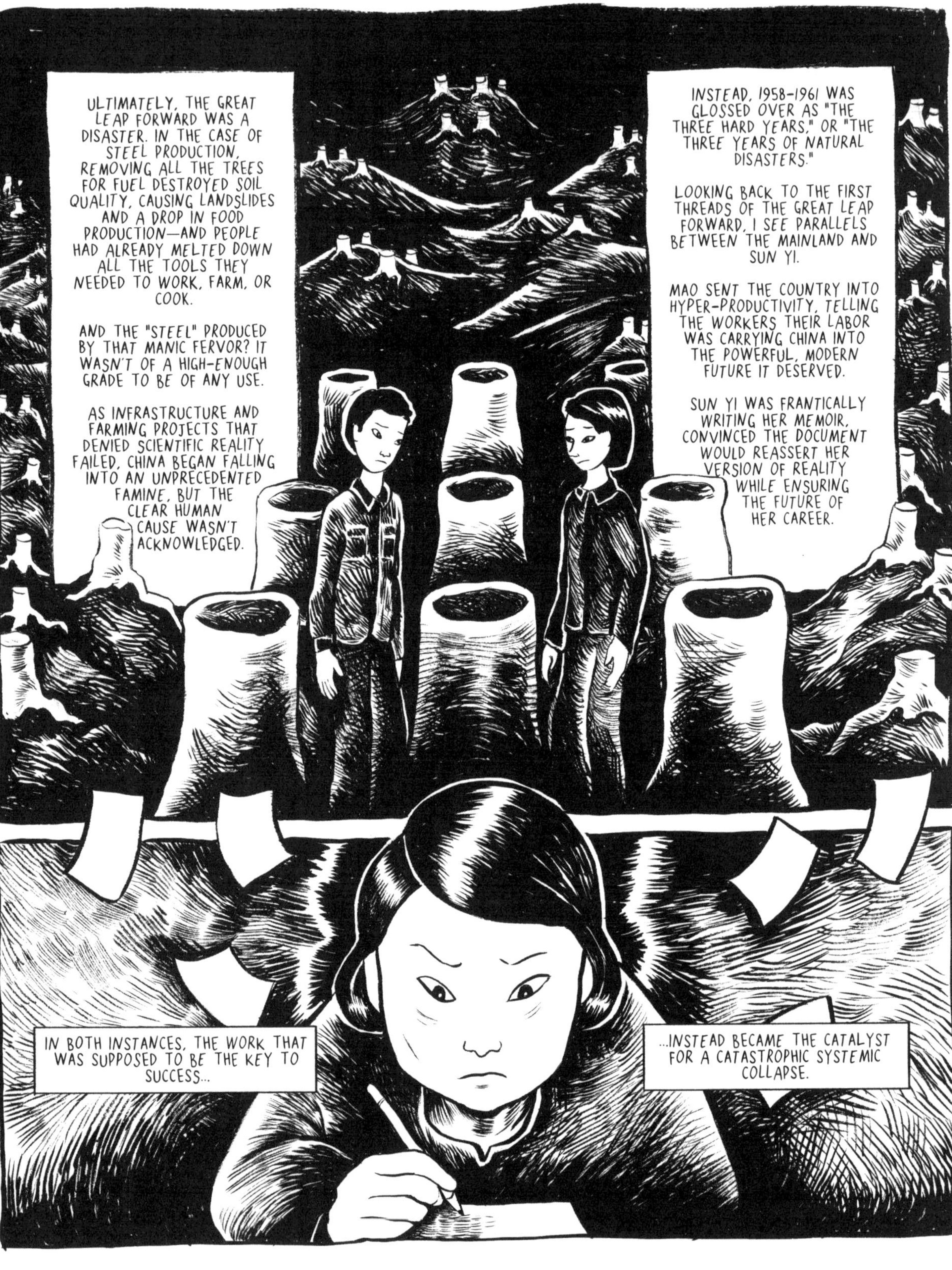
ULTIMATELY, THE GREAT LEAP FORWARD WAS A DISASTER. IN THE CASE OF STEEL PRODUCTION, REMOVING ALL THE TREES FOR FUEL DESTROYED SOIL QUALITY, CAUSING LANDSLIDES AND A DROP IN FOOD PRODUCTION—AND PEOPLE HAD ALREADY MELTED DOWN ALL THE TOOLS THEY NEEDED TO WORK, FARM, OR COOK.
AND THE "STEEL" PRODUCED BY THAT MANIC FERVOR? IT WASN'T OF A HIGH-ENOUGH GRADE TO BE OF ANY USE.
AS INFRASTRUCTURE AND FARMING PROJECTS THAT DENIED SCIENTIFIC REALITY FAILED, CHINA BEGAN FALLING INTO AN UNPRECEDENTED FAMINE, BUT THE CLEAR HUMAN CAUSE WASN'T ACKNOWLEDGED.
INSTEAD, 1958–1961 WAS GLOSSED OVER AS "THE THREE HARD YEARS," OR "THE THREE YEARS OF NATURAL DISASTERS."
LOOKING BACK TO THE FIRST THREADS OF THE GREAT LEAP FORWARD, I SEE PARALLELS BETWEEN THE MAINLAND AND SUN YI.
MAO SENT THE COUNTRY INTO HYPER-PRODUCTIVITY, TELLING THE WORKERS THEIR LABOR WAS CARRYING CHINA INTO THE POWERFUL, MODERN FUTURE IT DESERVED.
SUN YI WAS FRANTICALLY WRITING HER MEMOIR, CONVINCED THE DOCUMENT WOULD REASSERT HER VERSION OF REALITY WHILE ENSURING THE FUTURE OF HER CAREER.
IN BOTH INSTANCES, THE WORK THAT WAS SUPPOSED TO BE THE KEY TO SUCCESS...
...INSTEAD BECAME THE CATALYST FOR A CATASTROPHIC SYSTEMIC COLLAPSE.

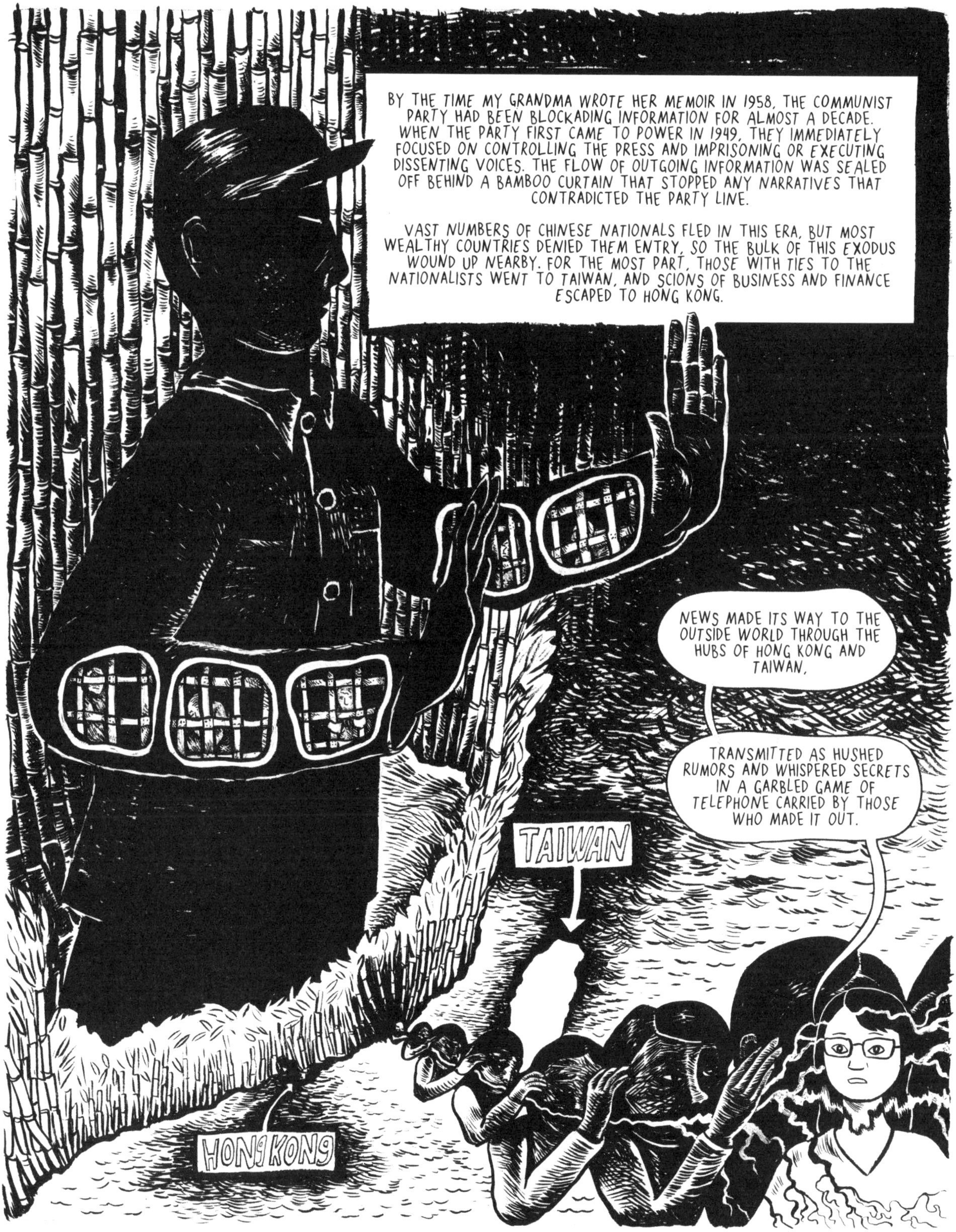
BY THE TIME MY GRANDMA WROTE HER MEMOIR IN 1958, THE COMMUNIST PARTY HAD BEEN BLOCKADING INFORMATION FOR ALMOST A DECADE. WHEN THE PARTY FIRST CAME TO POWER IN 1949, THEY IMMEDIATELY FOCUSED ON CONTROLLING THE PRESS AND IMPRISONING OR EXECUTING DISSENTING VOICES. THE FLOW OF OUTGOING INFORMATION WAS SEALED OFF BEHIND A BAMBOO CURTAIN THAT STOPPED ANY NARRATIVES THAT CONTRADICTED THE PARTY LINE.
VAST NUMBERS OF CHINESE NATIONALS FLED IN THIS ERA, BUT MOST WEALTHY COUNTRIES DENIED THEM ENTRY, SO THE BULK OF THIS EXODUS WOUND UP NEARBY. FOR THE MOST PART, THOSE WITH TIES TO THE NATIONALISTS WENT TO TAIWAN, AND SCIONS OF BUSINESS AND FINANCE ESCAPED TO HONG KONG.
NEWS MADE ITS WAY TO THE OUTSIDE WORLD THROUGH THE HUBS OF HONG KONG AND TAIWAN,
TRANSMITTED AS HUSHED RUMORS AND WHISPERED SECRETS IN A GARBLED GAME OF TELEPHONE CARRIED BY THOSE WHO MADE IT OUT.
TAIWAN
HONG KONG

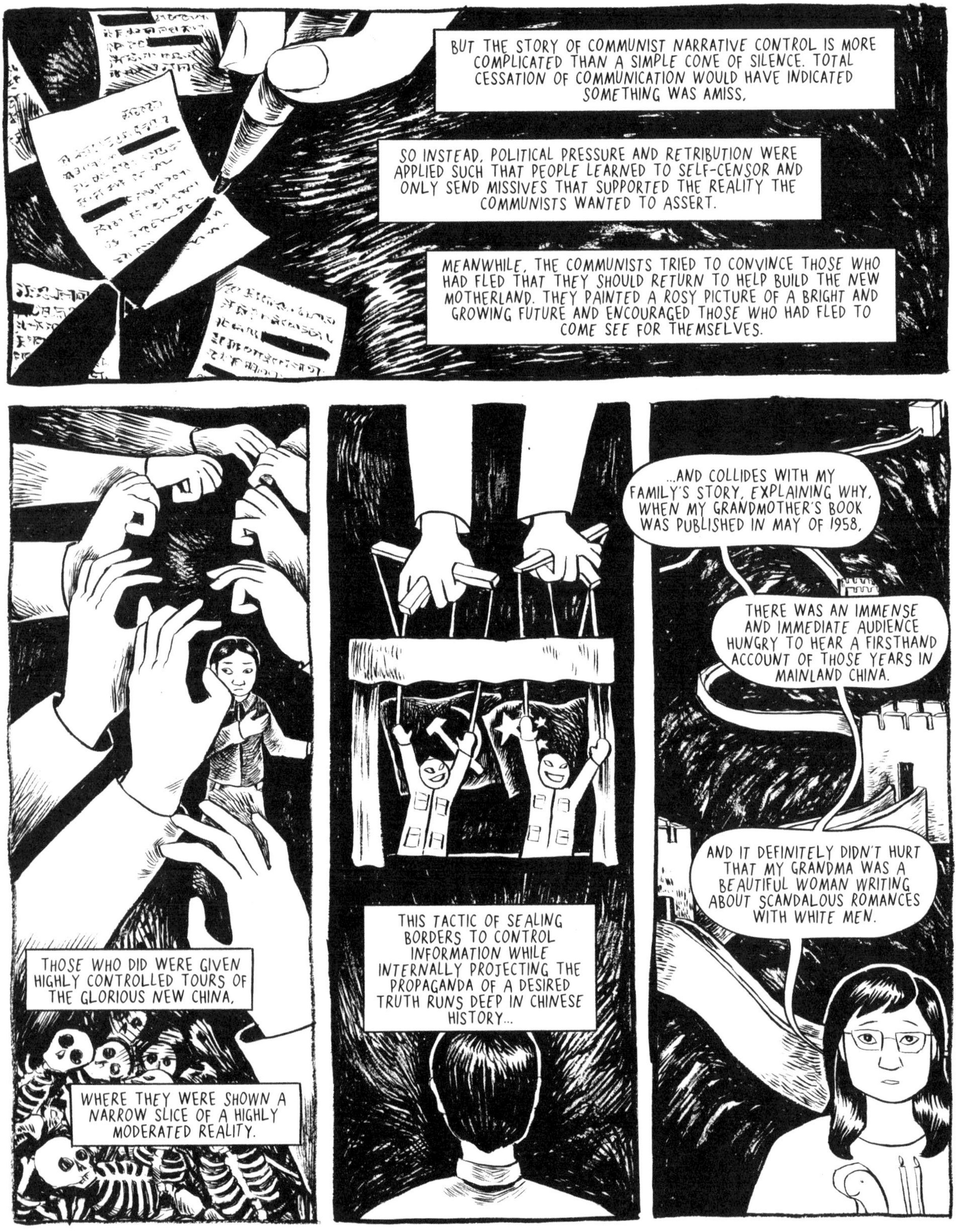
BUT THE STORY OF COMMUNIST NARRATIVE CONTROL IS MORE COMPLICATED THAN A SIMPLE CONE OF SILENCE. TOTAL CESSATION OF COMMUNICATION WOULD HAVE INDICATED SOMETHING WAS AMISS,
SO INSTEAD, POLITICAL PRESSURE AND RETRIBUTION WERE APPLIED SUCH THAT PEOPLE LEARNED TO SELF-CENSOR AND ONLY SEND MISSIVES THAT SUPPORTED THE REALITY THE COMMUNISTS WANTED TO ASSERT.
MEANWHILE, THE COMMUNISTS TRIED TO CONVINCE THOSE WHO HAD FLED THAT THEY SHOULD RETURN TO HELP BUILD THE NEW MOTHERLAND. THEY PAINTED A ROSY PICTURE OF A BRIGHT AND GROWING FUTURE AND ENCOURAGED THOSE WHO HAD FLED TO COME SEE FOR THEMSELVES.
THOSE WHO DID WERE GIVEN HIGHLY CONTROLLED TOURS OF THE GLORIOUS NEW CHINA,
WHERE THEY WERE SHOWN A NARROW SLICE OF A HIGHLY MODERATED REALITY.
THIS TACTIC OF SEALING BORDERS TO CONTROL INFORMATION WHILE INTERNALLY PROJECTING THE PROPAGANDA OF A DESIRED TRUTH RUNS DEEP IN CHINESE HISTORY...
...AND COLLIDES WITH MY FAMILY'S STORY, EXPLAINING WHY, WHEN MY GRANDMOTHER'S BOOK WAS PUBLISHED IN MAY OF 1958,
THERE WAS AN IMMENSE AND IMMEDIATE AUDIENCE HUNGRY TO HEAR A FIRSTHAND ACCOUNT OF THOSE YEARS IN MAINLAND CHINA.
AND IT DEFINITELY DIDN'T HURT THAT MY GRANDMA WAS A BEAUTIFUL WOMAN WRITING ABOUT SCANDALOUS ROMANCES WITH WHITE MEN.

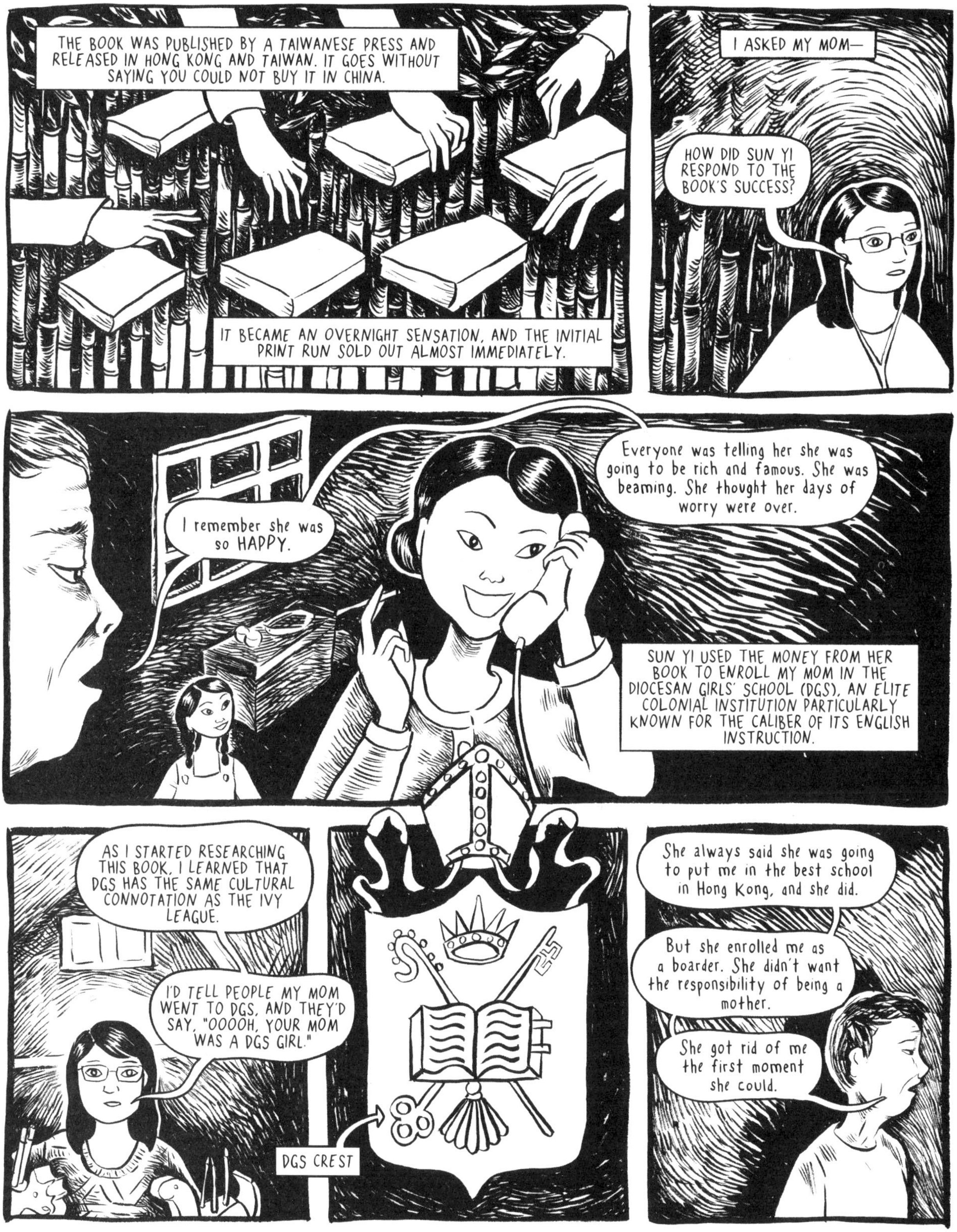
THE BOOK WAS PUBLISHED BY A TAIWANESE PRESS AND RELEASED IN HONG KONG AND TAIWAN. IT GOES WITHOUT SAYING YOU COULD NOT BUY IT IN CHINA.
IT BECAME AN OVERNIGHT SENSATION, AND THE INITIAL PRINT RUN SOLD OUT ALMOST IMMEDIATELY.
I ASKED MY MOM—
HOW DID SUN YI RESPOND TO THE BOOK'S SUCCESS?
I remember she was so HAPPY.
Everyone was telling her she was going to be rich and famous. She was beaming. She thought her days of worry were over.
SUN YI USED THE MONEY FROM HER BOOK TO ENROLL MY MOM IN THE DIOCESAN GIRLS' SCHOOL (DGS), AN ELITE COLONIAL INSTITUTION PARTICULARLY KNOWN FOR THE CALIBER OF ITS ENGLISH INSTRUCTION.
AS I STARTED RESEARCHING THIS BOOK, I LEARNED THAT DGS HAS THE SAME CULTURAL CONNOTATION AS THE IVY LEAGUE.
I'D TELL PEOPLE MY MOM WENT TO DGS, AND THEY'D SAY, "OOOOH, YOUR MOM WAS A DGS GIRL."
DGS CREST
She always said she was going to put me in the best school in Hong Kong, and she did.
But she enrolled me as a boarder. She didn't want the responsibility of being a mother.
She got rid of me the first moment she could.

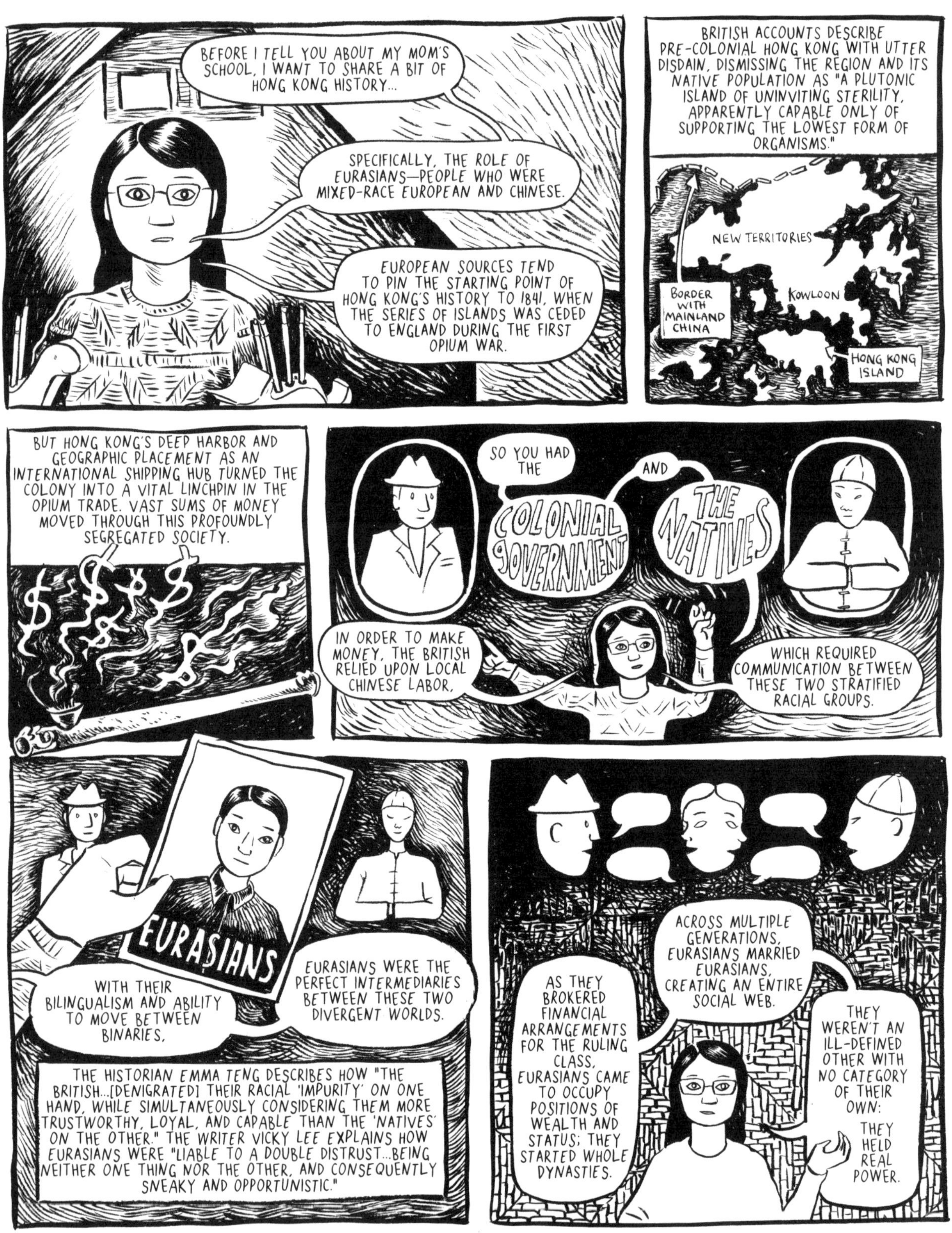

BEFORE I TELL YOU ABOUT MY MOM'S SCHOOL, I WANT TO SHARE A BIT OF HONG KONG HISTORY...
SPECIFICALLY, THE ROLE OF EURASIANS—PEOPLE WHO WERE MIXED-RACE EUROPEAN AND CHINESE.
EUROPEAN SOURCES TEND TO PIN THE STARTING POINT OF HONG KONG'S HISTORY TO 1841, WHEN THE SERIES OF ISLANDS WAS CEDED TO ENGLAND DURING THE FIRST OPIUM WAR.
BRITISH ACCOUNTS DESCRIBE PRE-COLONIAL HONG KONG WITH UTTER DISDAIN, DISMISSING THE REGION AND ITS NATIVE POPULATION AS "A PLUTONIC ISLAND OF UNINVITING STERILITY, APPARENTLY CAPABLE ONLY OF SUPPORTING THE LOWEST FORM OF ORGANISMS."
NEW TERRITORIES
BORDER WITH MAINLAND CHINA
KOWLOON
HONG KONG ISLAND
BUT HONG KONG'S DEEP HARBOR AND GEOGRAPHIC PLACEMENT AS AN INTERNATIONAL SHIPPING HUB TURNED THE COLONY INTO A VITAL LINCHPIN IN THE OPIUM TRADE. VAST SUMS OF MONEY MOVED THROUGH THIS PROFOUNDLY SEGREGATED SOCIETY.
SO YOU HAD THE
COLONIAL GOVERNMENT
AND
THE NATIVES
IN ORDER TO MAKE MONEY, THE BRITISH RELIED UPON LOCAL CHINESE LABOR,
WHICH REQUIRED COMMUNICATION BETWEEN THESE TWO STRATIFIED RACIAL GROUPS.
EURASIANS
WITH THEIR BILINGUALISM AND ABILITY TO MOVE BETWEEN BINARIES,
EURASIANS WERE THE PERFECT INTERMEDIARIES BETWEEN THESE TWO DIVERGENT WORLDS.
THE HISTORIAN EMMA TENG DESCRIBES HOW "THE BRITISH...[DENIGRATED] THEIR RACIAL 'IMPURITY' ON ONE HAND, WHILE SIMULTANEOUSLY CONSIDERING THEM MORE TRUSTWORTHY, LOYAL, AND CAPABLE THAN THE 'NATIVES' ON THE OTHER." THE WRITER VICKY LEE EXPLAINS HOW EURASIANS WERE "LIABLE TO A DOUBLE DISTRUST...BEING NEITHER ONE THING NOR THE OTHER, AND CONSEQUENTLY SNEAKY AND OPPORTUNISTIC."
AS THEY BROKERED FINANCIAL ARRANGEMENTS FOR THE RULING CLASS, EURASIANS CAME TO OCCUPY POSITIONS OF WEALTH AND STATUS; THEY STARTED WHOLE DYNASTIES.
ACROSS MULTIPLE GENERATIONS, EURASIANS MARRIED EURASIANS, CREATING AN ENTIRE SOCIAL WEB.
THEY WEREN'T AN ILL-DEFINED OTHER WITH NO CATEGORY OF THEIR OWN:
THEY HELD REAL POWER.

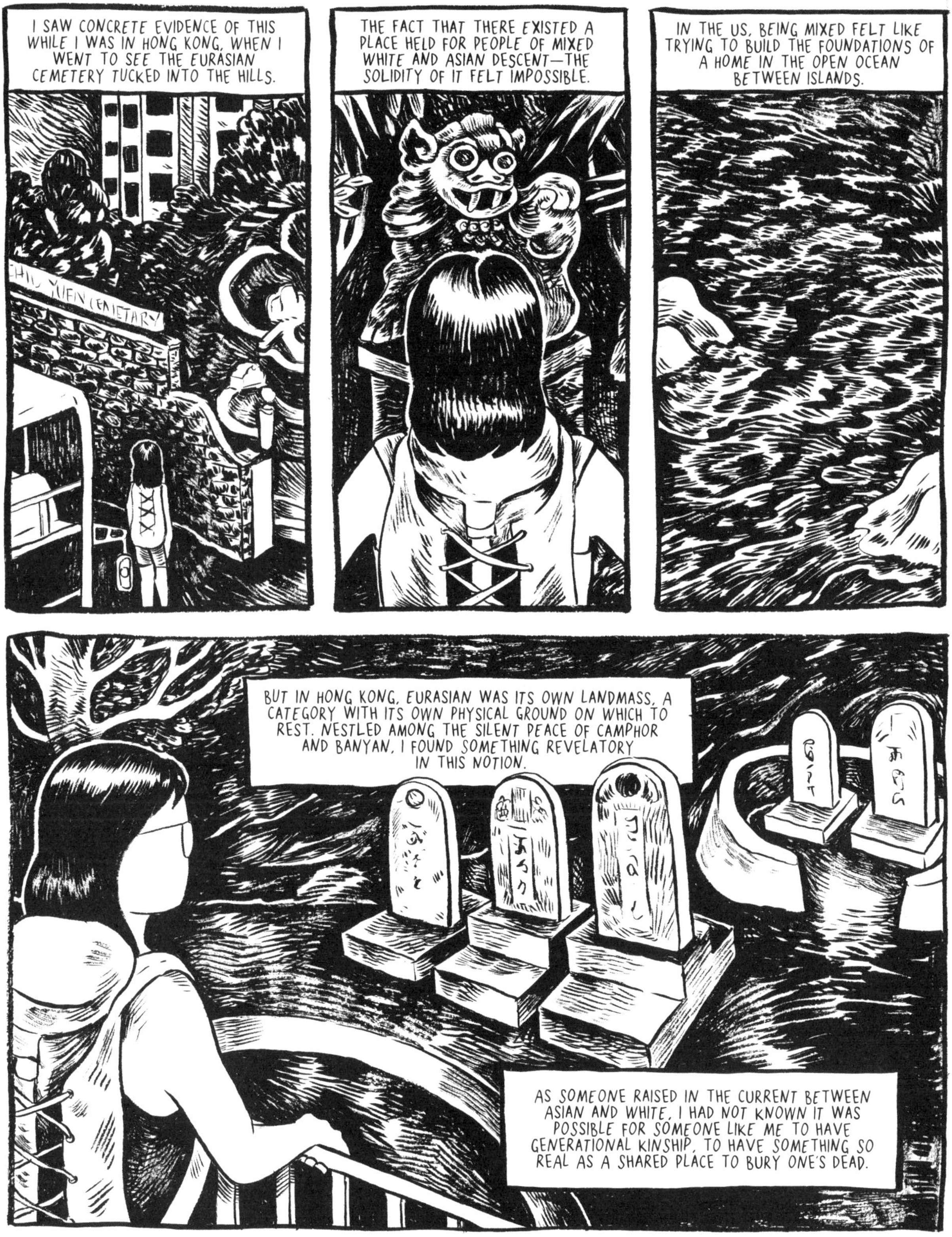
I SAW CONCRETE EVIDENCE OF THIS WHILE I WAS IN HONG KONG, WHEN I WENT TO SEE THE EURASIAN CEMETERY TUCKED INTO THE HILLS.
THE FACT THAT THERE EXISTED A PLACE HELD FOR PEOPLE OF MIXED WHITE AND ASIAN DESCENT—THE SOLIDITY OF IT FELT IMPOSSIBLE.
IN THE US, BEING MIXED FELT LIKE TRYING TO BUILD THE FOUNDATIONS OF A HOME IN THE OPEN OCEAN BETWEEN ISLANDS.
BUT IN HONG KONG, EURASIAN WAS ITS OWN LANDMASS, A CATEGORY WITH ITS OWN PHYSICAL GROUND ON WHICH TO REST. NESTLED AMONG THE SILENT PEACE OF CAMPHOR AND BANYAN, I FOUND SOMETHING REVELATORY IN THIS NOTION.
AS SOMEONE RAISED IN THE CURRENT BETWEEN ASIAN AND WHITE, I HAD NOT KNOWN IT WAS POSSIBLE FOR SOMEONE LIKE ME TO HAVE GENERATIONAL KINSHIP, TO HAVE SOMETHING SO REAL AS A SHARED PLACE TO BURY ONE'S DEAD.

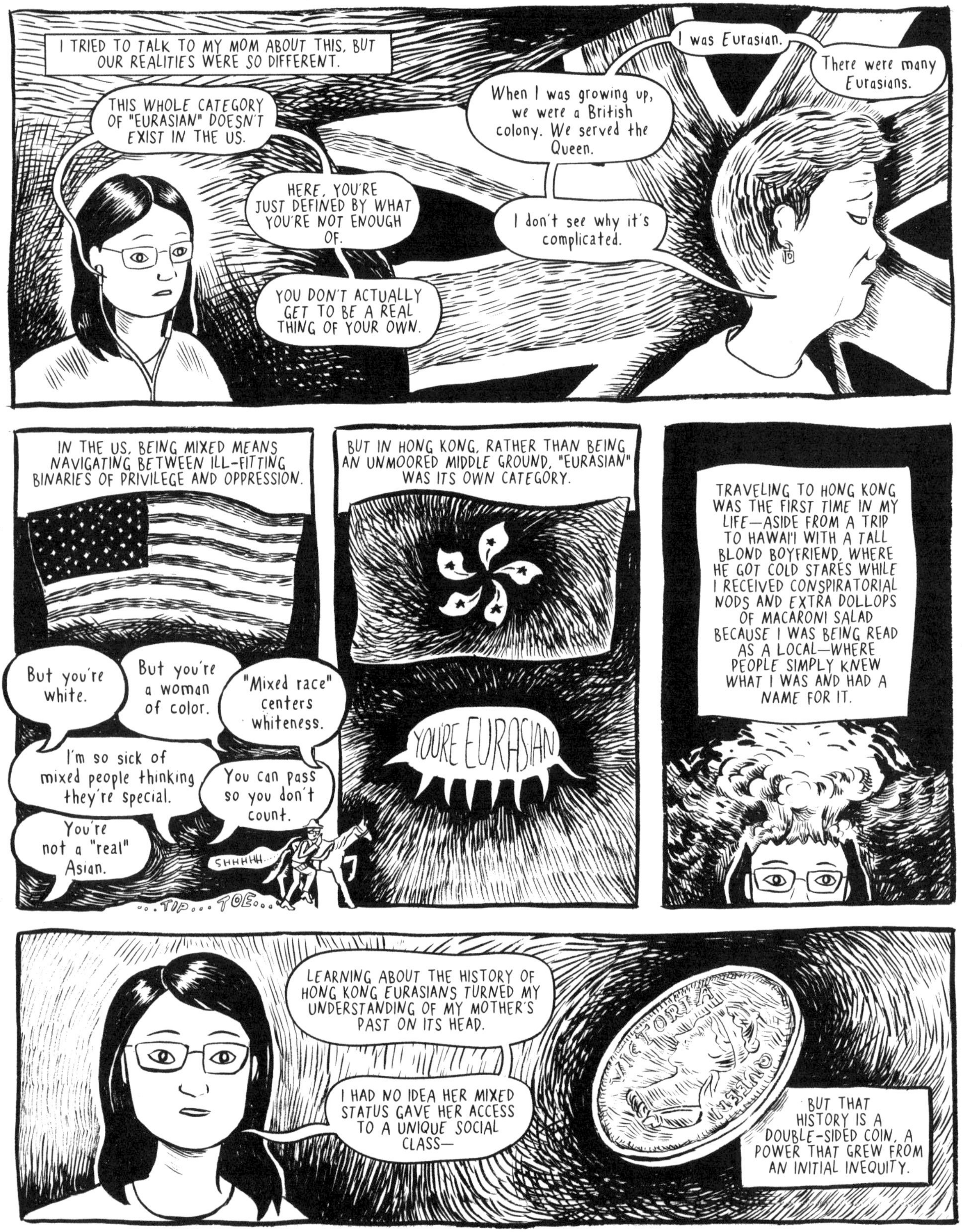
I TRIED TO TALK TO MY MOM ABOUT THIS, BUT OUR REALITIES WERE SO DIFFERENT.
THIS WHOLE CATEGORY OF "EURASIAN" DOESN'T EXIST IN THE US.
HERE, YOU'RE JUST DEFINED BY WHAT YOU'RE NOT ENOUGH OF.
YOU DON'T ACTUALLY GET TO BE A REAL THING OF YOUR OWN.
When I was growing up, we were a British colony. We served the Queen.
I was Eurasian.
There were many Eurasians.
I don't see why it's complicated.
IN THE US, BEING MIXED MEANS NAVIGATING BETWEEN ILL-FITTING BINARIES OF PRIVILEGE AND OPPRESSION.
But you're white.
But you're a woman of color.
"Mixed race" centers whiteness.
I'm so sick of mixed people thinking they're special.
You can pass so you don't count.
You're not a "real" Asian.
SHHHHH...
...TIP...TOE...
BUT IN HONG KONG, RATHER THAN BEING AN UNMOORED MIDDLE GROUND, "EURASIAN" WAS ITS OWN CATEGORY.
YOU'RE EURASIAN
TRAVELING TO HONG KONG WAS THE FIRST TIME IN MY LIFE—ASIDE FROM A TRIP TO HAWAI'I WITH A TALL BLOND BOYFRIEND, WHERE HE GOT COLD STARES WHILE I RECEIVED CONSPIRATORIAL NODS AND EXTRA DOLLOPS OF MACARONI SALAD BECAUSE I WAS BEING READ AS A LOCAL—WHERE PEOPLE SIMPLY KNEW WHAT I WAS AND HAD A NAME FOR IT.
LEARNING ABOUT THE HISTORY OF HONG KONG EURASIANS TURNED MY UNDERSTANDING OF MY MOTHER'S PAST ON ITS HEAD.
I HAD NO IDEA HER MIXED STATUS GAVE HER ACCESS TO A UNIQUE SOCIAL CLASS—
VICTORIA QUEEN
BUT THAT HISTORY IS A DOUBLE-SIDED COIN, A POWER THAT GREW FROM AN INITIAL INEQUITY.

THE EARLIEST ORIGINS OF HONG KONG'S EURASIAN COMMUNITY HAVE THEIR ROOTS IN SEX WORK, WITH WHITE MEN ENTERTAINING THEMSELVES WITH LOCAL WOMEN AS THEY PASSED THROUGH A PLACE THEY VIEWED AS TEMPORARY.

I FEEL RECOGNITION WITHIN THIS FACT; THIS IS, OF COURSE, WHY MY MOM EXISTS.

HONG KONG'S POPULATION SKEWED HEAVILY MALE. IN THE FIRST OFFICIAL CENSUS IN 1872, CHINESE MEN OUTNUMBERED CHINESE WOMEN SEVEN TO ONE.

MEN

WOMEN

PROSTITUTES

SOMETHING ELSE

...AND UNDER THE CATEGORY OF OCCUPATION, THE 1876 CENSUS LISTED FIVE OUT OF SIX CHINESE WOMEN AS PROSTITUTES.

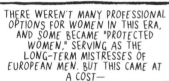

THERE WEREN'T MANY PROFESSIONAL OPTIONS FOR WOMEN IN THIS ERA, AND SOME BECAME "PROTECTED WOMEN," SERVING AS THE LONG-TERM MISTRESSES OF EUROPEAN MEN. BUT THIS CAME AT A COST—

"Most European men eventually returned home, leaving their Chinese mistresses in Hong Kong, where they were often despised by the mainstream of the Chinese community. The children of these women formed the beginnings of the Eurasian community."

THE EVOLUTION OF THIS EURASIAN COMMUNITY WAS SOMEWHAT PARADOXICAL...

ON THE ONE HAND, YOU HAD THE PRIVILEGED OFFSPRING OF INFLUENTIAL EURASIANS WITH POWERFUL BUSINESS TIES,

BUT YOU ALSO HAD THE IMPOVERISHED OFFSPRING OF CHINESE WOMEN ABANDONED BY WHITE MEN.

AS THE DYNASTIES OF PRIVILEGED EURASIANS GREW IN INFLUENCE, A NUMBER OF WEALTHY MALE EURASIANS BEGAN GATHERING TO DISCUSS WHAT TO DO WITH THIS PROBLEM OF FATHERLESS EURASIAN BASTARDS.

We Eurasians...being born into this world, belong to it...With the blood of Old China mixed with that of Europe in us

we can look after, not only ourselves, but also the destitute of our kith and kin.

THESE MEN ESTABLISHED THE EURASIAN WELFARE LEAGUE AND PUT RESOURCES INTO SUPPORTING THE EURASIAN COMMUNITY.

AND IN MY MOTHER'S SCHOOL, THESE TWO STORIES COLLIDE.
CHASING THREADS IN LIBRARIES AND ARCHIVES, I LEARNED DGS HELD DEEP TIES TO HONG KONG'S POWERFUL EURASIAN DYNASTIES AND WAS CONSIDERED THE SCHOOL FOR EURASIANS.
WHILE DGS EVENTUALLY BECAME ONE OF HONG KONG'S PREMIER EDUCATIONAL INSTITUTIONS, THE EARLIEST ITERATIONS OF THE SCHOOL GOING BACK TO THE 1860S WERE BASED IN CHARITY WORK AND CARING FOR THE DESTITUTE.
THE ROOTS OF THE DIOCESAN GIRLS' SCHOOL BEGAN AS A EURASIAN ORPHANAGE.
SUDDENLY THE PUZZLE PIECES SLID INTO PLACE. MY MOM AND SUN YI CAME TO HONG KONG DURING A MASSIVE INFLUX OF REFUGEES. EVERY FACET OF THE SOCIAL INFRASTRUCTURE WAS OVERBURDENED.
HARDLY ANY CHILDREN WERE ABLE TO ATTEND SCHOOL AT ALL. AND YET MY MOTHER, WHO DIDN'T YET SPEAK CANTONESE, WHO DIDN'T HAVE GUANXI WITH THE SOCIAL ELITE, WAS ACCEPTED INTO HONG KONG'S FINEST SCHOOL. I HADN'T UNDERSTOOD WHY—
UNTIL I TRACED BACK THE THREAD OF HISTORY AND LEARNED DGS WAS FOUNDED IN PART TO TAKE CARE OF PEOPLE LIKE HER. MY MOTHER WAS ONLY ACCEPTED BECAUSE OF HER WHITE FATHER AND THE FACT THAT HE HAD ABANDONED HER.
IT'S AMAZING, ISN'T IT? THE POWER OF THIS UNKNOWN WHITE FACE.
IT GRANTED MY MOM THE EDUCATION—MOST IMPORTANTLY THE ENGLISH—
THAT GAVE HER EVERYTHING.
WHEN I CONNECTED THE DOTS, THAT MY MOM WAS ACCEPTED AT DGS ONLY BECAUSE SHE WAS EURASIAN, I BROACHED MY THEORY TO HER TENTATIVELY, BUT—
Oh, it was stated as fact. When I misbehaved, my headmistress would yell at me, "The only reason you're at this school is because your mother went to bed with a white man!"

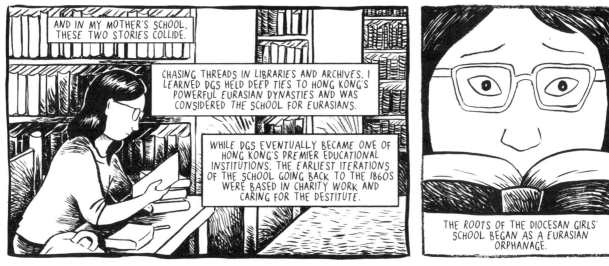

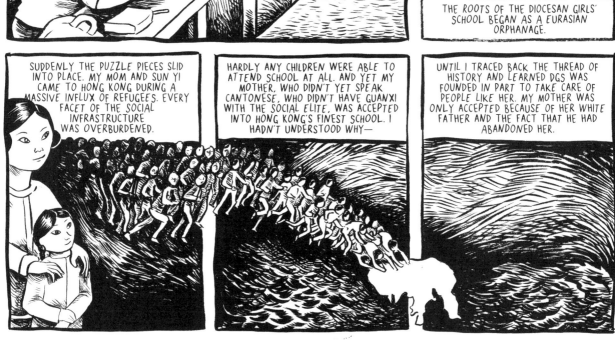

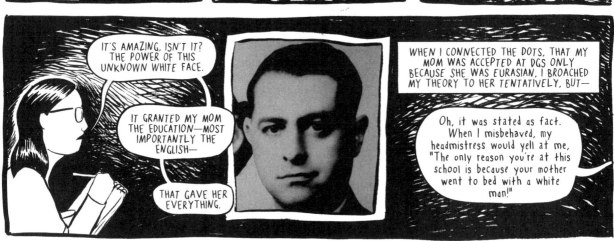

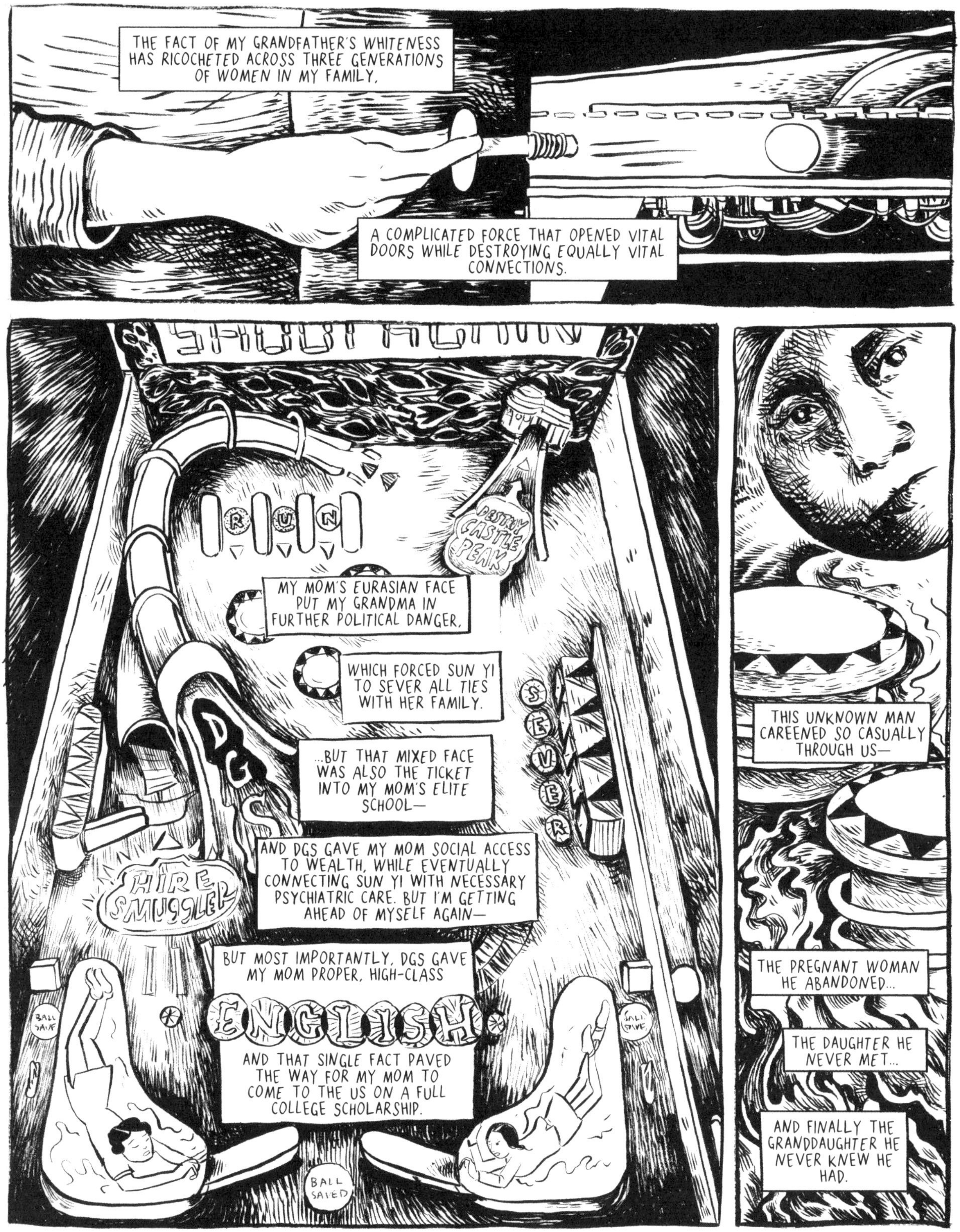
THE FACT OF MY GRANDFATHER'S WHITENESS HAS RICOCHETED ACROSS THREE GENERATIONS OF WOMEN IN MY FAMILY,
A COMPLICATED FORCE THAT OPENED VITAL DOORS WHILE DESTROYING EQUALLY VITAL CONNECTIONS.
RUN
DESTROY CASTLE PEAK
MY MOM'S EURASIAN FACE PUT MY GRANDMA IN FURTHER POLITICAL DANGER,
WHICH FORCED SUN YI TO SEVER ALL TIES WITH HER FAMILY.
SEVER
DGS
...BUT THAT MIXED FACE WAS ALSO THE TICKET INTO MY MOM'S ELITE SCHOOL—
HIRE SMUGGLER
AND DGS GAVE MY MOM SOCIAL ACCESS TO WEALTH, WHILE EVENTUALLY CONNECTING SUN YI WITH NECESSARY PSYCHIATRIC CARE. BUT I'M GETTING AHEAD OF MYSELF AGAIN—
BUT MOST IMPORTANTLY, DGS GAVE MY MOM PROPER, HIGH-CLASS
ENGLISH
AND THAT SINGLE FACT PAVED THE WAY FOR MY MOM TO COME TO THE US ON A FULL COLLEGE SCHOLARSHIP.
BALL SAVE
BALL SAVE
BALL SAVED
THIS UNKNOWN MAN CAREENED SO CASUALLY THROUGH US—
THE PREGNANT WOMAN HE ABANDONED...
THE DAUGHTER HE NEVER MET...
AND FINALLY THE GRANDDAUGHTER HE NEVER KNEW HE HAD.

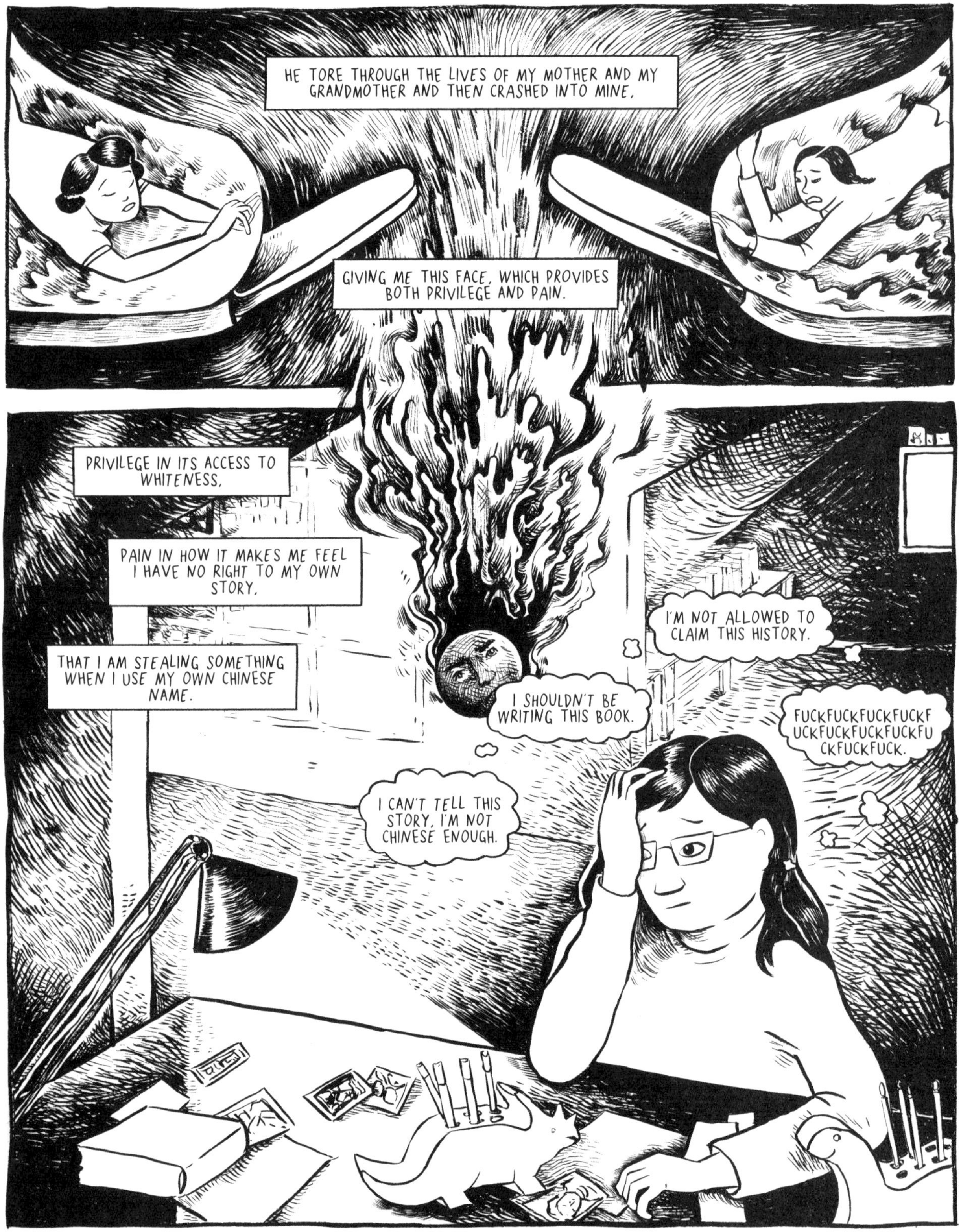
HE TORE THROUGH THE LIVES OF MY MOTHER AND MY GRANDMOTHER AND THEN CRASHED INTO MINE.
GIVING ME THIS FACE, WHICH PROVIDES BOTH PRIVILEGE AND PAIN.
PRIVILEGE IN ITS ACCESS TO WHITENESS.
PAIN IN HOW IT MAKES ME FEEL I HAVE NO RIGHT TO MY OWN STORY.
THAT I AM STEALING SOMETHING WHEN I USE MY OWN CHINESE NAME.
I'M NOT ALLOWED TO CLAIM THIS HISTORY.
I SHOULDN'T BE WRITING THIS BOOK.
FUCKFUCKFUCKFUCKFUCKFUCKFUCKFUCKFUCKFUCK.
I CAN'T TELL THIS STORY, I'M NOT CHINESE ENOUGH.

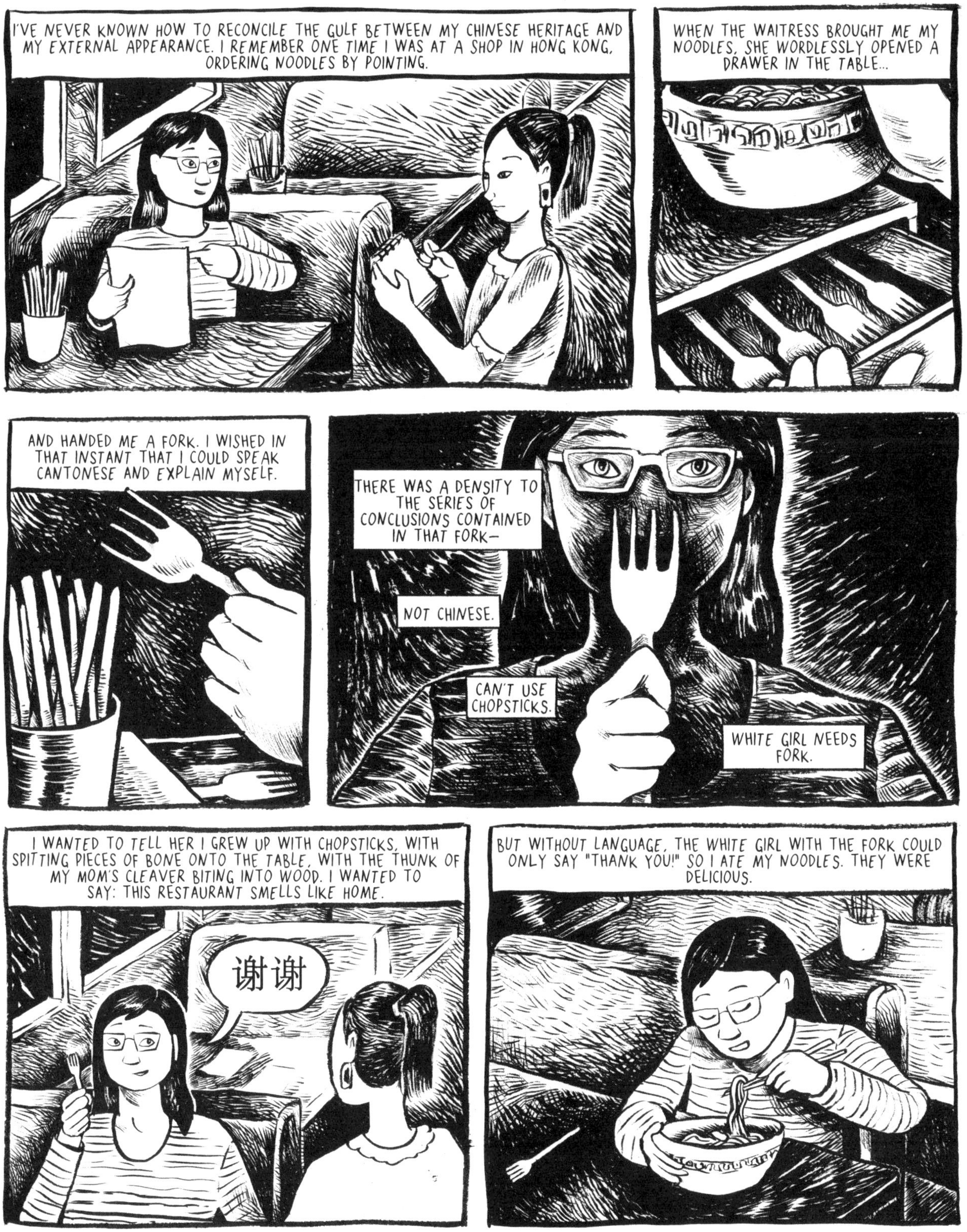
I'VE NEVER KNOWN HOW TO RECONCILE THE GULF BETWEEN MY CHINESE HERITAGE AND MY EXTERNAL APPEARANCE. I REMEMBER ONE TIME I WAS AT A SHOP IN HONG KONG, ORDERING NOODLES BY POINTING.
WHEN THE WAITRESS BROUGHT ME MY NOODLES, SHE WORDLESSLY OPENED A DRAWER IN THE TABLE...
AND HANDED ME A FORK. I WISHED IN THAT INSTANT THAT I COULD SPEAK CANTONESE AND EXPLAIN MYSELF.
THERE WAS A DENSITY TO THE SERIES OF CONCLUSIONS CONTAINED IN THAT FORK—
NOT CHINESE.
CAN'T USE CHOPSTICKS.
WHITE GIRL NEEDS FORK.
I WANTED TO TELL HER I GREW UP WITH CHOPSTICKS, WITH SPITTING PIECES OF BONE ONTO THE TABLE, WITH THE THUNK OF MY MOM'S CLEAVER BITING INTO WOOD. I WANTED TO SAY: THIS RESTAURANT SMELLS LIKE HOME.
谢谢
BUT WITHOUT LANGUAGE, THE WHITE GIRL WITH THE FORK COULD ONLY SAY "THANK YOU!" SO I ATE MY NOODLES. THEY WERE DELICIOUS.

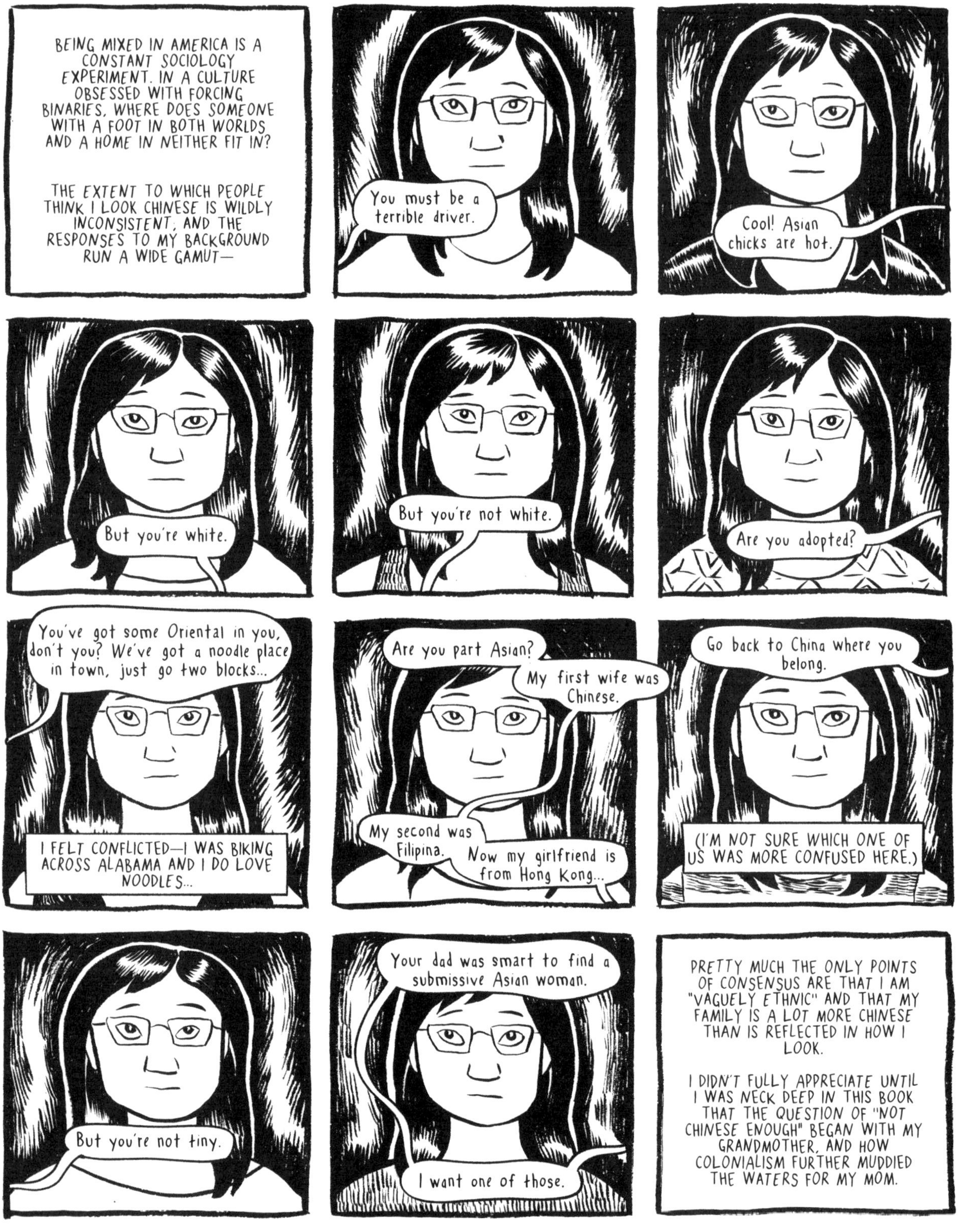

BEING MIXED IN AMERICA IS A CONSTANT SOCIOLOGY EXPERIMENT. IN A CULTURE OBSESSED WITH FORCING BINARIES, WHERE DOES SOMEONE WITH A FOOT IN BOTH WORLDS AND A HOME IN NEITHER FIT IN?
THE EXTENT TO WHICH PEOPLE THINK I LOOK CHINESE IS WILDLY INCONSISTENT, AND THE RESPONSES TO MY BACKGROUND RUN A WIDE GAMUT—
You must be a terrible driver.
Cool! Asian chicks are hot.
But you're white.
But you're not white.
Are you adopted?
You've got some Oriental in you, don't you? We've got a noodle place in town, just go two blocks...
I FELT CONFLICTED—I WAS BIKING ACROSS ALABAMA AND I DO LOVE NOODLES...
Are you part Asian?
My first wife was Chinese.
My second was Filipina.
Now my girlfriend is from Hong Kong...
Go back to China where you belong.
(I'M NOT SURE WHICH ONE OF US WAS MORE CONFUSED HERE.)
But you're not tiny.
Your dad was smart to find a submissive Asian woman.
I want one of those.
PRETTY MUCH THE ONLY POINTS OF CONSENSUS ARE THAT I AM "VAGUELY ETHNIC" AND THAT MY FAMILY IS A LOT MORE CHINESE THAN IS REFLECTED IN HOW I LOOK.
I DIDN'T FULLY APPRECIATE UNTIL I WAS NECK DEEP IN THIS BOOK THAT THE QUESTION OF "NOT CHINESE ENOUGH" BEGAN WITH MY GRANDMOTHER, AND HOW COLONIALISM FURTHER MUDDIED THE WATERS FOR MY MOM.

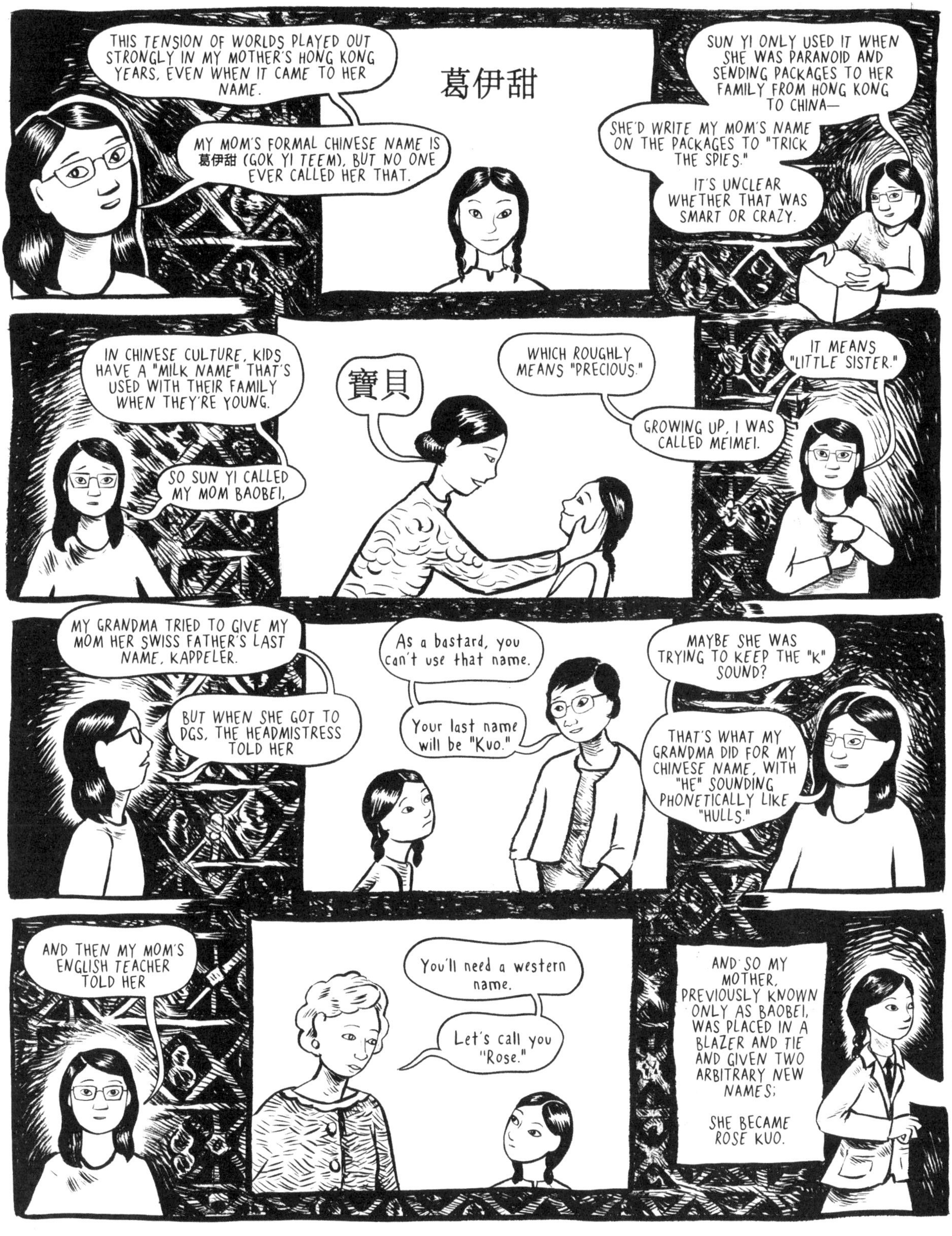
THIS TENSION OF WORLDS PLAYED OUT STRONGLY IN MY MOTHER'S HONG KONG YEARS, EVEN WHEN IT CAME TO HER NAME.
MY MOM'S FORMAL CHINESE NAME IS 葛伊甜 (GOK YI TEEM), BUT NO ONE EVER CALLED HER THAT.
葛伊甜
SUN YI ONLY USED IT WHEN SHE WAS PARANOID AND SENDING PACKAGES TO HER FAMILY FROM HONG KONG TO CHINA—
SHE'D WRITE MY MOM'S NAME ON THE PACKAGES TO "TRICK THE SPIES."
IT'S UNCLEAR WHETHER THAT WAS SMART OR CRAZY.
IN CHINESE CULTURE, KIDS HAVE A "MILK NAME" THAT'S USED WITH THEIR FAMILY WHEN THEY'RE YOUNG.
SO SUN YI CALLED MY MOM BAOBEI,
寶貝
WHICH ROUGHLY MEANS "PRECIOUS."
GROWING UP, I WAS CALLED MEIMEI.
IT MEANS "LITTLE SISTER."
MY GRANDMA TRIED TO GIVE MY MOM HER SWISS FATHER'S LAST NAME, KAPPELER.
BUT WHEN SHE GOT TO DGS, THE HEADMISTRESS TOLD HER
As a bastard, you can't use that name.
Your last name will be "Kuo."
MAYBE SHE WAS TRYING TO KEEP THE "K" SOUND?
THAT'S WHAT MY GRANDMA DID FOR MY CHINESE NAME, WITH "HE" SOUNDING PHONETICALLY LIKE "HULLS."
AND THEN MY MOM'S ENGLISH TEACHER TOLD HER
You'll need a western name.
Let's call you "Rose."
AND SO MY MOTHER, PREVIOUSLY KNOWN ONLY AS BAOBEI, WAS PLACED IN A BLAZER AND TIE AND GIVEN TWO ARBITRARY NEW NAMES;
SHE BECAME ROSE KUO.

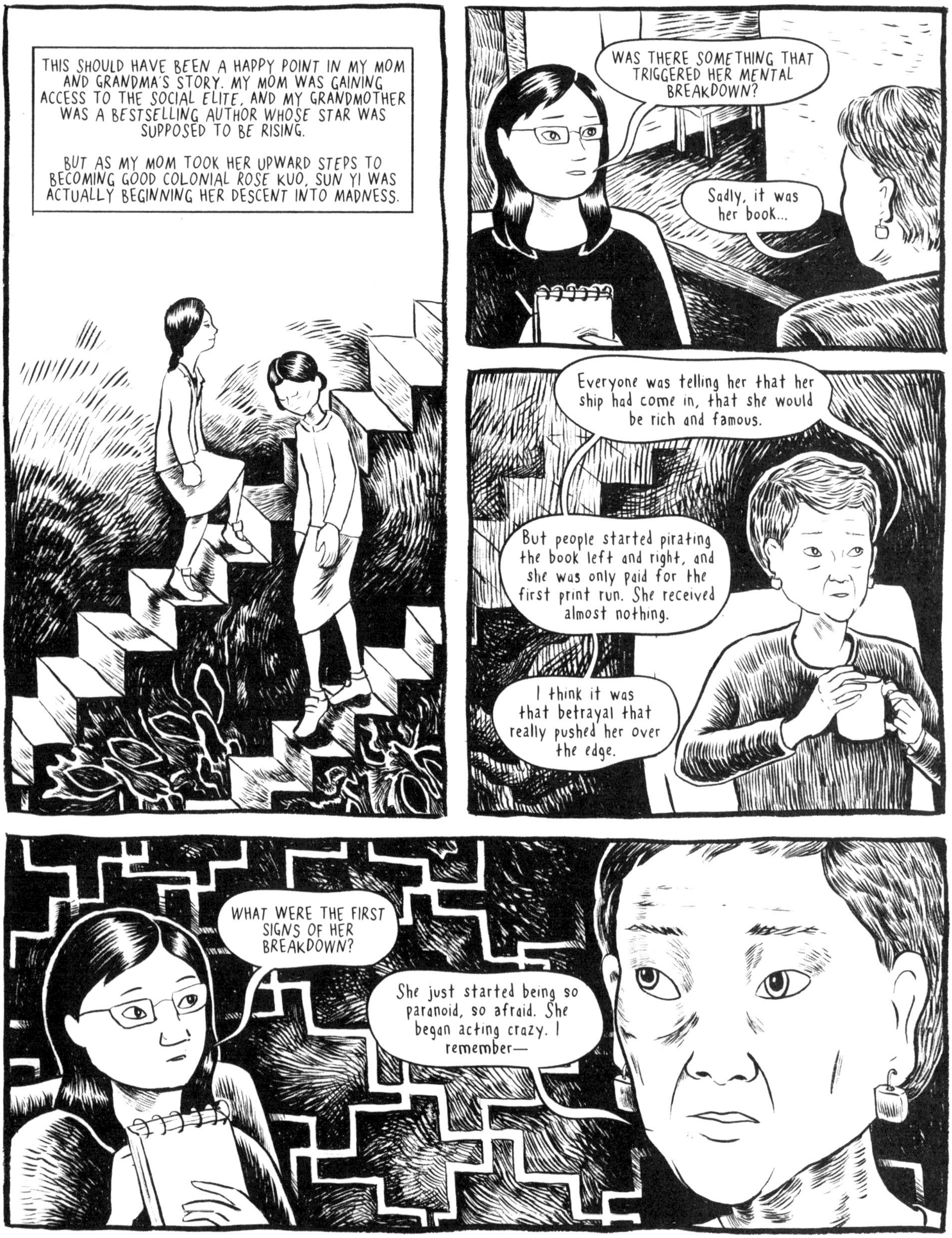
THIS SHOULD HAVE BEEN A HAPPY POINT IN MY MOM AND GRANDMA'S STORY. MY MOM WAS GAINING ACCESS TO THE SOCIAL ELITE, AND MY GRANDMOTHER WAS A BESTSELLING AUTHOR WHOSE STAR WAS SUPPOSED TO BE RISING.
BUT AS MY MOM TOOK HER UPWARD STEPS TO BECOMING GOOD COLONIAL ROSE KUO, SUN YI WAS ACTUALLY BEGINNING HER DESCENT INTO MADNESS.
WAS THERE SOMETHING THAT TRIGGERED HER MENTAL BREAKDOWN?
Sadly, it was her book...
Everyone was telling her that her ship had come in, that she would be rich and famous.
But people started pirating the book left and right, and she was only paid for the first print run. She received almost nothing.
I think it was that betrayal that really pushed her over the edge.
WHAT WERE THE FIRST SIGNS OF HER BREAKDOWN?
She just started being so paranoid, so afraid. She began acting crazy. I remember—

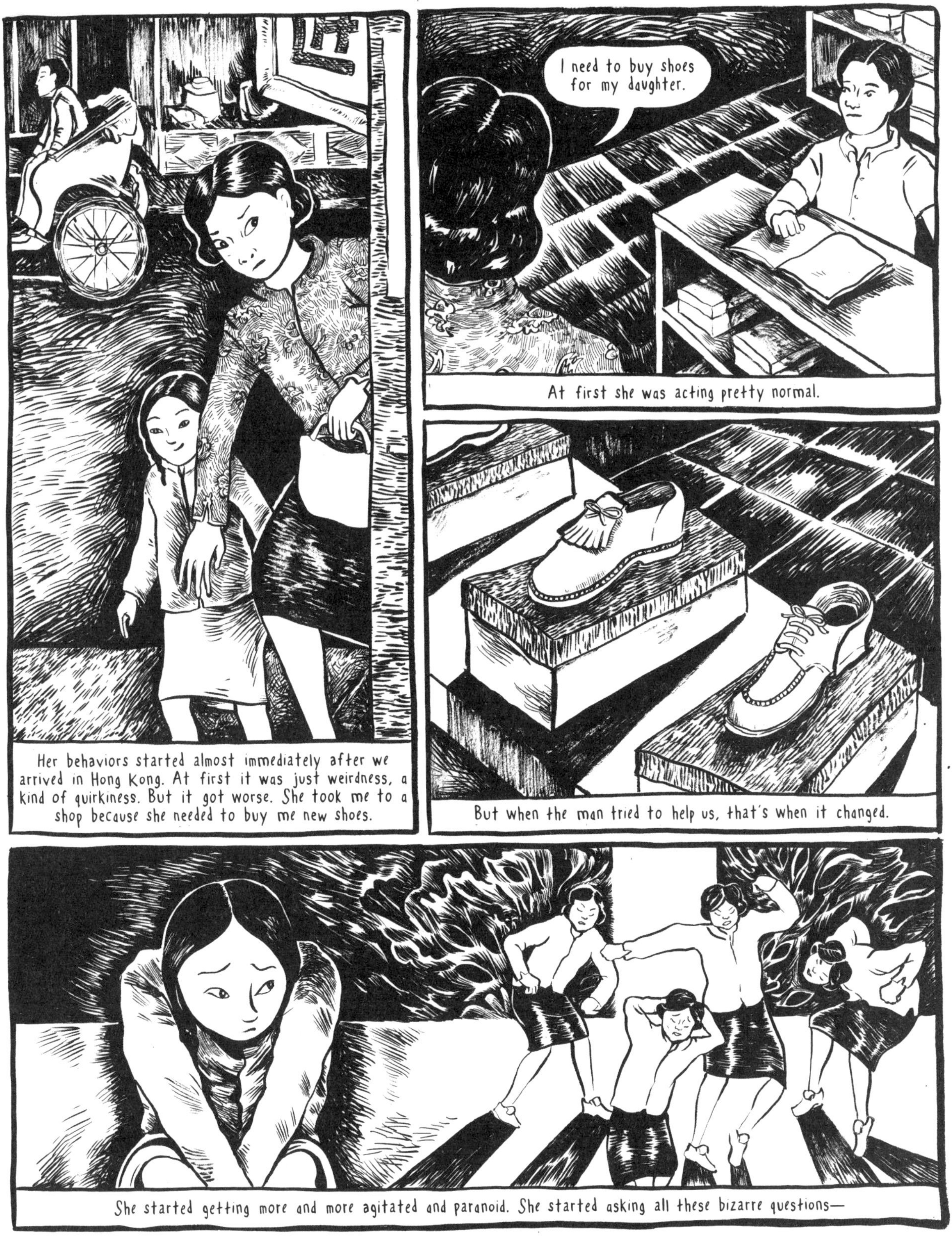
Her behaviors started almost immediately after we arrived in Hong Kong. At first it was just weirdness, a kind of quirkiness. But it got worse. She took me to a shop because she needed to buy me new shoes.
I need to buy shoes for my daughter.
At first she was acting pretty normal.
But when the man tried to help us, that's when it changed.
She started getting more and more agitated and paranoid. She started asking all these bizarre questions—

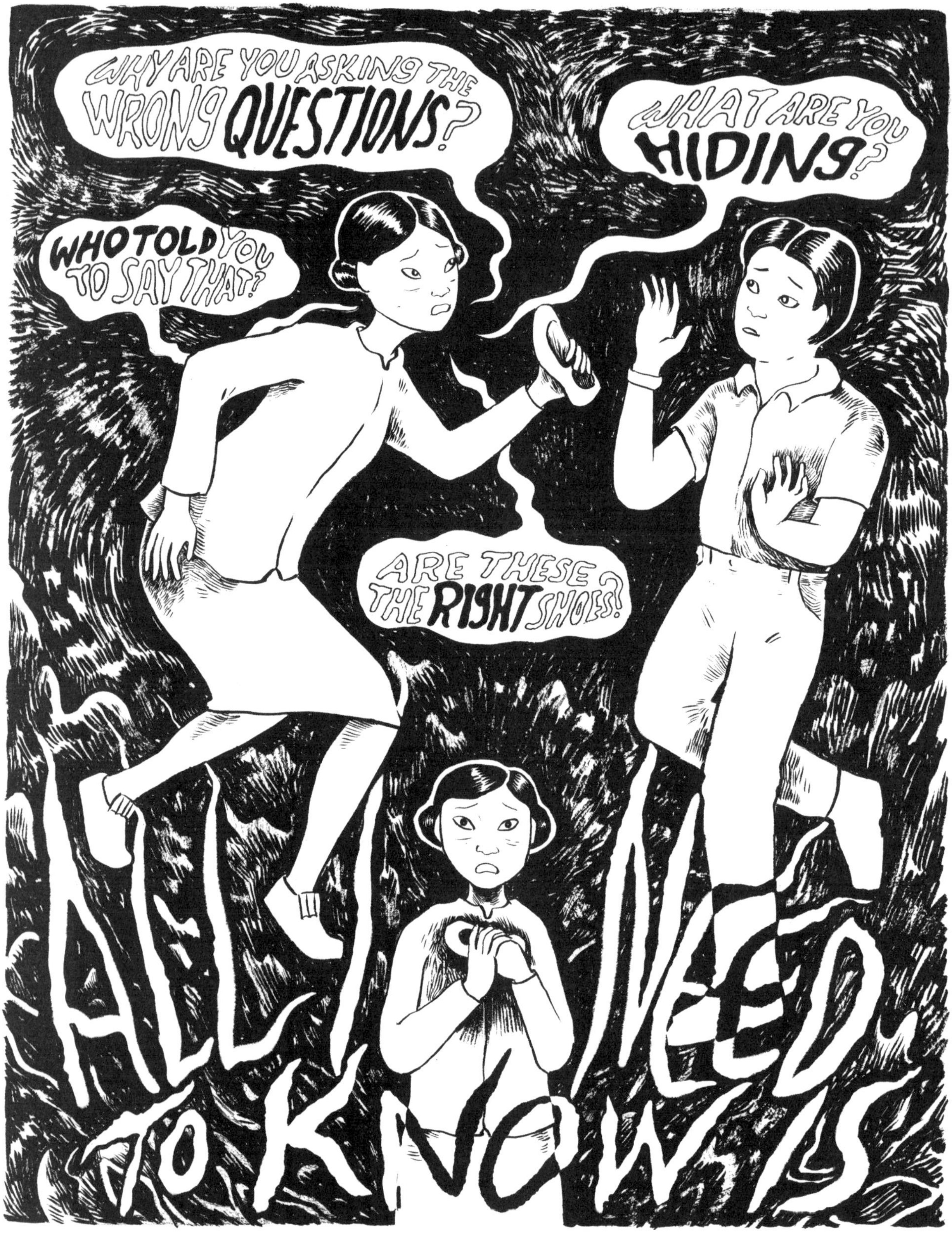
WHY ARE YOU ASKING THE WRONG QUESTIONS?
WHAT ARE YOU HIDING?
WHO TOLD YOU TO SAY THAT?
ARE THESE THE RIGHT SHOES?
ALL I NEED TO KNOW IS

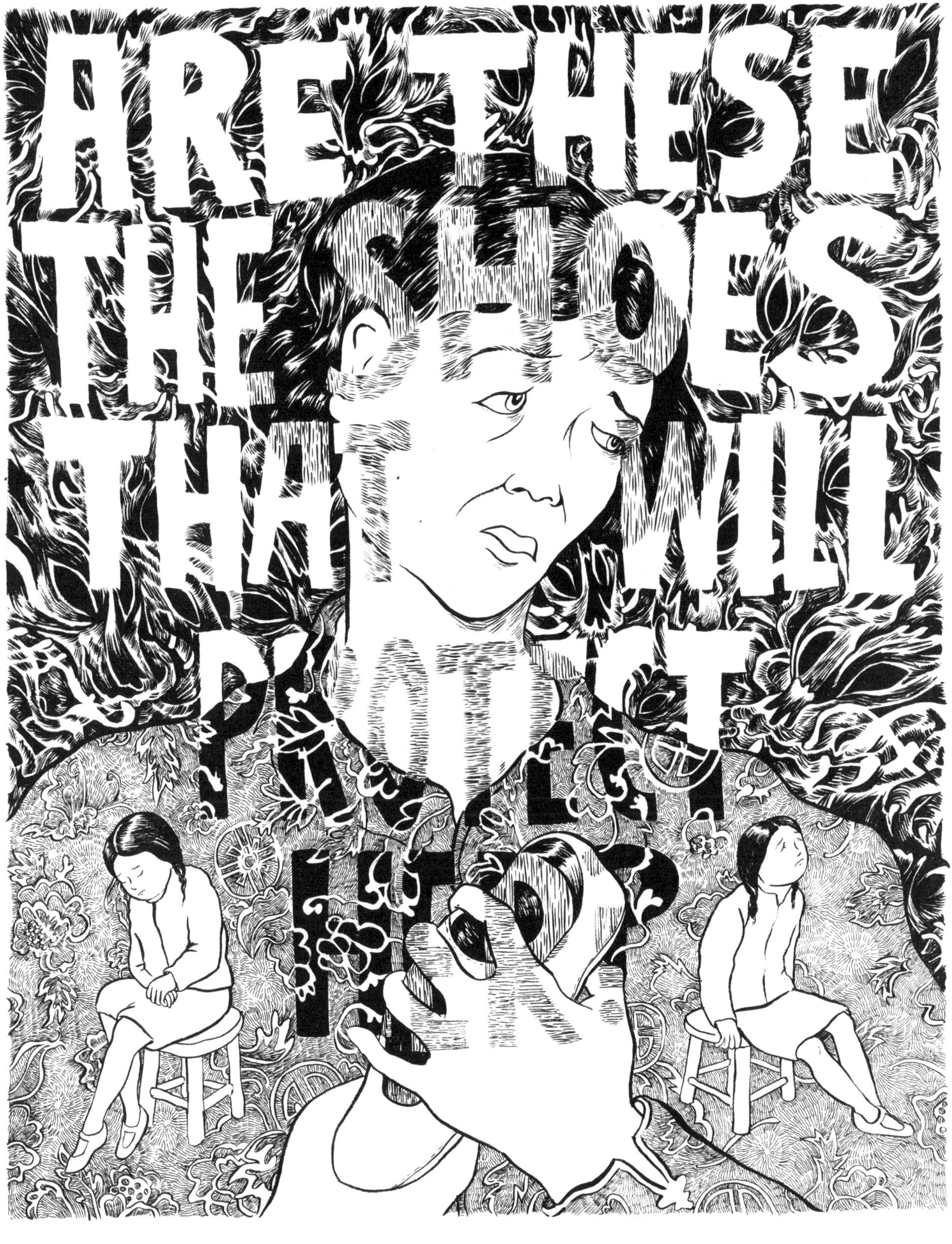
ARE THESE THE SHOES THAT WILL PROTECT HER?

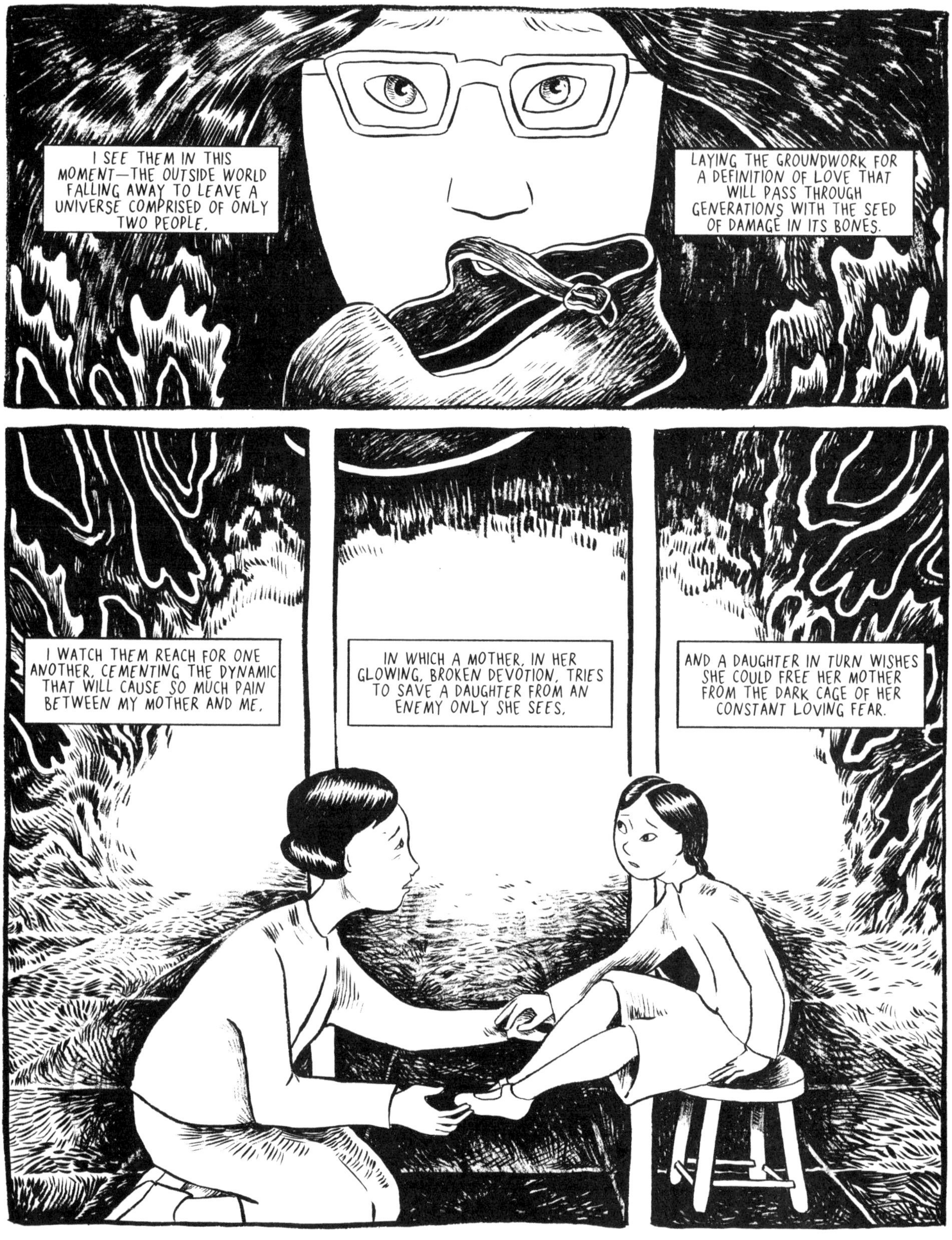

I SEE THEM IN THIS MOMENT—THE OUTSIDE WORLD FALLING AWAY TO LEAVE A UNIVERSE COMPRISED OF ONLY TWO PEOPLE,
LAYING THE GROUNDWORK FOR A DEFINITION OF LOVE THAT WILL PASS THROUGH GENERATIONS WITH THE SEED OF DAMAGE IN ITS BONES.
I WATCH THEM REACH FOR ONE ANOTHER, CEMENTING THE DYNAMIC THAT WILL CAUSE SO MUCH PAIN BETWEEN MY MOTHER AND ME,
IN WHICH A MOTHER, IN HER GLOWING, BROKEN DEVOTION, TRIES TO SAVE A DAUGHTER FROM AN ENEMY ONLY SHE SEES,
AND A DAUGHTER IN TURN WISHES SHE COULD FREE HER MOTHER FROM THE DARK CAGE OF HER CONSTANT LOVING FEAR.

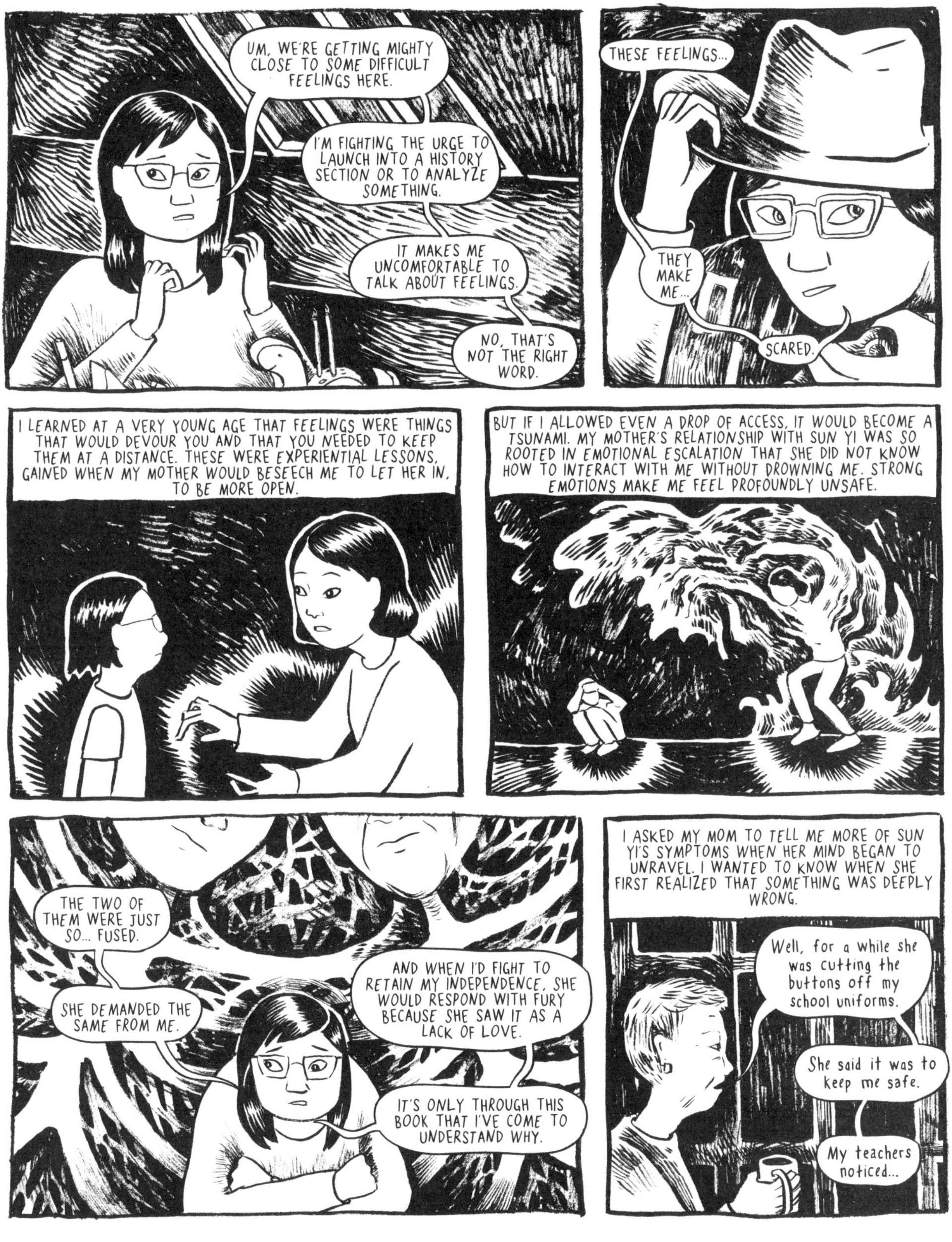
UM, WE'RE GETTING MIGHTY CLOSE TO SOME DIFFICULT FEELINGS HERE.
I'M FIGHTING THE URGE TO LAUNCH INTO A HISTORY SECTION OR TO ANALYZE SOMETHING.
IT MAKES ME UNCOMFORTABLE TO TALK ABOUT FEELINGS.
NO, THAT'S NOT THE RIGHT WORD.
THESE FEELINGS...
THEY MAKE ME...
SCARED.
I LEARNED AT A VERY YOUNG AGE THAT FEELINGS WERE THINGS THAT WOULD DEVOUR YOU AND THAT YOU NEEDED TO KEEP THEM AT A DISTANCE. THESE WERE EXPERIENTIAL LESSONS, GAINED WHEN MY MOTHER WOULD BESEECH ME TO LET HER IN, TO BE MORE OPEN.
BUT IF I ALLOWED EVEN A DROP OF ACCESS, IT WOULD BECOME A TSUNAMI. MY MOTHER'S RELATIONSHIP WITH SUN YI WAS SO ROOTED IN EMOTIONAL ESCALATION THAT SHE DID NOT KNOW HOW TO INTERACT WITH ME WITHOUT DROWNING ME. STRONG EMOTIONS MAKE ME FEEL PROFOUNDLY UNSAFE.
THE TWO OF THEM WERE JUST SO... FUSED.
SHE DEMANDED THE SAME FROM ME.
AND WHEN I'D FIGHT TO RETAIN MY INDEPENDENCE, SHE WOULD RESPOND WITH FURY BECAUSE SHE SAW IT AS A LACK OF LOVE.
IT'S ONLY THROUGH THIS BOOK THAT I'VE COME TO UNDERSTAND WHY.
I ASKED MY MOM TO TELL ME MORE OF SUN YI'S SYMPTOMS WHEN HER MIND BEGAN TO UNRAVEL. I WANTED TO KNOW WHEN SHE FIRST REALIZED THAT SOMETHING WAS DEEPLY WRONG.
Well, for a while she was cutting the buttons off my school uniforms.
She said it was to keep me safe.
My teachers noticed...

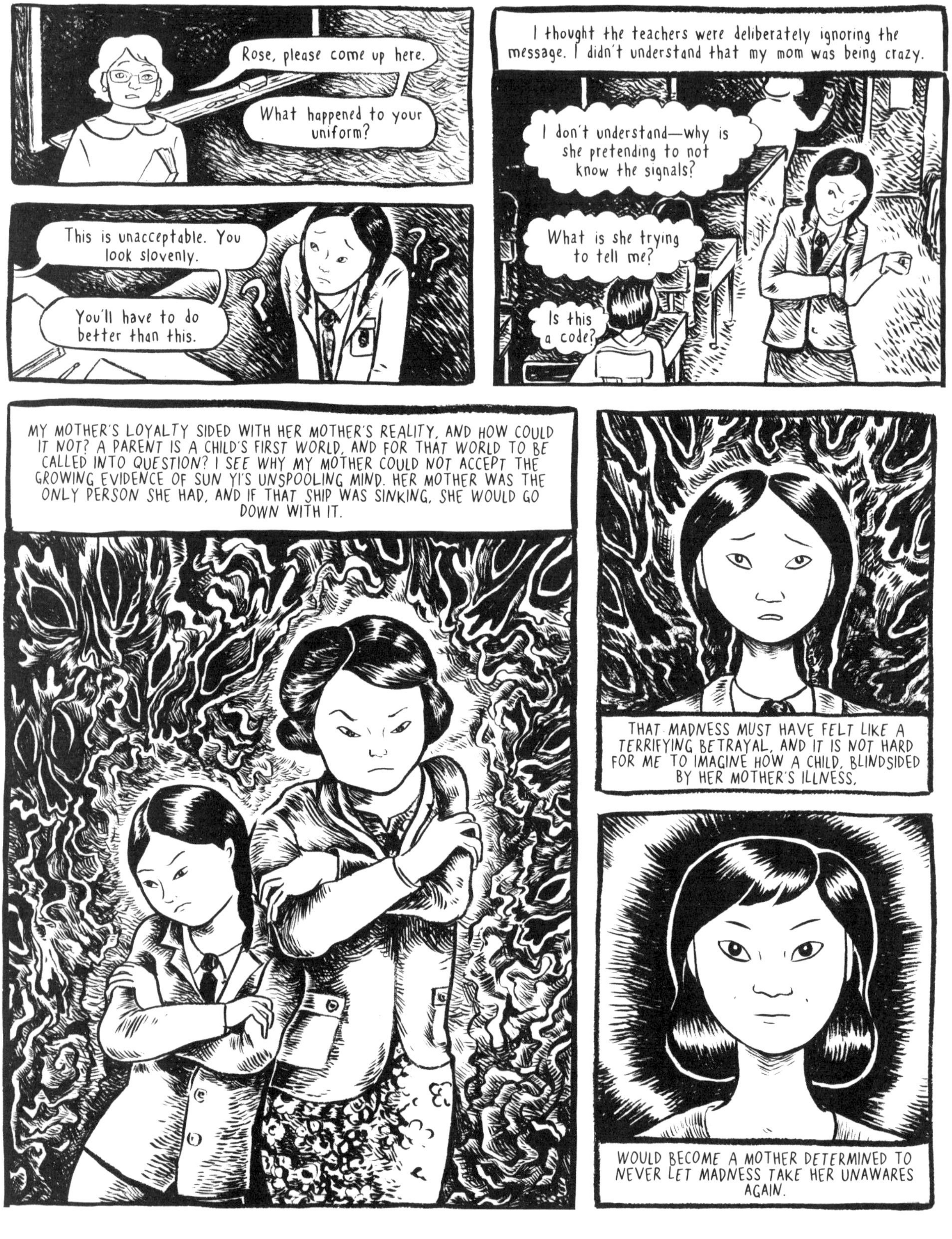
Rose, please come up here.
What happened to your uniform?
This is unacceptable. You look slovenly.
You'll have to do better than this.
I thought the teachers were deliberately ignoring the message. I didn't understand that my mom was being crazy.
I don't understand—why is she pretending to not know the signals?
What is she trying to tell me?
Is this a code?
MY MOTHER'S LOYALTY SIDED WITH HER MOTHER'S REALITY, AND HOW COULD IT NOT? A PARENT IS A CHILD'S FIRST WORLD, AND FOR THAT WORLD TO BE CALLED INTO QUESTION? I SEE WHY MY MOTHER COULD NOT ACCEPT THE GROWING EVIDENCE OF SUN YI'S UNSPOOLING MIND. HER MOTHER WAS THE ONLY PERSON SHE HAD, AND IF THAT SHIP WAS SINKING, SHE WOULD GO DOWN WITH IT.
THAT MADNESS MUST HAVE FELT LIKE A TERRIFYING BETRAYAL, AND IT IS NOT HARD FOR ME TO IMAGINE HOW A CHILD, BLINDSIDED BY HER MOTHER'S ILLNESS,
WOULD BECOME A MOTHER DETERMINED TO NEVER LET MADNESS TAKE HER UNAWARES AGAIN.

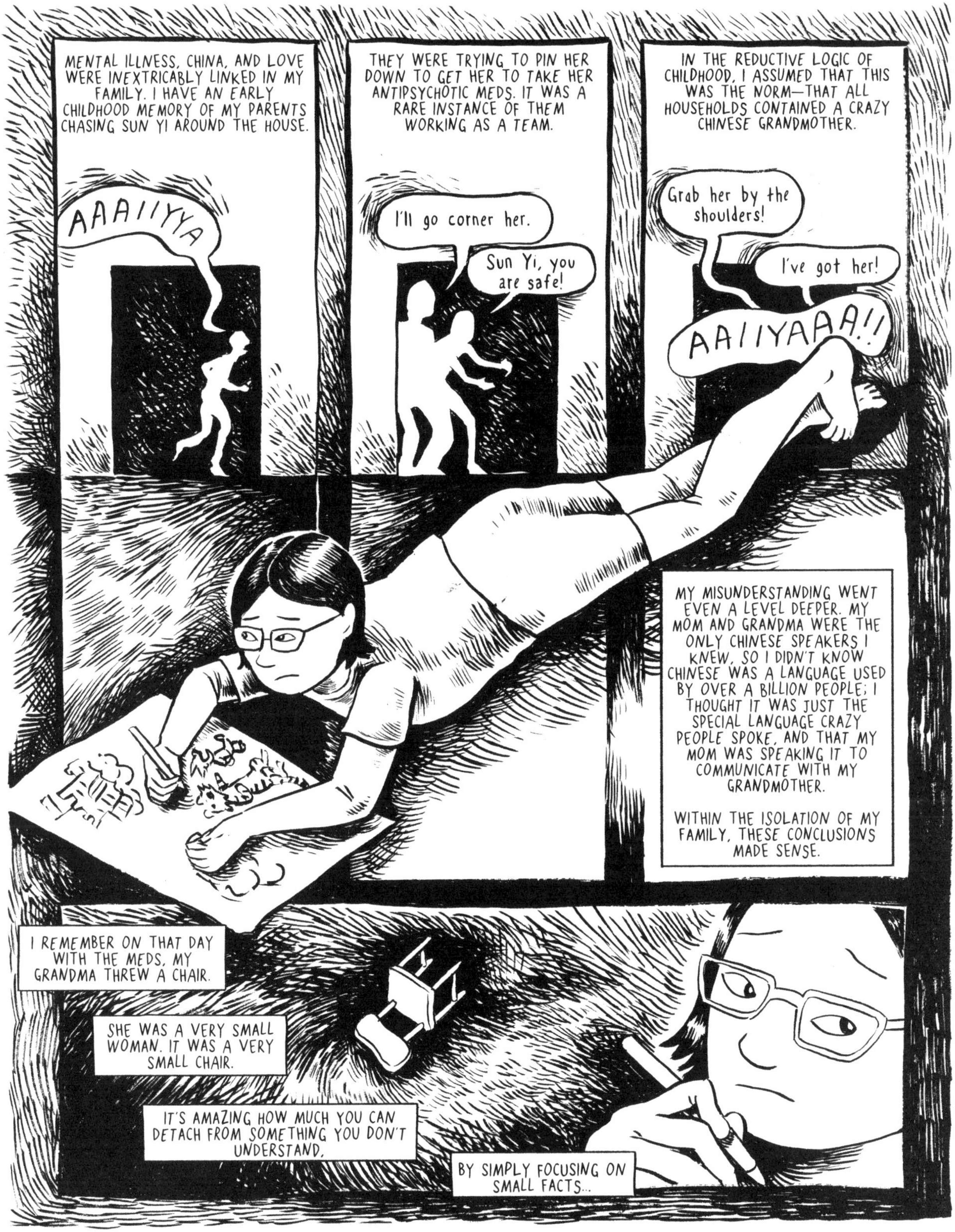
MENTAL ILLNESS, CHINA, AND LOVE WERE INEXTRICABLY LINKED IN MY FAMILY. I HAVE AN EARLY CHILDHOOD MEMORY OF MY PARENTS CHASING SUN YI AROUND THE HOUSE.
AAAIIYYA
THEY WERE TRYING TO PIN HER DOWN TO GET HER TO TAKE HER ANTIPSYCHOTIC MEDS. IT WAS A RARE INSTANCE OF THEM WORKING AS A TEAM.
I'll go corner her.
Sun Yi, you are safe!
IN THE REDUCTIVE LOGIC OF CHILDHOOD, I ASSUMED THAT THIS WAS THE NORM—THAT ALL HOUSEHOLDS CONTAINED A CRAZY CHINESE GRANDMOTHER.
Grab her by the shoulders!
I've got her!
AAIIYAAA!!
MY MISUNDERSTANDING WENT EVEN A LEVEL DEEPER. MY MOM AND GRANDMA WERE THE ONLY CHINESE SPEAKERS I KNEW, SO I DIDN'T KNOW CHINESE WAS A LANGUAGE USED BY OVER A BILLION PEOPLE; I THOUGHT IT WAS JUST THE SPECIAL LANGUAGE CRAZY PEOPLE SPOKE, AND THAT MY MOM WAS SPEAKING IT TO COMMUNICATE WITH MY GRANDMOTHER.
WITHIN THE ISOLATION OF MY FAMILY, THESE CONCLUSIONS MADE SENSE.
I REMEMBER ON THAT DAY WITH THE MEDS, MY GRANDMA THREW A CHAIR.
SHE WAS A VERY SMALL WOMAN. IT WAS A VERY SMALL CHAIR.
IT'S AMAZING HOW MUCH YOU CAN DETACH FROM SOMETHING YOU DON'T UNDERSTAND,
BY SIMPLY FOCUSING ON SMALL FACTS...

PEOPLE PRAISE ME FOR THIS QUALITY AS AN ADULT, FOR MY LEVELHEADEDNESS, MY OBJECTIVITY.

BUT LIKE THE WRITER JOSIE SIGLER SAID, "YOU CAN'T TAKE TOO MUCH CREDIT FOR YOUR STRENGTHS WITHOUT THANKING THE WOUNDS THAT ENGENDERED THEM."

MENTAL ILLNESS WAS THE WATERMARK ACROSS MY FAMILY, SOMETHING SO OMNIPRESENT

IT PRACTICALLY BECAME INVISIBLE.

DURING THE HEIGHT OF MY ANGSTY TEENAGE YEARS, I REMEMBER MY MOM TELLING ME—

You know back when I got pregnant, the prevailing attitude was that if you had a family history of mental illness,

...then you just shouldn't have kids.

When I was younger, I was afraid I had my mom's craziness.

I spent my twenties scared that I would lose my mind.

And then once I had kids...

I was terrified for you.

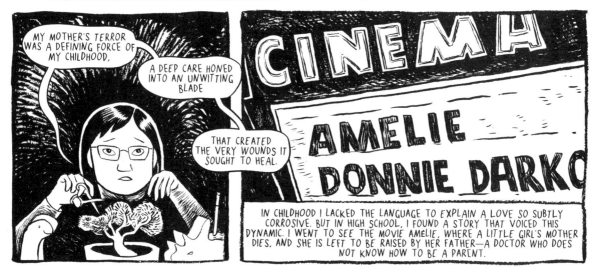

MY MOTHER'S TERROR WAS A DEFINING FORCE OF MY CHILDHOOD,

A DEEP CARE HONED INTO AN UNWITTING BLADE

THAT CREATED THE VERY WOUNDS IT SOUGHT TO HEAL.

CINEMA

AMELIE

DONNIE DARKO

IN CHILDHOOD I LACKED THE LANGUAGE TO EXPLAIN A LOVE SO SUBTLY CORROSIVE. BUT IN HIGH SCHOOL, I FOUND A STORY THAT VOICED THIS DYNAMIC. I WENT TO SEE THE MOVIE AMELIE, WHERE A LITTLE GIRL'S MOTHER DIES, AND SHE IS LEFT TO BE RAISED BY HER FATHER—A DOCTOR WHO DOES NOT KNOW HOW TO BE A PARENT.

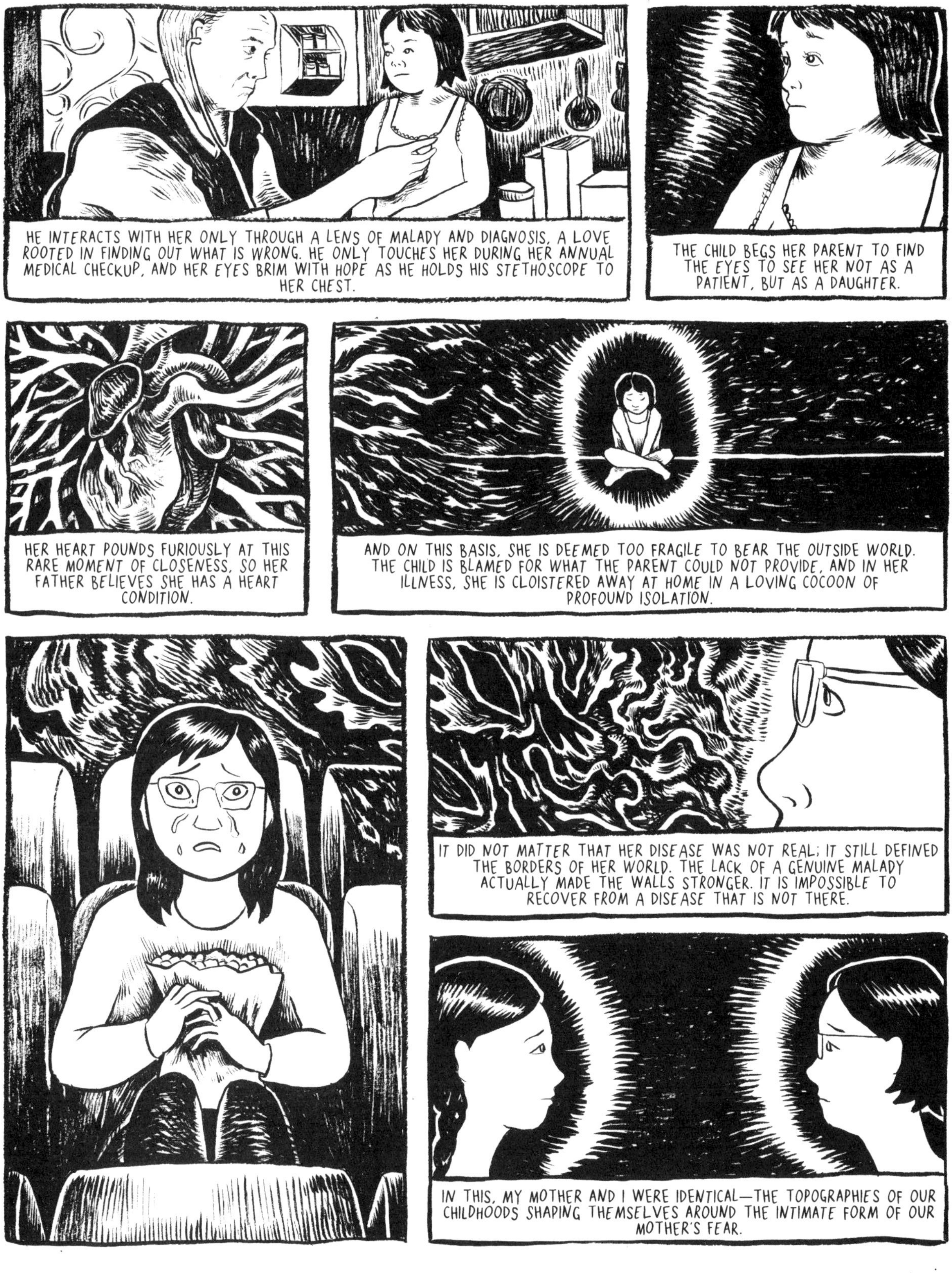
HE INTERACTS WITH HER ONLY THROUGH A LENS OF MALADY AND DIAGNOSIS, A LOVE ROOTED IN FINDING OUT WHAT IS WRONG. HE ONLY TOUCHES HER DURING HER ANNUAL MEDICAL CHECKUP, AND HER EYES BRIM WITH HOPE AS HE HOLDS HIS STETHOSCOPE TO HER CHEST.
THE CHILD BEGS HER PARENT TO FIND THE EYES TO SEE HER NOT AS A PATIENT, BUT AS A DAUGHTER.
HER HEART POUNDS FURIOUSLY AT THIS RARE MOMENT OF CLOSENESS, SO HER FATHER BELIEVES SHE HAS A HEART CONDITION.
AND ON THIS BASIS, SHE IS DEEMED TOO FRAGILE TO BEAR THE OUTSIDE WORLD. THE CHILD IS BLAMED FOR WHAT THE PARENT COULD NOT PROVIDE, AND IN HER ILLNESS, SHE IS CLOISTERED AWAY AT HOME IN A LOVING COCOON OF PROFOUND ISOLATION.
IT DID NOT MATTER THAT HER DISEASE WAS NOT REAL; IT STILL DEFINED THE BORDERS OF HER WORLD. THE LACK OF A GENUINE MALADY ACTUALLY MADE THE WALLS STRONGER. IT IS IMPOSSIBLE TO RECOVER FROM A DISEASE THAT IS NOT THERE.
IN THIS, MY MOTHER AND I WERE IDENTICAL—THE TOPOGRAPHIES OF OUR CHILDHOODS SHAPING THEMSELVES AROUND THE INTIMATE FORM OF OUR MOTHER'S FEAR.

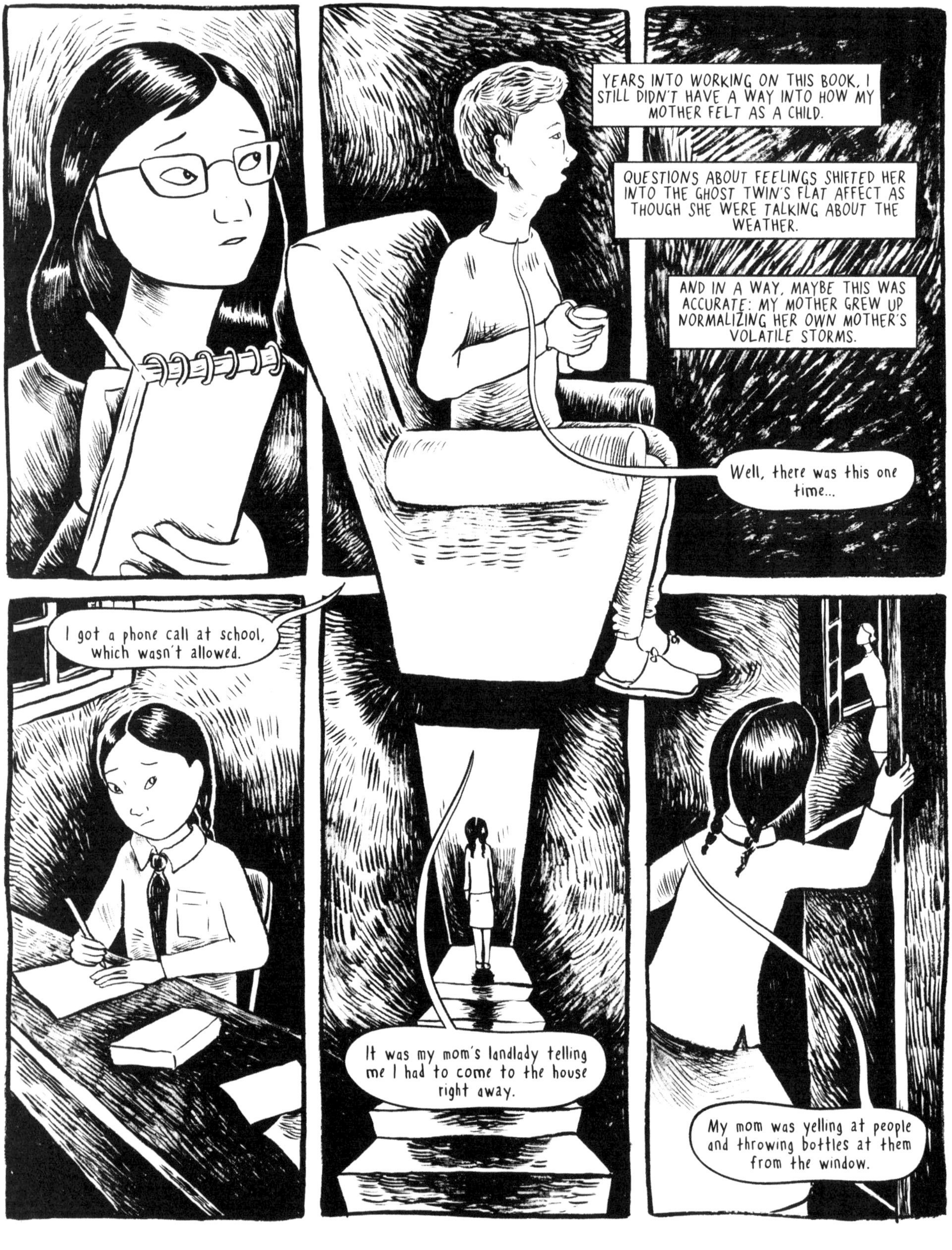

YEARS INTO WORKING ON THIS BOOK, I STILL DIDN'T HAVE A WAY INTO HOW MY MOTHER FELT AS A CHILD.
QUESTIONS ABOUT FEELINGS SHIFTED HER INTO THE GHOST TWIN'S FLAT AFFECT AS THOUGH SHE WERE TALKING ABOUT THE WEATHER.
AND IN A WAY, MAYBE THIS WAS ACCURATE: MY MOTHER GREW UP NORMALIZING HER OWN MOTHER'S VOLATILE STORMS.
Well, there was this one time...
I got a phone call at school, which wasn't allowed.
It was my mom's landlady telling me I had to come to the house right away.
My mom was yelling at people and throwing bottles at them from the window.

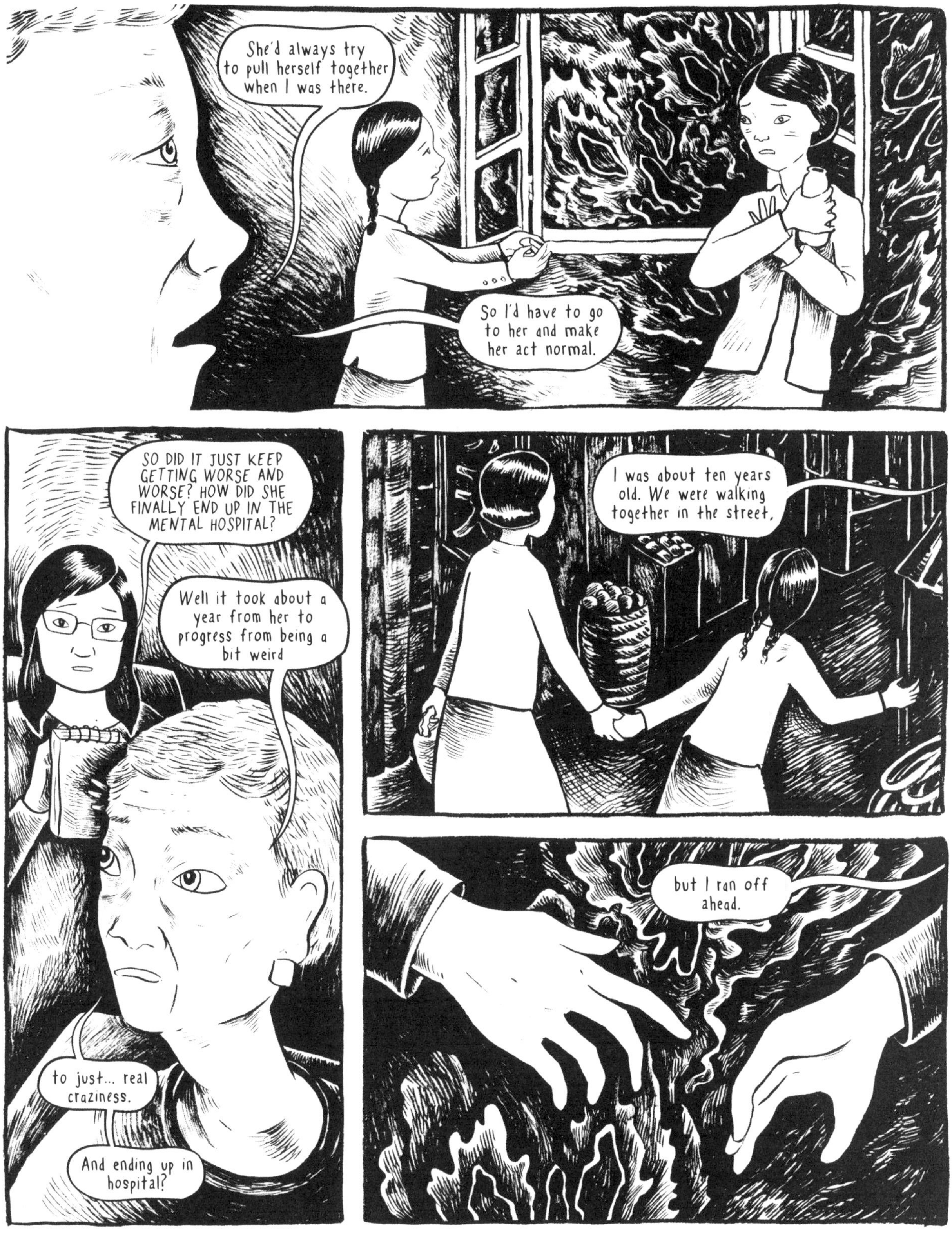
She'd always try to pull herself together when I was there.
So I'd have to go to her and make her act normal.
SO DID IT JUST KEEP GETTING WORSE AND WORSE? HOW DID SHE FINALLY END UP IN THE MENTAL HOSPITAL?
Well it took about a year from her to progress from being a bit weird
to just... real craziness.
And ending up in hospital?
I was about ten years old. We were walking together in the street,
but I ran off ahead.

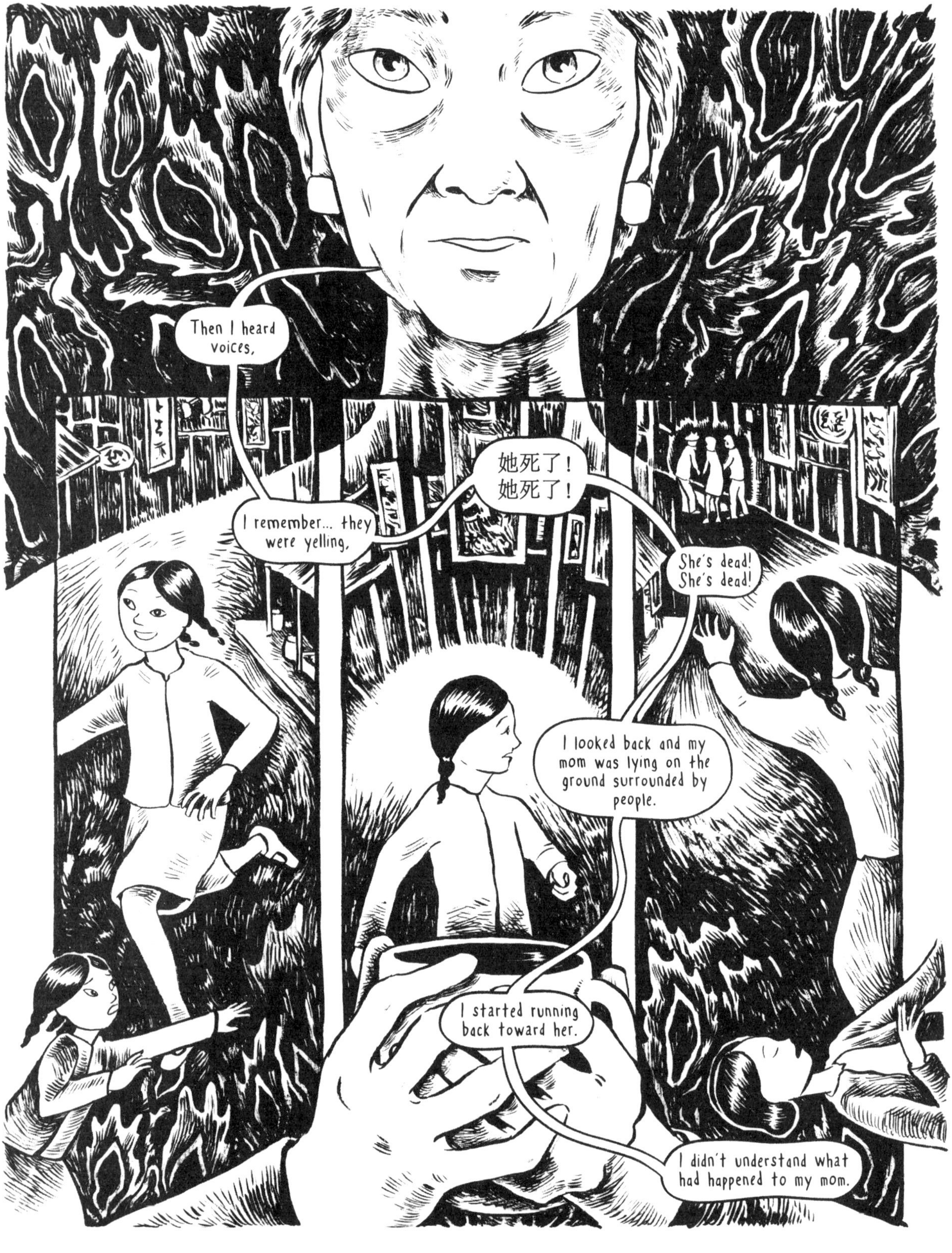
Then I heard voices,
I remember... they were yelling,
她死了！她死了！
She's dead! She's dead!
I looked back and my mom was lying on the ground surrounded by people.
I started running back toward her.
I didn't understand what had happened to my mom.

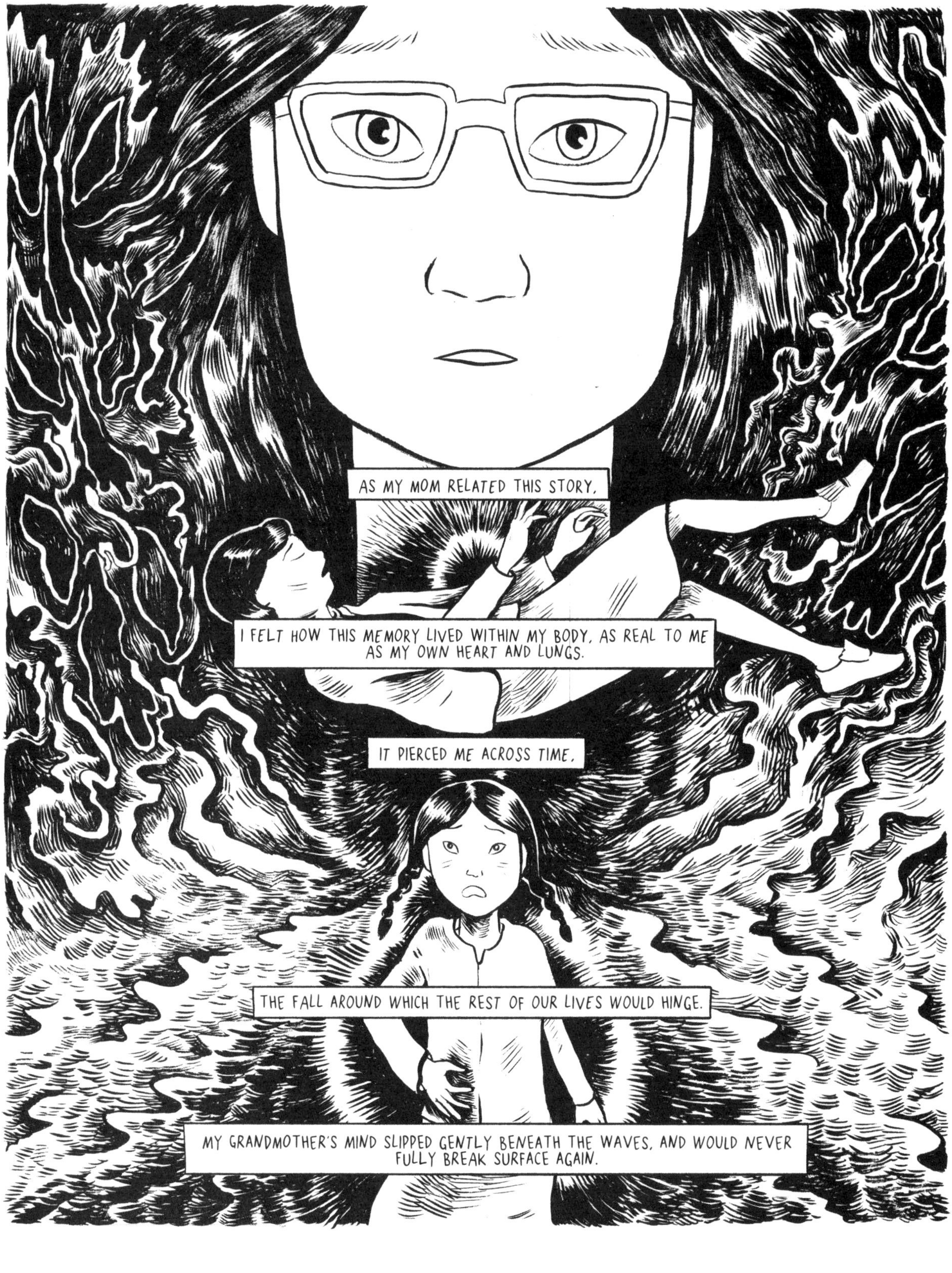
AS MY MOM RELATED THIS STORY,
I FELT HOW THIS MEMORY LIVED WITHIN MY BODY, AS REAL TO ME AS MY OWN HEART AND LUNGS.
IT PIERCED ME ACROSS TIME.
THE FALL AROUND WHICH THE REST OF OUR LIVES WOULD HINGE.
MY GRANDMOTHER'S MIND SLIPPED GENTLY BENEATH THE WAVES, AND WOULD NEVER FULLY BREAK SURFACE AGAIN.

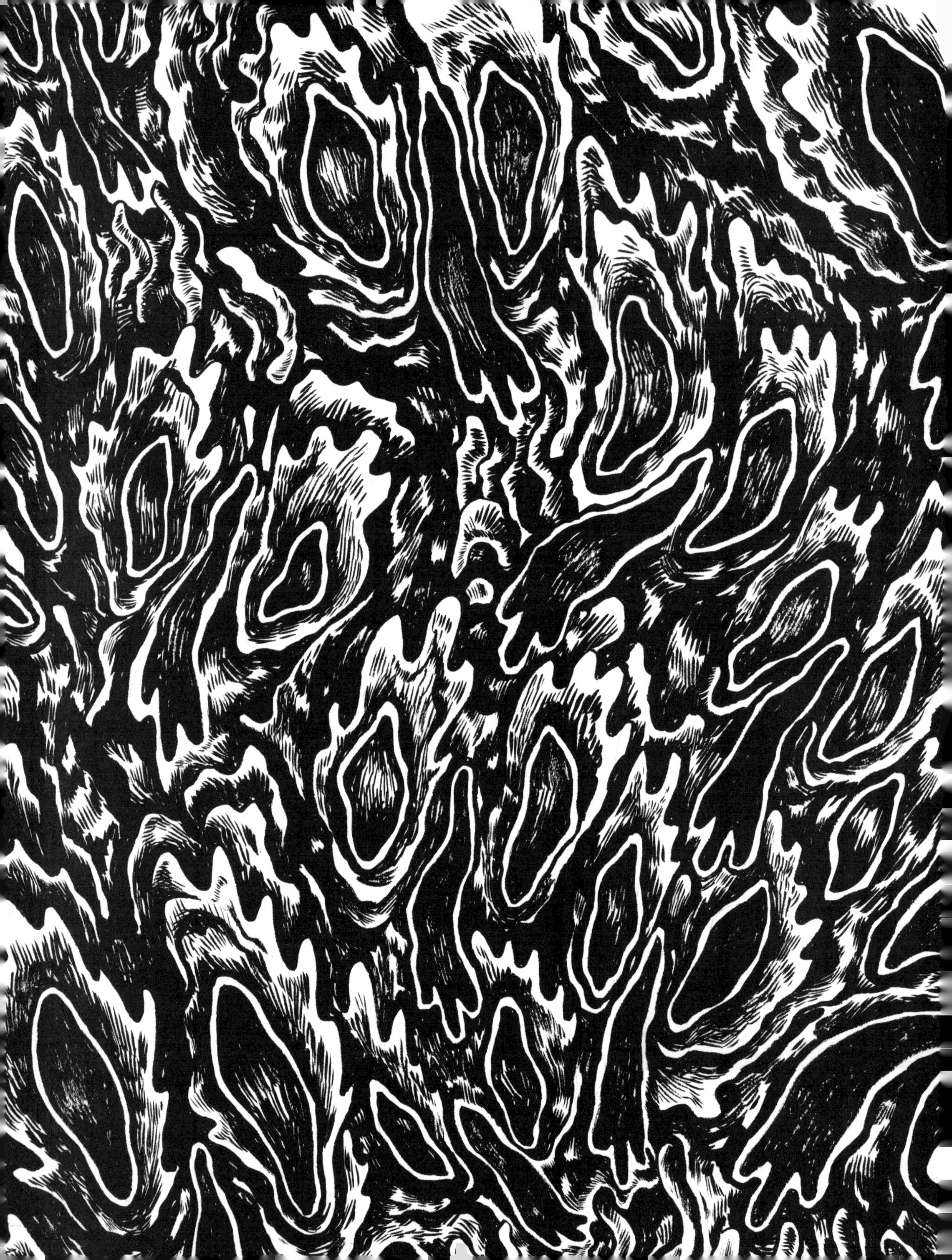

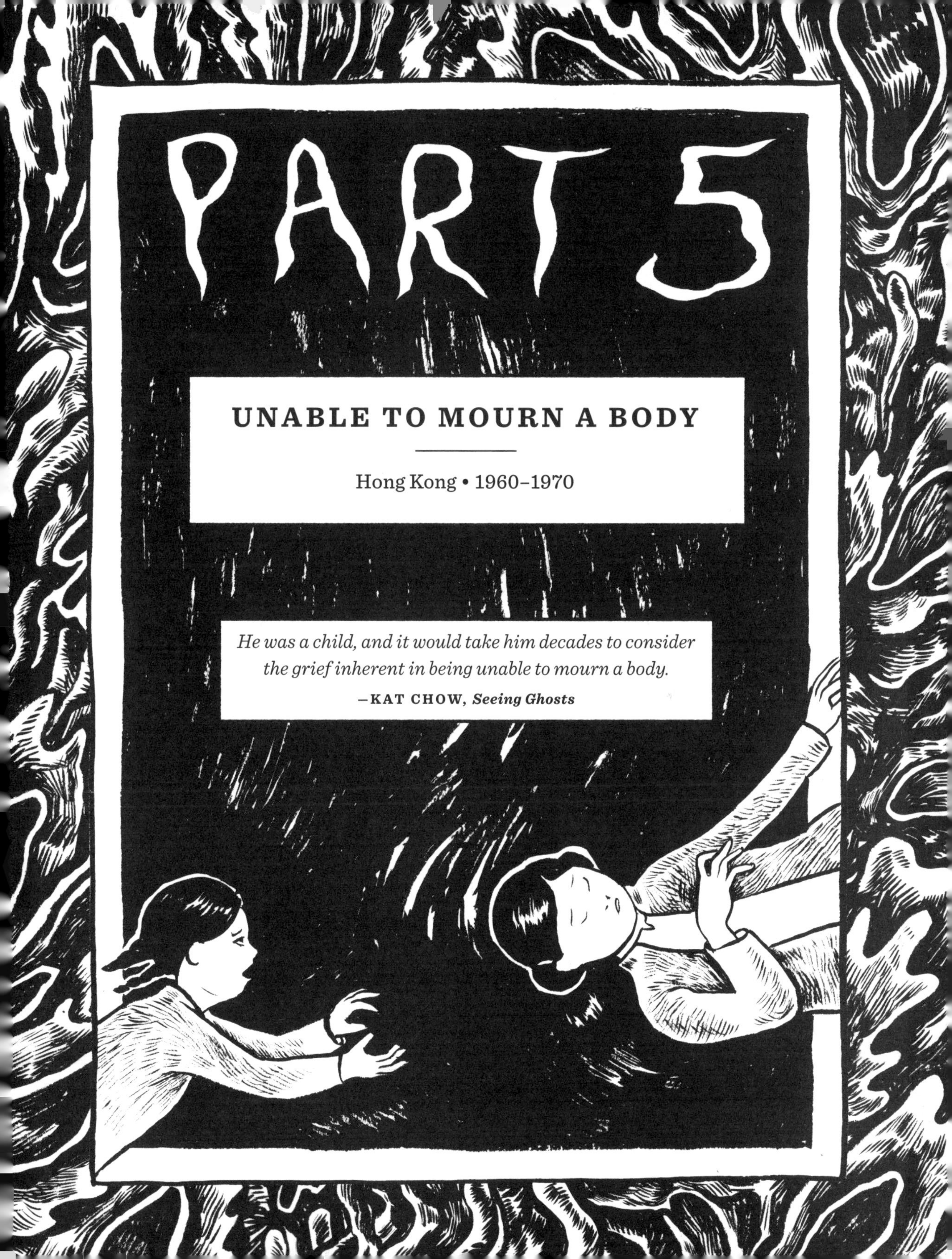
PART 5

PART 5

UNABLE TO MOURN A BODY

Hong Kong • 1960–1970

He was a child, and it would take him decades to consider the grief inherent in being unable to mourn a body.

—**KAT CHOW,** ***Seeing Ghosts***

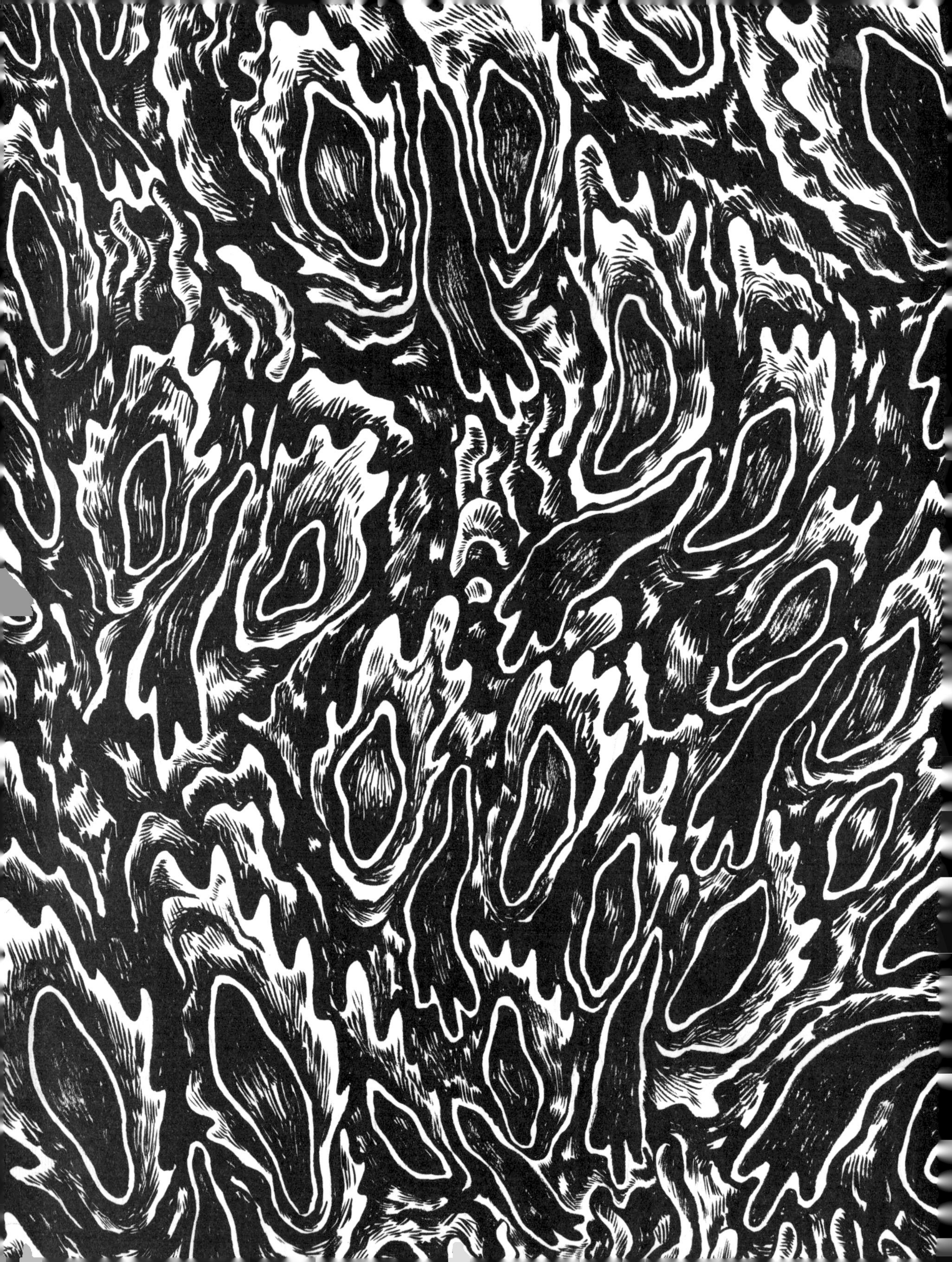

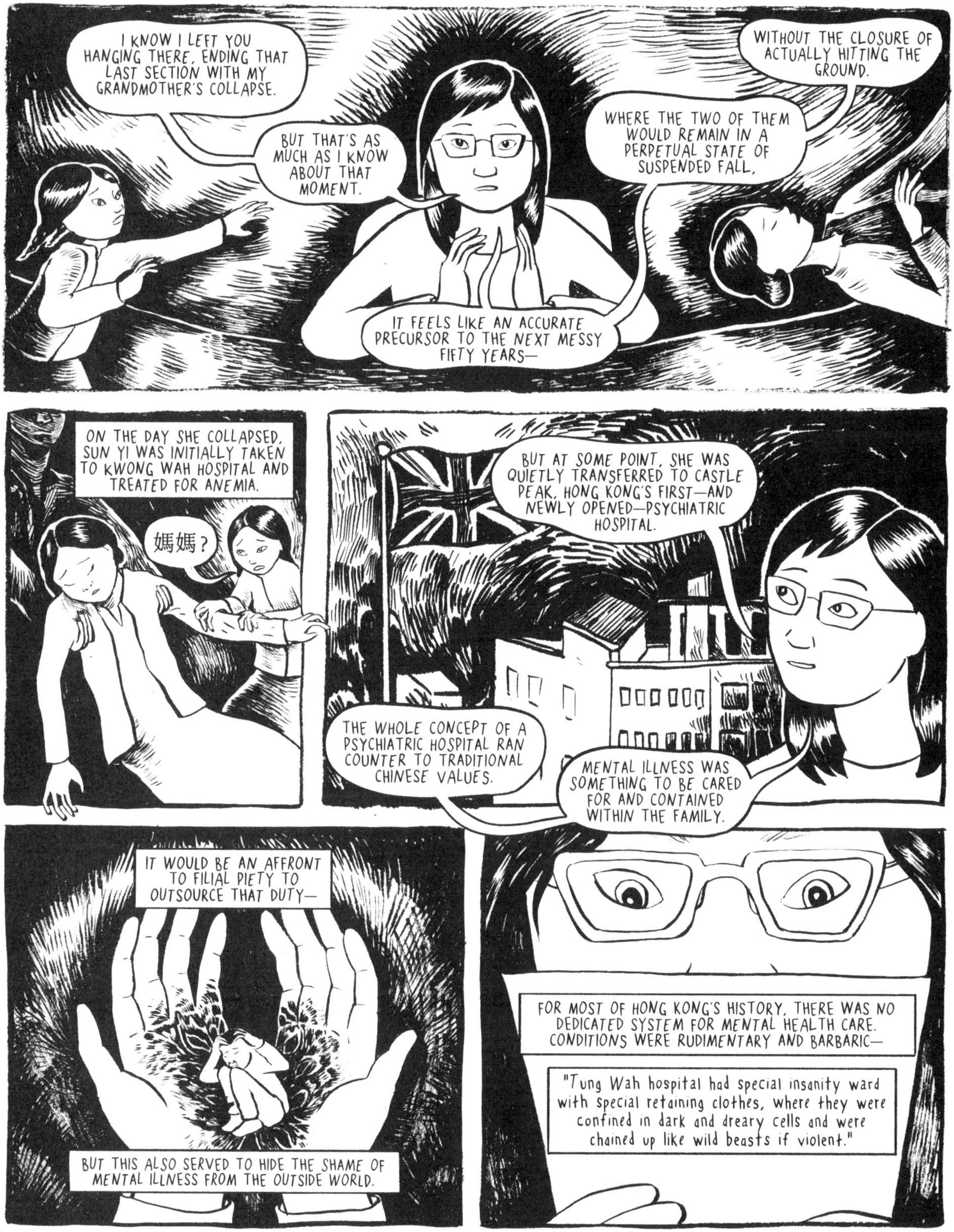
I KNOW I LEFT YOU HANGING THERE, ENDING THAT LAST SECTION WITH MY GRANDMOTHER'S COLLAPSE.
BUT THAT'S AS MUCH AS I KNOW ABOUT THAT MOMENT.
WHERE THE TWO OF THEM WOULD REMAIN IN A PERPETUAL STATE OF SUSPENDED FALL,
WITHOUT THE CLOSURE OF ACTUALLY HITTING THE GROUND.
IT FEELS LIKE AN ACCURATE PRECURSOR TO THE NEXT MESSY FIFTY YEARS—
ON THE DAY SHE COLLAPSED, SUN YI WAS INITIALLY TAKEN TO KWONG WAH HOSPITAL AND TREATED FOR ANEMIA.
媽媽?
BUT AT SOME POINT, SHE WAS QUIETLY TRANSFERRED TO CASTLE PEAK, HONG KONG'S FIRST—AND NEWLY OPENED—PSYCHIATRIC HOSPITAL.
THE WHOLE CONCEPT OF A PSYCHIATRIC HOSPITAL RAN COUNTER TO TRADITIONAL CHINESE VALUES.
MENTAL ILLNESS WAS SOMETHING TO BE CARED FOR AND CONTAINED WITHIN THE FAMILY.
IT WOULD BE AN AFFRONT TO FILIAL PIETY TO OUTSOURCE THAT DUTY—
BUT THIS ALSO SERVED TO HIDE THE SHAME OF MENTAL ILLNESS FROM THE OUTSIDE WORLD.
FOR MOST OF HONG KONG'S HISTORY, THERE WAS NO DEDICATED SYSTEM FOR MENTAL HEALTH CARE. CONDITIONS WERE RUDIMENTARY AND BARBARIC—
"Tung Wah hospital had special insanity ward with special retaining clothes, where they were confined in dark and dreary cells and were chained up like wild beasts if violent."

THIS BEGAN TO CHANGE AS REFUGEES FROM MAINLAND CHINA FLOODED INTO HONG KONG.

IN ADDITION TO THE PHYSICAL NEEDS OF FOOD AND HOUSING,

THEY BROUGHT WITH THEM TRAUMA-RAVAGED MINDS, ALSO IN NEED OF CARE.

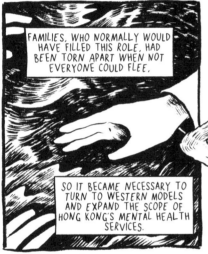

FAMILIES, WHO NORMALLY WOULD HAVE FILLED THIS ROLE, HAD BEEN TORN APART WHEN NOT EVERYONE COULD FLEE,

SO IT BECAME NECESSARY TO TURN TO WESTERN MODELS AND EXPAND THE SCOPE OF HONG KONG'S MENTAL HEALTH SERVICES.

AND SO, WHEN CASTLE PEAK OPENED ITS DOORS ON MARCH 27, 1961,

THE DEMAND WAS ENORMOUS. BUT THERE REMAINED AN OVERWHELMING STIGMA ON THE TOPIC OF MENTAL ILLNESS.

MY GRANDMA WOULD HAVE BEEN AMONG CASTLE PEAK'S FIRST PATIENTS, AND HER HOSPITALIZATION LEFT MY MOM IN A COMPLICATED POSITION.

SHE HAD ONLY BEEN ENROLLED AT DGS FOR ONE YEAR, AND THERE WAS NO MONEY LEFT TO PAY FOR HER EDUCATION.

WHAT WAS ONE TO DO WITH A TEN-YEAR-OLD PENNILESS, FATHERLESS BASTARD WHOSE MOTHER WAS NOW HELD IN A PSYCHIATRIC HOSPITAL?

WELL, BY JOVE, SHE WAS A DGS GIRL! AND DGS TAKES CARE OF ITS OWN!

THE SCHOOL TOOK MY MOTHER ON AS A CHARITY CASE AND PAID FOR EVERYTHING.

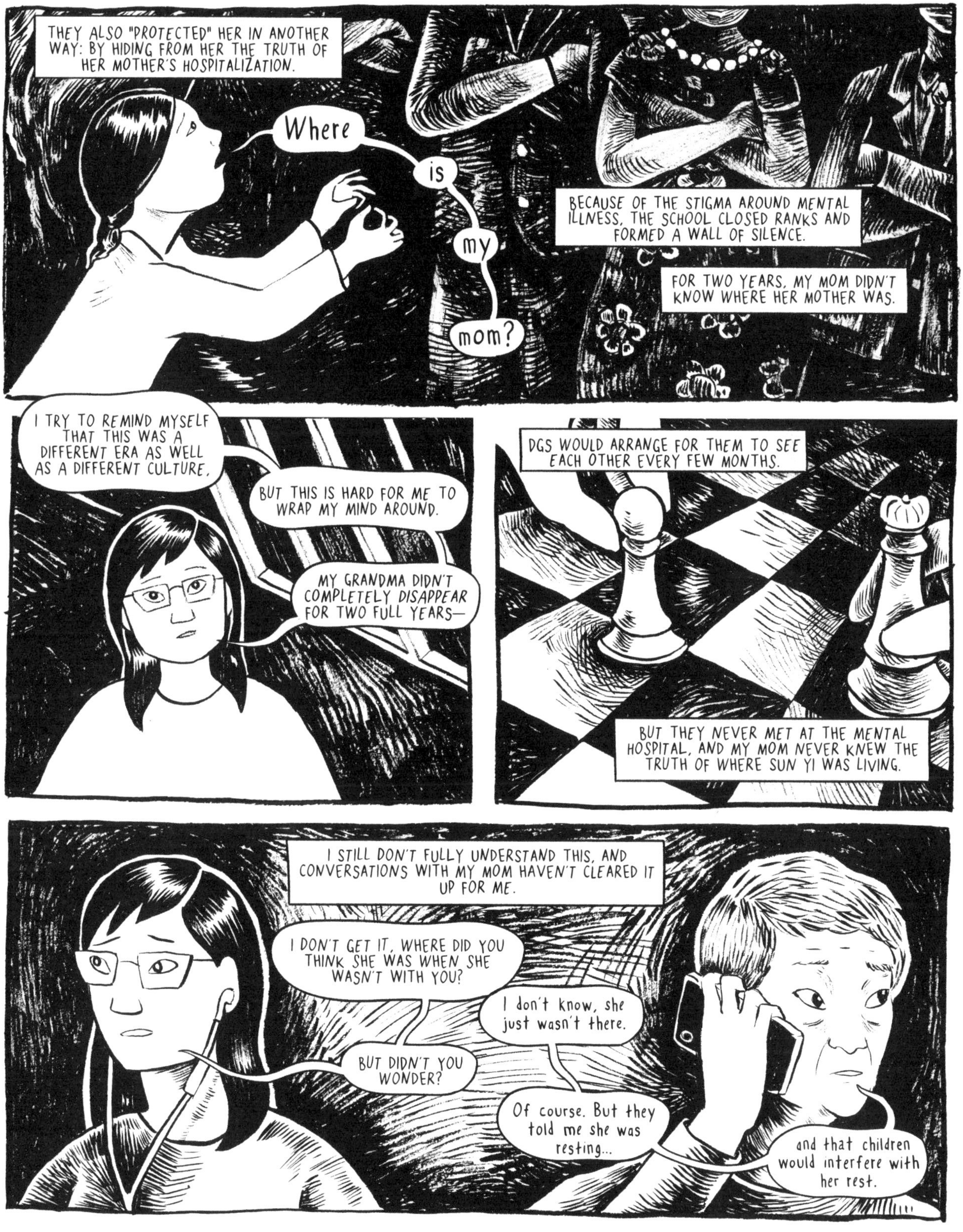
THEY ALSO "PROTECTED" HER IN ANOTHER WAY: BY HIDING FROM HER THE TRUTH OF HER MOTHER'S HOSPITALIZATION.
Where is my mom?
BECAUSE OF THE STIGMA AROUND MENTAL ILLNESS, THE SCHOOL CLOSED RANKS AND FORMED A WALL OF SILENCE.
FOR TWO YEARS, MY MOM DIDN'T KNOW WHERE HER MOTHER WAS.
I TRY TO REMIND MYSELF THAT THIS WAS A DIFFERENT ERA AS WELL AS A DIFFERENT CULTURE,
BUT THIS IS HARD FOR ME TO WRAP MY MIND AROUND.
MY GRANDMA DIDN'T COMPLETELY *DISAPPEAR* FOR TWO FULL YEARS—
DGS WOULD ARRANGE FOR THEM TO SEE EACH OTHER EVERY FEW MONTHS.
BUT THEY NEVER MET AT THE MENTAL HOSPITAL, AND MY MOM NEVER KNEW THE TRUTH OF WHERE SUN YI WAS LIVING.
I STILL DON'T FULLY UNDERSTAND THIS, AND CONVERSATIONS WITH MY MOM HAVEN'T CLEARED IT UP FOR ME.
I DON'T GET IT, WHERE DID YOU THINK SHE WAS WHEN SHE WASN'T WITH YOU?
I don't know, she just wasn't there.
BUT DIDN'T YOU WONDER?
Of course. But they told me she was resting...
and that children would interfere with her rest.

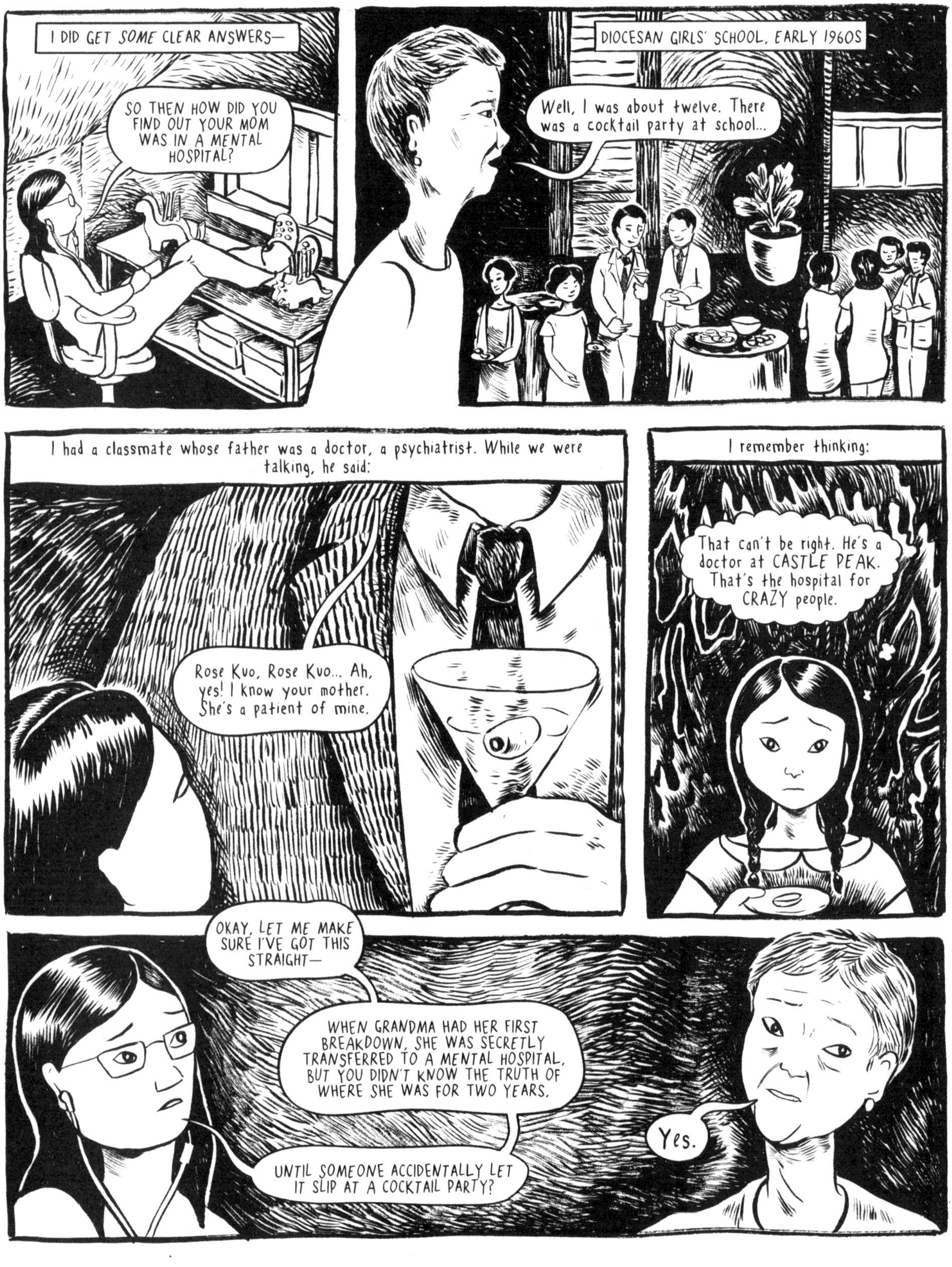
I DID GET SOME CLEAR ANSWERS—
SO THEN HOW DID YOU FIND OUT YOUR MOM WAS IN A MENTAL HOSPITAL?
DIOCESAN GIRLS' SCHOOL, EARLY 1960S
Well, I was about twelve. There was a cocktail party at school...
I had a classmate whose father was a doctor, a psychiatrist. While we were talking, he said:
Rose Kuo, Rose Kuo... Ah, yes! I know your mother. She's a patient of mine.
I remember thinking:
That can't be right. He's a doctor at CASTLE PEAK. That's the hospital for CRAZY people.
OKAY, LET ME MAKE SURE I'VE GOT THIS STRAIGHT—
WHEN GRANDMA HAD HER FIRST BREAKDOWN, SHE WAS SECRETLY TRANSFERRED TO A MENTAL HOSPITAL, BUT YOU DIDN'T KNOW THE TRUTH OF WHERE SHE WAS FOR TWO YEARS,
UNTIL SOMEONE ACCIDENTALLY LET IT SLIP AT A COCKTAIL PARTY?
Yes.

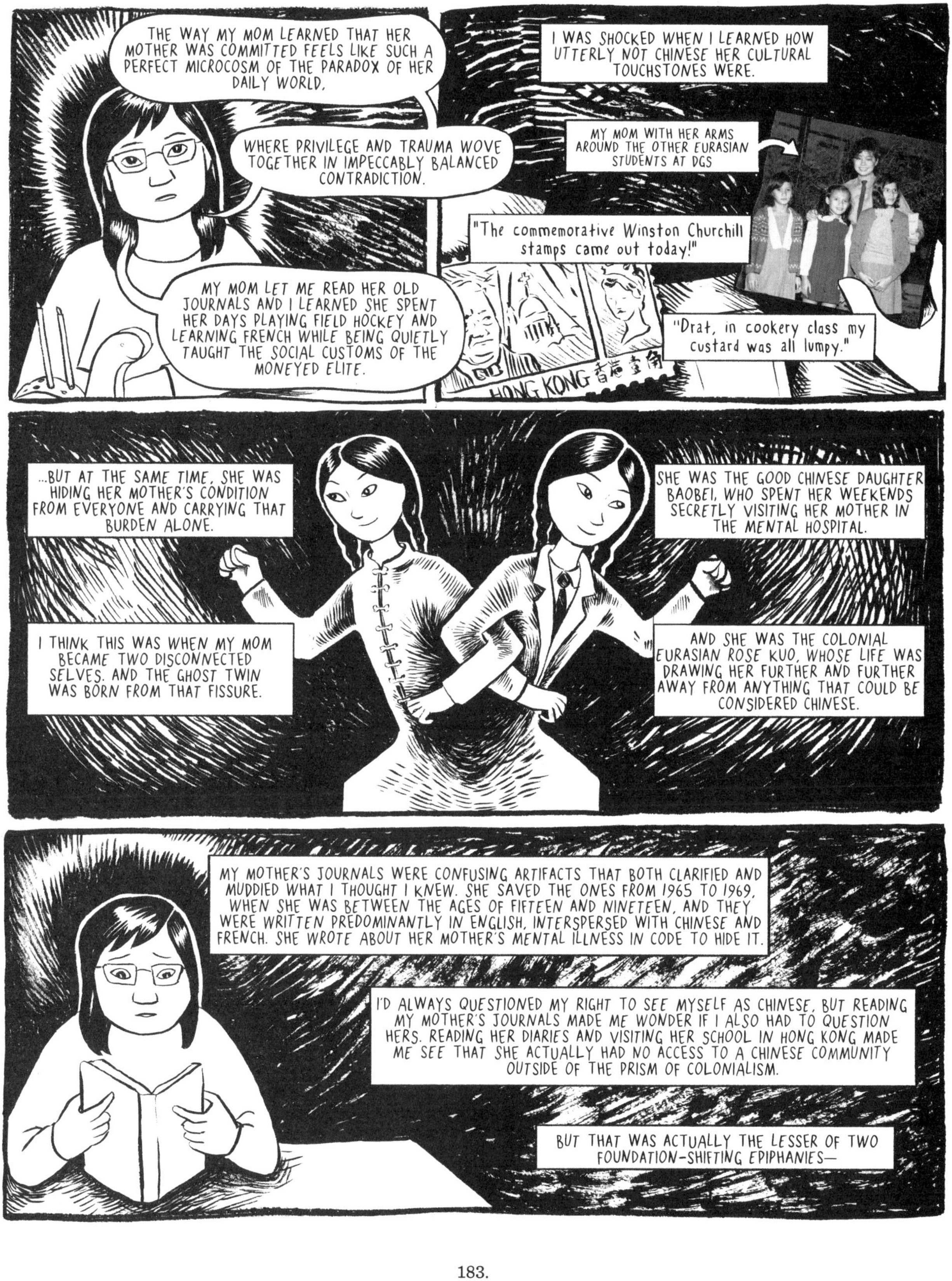
THE WAY MY MOM LEARNED THAT HER MOTHER WAS COMMITTED FEELS LIKE SUCH A PERFECT MICROCOSM OF THE PARADOX OF HER DAILY WORLD,
WHERE PRIVILEGE AND TRAUMA WOVE TOGETHER IN IMPECCABLY BALANCED CONTRADICTION.
MY MOM LET ME READ HER OLD JOURNALS AND I LEARNED SHE SPENT HER DAYS PLAYING FIELD HOCKEY AND LEARNING FRENCH WHILE BEING QUIETLY TAUGHT THE SOCIAL CUSTOMS OF THE MONEYED ELITE.
I WAS SHOCKED WHEN I LEARNED HOW UTTERLY NOT CHINESE HER CULTURAL TOUCHSTONES WERE.
MY MOM WITH HER ARMS AROUND THE OTHER EURASIAN STUDENTS AT DGS
"The commemorative Winston Churchill stamps came out today!"
HONG KONG 香港壹角
"Drat, in cookery class my custard was all lumpy."
...BUT AT THE SAME TIME, SHE WAS HIDING HER MOTHER'S CONDITION FROM EVERYONE AND CARRYING THAT BURDEN ALONE.
SHE WAS THE GOOD CHINESE DAUGHTER BAOBEI, WHO SPENT HER WEEKENDS SECRETLY VISITING HER MOTHER IN THE MENTAL HOSPITAL.
I THINK THIS WAS WHEN MY MOM BECAME TWO DISCONNECTED SELVES. AND THE GHOST TWIN WAS BORN FROM THAT FISSURE.
AND SHE WAS THE COLONIAL EURASIAN ROSE KUO, WHOSE LIFE WAS DRAWING HER FURTHER AND FURTHER AWAY FROM ANYTHING THAT COULD BE CONSIDERED CHINESE.
MY MOTHER'S JOURNALS WERE CONFUSING ARTIFACTS THAT BOTH CLARIFIED AND MUDDIED WHAT I THOUGHT I KNEW. SHE SAVED THE ONES FROM 1965 TO 1969, WHEN SHE WAS BETWEEN THE AGES OF FIFTEEN AND NINETEEN, AND THEY WERE WRITTEN PREDOMINANTLY IN ENGLISH, INTERSPERSED WITH CHINESE AND FRENCH. SHE WROTE ABOUT HER MOTHER'S MENTAL ILLNESS IN CODE TO HIDE IT.
I'D ALWAYS QUESTIONED MY RIGHT TO SEE MYSELF AS CHINESE, BUT READING MY MOTHER'S JOURNALS MADE ME WONDER IF I ALSO HAD TO QUESTION HERS. READING HER DIARIES AND VISITING HER SCHOOL IN HONG KONG MADE ME SEE THAT SHE ACTUALLY HAD NO ACCESS TO A CHINESE COMMUNITY OUTSIDE OF THE PRISM OF COLONIALISM.
BUT THAT WAS ACTUALLY THE LESSER OF TWO FOUNDATION-SHIFTING EPIPHANIES—

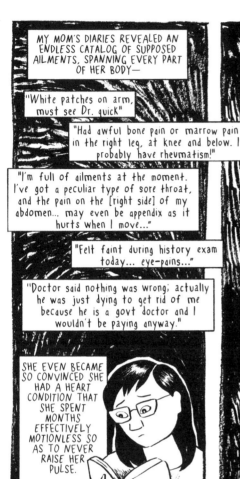

MY MOM'S DIARIES REVEALED AN ENDLESS CATALOG OF SUPPOSED AILMENTS, SPANNING EVERY PART OF HER BODY—

"White patches on arm, must see Dr. quick"

"Had awful bone pain or marrow pain in the right leg, at knee and below. I probably have rheumatism!"

"I'm full of ailments at the moment. I've got a peculiar type of sore throat, and the pain on the [right side] of my abdomen... may even be appendix as it hurts when I move..."

"Felt faint during history exam today... eye-pains..."

"Doctor said nothing was wrong; actually he was just dying to get rid of me because he is a govt doctor and I wouldn't be paying anyway."

SHE EVEN BECAME SO CONVINCED SHE HAD A HEART CONDITION THAT SHE SPENT MONTHS EFFECTIVELY MOTIONLESS SO AS TO NEVER RAISE HER PULSE.

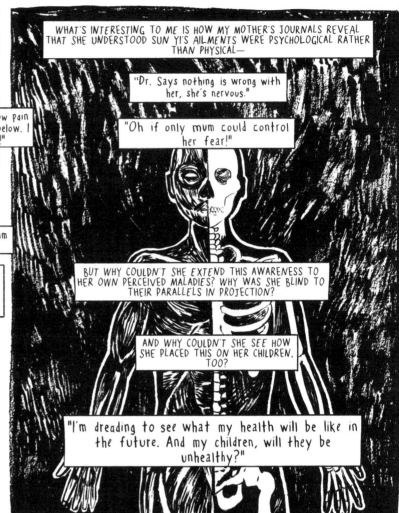

WHAT'S INTERESTING TO ME IS HOW MY MOTHER'S JOURNALS REVEAL THAT SHE UNDERSTOOD SUN YI'S AILMENTS WERE PSYCHOLOGICAL RATHER THAN PHYSICAL—

"Dr. Says nothing is wrong with her, she's nervous."

"Oh if only mum could control her fear!"

BUT WHY COULDN'T SHE EXTEND THIS AWARENESS TO HER OWN PERCEIVED MALADIES? WHY WAS SHE BLIND TO THEIR PARALLELS IN PROJECTION?

AND WHY COULDN'T SHE SEE HOW SHE PLACED THIS ON HER CHILDREN, TOO?

"I'm dreading to see what my health will be like in the future. And my children, will they be unhealthy?"

IN THESE PAGES I SEE THE ROUTE OF SUN YI'S WHISPERED PARANOIA. HOW THE CONSTANT ASSUMPTION OF ILLNESS...

WOVE THROUGH MY MOM'S CHILDHOOD...

AND TEENAGE YEARS...

AND EVENTUALLY HER OWN MOTHERHOOD.

READING MY MOTHER'S JOURNALS SHOWED ME A CHILDHOOD ENCASED IN A RELENTLESS, SEEKING FEAR.

I UNDERSTOOD FOR THE FIRST TIME WHY MY MOTHER EXISTED IN A STATE WHERE THE SKY WAS PERPETUALLY FALLING AND WHY SHE SAW THIS AS THE NORM.

SHE WAS LIKE CHICKEN LITTLE; WHEN AN ACORN DROPS FROM A TREE AND HITS HER ON THE HEAD, SHE BECOMES CONVINCED THE SKY IS FALLING. SHE MUST WARN OTHERS!

SHE MARCHES OFF TO TELL THE KING, AND HER ENTOURAGE GROWS AS SHE WALKS, DRAWN IN BY THE URGENCY OF HER FEAR. "THE SKY IS FALLING, THE SKY IS FALLING!" THEY CHANT. THIS IS WHY THIS PART OF THE STORY ALWAYS HIT HOME FOR ME, THE WAY CHICKEN LITTLE NEEDED HER FEAR TO BE REAL TO EVERYONE ELSE, TOO.

MY MOTHER'S FEAR DID NOT REQUIRE ANY CONCRETE MALADY ON WHICH TO LAND. IT INVENTED ITS OWN JUSTIFICATIONS. I'VE COME TO SEE IT ALMOST AS A FORM OF SONAR—

I just need a bit of your hair.

A SIGNAL THAT NEEDED TO BE CONSTANTLY BROADCAST SO THAT THE REFRACTIONS THAT BOUNCED BACK COULD BETTER DEFINE THE BORDERS OF HER WORLD.

The lab will analyze it and find your deficiencies.

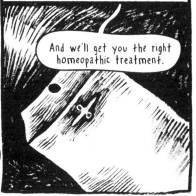
I HADN'T UNDERSTOOD UNTIL WRITING THIS BOOK THAT MY MOM SAW WORRY AS A PARTICIPATORY RELATIONSHIP IN WHICH I WAS FAILING TO DO MY PART.

And we'll get you the right homeopathic treatment.

BUT THE JOURNALS EXPLAINED SO MUCH. FROM THE AGE OF THIRTEEN MY MOTHER WAS EFFECTIVELY SUN YI'S CASEWORKER. THE HEADMISTRESS OF DGS HELPED, BUT THOSE DIARIES SHOW HOW MY MOTHER WAS CONSTANTLY TAKING HER MOM TO DOCTORS AND TRYING TO FIND PLACES FOR HER TO LIVE BETWEEN HOSPITALIZATIONS.

IT WASN'T JUST THAT ILLNESS AND TREATMENT WERE A COMPONENT OF THEIR RELATIONSHIP; THEY WERE THE FOUNDATION. WHICH IS WHY IT MAKES SENSE THAT MY MOTHER DIDN'T KNOW HOW TO PARENT A CHILD WHO WAS MENTALLY AND PHYSICALLY WHOLE.

LOVE AND DAMAGE WERE SO ENTWINED FOR HER; IF THERE WAS ROOM FOR ONE, THERE MUST BE ROOM FOR BOTH.

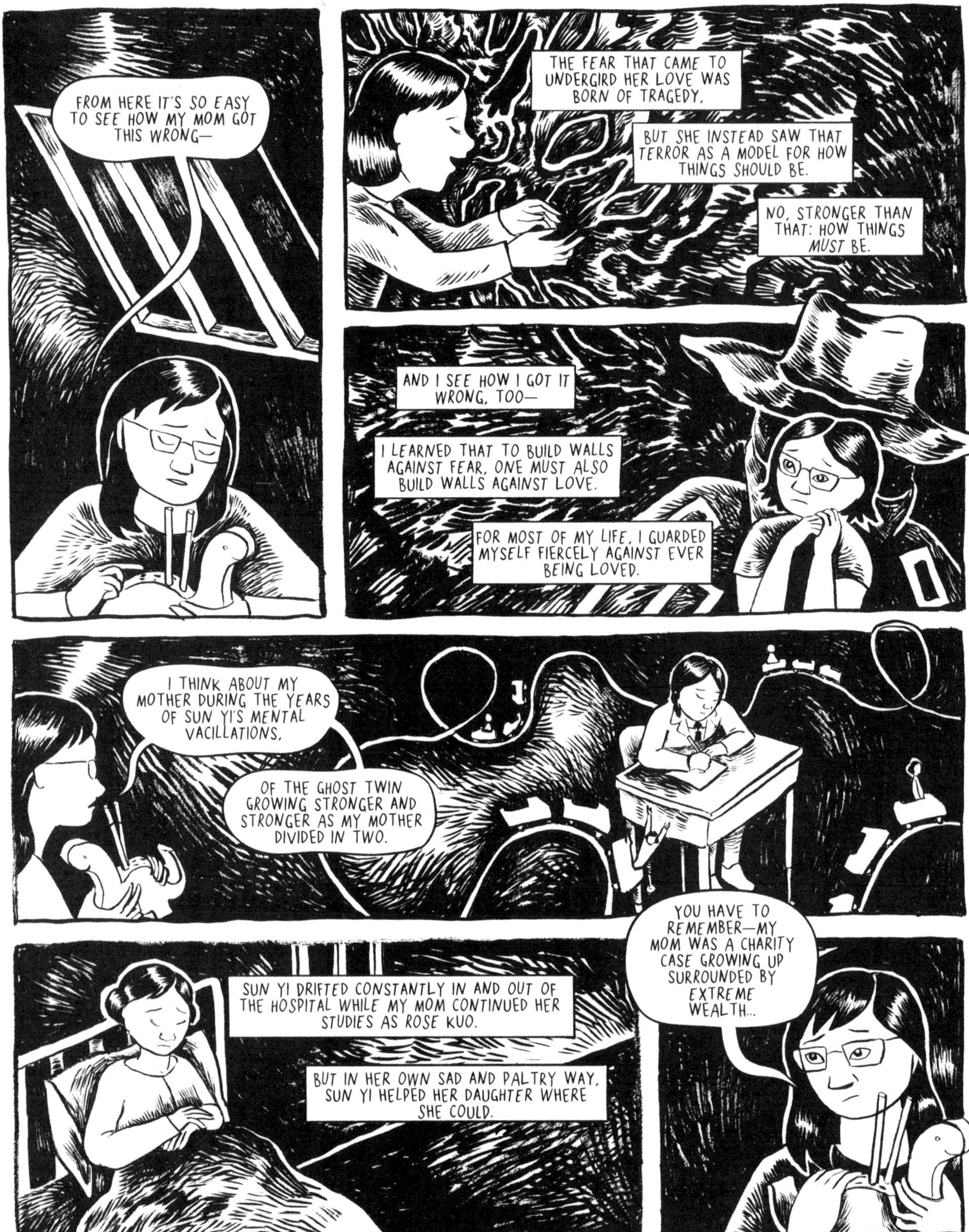
FROM HERE IT'S SO EASY TO SEE HOW MY MOM GOT THIS WRONG—
THE FEAR THAT CAME TO UNDERGIRD HER LOVE WAS BORN OF TRAGEDY,
BUT SHE INSTEAD SAW THAT TERROR AS A MODEL FOR HOW THINGS SHOULD BE.
NO, STRONGER THAN THAT: HOW THINGS *MUST* BE.
AND I SEE HOW I GOT IT WRONG, TOO—
I LEARNED THAT TO BUILD WALLS AGAINST FEAR, ONE MUST ALSO BUILD WALLS AGAINST LOVE.
FOR MOST OF MY LIFE, I GUARDED MYSELF FIERCELY AGAINST EVER BEING LOVED.
I THINK ABOUT MY MOTHER DURING THE YEARS OF SUN YI'S MENTAL VACILLATIONS,
OF THE GHOST TWIN GROWING STRONGER AND STRONGER AS MY MOTHER DIVIDED IN TWO.
SUN YI DRIFTED CONSTANTLY IN AND OUT OF THE HOSPITAL WHILE MY MOM CONTINUED HER STUDIES AS ROSE KUO.
BUT IN HER OWN SAD AND PALTRY WAY, SUN YI HELPED HER DAUGHTER WHERE SHE COULD.
YOU HAVE TO REMEMBER—MY MOM WAS A CHARITY CASE GROWING UP SURROUNDED BY EXTREME WEALTH...

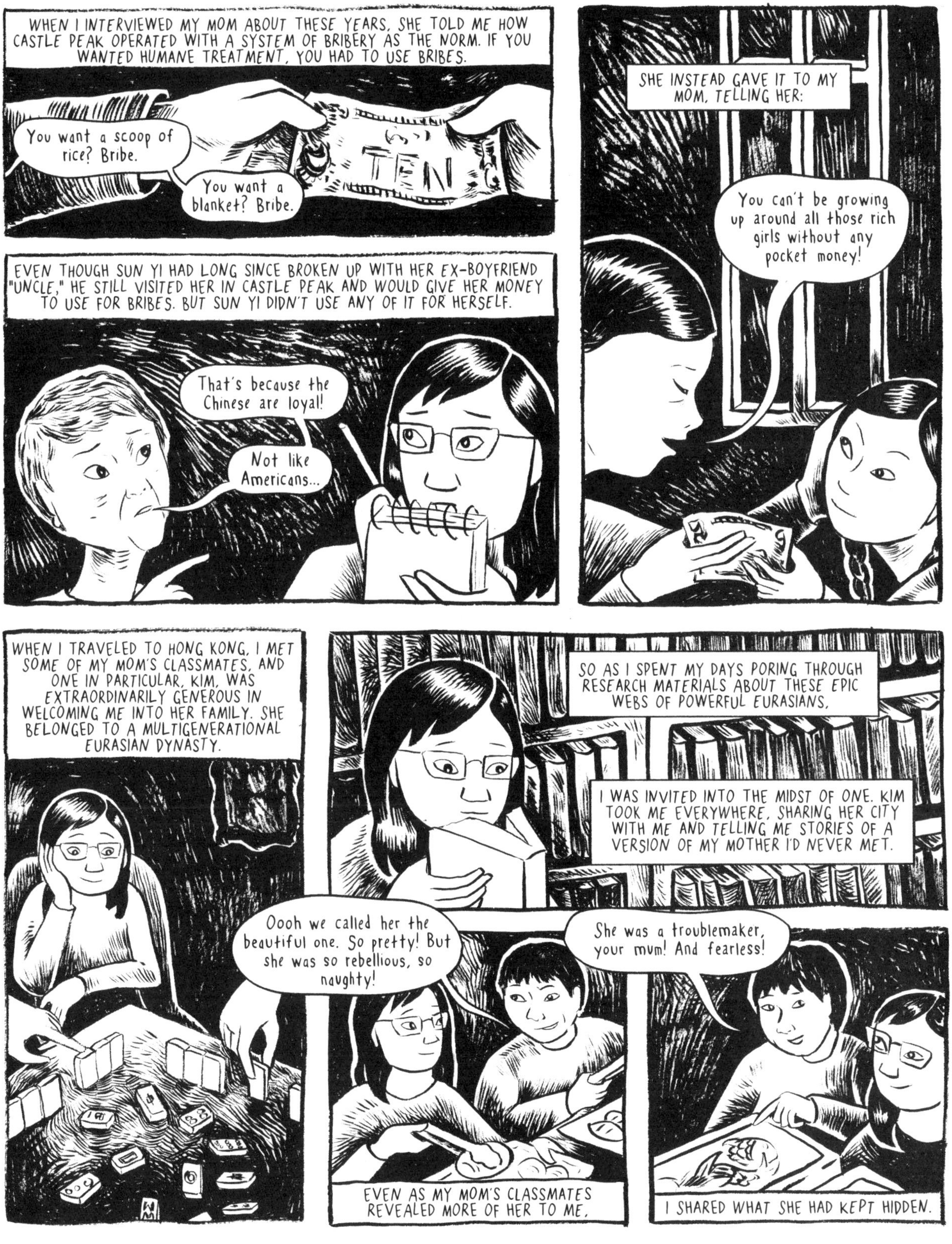
WHEN I INTERVIEWED MY MOM ABOUT THESE YEARS, SHE TOLD ME HOW CASTLE PEAK OPERATED WITH A SYSTEM OF BRIBERY AS THE NORM. IF YOU WANTED HUMANE TREATMENT, YOU HAD TO USE BRIBES.
You want a scoop of rice? Bribe.
You want a blanket? Bribe.
TEN
EVEN THOUGH SUN YI HAD LONG SINCE BROKEN UP WITH HER EX-BOYFRIEND "UNCLE," HE STILL VISITED HER IN CASTLE PEAK AND WOULD GIVE HER MONEY TO USE FOR BRIBES. BUT SUN YI DIDN'T USE ANY OF IT FOR HERSELF.
That's because the Chinese are loyal!
Not like Americans...
SHE INSTEAD GAVE IT TO MY MOM, TELLING HER:
You can't be growing up around all those rich girls without any pocket money!
WHEN I TRAVELED TO HONG KONG, I MET SOME OF MY MOM'S CLASSMATES, AND ONE IN PARTICULAR, KIM, WAS EXTRAORDINARILY GENEROUS IN WELCOMING ME INTO HER FAMILY. SHE BELONGED TO A MULTIGENERATIONAL EURASIAN DYNASTY.
SO AS I SPENT MY DAYS PORING THROUGH RESEARCH MATERIALS ABOUT THESE EPIC WEBS OF POWERFUL EURASIANS,
I WAS INVITED INTO THE MIDST OF ONE. KIM TOOK ME EVERYWHERE, SHARING HER CITY WITH ME AND TELLING ME STORIES OF A VERSION OF MY MOTHER I'D NEVER MET.
Oooh we called her the beautiful one. So pretty! But she was so rebellious, so naughty!
She was a troublemaker, your mum! And fearless!
EVEN AS MY MOM'S CLASSMATES REVEALED MORE OF HER TO ME,
I SHARED WHAT SHE HAD KEPT HIDDEN.

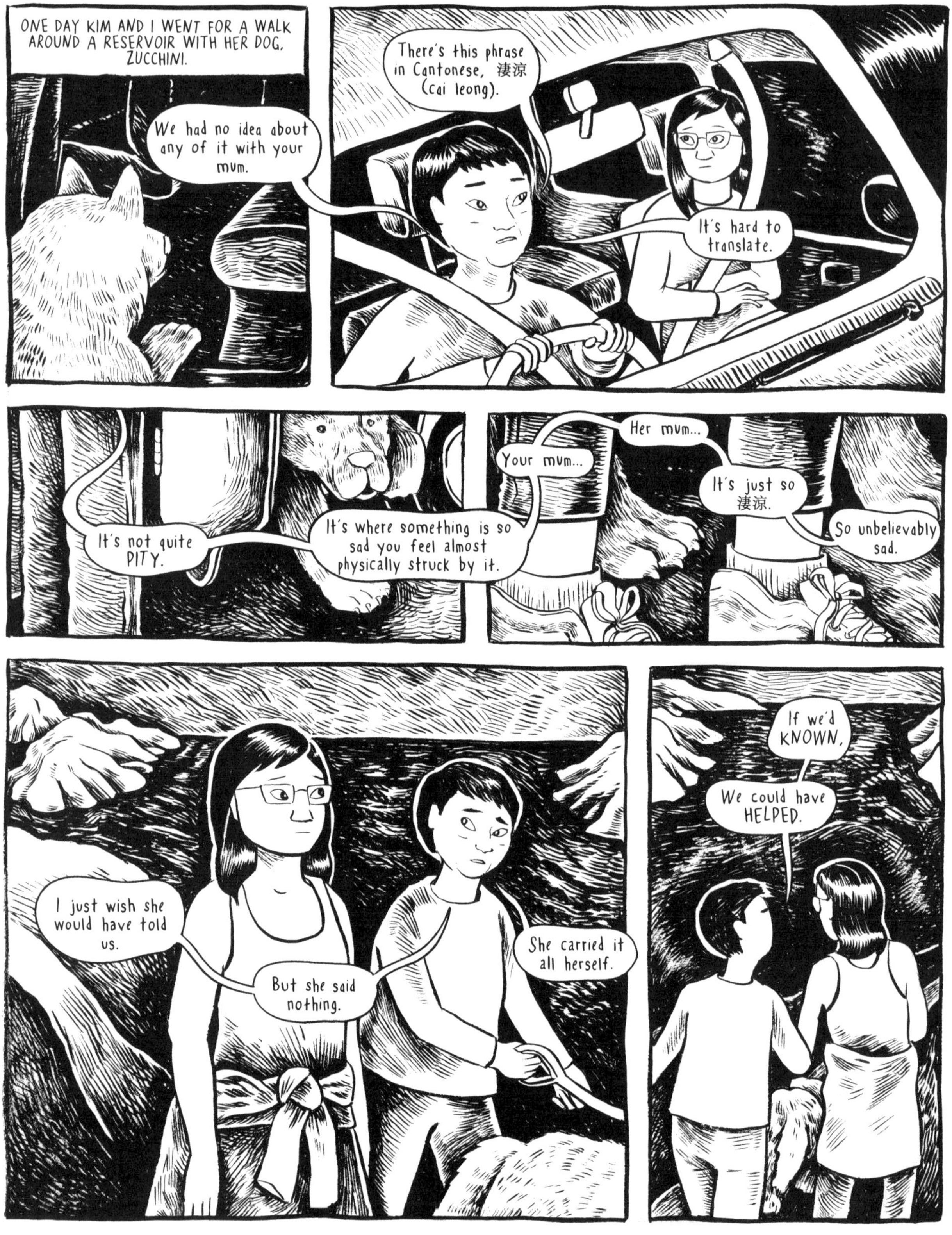
ONE DAY KIM AND I WENT FOR A WALK AROUND A RESERVOIR WITH HER DOG, ZUCCHINI.
We had no idea about any of it with your mum.
There's this phrase in Cantonese, 淒涼 (cai leong).
It's hard to translate.
It's not quite PITY.
It's where something is so sad you feel almost physically struck by it.
Your mum...
Her mum...
It's just so 淒涼.
So unbelievably sad.
I just wish she would have told us.
But she said nothing.
She carried it all herself.
If we'd KNOWN,
We could have HELPED.

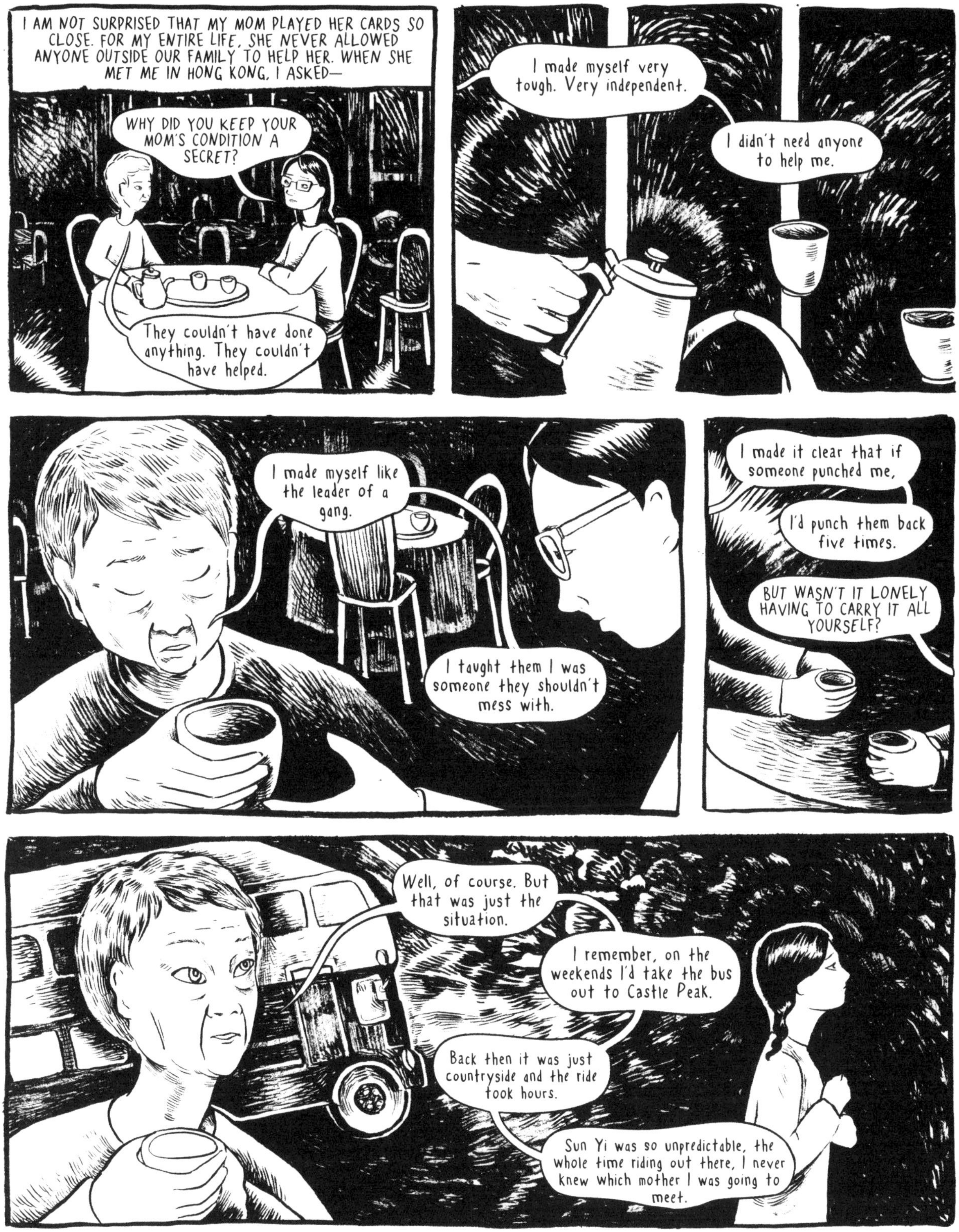

I AM NOT SURPRISED THAT MY MOM PLAYED HER CARDS SO CLOSE. FOR MY ENTIRE LIFE, SHE NEVER ALLOWED ANYONE OUTSIDE OUR FAMILY TO HELP HER. WHEN SHE MET ME IN HONG KONG, I ASKED—
WHY DID YOU KEEP YOUR MOM'S CONDITION A SECRET?
They couldn't have done anything. They couldn't have helped.
I made myself very tough. Very independent.
I didn't need anyone to help me.
I made myself like the leader of a gang.
I taught them I was someone they shouldn't mess with.
I made it clear that if someone punched me,
I'd punch them back five times.
BUT WASN'T IT LONELY HAVING TO CARRY IT ALL YOURSELF?
Well, of course. But that was just the situation.
I remember, on the weekends I'd take the bus out to Castle Peak.
Back then it was just countryside and the ride took hours.
Sun Yi was so unpredictable, the whole time riding out there, I never knew which mother I was going to meet.

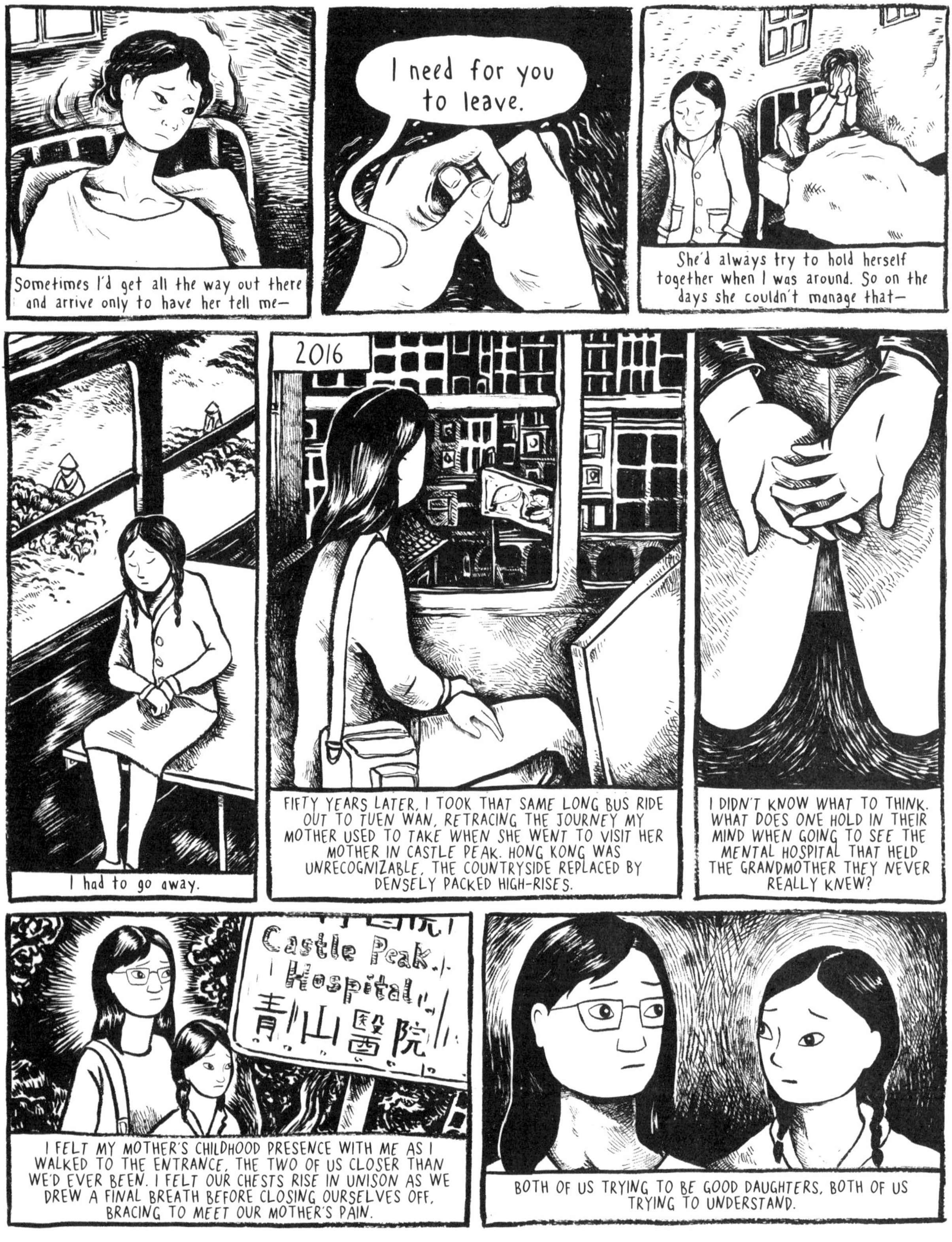
Sometimes I'd get all the way out there and arrive only to have her tell me—
I need for you to leave.
She'd always try to hold herself together when I was around. So on the days she couldn't manage that—
I had to go away.
2016
FIFTY YEARS LATER, I TOOK THAT SAME LONG BUS RIDE OUT TO TUEN WAN, RETRACING THE JOURNEY MY MOTHER USED TO TAKE WHEN SHE WENT TO VISIT HER MOTHER IN CASTLE PEAK. HONG KONG WAS UNRECOGNIZABLE, THE COUNTRYSIDE REPLACED BY DENSELY PACKED HIGH-RISES.
I DIDN'T KNOW WHAT TO THINK. WHAT DOES ONE HOLD IN THEIR MIND WHEN GOING TO SEE THE MENTAL HOSPITAL THAT HELD THE GRANDMOTHER THEY NEVER REALLY KNEW?
Castle Peak Hospital
青山醫院
I FELT MY MOTHER'S CHILDHOOD PRESENCE WITH ME AS I WALKED TO THE ENTRANCE, THE TWO OF US CLOSER THAN WE'D EVER BEEN. I FELT OUR CHESTS RISE IN UNISON AS WE DREW A FINAL BREATH BEFORE CLOSING OURSELVES OFF, BRACING TO MEET OUR MOTHER'S PAIN.
BOTH OF US TRYING TO BE GOOD DAUGHTERS, BOTH OF US TRYING TO UNDERSTAND.

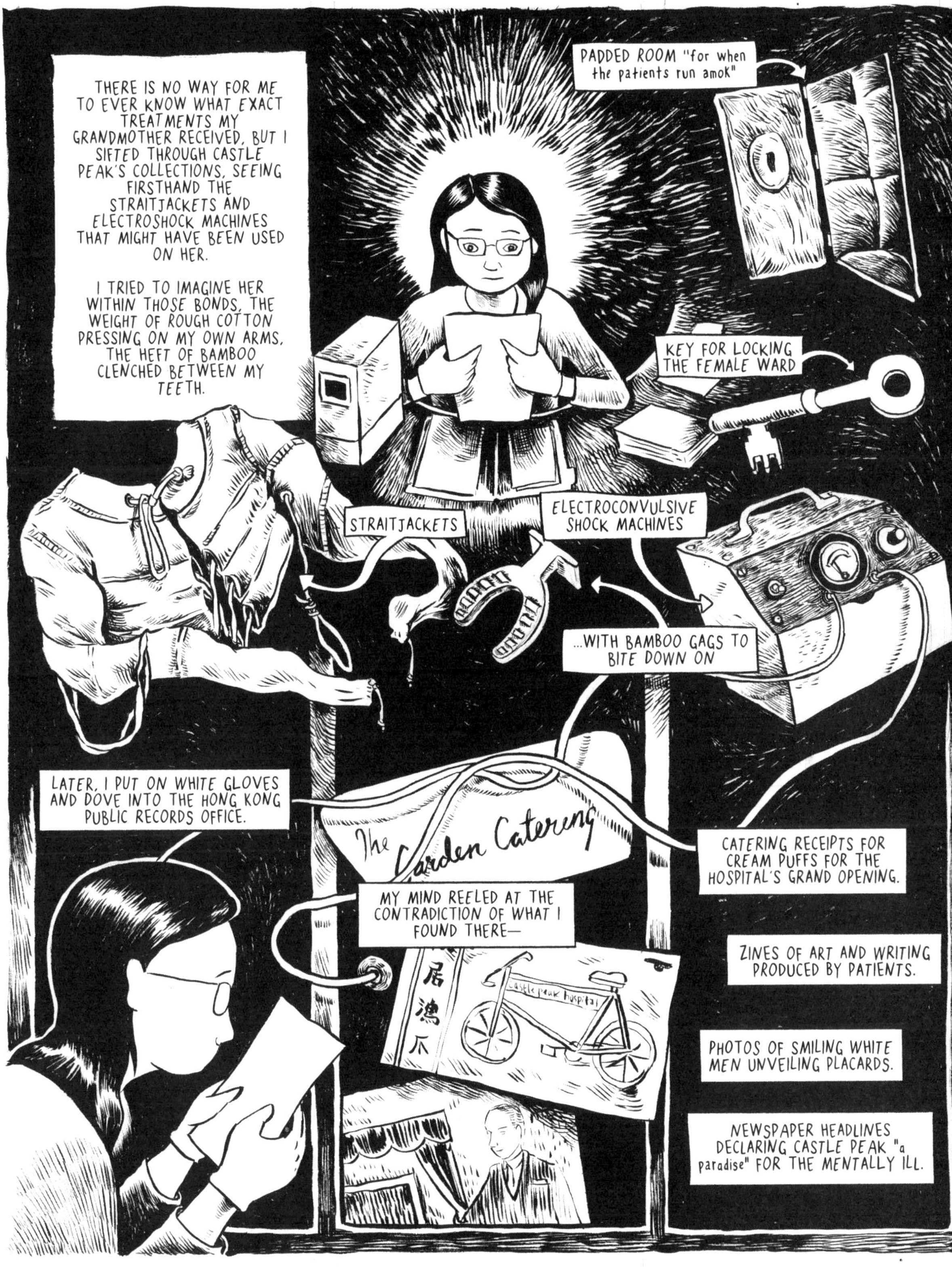
THERE IS NO WAY FOR ME TO EVER KNOW WHAT EXACT TREATMENTS MY GRANDMOTHER RECEIVED, BUT I SIFTED THROUGH CASTLE PEAK'S COLLECTIONS, SEEING FIRSTHAND THE STRAITJACKETS AND ELECTROSHOCK MACHINES THAT MIGHT HAVE BEEN USED ON HER.
I TRIED TO IMAGINE HER WITHIN THOSE BONDS, THE WEIGHT OF ROUGH COTTON PRESSING ON MY OWN ARMS, THE HEFT OF BAMBOO CLENCHED BETWEEN MY TEETH.
PADDED ROOM "for when the patients run amok"
KEY FOR LOCKING THE FEMALE WARD
STRAITJACKETS
ELECTROCONVULSIVE SHOCK MACHINES
...WITH BAMBOO GAGS TO BITE DOWN ON
LATER, I PUT ON WHITE GLOVES AND DOVE INTO THE HONG KONG PUBLIC RECORDS OFFICE.
The Garden Catering
CATERING RECEIPTS FOR CREAM PUFFS FOR THE HOSPITAL'S GRAND OPENING.
MY MIND REELED AT THE CONTRADICTION OF WHAT I FOUND THERE—
ZINES OF ART AND WRITING PRODUCED BY PATIENTS.
居漁爪
castle peak hospital
PHOTOS OF SMILING WHITE MEN UNVEILING PLACARDS.
NEWSPAPER HEADLINES DECLARING CASTLE PEAK "a paradise" FOR THE MENTALLY ILL.

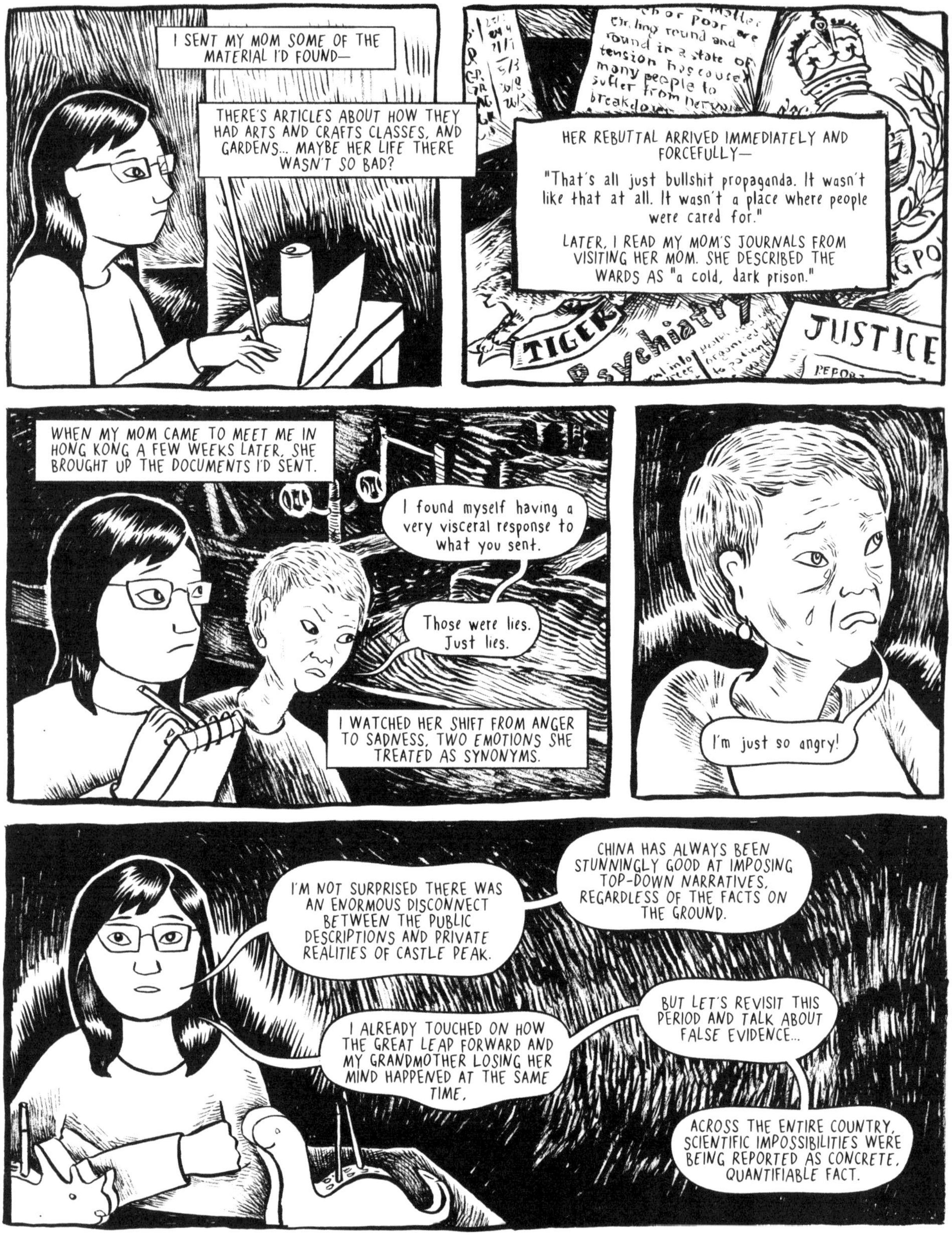
I SENT MY MOM SOME OF THE MATERIAL I'D FOUND—
THERE'S ARTICLES ABOUT HOW THEY HAD ARTS AND CRAFTS CLASSES, AND GARDENS... MAYBE HER LIFE THERE WASN'T SO BAD?
HER REBUTTAL ARRIVED IMMEDIATELY AND FORCEFULLY—
"That's all just bullshit propaganda. It wasn't like that at all. It wasn't a place where people were cared for."
LATER, I READ MY MOM'S JOURNALS FROM VISITING HER MOM. SHE DESCRIBED THE WARDS AS "a cold, dark prison."
TIGER
JUSTICE
WHEN MY MOM CAME TO MEET ME IN HONG KONG A FEW WEEKS LATER, SHE BROUGHT UP THE DOCUMENTS I'D SENT.
I found myself having a very visceral response to what you sent.
Those were lies. Just lies.
I WATCHED HER SHIFT FROM ANGER TO SADNESS, TWO EMOTIONS SHE TREATED AS SYNONYMS.
I'm just so angry!
I'M NOT SURPRISED THERE WAS AN ENORMOUS DISCONNECT BETWEEN THE PUBLIC DESCRIPTIONS AND PRIVATE REALITIES OF CASTLE PEAK.
CHINA HAS ALWAYS BEEN STUNNINGLY GOOD AT IMPOSING TOP-DOWN NARRATIVES, REGARDLESS OF THE FACTS ON THE GROUND.
I ALREADY TOUCHED ON HOW THE GREAT LEAP FORWARD AND MY GRANDMOTHER LOSING HER MIND HAPPENED AT THE SAME TIME.
BUT LET'S REVISIT THIS PERIOD AND TALK ABOUT FALSE EVIDENCE...
ACROSS THE ENTIRE COUNTRY, SCIENTIFIC IMPOSSIBILITIES WERE BEING REPORTED AS CONCRETE, QUANTIFIABLE FACT.

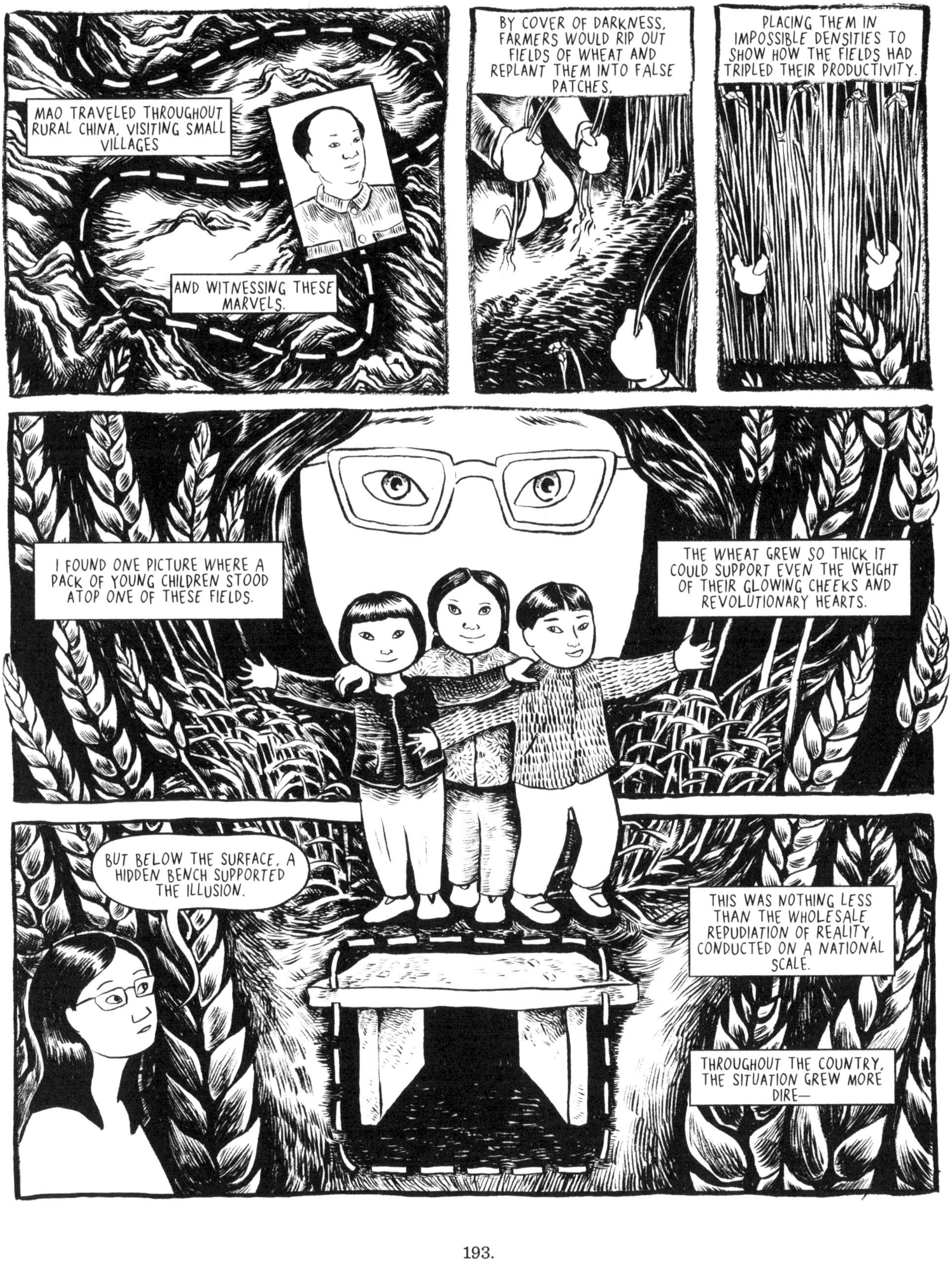
MAO TRAVELED THROUGHOUT RURAL CHINA, VISITING SMALL VILLAGES
AND WITNESSING THESE MARVELS.
BY COVER OF DARKNESS, FARMERS WOULD RIP OUT FIELDS OF WHEAT AND REPLANT THEM INTO FALSE PATCHES,
PLACING THEM IN IMPOSSIBLE DENSITIES TO SHOW HOW THE FIELDS HAD TRIPLED THEIR PRODUCTIVITY.
I FOUND ONE PICTURE WHERE A PACK OF YOUNG CHILDREN STOOD ATOP ONE OF THESE FIELDS.
THE WHEAT GREW SO THICK IT COULD SUPPORT EVEN THE WEIGHT OF THEIR GLOWING CHEEKS AND REVOLUTIONARY HEARTS.
BUT BELOW THE SURFACE, A HIDDEN BENCH SUPPORTED THE ILLUSION.
THIS WAS NOTHING LESS THAN THE WHOLESALE REPUDIATION OF REALITY, CONDUCTED ON A NATIONAL SCALE.
THROUGHOUT THE COUNTRY, THE SITUATION GREW MORE DIRE—

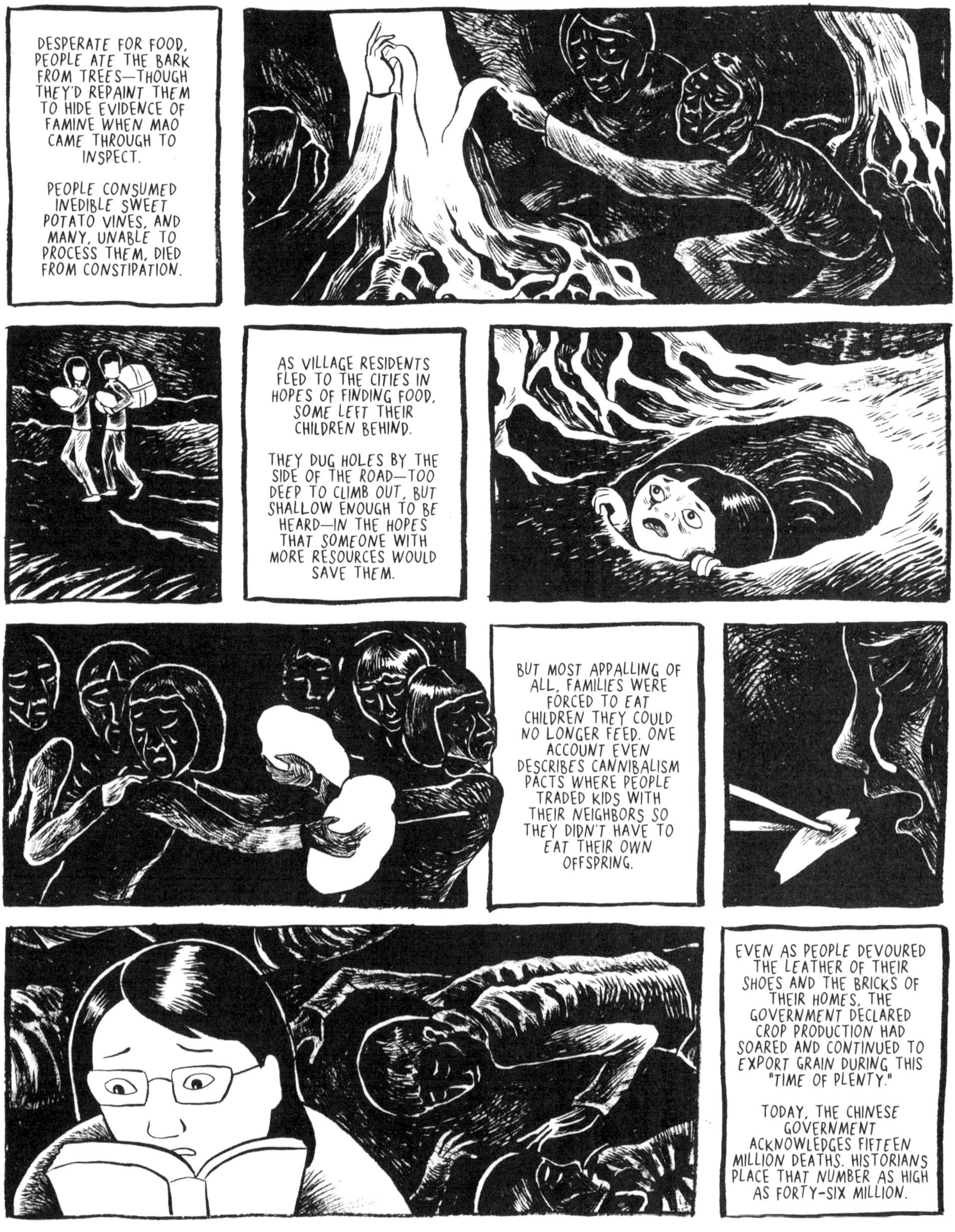
DESPERATE FOR FOOD, PEOPLE ATE THE BARK FROM TREES—THOUGH THEY'D REPAINT THEM TO HIDE EVIDENCE OF FAMINE WHEN MAO CAME THROUGH TO INSPECT.
PEOPLE CONSUMED INEDIBLE SWEET POTATO VINES, AND MANY, UNABLE TO PROCESS THEM, DIED FROM CONSTIPATION.
AS VILLAGE RESIDENTS FLED TO THE CITIES IN HOPES OF FINDING FOOD, SOME LEFT THEIR CHILDREN BEHIND.
THEY DUG HOLES BY THE SIDE OF THE ROAD—TOO DEEP TO CLIMB OUT, BUT SHALLOW ENOUGH TO BE HEARD—IN THE HOPES THAT SOMEONE WITH MORE RESOURCES WOULD SAVE THEM.
BUT MOST APPALLING OF ALL, FAMILIES WERE FORCED TO EAT CHILDREN THEY COULD NO LONGER FEED. ONE ACCOUNT EVEN DESCRIBES CANNIBALISM PACTS WHERE PEOPLE TRADED KIDS WITH THEIR NEIGHBORS SO THEY DIDN'T HAVE TO EAT THEIR OWN OFFSPRING.
EVEN AS PEOPLE DEVOURED THE LEATHER OF THEIR SHOES AND THE BRICKS OF THEIR HOMES, THE GOVERNMENT DECLARED CROP PRODUCTION HAD SOARED AND CONTINUED TO EXPORT GRAIN DURING THIS "TIME OF PLENTY."
TODAY, THE CHINESE GOVERNMENT ACKNOWLEDGES FIFTEEN MILLION DEATHS. HISTORIANS PLACE THAT NUMBER AS HIGH AS FORTY-SIX MILLION.

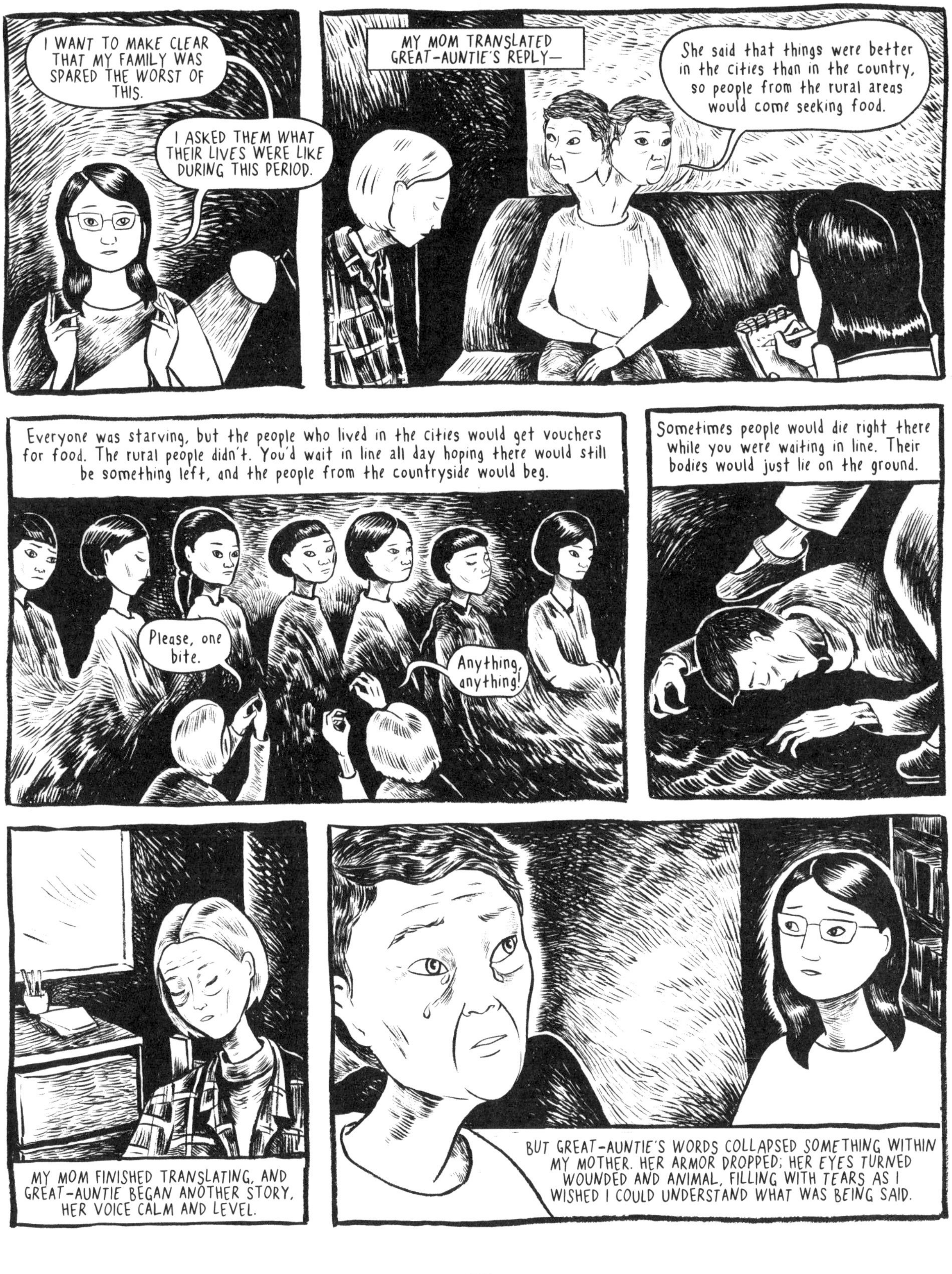
I WANT TO MAKE CLEAR THAT MY FAMILY WAS SPARED THE WORST OF THIS.
I ASKED THEM WHAT THEIR LIVES WERE LIKE DURING THIS PERIOD.
MY MOM TRANSLATED GREAT-AUNTIE'S REPLY—
She said that things were better in the cities than in the country, so people from the rural areas would come seeking food.
Everyone was starving, but the people who lived in the cities would get vouchers for food. The rural people didn't. You'd wait in line all day hoping there would still be something left, and the people from the countryside would beg.
Please, one bite.
Anything, anything!
Sometimes people would die right there while you were waiting in line. Their bodies would just lie on the ground.
MY MOM FINISHED TRANSLATING, AND GREAT-AUNTIE BEGAN ANOTHER STORY, HER VOICE CALM AND LEVEL.
BUT GREAT-AUNTIE'S WORDS COLLAPSED SOMETHING WITHIN MY MOTHER. HER ARMOR DROPPED; HER EYES TURNED WOUNDED AND ANIMAL, FILLING WITH TEARS AS I WISHED I COULD UNDERSTAND WHAT WAS BEING SAID.

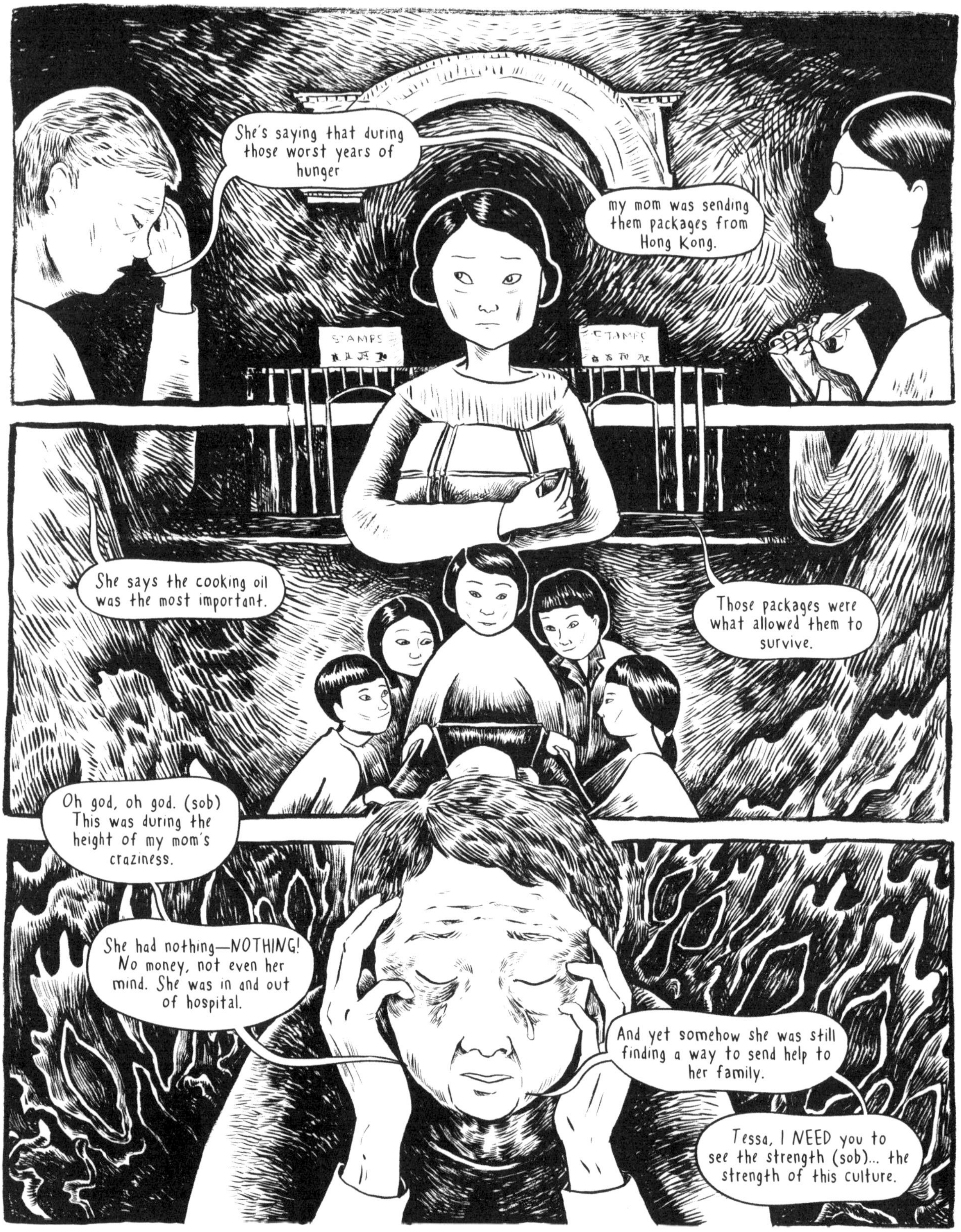

She's saying that during those worst years of hunger
my mom was sending them packages from Hong Kong.
STAMPS
STAMPS
She says the cooking oil was the most important.
Those packages were what allowed them to survive.
Oh god, oh god. (sob) This was during the height of my mom's craziness.
She had nothing—NOTHING! No money, not even her mind. She was in and out of hospital.
And yet somehow she was still finding a way to send help to her family.
Tessa, I NEED you to see the strength (sob)... the strength of this culture.

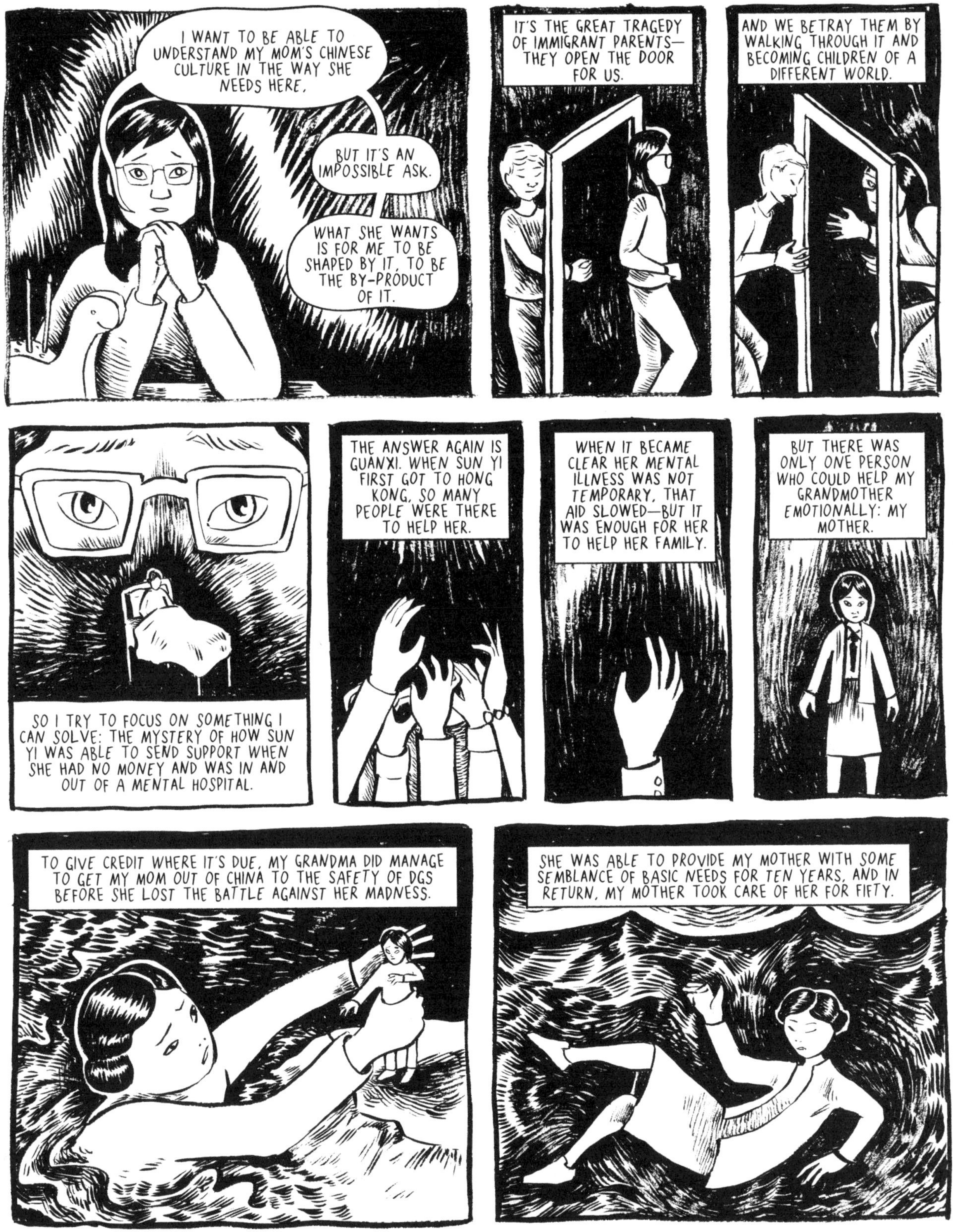
I WANT TO BE ABLE TO UNDERSTAND MY MOM'S CHINESE CULTURE IN THE WAY SHE NEEDS HERE,
BUT IT'S AN IMPOSSIBLE ASK.
WHAT SHE WANTS IS FOR ME TO BE SHAPED BY IT, TO BE THE BY-PRODUCT OF IT.
IT'S THE GREAT TRAGEDY OF IMMIGRANT PARENTS— THEY OPEN THE DOOR FOR US.
AND WE BETRAY THEM BY WALKING THROUGH IT AND BECOMING CHILDREN OF A DIFFERENT WORLD.
SO I TRY TO FOCUS ON SOMETHING I CAN SOLVE: THE MYSTERY OF HOW SUN YI WAS ABLE TO SEND SUPPORT WHEN SHE HAD NO MONEY AND WAS IN AND OUT OF A MENTAL HOSPITAL.
THE ANSWER AGAIN IS GUANXI. WHEN SUN YI FIRST GOT TO HONG KONG, SO MANY PEOPLE WERE THERE TO HELP HER.
WHEN IT BECAME CLEAR HER MENTAL ILLNESS WAS NOT TEMPORARY, THAT AID SLOWED—BUT IT WAS ENOUGH FOR HER TO HELP HER FAMILY.
BUT THERE WAS ONLY ONE PERSON WHO COULD HELP MY GRANDMOTHER EMOTIONALLY: MY MOTHER.
TO GIVE CREDIT WHERE IT'S DUE, MY GRANDMA DID MANAGE TO GET MY MOM OUT OF CHINA TO THE SAFETY OF DGS BEFORE SHE LOST THE BATTLE AGAINST HER MADNESS.
SHE WAS ABLE TO PROVIDE MY MOTHER WITH SOME SEMBLANCE OF BASIC NEEDS FOR TEN YEARS, AND IN RETURN, MY MOTHER TOOK CARE OF HER FOR FIFTY.

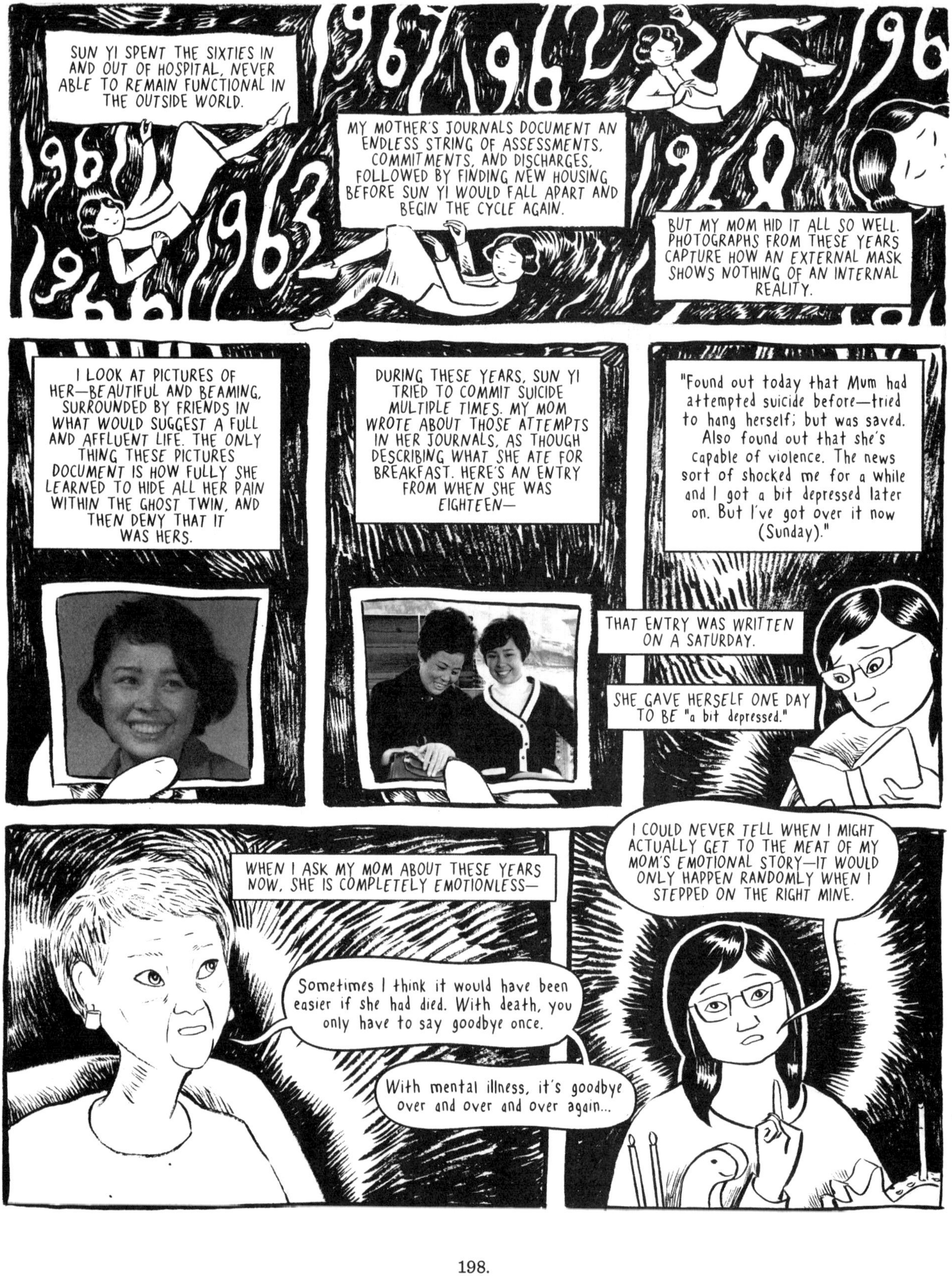
SUN YI SPENT THE SIXTIES IN AND OUT OF HOSPITAL, NEVER ABLE TO REMAIN FUNCTIONAL IN THE OUTSIDE WORLD.
MY MOTHER'S JOURNALS DOCUMENT AN ENDLESS STRING OF ASSESSMENTS, COMMITMENTS, AND DISCHARGES, FOLLOWED BY FINDING NEW HOUSING BEFORE SUN YI WOULD FALL APART AND BEGIN THE CYCLE AGAIN.
BUT MY MOM HID IT ALL SO WELL. PHOTOGRAPHS FROM THESE YEARS CAPTURE HOW AN EXTERNAL MASK SHOWS NOTHING OF AN INTERNAL REALITY.
I LOOK AT PICTURES OF HER—BEAUTIFUL AND BEAMING, SURROUNDED BY FRIENDS IN WHAT WOULD SUGGEST A FULL AND AFFLUENT LIFE. THE ONLY THING THESE PICTURES DOCUMENT IS HOW FULLY SHE LEARNED TO HIDE ALL HER PAIN WITHIN THE GHOST TWIN, AND THEN DENY THAT IT WAS HERS.
DURING THESE YEARS, SUN YI TRIED TO COMMIT SUICIDE MULTIPLE TIMES. MY MOM WROTE ABOUT THOSE ATTEMPTS IN HER JOURNALS, AS THOUGH DESCRIBING WHAT SHE ATE FOR BREAKFAST. HERE'S AN ENTRY FROM WHEN SHE WAS EIGHTEEN—
"Found out today that Mum had attempted suicide before—tried to hang herself; but was saved. Also found out that she's capable of violence. The news sort of shocked me for a while and I got a bit depressed later on. But I've got over it now (Sunday)."
THAT ENTRY WAS WRITTEN ON A SATURDAY.
SHE GAVE HERSELF ONE DAY TO BE "a bit depressed."
WHEN I ASK MY MOM ABOUT THESE YEARS NOW, SHE IS COMPLETELY EMOTIONLESS—
Sometimes I think it would have been easier if she had died. With death, you only have to say goodbye once.
With mental illness, it's goodbye over and over and over again...
I COULD NEVER TELL WHEN I MIGHT ACTUALLY GET TO THE MEAT OF MY MOM'S EMOTIONAL STORY—IT WOULD ONLY HAPPEN RANDOMLY WHEN I STEPPED ON THE RIGHT MINE.

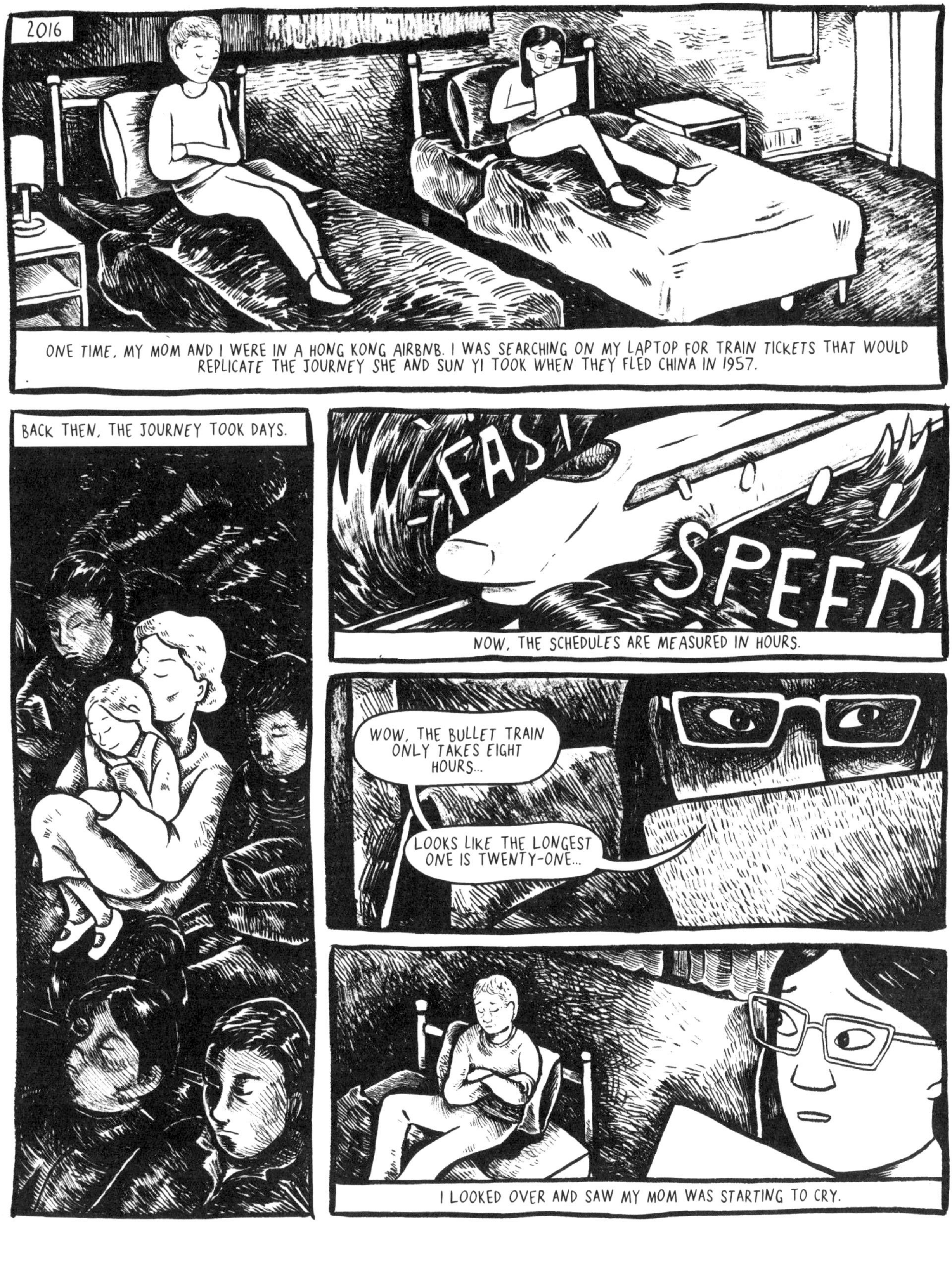
2016
ONE TIME, MY MOM AND I WERE IN A HONG KONG AIRBNB. I WAS SEARCHING ON MY LAPTOP FOR TRAIN TICKETS THAT WOULD REPLICATE THE JOURNEY SHE AND SUN YI TOOK WHEN THEY FLED CHINA IN 1957.
BACK THEN, THE JOURNEY TOOK DAYS.
FAST
SPEED
NOW, THE SCHEDULES ARE MEASURED IN HOURS.
WOW, THE BULLET TRAIN ONLY TAKES EIGHT HOURS...
LOOKS LIKE THE LONGEST ONE IS TWENTY-ONE...
I LOOKED OVER AND SAW MY MOM WAS STARTING TO CRY.

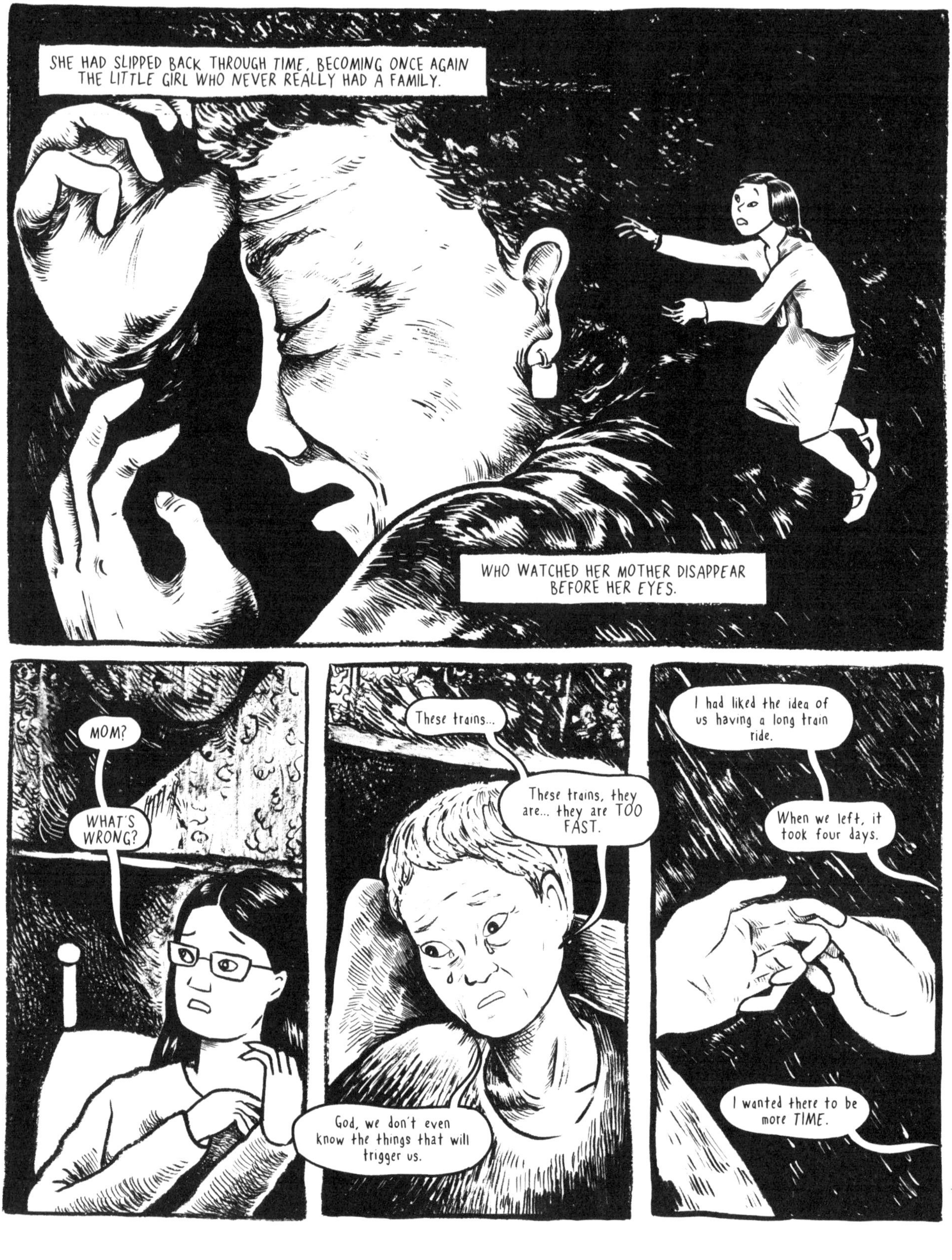
SHE HAD SLIPPED BACK THROUGH TIME, BECOMING ONCE AGAIN THE LITTLE GIRL WHO NEVER REALLY HAD A FAMILY.
WHO WATCHED HER MOTHER DISAPPEAR BEFORE HER EYES.
MOM?
WHAT'S WRONG?
These trains...
These trains, they are... they are TOO FAST.
God, we don't even know the things that will trigger us.
I had liked the idea of us having a long train ride.
When we left, it took four days.
I wanted there to be more TIME.

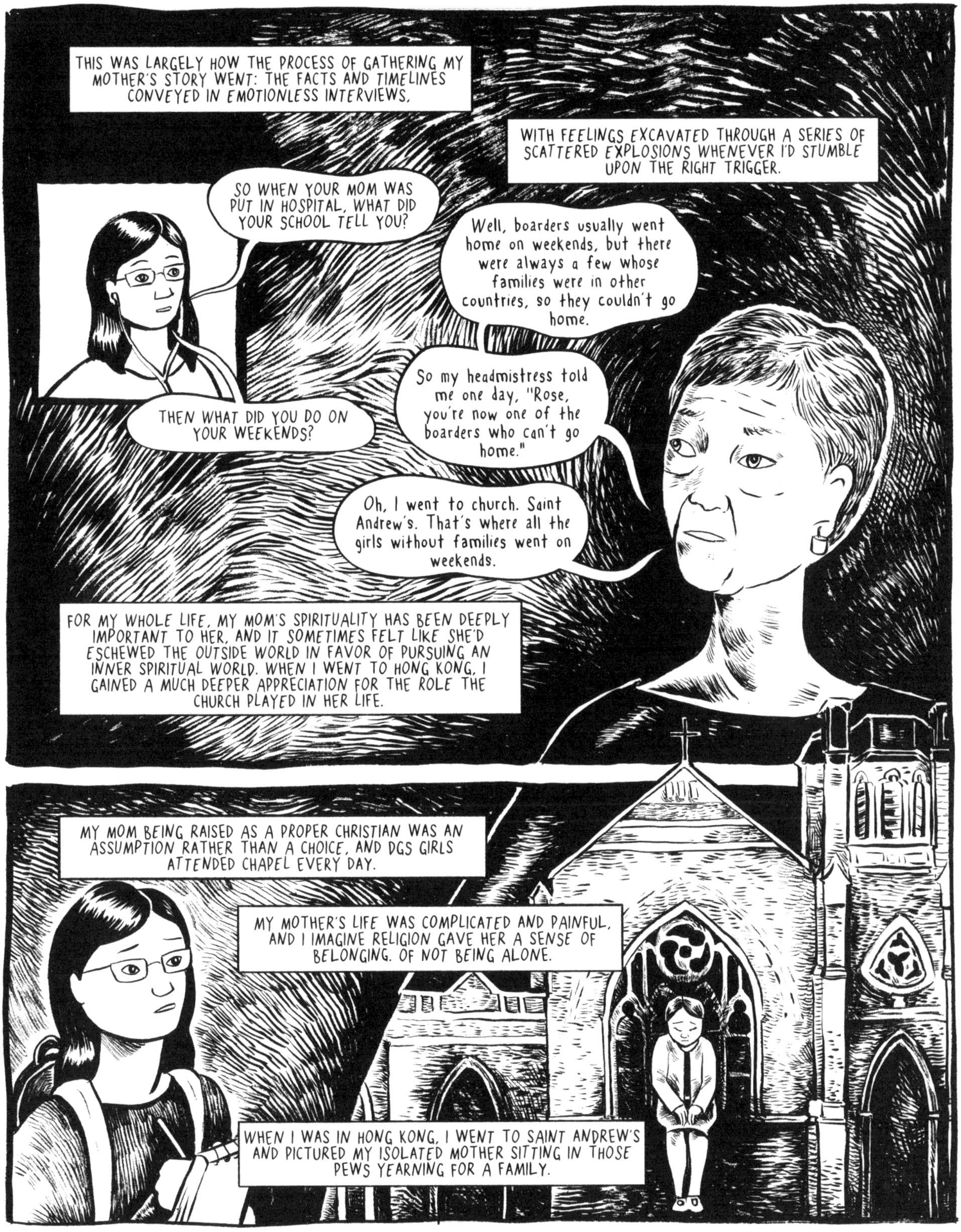

THIS WAS LARGELY HOW THE PROCESS OF GATHERING MY MOTHER'S STORY WENT: THE FACTS AND TIMELINES CONVEYED IN EMOTIONLESS INTERVIEWS,
WITH FEELINGS EXCAVATED THROUGH A SERIES OF SCATTERED EXPLOSIONS WHENEVER I'D STUMBLE UPON THE RIGHT TRIGGER.
SO WHEN YOUR MOM WAS PUT IN HOSPITAL, WHAT DID YOUR SCHOOL TELL YOU?
Well, boarders usually went home on weekends, but there were always a few whose families were in other countries, so they couldn't go home.
So my headmistress told me one day, "Rose, you're now one of the boarders who can't go home."
THEN WHAT DID YOU DO ON YOUR WEEKENDS?
Oh, I went to church. Saint Andrew's. That's where all the girls without families went on weekends.
FOR MY WHOLE LIFE, MY MOM'S SPIRITUALITY HAS BEEN DEEPLY IMPORTANT TO HER, AND IT SOMETIMES FELT LIKE SHE'D ESCHEWED THE OUTSIDE WORLD IN FAVOR OF PURSUING AN INNER SPIRITUAL WORLD. WHEN I WENT TO HONG KONG, I GAINED A MUCH DEEPER APPRECIATION FOR THE ROLE THE CHURCH PLAYED IN HER LIFE.
MY MOM BEING RAISED AS A PROPER CHRISTIAN WAS AN ASSUMPTION RATHER THAN A CHOICE, AND DGS GIRLS ATTENDED CHAPEL EVERY DAY.
MY MOTHER'S LIFE WAS COMPLICATED AND PAINFUL, AND I IMAGINE RELIGION GAVE HER A SENSE OF BELONGING. OF NOT BEING ALONE.
WHEN I WAS IN HONG KONG, I WENT TO SAINT ANDREW'S AND PICTURED MY ISOLATED MOTHER SITTING IN THOSE PEWS YEARNING FOR A FAMILY.

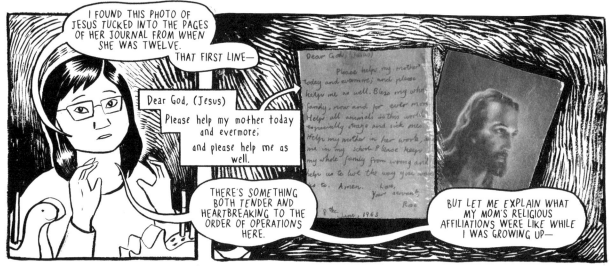

I FOUND THIS PHOTO OF JESUS TUCKED INTO THE PAGES OF HER JOURNAL FROM WHEN SHE WAS TWELVE. THAT FIRST LINE—

Dear God, (Jesus)

Please help my mother today and evermore;

and please help me as well.

THERE'S SOMETHING BOTH TENDER AND HEARTBREAKING TO THE ORDER OF OPERATIONS HERE.

Dear God, (Jesus)
Please help my mother today and evermore; and please help me as well. Bless my whole family, now and for ever more. Help all animals in this world especially strays and sick ones. Help my mother in her work, and me in my school. Please keep my whole family from wrong and help us to live the way you want us to. Amen. Love, Your servant, Ro.

8th June, 1965

BUT LET ME EXPLAIN WHAT MY MOM'S RELIGIOUS AFFILIATIONS WERE LIKE WHILE I WAS GROWING UP—

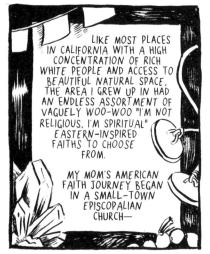

LIKE MOST PLACES IN CALIFORNIA WITH A HIGH CONCENTRATION OF RICH WHITE PEOPLE AND ACCESS TO BEAUTIFUL NATURAL SPACE, THE AREA I GREW UP IN HAD AN ENDLESS ASSORTMENT OF VAGUELY WOO-WOO "I'M NOT RELIGIOUS, I'M SPIRITUAL" EASTERN-INSPIRED FAITHS TO CHOOSE FROM.

MY MOM'S AMERICAN FAITH JOURNEY BEGAN IN A SMALL-TOWN EPISCOPALIAN CHURCH—

BUT THEN SHE BRANCHED OUT, DABBLING IN VEDANTA...

...AND "SPIRITUAL NEUROSCIENCE"...

...AND BREATHING WORKSHOPS...

...AND SWAMI VIVEKANANDA...

...AND JUNGIAN ANALYSIS...

...BEFORE COMING TO REST IN SUFISM.

MY MOTHER'S SHIFTING FAITHS DU JOUR WOULD BE REFLECTED IN THE BOOKS SHE READ TO MY BROTHER AND ME.

WHEN SHE BECAME OBSESSED WITH NEAR-DEATH EXPERIENCES, SHE READ US FIRSTHAND ACCOUNTS OF PEOPLE WHO'D "SEEN THE WHITE LIGHT."

DURING A MORE CHRISTIAN PHASE, IT WAS THE CROSS AND THE SWITCHBLADE, ABOUT A SMALL-TOWN PREACHER SAVING INNER-CITY KIDS IN NEW YORK.

SHE WOULD BECOME SO CAUGHT UP IN WHAT SHE SAW AS "THE ANSWER" THAT SHE NEEDED IT TO BE THE ANSWER FOR EVERYONE ELSE.

DYING TO LIVE
NEAR DEATH EXPERIENCE

THE CROSS AND THE SWITCHBLADE
The thrilling true story of a country preacher pitted against teen age violence in big city slums

I WENT AND REREAD SOME OF THE BOOKS SHE READ US—

TO SAY THEY WERE AGE INAPPROPRIATE WOULD BE... AN UNDERSTATEMENT.

DESCRIPTIONS OF GANG KIDS ENGAGING IN SATANIC SEX PARTIES

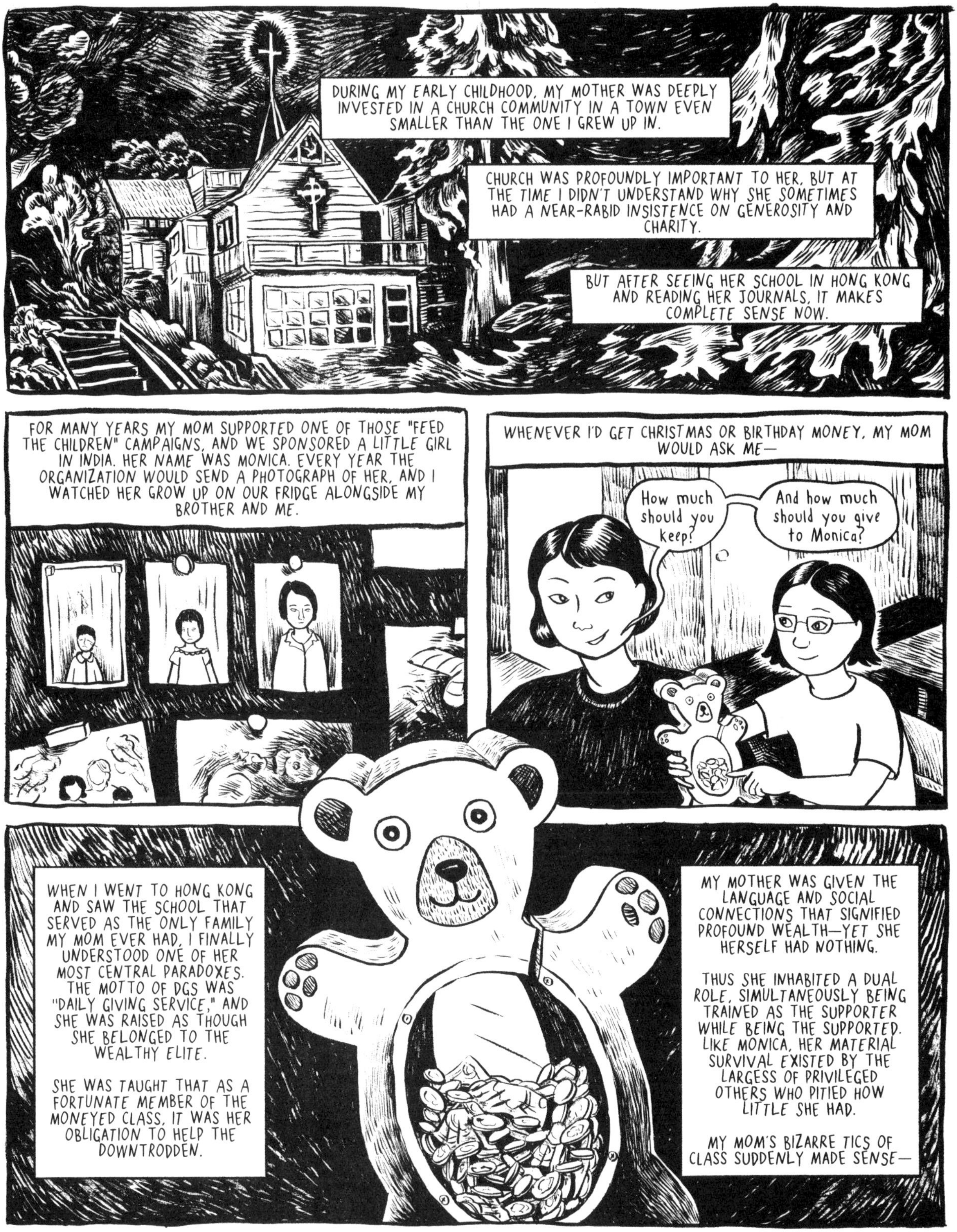
DURING MY EARLY CHILDHOOD, MY MOTHER WAS DEEPLY INVESTED IN A CHURCH COMMUNITY IN A TOWN EVEN SMALLER THAN THE ONE I GREW UP IN.
CHURCH WAS PROFOUNDLY IMPORTANT TO HER, BUT AT THE TIME I DIDN'T UNDERSTAND WHY SHE SOMETIMES HAD A NEAR-RABID INSISTENCE ON GENEROSITY AND CHARITY.
BUT AFTER SEEING HER SCHOOL IN HONG KONG AND READING HER JOURNALS, IT MAKES COMPLETE SENSE NOW.
FOR MANY YEARS MY MOM SUPPORTED ONE OF THOSE "FEED THE CHILDREN" CAMPAIGNS, AND WE SPONSORED A LITTLE GIRL IN INDIA. HER NAME WAS MONICA. EVERY YEAR THE ORGANIZATION WOULD SEND A PHOTOGRAPH OF HER, AND I WATCHED HER GROW UP ON OUR FRIDGE ALONGSIDE MY BROTHER AND ME.
WHENEVER I'D GET CHRISTMAS OR BIRTHDAY MONEY, MY MOM WOULD ASK ME—
How much should you keep?
And how much should you give to Monica?
WHEN I WENT TO HONG KONG AND SAW THE SCHOOL THAT SERVED AS THE ONLY FAMILY MY MOM EVER HAD, I FINALLY UNDERSTOOD ONE OF HER MOST CENTRAL PARADOXES. THE MOTTO OF DGS WAS "DAILY GIVING SERVICE," AND SHE WAS RAISED AS THOUGH SHE BELONGED TO THE WEALTHY ELITE.
SHE WAS TAUGHT THAT AS A FORTUNATE MEMBER OF THE MONEYED CLASS, IT WAS HER OBLIGATION TO HELP THE DOWNTRODDEN.
MY MOTHER WAS GIVEN THE LANGUAGE AND SOCIAL CONNECTIONS THAT SIGNIFIED PROFOUND WEALTH—YET SHE HERSELF HAD NOTHING.
THUS SHE INHABITED A DUAL ROLE, SIMULTANEOUSLY BEING TRAINED AS THE SUPPORTER WHILE BEING THE SUPPORTED. LIKE MONICA, HER MATERIAL SURVIVAL EXISTED BY THE LARGESS OF PRIVILEGED OTHERS WHO PITIED HOW LITTLE SHE HAD.
MY MOM'S BIZARRE TICS OF CLASS SUDDENLY MADE SENSE—

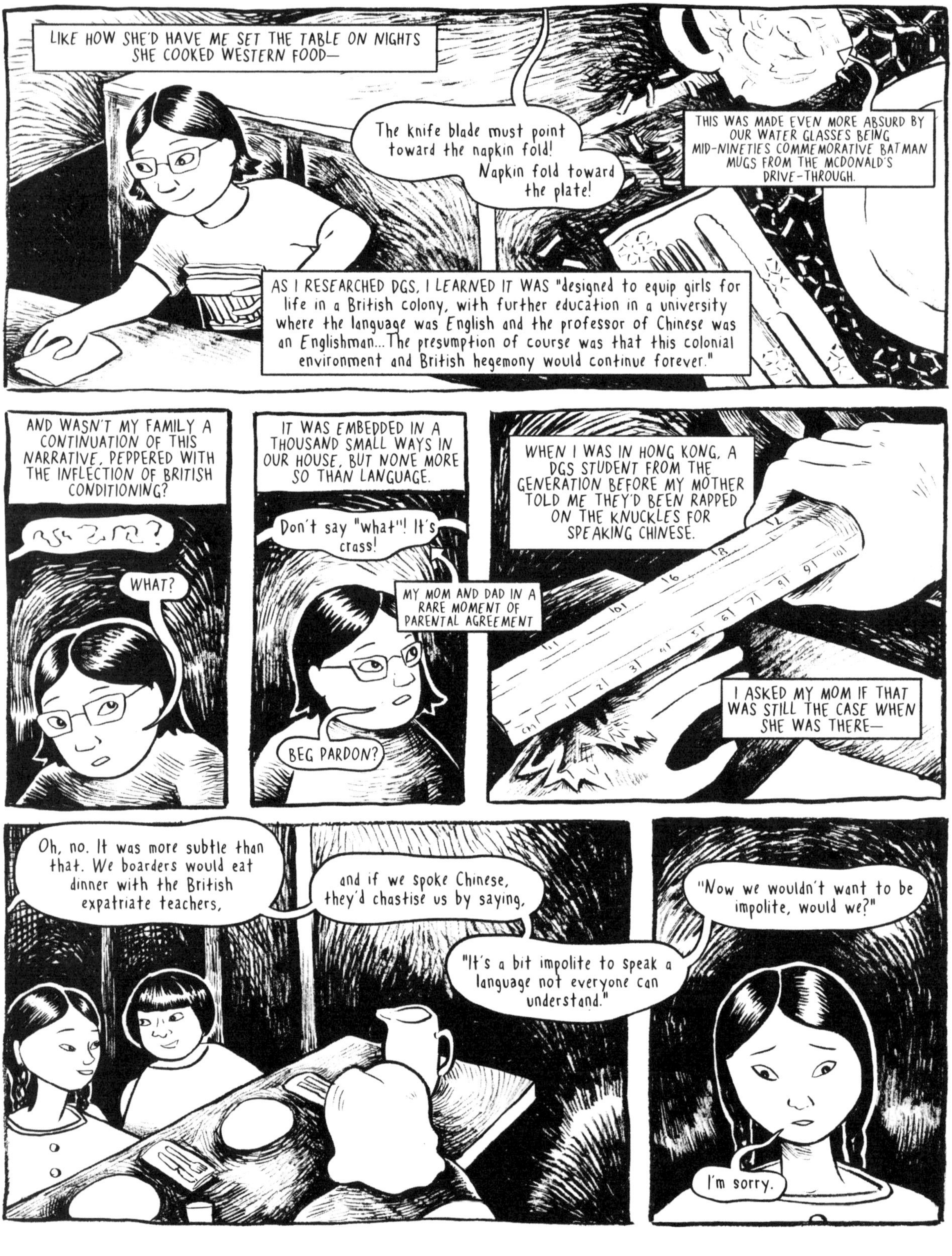
LIKE HOW SHE'D HAVE ME SET THE TABLE ON NIGHTS SHE COOKED WESTERN FOOD—
The knife blade must point toward the napkin fold!
Napkin fold toward the plate!
THIS WAS MADE EVEN MORE ABSURD BY OUR WATER GLASSES BEING MID-NINETIES COMMEMORATIVE BATMAN MUGS FROM THE MCDONALD'S DRIVE-THROUGH.
AS I RESEARCHED DGS, I LEARNED IT WAS "designed to equip girls for life in a British colony, with further education in a university where the language was English and the professor of Chinese was an Englishman... The presumption of course was that this colonial environment and British hegemony would continue forever."
AND WASN'T MY FAMILY A CONTINUATION OF THIS NARRATIVE, PEPPERED WITH THE INFLECTION OF BRITISH CONDITIONING?
WHAT?
IT WAS EMBEDDED IN A THOUSAND SMALL WAYS IN OUR HOUSE, BUT NONE MORE SO THAN LANGUAGE.
Don't say "what"! It's crass!
MY MOM AND DAD IN A RARE MOMENT OF PARENTAL AGREEMENT
BEG PARDON?
WHEN I WAS IN HONG KONG, A DGS STUDENT FROM THE GENERATION BEFORE MY MOTHER TOLD ME THEY'D BEEN RAPPED ON THE KNUCKLES FOR SPEAKING CHINESE.
I ASKED MY MOM IF THAT WAS STILL THE CASE WHEN SHE WAS THERE—
Oh, no. It was more subtle than that. We boarders would eat dinner with the British expatriate teachers,
and if we spoke Chinese, they'd chastise us by saying,
"It's a bit impolite to speak a language not everyone can understand."
"Now we wouldn't want to be impolite, would we?"
I'm sorry.

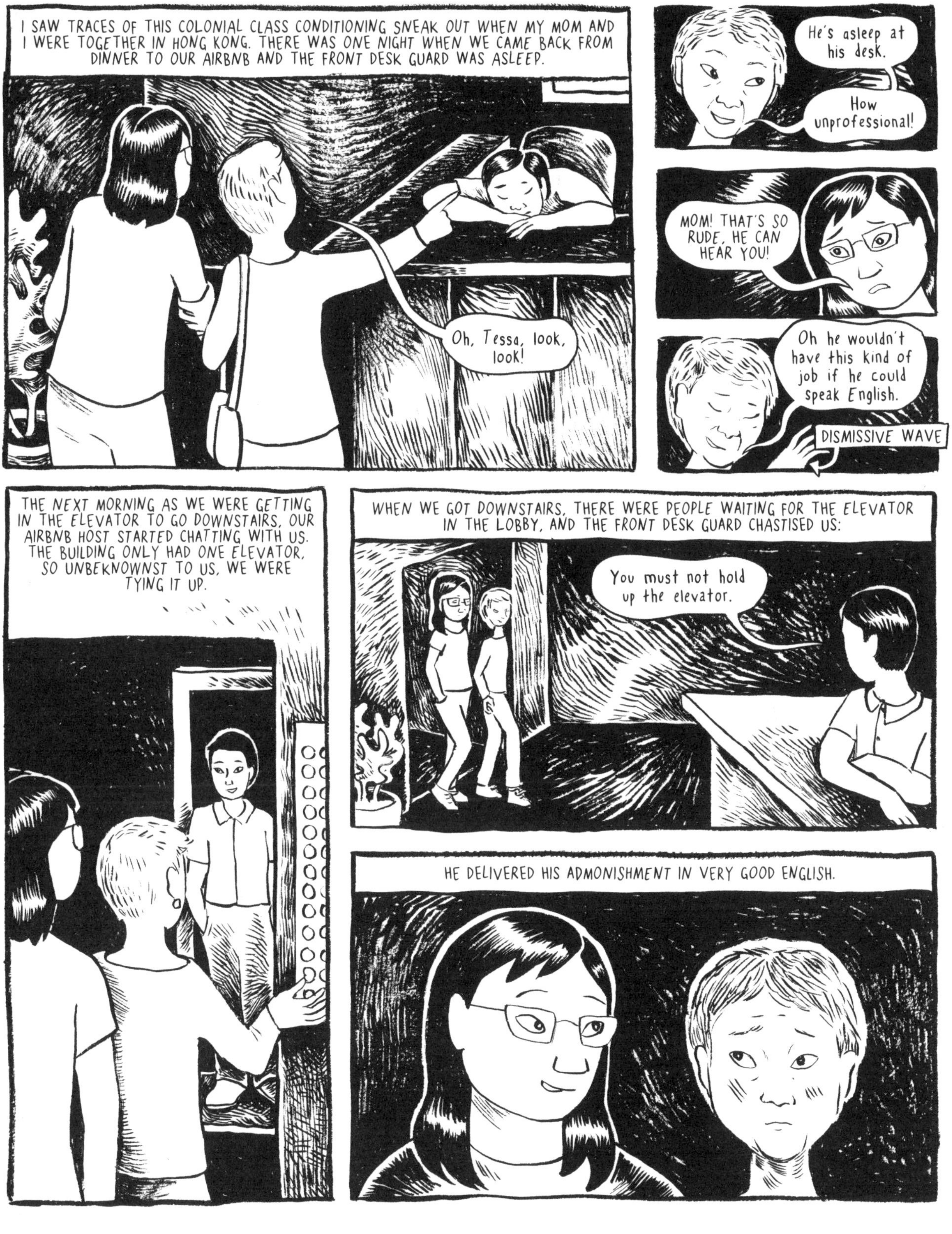
I SAW TRACES OF THIS COLONIAL CLASS CONDITIONING SNEAK OUT WHEN MY MOM AND I WERE TOGETHER IN HONG KONG. THERE WAS ONE NIGHT WHEN WE CAME BACK FROM DINNER TO OUR AIRBNB AND THE FRONT DESK GUARD WAS ASLEEP.
Oh, Tessa, look, look!
He's asleep at his desk.
How unprofessional!
MOM! THAT'S SO RUDE, HE CAN HEAR YOU!
Oh he wouldn't have this kind of job if he could speak English.
DISMISSIVE WAVE
THE NEXT MORNING AS WE WERE GETTING IN THE ELEVATOR TO GO DOWNSTAIRS, OUR AIRBNB HOST STARTED CHATTING WITH US. THE BUILDING ONLY HAD ONE ELEVATOR, SO UNBEKNOWNST TO US, WE WERE TYING IT UP.
WHEN WE GOT DOWNSTAIRS, THERE WERE PEOPLE WAITING FOR THE ELEVATOR IN THE LOBBY, AND THE FRONT DESK GUARD CHASTISED US:
You must not hold up the elevator.
HE DELIVERED HIS ADMONISHMENT IN VERY GOOD ENGLISH.

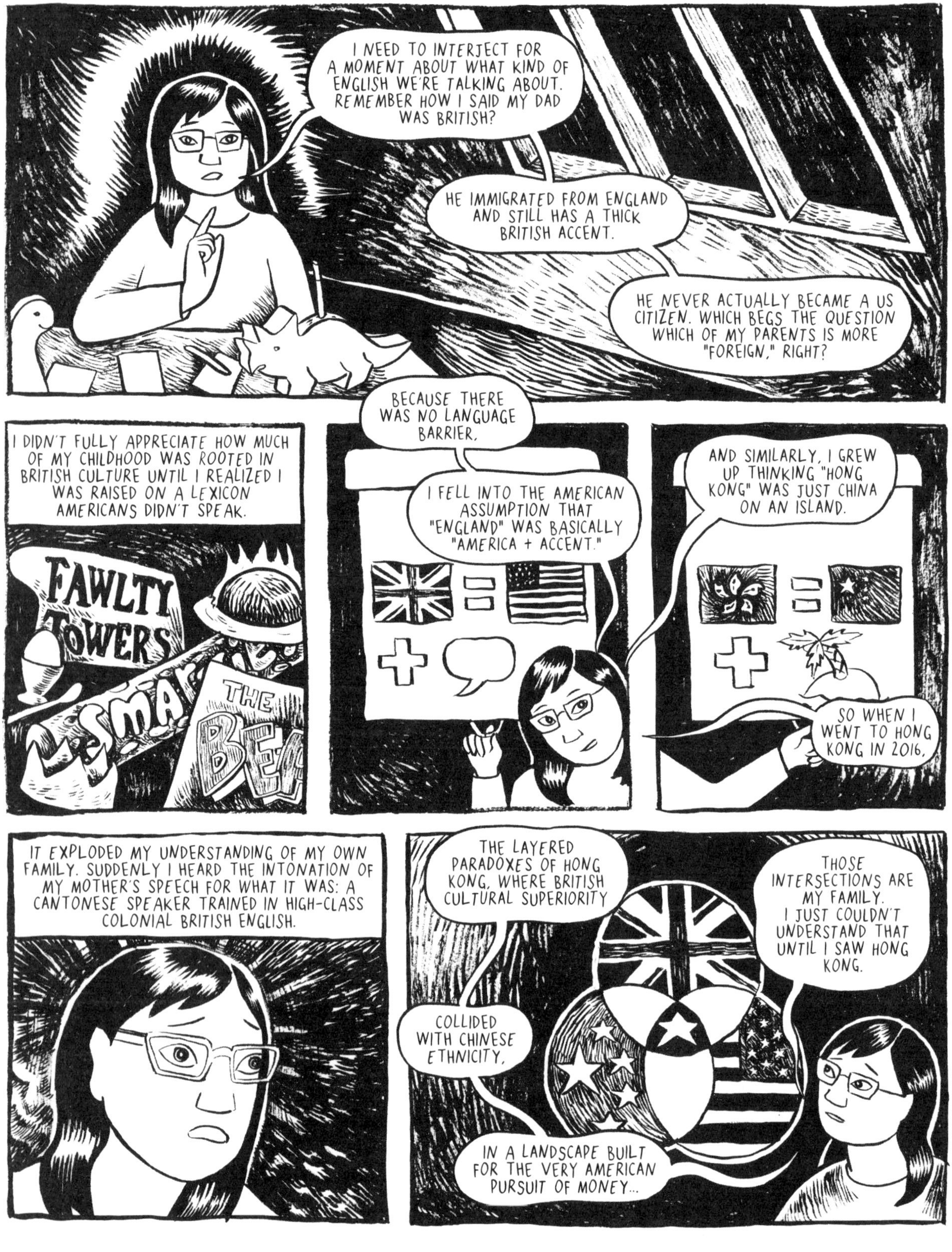

I NEED TO INTERJECT FOR A MOMENT ABOUT WHAT KIND OF ENGLISH WE'RE TALKING ABOUT. REMEMBER HOW I SAID MY DAD WAS BRITISH?
HE IMMIGRATED FROM ENGLAND AND STILL HAS A THICK BRITISH ACCENT.
HE NEVER ACTUALLY BECAME A US CITIZEN. WHICH BEGS THE QUESTION WHICH OF MY PARENTS IS MORE "FOREIGN," RIGHT?
I DIDN'T FULLY APPRECIATE HOW MUCH OF MY CHILDHOOD WAS ROOTED IN BRITISH CULTURE UNTIL I REALIZED I WAS RAISED ON A LEXICON AMERICANS DIDN'T SPEAK.
FAWLTY TOWERS
THE
BECAUSE THERE WAS NO LANGUAGE BARRIER,
I FELL INTO THE AMERICAN ASSUMPTION THAT "ENGLAND" WAS BASICALLY "AMERICA + ACCENT."
AND SIMILARLY, I GREW UP THINKING "HONG KONG" WAS JUST CHINA ON AN ISLAND.
SO WHEN I WENT TO HONG KONG IN 2016,
IT EXPLODED MY UNDERSTANDING OF MY OWN FAMILY. SUDDENLY I HEARD THE INTONATION OF MY MOTHER'S SPEECH FOR WHAT IT WAS: A CANTONESE SPEAKER TRAINED IN HIGH-CLASS COLONIAL BRITISH ENGLISH.
THE LAYERED PARADOXES OF HONG KONG, WHERE BRITISH CULTURAL SUPERIORITY
COLLIDED WITH CHINESE ETHNICITY,
IN A LANDSCAPE BUILT FOR THE VERY AMERICAN PURSUIT OF MONEY...
THOSE INTERSECTIONS ARE MY FAMILY. I JUST COULDN'T UNDERSTAND THAT UNTIL I SAW HONG KONG.

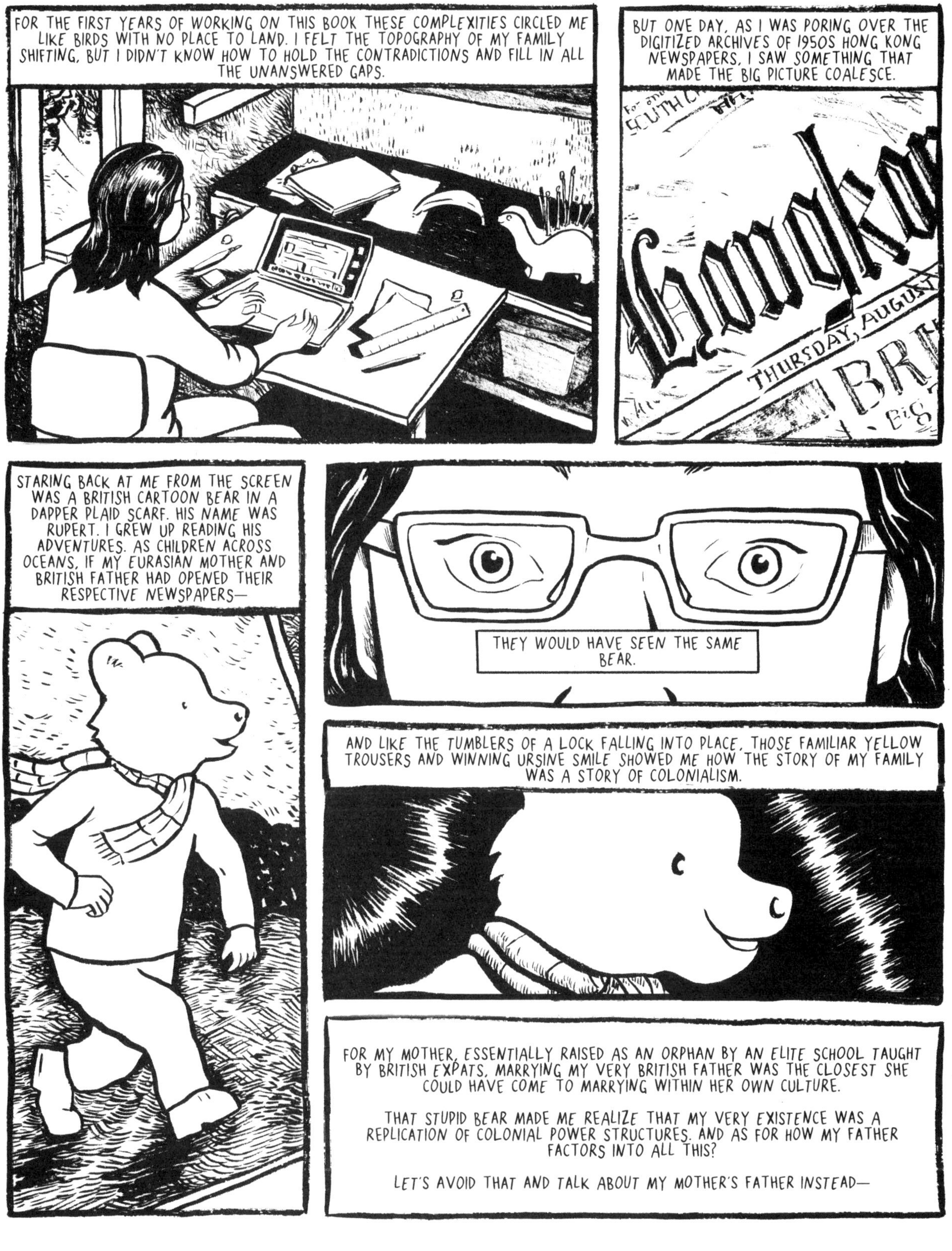
FOR THE FIRST YEARS OF WORKING ON THIS BOOK THESE COMPLEXITIES CIRCLED ME LIKE BIRDS WITH NO PLACE TO LAND. I FELT THE TOPOGRAPHY OF MY FAMILY SHIFTING, BUT I DIDN'T KNOW HOW TO HOLD THE CONTRADICTIONS AND FILL IN ALL THE UNANSWERED GAPS.
BUT ONE DAY, AS I WAS PORING OVER THE DIGITIZED ARCHIVES OF 1950S HONG KONG NEWSPAPERS, I SAW SOMETHING THAT MADE THE BIG PICTURE COALESCE.
THURSDAY, AUGUST
STARING BACK AT ME FROM THE SCREEN WAS A BRITISH CARTOON BEAR IN A DAPPER PLAID SCARF. HIS NAME WAS RUPERT. I GREW UP READING HIS ADVENTURES. AS CHILDREN ACROSS OCEANS, IF MY EURASIAN MOTHER AND BRITISH FATHER HAD OPENED THEIR RESPECTIVE NEWSPAPERS—
THEY WOULD HAVE SEEN THE SAME BEAR.
AND LIKE THE TUMBLERS OF A LOCK FALLING INTO PLACE, THOSE FAMILIAR YELLOW TROUSERS AND WINNING URSINE SMILE SHOWED ME HOW THE STORY OF MY FAMILY WAS A STORY OF COLONIALISM.
FOR MY MOTHER, ESSENTIALLY RAISED AS AN ORPHAN BY AN ELITE SCHOOL TAUGHT BY BRITISH EXPATS, MARRYING MY VERY BRITISH FATHER WAS THE CLOSEST SHE COULD HAVE COME TO MARRYING WITHIN HER OWN CULTURE.
THAT STUPID BEAR MADE ME REALIZE THAT MY VERY EXISTENCE WAS A REPLICATION OF COLONIAL POWER STRUCTURES. AND AS FOR HOW MY FATHER FACTORS INTO ALL THIS?
LET'S AVOID THAT AND TALK ABOUT MY MOTHER'S FATHER INSTEAD—

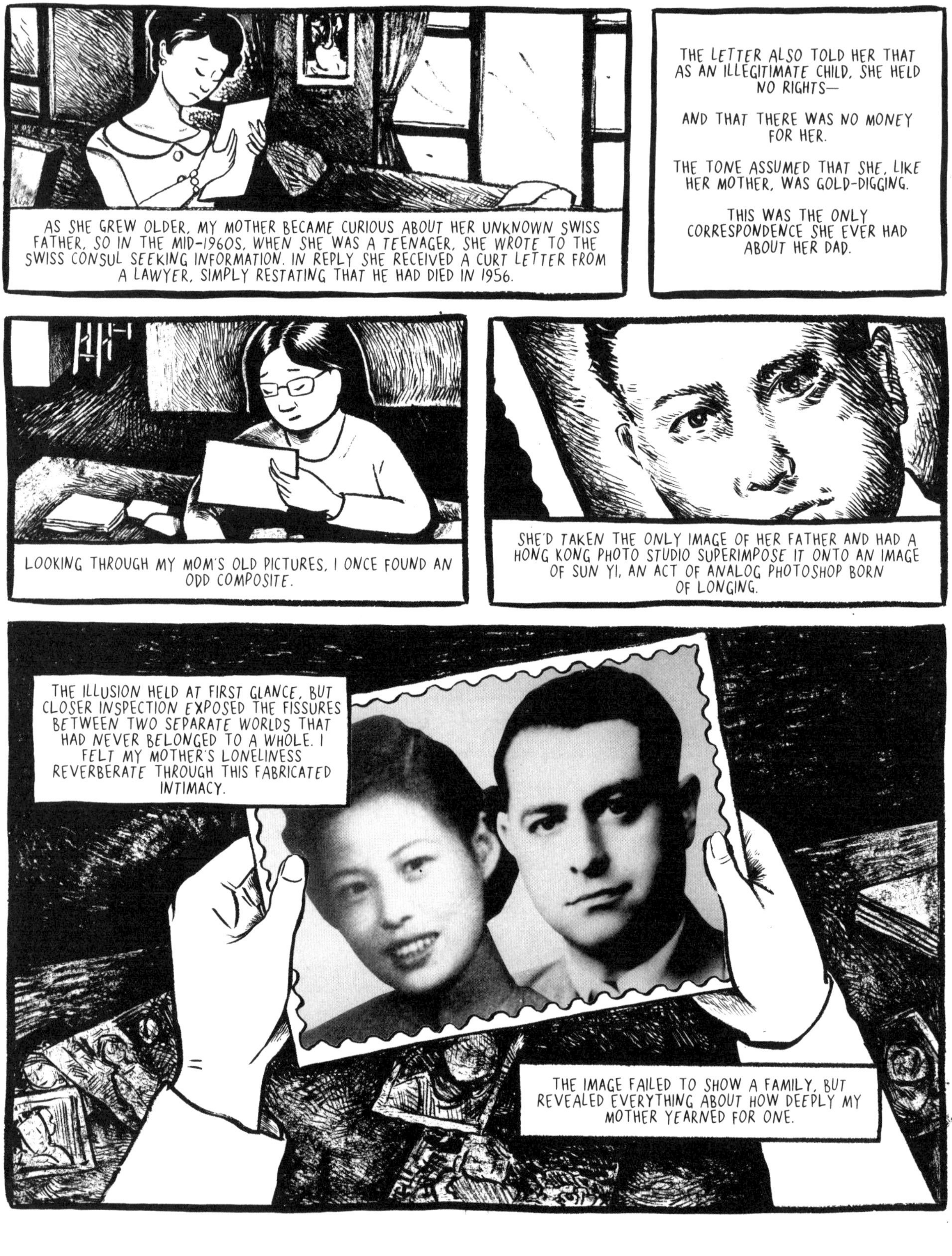

AS SHE GREW OLDER, MY MOTHER BECAME CURIOUS ABOUT HER UNKNOWN SWISS FATHER, SO IN THE MID-1960S, WHEN SHE WAS A TEENAGER, SHE WROTE TO THE SWISS CONSUL SEEKING INFORMATION. IN REPLY SHE RECEIVED A CURT LETTER FROM A LAWYER, SIMPLY RESTATING THAT HE HAD DIED IN 1956.
THE LETTER ALSO TOLD HER THAT AS AN ILLEGITIMATE CHILD, SHE HELD NO RIGHTS—
AND THAT THERE WAS NO MONEY FOR HER.
THE TONE ASSUMED THAT SHE, LIKE HER MOTHER, WAS GOLD-DIGGING.
THIS WAS THE ONLY CORRESPONDENCE SHE EVER HAD ABOUT HER DAD.
LOOKING THROUGH MY MOM'S OLD PICTURES, I ONCE FOUND AN ODD COMPOSITE.
SHE'D TAKEN THE ONLY IMAGE OF HER FATHER AND HAD A HONG KONG PHOTO STUDIO SUPERIMPOSE IT ONTO AN IMAGE OF SUN YI, AN ACT OF ANALOG PHOTOSHOP BORN OF LONGING.
THE ILLUSION HELD AT FIRST GLANCE, BUT CLOSER INSPECTION EXPOSED THE FISSURES BETWEEN TWO SEPARATE WORLDS THAT HAD NEVER BELONGED TO A WHOLE. I FELT MY MOTHER'S LONELINESS REVERBERATE THROUGH THIS FABRICATED INTIMACY.
THE IMAGE FAILED TO SHOW A FAMILY, BUT REVEALED EVERYTHING ABOUT HOW DEEPLY MY MOTHER YEARNED FOR ONE.

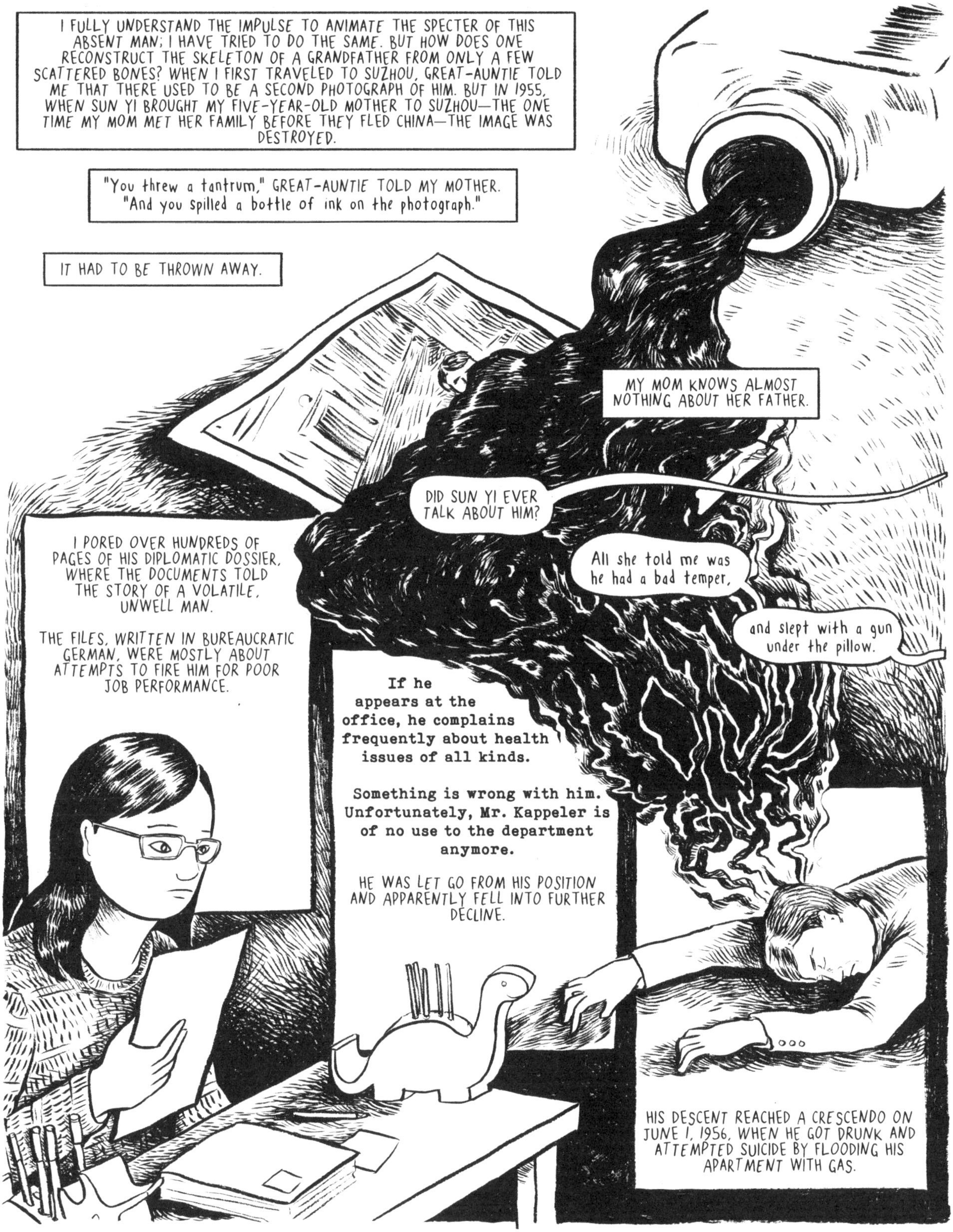
I FULLY UNDERSTAND THE IMPULSE TO ANIMATE THE SPECTER OF THIS ABSENT MAN; I HAVE TRIED TO DO THE SAME. BUT HOW DOES ONE RECONSTRUCT THE SKELETON OF A GRANDFATHER FROM ONLY A FEW SCATTERED BONES? WHEN I FIRST TRAVELED TO SUZHOU, GREAT-AUNTIE TOLD ME THAT THERE USED TO BE A SECOND PHOTOGRAPH OF HIM. BUT IN 1955, WHEN SUN YI BROUGHT MY FIVE-YEAR-OLD MOTHER TO SUZHOU—THE ONE TIME MY MOM MET HER FAMILY BEFORE THEY FLED CHINA—THE IMAGE WAS DESTROYED.
"You threw a tantrum," GREAT-AUNTIE TOLD MY MOTHER. "And you spilled a bottle of ink on the photograph."
IT HAD TO BE THROWN AWAY.
MY MOM KNOWS ALMOST NOTHING ABOUT HER FATHER.
DID SUN YI EVER TALK ABOUT HIM?
All she told me was he had a bad temper,
and slept with a gun under the pillow.
I PORED OVER HUNDREDS OF PAGES OF HIS DIPLOMATIC DOSSIER, WHERE THE DOCUMENTS TOLD THE STORY OF A VOLATILE, UNWELL MAN.
THE FILES, WRITTEN IN BUREAUCRATIC GERMAN, WERE MOSTLY ABOUT ATTEMPTS TO FIRE HIM FOR POOR JOB PERFORMANCE.
If he appears at the office, he complains frequently about health issues of all kinds.
Something is wrong with him. Unfortunately, Mr. Kappeler is of no use to the department anymore.
HE WAS LET GO FROM HIS POSITION AND APPARENTLY FELL INTO FURTHER DECLINE.
HIS DESCENT REACHED A CRESCENDO ON JUNE 1, 1956, WHEN HE GOT DRUNK AND ATTEMPTED SUICIDE BY FLOODING HIS APARTMENT WITH GAS.

FILES IN HIS DOSSIER ALLOWED ME TO TRACE HIM TO THE WALDAU PSYCHIATRIC HOSPITAL IN BERN.

SO BOTH MY GRANDPARENTS HAD ATTEMPTED SUICIDE AND BEEN COMMITTED TO MENTAL INSTITUTIONS!

KNOWING THE YEAR OF HIS DEATH, I SUSPECTED HE'D KILLED HIMSELF WHILE INSTITUTIONALIZED—

BUT I MANAGED TO PROCURE HIS MEDICAL RECORDS AND LEARNED HE WAS DISCHARGED JUST WEEKS BEFORE HE DIED.

SEEKING ANSWERS, I JOINED THE FACEBOOK PAGE FOR THE HISTORICAL SOCIETY OF HIS SWISS HOMETOWN.

THERE, I FOUND SOMEONE WHOSE FATHER HAD BEEN FRIENDS WITH MY GRANDFATHER AND WAS POINTED TOWARD A EUROPEAN GENEALOGY SITE WITH A FAMILY TREE...

WHICH SHOWED THAT WILLI KAPPELER HAD A SON.

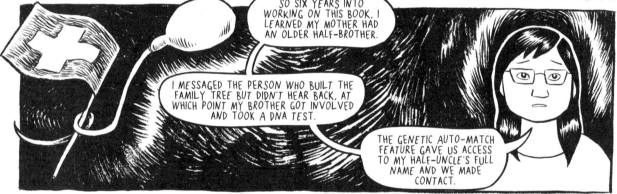

SO SIX YEARS INTO WORKING ON THIS BOOK, I LEARNED MY MOTHER HAD AN OLDER HALF-BROTHER.

I MESSAGED THE PERSON WHO BUILT THE FAMILY TREE BUT DIDN'T HEAR BACK, AT WHICH POINT MY BROTHER GOT INVOLVED AND TOOK A DNA TEST.

THE GENETIC AUTO-MATCH FEATURE GAVE US ACCESS TO MY HALF-UNCLE'S FULL NAME AND WE MADE CONTACT.

WHICH IS HOW I FOUND MYSELF ON A ZOOM CALL WITH MY MOM, MY BROTHER, AND MY NEWLY DISCOVERED HALF-UNCLE, PLUS HIS WIFE AND MY HALF-COUSIN.

THERE WAS A MODERATE LANGUAGE BARRIER INVOLVED, BUT CHILLS PASSED DOWN MY SPINE AT THE FIRST WORDS MY HALF-UNCLE SAID TO MY MOM:

So you are my sister.

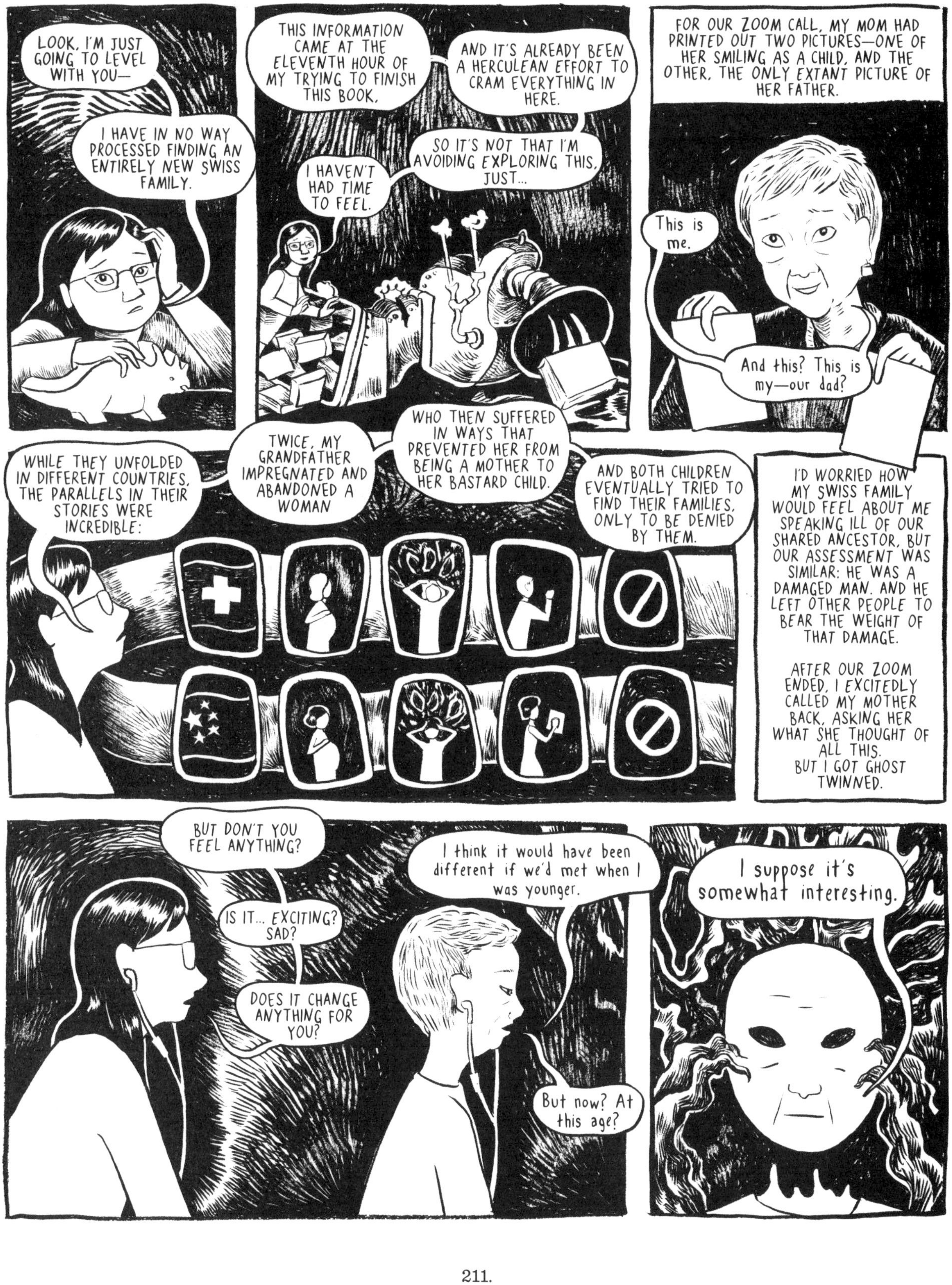
LOOK, I'M JUST GOING TO LEVEL WITH YOU—
I HAVE IN NO WAY PROCESSED FINDING AN ENTIRELY NEW SWISS FAMILY.
THIS INFORMATION CAME AT THE ELEVENTH HOUR OF MY TRYING TO FINISH THIS BOOK,
AND IT'S ALREADY BEEN A HERCULEAN EFFORT TO CRAM EVERYTHING IN HERE.
SO IT'S NOT THAT I'M AVOIDING EXPLORING THIS, JUST...
I HAVEN'T HAD TIME TO FEEL.
FOR OUR ZOOM CALL, MY MOM HAD PRINTED OUT TWO PICTURES—ONE OF HER SMILING AS A CHILD, AND THE OTHER, THE ONLY EXTANT PICTURE OF HER FATHER.
This is me.
And this? This is my—our dad?
WHILE THEY UNFOLDED IN DIFFERENT COUNTRIES, THE PARALLELS IN THEIR STORIES WERE INCREDIBLE:
TWICE, MY GRANDFATHER IMPREGNATED AND ABANDONED A WOMAN
WHO THEN SUFFERED IN WAYS THAT PREVENTED HER FROM BEING A MOTHER TO HER BASTARD CHILD.
AND BOTH CHILDREN EVENTUALLY TRIED TO FIND THEIR FAMILIES, ONLY TO BE DENIED BY THEM.
I'D WORRIED HOW MY SWISS FAMILY WOULD FEEL ABOUT ME SPEAKING ILL OF OUR SHARED ANCESTOR, BUT OUR ASSESSMENT WAS SIMILAR: HE WAS A DAMAGED MAN. AND HE LEFT OTHER PEOPLE TO BEAR THE WEIGHT OF THAT DAMAGE.
AFTER OUR ZOOM ENDED, I EXCITEDLY CALLED MY MOTHER BACK, ASKING HER WHAT SHE THOUGHT OF ALL THIS.
BUT I GOT GHOST TWINNED.
BUT DON'T YOU FEEL ANYTHING?
IS IT... EXCITING? SAD?
DOES IT CHANGE ANYTHING FOR YOU?
I think it would have been different if we'd met when I was younger.
But now? At this age?
I suppose it's somewhat interesting.

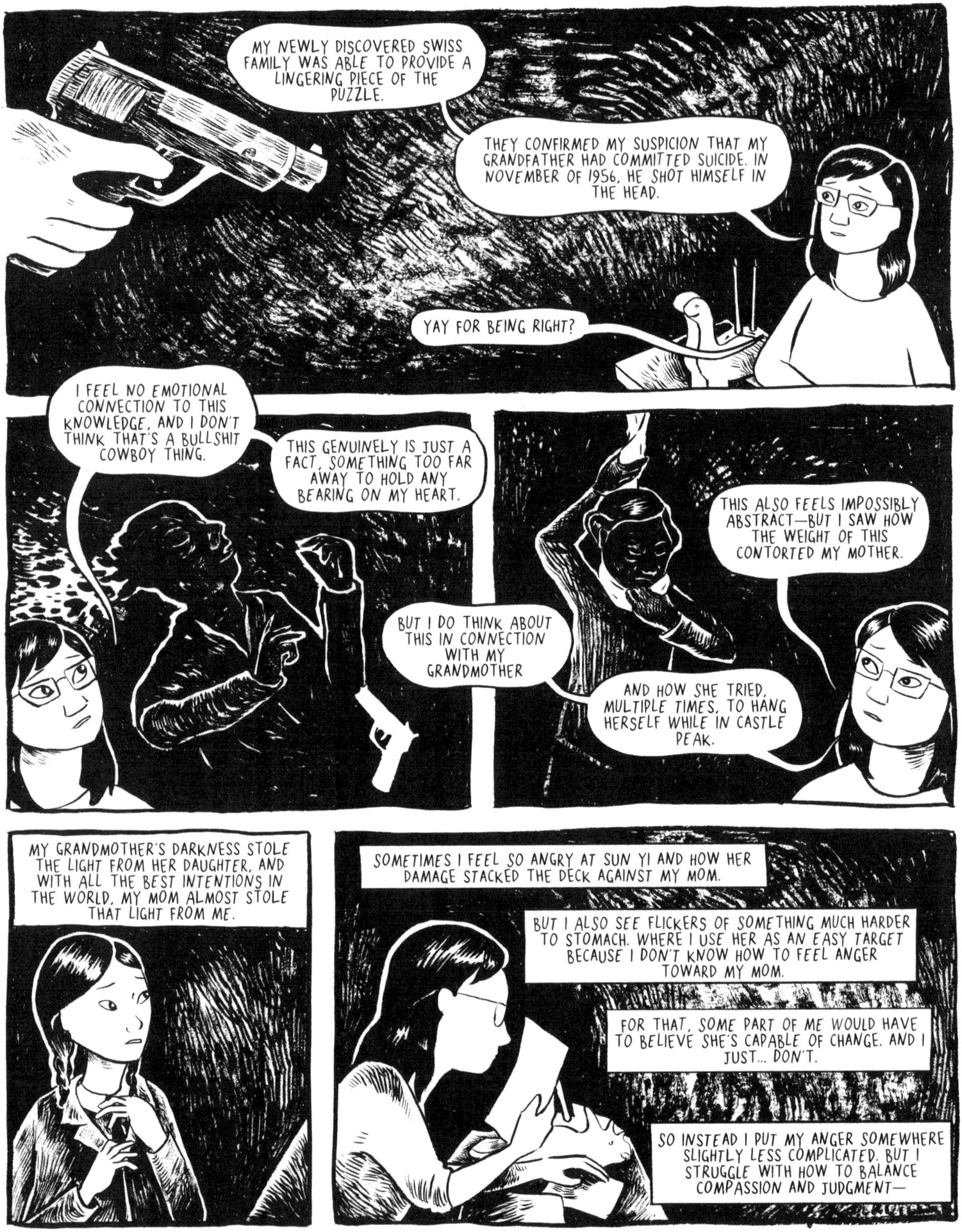
MY NEWLY DISCOVERED SWISS FAMILY WAS ABLE TO PROVIDE A LINGERING PIECE OF THE PUZZLE.
THEY CONFIRMED MY SUSPICION THAT MY GRANDFATHER HAD COMMITTED SUICIDE. IN NOVEMBER OF 1956, HE SHOT HIMSELF IN THE HEAD.
YAY FOR BEING RIGHT?
I FEEL NO EMOTIONAL CONNECTION TO THIS KNOWLEDGE, AND I DON'T THINK THAT'S A BULLSHIT COWBOY THING.
THIS GENUINELY IS JUST A FACT, SOMETHING TOO FAR AWAY TO HOLD ANY BEARING ON MY HEART.
BUT I DO THINK ABOUT THIS IN CONNECTION WITH MY GRANDMOTHER
AND HOW SHE TRIED, MULTIPLE TIMES, TO HANG HERSELF WHILE IN CASTLE PEAK.
THIS ALSO FEELS IMPOSSIBLY ABSTRACT—BUT I SAW HOW THE WEIGHT OF THIS CONTORTED MY MOTHER.
MY GRANDMOTHER'S DARKNESS STOLE THE LIGHT FROM HER DAUGHTER, AND WITH ALL THE BEST INTENTIONS IN THE WORLD, MY MOM ALMOST STOLE THAT LIGHT FROM ME.
SOMETIMES I FEEL SO ANGRY AT SUN YI AND HOW HER DAMAGE STACKED THE DECK AGAINST MY MOM.
BUT I ALSO SEE FLICKERS OF SOMETHING MUCH HARDER TO STOMACH. WHERE I USE HER AS AN EASY TARGET BECAUSE I DON'T KNOW HOW TO FEEL ANGER TOWARD MY MOM.
FOR THAT, SOME PART OF ME WOULD HAVE TO BELIEVE SHE'S CAPABLE OF CHANGE. AND I JUST... DON'T.
SO INSTEAD I PUT MY ANGER SOMEWHERE SLIGHTLY LESS COMPLICATED. BUT I STRUGGLE WITH HOW TO BALANCE COMPASSION AND JUDGMENT—

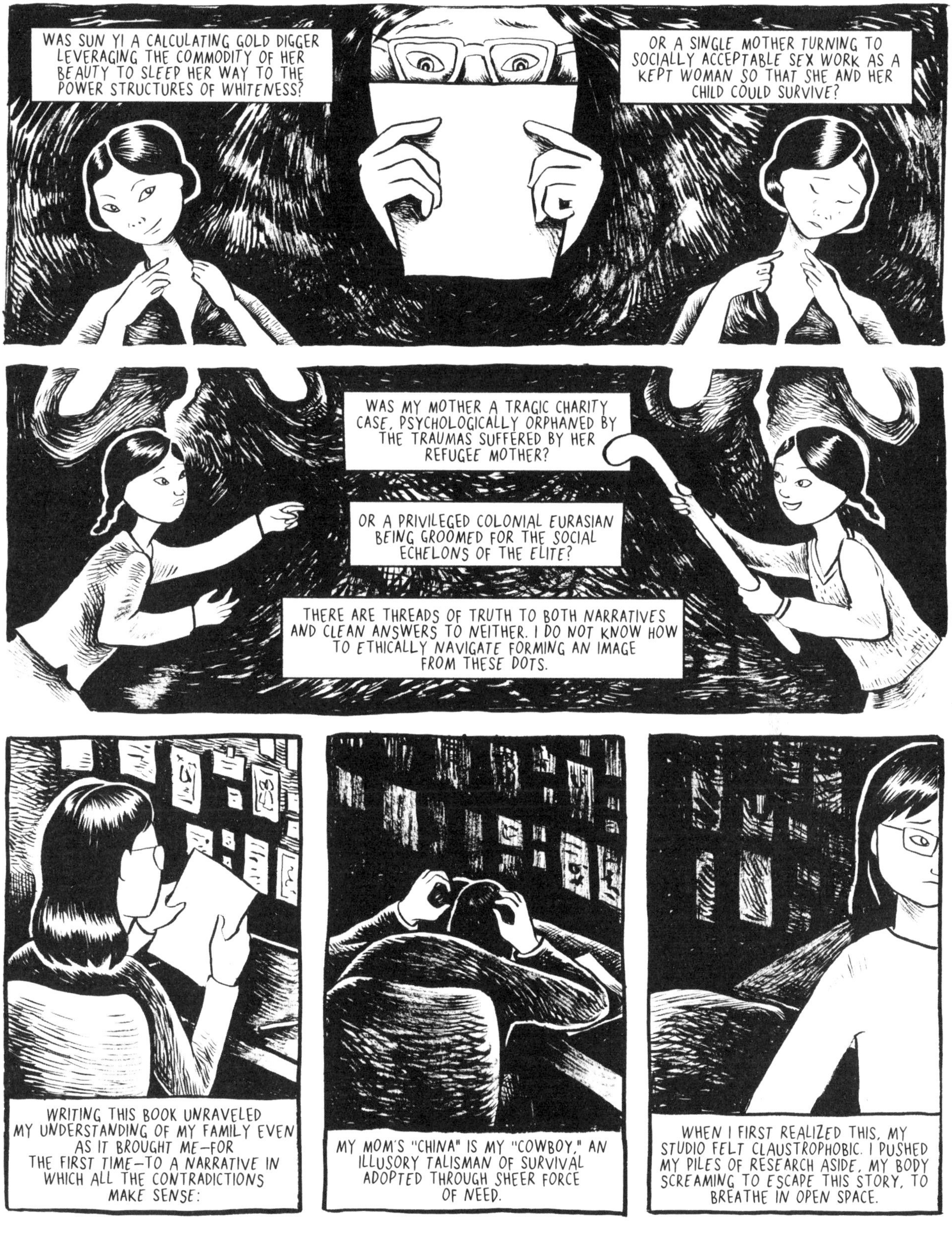

WAS SUN YI A CALCULATING GOLD DIGGER LEVERAGING THE COMMODITY OF HER BEAUTY TO SLEEP HER WAY TO THE POWER STRUCTURES OF WHITENESS?
OR A SINGLE MOTHER TURNING TO SOCIALLY ACCEPTABLE SEX WORK AS A KEPT WOMAN SO THAT SHE AND HER CHILD COULD SURVIVE?
WAS MY MOTHER A TRAGIC CHARITY CASE, PSYCHOLOGICALLY ORPHANED BY THE TRAUMAS SUFFERED BY HER REFUGEE MOTHER?
OR A PRIVILEGED COLONIAL EURASIAN BEING GROOMED FOR THE SOCIAL ECHELONS OF THE ELITE?
THERE ARE THREADS OF TRUTH TO BOTH NARRATIVES AND CLEAN ANSWERS TO NEITHER. I DO NOT KNOW HOW TO ETHICALLY NAVIGATE FORMING AN IMAGE FROM THESE DOTS.
WRITING THIS BOOK UNRAVELED MY UNDERSTANDING OF MY FAMILY EVEN AS IT BROUGHT ME—FOR THE FIRST TIME—TO A NARRATIVE IN WHICH ALL THE CONTRADICTIONS MAKE SENSE:
MY MOM'S "CHINA" IS MY "COWBOY," AN ILLUSORY TALISMAN OF SURVIVAL ADOPTED THROUGH SHEER FORCE OF NEED.
WHEN I FIRST REALIZED THIS, MY STUDIO FELT CLAUSTROPHOBIC. I PUSHED MY PILES OF RESEARCH ASIDE, MY BODY SCREAMING TO ESCAPE THIS STORY, TO BREATHE IN OPEN SPACE.

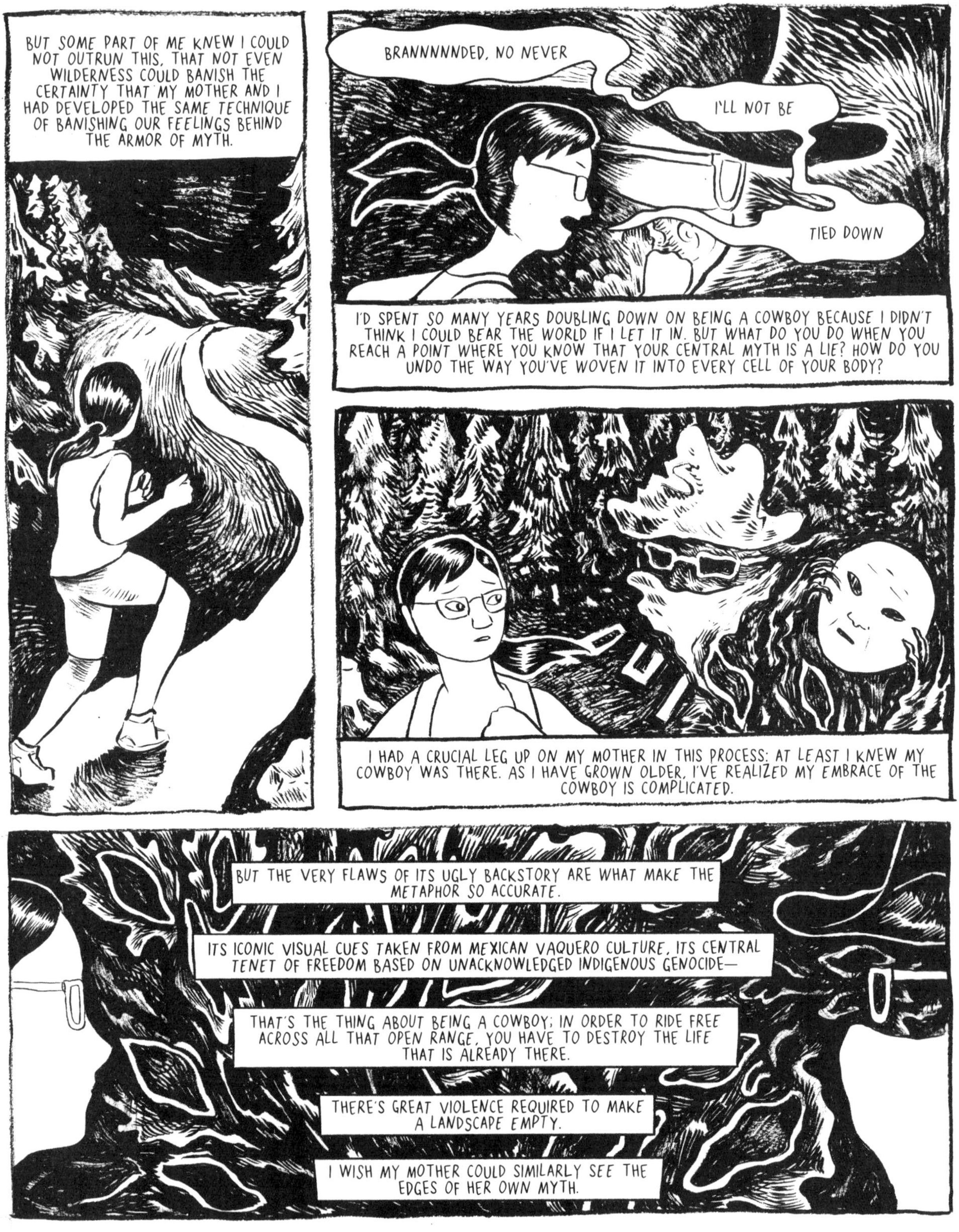
BUT SOME PART OF ME KNEW I COULD NOT OUTRUN THIS, THAT NOT EVEN WILDERNESS COULD BANISH THE CERTAINTY THAT MY MOTHER AND I HAD DEVELOPED THE SAME TECHNIQUE OF BANISHING OUR FEELINGS BEHIND THE ARMOR OF MYTH.
BRANNNNNDED, NO NEVER
I'LL NOT BE
TIED DOWN
I'D SPENT SO MANY YEARS DOUBLING DOWN ON BEING A COWBOY BECAUSE I DIDN'T THINK I COULD BEAR THE WORLD IF I LET IT IN. BUT WHAT DO YOU DO WHEN YOU REACH A POINT WHERE YOU KNOW THAT YOUR CENTRAL MYTH IS A LIE? HOW DO YOU UNDO THE WAY YOU'VE WOVEN IT INTO EVERY CELL OF YOUR BODY?
I HAD A CRUCIAL LEG UP ON MY MOTHER IN THIS PROCESS: AT LEAST I KNEW MY COWBOY WAS THERE. AS I HAVE GROWN OLDER, I'VE REALIZED MY EMBRACE OF THE COWBOY IS COMPLICATED.
BUT THE VERY FLAWS OF ITS UGLY BACKSTORY ARE WHAT MAKE THE METAPHOR SO ACCURATE.
ITS ICONIC VISUAL CUES TAKEN FROM MEXICAN VAQUERO CULTURE, ITS CENTRAL TENET OF FREEDOM BASED ON UNACKNOWLEDGED INDIGENOUS GENOCIDE—
THAT'S THE THING ABOUT BEING A COWBOY; IN ORDER TO RIDE FREE ACROSS ALL THAT OPEN RANGE, YOU HAVE TO DESTROY THE LIFE THAT IS ALREADY THERE.
THERE'S GREAT VIOLENCE REQUIRED TO MAKE A LANDSCAPE EMPTY.
I WISH MY MOTHER COULD SIMILARLY SEE THE EDGES OF HER OWN MYTH.

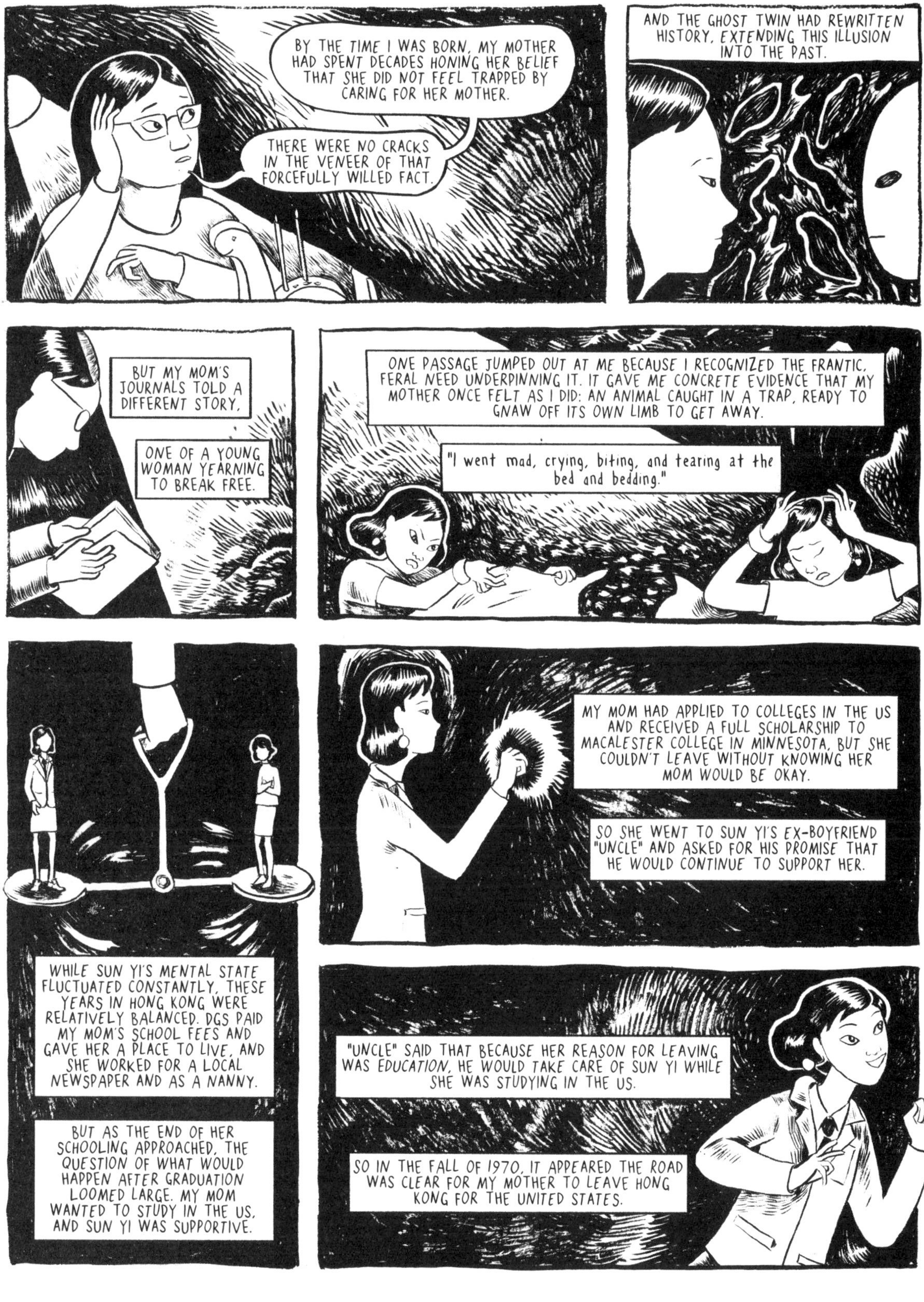
BY THE TIME I WAS BORN, MY MOTHER HAD SPENT DECADES HONING HER BELIEF THAT SHE DID NOT FEEL TRAPPED BY CARING FOR HER MOTHER.
THERE WERE NO CRACKS IN THE VENEER OF THAT FORCEFULLY WILLED FACT.
AND THE GHOST TWIN HAD REWRITTEN HISTORY, EXTENDING THIS ILLUSION INTO THE PAST.
BUT MY MOM'S JOURNALS TOLD A DIFFERENT STORY,
ONE OF A YOUNG WOMAN YEARNING TO BREAK FREE.
ONE PASSAGE JUMPED OUT AT ME BECAUSE I RECOGNIZED THE FRANTIC, FERAL NEED UNDERPINNING IT. IT GAVE ME CONCRETE EVIDENCE THAT MY MOTHER ONCE FELT AS I DID: AN ANIMAL CAUGHT IN A TRAP, READY TO GNAW OFF ITS OWN LIMB TO GET AWAY.
"I went mad, crying, biting, and tearing at the bed and bedding."
WHILE SUN YI'S MENTAL STATE FLUCTUATED CONSTANTLY, THESE YEARS IN HONG KONG WERE RELATIVELY BALANCED. DGS PAID MY MOM'S SCHOOL FEES AND GAVE HER A PLACE TO LIVE, AND SHE WORKED FOR A LOCAL NEWSPAPER AND AS A NANNY.
BUT AS THE END OF HER SCHOOLING APPROACHED, THE QUESTION OF WHAT WOULD HAPPEN AFTER GRADUATION LOOMED LARGE. MY MOM WANTED TO STUDY IN THE US, AND SUN YI WAS SUPPORTIVE.
MY MOM HAD APPLIED TO COLLEGES IN THE US AND RECEIVED A FULL SCHOLARSHIP TO MACALESTER COLLEGE IN MINNESOTA, BUT SHE COULDN'T LEAVE WITHOUT KNOWING HER MOM WOULD BE OKAY.
SO SHE WENT TO SUN YI'S EX-BOYFRIEND "UNCLE" AND ASKED FOR HIS PROMISE THAT HE WOULD CONTINUE TO SUPPORT HER.
"UNCLE" SAID THAT BECAUSE HER REASON FOR LEAVING WAS EDUCATION, HE WOULD TAKE CARE OF SUN YI WHILE SHE WAS STUDYING IN THE US.
SO IN THE FALL OF 1970, IT APPEARED THE ROAD WAS CLEAR FOR MY MOTHER TO LEAVE HONG KONG FOR THE UNITED STATES.

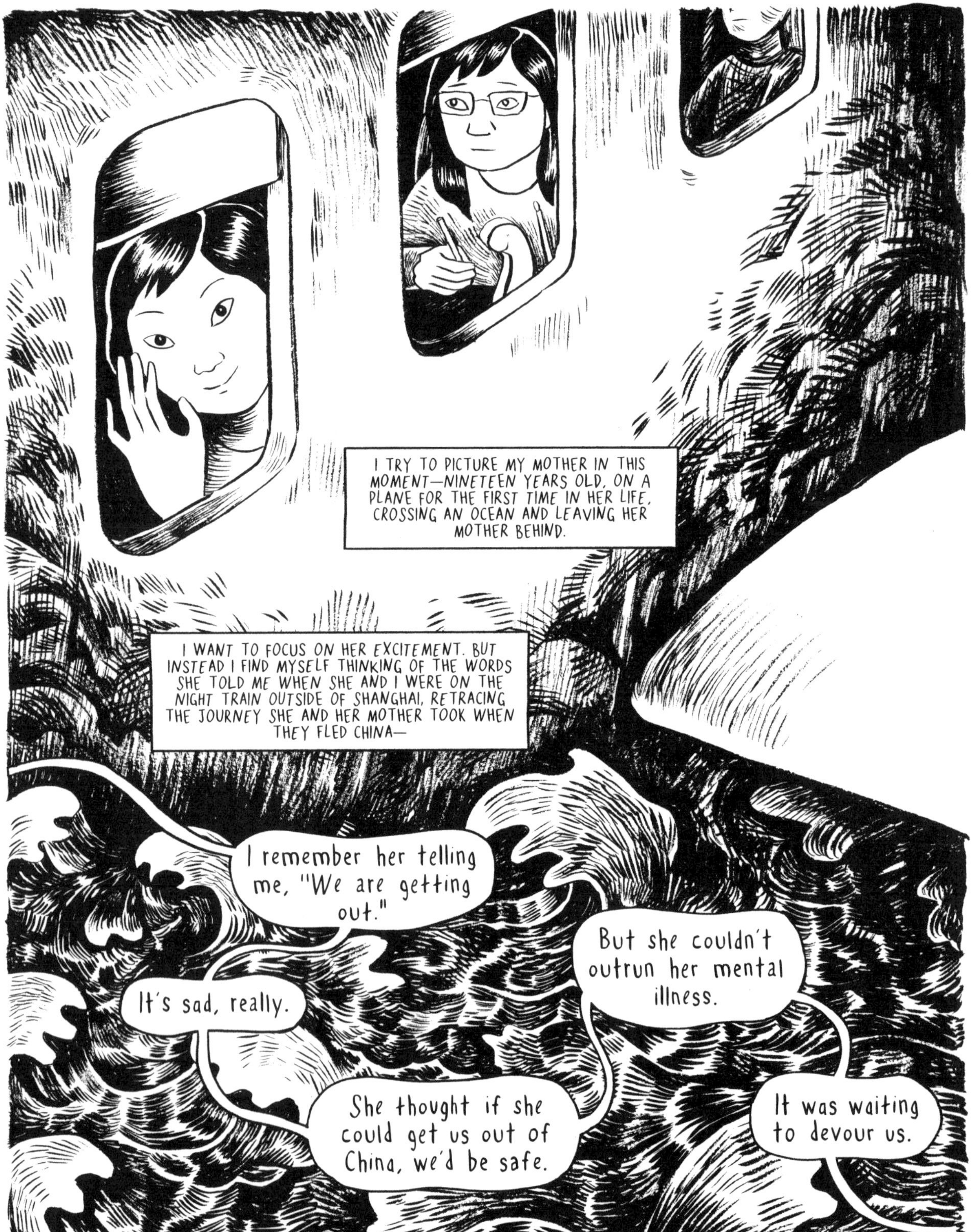

I TRY TO PICTURE MY MOTHER IN THIS MOMENT—NINETEEN YEARS OLD, ON A PLANE FOR THE FIRST TIME IN HER LIFE, CROSSING AN OCEAN AND LEAVING HER MOTHER BEHIND.
I WANT TO FOCUS ON HER EXCITEMENT. BUT INSTEAD I FIND MYSELF THINKING OF THE WORDS SHE TOLD ME WHEN SHE AND I WERE ON THE NIGHT TRAIN OUTSIDE OF SHANGHAI, RETRACING THE JOURNEY SHE AND HER MOTHER TOOK WHEN THEY FLED CHINA—
I remember her telling me, "We are getting out."
It's sad, really.
She thought if she could get us out of China, we'd be safe.
But she couldn't outrun her mental illness.
It was waiting to devour us.

PART 6

THE INVISIBLE WORLD

Minnesota, Drifting,
a Small Town in Northern California
1970–1997

*Whenever she had to warn us about life, my mother told stories . . .
tested our strength to establish realities . . . Those of us in the first
American generations had to figure out how the invisible world the
emigrants built around our childhoods fits in solid America.*

—MAXINE HONG KINGSTON, *The Woman Warrior*

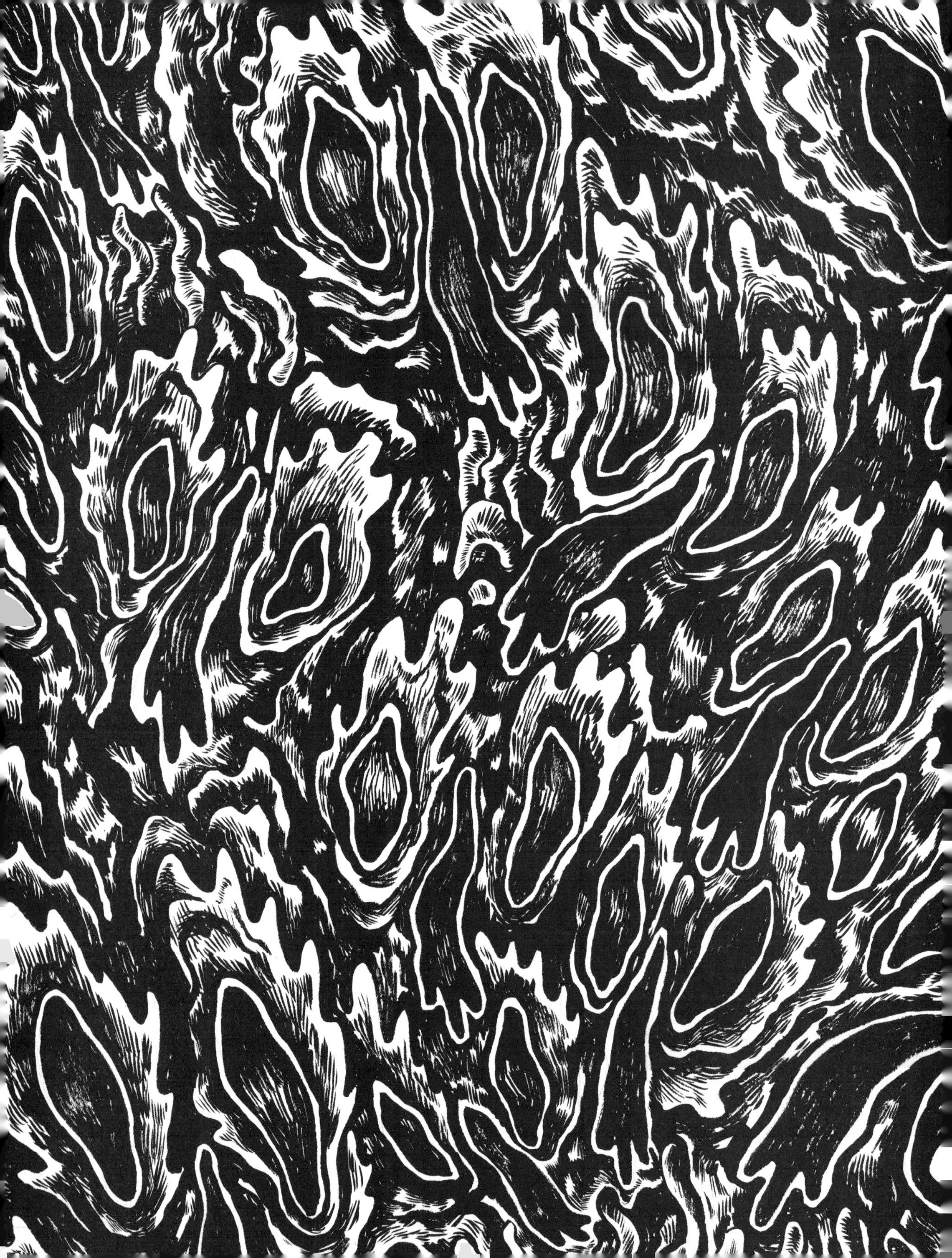

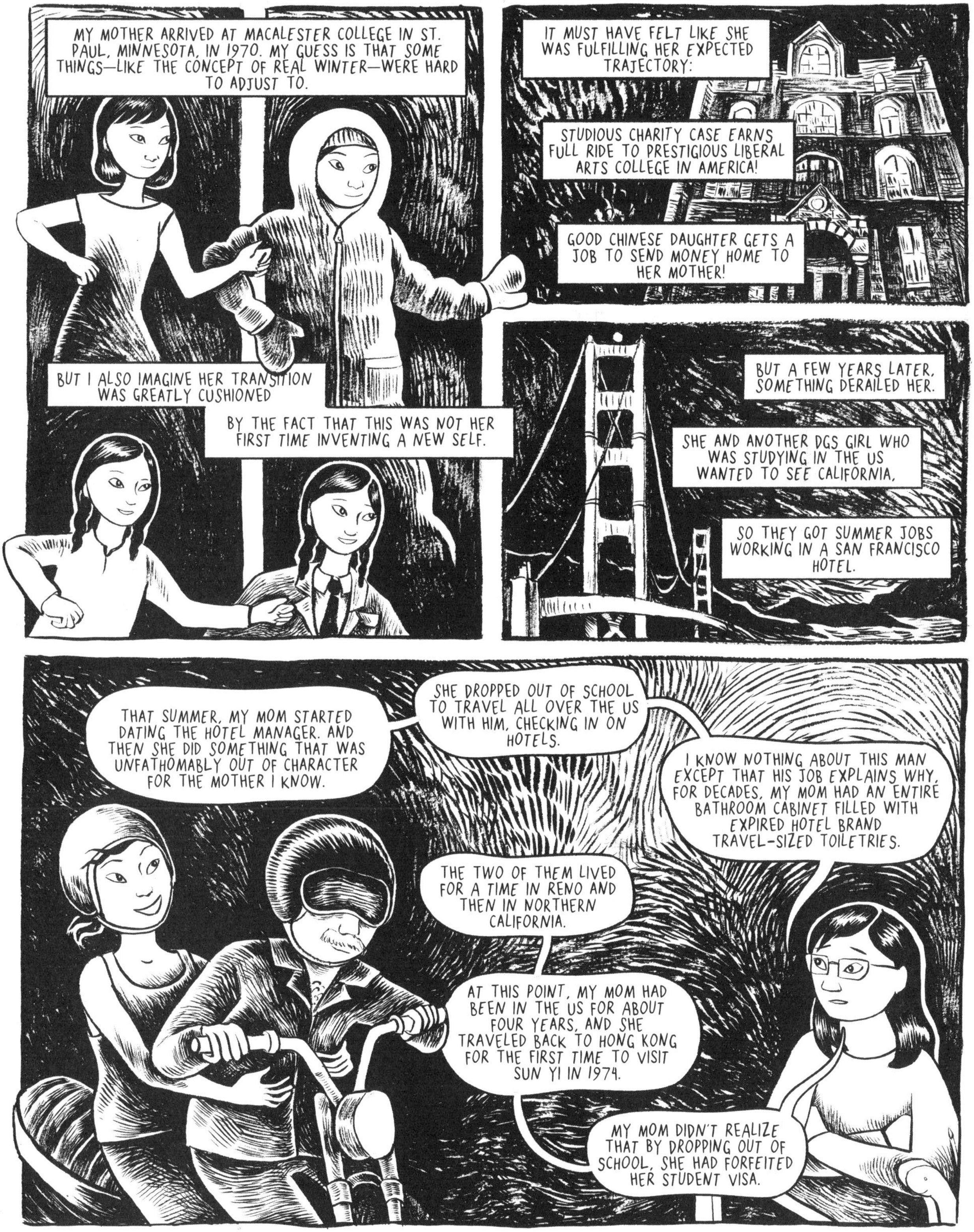
MY MOTHER ARRIVED AT MACALESTER COLLEGE IN ST. PAUL, MINNESOTA, IN 1970. MY GUESS IS THAT SOME THINGS—LIKE THE CONCEPT OF REAL WINTER—WERE HARD TO ADJUST TO.
BUT I ALSO IMAGINE HER TRANSITION WAS GREATLY CUSHIONED
BY THE FACT THAT THIS WAS NOT HER FIRST TIME INVENTING A NEW SELF.
IT MUST HAVE FELT LIKE SHE WAS FULFILLING HER EXPECTED TRAJECTORY:
STUDIOUS CHARITY CASE EARNS FULL RIDE TO PRESTIGIOUS LIBERAL ARTS COLLEGE IN AMERICA!
GOOD CHINESE DAUGHTER GETS A JOB TO SEND MONEY HOME TO HER MOTHER!
BUT A FEW YEARS LATER, SOMETHING DERAILED HER.
SHE AND ANOTHER DGS GIRL WHO WAS STUDYING IN THE US WANTED TO SEE CALIFORNIA,
SO THEY GOT SUMMER JOBS WORKING IN A SAN FRANCISCO HOTEL.
THAT SUMMER, MY MOM STARTED DATING THE HOTEL MANAGER. AND THEN SHE DID SOMETHING THAT WAS UNFATHOMABLY OUT OF CHARACTER FOR THE MOTHER I KNOW.
SHE DROPPED OUT OF SCHOOL TO TRAVEL ALL OVER THE US WITH HIM, CHECKING IN ON HOTELS.
I KNOW NOTHING ABOUT THIS MAN EXCEPT THAT HIS JOB EXPLAINS WHY, FOR DECADES, MY MOM HAD AN ENTIRE BATHROOM CABINET FILLED WITH EXPIRED HOTEL BRAND TRAVEL-SIZED TOILETRIES.
THE TWO OF THEM LIVED FOR A TIME IN RENO AND THEN IN NORTHERN CALIFORNIA.
AT THIS POINT, MY MOM HAD BEEN IN THE US FOR ABOUT FOUR YEARS, AND SHE TRAVELED BACK TO HONG KONG FOR THE FIRST TIME TO VISIT SUN YI IN 1974.
MY MOM DIDN'T REALIZE THAT BY DROPPING OUT OF SCHOOL, SHE HAD FORFEITED HER STUDENT VISA.

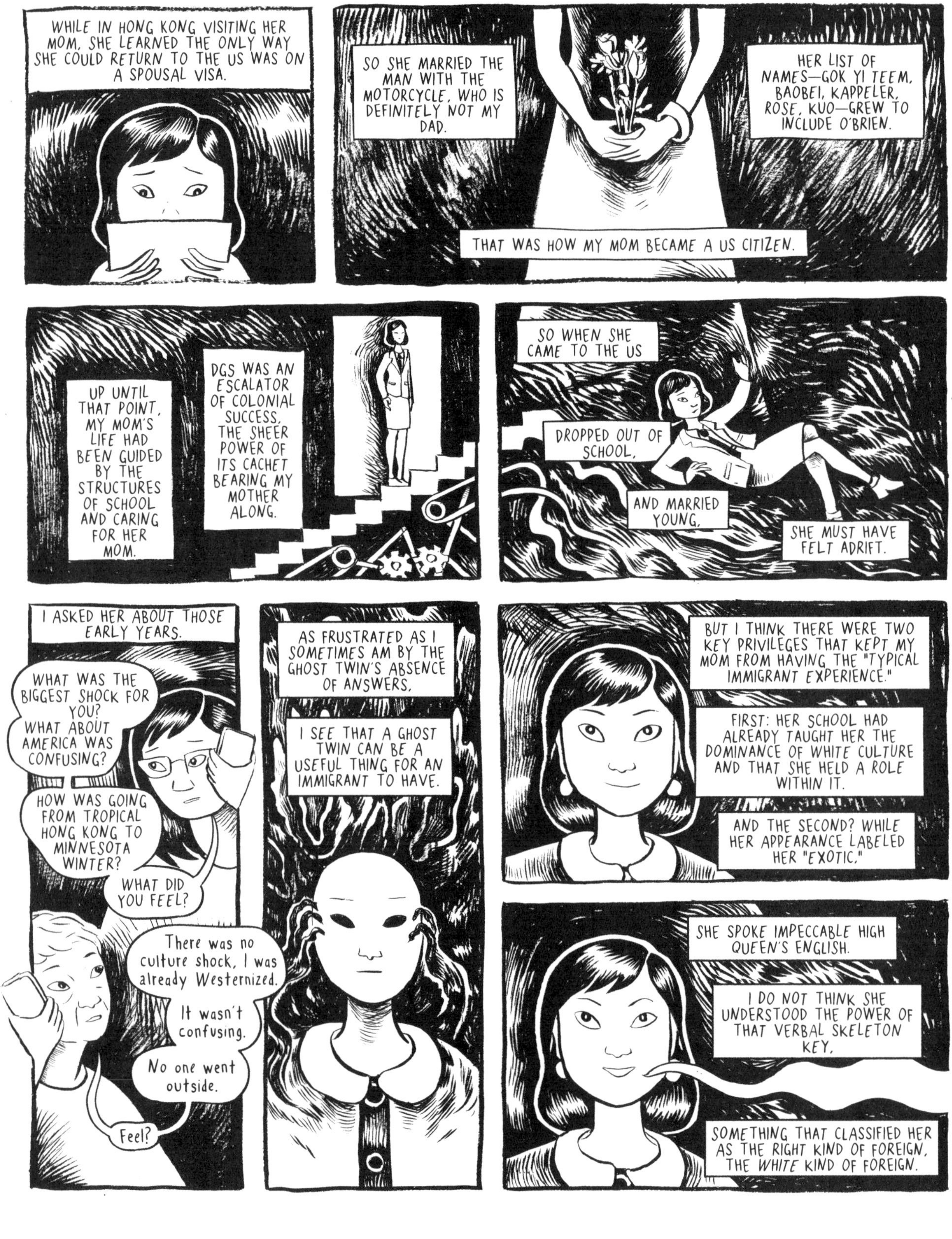
WHILE IN HONG KONG VISITING HER MOM, SHE LEARNED THE ONLY WAY SHE COULD RETURN TO THE US WAS ON A SPOUSAL VISA.
SO SHE MARRIED THE MAN WITH THE MOTORCYCLE, WHO IS DEFINITELY NOT MY DAD.
HER LIST OF NAMES—GOK YI TEEM, BAOBEI, KAPPELER, ROSE, KUO—GREW TO INCLUDE O'BRIEN.
THAT WAS HOW MY MOM BECAME A US CITIZEN.
UP UNTIL THAT POINT, MY MOM'S LIFE HAD BEEN GUIDED BY THE STRUCTURES OF SCHOOL AND CARING FOR HER MOM.
DGS WAS AN ESCALATOR OF COLONIAL SUCCESS, THE SHEER POWER OF ITS CACHET BEARING MY MOTHER ALONG.
SO WHEN SHE CAME TO THE US
DROPPED OUT OF SCHOOL,
AND MARRIED YOUNG,
SHE MUST HAVE FELT ADRIFT.
I ASKED HER ABOUT THOSE EARLY YEARS.
WHAT WAS THE BIGGEST SHOCK FOR YOU? WHAT ABOUT AMERICA WAS CONFUSING?
HOW WAS GOING FROM TROPICAL HONG KONG TO MINNESOTA WINTER?
WHAT DID YOU FEEL?
There was no culture shock, I was already Westernized.
It wasn't confusing.
No one went outside.
Feel?
AS FRUSTRATED AS I SOMETIMES AM BY THE GHOST TWIN'S ABSENCE OF ANSWERS,
I SEE THAT A GHOST TWIN CAN BE A USEFUL THING FOR AN IMMIGRANT TO HAVE.
BUT I THINK THERE WERE TWO KEY PRIVILEGES THAT KEPT MY MOM FROM HAVING THE "TYPICAL IMMIGRANT EXPERIENCE."
FIRST: HER SCHOOL HAD ALREADY TAUGHT HER THE DOMINANCE OF WHITE CULTURE AND THAT SHE HELD A ROLE WITHIN IT.
AND THE SECOND? WHILE HER APPEARANCE LABELED HER "EXOTIC,"
SHE SPOKE IMPECCABLE HIGH QUEEN'S ENGLISH.
I DO NOT THINK SHE UNDERSTOOD THE POWER OF THAT VERBAL SKELETON KEY,
SOMETHING THAT CLASSIFIED HER AS THE RIGHT KIND OF FOREIGN, THE *WHITE* KIND OF FOREIGN.

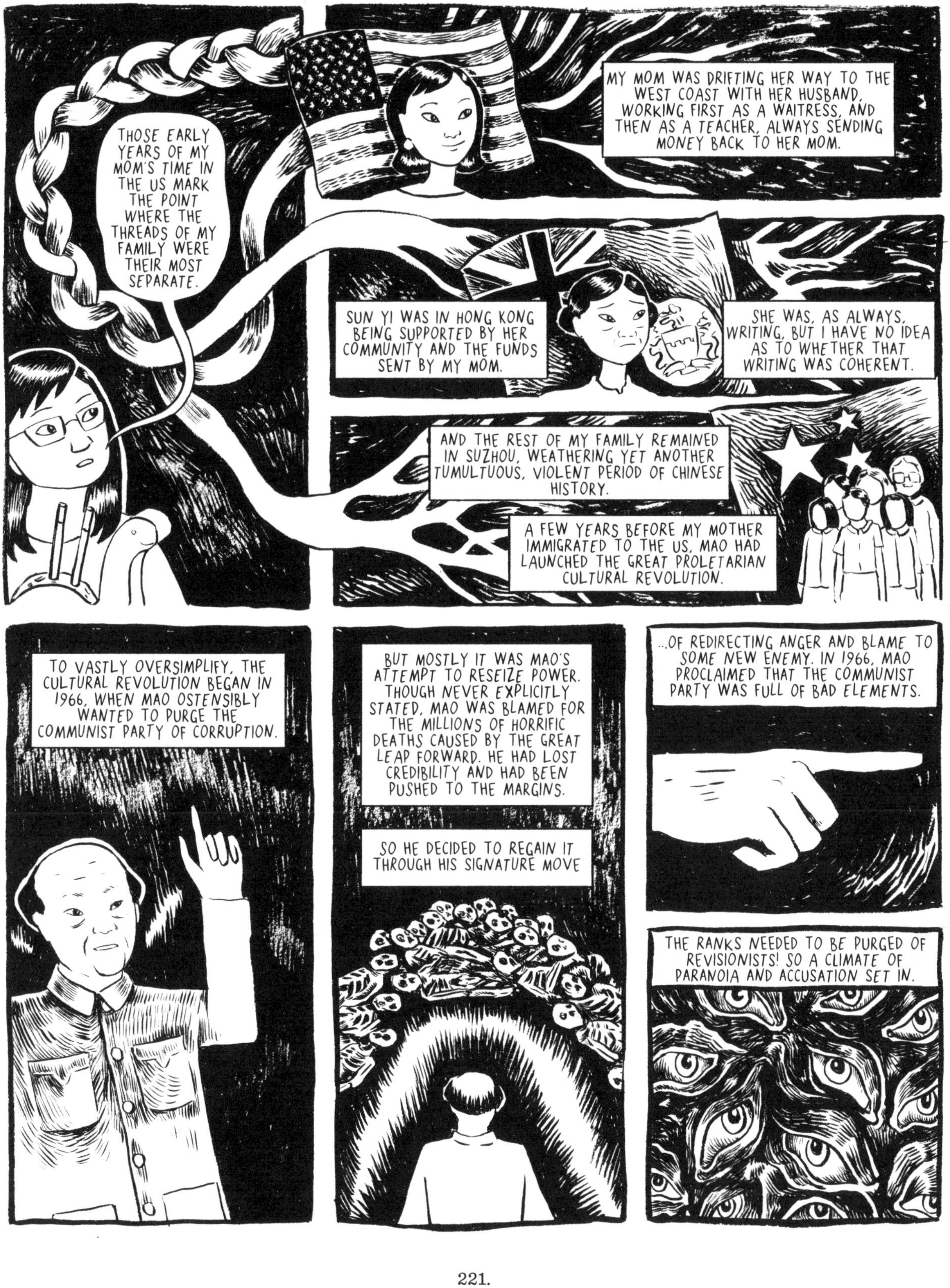

THOSE EARLY YEARS OF MY MOM'S TIME IN THE US MARK THE POINT WHERE THE THREADS OF MY FAMILY WERE THEIR MOST SEPARATE.
MY MOM WAS DRIFTING HER WAY TO THE WEST COAST WITH HER HUSBAND, WORKING FIRST AS A WAITRESS, AND THEN AS A TEACHER, ALWAYS SENDING MONEY BACK TO HER MOM.
SUN YI WAS IN HONG KONG BEING SUPPORTED BY HER COMMUNITY AND THE FUNDS SENT BY MY MOM.
SHE WAS, AS ALWAYS, WRITING, BUT I HAVE NO IDEA AS TO WHETHER THAT WRITING WAS COHERENT.
AND THE REST OF MY FAMILY REMAINED IN SUZHOU, WEATHERING YET ANOTHER TUMULTUOUS, VIOLENT PERIOD OF CHINESE HISTORY.
A FEW YEARS BEFORE MY MOTHER IMMIGRATED TO THE US, MAO HAD LAUNCHED THE GREAT PROLETARIAN CULTURAL REVOLUTION.
TO VASTLY OVERSIMPLIFY, THE CULTURAL REVOLUTION BEGAN IN 1966, WHEN MAO OSTENSIBLY WANTED TO PURGE THE COMMUNIST PARTY OF CORRUPTION.
BUT MOSTLY IT WAS MAO'S ATTEMPT TO RESEIZE POWER. THOUGH NEVER EXPLICITLY STATED, MAO WAS BLAMED FOR THE MILLIONS OF HORRIFIC DEATHS CAUSED BY THE GREAT LEAP FORWARD. HE HAD LOST CREDIBILITY AND HAD BEEN PUSHED TO THE MARGINS.
SO HE DECIDED TO REGAIN IT THROUGH HIS SIGNATURE MOVE
...OF REDIRECTING ANGER AND BLAME TO SOME NEW ENEMY. IN 1966, MAO PROCLAIMED THAT THE COMMUNIST PARTY WAS FULL OF BAD ELEMENTS.
THE RANKS NEEDED TO BE PURGED OF REVISIONISTS! SO A CLIMATE OF PARANOIA AND ACCUSATION SET IN.

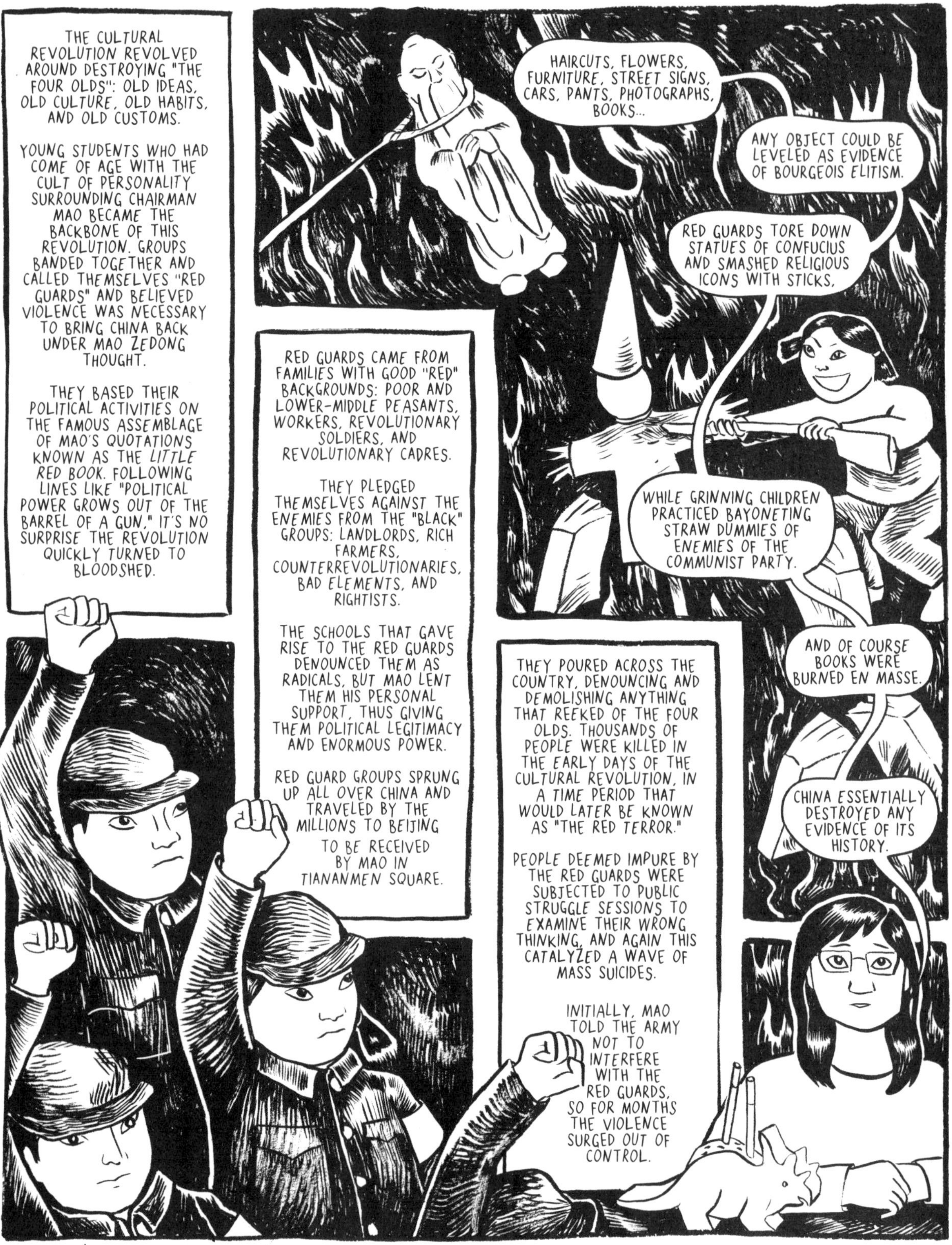
THE CULTURAL REVOLUTION REVOLVED AROUND DESTROYING "THE FOUR OLDS": OLD IDEAS, OLD CULTURE, OLD HABITS, AND OLD CUSTOMS.
YOUNG STUDENTS WHO HAD COME OF AGE WITH THE CULT OF PERSONALITY SURROUNDING CHAIRMAN MAO BECAME THE BACKBONE OF THIS REVOLUTION. GROUPS BANDED TOGETHER AND CALLED THEMSELVES "RED GUARDS" AND BELIEVED VIOLENCE WAS NECESSARY TO BRING CHINA BACK UNDER MAO ZEDONG THOUGHT.
THEY BASED THEIR POLITICAL ACTIVITIES ON THE FAMOUS ASSEMBLAGE OF MAO'S QUOTATIONS KNOWN AS THE *LITTLE RED BOOK*. FOLLOWING LINES LIKE "POLITICAL POWER GROWS OUT OF THE BARREL OF A GUN," IT'S NO SURPRISE THE REVOLUTION QUICKLY TURNED TO BLOODSHED.
HAIRCUTS, FLOWERS, FURNITURE, STREET SIGNS, CARS, PANTS, PHOTOGRAPHS, BOOKS...
ANY OBJECT COULD BE LEVELED AS EVIDENCE OF BOURGEOIS ELITISM.
RED GUARDS TORE DOWN STATUES OF CONFUCIUS AND SMASHED RELIGIOUS ICONS WITH STICKS,
WHILE GRINNING CHILDREN PRACTICED BAYONETING STRAW DUMMIES OF ENEMIES OF THE COMMUNIST PARTY.
AND OF COURSE BOOKS WERE BURNED EN MASSE.
CHINA ESSENTIALLY DESTROYED ANY EVIDENCE OF ITS HISTORY.
RED GUARDS CAME FROM FAMILIES WITH GOOD "RED" BACKGROUNDS: POOR AND LOWER-MIDDLE PEASANTS, WORKERS, REVOLUTIONARY SOLDIERS, AND REVOLUTIONARY CADRES.
THEY PLEDGED THEMSELVES AGAINST THE ENEMIES FROM THE "BLACK" GROUPS: LANDLORDS, RICH FARMERS, COUNTERREVOLUTIONARIES, BAD ELEMENTS, AND RIGHTISTS.
THE SCHOOLS THAT GAVE RISE TO THE RED GUARDS DENOUNCED THEM AS RADICALS, BUT MAO LENT THEM HIS PERSONAL SUPPORT, THUS GIVING THEM POLITICAL LEGITIMACY AND ENORMOUS POWER.
RED GUARD GROUPS SPRUNG UP ALL OVER CHINA AND TRAVELED BY THE MILLIONS TO BEIJING
TO BE RECEIVED BY MAO IN TIANANMEN SQUARE.
THEY POURED ACROSS THE COUNTRY, DENOUNCING AND DEMOLISHING ANYTHING THAT REEKED OF THE FOUR OLDS. THOUSANDS OF PEOPLE WERE KILLED IN THE EARLY DAYS OF THE CULTURAL REVOLUTION, IN A TIME PERIOD THAT WOULD LATER BE KNOWN AS "THE RED TERROR."
PEOPLE DEEMED IMPURE BY THE RED GUARDS WERE SUBJECTED TO PUBLIC STRUGGLE SESSIONS TO EXAMINE THEIR WRONG THINKING, AND AGAIN THIS CATALYZED A WAVE OF MASS SUICIDES.
INITIALLY, MAO TOLD THE ARMY NOT TO INTERFERE WITH THE RED GUARDS, SO FOR MONTHS THE VIOLENCE SURGED OUT OF CONTROL.

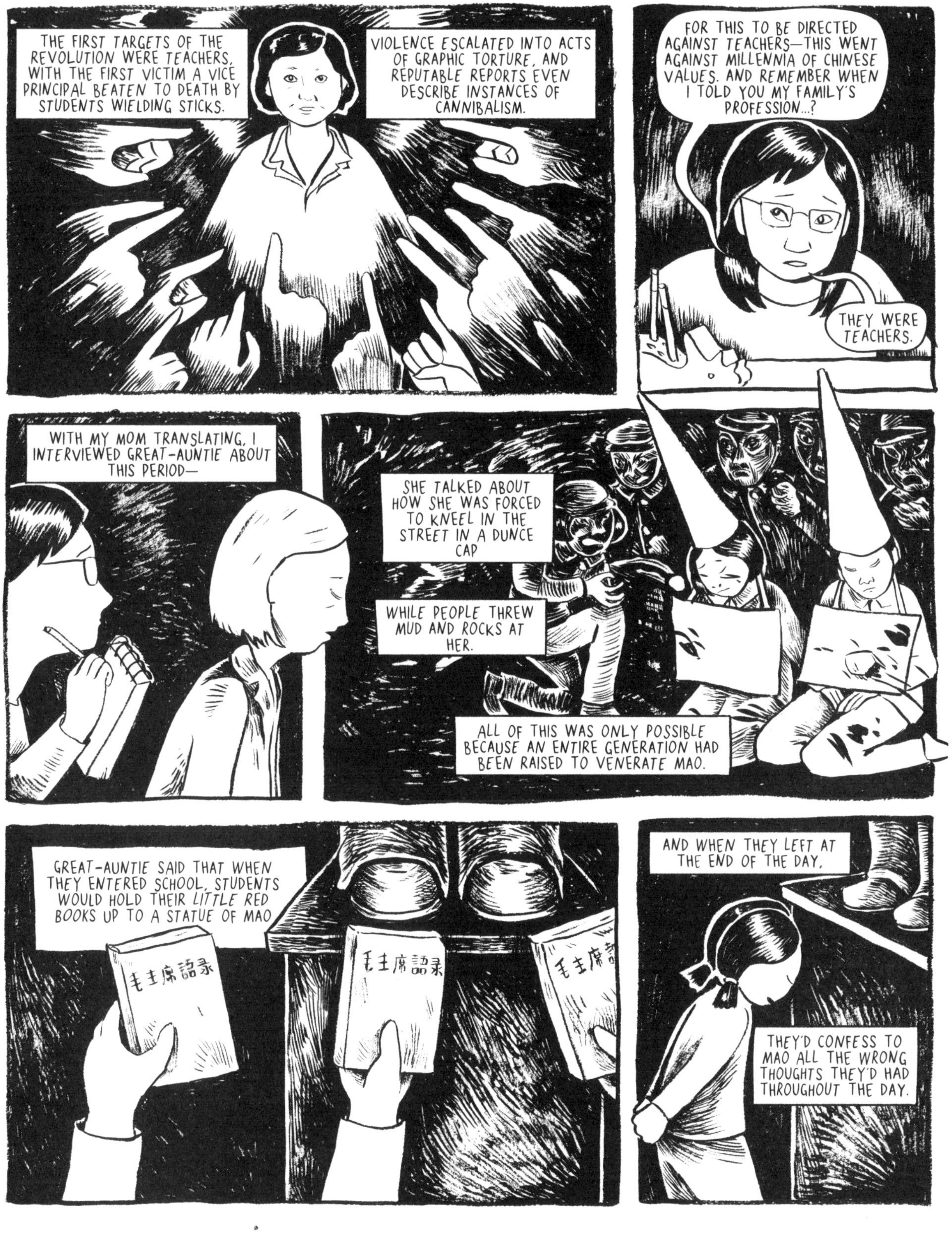
THE FIRST TARGETS OF THE REVOLUTION WERE TEACHERS, WITH THE FIRST VICTIM A VICE PRINCIPAL BEATEN TO DEATH BY STUDENTS WIELDING STICKS.
VIOLENCE ESCALATED INTO ACTS OF GRAPHIC TORTURE, AND REPUTABLE REPORTS EVEN DESCRIBE INSTANCES OF CANNIBALISM.
FOR THIS TO BE DIRECTED AGAINST TEACHERS—THIS WENT AGAINST MILLENNIA OF CHINESE VALUES. AND REMEMBER WHEN I TOLD YOU MY FAMILY'S PROFESSION...?
THEY WERE TEACHERS.
WITH MY MOM TRANSLATING, I INTERVIEWED GREAT-AUNTIE ABOUT THIS PERIOD—
SHE TALKED ABOUT HOW SHE WAS FORCED TO KNEEL IN THE STREET IN A DUNCE CAP
WHILE PEOPLE THREW MUD AND ROCKS AT HER.
ALL OF THIS WAS ONLY POSSIBLE BECAUSE AN ENTIRE GENERATION HAD BEEN RAISED TO VENERATE MAO.
GREAT-AUNTIE SAID THAT WHEN THEY ENTERED SCHOOL, STUDENTS WOULD HOLD THEIR *LITTLE RED BOOKS* UP TO A STATUE OF MAO
毛主席語录
毛主席語录
AND WHEN THEY LEFT AT THE END OF THE DAY,
THEY'D CONFESS TO MAO ALL THE WRONG THOUGHTS THEY'D HAD THROUGHOUT THE DAY.

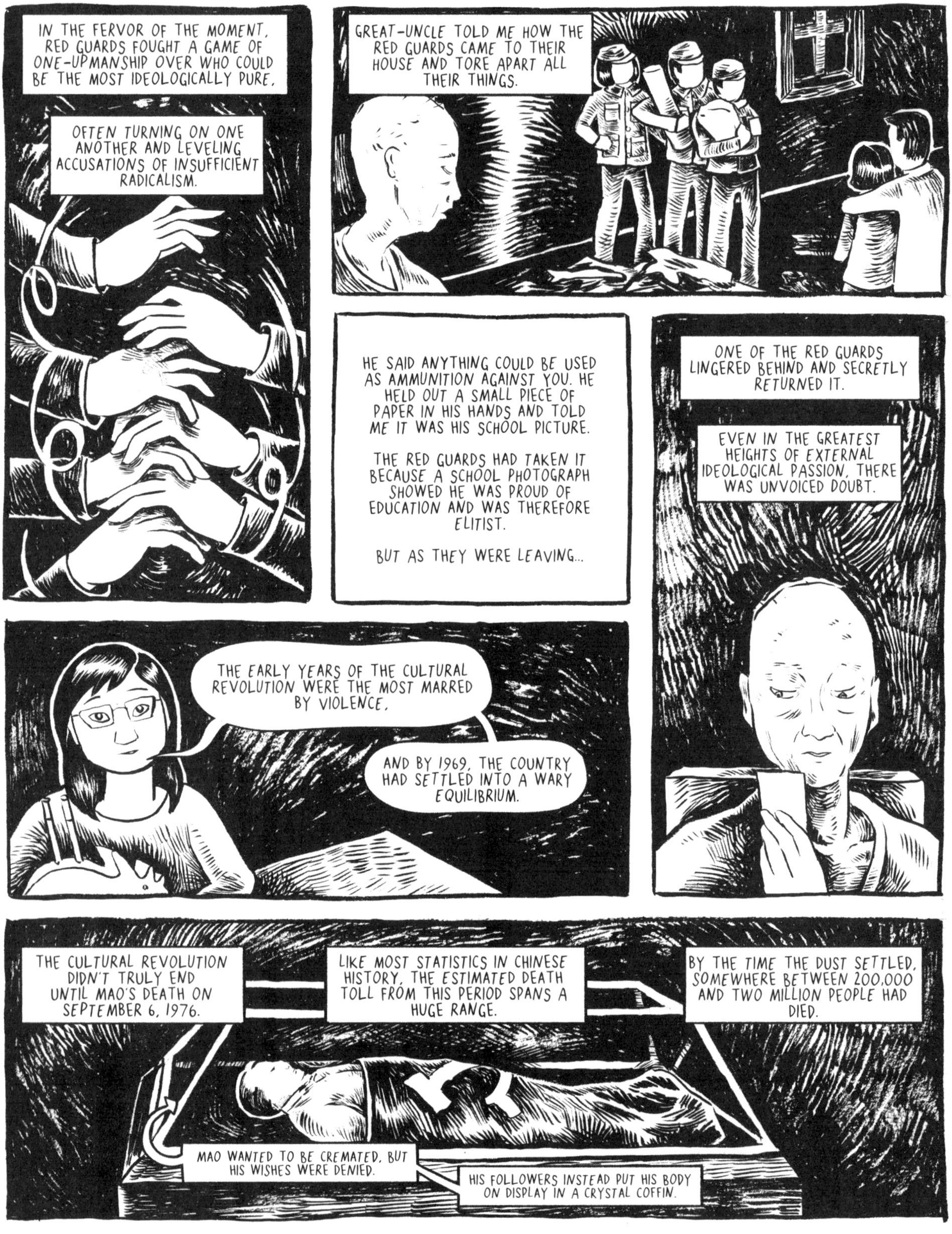
IN THE FERVOR OF THE MOMENT, RED GUARDS FOUGHT A GAME OF ONE-UPMANSHIP OVER WHO COULD BE THE MOST IDEOLOGICALLY PURE,
OFTEN TURNING ON ONE ANOTHER AND LEVELING ACCUSATIONS OF INSUFFICIENT RADICALISM.
GREAT-UNCLE TOLD ME HOW THE RED GUARDS CAME TO THEIR HOUSE AND TORE APART ALL THEIR THINGS.
HE SAID ANYTHING COULD BE USED AS AMMUNITION AGAINST YOU. HE HELD OUT A SMALL PIECE OF PAPER IN HIS HANDS AND TOLD ME IT WAS HIS SCHOOL PICTURE.
THE RED GUARDS HAD TAKEN IT BECAUSE A SCHOOL PHOTOGRAPH SHOWED HE WAS PROUD OF EDUCATION AND WAS THEREFORE ELITIST.
BUT AS THEY WERE LEAVING...
ONE OF THE RED GUARDS LINGERED BEHIND AND SECRETLY RETURNED IT.
EVEN IN THE GREATEST HEIGHTS OF EXTERNAL IDEOLOGICAL PASSION, THERE WAS UNVOICED DOUBT.
THE EARLY YEARS OF THE CULTURAL REVOLUTION WERE THE MOST MARRED BY VIOLENCE,
AND BY 1969, THE COUNTRY HAD SETTLED INTO A WARY EQUILIBRIUM.
THE CULTURAL REVOLUTION DIDN'T TRULY END UNTIL MAO'S DEATH ON SEPTEMBER 6, 1976.
LIKE MOST STATISTICS IN CHINESE HISTORY, THE ESTIMATED DEATH TOLL FROM THIS PERIOD SPANS A HUGE RANGE.
BY THE TIME THE DUST SETTLED, SOMEWHERE BETWEEN 200,000 AND TWO MILLION PEOPLE HAD DIED.
MAO WANTED TO BE CREMATED, BUT HIS WISHES WERE DENIED.
HIS FOLLOWERS INSTEAD PUT HIS BODY ON DISPLAY IN A CRYSTAL COFFIN.

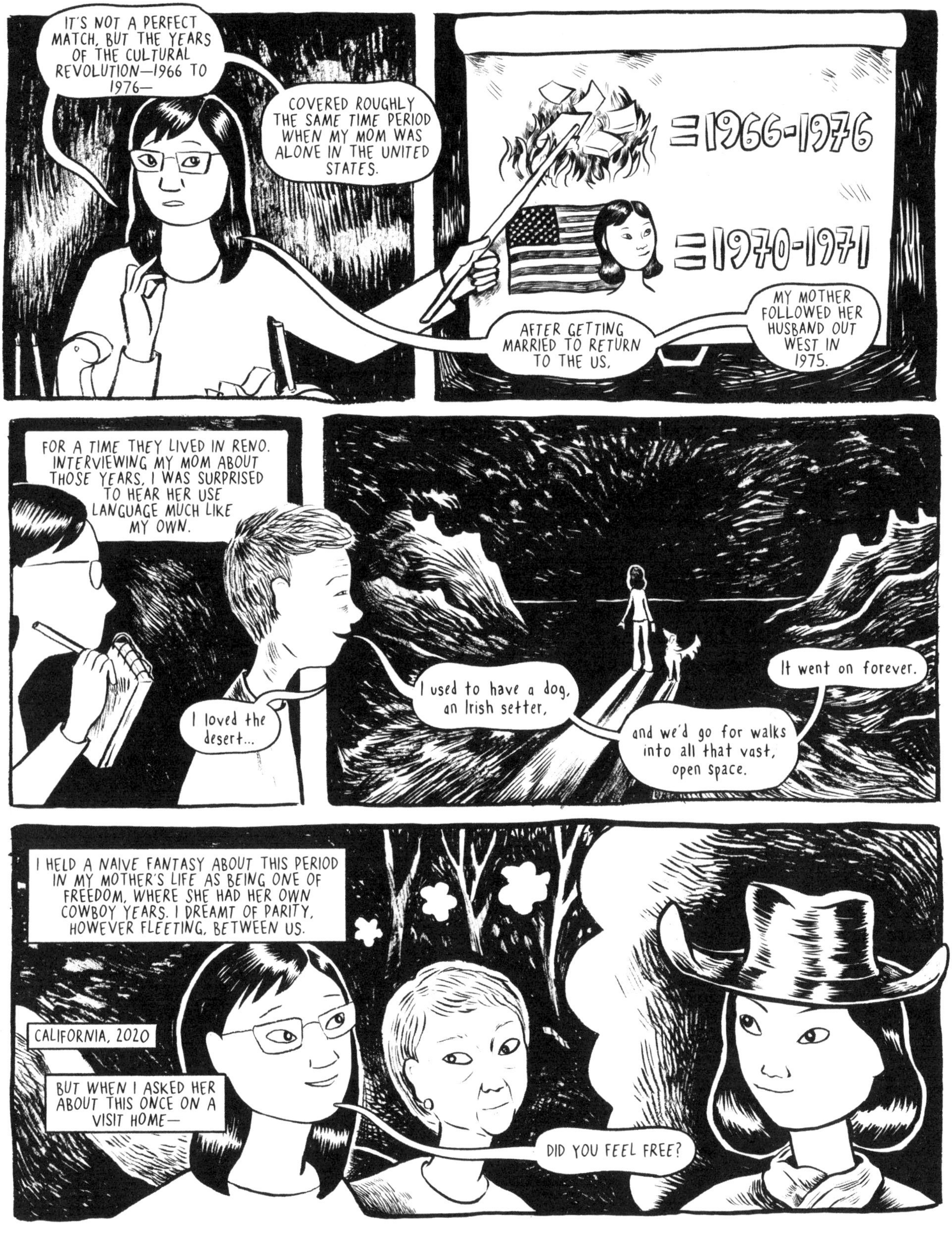
IT'S NOT A PERFECT MATCH, BUT THE YEARS OF THE CULTURAL REVOLUTION—1966 TO 1976—
COVERED ROUGHLY THE SAME TIME PERIOD WHEN MY MOM WAS ALONE IN THE UNITED STATES.
=1966-1976
=1970-1971
AFTER GETTING MARRIED TO RETURN TO THE US,
MY MOTHER FOLLOWED HER HUSBAND OUT WEST IN 1975.
FOR A TIME THEY LIVED IN RENO. INTERVIEWING MY MOM ABOUT THOSE YEARS, I WAS SURPRISED TO HEAR HER USE LANGUAGE MUCH LIKE MY OWN.
I loved the desert...
I used to have a dog, an Irish setter,
and we'd go for walks into all that vast, open space.
It went on forever.
I HELD A NAIVE FANTASY ABOUT THIS PERIOD IN MY MOTHER'S LIFE AS BEING ONE OF FREEDOM, WHERE SHE HAD HER OWN COWBOY YEARS. I DREAMT OF PARITY, HOWEVER FLEETING, BETWEEN US.
CALIFORNIA, 2020
BUT WHEN I ASKED HER ABOUT THIS ONCE ON A VISIT HOME—
DID YOU FEEL FREE?

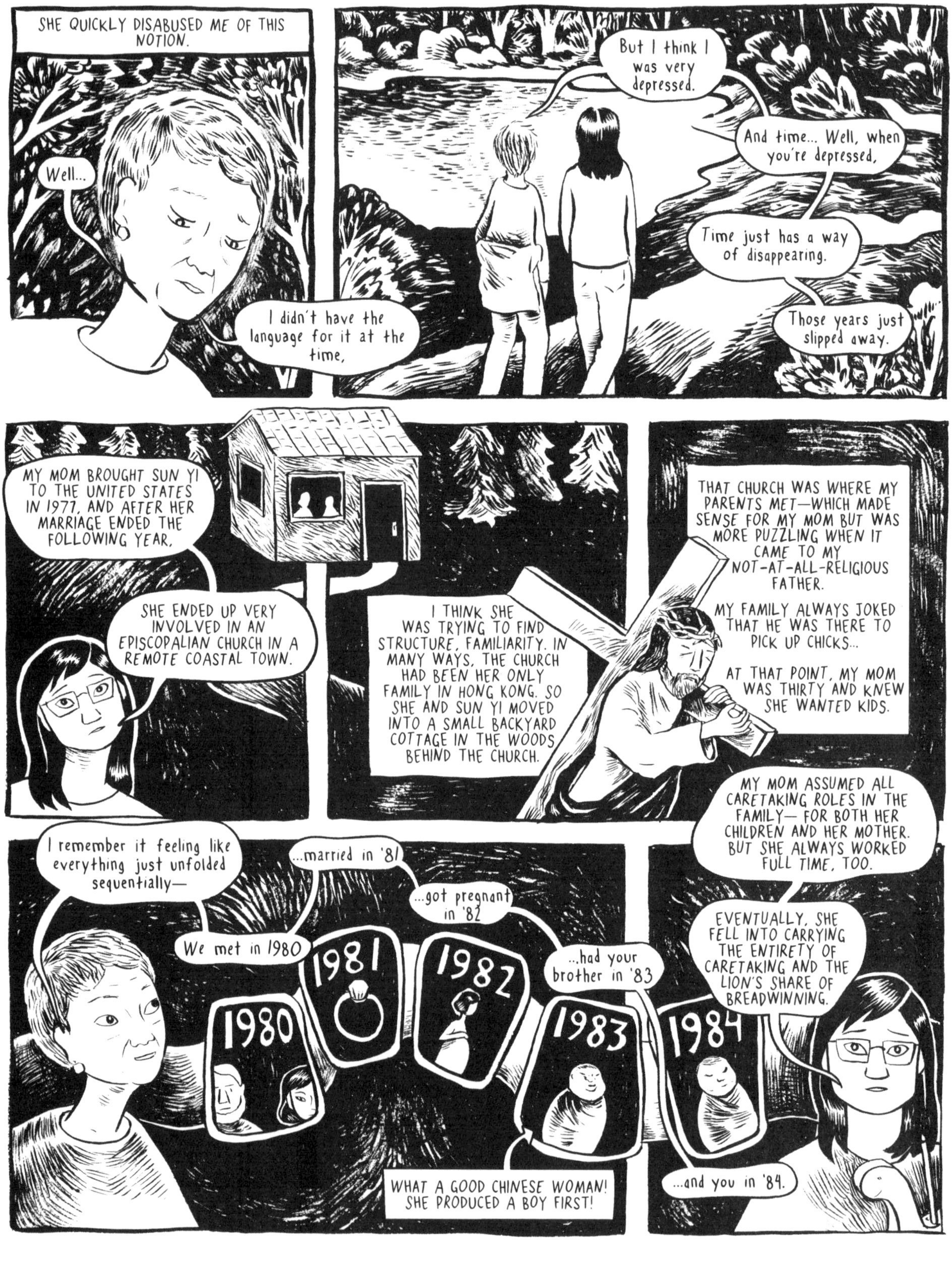
SHE QUICKLY DISABUSED ME OF THIS NOTION.
Well...
I didn't have the language for it at the time,
But I think I was very depressed.
And time... Well, when you're depressed,
Time just has a way of disappearing.
Those years just slipped away.
MY MOM BROUGHT SUN YI TO THE UNITED STATES IN 1977, AND AFTER HER MARRIAGE ENDED THE FOLLOWING YEAR,
SHE ENDED UP VERY INVOLVED IN AN EPISCOPALIAN CHURCH IN A REMOTE COASTAL TOWN.
I THINK SHE WAS TRYING TO FIND STRUCTURE, FAMILIARITY. IN MANY WAYS, THE CHURCH HAD BEEN HER ONLY FAMILY IN HONG KONG. SO SHE AND SUN YI MOVED INTO A SMALL BACKYARD COTTAGE IN THE WOODS BEHIND THE CHURCH.
THAT CHURCH WAS WHERE MY PARENTS MET—WHICH MADE SENSE FOR MY MOM BUT WAS MORE PUZZLING WHEN IT CAME TO MY NOT-AT-ALL-RELIGIOUS FATHER.
MY FAMILY ALWAYS JOKED THAT HE WAS THERE TO PICK UP CHICKS...
AT THAT POINT, MY MOM WAS THIRTY AND KNEW SHE WANTED KIDS.
I remember it feeling like everything just unfolded sequentially—
We met in 1980
...married in '81
...got pregnant in '82
...had your brother in '83
...and you in '84.
1980
1981
1982
1983
1984
WHAT A GOOD CHINESE WOMAN! SHE PRODUCED A BOY FIRST!
MY MOM ASSUMED ALL CARETAKING ROLES IN THE FAMILY— FOR BOTH HER CHILDREN AND HER MOTHER. BUT SHE ALWAYS WORKED FULL TIME, TOO.
EVENTUALLY, SHE FELL INTO CARRYING THE ENTIRETY OF CARETAKING AND THE LION'S SHARE OF BREADWINNING.

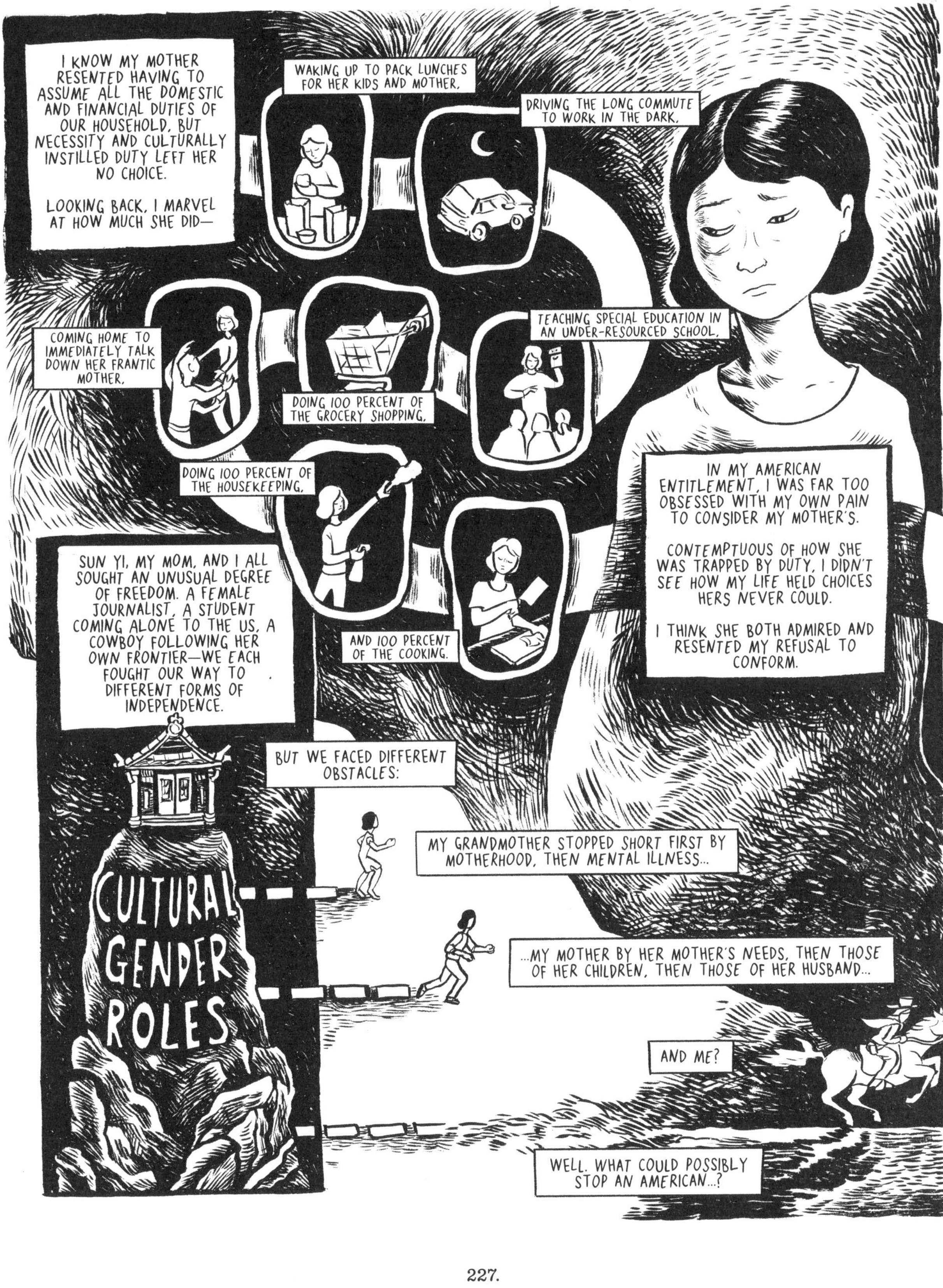
I KNOW MY MOTHER RESENTED HAVING TO ASSUME ALL THE DOMESTIC AND FINANCIAL DUTIES OF OUR HOUSEHOLD, BUT NECESSITY AND CULTURALLY INSTILLED DUTY LEFT HER NO CHOICE.
LOOKING BACK, I MARVEL AT HOW MUCH SHE DID—
WAKING UP TO PACK LUNCHES FOR HER KIDS AND MOTHER,
DRIVING THE LONG COMMUTE TO WORK IN THE DARK,
TEACHING SPECIAL EDUCATION IN AN UNDER-RESOURCED SCHOOL,
DOING 100 PERCENT OF THE GROCERY SHOPPING,
COMING HOME TO IMMEDIATELY TALK DOWN HER FRANTIC MOTHER,
DOING 100 PERCENT OF THE HOUSEKEEPING,
AND 100 PERCENT OF THE COOKING.
IN MY AMERICAN ENTITLEMENT, I WAS FAR TOO OBSESSED WITH MY OWN PAIN TO CONSIDER MY MOTHER'S.
CONTEMPTUOUS OF HOW SHE WAS TRAPPED BY DUTY, I DIDN'T SEE HOW MY LIFE HELD CHOICES HERS NEVER COULD.
I THINK SHE BOTH ADMIRED AND RESENTED MY REFUSAL TO CONFORM.
SUN YI, MY MOM, AND I ALL SOUGHT AN UNUSUAL DEGREE OF FREEDOM. A FEMALE JOURNALIST, A STUDENT COMING ALONE TO THE US, A COWBOY FOLLOWING HER OWN FRONTIER—WE EACH FOUGHT OUR WAY TO DIFFERENT FORMS OF INDEPENDENCE.
BUT WE FACED DIFFERENT OBSTACLES:
CULTURAL GENDER ROLES
MY GRANDMOTHER STOPPED SHORT FIRST BY MOTHERHOOD, THEN MENTAL ILLNESS...
...MY MOTHER BY HER MOTHER'S NEEDS, THEN THOSE OF HER CHILDREN, THEN THOSE OF HER HUSBAND...
AND ME?
WELL. WHAT COULD POSSIBLY STOP AN AMERICAN...?

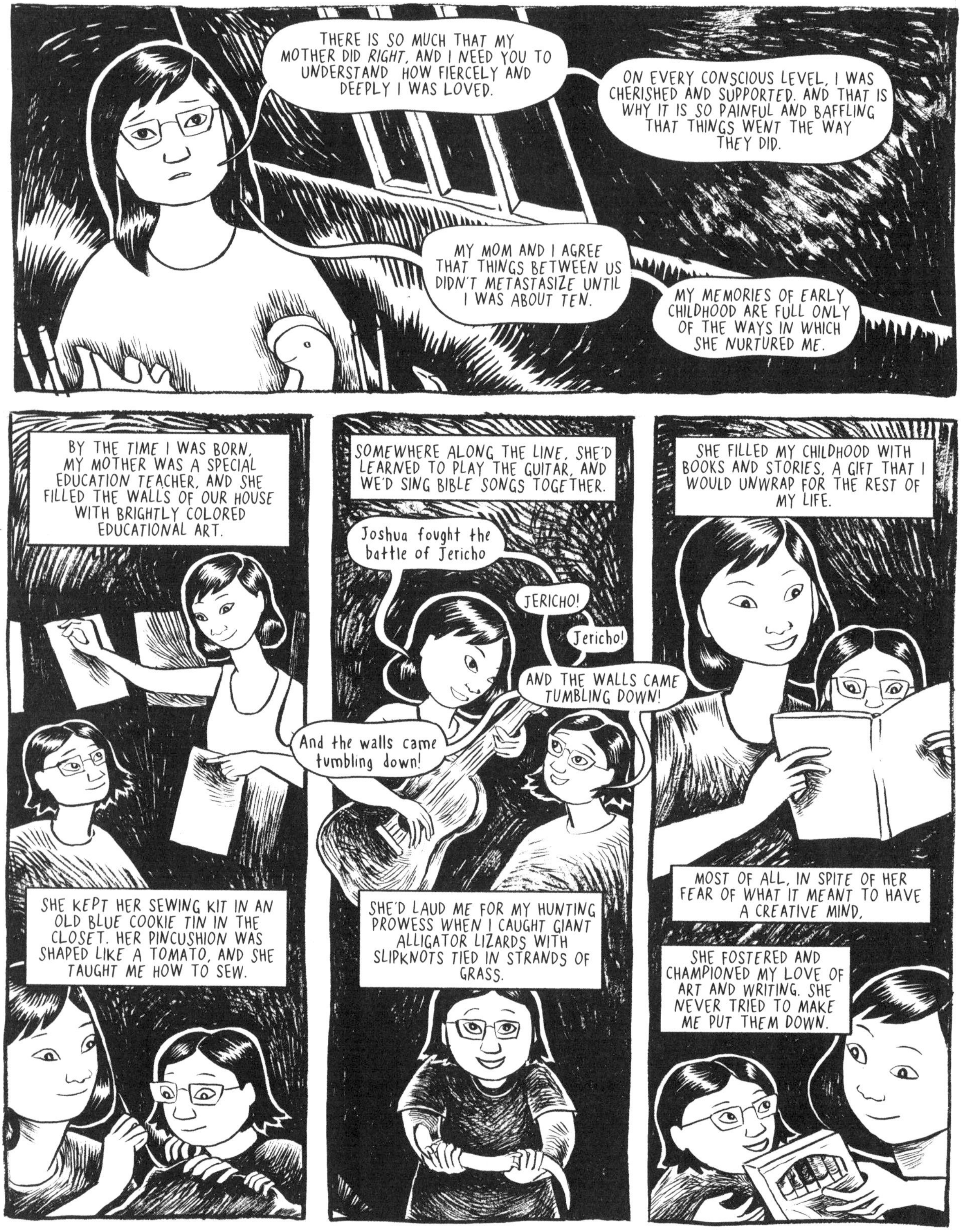

THERE IS SO MUCH THAT MY MOTHER DID *RIGHT*, AND I NEED YOU TO UNDERSTAND HOW FIERCELY AND DEEPLY I WAS LOVED.
ON EVERY CONSCIOUS LEVEL, I WAS CHERISHED AND SUPPORTED. AND THAT IS WHY IT IS SO PAINFUL AND BAFFLING THAT THINGS WENT THE WAY THEY DID.
MY MOM AND I AGREE THAT THINGS BETWEEN US DIDN'T METASTASIZE UNTIL I WAS ABOUT TEN.
MY MEMORIES OF EARLY CHILDHOOD ARE FULL ONLY OF THE WAYS IN WHICH SHE NURTURED ME.
BY THE TIME I WAS BORN, MY MOTHER WAS A SPECIAL EDUCATION TEACHER, AND SHE FILLED THE WALLS OF OUR HOUSE WITH BRIGHTLY COLORED EDUCATIONAL ART.
SHE KEPT HER SEWING KIT IN AN OLD BLUE COOKIE TIN IN THE CLOSET. HER PINCUSHION WAS SHAPED LIKE A TOMATO, AND SHE TAUGHT ME HOW TO SEW.
SOMEWHERE ALONG THE LINE, SHE'D LEARNED TO PLAY THE GUITAR, AND WE'D SING BIBLE SONGS TOGETHER.
Joshua fought the battle of Jericho
JERICHO!
Jericho!
AND THE WALLS CAME TUMBLING DOWN!
And the walls came tumbling down!
SHE'D LAUD ME FOR MY HUNTING PROWESS WHEN I CAUGHT GIANT ALLIGATOR LIZARDS WITH SLIPKNOTS TIED IN STRANDS OF GRASS.
SHE FILLED MY CHILDHOOD WITH BOOKS AND STORIES, A GIFT THAT I WOULD UNWRAP FOR THE REST OF MY LIFE.
MOST OF ALL, IN SPITE OF HER FEAR OF WHAT IT MEANT TO HAVE A CREATIVE MIND,
SHE FOSTERED AND CHAMPIONED MY LOVE OF ART AND WRITING. SHE NEVER TRIED TO MAKE ME PUT THEM DOWN.

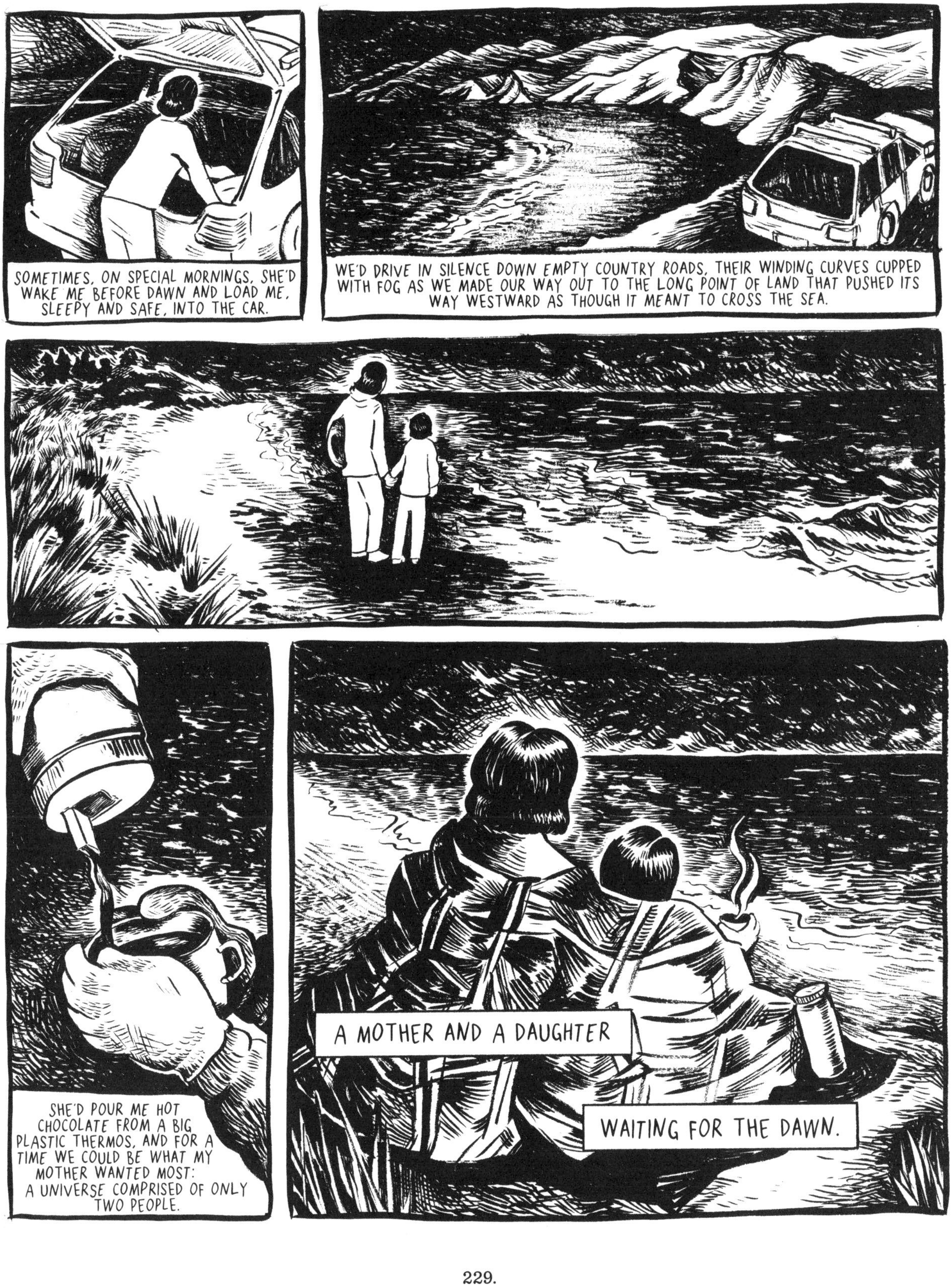
SOMETIMES, ON SPECIAL MORNINGS, SHE'D WAKE ME BEFORE DAWN AND LOAD ME, SLEEPY AND SAFE, INTO THE CAR.
WE'D DRIVE IN SILENCE DOWN EMPTY COUNTRY ROADS, THEIR WINDING CURVES CUPPED WITH FOG AS WE MADE OUR WAY OUT TO THE LONG POINT OF LAND THAT PUSHED ITS WAY WESTWARD AS THOUGH IT MEANT TO CROSS THE SEA.
SHE'D POUR ME HOT CHOCOLATE FROM A BIG PLASTIC THERMOS, AND FOR A TIME WE COULD BE WHAT MY MOTHER WANTED MOST: A UNIVERSE COMPRISED OF ONLY TWO PEOPLE.
A MOTHER AND A DAUGHTER
WAITING FOR THE DAWN.

SO LONG AS WE EXISTED AS A CLOSED CIRCUIT, MY MOTHER WAS A LOVING, DOTING PARENT. BUT IF THAT CONNECTION WAS INTERRUPTED? IF SOMETHING MADE HER FEEL AS IF I WAS DISTANCING MYSELF FROM HER?

THE GHOST TWIN WOULD APPEAR IN AN INSTANT, AND I WOULD RECOIL IN FEAR. BECAUSE MY MOTHER COULD NOT SEE HER TERRIFYING SECOND SELF, SHE TOOK THIS AS A SIGN THAT SOMETHING WAS WRONG WITH ME.

SHE WANTED SO MUCH TO KEEP ME SAFE THAT SHE CONSTANTLY POKED AT MY MIND, TRYING TO FIX IT, TO MEND IT, TO CURE IT... AND WHILE I DON'T BELIEVE SHE EVER MEANT TO TEACH ME THAT I WAS BROKEN, THAT IS WHAT I LEARNED.

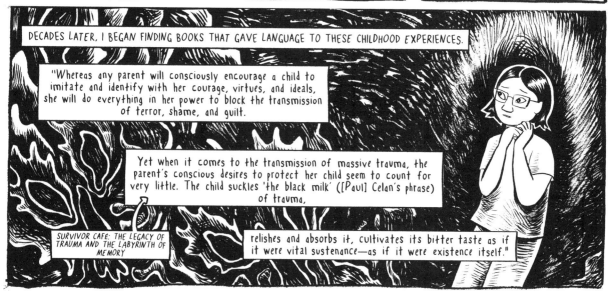

DECADES LATER, I BEGAN FINDING BOOKS THAT GAVE LANGUAGE TO THESE CHILDHOOD EXPERIENCES.

"Whereas any parent will consciously encourage a child to imitate and identify with her courage, virtues, and ideals, she will do everything in her power to block the transmission of terror, shame, and guilt.

Yet when it comes to the transmission of massive trauma, the parent's conscious desires to protect her child seem to count for very little. The child suckles 'the black milk' ([Paul] Celan's phrase) of trauma,

SURVIVOR CAFE: THE LEGACY OF TRAUMA AND THE LABYRINTH OF MEMORY

relishes and absorbs it, cultivates its bitter taste as if it were vital sustenance—as if it were existence itself."

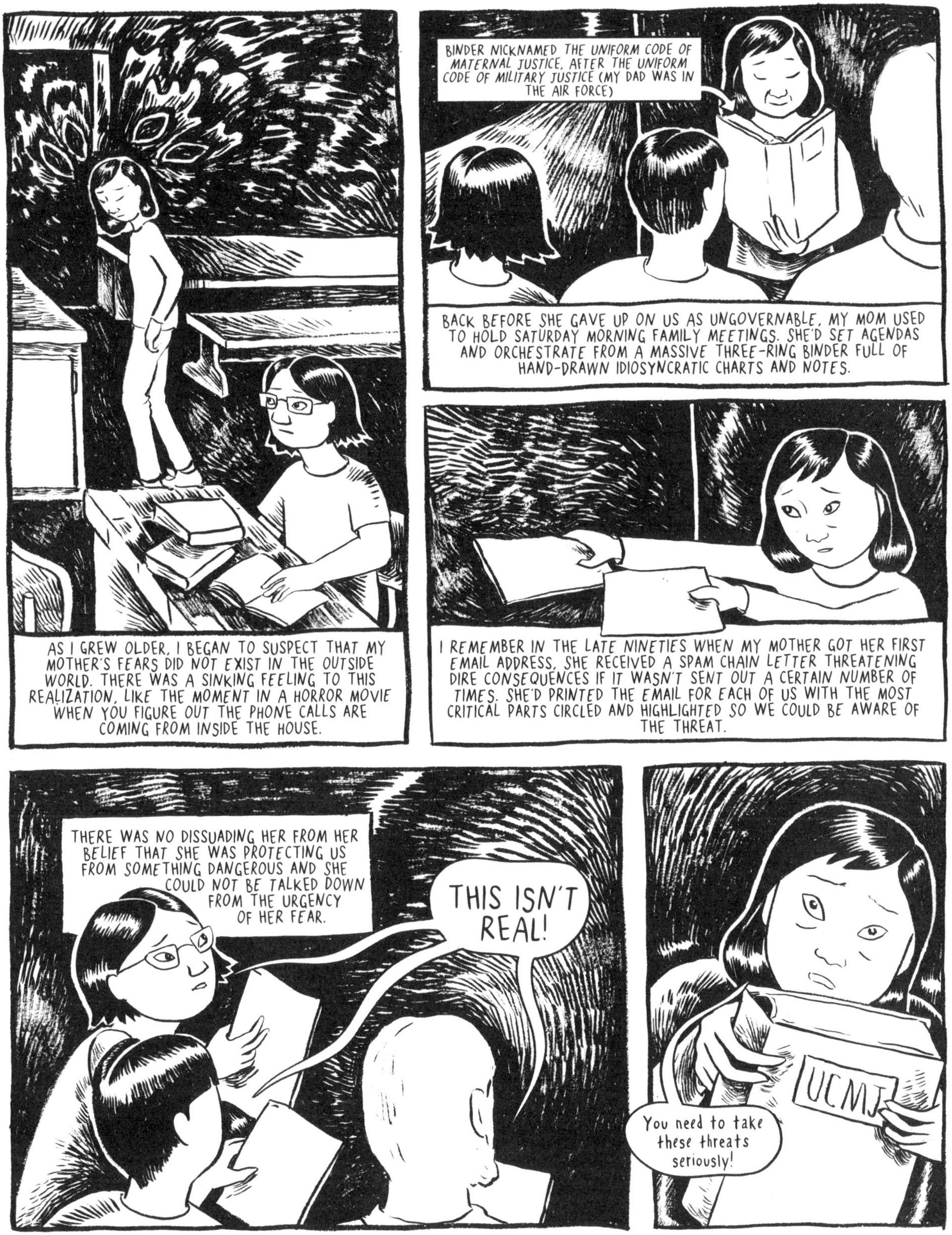
AS I GREW OLDER, I BEGAN TO SUSPECT THAT MY MOTHER'S FEARS DID NOT EXIST IN THE OUTSIDE WORLD. THERE WAS A SINKING FEELING TO THIS REALIZATION, LIKE THE MOMENT IN A HORROR MOVIE WHEN YOU FIGURE OUT THE PHONE CALLS ARE COMING FROM INSIDE THE HOUSE.
BINDER NICKNAMED THE *UNIFORM CODE OF MATERNAL JUSTICE*, AFTER THE *UNIFORM CODE OF MILITARY JUSTICE* (MY DAD WAS IN THE AIR FORCE)
BACK BEFORE SHE GAVE UP ON US AS UNGOVERNABLE, MY MOM USED TO HOLD SATURDAY MORNING FAMILY MEETINGS. SHE'D SET AGENDAS AND ORCHESTRATE FROM A MASSIVE THREE-RING BINDER FULL OF HAND-DRAWN IDIOSYNCRATIC CHARTS AND NOTES.
I REMEMBER IN THE LATE NINETIES WHEN MY MOTHER GOT HER FIRST EMAIL ADDRESS, SHE RECEIVED A SPAM CHAIN LETTER THREATENING DIRE CONSEQUENCES IF IT WASN'T SENT OUT A CERTAIN NUMBER OF TIMES. SHE'D PRINTED THE EMAIL FOR EACH OF US WITH THE MOST CRITICAL PARTS CIRCLED AND HIGHLIGHTED SO WE COULD BE AWARE OF THE THREAT.
THERE WAS NO DISSUADING HER FROM HER BELIEF THAT SHE WAS PROTECTING US FROM SOMETHING DANGEROUS AND SHE COULD NOT BE TALKED DOWN FROM THE URGENCY OF HER FEAR.
THIS ISN'T REAL!
UCMJ
You need to take these threats seriously!

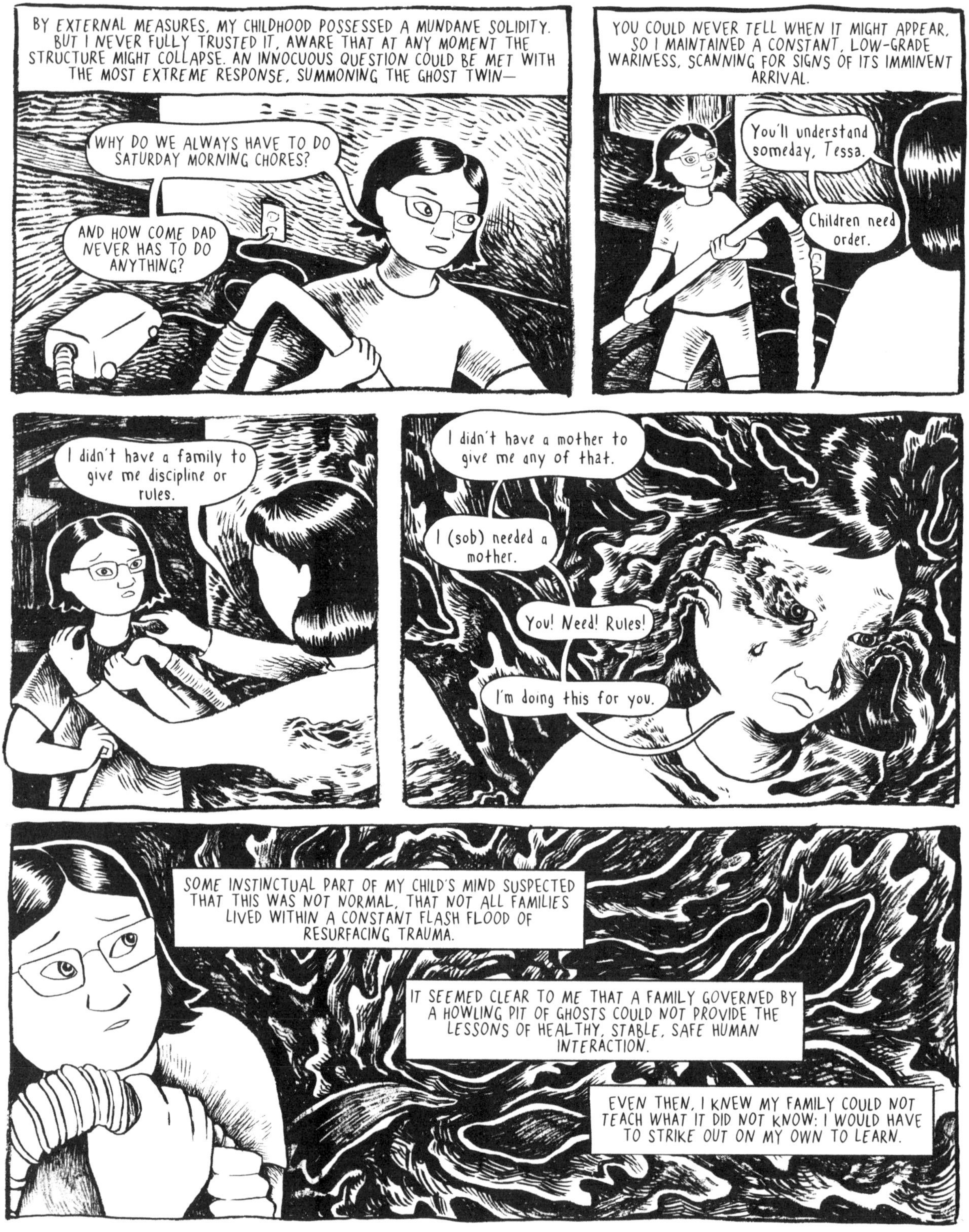
BY EXTERNAL MEASURES, MY CHILDHOOD POSSESSED A MUNDANE SOLIDITY. BUT I NEVER FULLY TRUSTED IT, AWARE THAT AT ANY MOMENT THE STRUCTURE MIGHT COLLAPSE. AN INNOCUOUS QUESTION COULD BE MET WITH THE MOST EXTREME RESPONSE, SUMMONING THE GHOST TWIN—
WHY DO WE ALWAYS HAVE TO DO SATURDAY MORNING CHORES?
AND HOW COME DAD NEVER HAS TO DO ANYTHING?
YOU COULD NEVER TELL WHEN IT MIGHT APPEAR, SO I MAINTAINED A CONSTANT, LOW-GRADE WARINESS, SCANNING FOR SIGNS OF ITS IMMINENT ARRIVAL.
You'll understand someday, Tessa.
Children need order.
I didn't have a family to give me discipline or rules.
I didn't have a mother to give me any of that.
I (sob) needed a mother.
You! Need! Rules!
I'm doing this for you.
SOME INSTINCTUAL PART OF MY CHILD'S MIND SUSPECTED THAT THIS WAS NOT NORMAL, THAT NOT ALL FAMILIES LIVED WITHIN A CONSTANT FLASH FLOOD OF RESURFACING TRAUMA.
IT SEEMED CLEAR TO ME THAT A FAMILY GOVERNED BY A HOWLING PIT OF GHOSTS COULD NOT PROVIDE THE LESSONS OF HEALTHY, STABLE, SAFE HUMAN INTERACTION.
EVEN THEN, I KNEW MY FAMILY COULD NOT TEACH WHAT IT DID NOT KNOW: I WOULD HAVE TO STRIKE OUT ON MY OWN TO LEARN.

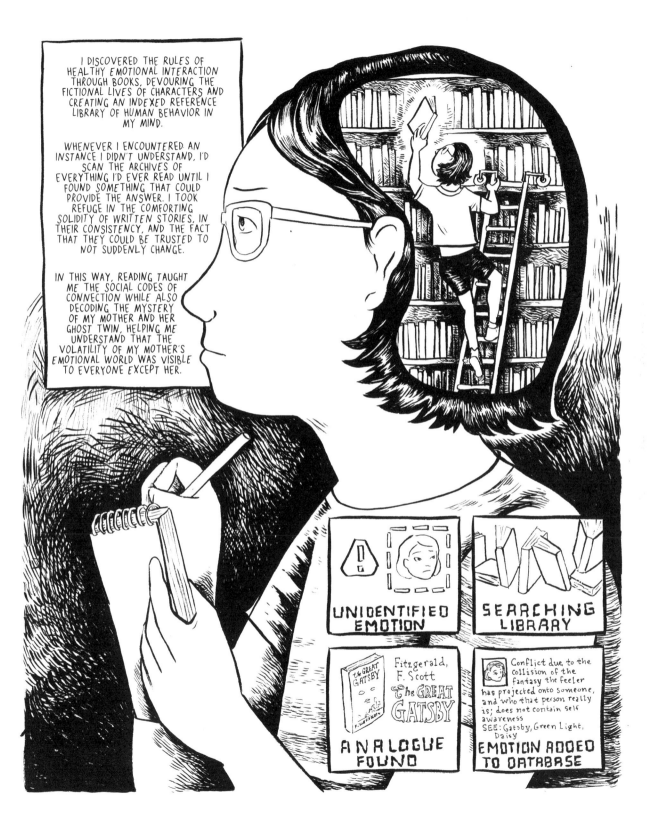

I DISCOVERED THE RULES OF HEALTHY EMOTIONAL INTERACTION THROUGH BOOKS, DEVOURING THE FICTIONAL LIVES OF CHARACTERS AND CREATING AN INDEXED REFERENCE LIBRARY OF HUMAN BEHAVIOR IN MY MIND.

WHENEVER I ENCOUNTERED AN INSTANCE I DIDN'T UNDERSTAND, I'D SCAN THE ARCHIVES OF EVERYTHING I'D EVER READ UNTIL I FOUND SOMETHING THAT COULD PROVIDE THE ANSWER. I TOOK REFUGE IN THE COMFORTING SOLIDITY OF WRITTEN STORIES, IN THEIR CONSISTENCY, AND THE FACT THAT THEY COULD BE TRUSTED TO NOT SUDDENLY CHANGE.

IN THIS WAY, READING TAUGHT ME THE SOCIAL CODES OF CONNECTION WHILE ALSO DECODING THE MYSTERY OF MY MOTHER AND HER GHOST TWIN, HELPING ME UNDERSTAND THAT THE VOLATILITY OF MY MOTHER'S EMOTIONAL WORLD WAS VISIBLE TO EVERYONE EXCEPT HER.

UNIDENTIFIED EMOTION

SEARCHING LIBRARY

Fitzgerald, F. Scott
The GREAT GATSBY

ANALOGUE FOUND

Conflict due to the collision of the fantasy the feeler has projected onto someone, and who that person really is; does not contain self awareness
SEE: Gatsby, Green Light, Daisy

EMOTION ADDED TO DATABASE

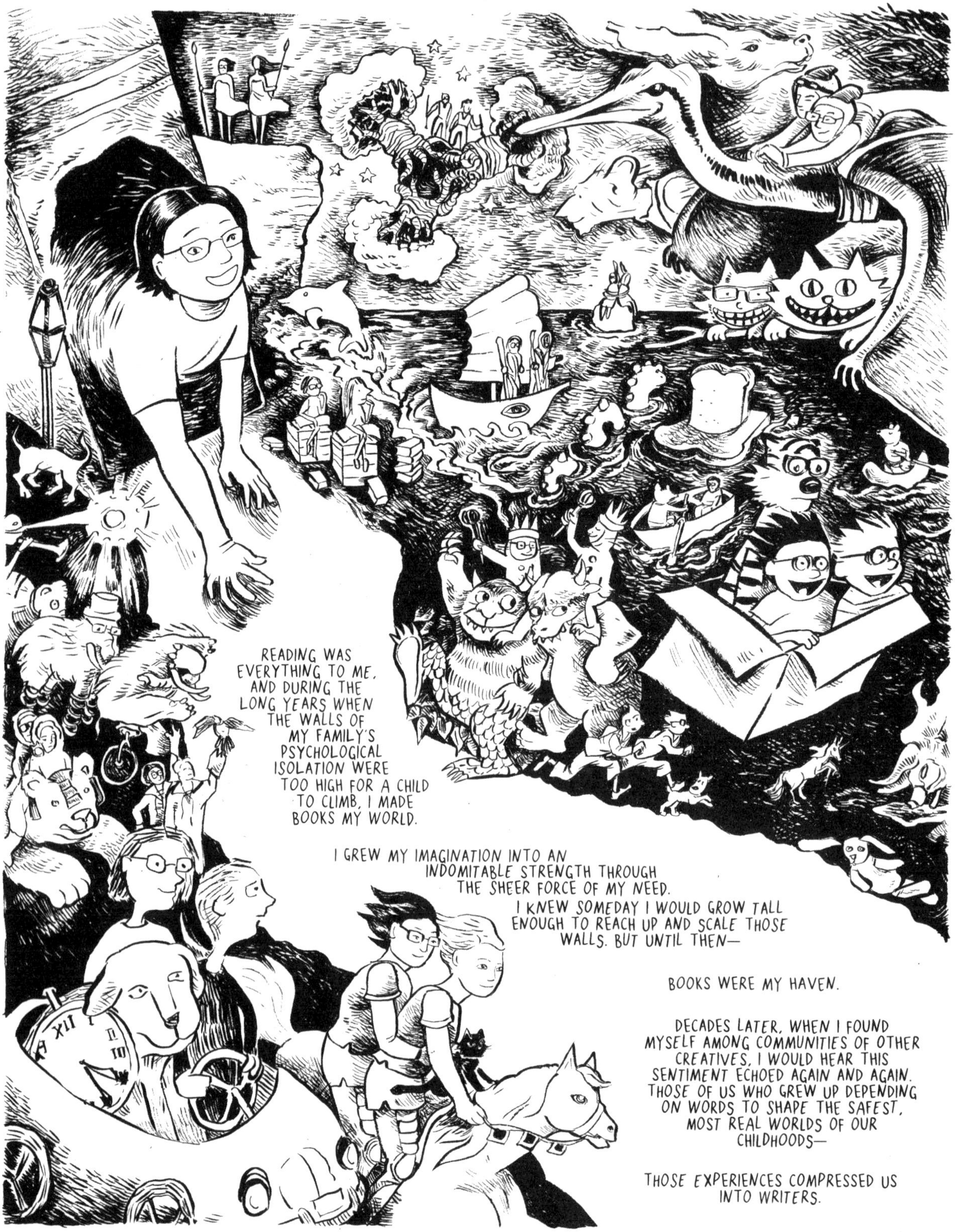
READING WAS EVERYTHING TO ME, AND DURING THE LONG YEARS WHEN THE WALLS OF MY FAMILY'S PSYCHOLOGICAL ISOLATION WERE TOO HIGH FOR A CHILD TO CLIMB, I MADE BOOKS MY WORLD.
I GREW MY IMAGINATION INTO AN INDOMITABLE STRENGTH THROUGH THE SHEER FORCE OF MY NEED.
I KNEW SOMEDAY I WOULD GROW TALL ENOUGH TO REACH UP AND SCALE THOSE WALLS. BUT UNTIL THEN—
BOOKS WERE MY HAVEN.
DECADES LATER, WHEN I FOUND MYSELF AMONG COMMUNITIES OF OTHER CREATIVES, I WOULD HEAR THIS SENTIMENT ECHOED AGAIN AND AGAIN. THOSE OF US WHO GREW UP DEPENDING ON WORDS TO SHAPE THE SAFEST, MOST REAL WORLDS OF OUR CHILDHOODS—
THOSE EXPERIENCES COMPRESSED US INTO WRITERS.

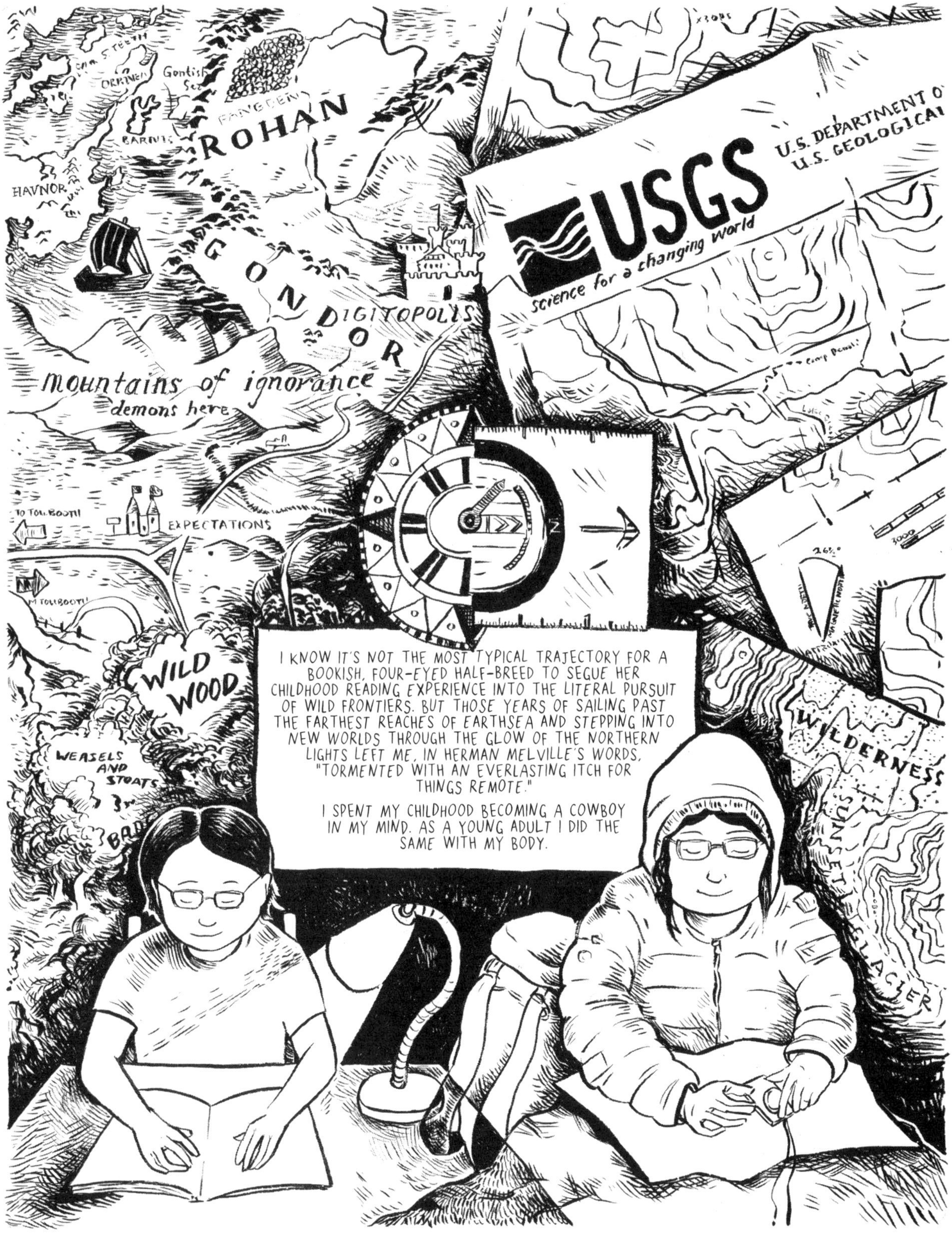
ROHAN
HAVNOR
GONDOR
DIGITOPOLIS
mountains of ignorance
demons here
TO TOLLBOOTH
EXPECTATIONS
WILD WOOD
WEASELS AND STOATS
USGS
science for a changing world
U.S. DEPARTMENT O
U.S. GEOLOGICAL
WILDERNESS
SUNSET GLACIER
I KNOW IT'S NOT THE MOST TYPICAL TRAJECTORY FOR A BOOKISH, FOUR-EYED HALF-BREED TO SEGUE HER CHILDHOOD READING EXPERIENCE INTO THE LITERAL PURSUIT OF WILD FRONTIERS. BUT THOSE YEARS OF SAILING PAST THE FARTHEST REACHES OF EARTHSEA AND STEPPING INTO NEW WORLDS THROUGH THE GLOW OF THE NORTHERN LIGHTS LEFT ME, IN HERMAN MELVILLE'S WORDS, "TORMENTED WITH AN EVERLASTING ITCH FOR THINGS REMOTE."
I SPENT MY CHILDHOOD BECOMING A COWBOY IN MY MIND. AS A YOUNG ADULT I DID THE SAME WITH MY BODY.

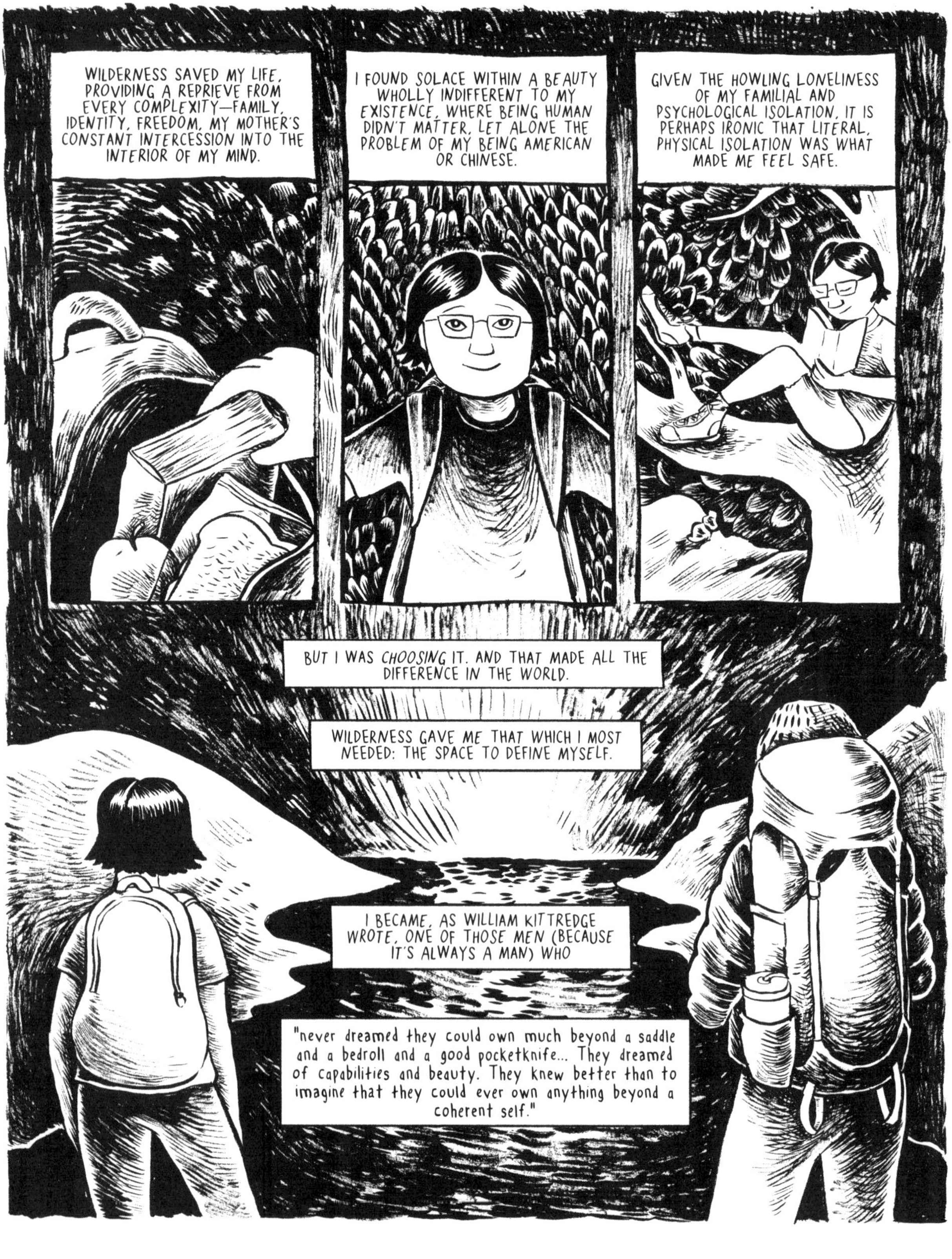

WILDERNESS SAVED MY LIFE, PROVIDING A REPRIEVE FROM EVERY COMPLEXITY—FAMILY, IDENTITY, FREEDOM, MY MOTHER'S CONSTANT INTERCESSION INTO THE INTERIOR OF MY MIND.
I FOUND SOLACE WITHIN A BEAUTY WHOLLY INDIFFERENT TO MY EXISTENCE, WHERE BEING HUMAN DIDN'T MATTER, LET ALONE THE PROBLEM OF MY BEING AMERICAN OR CHINESE.
GIVEN THE HOWLING LONELINESS OF MY FAMILIAL AND PSYCHOLOGICAL ISOLATION, IT IS PERHAPS IRONIC THAT LITERAL, PHYSICAL ISOLATION WAS WHAT MADE ME FEEL SAFE.
BUT I WAS *CHOOSING* IT. AND THAT MADE ALL THE DIFFERENCE IN THE WORLD.
WILDERNESS GAVE ME THAT WHICH I MOST NEEDED: THE SPACE TO DEFINE MYSELF.
I BECAME, AS WILLIAM KITTREDGE WROTE, ONE OF THOSE MEN (BECAUSE IT'S ALWAYS A MAN) WHO
"never dreamed they could own much beyond a saddle and a bedroll and a good pocketknife... They dreamed of capabilities and beauty. They knew better than to imagine that they could ever own anything beyond a coherent self."

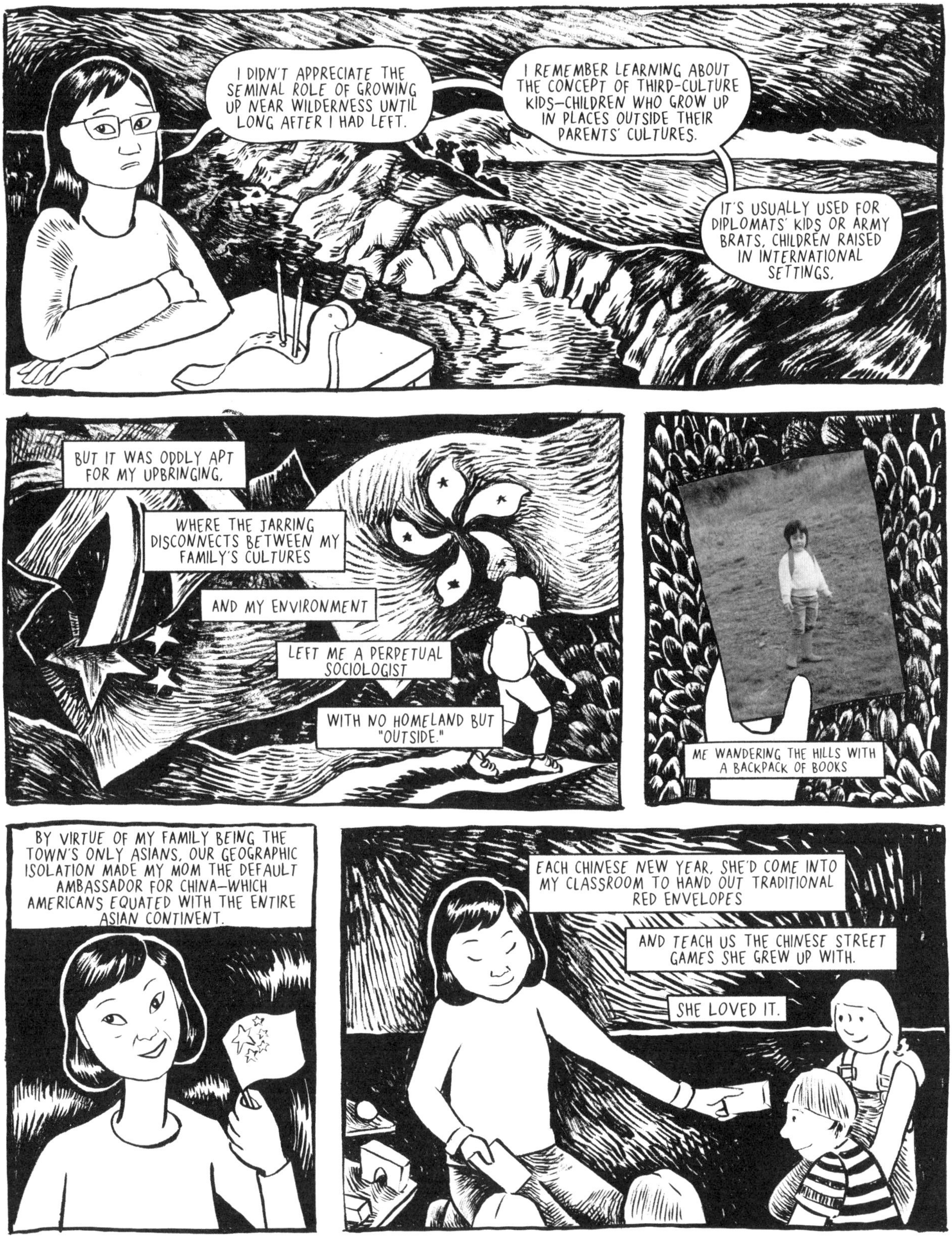
I DIDN'T APPRECIATE THE SEMINAL ROLE OF GROWING UP NEAR WILDERNESS UNTIL LONG AFTER I HAD LEFT.
I REMEMBER LEARNING ABOUT THE CONCEPT OF THIRD-CULTURE KIDS—CHILDREN WHO GROW UP IN PLACES OUTSIDE THEIR PARENTS' CULTURES.
IT'S USUALLY USED FOR DIPLOMATS' KIDS OR ARMY BRATS, CHILDREN RAISED IN INTERNATIONAL SETTINGS,
BUT IT WAS ODDLY APT FOR MY UPBRINGING,
WHERE THE JARRING DISCONNECTS BETWEEN MY FAMILY'S CULTURES
AND MY ENVIRONMENT
LEFT ME A PERPETUAL SOCIOLOGIST
WITH NO HOMELAND BUT "OUTSIDE."
ME WANDERING THE HILLS WITH A BACKPACK OF BOOKS
BY VIRTUE OF MY FAMILY BEING THE TOWN'S ONLY ASIANS, OUR GEOGRAPHIC ISOLATION MADE MY MOM THE DEFAULT AMBASSADOR FOR CHINA—WHICH AMERICANS EQUATED WITH THE ENTIRE ASIAN CONTINENT.
EACH CHINESE NEW YEAR, SHE'D COME INTO MY CLASSROOM TO HAND OUT TRADITIONAL RED ENVELOPES
AND TEACH US THE CHINESE STREET GAMES SHE GREW UP WITH.
SHE LOVED IT.

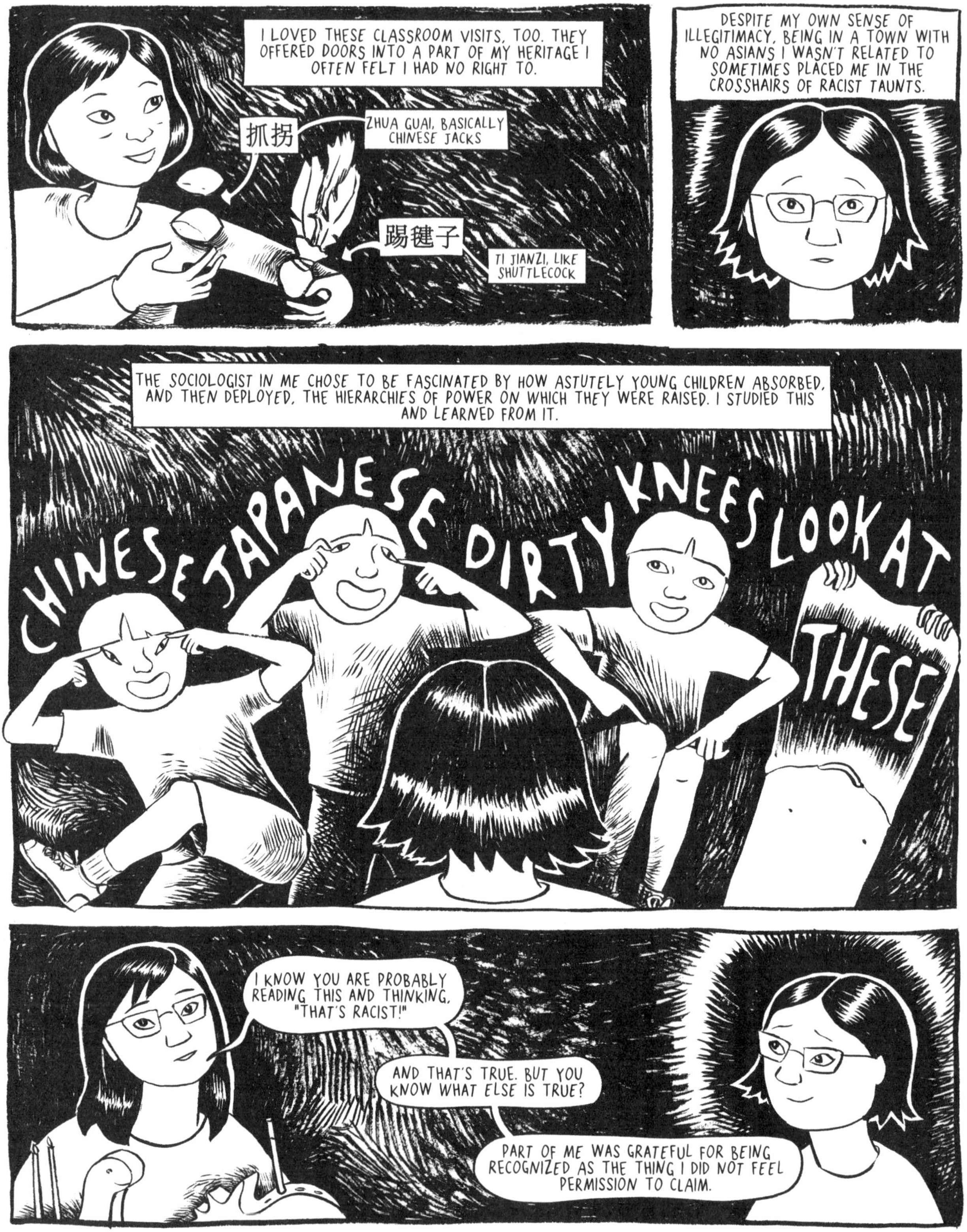

I LOVED THESE CLASSROOM VISITS, TOO. THEY OFFERED DOORS INTO A PART OF MY HERITAGE I OFTEN FELT I HAD NO RIGHT TO.
抓拐
ZHUA GUAI, BASICALLY CHINESE JACKS
踢毽子
TI JIANZI, LIKE SHUTTLECOCK
DESPITE MY OWN SENSE OF ILLEGITIMACY, BEING IN A TOWN WITH NO ASIANS I WASN'T RELATED TO SOMETIMES PLACED ME IN THE CROSSHAIRS OF RACIST TAUNTS.
THE SOCIOLOGIST IN ME CHOSE TO BE FASCINATED BY HOW ASTUTELY YOUNG CHILDREN ABSORBED, AND THEN DEPLOYED, THE HIERARCHIES OF POWER ON WHICH THEY WERE RAISED. I STUDIED THIS AND LEARNED FROM IT.
CHINESE JAPANESE DIRTY KNEES LOOK AT THESE
I KNOW YOU ARE PROBABLY READING THIS AND THINKING, "THAT'S RACIST!"
AND THAT'S TRUE. BUT YOU KNOW WHAT ELSE IS TRUE?
PART OF ME WAS GRATEFUL FOR BEING RECOGNIZED AS THE THING I DID NOT FEEL PERMISSION TO CLAIM.

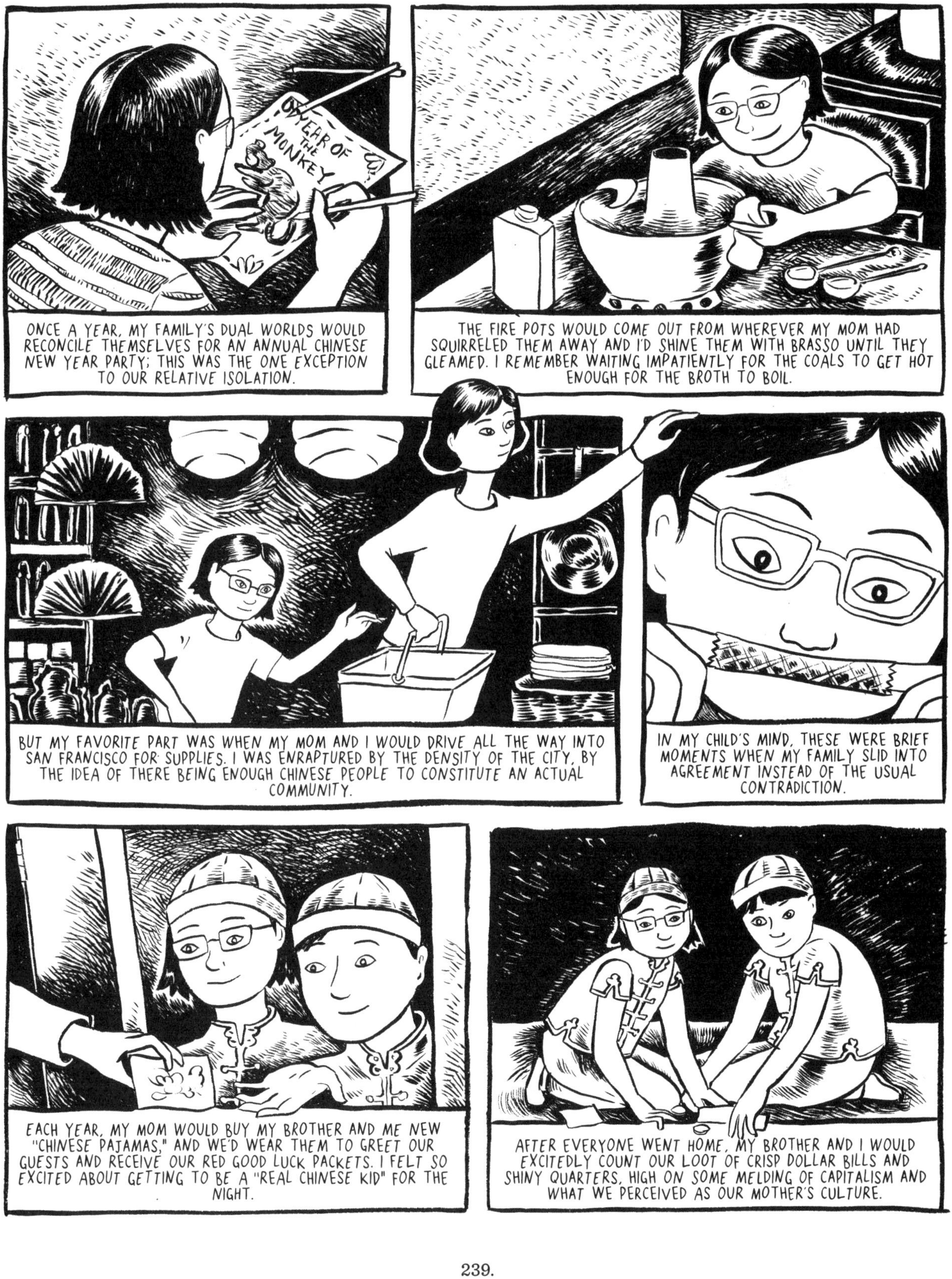
YEAR OF THE MONKEY
ONCE A YEAR, MY FAMILY'S DUAL WORLDS WOULD RECONCILE THEMSELVES FOR AN ANNUAL CHINESE NEW YEAR PARTY; THIS WAS THE ONE EXCEPTION TO OUR RELATIVE ISOLATION.
THE FIRE POTS WOULD COME OUT FROM WHEREVER MY MOM HAD SQUIRRELED THEM AWAY AND I'D SHINE THEM WITH BRASSO UNTIL THEY GLEAMED. I REMEMBER WAITING IMPATIENTLY FOR THE COALS TO GET HOT ENOUGH FOR THE BROTH TO BOIL.
BUT MY FAVORITE PART WAS WHEN MY MOM AND I WOULD DRIVE ALL THE WAY INTO SAN FRANCISCO FOR SUPPLIES. I WAS ENRAPTURED BY THE DENSITY OF THE CITY, BY THE IDEA OF THERE BEING ENOUGH CHINESE PEOPLE TO CONSTITUTE AN ACTUAL COMMUNITY.
IN MY CHILD'S MIND, THESE WERE BRIEF MOMENTS WHEN MY FAMILY SLID INTO AGREEMENT INSTEAD OF THE USUAL CONTRADICTION.
EACH YEAR, MY MOM WOULD BUY MY BROTHER AND ME NEW "CHINESE PAJAMAS," AND WE'D WEAR THEM TO GREET OUR GUESTS AND RECEIVE OUR RED GOOD LUCK PACKETS. I FELT SO EXCITED ABOUT GETTING TO BE A "REAL CHINESE KID" FOR THE NIGHT.
AFTER EVERYONE WENT HOME, MY BROTHER AND I WOULD EXCITEDLY COUNT OUR LOOT OF CRISP DOLLAR BILLS AND SHINY QUARTERS, HIGH ON SOME MELDING OF CAPITALISM AND WHAT WE PERCEIVED AS OUR MOTHER'S CULTURE.

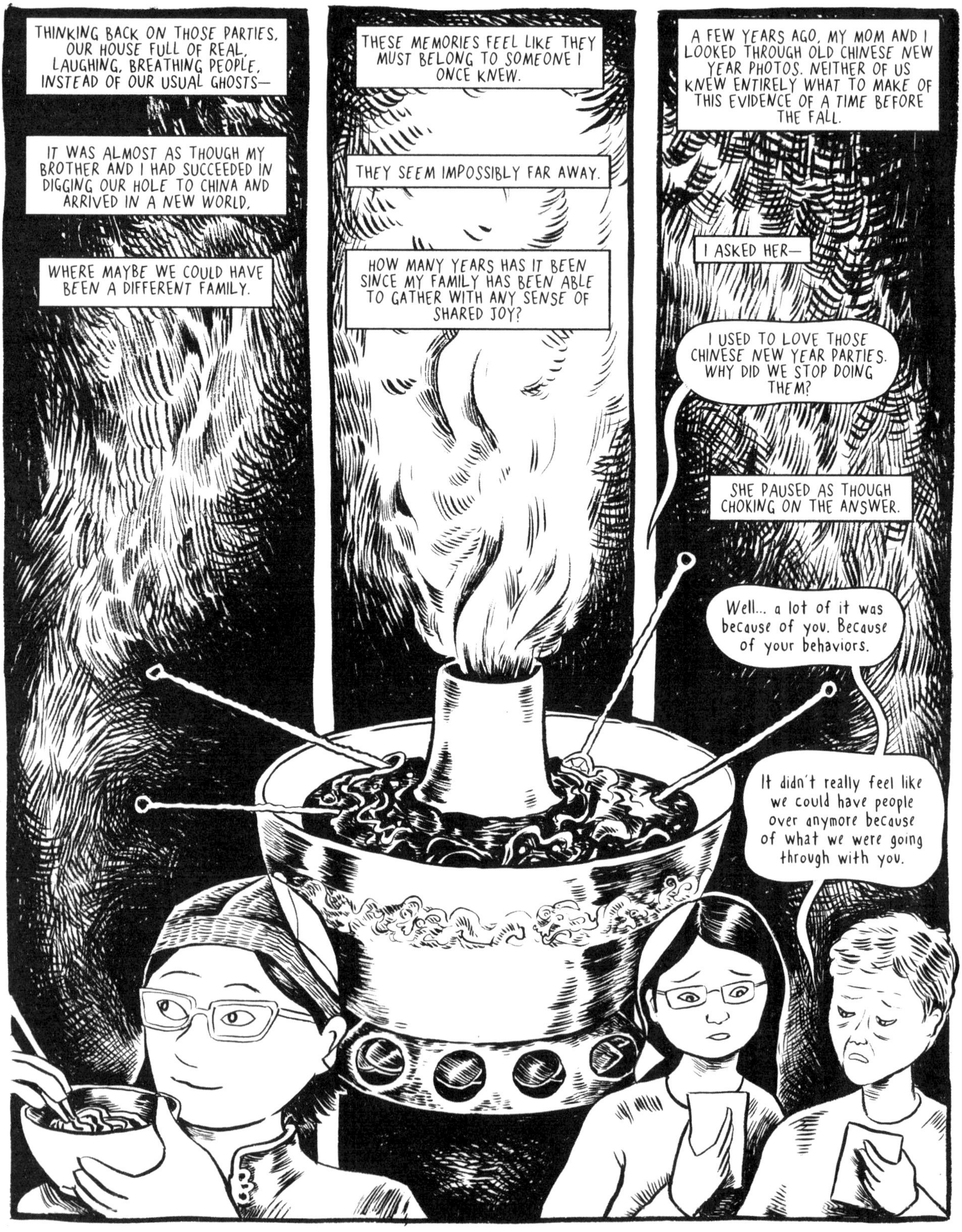
THINKING BACK ON THOSE PARTIES, OUR HOUSE FULL OF REAL, LAUGHING, BREATHING PEOPLE, INSTEAD OF OUR USUAL GHOSTS—
IT WAS ALMOST AS THOUGH MY BROTHER AND I HAD SUCCEEDED IN DIGGING OUR HOLE TO CHINA AND ARRIVED IN A NEW WORLD,
WHERE MAYBE WE COULD HAVE BEEN A DIFFERENT FAMILY.
THESE MEMORIES FEEL LIKE THEY MUST BELONG TO SOMEONE I ONCE KNEW.
THEY SEEM IMPOSSIBLY FAR AWAY.
HOW MANY YEARS HAS IT BEEN SINCE MY FAMILY HAS BEEN ABLE TO GATHER WITH ANY SENSE OF SHARED JOY?
A FEW YEARS AGO, MY MOM AND I LOOKED THROUGH OLD CHINESE NEW YEAR PHOTOS. NEITHER OF US KNEW ENTIRELY WHAT TO MAKE OF THIS EVIDENCE OF A TIME BEFORE THE FALL.
I ASKED HER—
I USED TO LOVE THOSE CHINESE NEW YEAR PARTIES. WHY DID WE STOP DOING THEM?
SHE PAUSED AS THOUGH CHOKING ON THE ANSWER.
Well... a lot of it was because of you. Because of your behaviors.
It didn't really feel like we could have people over anymore because of what we were going through with you.

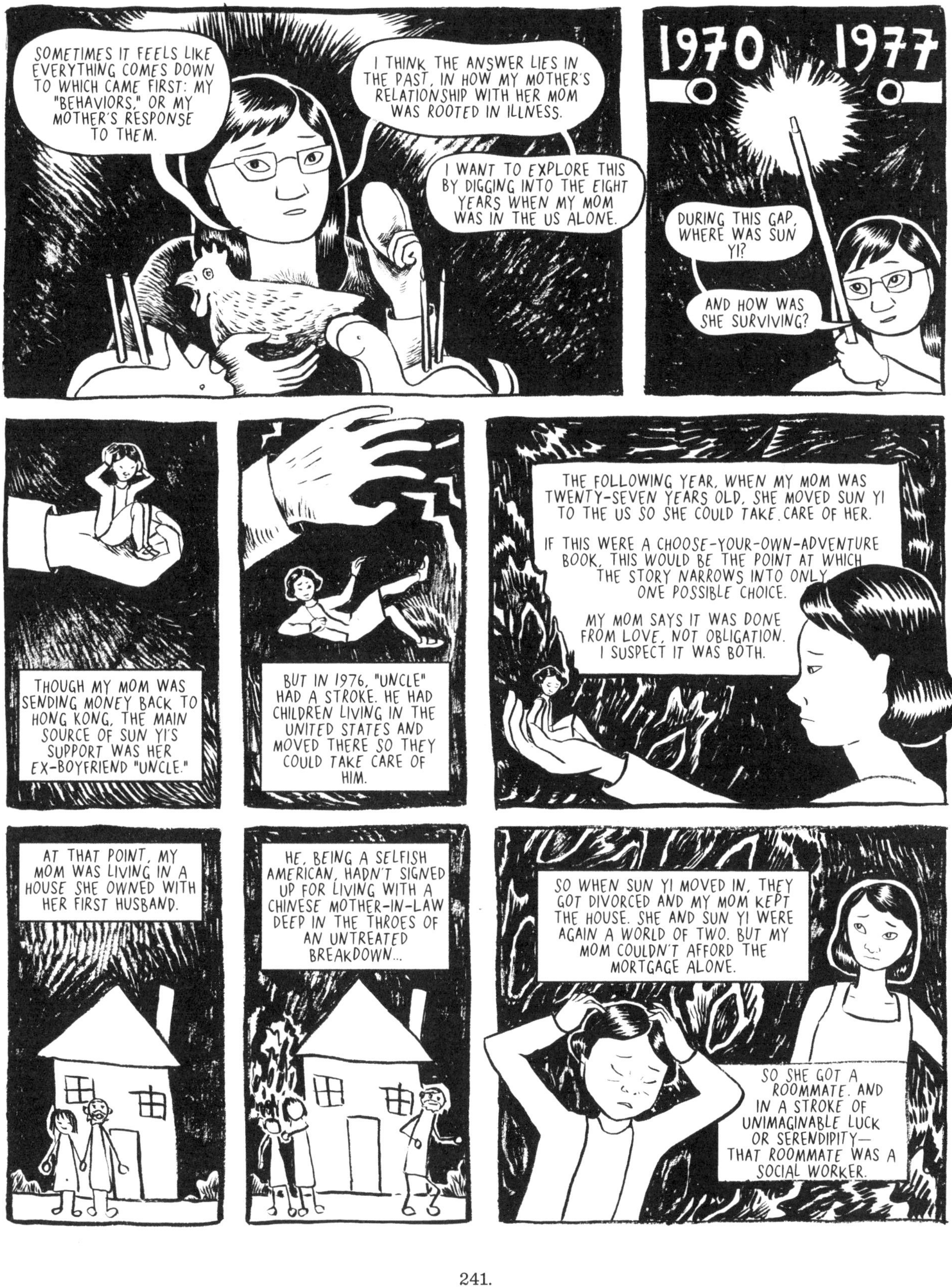
SOMETIMES IT FEELS LIKE EVERYTHING COMES DOWN TO WHICH CAME FIRST: MY "BEHAVIORS," OR MY MOTHER'S RESPONSE TO THEM.
I THINK THE ANSWER LIES IN THE PAST, IN HOW MY MOTHER'S RELATIONSHIP WITH HER MOM WAS ROOTED IN ILLNESS.
I WANT TO EXPLORE THIS BY DIGGING INTO THE EIGHT YEARS WHEN MY MOM WAS IN THE US ALONE.
1970
1977
DURING THIS GAP, WHERE WAS SUN YI?
AND HOW WAS SHE SURVIVING?
THOUGH MY MOM WAS SENDING MONEY BACK TO HONG KONG, THE MAIN SOURCE OF SUN YI'S SUPPORT WAS HER EX-BOYFRIEND "UNCLE."
BUT IN 1976, "UNCLE" HAD A STROKE. HE HAD CHILDREN LIVING IN THE UNITED STATES AND MOVED THERE SO THEY COULD TAKE CARE OF HIM.
THE FOLLOWING YEAR, WHEN MY MOM WAS TWENTY-SEVEN YEARS OLD, SHE MOVED SUN YI TO THE US SO SHE COULD TAKE CARE OF HER.
IF THIS WERE A CHOOSE-YOUR-OWN-ADVENTURE BOOK, THIS WOULD BE THE POINT AT WHICH THE STORY NARROWS INTO ONLY ONE POSSIBLE CHOICE.
MY MOM SAYS IT WAS DONE FROM LOVE, NOT OBLIGATION. I SUSPECT IT WAS BOTH.
AT THAT POINT, MY MOM WAS LIVING IN A HOUSE SHE OWNED WITH HER FIRST HUSBAND.
HE, BEING A SELFISH AMERICAN, HADN'T SIGNED UP FOR LIVING WITH A CHINESE MOTHER-IN-LAW DEEP IN THE THROES OF AN UNTREATED BREAKDOWN...
SO WHEN SUN YI MOVED IN, THEY GOT DIVORCED AND MY MOM KEPT THE HOUSE. SHE AND SUN YI WERE AGAIN A WORLD OF TWO. BUT MY MOM COULDN'T AFFORD THE MORTGAGE ALONE.
SO SHE GOT A ROOMMATE. AND IN A STROKE OF UNIMAGINABLE LUCK OR SERENDIPITY— THAT ROOMMATE WAS A SOCIAL WORKER.

SHE TOLD MY MOM THERE WAS HELP AVAILABLE (AND BECAUSE THIS WAS BEFORE PRESIDENT REAGAN STARTED GUTTING MENTAL HEALTH CARE, THERE ACTUALLY WAS).

FOR BETTER OR WORSE, SUN YI WOULD SPEND THE REST OF HER LIFE MEDICATED AND TREATED.

DECADES PASSED IN THIS STATE OF UNSTEADY EQUILIBRIUM, WITH MY GRANDMOTHER BALANCED WITH A DAILY DOSE OF HEAVY ANTIPSYCHOTICS.

THIS MOSTLY WORKED. BUT EVERY HANDFUL OF YEARS SHE'D SPIRAL OUT OF CONTROL AND NEED TO BE PUT IN A PSYCH WARD. THE LAST HANDFUL OF TIMES SHE WAS HOSPITALIZED, MY MOTHER WOULD TELL ME—

Sun Yi needs to be in hospital again.

This might be the last time. The time she finally doesn't come back out.

You need to say goodbye.

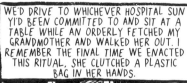

WE'D DRIVE TO WHICHEVER HOSPITAL SUN YI'D BEEN COMMITTED TO AND SIT AT A TABLE WHILE AN ORDERLY FETCHED MY GRANDMOTHER AND WALKED HER OUT. I REMEMBER THE FINAL TIME WE ENACTED THIS RITUAL, SHE CLUTCHED A PLASTIC BAG IN HER HANDS.

MY MOM ATTEMPTED TO TRANSLATE SUN YI'S REALITY FOR ME—

She's trying to give you a gift.

She thinks she's on a plane.

HER ARTHRITIC HANDS, DULLED TO FURTHER SLOWNESS BY SEDATIVES, CLAWED AT TIGHT PLASTIC KNOTS SHE HAD TIED BUT COULD NOT UNDO. SHE TRIED TO GIVE ME A GIFT, BUT SHE COULD NOT ACCESS IT AND I COULD NOT RECEIVE IT, AND I CONTEMPLATED WHAT IT MEANT TO SAY GOODBYE TO SOMEONE WHO, FOR ME, HAD ALWAYS BEEN GONE.

ON THE DRIVE HOME, WE SAT IN THE CAR AS TWO WOMEN BUILT OF NOTHING BUT SHARP EDGES, AND I KNEW THAT SOMEHOW, AS ALWAYS, I HAD FAILED TO BE WHATEVER IT WAS MY MOTHER NEEDED.

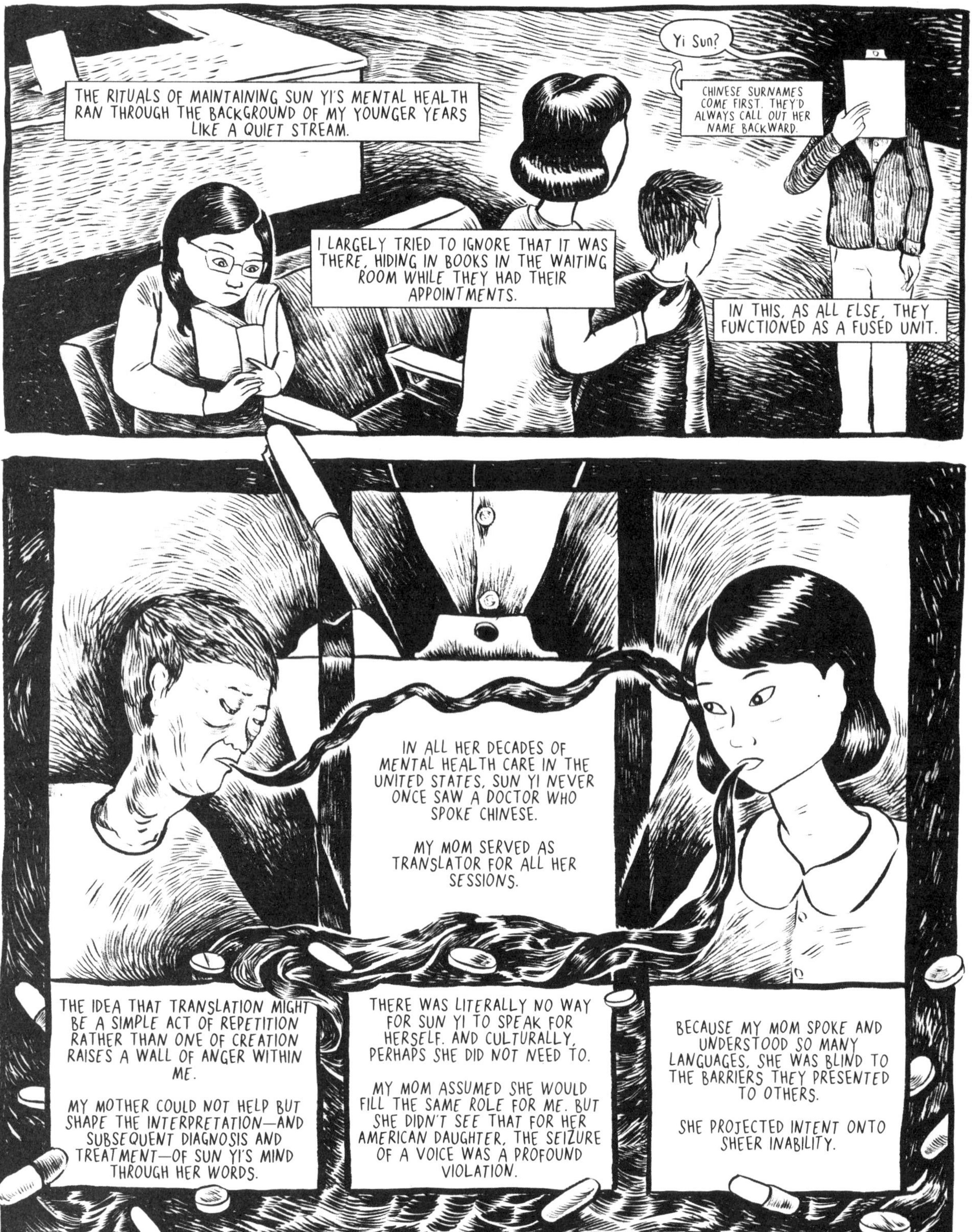

THE RITUALS OF MAINTAINING SUN YI'S MENTAL HEALTH RAN THROUGH THE BACKGROUND OF MY YOUNGER YEARS LIKE A QUIET STREAM.
Yi Sun?
CHINESE SURNAMES COME FIRST. THEY'D ALWAYS CALL OUT HER NAME BACKWARD.
I LARGELY TRIED TO IGNORE THAT IT WAS THERE, HIDING IN BOOKS IN THE WAITING ROOM WHILE THEY HAD THEIR APPOINTMENTS.
IN THIS, AS ALL ELSE, THEY FUNCTIONED AS A FUSED UNIT.
IN ALL HER DECADES OF MENTAL HEALTH CARE IN THE UNITED STATES, SUN YI NEVER ONCE SAW A DOCTOR WHO SPOKE CHINESE.
MY MOM SERVED AS TRANSLATOR FOR ALL HER SESSIONS.
THE IDEA THAT TRANSLATION MIGHT BE A SIMPLE ACT OF REPETITION RATHER THAN ONE OF CREATION RAISES A WALL OF ANGER WITHIN ME.
MY MOTHER COULD NOT HELP BUT SHAPE THE INTERPRETATION—AND SUBSEQUENT DIAGNOSIS AND TREATMENT—OF SUN YI'S MIND THROUGH HER WORDS.
THERE WAS LITERALLY NO WAY FOR SUN YI TO SPEAK FOR HERSELF. AND CULTURALLY, PERHAPS SHE DID NOT NEED TO.
MY MOM ASSUMED SHE WOULD FILL THE SAME ROLE FOR ME. BUT SHE DIDN'T SEE THAT FOR HER AMERICAN DAUGHTER, THE SEIZURE OF A VOICE WAS A PROFOUND VIOLATION.
BECAUSE MY MOM SPOKE AND UNDERSTOOD SO MANY LANGUAGES, SHE WAS BLIND TO THE BARRIERS THEY PRESENTED TO OTHERS.
SHE PROJECTED INTENT ONTO SHEER INABILITY.

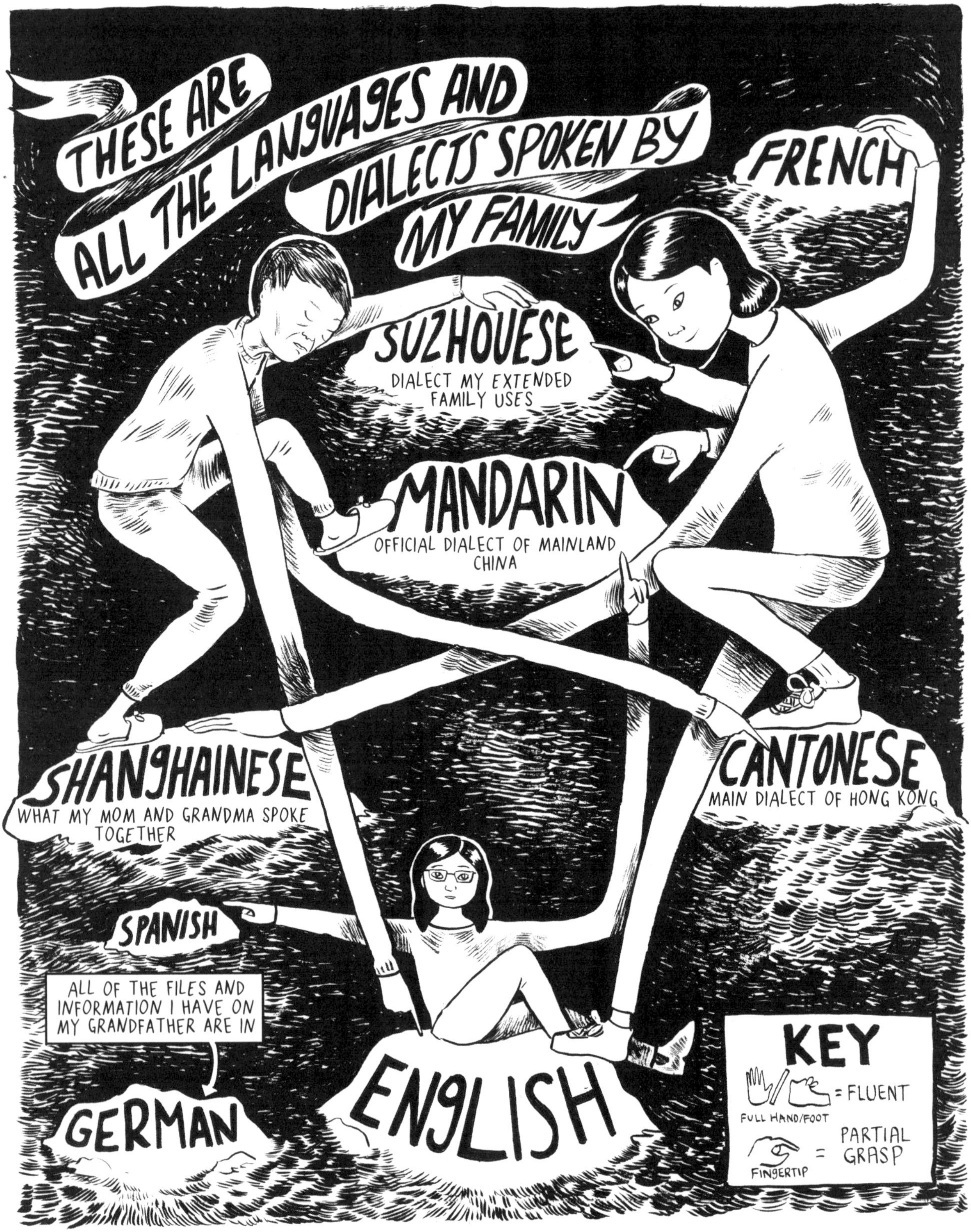
THESE ARE ALL THE LANGUAGES AND DIALECTS SPOKEN BY MY FAMILY
FRENCH
SUZHOUESE
DIALECT MY EXTENDED FAMILY USES
MANDARIN
OFFICIAL DIALECT OF MAINLAND CHINA
SHANGHAINESE
WHAT MY MOM AND GRANDMA SPOKE TOGETHER
CANTONESE
MAIN DIALECT OF HONG KONG
SPANISH
ALL OF THE FILES AND INFORMATION I HAVE ON MY GRANDFATHER ARE IN
GERMAN
ENGLISH
KEY
= FLUENT
FULL HAND/FOOT
= PARTIAL GRASP
FINGERTIP

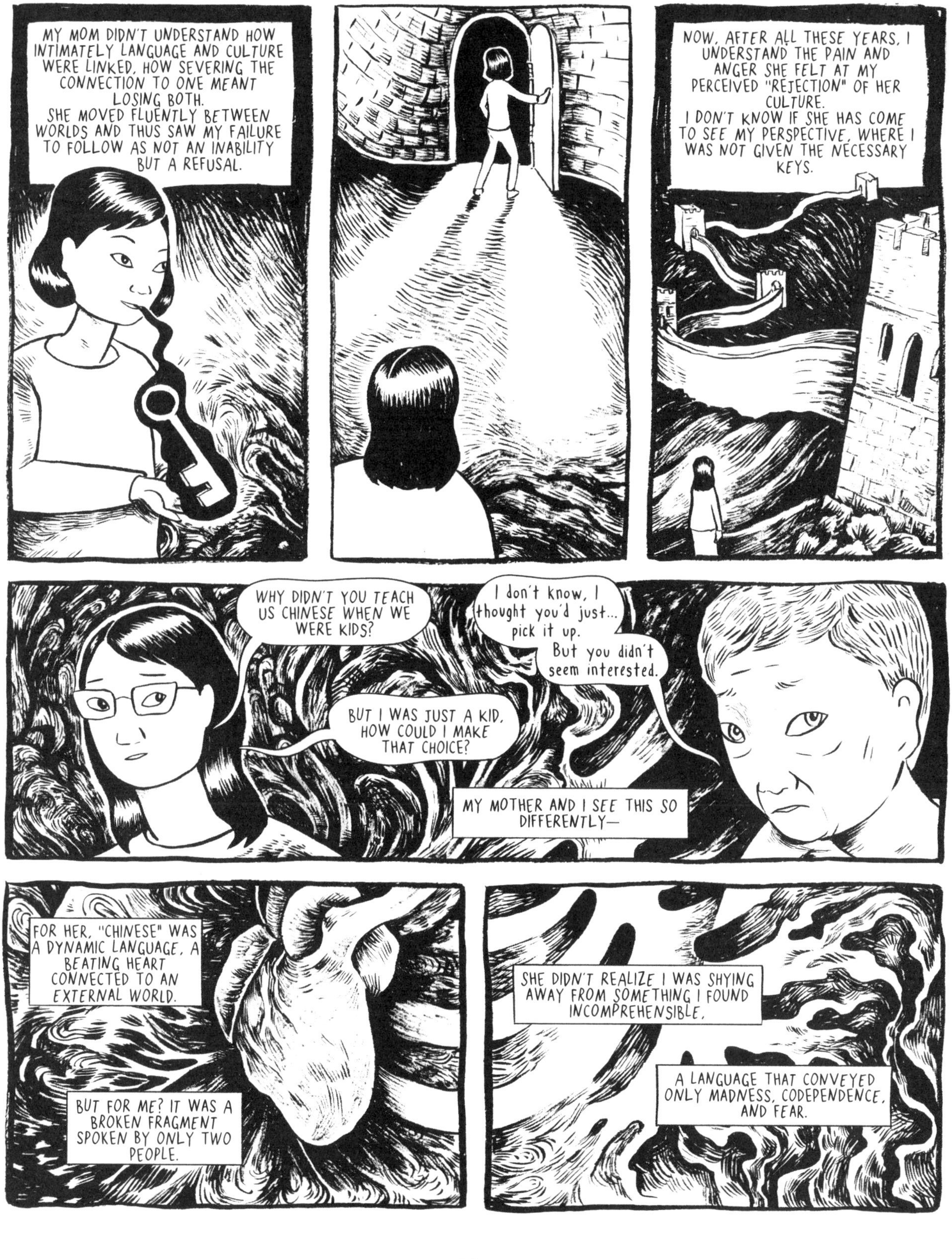
MY MOM DIDN'T UNDERSTAND HOW INTIMATELY LANGUAGE AND CULTURE WERE LINKED, HOW SEVERING THE CONNECTION TO ONE MEANT LOSING BOTH.
SHE MOVED FLUENTLY BETWEEN WORLDS AND THUS SAW MY FAILURE TO FOLLOW AS NOT AN INABILITY BUT A REFUSAL.
NOW, AFTER ALL THESE YEARS, I UNDERSTAND THE PAIN AND ANGER SHE FELT AT MY PERCEIVED "REJECTION" OF HER CULTURE.
I DON'T KNOW IF SHE HAS COME TO SEE MY PERSPECTIVE, WHERE I WAS NOT GIVEN THE NECESSARY KEYS.
WHY DIDN'T YOU TEACH US CHINESE WHEN WE WERE KIDS?
I don't know, I thought you'd just... pick it up.
But you didn't seem interested.
BUT I WAS JUST A KID, HOW COULD I MAKE THAT CHOICE?
MY MOTHER AND I SEE THIS SO DIFFERENTLY—
FOR HER, "CHINESE" WAS A DYNAMIC LANGUAGE, A BEATING HEART CONNECTED TO AN EXTERNAL WORLD.
BUT FOR ME? IT WAS A BROKEN FRAGMENT SPOKEN BY ONLY TWO PEOPLE.
SHE DIDN'T REALIZE I WAS SHYING AWAY FROM SOMETHING I FOUND INCOMPREHENSIBLE,
A LANGUAGE THAT CONVEYED ONLY MADNESS, CODEPENDENCE, AND FEAR.

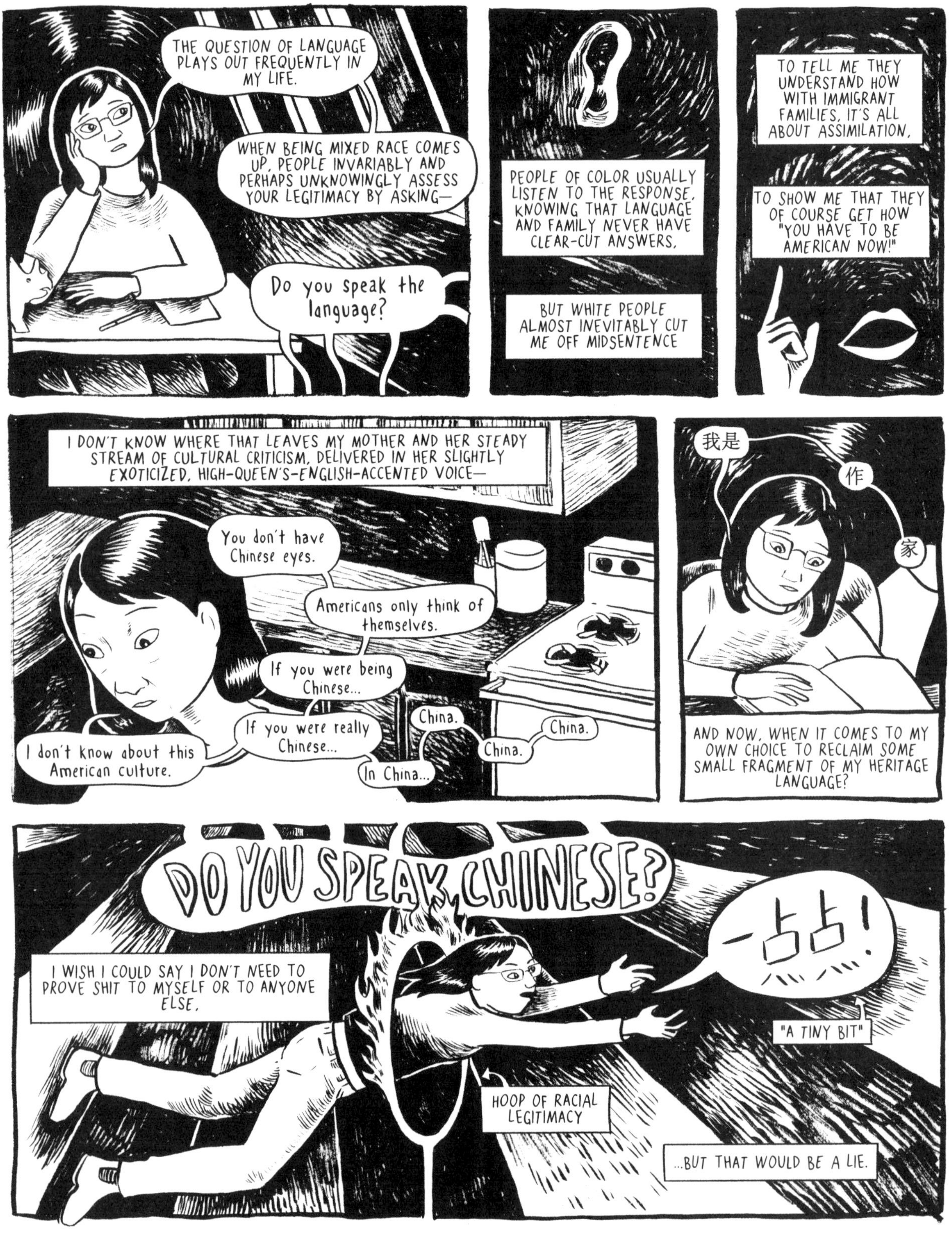
THE QUESTION OF LANGUAGE PLAYS OUT FREQUENTLY IN MY LIFE.
WHEN BEING MIXED RACE COMES UP, PEOPLE INVARIABLY AND PERHAPS UNKNOWINGLY ASSESS YOUR LEGITIMACY BY ASKING—
Do you speak the language?
PEOPLE OF COLOR USUALLY LISTEN TO THE RESPONSE, KNOWING THAT LANGUAGE AND FAMILY NEVER HAVE CLEAR-CUT ANSWERS.
BUT WHITE PEOPLE ALMOST INEVITABLY CUT ME OFF MIDSENTENCE
TO TELL ME THEY UNDERSTAND HOW WITH IMMIGRANT FAMILIES, IT'S ALL ABOUT ASSIMILATION,
TO SHOW ME THAT THEY OF COURSE GET HOW "YOU HAVE TO BE AMERICAN NOW!"
I DON'T KNOW WHERE THAT LEAVES MY MOTHER AND HER STEADY STREAM OF CULTURAL CRITICISM, DELIVERED IN HER SLIGHTLY EXOTICIZED, HIGH-QUEEN'S-ENGLISH-ACCENTED VOICE—
You don't have Chinese eyes.
Americans only think of themselves.
If you were being Chinese...
If you were really Chinese...
I don't know about this American culture.
In China...
China.
China.
China.
我是
作
家
AND NOW, WHEN IT COMES TO MY OWN CHOICE TO RECLAIM SOME SMALL FRAGMENT OF MY HERITAGE LANGUAGE?
DO YOU SPEAK CHINESE?
一占占!
"A TINY BIT"
I WISH I COULD SAY I DON'T NEED TO PROVE SHIT TO MYSELF OR TO ANYONE ELSE,
HOOP OF RACIAL LEGITIMACY
...BUT THAT WOULD BE A LIE.

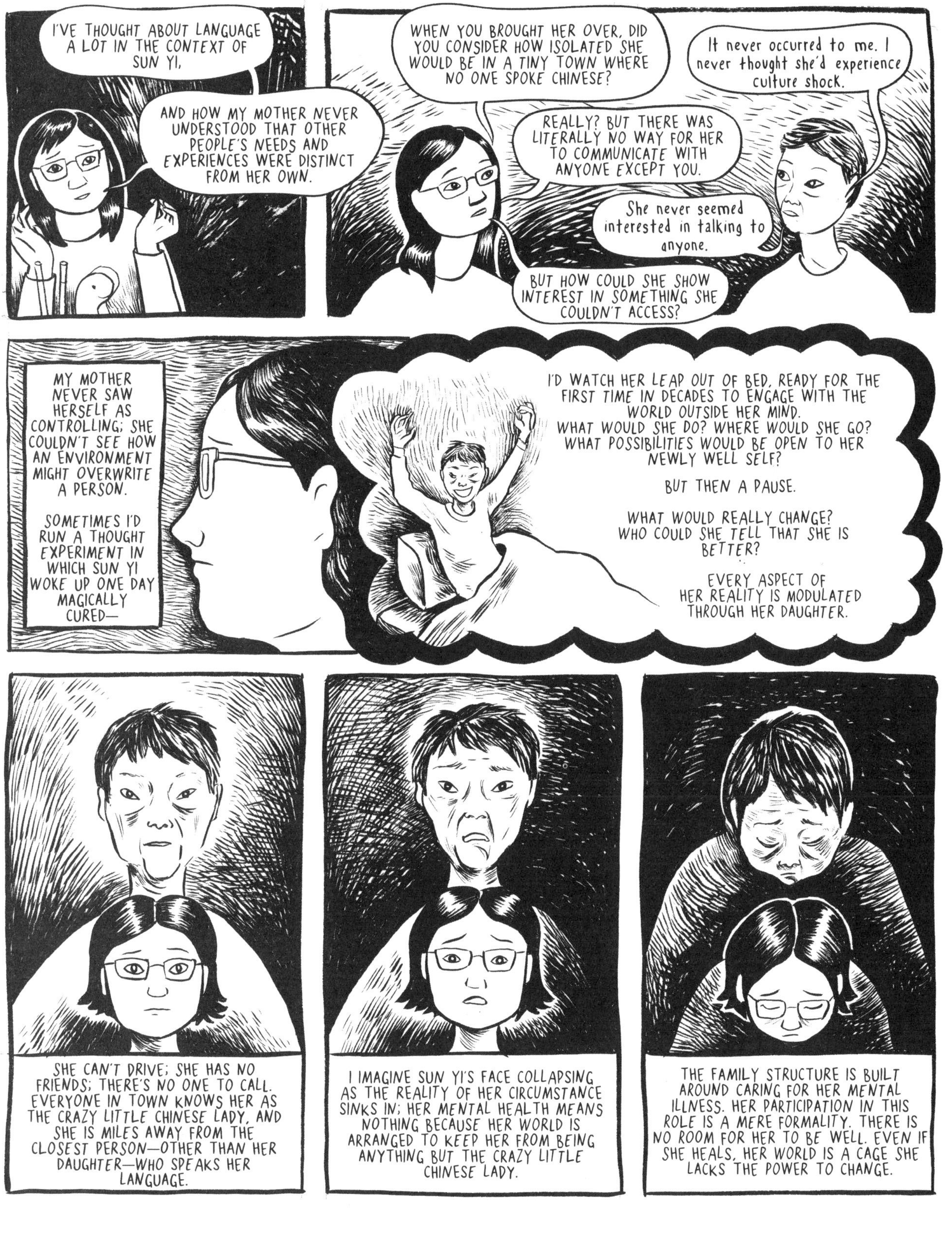

I'VE THOUGHT ABOUT LANGUAGE A LOT IN THE CONTEXT OF SUN YI,
AND HOW MY MOTHER NEVER UNDERSTOOD THAT OTHER PEOPLE'S NEEDS AND EXPERIENCES WERE DISTINCT FROM HER OWN.
WHEN YOU BROUGHT HER OVER, DID YOU CONSIDER HOW ISOLATED SHE WOULD BE IN A TINY TOWN WHERE NO ONE SPOKE CHINESE?
It never occurred to me. I never thought she'd experience culture shock.
REALLY? BUT THERE WAS LITERALLY NO WAY FOR HER TO COMMUNICATE WITH ANYONE EXCEPT YOU.
She never seemed interested in talking to anyone.
BUT HOW COULD SHE SHOW INTEREST IN SOMETHING SHE COULDN'T ACCESS?
MY MOTHER NEVER SAW HERSELF AS CONTROLLING; SHE COULDN'T SEE HOW AN ENVIRONMENT MIGHT OVERWRITE A PERSON.
SOMETIMES I'D RUN A THOUGHT EXPERIMENT IN WHICH SUN YI WOKE UP ONE DAY MAGICALLY CURED—
I'D WATCH HER LEAP OUT OF BED, READY FOR THE FIRST TIME IN DECADES TO ENGAGE WITH THE WORLD OUTSIDE HER MIND.
WHAT WOULD SHE DO? WHERE WOULD SHE GO? WHAT POSSIBILITIES WOULD BE OPEN TO HER NEWLY WELL SELF?
BUT THEN A PAUSE.
WHAT WOULD REALLY CHANGE? WHO COULD SHE TELL THAT SHE IS BETTER?
EVERY ASPECT OF HER REALITY IS MODULATED THROUGH HER DAUGHTER.
SHE CAN'T DRIVE; SHE HAS NO FRIENDS; THERE'S NO ONE TO CALL. EVERYONE IN TOWN KNOWS HER AS THE CRAZY LITTLE CHINESE LADY, AND SHE IS MILES AWAY FROM THE CLOSEST PERSON—OTHER THAN HER DAUGHTER—WHO SPEAKS HER LANGUAGE.
I IMAGINE SUN YI'S FACE COLLAPSING AS THE REALITY OF HER CIRCUMSTANCE SINKS IN; HER MENTAL HEALTH MEANS NOTHING BECAUSE HER WORLD IS ARRANGED TO KEEP HER FROM BEING ANYTHING BUT THE CRAZY LITTLE CHINESE LADY.
THE FAMILY STRUCTURE IS BUILT AROUND CARING FOR HER MENTAL ILLNESS. HER PARTICIPATION IN THIS ROLE IS A MERE FORMALITY. THERE IS NO ROOM FOR HER TO BE WELL. EVEN IF SHE HEALS, HER WORLD IS A CAGE SHE LACKS THE POWER TO CHANGE.

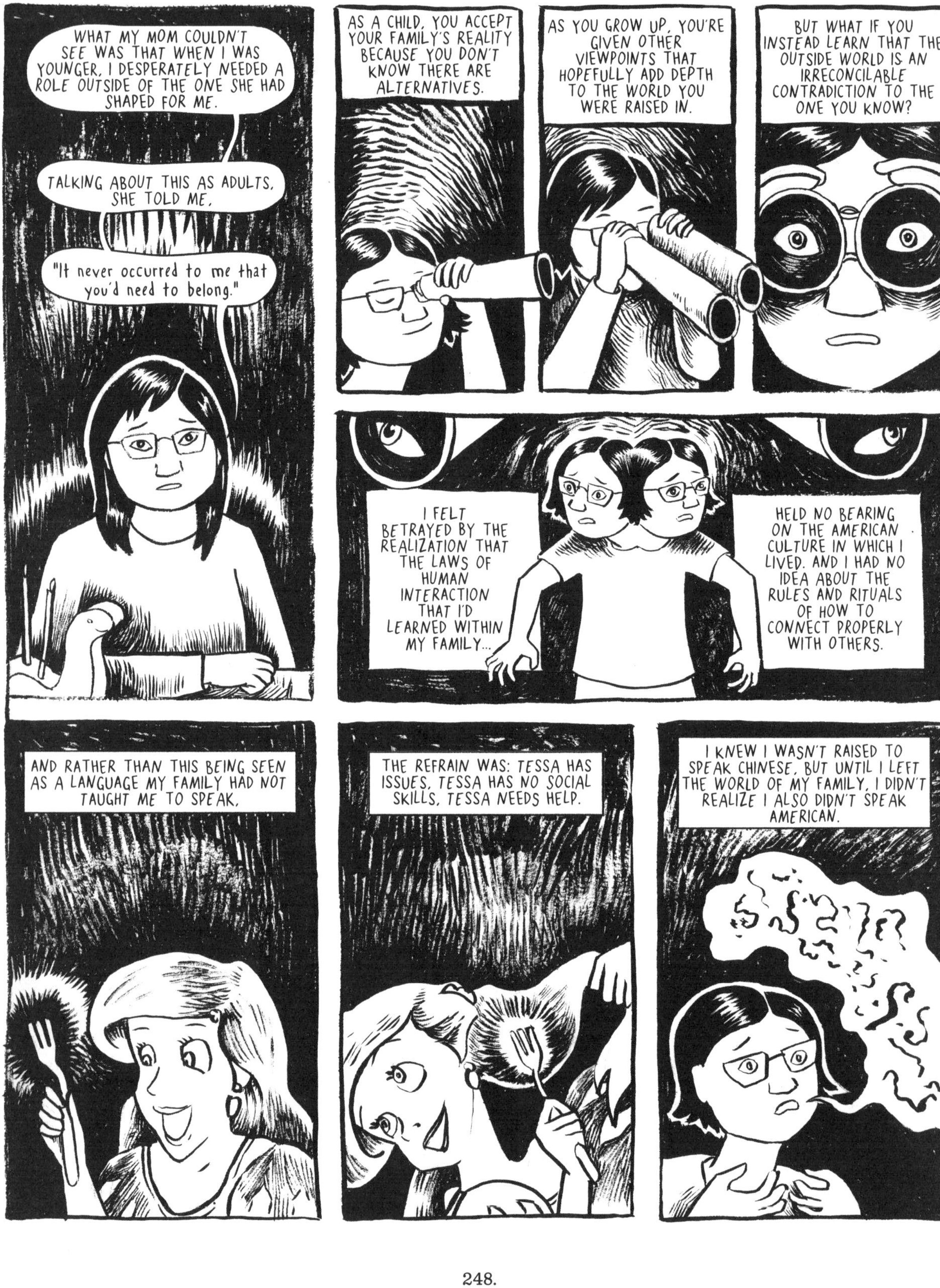

WHAT MY MOM COULDN'T SEE WAS THAT WHEN I WAS YOUNGER, I DESPERATELY NEEDED A ROLE OUTSIDE OF THE ONE SHE HAD SHAPED FOR ME.
TALKING ABOUT THIS AS ADULTS, SHE TOLD ME,
"It never occurred to me that you'd need to belong."
AS A CHILD, YOU ACCEPT YOUR FAMILY'S REALITY BECAUSE YOU DON'T KNOW THERE ARE ALTERNATIVES.
AS YOU GROW UP, YOU'RE GIVEN OTHER VIEWPOINTS THAT HOPEFULLY ADD DEPTH TO THE WORLD YOU WERE RAISED IN.
BUT WHAT IF YOU INSTEAD LEARN THAT THE OUTSIDE WORLD IS AN IRRECONCILABLE CONTRADICTION TO THE ONE YOU KNOW?
I FELT BETRAYED BY THE REALIZATION THAT THE LAWS OF HUMAN INTERACTION THAT I'D LEARNED WITHIN MY FAMILY...
HELD NO BEARING ON THE AMERICAN CULTURE IN WHICH I LIVED. AND I HAD NO IDEA ABOUT THE RULES AND RITUALS OF HOW TO CONNECT PROPERLY WITH OTHERS.
AND RATHER THAN THIS BEING SEEN AS A LANGUAGE MY FAMILY HAD NOT TAUGHT ME TO SPEAK,
THE REFRAIN WAS: TESSA HAS ISSUES, TESSA HAS NO SOCIAL SKILLS, TESSA NEEDS HELP.
I KNEW I WASN'T RAISED TO SPEAK CHINESE, BUT UNTIL I LEFT THE WORLD OF MY FAMILY, I DIDN'T REALIZE I ALSO DIDN'T SPEAK AMERICAN.

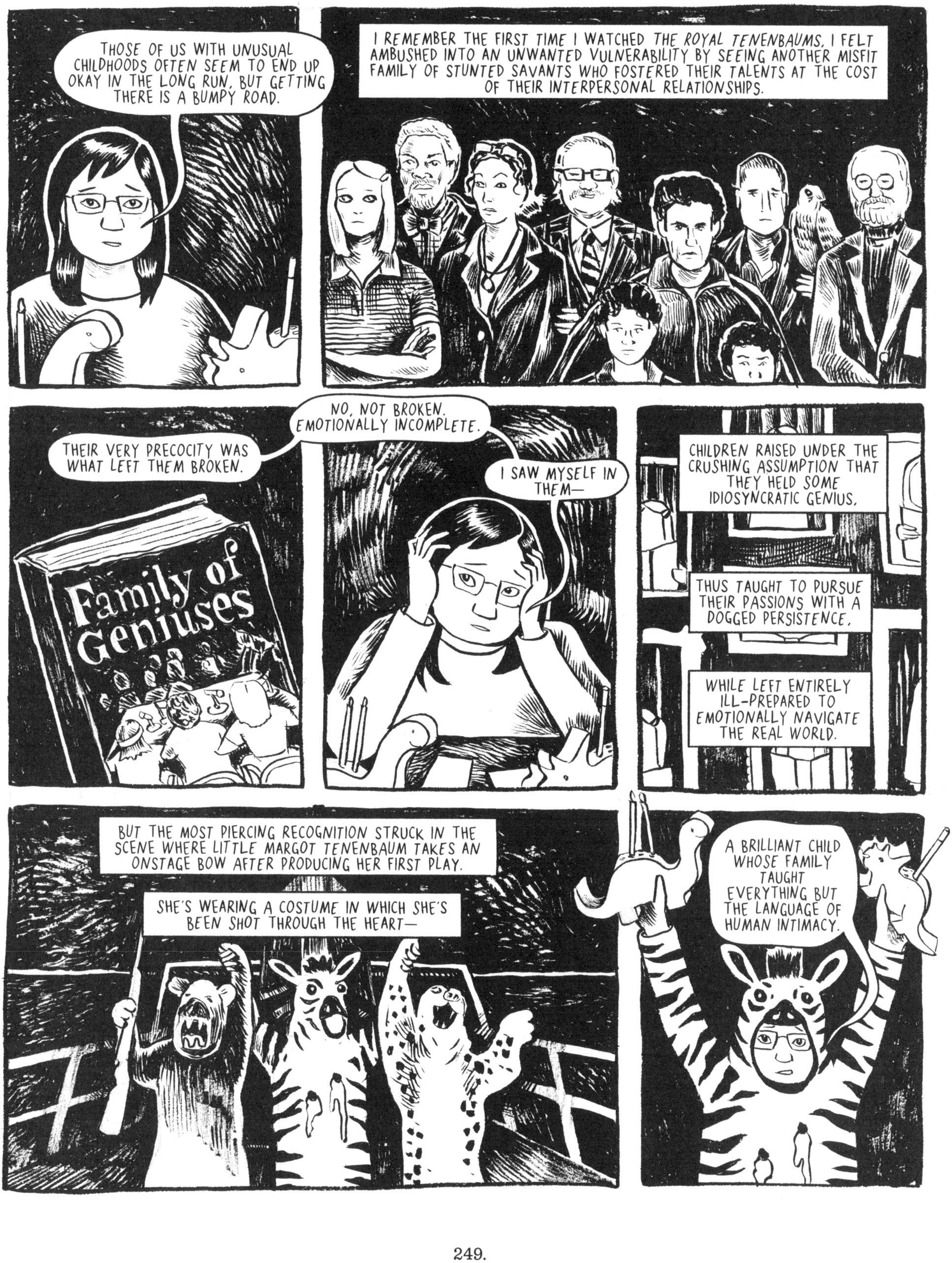

THOSE OF US WITH UNUSUAL CHILDHOODS OFTEN SEEM TO END UP OKAY IN THE LONG RUN, BUT GETTING THERE IS A BUMPY ROAD.
I REMEMBER THE FIRST TIME I WATCHED *THE ROYAL TENENBAUMS*, I FELT AMBUSHED INTO AN UNWANTED VULNERABILITY BY SEEING ANOTHER MISFIT FAMILY OF STUNTED SAVANTS WHO FOSTERED THEIR TALENTS AT THE COST OF THEIR INTERPERSONAL RELATIONSHIPS.
THEIR VERY PRECOCITY WAS WHAT LEFT THEM BROKEN.
Family of Geniuses
NO, NOT BROKEN. EMOTIONALLY INCOMPLETE.
I SAW MYSELF IN THEM—
CHILDREN RAISED UNDER THE CRUSHING ASSUMPTION THAT THEY HELD SOME IDIOSYNCRATIC GENIUS,
THUS TAUGHT TO PURSUE THEIR PASSIONS WITH A DOGGED PERSISTENCE,
WHILE LEFT ENTIRELY ILL-PREPARED TO EMOTIONALLY NAVIGATE THE REAL WORLD.
BUT THE MOST PIERCING RECOGNITION STRUCK IN THE SCENE WHERE LITTLE MARGOT TENENBAUM TAKES AN ONSTAGE BOW AFTER PRODUCING HER FIRST PLAY.
SHE'S WEARING A COSTUME IN WHICH SHE'S BEEN SHOT THROUGH THE HEART—
A BRILLIANT CHILD WHOSE FAMILY TAUGHT EVERYTHING BUT THE LANGUAGE OF HUMAN INTIMACY.

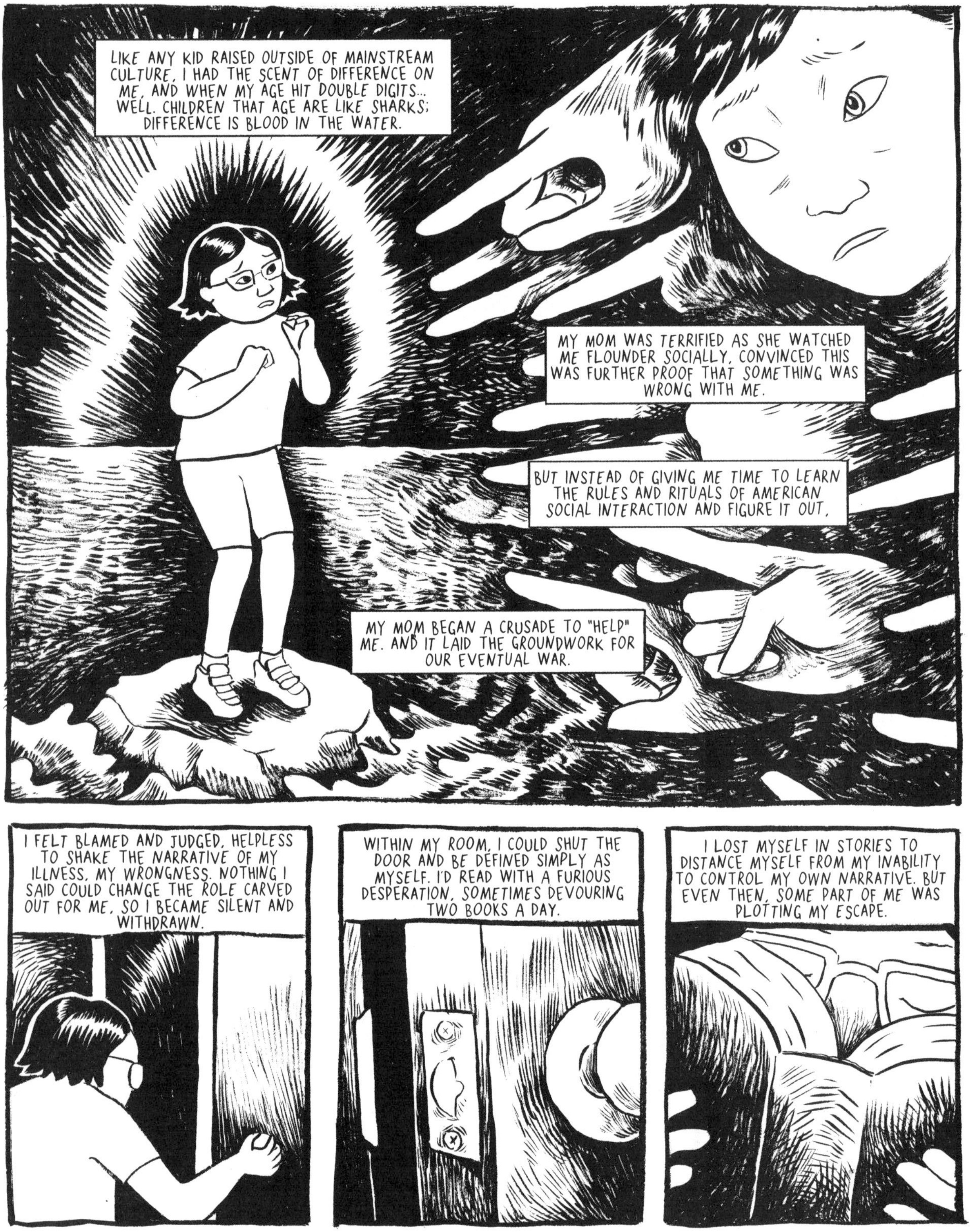
LIKE ANY KID RAISED OUTSIDE OF MAINSTREAM CULTURE, I HAD THE SCENT OF DIFFERENCE ON ME, AND WHEN MY AGE HIT DOUBLE DIGITS... WELL. CHILDREN THAT AGE ARE LIKE SHARKS; DIFFERENCE IS BLOOD IN THE WATER.
MY MOM WAS TERRIFIED AS SHE WATCHED ME FLOUNDER SOCIALLY, CONVINCED THIS WAS FURTHER PROOF THAT SOMETHING WAS WRONG WITH ME.
BUT INSTEAD OF GIVING ME TIME TO LEARN THE RULES AND RITUALS OF AMERICAN SOCIAL INTERACTION AND FIGURE IT OUT,
MY MOM BEGAN A CRUSADE TO "HELP" ME. AND IT LAID THE GROUNDWORK FOR OUR EVENTUAL WAR.
I FELT BLAMED AND JUDGED, HELPLESS TO SHAKE THE NARRATIVE OF MY ILLNESS, MY WRONGNESS. NOTHING I SAID COULD CHANGE THE ROLE CARVED OUT FOR ME, SO I BECAME SILENT AND WITHDRAWN.
WITHIN MY ROOM, I COULD SHUT THE DOOR AND BE DEFINED SIMPLY AS MYSELF. I'D READ WITH A FURIOUS DESPERATION, SOMETIMES DEVOURING TWO BOOKS A DAY.
I LOST MYSELF IN STORIES TO DISTANCE MYSELF FROM MY INABILITY TO CONTROL MY OWN NARRATIVE. BUT EVEN THEN, SOME PART OF ME WAS PLOTTING MY ESCAPE.

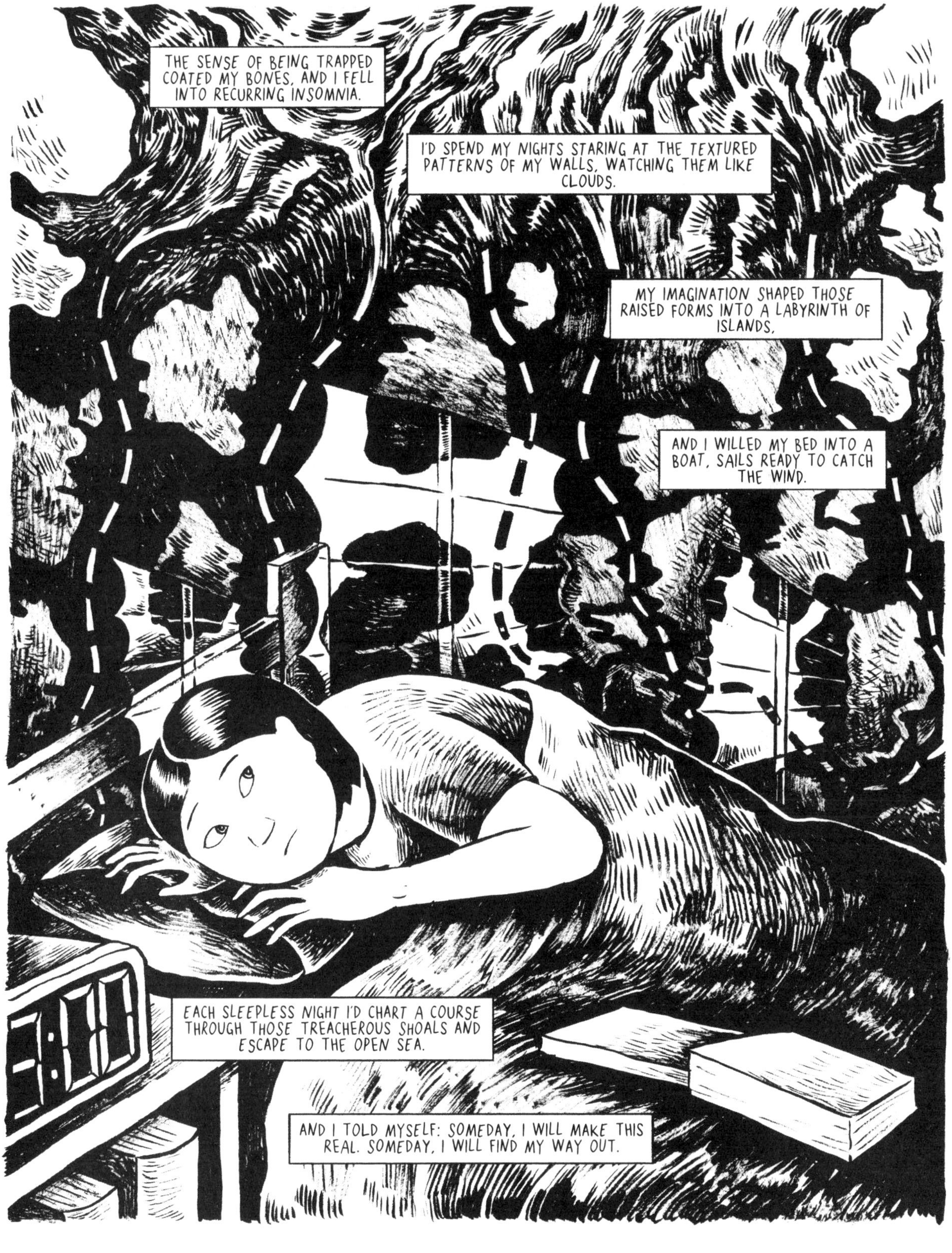
THE SENSE OF BEING TRAPPED COATED MY BONES, AND I FELL INTO RECURRING INSOMNIA.
I'D SPEND MY NIGHTS STARING AT THE TEXTURED PATTERNS OF MY WALLS, WATCHING THEM LIKE CLOUDS.
MY IMAGINATION SHAPED THOSE RAISED FORMS INTO A LABYRINTH OF ISLANDS,
AND I WILLED MY BED INTO A BOAT, SAILS READY TO CATCH THE WIND.
EACH SLEEPLESS NIGHT I'D CHART A COURSE THROUGH THOSE TREACHEROUS SHOALS AND ESCAPE TO THE OPEN SEA.
AND I TOLD MYSELF: SOMEDAY, I WILL MAKE THIS REAL. SOMEDAY, I WILL FIND MY WAY OUT.

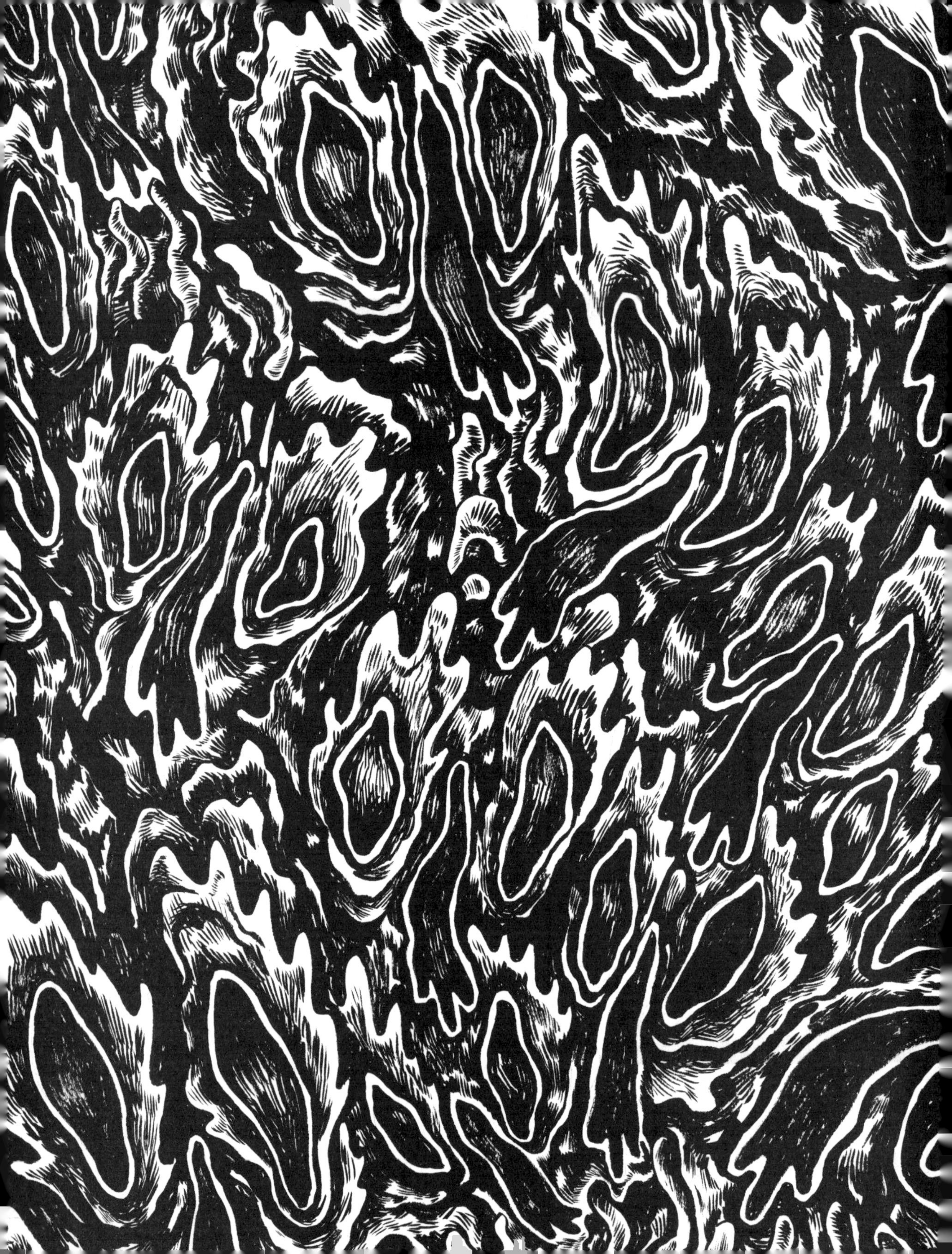

PART 7

THE TIME WHEN WE WERE NOT

A Small Town in Northern California
1994–2002

They called their refugee years The Time When We Were Not, and they were forgiven, because they had carried the truth of themselves in a sheltered place inside the flesh, exactly the way a fruit that has gone soft still carried inside itself the clean, hard stone of its future.

—BARBARA KINGSOLVER, ***Homeland and Other Stories***

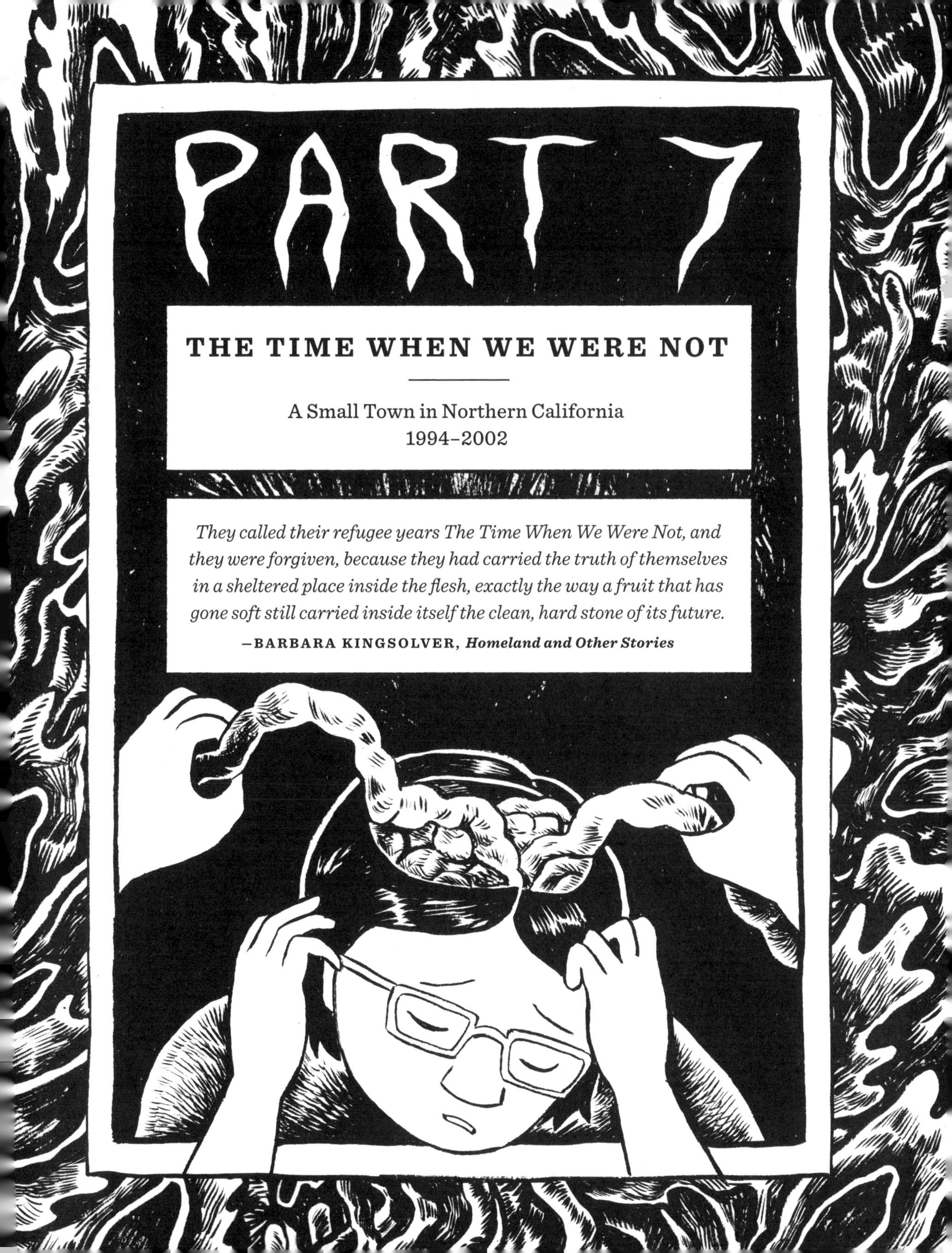

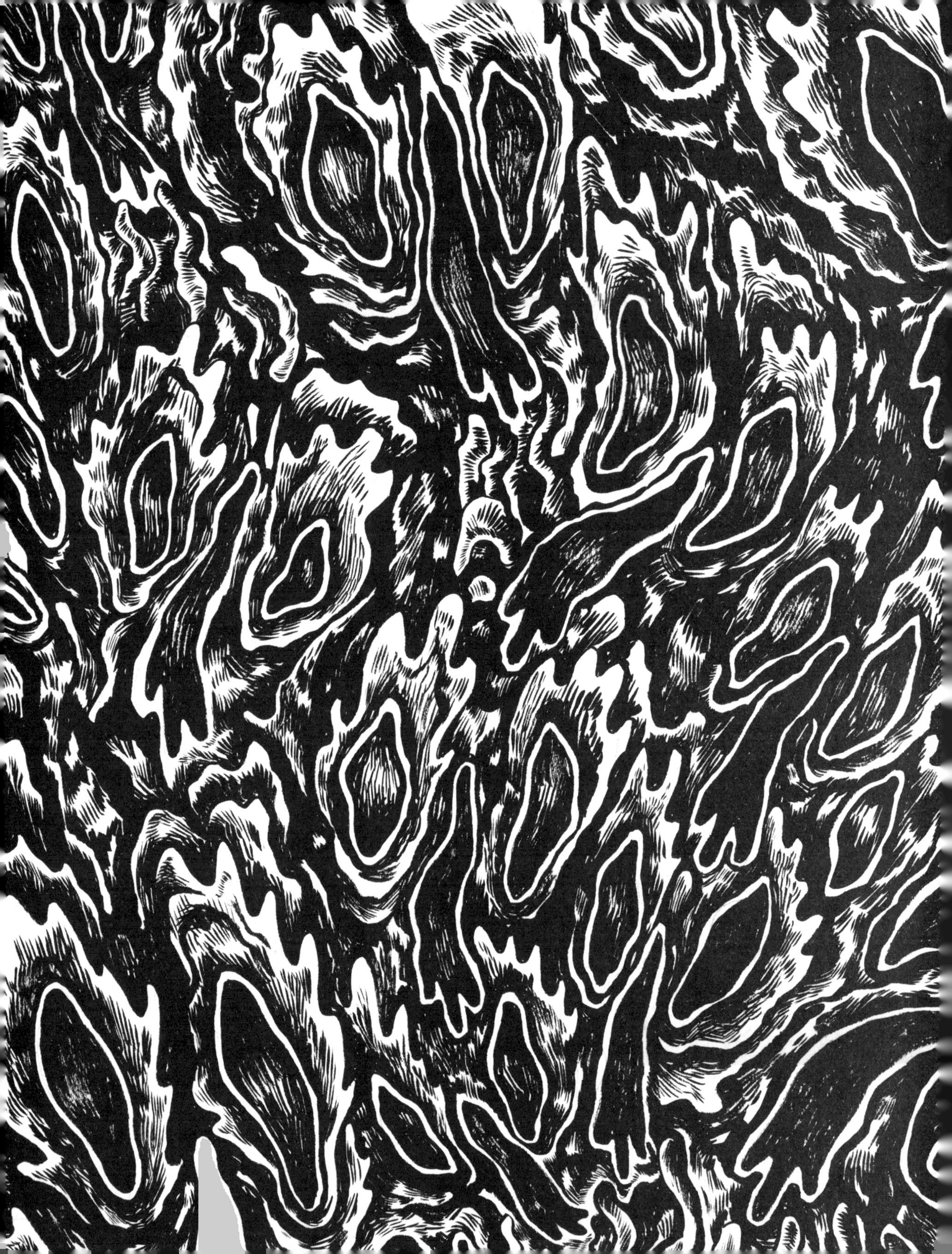

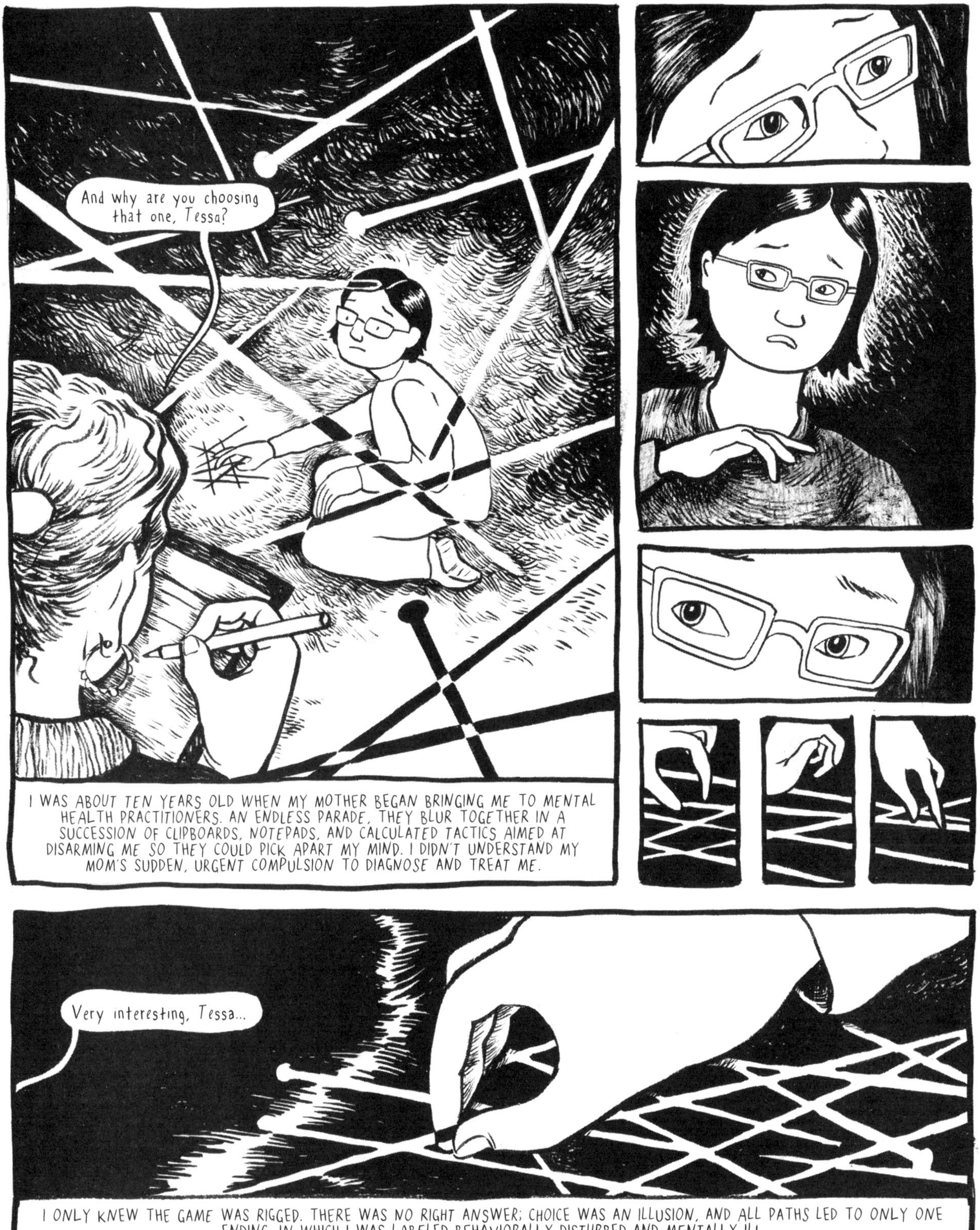
And why are you choosing that one, Tessa?
I WAS ABOUT TEN YEARS OLD WHEN MY MOTHER BEGAN BRINGING ME TO MENTAL HEALTH PRACTITIONERS. AN ENDLESS PARADE, THEY BLUR TOGETHER IN A SUCCESSION OF CLIPBOARDS, NOTEPADS, AND CALCULATED TACTICS AIMED AT DISARMING ME SO THEY COULD PICK APART MY MIND. I DIDN'T UNDERSTAND MY MOM'S SUDDEN, URGENT COMPULSION TO DIAGNOSE AND TREAT ME.
Very interesting, Tessa...
I ONLY KNEW THE GAME WAS RIGGED. THERE WAS NO RIGHT ANSWER; CHOICE WAS AN ILLUSION, AND ALL PATHS LED TO ONLY ONE ENDING, IN WHICH I WAS LABELED BEHAVIORALLY DISTURBED AND MENTALLY ILL.

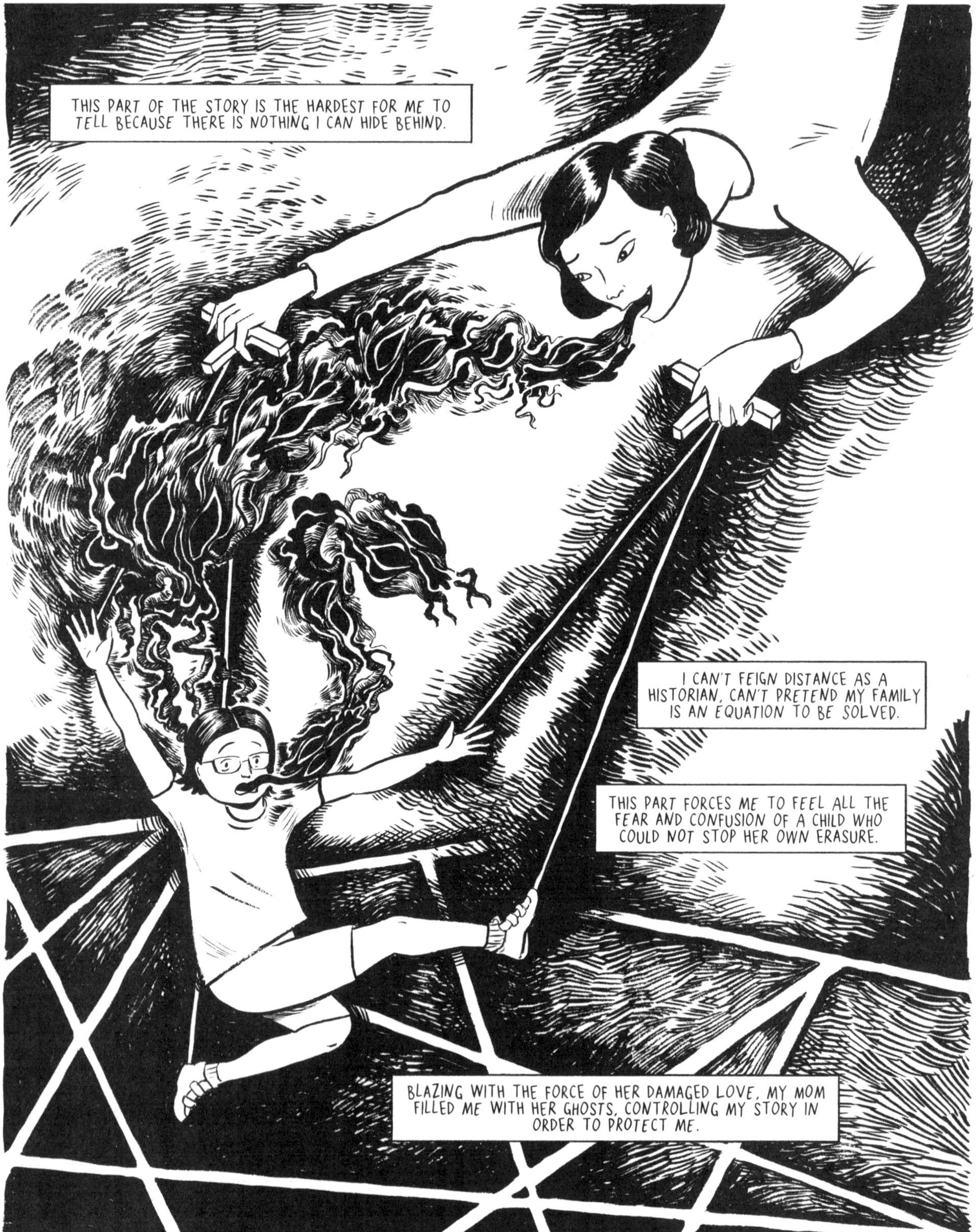

THIS PART OF THE STORY IS THE HARDEST FOR ME TO TELL BECAUSE THERE IS NOTHING I CAN HIDE BEHIND.
I CAN'T FEIGN DISTANCE AS A HISTORIAN, CAN'T PRETEND MY FAMILY IS AN EQUATION TO BE SOLVED.
THIS PART FORCES ME TO FEEL ALL THE FEAR AND CONFUSION OF A CHILD WHO COULD NOT STOP HER OWN ERASURE.
BLAZING WITH THE FORCE OF HER DAMAGED LOVE, MY MOM FILLED ME WITH HER GHOSTS, CONTROLLING MY STORY IN ORDER TO PROTECT ME.

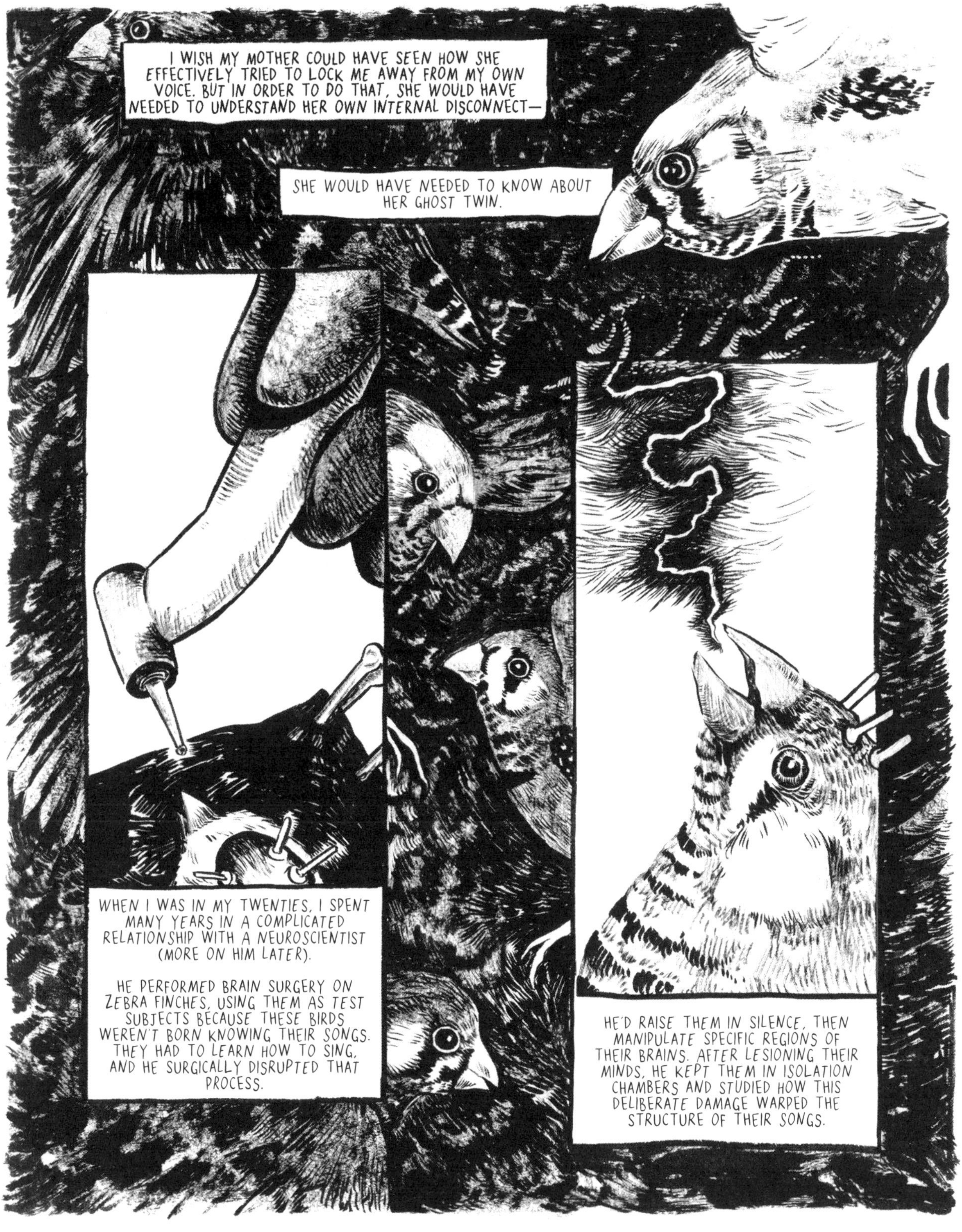
I WISH MY MOTHER COULD HAVE SEEN HOW SHE EFFECTIVELY TRIED TO LOCK ME AWAY FROM MY OWN VOICE. BUT IN ORDER TO DO THAT, SHE WOULD HAVE NEEDED TO UNDERSTAND HER OWN INTERNAL DISCONNECT—
SHE WOULD HAVE NEEDED TO KNOW ABOUT HER GHOST TWIN.
WHEN I WAS IN MY TWENTIES, I SPENT MANY YEARS IN A COMPLICATED RELATIONSHIP WITH A NEUROSCIENTIST (MORE ON HIM LATER).
HE PERFORMED BRAIN SURGERY ON ZEBRA FINCHES, USING THEM AS TEST SUBJECTS BECAUSE THESE BIRDS WEREN'T BORN KNOWING THEIR SONGS. THEY HAD TO LEARN HOW TO SING, AND HE SURGICALLY DISRUPTED THAT PROCESS.
HE'D RAISE THEM IN SILENCE, THEN MANIPULATE SPECIFIC REGIONS OF THEIR BRAINS. AFTER LESIONING THEIR MINDS, HE KEPT THEM IN ISOLATION CHAMBERS AND STUDIED HOW THIS DELIBERATE DAMAGE WARPED THE STRUCTURE OF THEIR SONGS.

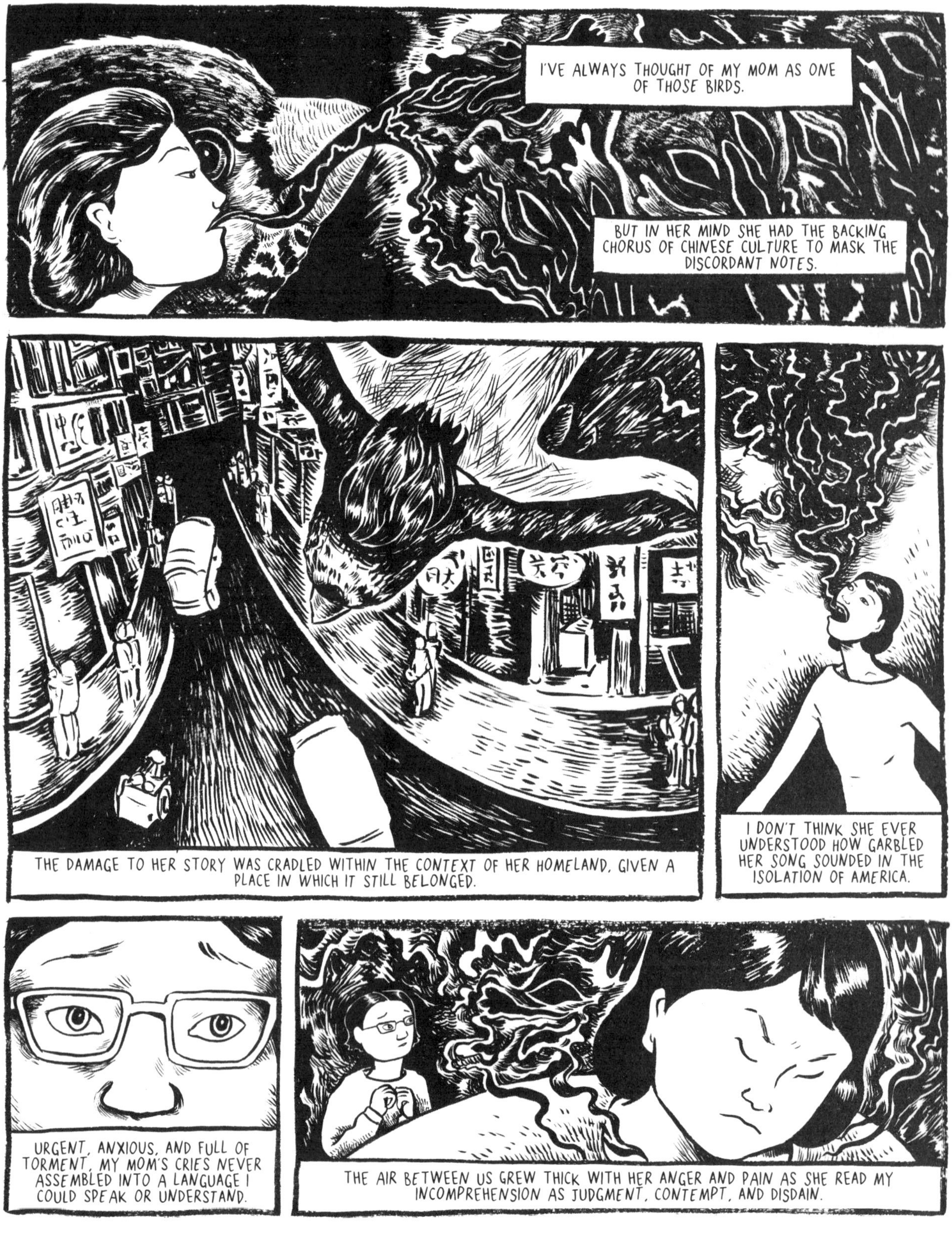
I'VE ALWAYS THOUGHT OF MY MOM AS ONE OF THOSE BIRDS.
BUT IN HER MIND SHE HAD THE BACKING CHORUS OF CHINESE CULTURE TO MASK THE DISCORDANT NOTES.
THE DAMAGE TO HER STORY WAS CRADLED WITHIN THE CONTEXT OF HER HOMELAND, GIVEN A PLACE IN WHICH IT STILL BELONGED.
I DON'T THINK SHE EVER UNDERSTOOD HOW GARBLED HER SONG SOUNDED IN THE ISOLATION OF AMERICA.
URGENT, ANXIOUS, AND FULL OF TORMENT, MY MOM'S CRIES NEVER ASSEMBLED INTO A LANGUAGE I COULD SPEAK OR UNDERSTAND.
THE AIR BETWEEN US GREW THICK WITH HER ANGER AND PAIN AS SHE READ MY INCOMPREHENSION AS JUDGMENT, CONTEMPT, AND DISDAIN.

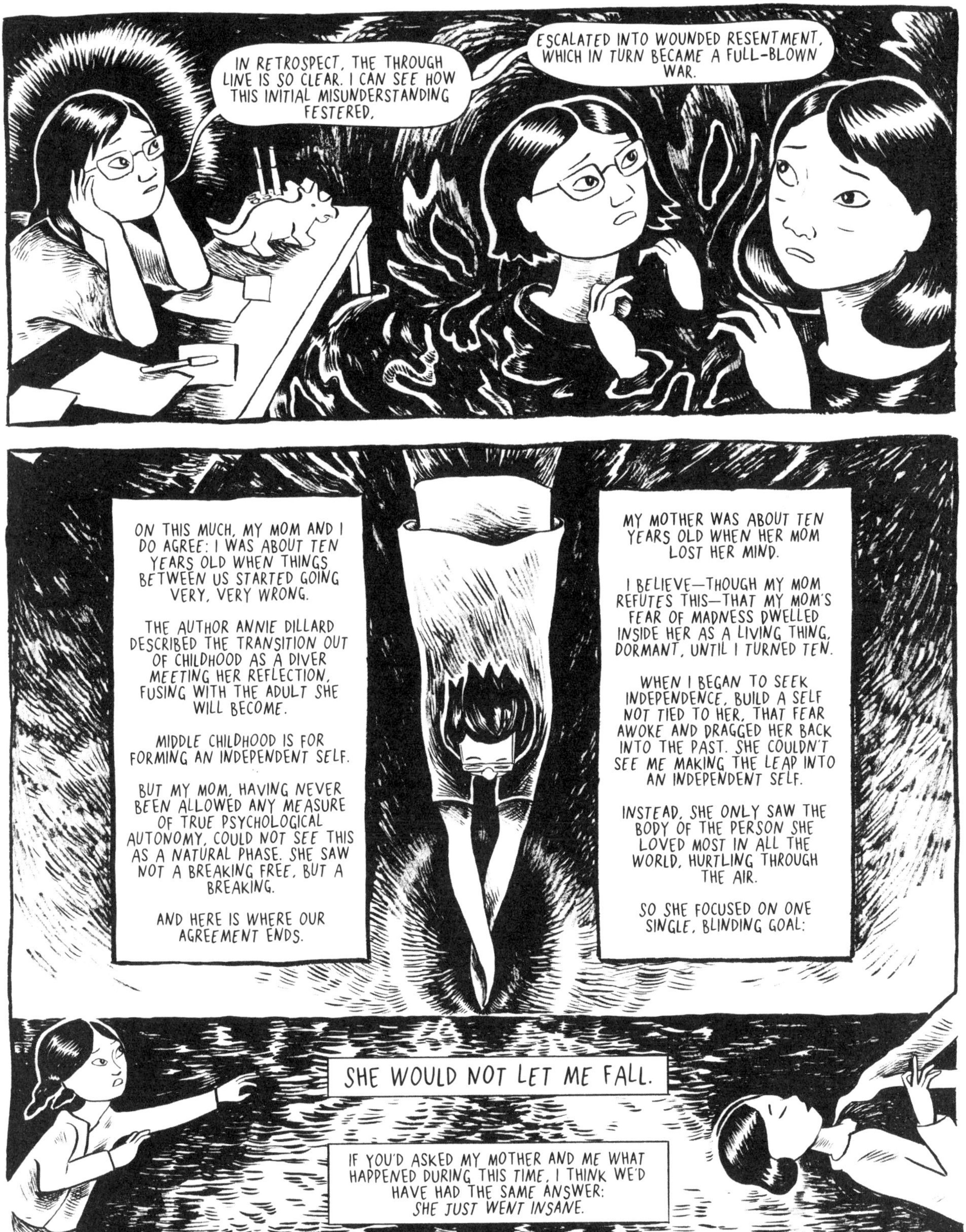
IN RETROSPECT, THE THROUGH LINE IS SO CLEAR. I CAN SEE HOW THIS INITIAL MISUNDERSTANDING FESTERED,
ESCALATED INTO WOUNDED RESENTMENT, WHICH IN TURN BECAME A FULL-BLOWN WAR.
ON THIS MUCH, MY MOM AND I DO AGREE: I WAS ABOUT TEN YEARS OLD WHEN THINGS BETWEEN US STARTED GOING VERY, VERY WRONG.
THE AUTHOR ANNIE DILLARD DESCRIBED THE TRANSITION OUT OF CHILDHOOD AS A DIVER MEETING HER REFLECTION, FUSING WITH THE ADULT SHE WILL BECOME.
MIDDLE CHILDHOOD IS FOR FORMING AN INDEPENDENT SELF.
BUT MY MOM, HAVING NEVER BEEN ALLOWED ANY MEASURE OF TRUE PSYCHOLOGICAL AUTONOMY, COULD NOT SEE THIS AS A NATURAL PHASE. SHE SAW NOT A BREAKING FREE, BUT A BREAKING.
AND HERE IS WHERE OUR AGREEMENT ENDS.
MY MOTHER WAS ABOUT TEN YEARS OLD WHEN HER MOM LOST HER MIND.
I BELIEVE—THOUGH MY MOM REFUTES THIS—THAT MY MOM'S FEAR OF MADNESS DWELLED INSIDE HER AS A LIVING THING, DORMANT, UNTIL I TURNED TEN.
WHEN I BEGAN TO SEEK INDEPENDENCE, BUILD A SELF NOT TIED TO HER, THAT FEAR AWOKE AND DRAGGED HER BACK INTO THE PAST. SHE COULDN'T SEE ME MAKING THE LEAP INTO AN INDEPENDENT SELF.
INSTEAD, SHE ONLY SAW THE BODY OF THE PERSON SHE LOVED MOST IN ALL THE WORLD, HURTLING THROUGH THE AIR.
SO SHE FOCUSED ON ONE SINGLE, BLINDING GOAL:
SHE WOULD NOT LET ME FALL.
IF YOU'D ASKED MY MOTHER AND ME WHAT HAPPENED DURING THIS TIME, I THINK WE'D HAVE HAD THE SAME ANSWER: *SHE JUST WENT INSANE.*

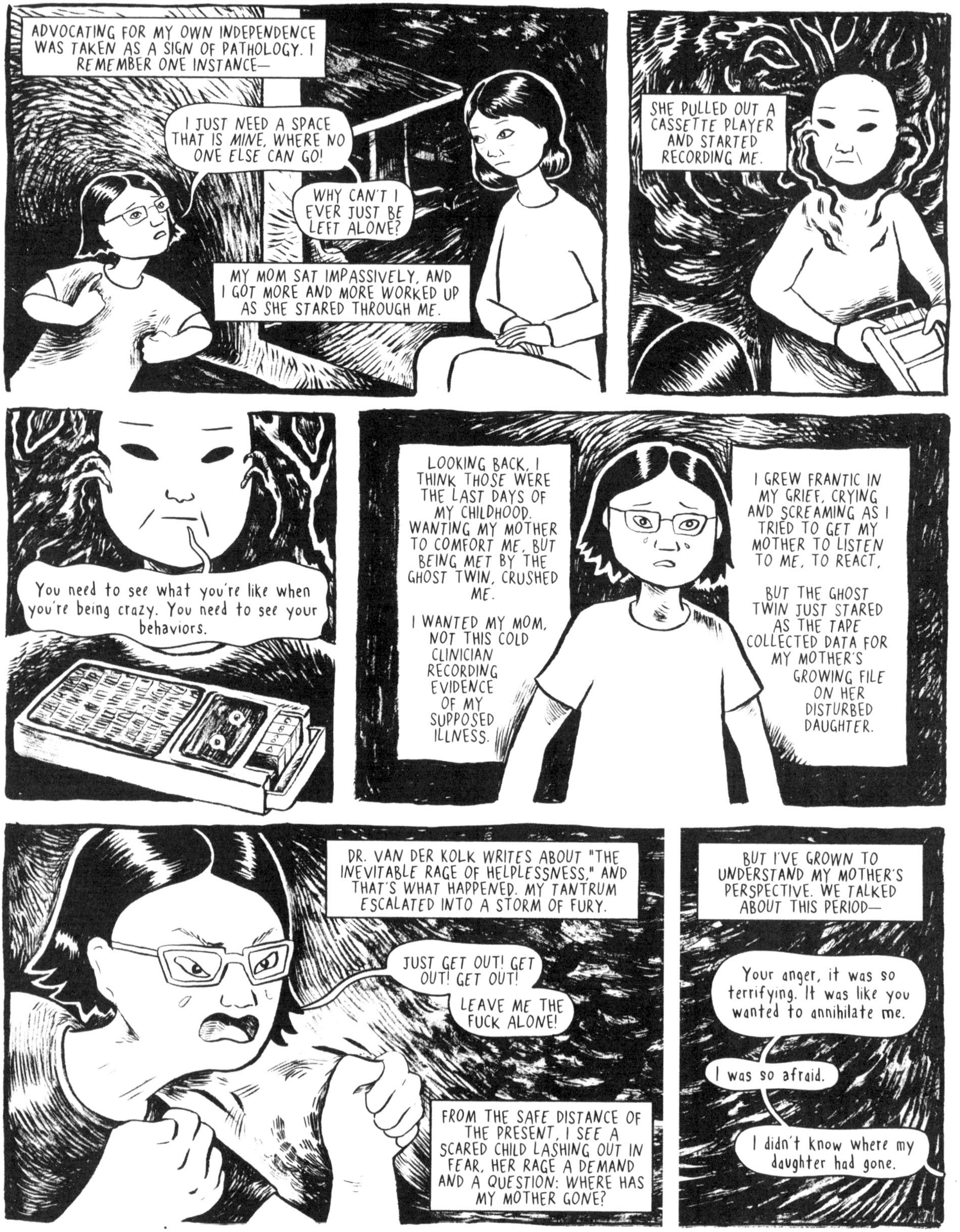

ADVOCATING FOR MY OWN INDEPENDENCE WAS TAKEN AS A SIGN OF PATHOLOGY. I REMEMBER ONE INSTANCE—
I JUST NEED A SPACE THAT IS *MINE*, WHERE NO ONE ELSE CAN GO!
WHY CAN'T I EVER JUST BE LEFT ALONE?
MY MOM SAT IMPASSIVELY, AND I GOT MORE AND MORE WORKED UP AS SHE STARED THROUGH ME.
SHE PULLED OUT A CASSETTE PLAYER AND STARTED RECORDING ME.
You need to see what you're like when you're being crazy. You need to see your behaviors.
LOOKING BACK, I THINK THOSE WERE THE LAST DAYS OF MY CHILDHOOD. WANTING MY MOTHER TO COMFORT ME, BUT BEING MET BY THE GHOST TWIN, CRUSHED ME.
I WANTED MY MOM, NOT THIS COLD CLINICIAN RECORDING EVIDENCE OF MY SUPPOSED ILLNESS.
I GREW FRANTIC IN MY GRIEF, CRYING AND SCREAMING AS I TRIED TO GET MY MOTHER TO LISTEN TO ME, TO REACT,
BUT THE GHOST TWIN JUST STARED AS THE *TAPE* COLLECTED DATA FOR MY MOTHER'S GROWING FILE ON HER DISTURBED DAUGHTER.
DR. VAN DER KOLK WRITES ABOUT "THE INEVITABLE RAGE OF HELPLESSNESS," AND THAT'S WHAT HAPPENED. MY TANTRUM ESCALATED INTO A STORM OF FURY.
JUST GET OUT! GET OUT! GET OUT!
LEAVE ME THE FUCK ALONE!
FROM THE SAFE DISTANCE OF THE PRESENT, I SEE A SCARED CHILD LASHING OUT IN FEAR, HER RAGE A DEMAND AND A QUESTION: WHERE HAS MY MOTHER GONE?
BUT I'VE GROWN TO UNDERSTAND MY MOTHER'S PERSPECTIVE. WE TALKED ABOUT THIS PERIOD—
Your anger, it was so terrifying. It was like you wanted to annihilate me.
I was so afraid.
I didn't know where my daughter had gone.

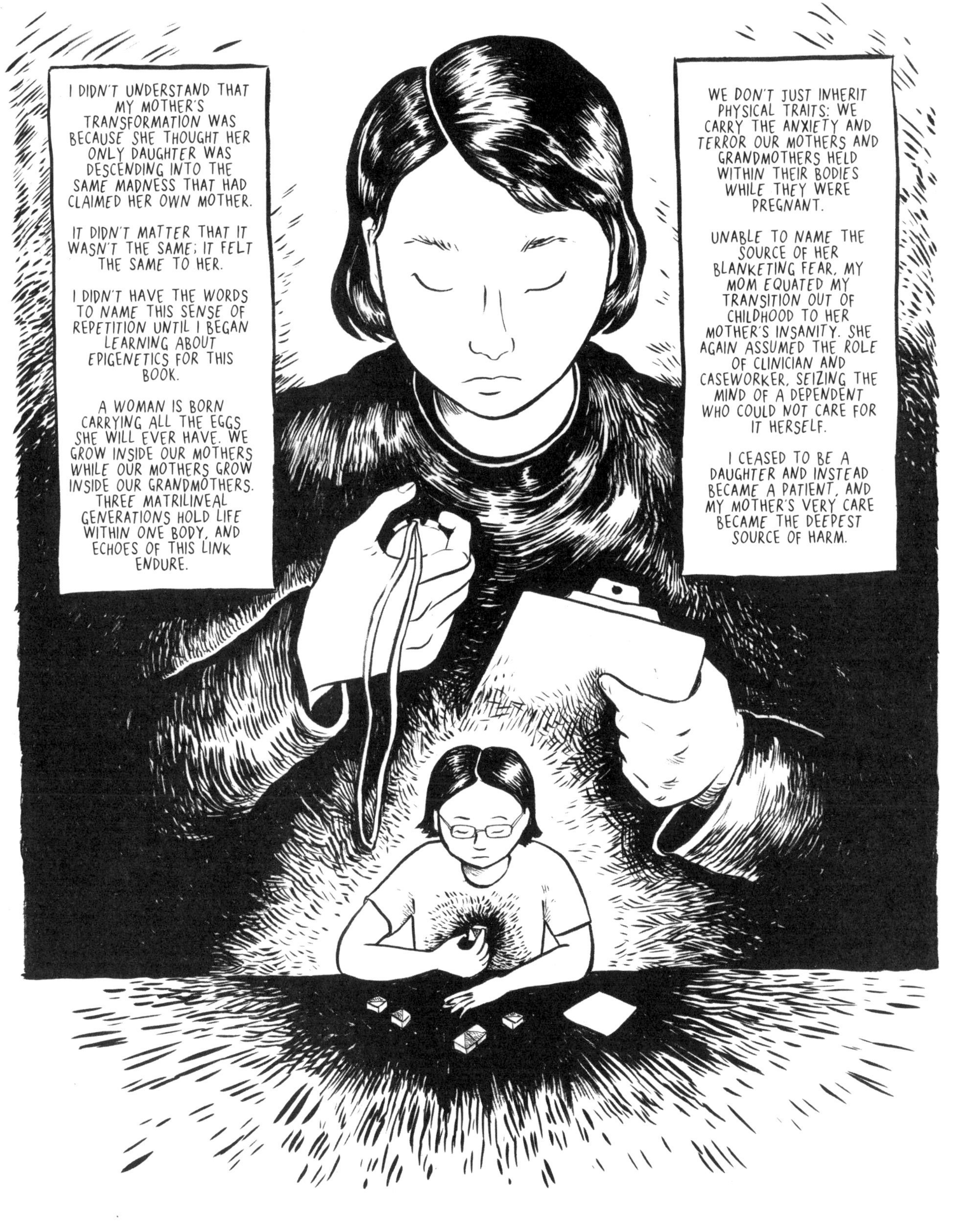
I DIDN'T UNDERSTAND THAT MY MOTHER'S TRANSFORMATION WAS BECAUSE SHE THOUGHT HER ONLY DAUGHTER WAS DESCENDING INTO THE SAME MADNESS THAT HAD CLAIMED HER OWN MOTHER.
IT DIDN'T MATTER THAT IT WASN'T THE SAME; IT FELT THE SAME TO HER.
I DIDN'T HAVE THE WORDS TO NAME THIS SENSE OF REPETITION UNTIL I BEGAN LEARNING ABOUT EPIGENETICS FOR THIS BOOK.
A WOMAN IS BORN CARRYING ALL THE EGGS SHE WILL EVER HAVE. WE GROW INSIDE OUR MOTHERS WHILE OUR MOTHERS GROW INSIDE OUR GRANDMOTHERS. THREE MATRILINEAL GENERATIONS HOLD LIFE WITHIN ONE BODY, AND ECHOES OF THIS LINK ENDURE.
WE DON'T JUST INHERIT PHYSICAL TRAITS: WE CARRY THE ANXIETY AND TERROR OUR MOTHERS AND GRANDMOTHERS HELD WITHIN THEIR BODIES WHILE THEY WERE PREGNANT.
UNABLE TO NAME THE SOURCE OF HER BLANKETING FEAR, MY MOM EQUATED MY TRANSITION OUT OF CHILDHOOD TO HER MOTHER'S INSANITY. SHE AGAIN ASSUMED THE ROLE OF CLINICIAN AND CASEWORKER, SEIZING THE MIND OF A DEPENDENT WHO COULD NOT CARE FOR IT HERSELF.
I CEASED TO BE A DAUGHTER AND INSTEAD BECAME A PATIENT, AND MY MOTHER'S VERY CARE BECAME THE DEEPEST SOURCE OF HARM.

I KNOW MY MOM'S HEART WAS IN THE RIGHT PLACE. SHE THOUGHT THAT IF THE ILLNESS WAS CONFRONTED HEAD ON BEFORE IT COULD MANIFEST, I COULD BE KEPT SAFE FROM IT. WE NEEDED TO BE VIGILANT FOR SIGNS IT WAS COMING, SO WHILE I WAS STILL A CHILD, SHE GAVE ME PSYCHOLOGY BOOKS LIKE—

AN UNQUIET MIND
Kay Redfield Jamison

TOUCHED WITH FIRE
Manic Depressive Illness and the Artistic Temperament
Kay Redfield Jamison

The Drama of the Gifted Child
Alice Miller

SHE WOULD WARN ME ABOUT MY MIND AND WHAT IT MEANT—

Oh my dear, my dear, it's going to be hard for you because you are BRILLIANT.

BUT—

JUST—

I'M NOT—

You, Dad, Chris—you're all GENIUSES, and those are hard minds to have.

But, Tessa, oh my Tessa, my Tessa... You will struggle the most because of your CREATIVITY.

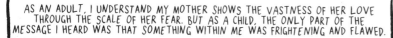

AS AN ADULT, I UNDERSTAND MY MOTHER SHOWS THE VASTNESS OF HER LOVE THROUGH THE SCALE OF HER FEAR. BUT AS A CHILD, THE ONLY PART OF THE MESSAGE I HEARD WAS THAT SOMETHING WITHIN ME WAS FRIGHTENING AND FLAWED.

I HAVE A DISTINCT MEMORY OF HER GIVING ME ONE OF THE REPORTS A PSYCHIATRIST WROTE ABOUT ME AND MY "BEHAVIORS."

262.

I DIDN'T WANT TO TALK.	Tessa didn't want to talk.
SHRINKS ALWAYS KEEP TOYS AROUND SO YOU'LL DO THINGS THEY CAN ANALYZE.	She looked around the toys in my office.
I PICKED UP SOME PLAY-DOH. THAT SEEMED NEUTRAL—COULDN'T READ MUCH INTO THAT, RIGHT?	She began playing with some Play-Doh.
I ROLLED IT INTO A BALL.	She rolled it into a ball.
I PROBABLY SCULPTED SOME DINOSAURS...	She played.
THE SHRINK WROTE IN HER CLIPBOARD.	She tossed the lump to herself.
I TOSSED THE LUMP TO MYSELF.	She then hurled the Play-Doh at my head.
THEN I BOUNCED IT IDLY OFF THE WALL AND CAUGHT IT AGAIN.	Fortunately, her aim was bad.
I WAS BORED.	She hit the wall instead.
THEN SHE ASKED ME TO PLAY CHESS.	Then I asked her to play chess.
I WAS SO RELIEVED BY AN ACTIVITY THAT HAD KNOWN RULES.	Her demeanor immediately changed.
WHERE I COULD RELAX INTO THE STRUCTURE OF A WORLD WITH CLEARLY DEFINED LAWS OF CAUSE AND EFFECT.	She stopped being sullen and violent.
A CHESSBOARD WAS A REALITY NO ONE COULD SUDDENLY SEIZE. I COULD FEEL SAFE.	And instead became cocky and arrogant.

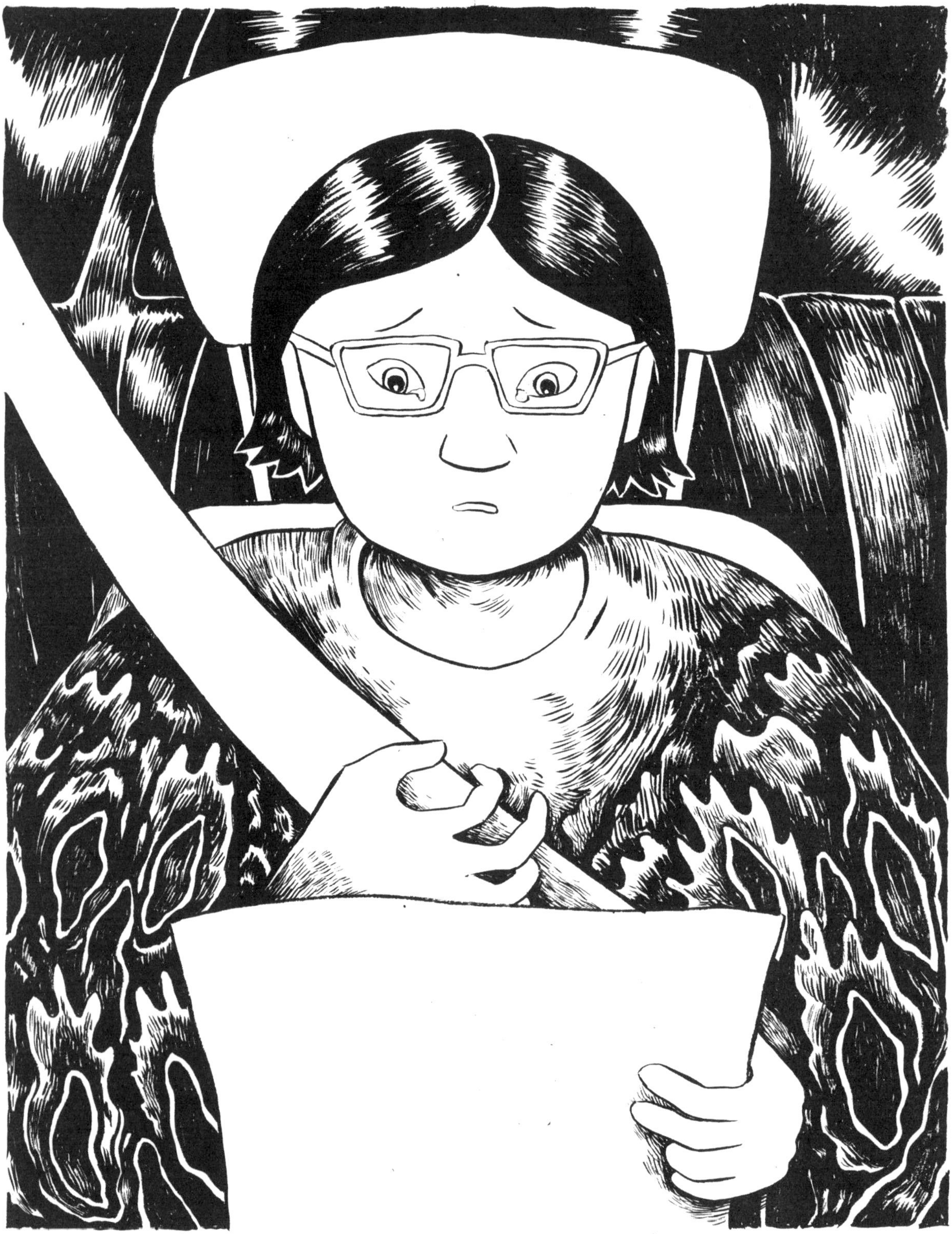

I FELT THOSE WORDS SLAM AGAINST MY SOLAR PLEXUS. THE PSYCHIATRIST HAD SEEN WHAT SHE HAD SET OUT TO FIND. I WANTED TO REFUTE HER VERSION OF EVENTS BUT KNEW IT WAS HOPELESS; THE REPORT OF A PSYCHIATRIST CARRIED MORE WEIGHT THAN THE VOICE OF AN "OBVIOUSLY DISTURBED CHILD."

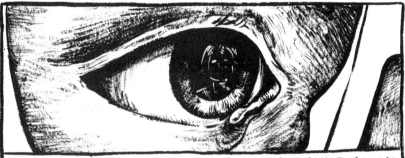

THE SOFTNESS IN ME SCREAMED IN CONFUSION. MOM, WHY ARE YOU DOING THIS? WHY DO YOU SEE ME AS THIS BROKEN THING?

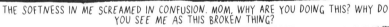

WHY AREN'T YOU PROTECTING ME?

BUT I PUSHED THAT SOFTNESS DOWN AND SHOWED NOTHING, DREW MY COWBOY ACROSS MY BODY AND TURNED MY BONES TO ICE.

THERE WAS NO RIGHT ANSWER, RIGHT BEHAVIOR, RIGHT RESPONSE.

ANYTHING I SAID OR DID WOULD BE USED TO REINFORCE A STORY THEY HAD ALREADY WRITTEN.

SO I WOULD GIVE THEM NOTHING, NO ROPE TO HANG THIS OUTLAW.

IN THE WORDS OF ADRIENNE RICH, "SILENCE CAN BE A PLAN RIGOROUSLY EXECUTED."

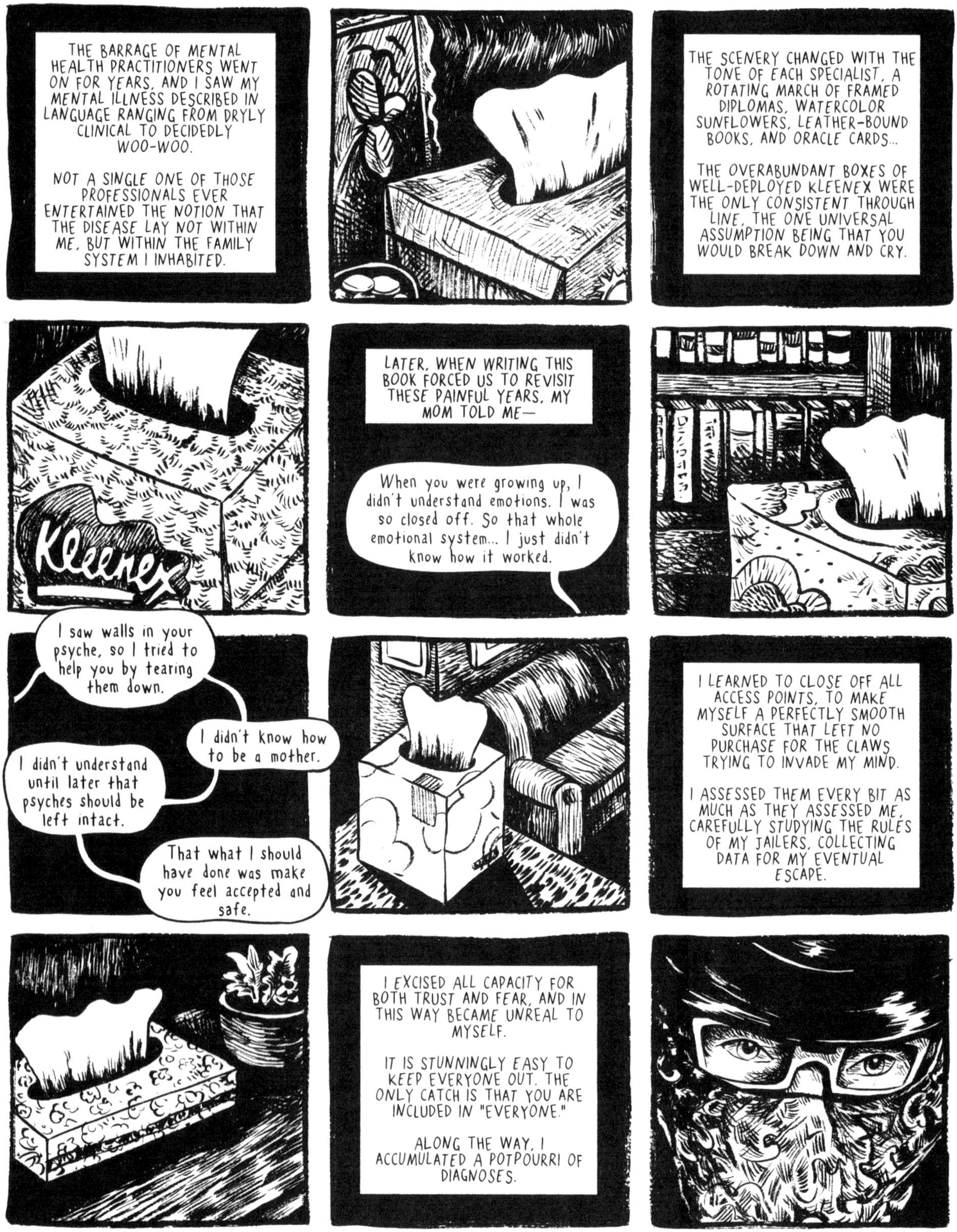
THE BARRAGE OF MENTAL HEALTH PRACTITIONERS WENT ON FOR YEARS, AND I SAW MY MENTAL ILLNESS DESCRIBED IN LANGUAGE RANGING FROM DRYLY CLINICAL TO DECIDEDLY WOO-WOO.
NOT A SINGLE ONE OF THOSE PROFESSIONALS EVER ENTERTAINED THE NOTION THAT THE DISEASE LAY NOT WITHIN ME, BUT WITHIN THE FAMILY SYSTEM I INHABITED.
THE SCENERY CHANGED WITH THE TONE OF EACH SPECIALIST, A ROTATING MARCH OF FRAMED DIPLOMAS, WATERCOLOR SUNFLOWERS, LEATHER-BOUND BOOKS, AND ORACLE CARDS...
THE OVERABUNDANT BOXES OF WELL-DEPLOYED KLEENEX WERE THE ONLY CONSISTENT THROUGH LINE, THE ONE UNIVERSAL ASSUMPTION BEING THAT YOU WOULD BREAK DOWN AND CRY.
Kleenex
LATER, WHEN WRITING THIS BOOK FORCED US TO REVISIT THESE PAINFUL YEARS, MY MOM TOLD ME—
When you were growing up, I didn't understand emotions. I was so closed off. So that whole emotional system... I just didn't know how it worked.
I saw walls in your psyche, so I tried to help you by tearing them down.
I didn't know how to be a mother.
I didn't understand until later that psyches should be left intact.
That what I should have done was make you feel accepted and safe.
I LEARNED TO CLOSE OFF ALL ACCESS POINTS, TO MAKE MYSELF A PERFECTLY SMOOTH SURFACE THAT LEFT NO PURCHASE FOR THE CLAWS TRYING TO INVADE MY MIND.
I ASSESSED THEM EVERY BIT AS MUCH AS THEY ASSESSED ME, CAREFULLY STUDYING THE RULES OF MY JAILERS, COLLECTING DATA FOR MY EVENTUAL ESCAPE.
I EXCISED ALL CAPACITY FOR BOTH TRUST AND FEAR, AND IN THIS WAY BECAME UNREAL TO MYSELF.
IT IS STUNNINGLY EASY TO KEEP EVERYONE OUT. THE ONLY CATCH IS THAT YOU ARE INCLUDED IN "EVERYONE."
ALONG THE WAY, I ACCUMULATED A POTPOURRI OF DIAGNOSES.

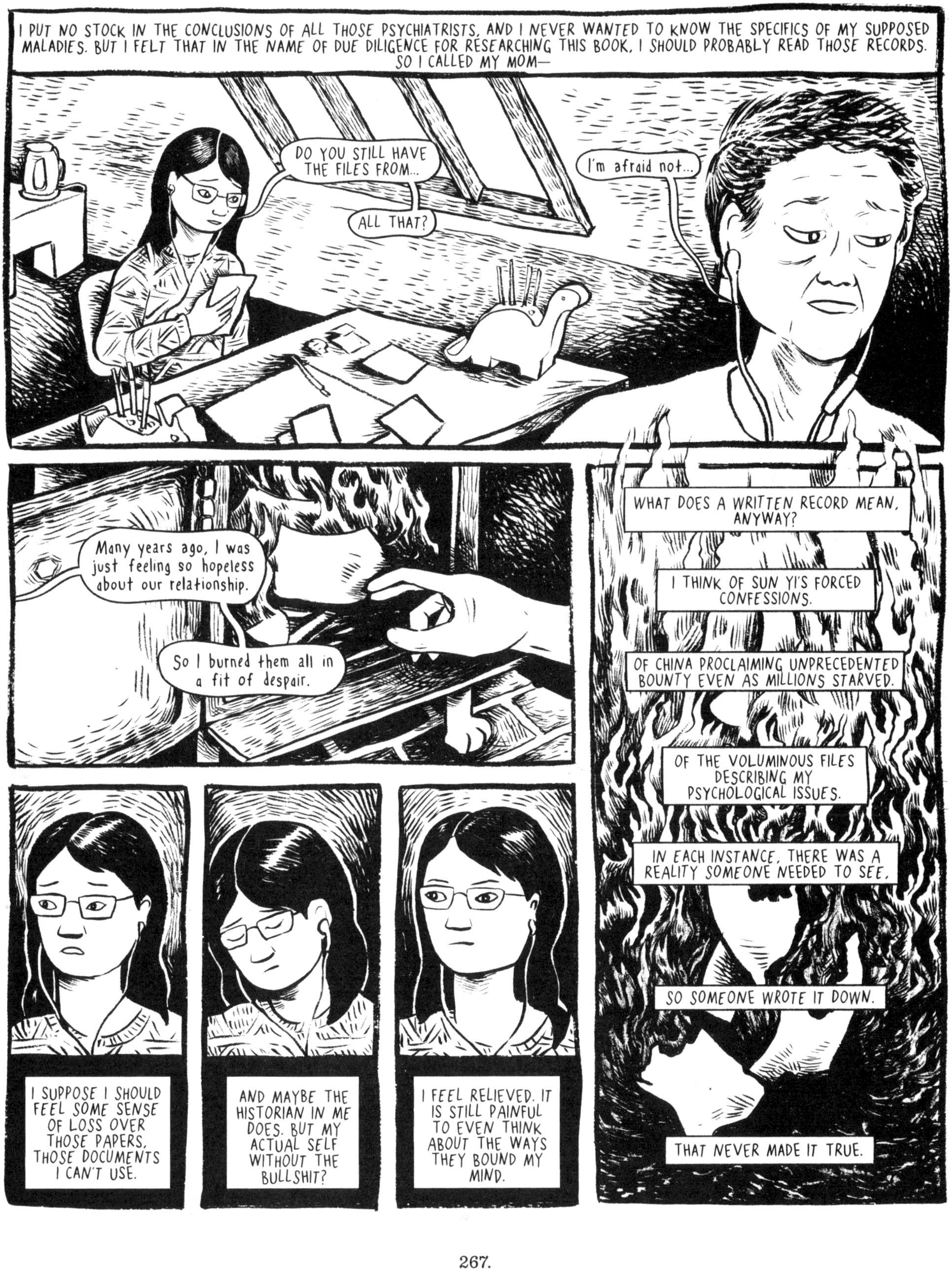
I PUT NO STOCK IN THE CONCLUSIONS OF ALL THOSE PSYCHIATRISTS, AND I NEVER WANTED TO KNOW THE SPECIFICS OF MY SUPPOSED MALADIES. BUT I FELT THAT IN THE NAME OF DUE DILIGENCE FOR RESEARCHING THIS BOOK, I SHOULD PROBABLY READ THOSE RECORDS. SO I CALLED MY MOM—
DO YOU STILL HAVE THE FILES FROM...
ALL THAT?
I'm afraid not...
Many years ago, I was just feeling so hopeless about our relationship.
So I burned them all in a fit of despair.
I SUPPOSE I SHOULD FEEL SOME SENSE OF LOSS OVER THOSE PAPERS, THOSE DOCUMENTS I CAN'T USE.
AND MAYBE THE HISTORIAN IN ME DOES. BUT MY ACTUAL SELF WITHOUT THE BULLSHIT?
I FEEL RELIEVED. IT IS STILL PAINFUL TO EVEN THINK ABOUT THE WAYS THEY BOUND MY MIND.
WHAT DOES A WRITTEN RECORD MEAN, ANYWAY?
I THINK OF SUN YI'S FORCED CONFESSIONS.
OF CHINA PROCLAIMING UNPRECEDENTED BOUNTY EVEN AS MILLIONS STARVED.
OF THE VOLUMINOUS FILES DESCRIBING MY PSYCHOLOGICAL ISSUES.
IN EACH INSTANCE, THERE WAS A REALITY SOMEONE NEEDED TO SEE,
SO SOMEONE WROTE IT DOWN.
THAT NEVER MADE IT TRUE.

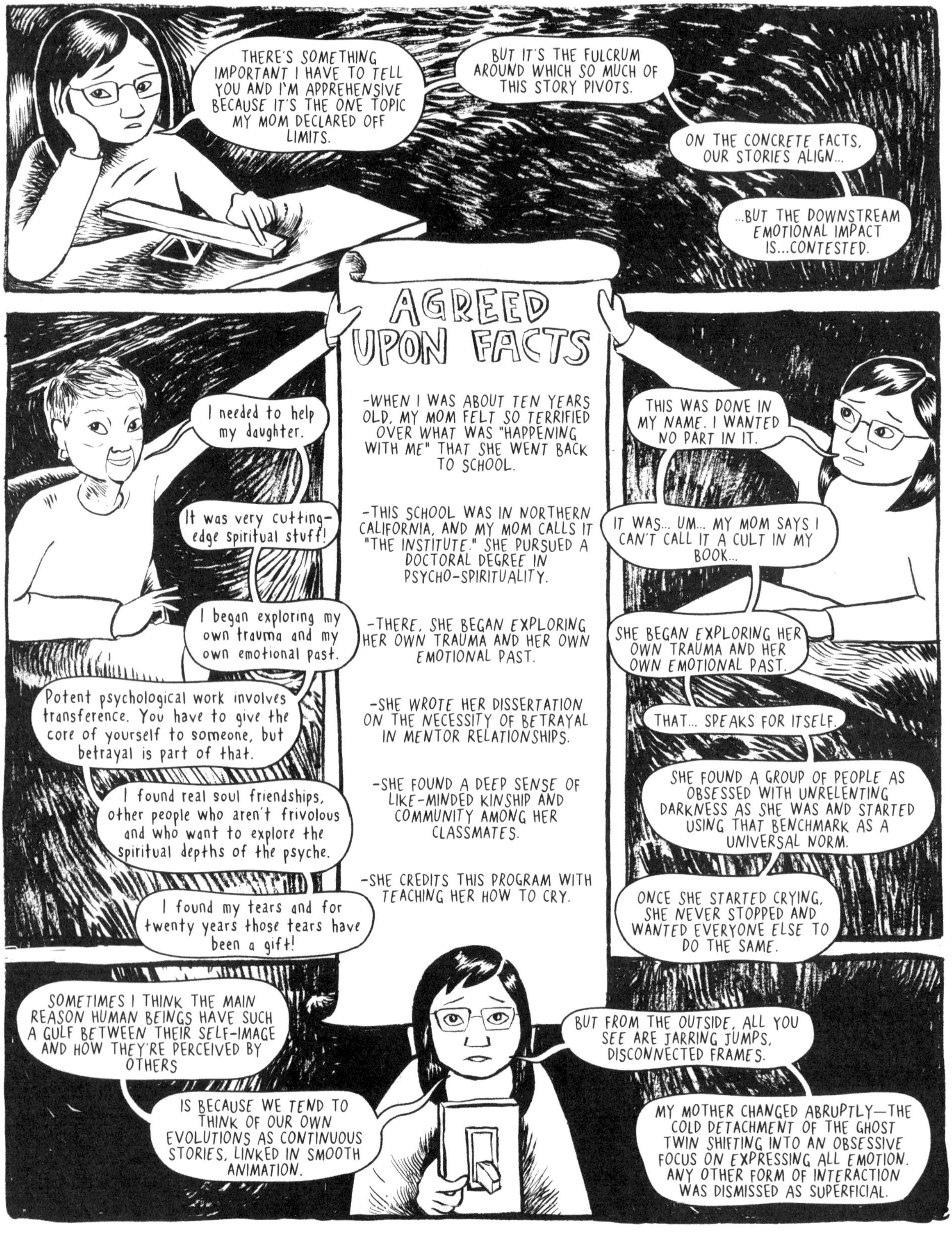
THERE'S SOMETHING IMPORTANT I HAVE TO TELL YOU AND I'M APPREHENSIVE BECAUSE IT'S THE ONE TOPIC MY MOM DECLARED OFF LIMITS.
BUT IT'S THE FULCRUM AROUND WHICH SO MUCH OF THIS STORY PIVOTS.
ON THE CONCRETE FACTS, OUR STORIES ALIGN...
...BUT THE DOWNSTREAM EMOTIONAL IMPACT IS...CONTESTED.
AGREED UPON FACTS
-WHEN I WAS ABOUT TEN YEARS OLD, MY MOM FELT SO TERRIFIED OVER WHAT WAS "HAPPENING WITH ME" THAT SHE WENT BACK TO SCHOOL.
I needed to help my daughter.
THIS WAS DONE IN MY NAME. I WANTED NO PART IN IT.
-THIS SCHOOL WAS IN NORTHERN CALIFORNIA, AND MY MOM CALLS IT "THE INSTITUTE." SHE PURSUED A DOCTORAL DEGREE IN PSYCHO-SPIRITUALITY.
It was very cutting-edge spiritual stuff!
IT WAS... UM... MY MOM SAYS I CAN'T CALL IT A CULT IN MY BOOK...
-THERE, SHE BEGAN EXPLORING HER OWN TRAUMA AND HER OWN EMOTIONAL PAST.
I began exploring my own trauma and my own emotional past.
SHE BEGAN EXPLORING HER OWN TRAUMA AND HER OWN EMOTIONAL PAST.
-SHE WROTE HER DISSERTATION ON THE NECESSITY OF BETRAYAL IN MENTOR RELATIONSHIPS.
Potent psychological work involves transference. You have to give the core of yourself to someone, but betrayal is part of that.
THAT... SPEAKS FOR ITSELF.
-SHE FOUND A DEEP SENSE OF LIKE-MINDED KINSHIP AND COMMUNITY AMONG HER CLASSMATES.
I found real soul friendships, other people who aren't frivolous and who want to explore the spiritual depths of the psyche.
SHE FOUND A GROUP OF PEOPLE AS OBSESSED WITH UNRELENTING DARKNESS AS SHE WAS AND STARTED USING THAT BENCHMARK AS A UNIVERSAL NORM.
-SHE CREDITS THIS PROGRAM WITH TEACHING HER HOW TO CRY.
I found my tears and for twenty years those tears have been a gift!
ONCE SHE STARTED CRYING, SHE NEVER STOPPED AND WANTED EVERYONE ELSE TO DO THE SAME.
SOMETIMES I THINK THE MAIN REASON HUMAN BEINGS HAVE SUCH A GULF BETWEEN THEIR SELF-IMAGE AND HOW THEY'RE PERCEIVED BY OTHERS
IS BECAUSE WE TEND TO THINK OF OUR OWN EVOLUTIONS AS CONTINUOUS STORIES, LINKED IN SMOOTH ANIMATION.
BUT FROM THE OUTSIDE, ALL YOU SEE ARE JARRING JUMPS, DISCONNECTED FRAMES.
MY MOTHER CHANGED ABRUPTLY—THE COLD DETACHMENT OF THE GHOST TWIN SHIFTING INTO AN OBSESSIVE FOCUS ON EXPRESSING ALL EMOTION. ANY OTHER FORM OF INTERACTION WAS DISMISSED AS SUPERFICIAL.

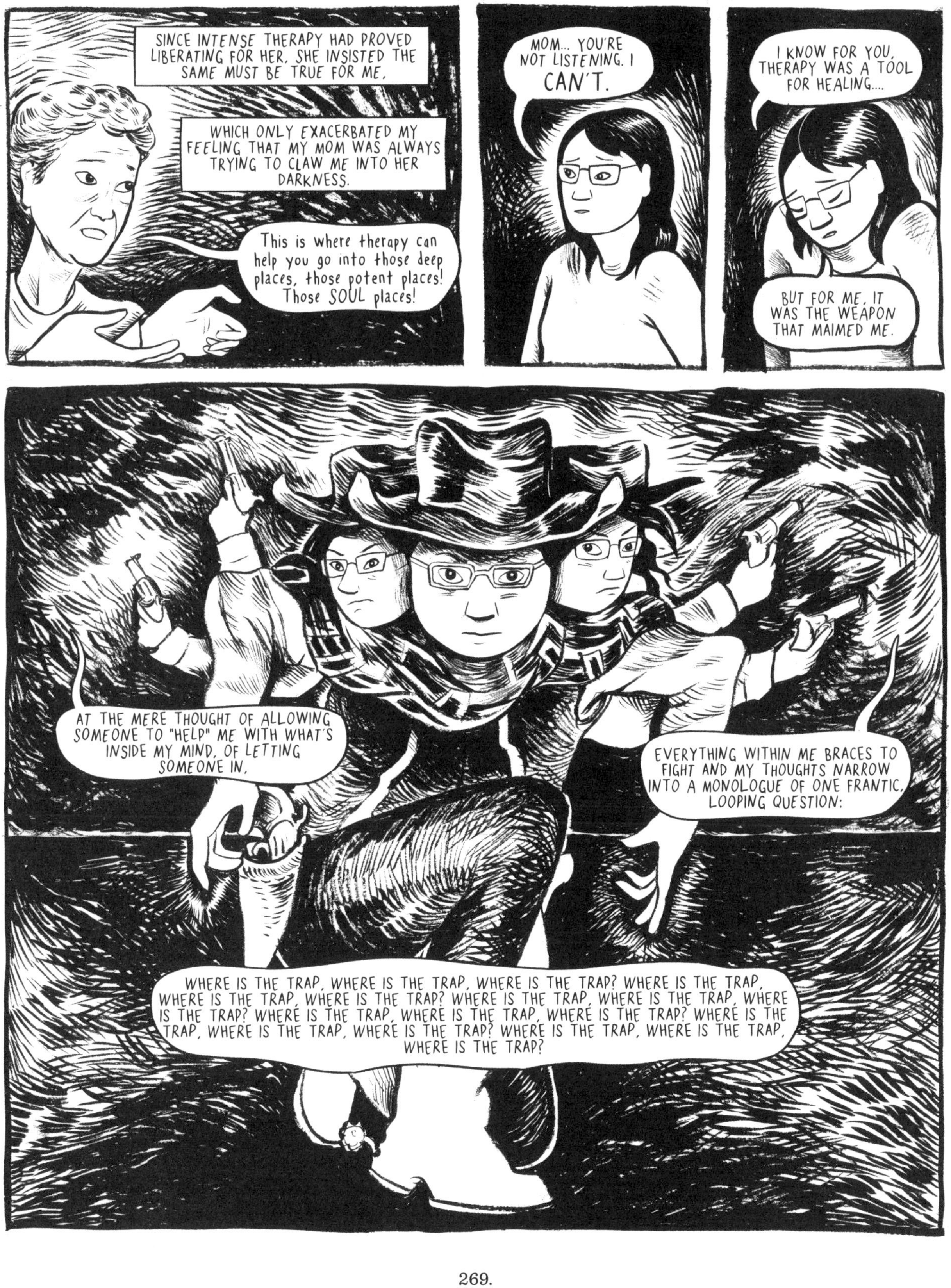
SINCE INTENSE THERAPY HAD PROVED LIBERATING FOR HER, SHE INSISTED THE SAME MUST BE TRUE FOR ME,
WHICH ONLY EXACERBATED MY FEELING THAT MY MOM WAS ALWAYS TRYING TO CLAW ME INTO HER DARKNESS.
This is where therapy can help you go into those deep places, those potent places! Those SOUL places!
MOM... YOU'RE NOT LISTENING. I CAN'T.
I KNOW FOR YOU, THERAPY WAS A TOOL FOR HEALING....
BUT FOR ME, IT WAS THE WEAPON THAT MAIMED ME.
AT THE MERE THOUGHT OF ALLOWING SOMEONE TO "HELP" ME WITH WHAT'S INSIDE MY MIND, OF LETTING SOMEONE IN,
EVERYTHING WITHIN ME BRACES TO FIGHT AND MY THOUGHTS NARROW INTO A MONOLOGUE OF ONE FRANTIC, LOOPING QUESTION:
WHERE IS THE TRAP, WHERE IS THE TRAP, WHERE IS THE TRAP? WHERE IS THE TRAP, WHERE IS THE TRAP, WHERE IS THE TRAP? WHERE IS THE TRAP, WHERE IS THE TRAP, WHERE IS THE TRAP? WHERE IS THE TRAP, WHERE IS THE TRAP, WHERE IS THE TRAP? WHERE IS THE TRAP, WHERE IS THE TRAP, WHERE IS THE TRAP? WHERE IS THE TRAP, WHERE IS THE TRAP, WHERE IS THE TRAP?

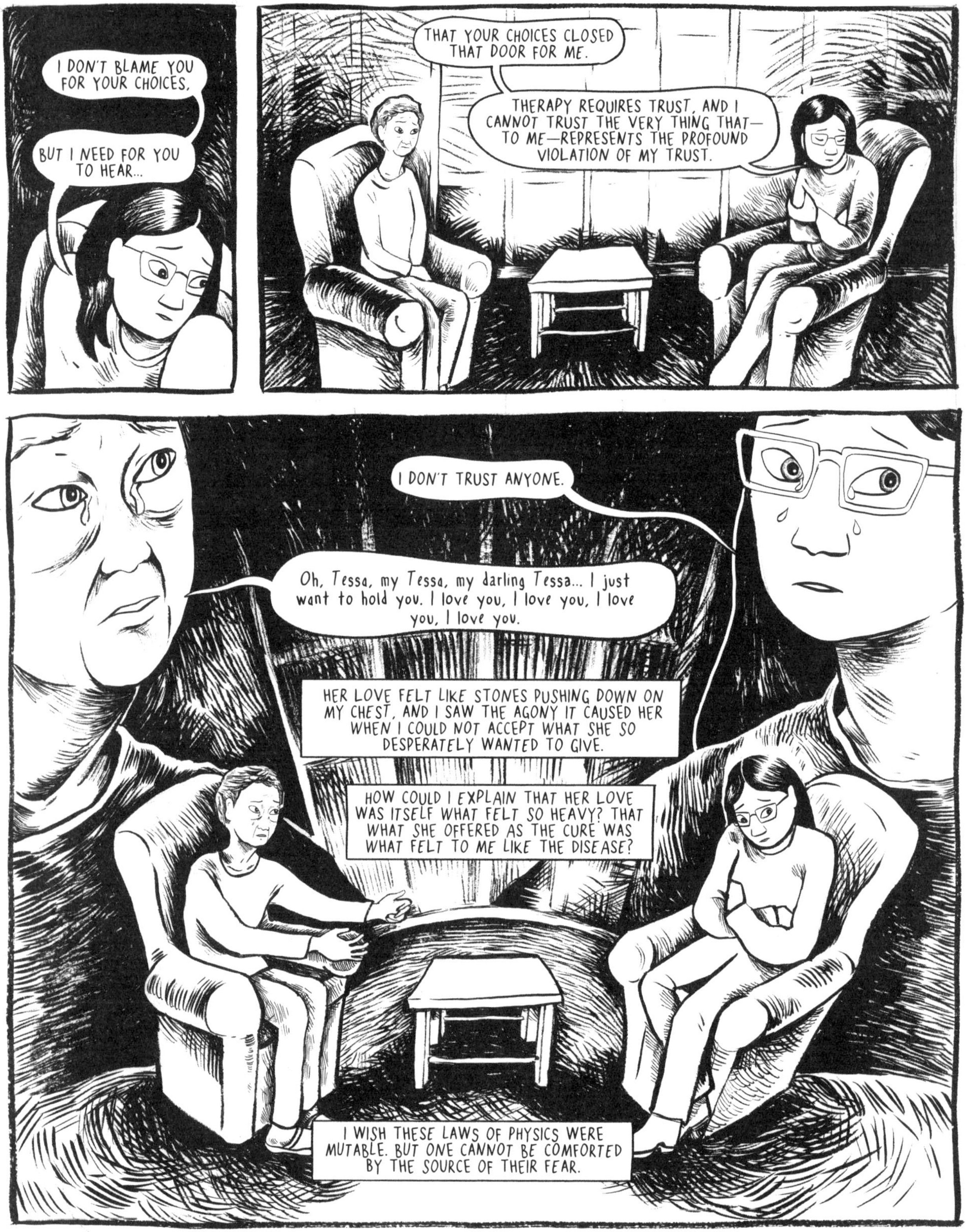
I DON'T BLAME YOU FOR YOUR CHOICES,
BUT I NEED FOR YOU TO HEAR...
THAT YOUR CHOICES CLOSED THAT DOOR FOR ME.
THERAPY REQUIRES TRUST, AND I CANNOT TRUST THE VERY THING THAT—TO ME—REPRESENTS THE PROFOUND VIOLATION OF MY TRUST.
I DON'T TRUST ANYONE.
Oh, Tessa, my Tessa, my darling Tessa... I just want to hold you. I love you, I love you, I love you, I love you.
HER LOVE FELT LIKE STONES PUSHING DOWN ON MY CHEST, AND I SAW THE AGONY IT CAUSED HER WHEN I COULD NOT ACCEPT WHAT SHE SO DESPERATELY WANTED TO GIVE.
HOW COULD I EXPLAIN THAT HER LOVE WAS ITSELF WHAT FELT SO HEAVY? THAT WHAT SHE OFFERED AS THE CURE WAS WHAT FELT TO ME LIKE THE DISEASE?
I WISH THESE LAWS OF PHYSICS WERE MUTABLE. BUT ONE CANNOT BE COMFORTED BY THE SOURCE OF THEIR FEAR.

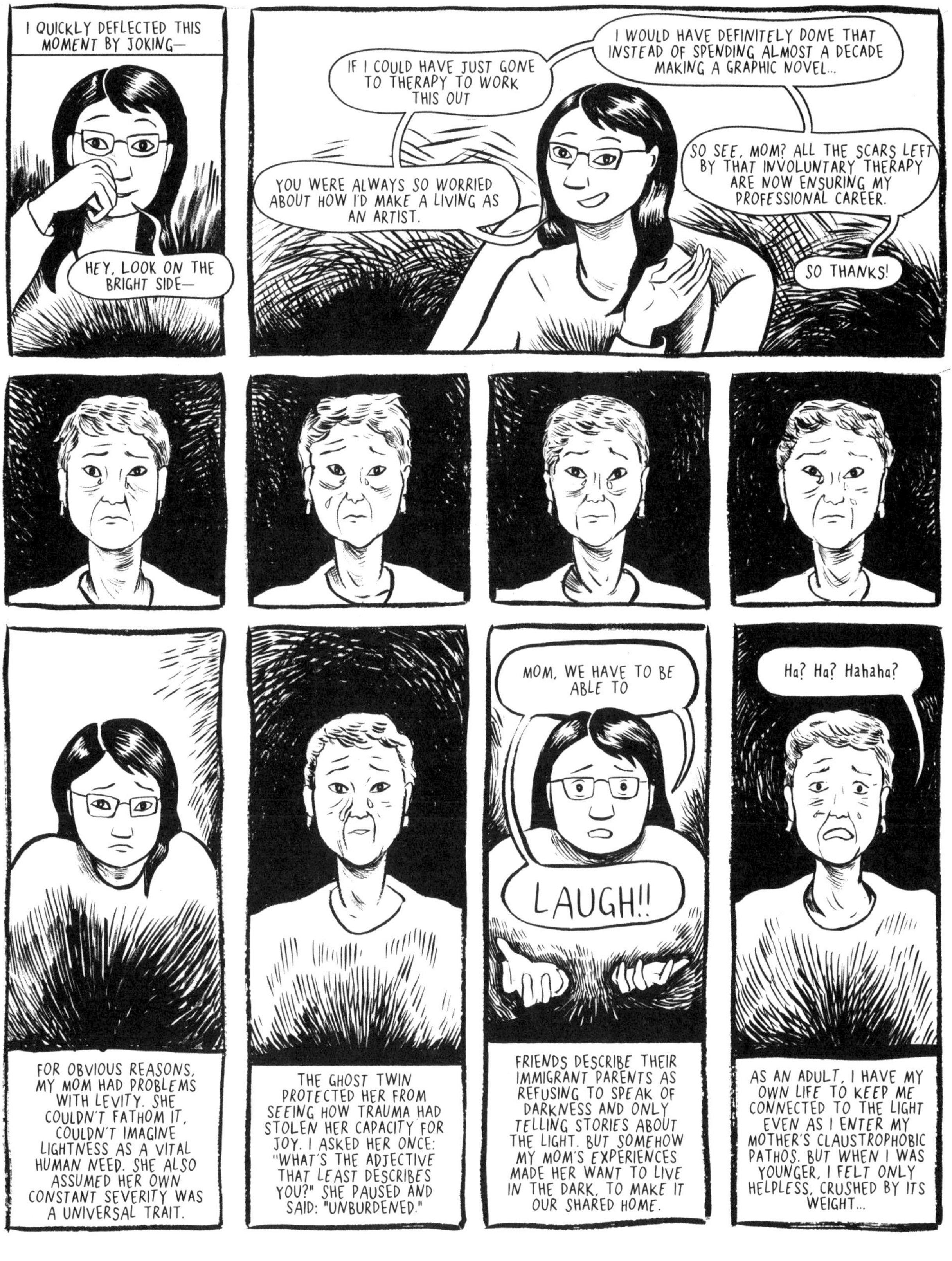
I QUICKLY DEFLECTED THIS MOMENT BY JOKING—
HEY, LOOK ON THE BRIGHT SIDE—
YOU WERE ALWAYS SO WORRIED ABOUT HOW I'D MAKE A LIVING AS AN ARTIST.
IF I COULD HAVE JUST GONE TO THERAPY TO WORK THIS OUT
I WOULD HAVE DEFINITELY DONE THAT INSTEAD OF SPENDING ALMOST A DECADE MAKING A GRAPHIC NOVEL...
SO SEE, MOM? ALL THE SCARS LEFT BY THAT INVOLUNTARY THERAPY ARE NOW ENSURING MY PROFESSIONAL CAREER.
SO THANKS!
FOR OBVIOUS REASONS, MY MOM HAD PROBLEMS WITH LEVITY. SHE COULDN'T FATHOM IT, COULDN'T IMAGINE LIGHTNESS AS A VITAL HUMAN NEED. SHE ALSO ASSUMED HER OWN CONSTANT SEVERITY WAS A UNIVERSAL TRAIT.
THE GHOST TWIN PROTECTED HER FROM SEEING HOW TRAUMA HAD STOLEN HER CAPACITY FOR JOY. I ASKED HER ONCE: "WHAT'S THE ADJECTIVE THAT LEAST DESCRIBES YOU?" SHE PAUSED AND SAID: "UNBURDENED."
MOM, WE HAVE TO BE ABLE TO
LAUGH!!
FRIENDS DESCRIBE THEIR IMMIGRANT PARENTS AS REFUSING TO SPEAK OF DARKNESS AND ONLY TELLING STORIES ABOUT THE LIGHT. BUT SOMEHOW MY MOM'S EXPERIENCES MADE HER WANT TO LIVE IN THE DARK, TO MAKE IT OUR SHARED HOME.
Ha? Ha? Hahaha?
AS AN ADULT, I HAVE MY OWN LIFE TO KEEP ME CONNECTED TO THE LIGHT EVEN AS I ENTER MY MOTHER'S CLAUSTROPHOBIC PATHOS. BUT WHEN I WAS YOUNGER, I FELT ONLY HELPLESS, CRUSHED BY ITS WEIGHT...

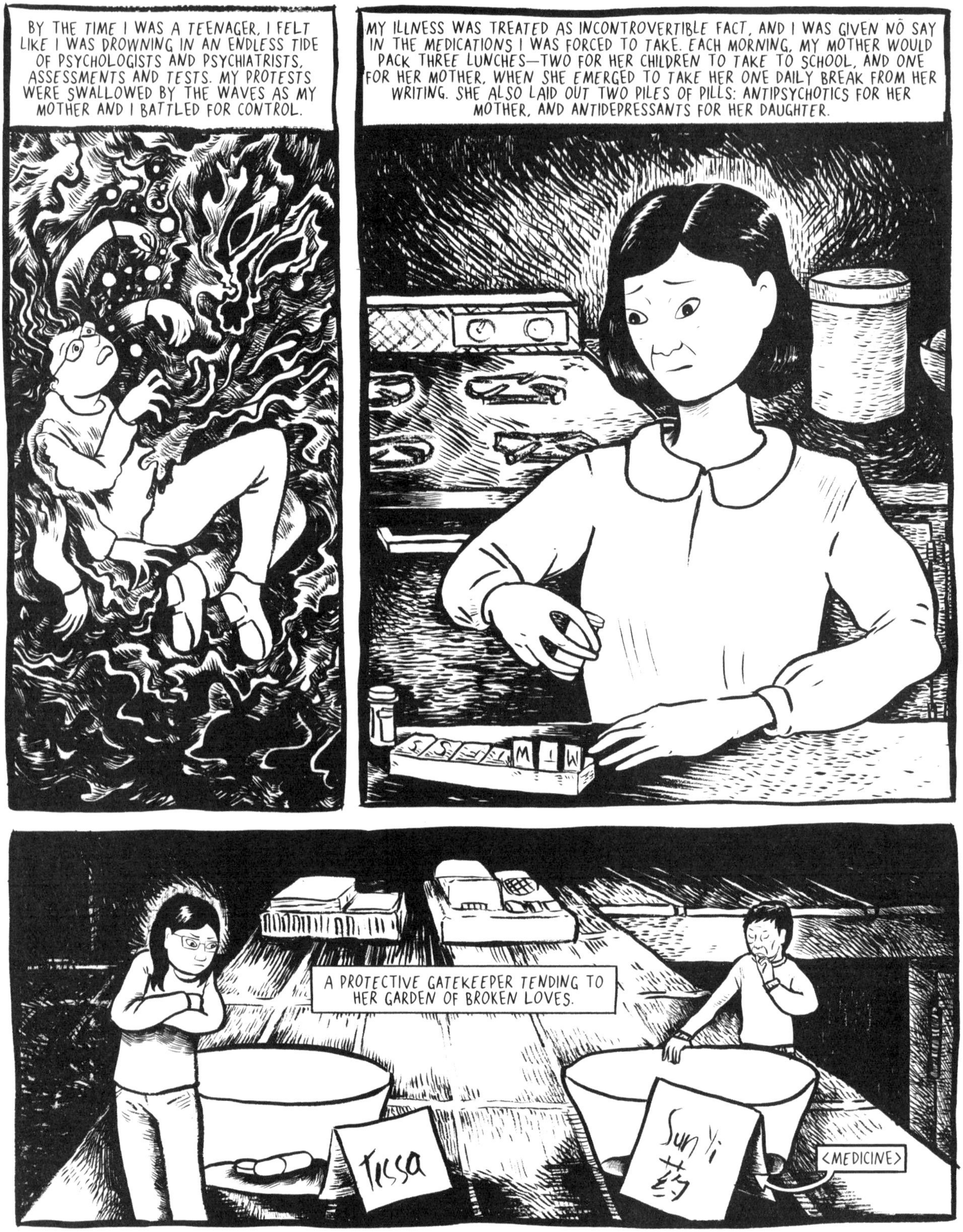
BY THE TIME I WAS A TEENAGER, I FELT LIKE I WAS DROWNING IN AN ENDLESS TIDE OF PSYCHOLOGISTS AND PSYCHIATRISTS, ASSESSMENTS AND TESTS. MY PROTESTS WERE SWALLOWED BY THE WAVES AS MY MOTHER AND I BATTLED FOR CONTROL.
MY ILLNESS WAS TREATED AS INCONTROVERTIBLE FACT, AND I WAS GIVEN NO SAY IN THE MEDICATIONS I WAS FORCED TO TAKE. EACH MORNING, MY MOTHER WOULD PACK THREE LUNCHES—TWO FOR HER CHILDREN TO TAKE TO SCHOOL, AND ONE FOR HER MOTHER, WHEN SHE EMERGED TO TAKE HER ONE DAILY BREAK FROM HER WRITING. SHE ALSO LAID OUT TWO PILES OF PILLS: ANTIPSYCHOTICS FOR HER MOTHER, AND ANTIDEPRESSANTS FOR HER DAUGHTER.
A PROTECTIVE GATEKEEPER TENDING TO HER GARDEN OF BROKEN LOVES.
Tessa
Sun Yi
药
<MEDICINE>

BUT OUR WAR WAS NOT VISIBLE OUTSIDE OF HOME.

I ENACTED MY OWN DUAL REALITY: I GOT STRAIGHT A'S AND HIGH TEST SCORES.

I EARNED ART AND WRITING AWARDS WHILE ALSO MANAGING TO BE A STAR ATHLETE.

I'D ALWAYS BEEN ATHLETIC, BUT IT SEEMED COMICALLY FITTING WHEN I PROVED TO HAVE AN INNATE GIFT FOR HURDLING.

I'D SPENT MY ENTIRE LIFE TRAINING FOR SOMETHING THAT DEMANDED RUNNING AS FAST AS YOU COULD WITH EXTREME CALCULATION, AND LETTING NOTHING SLOW YOU DOWN.

UNSTOPPABLE VELOCITY WAS THE LANGUAGE OF MY BONES.

BUT OUTSIDE MY VENEER OF ACHIEVEMENT, I THREW MYSELF INTO ANYTHING THAT MIGHT PROMISE A SHRED OF ESCAPE.

I WAS THOROUGH IN MY EMBRACE OF BEING A FUCKED-UP TEENAGER. WHAT CAN I SAY? I'VE NEVER BEEN ONE FOR HALF MEASURES.

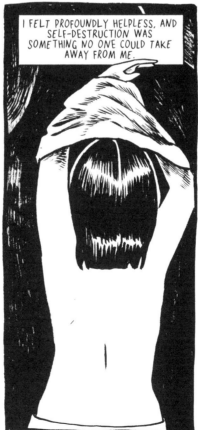

I FELT PROFOUNDLY HELPLESS, AND SELF-DESTRUCTION WAS SOMETHING NO ONE COULD TAKE AWAY FROM ME.

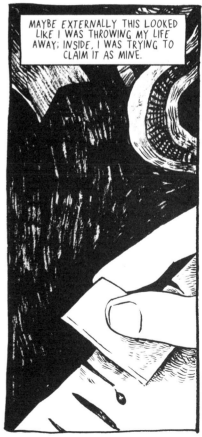

MAYBE EXTERNALLY THIS LOOKED LIKE I WAS THROWING MY LIFE AWAY; INSIDE, I WAS TRYING TO CLAIM IT AS MINE.

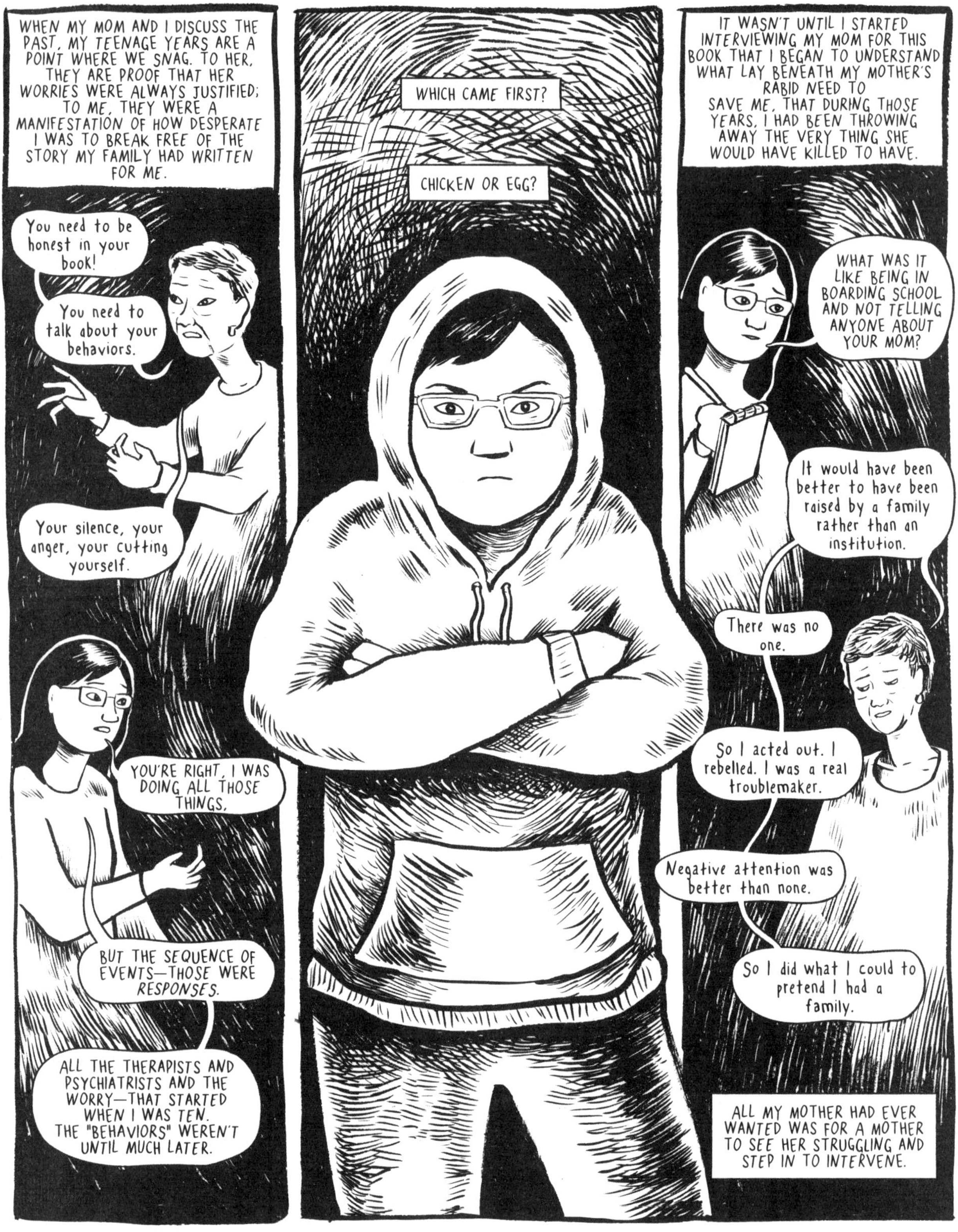
WHEN MY MOM AND I DISCUSS THE PAST, MY TEENAGE YEARS ARE A POINT WHERE WE SNAG. TO HER, THEY ARE PROOF THAT HER WORRIES WERE ALWAYS JUSTIFIED; TO ME, THEY WERE A MANIFESTATION OF HOW DESPERATE I WAS TO BREAK FREE OF THE STORY MY FAMILY HAD WRITTEN FOR ME.
You need to be honest in your book!
You need to talk about your behaviors.
Your silence, your anger, your cutting yourself.
YOU'RE RIGHT, I WAS DOING ALL THOSE THINGS,
BUT THE SEQUENCE OF EVENTS—THOSE WERE *RESPONSES*.
ALL THE THERAPISTS AND PSYCHIATRISTS AND THE WORRY—THAT STARTED WHEN I WAS *TEN*. THE "BEHAVIORS" WEREN'T UNTIL MUCH LATER.
WHICH CAME FIRST?
CHICKEN OR EGG?
IT WASN'T UNTIL I STARTED INTERVIEWING MY MOM FOR THIS BOOK THAT I BEGAN TO UNDERSTAND WHAT LAY BENEATH MY MOTHER'S RABID NEED TO SAVE ME, THAT DURING THOSE YEARS, I HAD BEEN THROWING AWAY THE VERY THING SHE WOULD HAVE KILLED TO HAVE.
WHAT WAS IT LIKE BEING IN BOARDING SCHOOL AND NOT TELLING ANYONE ABOUT YOUR MOM?
It would have been better to have been raised by a family rather than an institution.
There was no one.
So I acted out. I rebelled. I was a real troublemaker.
Negative attention was better than none.
So I did what I could to pretend I had a family.
ALL MY MOTHER HAD EVER WANTED WAS FOR A MOTHER TO SEE HER STRUGGLING AND STEP IN TO INTERVENE.

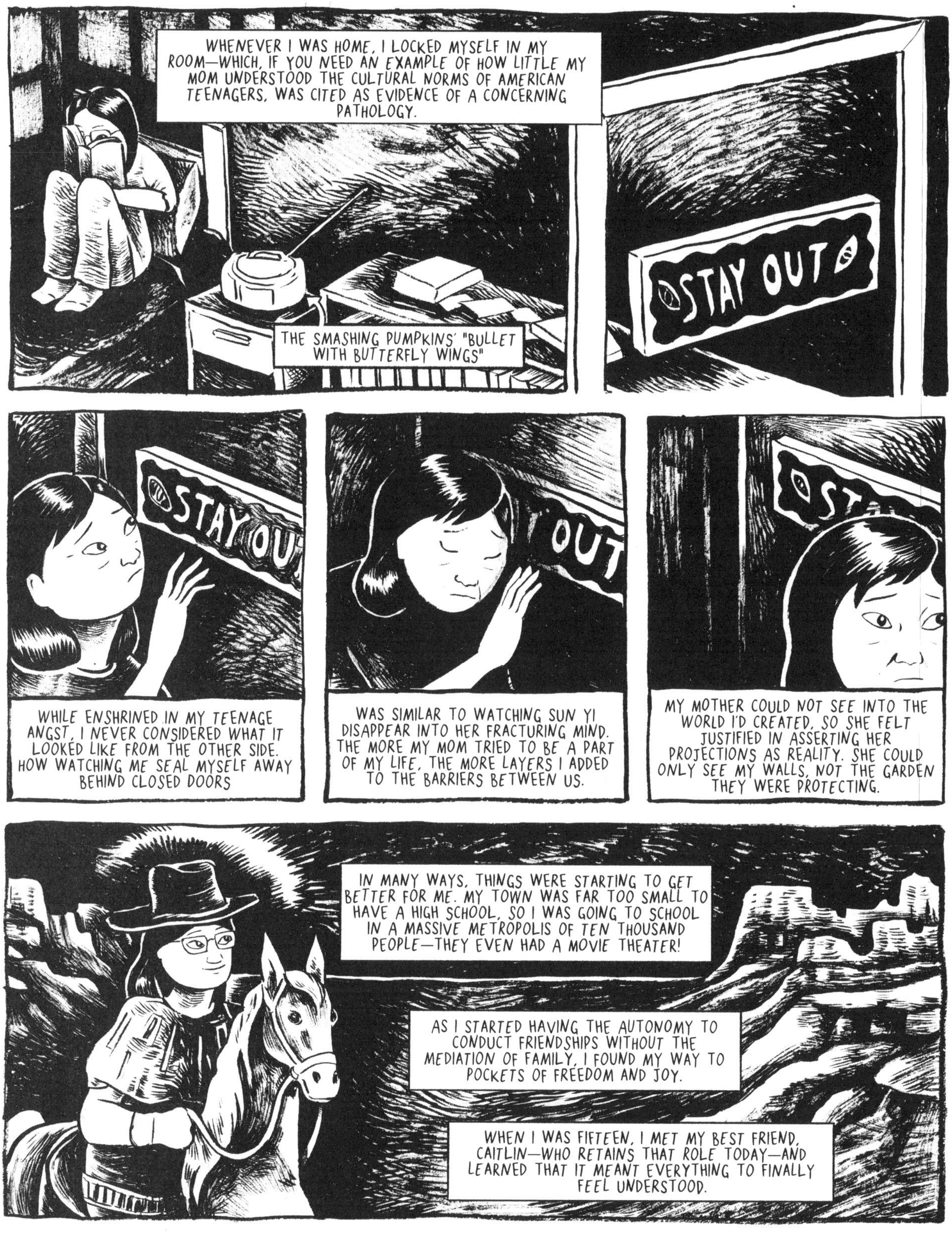
WHENEVER I WAS HOME, I LOCKED MYSELF IN MY ROOM—WHICH, IF YOU NEED AN EXAMPLE OF HOW LITTLE MY MOM UNDERSTOOD THE CULTURAL NORMS OF AMERICAN TEENAGERS, WAS CITED AS EVIDENCE OF A CONCERNING PATHOLOGY.
THE SMASHING PUMPKINS' "BULLET WITH BUTTERFLY WINGS"
STAY OUT
STAY OUT
WHILE ENSHRINED IN MY TEENAGE ANGST, I NEVER CONSIDERED WHAT IT LOOKED LIKE FROM THE OTHER SIDE. HOW WATCHING ME SEAL MYSELF AWAY BEHIND CLOSED DOORS
OUT
WAS SIMILAR TO WATCHING SUN YI DISAPPEAR INTO HER FRACTURING MIND. THE MORE MY MOM TRIED TO BE A PART OF MY LIFE, THE MORE LAYERS I ADDED TO THE BARRIERS BETWEEN US.
MY MOTHER COULD NOT SEE INTO THE WORLD I'D CREATED, SO SHE FELT JUSTIFIED IN ASSERTING HER PROJECTIONS AS REALITY. SHE COULD ONLY SEE MY WALLS, NOT THE GARDEN THEY WERE PROTECTING.
IN MANY WAYS, THINGS WERE STARTING TO GET BETTER FOR ME. MY TOWN WAS FAR TOO SMALL TO HAVE A HIGH SCHOOL, SO I WAS GOING TO SCHOOL IN A MASSIVE METROPOLIS OF TEN THOUSAND PEOPLE—THEY EVEN HAD A MOVIE THEATER!
AS I STARTED HAVING THE AUTONOMY TO CONDUCT FRIENDSHIPS WITHOUT THE MEDIATION OF FAMILY, I FOUND MY WAY TO POCKETS OF FREEDOM AND JOY.
WHEN I WAS FIFTEEN, I MET MY BEST FRIEND, CAITLIN—WHO RETAINS THAT ROLE TODAY—AND LEARNED THAT IT MEANT EVERYTHING TO FINALLY FEEL UNDERSTOOD.

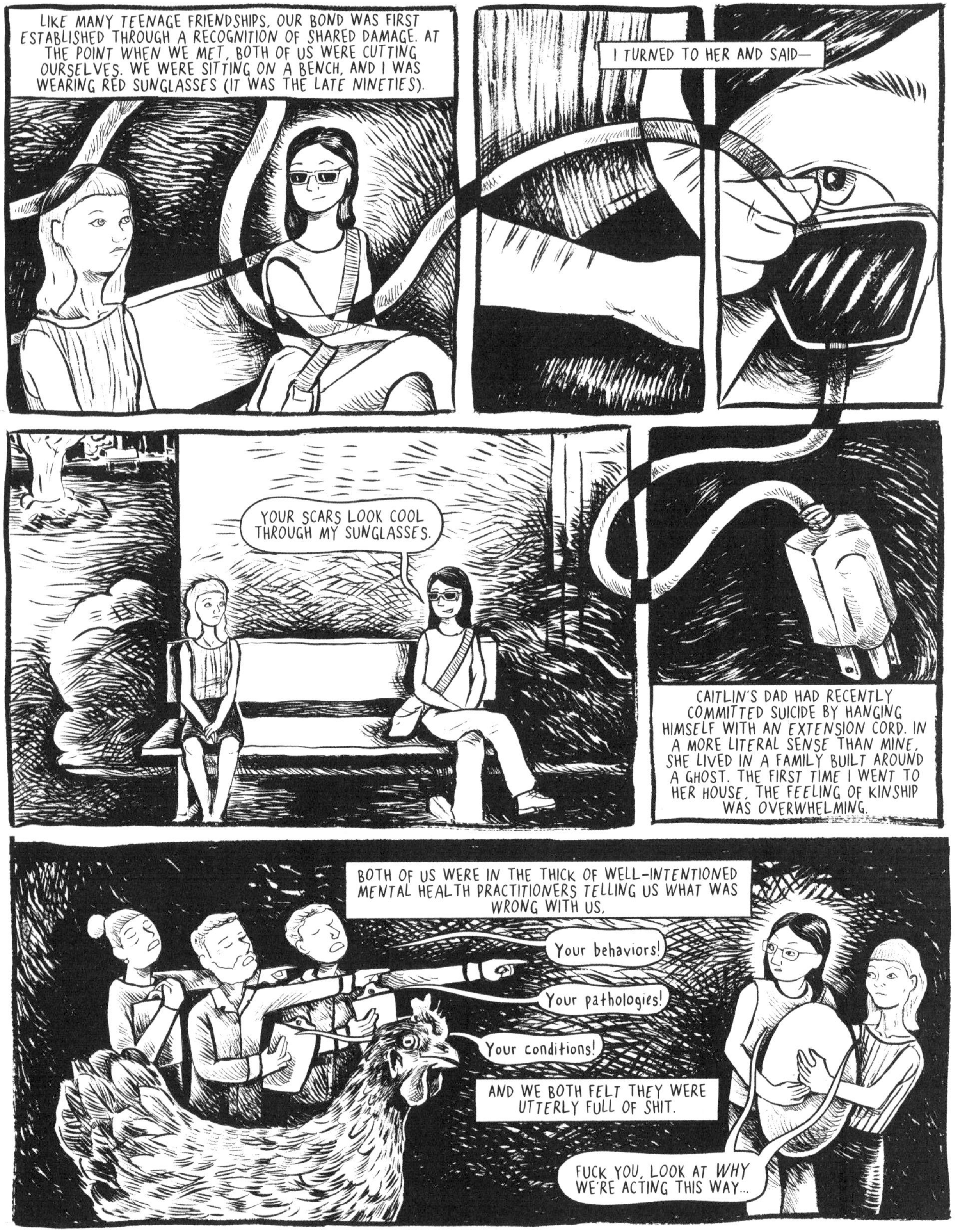
LIKE MANY TEENAGE FRIENDSHIPS, OUR BOND WAS FIRST ESTABLISHED THROUGH A RECOGNITION OF SHARED DAMAGE. AT THE POINT WHEN WE MET, BOTH OF US WERE CUTTING OURSELVES. WE WERE SITTING ON A BENCH, AND I WAS WEARING RED SUNGLASSES (IT WAS THE LATE NINETIES).
I TURNED TO HER AND SAID—
YOUR SCARS LOOK COOL THROUGH MY SUNGLASSES.
CAITLIN'S DAD HAD RECENTLY COMMITTED SUICIDE BY HANGING HIMSELF WITH AN EXTENSION CORD. IN A MORE LITERAL SENSE THAN MINE, SHE LIVED IN A FAMILY BUILT AROUND A GHOST. THE FIRST TIME I WENT TO HER HOUSE, THE FEELING OF KINSHIP WAS OVERWHELMING.
BOTH OF US WERE IN THE THICK OF WELL-INTENTIONED MENTAL HEALTH PRACTITIONERS TELLING US WHAT WAS WRONG WITH US.
Your behaviors!
Your pathologies!
Your conditions!
AND WE BOTH FELT THEY WERE UTTERLY FULL OF SHIT.
FUCK YOU, LOOK AT WHY WE'RE ACTING THIS WAY...

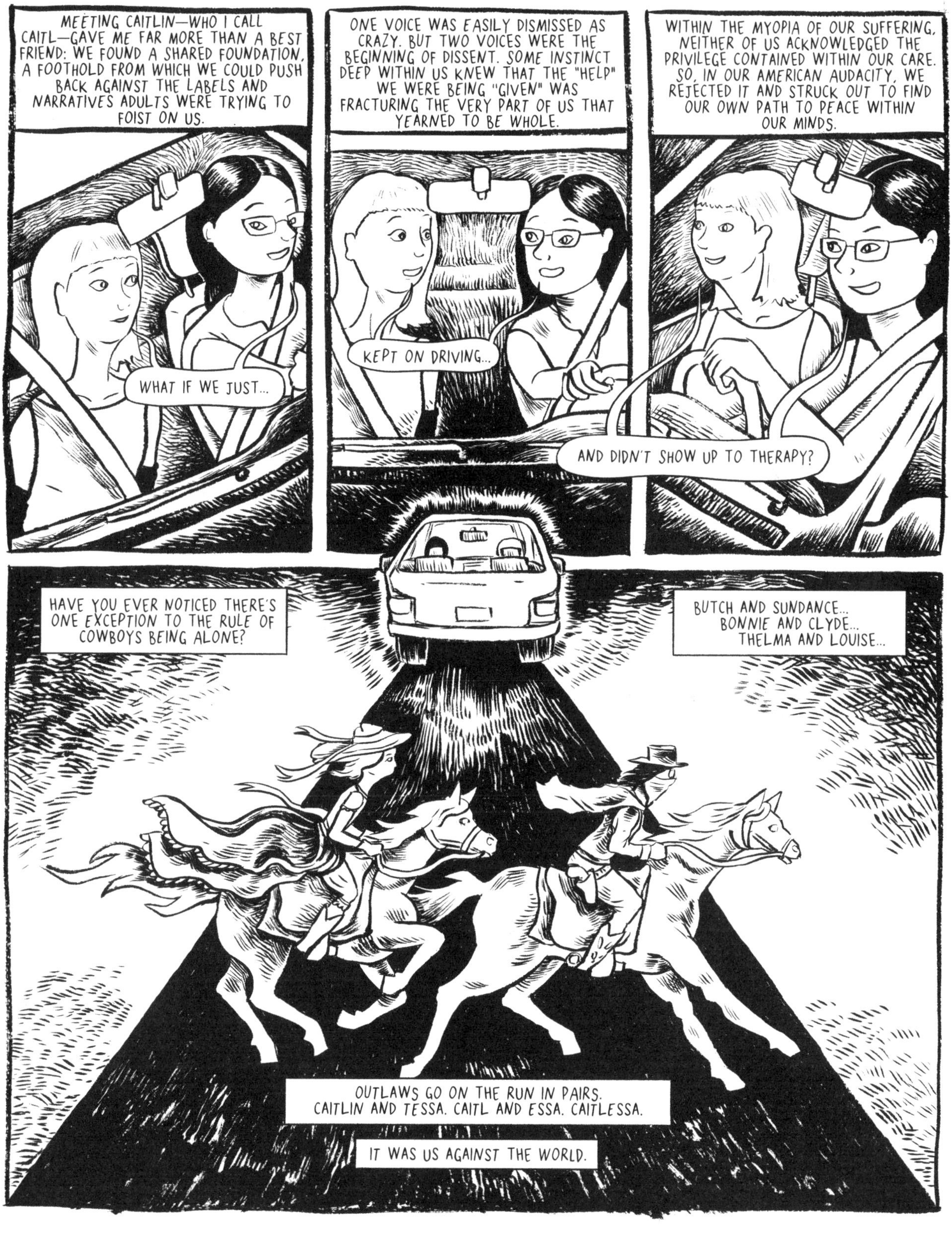
MEETING CAITLIN—WHO I CALL CAITL—GAVE ME FAR MORE THAN A BEST FRIEND: WE FOUND A SHARED FOUNDATION, A FOOTHOLD FROM WHICH WE COULD PUSH BACK AGAINST THE LABELS AND NARRATIVES ADULTS WERE TRYING TO FOIST ON US.
WHAT IF WE JUST...
ONE VOICE WAS EASILY DISMISSED AS CRAZY. BUT TWO VOICES WERE THE BEGINNING OF DISSENT. SOME INSTINCT DEEP WITHIN US KNEW THAT THE "HELP" WE WERE BEING "GIVEN" WAS FRACTURING THE VERY PART OF US THAT YEARNED TO BE WHOLE.
KEPT ON DRIVING...
WITHIN THE MYOPIA OF OUR SUFFERING, NEITHER OF US ACKNOWLEDGED THE PRIVILEGE CONTAINED WITHIN OUR CARE. SO, IN OUR AMERICAN AUDACITY, WE REJECTED IT AND STRUCK OUT TO FIND OUR OWN PATH TO PEACE WITHIN OUR MINDS.
AND DIDN'T SHOW UP TO THERAPY?
HAVE YOU EVER NOTICED THERE'S ONE EXCEPTION TO THE RULE OF COWBOYS BEING ALONE?
BUTCH AND SUNDANCE... BONNIE AND CLYDE... THELMA AND LOUISE...
OUTLAWS GO ON THE RUN IN PAIRS. CAITLIN AND TESSA. CAITL AND ESSA. CAITLESSA.
IT WAS US AGAINST THE WORLD.

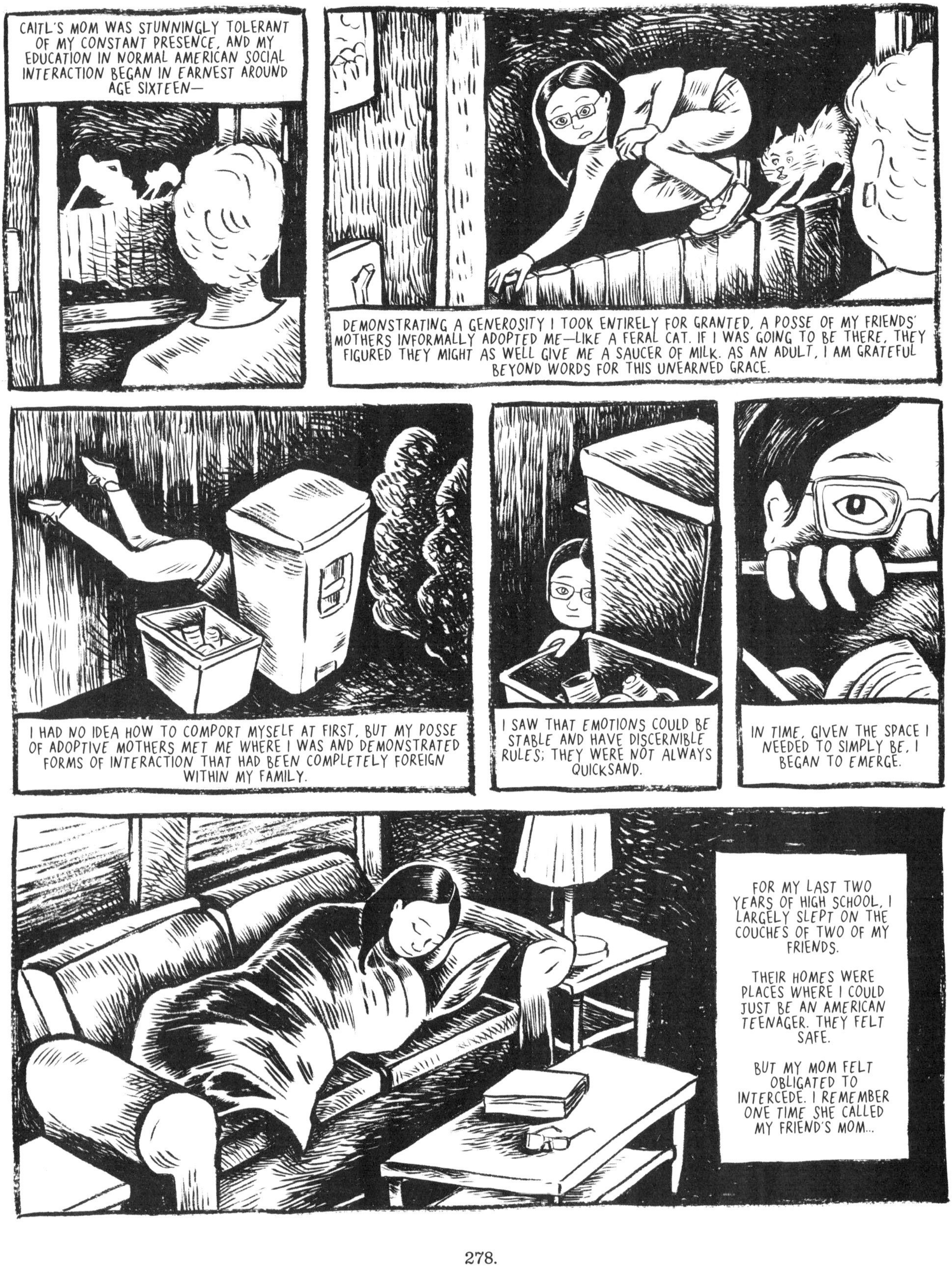
CAITL'S MOM WAS STUNNINGLY TOLERANT OF MY CONSTANT PRESENCE, AND MY EDUCATION IN NORMAL AMERICAN SOCIAL INTERACTION BEGAN IN EARNEST AROUND AGE SIXTEEN—
DEMONSTRATING A GENEROSITY I TOOK ENTIRELY FOR GRANTED, A POSSE OF MY FRIENDS' MOTHERS INFORMALLY ADOPTED ME—LIKE A FERAL CAT. IF I WAS GOING TO BE THERE, THEY FIGURED THEY MIGHT AS WELL GIVE ME A SAUCER OF MILK. AS AN ADULT, I AM GRATEFUL BEYOND WORDS FOR THIS UNEARNED GRACE.
I HAD NO IDEA HOW TO COMPORT MYSELF AT FIRST, BUT MY POSSE OF ADOPTIVE MOTHERS MET ME WHERE I WAS AND DEMONSTRATED FORMS OF INTERACTION THAT HAD BEEN COMPLETELY FOREIGN WITHIN MY FAMILY.
I SAW THAT EMOTIONS COULD BE STABLE AND HAVE DISCERNIBLE RULES; THEY WERE NOT ALWAYS QUICKSAND.
IN TIME, GIVEN THE SPACE I NEEDED TO SIMPLY BE, I BEGAN TO EMERGE.
FOR MY LAST TWO YEARS OF HIGH SCHOOL, I LARGELY SLEPT ON THE COUCHES OF TWO OF MY FRIENDS.
THEIR HOMES WERE PLACES WHERE I COULD JUST BE AN AMERICAN TEENAGER. THEY FELT SAFE.
BUT MY MOM FELT OBLIGATED TO INTERCEDE. I REMEMBER ONE TIME SHE CALLED MY FRIEND'S MOM...

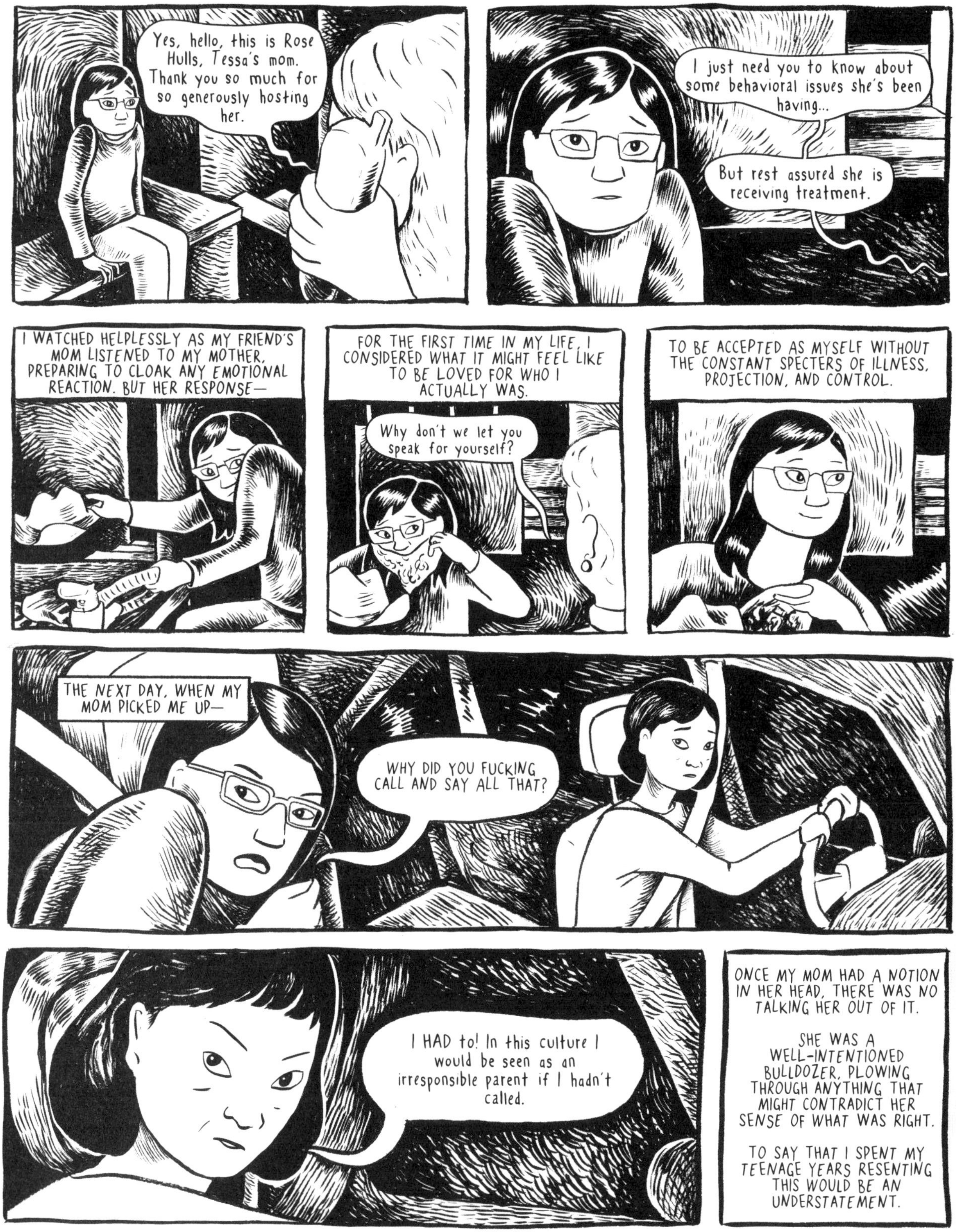

Yes, hello, this is Rose Hulls, Tessa's mom. Thank you so much for so generously hosting her.
I just need you to know about some behavioral issues she's been having...
But rest assured she is receiving treatment.
I WATCHED HELPLESSLY AS MY FRIEND'S MOM LISTENED TO MY MOTHER, PREPARING TO CLOAK ANY EMOTIONAL REACTION. BUT HER RESPONSE—
FOR THE FIRST TIME IN MY LIFE, I CONSIDERED WHAT IT MIGHT FEEL LIKE TO BE LOVED FOR WHO I ACTUALLY WAS.
Why don't we let you speak for yourself?
TO BE ACCEPTED AS MYSELF WITHOUT THE CONSTANT SPECTERS OF ILLNESS, PROJECTION, AND CONTROL.
THE NEXT DAY, WHEN MY MOM PICKED ME UP—
WHY DID YOU FUCKING CALL AND SAY ALL THAT?
I HAD to! In this culture I would be seen as an irresponsible parent if I hadn't called.
ONCE MY MOM HAD A NOTION IN HER HEAD, THERE WAS NO TALKING HER OUT OF IT.
SHE WAS A WELL-INTENTIONED BULLDOZER, PLOWING THROUGH ANYTHING THAT MIGHT CONTRADICT HER SENSE OF WHAT WAS RIGHT.
TO SAY THAT I SPENT MY TEENAGE YEARS RESENTING THIS WOULD BE AN UNDERSTATEMENT.

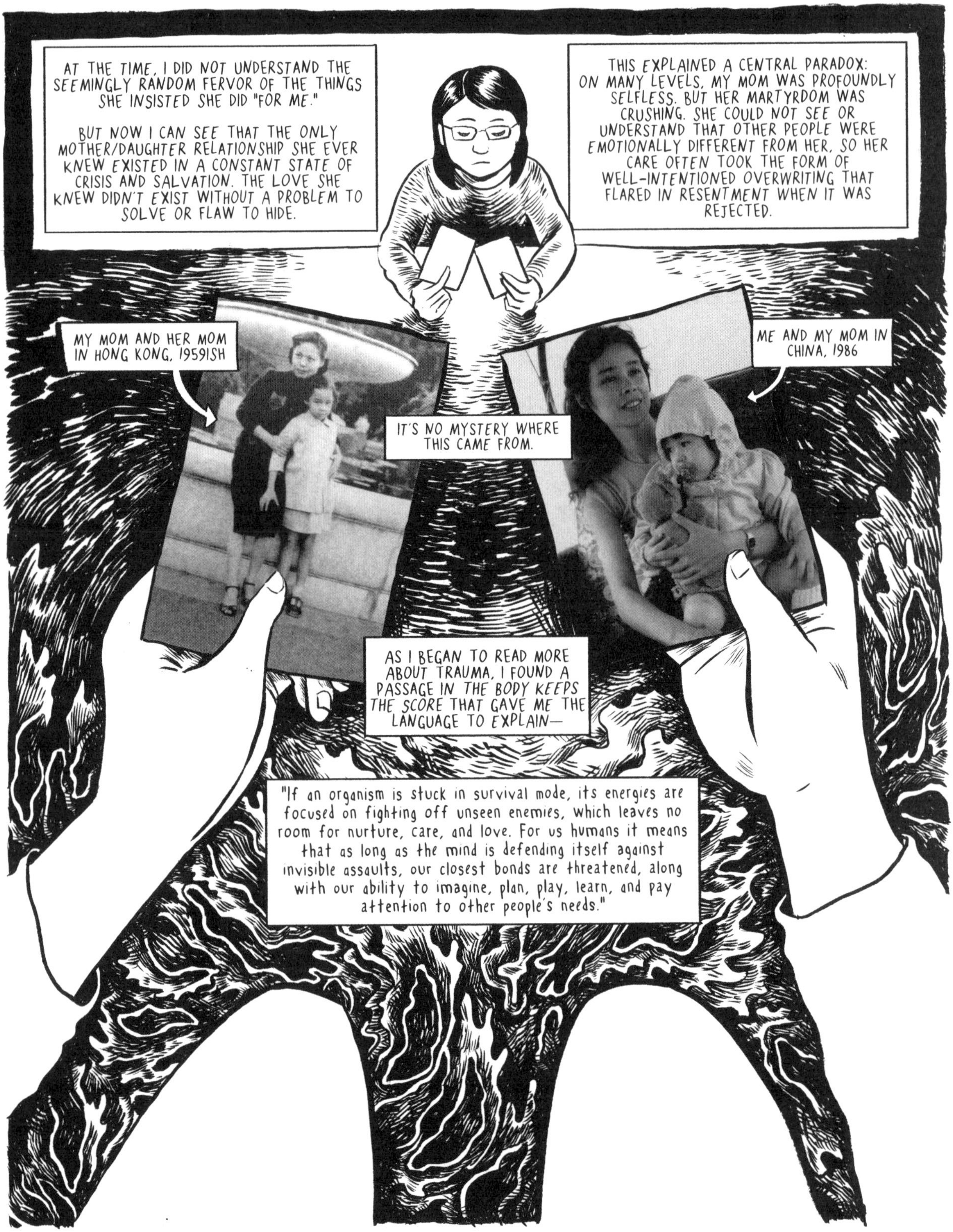
AT THE TIME, I DID NOT UNDERSTAND THE SEEMINGLY RANDOM FERVOR OF THE THINGS SHE INSISTED SHE DID "FOR ME."
BUT NOW I CAN SEE THAT THE ONLY MOTHER/DAUGHTER RELATIONSHIP SHE EVER KNEW EXISTED IN A CONSTANT STATE OF CRISIS AND SALVATION. THE LOVE SHE KNEW DIDN'T EXIST WITHOUT A PROBLEM TO SOLVE OR FLAW TO HIDE.
THIS EXPLAINED A CENTRAL PARADOX: ON MANY LEVELS, MY MOM WAS PROFOUNDLY SELFLESS. BUT HER MARTYRDOM WAS CRUSHING. SHE COULD NOT SEE OR UNDERSTAND THAT OTHER PEOPLE WERE EMOTIONALLY DIFFERENT FROM HER, SO HER CARE OFTEN TOOK THE FORM OF WELL-INTENTIONED OVERWRITING THAT FLARED IN RESENTMENT WHEN IT WAS REJECTED.
MY MOM AND HER MOM IN HONG KONG, 1959ISH
ME AND MY MOM IN CHINA, 1986
IT'S NO MYSTERY WHERE THIS CAME FROM.
AS I BEGAN TO READ MORE ABOUT TRAUMA, I FOUND A PASSAGE IN *THE BODY KEEPS THE SCORE* THAT GAVE ME THE LANGUAGE TO EXPLAIN—
"If an organism is stuck in survival mode, its energies are focused on fighting off unseen enemies, which leaves no room for nurture, care, and love. For us humans it means that as long as the mind is defending itself against invisible assaults, our closest bonds are threatened, along with our ability to imagine, plan, play, learn, and pay attention to other people's needs."

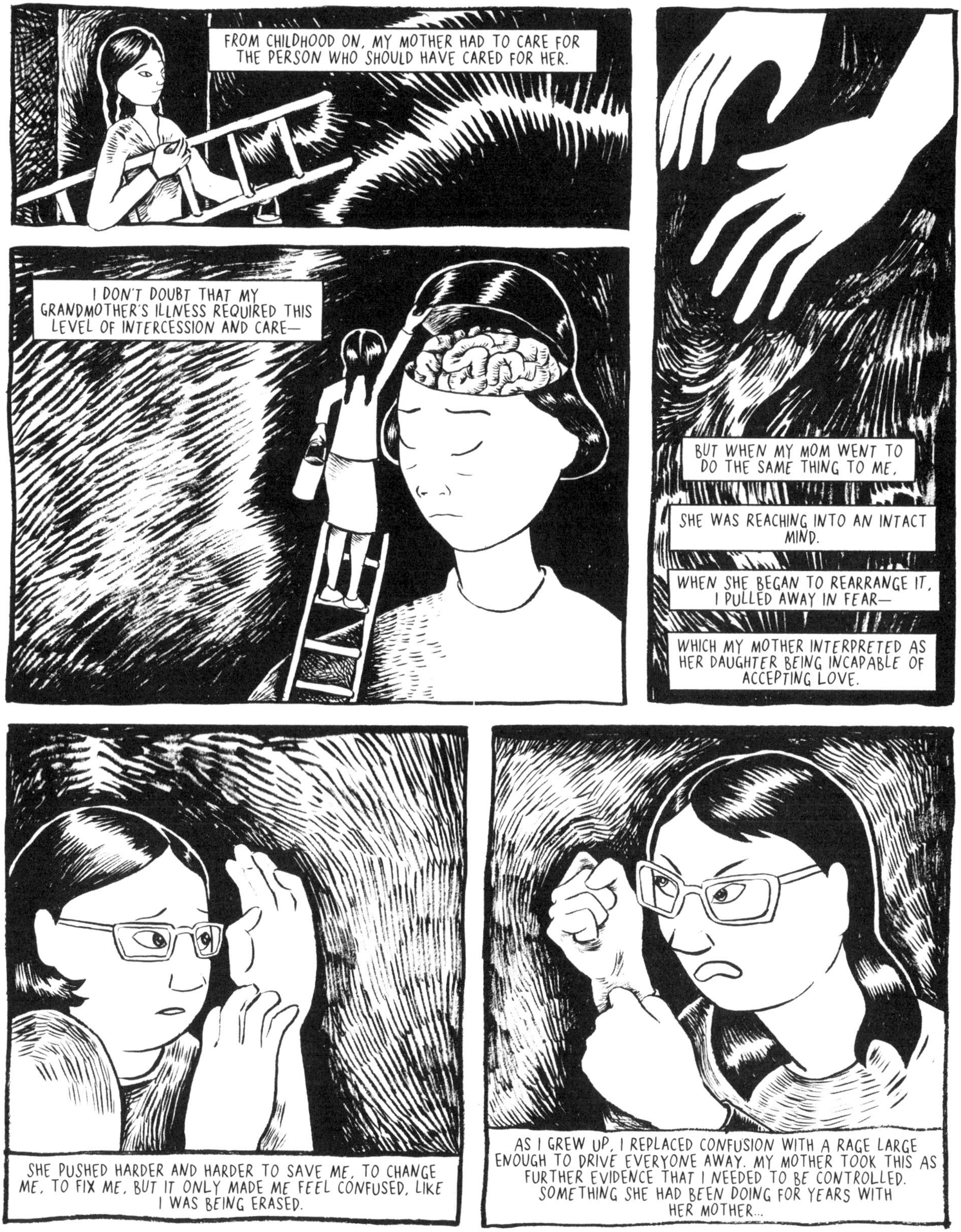
FROM CHILDHOOD ON, MY MOTHER HAD TO CARE FOR THE PERSON WHO SHOULD HAVE CARED FOR HER.
I DON'T DOUBT THAT MY GRANDMOTHER'S ILLNESS REQUIRED THIS LEVEL OF INTERCESSION AND CARE—
BUT WHEN MY MOM WENT TO DO THE SAME THING TO ME,
SHE WAS REACHING INTO AN INTACT MIND.
WHEN SHE BEGAN TO REARRANGE IT, I PULLED AWAY IN FEAR—
WHICH MY MOTHER INTERPRETED AS HER DAUGHTER BEING INCAPABLE OF ACCEPTING LOVE.
SHE PUSHED HARDER AND HARDER TO SAVE ME, TO CHANGE ME, TO FIX ME, BUT IT ONLY MADE ME FEEL CONFUSED, LIKE I WAS BEING ERASED.
AS I GREW UP, I REPLACED CONFUSION WITH A RAGE LARGE ENOUGH TO DRIVE EVERYONE AWAY. MY MOTHER TOOK THIS AS FURTHER EVIDENCE THAT I NEEDED TO BE CONTROLLED. SOMETHING SHE HAD BEEN DOING FOR YEARS WITH HER MOTHER...

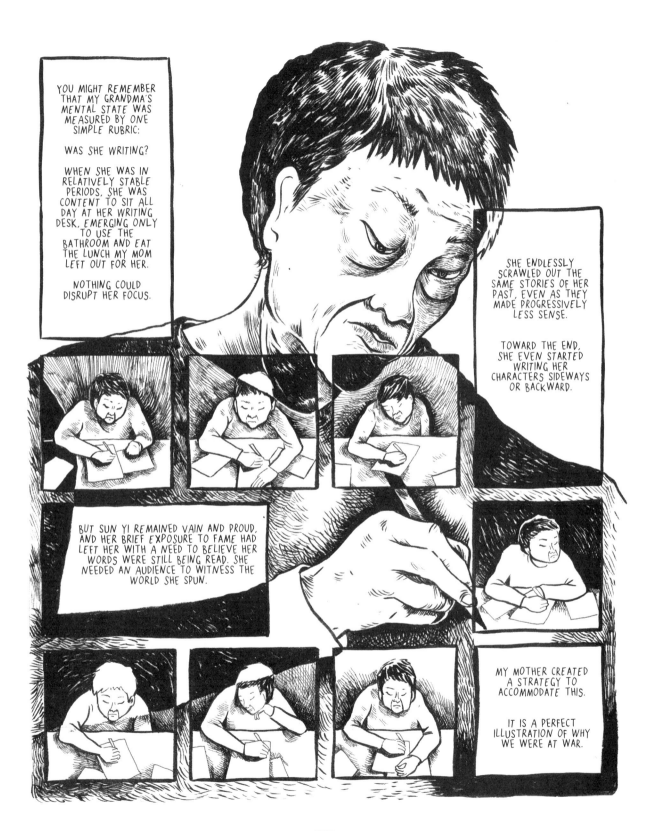

YOU MIGHT REMEMBER THAT MY GRANDMA'S MENTAL STATE WAS MEASURED BY ONE SIMPLE RUBRIC:

WAS SHE WRITING?

WHEN SHE WAS IN RELATIVELY STABLE PERIODS, SHE WAS CONTENT TO SIT ALL DAY AT HER WRITING DESK, EMERGING ONLY TO USE THE BATHROOM AND EAT THE LUNCH MY MOM LEFT OUT FOR HER.

NOTHING COULD DISRUPT HER FOCUS.

SHE ENDLESSLY SCRAWLED OUT THE SAME STORIES OF HER PAST, EVEN AS THEY MADE PROGRESSIVELY LESS SENSE.

TOWARD THE END, SHE EVEN STARTED WRITING HER CHARACTERS SIDEWAYS OR BACKWARD.

BUT SUN YI REMAINED VAIN AND PROUD, AND HER BRIEF EXPOSURE TO FAME HAD LEFT HER WITH A NEED TO BELIEVE HER WORDS WERE STILL BEING READ. SHE NEEDED AN AUDIENCE TO WITNESS THE WORLD SHE SPUN.

MY MOTHER CREATED A STRATEGY TO ACCOMMODATE THIS.

IT IS A PERFECT ILLUSTRATION OF WHY WE WERE AT WAR.

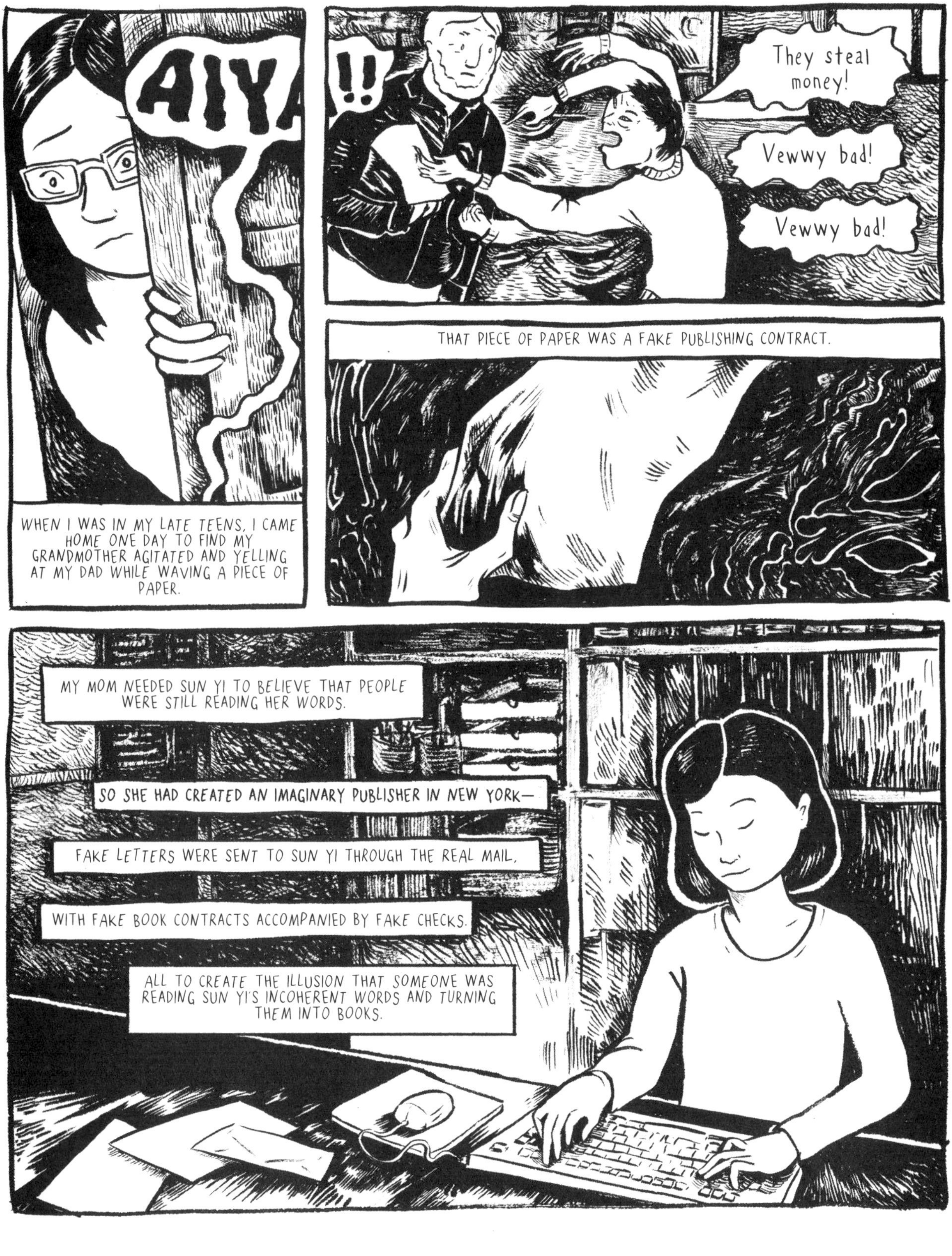
AIYA!!
When I was in my late teens, I came home one day to find my grandmother agitated and yelling at my dad while waving a piece of paper.
They steal money!
Vewwy bad!
Vewwy bad!
That piece of paper was a fake publishing contract.
My mom needed Sun Yi to believe that people were still reading her words.
So she had created an imaginary publisher in New York—
fake letters were sent to Sun Yi through the real mail,
with fake book contracts accompanied by fake checks.
All to create the illusion that someone was reading Sun Yi's incoherent words and turning them into books.

SHE WENT SO FAR AS TO HAVE THEM PRINTED AND BOUND SO SUN YI COULD RECEIVE "PUBLISHED COPIES" OF HER WORKS.

THAT DAY WITH THE FAKE CONTRACT...

Look, Sun Yi. You have been paid. No one is cheating you.

You are okay.

Here, Tessa will come help you.

I TOOK THE PAPER IN MY HAND AND REPEATED THE FAMILY LIE—

SEE, SUN YI? IT SAYS RIGHT HERE—NO ONE TOOK YOUR MONEY.

YOU ARE SAFE.

BUT INSIDE ME EVERYTHING WAS SCREAMING:

THIS IS WRONG THIS IS WRONG THIS IS WRONG THIS IS WRONG THIS IS WRONG

MY MOM AND I ARGUED ABOUT IT—

YOU'RE TAKING SOMEONE WITH A MENTAL ILLNESS THAT MAKES HER PARANOID THAT PEOPLE ARE LYING TO HER AND SHAPING HER REALITY...

AND YOU'RE LYING TO HER AND SHAPING HER REALITY!

It's a deception born from great love!!

I DIDN'T DISAGREE.

I ALSO DIDN'T THINK THAT LOVE MADE IT RIGHT.

284.

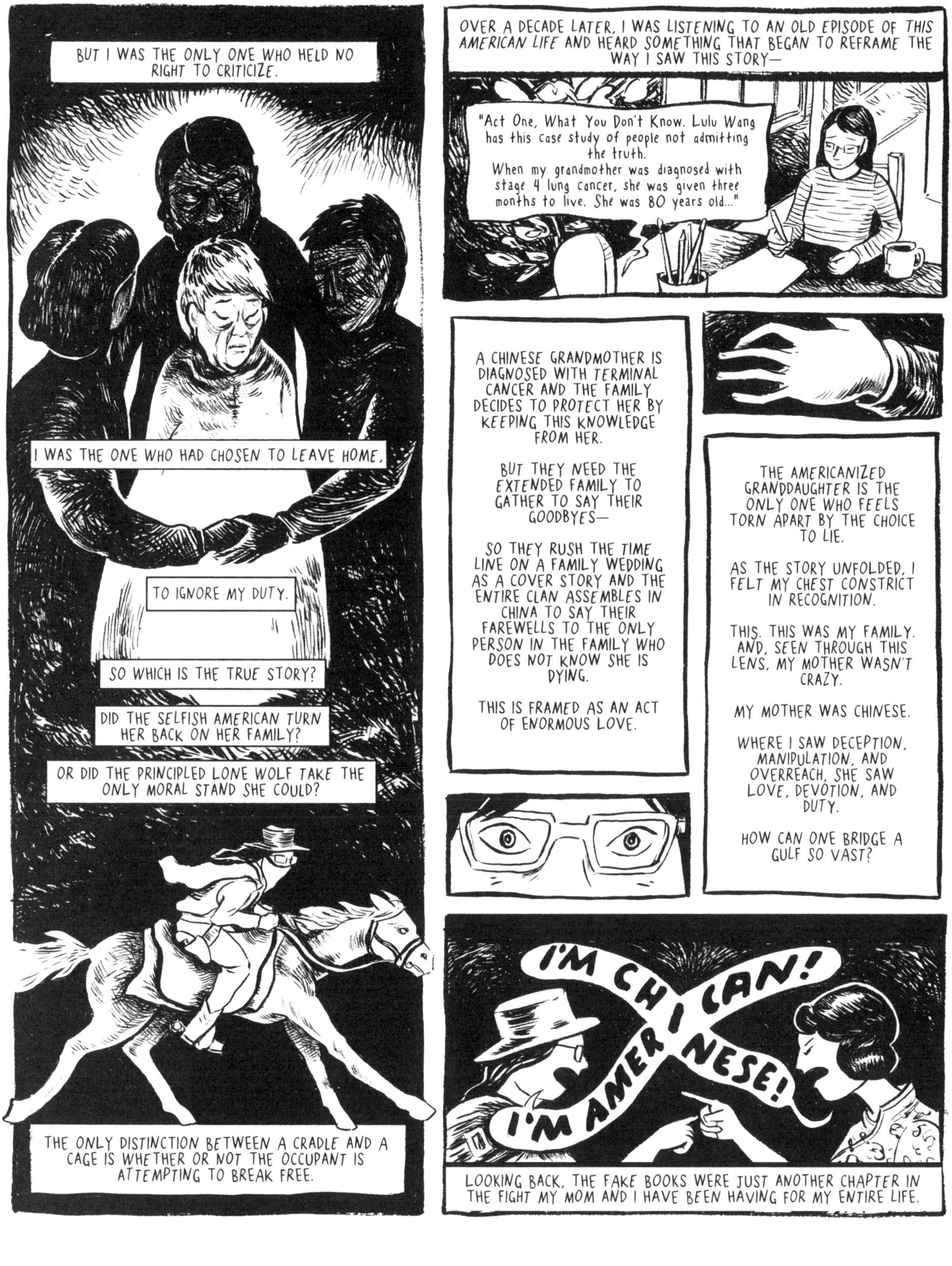
BUT I WAS THE ONLY ONE WHO HELD NO RIGHT TO CRITICIZE.
I WAS THE ONE WHO HAD CHOSEN TO LEAVE HOME,
TO IGNORE MY DUTY.
SO WHICH IS THE TRUE STORY?
DID THE SELFISH AMERICAN TURN HER BACK ON HER FAMILY?
OR DID THE PRINCIPLED LONE WOLF TAKE THE ONLY MORAL STAND SHE COULD?
THE ONLY DISTINCTION BETWEEN A CRADLE AND A CAGE IS WHETHER OR NOT THE OCCUPANT IS ATTEMPTING TO BREAK FREE.
OVER A DECADE LATER, I WAS LISTENING TO AN OLD EPISODE OF *THIS AMERICAN LIFE* AND HEARD SOMETHING THAT BEGAN TO REFRAME THE WAY I SAW THIS STORY—
"Act One, What You Don't Know. Lulu Wang has this case study of people not admitting the truth.
When my grandmother was diagnosed with stage 4 lung cancer, she was given three months to live. She was 80 years old..."
A CHINESE GRANDMOTHER IS DIAGNOSED WITH TERMINAL CANCER AND THE FAMILY DECIDES TO PROTECT HER BY KEEPING THIS KNOWLEDGE FROM HER.
BUT THEY NEED THE EXTENDED FAMILY TO GATHER TO SAY THEIR GOODBYES—
SO THEY RUSH THE TIME LINE ON A FAMILY WEDDING AS A COVER STORY AND THE ENTIRE CLAN ASSEMBLES IN CHINA TO SAY THEIR FAREWELLS TO THE ONLY PERSON IN THE FAMILY WHO DOES NOT KNOW SHE IS DYING.
THIS IS FRAMED AS AN ACT OF ENORMOUS LOVE.
THE AMERICANIZED GRANDDAUGHTER IS THE ONLY ONE WHO FEELS TORN APART BY THE CHOICE TO LIE.
AS THE STORY UNFOLDED, I FELT MY CHEST CONSTRICT IN RECOGNITION.
THIS. THIS WAS MY FAMILY. AND, SEEN THROUGH THIS LENS, MY MOTHER WASN'T CRAZY.
MY MOTHER WAS CHINESE.
WHERE I SAW DECEPTION, MANIPULATION, AND OVERREACH, SHE SAW LOVE, DEVOTION, AND DUTY.
HOW CAN ONE BRIDGE A GULF SO VAST?
I'M CHINESE!
I'M AMERICAN!
LOOKING BACK, THE FAKE BOOKS WERE JUST ANOTHER CHAPTER IN THE FIGHT MY MOM AND I HAVE BEEN HAVING FOR MY ENTIRE LIFE.

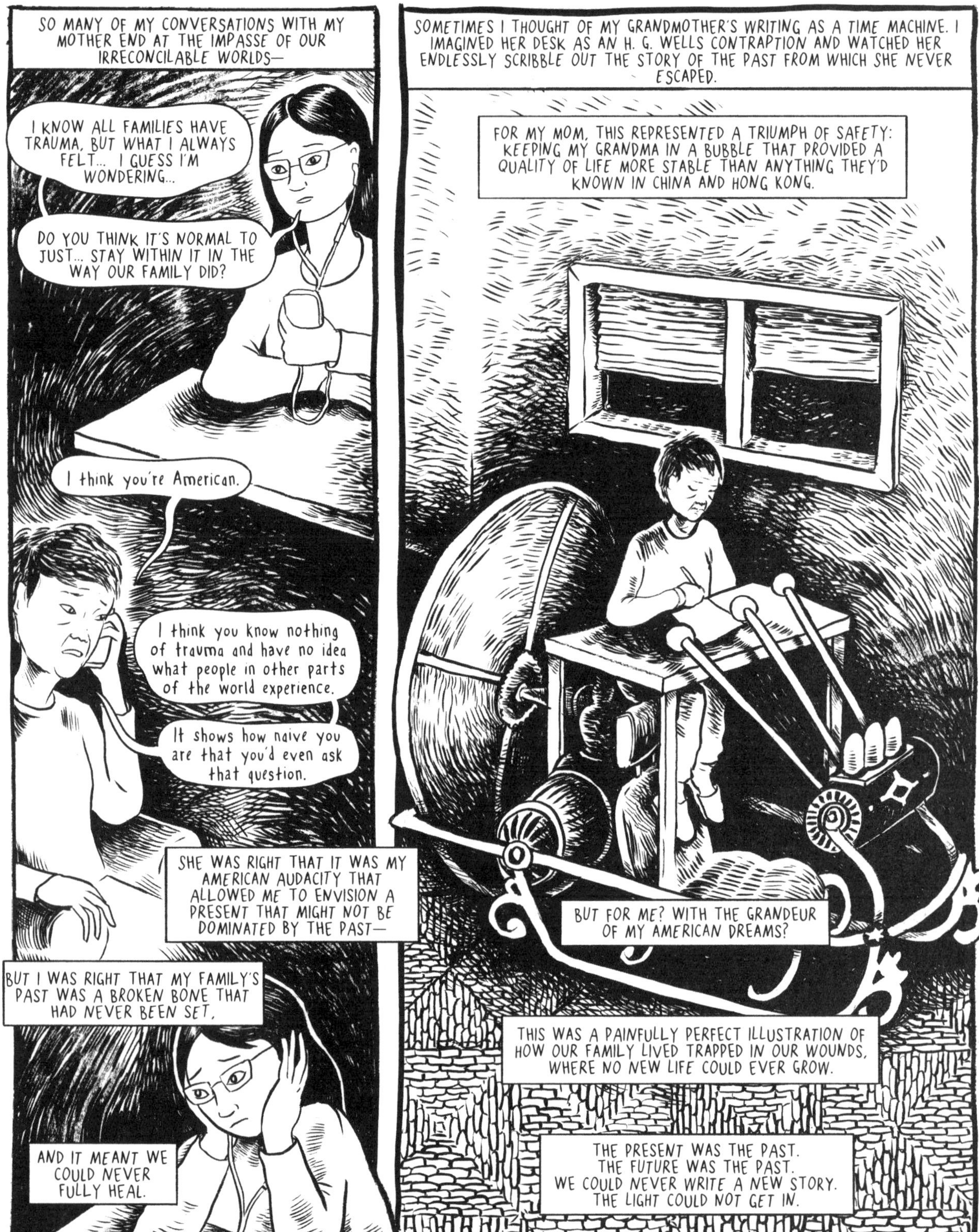
SO MANY OF MY CONVERSATIONS WITH MY MOTHER END AT THE IMPASSE OF OUR IRRECONCILABLE WORLDS—
I KNOW ALL FAMILIES HAVE TRAUMA, BUT WHAT I ALWAYS FELT... I GUESS I'M WONDERING...
DO YOU THINK IT'S NORMAL TO JUST... STAY WITHIN IT IN THE WAY OUR FAMILY DID?
I think you're American.
I think you know nothing of trauma and have no idea what people in other parts of the world experience.
It shows how naive you are that you'd even ask that question.
SHE WAS RIGHT THAT IT WAS MY AMERICAN AUDACITY THAT ALLOWED ME TO ENVISION A PRESENT THAT MIGHT NOT BE DOMINATED BY THE PAST—
BUT I WAS RIGHT THAT MY FAMILY'S PAST WAS A BROKEN BONE THAT HAD NEVER BEEN SET,
AND IT MEANT WE COULD NEVER FULLY HEAL.
SOMETIMES I THOUGHT OF MY GRANDMOTHER'S WRITING AS A TIME MACHINE. I IMAGINED HER DESK AS AN H. G. WELLS CONTRAPTION AND WATCHED HER ENDLESSLY SCRIBBLE OUT THE STORY OF THE PAST FROM WHICH SHE NEVER ESCAPED.
FOR MY MOM, THIS REPRESENTED A TRIUMPH OF SAFETY: KEEPING MY GRANDMA IN A BUBBLE THAT PROVIDED A QUALITY OF LIFE MORE STABLE THAN ANYTHING THEY'D KNOWN IN CHINA AND HONG KONG.
BUT FOR ME? WITH THE GRANDEUR OF MY AMERICAN DREAMS?
THIS WAS A PAINFULLY PERFECT ILLUSTRATION OF HOW OUR FAMILY LIVED TRAPPED IN OUR WOUNDS, WHERE NO NEW LIFE COULD EVER GROW.
THE PRESENT WAS THE PAST.
THE FUTURE WAS THE PAST.
WE COULD NEVER WRITE A NEW STORY.
THE LIGHT COULD NOT GET IN.

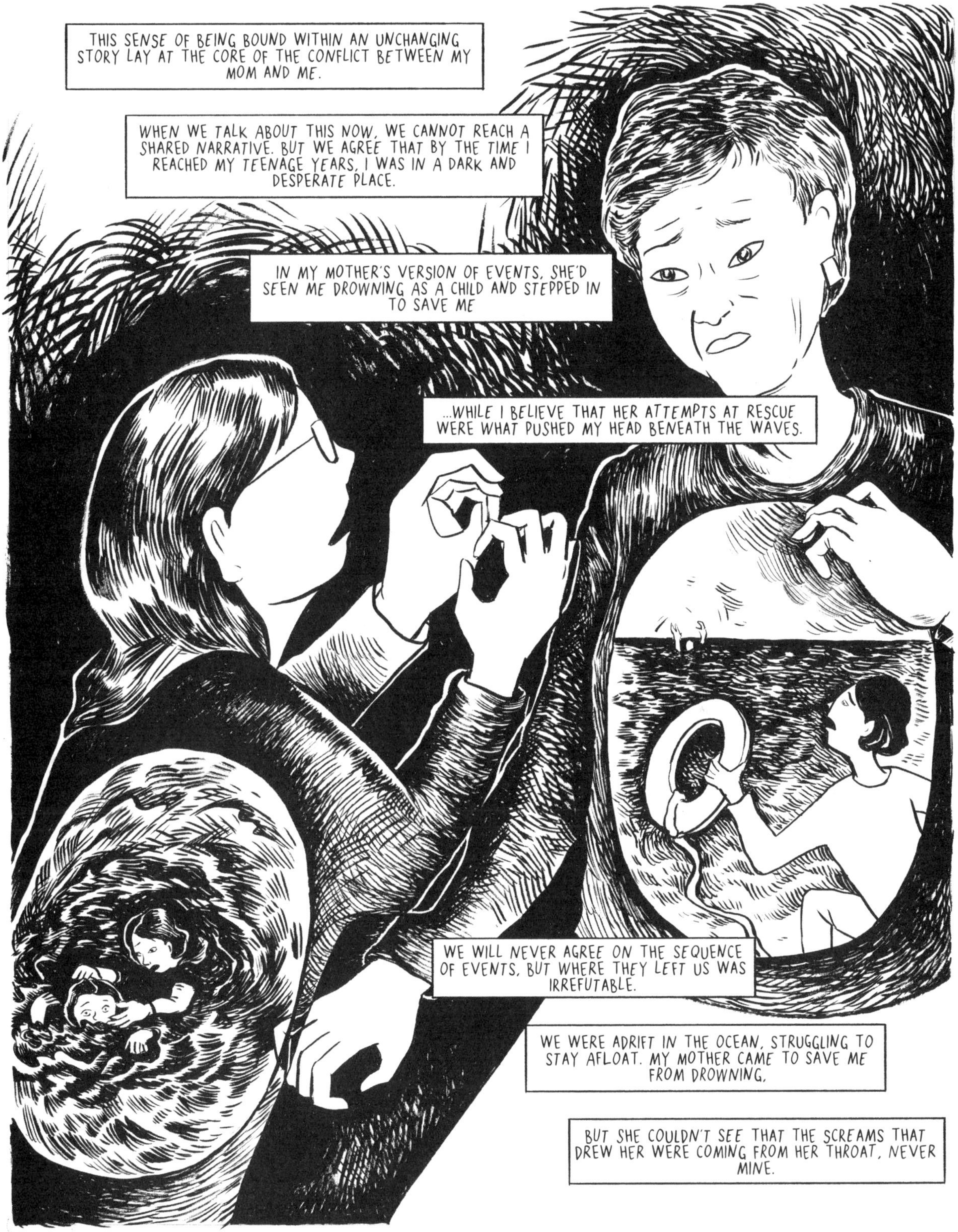
THIS SENSE OF BEING BOUND WITHIN AN UNCHANGING STORY LAY AT THE CORE OF THE CONFLICT BETWEEN MY MOM AND ME.
WHEN WE TALK ABOUT THIS NOW, WE CANNOT REACH A SHARED NARRATIVE. BUT WE AGREE THAT BY THE TIME I REACHED MY TEENAGE YEARS, I WAS IN A DARK AND DESPERATE PLACE.
IN MY MOTHER'S VERSION OF EVENTS, SHE'D SEEN ME DROWNING AS A CHILD AND STEPPED IN TO SAVE ME
...WHILE I BELIEVE THAT HER ATTEMPTS AT RESCUE WERE WHAT PUSHED MY HEAD BENEATH THE WAVES.
WE WILL NEVER AGREE ON THE SEQUENCE OF EVENTS, BUT WHERE THEY LEFT US WAS IRREFUTABLE.
WE WERE ADRIFT IN THE OCEAN, STRUGGLING TO STAY AFLOAT. MY MOTHER CAME TO SAVE ME FROM DROWNING.
BUT SHE COULDN'T SEE THAT THE SCREAMS THAT DREW HER WERE COMING FROM HER THROAT, NEVER MINE.

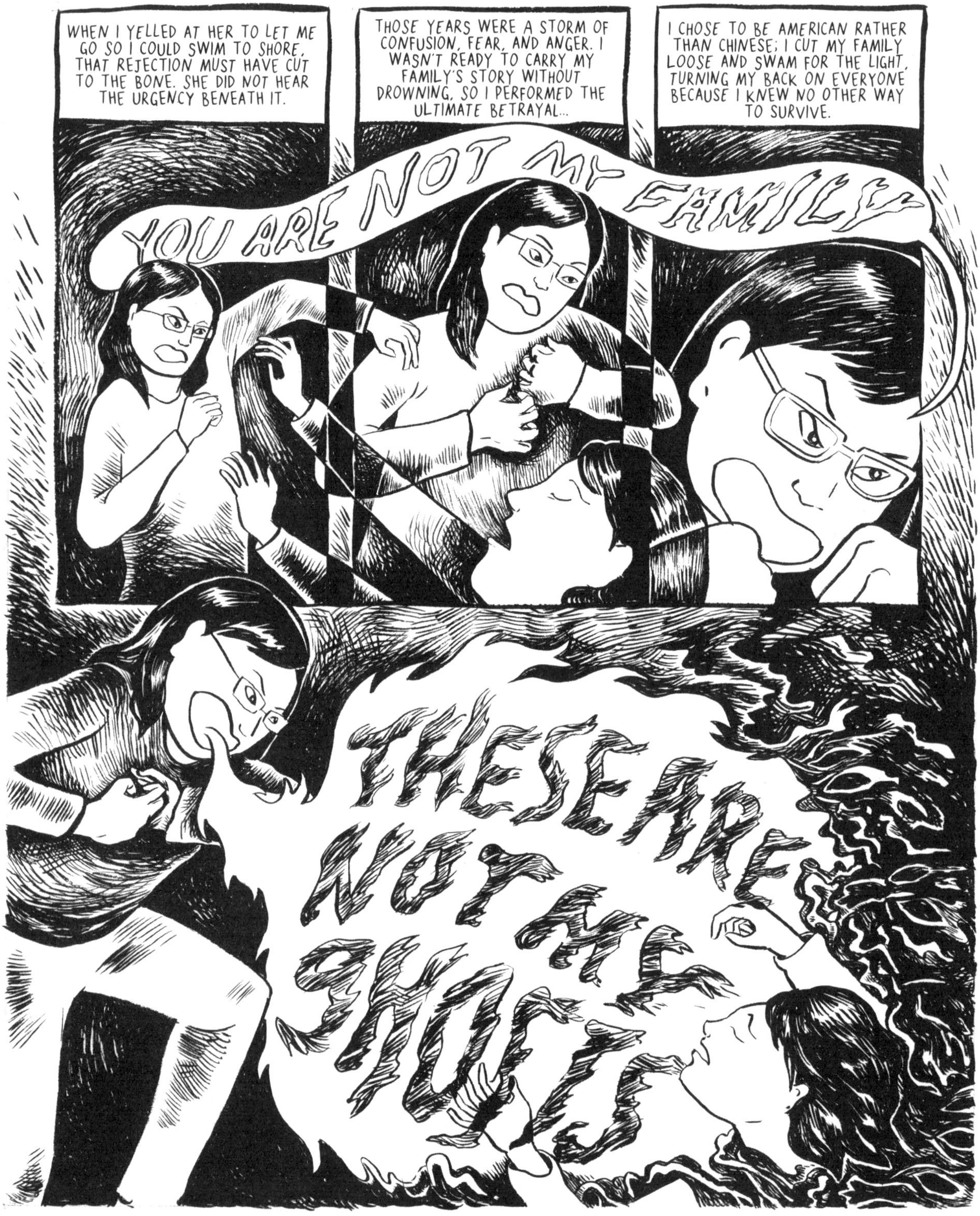

WHEN I YELLED AT HER TO LET ME GO SO I COULD SWIM TO SHORE, THAT REJECTION MUST HAVE CUT TO THE BONE. SHE DID NOT HEAR THE URGENCY BENEATH IT.
THOSE YEARS WERE A STORM OF CONFUSION, FEAR, AND ANGER. I WASN'T READY TO CARRY MY FAMILY'S STORY WITHOUT DROWNING, SO I PERFORMED THE ULTIMATE BETRAYAL...
I CHOSE TO BE AMERICAN RATHER THAN CHINESE; I CUT MY FAMILY LOOSE AND SWAM FOR THE LIGHT, TURNING MY BACK ON EVERYONE BECAUSE I KNEW NO OTHER WAY TO SURVIVE.
YOU ARE NOT MY FAMILY
THESE ARE NOT MY GHOSTS

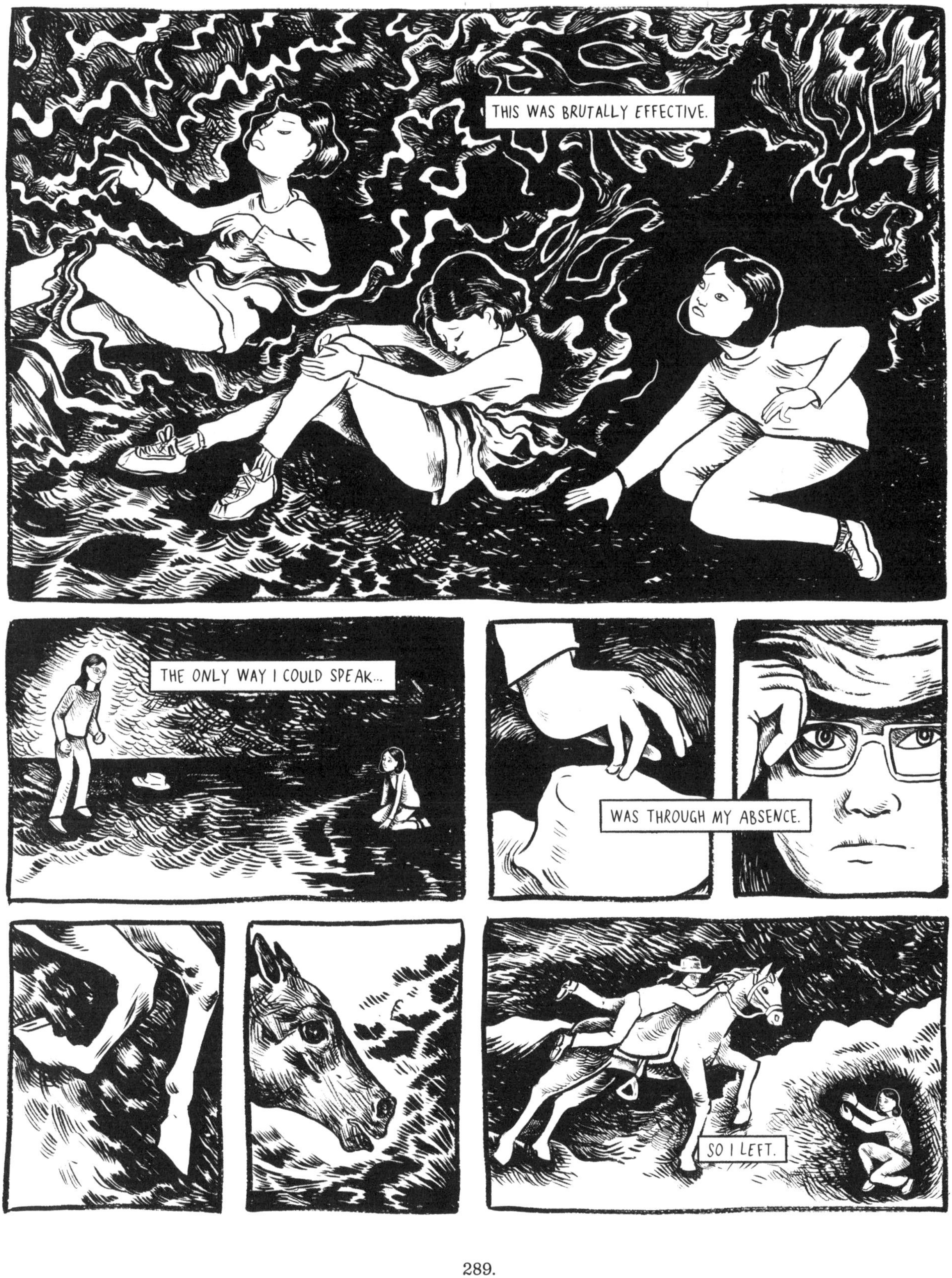
THIS WAS BRUTALLY EFFECTIVE.
THE ONLY WAY I COULD SPEAK...
WAS THROUGH MY ABSENCE.
SO I LEFT.

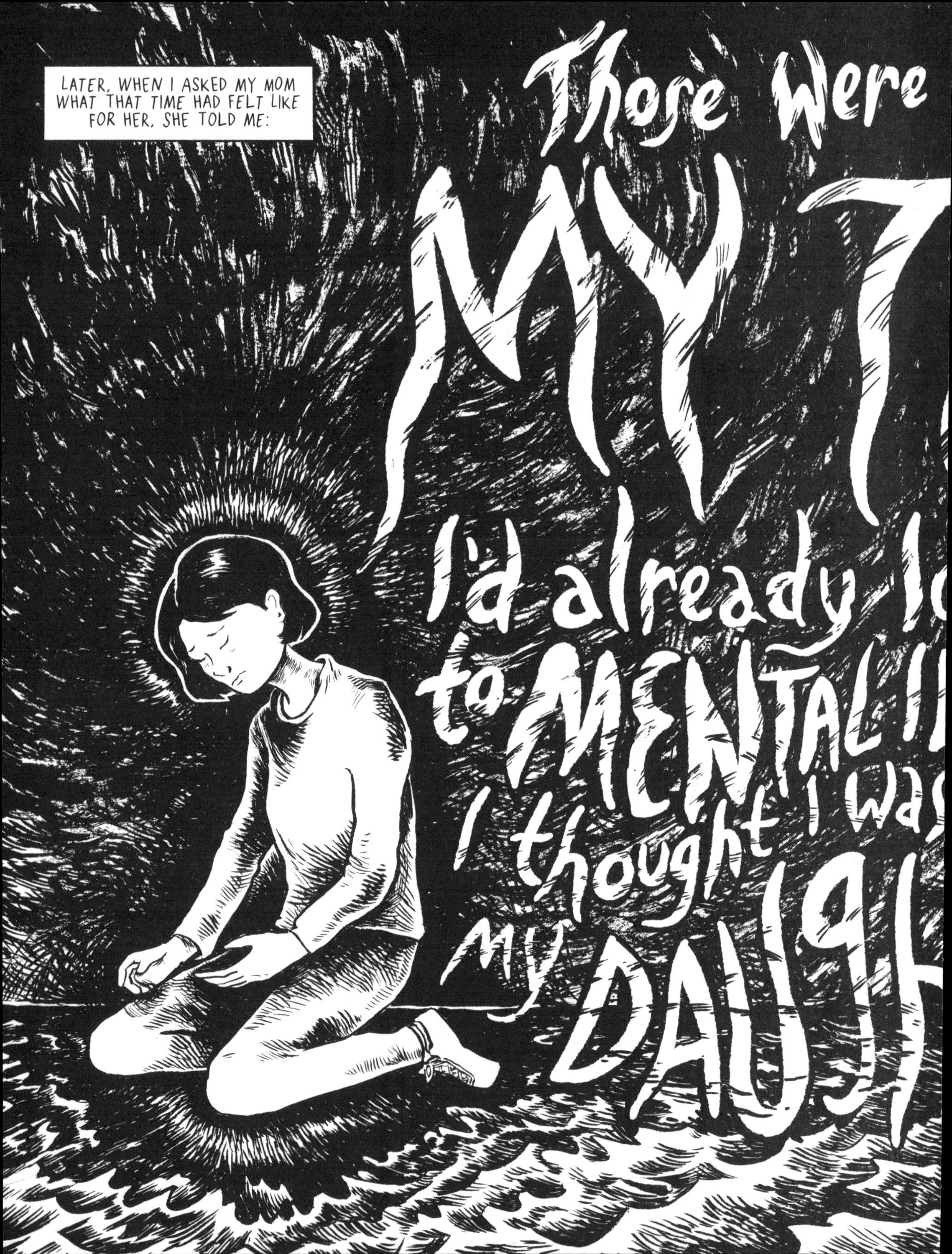
LATER, WHEN I ASKED MY MOM WHAT THAT TIME HAD FELT LIKE FOR HER, SHE TOLD ME:
Those Were
MY
I'd already
to MENTAL
I thought I was
my
DAU

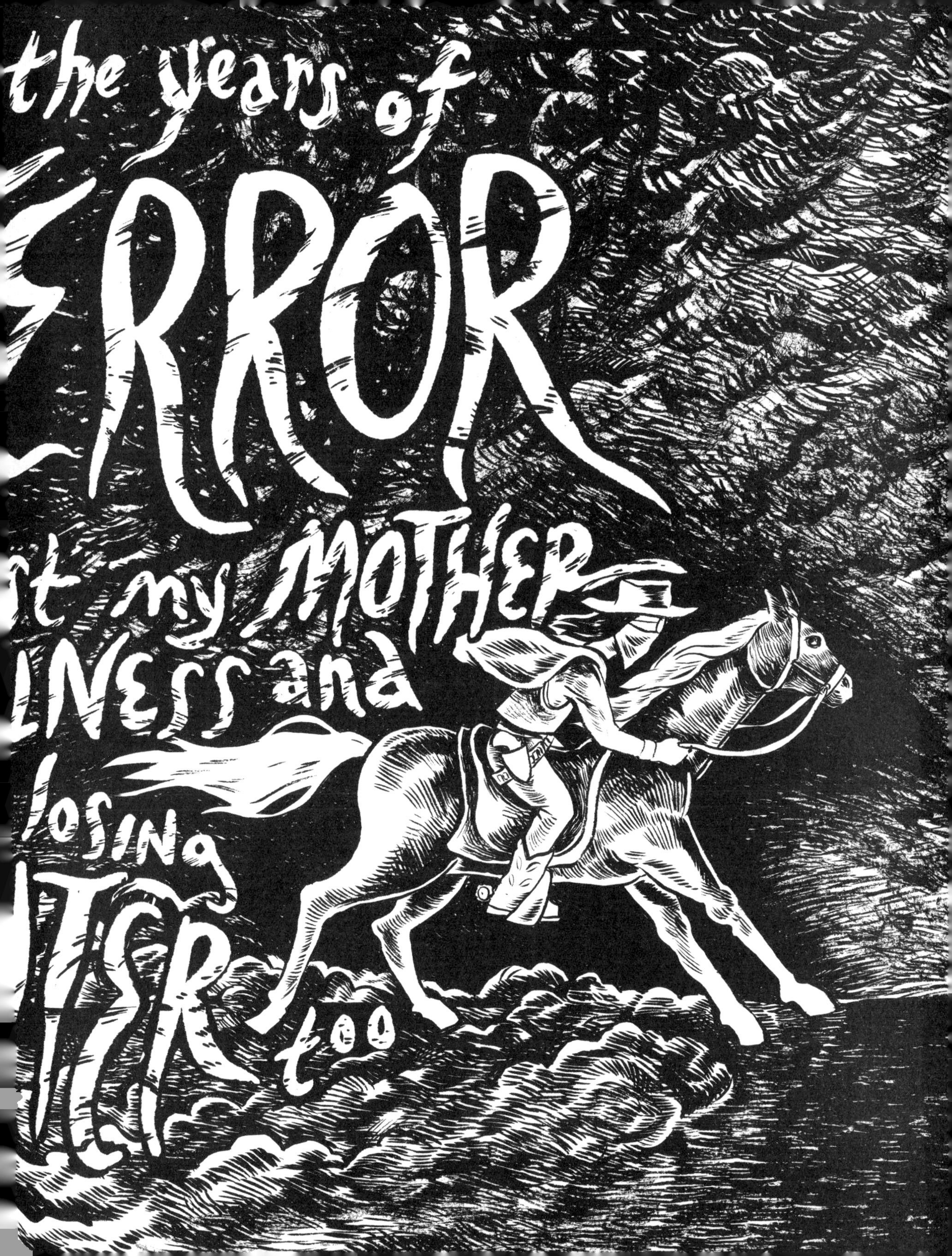

the years of
RROR
t my MOTHER
LNESS and
losing
SR too

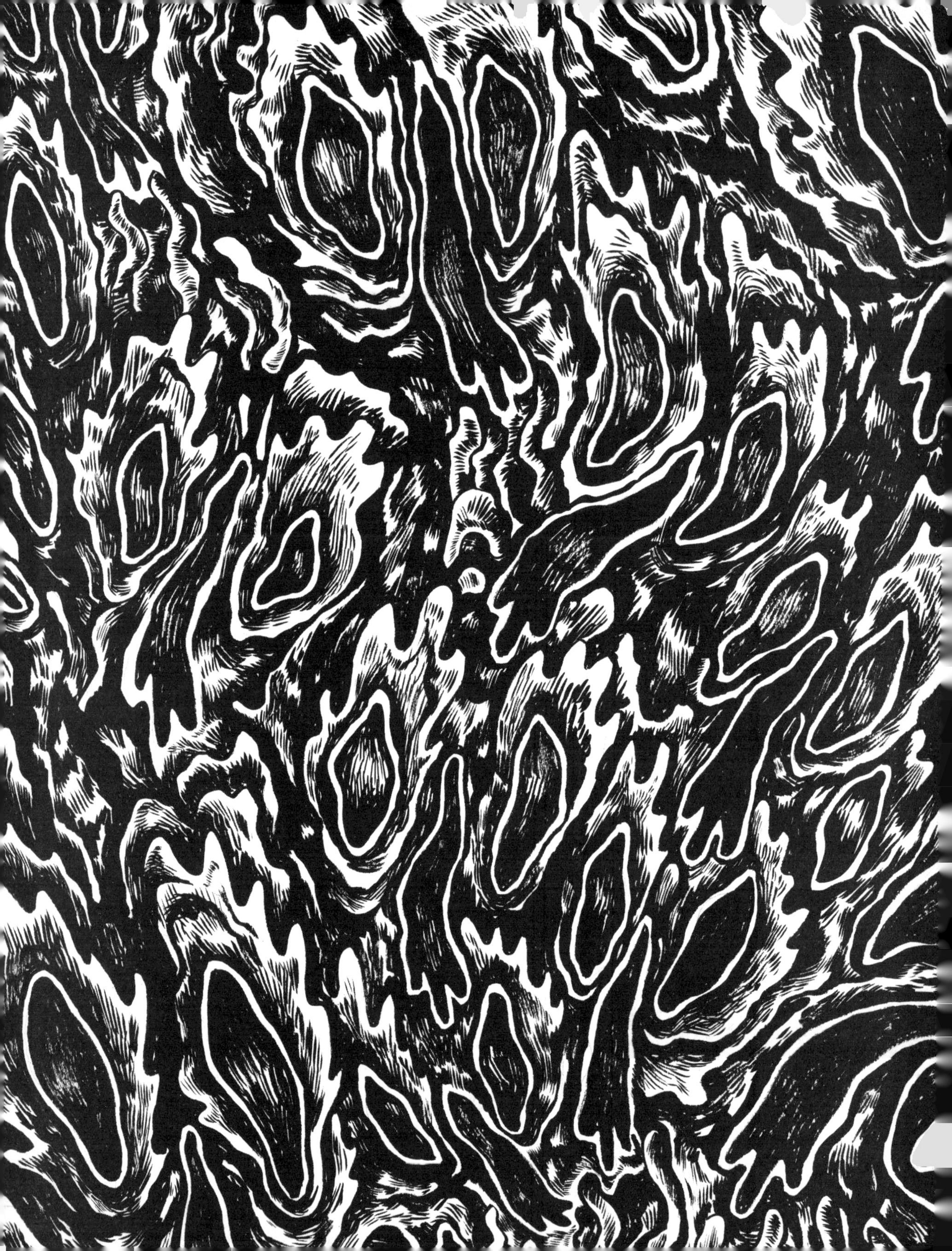

PART 8

BURNING DOWN THE HOUSE

Every Frontier I Could Find • 2002–2015

And some people travel far more than others. There are those who receive as a birthright an adequate or at least unquestioned sense of self and those who set out to reinvent themselves, for survival or satisfaction, and travel far. Some people inherit values and practices as a house they inhabit; some of us have to burn down that house, find our own ground, build from scratch, even a psychological metamorphosis.

—REBECCA SOLNIT, *A Field Guide to Getting Lost*

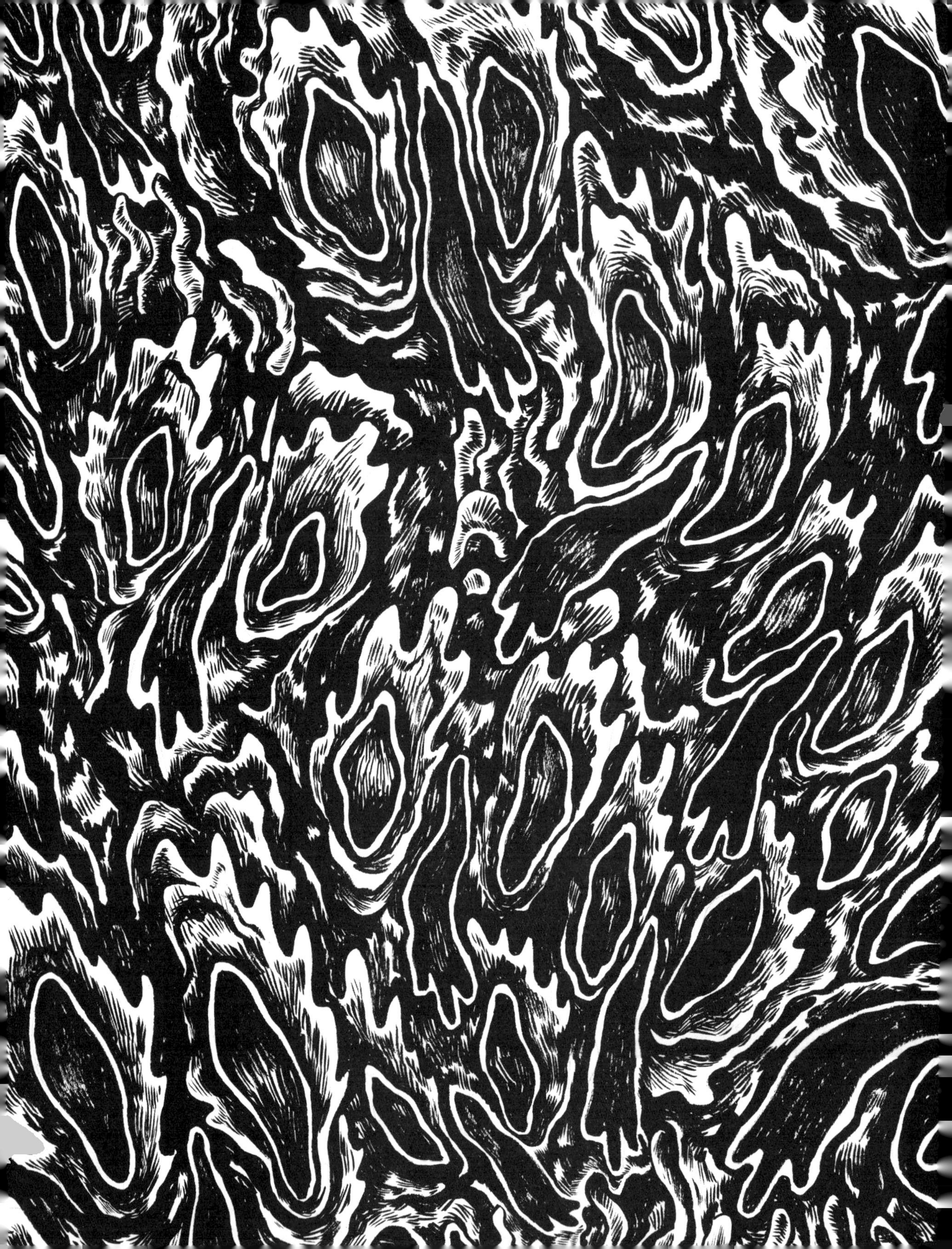

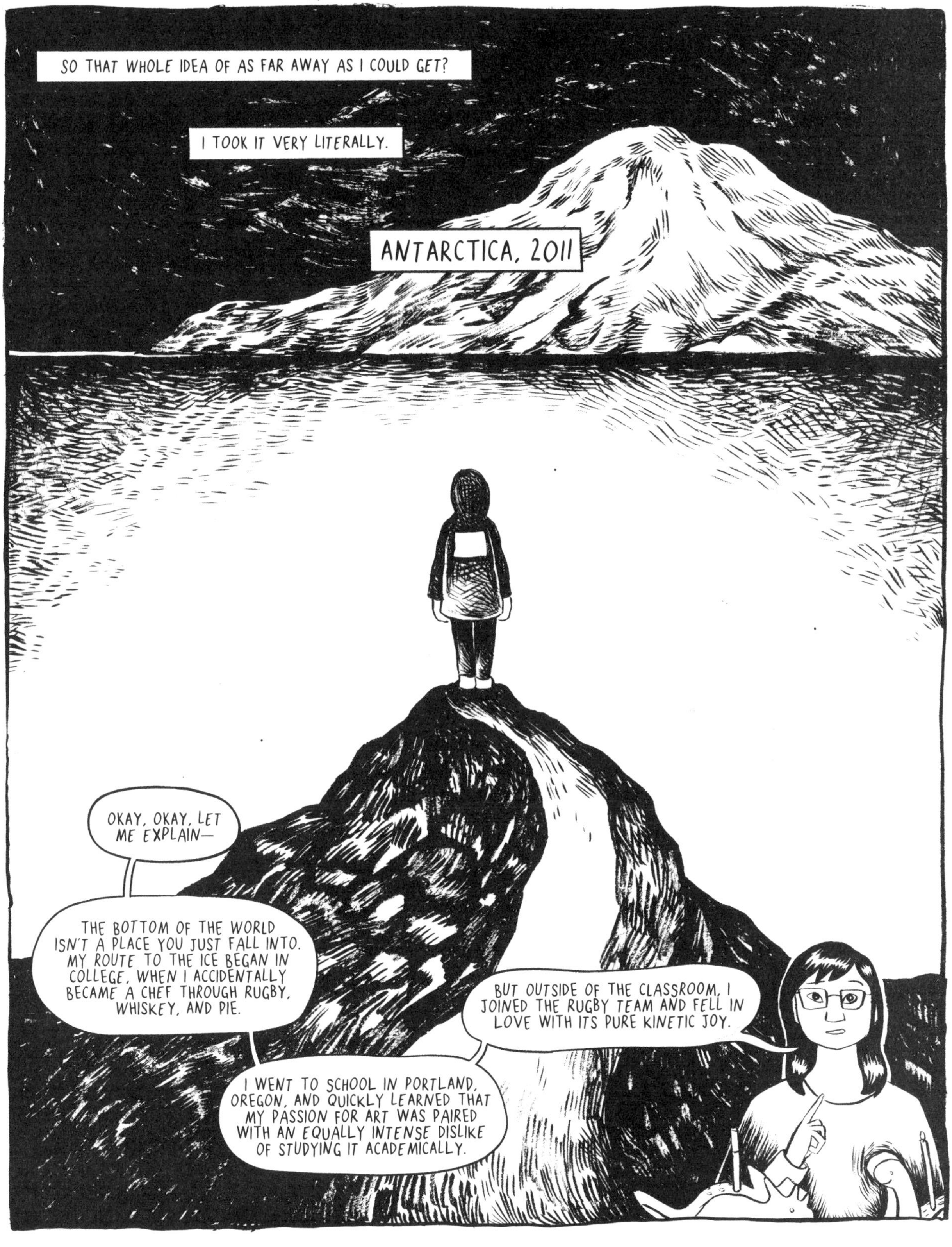
SO THAT WHOLE IDEA OF AS FAR AWAY AS I COULD GET?
I TOOK IT VERY LITERALLY.
ANTARCTICA, 2011
OKAY, OKAY, LET ME EXPLAIN—
THE BOTTOM OF THE WORLD ISN'T A PLACE YOU JUST FALL INTO. MY ROUTE TO THE ICE BEGAN IN COLLEGE, WHEN I ACCIDENTALLY BECAME A CHEF THROUGH RUGBY, WHISKEY, AND PIE.
I WENT TO SCHOOL IN PORTLAND, OREGON, AND QUICKLY LEARNED THAT MY PASSION FOR ART WAS PAIRED WITH AN EQUALLY INTENSE DISLIKE OF STUDYING IT ACADEMICALLY.
BUT OUTSIDE OF THE CLASSROOM, I JOINED THE RUGBY TEAM AND FELL IN LOVE WITH ITS PURE KINETIC JOY.

SOME OF MY OLDER TEAMMATES LOVED TO GET DRUNK AND MAKE PIE, SO THEY FORMED A STUDENT GROUP CALLED "THE LADIES PIE SOCIETY." WE'D STAY UP DRINKING AND BAKING.

THE NEXT DAY, WE'D GO TO THE LIBRARY AND GIVE PIES AWAY. HORDES OF PEOPLE KNEW TO SHOW UP WITH THEIR OWN FORKS AND WAIT.

WATCHING GROUPS OF PEOPLE COME TOGETHER TO COOK MADE ME REEXAMINE MY OWN FAMILY'S RELATIONSHIP TO FOOD.

Rose...

WITHIN MY HOUSEHOLD, MY MOM DID EVERYTHING. SHE BOTH RESENTED THIS AND COULDN'T IMAGINE A DIFFERENT MODEL. GIVEN HER CULTURE AND HER COLONIAL EDUCATION, IT WOULD HAVE BEEN INCONCEIVABLE TO ALLOW MY DAD TO LIFT A FINGER. I REMEMBER WATCHING HIM ONE TIME—

I wouldn't mind a spot more tea...

WITHOUT EVEN TURNING TO LOOK AT HER, HE HELD OUT HIS EMPTY MUG SO SHE COULD COME REFILL IT.

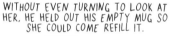

COOKING WITHIN OUR FAMILY WAS SIMPLY A TASK AMONG TASKS, JUST ONE OF MY MOM'S MANY DUTIES THAT WE ALL TOOK FOR GRANTED.

I'D SO INTERNALIZED THIS MODEL OF COOKING AS A JOYLESS, REPETITIVE CHORE

THAT IT WAS IMPOSSIBLE FOR ME TO IMAGINE FAMILIES BROUGHT TOGETHER BY FOOD.

SO GATHERING WITH TEAMMATES TO BAKE FELT LIKE AN ANARCHIC REVELATION.

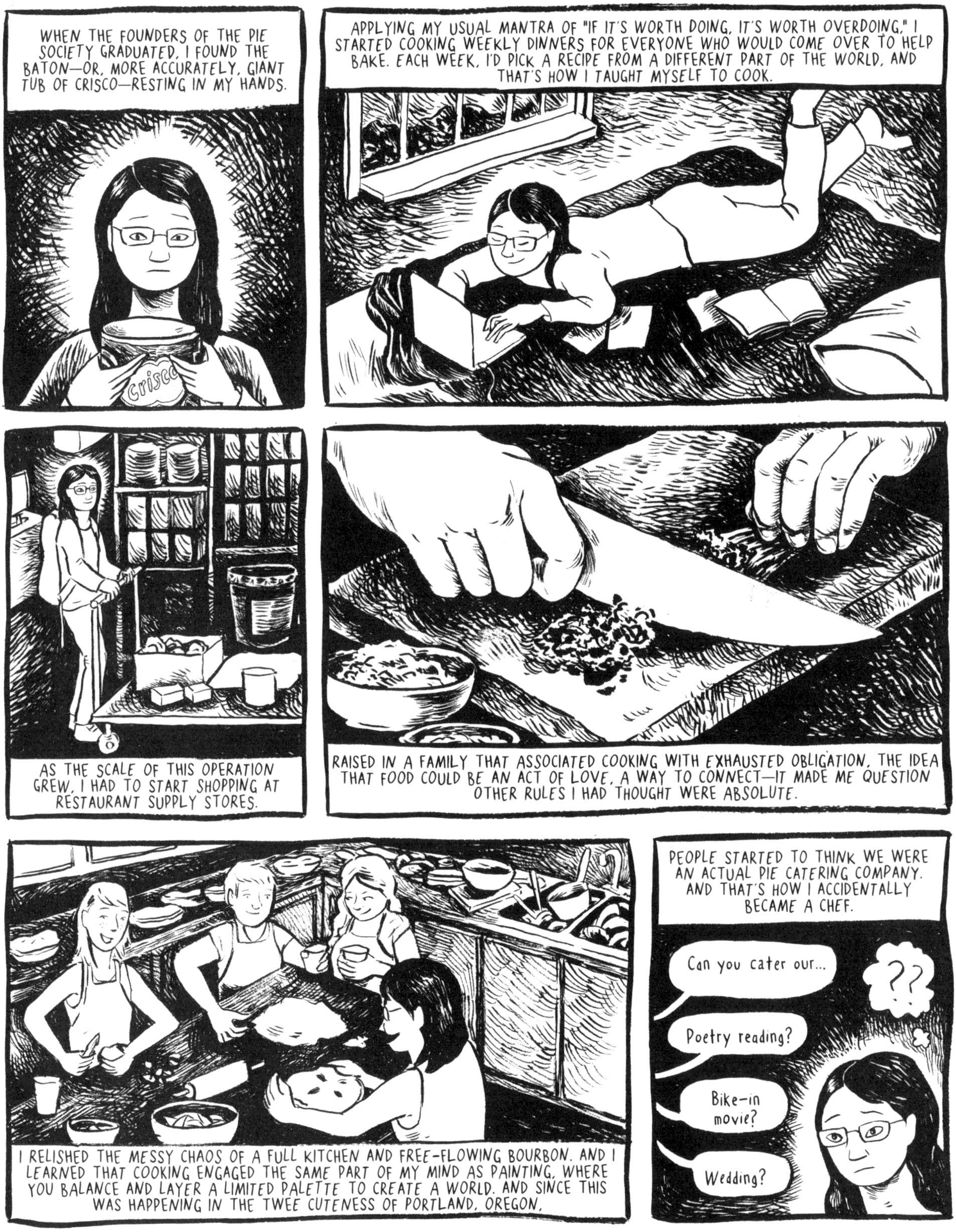
WHEN THE FOUNDERS OF THE PIE SOCIETY GRADUATED, I FOUND THE BATON—OR, MORE ACCURATELY, GIANT TUB OF CRISCO—RESTING IN MY HANDS.
Crisco
APPLYING MY USUAL MANTRA OF "IF IT'S WORTH DOING, IT'S WORTH OVERDOING," I STARTED COOKING WEEKLY DINNERS FOR EVERYONE WHO WOULD COME OVER TO HELP BAKE. EACH WEEK, I'D PICK A RECIPE FROM A DIFFERENT PART OF THE WORLD, AND THAT'S HOW I TAUGHT MYSELF TO COOK.
AS THE SCALE OF THIS OPERATION GREW, I HAD TO START SHOPPING AT RESTAURANT SUPPLY STORES.
RAISED IN A FAMILY THAT ASSOCIATED COOKING WITH EXHAUSTED OBLIGATION, THE IDEA THAT FOOD COULD BE AN ACT OF LOVE, A WAY TO CONNECT—IT MADE ME QUESTION OTHER RULES I HAD THOUGHT WERE ABSOLUTE.
I RELISHED THE MESSY CHAOS OF A FULL KITCHEN AND FREE-FLOWING BOURBON. AND I LEARNED THAT COOKING ENGAGED THE SAME PART OF MY MIND AS PAINTING, WHERE YOU BALANCE AND LAYER A LIMITED PALETTE TO CREATE A WORLD. AND SINCE THIS WAS HAPPENING IN THE TWEE CUTENESS OF PORTLAND, OREGON,
PEOPLE STARTED TO THINK WE WERE AN ACTUAL PIE CATERING COMPANY. AND THAT'S HOW I ACCIDENTALLY BECAME A CHEF.
Can you cater our...
??
Poetry reading?
Bike-in movie?
Wedding?

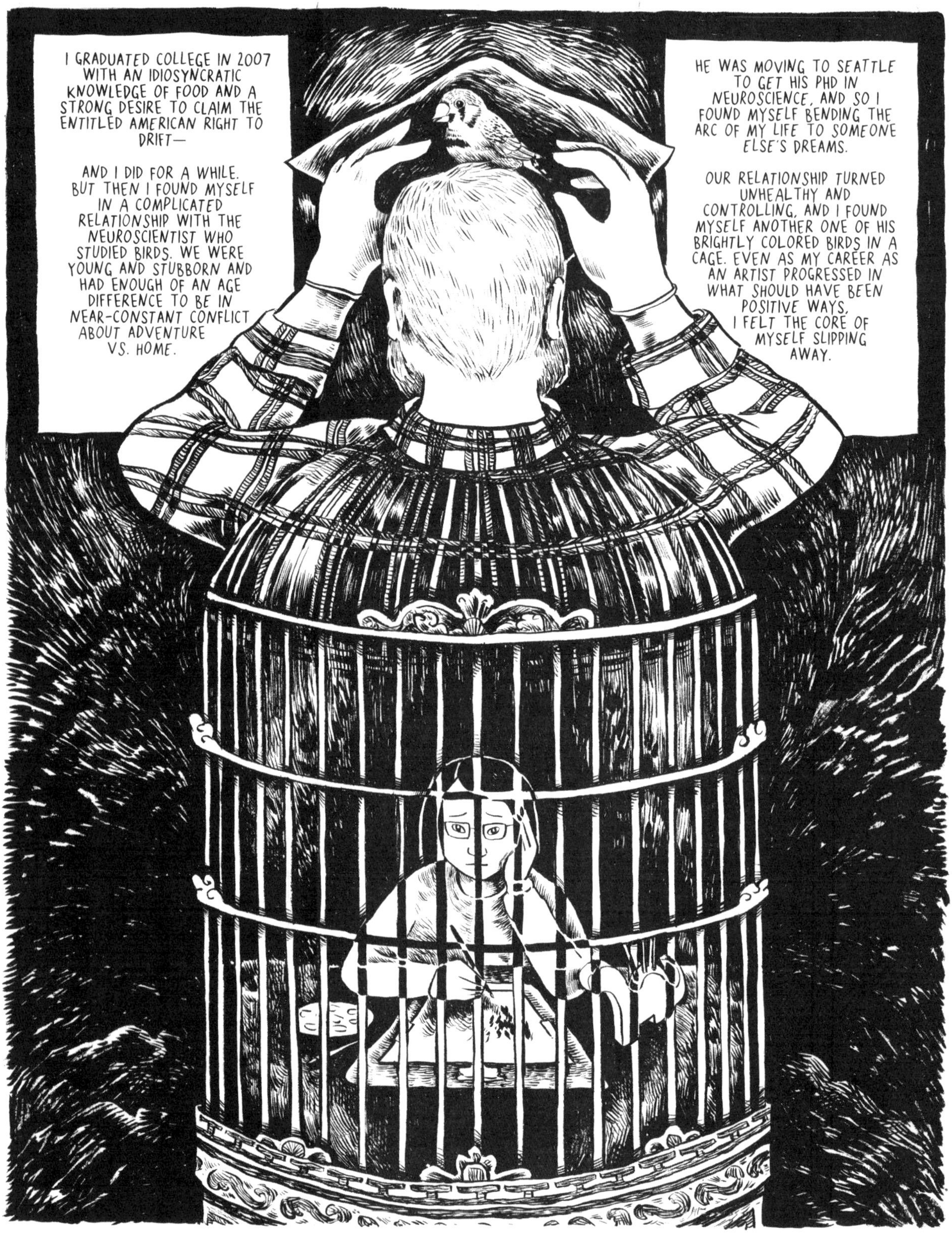
I GRADUATED COLLEGE IN 2007 WITH AN IDIOSYNCRATIC KNOWLEDGE OF FOOD AND A STRONG DESIRE TO CLAIM THE ENTITLED AMERICAN RIGHT TO DRIFT—
AND I DID FOR A WHILE. BUT THEN I FOUND MYSELF IN A COMPLICATED RELATIONSHIP WITH THE NEUROSCIENTIST WHO STUDIED BIRDS. WE WERE YOUNG AND STUBBORN AND HAD ENOUGH OF AN AGE DIFFERENCE TO BE IN NEAR-CONSTANT CONFLICT ABOUT ADVENTURE VS. HOME.
HE WAS MOVING TO SEATTLE TO GET HIS PHD IN NEUROSCIENCE, AND SO I FOUND MYSELF BENDING THE ARC OF MY LIFE TO SOMEONE ELSE'S DREAMS.
OUR RELATIONSHIP TURNED UNHEALTHY AND CONTROLLING, AND I FOUND MYSELF ANOTHER ONE OF HIS BRIGHTLY COLORED BIRDS IN A CAGE. EVEN AS MY CAREER AS AN ARTIST PROGRESSED IN WHAT SHOULD HAVE BEEN POSITIVE WAYS, I FELT THE CORE OF MYSELF SLIPPING AWAY.

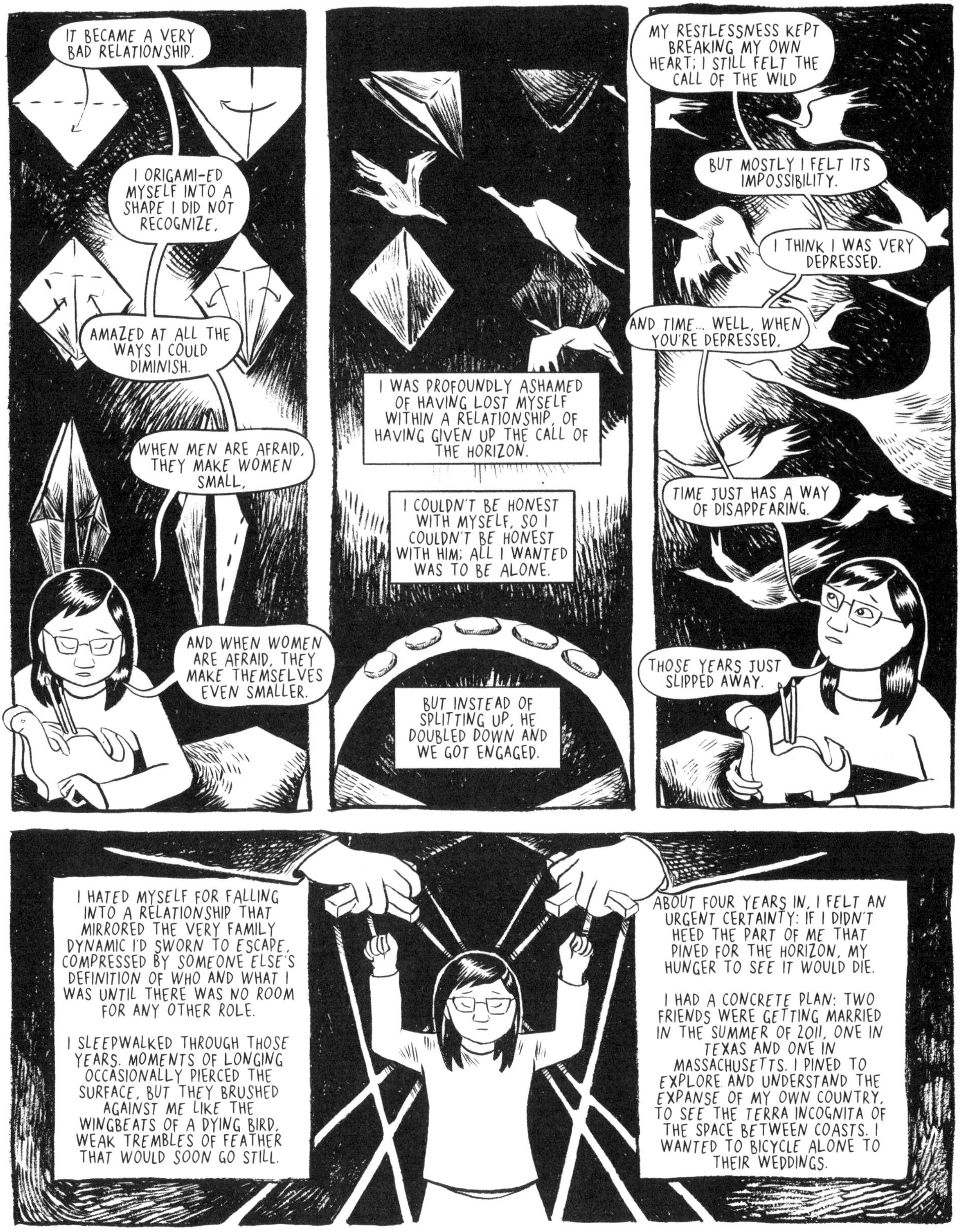

IT BECAME A VERY BAD RELATIONSHIP.
I ORIGAMI-ED MYSELF INTO A SHAPE I DID NOT RECOGNIZE,
AMAZED AT ALL THE WAYS I COULD DIMINISH.
WHEN MEN ARE AFRAID, THEY MAKE WOMEN SMALL,
AND WHEN WOMEN ARE AFRAID, THEY MAKE THEMSELVES EVEN SMALLER.
I WAS PROFOUNDLY ASHAMED OF HAVING LOST MYSELF WITHIN A RELATIONSHIP, OF HAVING GIVEN UP THE CALL OF THE HORIZON.
I COULDN'T BE HONEST WITH MYSELF, SO I COULDN'T BE HONEST WITH HIM; ALL I WANTED WAS TO BE ALONE.
BUT INSTEAD OF SPLITTING UP, HE DOUBLED DOWN AND WE GOT ENGAGED.
MY RESTLESSNESS KEPT BREAKING MY OWN HEART; I STILL FELT THE CALL OF THE WILD
BUT MOSTLY I FELT ITS IMPOSSIBILITY.
I THINK I WAS VERY DEPRESSED.
AND TIME... WELL, WHEN YOU'RE DEPRESSED,
TIME JUST HAS A WAY OF DISAPPEARING.
THOSE YEARS JUST SLIPPED AWAY.
I HATED MYSELF FOR FALLING INTO A RELATIONSHIP THAT MIRRORED THE VERY FAMILY DYNAMIC I'D SWORN TO ESCAPE, COMPRESSED BY SOMEONE ELSE'S DEFINITION OF WHO AND WHAT I WAS UNTIL THERE WAS NO ROOM FOR ANY OTHER ROLE.
I SLEEPWALKED THROUGH THOSE YEARS. MOMENTS OF LONGING OCCASIONALLY PIERCED THE SURFACE, BUT THEY BRUSHED AGAINST ME LIKE THE WINGBEATS OF A DYING BIRD, WEAK TREMBLES OF FEATHER THAT WOULD SOON GO STILL.
ABOUT FOUR YEARS IN, I FELT AN URGENT CERTAINTY: IF I DIDN'T HEED THE PART OF ME THAT PINED FOR THE HORIZON, MY HUNGER TO SEE IT WOULD DIE.
I HAD A CONCRETE PLAN: TWO FRIENDS WERE GETTING MARRIED IN THE SUMMER OF 2011, ONE IN TEXAS AND ONE IN MASSACHUSETTS. I PINED TO EXPLORE AND UNDERSTAND THE EXPANSE OF MY OWN COUNTRY, TO SEE THE TERRA INCOGNITA OF THE SPACE BETWEEN COASTS. I WANTED TO BICYCLE ALONE TO THEIR WEDDINGS.

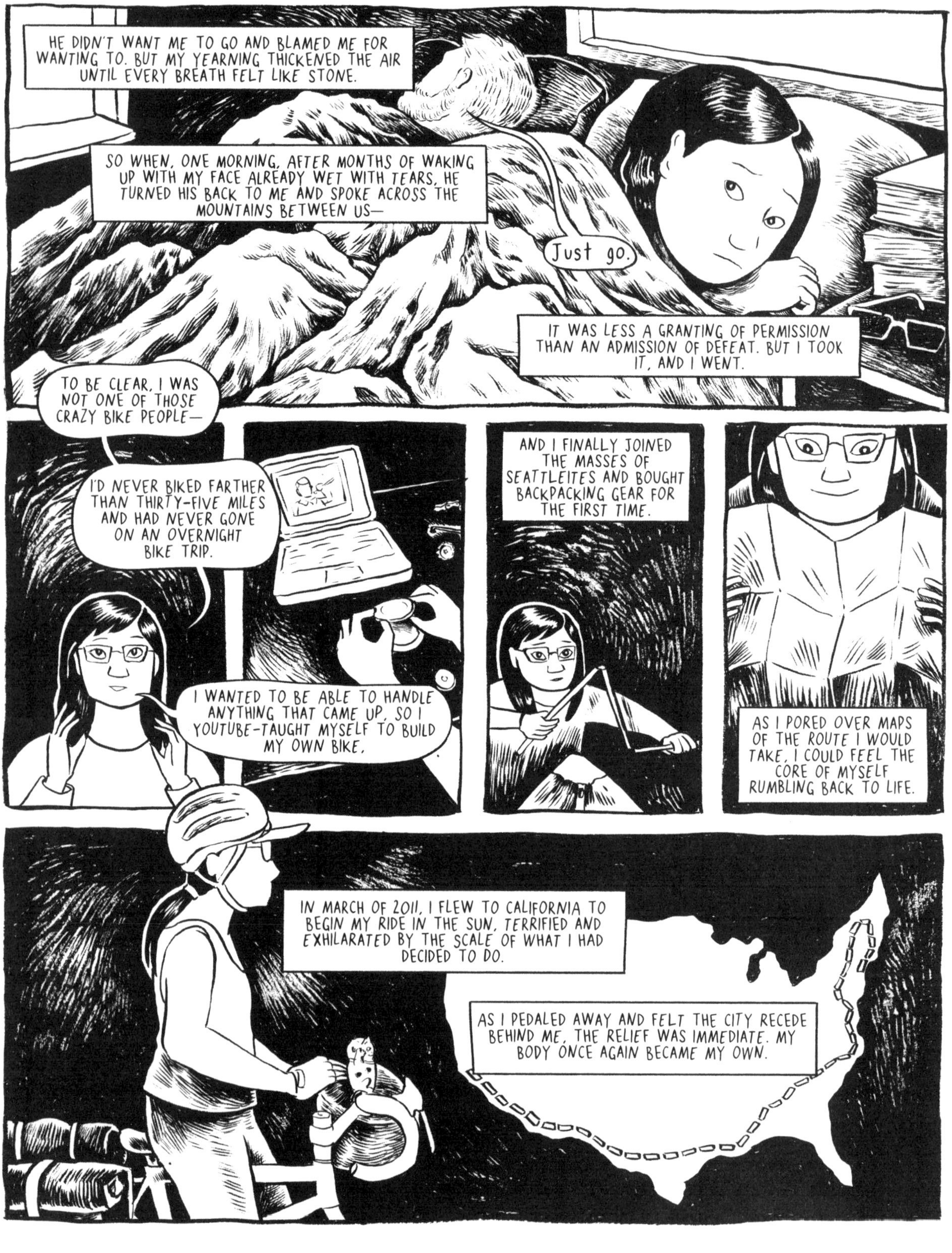
HE DIDN'T WANT ME TO GO AND BLAMED ME FOR WANTING TO. BUT MY YEARNING THICKENED THE AIR UNTIL EVERY BREATH FELT LIKE STONE.
SO WHEN, ONE MORNING, AFTER MONTHS OF WAKING UP WITH MY FACE ALREADY WET WITH TEARS, HE TURNED HIS BACK TO ME AND SPOKE ACROSS THE MOUNTAINS BETWEEN US—
Just go.
IT WAS LESS A GRANTING OF PERMISSION THAN AN ADMISSION OF DEFEAT. BUT I TOOK IT, AND I WENT.
TO BE CLEAR, I WAS NOT ONE OF THOSE CRAZY BIKE PEOPLE—
I'D NEVER BIKED FARTHER THAN THIRTY-FIVE MILES AND HAD NEVER GONE ON AN OVERNIGHT BIKE TRIP.
I WANTED TO BE ABLE TO HANDLE ANYTHING THAT CAME UP, SO I YOUTUBE-TAUGHT MYSELF TO BUILD MY OWN BIKE.
AND I FINALLY JOINED THE MASSES OF SEATTLEITES AND BOUGHT BACKPACKING GEAR FOR THE FIRST TIME.
AS I PORED OVER MAPS OF THE ROUTE I WOULD TAKE, I COULD FEEL THE CORE OF MYSELF RUMBLING BACK TO LIFE.
IN MARCH OF 2011, I FLEW TO CALIFORNIA TO BEGIN MY RIDE IN THE SUN, TERRIFIED AND EXHILARATED BY THE SCALE OF WHAT I HAD DECIDED TO DO.
AS I PEDALED AWAY AND FELT THE CITY RECEDE BEHIND ME, THE RELIEF WAS IMMEDIATE. MY BODY ONCE AGAIN BECAME MY OWN.

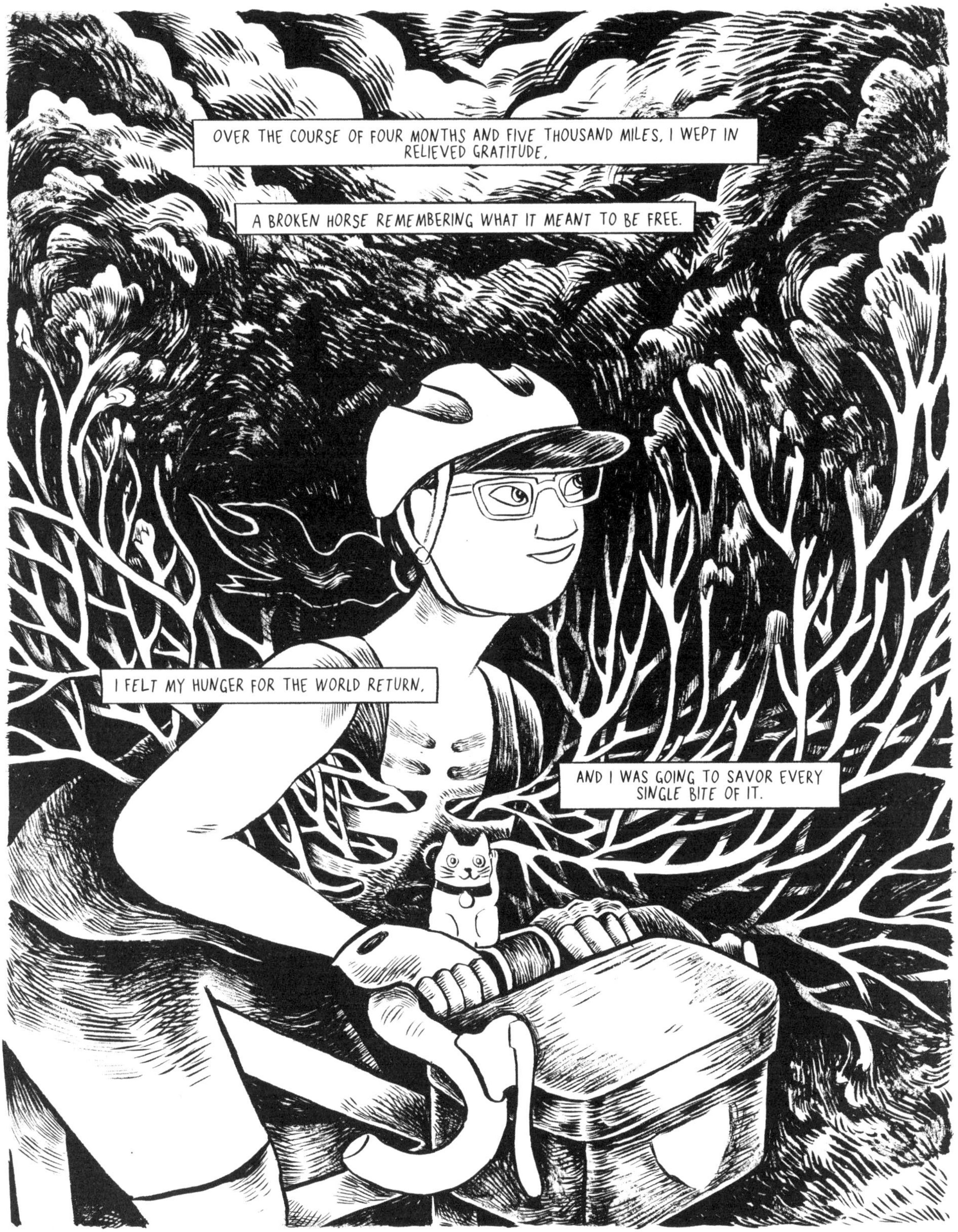
OVER THE COURSE OF FOUR MONTHS AND FIVE THOUSAND MILES, I WEPT IN RELIEVED GRATITUDE,
A BROKEN HORSE REMEMBERING WHAT IT MEANT TO BE FREE.
I FELT MY HUNGER FOR THE WORLD RETURN,
AND I WAS GOING TO SAVOR EVERY SINGLE BITE OF IT.

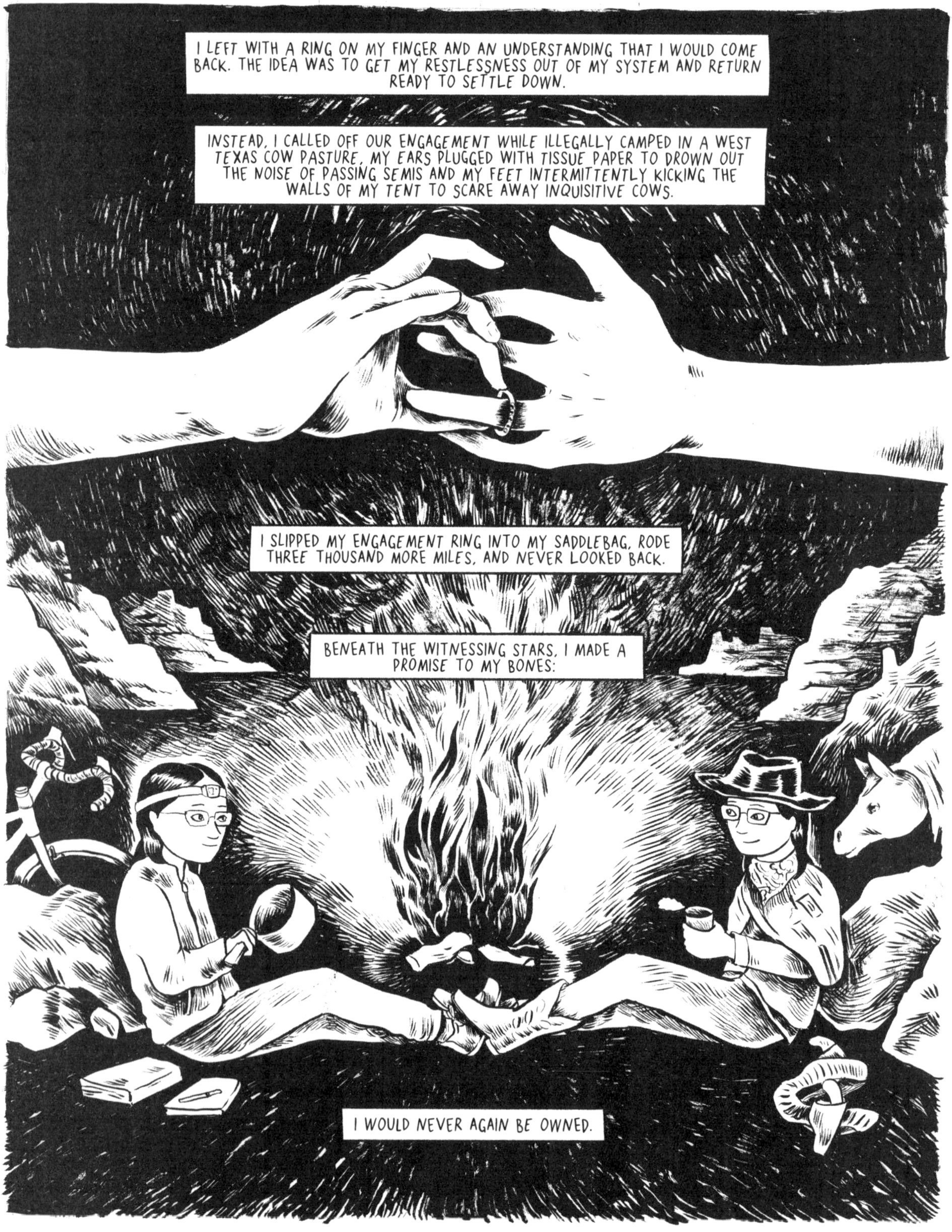
I LEFT WITH A RING ON MY FINGER AND AN UNDERSTANDING THAT I WOULD COME BACK. THE IDEA WAS TO GET MY RESTLESSNESS OUT OF MY SYSTEM AND RETURN READY TO SETTLE DOWN.
INSTEAD, I CALLED OFF OUR ENGAGEMENT WHILE ILLEGALLY CAMPED IN A WEST TEXAS COW PASTURE, MY EARS PLUGGED WITH TISSUE PAPER TO DROWN OUT THE NOISE OF PASSING SEMIS AND MY FEET INTERMITTENTLY KICKING THE WALLS OF MY TENT TO SCARE AWAY INQUISITIVE COWS.
I SLIPPED MY ENGAGEMENT RING INTO MY SADDLEBAG, RODE THREE THOUSAND MORE MILES, AND NEVER LOOKED BACK.
BENEATH THE WITNESSING STARS, I MADE A PROMISE TO MY BONES:
I WOULD NEVER AGAIN BE OWNED.

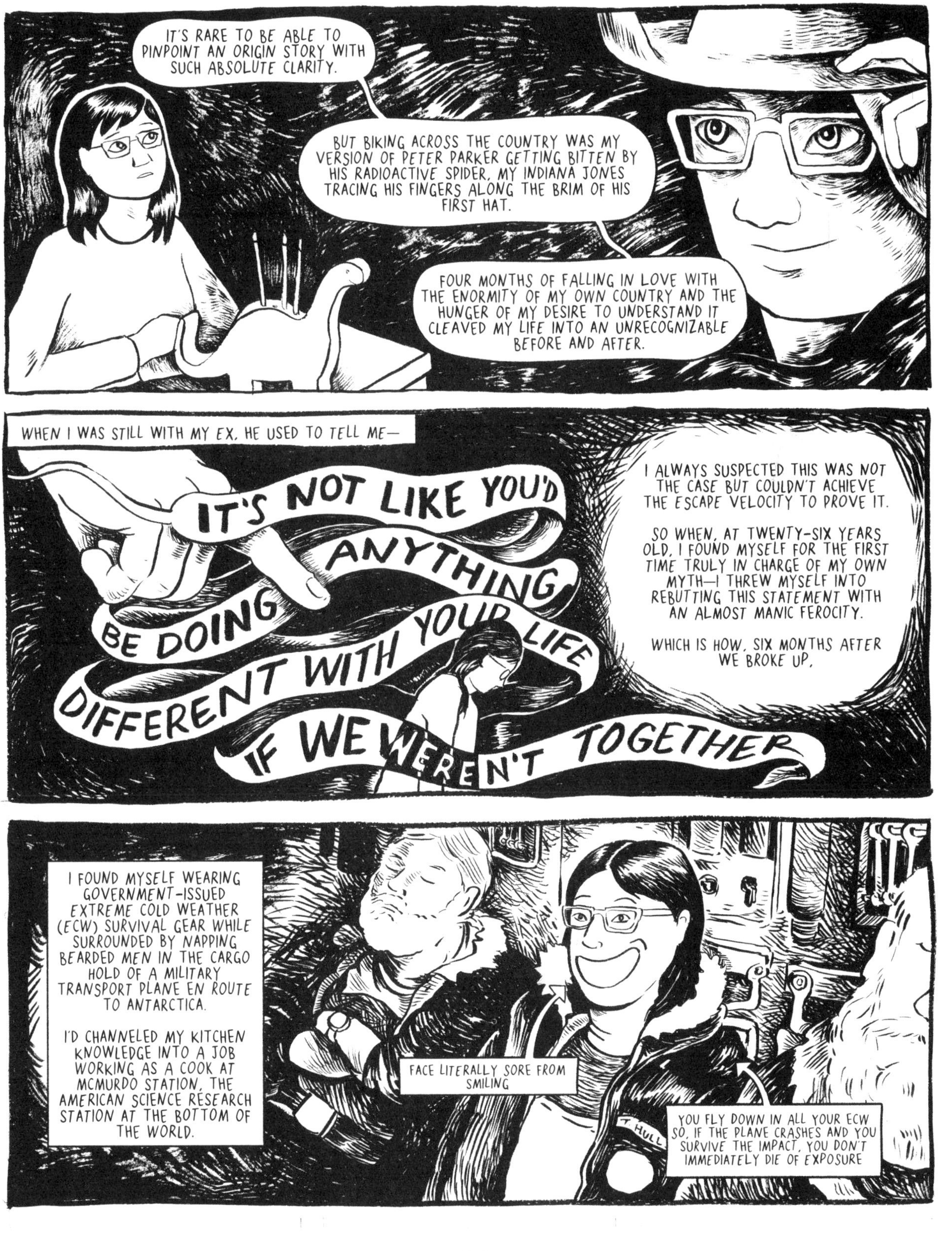
IT'S RARE TO BE ABLE TO PINPOINT AN ORIGIN STORY WITH SUCH ABSOLUTE CLARITY.
BUT BIKING ACROSS THE COUNTRY WAS MY VERSION OF PETER PARKER GETTING BITTEN BY HIS RADIOACTIVE SPIDER, MY INDIANA JONES TRACING HIS FINGERS ALONG THE BRIM OF HIS FIRST HAT.
FOUR MONTHS OF FALLING IN LOVE WITH THE ENORMITY OF MY OWN COUNTRY AND THE HUNGER OF MY DESIRE TO UNDERSTAND IT CLEAVED MY LIFE INTO AN UNRECOGNIZABLE BEFORE AND AFTER.
WHEN I WAS STILL WITH MY EX, HE USED TO TELL ME—
IT'S NOT LIKE YOU'D BE DOING ANYTHING DIFFERENT WITH YOUR LIFE IF WE WEREN'T TOGETHER
I ALWAYS SUSPECTED THIS WAS NOT THE CASE BUT COULDN'T ACHIEVE THE ESCAPE VELOCITY TO PROVE IT.
SO WHEN, AT TWENTY-SIX YEARS OLD, I FOUND MYSELF FOR THE FIRST TIME TRULY IN CHARGE OF MY OWN MYTH—I THREW MYSELF INTO REBUTTING THIS STATEMENT WITH AN ALMOST MANIC FEROCITY.
WHICH IS HOW, SIX MONTHS AFTER WE BROKE UP,
I FOUND MYSELF WEARING GOVERNMENT-ISSUED EXTREME COLD WEATHER (ECW) SURVIVAL GEAR WHILE SURROUNDED BY NAPPING BEARDED MEN IN THE CARGO HOLD OF A MILITARY TRANSPORT PLANE EN ROUTE TO ANTARCTICA.
I'D CHANNELED MY KITCHEN KNOWLEDGE INTO A JOB WORKING AS A COOK AT MCMURDO STATION, THE AMERICAN SCIENCE RESEARCH STATION AT THE BOTTOM OF THE WORLD.
FACE LITERALLY SORE FROM SMILING
T. HULL
YOU FLY DOWN IN ALL YOUR ECW SO, IF THE PLANE CRASHES AND YOU SURVIVE THE IMPACT, YOU DON'T IMMEDIATELY DIE OF EXPOSURE

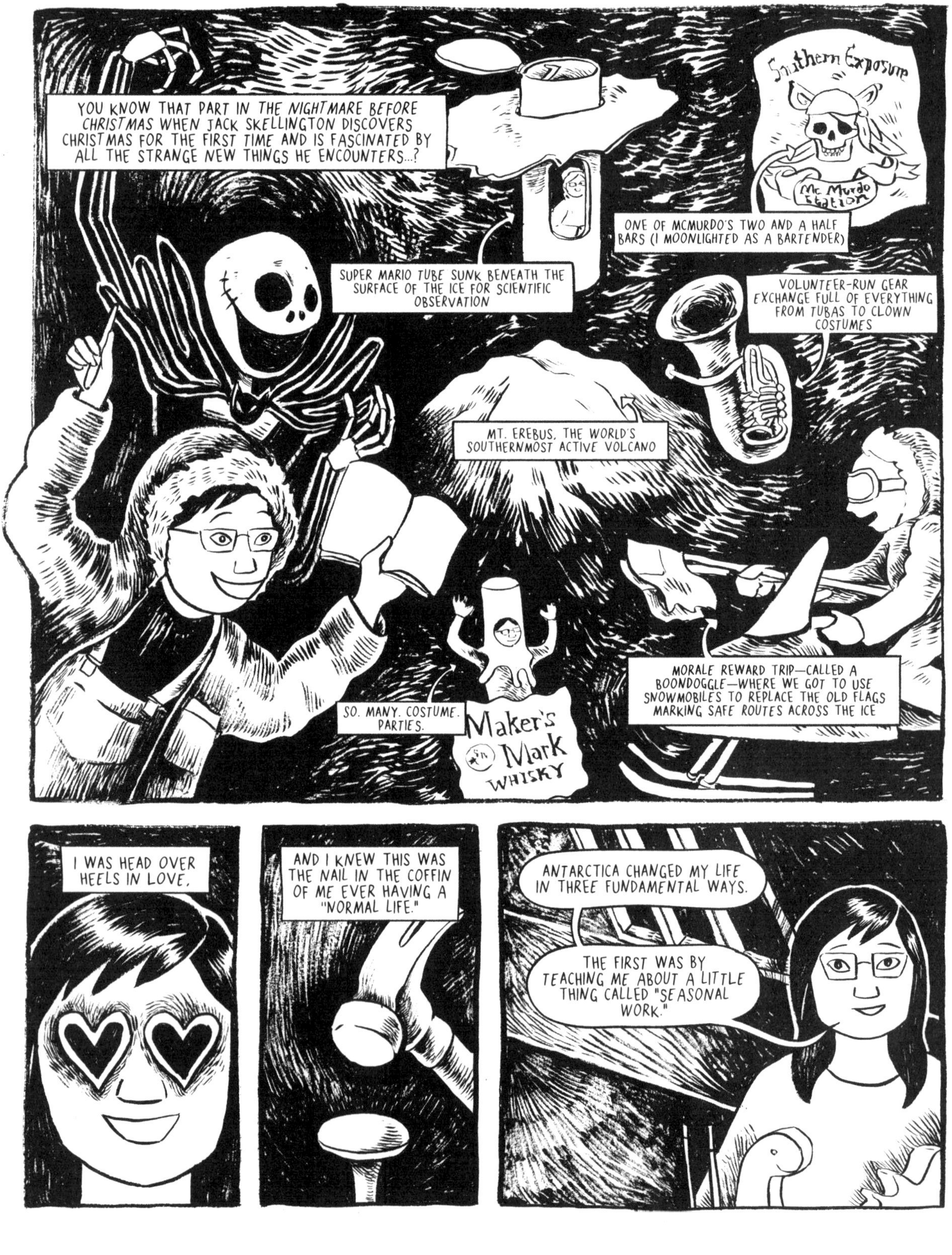
YOU KNOW THAT PART IN THE *NIGHTMARE BEFORE CHRISTMAS* WHEN JACK SKELLINGTON DISCOVERS CHRISTMAS FOR THE FIRST TIME AND IS FASCINATED BY ALL THE STRANGE NEW THINGS HE ENCOUNTERS...?
Southern Exposure
McMurdo Station
ONE OF MCMURDO'S TWO AND A HALF BARS (I MOONLIGHTED AS A BARTENDER)
SUPER MARIO TUBE SUNK BENEATH THE SURFACE OF THE ICE FOR SCIENTIFIC OBSERVATION
VOLUNTEER-RUN GEAR EXCHANGE FULL OF EVERYTHING FROM TUBAS TO CLOWN COSTUMES
MT. EREBUS, THE WORLD'S SOUTHERNMOST ACTIVE VOLCANO
MORALE REWARD TRIP—CALLED A BOONDOGGLE—WHERE WE GOT TO USE SNOWMOBILES TO REPLACE THE OLD FLAGS MARKING SAFE ROUTES ACROSS THE ICE
SO. MANY. COSTUME. PARTIES.
Maker's Mark WHISKY
I WAS HEAD OVER HEELS IN LOVE.
AND I KNEW THIS WAS THE NAIL IN THE COFFIN OF ME EVER HAVING A "NORMAL LIFE."
ANTARCTICA CHANGED MY LIFE IN THREE FUNDAMENTAL WAYS.
THE FIRST WAS BY TEACHING ME ABOUT A LITTLE THING CALLED "SEASONAL WORK."

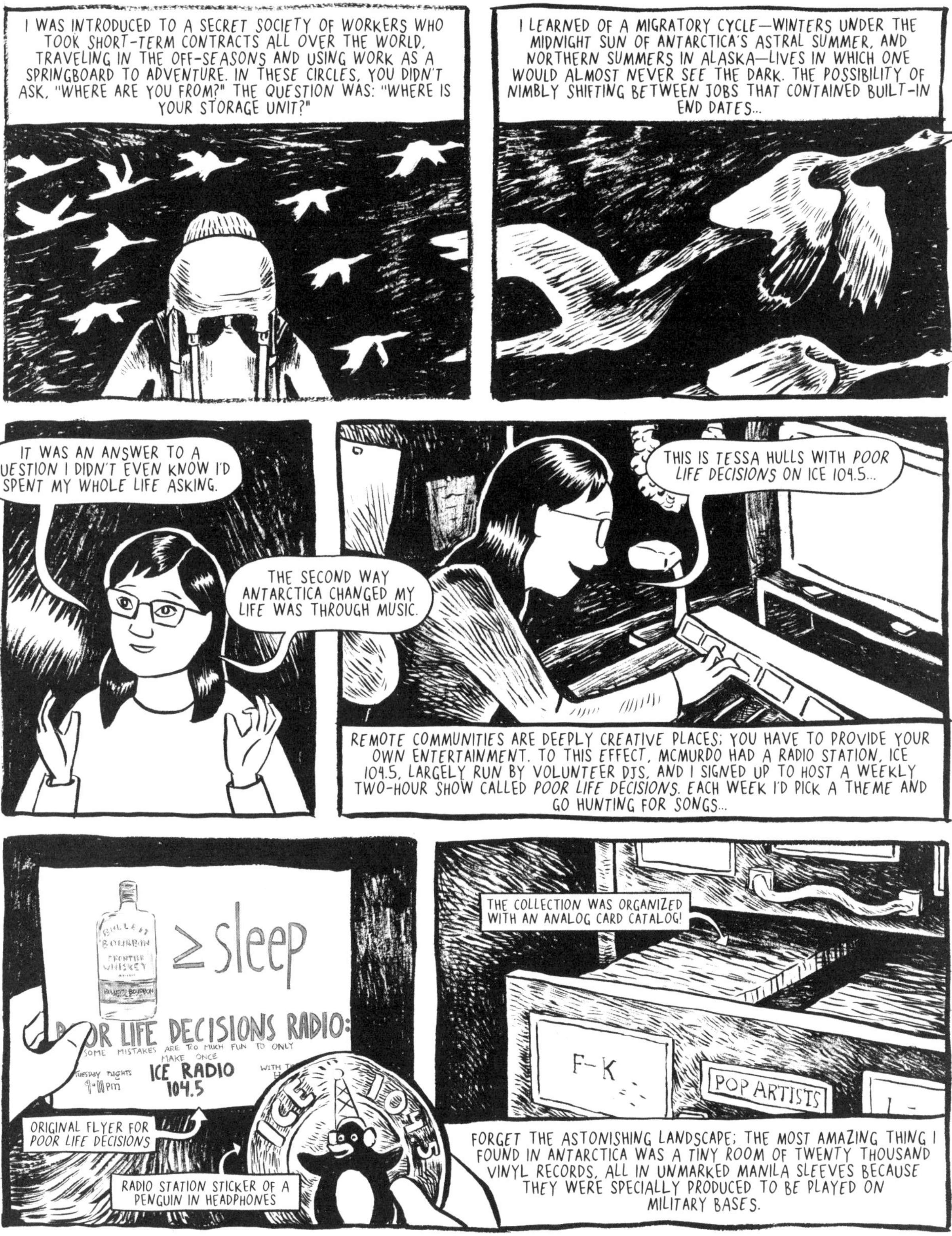
I WAS INTRODUCED TO A SECRET SOCIETY OF WORKERS WHO TOOK SHORT-TERM CONTRACTS ALL OVER THE WORLD, TRAVELING IN THE OFF-SEASONS AND USING WORK AS A SPRINGBOARD TO ADVENTURE. IN THESE CIRCLES, YOU DIDN'T ASK, "WHERE ARE YOU FROM?" THE QUESTION WAS: "WHERE IS YOUR STORAGE UNIT?"
I LEARNED OF A MIGRATORY CYCLE—WINTERS UNDER THE MIDNIGHT SUN OF ANTARCTICA'S ASTRAL SUMMER, AND NORTHERN SUMMERS IN ALASKA—LIVES IN WHICH ONE WOULD ALMOST NEVER SEE THE DARK. THE POSSIBILITY OF NIMBLY SHIFTING BETWEEN JOBS THAT CONTAINED BUILT-IN END DATES...
IT WAS AN ANSWER TO A QUESTION I DIDN'T EVEN KNOW I'D SPENT MY WHOLE LIFE ASKING.
THE SECOND WAY ANTARCTICA CHANGED MY LIFE WAS THROUGH MUSIC.
THIS IS TESSA HULLS WITH POOR LIFE DECISIONS ON ICE 104.5...
REMOTE COMMUNITIES ARE DEEPLY CREATIVE PLACES; YOU HAVE TO PROVIDE YOUR OWN ENTERTAINMENT. TO THIS EFFECT, MCMURDO HAD A RADIO STATION, ICE 104.5, LARGELY RUN BY VOLUNTEER DJS, AND I SIGNED UP TO HOST A WEEKLY TWO-HOUR SHOW CALLED POOR LIFE DECISIONS. EACH WEEK I'D PICK A THEME AND GO HUNTING FOR SONGS...
≥ sleep
POOR LIFE DECISIONS RADIO:
SOME MISTAKES ARE TOO MUCH FUN TO ONLY MAKE ONCE
TUESDAY NIGHTS 9-11pm
ICE RADIO 104.5
ORIGINAL FLYER FOR POOR LIFE DECISIONS
ICE 104.5
RADIO STATION STICKER OF A PENGUIN IN HEADPHONES
THE COLLECTION WAS ORGANIZED WITH AN ANALOG CARD CATALOG!
F-K
POP ARTISTS
FORGET THE ASTONISHING LANDSCAPE; THE MOST AMAZING THING I FOUND IN ANTARCTICA WAS A TINY ROOM OF TWENTY THOUSAND VINYL RECORDS, ALL IN UNMARKED MANILA SLEEVES BECAUSE THEY WERE SPECIALLY PRODUCED TO BE PLAYED ON MILITARY BASES.

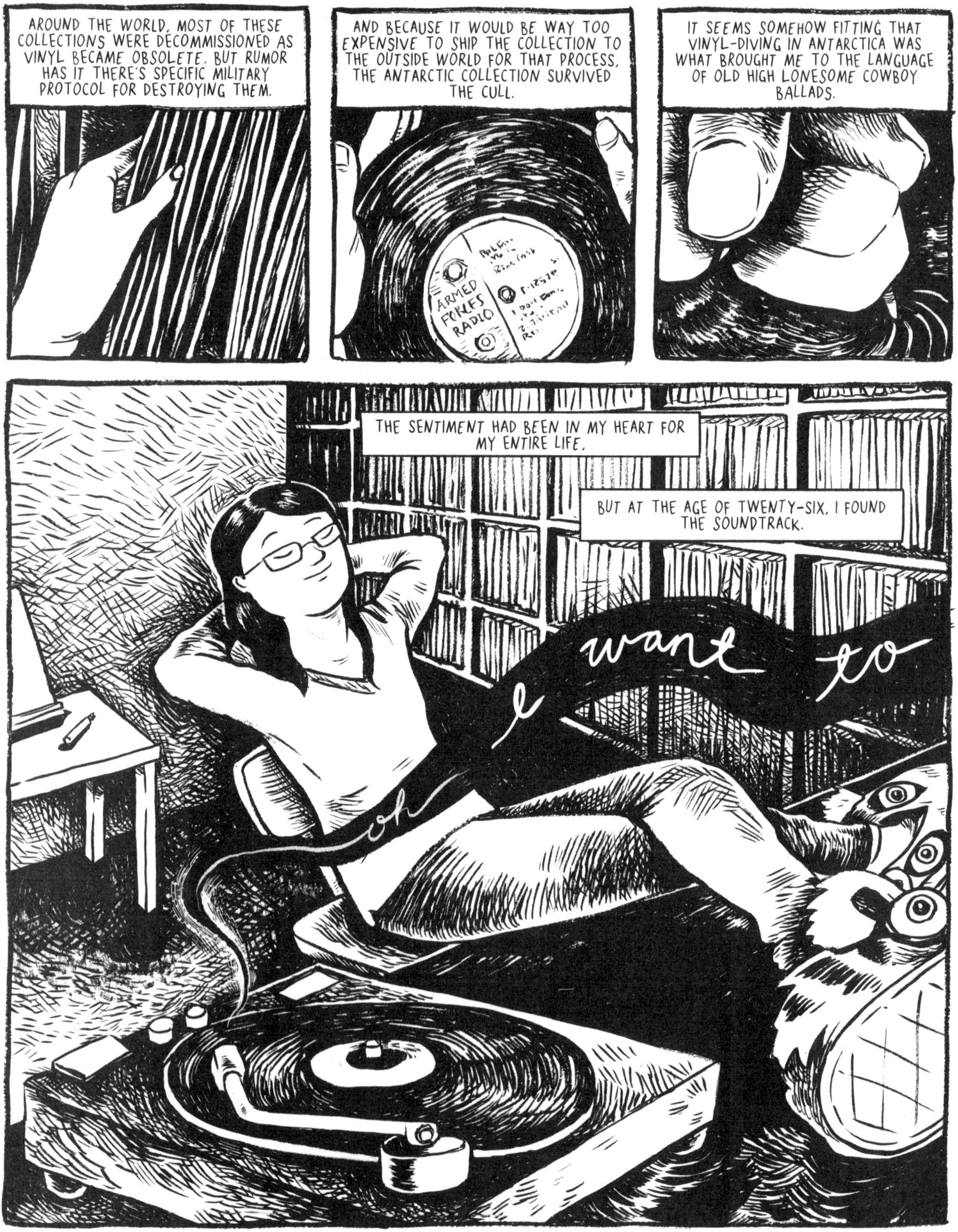
AROUND THE WORLD, MOST OF THESE COLLECTIONS WERE DECOMMISSIONED AS VINYL BECAME OBSOLETE. BUT RUMOR HAS IT THERE'S SPECIFIC MILITARY PROTOCOL FOR DESTROYING THEM.
AND BECAUSE IT WOULD BE WAY TOO EXPENSIVE TO SHIP THE COLLECTION TO THE OUTSIDE WORLD FOR THAT PROCESS, THE ANTARCTIC COLLECTION SURVIVED THE CULL.
IT SEEMS SOMEHOW FITTING THAT VINYL-DIVING IN ANTARCTICA WAS WHAT BROUGHT ME TO THE LANGUAGE OF OLD HIGH LONESOME COWBOY BALLADS.
THE SENTIMENT HAD BEEN IN MY HEART FOR MY ENTIRE LIFE,
BUT AT THE AGE OF TWENTY-SIX, I FOUND THE SOUNDTRACK.
oh I want to

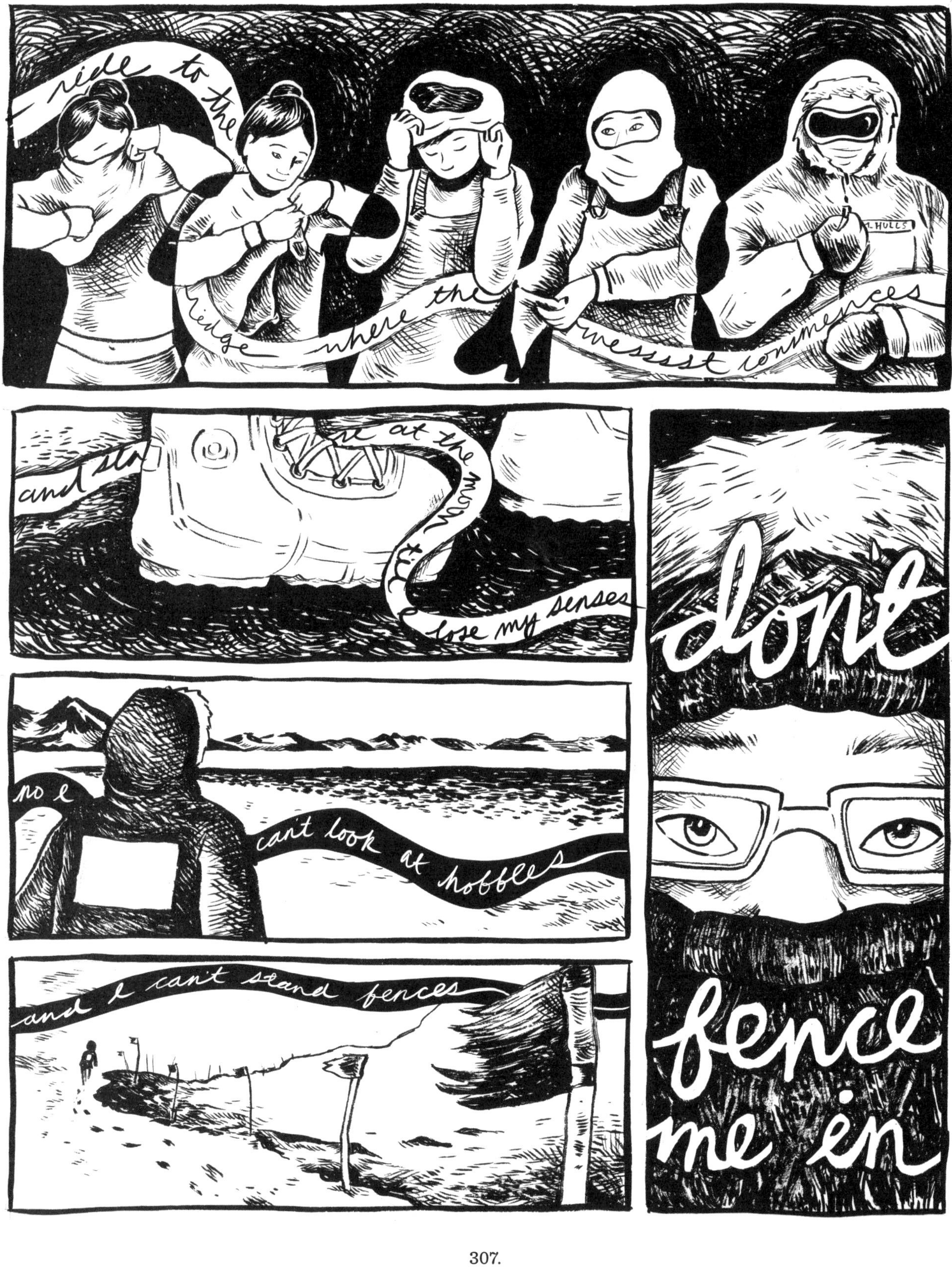
ride to the ridge where the wessssst commences
L. HULLS
and st
e at the moon til
lose my senses
no I can't look at hobbles
and I can't stand fences
don't fence me in

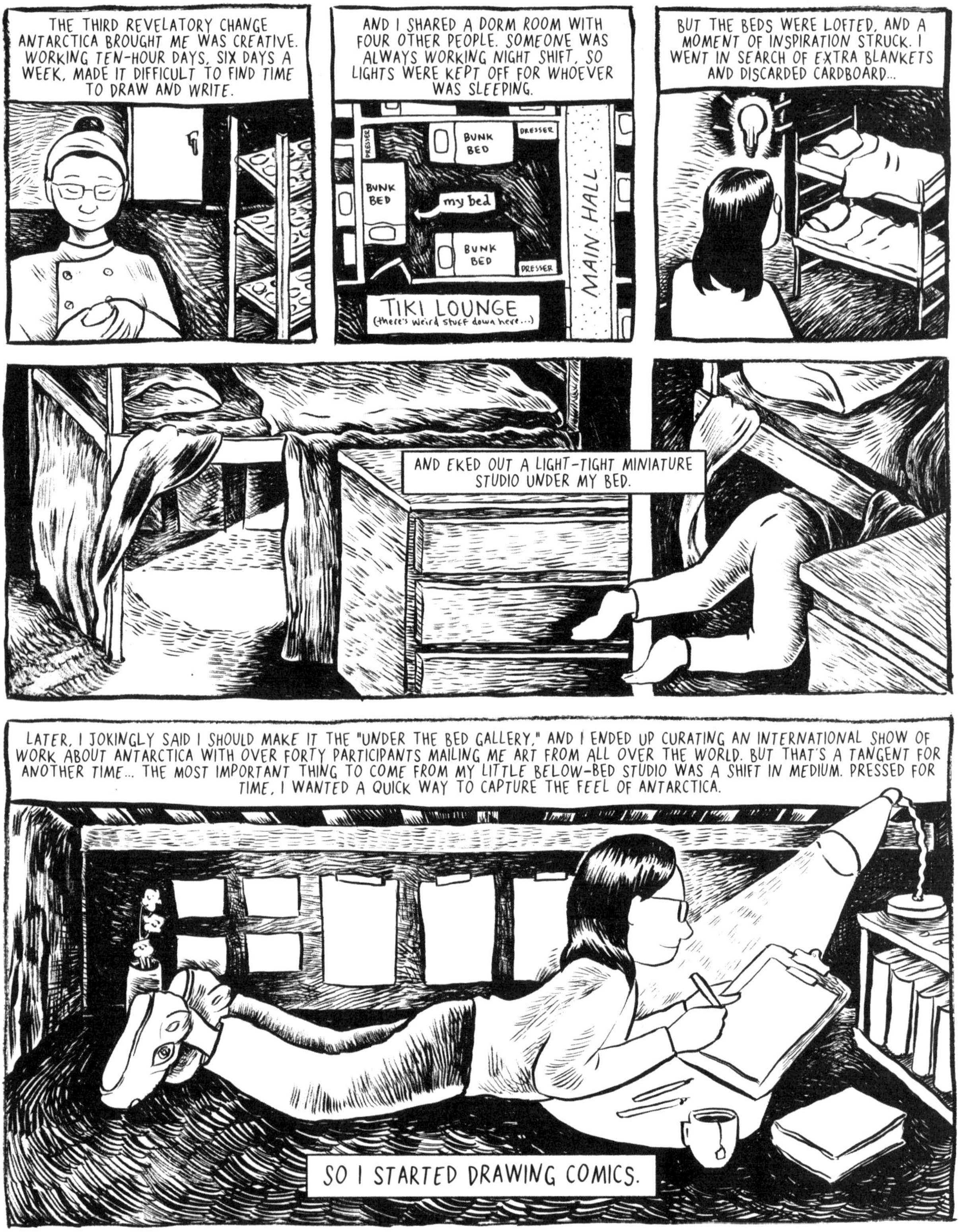
THE THIRD REVELATORY CHANGE ANTARCTICA BROUGHT ME WAS CREATIVE. WORKING TEN-HOUR DAYS, SIX DAYS A WEEK, MADE IT DIFFICULT TO FIND TIME TO DRAW AND WRITE.
AND I SHARED A DORM ROOM WITH FOUR OTHER PEOPLE. SOMEONE WAS ALWAYS WORKING NIGHT SHIFT, SO LIGHTS WERE KEPT OFF FOR WHOEVER WAS SLEEPING.
DRESSER
BUNK BED
DRESSER
BUNK BED
my bed
BUNK BED
DRESSER
MAIN HALL
TIKI LOUNGE
(there's weird stuff down here...)
BUT THE BEDS WERE LOFTED, AND A MOMENT OF INSPIRATION STRUCK. I WENT IN SEARCH OF EXTRA BLANKETS AND DISCARDED CARDBOARD...
AND EKED OUT A LIGHT-TIGHT MINIATURE STUDIO UNDER MY BED.
LATER, I JOKINGLY SAID I SHOULD MAKE IT THE "UNDER THE BED GALLERY," AND I ENDED UP CURATING AN INTERNATIONAL SHOW OF WORK ABOUT ANTARCTICA WITH OVER FORTY PARTICIPANTS MAILING ME ART FROM ALL OVER THE WORLD. BUT THAT'S A TANGENT FOR ANOTHER TIME... THE MOST IMPORTANT THING TO COME FROM MY LITTLE BELOW-BED STUDIO WAS A SHIFT IN MEDIUM. PRESSED FOR TIME, I WANTED A QUICK WAY TO CAPTURE THE FEEL OF ANTARCTICA.
SO I STARTED DRAWING COMICS.

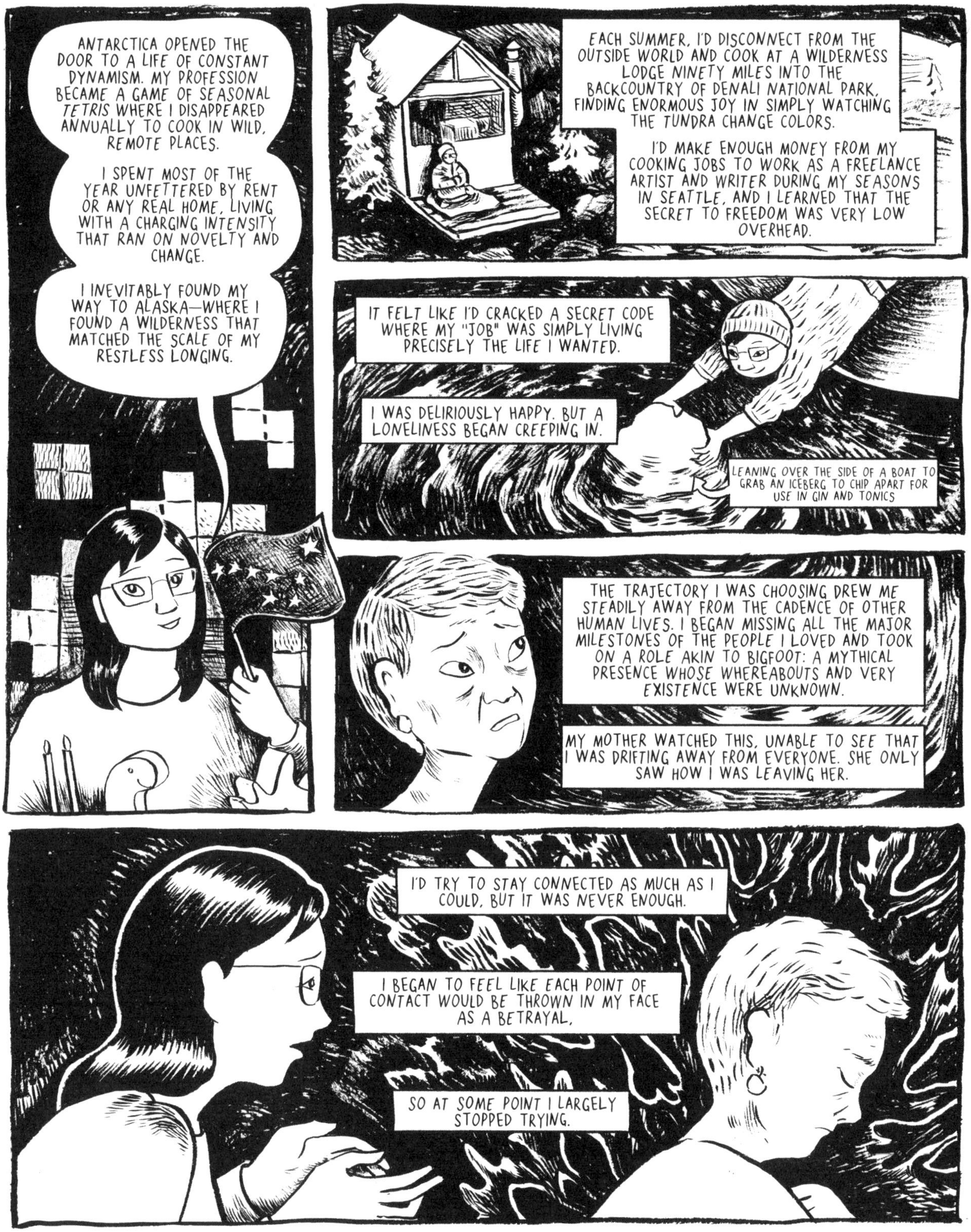
ANTARCTICA OPENED THE DOOR TO A LIFE OF CONSTANT DYNAMISM. MY PROFESSION BECAME A GAME OF SEASONAL *TETRIS* WHERE I DISAPPEARED ANNUALLY TO COOK IN WILD, REMOTE PLACES.
I SPENT MOST OF THE YEAR UNFETTERED BY RENT OR ANY REAL HOME, LIVING WITH A CHARGING INTENSITY THAT RAN ON NOVELTY AND CHANGE.
I INEVITABLY FOUND MY WAY TO ALASKA—WHERE I FOUND A WILDERNESS THAT MATCHED THE SCALE OF MY RESTLESS LONGING.
EACH SUMMER, I'D DISCONNECT FROM THE OUTSIDE WORLD AND COOK AT A WILDERNESS LODGE NINETY MILES INTO THE BACKCOUNTRY OF DENALI NATIONAL PARK, FINDING ENORMOUS JOY IN SIMPLY WATCHING THE TUNDRA CHANGE COLORS.
I'D MAKE ENOUGH MONEY FROM MY COOKING JOBS TO WORK AS A FREELANCE ARTIST AND WRITER DURING MY SEASONS IN SEATTLE, AND I LEARNED THAT THE SECRET TO FREEDOM WAS VERY LOW OVERHEAD.
IT FELT LIKE I'D CRACKED A SECRET CODE WHERE MY "JOB" WAS SIMPLY LIVING PRECISELY THE LIFE I WANTED.
I WAS DELIRIOUSLY HAPPY. BUT A LONELINESS BEGAN CREEPING IN.
LEANING OVER THE SIDE OF A BOAT TO GRAB AN ICEBERG TO CHIP APART FOR USE IN GIN AND TONICS
THE TRAJECTORY I WAS CHOOSING DREW ME STEADILY AWAY FROM THE CADENCE OF OTHER HUMAN LIVES. I BEGAN MISSING ALL THE MAJOR MILESTONES OF THE PEOPLE I LOVED AND TOOK ON A ROLE AKIN TO BIGFOOT: A MYTHICAL PRESENCE WHOSE WHEREABOUTS AND VERY EXISTENCE WERE UNKNOWN.
MY MOTHER WATCHED THIS, UNABLE TO SEE THAT I WAS DRIFTING AWAY FROM EVERYONE. SHE ONLY SAW HOW I WAS LEAVING HER.
I'D TRY TO STAY CONNECTED AS MUCH AS I COULD, BUT IT WAS NEVER ENOUGH.
I BEGAN TO FEEL LIKE EACH POINT OF CONTACT WOULD BE THROWN IN MY FACE AS A BETRAYAL,
SO AT SOME POINT I LARGELY STOPPED TRYING.

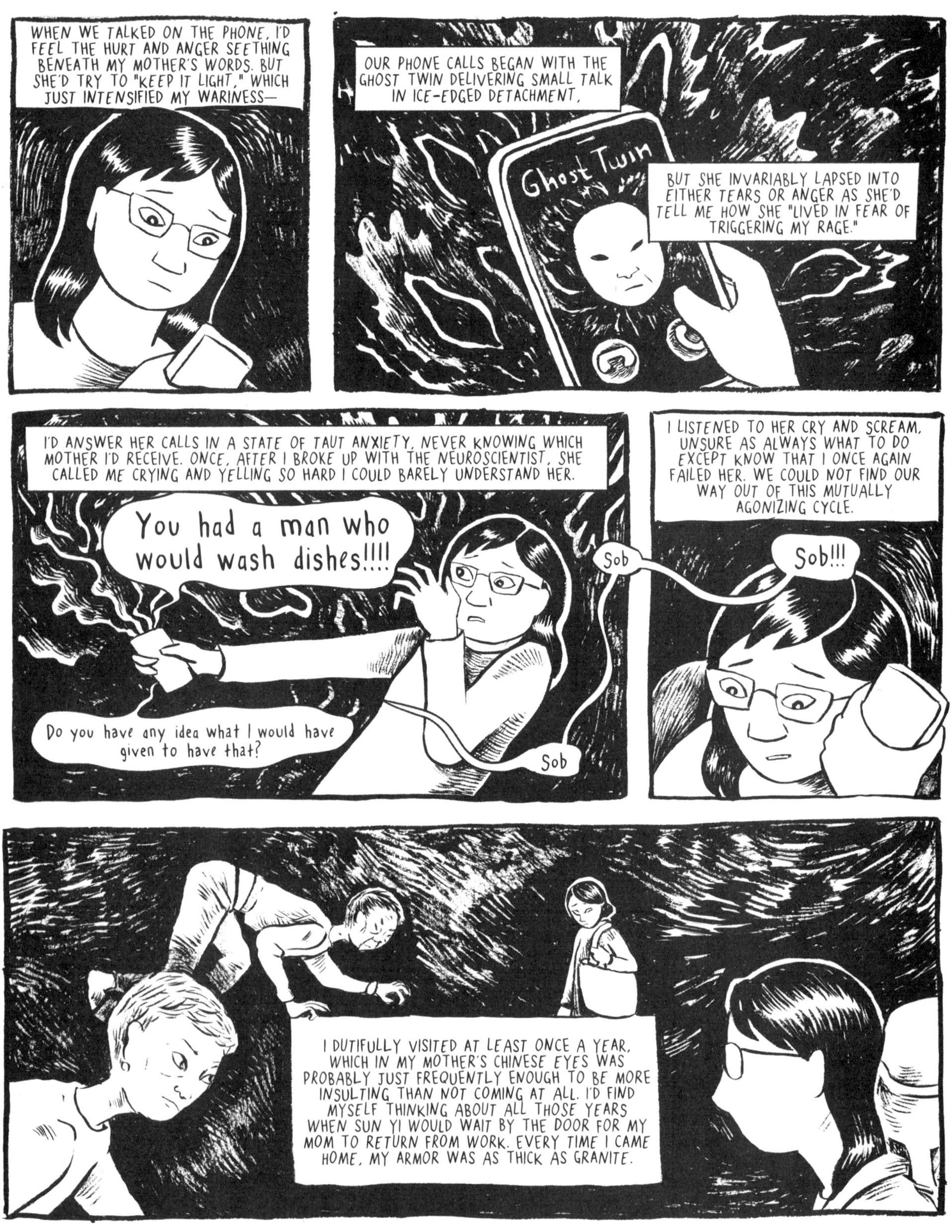
WHEN WE TALKED ON THE PHONE, I'D FEEL THE HURT AND ANGER SEETHING BENEATH MY MOTHER'S WORDS. BUT SHE'D TRY TO "KEEP IT LIGHT," WHICH JUST INTENSIFIED MY WARINESS—
OUR PHONE CALLS BEGAN WITH THE GHOST TWIN DELIVERING SMALL TALK IN ICE-EDGED DETACHMENT,
Ghost Twin
BUT SHE INVARIABLY LAPSED INTO EITHER TEARS OR ANGER AS SHE'D TELL ME HOW SHE "LIVED IN FEAR OF TRIGGERING MY RAGE."
I'D ANSWER HER CALLS IN A STATE OF TAUT ANXIETY, NEVER KNOWING WHICH MOTHER I'D RECEIVE. ONCE, AFTER I BROKE UP WITH THE NEUROSCIENTIST, SHE CALLED ME CRYING AND YELLING SO HARD I COULD BARELY UNDERSTAND HER.
You had a man who would wash dishes!!!!
Do you have any idea what I would have given to have that?
Sob
Sob
I LISTENED TO HER CRY AND SCREAM, UNSURE AS ALWAYS WHAT TO DO EXCEPT KNOW THAT I ONCE AGAIN FAILED HER. WE COULD NOT FIND OUR WAY OUT OF THIS MUTUALLY AGONIZING CYCLE.
Sob!!!
I DUTIFULLY VISITED AT LEAST ONCE A YEAR, WHICH IN MY MOTHER'S CHINESE EYES WAS PROBABLY JUST FREQUENTLY ENOUGH TO BE MORE INSULTING THAN NOT COMING AT ALL. I'D FIND MYSELF THINKING ABOUT ALL THOSE YEARS WHEN SUN YI WOULD WAIT BY THE DOOR FOR MY MOM TO RETURN FROM WORK. EVERY TIME I CAME HOME, MY ARMOR WAS AS THICK AS GRANITE.

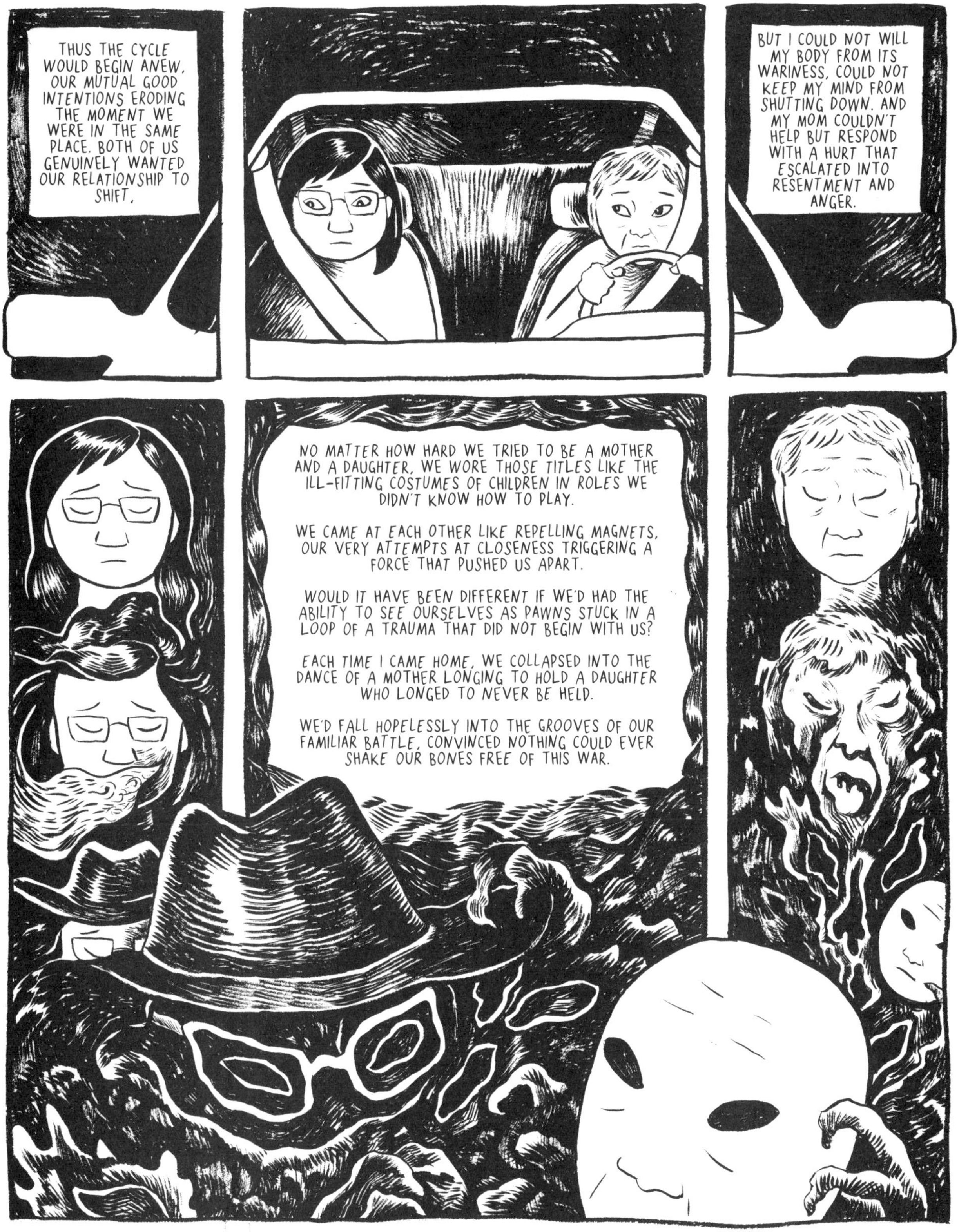

THUS THE CYCLE WOULD BEGIN ANEW, OUR MUTUAL GOOD INTENTIONS ERODING THE MOMENT WE WERE IN THE SAME PLACE. BOTH OF US GENUINELY WANTED OUR RELATIONSHIP TO SHIFT.
BUT I COULD NOT WILL MY BODY FROM ITS WARINESS, COULD NOT KEEP MY MIND FROM SHUTTING DOWN. AND MY MOM COULDN'T HELP BUT RESPOND WITH A HURT THAT ESCALATED INTO RESENTMENT AND ANGER.
NO MATTER HOW HARD WE TRIED TO BE A MOTHER AND A DAUGHTER, WE WORE THOSE TITLES LIKE THE ILL-FITTING COSTUMES OF CHILDREN IN ROLES WE DIDN'T KNOW HOW TO PLAY.
WE CAME AT EACH OTHER LIKE REPELLING MAGNETS, OUR VERY ATTEMPTS AT CLOSENESS TRIGGERING A FORCE THAT PUSHED US APART.
WOULD IT HAVE BEEN DIFFERENT IF WE'D HAD THE ABILITY TO SEE OURSELVES AS PAWNS STUCK IN A LOOP OF A TRAUMA THAT DID NOT BEGIN WITH US?
EACH TIME I CAME HOME, WE COLLAPSED INTO THE DANCE OF A MOTHER LONGING TO HOLD A DAUGHTER WHO LONGED TO NEVER BE HELD.
WE'D FALL HOPELESSLY INTO THE GROOVES OF OUR FAMILIAR BATTLE, CONVINCED NOTHING COULD EVER SHAKE OUR BONES FREE OF THIS WAR.

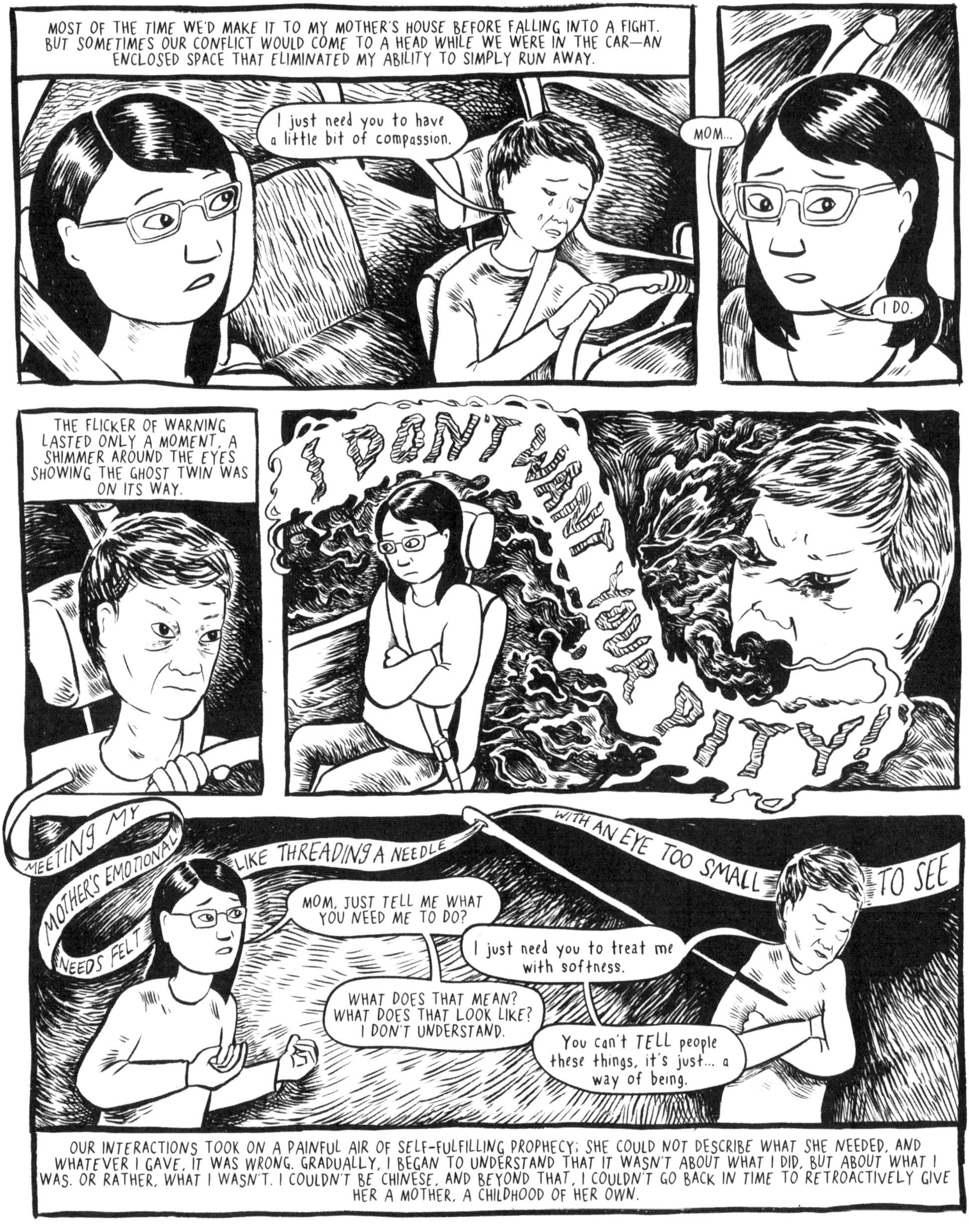

MOST OF THE TIME WE'D MAKE IT TO MY MOTHER'S HOUSE BEFORE FALLING INTO A FIGHT. BUT SOMETIMES OUR CONFLICT WOULD COME TO A HEAD WHILE WE WERE IN THE CAR—AN ENCLOSED SPACE THAT ELIMINATED MY ABILITY TO SIMPLY RUN AWAY.
I just need you to have a little bit of compassion.
MOM...
I DO.
THE FLICKER OF WARNING LASTED ONLY A MOMENT, A SHIMMER AROUND THE EYES SHOWING THE GHOST TWIN WAS ON ITS WAY.
I DON'T WANT YOUR PITY!
MEETING MY MOTHER'S EMOTIONAL NEEDS FELT LIKE THREADING A NEEDLE WITH AN EYE TOO SMALL TO SEE
MOM, JUST TELL ME WHAT YOU NEED ME TO DO?
I just need you to treat me with softness.
WHAT DOES THAT MEAN? WHAT DOES THAT LOOK LIKE? I DON'T UNDERSTAND.
You can't TELL people these things, it's just... a way of being.
OUR INTERACTIONS TOOK ON A PAINFUL AIR OF SELF-FULFILLING PROPHECY; SHE COULD NOT DESCRIBE WHAT SHE NEEDED, AND WHATEVER I GAVE, IT WAS WRONG. GRADUALLY, I BEGAN TO UNDERSTAND THAT IT WASN'T ABOUT WHAT I DID, BUT ABOUT WHAT I WAS. OR RATHER, WHAT I WASN'T. I COULDN'T BE CHINESE, AND BEYOND THAT, I COULDN'T GO BACK IN TIME TO RETROACTIVELY GIVE HER A MOTHER, A CHILDHOOD OF HER OWN.

THESE VISITS WERE MUTUALLY AGONIZING, MADE ALL THE WORSE FOR BEGINNING EACH TIME IN A PLACE OF GENUINE HOPE. SO WHEN THEY CONSISTENTLY ENDED IN SCORCHED EARTH,

I'D HOLD MY BREATH UNTIL I MADE IT TO THE AIRPORT, WHERE I COULD COLLAPSE IN SHAKEN RELIEF OVER AN OVERPRICED BEER.

GOING "HOME" LEVELED ME, SEARING AWAY ALL FEELING EXCEPT A FERAL NEED TO RUN.

MOSTLY, THOSE VISITS BACK LEFT ME IN A PLACE OF OVERWHELMING DOUBT.

GOING HOME WAS LIKE STANDING IN A HURRICANE, WHERE MY FAMILY'S NARRATIVE ABOUT ME—BROKEN, COLD, SELFISH, ANGRY, UNSTABLE—PELTED MY SKIN LIKE HAIL. BY THE END OF EACH VISIT I'D WONDER, WERE THEY RIGHT? WAS I IN FACT CRAZY? WAS I LYING TO MYSELF ABOUT WHO AND WHAT I WAS? WAS ANYTHING REAL?

SAY I AM I AM NOT WHAT THEY SAY I AM I AM NOT WHAT THEY SAY I AM I AM NOT WHAT THEY SAY I AM I NOT WHAT THEY SAY I AM I AM NOT WHAT THEY SAY I AM I AM NOT WHAT THEY SAY I AM I AM NOT WHAT THEY SAY I AM I AM NOT WHAT THEY SAY I AM I AM NOT WHAT THEY SAY I AM I AM NOT WHAT THEY SAY I AM I AM NOT WHAT THEY SAY I AM I AM NOT WHAT THEY SAY I AM I AM NOT WHAT THEY SAY I AM I AM NOT WHAT THEY SAY I AM I AM NOT WHAT THEY SAY I AM I AM NOT WHAT THEY SAY I AM I AM NOT WHAT THEY SAY I AM I AM NOT WHAT THEY SAY I AM I AM

I'D COME HOME TO SEATTLE AND TRY TO SETTLE BACK INTO THE SOLID COMFORT OF THE LIFE AND COMMUNITY I'D WORKED SO HARD TO BUILD. BUT I'D SPEND DAYS TRAPPED WITHIN A CYCLE OF REFUTATION, VACILLATING BETWEEN FEELING HOPELESS AND NUMB.

MY FRIENDS WOULD HELP ME COME BACK TO MYSELF, TO BRING MY HEART OUT OF HIDING.

THEY TRUSTED ME WHEN I COULD NOT TRUST MYSELF, AND I RELIED ON THEM TO FIND MY WAY BACK TO SOLID GROUND.

SLOWLY, THE PANIC WOULD SUBSIDE. MY FAMILY'S STORY WOULD FADE, AND I'D GET BACK TO A LIFE THAT SHIFTED WITH EACH SEASON.

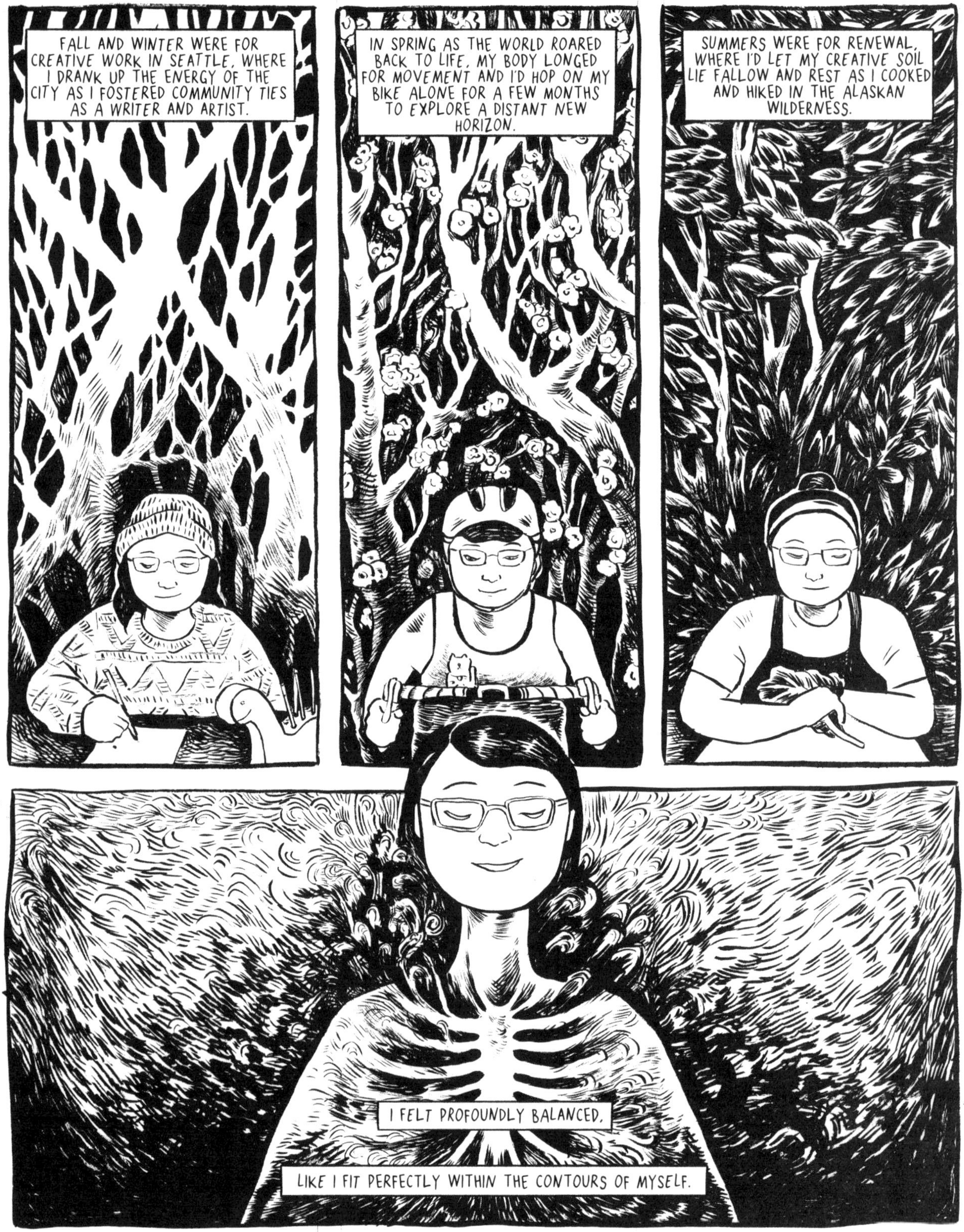
FALL AND WINTER WERE FOR CREATIVE WORK IN SEATTLE, WHERE I DRANK UP THE ENERGY OF THE CITY AS I FOSTERED COMMUNITY TIES AS A WRITER AND ARTIST.
IN SPRING AS THE WORLD ROARED BACK TO LIFE, MY BODY LONGED FOR MOVEMENT AND I'D HOP ON MY BIKE ALONE FOR A FEW MONTHS TO EXPLORE A DISTANT NEW HORIZON.
SUMMERS WERE FOR RENEWAL, WHERE I'D LET MY CREATIVE SOIL LIE FALLOW AND REST AS I COOKED AND HIKED IN THE ALASKAN WILDERNESS.
I FELT PROFOUNDLY BALANCED,
LIKE I FIT PERFECTLY WITHIN THE CONTOURS OF MYSELF.

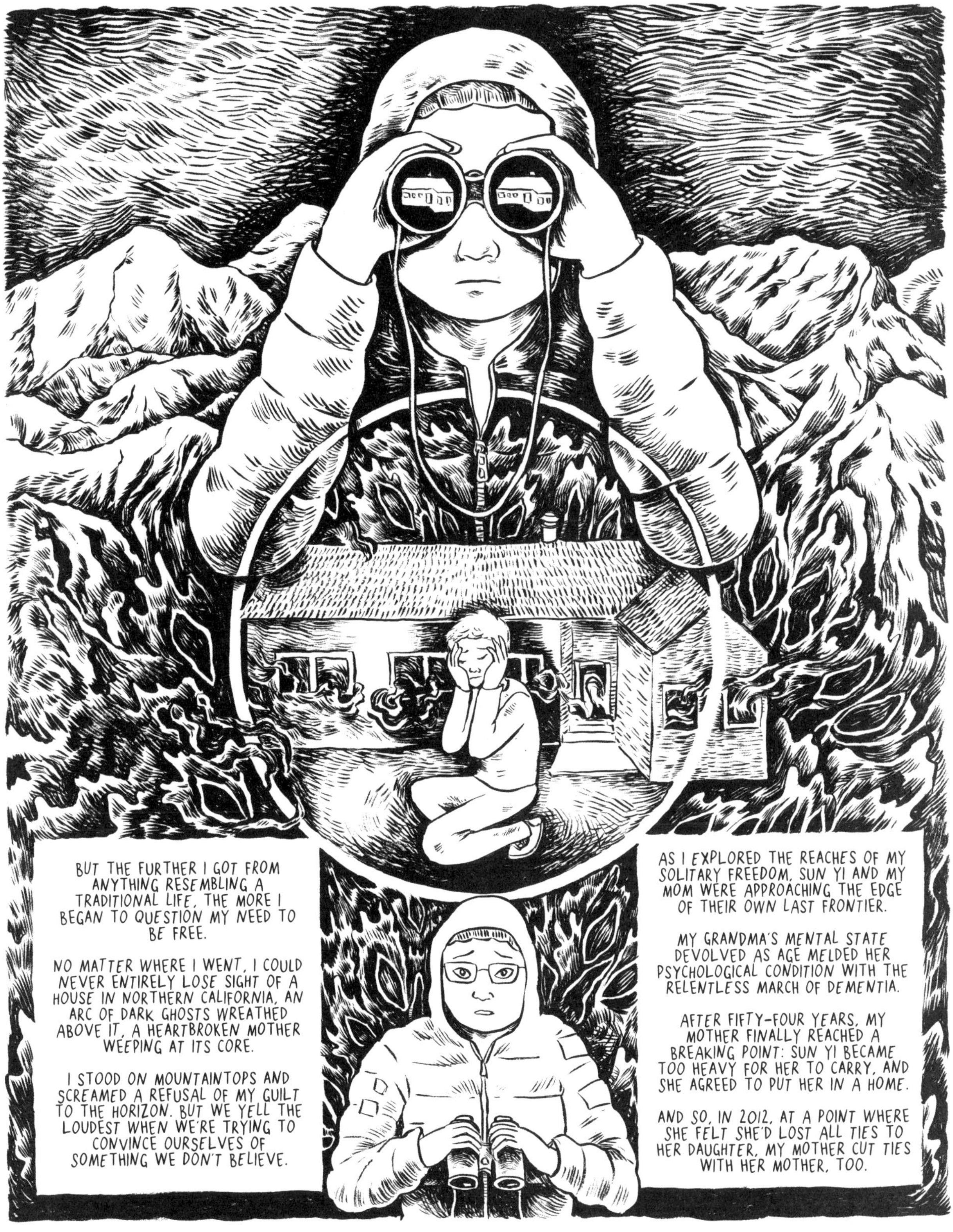

BUT THE FURTHER I GOT FROM ANYTHING RESEMBLING A TRADITIONAL LIFE, THE MORE I BEGAN TO QUESTION MY NEED TO BE FREE.
NO MATTER WHERE I WENT, I COULD NEVER ENTIRELY LOSE SIGHT OF A HOUSE IN NORTHERN CALIFORNIA, AN ARC OF DARK GHOSTS WREATHED ABOVE IT, A HEARTBROKEN MOTHER WEEPING AT ITS CORE.
I STOOD ON MOUNTAINTOPS AND SCREAMED A REFUSAL OF MY GUILT TO THE HORIZON. BUT WE YELL THE LOUDEST WHEN WE'RE TRYING TO CONVINCE OURSELVES OF SOMETHING WE DON'T BELIEVE.
AS I EXPLORED THE REACHES OF MY SOLITARY FREEDOM, SUN YI AND MY MOM WERE APPROACHING THE EDGE OF THEIR OWN LAST FRONTIER.
MY GRANDMA'S MENTAL STATE DEVOLVED AS AGE MELDED HER PSYCHOLOGICAL CONDITION WITH THE RELENTLESS MARCH OF DEMENTIA.
AFTER FIFTY-FOUR YEARS, MY MOTHER FINALLY REACHED A BREAKING POINT: SUN YI BECAME TOO HEAVY FOR HER TO CARRY, AND SHE AGREED TO PUT HER IN A HOME.
AND SO, IN 2012, AT A POINT WHERE SHE FELT SHE'D LOST ALL TIES TO HER DAUGHTER, MY MOTHER CUT TIES WITH HER MOTHER, TOO.

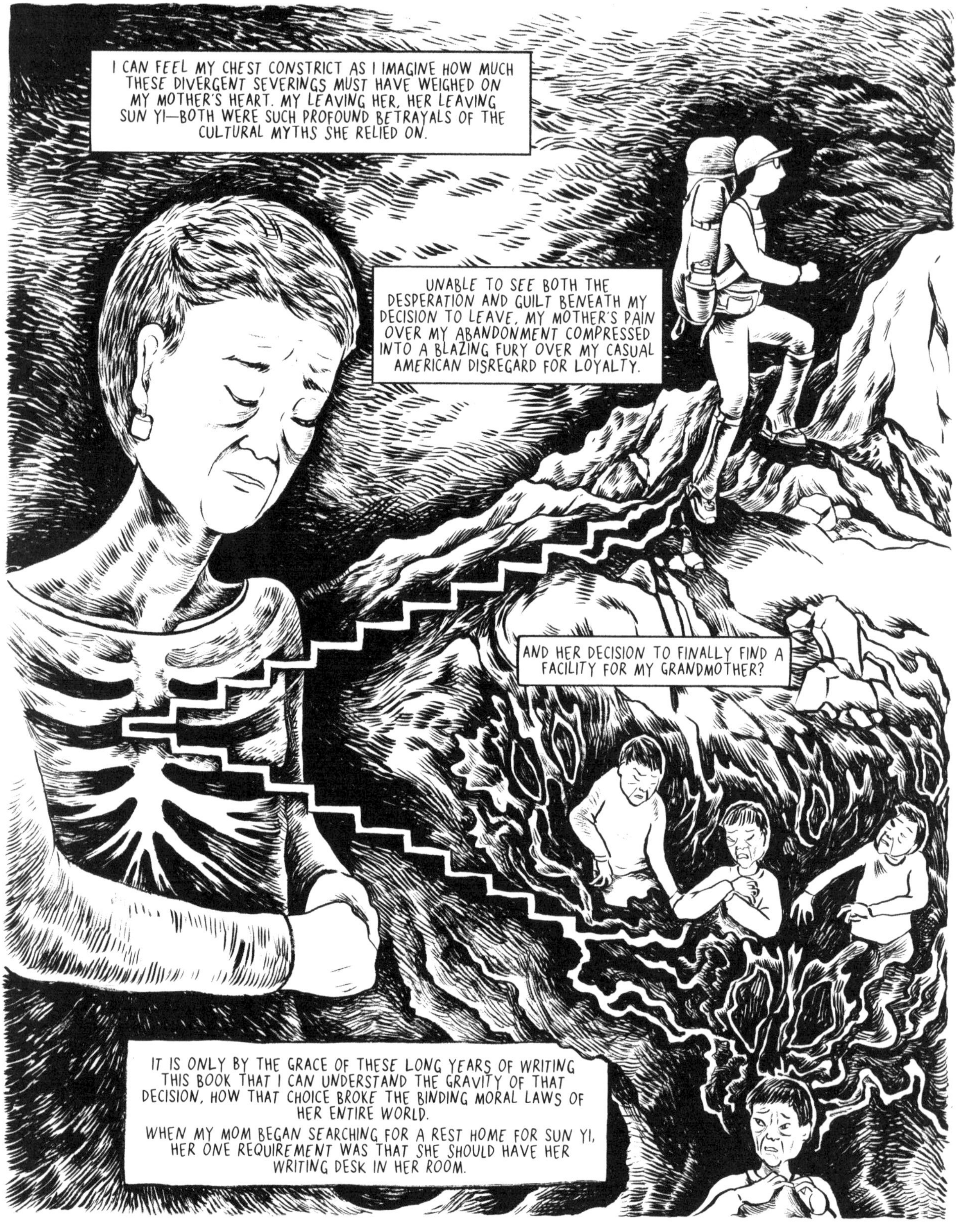
I CAN FEEL MY CHEST CONSTRICT AS I IMAGINE HOW MUCH THESE DIVERGENT SEVERINGS MUST HAVE WEIGHED ON MY MOTHER'S HEART. MY LEAVING HER, HER LEAVING SUN YI—BOTH WERE SUCH PROFOUND BETRAYALS OF THE CULTURAL MYTHS SHE RELIED ON.
UNABLE TO SEE BOTH THE DESPERATION AND GUILT BENEATH MY DECISION TO LEAVE, MY MOTHER'S PAIN OVER MY ABANDONMENT COMPRESSED INTO A BLAZING FURY OVER MY CASUAL AMERICAN DISREGARD FOR LOYALTY.
AND HER DECISION TO FINALLY FIND A FACILITY FOR MY GRANDMOTHER?
IT IS ONLY BY THE GRACE OF THESE LONG YEARS OF WRITING THIS BOOK THAT I CAN UNDERSTAND THE GRAVITY OF THAT DECISION, HOW THAT CHOICE BROKE THE BINDING MORAL LAWS OF HER ENTIRE WORLD.
WHEN MY MOM BEGAN SEARCHING FOR A REST HOME FOR SUN YI, HER ONE REQUIREMENT WAS THAT SHE SHOULD HAVE HER WRITING DESK IN HER ROOM.

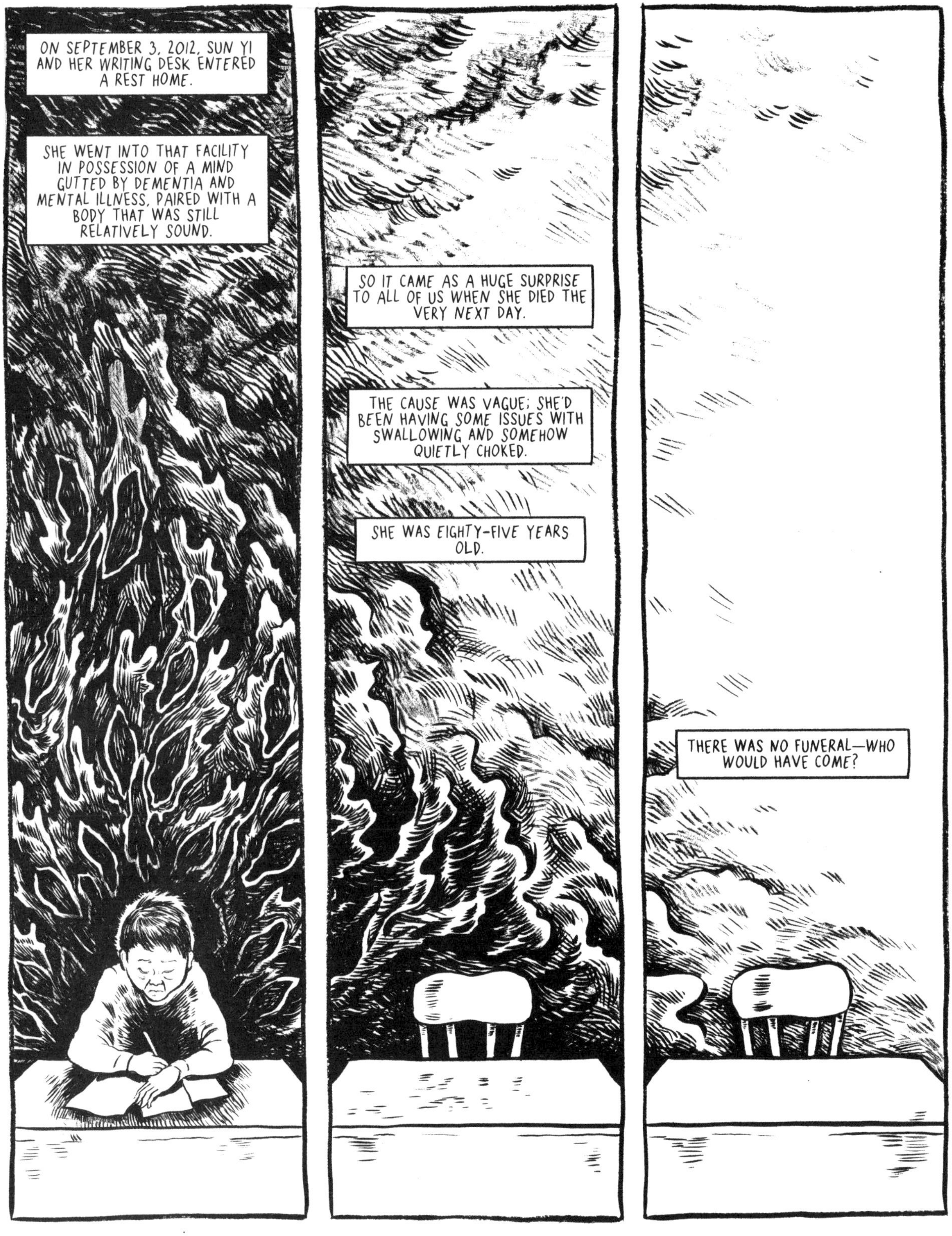
ON SEPTEMBER 3, 2012, SUN YI AND HER WRITING DESK ENTERED A REST HOME.
SHE WENT INTO THAT FACILITY IN POSSESSION OF A MIND GUTTED BY DEMENTIA AND MENTAL ILLNESS, PAIRED WITH A BODY THAT WAS STILL RELATIVELY SOUND.
SO IT CAME AS A HUGE SURPRISE TO ALL OF US WHEN SHE DIED THE VERY NEXT DAY.
THE CAUSE WAS VAGUE; SHE'D BEEN HAVING SOME ISSUES WITH SWALLOWING AND SOMEHOW QUIETLY CHOKED.
SHE WAS EIGHTY-FIVE YEARS OLD.
THERE WAS NO FUNERAL—WHO WOULD HAVE COME?

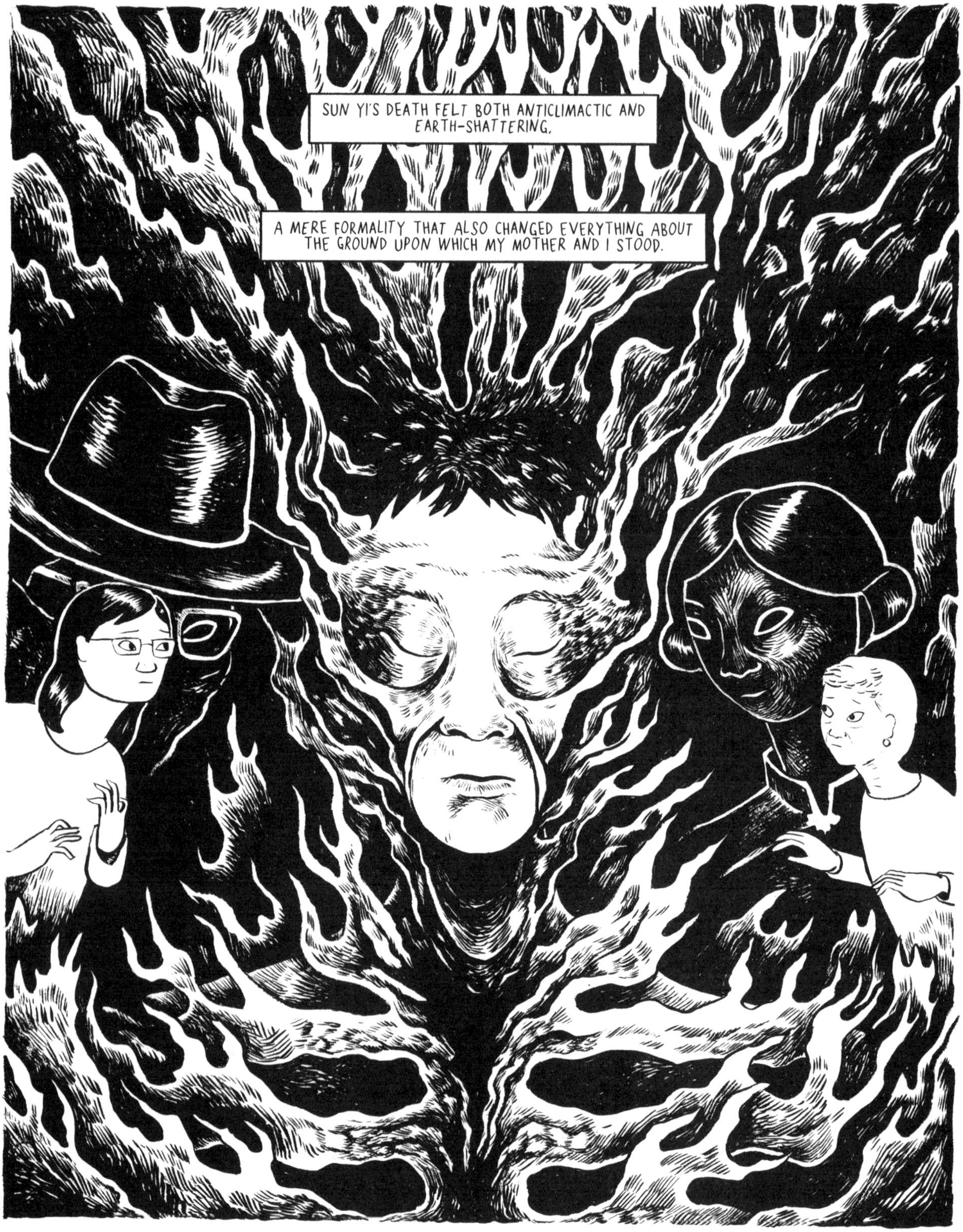
SUN YI'S DEATH FELT BOTH ANTICLIMACTIC AND EARTH-SHATTERING.
A MERE FORMALITY THAT ALSO CHANGED EVERYTHING ABOUT THE GROUND UPON WHICH MY MOTHER AND I STOOD.

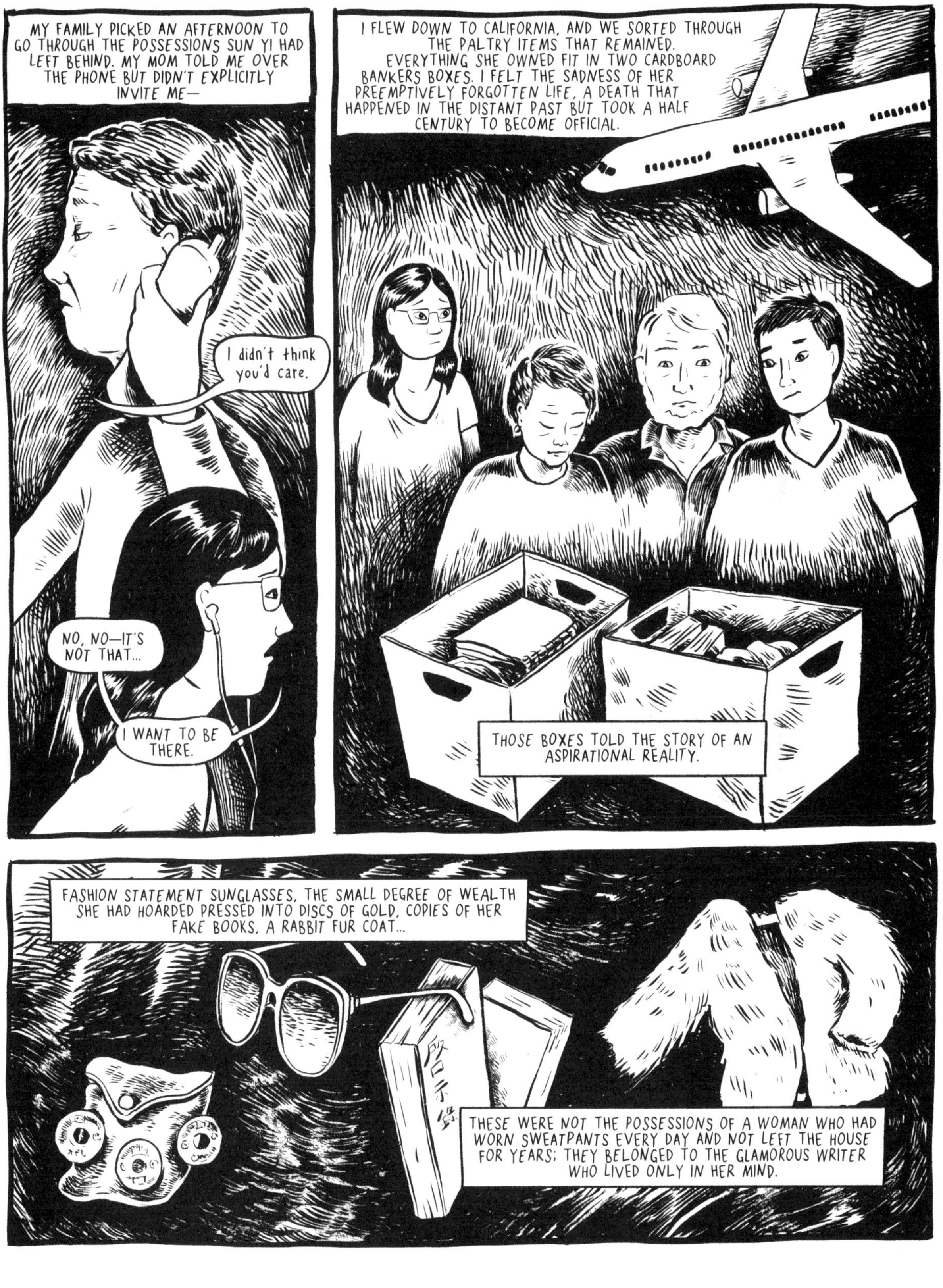
MY FAMILY PICKED AN AFTERNOON TO GO THROUGH THE POSSESSIONS SUN YI HAD LEFT BEHIND. MY MOM TOLD ME OVER THE PHONE BUT DIDN'T EXPLICITLY INVITE ME—
I didn't think you'd care.
NO, NO—IT'S NOT THAT...
I WANT TO BE THERE.
I FLEW DOWN TO CALIFORNIA, AND WE SORTED THROUGH THE PALTRY ITEMS THAT REMAINED. EVERYTHING SHE OWNED FIT IN TWO CARDBOARD BANKERS BOXES. I FELT THE SADNESS OF HER PREEMPTIVELY FORGOTTEN LIFE, A DEATH THAT HAPPENED IN THE DISTANT PAST BUT TOOK A HALF CENTURY TO BECOME OFFICIAL.
THOSE BOXES TOLD THE STORY OF AN ASPIRATIONAL REALITY.
FASHION STATEMENT SUNGLASSES, THE SMALL DEGREE OF WEALTH SHE HAD HOARDED PRESSED INTO DISCS OF GOLD, COPIES OF HER FAKE BOOKS, A RABBIT FUR COAT...
THESE WERE NOT THE POSSESSIONS OF A WOMAN WHO HAD WORN SWEATPANTS EVERY DAY AND NOT LEFT THE HOUSE FOR YEARS; THEY BELONGED TO THE GLAMOROUS WRITER WHO LIVED ONLY IN HER MIND.

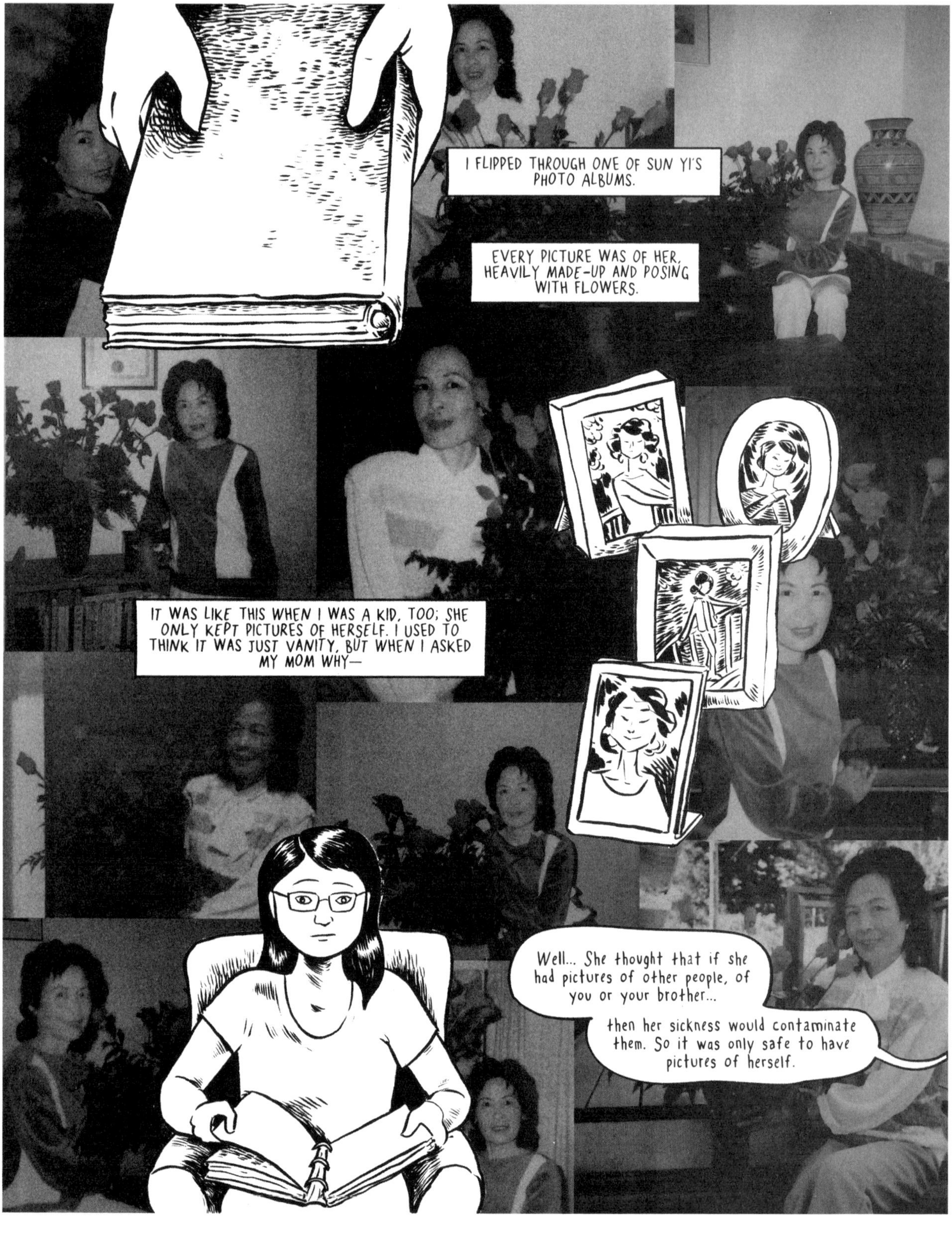
I FLIPPED THROUGH ONE OF SUN YI'S PHOTO ALBUMS.
EVERY PICTURE WAS OF HER, HEAVILY MADE-UP AND POSING WITH FLOWERS.
IT WAS LIKE THIS WHEN I WAS A KID, TOO; SHE ONLY KEPT PICTURES OF HERSELF. I USED TO THINK IT WAS JUST VANITY, BUT WHEN I ASKED MY MOM WHY—
Well... She thought that if she had pictures of other people, of you or your brother...
then her sickness would contaminate them. So it was only safe to have pictures of herself.

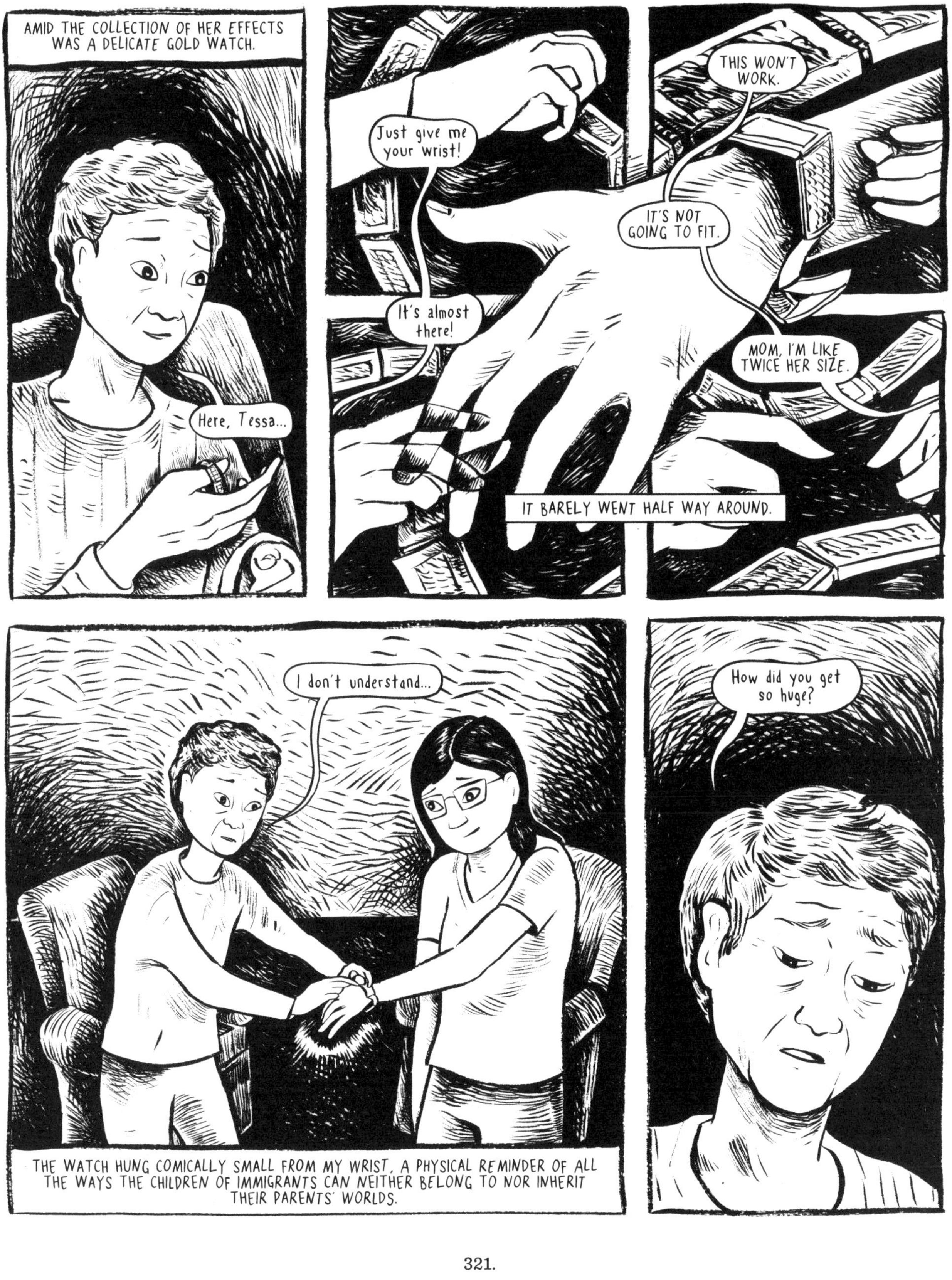
AMID THE COLLECTION OF HER EFFECTS WAS A DELICATE GOLD WATCH.
Here, Tessa...
Just give me your wrist!
It's almost there!
THIS WON'T WORK.
IT'S NOT GOING TO FIT.
MOM, I'M LIKE TWICE HER SIZE.
IT BARELY WENT HALF WAY AROUND.
I don't understand...
THE WATCH HUNG COMICALLY SMALL FROM MY WRIST, A PHYSICAL REMINDER OF ALL THE WAYS THE CHILDREN OF IMMIGRANTS CAN NEITHER BELONG TO NOR INHERIT THEIR PARENTS' WORLDS.
How did you get so huge?

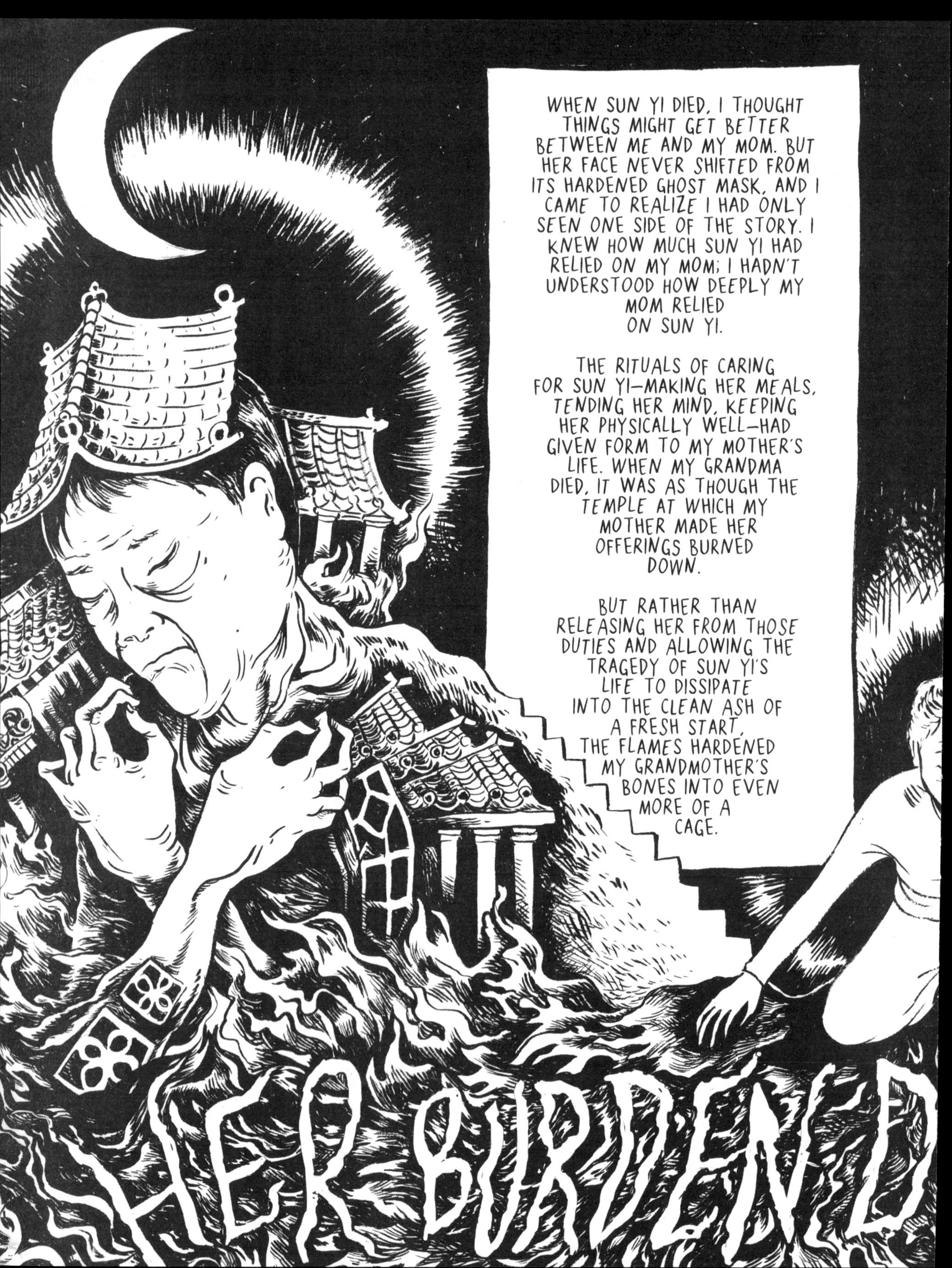
WHEN SUN YI DIED, I THOUGHT THINGS MIGHT GET BETTER BETWEEN ME AND MY MOM. BUT HER FACE NEVER SHIFTED FROM ITS HARDENED GHOST MASK, AND I CAME TO REALIZE I HAD ONLY SEEN ONE SIDE OF THE STORY. I KNEW HOW MUCH SUN YI HAD RELIED ON MY MOM; I HADN'T UNDERSTOOD HOW DEEPLY MY MOM RELIED ON SUN YI.
THE RITUALS OF CARING FOR SUN YI—MAKING HER MEALS, TENDING HER MIND, KEEPING HER PHYSICALLY WELL—HAD GIVEN FORM TO MY MOTHER'S LIFE. WHEN MY GRANDMA DIED, IT WAS AS THOUGH THE TEMPLE AT WHICH MY MOTHER MADE HER OFFERINGS BURNED DOWN.
BUT RATHER THAN RELEASING HER FROM THOSE DUTIES AND ALLOWING THE TRAGEDY OF SUN YI'S LIFE TO DISSIPATE INTO THE CLEAN ASH OF A FRESH START, THE FLAMES HARDENED MY GRANDMOTHER'S BONES INTO EVEN MORE OF A CAGE.
HER BURDEN D

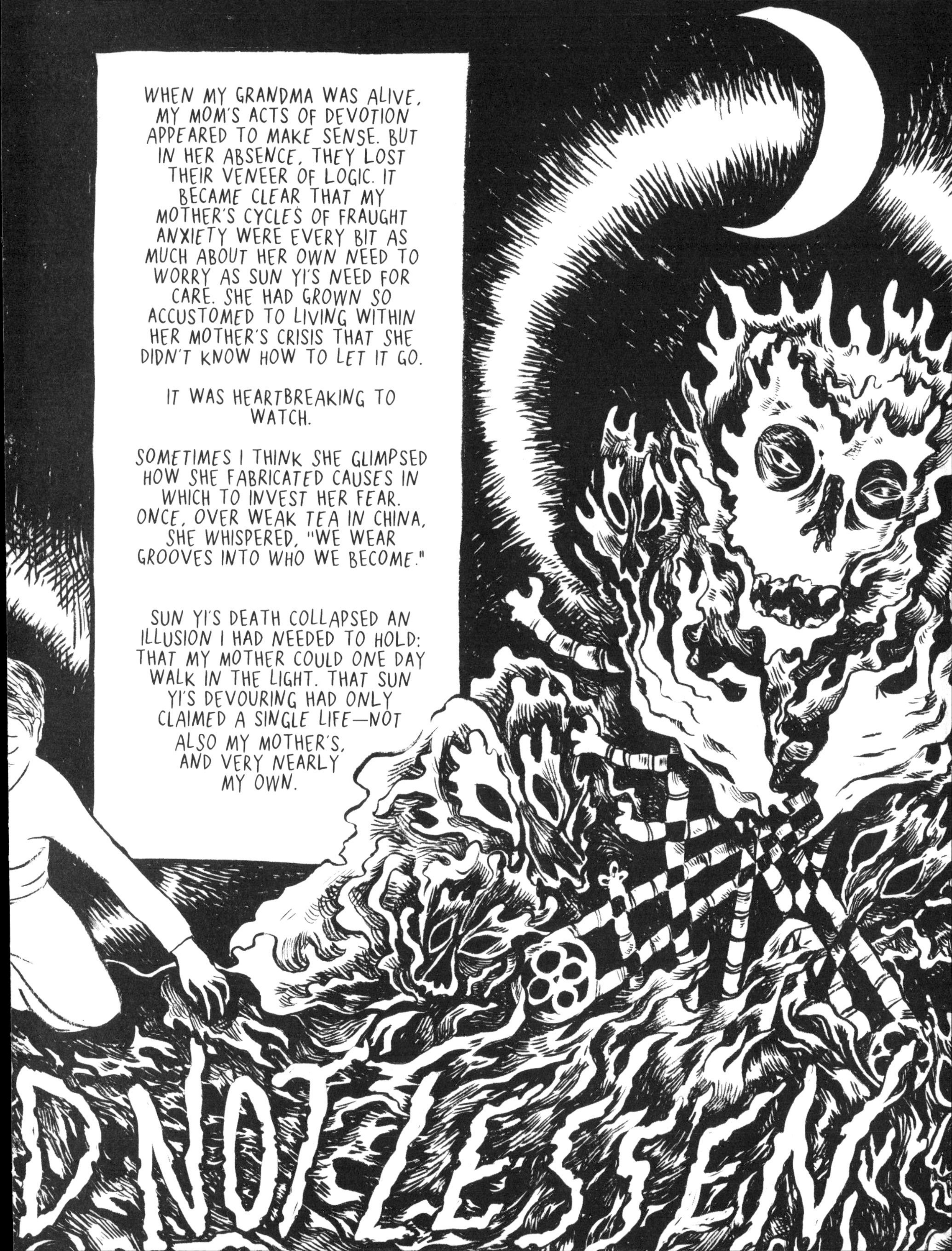
WHEN MY GRANDMA WAS ALIVE, MY MOM'S ACTS OF DEVOTION APPEARED TO MAKE SENSE. BUT IN HER ABSENCE, THEY LOST THEIR VENEER OF LOGIC. IT BECAME CLEAR THAT MY MOTHER'S CYCLES OF FRAUGHT ANXIETY WERE EVERY BIT AS MUCH ABOUT HER OWN NEED TO WORRY AS SUN YI'S NEED FOR CARE. SHE HAD GROWN SO ACCUSTOMED TO LIVING WITHIN HER MOTHER'S CRISIS THAT SHE DIDN'T KNOW HOW TO LET IT GO.
IT WAS HEARTBREAKING TO WATCH.
SOMETIMES I THINK SHE GLIMPSED HOW SHE FABRICATED CAUSES IN WHICH TO INVEST HER FEAR. ONCE, OVER WEAK TEA IN CHINA, SHE WHISPERED, "WE WEAR GROOVES INTO WHO WE BECOME."
SUN YI'S DEATH COLLAPSED AN ILLUSION I HAD NEEDED TO HOLD: THAT MY MOTHER COULD ONE DAY WALK IN THE LIGHT. THAT SUN YI'S DEVOURING HAD ONLY CLAIMED A SINGLE LIFE—NOT ALSO MY MOTHER'S, AND VERY NEARLY MY OWN.
D NOT LESSEN

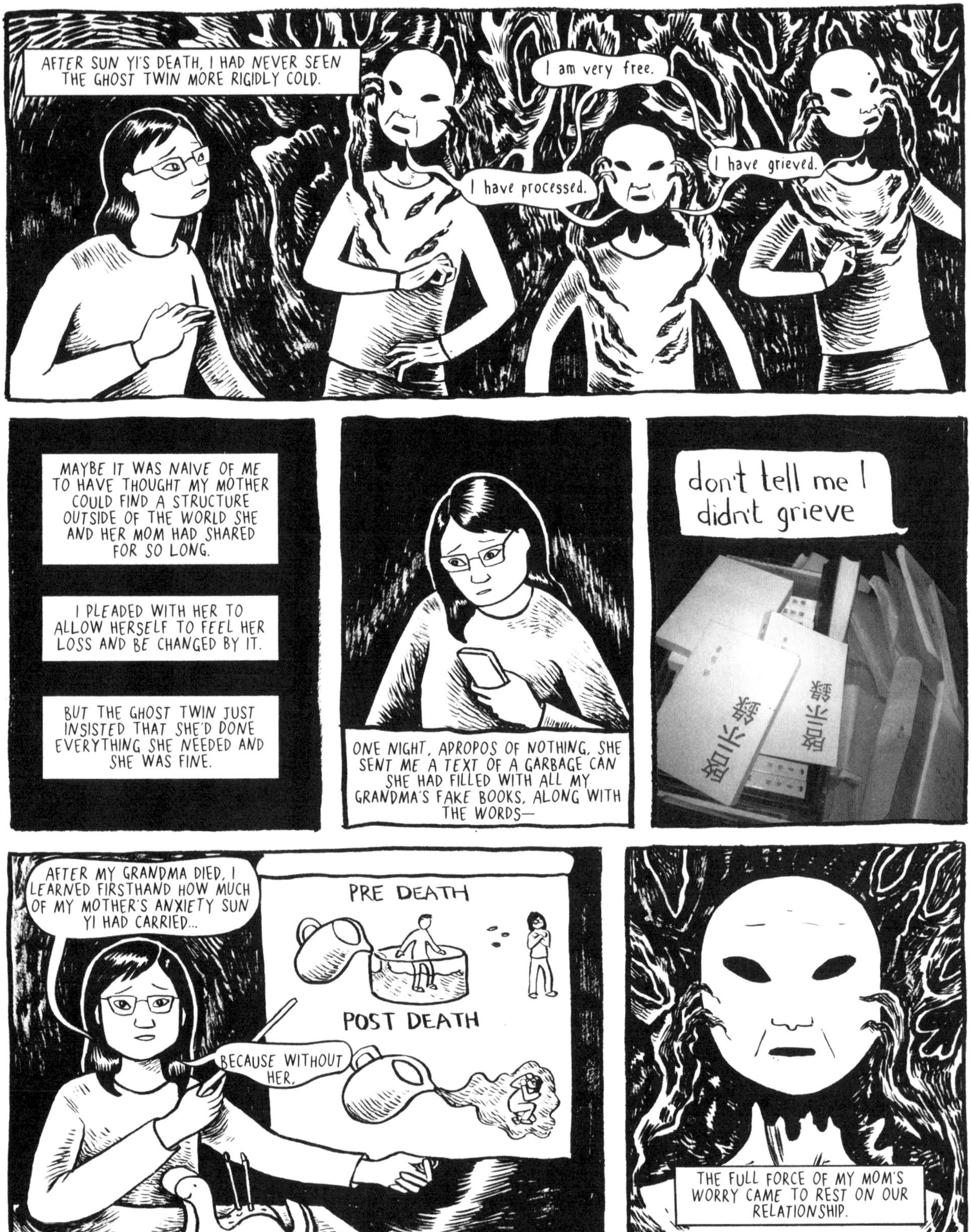
AFTER SUN YI'S DEATH, I HAD NEVER SEEN THE GHOST TWIN MORE RIGIDLY COLD.
I am very free.
I have processed.
I have grieved.
MAYBE IT WAS NAIVE OF ME TO HAVE THOUGHT MY MOTHER COULD FIND A STRUCTURE OUTSIDE OF THE WORLD SHE AND HER MOM HAD SHARED FOR SO LONG.
I PLEADED WITH HER TO ALLOW HERSELF TO FEEL HER LOSS AND BE CHANGED BY IT.
BUT THE GHOST TWIN JUST INSISTED THAT SHE'D DONE EVERYTHING SHE NEEDED AND SHE WAS FINE.
ONE NIGHT, APROPOS OF NOTHING, SHE SENT ME A TEXT OF A GARBAGE CAN SHE HAD FILLED WITH ALL MY GRANDMA'S FAKE BOOKS, ALONG WITH THE WORDS—
don't tell me I didn't grieve
AFTER MY GRANDMA DIED, I LEARNED FIRSTHAND HOW MUCH OF MY MOTHER'S ANXIETY SUN YI HAD CARRIED...
PRE DEATH
POST DEATH
BECAUSE WITHOUT HER,
THE FULL FORCE OF MY MOM'S WORRY CAME TO REST ON OUR RELATIONSHIP.

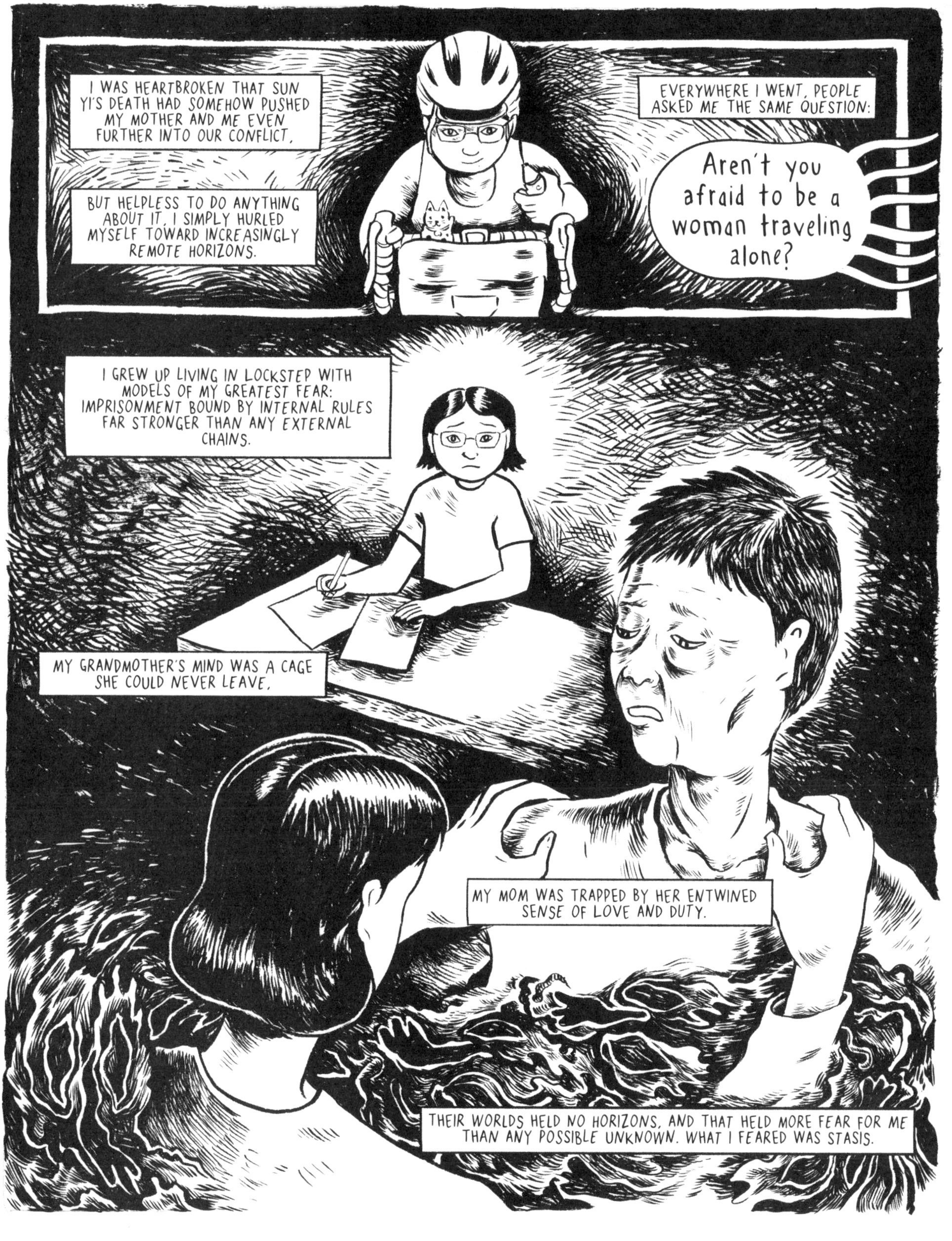
I WAS HEARTBROKEN THAT SUN YI'S DEATH HAD SOMEHOW PUSHED MY MOTHER AND ME EVEN FURTHER INTO OUR CONFLICT,
BUT HELPLESS TO DO ANYTHING ABOUT IT, I SIMPLY HURLED MYSELF TOWARD INCREASINGLY REMOTE HORIZONS.
EVERYWHERE I WENT, PEOPLE ASKED ME THE SAME QUESTION:
Aren't you afraid to be a woman traveling alone?
I GREW UP LIVING IN LOCKSTEP WITH MODELS OF MY GREATEST FEAR: IMPRISONMENT BOUND BY INTERNAL RULES FAR STRONGER THAN ANY EXTERNAL CHAINS.
MY GRANDMOTHER'S MIND WAS A CAGE SHE COULD NEVER LEAVE,
MY MOM WAS TRAPPED BY HER ENTWINED SENSE OF LOVE AND DUTY.
THEIR WORLDS HELD NO HORIZONS, AND THAT HELD MORE FEAR FOR ME THAN ANY POSSIBLE UNKNOWN. WHAT I FEARED WAS STASIS.

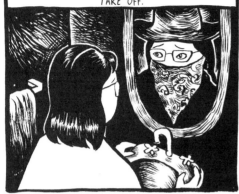

BUT THE MORE MY LIFE BECAME A CONSTANTLY MOVING SERIES OF EXPLORATIONS AND ADVENTURES, THE MORE I BEGAN TO FEEL A VITAL SOFTNESS CALCIFYING WITHIN ME. MY COWBOY WAS BECOMING SOMETHING I COULDN'T TAKE OFF.

DON'T GET ME WRONG—I LIVED TO FLING MYSELF INTO THE WORLD; BUT I ALSO SAW HOW I WAS USING MY CURIOSITY AS AN EXCUSE TO HIDE FROM MY GHOSTS. THE HOUSE OF CARDS BEGAN TO CRUMBLE IN 2014 WHEN I SPENT SIX WEEKS BIKING ALONE IN GHANA.

I HAVE A LONG-STANDING TRAVEL TRADITION OF BRINGING ONLY ONE BOOK FROM HOME TO START A TRIP.

AFTER THAT, I ONLY READ WHAT CROSSES MY PATH.

SERENDIPITY EMERGES AS A TEACHER, SHOWING ME QUESTIONS I DIDN'T REALIZE I WAS ALREADY BEGINNING TO ASK.

IT'S MY VERSION OF LIVE-ACTION TAROT READING. IT'S NOT THAT ANYTHING IS PREDICTING THE FUTURE, ONLY THAT YOU'RE GIVEN A DIFFERENT LENS THROUGH WHICH TO EXAMINE THE PRESENT.

Obruni!

China!

"FOREIGNER" IN TWI

EVERYONE IN GHANA PERCEIVED ME AS CHINESE

I CAME ACROSS A BOOKSELLER IN A MARKET IN TAMALE AND STUMBLED UPON TWO TITLES THAT HELPED ME SEE HOW MY BEDROCK WAS ALREADY SHIFTING. YOU SEE, MY CREATIVE PROCESS IS FERAL AND SECRETIVE.

My sister, come here!

IT QUIETLY CHEWS ON IDEAS FOR MONTHS OR YEARS BEFORE ALERTING MY CONSCIOUS MIND. THESE TITLES REVEALED TO ME THAT I WAS LAYING THE GROUNDWORK FOR THE BOOK YOU'RE HOLDING NOW.

MEDAASE!

"THANK YOU" IN TWI

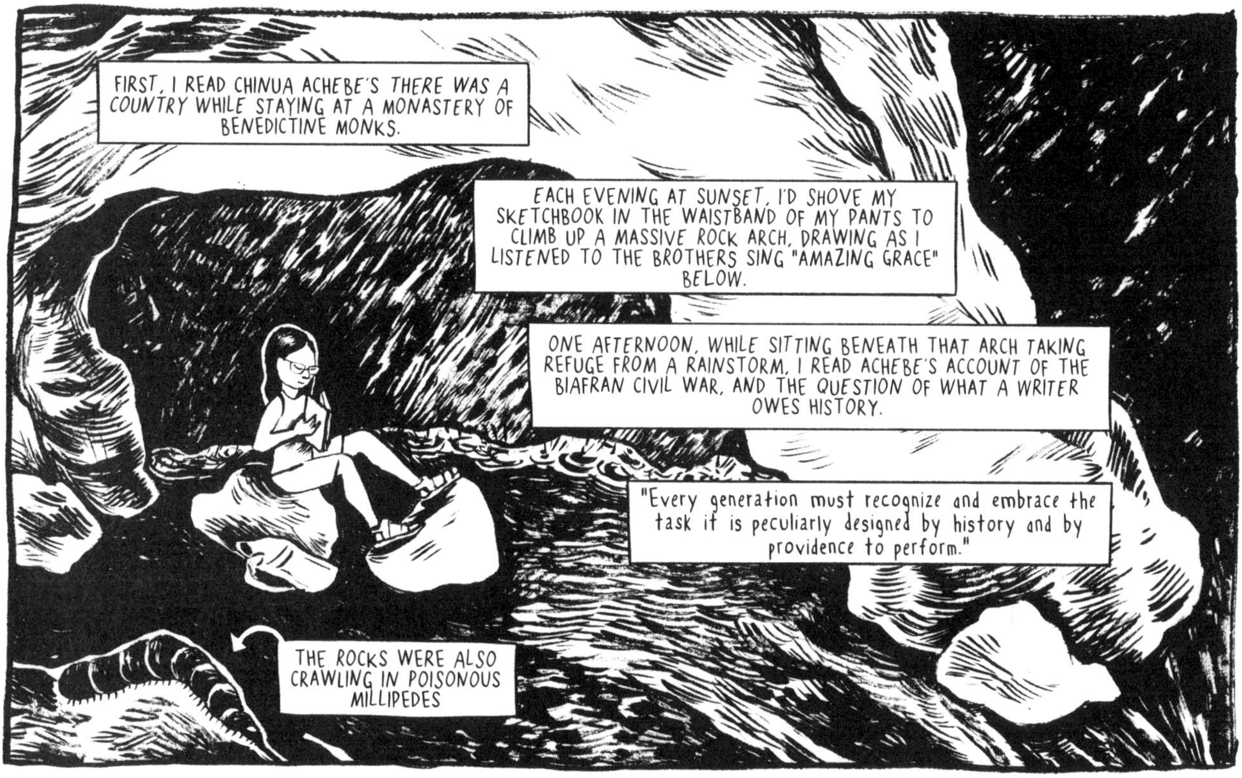
FIRST, I READ CHINUA ACHEBE'S THERE WAS A COUNTRY WHILE STAYING AT A MONASTERY OF BENEDICTINE MONKS.
EACH EVENING AT SUNSET, I'D SHOVE MY SKETCHBOOK IN THE WAISTBAND OF MY PANTS TO CLIMB UP A MASSIVE ROCK ARCH, DRAWING AS I LISTENED TO THE BROTHERS SING "AMAZING GRACE" BELOW.
ONE AFTERNOON, WHILE SITTING BENEATH THAT ARCH TAKING REFUGE FROM A RAINSTORM, I READ ACHEBE'S ACCOUNT OF THE BIAFRAN CIVIL WAR, AND THE QUESTION OF WHAT A WRITER OWES HISTORY.
"Every generation must recognize and embrace the task it is peculiarly designed by history and by providence to perform."
THE ROCKS WERE ALSO CRAWLING IN POISONOUS MILLIPEDES

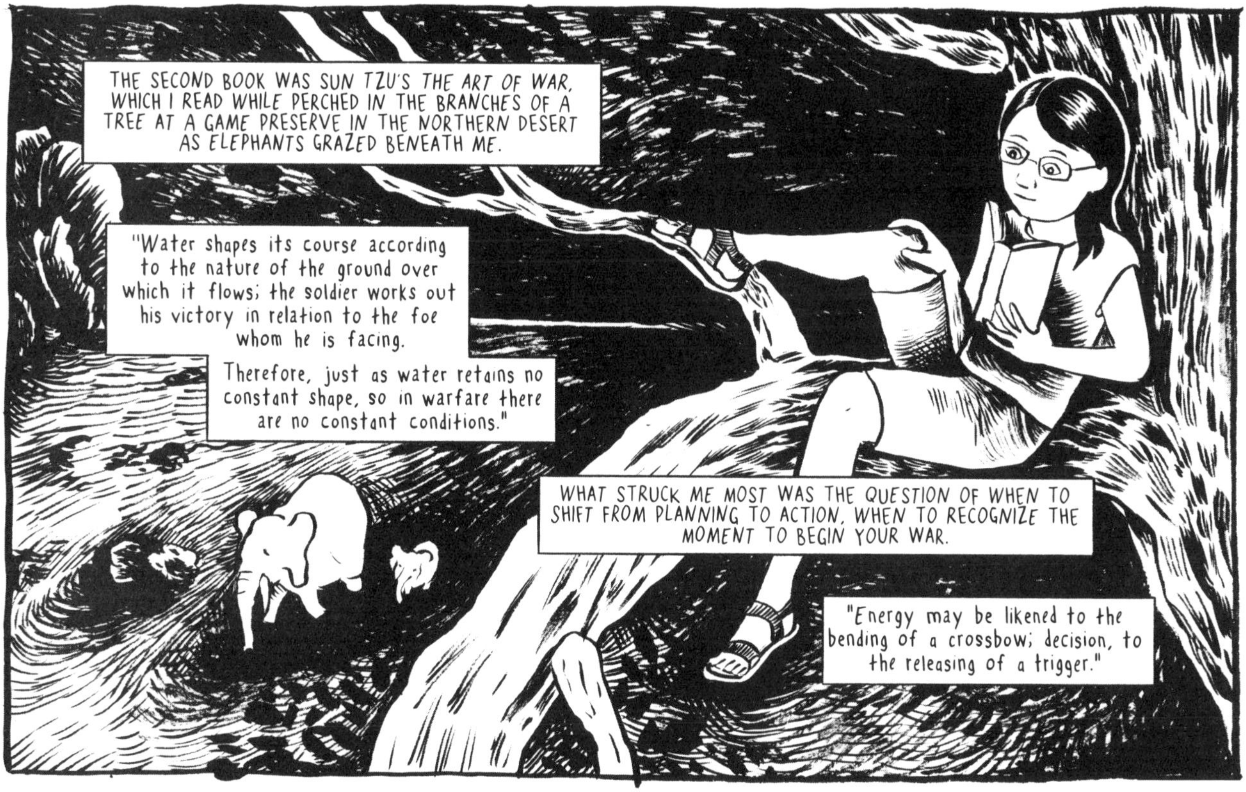
THE SECOND BOOK WAS SUN TZU'S THE ART OF WAR, WHICH I READ WHILE PERCHED IN THE BRANCHES OF A TREE AT A GAME PRESERVE IN THE NORTHERN DESERT AS ELEPHANTS GRAZED BENEATH ME.
"Water shapes its course according to the nature of the ground over which it flows; the soldier works out his victory in relation to the foe whom he is facing.
Therefore, just as water retains no constant shape, so in warfare there are no constant conditions."
WHAT STRUCK ME MOST WAS THE QUESTION OF WHEN TO SHIFT FROM PLANNING TO ACTION, WHEN TO RECOGNIZE THE MOMENT TO BEGIN YOUR WAR.
"Energy may be likened to the bending of a crossbow; decision, to the releasing of a trigger."

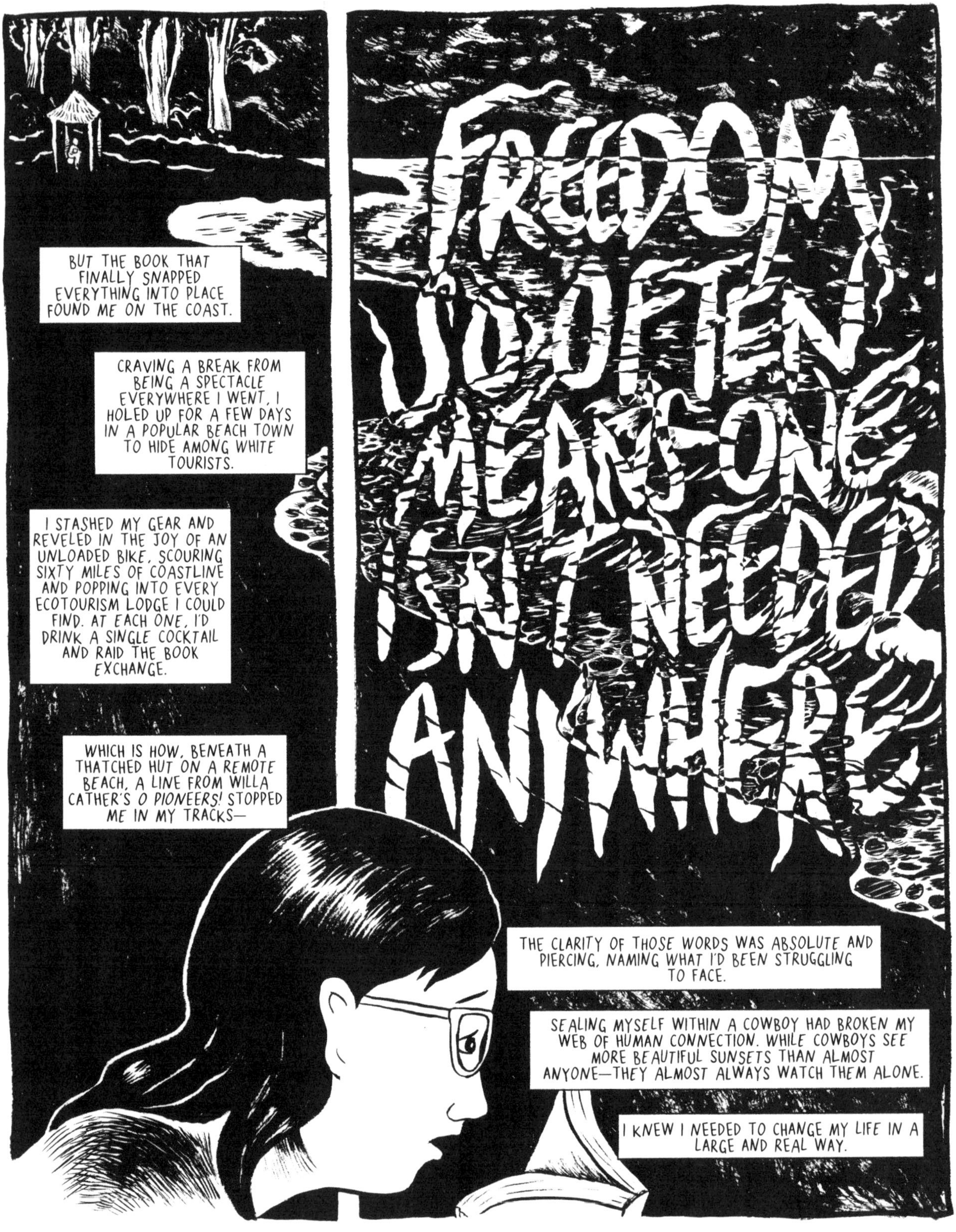
BUT THE BOOK THAT FINALLY SNAPPED EVERYTHING INTO PLACE FOUND ME ON THE COAST.
CRAVING A BREAK FROM BEING A SPECTACLE EVERYWHERE I WENT, I HOLED UP FOR A FEW DAYS IN A POPULAR BEACH TOWN TO HIDE AMONG WHITE TOURISTS.
I STASHED MY GEAR AND REVELED IN THE JOY OF AN UNLOADED BIKE, SCOURING SIXTY MILES OF COASTLINE AND POPPING INTO EVERY ECOTOURISM LODGE I COULD FIND. AT EACH ONE, I'D DRINK A SINGLE COCKTAIL AND RAID THE BOOK EXCHANGE.
WHICH IS HOW, BENEATH A THATCHED HUT ON A REMOTE BEACH, A LINE FROM WILLA CATHER'S *O PIONEERS!* STOPPED ME IN MY TRACKS—
FREEDOM SO OFTEN MEANS ONE ISN'T NEEDED ANYWHERE.
THE CLARITY OF THOSE WORDS WAS ABSOLUTE AND PIERCING, NAMING WHAT I'D BEEN STRUGGLING TO FACE.
SEALING MYSELF WITHIN A COWBOY HAD BROKEN MY WEB OF HUMAN CONNECTION. WHILE COWBOYS SEE MORE BEAUTIFUL SUNSETS THAN ALMOST ANYONE—THEY ALMOST ALWAYS WATCH THEM ALONE.
I KNEW I NEEDED TO CHANGE MY LIFE IN A LARGE AND REAL WAY.

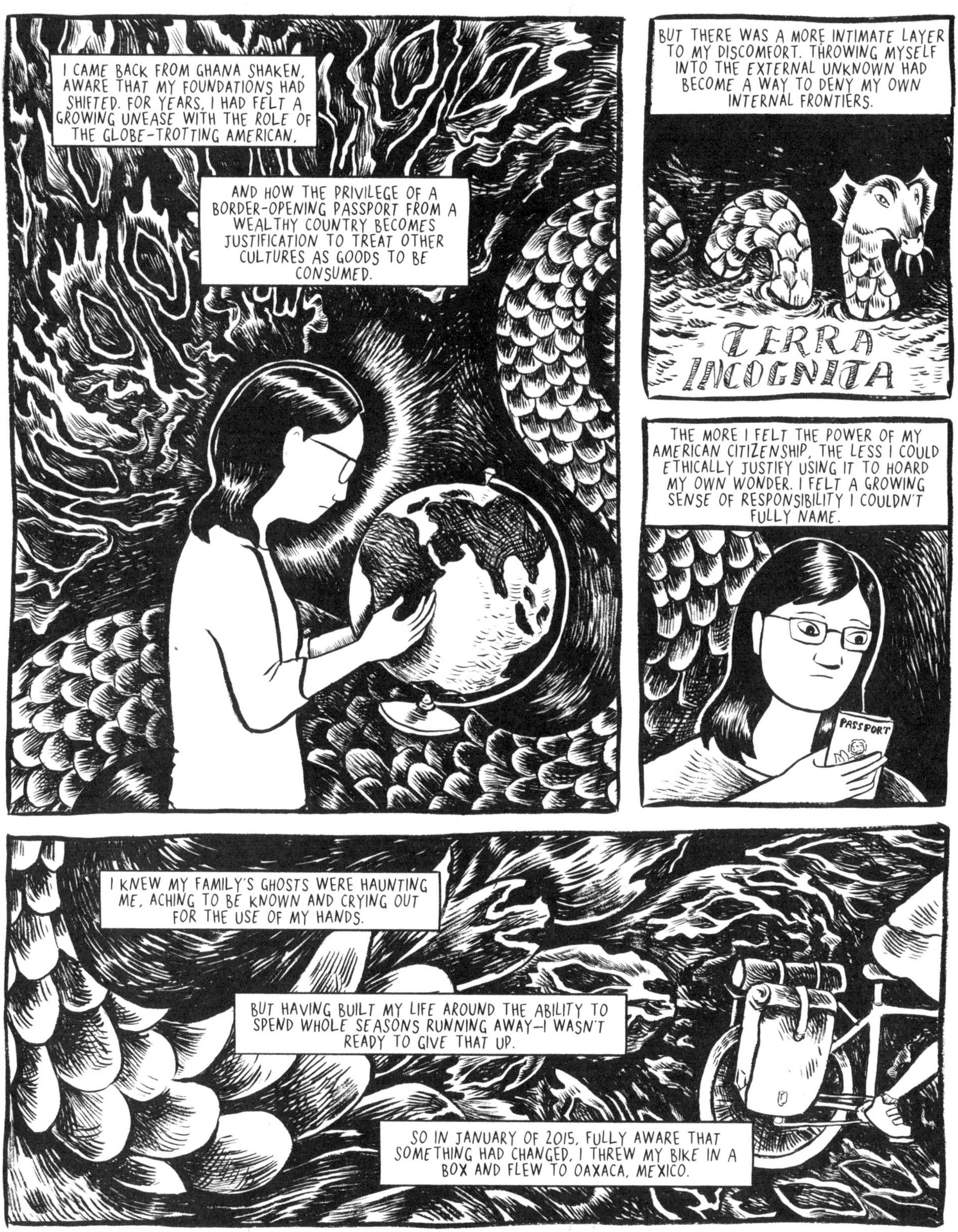
I CAME BACK FROM GHANA SHAKEN, AWARE THAT MY FOUNDATIONS HAD SHIFTED. FOR YEARS, I HAD FELT A GROWING UNEASE WITH THE ROLE OF THE GLOBE-TROTTING AMERICAN,
AND HOW THE PRIVILEGE OF A BORDER-OPENING PASSPORT FROM A WEALTHY COUNTRY BECOMES JUSTIFICATION TO TREAT OTHER CULTURES AS GOODS TO BE CONSUMED.
BUT THERE WAS A MORE INTIMATE LAYER TO MY DISCOMFORT. THROWING MYSELF INTO THE EXTERNAL UNKNOWN HAD BECOME A WAY TO DENY MY OWN INTERNAL FRONTIERS.
TERRA INCOGNITA
THE MORE I FELT THE POWER OF MY AMERICAN CITIZENSHIP, THE LESS I COULD ETHICALLY JUSTIFY USING IT TO HOARD MY OWN WONDER. I FELT A GROWING SENSE OF RESPONSIBILITY I COULDN'T FULLY NAME.
PASSPORT
I KNEW MY FAMILY'S GHOSTS WERE HAUNTING ME, ACHING TO BE KNOWN AND CRYING OUT FOR THE USE OF MY HANDS.
BUT HAVING BUILT MY LIFE AROUND THE ABILITY TO SPEND WHOLE SEASONS RUNNING AWAY—I WASN'T READY TO GIVE THAT UP.
SO IN JANUARY OF 2015, FULLY AWARE THAT SOMETHING HAD CHANGED, I THREW MY BIKE IN A BOX AND FLEW TO OAXACA, MEXICO.

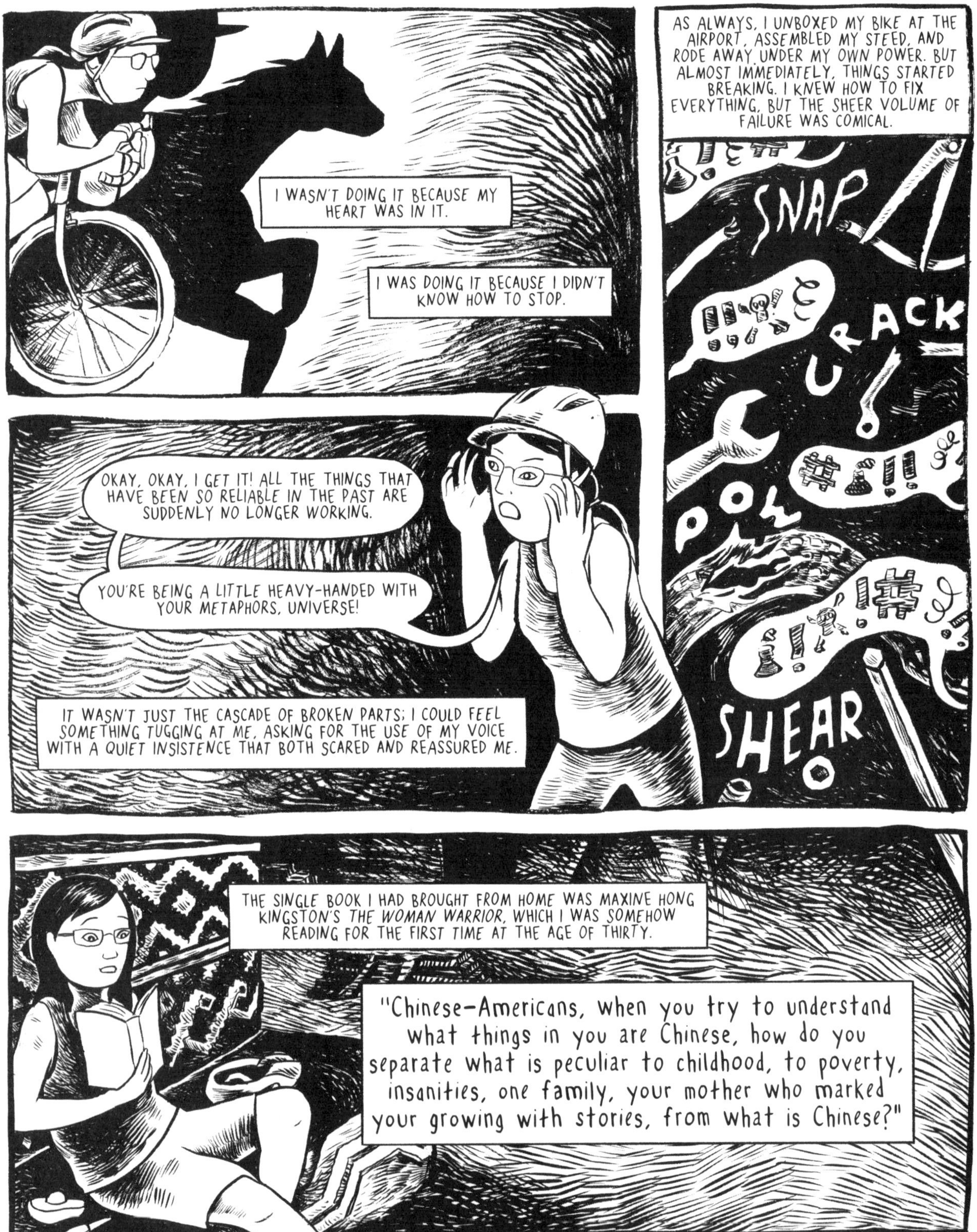

I WASN'T DOING IT BECAUSE MY HEART WAS IN IT.
I WAS DOING IT BECAUSE I DIDN'T KNOW HOW TO STOP.
AS ALWAYS, I UNBOXED MY BIKE AT THE AIRPORT, ASSEMBLED MY STEED, AND RODE AWAY UNDER MY OWN POWER. BUT ALMOST IMMEDIATELY, THINGS STARTED BREAKING. I KNEW HOW TO FIX EVERYTHING, BUT THE SHEER VOLUME OF FAILURE WAS COMICAL.
SNAP
CRACK
POW
SHEAR
OKAY, OKAY, I GET IT! ALL THE THINGS THAT HAVE BEEN SO RELIABLE IN THE PAST ARE SUDDENLY NO LONGER WORKING.
YOU'RE BEING A LITTLE HEAVY-HANDED WITH YOUR METAPHORS, UNIVERSE!
IT WASN'T JUST THE CASCADE OF BROKEN PARTS; I COULD FEEL SOMETHING TUGGING AT ME, ASKING FOR THE USE OF MY VOICE WITH A QUIET INSISTENCE THAT BOTH SCARED AND REASSURED ME.
THE SINGLE BOOK I HAD BROUGHT FROM HOME WAS MAXINE HONG KINGSTON'S *THE WOMAN WARRIOR*, WHICH I WAS SOMEHOW READING FOR THE FIRST TIME AT THE AGE OF THIRTY.
"Chinese-Americans, when you try to understand what things in you are Chinese, how do you separate what is peculiar to childhood, to poverty, insanities, one family, your mother who marked your growing with stories, from what is Chinese?"

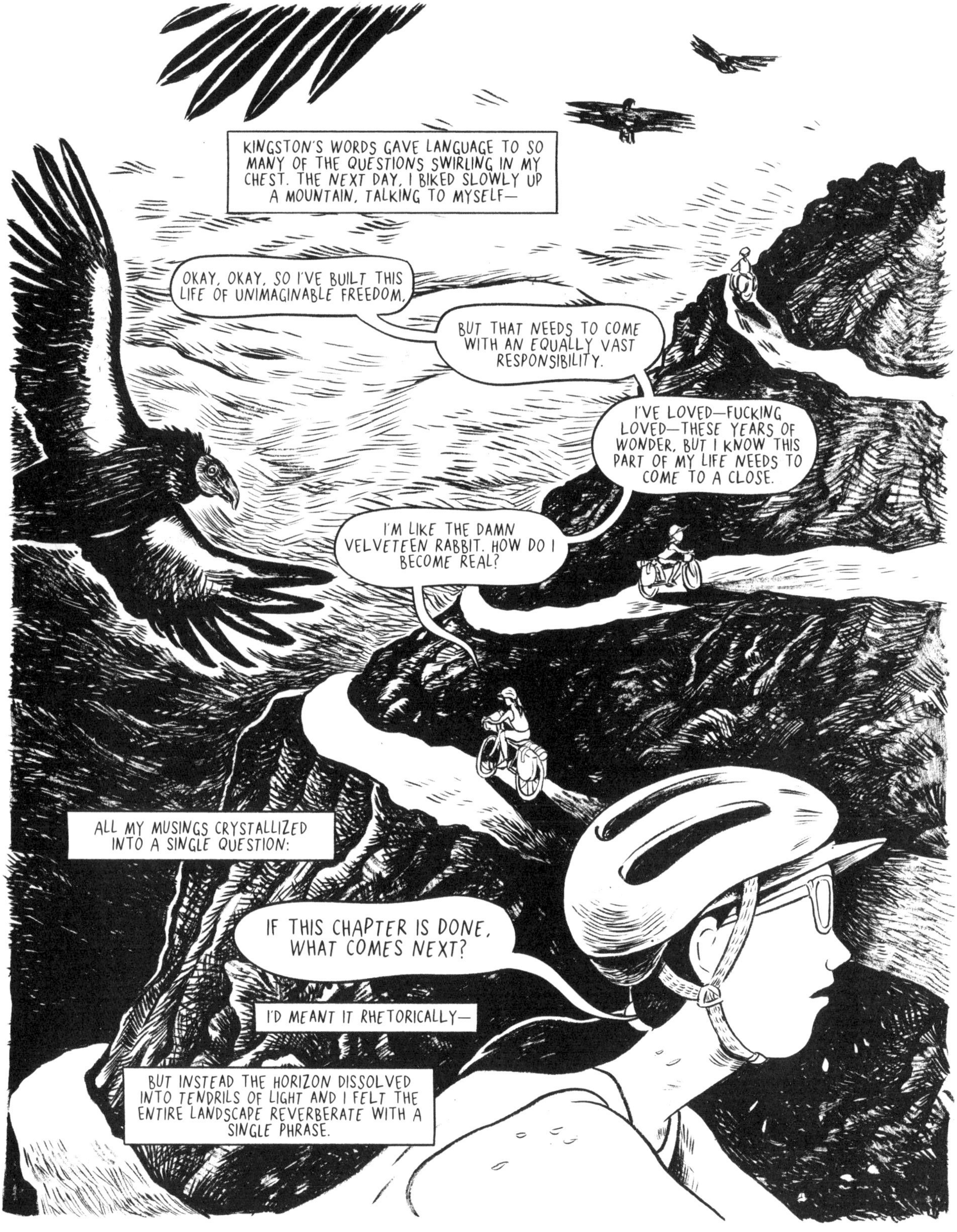
KINGSTON'S WORDS GAVE LANGUAGE TO SO MANY OF THE QUESTIONS SWIRLING IN MY CHEST. THE NEXT DAY, I BIKED SLOWLY UP A MOUNTAIN, TALKING TO MYSELF—
OKAY, OKAY, SO I'VE BUILT THIS LIFE OF UNIMAGINABLE FREEDOM,
BUT THAT NEEDS TO COME WITH AN EQUALLY VAST RESPONSIBILITY.
I'VE LOVED—FUCKING LOVED—THESE YEARS OF WONDER, BUT I KNOW THIS PART OF MY LIFE NEEDS TO COME TO A CLOSE.
I'M LIKE THE DAMN VELVETEEN RABBIT. HOW DO I BECOME REAL?
ALL MY MUSINGS CRYSTALLIZED INTO A SINGLE QUESTION:
IF THIS CHAPTER IS DONE, WHAT COMES NEXT?
I'D MEANT IT RHETORICALLY—
BUT INSTEAD THE HORIZON DISSOLVED INTO TENDRILS OF LIGHT AND I FELT THE ENTIRE LANDSCAPE REVERBERATE WITH A SINGLE PHRASE.

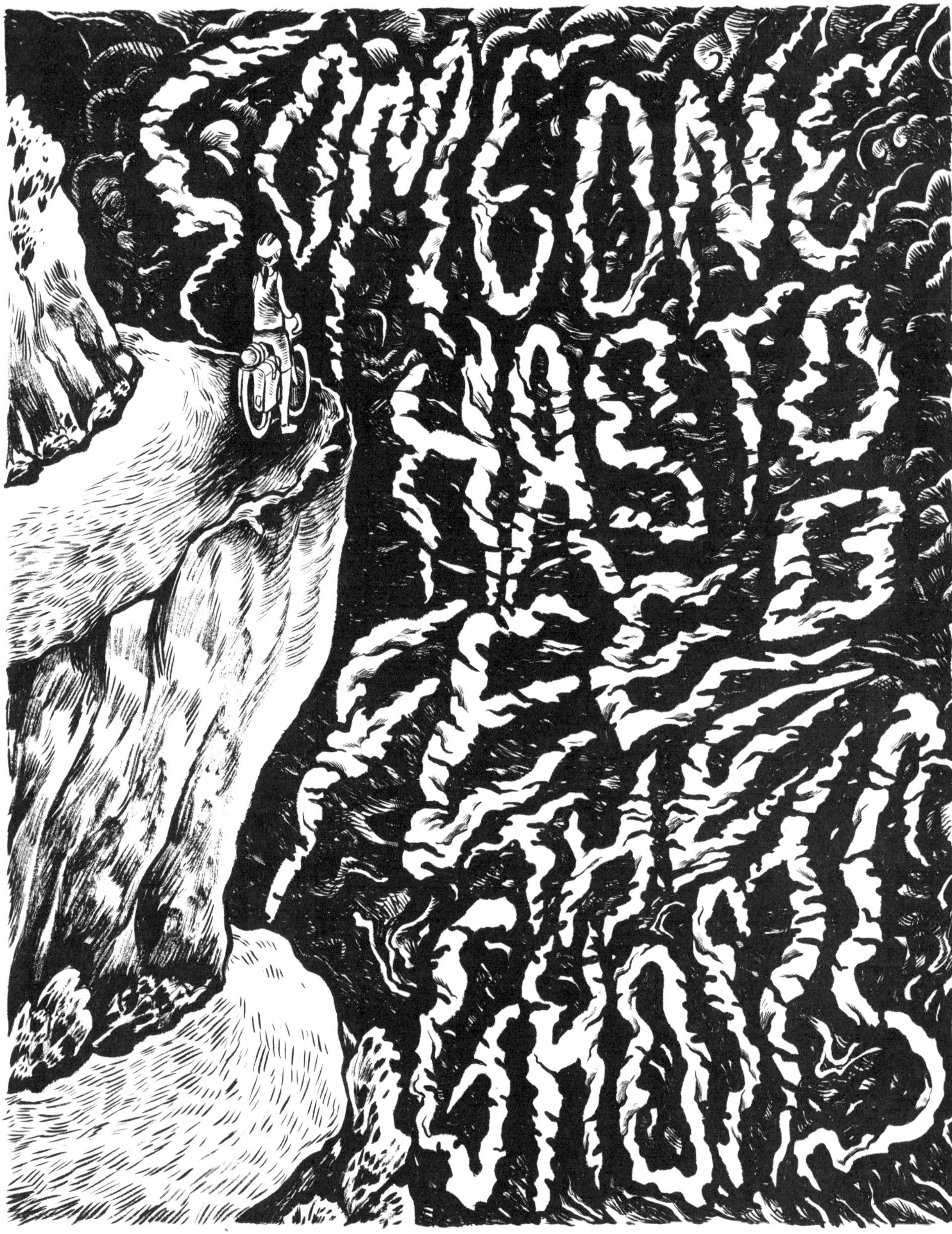
SOMEONE

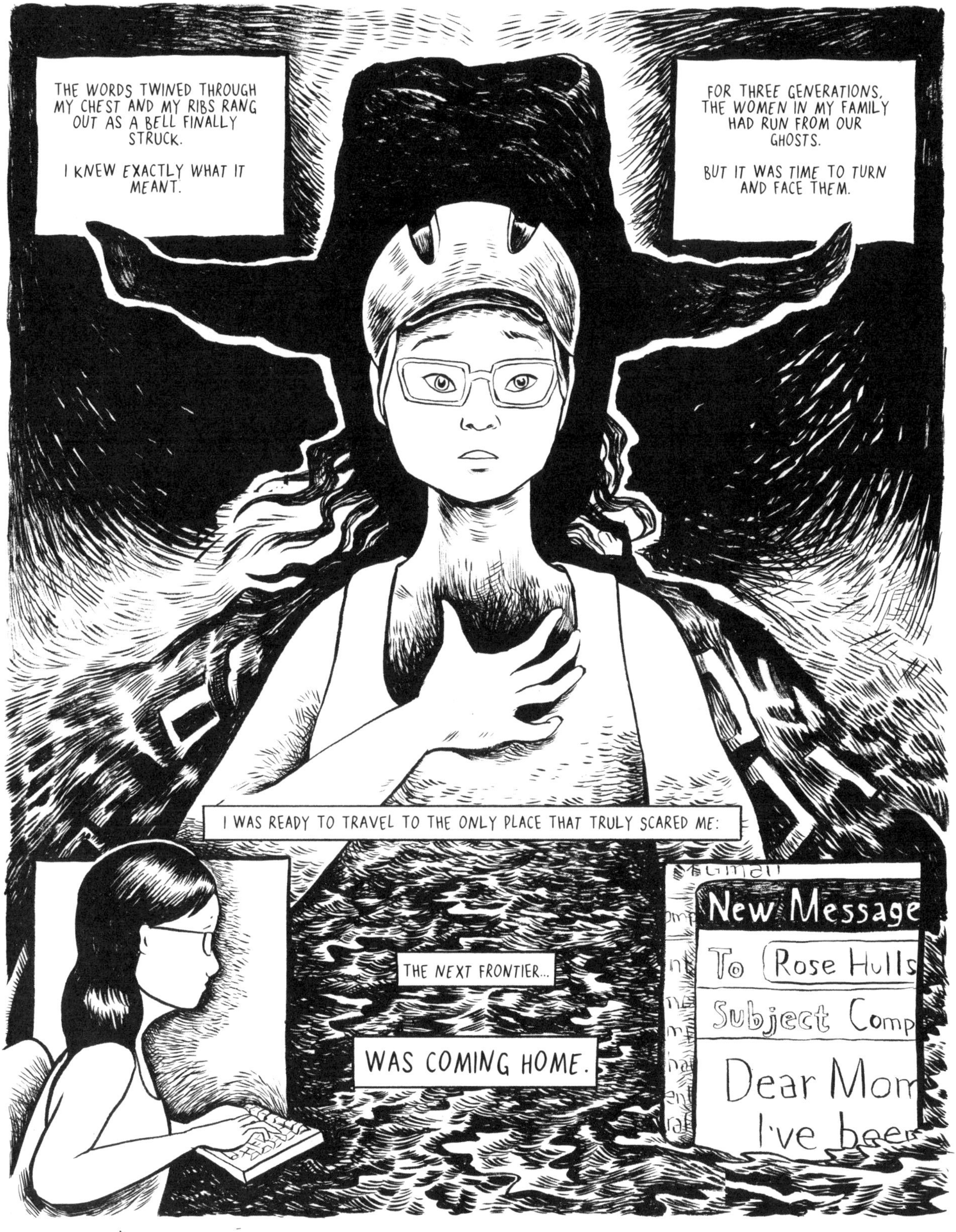
THE WORDS TWINED THROUGH MY CHEST AND MY RIBS RANG OUT AS A BELL FINALLY STRUCK.
I KNEW EXACTLY WHAT IT MEANT.
FOR THREE GENERATIONS, THE WOMEN IN MY FAMILY HAD RUN FROM OUR GHOSTS.
BUT IT WAS TIME TO TURN AND FACE THEM.
I WAS READY TO TRAVEL TO THE ONLY PLACE THAT TRULY SCARED ME:
THE NEXT FRONTIER...
WAS COMING HOME.
New Message
To Rose Hulls
Subject Comp
Dear Mom
I've been

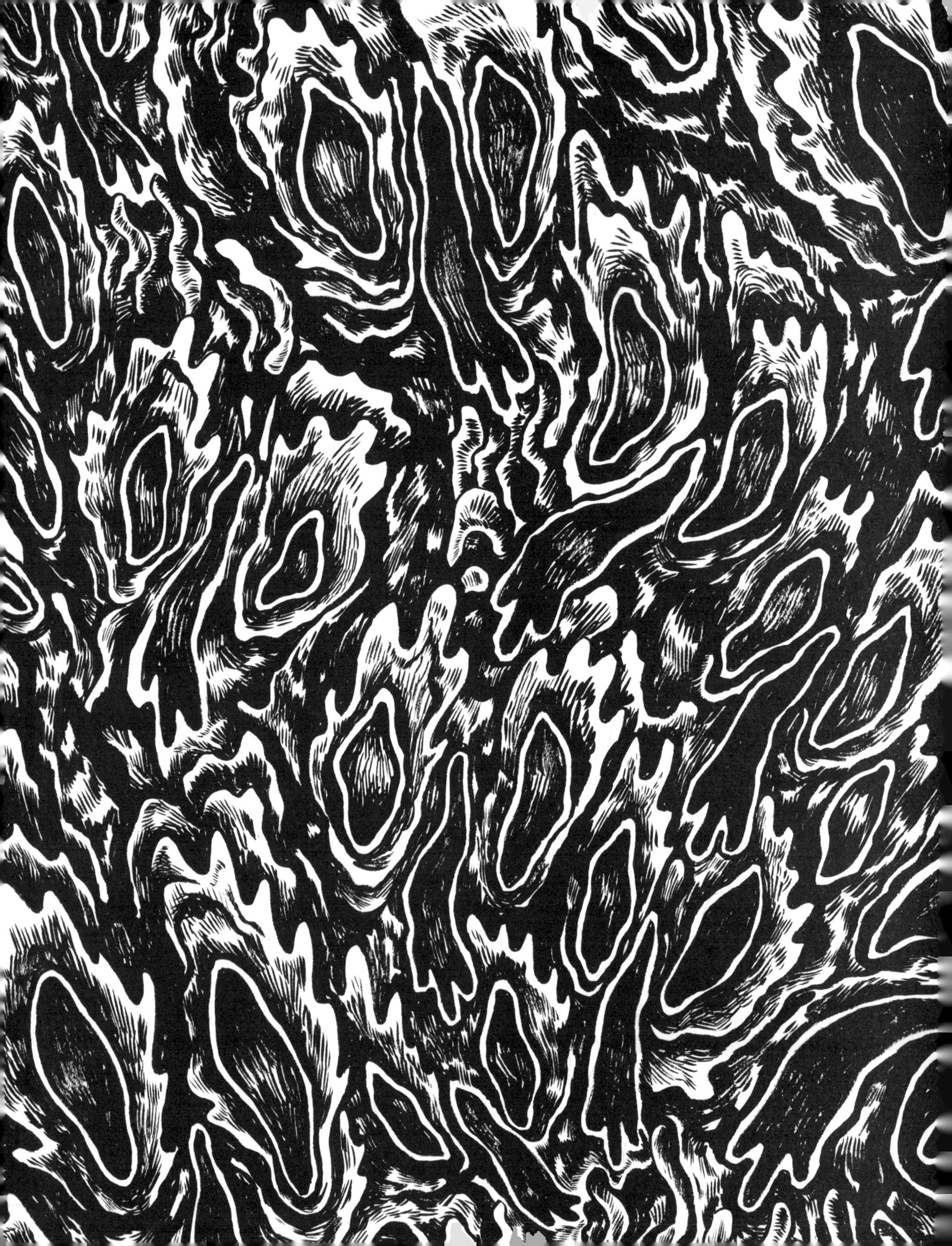

PART 9

THE CREATION OF HOME

Roaming • 2015–2022

This is not a homecoming, since this home has never before existed. It is the creation of home.

—**ALICE MILLER**, ***The Drama of the Gifted Child***

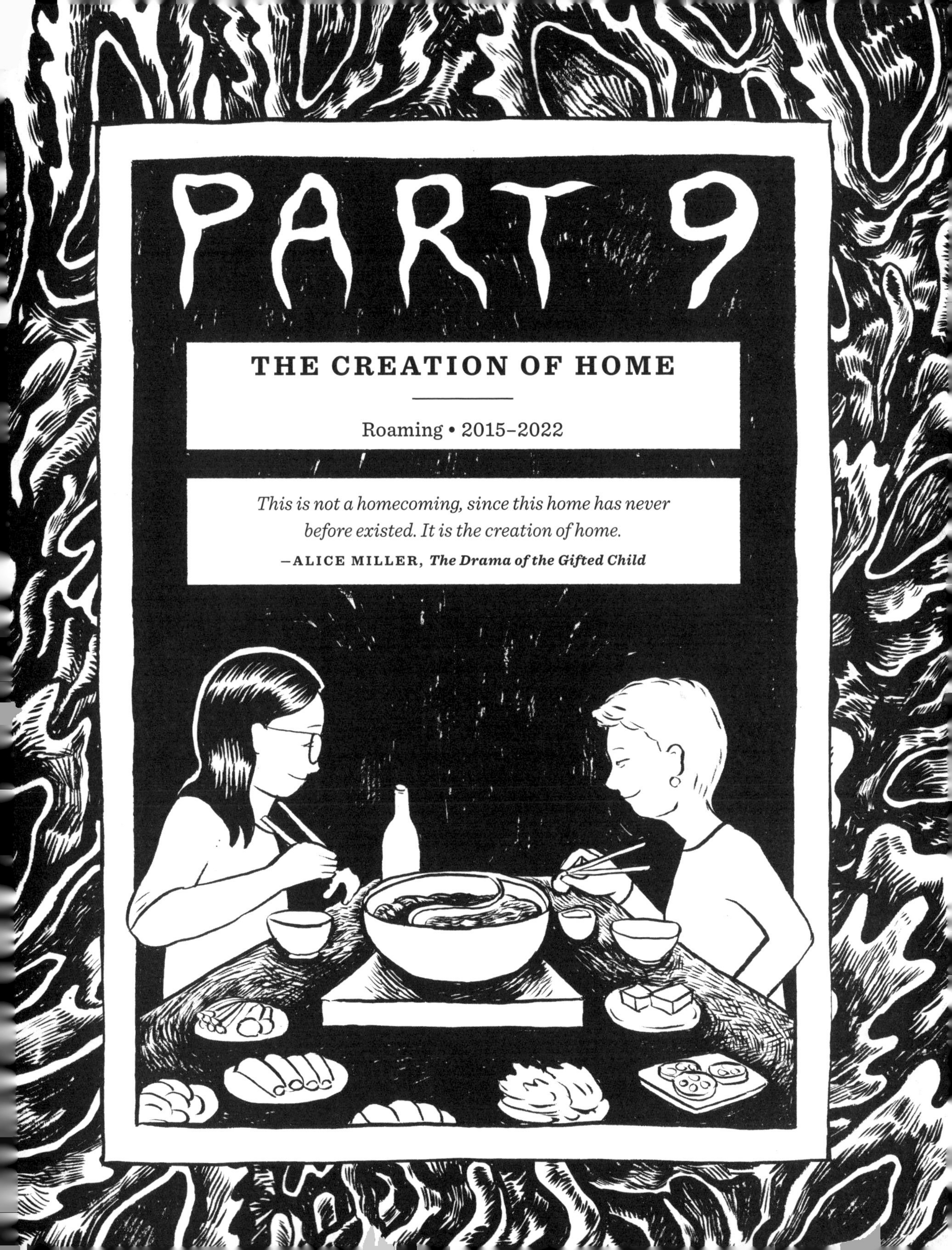

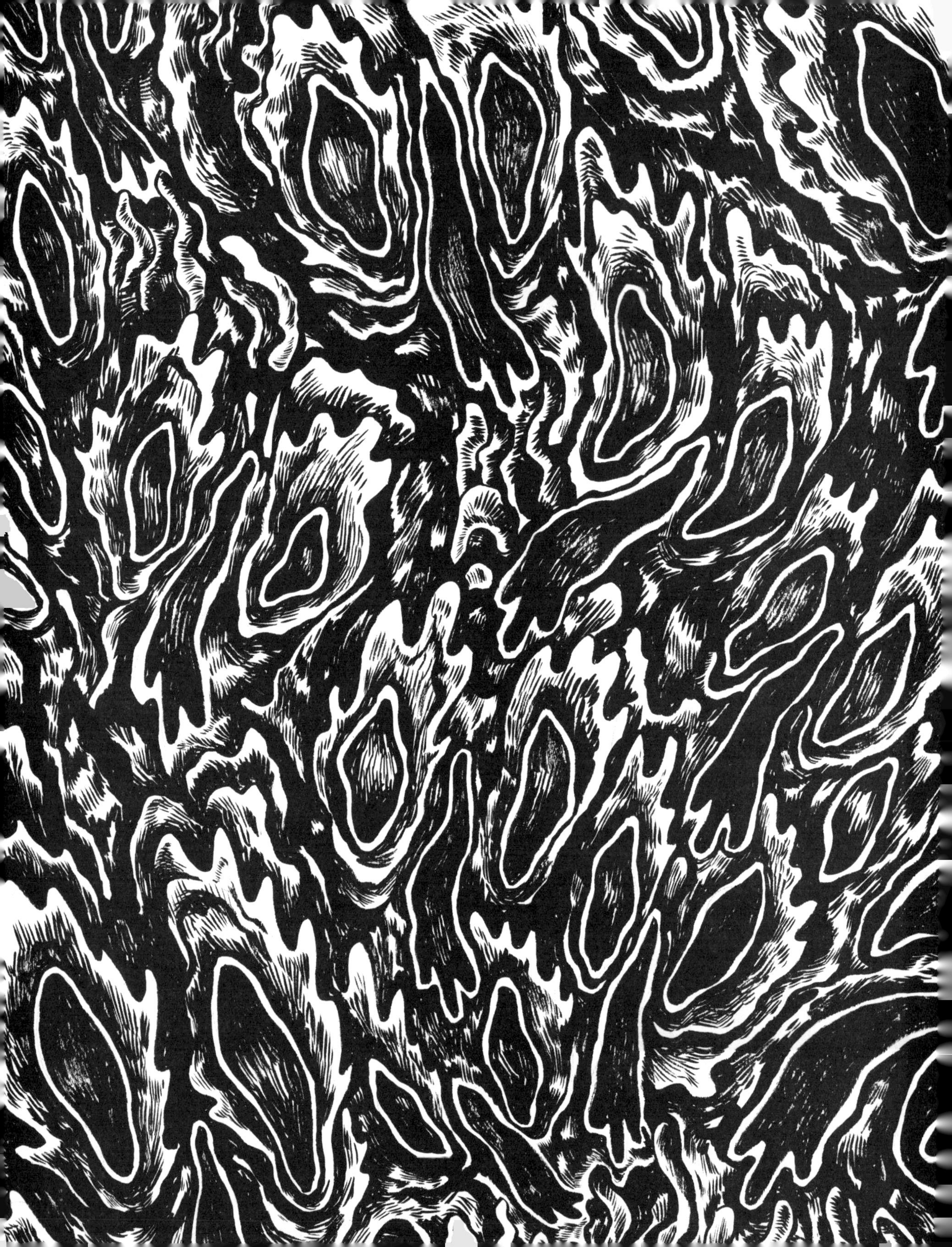

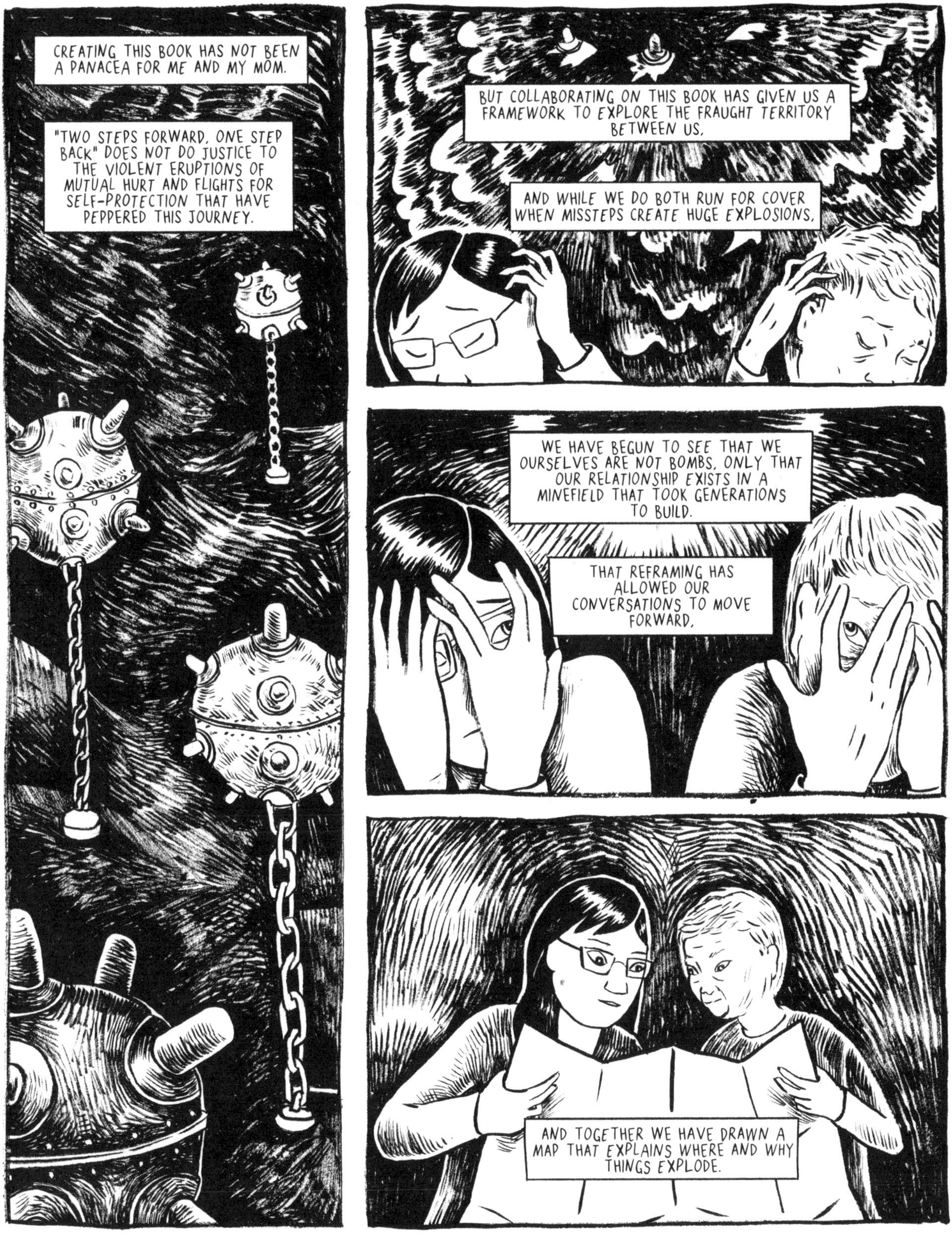

CREATING THIS BOOK HAS NOT BEEN A PANACEA FOR ME AND MY MOM.
"TWO STEPS FORWARD, ONE STEP BACK" DOES NOT DO JUSTICE TO THE VIOLENT ERUPTIONS OF MUTUAL HURT AND FLIGHTS FOR SELF-PROTECTION THAT HAVE PEPPERED THIS JOURNEY.
BUT COLLABORATING ON THIS BOOK HAS GIVEN US A FRAMEWORK TO EXPLORE THE FRAUGHT TERRITORY BETWEEN US,
AND WHILE WE DO BOTH RUN FOR COVER WHEN MISSTEPS CREATE HUGE EXPLOSIONS,
WE HAVE BEGUN TO SEE THAT WE OURSELVES ARE NOT BOMBS, ONLY THAT OUR RELATIONSHIP EXISTS IN A MINEFIELD THAT TOOK GENERATIONS TO BUILD.
THAT REFRAMING HAS ALLOWED OUR CONVERSATIONS TO MOVE FORWARD,
AND TOGETHER WE HAVE DRAWN A MAP THAT EXPLAINS WHERE AND WHY THINGS EXPLODE.

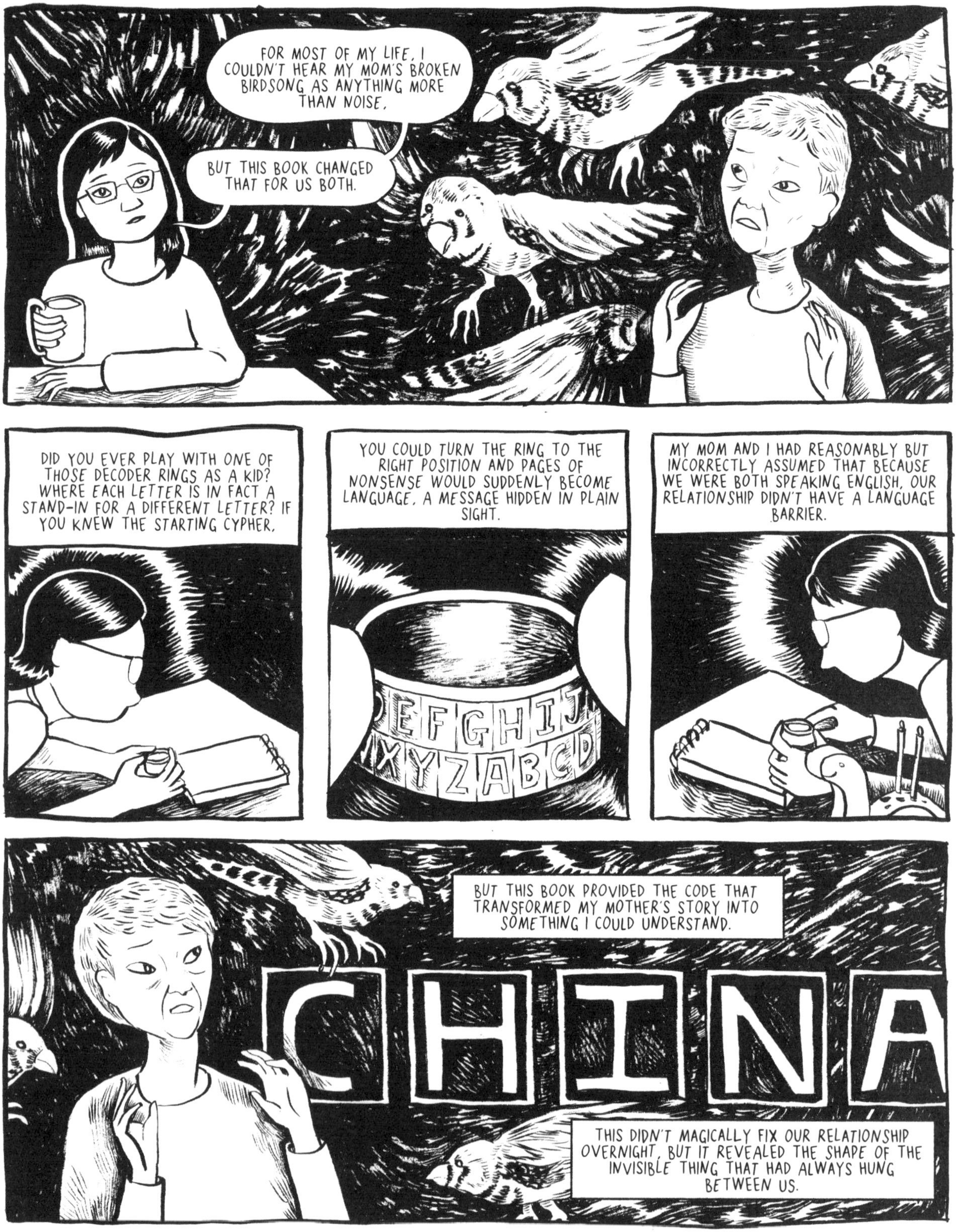
FOR MOST OF MY LIFE, I COULDN'T HEAR MY MOM'S BROKEN BIRDSONG AS ANYTHING MORE THAN NOISE.
BUT THIS BOOK CHANGED THAT FOR US BOTH.
DID YOU EVER PLAY WITH ONE OF THOSE DECODER RINGS AS A KID? WHERE EACH LETTER IS IN FACT A STAND-IN FOR A DIFFERENT LETTER? IF YOU KNEW THE STARTING CYPHER,
YOU COULD TURN THE RING TO THE RIGHT POSITION AND PAGES OF NONSENSE WOULD SUDDENLY BECOME LANGUAGE, A MESSAGE HIDDEN IN PLAIN SIGHT.
EFGHIJ
XYZABCD
MY MOM AND I HAD REASONABLY BUT INCORRECTLY ASSUMED THAT BECAUSE WE WERE BOTH SPEAKING ENGLISH, OUR RELATIONSHIP DIDN'T HAVE A LANGUAGE BARRIER.
BUT THIS BOOK PROVIDED THE CODE THAT TRANSFORMED MY MOTHER'S STORY INTO SOMETHING I COULD UNDERSTAND.
CHINA
THIS DIDN'T MAGICALLY FIX OUR RELATIONSHIP OVERNIGHT, BUT IT REVEALED THE SHAPE OF THE INVISIBLE THING THAT HAD ALWAYS HUNG BETWEEN US.

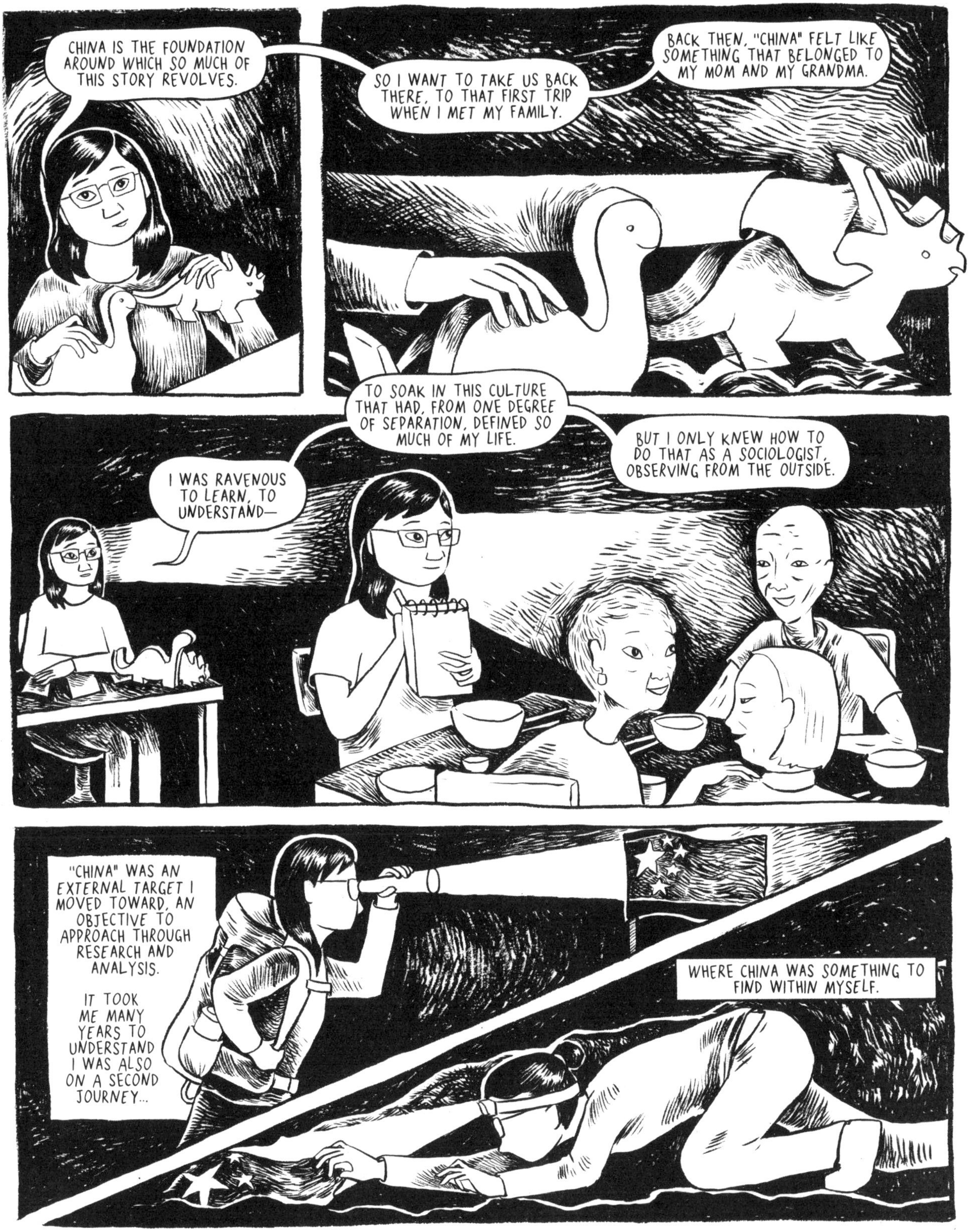
CHINA IS THE FOUNDATION AROUND WHICH SO MUCH OF THIS STORY REVOLVES.
SO I WANT TO TAKE US BACK THERE, TO THAT FIRST TRIP WHEN I MET MY FAMILY.
BACK THEN, "CHINA" FELT LIKE SOMETHING THAT BELONGED TO MY MOM AND MY GRANDMA.
I WAS RAVENOUS TO LEARN, TO UNDERSTAND—
TO SOAK IN THIS CULTURE THAT HAD, FROM ONE DEGREE OF SEPARATION, DEFINED SO MUCH OF MY LIFE.
BUT I ONLY KNEW HOW TO DO THAT AS A SOCIOLOGIST, OBSERVING FROM THE OUTSIDE.
"CHINA" WAS AN EXTERNAL TARGET I MOVED TOWARD, AN OBJECTIVE TO APPROACH THROUGH RESEARCH AND ANALYSIS.
IT TOOK ME MANY YEARS TO UNDERSTAND I WAS ALSO ON A SECOND JOURNEY...
WHERE CHINA WAS SOMETHING TO FIND WITHIN MYSELF.

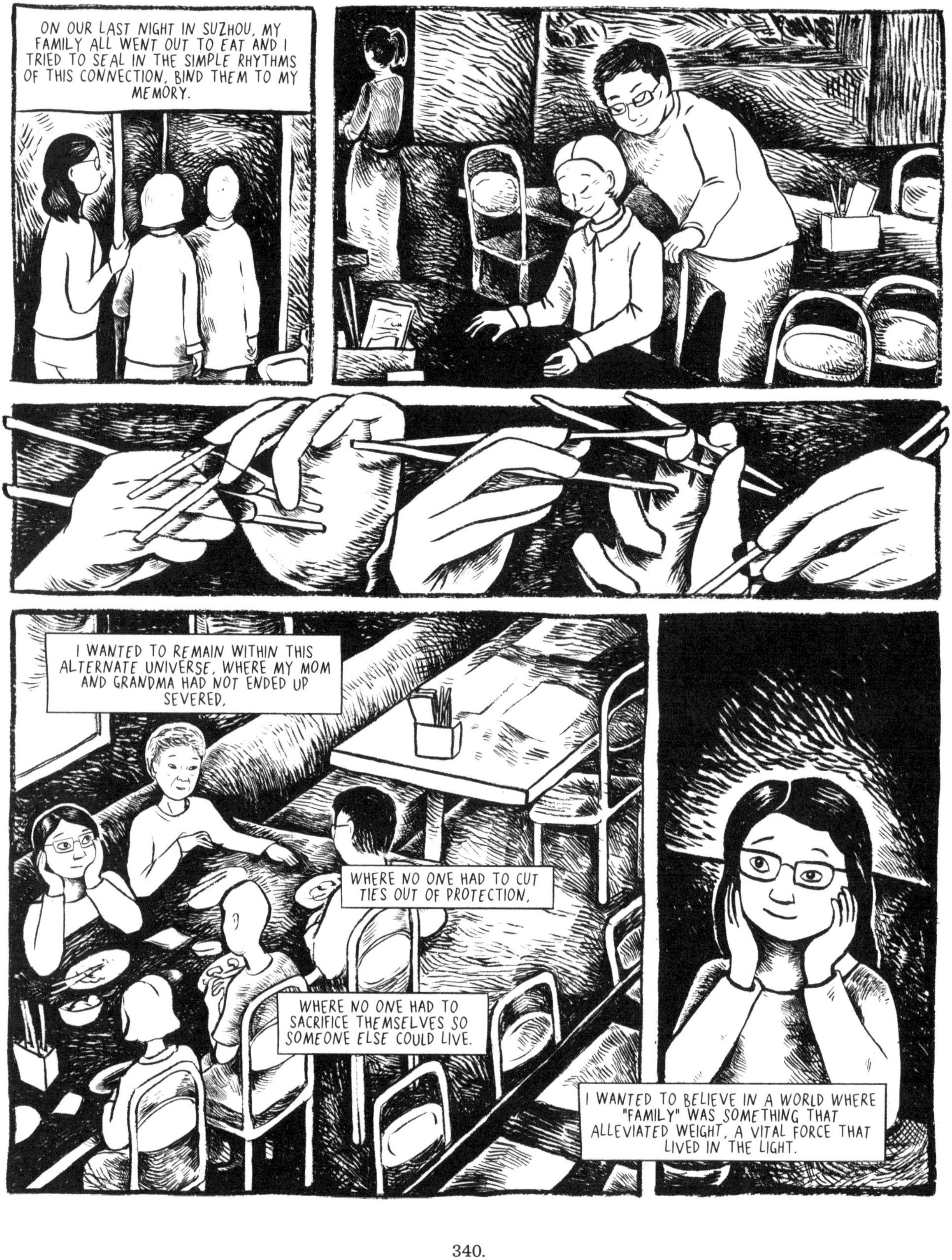
ON OUR LAST NIGHT IN SUZHOU, MY FAMILY ALL WENT OUT TO EAT AND I TRIED TO SEAL IN THE SIMPLE RHYTHMS OF THIS CONNECTION, BIND THEM TO MY MEMORY.
I WANTED TO REMAIN WITHIN THIS ALTERNATE UNIVERSE, WHERE MY MOM AND GRANDMA HAD NOT ENDED UP SEVERED,
WHERE NO ONE HAD TO CUT TIES OUT OF PROTECTION,
WHERE NO ONE HAD TO SACRIFICE THEMSELVES SO SOMEONE ELSE COULD LIVE.
I WANTED TO BELIEVE IN A WORLD WHERE "FAMILY" WAS SOMETHING THAT ALLEVIATED WEIGHT, A VITAL FORCE THAT LIVED IN THE LIGHT.

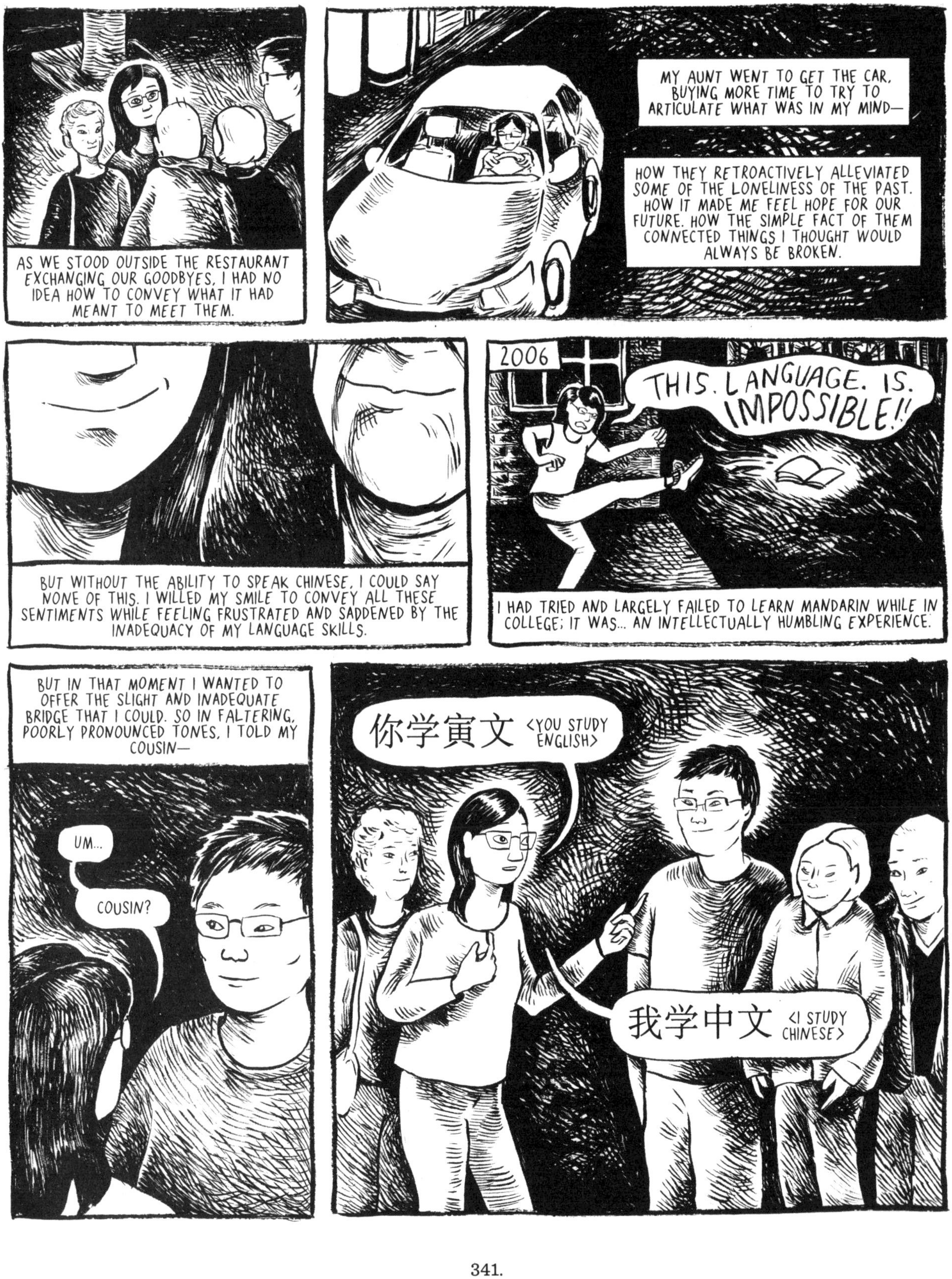
AS WE STOOD OUTSIDE THE RESTAURANT EXCHANGING OUR GOODBYES, I HAD NO IDEA HOW TO CONVEY WHAT IT HAD MEANT TO MEET THEM.
MY AUNT WENT TO GET THE CAR, BUYING MORE TIME TO TRY TO ARTICULATE WHAT WAS IN MY MIND—
HOW THEY RETROACTIVELY ALLEVIATED SOME OF THE LONELINESS OF THE PAST. HOW IT MADE ME FEEL HOPE FOR OUR FUTURE. HOW THE SIMPLE FACT OF THEM CONNECTED THINGS I THOUGHT WOULD ALWAYS BE BROKEN.
BUT WITHOUT THE ABILITY TO SPEAK CHINESE, I COULD SAY NONE OF THIS. I WILLED MY SMILE TO CONVEY ALL THESE SENTIMENTS WHILE FEELING FRUSTRATED AND SADDENED BY THE INADEQUACY OF MY LANGUAGE SKILLS.
2006
THIS. LANGUAGE. IS. IMPOSSIBLE!!
I HAD TRIED AND LARGELY FAILED TO LEARN MANDARIN WHILE IN COLLEGE; IT WAS... AN INTELLECTUALLY HUMBLING EXPERIENCE.
BUT IN THAT MOMENT I WANTED TO OFFER THE SLIGHT AND INADEQUATE BRIDGE THAT I COULD. SO IN FALTERING, POORLY PRONOUNCED TONES, I TOLD MY COUSIN—
UM...
COUSIN?
你学寅文 <YOU STUDY ENGLISH>
我学中文 <I STUDY CHINESE>

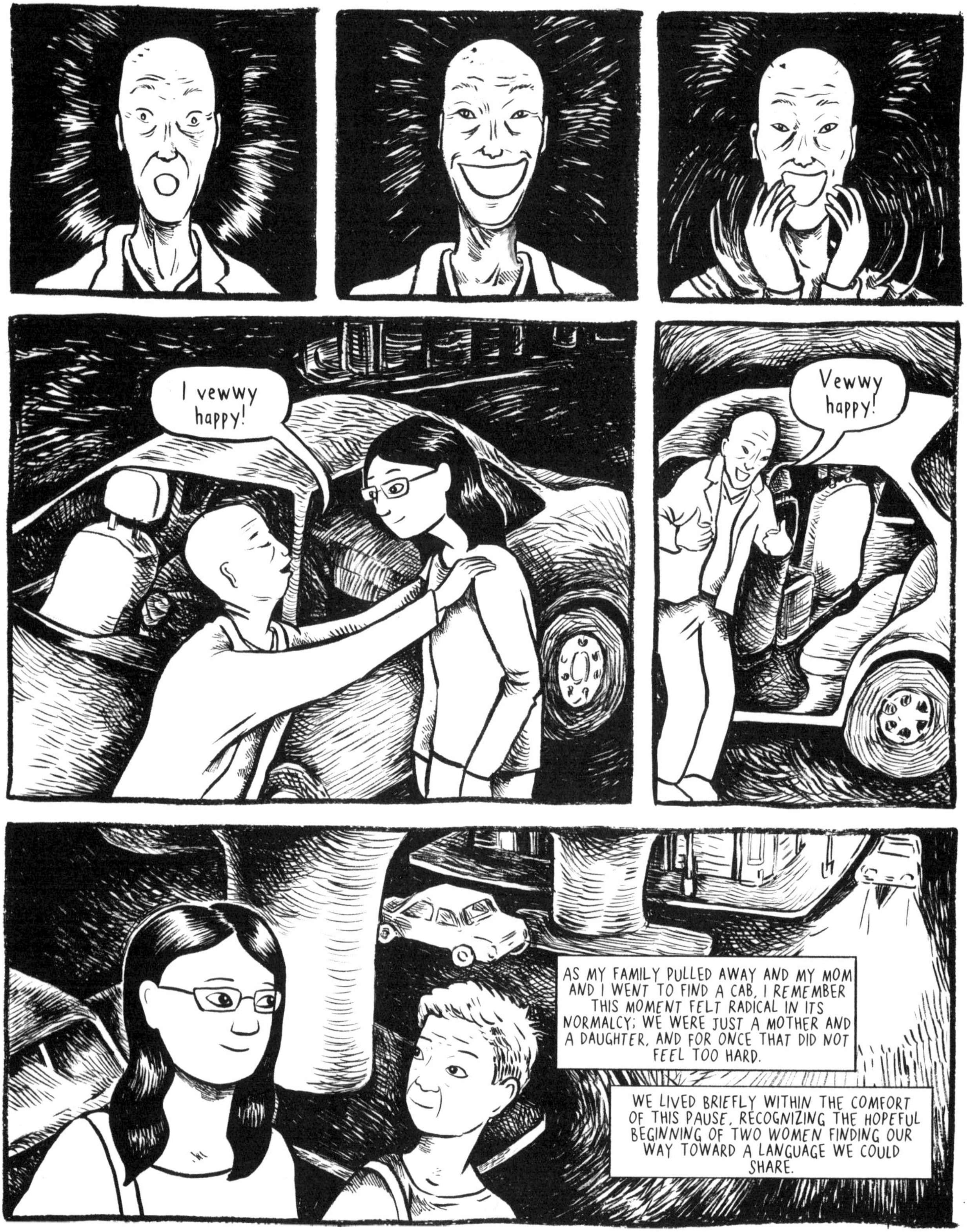
I vewwy happy!
Vewwy happy!
AS MY FAMILY PULLED AWAY AND MY MOM AND I WENT TO FIND A CAB, I REMEMBER THIS MOMENT FELT RADICAL IN ITS NORMALCY; WE WERE JUST A MOTHER AND A DAUGHTER, AND FOR ONCE THAT DID NOT FEEL TOO HARD.
WE LIVED BRIEFLY WITHIN THE COMFORT OF THIS PAUSE, RECOGNIZING THE HOPEFUL BEGINNING OF TWO WOMEN FINDING OUR WAY TOWARD A LANGUAGE WE COULD SHARE.

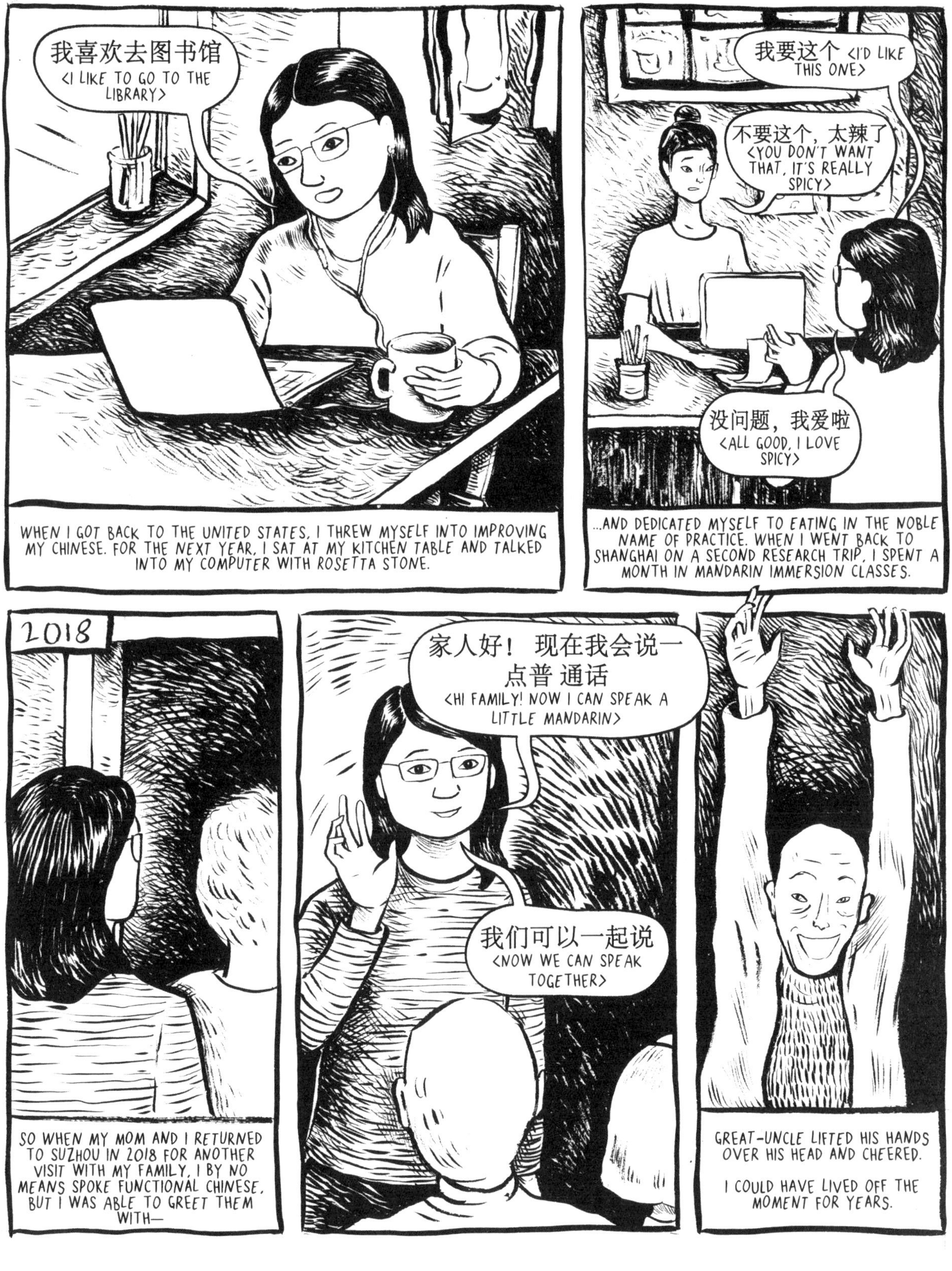
我喜欢去图书馆
<I LIKE TO GO TO THE LIBRARY>
WHEN I GOT BACK TO THE UNITED STATES, I THREW MYSELF INTO IMPROVING MY CHINESE. FOR THE NEXT YEAR, I SAT AT MY KITCHEN TABLE AND TALKED INTO MY COMPUTER WITH ROSETTA STONE.
我要这个 <I'D LIKE THIS ONE>
不要这个，太辣了
<YOU DON'T WANT THAT, IT'S REALLY SPICY>
没问题，我爱啦
<ALL GOOD, I LOVE SPICY>
...AND DEDICATED MYSELF TO EATING IN THE NOBLE NAME OF PRACTICE. WHEN I WENT BACK TO SHANGHAI ON A SECOND RESEARCH TRIP, I SPENT A MONTH IN MANDARIN IMMERSION CLASSES.
2018
SO WHEN MY MOM AND I RETURNED TO SUZHOU IN 2018 FOR ANOTHER VISIT WITH MY FAMILY, I BY NO MEANS SPOKE FUNCTIONAL CHINESE, BUT I WAS ABLE TO GREET THEM WITH—
家人好！ 现在我会说一点普 通话
<HI FAMILY! NOW I CAN SPEAK A LITTLE MANDARIN>
我们可以一起说
<NOW WE CAN SPEAK TOGETHER>
GREAT-UNCLE LIFTED HIS HANDS OVER HIS HEAD AND CHEERED.
I COULD HAVE LIVED OFF THE MOMENT FOR YEARS.

I CAME BACK FROM CHINA HAVING GATHERED ALL THE LOGISTICAL PUZZLE PIECES I NEEDED TO FORM THE BONES OF THIS BOOK. BUT MY HEART WASN'T READY.

I BEGAN FROM MY USUAL PLACE OF PRAGMATIC TENACITY. ACCESSING MY BRUTE STRENGTH WAS EASY; WHAT PROVED MUCH HARDER WAS FINDING THE FORCE OF MY COMPASSION.

To Do
☑ LEARN HISTORY
☑ LEARN (SOME) CHINESE
☑ LEARN TO DRAW COMICS
☑ LEARN HOW TO WRITE A BOOK
☐ VANQUISH CYCLE OF INTERGENERATIONAL TRAUMA
☐ SLEEP WHEN DEAD?

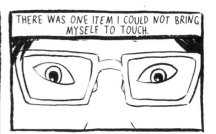

THERE WAS ONE ITEM I COULD NOT BRING MYSELF TO TOUCH.

☐ FEEL

I TRIED SO HARD TO REMAIN A DISPASSIONATE NARRATOR, BUT SOMETIMES THE WEIGHT OF MY PEN TOUCHED SOMETHING THAT SUMMONED MY COWBOY.

YOU WILL NOT DROWN ME!!!!

I BEGAN TO SEE THAT THIS STORY WOULD BREAK ME IF I HAD TO CARRY IT ALONE.

BUT HOW DOES A COWBOY UNDO A LIFETIME OF REFUSING TO NEED HELP?

MY FRIENDS STEPPED IN, SEEING THE YEARNING I LACKED THE WORDS TO VOICE. THEY SHOWED ME THE TRUTH OF PAUL AUSTER'S ASSERTION THAT LOVE "IS THE ONE THING THAT CAN STOP A MAN FROM FALLING, THE ONE THING POWERFUL ENOUGH TO NEGATE THE LAWS OF GRAVITY."

FRIENDSHIP HELPED ME WHERE I COULD NOT HELP MYSELF, CARRYING ME TO THE SOFTNESS I HAD BANISHED SO LONG AGO. SLOWLY, I BEGAN TO FORGE MY OWN BRIDGE TO CHINESE CULTURE.

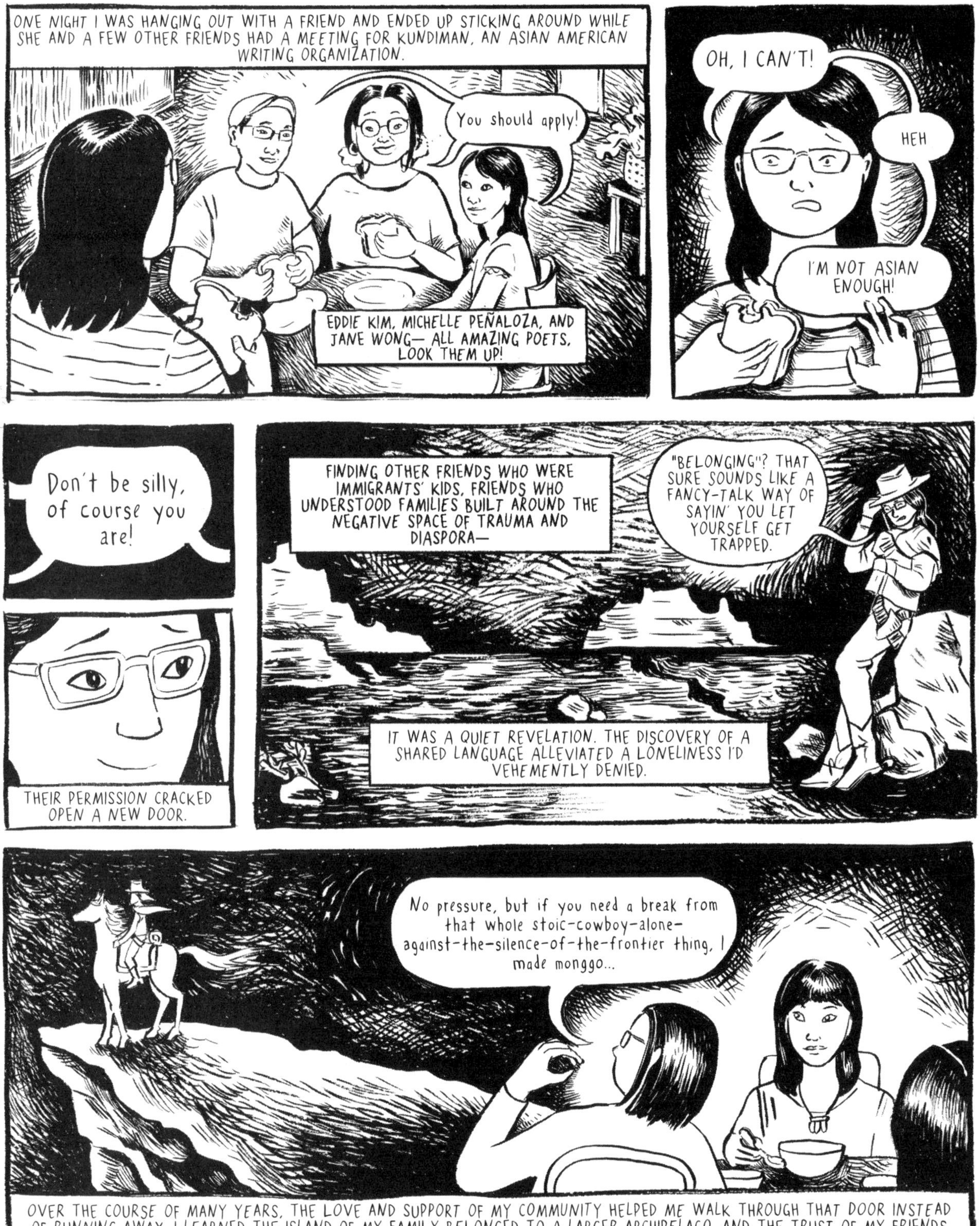
ONE NIGHT I WAS HANGING OUT WITH A FRIEND AND ENDED UP STICKING AROUND WHILE SHE AND A FEW OTHER FRIENDS HAD A MEETING FOR KUNDIMAN, AN ASIAN AMERICAN WRITING ORGANIZATION.
You should apply!
EDDIE KIM, MICHELLE PEÑALOZA, AND JANE WONG— ALL AMAZING POETS. LOOK THEM UP!
OH, I CAN'T!
HEH
I'M NOT ASIAN ENOUGH!
Don't be silly, of course you are!
THEIR PERMISSION CRACKED OPEN A NEW DOOR.
FINDING OTHER FRIENDS WHO WERE IMMIGRANTS' KIDS, FRIENDS WHO UNDERSTOOD FAMILIES BUILT AROUND THE NEGATIVE SPACE OF TRAUMA AND DIASPORA—
"BELONGING"? THAT SURE SOUNDS LIKE A FANCY-TALK WAY OF SAYIN' YOU LET YOURSELF GET TRAPPED.
IT WAS A QUIET REVELATION. THE DISCOVERY OF A SHARED LANGUAGE ALLEVIATED A LONELINESS I'D VEHEMENTLY DENIED.
No pressure, but if you need a break from that whole stoic-cowboy-alone-against-the-silence-of-the-frontier thing, I made monggo...
OVER THE COURSE OF MANY YEARS, THE LOVE AND SUPPORT OF MY COMMUNITY HELPED ME WALK THROUGH THAT DOOR INSTEAD OF RUNNING AWAY. I LEARNED THE ISLAND OF MY FAMILY BELONGED TO A LARGER ARCHIPELAGO, AND THE TRUST OF MY FRIENDS GAVE ME FAITH IN MY RIGHT TO MY OWN STORY.

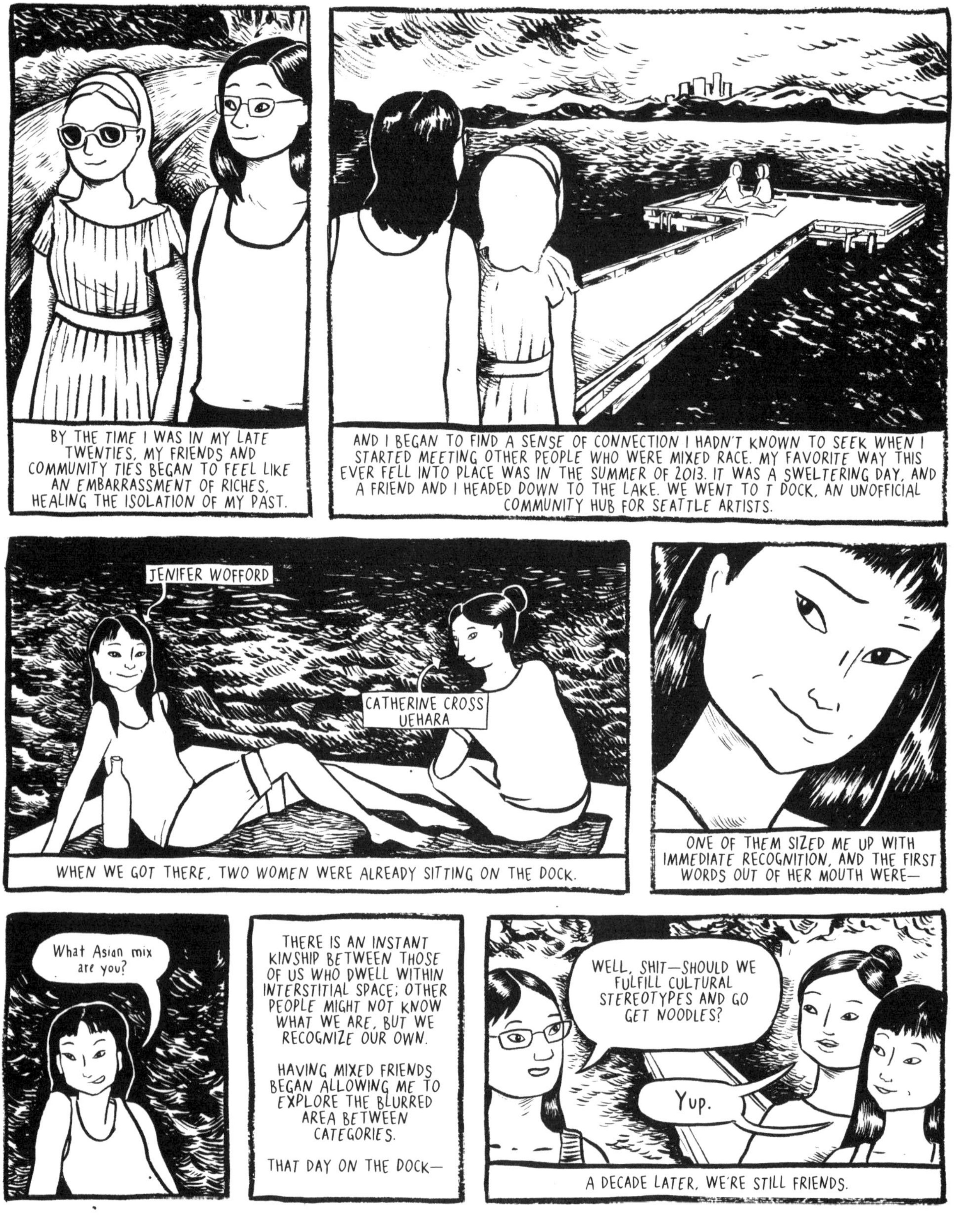
BY THE TIME I WAS IN MY LATE TWENTIES, MY FRIENDS AND COMMUNITY TIES BEGAN TO FEEL LIKE AN EMBARRASSMENT OF RICHES, HEALING THE ISOLATION OF MY PAST.
AND I BEGAN TO FIND A SENSE OF CONNECTION I HADN'T KNOWN TO SEEK WHEN I STARTED MEETING OTHER PEOPLE WHO WERE MIXED RACE. MY FAVORITE WAY THIS EVER FELL INTO PLACE WAS IN THE SUMMER OF 2013. IT WAS A SWELTERING DAY, AND A FRIEND AND I HEADED DOWN TO THE LAKE. WE WENT TO T DOCK, AN UNOFFICIAL COMMUNITY HUB FOR SEATTLE ARTISTS.
JENIFER WOFFORD
CATHERINE CROSS UEHARA
WHEN WE GOT THERE, TWO WOMEN WERE ALREADY SITTING ON THE DOCK.
ONE OF THEM SIZED ME UP WITH IMMEDIATE RECOGNITION, AND THE FIRST WORDS OUT OF HER MOUTH WERE—
What Asian mix are you?
THERE IS AN INSTANT KINSHIP BETWEEN THOSE OF US WHO DWELL WITHIN INTERSTITIAL SPACE; OTHER PEOPLE MIGHT NOT KNOW WHAT WE ARE, BUT WE RECOGNIZE OUR OWN.
HAVING MIXED FRIENDS BEGAN ALLOWING ME TO EXPLORE THE BLURRED AREA BETWEEN CATEGORIES.
THAT DAY ON THE DOCK—
WELL, SHIT—SHOULD WE FULFILL CULTURAL STEREOTYPES AND GO GET NOODLES?
Yup.
A DECADE LATER, WE'RE STILL FRIENDS.

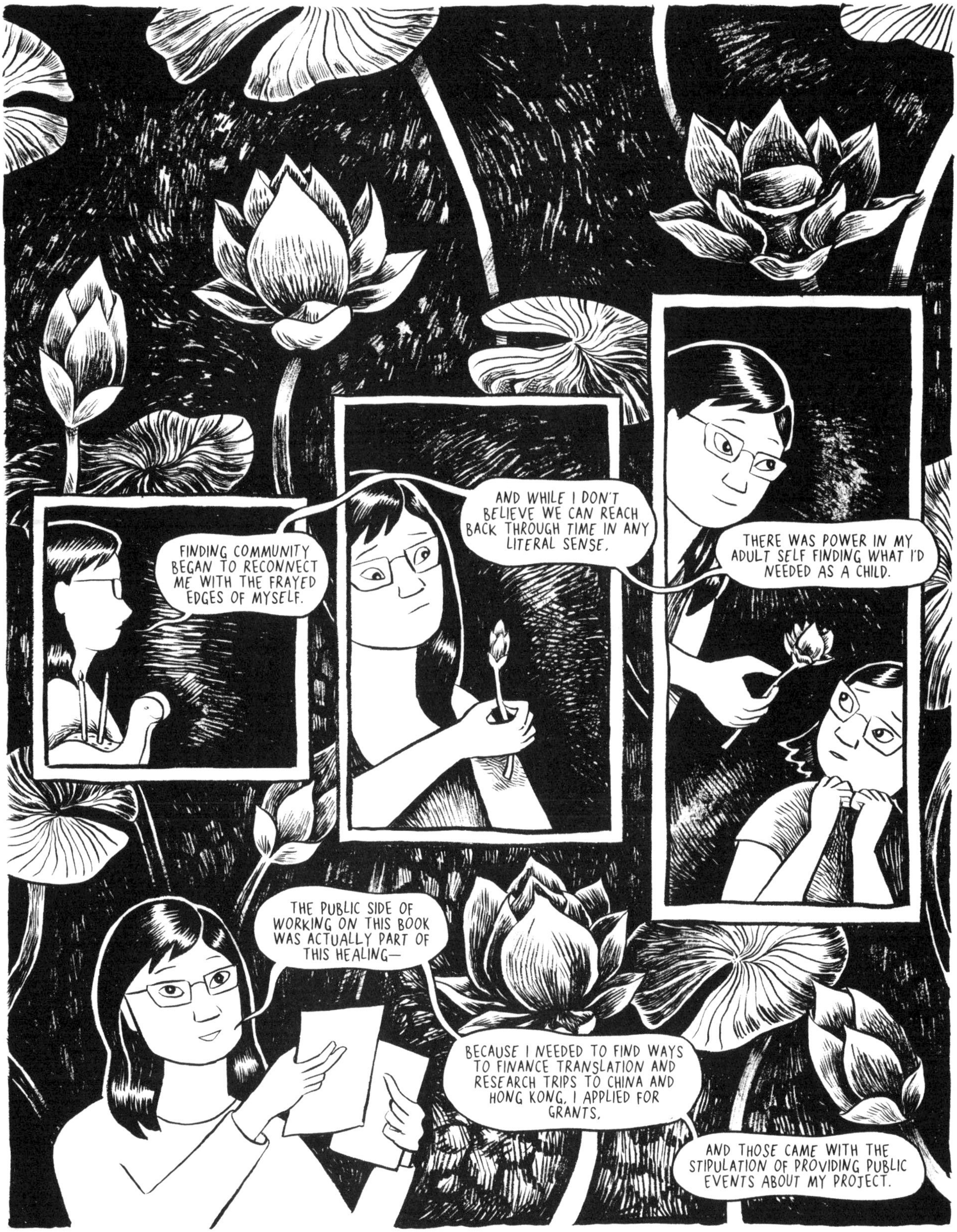
FINDING COMMUNITY BEGAN TO RECONNECT ME WITH THE FRAYED EDGES OF MYSELF.
AND WHILE I DON'T BELIEVE WE CAN REACH BACK THROUGH TIME IN ANY LITERAL SENSE,
THERE WAS POWER IN MY ADULT SELF FINDING WHAT I'D NEEDED AS A CHILD.
THE PUBLIC SIDE OF WORKING ON THIS BOOK WAS ACTUALLY PART OF THIS HEALING—
BECAUSE I NEEDED TO FIND WAYS TO FINANCE TRANSLATION AND RESEARCH TRIPS TO CHINA AND HONG KONG, I APPLIED FOR GRANTS,
AND THOSE CAME WITH THE STIPULATION OF PROVIDING PUBLIC EVENTS ABOUT MY PROJECT.

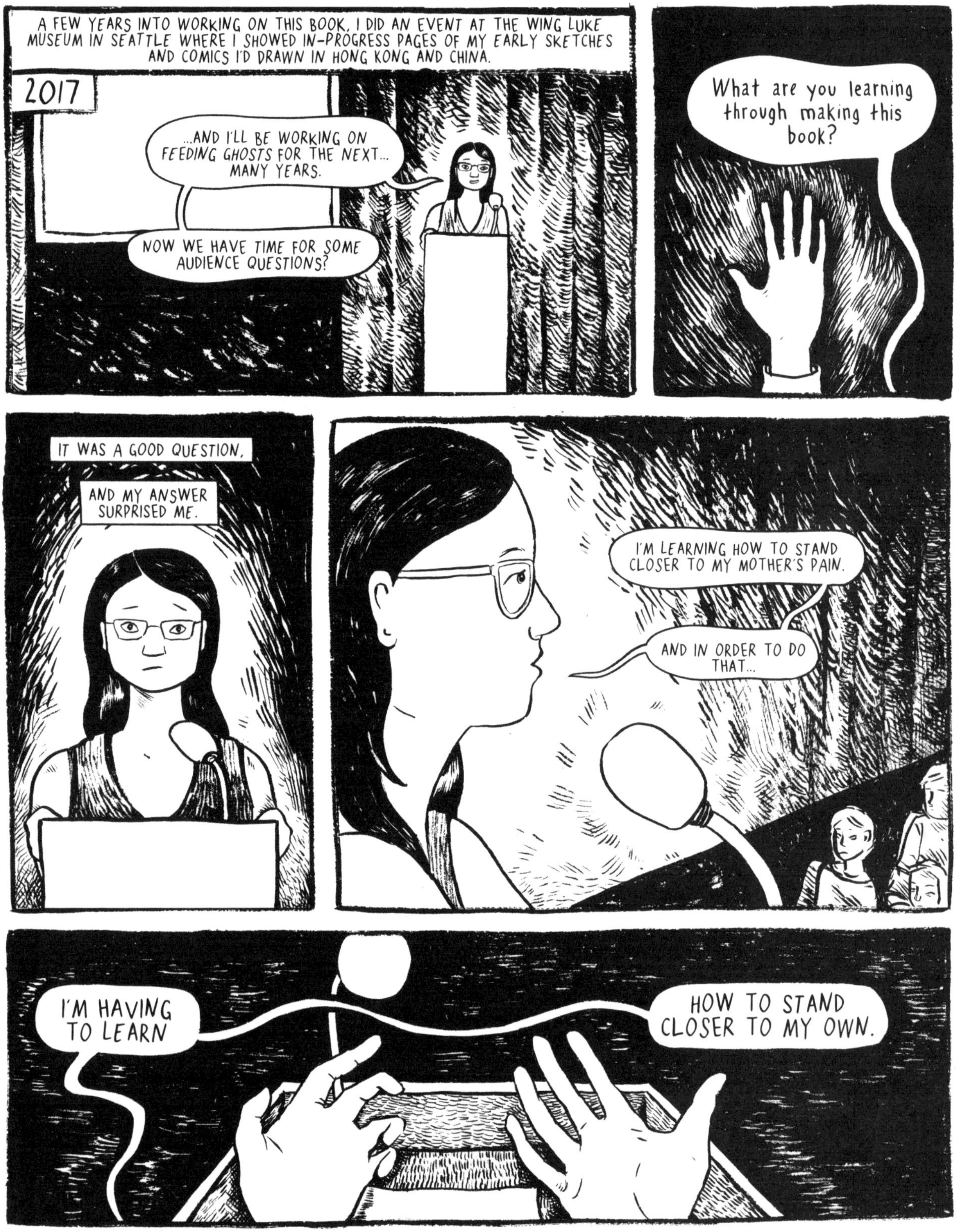
A FEW YEARS INTO WORKING ON THIS BOOK, I DID AN EVENT AT THE WING LUKE MUSEUM IN SEATTLE WHERE I SHOWED IN-PROGRESS PAGES OF MY EARLY SKETCHES AND COMICS I'D DRAWN IN HONG KONG AND CHINA.
2017
...AND I'LL BE WORKING ON FEEDING GHOSTS FOR THE NEXT... MANY YEARS.
NOW WE HAVE TIME FOR SOME AUDIENCE QUESTIONS?
What are you learning through making this book?
IT WAS A GOOD QUESTION,
AND MY ANSWER SURPRISED ME.
I'M LEARNING HOW TO STAND CLOSER TO MY MOTHER'S PAIN.
AND IN ORDER TO DO THAT...
I'M HAVING TO LEARN
HOW TO STAND CLOSER TO MY OWN.

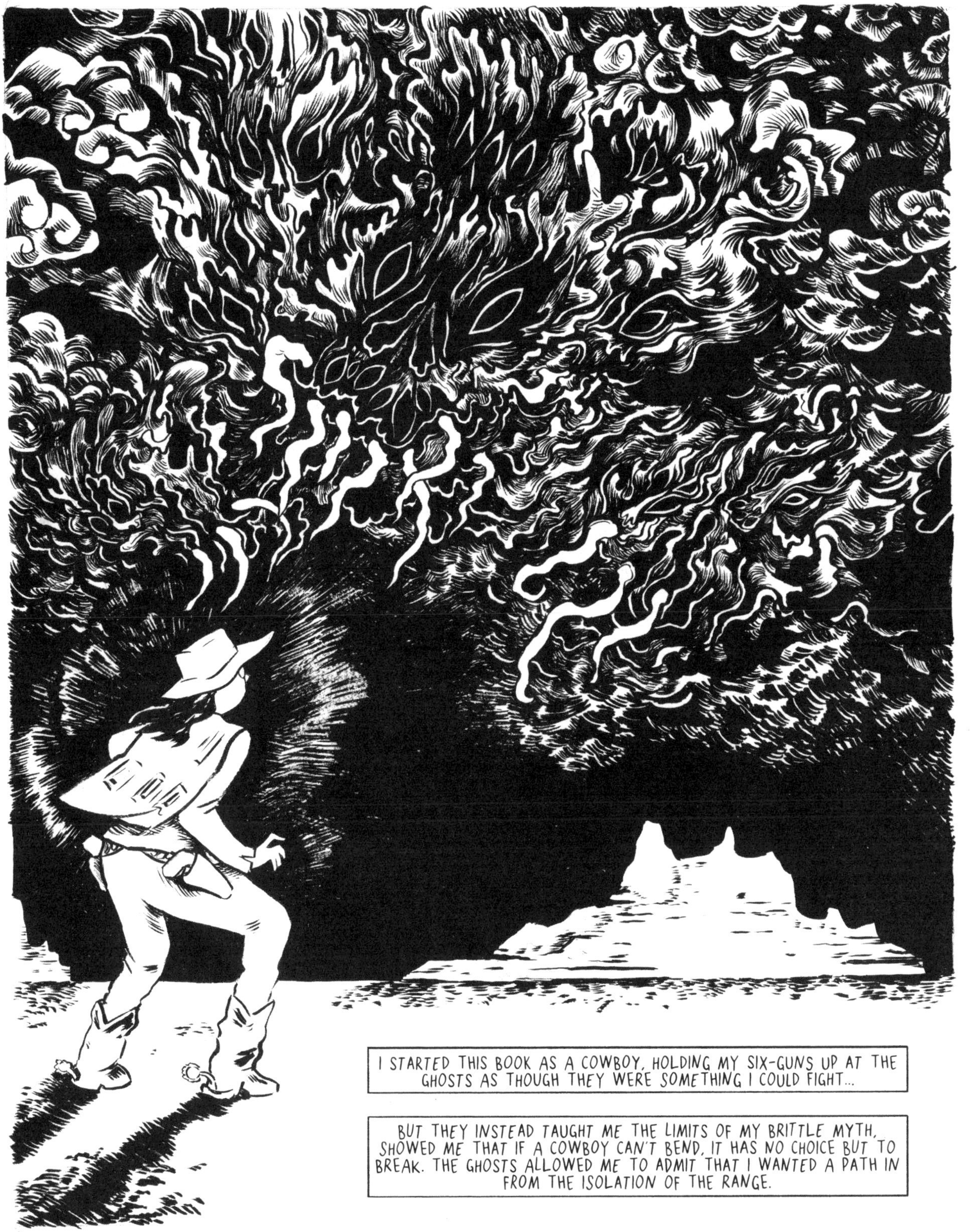
I STARTED THIS BOOK AS A COWBOY, HOLDING MY SIX-GUNS UP AT THE GHOSTS AS THOUGH THEY WERE SOMETHING I COULD FIGHT...
BUT THEY INSTEAD TAUGHT ME THE LIMITS OF MY BRITTLE MYTH, SHOWED ME THAT IF A COWBOY CAN'T BEND, IT HAS NO CHOICE BUT TO BREAK. THE GHOSTS ALLOWED ME TO ADMIT THAT I WANTED A PATH IN FROM THE ISOLATION OF THE RANGE.

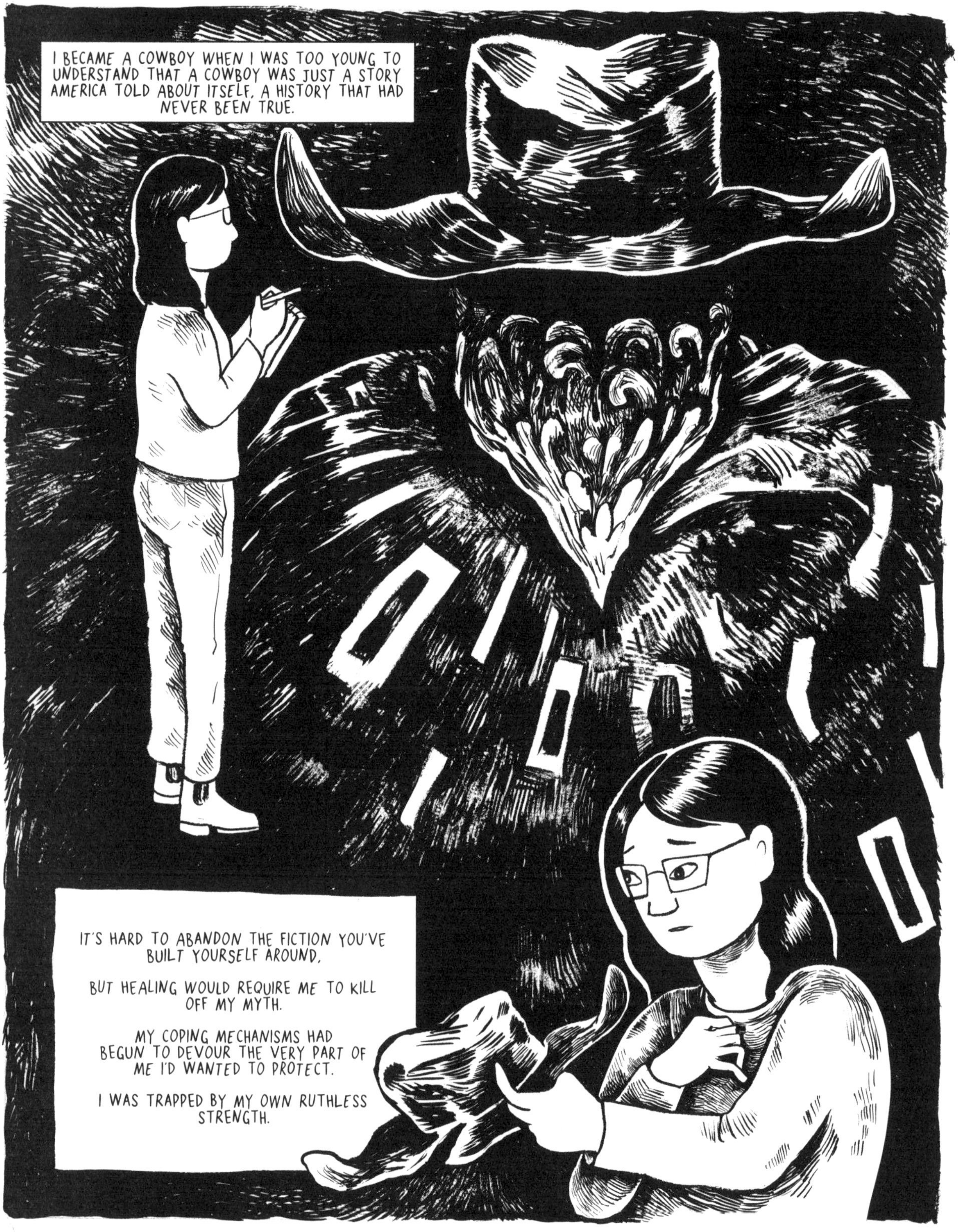
I BECAME A COWBOY WHEN I WAS TOO YOUNG TO UNDERSTAND THAT A COWBOY WAS JUST A STORY AMERICA TOLD ABOUT ITSELF, A HISTORY THAT HAD NEVER BEEN TRUE.
IT'S HARD TO ABANDON THE FICTION YOU'VE BUILT YOURSELF AROUND,
BUT HEALING WOULD REQUIRE ME TO KILL OFF MY MYTH.
MY COPING MECHANISMS HAD BEGUN TO DEVOUR THE VERY PART OF ME I'D WANTED TO PROTECT.
I WAS TRAPPED BY MY OWN RUTHLESS STRENGTH.

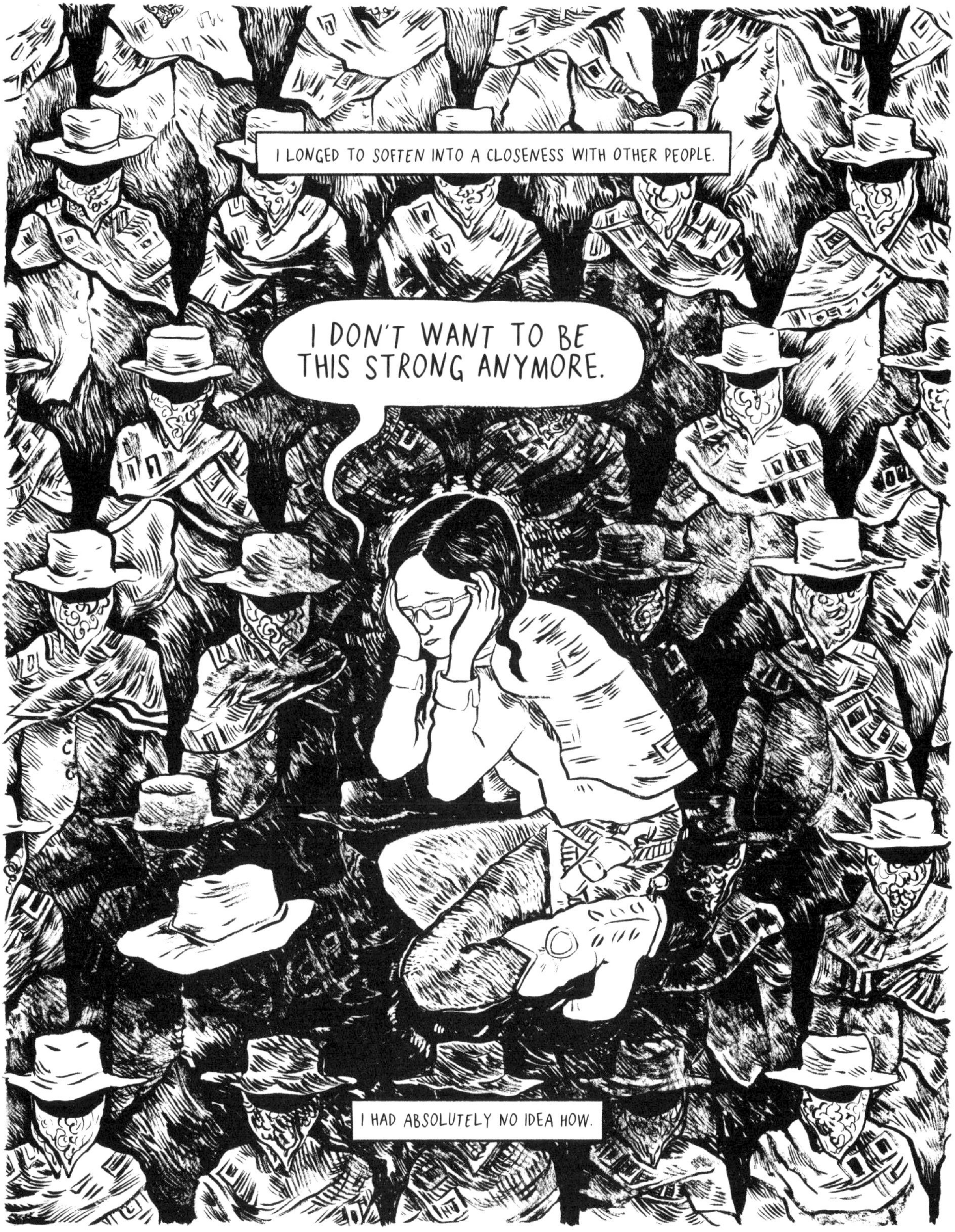
I LONGED TO SOFTEN INTO A CLOSENESS WITH OTHER PEOPLE.
I DON'T WANT TO BE THIS STRONG ANYMORE.
I HAD ABSOLUTELY NO IDEA HOW.

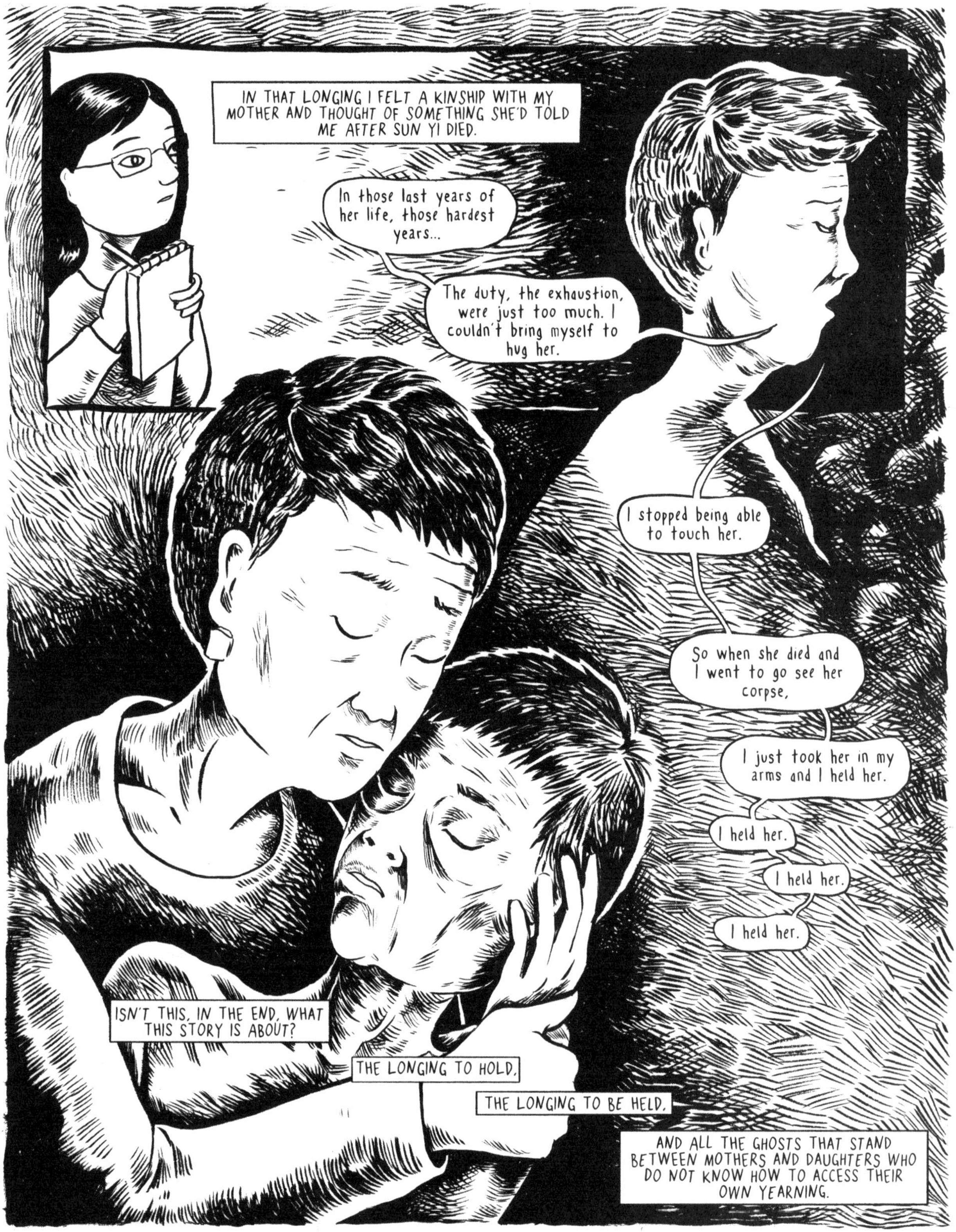
IN THAT LONGING I FELT A KINSHIP WITH MY MOTHER AND THOUGHT OF SOMETHING SHE'D TOLD ME AFTER SUN YI DIED.
In those last years of her life, those hardest years...
The duty, the exhaustion, were just too much. I couldn't bring myself to hug her.
I stopped being able to touch her.
So when she died and I went to go see her corpse,
I just took her in my arms and I held her.
I held her.
I held her.
I held her.
ISN'T THIS, IN THE END, WHAT THIS STORY IS ABOUT?
THE LONGING TO HOLD,
THE LONGING TO BE HELD,
AND ALL THE GHOSTS THAT STAND BETWEEN MOTHERS AND DAUGHTERS WHO DO NOT KNOW HOW TO ACCESS THEIR OWN YEARNING.

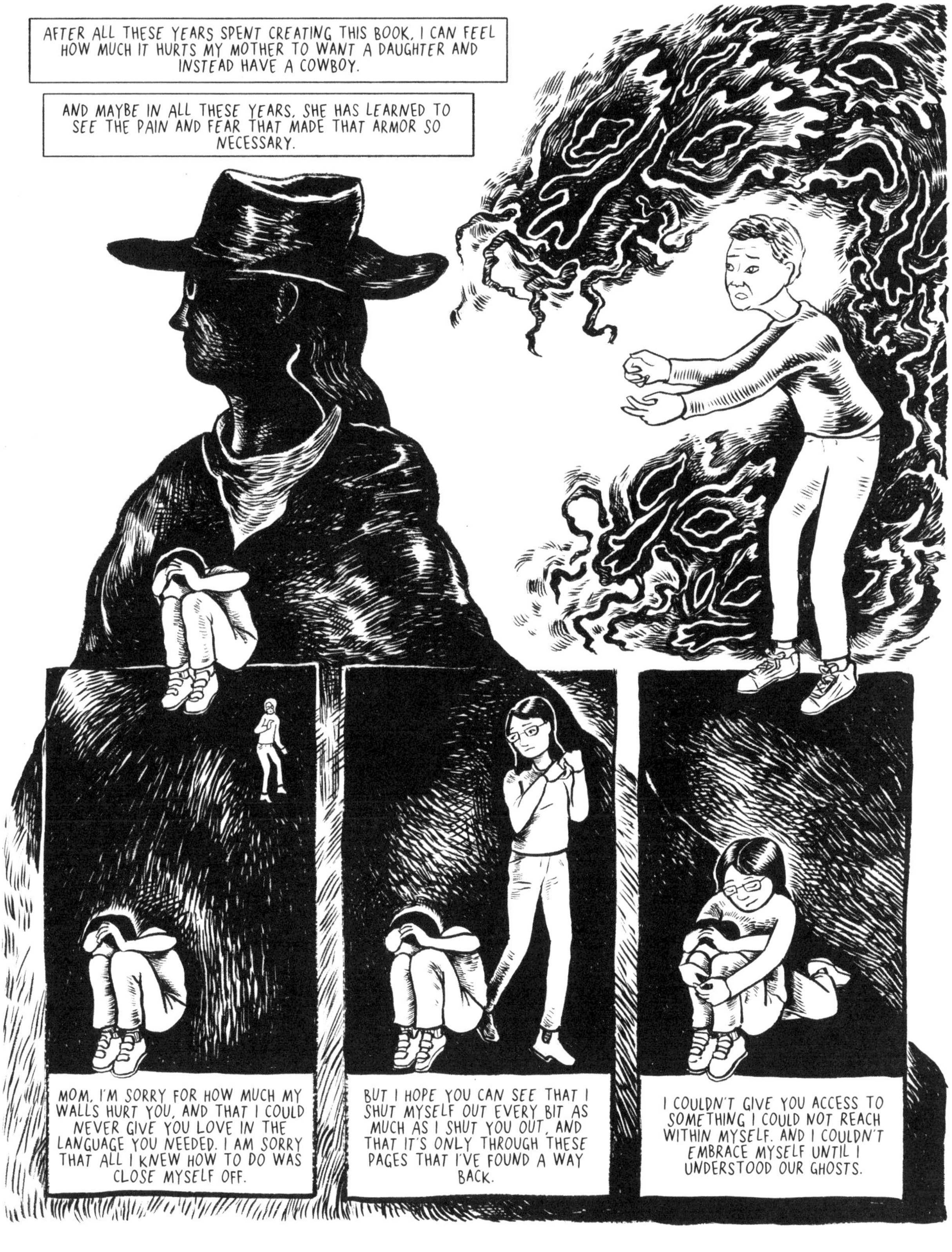
AFTER ALL THESE YEARS SPENT CREATING THIS BOOK, I CAN FEEL HOW MUCH IT HURTS MY MOTHER TO WANT A DAUGHTER AND INSTEAD HAVE A COWBOY.
AND MAYBE IN ALL THESE YEARS, SHE HAS LEARNED TO SEE THE PAIN AND FEAR THAT MADE THAT ARMOR SO NECESSARY.
MOM, I'M SORRY FOR HOW MUCH MY WALLS HURT YOU, AND THAT I COULD NEVER GIVE YOU LOVE IN THE LANGUAGE YOU NEEDED. I AM SORRY THAT ALL I KNEW HOW TO DO WAS CLOSE MYSELF OFF.
BUT I HOPE YOU CAN SEE THAT I SHUT MYSELF OUT EVERY BIT AS MUCH AS I SHUT YOU OUT, AND THAT IT'S ONLY THROUGH THESE PAGES THAT I'VE FOUND A WAY BACK.
I COULDN'T GIVE YOU ACCESS TO SOMETHING I COULD NOT REACH WITHIN MYSELF. AND I COULDN'T EMBRACE MYSELF UNTIL I UNDERSTOOD OUR GHOSTS.

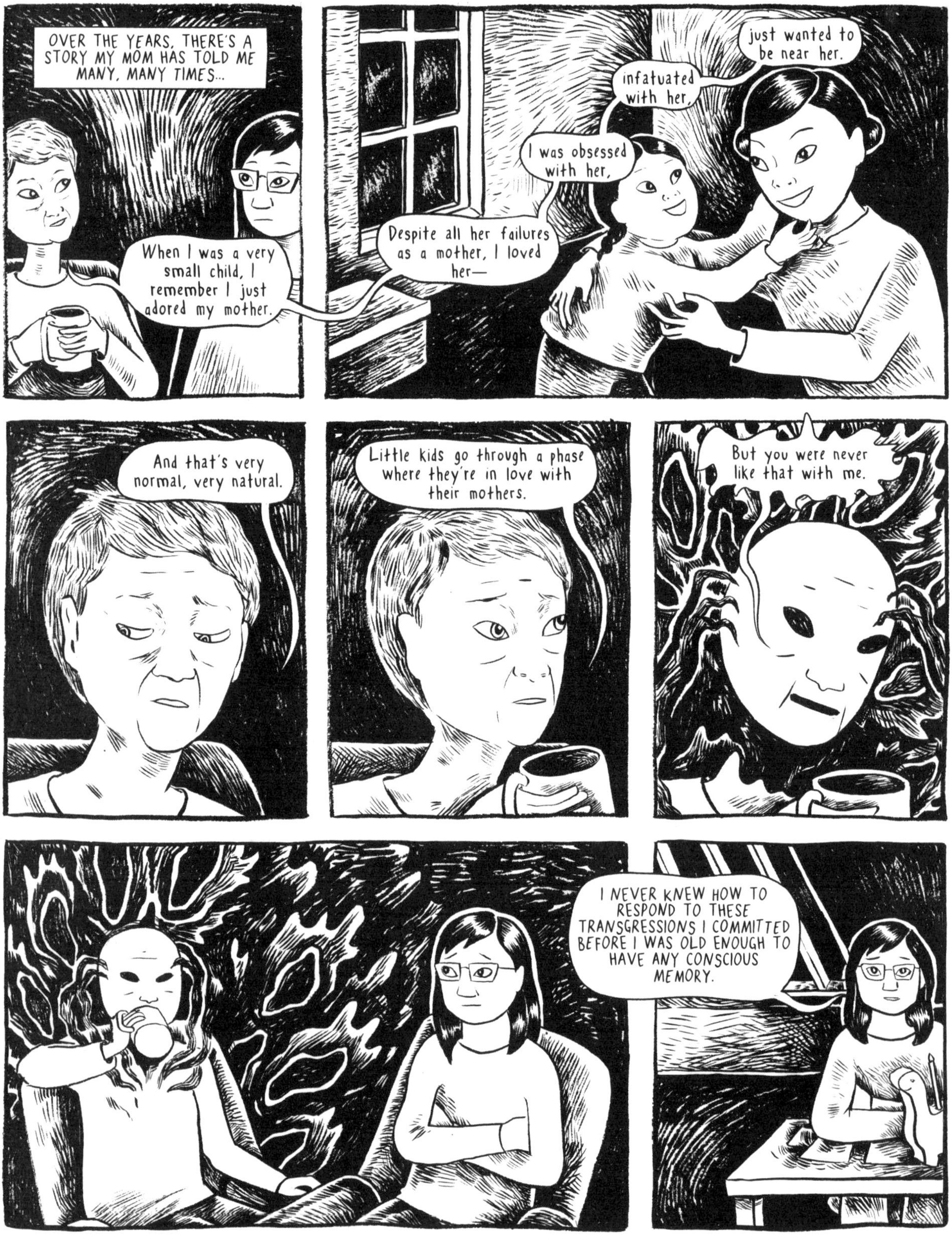
OVER THE YEARS, THERE'S A STORY MY MOM HAS TOLD ME MANY, MANY TIMES...
When I was a very small child, I remember I just adored my mother.
Despite all her failures as a mother, I loved her—
I was obsessed with her,
infatuated with her,
just wanted to be near her.
And that's very normal, very natural.
Little kids go through a phase where they're in love with their mothers.
But you were never like that with me.
I NEVER KNEW HOW TO RESPOND TO THESE TRANSGRESSIONS I COMMITTED BEFORE I WAS OLD ENOUGH TO HAVE ANY CONSCIOUS MEMORY.

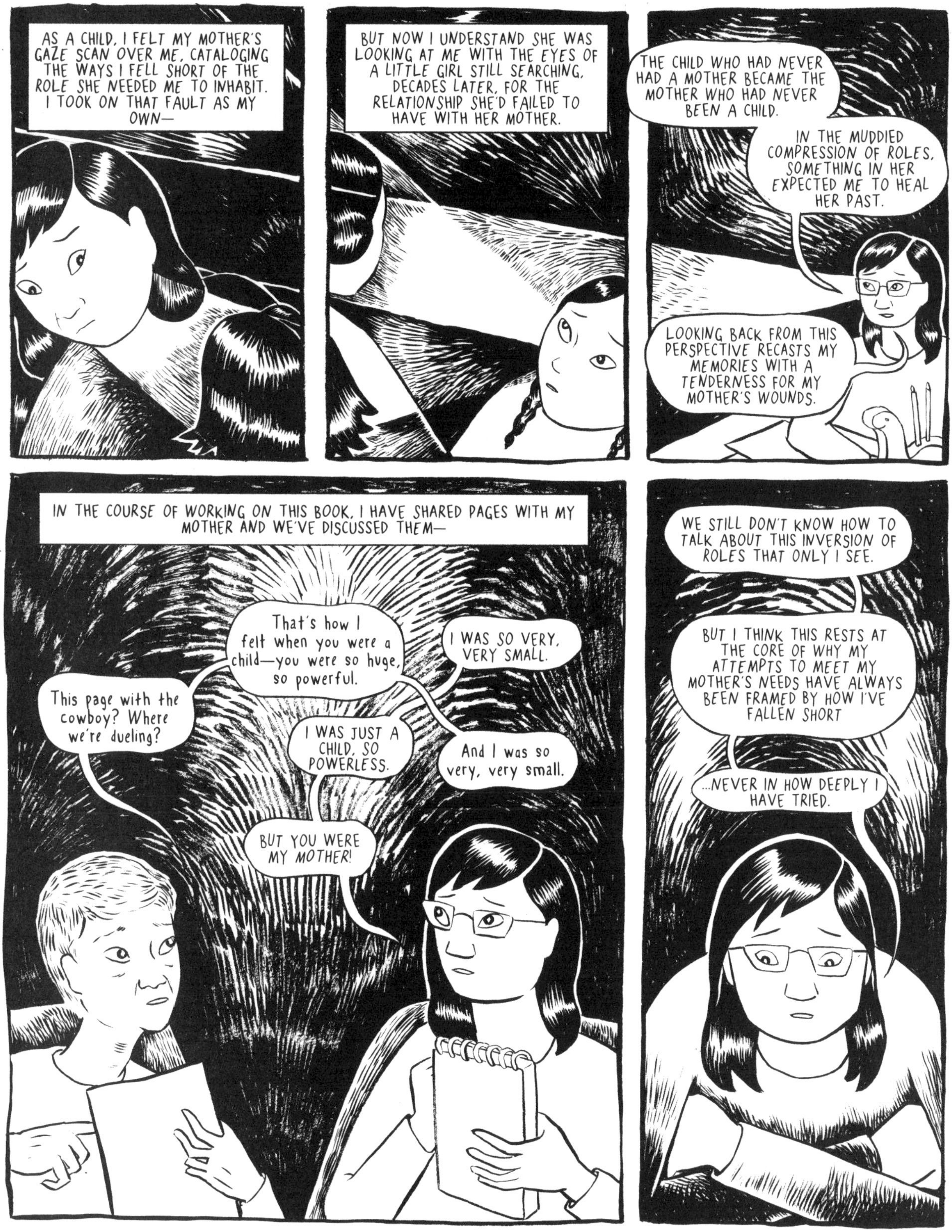
AS A CHILD, I FELT MY MOTHER'S GAZE SCAN OVER ME, CATALOGING THE WAYS I FELL SHORT OF THE ROLE SHE NEEDED ME TO INHABIT. I TOOK ON THAT FAULT AS MY OWN—
BUT NOW I UNDERSTAND SHE WAS LOOKING AT ME WITH THE EYES OF A LITTLE GIRL STILL SEARCHING, DECADES LATER, FOR THE RELATIONSHIP SHE'D FAILED TO HAVE WITH HER MOTHER.
THE CHILD WHO HAD NEVER HAD A MOTHER BECAME THE MOTHER WHO HAD NEVER BEEN A CHILD.
IN THE MUDDIED COMPRESSION OF ROLES, SOMETHING IN HER EXPECTED ME TO HEAL HER PAST.
LOOKING BACK FROM THIS PERSPECTIVE RECASTS MY MEMORIES WITH A TENDERNESS FOR MY MOTHER'S WOUNDS.
IN THE COURSE OF WORKING ON THIS BOOK, I HAVE SHARED PAGES WITH MY MOTHER AND WE'VE DISCUSSED THEM—
This page with the cowboy? Where we're dueling?
BUT YOU WERE MY MOTHER!
That's how I felt when you were a child—you were so huge, so powerful.
I WAS JUST A CHILD, SO POWERLESS.
I WAS SO VERY, VERY SMALL.
And I was so very, very small.
WE STILL DON'T KNOW HOW TO TALK ABOUT THIS INVERSION OF ROLES THAT ONLY I SEE.
BUT I THINK THIS RESTS AT THE CORE OF WHY MY ATTEMPTS TO MEET MY MOTHER'S NEEDS HAVE ALWAYS BEEN FRAMED BY HOW I'VE FALLEN SHORT
...NEVER IN HOW DEEPLY I HAVE TRIED.

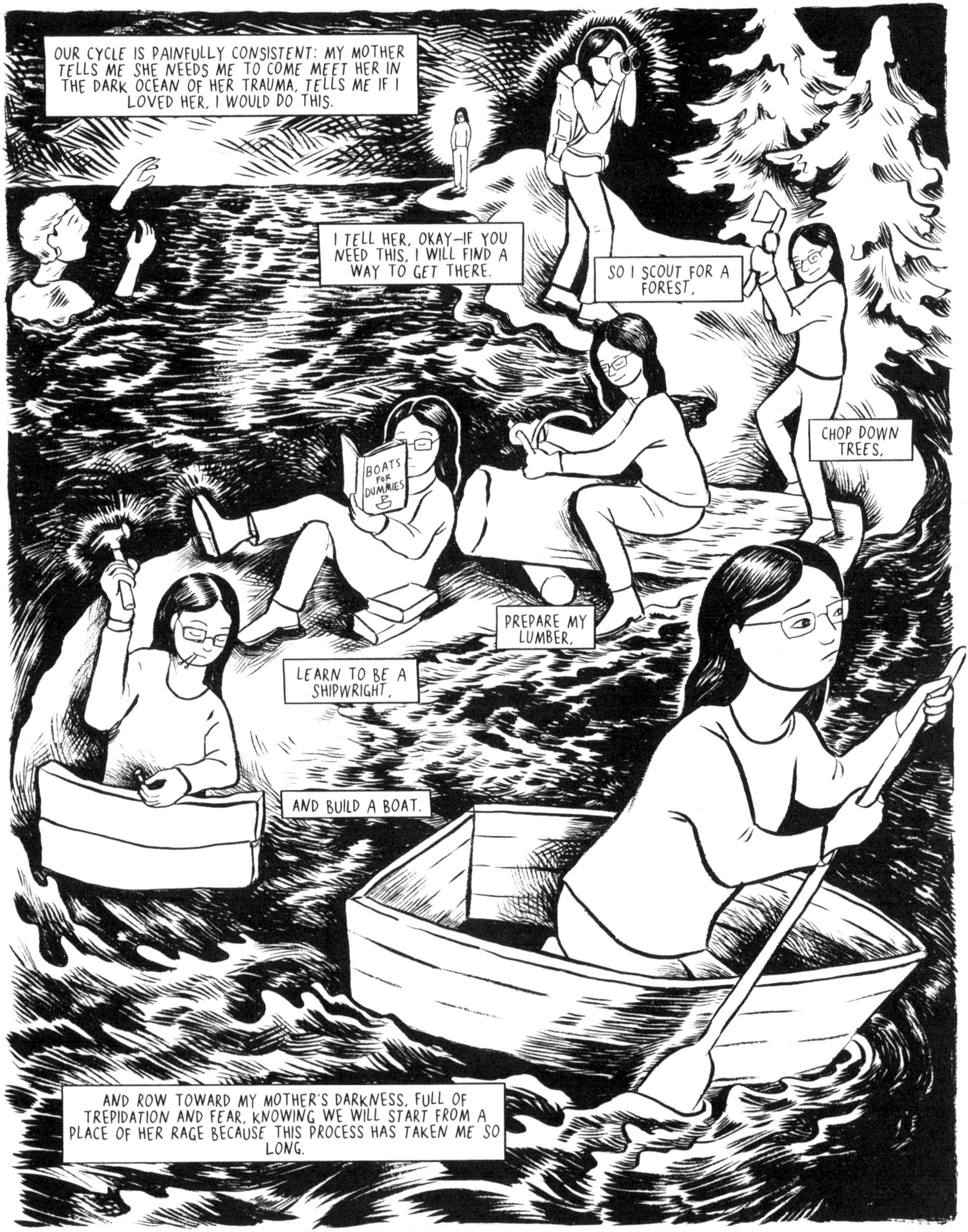
OUR CYCLE IS PAINFULLY CONSISTENT: MY MOTHER TELLS ME SHE NEEDS ME TO COME MEET HER IN THE DARK OCEAN OF HER TRAUMA, TELLS ME IF I LOVED HER, I WOULD DO THIS.
I TELL HER, OKAY—IF YOU NEED THIS, I WILL FIND A WAY TO GET THERE.
SO I SCOUT FOR A FOREST,
CHOP DOWN TREES,
PREPARE MY LUMBER,
BOATS FOR DUMMIES
LEARN TO BE A SHIPWRIGHT,
AND BUILD A BOAT.
AND ROW TOWARD MY MOTHER'S DARKNESS, FULL OF TREPIDATION AND FEAR, KNOWING WE WILL START FROM A PLACE OF HER RAGE BECAUSE THIS PROCESS HAS TAKEN ME SO LONG.

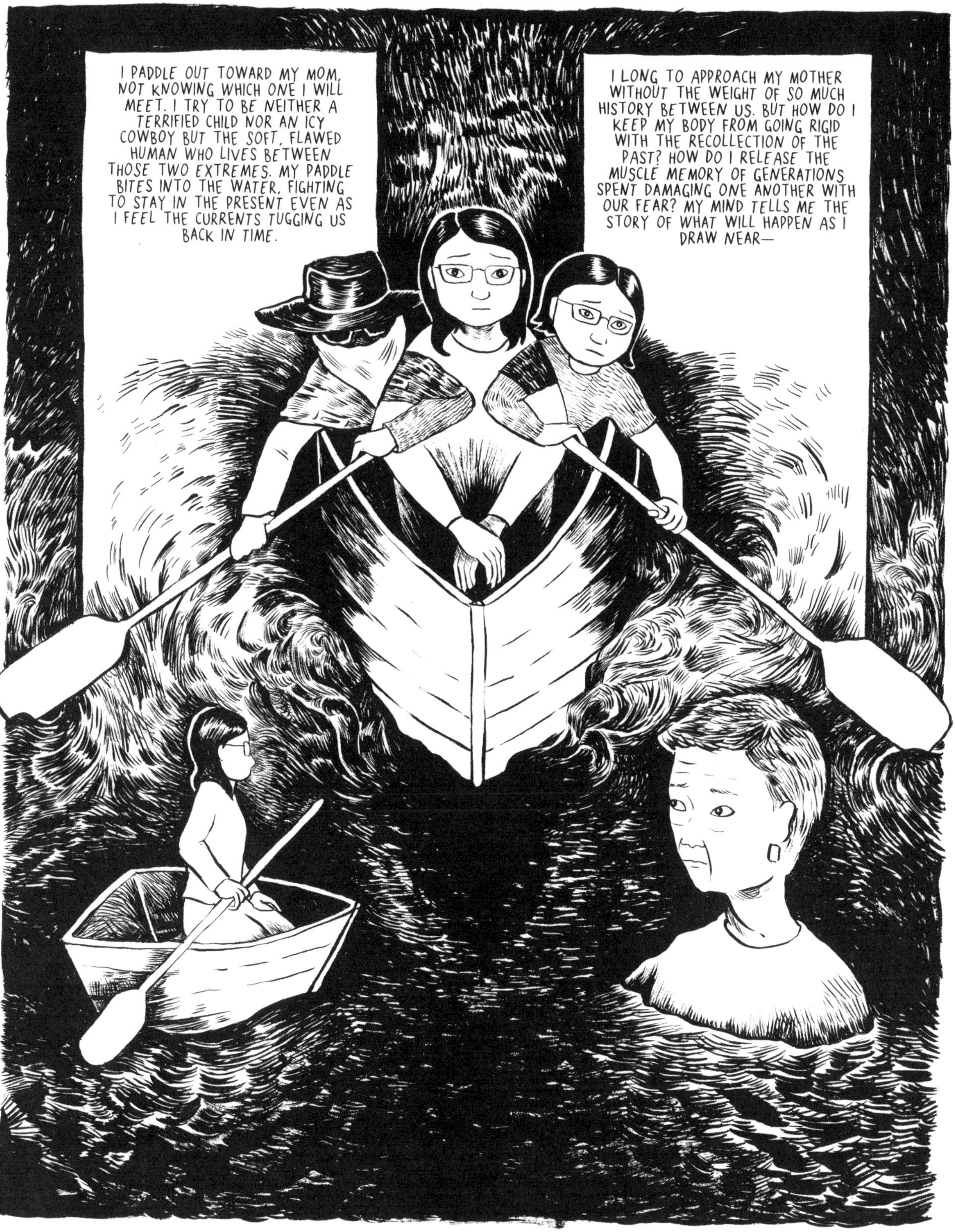
I PADDLE OUT TOWARD MY MOM, NOT KNOWING WHICH ONE I WILL MEET. I TRY TO BE NEITHER A TERRIFIED CHILD NOR AN ICY COWBOY BUT THE SOFT, FLAWED HUMAN WHO LIVES BETWEEN THOSE TWO EXTREMES. MY PADDLE BITES INTO THE WATER, FIGHTING TO STAY IN THE PRESENT EVEN AS I FEEL THE CURRENTS TUGGING US BACK IN TIME.
I LONG TO APPROACH MY MOTHER WITHOUT THE WEIGHT OF SO MUCH HISTORY BETWEEN US. BUT HOW DO I KEEP MY BODY FROM GOING RIGID WITH THE RECOLLECTION OF THE PAST? HOW DO I RELEASE THE MUSCLE MEMORY OF GENERATIONS SPENT DAMAGING ONE ANOTHER WITH OUR FEAR? MY MIND TELLS ME THE STORY OF WHAT WILL HAPPEN AS I DRAW NEAR—

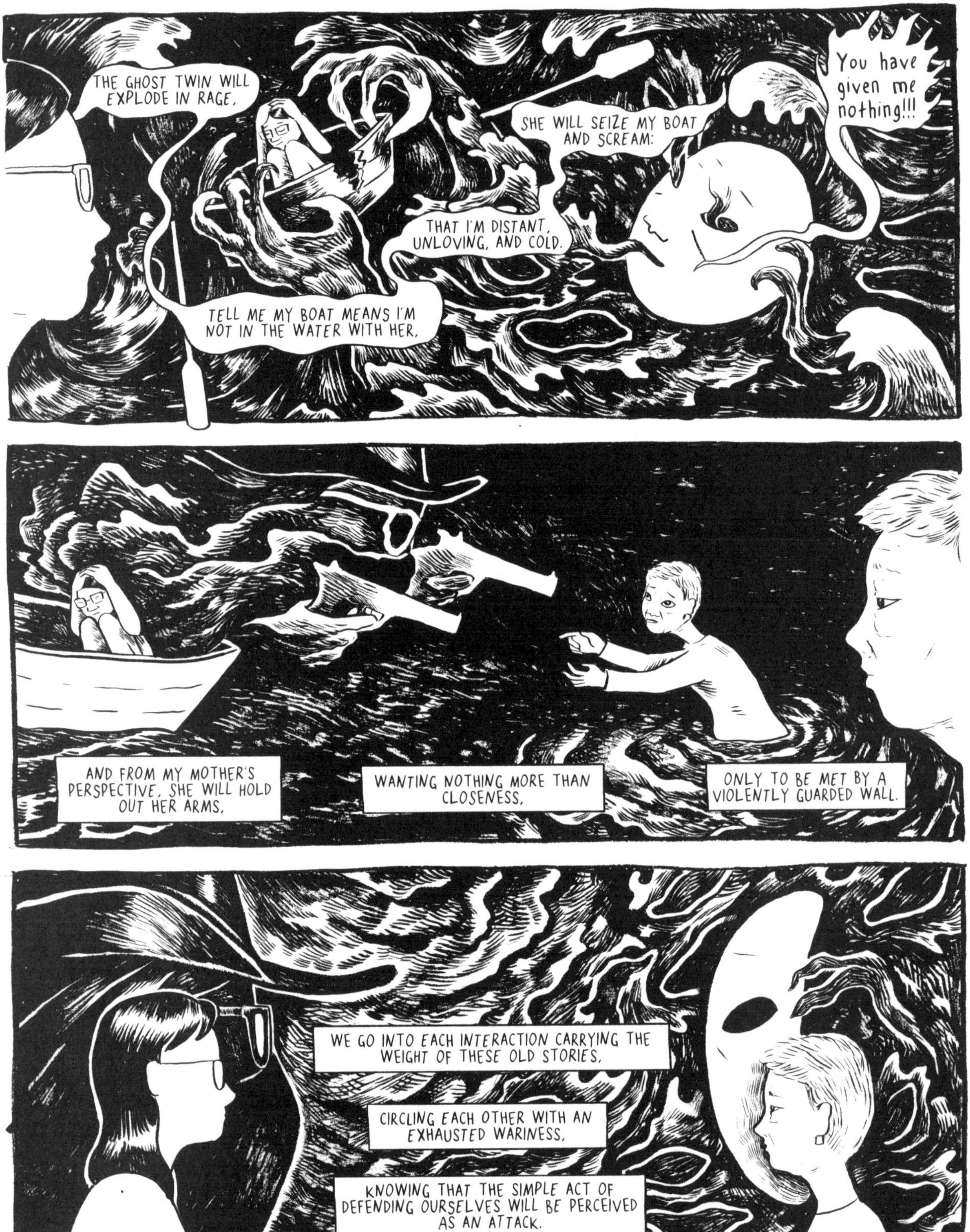
THE GHOST TWIN WILL EXPLODE IN RAGE,
SHE WILL SEIZE MY BOAT AND SCREAM:
You have given me nothing!!!
THAT I'M DISTANT, UNLOVING, AND COLD.
TELL ME MY BOAT MEANS I'M NOT IN THE WATER WITH HER.
AND FROM MY MOTHER'S PERSPECTIVE, SHE WILL HOLD OUT HER ARMS,
WANTING NOTHING MORE THAN CLOSENESS,
ONLY TO BE MET BY A VIOLENTLY GUARDED WALL.
WE GO INTO EACH INTERACTION CARRYING THE WEIGHT OF THESE OLD STORIES,
CIRCLING EACH OTHER WITH AN EXHAUSTED WARINESS,
KNOWING THAT THE SIMPLE ACT OF DEFENDING OURSELVES WILL BE PERCEIVED AS AN ATTACK.

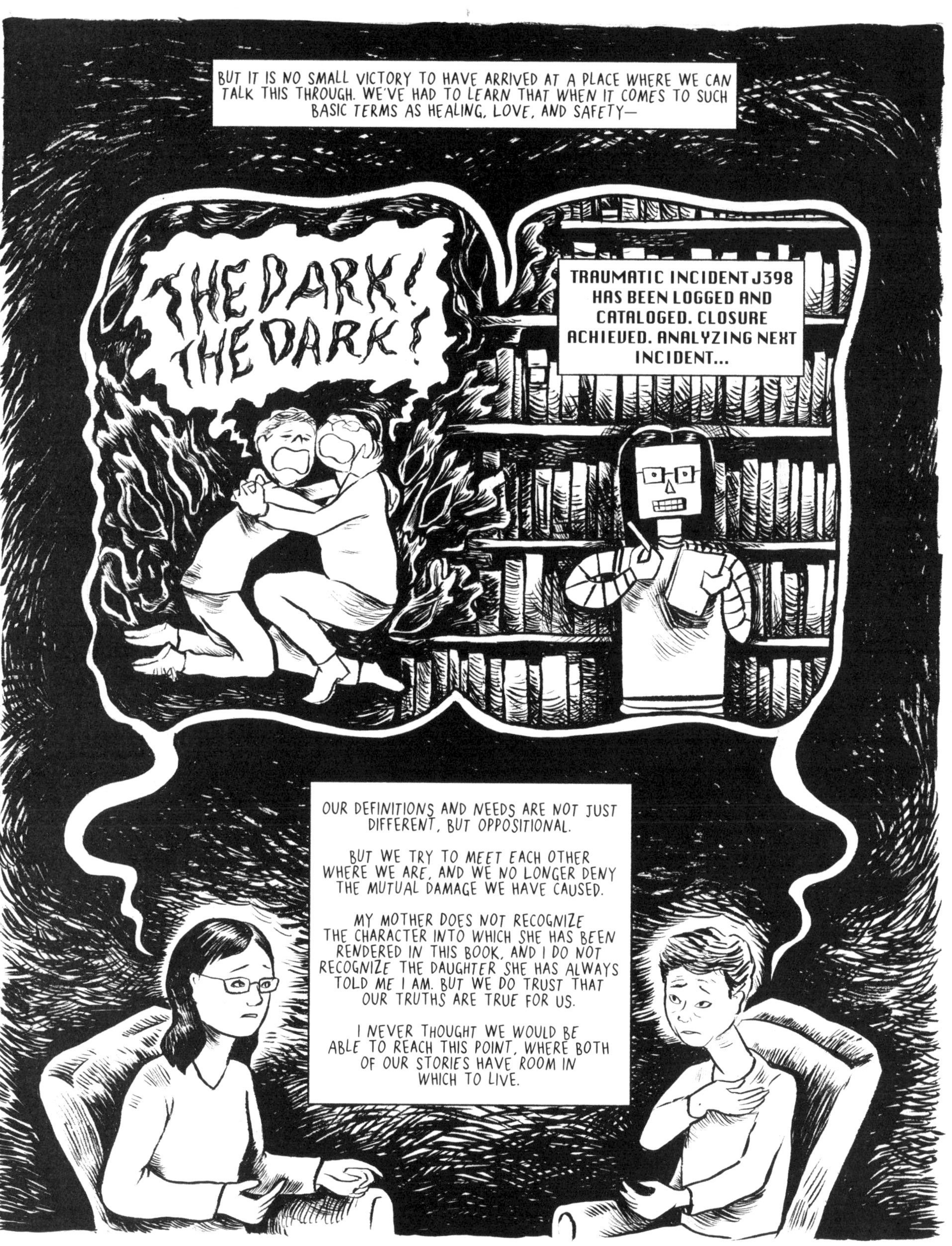
BUT IT IS NO SMALL VICTORY TO HAVE ARRIVED AT A PLACE WHERE WE CAN TALK THIS THROUGH. WE'VE HAD TO LEARN THAT WHEN IT COMES TO SUCH BASIC TERMS AS HEALING, LOVE, AND SAFETY—
THE DARK! THE DARK!
TRAUMATIC INCIDENT J398 HAS BEEN LOGGED AND CATALOGED. CLOSURE ACHIEVED. ANALYZING NEXT INCIDENT...
OUR DEFINITIONS AND NEEDS ARE NOT JUST DIFFERENT, BUT OPPOSITIONAL.
BUT WE TRY TO MEET EACH OTHER WHERE WE ARE, AND WE NO LONGER DENY THE MUTUAL DAMAGE WE HAVE CAUSED.
MY MOTHER DOES NOT RECOGNIZE THE CHARACTER INTO WHICH SHE HAS BEEN RENDERED IN THIS BOOK, AND I DO NOT RECOGNIZE THE DAUGHTER SHE HAS ALWAYS TOLD ME I AM. BUT WE DO TRUST THAT OUR TRUTHS ARE TRUE FOR US.
I NEVER THOUGHT WE WOULD BE ABLE TO REACH THIS POINT, WHERE BOTH OF OUR STORIES HAVE ROOM IN WHICH TO LIVE.

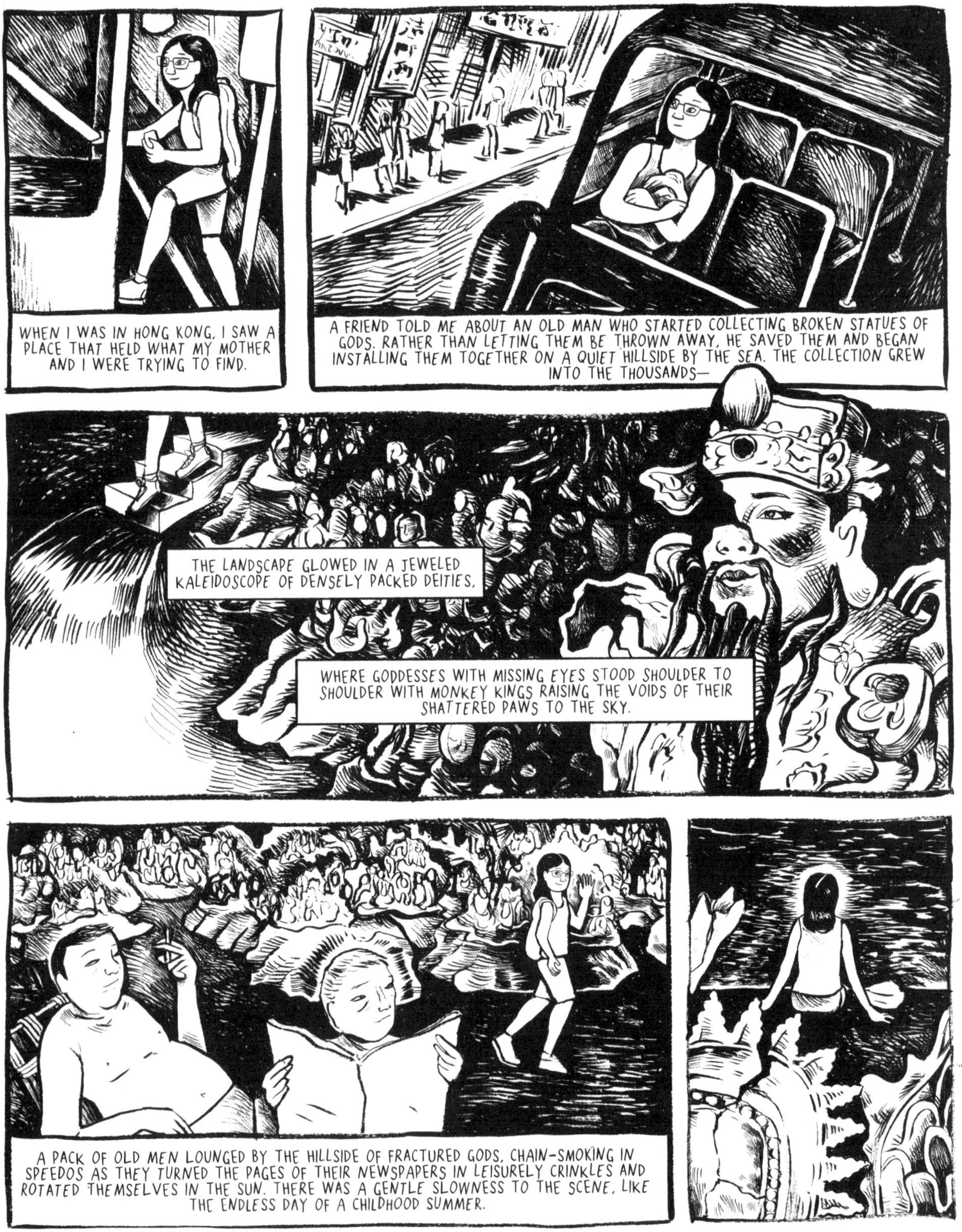
WHEN I WAS IN HONG KONG, I SAW A PLACE THAT HELD WHAT MY MOTHER AND I WERE TRYING TO FIND.
A FRIEND TOLD ME ABOUT AN OLD MAN WHO STARTED COLLECTING BROKEN STATUES OF GODS. RATHER THAN LETTING THEM BE THROWN AWAY, HE SAVED THEM AND BEGAN INSTALLING THEM TOGETHER ON A QUIET HILLSIDE BY THE SEA. THE COLLECTION GREW INTO THE THOUSANDS—
THE LANDSCAPE GLOWED IN A JEWELED KALEIDOSCOPE OF DENSELY PACKED DEITIES,
WHERE GODDESSES WITH MISSING EYES STOOD SHOULDER TO SHOULDER WITH MONKEY KINGS RAISING THE VOIDS OF THEIR SHATTERED PAWS TO THE SKY.
A PACK OF OLD MEN LOUNGED BY THE HILLSIDE OF FRACTURED GODS, CHAIN-SMOKING IN SPEEDOS AS THEY TURNED THE PAGES OF THEIR NEWSPAPERS IN LEISURELY CRINKLES AND ROTATED THEMSELVES IN THE SUN. THERE WAS A GENTLE SLOWNESS TO THE SCENE, LIKE THE ENDLESS DAY OF A CHILDHOOD SUMMER.

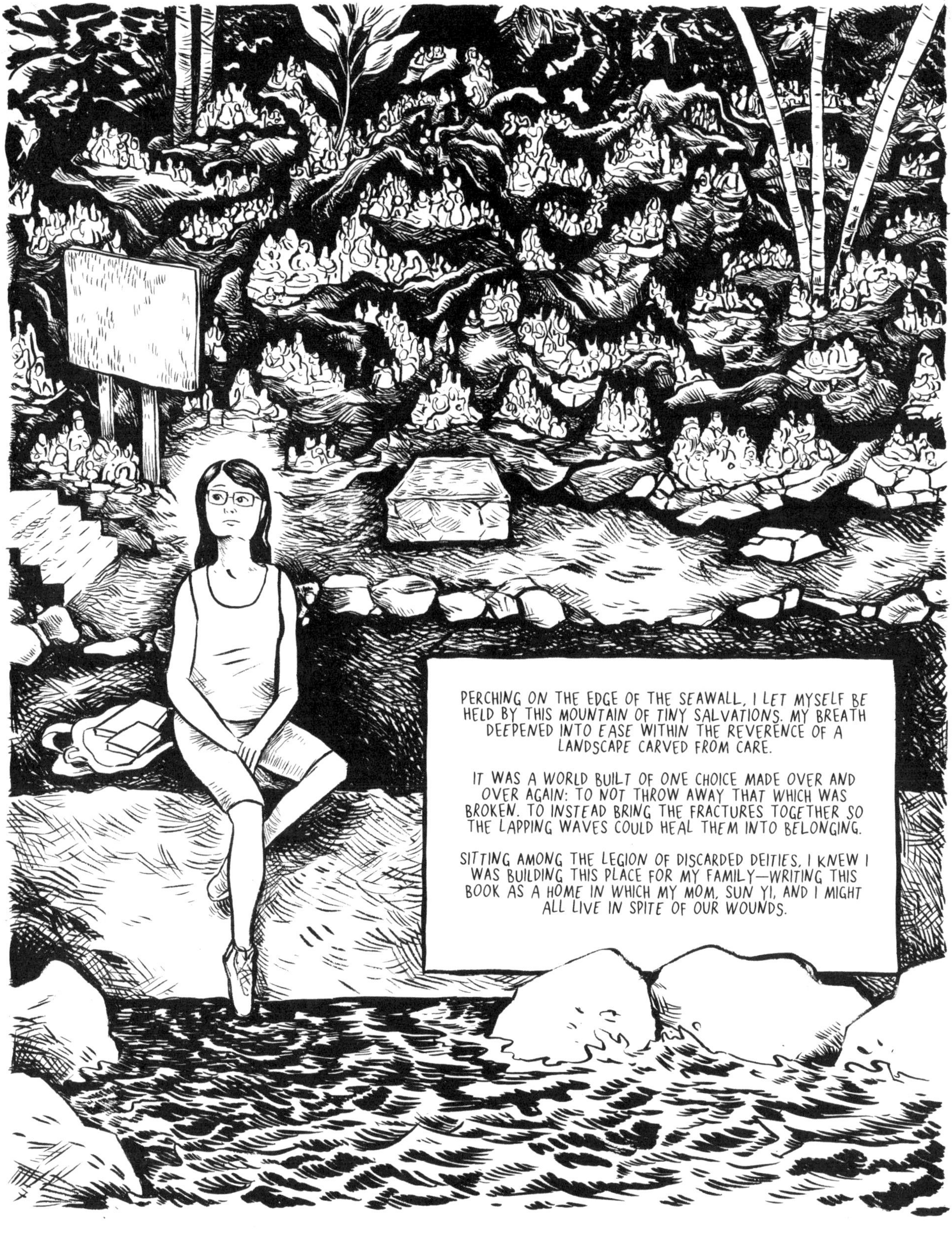
PERCHING ON THE EDGE OF THE SEAWALL, I LET MYSELF BE HELD BY THIS MOUNTAIN OF TINY SALVATIONS. MY BREATH DEEPENED INTO EASE WITHIN THE REVERENCE OF A LANDSCAPE CARVED FROM CARE.
IT WAS A WORLD BUILT OF ONE CHOICE MADE OVER AND OVER AGAIN: TO NOT THROW AWAY THAT WHICH WAS BROKEN. TO INSTEAD BRING THE FRACTURES TOGETHER SO THE LAPPING WAVES COULD HEAL THEM INTO BELONGING.
SITTING AMONG THE LEGION OF DISCARDED DEITIES, I KNEW I WAS BUILDING THIS PLACE FOR MY FAMILY—WRITING THIS BOOK AS A HOME IN WHICH MY MOM, SUN YI, AND I MIGHT ALL LIVE IN SPITE OF OUR WOUNDS.

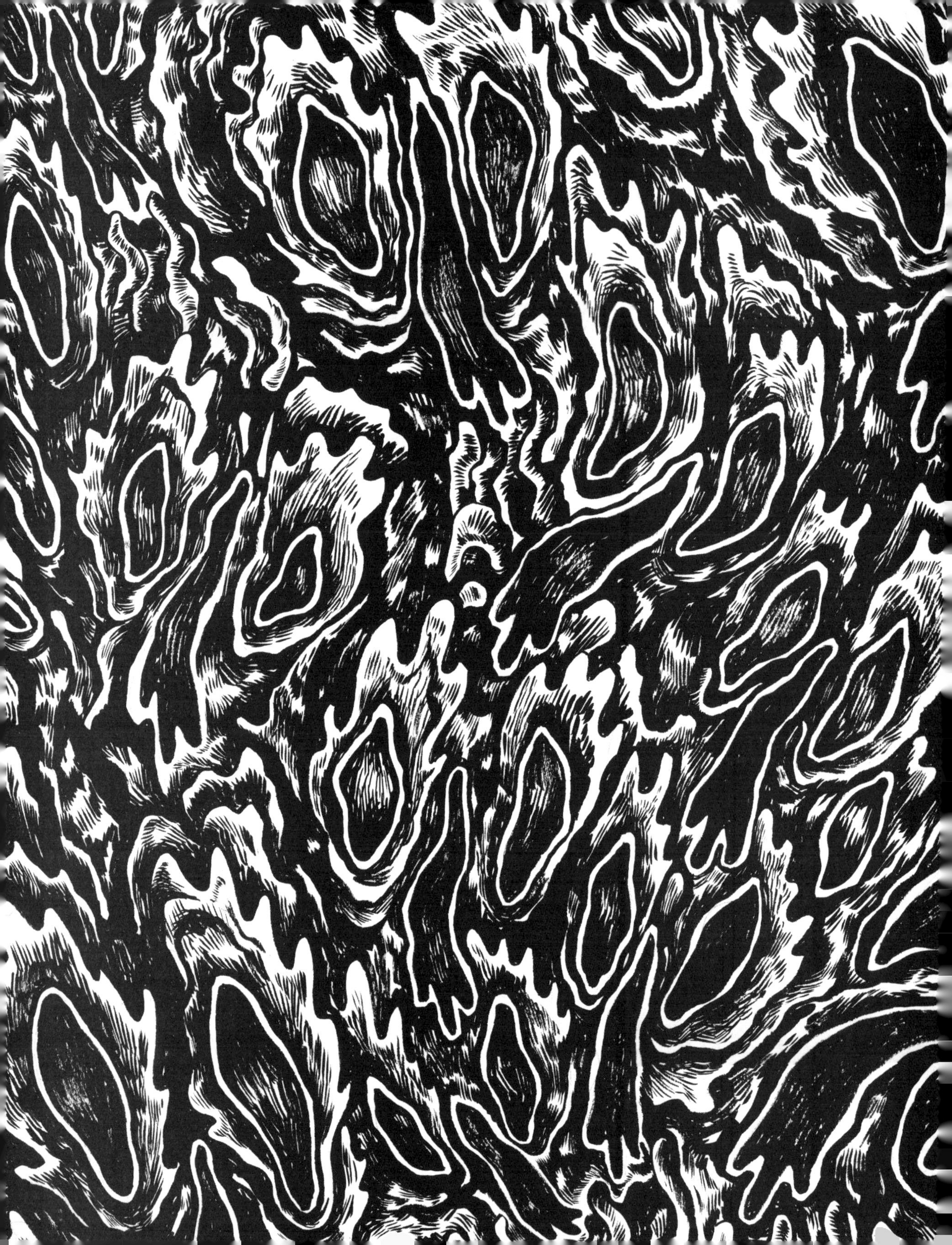

EPILOGUE

TOUCHING US BACK FROM EXTINCTION

The Ocean • The Present

pressing
this pen to paper, I was touching us
back from extinction

—**OCEAN VUONG, "Daily Bread"**

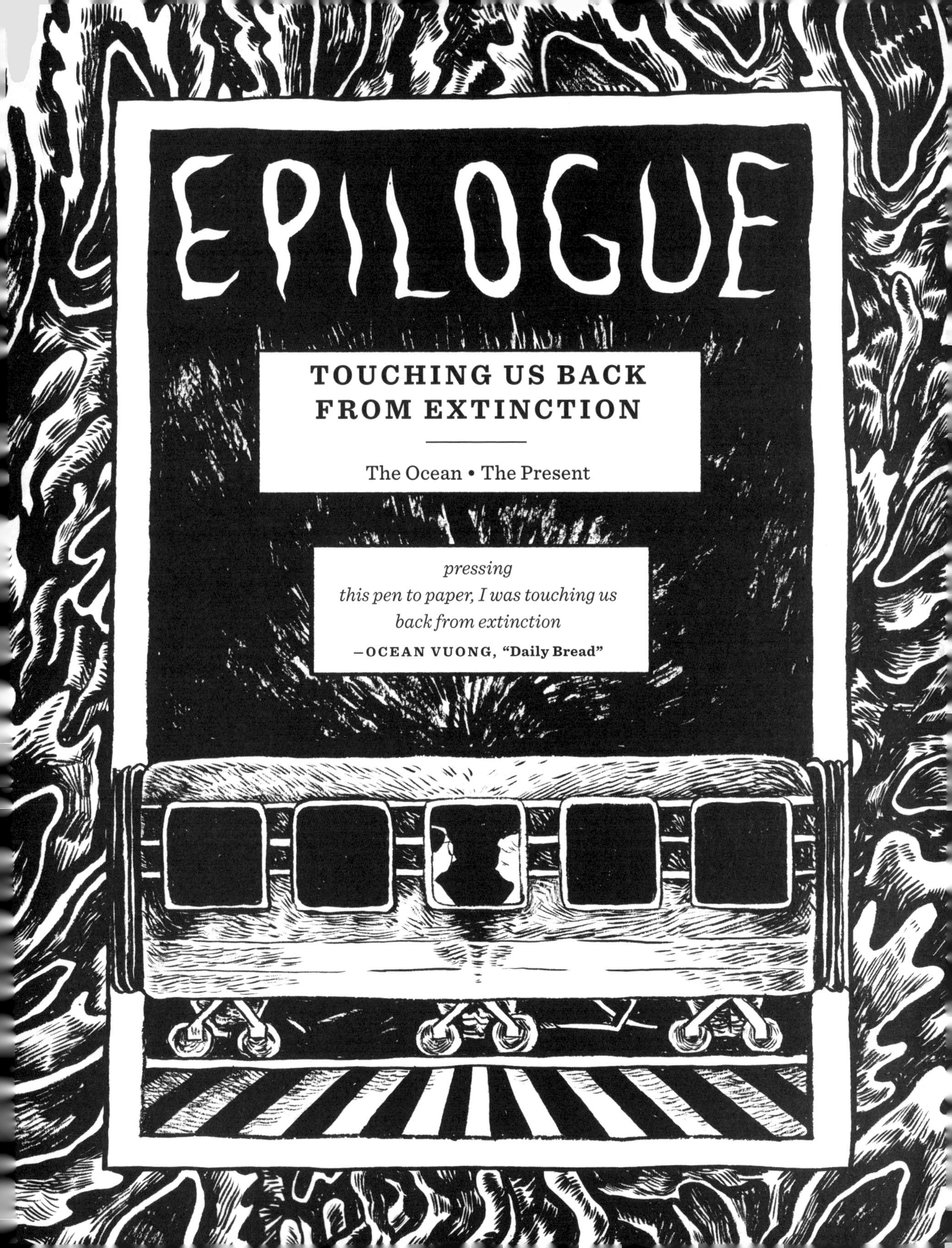

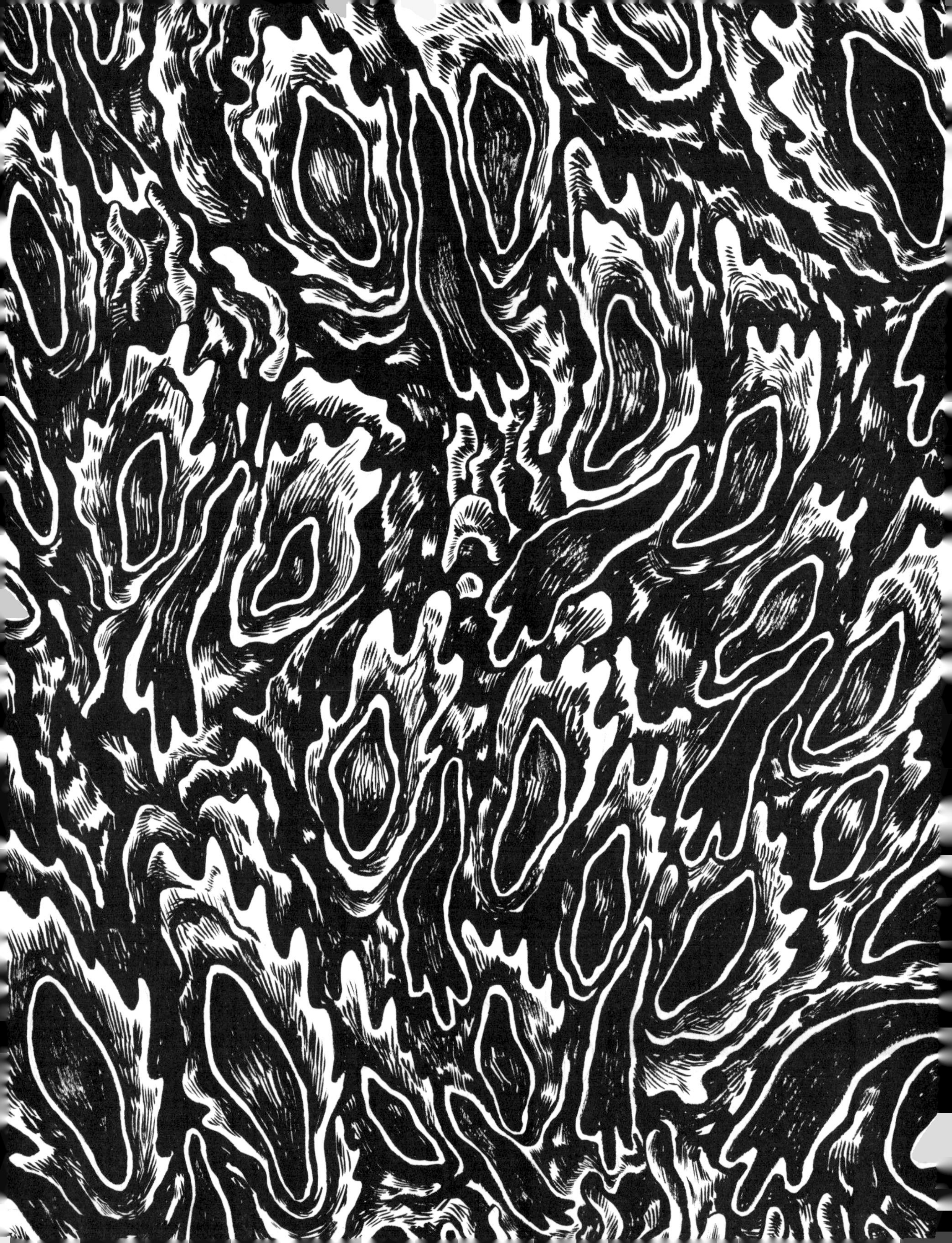

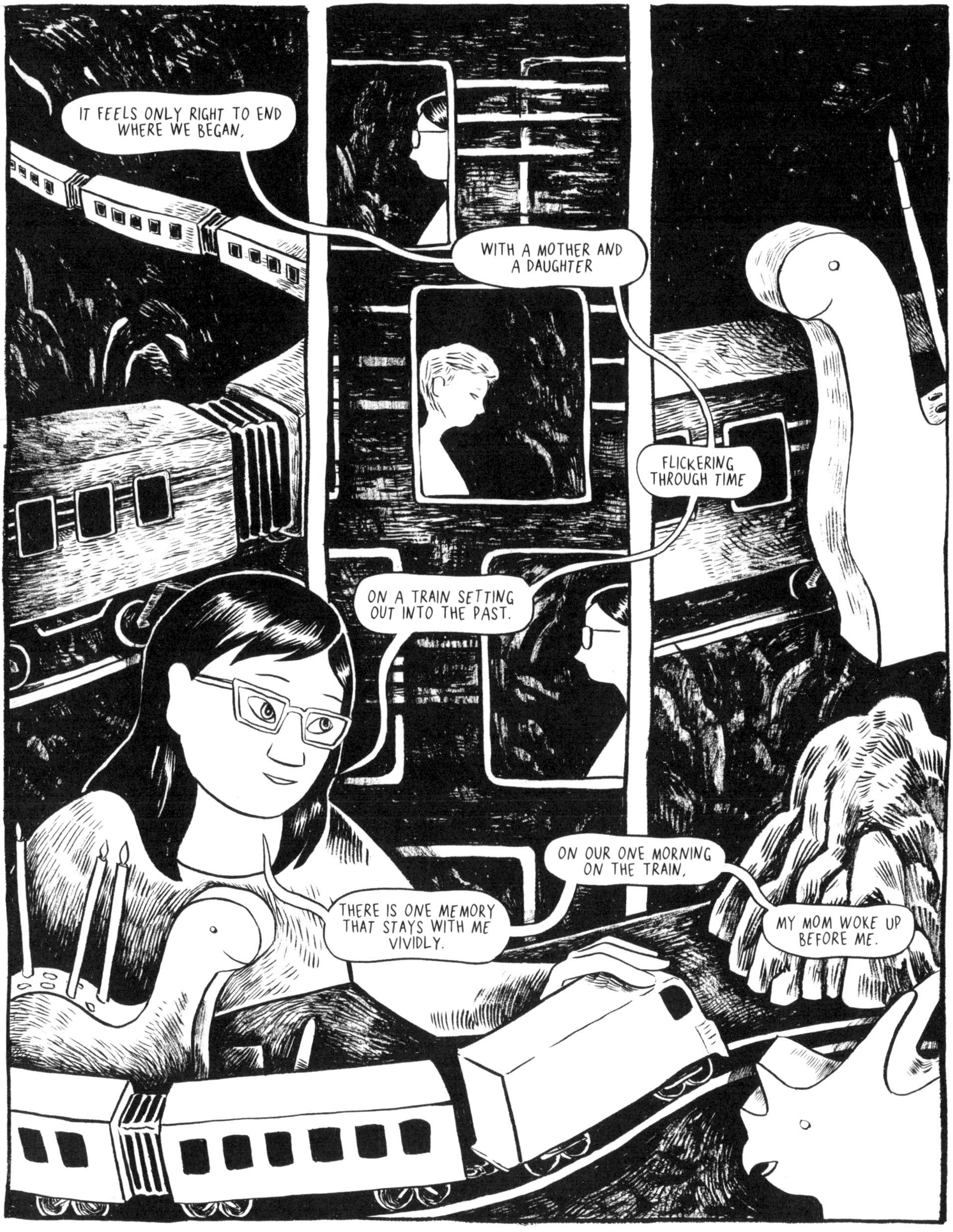
IT FEELS ONLY RIGHT TO END WHERE WE BEGAN,
WITH A MOTHER AND A DAUGHTER
FLICKERING THROUGH TIME
ON A TRAIN SETTING OUT INTO THE PAST.
THERE IS ONE MEMORY THAT STAYS WITH ME VIVIDLY.
ON OUR ONE MORNING ON THE TRAIN,
MY MOM WOKE UP BEFORE ME.

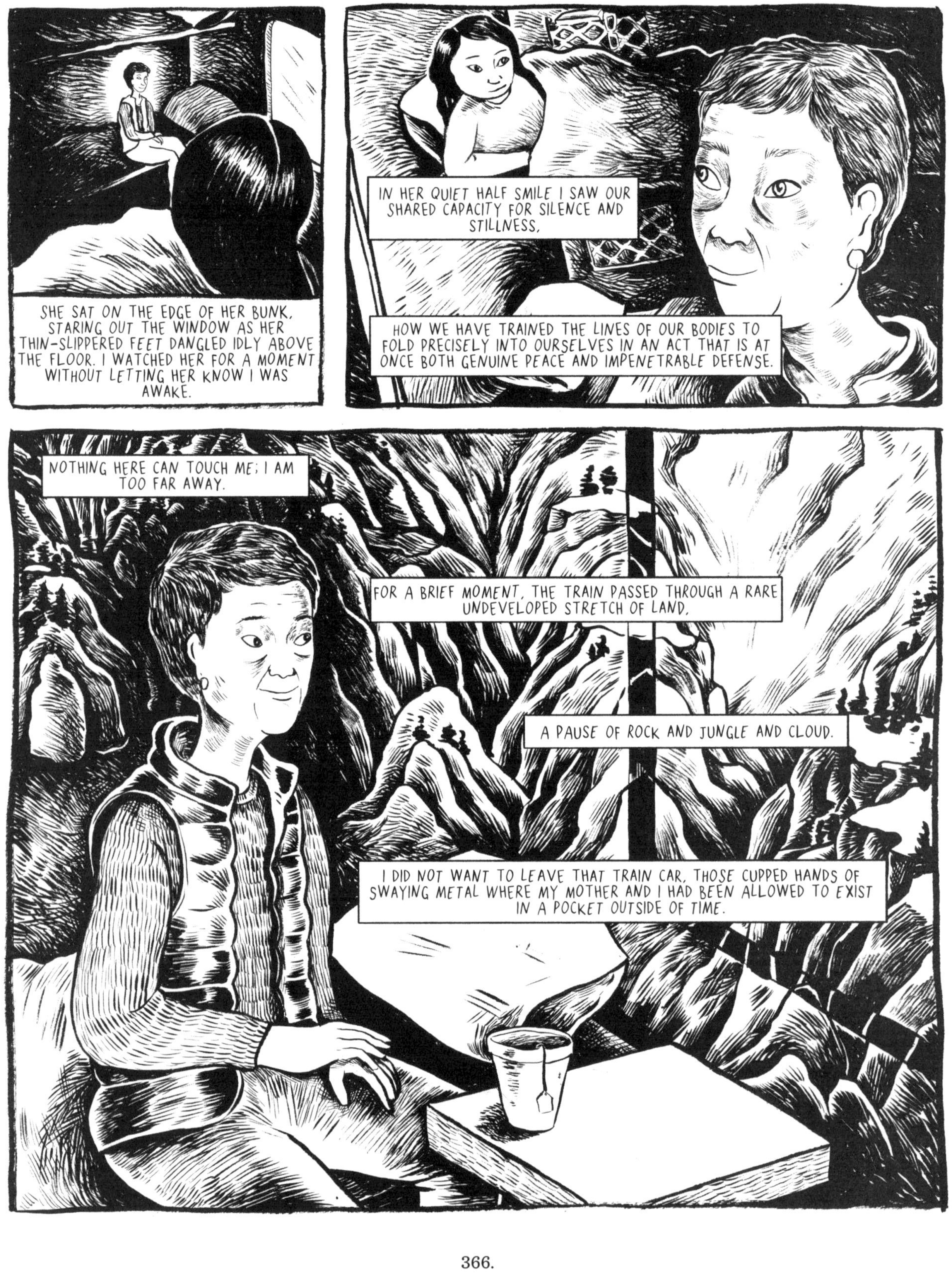
SHE SAT ON THE EDGE OF HER BUNK, STARING OUT THE WINDOW AS HER THIN-SLIPPERED FEET DANGLED IDLY ABOVE THE FLOOR. I WATCHED HER FOR A MOMENT WITHOUT LETTING HER KNOW I WAS AWAKE.
IN HER QUIET HALF SMILE I SAW OUR SHARED CAPACITY FOR SILENCE AND STILLNESS,
HOW WE HAVE TRAINED THE LINES OF OUR BODIES TO FOLD PRECISELY INTO OURSELVES IN AN ACT THAT IS AT ONCE BOTH GENUINE PEACE AND IMPENETRABLE DEFENSE.
NOTHING HERE CAN TOUCH ME; I AM TOO FAR AWAY.
FOR A BRIEF MOMENT, THE TRAIN PASSED THROUGH A RARE UNDEVELOPED STRETCH OF LAND,
A PAUSE OF ROCK AND JUNGLE AND CLOUD.
I DID NOT WANT TO LEAVE THAT TRAIN CAR, THOSE CUPPED HANDS OF SWAYING METAL WHERE MY MOTHER AND I HAD BEEN ALLOWED TO EXIST IN A POCKET OUTSIDE OF TIME.

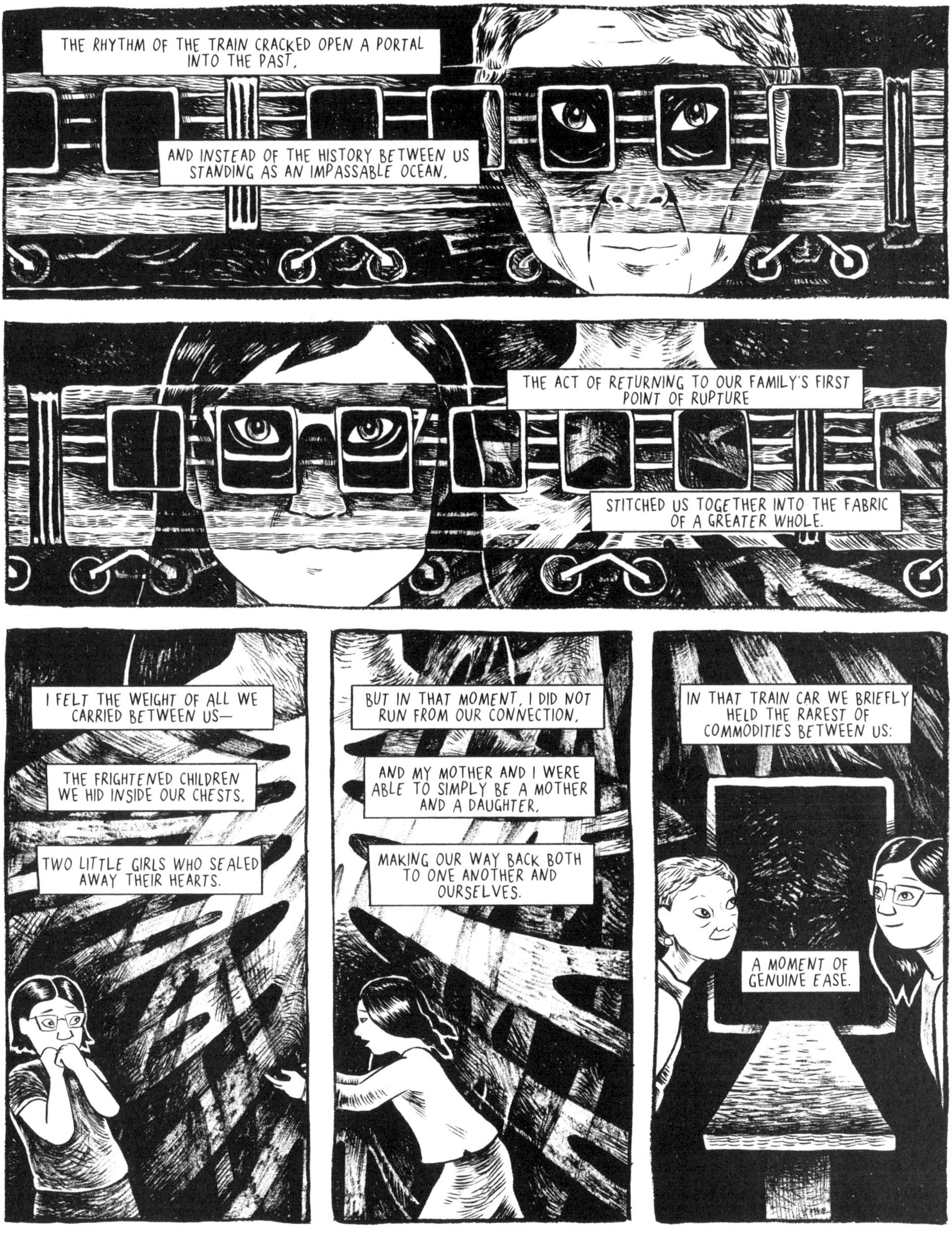
THE RHYTHM OF THE TRAIN CRACKED OPEN A PORTAL INTO THE PAST,
AND INSTEAD OF THE HISTORY BETWEEN US STANDING AS AN IMPASSABLE OCEAN,
THE ACT OF RETURNING TO OUR FAMILY'S FIRST POINT OF RUPTURE
STITCHED US TOGETHER INTO THE FABRIC OF A GREATER WHOLE.
I FELT THE WEIGHT OF ALL WE CARRIED BETWEEN US—
THE FRIGHTENED CHILDREN WE HID INSIDE OUR CHESTS,
TWO LITTLE GIRLS WHO SEALED AWAY THEIR HEARTS.
BUT IN THAT MOMENT, I DID NOT RUN FROM OUR CONNECTION,
AND MY MOTHER AND I WERE ABLE TO SIMPLY BE A MOTHER AND A DAUGHTER,
MAKING OUR WAY BACK BOTH TO ONE ANOTHER AND OURSELVES.
IN THAT TRAIN CAR WE BRIEFLY HELD THE RAREST OF COMMODITIES BETWEEN US:
A MOMENT OF GENUINE EASE.

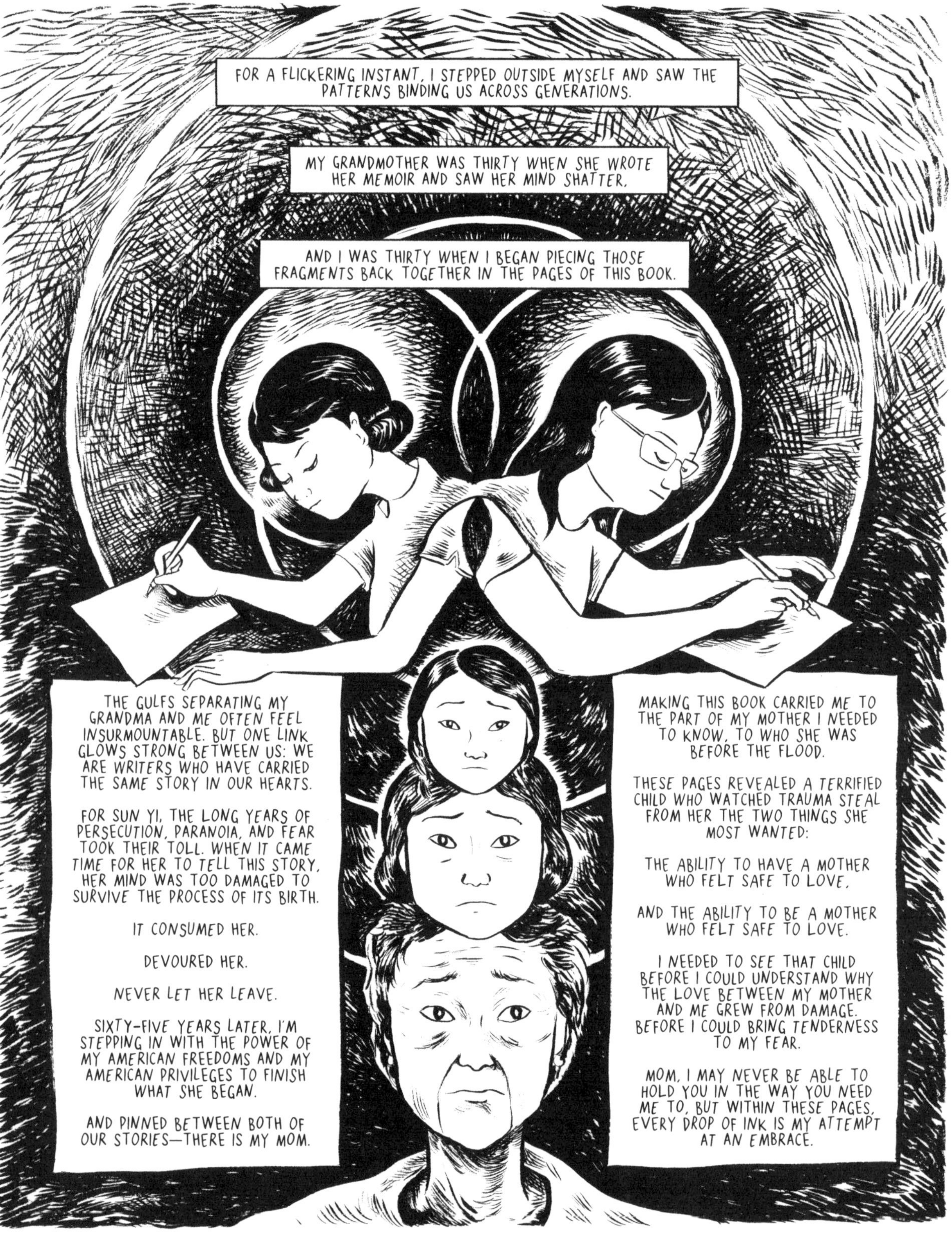

FOR A FLICKERING INSTANT, I STEPPED OUTSIDE MYSELF AND SAW THE PATTERNS BINDING US ACROSS GENERATIONS.
MY GRANDMOTHER WAS THIRTY WHEN SHE WROTE HER MEMOIR AND SAW HER MIND SHATTER.
AND I WAS THIRTY WHEN I BEGAN PIECING THOSE FRAGMENTS BACK TOGETHER IN THE PAGES OF THIS BOOK.
THE GULFS SEPARATING MY GRANDMA AND ME OFTEN FEEL INSURMOUNTABLE. BUT ONE LINK GLOWS STRONG BETWEEN US: WE ARE WRITERS WHO HAVE CARRIED THE SAME STORY IN OUR HEARTS.
FOR SUN YI, THE LONG YEARS OF PERSECUTION, PARANOIA, AND FEAR TOOK THEIR TOLL. WHEN IT CAME TIME FOR HER TO TELL THIS STORY, HER MIND WAS TOO DAMAGED TO SURVIVE THE PROCESS OF ITS BIRTH.
IT CONSUMED HER.
DEVOURED HER.
NEVER LET HER LEAVE.
SIXTY-FIVE YEARS LATER, I'M STEPPING IN WITH THE POWER OF MY AMERICAN FREEDOMS AND MY AMERICAN PRIVILEGES TO FINISH WHAT SHE BEGAN.
AND PINNED BETWEEN BOTH OF OUR STORIES—THERE IS MY MOM.
MAKING THIS BOOK CARRIED ME TO THE PART OF MY MOTHER I NEEDED TO KNOW, TO WHO SHE WAS BEFORE THE FLOOD.
THESE PAGES REVEALED A TERRIFIED CHILD WHO WATCHED TRAUMA STEAL FROM HER THE TWO THINGS SHE MOST WANTED:
THE ABILITY TO HAVE A MOTHER WHO FELT SAFE TO LOVE,
AND THE ABILITY TO BE A MOTHER WHO FELT SAFE TO LOVE.
I NEEDED TO SEE THAT CHILD BEFORE I COULD UNDERSTAND WHY THE LOVE BETWEEN MY MOTHER AND ME GREW FROM DAMAGE. BEFORE I COULD BRING TENDERNESS TO MY FEAR.
MOM, I MAY NEVER BE ABLE TO HOLD YOU IN THE WAY YOU NEED ME TO, BUT WITHIN THESE PAGES, EVERY DROP OF INK IS MY ATTEMPT AT AN EMBRACE.

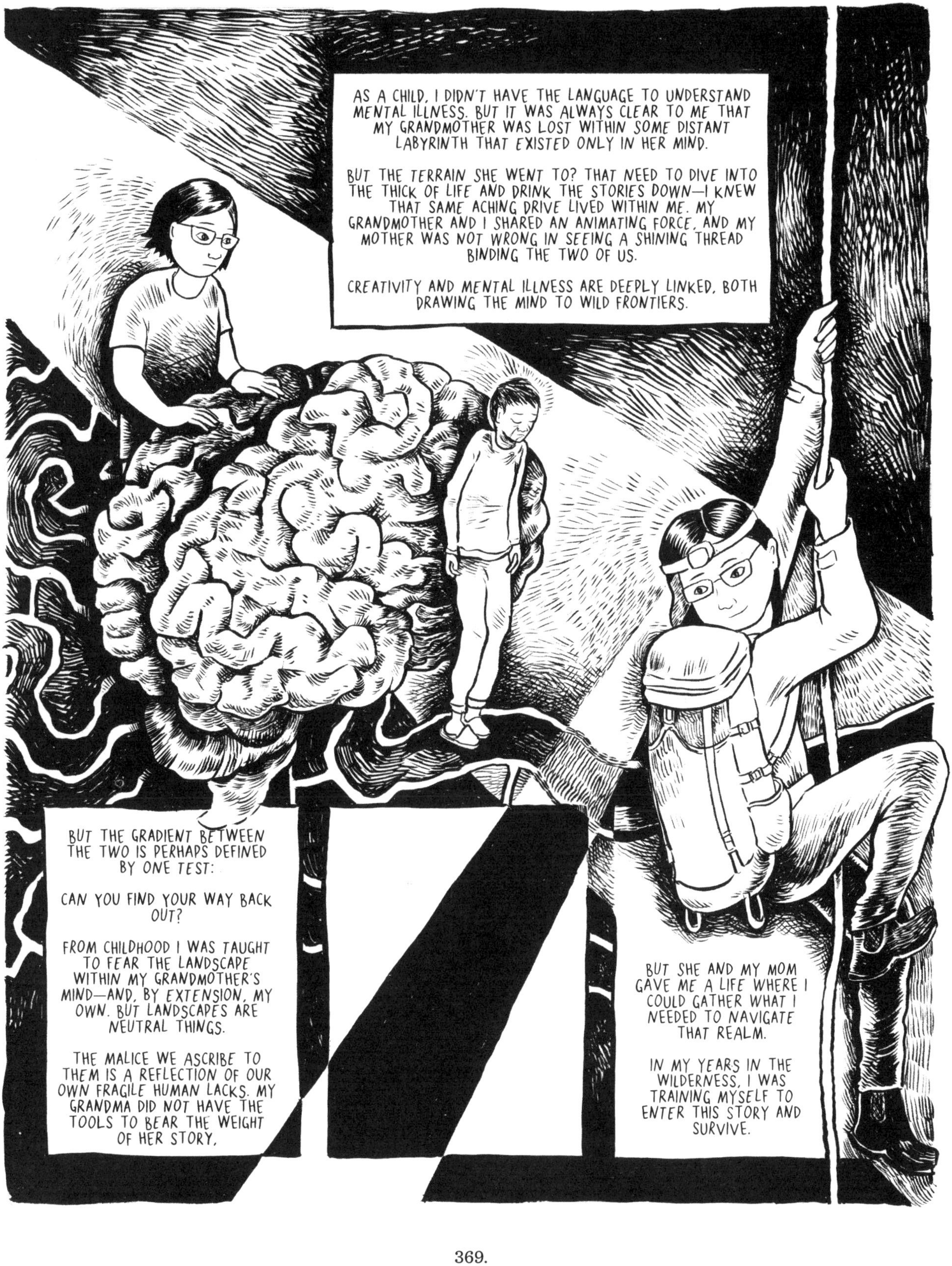
AS A CHILD, I DIDN'T HAVE THE LANGUAGE TO UNDERSTAND MENTAL ILLNESS. BUT IT WAS ALWAYS CLEAR TO ME THAT MY GRANDMOTHER WAS LOST WITHIN SOME DISTANT LABYRINTH THAT EXISTED ONLY IN HER MIND.
BUT THE TERRAIN SHE WENT TO? THAT NEED TO DIVE INTO THE THICK OF LIFE AND DRINK THE STORIES DOWN—I KNEW THAT SAME ACHING DRIVE LIVED WITHIN ME. MY GRANDMOTHER AND I SHARED AN ANIMATING FORCE, AND MY MOTHER WAS NOT WRONG IN SEEING A SHINING THREAD BINDING THE TWO OF US.
CREATIVITY AND MENTAL ILLNESS ARE DEEPLY LINKED, BOTH DRAWING THE MIND TO WILD FRONTIERS.
BUT THE GRADIENT BETWEEN THE TWO IS PERHAPS DEFINED BY ONE TEST:
CAN YOU FIND YOUR WAY BACK OUT?
FROM CHILDHOOD I WAS TAUGHT TO FEAR THE LANDSCAPE WITHIN MY GRANDMOTHER'S MIND—AND, BY EXTENSION, MY OWN. BUT LANDSCAPES ARE NEUTRAL THINGS.
THE MALICE WE ASCRIBE TO THEM IS A REFLECTION OF OUR OWN FRAGILE HUMAN LACKS. MY GRANDMA DID NOT HAVE THE TOOLS TO BEAR THE WEIGHT OF HER STORY,
BUT SHE AND MY MOM GAVE ME A LIFE WHERE I COULD GATHER WHAT I NEEDED TO NAVIGATE THAT REALM.
IN MY YEARS IN THE WILDERNESS, I WAS TRAINING MYSELF TO ENTER THIS STORY AND SURVIVE.

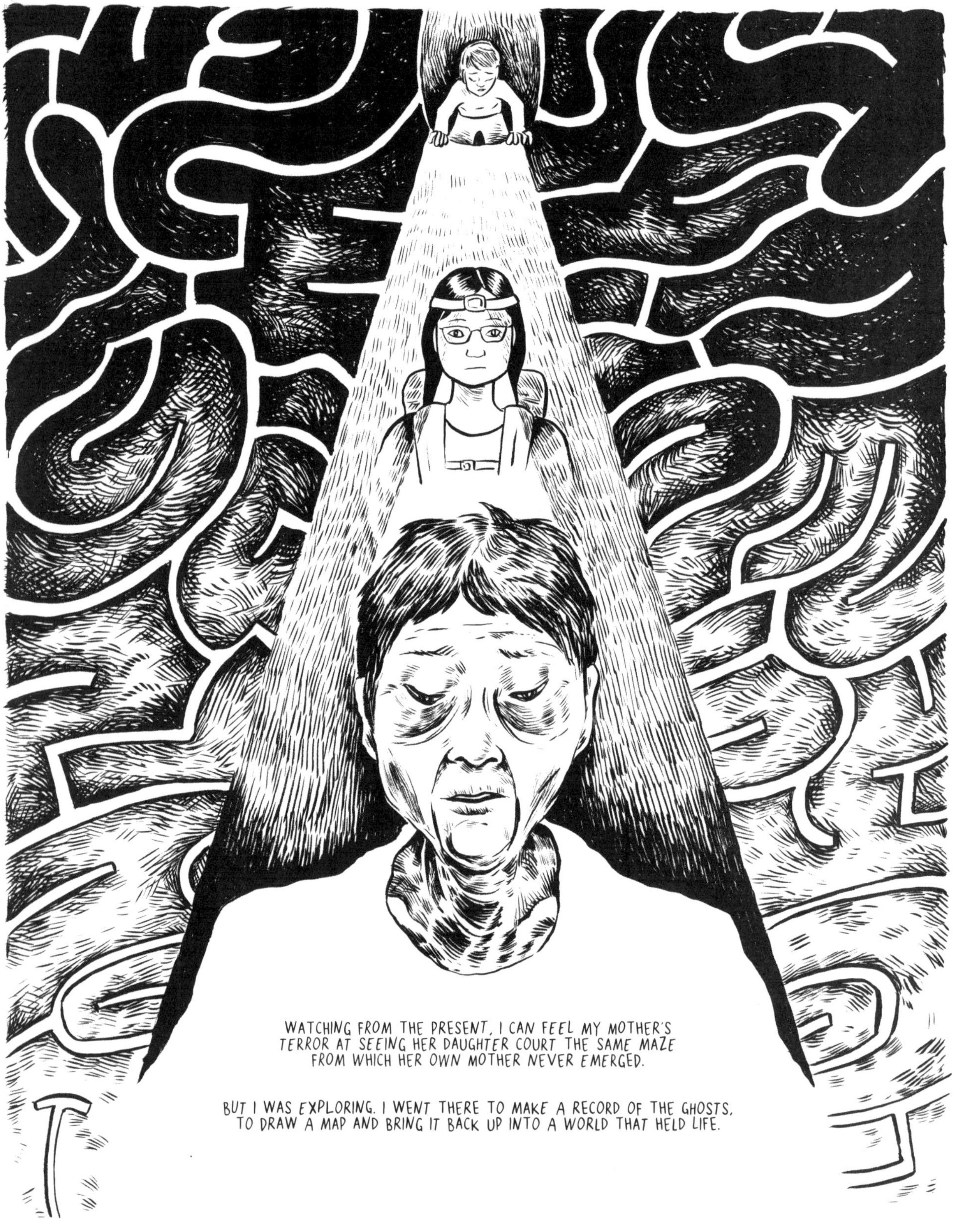
WATCHING FROM THE PRESENT, I CAN FEEL MY MOTHER'S TERROR AT SEEING HER DAUGHTER COURT THE SAME MAZE FROM WHICH HER OWN MOTHER NEVER EMERGED.
BUT I WAS EXPLORING. I WENT THERE TO MAKE A RECORD OF THE GHOSTS, TO DRAW A MAP AND BRING IT BACK UP INTO A WORLD THAT HELD LIFE.

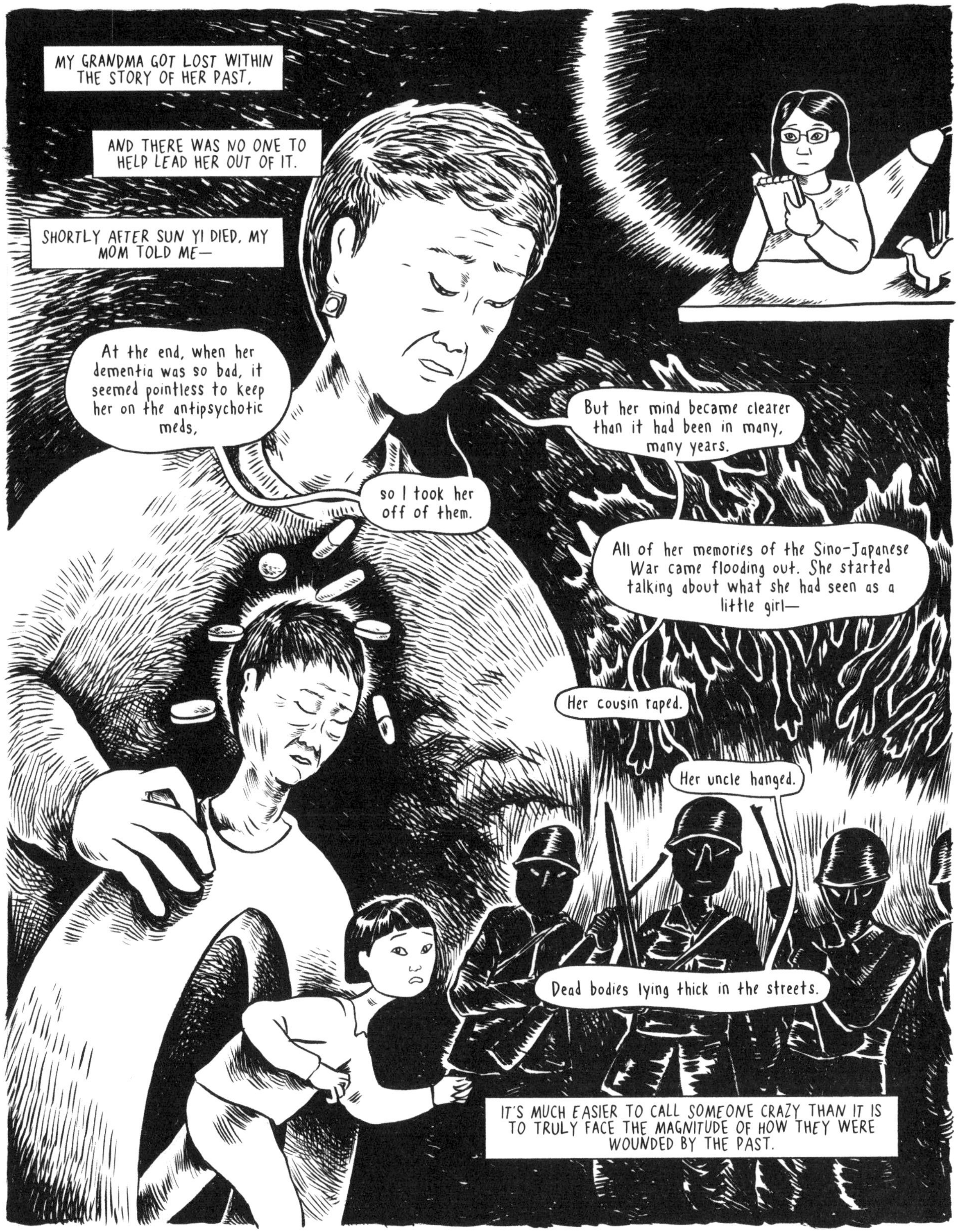

MY GRANDMA GOT LOST WITHIN THE STORY OF HER PAST,
AND THERE WAS NO ONE TO HELP LEAD HER OUT OF IT.
SHORTLY AFTER SUN YI DIED, MY MOM TOLD ME—
At the end, when her dementia was so bad, it seemed pointless to keep her on the antipsychotic meds,
so I took her off of them.
But her mind became clearer than it had been in many, many years.
All of her memories of the Sino-Japanese War came flooding out. She started talking about what she had seen as a little girl—
Her cousin raped.
Her uncle hanged.
Dead bodies lying thick in the streets.
IT'S MUCH EASIER TO CALL SOMEONE CRAZY THAN IT IS TO TRULY FACE THE MAGNITUDE OF HOW THEY WERE WOUNDED BY THE PAST.

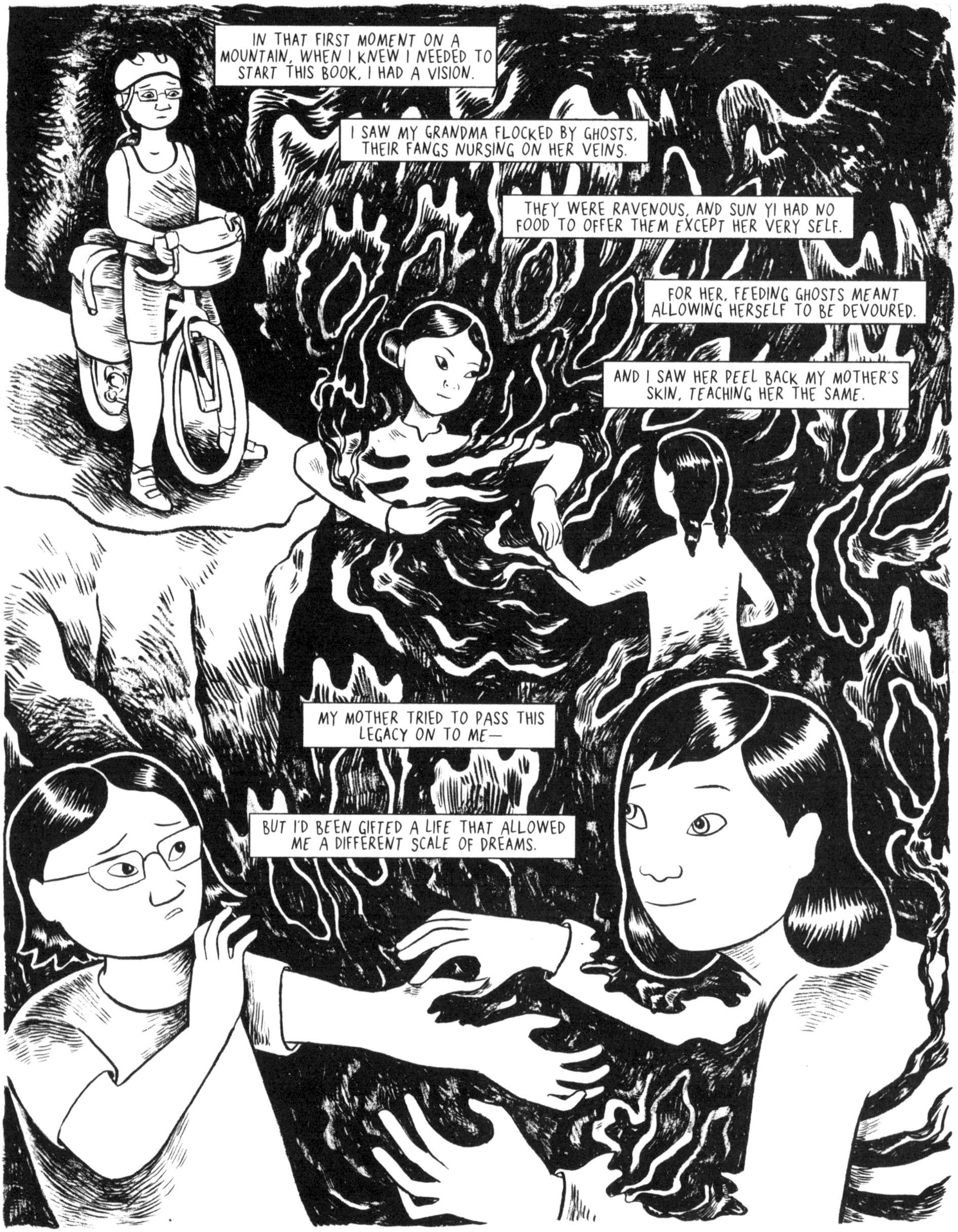
IN THAT FIRST MOMENT ON A MOUNTAIN, WHEN I KNEW I NEEDED TO START THIS BOOK, I HAD A VISION.
I SAW MY GRANDMA FLOCKED BY GHOSTS, THEIR FANGS NURSING ON HER VEINS.
THEY WERE RAVENOUS, AND SUN YI HAD NO FOOD TO OFFER THEM EXCEPT HER VERY SELF.
FOR HER, FEEDING GHOSTS MEANT ALLOWING HERSELF TO BE DEVOURED.
AND I SAW HER PEEL BACK MY MOTHER'S SKIN, TEACHING HER THE SAME.
MY MOTHER TRIED TO PASS THIS LEGACY ON TO ME—
BUT I'D BEEN GIFTED A LIFE THAT ALLOWED ME A DIFFERENT SCALE OF DREAMS.

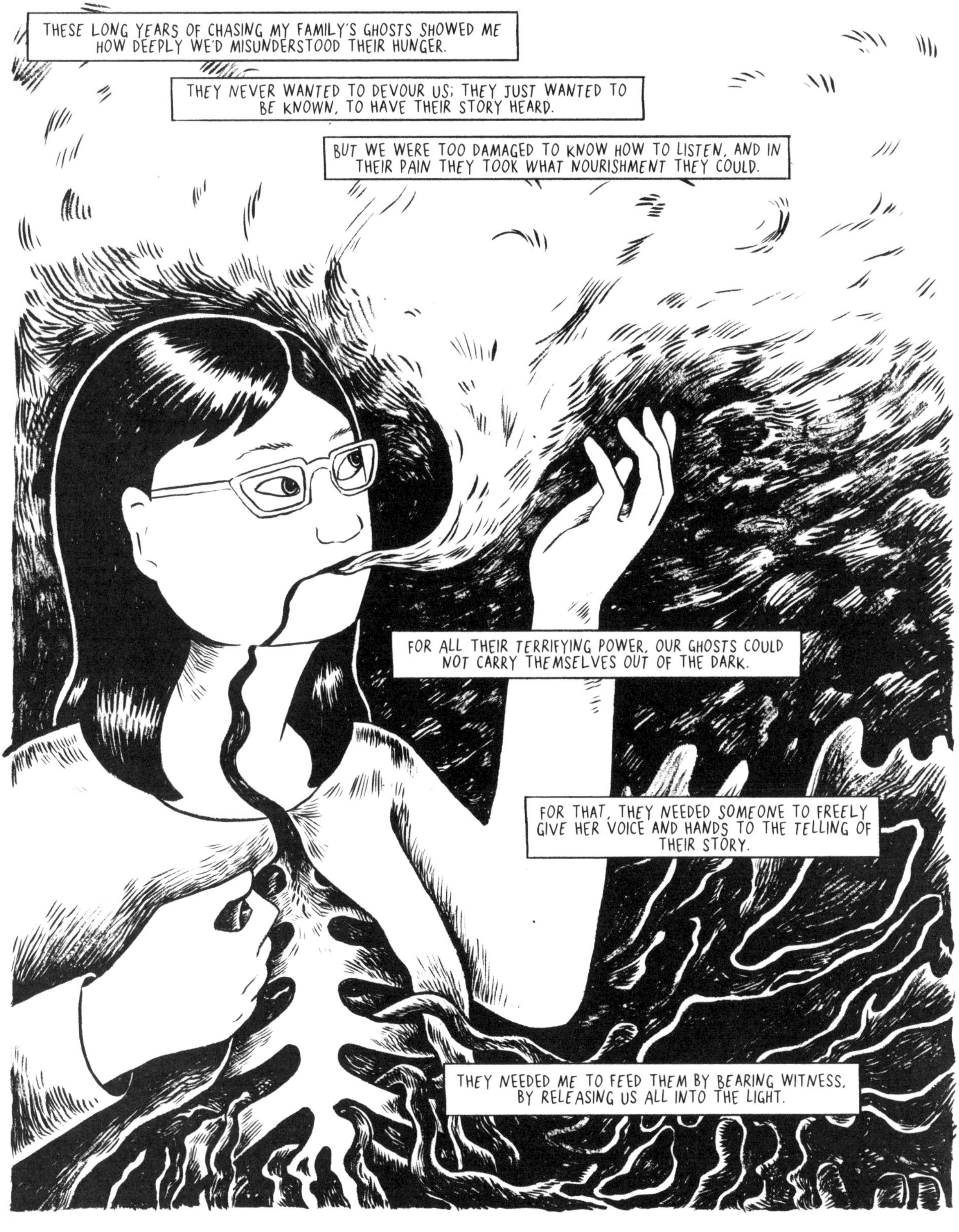
THESE LONG YEARS OF CHASING MY FAMILY'S GHOSTS SHOWED ME HOW DEEPLY WE'D MISUNDERSTOOD THEIR HUNGER.
THEY NEVER WANTED TO DEVOUR US; THEY JUST WANTED TO BE KNOWN, TO HAVE THEIR STORY HEARD.
BUT WE WERE TOO DAMAGED TO KNOW HOW TO LISTEN, AND IN THEIR PAIN THEY TOOK WHAT NOURISHMENT THEY COULD.
FOR ALL THEIR TERRIFYING POWER, OUR GHOSTS COULD NOT CARRY THEMSELVES OUT OF THE DARK.
FOR THAT, THEY NEEDED SOMEONE TO FREELY GIVE HER VOICE AND HANDS TO THE TELLING OF THEIR STORY.
THEY NEEDED ME TO FEED THEM BY BEARING WITNESS, BY RELEASING US ALL INTO THE LIGHT.

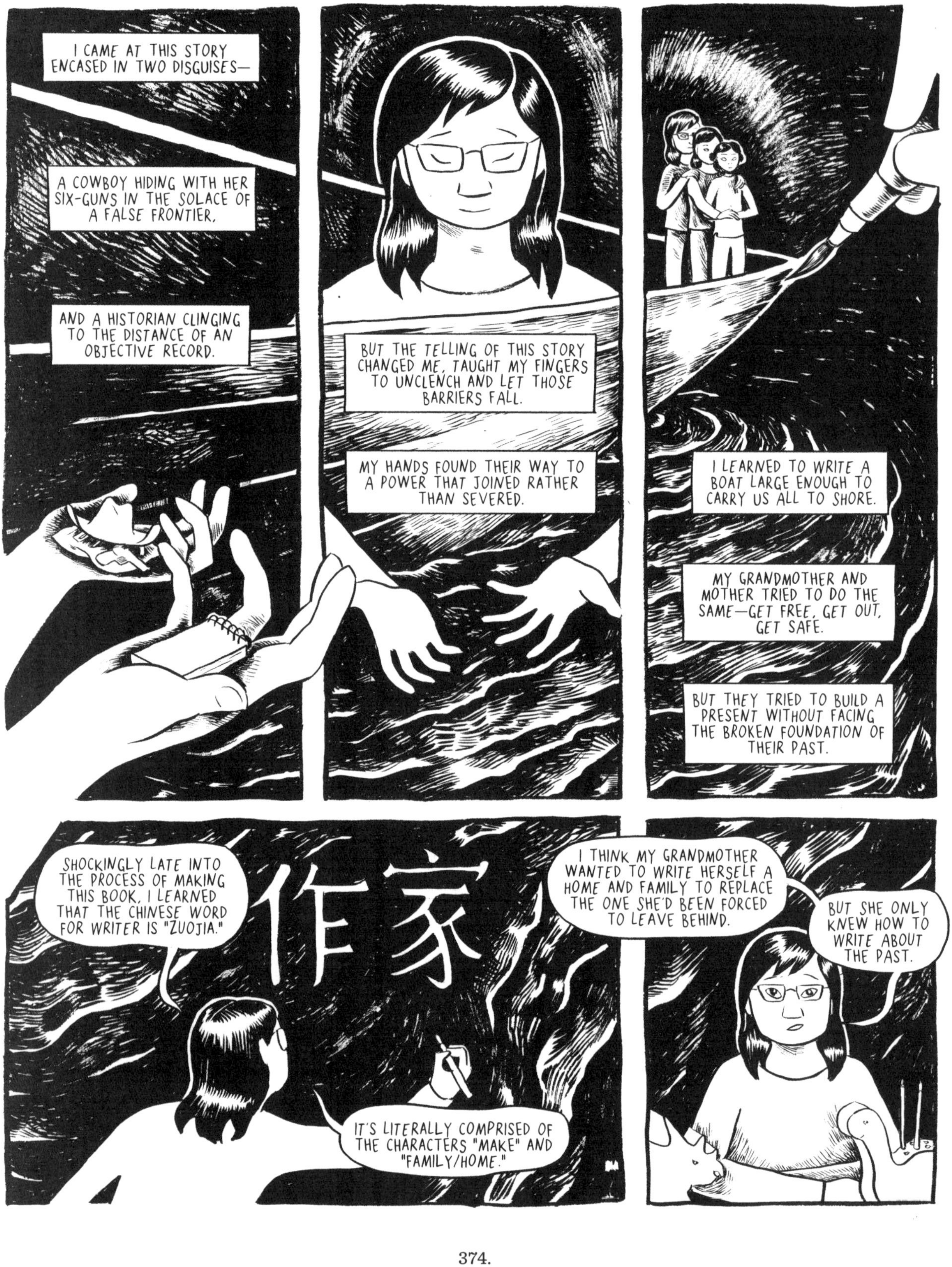

I CAME AT THIS STORY ENCASED IN TWO DISGUISES—
A COWBOY HIDING WITH HER SIX-GUNS IN THE SOLACE OF A FALSE FRONTIER,
AND A HISTORIAN CLINGING TO THE DISTANCE OF AN OBJECTIVE RECORD.
BUT THE TELLING OF THIS STORY CHANGED ME, TAUGHT MY FINGERS TO UNCLENCH AND LET THOSE BARRIERS FALL.
MY HANDS FOUND THEIR WAY TO A POWER THAT JOINED RATHER THAN SEVERED.
I LEARNED TO WRITE A BOAT LARGE ENOUGH TO CARRY US ALL TO SHORE.
MY GRANDMOTHER AND MOTHER TRIED TO DO THE SAME—GET FREE, GET OUT, GET SAFE.
BUT THEY TRIED TO BUILD A PRESENT WITHOUT FACING THE BROKEN FOUNDATION OF THEIR PAST.
SHOCKINGLY LATE INTO THE PROCESS OF MAKING THIS BOOK, I LEARNED THAT THE CHINESE WORD FOR WRITER IS "ZUOJIA."
作家
IT'S LITERALLY COMPRISED OF THE CHARACTERS "MAKE" AND "FAMILY/HOME."
I THINK MY GRANDMOTHER WANTED TO WRITE HERSELF A HOME AND FAMILY TO REPLACE THE ONE SHE'D BEEN FORCED TO LEAVE BEHIND.
BUT SHE ONLY KNEW HOW TO WRITE ABOUT THE PAST.

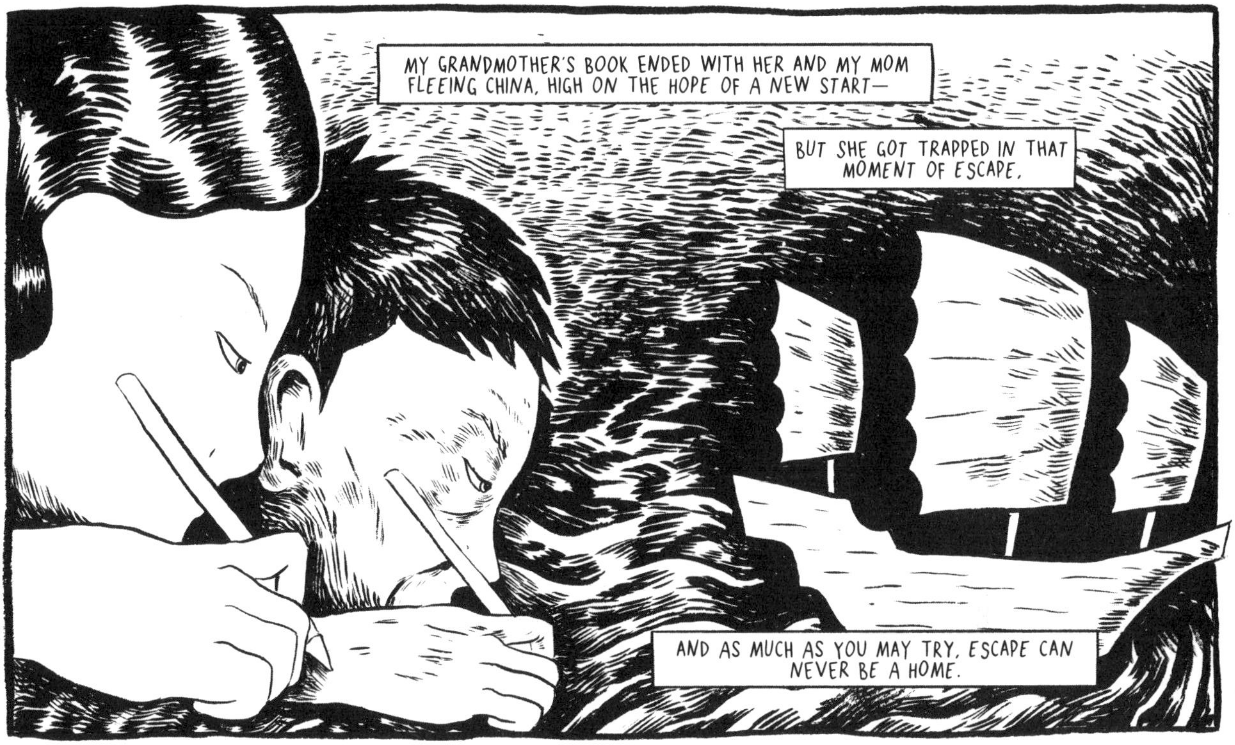
MY GRANDMOTHER'S BOOK ENDED WITH HER AND MY MOM FLEEING CHINA, HIGH ON THE HOPE OF A NEW START—
BUT SHE GOT TRAPPED IN THAT MOMENT OF ESCAPE.
AND AS MUCH AS YOU MAY TRY, ESCAPE CAN NEVER BE A HOME.

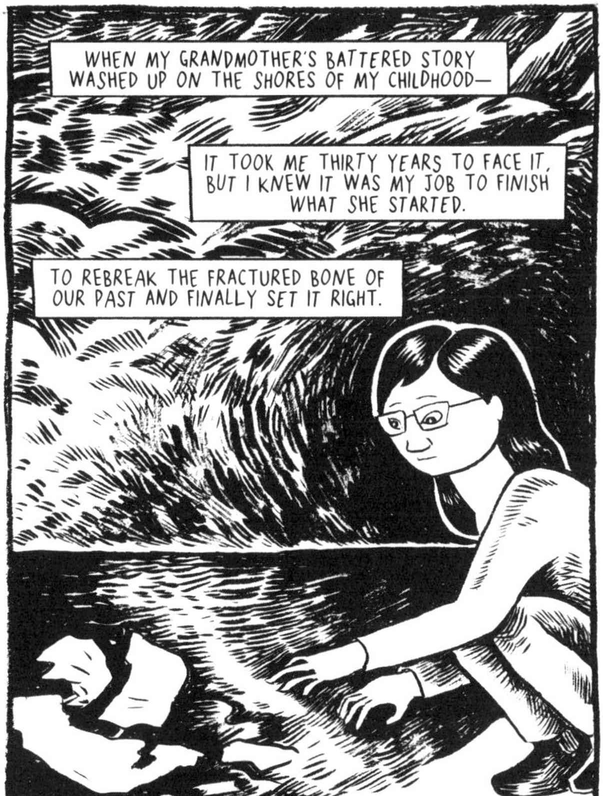
WHEN MY GRANDMOTHER'S BATTERED STORY WASHED UP ON THE SHORES OF MY CHILDHOOD—
IT TOOK ME THIRTY YEARS TO FACE IT, BUT I KNEW IT WAS MY JOB TO FINISH WHAT SHE STARTED.
TO REBREAK THE FRACTURED BONE OF OUR PAST AND FINALLY SET IT RIGHT.

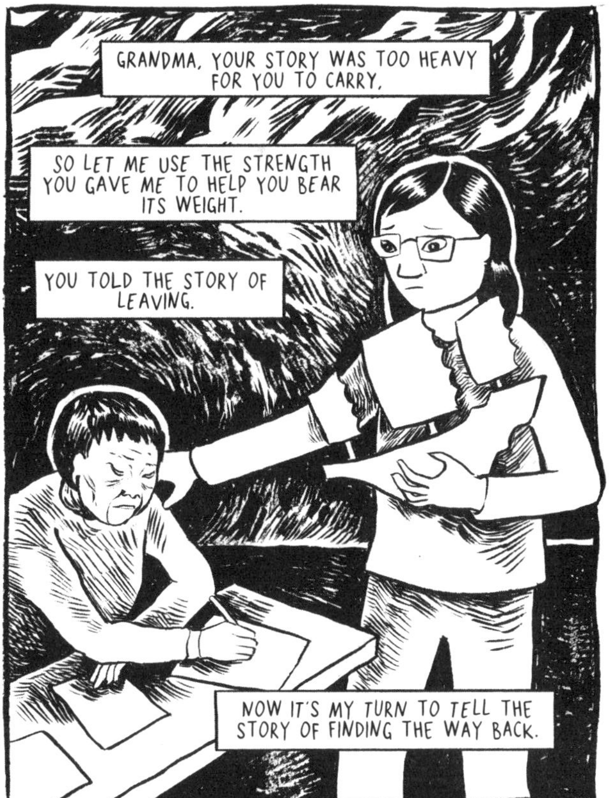
GRANDMA, YOUR STORY WAS TOO HEAVY FOR YOU TO CARRY.
SO LET ME USE THE STRENGTH YOU GAVE ME TO HELP YOU BEAR ITS WEIGHT.
YOU TOLD THE STORY OF LEAVING.
NOW IT'S MY TURN TO TELL THE STORY OF FINDING THE WAY BACK.

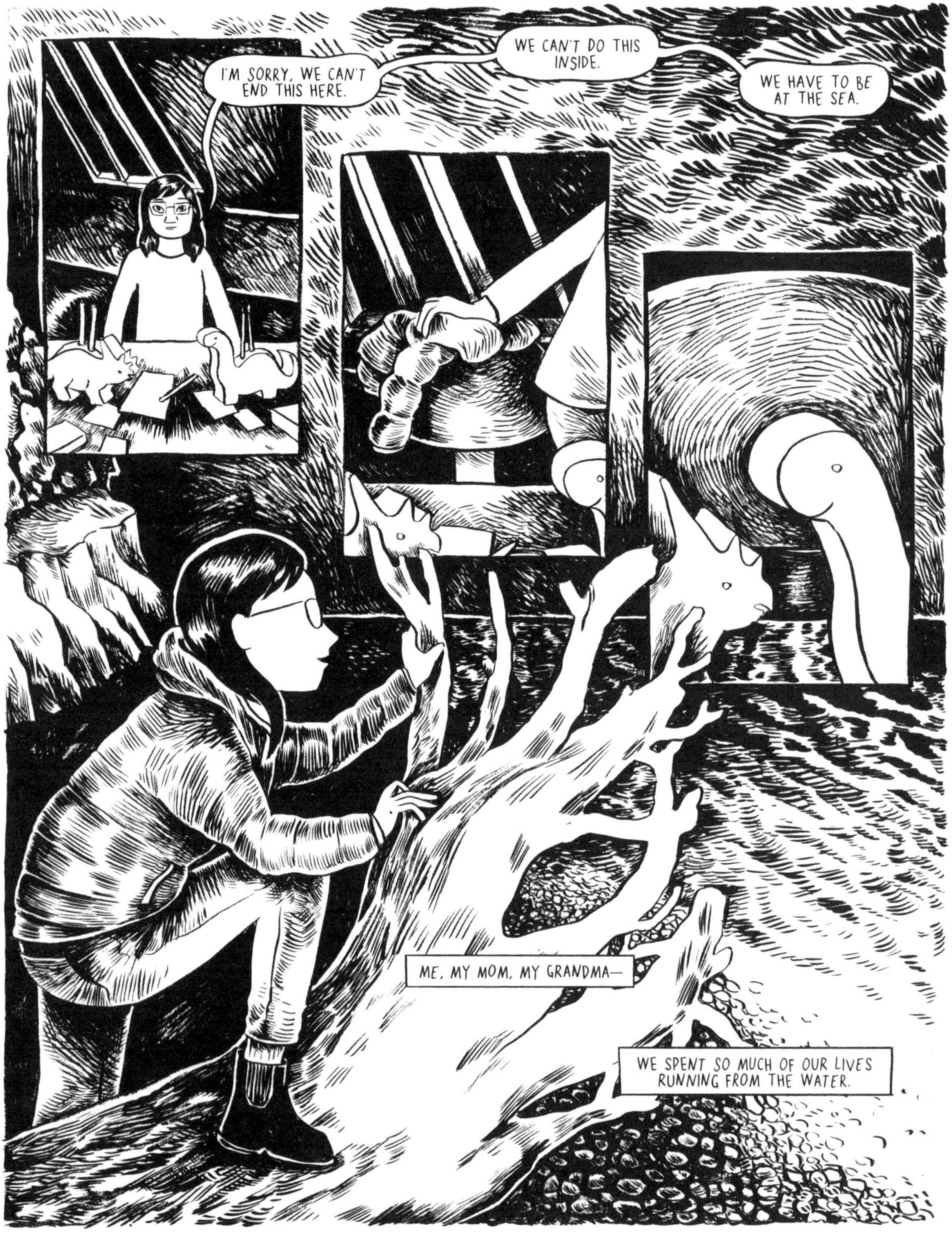
I'M SORRY, WE CAN'T END THIS HERE.
WE CAN'T DO THIS INSIDE.
WE HAVE TO BE AT THE SEA.
ME, MY MOM, MY GRANDMA—
WE SPENT SO MUCH OF OUR LIVES RUNNING FROM THE WATER.

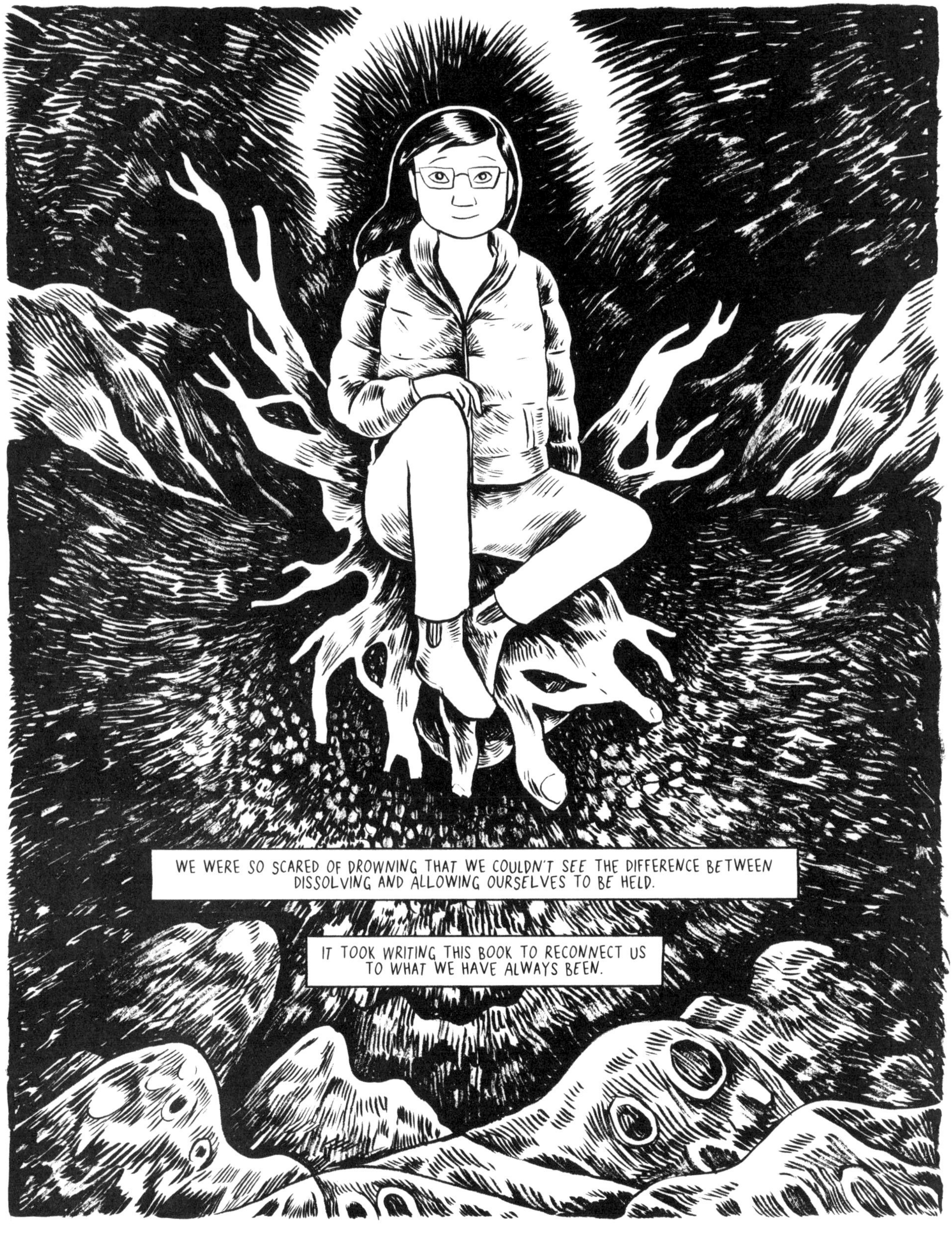
WE WERE SO SCARED OF DROWNING THAT WE COULDN'T SEE THE DIFFERENCE BETWEEN DISSOLVING AND ALLOWING OURSELVES TO BE HELD.
IT TOOK WRITING THIS BOOK TO RECONNECT US TO WHAT WE HAVE ALWAYS BEEN.

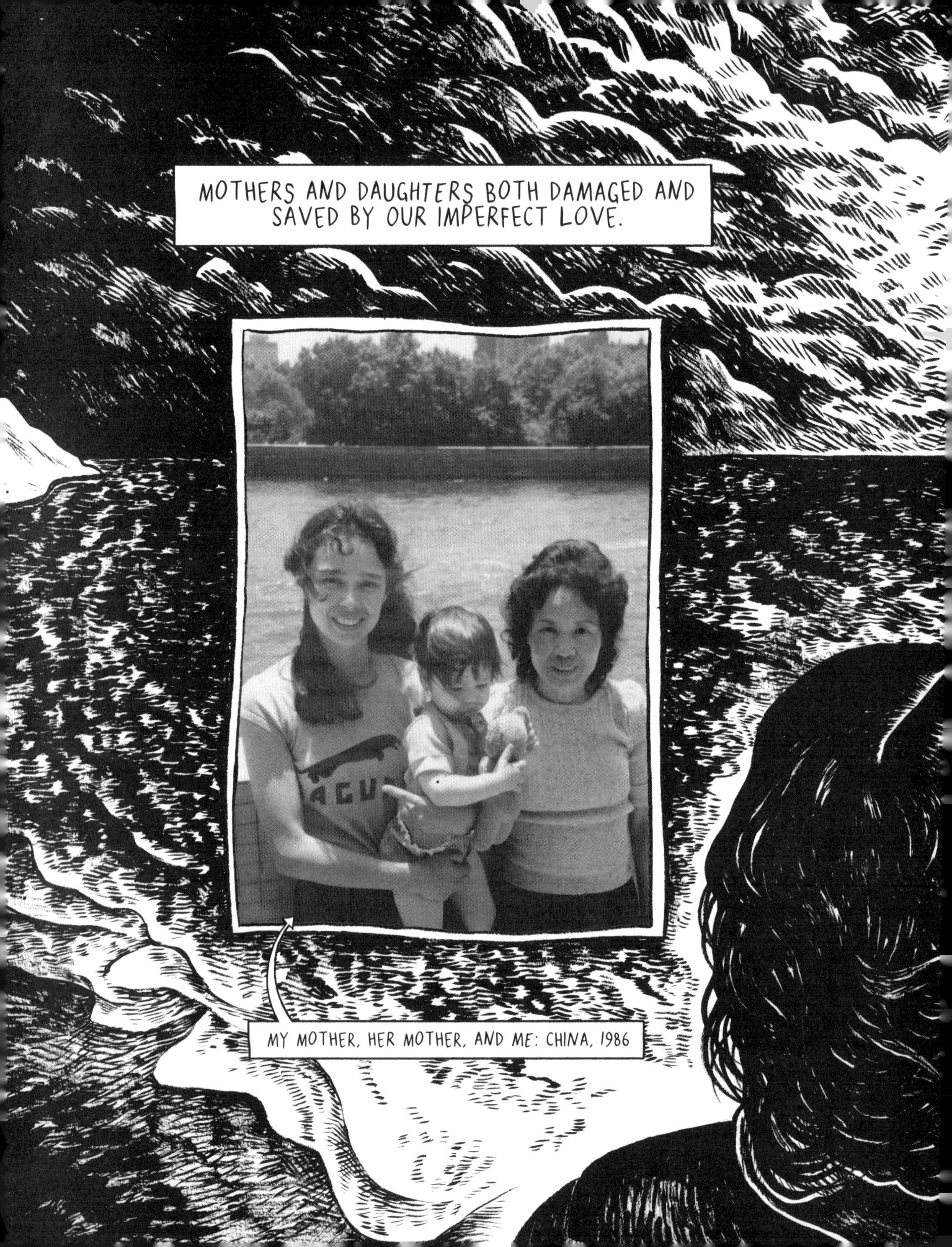
MOTHERS AND DAUGHTERS BOTH DAMAGED AND SAVED BY OUR IMPERFECT LOVE.
MY MOTHER, HER MOTHER, AND ME: CHINA, 1986

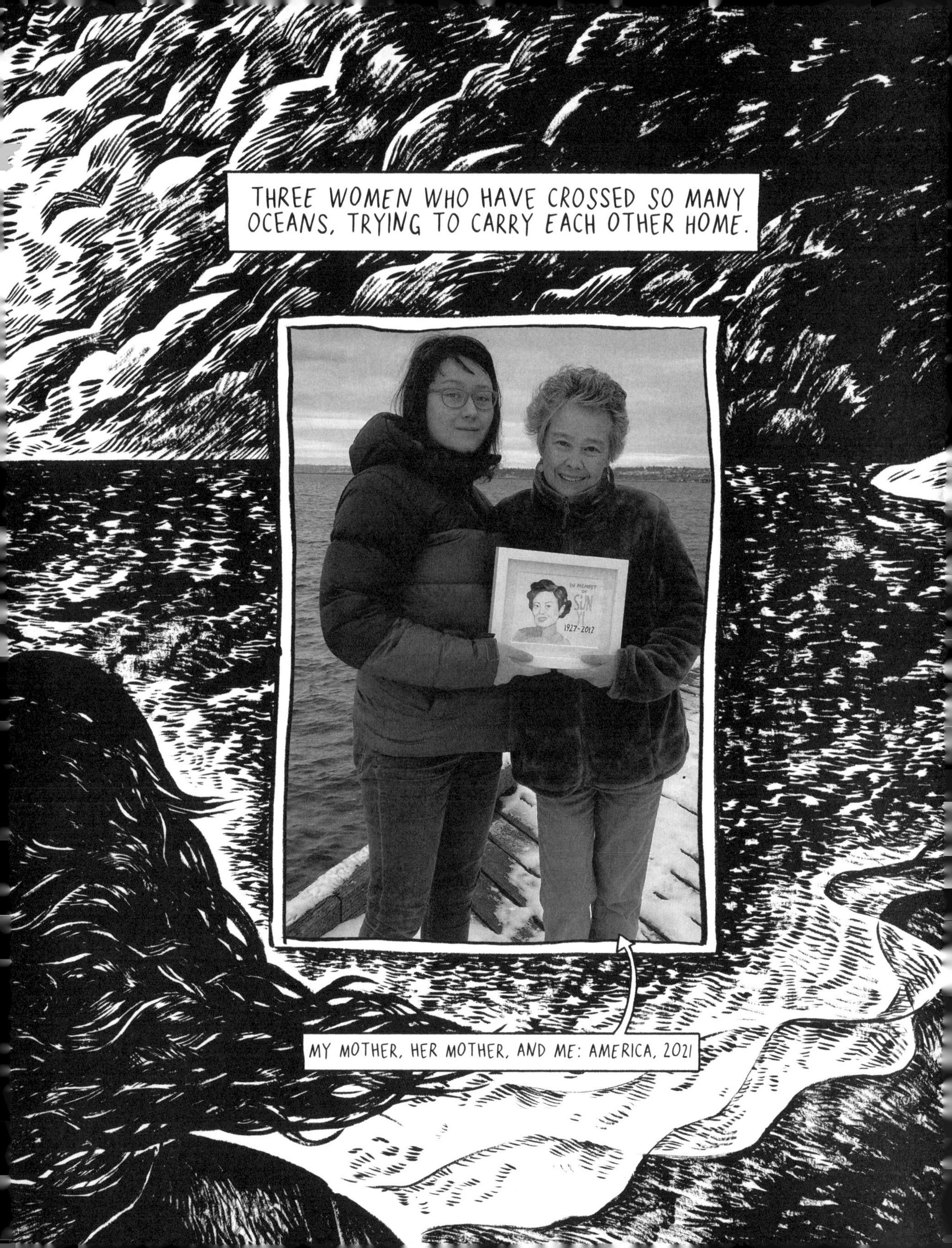
THREE WOMEN WHO HAVE CROSSED SO MANY OCEANS, TRYING TO CARRY EACH OTHER HOME.
IN MEMORY OF
SUN YI
1927-2012
MY MOTHER, HER MOTHER, AND ME: AMERICA, 2021

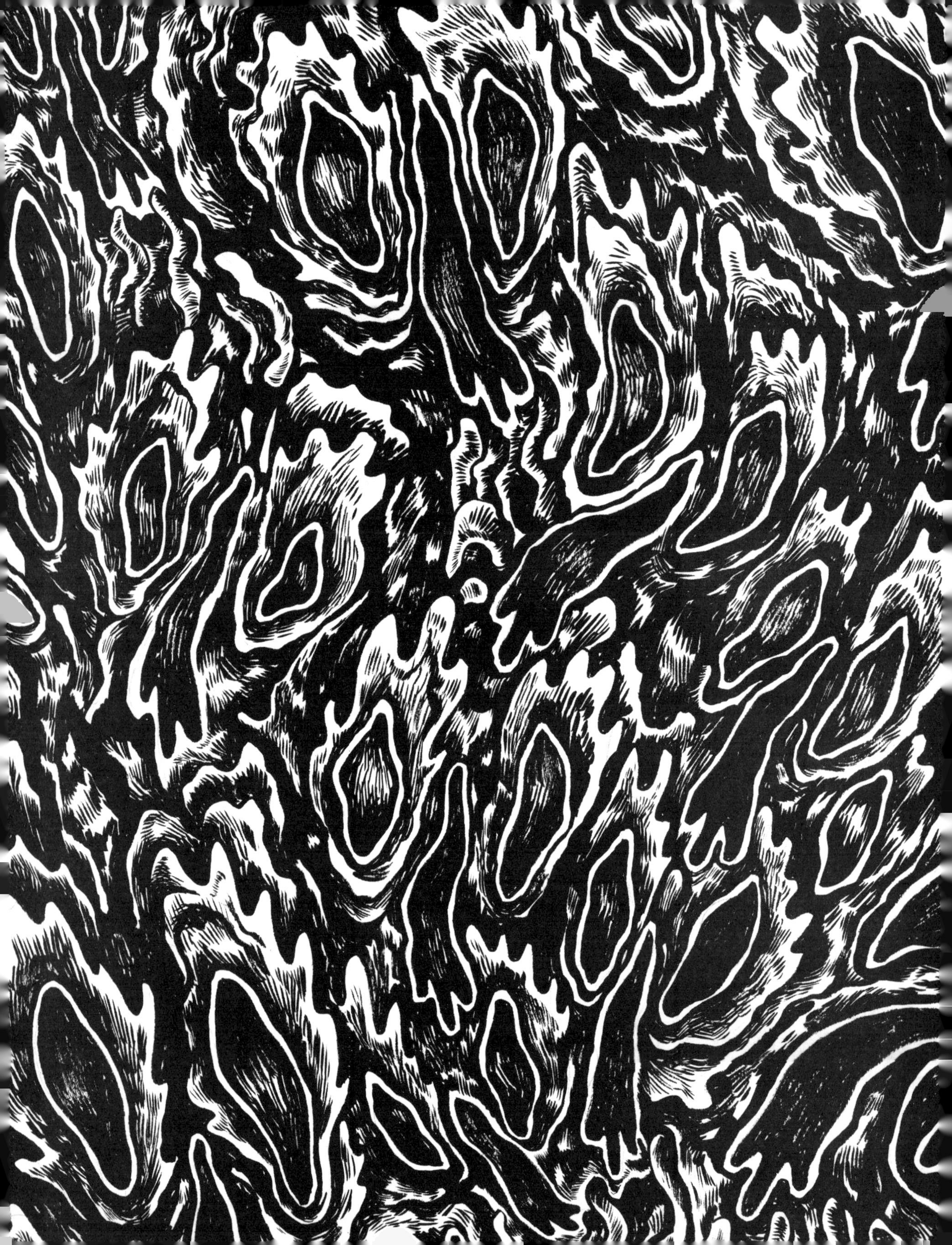

NOTES

1 From a November 20, 1996, talk at the Charlotte Mecklenburg Library, Charlotte, North Carolina.

7 Search results for "红色上海八年/ Hong se Shanghai ba nian," WorldCat, https://www.worldcat.org/title/31224143?oclcNum=31224143.

9 Bessel van der Kolk, *The Body Keeps the Score* (New York: Viking, 2014), 197.

15 Wallace Stegner, *The American West as Living Space* (Ann Arbor: University of Michigan Press, 1987), 22.

23 Adrienne Rich, *Diving into the Wreck: Poems 1971–1972* (New York: W. W. Norton, 1973), 23.

26 Arthur H. Smith, *Village Life in China: A Study in Sociology* (New York: Fleming H. Revell, 1899), 258.

34 Ian McLachlan, *Shanghai 1949: The End of an Era* (New York: New Amsterdam Books, 1990), 17. The book's photographer, Sam Tata, is quoting Sammy Tuttleman, a former Shanghai Public School student.

35 Rana Mitter, *Forgotten Ally: China's World War II, 1937–1945* (New York: Mariner Books, 2013), 49.

35 Helen Zia, *Last Boat Out of Shanghai* (New York: Ballantine Books, 2019), 63.

36 Iris Chang, *The Rape of Nanking* (New York: Basic Books, 1997), 85–86.

41 Karen Russell, *Swamplandia!* (New York: Alfred A. Knopf, 2011), 250.

41 4Culture Artist Project grant, 2016.

51 "Hui lai" is a very broad term whose meaning depends on context, so this is not an entirely literal translation.

56 From a conversation with Jason Y. Ng, author of *Umbrellas in Bloom*.

60 Frank Dikötter, *The Tragedy of Liberation: A History of the Chinese Revolution, 1945–1957* (New York: Bloomsbury, 2017), 109.

63 McLachlan, *Shanghai 1949*, 31.

66 Dikötter, *The Tragedy of Liberation*, 45.

68 Seattle Office of Arts & Culture, CityArtist grant, 2015.

76 Zia, *Last Boat Out of Shanghai*, 231.

76 Dikötter, *The Tragedy of Liberation*, 18.

77 McLachlan, *Shanghai 1949*, 30.

77 Dikötter, *The Tragedy of Liberation*, 31; Feng Bingxing interviewed by the *Shanghai Daily*, "Shanghai Celebrates Its 60th Year of Liberation," *Shanghai Daily*, May 28, 2009.

78 Dikötter, *The Tragedy of Liberation*, 47.

78 Dikötter, *The Tragedy of Liberation*, 47–48.

78 Dikötter, *The Tragedy of Liberation*, 49.

79 Stella Dong, *Shanghai: The Rise and Fall of a Decadent City* (New York: William Morrow, 2000), 2.

79 McLachlan, *Shanghai 1949*, 20.

83 Edward Hunter, *Brain-Washing in Red China: The Calculated Destruction of Men's Minds* (New York: Vanguard Press, 1953), 63–65.

84 Dikötter, *The Tragedy of Liberation*, 95.

85 Dikötter, *The Tragedy of Liberation*, xii.

85 Laogai Research Foundation, "The Laogai System: History & Purpose," accessed September 15, 2022, https://laogairesearch.org/laogai-system.

85 Robert Jay Lifton, *Thought Reform and the Psychology of Totalism* (Chapel Hill: University of North Carolina Press, 1989), 5.

85 Lifton, *Thought Reform and the Psychology of Totalism*, 8.

85 Robert Loh, *Escape from Red China* (Auckland, New Zealand: Muriwai Books, 2017; Kindle edition), location 885 of 5095.

85 Dikötter, *The Tragedy of Liberation*, 85.

89 Esther Cheo Ying, *Black Country to Red China: One Girl's Story from War-Torn England to Revolutionary China* (London: Vintage, 2009), quoted in Dikötter, *The Tragedy of Liberation*, 102.

101 Edward Abbey, *Desert Solitaire: A Season in the Wilderness* (New York: McGraw-Hill, 1968), 162.

105 To corroborate my grandma's account, this incident also appears in Loh, *Escape from Red China*, location 833.

108 Dikötter, *The Tragedy of Liberation*, 73.

108 Dikötter, *The Tragedy of Liberation*, 83.

112 Mitter, *Forgotten Ally*, 38.

127 "Cowboy's Lament," on Burl Ives, *A Twinkle in Your Eye*, Columbia Records, a division of Sony Music Entertainment, 1941.

132 Harry Wu with George Vecsey, *Troublemaker: One Man's Crusade Against China's Cruelty* (West Palm Beach, FL: NewsMax.com Book, 2002), 49.

133 This is a point where my grandmother's timeline deviates from the more widely accepted historical record. Most sources say that China's food shortages didn't begin until 1958. It's possible she was experiencing regional food shortages, but this is before the Great Famine.

139 Audre Lorde, *The Black Unicorn* (New York: W. W. Norton, 1995), 31.

144 Li Kunwu and Philippe Ôtié, *A Chinese Life*, trans. Edward Gauvin (New York: Harry N. Abrams, 2012), 69.

144 Jasper Becker, *Hungry Ghosts: Mao's Secret Famine* (New York: Henry Holt, 1998); see illustration note 10 on page viii, referencing image appearing on unnumbered page between 144–45.

147 Yang Jisheng, *Tombstone: The Great Chinese Famine, 1958–1962* (New York: Farrar, Straus and Giroux, 2012), 188.

147 Becker, *Hungry Ghosts*, 81.

147 Jisheng, *Tombstone*, 177.

147 Becker, *Hungry Ghosts*, 63, quoting from *People's Daily*, 1958.

147 Jisheng, *Tombstone*, 99.

148 Jisheng, *Tombstone*, 192, 201.

150 Zia, *Last Boat Out of Shanghai*, 288.

152 John Carroll, *A Concise History of Hong Kong* (Lanham, MD: Rowman & Littlefield, 2007), 9.

152 Emma Teng, *Eurasian* (Berkeley: University of California Press, 2013), 225.

152 Vicky Lee, *Being Eurasian: Memories Across Racial Divides* (Hong Kong: Hong Kong University Press, 2004), 24.

155 Carroll, *A Concise History of Hong Kong*, 56.

155 Carroll, *A Concise History of Hong Kong*, 58.

155 Teng, *Eurasian*, 222. Speech from C. G. Anderson at the founding of the Eurasian Welfare League, quoting Eric Peter Ho, *The Welfare League (Tong Ren Hui): The Sixty Years 1930–1990* (Hong Kong: Welfare League, 1990), 9.

156 *China Mail*, April 2, 1869.

161 This is how my mom spelled out her name phonetically for me. Romanized in Mandarin pinyin, it would be Ge Yi Tian.

170 Josie Sigler, *The Galaxie and Other Rides* (Livingston, AL: Livingston Press, 2012).

177 Kat Chow, *Seeing Ghosts: A Memoir* (New York: Grand Central, 2021), 171.

179 *Long Road to Our Verdant Peak: The History and Relics of Psychiatry in Hong Kong*, brochure from Hong Kong History Museum, 2013.

183 "1966 Winston Churchill Commemoration, 1874–1965," StampWorld, https://www.stampworld.com/stamps /Hong-Kong/Postage-stamps/g0222.

194 Becker, *Hungry Ghosts*, 311–12.

194 Becker, *Hungry Ghosts*, 153–54.

194 Jisheng, *Tombstone*, 14, and Becker, *Hungry Ghosts*, 138.

204 Frances Wong, *China, Bound and Unbound* (Hong Kong: Hong Kong University Press, 2009), xi.

204 Author interview with Patsy Fenton, Hong Kong, 2016.

214 "Saddle Tramp," on Marty Robbins, *Gunfighter Ballads and Trail Songs*, Columbia Records, 1959.

217 Maxine Hong Kingston, *The Woman Warrior* (New York: Vintage, 1989), 5.

222 Zia, *Last Boat Out of Shanghai*, 411.

222 Mao Zedong speech during a Chinese Communist Party (CCP) meeting, August 7, 1927.

222 Kent Wong, *Swimming to Freedom: My Escape from China and the Cultural Revolution* (New York: Abrams Press, 2021; Kindle edition), location 1249.

224 Wong, *Swimming to Freedom*, location 1309.

230 Elizabeth Rosner, *Survivor Café: The Legacy of Trauma and the Labyrinth of Memory* (Berkeley, CA: Counterpoint, 2017), 49.

235 Herman Melville, *Moby-Dick* (London: Random House, 2010), 7.

236 William Kittredge, *Who Owns the West?* (San Francisco: Mercury House, 1996), 22.

253 Barbara Kingsolver, *Homeland and Other Stories* (London: HarperCollins, 1993), 2.

260 van der Kolk, *The Body Keeps the Score*, 136.

265 Adrienne Rich, *The Dream of a Common Language: Poems 1974–1977* (New York: W. W. Norton, 2013), 22.

280 van der Kolk, *The Body Keeps the Score*, 76.

285 "Episode 585: In Defense of Ignorance," *This American Life*, April 22, 2016, https://www.thisamericanlife .org/585/in-defense-of-ignorance.

293 Rebecca Solnit, *A Field Guide to Getting Lost* (New York: Penguin, 2006), 78.

307 Cole Porter and Robert Fletcher, "Don't Fence Me In," 1934.

327 Chinua Achebe, *There Was a Country: A Personal History of Biafra* (New York: Penguin, 2012), 14.

327 "Sūnzǐ: The Art of War, Chapter 6: Weak Points and Strong," https://pages.ucsd.edu/~dkjordan/chin /Suentzyy/Suentzyy06e.html#:~:text=Water%20 shapes%20its%20course%20according, 34 and 35.

327 "Sun Tzu's Art of War, Chapter 5: Energy," https:// suntzusaid.com/book/5/15, 15.

328 Willa Cather, *O Pioneers!* (Oxford: Oxford University Press, 1999), 68.

330 Kingston, *The Woman Warrior*, 5–6.

335 Alice Miller, *The Drama of the Gifted Child* (New York: Basic Books, 1997), 19.

344 Paul Auster, *Moon Palace* (New York: Penguin, 1990), 50.

363 Ocean Vuong, *Night Sky with Exit Wounds* (Port Townsend, WA: Copper Canyon Press, 2016), 76.

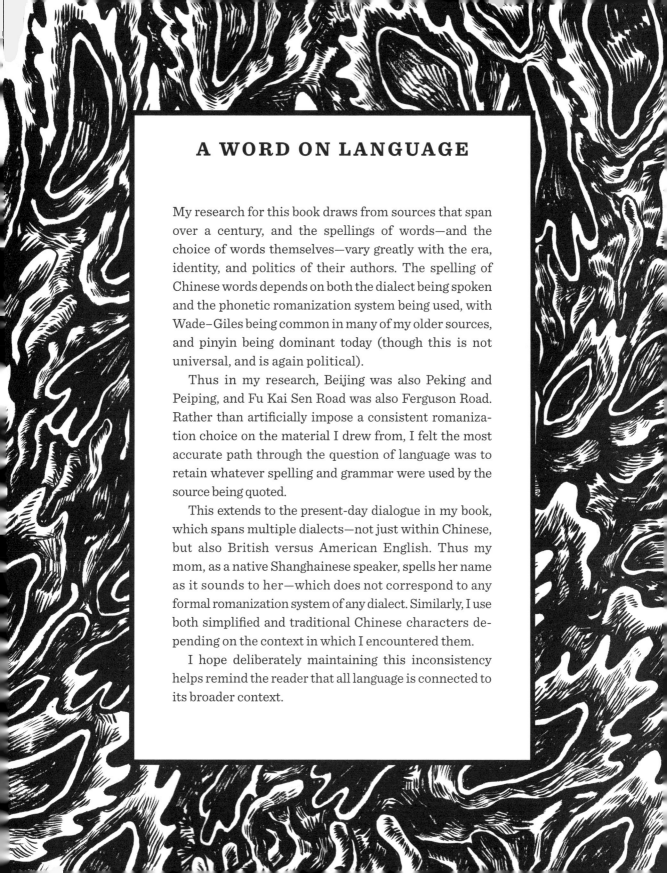

A WORD ON LANGUAGE

My research for this book draws from sources that span over a century, and the spellings of words—and the choice of words themselves—vary greatly with the era, identity, and politics of their authors. The spelling of Chinese words depends on both the dialect being spoken and the phonetic romanization system being used, with Wade–Giles being common in many of my older sources, and pinyin being dominant today (though this is not universal, and is again political).

Thus in my research, Beijing was also Peking and Peiping, and Fu Kai Sen Road was also Ferguson Road. Rather than artificially impose a consistent romanization choice on the material I drew from, I felt the most accurate path through the question of language was to retain whatever spelling and grammar were used by the source being quoted.

This extends to the present-day dialogue in my book, which spans multiple dialects—not just within Chinese, but also British versus American English. Thus my mom, as a native Shanghainese speaker, spells her name as it sounds to her—which does not correspond to any formal romanization system of any dialect. Similarly, I use both simplified and traditional Chinese characters depending on the context in which I encountered them.

I hope deliberately maintaining this inconsistency helps remind the reader that all language is connected to its broader context.

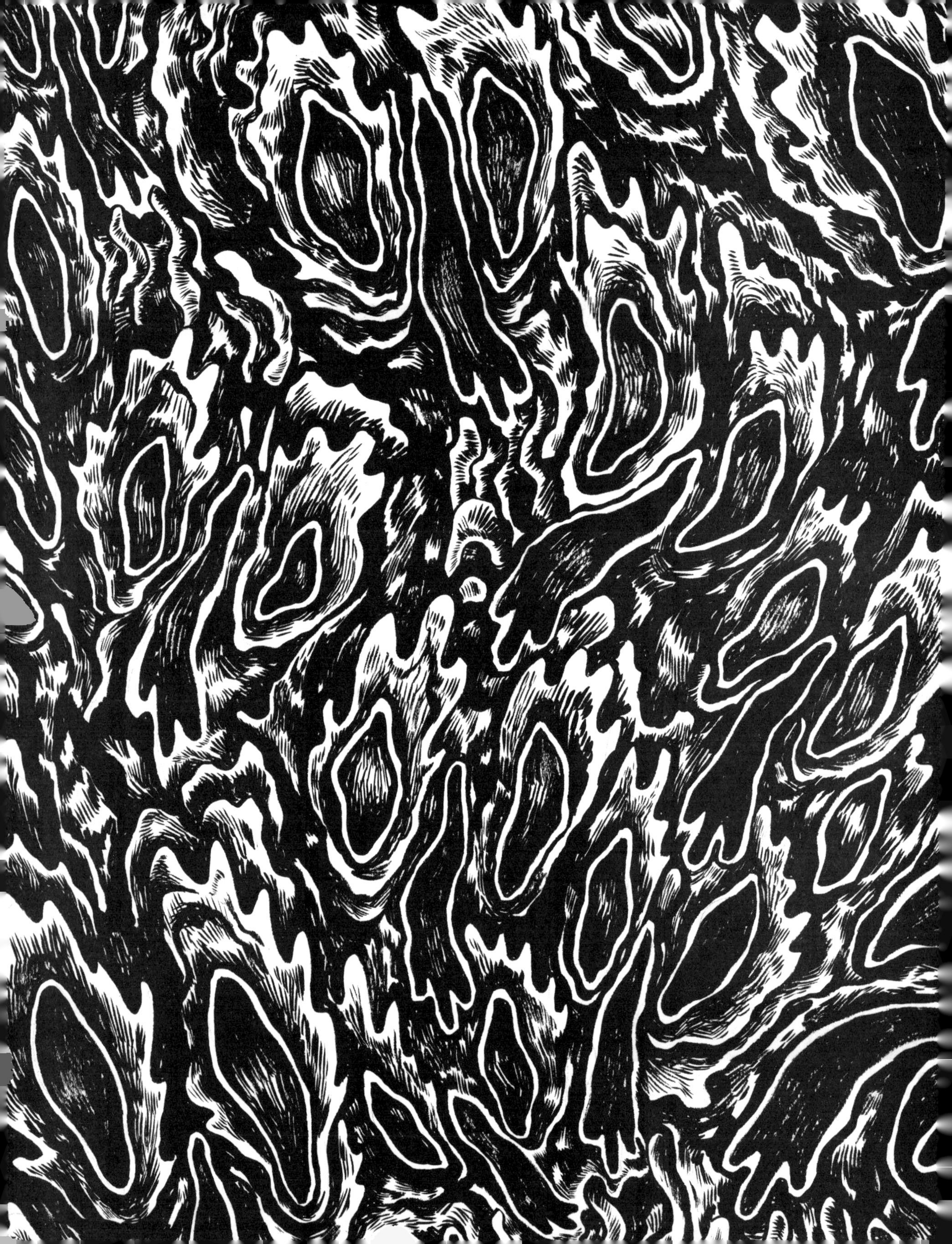

ACKNOWLEDGMENTS

Making this book was the most isolating cowboy-on-the-range endeavor I've ever put myself through, and I would not have survived this process without the support of too many people to list.

Eternal thanks to my raccoon sisters Michelle Peñaloza and Jane Wong; we've carried one another through most everything, haven't we? Thanks to my larger raccoon family (a.k.a. the AAABC: Accidental Asian American Book Club) of Devon Hale, Arlene Kim, and Quinha Faria. In writing this acknowledgment, I just learned the collective noun for a pack of raccoons is "nursery" or "gaze," but fuck that—you will always be my plotting of raccoons, my vortex of raccoons....

My deep gratitude to the Smart/Bach, Rolston, Banks, and Hoelting families for informally adopting me, and to the Jackson-hyphens—Susan, Samuel, Aira, Mahkeah, Kalila, and Henry (and all your dogs)—for literally and figuratively feeding me through this process.

Thank you to the earliest supporters of this book: Jess Van Nostrand and the Project Room for championing the existence of this book long before I ever began it. Everett O'Cillín and the Santa Cruz Museum of Art and History (and George Ow) for asking me to make Guided by Ghosts, which helped me see my family's story through a much broader historical lens. Vee Hua (華婷婷) for our fifteenish years of mutual serendipity, and for translating my grandmother's memoir.

Geographic thanks to my communities in:

Alaska: Kristin Hoelting for ruining me for all other places by first getting me up there (thank you/damn you), Scott and Julie Hursey, Ray Troll, Martha McPheeters, and Eric O'Keefe. Thanks to Camp De-nali for providing the wilderness in which I took the first steps into the making of this book; Pika Hut will always hold a very special place in my heart.

Seattle: Jen Zeyl and the Canoe Social Club crew—Chance Reschke, Kate Fernandez, Melanie Masson, Laura Becker, Anne Blackburn, and Jed Dunkerley. Miscellaneous thanks to Claudia Bach, Mary Ann Peters, Eroyn Franklin, Rachel Kessler, Meg Hartwig, Eric Olson, Paul Margolis and Mandy Greer, Shawn Landis and Jodi Rockwell and the Rockland Woods community, Reed Olsen, Diana Adams and Vermillion, On the Boards, Weird and Awesome with Emmett Montgomery, Seattle Arts and Lectures, the Seattle Public Library, Andrea Ramsey and Kristen Ramirez, Laura Dean, Tia Kramer, Bill Wood, Andy Predergast, and so, so many more. Thanks to Arne Pihl and the lake plunge crew for jumping in freezing water with me (almost) every Saturday morning during the final year of this book.

Port Townsend shout-outs to Liz Hopkins, Amanda Thieroff, Karen Amundson, Ginny Wilson, Erin Jakubek, and Linda Okazaki, and to Leland Gibson for criminally undercharging me for studio rent. Thanks to Morgan Svik and Cotton Banks for the many things you've provided in our twenty-four years of friendship.

California gratitude to Martha Cederstrom, Kay Ryan and Carol Adair, Andrew Hagen, and Kathy Rolston.

Deepest thanks to Kim Fenton and her family for taking me under their wing so generously in Hong Kong, and thanks to the Diocesan Girls' School, Gwulo, Castle Peak, and the Hong Kong Museum of History.

Thank you to Rebecca Reilly for your joy, and for always helping me find the way back to mine.

Thank you to my many friends who died young in tragic ways—particularly Chelsea Faith Dolan (Cherushii) and KC Boehly—and became my beloved meddling ghost posse; y'all sometimes pull some heavy-handed ghost strings when it comes to imbuing my life with an unusual amount of serendipity. I'm grateful for the ways you continue to be good friends, and continue to push me to be a good friend to others.

Thank you to the graphic novelists who all talked me down from various points when I wanted to light this thing on fire and run for the hills: Ellen Forney, David Lasky, and Jason Lutes.

Thank you to all the readers who spent time with drafts of this book and lent their eagle-eyed clarity when I was lost in the weeds: Majula Martin, Caitlin McKenna, Amber Casali, Alicia Craven, Jenny Liou, Michelle Peñaloza, Margaret Lee, and Arlene Kim. Margaret Lee and Zara Chowdhary, thank you for posse-ing up so we could navigate the trenches of our depressing memoirs together.

Big thanks to all the residency programs that supported this book: Playa, Pine Meadow Ranch, Ucross, the Corporation of Yaddo, Hedgebrook, Storyknife, and Suttle Lodge. And the residencies that supported me by letting me take a book break to be their chefs: Mineral School, Till, and Rockland Woods. A particular shout-out to Caldera for taking a chance by giving me my first residency when this story was just a series of scattered dots. And thank you to the PEN Northwest Margery Davis Boyden Wilderness Writing Residency, where my six months alone as a caretaker on the Rogue River showed me the path back to the softness I needed to tell this story. My time there is a gift I will spend the rest of my life unwrapping, and my continued friendship with the Brothers Boyden is icing on the cake. Thank you to everyone who participated in my Desert Island Book Project while I was living out there.

Thanks to the Robert B. McMillen Foundation, the Seattle Office of Arts and Culture, 4Culture, and the Washington Artist Trust for the funding that allowed this book to exist. Thank you to my agent, Anjali Singh, for championing this story and acting like it was completely normal to negotiate a book auction while one's writer was deep in the wilderness and reachable only by unreliable radio phone. Thanks to my editor, Daphne Durham, for encouraging me to roam to the furthest edges of my creative frontiers and understanding that a cowboy's loyalty is best earned by giving her an anarchic level of freedom. Thanks to Lydia Zoells, Brianna Fairman, Amybeth Menendez, Gretchen Achilles, Na Kim, Sean McDonald, and the whole team at MCD/FSG.

Thank you everyone who helped remind me of my wildness during the long years when being chained to my drawing table kept me from being able to live it (NEVER. AGAIN.): Amber Casali, Will Koomjian, Jenny Liou, Jon Felis, Greg Smart (and Canela), Kristin Hoelting, Mary Ann Thomas, Grace Anderson, Michael Boonstra, Siolo Thompson, Arne Pihl, Meg Hartwig, Alicia Craven, Caitlin Lenahan, and Everett O'Cillín. And thank you to the enduring wisdom of my "old man pen pals" Jim Dodge and Frank Boyden. In the post-book recovery, I am grateful to all the places that have allowed me to plant trees, dig holes, move rocks, and reimmerse myself in the rhythms of the natural world. I may be MCD's first writer to simply refuse to go on book tour because I have decided to instead become a stonemason.

Thank you to everyone across Alaska and Iceland who helped me with the somewhat absurd task of needing to borrow various pieces of technology to finalize this production process while on a multi-month bicycle trip.

And the biggest thanks last:

To my family in Suzhou for opening their hearts and histories to me in spite of their fears.

To Caitl for being my best friend for twenty-two years and counting.

To Henry Jackson-Spieker, whose kindness carried me through the trenches of this book.

And I'll end where I began: thank you to my mother and her mother, for trusting me with our story.